MARKETING

AN INTRODUCTION

CANADIAN 6 EDITION

MARKETING

AN INTRODUCTION

CANADIAN **6** EDITION

GARY ARMSTRONG

University of North Carolina

PHILIP KOTLER

Northwestern University

VALERIE TRIFTS

Dalhousie University

LILLY ANNE BUCHWITZ

Wilfrid Laurier University

CONTRIBUTING AUTHOR:

DAVID GAUDET

SAIT Polytechnic

Toronto

Editorial Director: Claudine O'Donnell
Acquisitions Editor: Carolin Sweig
Marketing Manager: Lisa Gillis
Program Manager: Karen Townsend
Project Manager: Jessica Hellen
Developmental Editor: Paul Donnelly
Media Editor: Simon Bailey
Media Developer: Kelli Cadet
Production Services: iEnergizer Aptara®, Ltd.
Permissions Project Manager: Joanne Tang
Photo and Text Permissions Research: Rachel Irwin
Interior and Cover Designer: Anthony Leung
Cover Image: HOCO Entertainment and Resorts
Vice-President, Cross Media and Publishing Services: Gary Bennett

Credits and acknowledgments for material borrowed from other sources and reproduced, with permission, in this textbook appear on the appropriate page within the text.

Library and Archives Canada Cataloguing in Publication

Armstrong, Gary, author
　　Marketing : an introduction / Gary Armstrong, University of North Carolina, Philip Kotler, Northwestern University, Valerie Trifts, Dalhousie University, Lilly Anne Buchwitz, Humber College ; contributing author, David Gaudet, SAIT Polytechnic. — Sixth Canadian edition.
　　ISBN 978-0-13-409580-6 (paperback)
　　1. Marketing—Textbooks. 2. Marketing—Canada—Textbooks.
I. Kotler, Philip, author　II. Trifts, Valerie, author　III. Buchwitz, Lilly Anne, author
IV. Gaudet, David (Professor), author　V. Title.

HF5415.M295 2015　　　　　　658.8　　　　　　C2015-907141-0

ISBN: 978-0-13-409580-6

KV 08.06.2018 1547

Brief Contents

Brief Contents

Contents

PART 2 UNDERSTANDING THE MARKETPLACE AND CONSUMERS 116

**PART 3 DESIGNING A CUSTOMER-DRIVEN MARKETING STRATEGY
AND MARKETING MIX 236**

10   Pricing: Understanding and Capturing Customer Value   351

About the Authors

GARY ARMSTRONG is Crist W. Blackwell Distinguished Professor Emeritus of Undergraduate Education in the Kenan-Flagler Business School at the University of North Carolina at Chapel Hill. He holds undergraduate and master's degrees in business from Wayne State University in Detroit, and he received his Ph.D. in marketing from Northwestern University. Dr. Armstrong has contributed numerous articles to leading business journals. As a consultant and researcher, he has worked with many companies on marketing research, sales management, and marketing strategy.

But Professor Armstrong's first love has always been teaching. His long-held Blackwell Distinguished Professorship is the only permanent endowed professorship for distinguished undergraduate teaching at the University of North Carolina at Chapel Hill. He has been very active in the teaching and administration of Kenan-Flagler's undergraduate program. His administrative posts have included chair of marketing, associate director of the undergraduate business program, director of the business honors program, and many others. Through the years, he has worked closely with business student groups and has received several campus-wide and Business School teaching awards. He is the only repeat recipient of the school's highly regarded Award for Excellence in Undergraduate Teaching, which he received three times. Most recently, Professor Armstrong received the UNC Board of Governors Award for Excellence in Teaching, the highest teaching honour bestowed by the sixteen-campus University of North Carolina system.

PHILIP KOTLER is S. C. Johnson & Son Distinguished Professor of International Marketing at the Kellogg School of Management, Northwestern University. He received his master's degree at the University of Chicago and his Ph.D. at M.I.T., both in economics. Dr. Kotler is author of *Marketing Management* (Pearson Prentice Hall), now in its 13th edition and the world's most widely used marketing textbook in graduate schools of business worldwide. He has authored dozens of other successful books and has written more than 100 articles in leading journals. He is the only three-time winner of the coveted Alpha Kappa Psi award for the best annual article in the *Journal of Marketing*.

Professor Kotler was named the first recipient of two major awards: the Distinguished Marketing Educator of the Year Award given by the American Marketing Association and the Philip Kotler Award for Excellence in Health Care Marketing presented by the Academy for Health Care Services Marketing. His numerous other major honours include the Sales and Marketing Executives International Marketing Educator of the Year Award; The European Association of Marketing Consultants and Trainers Marketing Excellence Award; the Charles Coolidge Parlin Marketing Research Award; and the Paul D. Converse Award, given by the American Marketing Association to honour "outstanding contributions to science in marketing." In a recent *Financial Times* poll of 1000 senior executives across the world, Professor Kotler was ranked as the fourth "most influential business writer/guru" of the 21st century.

Dr. Kotler has served as chairman of the College on Marketing of the Institute of Management Sciences, a director of the American Marketing Association, and a trustee of the Marketing Science Institute. He has consulted with many major U.S. and international companies in the areas of marketing strategy and planning, marketing organization, and international marketing. He has travelled and lectured extensively throughout Europe, Asia, and South America, advising companies and governments about global marketing practices and opportunities.

VALERIE TRIFTS is an associate professor of marketing at Dalhousie University, Rowe School of Business, in Halifax. She received her undergraduate business degree from the University of Prince Edward Island, her MBA from Saint Mary's University, and her Ph.D. in marketing from the University of Alberta. Her research spans a broad range of topics, but her primary research interests are in the area of consumer information search and decision making. Specifically, she is interested in how firms can benefit from strategically providing their customers with information about competitors, as well as in exploring individual difference variables that influence search behaviour. More recently, she has begun to explore how personalization technologies can be leveraged online to customize digital media products for individual consumers. She is also involved in interdisciplinary work in the fields of transportation research and business ethics. She integrates her research into a variety of courses she has taught, including introduction to marketing, consumer behaviour, Internet marketing, and marketing research at both the undergraduate and graduate levels. Her research has been published in *Marketing Science*, the *Journal of Consumer Psychology*, the *Journal of Marketing Theory and Practice*, and *Transportation Research: Part E*. She has presented at numerous academic conferences and has been funded by the Social Sciences and Humanities Research Council of Canada.

LILLY ANNE BUCHWITZ is an author, teacher, and expert in the field of Internet marketing and advertising who became an academic after 15 years in the professional world of high-tech product and Internet marketing. In the early days of the Internet, she was the marketing manager for the Open Text Index, one of the original Internet search engines developed by Canadian software company Open Text, where she became notorious for developing paid search advertising in 1996. She later worked for the Internet start-up that became About.com, helped launch Internet advertising network DoubleClick in Canada, and was the Internet marketing manager for Chapters Online. Her professional activities eventually led her to teaching and research in the still-developing field of Internet advertising, which eventually became the subject of her Ph.D. dissertation. She has undergraduate degrees in English literature and education from McGill University, and an MBA from Wilfrid Laurier University. She began her university teaching career at the University of New Brunswick in its emerging e-commerce program in St. John, as well as in its business education program in Beijing, China. Since then she has taught marketing communications, advertising, and Internet marketing at Brock University, Wilfrid Laurier University, and San Jose State University. Today she is a writer, speaker, and professor at Humber College in Toronto.

DAVID GAUDET is an instructor at SAIT Polytechnic and the University of Calgary, and an active business owner/consultant, operating in a diverse number of industries. Holding an MBA with high distinction, from the University of Southern Queensland, Australia, he develops and delivers business courses in subjects ranging from accounting to marketing. His embracement of new technologies and integration of social media into his teaching have made him an early adopter and pioneer of flipped classroom methodology, and a regular speaker at the annual NISOD Conference in Austin, Texas, supported by the University of Texas.

Gaudet's professional career began in broadcasting, after earning his diploma of Applied Arts in 1983. He went on to assist in the successful launch of multiple radio stations, and ultimately held down programming duties in some of the country's most listened to and influential rock radio outlets. His passion for media converged with his entrepreneurial DNA in the early 90's when he started his first business, a media market research company, providing listener/viewer data to clients. He has added a plethora of marketing services to his portfolio over the last 25 years, providing corporate communications, project management, business analysis, crisis communications, media training, public relations, copywriting, web design, content management and strategic planning all under his third business startup, "Triceratops Brand Logic Inc".

Preface

The Sixth Canadian Edition of *Marketing: An Introduction:* Creating More Value for You!

Top marketers all share a common goal: putting consumers at the heart of marketing. Today's marketing is all about creating customer value and engagement in a fast-changing, increasingly digital and social marketplace.

Marketing starts with understanding consumer needs and wants, deciding which target markets the organization can serve best, and developing a compelling value proposition by which the organization can attract, keep, and grow targeted consumers. Then, more than just making a sale, today's marketers want to engage customers and build deep customer relationships that make their brands a meaningful part of consumers' conversations and lives. In this digital age, to go along with their tried-and-true traditional marketing methods, marketers have access to a dazzling set of new customer relationship–building tools—from the Internet, smartphones, and tablets to online, mobile, and social media—for engaging customers any time, anyplace to shape brand conversations, experiences, and community. If marketers do these things well, they will reap the rewards in terms of market share, profits, and customer equity. In the sixth Canadian edition of *Marketing: An Introduction*, you'll learn how *customer value* and *customer engagement* drive every good marketing strategy.

Marketing: An Introduction makes learning and teaching marketing more productive and enjoyable than ever. The sixth Canadian edition's streamlined approach strikes an effective balance between depth of coverage and ease of learning. Unlike more abbreviated texts, it provides complete and timely coverage of all the latest marketing thinking and practice. And unlike longer, more complex texts, its moderate length makes it easy to digest in a given semester.

Marketing: An Introduction's approachable organization, style, and design are well suited to beginning marketing students. The sixth Canadian edition's learning design helps students to learn, link, and apply important concepts. Its simple organization and writing style present even the most advanced topics in an approachable, exciting way. The sixth Canadian edition brings marketing to life with deep and relevant examples and illustrations throughout. And when combined with MyMarketingLab, our online homework and personalized study tool, *Marketing: An Introduction* ensures that students will come to class well prepared and leave class with a richer understanding of basic marketing concepts, strategies, and practices.

What's New in the Sixth Canadian Edition?

We've thoroughly revised the sixth Canadian edition of *Marketing: An Introduction* to reflect the major trends and forces impacting marketing in this digital age of customer value, engagement, and relationships. Here are just some of the changes you'll find in this edition:

- More than any other developments, sweeping new **online, social media, mobile, and other digital technologies** are now affecting how marketers, brands, and customers engage with each other. The sixth Canadian edition features new and revised discussions and examples of the explosive impact of exciting *new digital marketing technologies* shaping marketing strategy and practice—from online, mobile, and social media engagement technologies discussed in Chapters 1, 6, 12, 13, and 15 to "online listening" and research tools in Chapter 5, online influence and brand communities in Chapter 6, and location-based marketing in Chapter 8, to the use of social media in business-to-business marketing and sales in Chapters 7 and 14, and to consumer Web, social media, and mobile marketing, as well as other new communications technologies, in Chapters 1, 6, 13, 15, and throughout.

A new Chapter 1 section, *The Digital Age: Online, Mobile, and Social Media Marketing*, introduces the exciting new developments in digital and social media marketing. A completely revised Chapter 15, *Direct, Online, Social Media, and Mobile Marketing*, digs deeply into digital marketing tools such as websites, social media, mobile ads and apps, online video, email, blogs, and other digital platforms that engage consumers anywhere, any time via their computers, smartphones, tablets, Internet-ready TVs, and other digital devices. The sixth Canadian edition is packed with new stories and examples illustrating how companies employ digital technology to gain competitive advantage—from traditional marketing all-stars such as Nike, P&G, Southwest, and McDonald's to new-age digital competitors such as Google, Amazon.com, Apple, Netflix, Pinterest, and Facebook.

- The sixth Canadian edition features completely new and revised coverage of the emerging trend toward **customer engagement marketing**—building direct and continuous customer involvement in shaping brands, brand conversations, brand experiences, and brand community. The Internet and social media have created better-informed, more-connected, and more-empowered consumers. Thus, today's marketers must now *engage* consumers rather than interrupting them. Marketers are augmenting their mass-media marketing efforts with a rich mix of online, mobile, and social media marketing that promotes deep consumer involvement and a sense of customer community surrounding their brands. Today's new engagement-building tools include everything from websites, blogs, in-person events, and video sharing to online communities and social media such as Facebook, YouTube, Pinterest, Twitter, and a company's own social networking sites.

In all, today's more engaged consumers are giving as much as they get in the form of two-way brand relationships. The sixth Canadian edition contains substantial new material on **customer engagement** and related developments such as **consumer empowerment, crowdsourcing, customer co-creation,** and **consumer-generated marketing**. A new Chapter 1 section—*Engaging Customers*—introduces customer engagement marketing. This and other related customer engagement topics are presented in Chapter 1 (new sections: *Customer Engagement and Today's Digital and Social Media* and *Consumer-Generated Marketing*), Chapter 5 (qualitative approaches to gaining deeper customer insights), Chapter 6 (managing online influence and customer community through digital and social media marketing), Chapter 8 (crowdsourcing and customer-driven new-product development), Chapter 13 (the new, more engaging marketing communications model), and Chapter 15 (direct digital, online, social media, and mobile marketing).

- The sixth Canadian edition continues to build on and extend the innovative **customer value framework** from previous editions. The customer value model presented in the first chapter is fully integrated throughout the remainder of the book. No other marketing text presents such a clear and compelling customer value approach.

- The sixth Canadian edition provides revised and expanded coverage of developments in the fast-changing area of **integrated marketing communications**. It tells how marketers are blending the new digital and social media tools—everything from Internet and mobile marketing to blogs, viral videos, and social media—with traditional media to create more targeted, personal, and engaging customer relationships. Marketers are no longer simply creating integrated promotion programs; they are practising *marketing content management* in paid, owned, earned, and shared media. No other text provides more current or encompassing coverage of these exciting developments.

- Revised coverage in the sixth Canadian edition shows how companies and consumers continue to deal with **marketing in an uncertain economy** in the lingering aftermath of the recession. Starting with a section in Chapter 1 and continuing with revised discussions in Chapters 4, 10, and elsewhere throughout the text, the sixth Canadian edition shows how now, even as the economy recovers, marketers must focus on creating customer value and sharpening their value propositions in this era of more sensible consumption.

- New material throughout the sixth Canadian edition highlights the increasing importance of **sustainable marketing**. The discussion begins in Chapter 1 and continues in more detail in Chapter 3, which pulls marketing concepts together under a sustainable marketing framework. Frequent discussions and examples showing how sustainable marketing calls for socially and environmentally responsible actions that meet both the immediate and the future needs of customers, companies, and society as a whole are presented throughout the text.

- The sixth Canadian edition provides new discussions and examples of the growth in **global marketing.** As the world becomes a smaller, more competitive place, marketers face new global marketing challenges and opportunities, especially in fast-growing emerging markets such as China, India, Africa, and others. You'll find much new coverage of global marketing throughout the text, starting in Chapter 1 and discussed fully in Chapter 16.

- The sixth Canadian edition continues its emphasis on **measuring and managing return on marketing**, including many new end-of-chapter financial and quantitative marketing exercises that let students apply analytical thinking to relevant concepts in each chapter and link chapter concepts to the text's innovative and comprehensive Appendix 3, *Marketing by the Numbers*.

- The sixth Canadian edition continues to engage students with this title's most unique feature, **the comprehensive case**. For this edition, we are offering two cases, one with a business-to-consumer (B-to-C) focus and one with a business-to-business (B-to-B) focus. Used to further illustrate a chapter's key learnings, the B-to-C case runs throughout the book, and examines Boston Pizza's marketing strategy as it relates to the content being discussed.

- The B-to-B comprehensive case, featuring Farmers Edge, is available. Contact your local Pearson sales representative for more details.

- The sixth Canadian edition provides new end-of-chapter company cases by which students can apply what they learn to actual company situations. Additionally, all of the chapter-opening stories and MARKETING@WORK highlights in the sixth Canadian edition are either new or revised for currency.

Five Major Customer Value and Engagement Themes

The sixth Canadian edition of *Marketing: An Introduction* builds on five major customer value and engagement themes:

1. ***Creating value for customers in order to capture value from customers in return.*** Today's marketers must be good at *creating customer value*, *engaging customers*, and *managing customer relationships*. Outstanding marketing companies understand the marketplace and customer needs, design value-creating marketing strategies, develop integrated marketing programs that engage customers and deliver value and satisfaction, and build strong customer relationships and brand community. In return, they capture value from customers in the form of sales, profits, and customer equity.

   This innovative *customer value framework* is introduced at the start of Chapter 1 in a five-step marketing process model, which details how marketing *creates* customer value and engagement and *captures* value in return. The framework is carefully explained in the first two chapters and then integrated throughout the remainder of the text.

2. ***Customer engagement and today's digital and social media.*** New digital and social media have taken today's marketing by storm, dramatically changing how companies and brands engage consumers and how consumers connect and influence each other's brand behaviours. The sixth Canadian edition introduces and thoroughly explores the contemporary concept of *customer engagement marketing* and the exciting new digital and social media technologies that help brands to engage customers more deeply and interactively. It starts with two major new Chapter 1 sections: *Customer Engagement and Today's Digital and Social Media* and *The Digital Age: Online, Mobile, and Social Media*. A completely revised Chapter 15, *Direct, Online, Social Media, and Mobile Marketing*, summarizes the latest developments in digital engagement and relationship-building tools. Everywhere in between, you'll find revised and expanded coverage of the exploding use of digital and social tools to create customer engagement and build brand community.

3. ***Building and managing strong brands to create brand equity.*** Well-positioned brands with strong brand equity provide the basis upon which to build profitable customer relationships. Today's marketers must position their brands powerfully and manage them well to create valued customer brand experiences. The sixth Canadian edition provides a deep focus on brands, anchored by the discussion in Chapter 9.

4. ***Measuring and managing return on marketing.*** Especially in uneven economic times, marketing managers must ensure that their marketing dollars are being well spent. In the past, many marketers spent freely on big, expensive marketing programs, often without thinking carefully about the financial returns on their spending. But all that has changed rapidly. "Marketing accountability"—measuring and managing marketing return on investment—has now become an important part of strategic marketing decision making. This emphasis on marketing accountability is addressed in Chapter 2; Appendix 3, *Marketing by the Numbers*; and throughout the sixth Canadian edition.

5. ***Sustainable marketing around the globe.*** As new technologies make the world an increasingly smaller and more fragile place, marketers must be good at marketing their brands globally and in sustainable ways. New material throughout the sixth Canadian edition emphasizes the concepts of *global marketing* and *sustainable marketing*—meeting the present needs of consumers and businesses while also preserving or enhancing the ability of future generations to meet their needs. This edition integrates global marketing and sustainability topics throughout the text. It provides focused coverage on each topic in Chapters 16 and 3, respectively.

Real Experiences: MARKETING@WORK

Marketing: An Introduction, sixth Canadian edition, guides new marketing students down the intriguing, discovery-laden road to learning marketing in an applied and practical way. The text takes a practical marketing-management approach, providing countless in-depth, real-life examples and stories that engage students with basic marketing concepts and bring the marketing journey to life. Every chapter contains an opening story plus *Marketing@Work* highlight features that reveal the drama of modern marketing. Students learn, for example, about the following:

- Loblaw's Joe Fresh brand is creating exceptional value for its customers.
- Nike's outstanding success results from more than just making and selling good sports gear. It's based on a customer-focused strategy through which Nike creates brand engagement and close brand community with and among its customers.
- Sony's dizzying fall from market leadership provides a cautionary tale of what can happen when a company—even a dominant marketing leader—fails to adapt to its changing environment.
- Chipotle's sustainability mission isn't an add-on, created just to position the company as "socially responsible"—doing good is ingrained in everything the company does.
- At T-shirt and apparel maker Life is good, engagement and social media are about building meaningful customer engagement, measured by the depth of consumer commenting and community that surround the brand.
- Giant social network Facebook promises to become one of the world's most powerful and profitable digital marketers—but it's just getting started.
- Innovator Samsung has transformed itself by creating a seemingly endless flow of inspired new products that feature stunning design, innovative technology, life-enriching features, and a big dose of "Wow!"
- The explosion of the Internet, social media, mobile devices, and other technologies has some marketers asking, "Who needs face-to-face selling anymore?"
- For Coca-Cola, marketing in Africa is like "sticking its hand into a bees' nest to get some honey."
- Under its "Conscious Consumption" mission, outdoor apparel and gear maker Patagonia takes sustainability to new extremes by telling consumers to buy *less*.

Beyond such features, each chapter is packed with countless real, engaging, and timely examples that reinforce key concepts. No other text brings marketing to life like the sixth Canadian edition of *Marketing: An Introduction*.

Canada Goose: Authenticity Is Key to Customer Value

In 1957, Sam Tick founded Metro Sportswear, which produced a modest line of jackets and woollen shirts in a small manufacturing facility in Toronto. The 1970s saw the business expand to include the production of custom-ordered down-filled coats for the Canadian Rangers, city police forces, and other government workers. In 1985, the company was renamed Snow Goose, and in the early 1990s it began selling its products in Europe under the name Canada Goose. By the late 1990s the modern era of Canada Goose had begun and the real expansion of the brand began. Over the past 10 years or so, Canada Goose parka sales have soared within Canada and in more than 40 other countries worldwide. In fact, Canada Goose placed 102nd on the 2014 Profit 500 list of fastest growing Canadian companies, with a 641 percent growth in revenues over the previous five years.

How did Canada Goose achieve such phenomenal growth? A number of factors have contributed to the company's success. First, Canada Goose very carefully chose spokespeople who were highly credible users of the brand. Lance Mackey, a four-time Iditarod and Yukon Quest champion, grew up in Alaska and is known as one of the best dogsled mushers in the world. Ray Zahab, ultra marathon runner and adventurer, and Laurie Skreslet, the first Canadian to reach the summit of Mount Everest, also joined the list of Canada Goose spokespeople. These individuals have enormous credibility with the company's core customer segment, which consists of polar expeditioners, oil riggers, and police departments alike. Well-known Canadian athletes have also joined the list of "Goose People," including Olympic soccer player Karina LeBlanc, Toronto Raptors NBA player Amir Johnson, and tennis superstar Milos Raonic.

Rather than using traditional advertising campaigns to develop brand awareness, Canada Goose relied on consumer-driven marketing tactics to build its brand. In the early stages of the company's marketing efforts, product was placed on people who worked outside in cold environments, such as bouncers at nightclubs or doormen at hotels, who could give the brand credibility. Today, Canada Goose still employs several nontraditional forms of promotion to build brand awareness, from supplying Fairmont Hotels' doormen and valets with Expedition parkas to running a Canada Goose coat check at Toronto Maple Leafs and Toronto Raptors games, where fans are offered the chance to try on parkas while checking their own garments.

Celebrities caught on camera and actors in feature films wearing the brand have also contributed to Canada Goose's success. Hayden Christensen was photographed wearing one at the Vancouver 2010 Winter Olympics. Daniel Radcliffe is often spotted wearing his Canada Goose parka. The brand has been used in the film industry for decades behind the scenes, but now appears on screen as well in such movies as *The Day After Tomorrow, Eight Below, National Treasure, Good Luck Chuck,* and *Whiteout.*

While Canada Goose has long been a bestseller in Europe, it has also been successful in the highly competitive U.S. fashion market. It currently sells its products at premium department stores such as Barneys and Saks Fifth Avenue and is expanding its product offerings via collaborations with Italian cashmere and wool manufacturer Loro Piana and Japanese designer Yuki Matsuda.

Canada Goose is a company that has always chosen its own path and stayed true to its brand. As a result, it has attracted a diverse base of customers who are interested in everything from function to fashion. This is perhaps the biggest reason why Canada Goose has been able to build lasting customer relationships by creating superior customer value and satisfaction. Customers know what to expect when they buy a Canada Goose product. For example, despite the growing trend in the textile industry to ship production to overseas markets, Canada Goose still manufactures approximately 250 000 parkas per year at its plant in Toronto. An in-house designer cuts the fabric, and dozens of

Exhibit 1.6 Quality, functionality, and style are central to the Canada Goose brand and are key to building customer-perceived value.

Kevin Van Paassen/The Globe and Mail/CP

DISCUSSION QUESTIONS

1. Name and briefly describe the elements of an organization's microenvironment and discuss how they affect marketing.

2. What is demography, and why is it so important for marketers?

3. Who are the Millennials, and why are they of so much interest to marketers?

4. Discuss trends in the natural environment of which marketers must be aware, and provide examples of companies' responses to them.

5. Compare and contrast core beliefs/values and secondary beliefs/values. Provide an example of each and discuss the potential impact marketers have on each.

6. How should marketers respond to the changing environment?

CRITICAL THINKING EXERCISES

1. Research a current or emerging change in the legal or regulatory environment affecting marketing. Explain its impact on marketing and how companies are reacting to the law or regulation.

2. Cause-related marketing has grown considerably over the past 10 years. Visit www.causemarketingforum.com to learn about companies that have won Halo Awards for outstanding cause-related marketing programs. Present an award-winning case study to your class.

ONLINE, MOBILE, AND SOCIAL MEDIA MARKETING

If you have a great product idea but no money, never fear: There's Kickstarter, an online crowdfunding site. Founded in 2008, Kickstarter enables companies to raise money from multiple individuals; since its founding, it has helped launch more than 91 000 projects. For example, when Pebble Technology Corporation created a "smart" wristwatch called Pebble, which works with iPhones or Android phones, it didn't have the funding to produce and market the device. So young CEO Eric Migicovsky turned to Kickstarter for crowdfunding. His modest goal was to raise US$100 000—but the company raised US$1 million in only one day and a total of US$10.27 million in just over one month! Nearly 70 000 people pre-ordered the $115 watch, and Pebble had to deliver on the promise. Kickstarter takes a 5 percent fee on the total funds raised, with Amazon Payments handling the processing of the funds. Kickstarter charges pledgers' credit cards, and the project creator receives the funds within only a few weeks.

The JOBS Act legislation in the United States, signed into law in 2012, provides a legal framework for this type of financing, which is expected grow even faster as a result. (Canadian legislators have been slow to regulate the crowdfunding industry, although a few provinces have proposed guidelines to do so.) However, Kickstarter and similar sites don't guarantee that the projects will be delivered as promised, and some people are concerned that *crowdfunding* will beget *crowdfrauding.*

QUESTIONS

1. Find another crowdfunding site and describe two projects featured on that site.

2. Learn more about the JOBS Act and how it impacts crowdfunding for start-up businesses. What protections are in place for investors with regard to crowdfrauding? What types of regulation exists in Canada for Canadian start-ups?

THINK LIKE A MARKETING MANAGER

Customer loyalty for online travel companies is low because the average consumer checks several different travel sites for the best prices on air travel, hotels, and rental cars before booking. With consumers highly motivated to make their selections based on price, online travel companies are trying to figure out other ways to differentiate themselves from the competition.

QUESTIONS

1. What macroenvironmental forces do you think are having the greatest positive and negative impact on online travel companies?

2. What do you think will be the most significant environmental issues facing the online travel industry in the next five years?

Valuable Learning Aids

A wealth of chapter-opening, within-chapter, and end-of-chapter learning devices helps students to engage with marketing by learning, linking, and applying major concepts:

- **Chapter openers.** Each active and integrative chapter-opening spread features an outline of chapter contents and learning objectives, a brief *Previewing the Concepts* section that introduces chapter concepts, and an opening vignette—an engaging, deeply developed, illustrated, and annotated marketing story that introduces the chapter material and sparks student interest.

- **Marketing@Work highlights.** Each chapter contains two highlight features that provide an in-depth look at the real marketing practices of large and small companies.

- **Reviewing the Concepts.** A summary at the end of each chapter reviews major chapter concepts and links them to chapter objectives.

- **Discussion Questions and Critical Thinking Exercises.** These sections at the end of each chapter help students keep track of and apply what they've learned in the chapter.

- **Applications and End-of-Chapter Cases.** Brief *Online, Mobile, and Social Media Marketing; Think Like a Marketing Manager; Marketing Ethics;* and *Marketing by the Numbers* sections at the end of each chapter provide short application cases that facilitate discussion of current issues and company situations in areas such as digital and social media marketing, ethics, and financial marketing analysis. The *End-of-Chapter Case* feature provides many new company cases for further analysis.

Additional resources include the following:

- **General Company Information: Boston Pizza.** Appendix 1 tells the story of Boston Pizza and illustrates how its marketing strategy has been a key element of its success.

- **Abbreviated Sample Marketing Plan: Boston Pizza.** Appendix 2 contains a sample marketing plan that helps students apply important marketing planning concepts.

- **Marketing by the Numbers.** An innovative Appendix 3 provides students with a comprehensive introduction to the marketing financial analysis that helps to guide, assess, and support marketing decisions.

More than ever before, the sixth Canadian edition of *Marketing: An Introduction* provides an effective and enjoyable total package for engaging students and moving them down the road to learning marketing!

Comprehensive Case: Boston Pizza

Despite its name, Boston Pizza is a purely Canadian success story. Well, Canadian–Greek success story, as it was Greek Gus Agioritis who opened the first BP restaurant in 1964 in Edmonton. It is still the subject of debate as to why "Boston" was chosen as the name of the now international Canadian chain. That seems inconsequential, however, as Boston Pizza has reached iconic status as Canada's casual family dining establishment meets sports bar hangout. With a 400-store milestone now in sight, and its 50th anniversary in the rear-view mirror, BP signs hover alongside Tim Hortons and Canadian Tire as this country's most familiar brands. From small things, big things one day do come.

We've used Boston Pizza as our comprehensive case in the sixth Canadian edition. This case material can be found in three key areas of the text:

1. *Comprehensive Cases: Boston Pizza.* At the end of each chapter is a short case about the company that illustrates how it employs the topics covered in that chapter.

2. *Appendix 1—General Company Information: Boston Pizza.* This appendix tells the story of Boston Pizza and illustrates how its marketing strategy has been a key element of its success.

3. *Appendix 2—Abbreviated Sample Marketing Plan: Boston Pizza.* Our second appendix contains a sample Boston Pizza marketing plan that helps you see how marketing concepts translate into real-life marketing strategies.

An alternative Comprehensive Case featuring Farmers Edge (which includes alternative Appendices 1 and 2) is available. Contact your local Pearson sales representative for more details.

BOSTON PIZZA COMPREHENSIVE CASE

The Wings Two-Four

Consumer behaviour is one of the most important concepts in marketing, and it focuses squarely on the importance of knowing your market—right down to personal habits, traits, and preferences. Successful Canadian consumer brands such as Tim Hortons, Canadian Tire, and Boston Pizza have stood the test of time because, above all else, they were built by Canadians for Canadians. And that identity has never been forgotten.

In early 2015, as Boston Pizza began the second half of its first century, it launched a brand-new promotional campaign called "We'll Make You a Fan." More than just a catchy tagline coined by an ad agency, the statement deliberately lends itself to multiple interpretations. While one intent was to emphasize BP's commitment to earn consumers' business, another was to reinforce BP's position in the sports bar category. And what better way to resonate with the quintessential Canadian sports fan than with a quintessential and uniquely Canadian icon—the two-four?

"If there's one thing Canadians know and love, it's the two-four. It's a part of our culture, especially during playoffs and summer weekends. But, until now, Canadians have never been able to eat one," said Steve Silverstone, Boston Pizza International's executive vice-president of marketing. "Unlike other two-fours, Canadians can crack open a Wings Two-Four virtually anywhere, any time they want. It really is the perfect union of BP's famous wings and the ubiquitous two-four." BP cleverly tied the chicken wing two-four with a hockey-glove-shaped pitcher to serve Molson Canadian beer during the 2015 Stanley Cup Playoffs.

Consumers have a lot of choices in where to eat out, and what to eat once they get there. Understanding the psychological triggers, such as the Canadian hockey fan's emotional tie to the social aspect of watching the playoffs, helps develop product and promotional ideas, and ultimately assists fans and foodies in their purchase decision.

QUESTIONS

1. Using the steps in the consumer purchase decision process, describe the thought process that a guest at Boston Pizza's Sports Bar might go through before deciding on the Wings Two-Four.
2. While the purchase decision has five known steps, a variety of decision influencers come into play as well. List these categories and provide an example as it pertains to a diner at Boston Pizza.

229

Abbreviated Sample Marketing Plan: Boston Pizza

This appendix provides a sample marketing plan for a new product offered by Boston Pizza. Deciding on a new product is no small feat, and it's a decision that is not made lightly. Although its main product is in its name, Boston Pizza continually monitors trends, listens to its customers, and updates its menu accordingly. Over its first 50 years, BP's menu has grown from pizza and spaghetti to a wide range of appetizers and main courses, expanding far beyond the original product offering as the demands of its customers have evolved. This is typically the origin of a new product idea for Boston Pizza, which must keep with the times in order to stay in business. But how are new product ideas fully developed, and how do they come to market?

Although a SWOT analysis appears several pages into a marketing plan, it's actually one of the first tasks required in product development. The determination of a new product idea either results from, or is validated by, a thorough SWOT analysis, followed by brainstorming ideas based on what the SWOT analysis reveals. For instance, if Boston Pizza were faced with a competitive threat, whereby fast-casual, quick-service, and family restaurants had introduced a product type that BP didn't currently carry, it would compel the marketing team to at least consider its suitability for BP's menu.

This situation might be compounded by a social opportunity identified by demand among BP's target market for a similar product. However, there may be hindrances exposed through the SWOT process as well, such as a specific weakness that BP would have to fix in order to proceed in developing the product idea. The main takeaway is that a thorough SWOT analysis is one of the first steps toward discovering an appropriate new-product idea.

After executing a SWOT analysis, the new-product development process must be deep and rigorous. While Boston Pizza may introduce several new menu items in any given year, none of them arrive on a guest's table without having been subjected to the checkpoints in this process. We recommend that you review Chapter 8, Developing and Managing Products and Services, as you go through the following example. The steps covered in that chapter, coupled with management's thorough analysis of Boston Pizza's current situation, can provide a number of plausible new product ideas.

Finally, whatever the new product idea is, management must ensure that it's consistent with the Boston Pizza brand—an intangible quality that speaks to the essence of the company. Typical Boston Pizza offerings exemplify such descriptors as *family-oriented, high quality, hearty,* and *delicious.* That's why nachos and wings make it in while other offerings, despite being trendy and healthy, would not make the cut.

What follows is marketing plan for a hypothetical new-product launch for Boston Pizza. This plan is structured using sections and sequencing similar to those of an actual marketing plan, but in no way are these reflective of Boston Pizza's objectives or strategies, which remain confidential. As such, everything that follows should be treated as a guideline only. The sample in part draws from the primary and secondary research used in the creation of the text's end-of-chapter comprehensive cases, but, again, it's not intended to represent Boston Pizza's actual marketing plan. It is deliberately hypothetical.

621

Teaching and Learning Support

A successful marketing course requires more than a well-written book. Today's classroom requires a dedicated teacher and a fully integrated teaching package. A total package of teaching and learning supplements extends this edition's emphasis on effective teaching and learning. The following aids support *Marketing: An Introduction*.

Farmers Edge. This alternative B-to-B comprehensive case (which includes alternative Appendices 1 and 2) is available and can be included in your text. Your local Pearson sales representative can provide you with more details.

Instructor's Resource Manual. This invaluable resource not only includes chapter-by-chapter teaching strategies; it also features notes about the PowerPoint slides. This supplement is available through Pearson Canada's online catalogue at catalogue.pearsoned.ca

Computerized Test Bank. Pearson's computerized test banks allow instructors to filter and select questions to create quizzes, tests, or homework. Instructors can revise questions or add their own, and may be able to choose print or online options. These questions are also available in Microsoft Word format.

PowerPoint Presentations. Point slides are available with this edition that help bring marketing concepts to life. The PowerPoints are also available to instructors through Pearson Canada's online catalogue at catalogue.pearsoned.ca

Learning Solutions Managers. Pearson's Learning Solutions Managers work with faculty and campus course designers to ensure that Pearson technology products, assessment tools, and online course materials are tailored to meet your specific needs. This highly qualified team is dedicated to helping schools take full advantage of a wide range of educational resources by assisting in the integration of a variety of instructional materials and media formats. Your local Pearson Canada sales representative can provide you with more details on this service program.

Pearson eText

The Pearson eText gives students access to their textbook any time, anywhere. In addition to enabling note taking, highlighting, and bookmarking, the Pearson eText offers interactive and sharing features. Rich media options may include videos, animations, interactive figures, and built-in assessments, all embedded in the text. Instructors can share their comments or highlights, and students can add their own, creating a tight community of learners within the class.

The Pearson eText may include a responsive design for easy viewing on smartphones and tablets. Many of these eTexts now have configurable reading settings, including resizable type and night-reading mode.

MyMarketingLab Resources

MyMarketingLab delivers **proven results** in helping individual students succeed. It provides **engaging experiences** that personalize, stimulate, and measure learning for each student. For the second Canadian edition, MyMarketingLab includes powerful new learning resources, including a new set of online lesson presentations to help students work through and master key business topics, a completely restructured Study Plan for student self-study, and a wealth of engaging assessment and teaching aids to help students and instructors explore unique learning pathways. MyMarketingLab online resources include:

- *NEW Interactive Lesson Presentations.* Students can now study key chapter topics and work through interactive assessments to test their knowledge and mastery of business concepts. Each presentation allows students to explore through expertly designed steps of reading, practising, and testing to ensure that students not only experience the content, but truly engage with each topic. Instructors also have the ability to assign quizzes, projects, and follow-up discussion questions relating to the online lessons to further develop the valuable learning experiences from the presentations.

- *NEW Study Plan.* MyMarketingLab offers students an engaging and focused self-study experience that is driven by a powerful new Study Plan. Students work through assessments in each chapter to gauge their understanding and target the topics that require additional practice. Along the way, they are recognized for their mastery of each topic and guided toward resources in areas that they might be struggling to understand.

- *NEW Dynamic Study Modules.* These new study modules allow students to work through groups of questions and check their understanding of foundational business topics. As students work through questions, the Dynamic Study Modules assess their knowledge and only show questions that still require practice. Dynamic Study Modules can be completed online using your computer, tablet, or mobile device.

- *Decision-Making Simulations.* Decision-Making Mini-Simulations walk students through key marketing decision-making scenarios to help them understand how marketing decisions are made. Students are asked to make important decisions relating to core marketing concepts. At each point, students receive feedback to help them understand the implications of their choices in the marketing environment. These simulations can now be assigned by instructors and graded directly through MyMarketingLab.

- *NEW Video Library & Exercises.* Robust video library with over 1000 videos that include easy-to-assign assessments. The video library also includes the ability for instructors to add YouTube or other video sources, allows for students to upload video submissions, and has polling and teamwork functions. Engaging videos explore business topics related to the theory students are learning in class; quizzes then assess students' comprehension of the concepts covered in each video.

- *Writing Assignments.* Each assisted-graded writing assignment is based on a question from the text and provides the perfect framework for instructors to efficiently assign, review, and grade students' written work. Questions are accompanied by a clickable rubric that allows instructors to review written work, provide immediate feedback, and assign a grade quickly and consistently.

- *NEW Learning Catalytics.* Learning Catalytics is a "bring your own device" student engagement, assessment, and classroom intelligence system. It allows instructors to engage students in class with a variety of question types designed to gauge student understanding.

- *Glossary Flashcards.* The Glossary Flashcards provide a targeted review of the Key Terms in each chapter. They allow learners to select the specific terms and chapters that they would like to study. The cards can also be sorted by Key Term or by definition to give students greater flexibility when studying.

- *NEW Canadian Sketch Animation Series.* Explore a NEW animation series that presents key marketing and business concepts from a uniquely Canadian perspective. This interesting and lively series of videos will help your students grasp course concepts that they find difficult.
- *NEW Marketing Metrics Activities.* This unique assignment type allows your students to practise their marketing metrics and analytics skills, improving their understanding of the quantitative aspects of marketing.

Acknowledgments

Writing a textbook, even when it is a new edition of a previous work, is a long, long process that requires a hard-working and dedicated team of people. On behalf of Gary Armstrong, Philip Kotler, and Lilly Anne Buchwitz, I would like to acknowledge the incredible team of editors, writers, and designers at Pearson without whom you would not be holding this book in your hands: Claudine O'Donnell, editor-in-chief; Carolin Sweig, acquisitions editor; Karen Townsend, program manager, Paul Donnelly, developmental editor; Jessica Hellen, project manager; Karen Alliston, copy editor; and Jessica McInnis, marketing manager.

There were many marketing instructors and professors at schools across Canada who provided valuable comments and suggestions for this edition. In particular, I would like to thank:

Di Best, *Nova Scotia Community College*

Francie Deveau, *Langara College*

Dawit Eshetu, *Niagara College*

Paul Leigh, *Kwantlen Polytechnic University*

Andrea Rennie, *Seneca College*

Mark Valvasori, *Mohawk College*

Jarrett Vaughan, *Langara College*

Duane Weaver, *Vancouver Island University*

Anne Marie Webb-Hughes, *British Columbia Institute of Technology*

" We owe many thanks to our families for their constant support and encouragement. To them, we dedicate this book. "

—Valerie Trifts

" To all my past, present, and future marketing and advertising students at Wilfrid Laurier University, Brock University, San Jose State University, and Humber College. You make me a better teacher every day. "

—Lilly Buchwitz

Jason Merritt/Getty Images

AFTER STUDYING THIS CHAPTER, YOU SHOULD BE ABLE TO

1 define marketing and outline the steps in the marketing process

2 explain the importance of understanding customers and the marketplace, and identify the five core marketplace concepts

3 identify the key elements of a customer-driven marketing strategy and discuss the marketing management orientations that guide marketing strategy

4 discuss customer relationship management and identify strategies for creating value *for* customers and capturing value *from* customers in return

5 describe the major trends and forces that are changing the marketing landscape in this age of relationships

Marketing: Creating and Capturing Customer Value

PREVIEWING THE CONCEPTS

This chapter introduces you to the basic concepts of marketing. We start with the question, What *is* marketing? Simply put, marketing is managing profitable customer relationships. The aim of marketing is to create value *for* customers and to capture value *from* customers in return. Next, we discuss the five steps in the marketing process—from understanding customer needs to designing customer-driven marketing strategies and integrated marketing programs, to building customer relationships and capturing value for the firm. Finally, we discuss the major trends and forces affecting marketing in this age of customer relationships. Understanding these basic concepts and forming your own ideas about what they really mean to you will give you a solid foundation for all that follows.

Let's start with a good story about marketing in action at Loblaw, whose clothing line, Joe Fresh, has become one of Canada's most successful apparel brands. The secret to Joe Fresh's success? It's really no secret at all: Creating customer value through its "Fresh style. Fresh price" philosophy is what keeps customers coming back. You'll see this theme of creating customer value to capture value in return repeated throughout this chapter and throughout the text.

LOBLAW'S DEVELOPMENT OF JOE FRESH: HOW "FRESH" IS CREATING VALUE FOR ITS CUSTOMERS

In the ever-changing and highly competitive fashion industry, Canadian brand Joe Fresh stands out as one of the best success stories in Canadian retail. How has it done that? By providing customers with fresh and affordable fashion in a retail setting where they shop every week—the grocery store!

As the largest food distributor and leading provider of general merchandise, drugstore, and financial products and services in Canada, Loblaw Companies operates more than 1050 stores under 22 different banners, including Superstore, Loblaw, Provigo, and Save Easy, to name a few. More than 14 million Canadians shop at a Loblaw store every week.

In an effort to compete with large U.S.-based retailers such as Walmart and Target, Loblaw began an aggressive expansion strategy to better satisfy the needs of its customers. In 2012, Loblaw spent approximately $40 million on customer-friendly initiatives such as pricing, store execution, and customer service in order to set itself apart from rivals like Sobeys and Walmart. And its strategy appears to be paying off, both financially and in terms of customer satisfaction. Corporate revenues in the first quarter of 2013 topped $7.2 billion, an increase of over 3.8 percent from the first quarter of 2012, and marketing research polls continue to show significant gains in in-store customer satisfaction for the company. In July 2013, Loblaw also announced what may be one of the largest mergers in Canadian retail history: a $12.4 billion deal to take over Canada's biggest drugstore chain, Shoppers Drug Mart. By 2015, Loblaw had grown to become one of Canada's largest private-sector employers, with approximately 192 000 full- and part-time employees; its second-quarter revenue had reached $10.5 billion.

Since the introduction of The Decadent Chocolate Chip Cookie, Loblaw has continued to provide the Canadian marketplace with a number of brands, such as PC GREEN, PC Organics, and PC Blue Menu. In fact, three of Canada's top brands include Loblaw's Life Brand, no name, and President's Choice brands. But perhaps the company's most successful (and, some would argue, surprising) brand creation is Joe Fresh, which helps set the shopping experience apart from other grocery stores and has grown to become the largest apparel brand in Canada in terms of both units sold and dollars.

Joe Fresh was launched in 2006, when Loblaw hired designer Joe Mimran (the designer of the Alfred Sung and Club Monaco labels) to create an affordable brand to be sold in the Canadian grocery stores. His involvement in the project, as well as the company's decision to hold its own fashion shows twice yearly, gave instant credibility to the Joe Fresh brand and led to rapid success in a very short time frame. In its first year alone, Joe Fresh was launched in over 100 retail locations in Canada, and by its third year it had grown to over 330 stores. After the hugely successful launch of the women's clothing line, Joe Fresh expanded to children's wear. "Kids and food shopping really go hand-in-hand," Mimran says, and "there is no better place for the mom to shop for kids' apparel than in the food store." The brand has further expanded to include menswear and a line of cosmetics.

In 2010, Joe Fresh launched its first stand-alone store in downtown Vancouver, targeting the younger fashionista market. Like everything else about the Joe Fresh brand, the stand-alone store concept was an instant success, and the company now operates 16 such stores in Canada. But Joe Fresh set its sights on an even more aggressive expansion strategy: entry into the highly competitive U.S. marketplace. Five years after the initial launch in Canada, the Joe Fresh brand was poised to take the United States by storm. It opened its first U.S.-based stand-alone store in March 2012 on Fifth Avenue in New York City. It was the brand's biggest store, with the largest assortment of merchandise, and it made the Joe Fresh brand visible to the entire world. It even prompted New York's then-mayor Michael Bloomberg to remark that it was "the greatest Canadian export since Justin Bieber." Since then, Joe Fresh has opened five other U.S.-based stand-alone stores and currently sells its merchandise in over 650 JCPenney stores across the United States. It appears that this brand truly resonates with consumers.

But what is it that makes Joe Fresh so successful? Although price is a key differentiator, what really makes the brand work is that it's highly accessible, and its styles are constantly changing to meet the demands of consumers. In fact, new product arrives at the stores every four weeks to maintain the brand's relevancy in the fickle fashion market. The company realized quickly that customers were in the store on a weekly basis, so the assortment had to constantly change to stay "fresh."

However, the company did face an initial challenge of selling clothing in a grocery store, as customers had to adapt their buying habits. "We quickly realized we couldn't merchandise like a grocery store," said Craig Hutchinson, senior vice-president of marketing and public relations (PR). Joe Fresh's success as a major fashion brand came about largely as a result of extensive PR efforts, with over 1 billion PR hits in the brand's first five years.

Joe Fresh maintains a consistent style and image in all its promotional materials and ties its brand to its original music. The 2013 spring collection premiered at Toronto's Fashion Week. "It's the ultimate compliment when people want to come and see what we're up to," said Joe Mimran. "It's not something you would normally expect from a brand that trades at these price points and that trades the way we do—in supermarkets." And, as he went on to explain, "We tend to be a brand that filters the trends and offers it to consumers. We distill it more and are a little more realistic about our customer base." In essence, Joe Fresh has succeeded by providing customers with value—perceived customer value based on providing affordable high fashion that is accessible and constantly changing to meet customers' lifestyles.

Despite the departure of founder Joe Mimran in early 2015, the future of the Joe Fresh brand looks bright. For example, Aldo Group, one of Canada's largest shoe retailers, has signed a deal to design a shoe line exclusively for Joe Fresh. And at Toronto's 2015 Fashion Week, Joe Fresh announced that it was investing in Canada's fashion future by donating $1 million to Ryerson University's Fashion Zone in order to create Canada's first fashion innovation centre. Finally, Loblaw's continued commitment to the Save the Children Bangladesh and the Centre for Rehabilitation of the Paralysed after the 2013 factory collapse in Bangladesh certainly extends the creation and capturing of customer value well beyond merely making a great product.[1]

TODAY'S successful companies have one thing in common: Like Loblaw, they are strongly customer focused and heavily committed to marketing. These companies share a passion for understanding and satisfying customer needs in well-defined target markets. They motivate everyone in the organization to help build lasting customer relationships based on creating value.

Customer relationships and value have become especially important. Facing dramatic technological advances and deep economic, social, and environmental challenges, today's customers are relating digitally with companies and each other, spending more carefully, and reassessing their relationships with brands. Digital, mobile, and social media developments have revolutionized how consumers shop and interact, in turn calling for new marketing strategies and tactics. In these fast-changing times, it's more important than ever to build strong customer relationships based on real and enduring customer value.

We'll discuss the exciting new challenges facing both customers and marketers later in the chapter. But first, let's introduce the basics of marketing.

What Is Marketing? LO1

←●– **Simulate** on MyMarketingLab

What is Marketing?

Marketing, more than any other business function, deals with customers. Although we will soon explore more-detailed definitions of marketing, perhaps the simplest definition is this one: *Marketing is managing profitable customer relationships.* The twofold goal of marketing is to attract new customers by promising superior value and to keep and grow current customers by delivering satisfaction.

For example, McDonald's fulfills its "i'm lovin' it" motto by being "our customers' favourite place and way to eat" the world over, giving it nearly as much market share as its nearest four competitors combined. Walmart has become the world's largest retailer—and the world's second-largest company—by delivering on its promise, "Save Money. Live Better." Facebook has attracted more than a billion active web and mobile users worldwide

Justin Lewis/Getty Images

Exhibit 1.1 Marketing is all around you, in good old traditional forms and in a host of new forms, from websites and mobile phone apps to videos and online social media.

by helping them to "connect and share" with the people in their lives."[2]

Sound marketing is critical to the success of every organization. Large for-profit firms, such as Google, Procter & Gamble, Toyota, and Microsoft, use marketing. But so do not-for-profit organizations, such as universities, hospitals, museums, symphony orchestras, and even churches.

You already know a lot about marketing—it's all around you. Marketing comes to you in the good old traditional forms: You see it in the abundance of products at your nearby shopping mall and in the ads that fill your TV screen, spice up your magazines, or stuff your mailbox. But in recent years, marketers have assembled a host of new marketing approaches: everything from imaginative websites and mobile phone apps to blogs, online videos, and social media. These new approaches do more than just blast out messages to the masses. They reach you directly, personally, and interactively. Today's marketers want to become a part of your life and enrich your experiences with their brands—to help you *live* their brands.

Whether at home, at school, where you work, or where you play, you see marketing in almost everything you do. Yet there is much more to marketing than meets the consumer's casual eye. Behind it all is a massive network of people and activities competing for your attention and purchases. This book will give you a complete introduction to the basic concepts and practices of today's marketing. In this chapter, we begin by defining marketing and the marketing process.

Marketing Defined

What *is* marketing? Many people think of marketing as only selling and advertising. We are bombarded every day with TV commercials, catalogues, spiels from salespeople, and online pitches. However, selling and advertising are only the tip of the marketing iceberg.

Today, marketing must be understood not in the old sense of making a sale—"telling and selling"—but in the new sense of *satisfying customer needs*. If the marketer engages consumers effectively, understands their needs, develops products that provide superior customer value, and prices, distributes, and promotes them well, these products will sell easily. In fact, according to management guru Peter Drucker, "The aim of marketing is to make selling unnecessary."[3] Selling and advertising are only part of a larger *marketing mix*—a set of marketing tools that work together to satisfy customer needs and build customer relationships.

Broadly defined, marketing is a social and managerial process by which individuals and organizations obtain what they need and want through creating and exchanging value with others. In a narrower business context, marketing involves building profitable, value-laden exchange relationships with customers. Hence, we define **marketing** as the process by which companies create value for customers and build strong customer relationships in order to capture value from customers in return.[4]

Marketing

The process by which companies create value for customers and build strong customer relationships in order to capture value from customers in return.

The Marketing Process

Figure 1.1 presents a simple, five-step model of the marketing process for creating and capturing customer value. In the first four steps, companies work to understand consumers, create customer value, and build strong customer relationships. In the final step, companies reap the rewards of creating superior customer value. By creating value *for*

FIGURE 1.1 A Simple Model of the Marketing Process

consumers, they in turn capture value *from* consumers in the form of sales, profits, and long-term customer equity.

In this chapter and the next, we will examine the five steps of this simple model of marketing. In this chapter, we review each step but focus more on the customer relationship steps—understanding customers, building customer relationships, and capturing value from customers. In Chapter 2, we look more deeply into the second and third steps—designing value-creating marketing strategies and constructing marketing programs.

Understanding the Marketplace and Customer Needs LO2

As a first step, marketers need to understand customer needs and wants and the marketplace in which they operate. We examine five core customer and marketplace concepts: (1) *needs, wants, and demands*; (2) *market offerings (products, services, and experiences)*; (3) *value and satisfaction*; (4) *exchanges and relationships*; and (5) *markets*.

Customer Needs, Wants, and Demands

The most basic concept underlying marketing is that of human needs. Human **needs** are states of felt deprivation. They include basic *physical* needs for food, clothing, warmth, and safety; *social* needs for belonging and affection; and *individual* needs for knowledge and self-expression. Marketers did not create these needs; they are a basic part of the human makeup.

Wants are the form human needs take as they are shaped by culture and individual personality. A Canadian *needs* food but *wants* a breakfast sandwich and a large double-double from Tim Hortons. Wants are shaped by one's society and are described in terms of objects that will satisfy those needs. When backed by buying power, wants become **demands**. Given their wants and resources, people demand products and services with benefits that add up to the most value and satisfaction.

Outstanding marketing companies go to great lengths to learn about and understand their customers' needs, wants, and demands. They conduct consumer research, analyze mountains of customer data, and observe customers as they shop and interact, offline and online. People at all levels of the company—including top management—stay close to customers. For example, Kroger chairman and CEO David Dillon regularly dons blue jeans and roams the aisles of local Kroger supermarkets, blending in with and talking to other shoppers. Similarly, Walmart president and CEO Michael Duke and his entire executive team make regular store and in-home visits with customers to get to know them and understand their needs. Top McDonald's marketers hold frequent Twitter chats, connecting directly with McDonald's Twitter followers, both fans and critics, to learn their thoughts about topics ranging from nutrition and sustainability to products and brand promotions.[5]

Needs
States of felt deprivation.

Wants
The form human needs take as they are shaped by culture and individual personality.

Demands
Human wants that are backed by buying power.

Tom Hanson/CP

Exhibit 1.2 Market offerings are not limited to physical products: The David Suzuki Foundation powerfully markets the idea that government, businesses, and individuals can be involved in creating a healthy and sustainable environment.

Market offerings
Some combination of products, services, information, or experiences offered to a market to satisfy a need or want.

Marketing myopia
The mistake of paying more attention to the specific products a company offers than to the benefits and experiences produced by these products.

Market Offerings—Products, Services, and Experiences

Consumers' needs and wants are fulfilled through **market offerings**—some combination of products, services, information, or experiences offered to a market to satisfy a need or a want. Market offerings are not limited to physical *products*. They also include *services*—activities or benefits offered for sale that are essentially intangible and do not result in the ownership of anything. Examples include banking, airline, hotel, retailing, and home repair services.

More broadly, market offerings also include other entities, such as *persons*, *places*, *organizations*, *information*, and *ideas*. For example, the David Suzuki Foundation powerfully markets the idea that individuals and organizations can be involved in creating a healthy and sustainable environment. Travel Alberta markets the province as one of the most beautiful tourist destinations in the world. And with its recent "Take the Pledge" campaign, Sport Nova Scotia markets the precepts of fair play and sportsmanship.

Many sellers make the mistake of paying more attention to the specific products they offer than to the benefits and experiences produced by these products. These sellers suffer from **marketing myopia**. They are so taken with their products that they focus only on existing wants and lose sight of underlying customer needs.[6] They forget that a product is only a tool to solve a consumer problem. A manufacturer of quarter-inch drill bits may think that the customer needs a drill bit. But what the customer *really* needs is a quarter-inch hole. These sellers will have trouble if a new product comes along that serves the customer's need better or less expensively. The customer will have the same *need* but will *want* the new product.

Smart marketers look beyond the attributes of the products and services they sell. By orchestrating several services and products, they create *brand experiences* for consumers. For example, you don't just visit Walt Disney World Resort; you immerse yourself and your family in a world of wonder, a world where dreams come true and things still work the way they should. You're "in the heart of the magic!" says Disney.

Similarly, Angry Birds is much more than just a mobile game app. To more than 200 million fans in 116 countries, it's a deeply involving experience. As one observers puts it, "Angry Birds land is a state of mind—a

Archivo CEET GDA Photo Service/Newscom

Exhibit 1.3 Marketing experiences: More than just a mobile game app, Angry Birds is "a digital immersion in addictively cheerful destruction." Creator Rovio plans to expand the Angry Birds experience through animated videos, licensed products, and even Angry Birds–branded playgrounds and activity parks.

digital immersion in addictively cheerful destruction, a refuge from the boredom of subway commutes and doctors' waiting rooms, where the fine art of sling-shotting tiny brightly hued birds at wooden fortresses to vanquish pigs taking shelter inside makes eminent sense and is immensely satisfying." The game's creator, Rovio Entertainment, plans to expand the Angry Birds experience through everything from animated short videos (called *Angry Birds Toons*) and 3-D animated movies to a growing list of licensed toys, apparel, yard art, and even Angry Birds–branded playgrounds and activity parks.[7]

Customer Value and Satisfaction

Consumers usually face a broad array of products and services that might satisfy a given need. How do they choose among these many market offerings? Customers form expectations about the value and satisfaction that various market offerings will deliver and buy accordingly. Satisfied customers buy again and tell others about their good experiences. Dissatisfied customers often switch to competitors and disparage the product to others.

Marketers must be careful to set the right level of expectations. If they set expectations too low, they may satisfy those who buy but fail to attract enough buyers. If they set expectations too high, buyers will be disappointed. Customer value and customer satisfaction are key building blocks for developing and managing customer relationships. We will revisit these core concepts later in the chapter.

Exchanges and Relationships

Marketing occurs when people decide to satisfy their needs and wants through exchange relationships. **Exchange** is the act of obtaining a desired object from someone by offering something in return. In the broadest sense, the marketer tries to bring about a response to some market offering. The response may be more than simply buying or trading products and services. A political candidate, for instance, wants votes; a church wants membership; an orchestra wants an audience; and a social action group wants idea acceptance.

Exchange
The act of obtaining a desired object from someone by offering something in return.

Marketing consists of actions taken to create, maintain, and grow desirable exchange *relationships* with target audiences involving a product, service, idea, or other object. Companies want to build strong relationships by consistently delivering superior customer value. We will expand on the important concept of managing customer relationships later in the chapter.

Markets

The concepts of exchange and relationships lead to the concept of a market. A **market** is the set of actual and potential buyers of a product or service. These buyers share a particular need or want that can be satisfied through exchange relationships.

Market
The set of all actual and potential buyers of a product or service.

Marketing means managing markets to bring about profitable customer relationships. However, creating these relationships takes work. Sellers must search for buyers, identify their needs, design good market offerings, set prices for them, promote them, and store and deliver them. Activities such as consumer research, product development, communication, distribution, pricing, and service are core marketing activities.

Although we normally think of marketing as being carried out by sellers, buyers also carry out marketing. Consumers market when they search for products, interact with companies to obtain information, and make their purchases. In fact, today's digital technologies, from websites and smartphone apps to the explosion of social media, have empowered consumers and made marketing a truly two-way affair. Thus, in addition to customer relationship management, today's marketers must deal effectively with *customer-managed relationships*. Marketers are no longer asking only "How can we influence our customers?" but also "How can our customers influence us?" and even "How can our customers influence each other?"

FIGURE 1.2 A Modern Marketing System

Figure 1.2 shows the main elements in a marketing system. Marketing involves serving a market of final consumers in the face of competitors. The company and competitors research the market and interact with consumers to understand their needs. Then they create and send their market offerings and messages to consumers, either directly or through marketing intermediaries. Each party in the system is affected by major environmental forces (demographic, economic, natural, technological, political, and social/cultural).

Each party in the system adds value for the next level. The arrows represent relationships that must be developed and managed. Thus, a company's success at building profitable relationships depends not only on its own actions but also on how well the entire system serves the needs of final consumers. Walmart cannot fulfill its promise of low prices unless its suppliers provide merchandise at low costs. And Ford cannot deliver a high-quality car-ownership experience unless its dealers provide outstanding sales and service.

◀●▶ **Simulate** on MyMarketingLab

Service Marketing

Marketing management
The art and science of choosing target markets and building profitable relationships with them.

Designing a Customer-Driven Marketing Strategy LO3

Once it fully understands consumers and the marketplace, marketing management can design a customer-driven marketing strategy. We define **marketing management** as the art and science of choosing target markets and building profitable relationships with them. The marketing manager's aim is to find, attract, keep, and grow target customers by creating, delivering, and communicating superior customer value.

To design a winning marketing strategy, the marketing manager must answer two important questions: *What customers will we serve (what's our target market)?* and *How can we serve these customers best (what's our value proposition)?* We will discuss these marketing strategy concepts briefly here and then look at them in more detail in Chapter 2.

Selecting Customers to Serve

The company must first decide *whom* it will serve. It does this by dividing the market into segments of customers (*market segmentation*) and selecting which segments it will go after (*target marketing*). Some people think of marketing management as finding as many customers as possible and increasing demand. But marketing managers know that they cannot serve all customers in every way. By trying to serve all customers, they may not serve any customers well. Instead, the company wants to select only those customers whom it can serve well and profitably. For example, Holt Renfrew profitably targets affluent professionals; Dollarama profitably targets families with more modest means.

Ultimately, marketing managers must decide which customers they want to target and the level, timing, and nature of their demand. Simply put, marketing management is *customer management* and *demand management*.

Choosing a Value Proposition

The company must also decide how it will serve targeted customers—how it will *differentiate and position* itself in the marketplace. A brand's *value proposition* is the set of benefits or values it promises to deliver to consumers to satisfy their needs. Facebook helps you "connect and share with the people in your life," whereas YouTube "provides a place for people to connect, inform, and inspire others across the globe." BMW promises "the ultimate driving machine," whereas the diminutive smart car suggests that you "Open your mind to the car that challenges the status quo." New Balance's Minimus shoes are "like barefoot only better"; and with Vibram FiveFingers shoes, "You are the technology."

Exhibit 1.4 **Value propositions:** With Vibram FiveFingers shoes, "You are the technology."

Vibram USA, Inc.

Such value propositions differentiate one brand from another. They answer the customer's question, "Why should I buy your brand rather than a competitor's?" Companies must design strong value propositions that give them the greatest advantage in their target markets. For example, Vibram FiveFingers shoes promise the best of two worlds—running with shoes and without: "You get all the health and performance benefits of barefoot running combined with a Vibram sole that protects you from elements and obstacles in your path." With Vibram FiveFingers shoes, "The more it looks like a foot, the more it acts like a foot."

Marketing Management Orientations

Marketing management wants to design strategies that will build profitable relationships with target consumers. But what *philosophy* should guide these marketing strategies? What weight should be given to the interests of customers, the organization, and society? Very often, these interests conflict.

There are five alternative concepts under which organizations design and carry out their marketing strategies: the *production, product, selling, marketing,* and *societal marketing concepts.*

The Production Concept The **production concept** holds that consumers will favour products that are available and highly affordable. Therefore, management should focus on improving production and distribution efficiency. This concept is one of the oldest orientations that guide sellers.

The production concept is still a useful philosophy in some situations. For example, both personal computer maker Lenovo and home appliance maker Haier dominate the highly competitive, price-sensitive Chinese market through low labour costs, high production efficiency, and mass distribution. However, although useful in some situations, the production concept can lead to marketing myopia. Companies adopting this orientation run a major risk of focusing too narrowly on their own operations and losing sight of the real objective—satisfying customer needs and building customer relationships.

The Product Concept The **product concept** holds that consumers will favour products that offer the most in quality, performance, and innovative features. Under this concept, marketing strategy focuses on making continual product improvements.

Production concept
The idea that consumers will favour products that are available and highly affordable; therefore, the organization should focus on improving production and distribution efficiency.

Product concept
The idea that consumers will favour products that offer the most quality, performance, and features; therefore, the organization should devote its energy to making continual product improvements.

Product quality and improvement are important parts of most marketing strategies. However, focusing *only* on the company's products can also lead to marketing myopia. For example, some manufacturers believe that if they can "build a better mousetrap, the world will beat a path to their door." But they are often rudely shocked. Buyers may be looking for a better solution to a mouse problem but not necessarily for a better mousetrap. The better solution might be a chemical spray, an exterminating service, a house cat, or something else that suits their needs even better than a mousetrap. Furthermore, a better mousetrap will not sell unless the manufacturer designs, packages, and prices it attractively; places it in convenient distribution channels; brings it to the attention of people who need it; and convinces buyers that it is a better product.

Selling concept
The idea that consumers will not buy enough of the firm's products unless the firm undertakes a large-scale selling and promotion effort.

The Selling Concept Many companies follow the **selling concept**, which holds that consumers will not buy enough of the firm's products unless it undertakes a large-scale selling and promotion effort. The selling concept is typically practised with unsought goods—those that buyers do not normally think of buying, such as insurance or burial plots. These industries must be good at tracking down prospects and selling them on a product's benefits.

Such aggressive selling, however, carries high risks. It focuses on creating sales transactions rather than on building long-term, profitable customer relationships. The aim is often to sell what the company makes rather than making what the market wants. It assumes that customers who are coaxed into buying the product will like it. Or, if they don't like it, they will possibly forget their disappointment and buy it again later. These are usually poor assumptions.

Marketing concept
A philosophy in which achieving organizational goals depends on knowing the needs and wants of target markets and delivering the desired satisfactions better than competitors do.

The Marketing Concept The **marketing concept** holds that achieving organizational goals depends on knowing the needs and wants of target markets and delivering the desired satisfactions better than competitors do. Under the marketing concept, customer focus and value are the *paths* to sales and profits. Instead of a product-centred *make-and-sell* philosophy, the marketing concept is a customer-centred *sense-and-respond* philosophy. The job is not to find the right customers for your product but to find the right products for your customers.

Figure 1.3 contrasts the selling concept and the marketing concept. The selling concept takes an *inside-out* perspective. It starts with the factory, focuses on the company's existing products, and calls for heavy selling and promotion to obtain profitable sales. It focuses primarily on customer conquest—getting short-term sales with little concern about who buys or why.

In contrast, the marketing concept takes an *outside-in* perspective. As Herb Kelleher, the colourful founder of Southwest Airlines, once put it, "We don't have a marketing department; we have a customer department." The marketing concept starts with a well-defined market, focuses on customer needs, and integrates all the marketing activities that

FIGURE 1.3 · The Selling and Marketing Concepts Contrasted

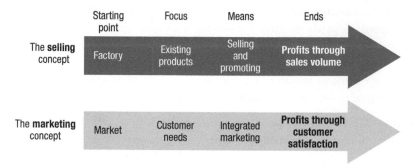

affect customers. In turn, it yields profits by creating relationships with the right customers based on customer value and satisfaction.

Implementing the marketing concept often means more than simply responding to customers' stated desires and obvious needs. *Customer-driven* companies research customers deeply to learn about their desires, gather new product ideas, and test product improvements. Such customer-driven marketing usually works well when a clear need exists and when customers know what they want.

In many cases, however, customers *don't* know what they want or even what is possible. As Henry Ford once remarked, "If I'd asked people what they wanted, they would have said faster horses."[8] For example, even 20 years ago, how many consumers would have thought to ask for now-commonplace products such as tablet computers, smartphones, digital cameras, 24-hour online buying, and GPS systems in their cars? Such situations call for *customer-driven* marketing—understanding customer needs even better than customers themselves do and creating products and services that meet both existing and latent needs, now and in the future. As an executive at 3M put it, "Our goal is to lead customers where they want to go before *they* know where they want to go."

The Societal Marketing Concept The **societal marketing concept** questions whether the pure marketing concept overlooks possible conflicts between consumer *short-run wants* and consumer *long-run welfare*. Is a firm that satisfies the immediate needs and wants of target markets always doing what's best for its consumers in the long run? The societal marketing concept holds that marketing strategy should deliver value to customers in a way that maintains or improves both the consumer's *and society's* well-being. It calls for *sustainable marketing*—socially and environmentally responsible marketing that meets the present needs of consumers and businesses while also preserving or enhancing the ability of future generations to meet their needs.

Even more broadly, many leading business and marketing thinkers are now preaching the concept of *shared value*, which recognizes that societal needs, not just economic needs, define markets.[9] The concept of shared value focuses on creating economic value in a way that also creates value for society. A growing number of companies known for their hard-nosed approaches to business—such as GE, Google, IBM, Intel, Johnson & Johnson, Nestlé, Unilever, and Walmart—are rethinking the interactions between society and corporate performance. They are concerned not just with short-term economic gains, but with the well-being of their customers, the depletion of natural resources vital to their businesses, the viability of key suppliers, and the economic well-being of the communities in which they produce and sell. One prominent marketer calls this "Marketing 3.0." "Marketing 3.0 organizations are values-driven," he says. "I'm not talking about being value-driven. I'm talking about 'values' plural, where values amount to caring about the state of the world."[10]

As Figure 1.4 shows, companies should balance three considerations in setting their

Societal marketing concept
The idea that a company's marketing decisions should consider consumers' wants, the company's requirements, consumers' long-run interests, and society's long-run interests.

Royal Bank of Canada

Exhibit 1.5 The societal marketing concept: RBC takes a leadership role in responsibility to the community and environmental sustainability. For example, its Blue Water Project has committed $50 million to help provide access to clean water now and for future generations.

FIGURE 1.4 The Considerations Underlying the Societal Marketing Concept

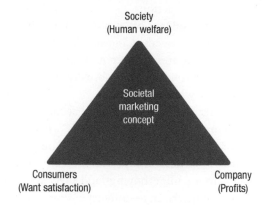

marketing strategies: company profits, consumer wants, *and* society's interests. RBC does this well:

> RBC seeks more than just short-run sales and profits. Its underlying philosophy is to operate with integrity at all times and strive to have a positive impact around the globe. The firm supports many worthy causes that make real differences in people's lives, with an emphasis on children and youth, sports, emerging artists, diversity, and inclusion. RBC has also established its own environmental policy in the areas of climate change, biodiversity, and fresh water. For example, the RBC Blue Water Project is a 10-year global charitable commitment of $50 million to help provide access to drinkable, swimmable, fishable water, now and for future generations. To date, the company has pledged over $41 million to more than 700 charitable organizations worldwide that protect watersheds and promote access to clean drinking water.[11]

Preparing an Integrated Marketing Plan and Program

The company's marketing strategy outlines which customers it will serve and how it will create value for these customers. Next, the marketer develops an integrated marketing program that will actually deliver the intended value to target customers. The marketing program builds customer relationships by transforming the marketing strategy into action. It consists of the firm's *marketing mix*: the set of marketing tools the firm uses to implement its marketing strategy.

The major marketing mix tools are classified into four broad groups, called the *four Ps* of marketing: product, price, place, and promotion. To deliver on its value proposition, the firm must first create a need-satisfying market offering (product). It must then decide how much it will charge for the offering (price) and how it will make the offering available to target consumers (place). Finally, it must communicate with target customers about the offering and persuade them of its merits (promotion). The firm must blend each marketing mix tool into a comprehensive integrated marketing program that communicates and delivers the intended value to chosen customers. We will explore marketing programs and the marketing mix in much more detail in later chapters.

◄●▶ **Simulate** on MyMarketingLab ## Building Customer Relationships LO4

Service Marketing

The first three steps in the marketing process—understanding the marketplace and customer needs, designing a customer-driven marketing strategy, and constructing a marketing program—all lead up to the fourth and most important step: building and managing profitable customer relationships. We first discuss the basics of customer relationship management. Then, we examine how companies go about engaging customers on a deeper level in this age of digital and social marketing.

Customer Relationship Management

Customer relationship management is perhaps the most important concept of modern marketing. In the broadest sense, **customer relationship management** is the overall process of building and maintaining profitable customer relationships by delivering superior customer value and satisfaction. It deals with all aspects of acquiring, keeping, and growing customers.

Relationship Building Blocks: Customer Value and Satisfaction The key to building lasting customer relationships is to create superior customer value and satisfaction. Satisfied customers are more likely to be loyal customers and give the company a larger share of their business.

CUSTOMER VALUE Attracting and retaining customers can be a difficult task. Customers often face a bewildering array of products and services from which to choose. A customer buys from the firm that offers the highest **customer-perceived value**—the customer's evaluation of the difference between all the benefits and all the costs of a market offering relative to those of competing offers. Importantly, customers often do not judge values and costs "accurately" or "objectively." They act on *perceived* value.

To some consumers, value might mean sensible products at affordable prices. To other consumers, however, value might mean paying more to get more. For example, a top-of-the-line Weber Summit E-670 barbecue grill carries a suggested retail price of US$2600, more than five times the price of competitor Char-Broil's best grill. According to Weber, the stainless-steel Summit grill "embraces true grilling luxury with the highest quality materials, exclusive features, and stunning looks." However, Weber's marketing also suggests that the grill is a real value, even at the premium price. For the money, you get practical features such as all-stainless-steel construction, spacious cooking and work areas, lighted control knobs, a tuck-away motorized rotisserie system, and an LED tank scale that lets you know how much propane you have left in the tank. Is the Weber Summit grill worth the premium price compared with less expensive grills? To many consumers, the answer is no. But to the target segment of affluent, hard-core grillers, the answer is yes.[12] (For another example of customer-perceived value, see Marketing@Work 1.1.)

CUSTOMER SATISFACTION Customer satisfaction depends on the product's perceived performance relative to a buyer's expectations. If the product's performance falls short of expectations, the customer is dissatisfied. If performance matches expectations, the customer is satisfied. If performance exceeds expectations, the customer is highly satisfied or delighted.

Outstanding marketing companies go out of their way to keep important customers satisfied. Most studies show that higher levels of customer satisfaction lead to greater customer loyalty, which in turn results in better company performance. Smart companies aim to delight customers by promising only what they can deliver and then delivering more than they promise. Delighted customers not only make repeat purchases but also become willing marketing partners and "customer evangelists" who spread the word about their good experiences to others.

For companies interested in delighting customers, exceptional value and service become part of the overall company culture. For example, year after year, JetBlue ranks at or near the top of the airline industry in terms of customer satisfaction. The company's slogan—"JetBlue: YOU ABOVE ALL"—tells customers that they are at the heart of the company's strategy and culture:

> JetBlue has an evangelistic zeal for creating first-rate, customer-satisfying experiences. At JetBlue, customer care starts with basic amenities that exceed customer expectations, especially for a low-cost carrier—leather coach seats with extra leg room, free premium snacks, free satellite TV. But it's the *human* touch that really makes JetBlue special. JetBlue employees not only *know* the company's core values—safety, integrity, caring, passion, and fun—they *live* them. Those heart-felt values result in outstanding customer experiences, making JetBlue

Customer relationship management
The overall process of building and maintaining profitable customer relationships by delivering superior customer value and satisfaction.

Customer-perceived value
The customer's evaluation of the difference between all the benefits and all the costs of a marketing offer relative to those of competing offers.

Customer satisfaction
The extent to which a product's perceived performance matches a buyer's expectations.

MARKETING@WORK   1.1

Canada Goose: Authenticity Is Key to Customer Value

In 1957, Sam Tick founded Metro Sportswear, which produced a modest line of jackets and woollen shirts in a small manufacturing facility in Toronto. The 1970s saw the business expand to include the production of custom-ordered down-filled coats for the Canadian Rangers, city police forces, and other government workers. In 1985, the company was renamed Snow Goose, and in the early 1990s it began selling its products in Europe under the name Canada Goose. By the late 1990s the modern era of Canada Goose had begun and the real expansion of the brand began. Over the past 10 years or so, Canada Goose parka sales have soared within Canada and in more than 40 other countries worldwide. In fact, Canada Goose placed 102nd on the 2014 Profit 500 list of fastest growing Canadian companies, with a 641 percent growth in revenues over the previous five years.

How did Canada Goose achieve such phenomenal growth? A number of factors have contributed to the company's success. First, Canada Goose very carefully chose spokespeople who were highly credible users of the brand. Lance Mackey, a four-time Iditarod and Yukon Quest champion, grew up in Alaska and is known as one of the best dogsled mushers in the world. Ray Zahab, ultra marathon runner and adventurer, and Laurie Skreslet, the first Canadian to reach the summit of Mount Everest, also joined the list of Canada Goose spokespeople. These individuals have enormous credibility with the company's core customer segment, which consists of polar expeditioners, oil riggers, and police departments alike. Well-known Canadian athletes have also joined the list of "Goose People," including Olympic soccer player Karina LeBlanc, Toronto Raptors NBA player Amir Johnson, and tennis superstar Milos Raonic.

Rather than using traditional advertising campaigns to develop brand awareness, Canada Goose relied on consumer-driven marketing tactics to build its brand. In the early stages of the company's marketing efforts, product was placed on people who worked outside in cold environments, such as bouncers at nightclubs or doormen at hotels, who could give the brand credibility. Today, Canada Goose still employs several nontraditional forms of promotion to build brand awareness, from supplying Fairmont Hotels' doormen and valets with Expedition parkas to running a Canada Goose coat check at Toronto Maple Leafs and Toronto Raptors games, where fans are offered the chance to try on parkas while checking their own garments.

Celebrities caught on camera and actors in feature films wearing the brand have also contributed to Canada Goose's success. Hayden Christensen was photographed wearing one at the Vancouver 2010 Winter Olympics. Daniel Radcliffe is often spotted wearing his Canada Goose parka. The brand has been used in the film industry for decades behind the scenes, but now appears on screen as well in such movies as *The Day After Tomorrow*, *Eight Below*, *National Treasure*, *Good Luck Chuck*, and *Whiteout*.

While Canada Goose has long been a bestseller in Europe, it has also been successful in the highly competitive U.S. fashion market. It currently sells its products at premium department stores such as Barneys and Saks Fifth Avenue and is expanding its product offerings via collaborations with Italian cashmere and wool manufacturer Loro Piana and Japanese designer Yuki Matsuda.

Canada Goose is a company that has always chosen its own path and stayed true to its brand. As a result, it has attracted a diverse base of customers who are interested in everything from function to fashion. This is perhaps the biggest reason why Canada Goose has been able to build lasting customer relationships by creating superior customer value and satisfaction. Customers know what to expect when they buy a Canada Goose product. For example, despite the growing trend in the textile industry to ship production to overseas markets, Canada Goose still manufactures approximately 250 000 parkas per year at its plant in Toronto. An in-house designer cuts the fabric, and dozens of

Exhibit 1.6 Quality, functionality, and style are central to the Canada Goose brand and are key to building customer-perceived value.

Kevin Van Paassen/The Globe and Mail/CP

sewers assemble the coats in much the same way as they did in the beginning. While the production of some accessories, such as gloves and mittens, has been moved to overseas plants, the company opted not to move its manufacturing of coats to Asia because it realized early on that having its clothes made in Canada was integral to the authenticity of its brand.

Canada Goose has also faced criticism from animal rights groups protesting the use of coyote fur on its hoods and down feathers in its coats. The company adheres to very strict policies on the ethical procurement of these materials, which it outlines clearly on its corporate website. Because animal products are central to the quality and warmth of Canada Goose coats, the company has

opted to continue their use and to do so in an ethical and sustainable manner.

Quality, functionality, and style are central to the Canada Goose brand, and maintaining these properties is key to the brand's authenticity. What does this mean for the customers' perceived value of the Canada Goose brand? It depends on whom you ask. While some consumers would question Canada Goose's hefty price tag and point to less expensive alternatives such as The North Face or Columbia, rarely would Canada Goose customers question the value of their chosen brand. For the extreme-weather consumer, perceived value comes from the brand's functionality and protection from severe weather conditions. For the fashion-conscious consumer, the appeal is

more than just about warmth. The premium pricing and limited availability (Canada Goose has deliberately under-supplied the market to protect against oversaturation) have led to Canada Goose becoming a symbol of status and wealth. So, whether you ask an adventurer trekking to the North Pole or a student trekking across the University of Alberta's campus if purchasing a Canada Goose jacket was worth it, the answer will most likely be yes!

Sources: Grant Robertson, "Year of the Goose," *Globe and Mail*, February 25, 2010, www.theglobeandmail.com/report-onbusiness/rob-magazine/year-of-the-goose/article1480120; David Kaufman, "Northern Exposure," *Financial Times*, January 13, 2012, www.ft.com/cms/s/2/b18d3dc8-36fb-11e1-b741-00144feabdc0.html#axzz1jSZ6VwAz; "Profit 500 Canada's Fastest-Growing Companies," www.profitguide.com/microsite/profit500/2014; and Canada Goose's corporate website, www.canada-goose.com.

customers the most satisfied and enthusiastic of any in the airline industry.

In fact, JetBlue often lets its customers do the talking. For example, its "Experience JetBlue" website and *Blue Tales* blog feature real first-person testimonials from devoted fans. And in a former advertising campaign, called "Sincerely, JetBlue," actual customers gave voice to specific service heroics by dedicated JetBlue employees. For example, customer Brian related how a JetBlue flight attendant dashed from the plane just before takeoff to retrieve a brand-new iPod he'd left in a rental car. And the Steins from Darien, Connecticut, told how they arrived late at night for a family vacation in Florida with their three very tired small children only to learn that their hotel wouldn't take them in. "Out of nowhere we heard a voice from behind us, go ahead, take my room," the Steins recalled. "A superhero in a JetBlue pilot's uniform, who sacrificed his room graciously, saved our night. And we slept like babies. Thank you, JetBlue." So, JetBlue really means it when it tells customers, YOU ABOVE ALL. It "gets us back to our DNA, our original mission, bringing humanity back to air travel," says JetBlue's senior VP of marketing.[13]

Despite continual improvements, Canadian airlines have not fared well on recent customer satisfaction surveys compared with their American counterparts. For example, the JD Power 2014 North American Airline Satisfaction Study ranks Air Canada at the segment average for traditional airlines, while WestJet ranked below the average in the low-cost airlines segment on customer satisfaction.[14] However, a company doesn't need to have over-the-top service to

Exhibit 1.7 Creating customer satisfaction: JetBlue creates first-rate, customer-satisfying experiences. Its slogan—JetBlue: YOU ABOVE ALL—tells customers that they are at the very heart of JetBlue's strategy and culture.

create customer delight. For example, no-frills grocery chain Aldi has highly satisfied customers, even though they have to bag their own groceries and can't use credits cards. Aldi's everyday very low pricing on good-quality products delights customers and keeps them coming back. In other words, customer satisfaction comes not just from service heroics, but from how well a company delivers on its basic value proposition and helps customers solve their buying problems.

Although a customer-centred firm seeks to deliver high customer satisfaction relative to competitors, it does not attempt to *maximize* customer satisfaction. A company can always increase customer satisfaction by lowering its prices or increasing its services. But this may result in lower profits. Thus, the purpose of marketing is to generate customer value profitably. This requires a very delicate balance: The marketer must continue to generate more customer value and satisfaction but not "give away the house."

Customer Relationship Levels and Tools Companies can build customer relationships at many levels, depending on the nature of the target market. At one extreme, a company with many low-margin customers may seek to develop *basic relationships* with them. For example, Procter & Gamble's Tide detergent division doesn't phone or call on all of its consumers to get to know them personally. Instead, P&G creates relationships through brand-building advertising, websites, and social media presence. At the other extreme, in markets with few customers and high margins, sellers want to create *full partnerships* with key customers. For example, P&G sales representatives work closely with the Walmart, Kroger, and other large retailers that sell Tide. In between these two extremes, other levels of customer relationships are appropriate.

Beyond offering consistently high value and satisfaction, marketers can use specific marketing tools to develop stronger bonds with customers. For example, many companies offer *frequency marketing programs* that reward customers who buy frequently or in large amounts. Airlines offer frequent-flyer programs, hotels give room upgrades to frequent guests, and supermarkets give patronage discounts to "very important customers." These days, almost every brand has a loyalty rewards program. For example, fast-casual restaurant Panera has a MyPanera loyalty program that surprises frequent customers with things like complimentary bakery-café items, exclusive tastings and demonstrations, and invitations to special events. Almost half of all Panera purchases are logged on MyPanera cards. The program not only lets Panera track individual customer purchases; it also lets the company build unique relationships with each MyPanera member.[15]

Courtesy Gary Armstrong

Exhibit 1.8 **Relationship marketing tools:** The MyPanera loyalty rewards program not only lets Panera track individual customer purchases; it also lets the company build unique relationships with each MyPanera member.

Other companies sponsor *club marketing programs* that offer members special benefits and create member communities. For example, Apple encourages customers to form local Apple user groups. More than 800 registered Apple user groups worldwide offer monthly meetings, a newsletter, advice on technical issues, training classes, product discounts, and a forum for swapping ideas and stories with like-minded Apple fans. Similarly, buy one of those Weber grills and you can join the Weber Nation—"the site for real people who love their Weber grills." Membership gets you exclusive access to online grilling classes, an interactive recipe box, grilling tips and 24/7 telephone support, audio and video podcasts, straight-talk forums for interacting with other grilling fanatics, and even a chance to star in a Weber TV commercial. "Become a spatula-carrying member today," says Weber.[16]

Engaging Customers

Significant changes are occurring in the nature of customer–brand relationships. Today's digital technologies have not only profoundly changed the ways we relate to one another, but have also had a huge impact on how companies and brands connect with customers, and how customers connect with and influence each other's brand behaviours.

Customer Engagement and Today's Digital and Social Media The digital age has spawned a dazzling set of new customer relationship–building tools, from websites, online ads and videos, mobile ads and apps, and blogs to online communities and the major social networks such as Twitter, Facebook, YouTube, Instagram, and Pinterest.

Yesterday's companies focused mostly on mass-marketing to broad segments of customers at arm's length. By contrast, today's companies are using online, mobile, and social media to refine their targeting and to engage customers more deeply and interactively. The *old marketing* involved marketing brands *to* consumers. The *new marketing*, known as **customer-engagement marketing**, fosters direct and continual customer involvement in shaping brand conversations, brand experiences, and brand community. Customer-engagement marketing goes beyond just selling a brand to consumers. Its goal is to make the brand a meaningful part of consumers' conversations and lives.

The burgeoning Internet and social media have given a huge boost to customer-engagement marketing. Today's consumers are better informed, more connected, and more empowered than ever before. Newly empowered consumers have more information about brands, and they have a wealth of digital platforms for airing and sharing their brand views with others. Thus, marketers are now embracing not only customer relationship management, but also *customer-managed relationships*, in which customers connect with companies and with each other to help forge their own brand experiences.

Greater consumer empowerment means that companies can no longer rely on marketing by *intrusion*. Instead, they must practise marketing by *attraction*—creating market offerings and messages that engage consumers rather than interrupt them. Hence, most marketers now augment their mass-media marketing efforts with a rich mix of online, mobile, and social media marketing that promotes brand–consumer engagement and conversation.

For example, companies post their latest ads and videos on social media sites, hoping they'll go viral. They maintain an extensive presence on Twitter, YouTube, Facebook, Google+, Pinterest, and other social media to create brand buzz. They launch their own blogs, mobile apps, online microsites, and consumer-generated review systems, all with the aim of engaging customers on a more personal, interactive level.

Take Twitter, for example. Organizations ranging from Dell, West 49, lululemon, and Dalhousie University to the Edmonton Oilers and Tourism PEI have created Twitter pages and promotions. They use tweets to start conversations with and between Twitter's more than 316 million monthly active users, address customer service issues, research customer reactions, and drive traffic to relevant articles, web and mobile marketing sites, contests, videos, and other brand activities.

Similarly, almost every company has something going on Facebook these days. Starbucks has more than 34 million Facebook fans; Coca-Cola has more than 61 million. And every major

Customer-engagement marketing Making the brand a meaningful part of consumers' conversations and lives by fostering direct and continual customer involvement in shaping brand conversations, experiences, and community.

Exhibit 1.9 Customer engagement and social media: Hertz's "Share It Up" social media campaign gave larger discounts to customers who shared Hertz coupons with social network friends. At least 45 percent of users who saw the coupons ended up sharing them.

Hertz Systems Inc.

marketer has a YouTube channel where the brand and its fans post current ads and other entertaining or informative videos. Artful use of social media can get consumers involved with and talking about a brand.

Rental car company Hertz uses a broad range of digital and social media to engage its customers and boost sales:

> A recent Hertz study found that consumers who engage in social conversations about the brand are 30 percent more likely to make a purchase than those who don't. And customers who engage in Hertz-related social activity in early stages of the rental process are four times more likely to visit Hertz's site. So, Hertz now incorporates social media in almost all of its marketing, such as Twitter hashtags, links to major social media, and sharing features. For example, Hertz's Twitter feed is a 140-character customer-service line that tends to each problem and question posted by members. On the brand's Facebook and Google+ pages, Hertz posts specials, such as waiving the young driver fee for car rentals during the spring break season. On its "Traveling at the Speed of Hertz" YouTube channel, Hertz posts its latest commercials as well as videos about new features such as its ExpressRent Interactive Kiosks. More than just creating conversations, Hertz also uses the social media to help build sales. Last year, the brand ran a "Share It Up" campaign on Facebook using social coupons to increase visibility. Users who shared the coupons with friends on Facebook and other social networks earned larger discounts based on how often they shared the coupon with friends. At least 45 percent of users who saw the coupon ended up sharing it.[17]

The key to engagement marketing is to find ways to enter consumers' conversations with engaging and relevant brand messages. Simply posting a humorous video, creating a social media page, or hosting a blog isn't enough. Successful engagement marketing means making relevant and genuine contributions to consumers' lives and conversations. According to David Oksman, chief marketer for T-shirt and apparel maker Life is good, Inc., engagement and social media are "about deep meaningful relationships that go beyond the product you are selling. The real depth of engagement is in the commenting and community that go on [around the brand]."[18] (See Marketing@Work 1.2.)

Consumer-Generated Marketing A growing form of customer-engagement marketing is **consumer-generated marketing**, by which consumers themselves are playing a bigger role in shaping their own brand experiences and those of others. This might happen through uninvited consumer-to-consumer exchanges in blogs, video-sharing sites, social media, and other digital forums. But companies themselves are increasingly inviting consumers to play a more active role in shaping products and brand content.

Consumer-generated marketing
Brand exchanges created by consumers themselves—both invited and uninvited—by which consumers are playing an increasing role in shaping their own brand experiences and those of other consumers.

Some companies ask consumers for new product and service ideas. For example, at its My Starbucks Idea site, Starbucks collects ideas from customers on new products, store changes, and just about anything else that might make their Starbucks experience better. "You know better than anyone else what you want from Starbucks," says the company website. "So tell us. What's your Starbucks idea? Revolutionary or simple—we want to hear it." The site invites customers to share their ideas, vote on and discuss the ideas of others, and see which ideas Starbucks has implemented.[19]

Other companies are inviting customers to play an active role in shaping ads. For example, for the past seven years, PepsiCo's Doritos brand has held a "Crash the Super Bowl" contest in which it invites 30-second ads from consumers and runs the best ones during the game. The consumer-generated ads have been a huge success. Last year, from more than 3500 entries, Doritos aired two fan-produced ads during the Super Bowl. Past campaigns have produced numerous top-place finishers in the *USA Today* Ad Meter rankings, earning their creators $1 million in cash prizes from PepsiCo's Frito-Lay division. Both of last year's ads finished in the top six, and the contest was again deemed a huge success. For the first time, Doritos moved the campaign from the brand's website to Facebook. Thanks to Facebook's viral capabilities, the five finalist Doritos ads captured more than 100 million views. In addition, the number of Doritos Facebook fans

MARKETING@WORK 1.2

Life Is Good, Inc.: Engaging Customers and Spreading Optimism

Building customer engagement may sound simple at first. But meaningful engagement involves much more than just tacking a buzzword onto a mission statement or setting up social media pages. The fibres of true customer engagement are woven deeply into the company and brand culture.

For starters, a brand must have a story to tell—an authentic, engagement-worthy sense of purpose that goes beyond the product. Then, rather than force-feeding the brand to customers, the company must engage them on their own terms, letting them help shape and share their own brand experiences. Finally, weaving the brand into customers' lives requires going where customers congregate. Increasingly, that means meeting up with customers in the digital world with social media.

All of these customer-engagement essentials seem to come naturally to T-shirt and apparel maker Life is good. The brand was founded with a deeply felt sense of purpose: spreading the power of optimism. "Optimism is where everything begins for us," says David Oksman, head of marketing at Life is good. "Optimism is not a strategy. It's ingrained in who we are."

In fact, Life is good doesn't even consider itself a clothing company. Instead, it's a lifestyle brand that spreads the power of optimism. As Oksman puts it, "Many companies might say, 'We have a great T-shirt, it's good quality, and it's got a fun saying on it.' That's not how we think. For us, it's rallying people around the belief [in] the power of optimism . . . everything spirals out from there." The company backs its optimism philosophy with good deeds. For example, it donates 10 percent of its net profits each year to the Life is good Foundation to help kids in need.

It all started with founders Bert and John Jacobs selling T-shirts out of an old van at colleges and street fairs. After five years, with little to show for their efforts and on the verge of closing up shop, the brothers gathered friends at their apartment to get feedback on a new set of designs. The friends overwhelmingly chose

Jake—the now-familiar beret-wearing, happy-go-lucky stick figure—and the slogan "Life is good." Jake has now become a pop-culture icon. And the company's apparel has become a canvas for the optimistic Life is good message.

Life is good's infectious philosophy is a powerfully engaging one that people want to embrace and pass along to others. As Oksman explains, "The brand is about helping people to open up, create relationships, and connect with other people. We think engagement . . . spreading optimism . . . is what we do."

Such fundamental Life is good concepts—connecting, sharing, spreading optimism—don't lend themselves well to traditional apparel marketing that pushes products and messages out to the masses. Instead, the Jacobs brothers understood that nurturing the Life is good brand would require letting customers interact with and share the brand on their own terms. For example, every year the brand holds a Life is good Festival that draws tens of thousands of fans with family-friendly activities and an all-star entertainment lineup.

More recently, as all things digital have exploded onto the marketing scene, social media have become a perfect fit for sharing the Life is good mission with customers. Today, the company fosters a community of Optimists with more than 1.7 million Facebook fans, 172 000 Twitter followers, 34 Pinterest boards, and an active YouTube channel. Life is good Radio provides a 24/7 playlist, because—as the site tells us—"Good tunes and good vibes go hand in hand."

But the strongest platform for engaging customers is the brand's own website, Lifeisgood.com. For example, the site's "Good Vibes" section gives brand fans a "breath of fresh share." One of the most active customer-engagement sites found anywhere online, Good Vibes is home to a thriving community of optimists. It's a place where fans can share photos, videos, and stories showing the brand's role in their trials, triumphs, and optimism. The postings

illustrate the depth of engagement and inspiration the Life is good brand engenders. Here are just a few examples from the hundreds, even thousands, of user-generated postings you'll find at the Lifeisgood.com Good Vibes section:

- *Jake and Jackie.* A photo of a couple's forearms, one featuring a colourful tattoo of Jake, the other a tattoo of his female counterpart Jackie, each with the Life is good tagline. "Here are pictures of our tattoos," says the couple. "Life is truly good!"

- *Love Is in the Air.* A couple holding up a Life is good banner, proclaiming "We used this pic [to spread] news of our engagement!!"

- *Thanks from Sebeta!* A picture of two young boys with the caption, "A couple of the blind students at the Sebeta School for the Blind in Sebeta, Ethiopia, rocking in their new Life is good shirts!"

- *Snowshoeing the Winter Away.* A picture posted by a registered nurse from northeast Washington of herself in a wintry forest. "At age 54 I learned to downhill ski," she says, "and this year, at age 59, I put on my first pair of snowshoes. As an RN for 40 years, I have seen way too many lives end early. So to honor those [whose] years were short, I am living my life to the fullest and it is good!"

- *All the Way Full.* A photo of a family of four on the beach accompanied by this story: "Throughout my Grace's treatment for a malignant brain tumor, we looked for silver linings. A friend gave me one of your shirts—HALF FULL—and it entered heavy rotation in my wardrobe. Grace loves the softness of the shirt, which was particularly nice against chemo-sore skin. Though only five at the time of her diagnosis, Grace understood fully the meaning of the shirt, and declared, "But Mommy, you're not HALF FULL, you're ALL THE WAY FULL!" And so ALL THE WAY FULL is how we're getting through cancer. This June,

The Life is Good Company

Exhibit 1.10 Engaging customers: Life is good starts with a deeply felt, engagement-worthy sense of purpose: spreading the power of optimism. Then, "the real depth of engagement is in the commenting and community that go on around the brand."

Grace will be two years beyond the end of treatment. We wanted to make sure you knew the significance your positivity has played in our lives."

These kinds of interactions from brand lovers are customer engagement at its best. In the end, the brand belongs to those who use and share it. Says Oksman, "We don't solicit [the stories] at all. Ultimately, we don't own optimism, our community does. So we want to create tools to let our consumers engage." True engagement is

"about deep meaningful relationships that go beyond the product you are selling. The real depth of engagement is in the commenting and community that go on [around the brand]."

Today, Life is good products are sold at more than 3500 retailers in the United States, including six company-owned stores and the Lifeisgood.com website. The privately owned company's revenues are estimated at well over US$100 million per year. But the brand's impact on its customers' lives goes well beyond its sales revenues. If optimism sells, so does customer engagement. For both the brand and its customers, Life is good.

Sources: Based on information from Gordon Wyner, "Getting Engaged," *Marketing Management*, Fall 2012, pp. 4–9; Bob Garfield and Doug Levy, "The Dawn of the Relationship Era," *Advertising Age*, January 2, 2012, pp. 1, 8–11; David Aponovich, "Powered by People, Fueled by Optimism," *Fast Company*, July 18, 2012, www.fastcompany.com/1842834/life-good-powered-people-fueled-optimism; "Bert and John Jacobs Deliver Commencement Address at 94th Annual Bentley University Ceremony," *Wall Street Journal*, March 18, 2012, http://online.wsj.com/article/PR-CO-20130318-909680.html?mod=crnews; and www.lifeisgood.com and www.lifeisgood.com/good-vibes, accessed November 2013.

pushed past the 4 million mark during the campaign. According to Frito-Lay's VP of marketing, "People like to talk about the videos, and [Facebook] reaches their circle of friends." The real value of such engagement lies in the fact that consumers are seeking out and sharing the brand messages rather than being unwilling recipients.[20]

Despite the successes, however, harnessing consumer-generated content can be a time-consuming and costly process, and companies may find it difficult to glean even a little gold from all the garbage. For example, when Heinz invited consumers to submit homemade ads for its ketchup on its YouTube page, it ended up sifting through more than 8000 entries, of which it posted nearly 4000. Some of the amateur ads were very good—entertaining and potentially effective. Most, however, were so-so at best, and others were downright dreadful. In one ad, a contestant chugged ketchup straight from the bottle. In another, the would-be filmmaker brushed his teeth, washed his hair, and shaved his face with Heinz's product.[21]

As consumers become more connected and empowered, and as the boom in digital and social media technologies continues, consumer brand engagement—whether invited by marketers or not—will be an increasingly important marketing force. Through a profusion of consumer-generated videos, shared reviews, blogs, apps, and websites, consumers are playing a growing role in shaping

© H.J. Heinz Company, used with permission

Exhibit 1.11 Harnessing consumer-generated marketing: When H.J. Heinz invited consumers to submit homemade ads for its ketchup brand on YouTube, it received more than 8000 entries—some very good but most only so-so or even downright dreadful.

their own and other consumers' brand experiences. Engaged consumers are now having a say in everything from product design, usage, and packaging to brand messaging, pricing, and distribution. Brands must embrace this new consumer empowerment and master the new digital and social media relationship tools or risk being left behind.

Partner Relationship Management

When it comes to creating customer value and building strong customer relationships, today's marketers know that they can't go it alone. They must work closely with a variety of marketing partners. In addition to being good at *customer relationship management*, marketers must be good at **partner relationship management**—working closely with others inside and outside the company to jointly bring more value to customers.

Traditionally, marketers have been charged with understanding customers and representing customer needs to different company departments. However, in today's more connected world, every functional area in the organization can interact with customers. The new thinking is that—no matter what your job is in a company—you must understand marketing and be customer focused. Rather than letting each department go its own way, firms must link all departments in the cause of creating customer value.

Marketers must also partner with suppliers, channel partners, and others outside the company. Marketing channels consist of distributors, retailers, and others who connect the company to its buyers. The *supply chain* describes a longer channel, stretching from raw materials to components to final products that are carried to final buyers. Through *supply chain management*, companies today are strengthening their connections with partners all along the supply chain. They know that their fortunes rest on more than just how well they perform. Success at delivering customer value rests on how well their entire supply chain performs against competitors' supply chains.

> **Partner relationship management**
> Working closely with partners in other company departments and outside the company to jointly bring greater value to customers.

Capturing Value from Customers

The first four steps in the marketing process outlined in Figure 1.1 involve building customer relationships by creating and delivering superior customer value. The final step involves capturing value in return in the form of sales, market share, and profits. By creating superior customer value, a firm creates highly satisfied customers who stay loyal and buy more. This, in turn, means greater long-run returns for the firm. Here, we discuss the outcomes of creating customer value: customer loyalty and retention, share of market and share of customer, and customer equity.

Creating Customer Loyalty and Retention

Good customer relationship management creates customer satisfaction. In turn, satisfied customers remain loyal and talk favourably to others about the company and its products. Studies show big differences in the loyalty of customers who are less satisfied, somewhat satisfied, and completely satisfied. Even a slight drop from complete satisfaction can create an enormous drop in loyalty. Thus, the aim of customer relationship management is to create not only customer satisfaction but also customer delight.

Keeping customers loyal makes good economic sense. Loyal customers spend more and stay around longer. Research also shows that it's five times cheaper to keep an old customer than acquire a new one. Conversely, customer defections can be costly. Losing a customer means losing more than a single sale. It means losing the entire stream of purchases that the customer would make over a lifetime of patronage. For example, here is a classic illustration of **customer lifetime value**:

> **Customer lifetime value**
> The value of the entire stream of purchases a customer makes over a lifetime of patronage.

Courtesy of Stew Leonard's

Exhibit 1.12 Customer lifetime value: To keep customers coming back, Stew Leonard's has created the "Disneyland of dairy stores." Rule #1—The customer is always right. Rule #2—If the customer is ever wrong, reread Rule #1.

Stew Leonard, who operates a highly profitable four-store supermarket in Connecticut and New York, once said that he sees US$50 000 flying out of his store every time he sees a sulking customer. Why? Because his average customer spends about $100 a week, shops 50 weeks a year, and remains in the area for about 10 years. If this customer has an unhappy experience and switches to another supermarket, Stew Leonard's has lost US$50 000 in lifetime revenue. The loss can be much greater if the disappointed customer shares the bad experience with other customers and causes them to defect.

To keep customers coming back, Stew Leonard's has created what the *New York Times* has dubbed the "Disneyland of dairy stores," complete with costumed characters, scheduled entertainment, a petting zoo, and animatronics throughout the store. From its humble beginnings as a small dairy store in 1969, Stew Leonard's has grown at an amazing pace. It's built 29 additions onto the original store, which now serves more than 300 000 customers each week. This legion of loyal shoppers is largely a result of the store's passionate approach to customer service. "Rule #1: The customer is always right. Rule #2: If the customer is ever wrong, reread rule #1."[22]

Stew Leonard is not alone in assessing customer lifetime value. Lexus, for example, estimates that a single satisfied and loyal customer is worth more than US$600 000 in lifetime sales. And the estimated lifetime value of a young mobile phone consumer is US$26 000.[23] In fact, a company can lose money on a specific transaction but still benefit greatly from a long-term relationship. This means that companies must aim high in building customer relationships. Customer delight creates an emotional relationship with a brand, not just a rational preference. And that relationship keeps customers coming back.

Growing Share of Customer

Share of customer

The portion of the customer's purchasing that a company gets in its product categories.

Beyond simply retaining good customers to capture customer lifetime value, good customer relationship management can help marketers increase their **share of customer**—the share they get of the customer's purchasing in their product categories. Thus, banks want to increase "share of wallet." Supermarkets and restaurants want to get more "share of stomach." Car companies want to increase "share of garage," and airlines want greater "share of travel."

To increase share of customer, firms can offer greater variety to current customers. Or they can create programs to cross-sell and up-sell in order to market more products and services to existing customers. For example, Amazon.com is highly skilled at leveraging relationships with its 188 million customers to increase its share of each customer's spending budget:

Once they log on to Amazon.com, customers often buy more than they intend. And Amazon does all it can to help make that happen. The online giant continues to broaden its merchandise assortment, creating an ideal spot for one-stop shopping. And based on each customer's purchase and search history, the company recommends related products that might be of interest. This recommendation system influences up to 30 percent of all sales. Amazon's ingenious Amazon Prime two-day shipping program has also helped boost its share of customers' wallets. For an annual fee of $79, Prime members receive delivery of all their purchases within two days, whether it's a single paperback book or a 60-inch HDTV. According to one analyst, the ingenious Amazon Prime program "converts casual shoppers, who gorge on the gratification of having purchases reliably appear two days after the order, into Amazon addicts." As a result, after signing up for Prime, shoppers more than triple their annual Amazon.com purchases. A Prime member is about eight times more valuable to Amazon than a non-Prime member.[24]

Building Customer Equity

We can now see the importance of not only acquiring customers but also keeping and growing them. After all, the value of a company comes from the value of its current and future customers. Customer relationship management therefore takes a long-term view: Companies want not only to create profitable customers but also to "own" them for life, earn a greater share of their purchases, and capture their customer lifetime value.

What Is Customer Equity? The ultimate aim of customer relationship management is to produce high *customer equity*.[25] **Customer equity** is the total combined customer lifetime values of all the company's current and potential customers. As such, it's a measure of the future value of the company's customer base. Clearly, the more loyal the firm's profitable customers, the higher its customer equity. Customer equity may be a better measure of a firm's performance than current sales or market share. Whereas sales and market share reflect the past, customer equity suggests the future. Consider Cadillac:

> In the 1970s and 1980s, Cadillac had some of the most loyal customers in the industry. To an entire generation of car buyers, the name *Cadillac* defined "The Standard of the World." Cadillac's share of the luxury car market reached a whopping 51 percent in 1976, and based on market share and sales, the brand's future looked rosy. However, measures of customer equity would have painted a bleaker picture. Cadillac customers were getting older (average age 60) and average customer lifetime value was falling. Many Cadillac buyers were on their last cars. Thus, although Cadillac's market share was good, its customer equity was not.
>
> Compare this with BMW. Its more youthful and vigorous image didn't win BMW the early market share war. However, it did win BMW younger customers (average age about 40) with higher customer lifetime values. The result: In the years that followed, BMW's market share and profits soared while Cadillac's fortunes eroded badly. BMW overtook Cadillac in the 1980s. In recent years, Cadillac has struggled to make the Caddy cool again with edgier, high-performance designs that target a younger generation of consumers. The brand now positions itself as "The New Standard of the World" with marketing pitches based on "power, performance, and design." Nonetheless, for the past decade, Cadillac's share of the luxury car market has stagnated. The moral: Marketers should care not just about current sales and market share; customer lifetime value and customer equity are the name of the game.[26]

Building the Right Relationships with the Right Customers Companies should manage customer equity carefully. They should view customers as assets that need to be managed and maximized. But not all customers, not even all loyal customers, are good investments. Surprisingly, some loyal customers can be unprofitable, and some disloyal customers can be profitable. Which customers should the company acquire and retain?

The company can classify customers according to their potential profitability and manage its relationships with them accordingly. Figure 1.5 classifies customers into one of four relationship groups, according to their profitability and projected loyalty.[27] Each group requires a different relationship management strategy.

Strangers show low potential profitability and little projected loyalty. There is little fit between the company's offerings and their needs. The relationship management strategy for these customers is simple: Don't invest anything in them.

Customer equity
The total combined customer lifetime values of all the company's customers.

Exhibit 1.13 Managing customer equity: To increase customer lifetime value, Cadillac is trying to make the Caddy cool again with edgier, high-performance designs that target a younger generation of consumers.

© Transtock/Corbis

FIGURE 1.5 Customer Relationship Groups

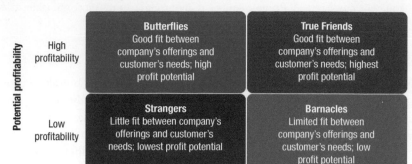

Butterflies are potentially profitable but not loyal. There is a good fit between the company's offerings and their needs. However, like real butterflies, we can enjoy them for only a short while and then they're gone. (One example is stock market investors who trade shares often and in large amounts but who enjoy hunting out the best deals without building a regular relationship with any single brokerage company.) Efforts to convert butterflies into loyal customers are rarely successful. Instead, the company should enjoy the butterflies for the moment. It should create satisfying and profitable transactions with them, capturing as much of their business as possible in the short time during which they buy from the company. Then, it should cease investing in them until the next time around.

True friends are both profitable and loyal. There is a strong fit between their needs and the company's offerings. The firm wants to make continual relationship investments to delight these customers and nurture, retain, and grow them. It wants to turn true friends into *true believers*, who come back regularly and tell others about their good experiences with the company.

Barnacles are highly loyal but not very profitable. There is a limited fit between their needs and the company's offerings. (One example is smaller bank customers who bank regularly but do not generate enough returns to cover the costs of maintaining their accounts.) Like barnacles on the hull of a ship, they create drag. Barnacles are perhaps the most problematic customers. The company might be able to improve their profitability by selling them more, raising their fees, or reducing service to them. However, if they cannot be made profitable, they should be "fired."

The point here is an important one: Different types of customers require different relationship management strategies. The goal is to build the *right relationships* with the *right customers.*

The Changing Marketing Landscape LO5

Every day, dramatic changes are occurring in the marketplace. Richard Love of HP observed, "The pace of change is so rapid that the ability to change has now become a competitive advantage." Yogi Berra, the legendary New York Yankees catcher and manager, summed it up more simply when he said, "The future ain't what it used to be." As the marketplace changes, so must those who serve it.

In this section, we examine the major trends and forces that are changing the marketing landscape and challenging marketing strategy. We look at five major developments:

the digital age, the changing economic environment, the growth of not-for-profit marketing, rapid globalization, and the call for more ethics and social responsibility.

The Digital Age: Online, Mobile, and Social Media Marketing

The explosive growth in digital technology has fundamentally changed the way we live—how we communicate, share information, access entertainment, and shop. By 2016, an estimated 3 billion people—more than 40 percent of the world's population—will be online. A majority of them will be using smartphones and other mobile devices to access the Web. More than 55 percent of Canadians now own smartphones, with the majority using them to access social media sites. These numbers will only grow as digital technology rockets into the future.[28]

Most consumers are totally smitten with all things digital. For example, according to one study, more than half of Americans keep their mobile phone next to them when they sleep—they say it's the first thing they touch when they get up in the morning and the last thing they touch at night. Favourite online and mobile destinations include the profusion of websites and social media that have sprung up. Americans who use social media spend an average of 3.2 hours per day doing so.[29] Canadian studies reveal similar patterns. In fact, one online poll of 28 000 smartphone owners found that they spent approximately 86 percent of their free time staring at one of their many screens, including smartphones, TVs, computers, or tablets. This translates to approximately 7 hours of screen time per day![30]

The consumer love affair with digital and mobile technology makes it fertile ground for marketers trying to engage customers. So it's no surprise that rapid advances in digital and social media have taken the marketing world by storm. **Digital and social media marketing** involves using digital marketing tools such as websites, social media, mobile ads and apps, online video, email, blogs, and other digital platforms that engage consumers anywhere, any time via their computers, smartphones, tablets, Internet-ready TVs, and other digital devices. These days, it seems that every company is reaching out to customers with multiple websites, newsy tweets and Facebook pages, viral ads and videos posted on YouTube, rich-media emails, and mobile apps that solve consumer problems and help them shop.

At the most basic level, marketers set up company and brand websites that provide information and promote the company's products. Many of these sites also serve as online brand communities, where customers can congregate and exchange brand-related interests and information. For example, Mountain Dew's "This Is How We Dew" site serves as a lifestyle hub where the brand's super-passionate fans can check out the latest Mountain Dew ads and videos, vote on new flavours, follow the adventures of Mountain Dew's amateur skateboarding team, "chase the taste" with NASCAR driver Dale Earnhardt, Jr., or just check out the Mountain Dew product lineup.[31]

Beyond brand sites, most companies are also integrating social and mobile media into their marketing mixes.

Social Media Marketing It's hard to find a brand site, or even a traditional media ad, that doesn't feature links to the brand's Facebook, Twitter, Google+, YouTube, Pinterest, Instagram, or other social media sites. Social media provide exciting opportunities to extend customer engagement and get people talking about a brand. Nearly 90 percent of all U.S. companies now use social media as part of their marketing

Digital and social media marketing The use of digital marketing tools such as websites, social media, mobile apps and ads, online video, email, and blogs in order to engage consumers anywhere and at any time via their digital devices.

Exhibit 1.14 Social media marketing: It's hard to find a brand that doesn't feature Facebook, Twitter, Google+, Pinterest, Instagram, YouTube, and other social media sites.

© Anatoli Babii/Alamy

mixes. By various estimates, social media spending accounts for about 10 percent of marketing budgets and will rise to an estimated nearly 20 percent within the next five years.[32]

Some social media are huge—Facebook has more than 1 billion members; Twitter has more than 316 million active users per month. Reddit, the online social news community, has nearly 63 million unique visitors a month from 174 countries. But more focused social media sites are also thriving, such as CafeMom, an online community of 10 million moms who exchange advice, entertainment, and commiseration at the community's online, Facebook, Twitter, Pinterest, YouTube, Google+, and mobile sites. Online social networks provide a digital home where people can connect and share important information and moments in their lives.

Using social media might involve something as simple as a contest or promotion to garner Facebook Likes, tweets, or YouTube postings. For example, when Boylan Bottling Company ran Facebook promotions giving free bottles of its Shirley Temple soda to consumers who shared the promotion with others, Facebook chatter about the brand jumped to five times the normal volume. But more than just Likes, tweets, or video posts, the goal of most social media campaigns is *social sharing*: getting people to talk with others and pass along their positive brand experiences. As Boylan Bottling's CEO puts it, "We've done some advertising to get Facebook Likes . . . but we've found that Facebook is a better place to percolate a frenzy around our brand."[33]

Method, maker of eco-friendly household cleaning and personal care products, relies *exclusively* on social media to promote its products and engage customers. Its quirky, zero-dollar global brand campaign—Clean Happy—is built entirely around 90-second brand videos posted on YouTube, Facebook, Twitter, and Method's blogger network. "We are the people against dirty," the videos proclaim. "Join us and clean happy." Social media work well for smaller brands like Method, which has an engaging eco-based story to tell. "The brands we compete against thrive in a 30-second spot world . . . but we can't afford to go there yet," says Method's co-founder Eric Ryan. However, "brands [like ours] that have stories to tell have an advantage [in social media]."[34]

Exhibit 1.15 Mobile marketing: PEDIGREE and Walmart ran a mobile campaign to promote the retailer as a place to shop for pet food while also improving the brand's sales. Customers used their phones to scan QR codes in ads or on packages in stores.

Mobile Marketing Mobile marketing is perhaps the fastest growing digital marketing platform. A 2014 survey of Canadian smartphone owners found that 70 percent of them use their phones for shopping-related activities—browsing product information through apps or the mobile Web, making in-store price comparisons, reading online product reviews, finding and redeeming coupons, and more.[35] Smartphones are ever-present, always on, finely targeted, and highly personal. This makes them ideal for engaging customers any time, anywhere as they move through the buying process. For example, Starbucks customers can use their mobile devices for everything from finding the nearest Starbucks and learning about new products to placing and paying for orders.

Marketers use mobile channels to stimulate immediate buying, make shopping easier, enrich the brand experience, or all of these. For example, P&G recently used mobile marketing to boost sampling through vending machines—called Freebies—that it placed in Walmart stores. To get a sample of, say, Tide Pods, customers first used their mobile phones in the store to check into the Tide Pods Facebook site, where they received product information and marketing.

Walmart and PEDIGREE joined forces to run a mobile-based "Pets Love Walmart" campaign to promote the retailer as a place to shop for pet food while also improving the brand's sales:

> Prior to the "Pets Love Walmart" campaign, of the 90 million pet owners who shop weekly at Walmart, fewer than 60 percent were buying pet food from the retailer. That left plenty of opportunity to capture more sales. When shoppers used their phones in stores to scan QR codes on PEDIGREE pet food packages, a "bowl of food" was donated directly to a pet shelter. The code also sent shoppers to a mobile site within Walmart.com, where they found promotional offers, information about pet care and Walmart's in-store pet education events, and a link to make additional charitable donations to local pet shelters. The award-winning mobile campaign boosted PEDIGREE brand sales in Walmart stores by 25 percent and caused a 15-point jump in customer agreement with the statement "Walmart is the first place I think of for pet supplies."[36]

Although online, social media, and mobile marketing offer huge potential, most marketers are still learning how to use them effectively. The key is to blend the new digital approaches with traditional marketing to create a smoothly integrated marketing strategy and mix. We will examine digital and social media marketing throughout the text—it touches almost every area of marketing strategy and tactics. Then, after we've covered the marketing basics, we'll look more deeply into direct and digital marketing in Chapter 15.

The Changing Economic Environment

The Great Recession of 2008–2009 and its aftermath hit consumers hard. After two decades of overspending, new economic realities forced consumers to bring their consumption back in line with their incomes and rethink their buying priorities.

In today's post-recession era, consumer incomes and spending are again on the rise. However, even as the economy has strengthened, rather than reverting to their old free-spending ways, Canadians are now showing an enthusiasm for frugality not seen in decades. Sensible consumption has made a comeback, and it appears to be here to stay. The new consumer spending values emphasize simpler living and more value for the dollar. Despite their rebounding means, consumers continue to buy less, clip more coupons, swipe their credit cards less, and put more in the bank.

Many consumers are reconsidering their very definition of the good life. "People are finding happiness in old-fashioned virtues—thrift, savings, do-it-yourself projects, self-improvement, hard work, faith, and community," says one consumer behaviour expert. "We are moving from mindless to mindful consumption." The new, more frugal spending values don't mean that people have resigned themselves to lives of deprivation. As the economy has improved, consumers are indulging in luxuries and bigger-ticket purchases again, just more sensibly. "Luxury is [again] on the 'to-do' list," says the expert, "but people are taking a more mindful approach to where, how, and on what they spend."[37]

In response, companies in all industries—from discounters such as Target to luxury brands such as Lexus and De Beers diamonds—have realigned their marketing strategies with the new economic realities. More than ever, marketers are emphasizing the *value* in their value propositions. They are focusing on value-for-the-money, practicality, and durability in their product offerings and marketing pitches.

For example, for years discount retailer Target focused increasingly on the "Expect More" side of its "Expect More. Pay Less" value proposition. Its carefully cultivated "upscale discounter" image successfully differentiated it from Walmart's more hard-nosed "lowest price" position. But when the economy soured, many consumers worried that Target's trendier assortments and hip marketing also meant higher prices.

Exhibit 1.16 Canadians are now showing an enthusiasm for frugality not seen in decades. More sensible spending might be here to stay.

Rangizzz/Shutterstock

So Target has shifted its balance more toward the "Pay Less" half of the slogan, making certain that its prices are in line with Walmart's and that customers know it. Although still trendy, Target's marketing now emphasizes more practical price and savings appeals.[38]

At the other extreme, even diamond marketer De Beers has adjusted its value proposition to these more sensible times. One De Beers ad, headlined "Here's to Less," makes that next diamond purchase seem—what else—downright practical. Although a diamond purchase might be spendy up front, the ad points out, it's something you'll never have to replace or throw away. As the old James Bond thriller suggests, a diamond is forever.

In adjusting to the new economy, companies may be tempted to cut their marketing budgets and slash prices in an effort to coax more frugal customers into opening their wallets. However, although cutting costs and offering selected discounts can be important marketing tactics, smart marketers understand that making cuts in the wrong places can damage long-term brand images and customer relationships. The challenge is to balance the brand's value proposition with the current times while also enhancing its long-term equity. Thus, rather than slashing prices in uncertain economic times, many marketers hold the line on prices and instead explain why their brands were worth it.

The Growth of Not-for-Profit Marketing

In recent years, marketing has also become a major part of the strategies of many not-for-profit organizations, such as universities, hospitals, museums, zoos, symphony orchestras, and even churches. The nation's not-for-profits face stiff competition for support and membership. Sound marketing can help them attract membership, funds, and support. Consider the marketing efforts behind the success of Bust a Move for Breast Health:

> A grassroots initiative that began in Halifax in 2010, Bust a Move for Breast Health is poised to take the country by storm. The one-day fundraising event was established by the Queen Elizabeth II (QEII) Foundation and IWK Health Centre to fund an integrated, world-class Breast Health Centre in Nova Scotia. Participants enter as a team or individual and are required to raise $1000 through sponsorships. In return, they experience an unforgettable day, which includes six hours of exercise with leading fitness trainers, music and entertainment, and plenty of fun. The success of this event stems from the way QEII and IWK were able to reach out to potential participants. They quickly realized that everyone in the local community has been or knows someone who has been affected by breast cancer. Using social media sites like Facebook and Twitter and backed by TV ads, word of the event quickly spread in the local community. Celebrity hosts Richard Simmons (2010), Paula Abdul (2011), and Canadian comedian Andrea Martin (2012) brought instant publicity to the events and helped raise awareness across the country. While it continues in other cities (Edmonton raised over $435 000 in 2015, bringing the four-year total to $1.2 million), the event held in 2014 marked the final one for Halifax, raising more than $5 million over five years to help create the Breast Health Centre for Atlantic Canadians. The movement has expanded to other Canadian cities, including St. John's, Ottawa, London, Saskatoon, Edmonton, Calgary, and Vancouver, and as far away as Brisbane, Australia.[39]

Exhibit 1.17 **Not-for-profit marketing:** What began as a grassroots initiative in Halifax by the QEII Foundation and the IWK Health Centre, Bust a Move for Breast Health has now raised millions of dollars for breast health in several Canadian cities and has expanded to Australia.

Xinhua/Sipa USA/Newscom

Government agencies have also shown an increased interest in marketing. For example, both the Canadian military and the Royal Canadian Mounted Police have marketing plans to attract recruits to their different services, and various government agencies are now designing *social marketing campaigns* to encourage energy conservation and concern for the environment or to discourage smoking, excessive drinking, and drug use. Reports show that the Canadian government ad expenditure has nearly tripled in recent years, peaking at $136.3 million in 2009–2010 (with a large push to promote the Economic Action Plan), then dropping to $75.2 million in 2013–2014.[40]

Rapid Globalization

As they are redefining their customer relationships, marketers are also taking a fresh look at the ways in which they relate with the broader world around them. Today, almost every company, large or small, is touched in some way by global competition. A neighbourhood florist buys its flowers from Mexican nurseries, and a large U.S. electronics manufacturer competes in its home markets with giant Korean rivals. A fledgling Internet retailer finds itself receiving orders from all over the world at the same time that a Canadian consumer goods producer introduces new products into emerging markets abroad.

North American firms have been challenged at home by the skilful marketing of European and Asian multinationals. Companies such as Toyota, Nestlé, and Samsung have often outperformed their North American counterparts. Similarly, Canadian companies in a wide range of industries have developed truly global operations, making and selling their products worldwide. Quebec-based Bombardier has become a leader in the aviation and rail transportation industries, with manufacturing, engineering, and service facilities throughout the world. British Columbia–based lululemon, a yoga-inspired athletic apparel company, manufactures its products in seven countries and operates 302 stores in Canada, the United States, Australia, China, New Zealand, and the United Kingdom. Today, companies are not only trying to sell more of their locally produced goods in international markets; they're also buying more supplies and components abroad.

Thus, managers in countries around the world are increasingly taking a global, not just local, view of the company's industry, competitors, and opportunities. They are asking: What is global marketing? How does it differ from domestic marketing? How do global competitors and forces affect our business? To what extent should we "go global"? We will discuss the global marketplace in more detail in Chapter 16.

Sustainable Marketing: The Call for More Environmental and Social Responsibility

Marketers are re-examining their relationships with social values and responsibilities and with the very Earth that sustains us. As the worldwide consumerism and environmentalism movements mature, today's marketers are being called on to develop *sustainable marketing* practices. Corporate ethics and social responsibility have become hot

Sean Gallup/Getty Images

Exhibit 1.18 Companies in a wide range of industries have developed truly global operations. Quebec-based Bombardier has become a leader in the aviation and rail transportation industries, with manufacturing, engineering, and service facilities throughout the world.

Property of Patagonia, Inc. Used with permission

Exhibit 1.19 Sustainable marketing: Patagonia believes in "using business to inspire solutions to the environmental crisis." It backs these words by pledging at least 1 percent of its sales or 10 percent of its profits, whichever is greater, to the protection of the natural environment.

topics for almost every business. And few companies can ignore the renewed and very demanding environmental movement. Every company action can affect customer relationships. Today's customers expect companies to deliver value in a socially and environmentally responsible way.

The social responsibility and environmental movements will place even stricter demands on companies in the future. Some companies resist these movements, budging only when forced by legislation or organized consumer outcries. Forward-looking companies, however, readily accept their responsibilities to the world around them. They view sustainable marketing as an opportunity to do well by doing good. They seek ways to profit by serving immediate needs and the best long-run interests of their customers and communities.

Some companies, such as Patagonia, Ben & Jerry's, Timberland, Method, and others, practise *caring capitalism*, setting themselves apart by being civic minded and responsible. They build social responsibility and action into their company value and mission statements. For example, when it comes to environmental responsibility, outdoor gear marketer Patagonia is "committed to the core." "Those of us who work here share a strong commitment to protecting undomesticated lands and waters," says the company's website. "We believe in using business to inspire solutions to the environmental crisis." Patagonia backs these words with actions. Each year it pledges at least 1 percent of its sales or 10 percent of its profits, whichever is greater, to the protection of the natural environment.[41] We will revisit the topic of sustainable marketing in greater detail in Chapter 3.

So, What Is Marketing? Pulling It All Together

At the start of this chapter, Figure 1.1 presented a simple model of the marketing process. Now that we've discussed all the steps in the process, Figure 1.6 presents an expanded model that will help you pull it all together. What is marketing? Simply put, marketing is the process of building profitable customer relationships by creating value for customers and capturing value in return.

The first four steps of the marketing process focus on creating value for customers. The company first gains a full understanding of the marketplace by researching customer needs and managing marketing information. It then designs a customer-driven marketing strategy based on the answers to two simple questions. The first question is "What consumers will we serve?" (market segmentation and targeting). Good marketing companies know that they cannot serve all customers in every way. Instead, they need to focus their resources on the customers they can serve best and most profitably. The second marketing strategy question is "How can we best serve targeted customers?" (differentiation and positioning). Here, the marketer outlines a value proposition that spells out what values the company will deliver to win target customers.

With its marketing strategy chosen, the company now constructs an integrated marketing program—consisting of a blend of the four marketing mix elements, the four *P*s—that transforms the marketing strategy into real value for customers. The company develops product offers and creates strong brand identities for them. It prices these offers to create real customer value and distributes the offers to make them available to target consumers. Finally, the company designs promotion programs that communicate the value proposition to target customers and persuade them to act on the market offering.

Perhaps the most important step in the marketing process involves building value-laden, profitable relationships with target customers. Throughout the process, marketers practise customer relationship management to create customer satisfaction and delight. They engage customers in the process of creating brand conversations, experiences, and community. In creating customer value and relationships, however, the company cannot go it alone. It must work closely with marketing partners both inside the company and throughout its marketing system. Thus, beyond practising good customer relationship

FIGURE 1.6 An Expanded Model of the Marketing Process

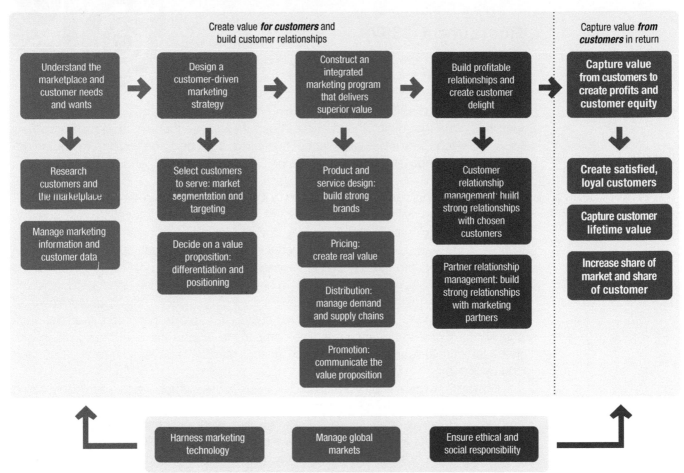

management and customer-engagement marketing, firms must also practise good partner relationship management.

The first four steps in the marketing process create value *for* customers. In the final step, the company reaps the rewards of its strong customer relationships by capturing value *from* customers. Delivering superior customer value creates highly satisfied customers who will buy more and buy again. This helps the company capture customer lifetime value and greater share of customer. The result is increased long-term customer equity for the firm.

Finally, in the face of today's changing marketing landscape, companies must take into account three additional factors. In building customer and partner relationships, they must harness marketing technologies in the new digital age, take advantage of global opportunities, and ensure that they act in an environmentally and socially responsible way. Figure 1.6 provides a good road map to future chapters of this text. Chapter 2 continues this chapter's introduction to the marketing process, with a focus on building customer relationships and capturing value from customers. Chapter 3 focuses on understanding the impact marketing has on society and the ethical concerns associated with marketing practice. Chapters 4, 5, and 6 address the first step of the marketing process—understanding the marketing environment, managing marketing information, and understanding consumer and business buyer behaviour. In Chapter 7, we look more deeply into the two major marketing strategy decisions: selecting which customers to serve (segmentation and targeting) and deciding on a value proposition (differentiation and positioning). Chapters 8 through 15 discuss the marketing mix variables, one by one. Finally, Chapter 16 examines global marketing in more detail.

Restaurant #367

November 3, 2014, was just another day in Fergus, Ontario, a short drive up Highway 6 from Hamilton. Just another day to most folks in Fergus, but to Boston Pizza, Canada's largest casual dining chain, it marked the opening of the chain's 367th location. While that might sound a little "been-there-done-that-ish," it did not stop Paul Pascal, Boston Pizza's vice-president of marketing, from being on location to cut the ribbon along with new store owners Katherine Brasch, Jim Silburn, and Michael Mattioli as well as local dignitaries, restaurant employees, and Fergus locals.

"We really see ourselves as independent business owners in the local community," said Pascal, emphasizing the uniqueness of every Boston Pizza location from coast to coast. Non-coincidentally, that is exactly how the iconic pizza chain began in the early 1960s: as the stand-alone Edmonton operation of Greek immigrant Gus Agioritis. Then, in 1973, it morphed into the branded enterprise through the vision of RCMP officer turned entrepreneur Jim Treliving, who opened 16 new restaurants leading up to 1983, when he and business partner George Melville bought the company. By 1986 there were over 30 locations in western Canada, and BP had successfully bid to become the official pizza supplier for Expo 86 in Vancouver. The company leveraged the brand association with that international event to grow across Canada, reaching 95 restaurants by 1995, and 300 by 2010.

Boston Pizza's value proposition to customers is quite simple—a fun, affordable dining experience, coupled with an adjoining sports bar featuring parallel product offerings and ambience. However, its value to the communities where it's established goes deeper. Local sports teams and charities are always beneficiaries of BP, along with its quantifiable contribution to local economies. Meanwhile, back in Fergus, employees were enacting this corporate value—donating $4100 worth of opening week tips to the local chapter of Big Brothers Big Sisters.

To Boston Pizza and all its stakeholders, value is a lot like their pizzas—every slice is a reflection of the brand.

QUESTIONS

1. What is Boston Pizza's value proposition?
2. Does Boston Pizza's value proposition extend beyond customers and into the community in which it has a location?
3. To which market segments does Boston Pizza appeal?

REVIEWING THE CONCEPTS

 Define marketing and outline the steps in the marketing process.

Marketing is the process by which companies create value for customers and build strong customer relationships in order to capture value from customers in return. The marketing process involves five steps. The first four steps create value *for* customers. First, marketers need to understand the marketplace and customer needs and wants. Next, marketers design a customer-driven marketing strategy with the goal of getting, keeping, and growing target customers. In the third step, marketers construct a marketing program that actually delivers superior value. All of these steps form the basis for the fourth step, building profitable customer relationships and creating customer delight. In the final step, the company reaps the rewards of strong customer relationships by capturing value *from* customers.

 Explain the importance of understanding customers and the marketplace, and identify the five core marketplace concepts.

Outstanding marketing companies go to great lengths to learn about and understand their customers' *needs*, *wants*, and *demands*. This understanding helps them design want-satisfying market offerings and build value-laden customer relationships by which they can capture *customer lifetime value* and greater *share of customer*. The result is increased long-term *customer equity* for the firm.

The core marketplace concepts are needs, wants, and demands; market offerings (products, services, and experiences); value and satisfaction; exchange and relationships; and markets. Wants are the form taken by human needs when shaped by culture and individual personality. When backed by buying power, wants become demands. Companies address needs by putting forth a value proposition, a set of benefits that they promise to consumers to satisfy their needs. The value proposition is fulfilled through a market offering, which delivers customer value and satisfaction, resulting in long-term exchange relationships with customers.

 Identify the key elements of a customer-driven marketing strategy and discuss the marketing management orientations that guide marketing strategy.

To design a winning marketing strategy, the company must first decide whom it will serve. It does this by dividing the market into segments of customers (*market segmentation*)

and selecting which segments it will cultivate (*target marketing*). Next, the company must decide *how* it will serve targeted customers (how it will *differentiate and position* itself in the marketplace).

Marketing management can adopt one of five competing market orientations. The *production concept* holds that management's task is to improve production efficiency and bring down prices. The *product concept* holds that consumers favour products that offer the most in quality, performance, and innovative features; thus, little promotional effort is required. The *selling concept* holds that consumers will not buy enough of an organization's products unless it undertakes a large-scale selling and promotion effort. The *marketing concept* holds that achieving organizational goals depends on determining the needs and wants of target markets and delivering the desired satisfactions more effectively and efficiently than competitors do. The *societal marketing concept* holds that generating customer satisfaction *and* long-run societal well-being through sustainable marketing strategies are key to both achieving the company's goals and fulfilling its responsibilities.

 Discuss customer relationship management and identify strategies for creating value *for* customers and capturing value *from* customers in return.

Broadly defined, *customer relationship management* is the process of building and maintaining profitable customer relationships by delivering superior customer value and satisfaction. *Customer-engagement marketing* aims to make a brand a meaningful part of consumers' conversations and lives through direct and continual customer involvement in shaping brand conversations, experiences, and community. The aim of customer relationship management and customer engagement is to produce high *customer equity*: the total combined customer lifetime values of all the company's customers. The key to building lasting relationships is the creation of superior *customer value* and *satisfaction*.

Companies want to not only acquire profitable customers but also build relationships that will keep them and grow "share of customer." Different types of customers require different customer relationship management strategies. The marketer's aim is to build the *right relationships* with the *right customers*. In return for creating value *for* targeted customers, the company captures value *from* customers in the form of profits and customer equity.

In building customer relationships, good marketers realize that they cannot go it alone. They must work closely with marketing partners inside and outside the company. In addition to being good at customer relationship management, they must be good at *partner relationship management*.

 Describe the major trends and forces that are changing the marketing landscape in this age of relationships.

Dramatic changes are occurring in the marketing arena. The digital age has created exciting new ways to learn about and relate to individual customers. As a result, advances in digital and social media have taken the marketing world by storm. Online, social media, and mobile marketing offer exciting new opportunities to target customers more selectively and engage them more deeply. Although the new digital and social media offer huge potential, most marketers are still learning how to use them effectively. The key is to blend the new digital approaches with traditional marketing to create a smoothly integrated marketing strategy and mix.

The Great Recession hit consumers hard, causing them to rethink their buying priorities and bring their consumption back in line with their incomes. Even as the post-recession economy has strengthened, consumers are now showing an enthusiasm for frugality not seen in decades. Sensible consumption has made a comeback, and it appears to be here to stay. More than ever, marketers must now emphasize the *value* in their value propositions. The challenge is to balance a brand's value proposition with current times while also enhancing its long-term equity.

In recent years, marketing has become a major part of the strategies for many not-for-profit organizations, such as universities, hospitals, museums, zoos, symphony orchestras, and even churches. Also, in an increasingly smaller world, many marketers are now connected *globally* with their customers and marketing partners. Today, almost every company, large or small, is touched in some way by global competition. Finally, today's marketers are also re-examining their ethical and societal responsibilities. Marketers are being called on to take greater responsibility for the social and environmental impacts of their actions.

Pulling it all together, as discussed throughout the chapter, the major new developments in marketing can be summed up in a single concept: *creating and capturing customer value*. Today, marketers of all kinds are taking advantage of new opportunities for building value-laden relationships with their customers, their marketing partners, and the world around them.

MyMarketingLab

Study, practise, and explore real marketing situations with these helpful resources:

- **Interactive Lesson Presentations:** Work through interactive presentations and assessments to test your knowledge of marketing concepts.
- **Study Plan:** Check your understanding of chapter concepts with self-study quizzes.
- **Dynamic Study Modules:** Work through adaptive study modules on your computer, tablet, or mobile device.
- **Simulations:** Practise decision-making in simulated marketing environments.

DISCUSSION QUESTIONS

1. Define *marketing* and outline the steps in the marketing process.

2. What is marketing myopia, and how can it be avoided?

3. What is customer-engagement marketing, and how is it related to the surge in digital and social media technologies?

4. What is consumer-generated marketing? Describe examples of both invited and uninvited consumer exchanges.

5. Discuss trends impacting marketing and the implications of these trends on how marketers deliver value to customers.

CRITICAL THINKING EXERCISES

1. Select a publicly traded company and research how much was spent on marketing activities in the most recent year of available data. What percentage of sales does marketing expenditures represent for the company? Have these expenditures increased or decreased over the past five years? Write a brief report of your findings.

2. Go to the website of a company, organization, or specific brand that has a link to Facebook, Google+, YouTube, Twitter, and/or Pinterest. Click on the links and describe how that company is using social media to market its products. Evaluate its effectiveness in creating customer engagement.

3. Search the Internet for salary information regarding jobs in marketing; for example, look for sites such as www.pay-scale.com/research/CA/Country=Canada/Salary. What is the national average salary for five different jobs in marketing? How do the averages compare in different areas of the country? Write a brief report on your findings.

ONLINE, MOBILE, AND SOCIAL MEDIA MARKETING

Eight years after the launch of its wildly successful Xbox 360, Microsoft finally launched its new Xbox One at the end of 2013. The company hoped the new console would turn around the 71 percent plunge in profits it experienced in 2012. The Xbox One touts a Blu-ray video player, voice-activated on-demand movies and TV, Skype calling, and social media integration. Smart-TV features customize menus for each player and tailor content for individual users. Xbox Live's 48 million members are able to interact on social media during special televised events such as the Olympics, Super Bowl, Oscars, and other special programming. Games have greater artificial intelligence, enabling players to feel as if the virtual athletes are making decisions on their own. Sports data such as daily performance and injury updates feed into online games, such as *Madden NFL*, mirroring their real-world counterparts. Players are able to augment live televised games with fantasy football stats that can be shared with friends via Skype and Microsoft's Smart-Glass apps. One thing the Xbox One isn't able to do is play old games. Competitor Sony plans to come out with its PlayStation 4 that will have touch sensors in its controller and allow players to play any game—current or old—instantly over the Internet. Both companies are banking on more digital and social media applications to save them from the fate competitor Nintendo faced with its failed Wii U console, which it introduced in 2012.

QUESTIONS

1. Debate whether these new features in game consoles are enough to survive against the growth of smartphone and tablet apps that offer free or inexpensive games.

2. Brainstorm three new game console features incorporating digital, mobile, or social media technology to encourage consumer interaction and engagement with gaming.

THINK LIKE A MARKETING MANAGER

Boathouse is a leading Canadian specialty retailer specializing in active lifestyle apparel and equipment, catering to outdoor thrill seekers and sports enthusiasts alike. What began as a small business in St. Catharines has grown to over 80 retail locations across Canada and an online store, Boathousestores.com. The company also has an active presence on social media. Visit Boathouse's website and social media pages and answer the following questions.

QUESTIONS

1. Suppose you are the marketing manager at Boathouse. How would you describe your value proposition?

2. What specific elements of Boathouse's website and social media presence help create customer loyalty? What other ways could the company build relationships with its customers?

MARKETING ETHICS

With two-thirds of adults and one-third of school-aged children in the United States overweight or obese, the mayor of New York City, Michael Bloomberg, took action against the soft drink industry. Mayor Bloomberg banned big sugary drinks such as 7-Eleven's mammoth 32-ounce "Big Gulp." The ban put a 16-ounce cap on fountain and bottled drinks sold at restaurants, theatres, and sporting events. Although the ban applied to drinks having more than 25 calories per 8 ounces, it did not apply to 100 percent juice or milk-based beverages. Establishments serving fountain drinks feared a significant revenue drop because these drinks are often marked up at 10 to 15 times their cost. Many consumers opposed the ban because they perceived it as further encroachment of the "nanny state." Even though this ban did not go into effect because a judge ruled that Mayor Bloomberg did not have jurisdiction to impose it, he had already banned smoking in public parks and trans fats in restaurant foods, and had required chain restaurants to include calorie information on menus. New York isn't the only city that has taken action. The San Francisco city council passed the Healthy Food Incentive Ordinance, banning toys inside children's meals that do not meet strict nutritional standards. This leads many to ask, "What's next?"

QUESTIONS

1. Should marketers embrace the societal marketing concept with respect to foods or products that could be harmful to consumers? Discuss an example of a company embracing the societal marketing concept with respect to the obesity epidemic.

2. Is government intervention even necessary, given the overall decline in demand for soft drinks? Why or why not?

MARKETING BY THE NUMBERS

Consumer consumption makes up a large portion of the U.S. gross domestic product (GDP). The American Customer Satisfaction Index (ACSI) is an economic barometer of consumers' satisfaction with goods and services across many sectors of the economy. The company that produces the index interviews nearly 80 000 Americans annually to create a national, sector, industry, and company satisfaction index. The ACSI benchmarks 10 economic sectors, 43 industries, and hundreds of companies and federal and local government sectors. Although the sales and profit data are historical, the ACSI is considered a leading economic indicator of macroeconomic growth. Marketers use this index to measure the pulse of the consumer. Research has shown it to be a predictor of GDP and personal consumption expenditure (PCE) growth, and even stock market performance.

QUESTIONS

1. Visit www.theacsi.org and learn about the American Customer Satisfaction Index (ACSI). Write a report explaining the index and compare indices for five different industries along with the national average. Are there differences in customer satisfaction among industries? Explain why or why not.

2. The Customer Satisfaction Index (CSI) is measured similarly in other countries. Find another country's CSI and compare results to the American Customer Satisfaction Index (ACSI). Are U.S. consumers more or less satisfied than consumers in the other country? Are trends in the national score similar?

PINTEREST: REVOLUTIONIZING THE WEB—AGAIN

In less than two years after its 2010 launch, Pinterest reached the milestone of 10 million unique monthly visitors—faster than any other site in history. At that time, it was driving more traffic than Google+, YouTube, and LinkedIn combined. One year later, it reached 50 million unique monthly visitors. Pinterest is still growing so fast that trying to quantify its success with such a number seems pointless.

Rather, the impact of this brash young start-up can be observed in much more substantial ways. In fact, Pinterest seems to have accomplished the unlikely feat of revolutionizing the Web—something that seems to happen every couple of years. Like Amazon, Google, Facebook, and others before it, Pinterest has put businesses and other websites everywhere on notice that they'd better orient themselves around its platform or be left behind. And like the other Internet revolutionists before, Pinterest's impact has caused even the top dogs to stop and take notice. Indeed, Pinterest is changing web design. It is also changing e-commerce. And it looks like Pinterest has solved one of the Internet's biggest problems.

THE DISCOVERY PROBLEM

At first blush, Pinterest may sound like any other social media site, full of people sharing images and commenting on them. Founder and CEO Ben Silbermann's big idea for Pinterest came as he and college buddy Paul Sciarra struggled to make a business out of their first product, a shopping app called Tote. Although Tote failed to take off, it revealed a pent-up need among Internet users. Tote users didn't buy things (kind of a necessity for a shopping app). But they did email themselves pictures of products to view later.

Silbermann—a lifetime collector of "stuff"—could identify with that. As a boy, he had a particular fascination with collecting bugs. "I really liked insects," he says. "All kinds: flies, grasshoppers, weevils." He spent his youth collecting, pinning, drying, tagging—creating his own private museum of natural history. So when Silbermann and Sciarra met Pinterest's third co-founder, Evan Sharp, the idea of a digital collection—of books, clothes, or even insects—as a powerful medium for self-expression began to take shape.

As the three began working on developing Pinterest, something about all-things-Internet bothered Silbermann. Despite the seemingly infinite possibilities for exploration, expression, and creation, he felt that the Internet was organized in a way that boxed people in. For starters, the nature of "search" in any online context may seem to promote discovery, but it actually stunts it. For example, Google depends on finely tuned queries in order to yield useful results. Try to find something when you're not quite sure what you want—say, "nice Father's Day gift" or even "very special Father's Day gift"—and Google isn't really much help. The bottom line is, if you try talking to Google as you would talk to a friend or a department store clerk, it won't know where to begin.

The belief that discovery is a problem on the Internet isn't original to Silbermann. In fact, it's an issue that many digital designers have struggled with since the launch of the Web, but no one has seemed to be able to solve. Take Amazon, for example. As successful as it is, Amazon's entire structure is set up like every other commerce site—a detailed system of menus and categories. To browse for something, users must function within this structure while at the same time being pulled in dozens of different directions by suggested items and competing products.

"You spend three hours buying a $20 toaster," says Barry Schwartz, psychology professor and author of *The Paradox of Choice*. "Amazon and Google pretty much stink at browsing," echoes Leland Rechis, director of product experience at Etsy. But Amazon and Google are not alone. The entire Internet is structured as a series of ever-more-specific menus, inconsistent with how the human mind works. The types of free-associative leaps that happen naturally as people walk through shopping malls, meander through a museum, or even drive down the street are nearly impossible online.

As Silbermann and his co-founders worked to sketch out Pinterest, the three were intent on eliminating another limiting characteristic of online design. Social networks are all organized around feeds—lines of text or images organized by time. This setup makes it impossible to browse multiple images at once. The Pinterest team wanted to change this. "We were really excited about bringing something that wasn't immediate and real time, something that wasn't a chronological feed," says Sharp. They pictured a grid of images rather than the directories, time stamps, and pagination so commonly imposed by the

Web. The goal for Pinterest was to create an interface that would feel more like visiting a store or a museum.

As Pinterest took shape, there was no question in the minds of its creators that it was to be a social network at its core. As such, Silbermann's ability to look beyond the tunnel vision of social media entrepreneurship set Pinterest apart from the pack in yet another way. Although the current social Web is frequented by millions, most of them are observers, not creators; they're taking part in the experience on only one level. Not everyone is a photographer, a filmmaker, or a broadcaster. "Most people don't have anything witty to say on Twitter or anything gripping to put on Facebook, but a lot of them are really interesting people," Silbermann says. "They have awesome taste in books or furniture or design, but there was no way to share that."

SOMETHING COMPLETELY DIFFERENT

The Pinterest team's focus on solving some of the most limiting characteristics of the Internet yielded fruit. When Pinterest launched in March 2010, it was widely hailed as one of the most visually stunning sites ever. Silbermann, Sciarra, and Sharp went through 50 working versions of the site, painstakingly tweaking column widths, layouts, and ways of presenting pictures to perfection. "From the beginning, we were aware that if we were going to get somebody to spend all this time putting together a collection, at the very least, the collection had to be beautiful," Silbermann says. Pinterest's grid—interlocking images of fixed width and varying heights—is a key element of its design; the grid rearranges itself every time a new image is pinned, meaning users rarely see the same home page twice.

Pinterest also bucked conventional online design in other ways. At a time when "gamification" was hot, Pinterest displayed no elements of competition. There is no leader board or any other means of identifying the most popular pinners. Pinterest also did away with page views—the predominant metric for illustrating growth and momentum. Rather, Pinterest's "infinite scroll" automatically loads more images as the user expands the browser or scrolls downward. With almost no time spent clicking or waiting for pages to load, this feature has proven addictive for many.

"When you open up Pinterest," Silbermann says, "you should feel like you've walked into a building full of stuff that only you are interested in. Everything should feel handpicked for you." As Pinterest debuted, it was obvious that Silbermann and his cohorts had succeeded. Pinterest page after Pinterest page has the feel of a collection designed by someone to reflect his or her own needs,

ambitions, and desires. It's as if each person is saying, "Here are the beautiful things that make me who I am— or who I want to be." And there is no single theme to a pinboard. Pinterest is a place where young women plan their weddings, individuals create the ultimate wish list of food dishes, and couples assemble furniture sets for their new home. And departing from other social networks, every Pinterest homepage is an ever-changing collage that is the sum of each user's choices.

Given that Pinterest's design has departed from Internet convention in so many ways, it's only natural that its growth dynamics would break from present trends. In the United States, most successful social services spread through early adopters on the nation's coasts, then break through to the masses. But Pinterest's growth has been scattered throughout the heartland, driven by such unlikely cohorts as the "bloggernacle" of tech-savvy young Mormons. Additionally, nearly 80 percent of Pinterest's users are women, most between the ages of 25 and 54—another demographic not normally associated with fast-growing social media sites.

HOPE FOR MONETIZATION

Perhaps the biggest splash that Pinterest has made in the Internet pool is its huge influence on consumer purchasing. Although many dot-coms have made a profit by selling online, the digital world in general still struggles with turning eyeballs into dollars. Even Facebook, although it turns a profit, prompts relatively few of its 1-billion-plus members to open their wallets.

But something about the combination of Pinterest's elegant design and smart social dynamics has users shopping like mad. According to e-commerce tracker RichRelevance, the average sale resulting from a Pinterest user following an image back to its source and then buying an item is $180. For Facebook users, it's only $80. And for tweeters, it's only $70. Companies are already jumping on this opportunity. One of the primary ways brands are driving traffic to their own Pinterest or external site is by paying opinion leaders to pin an image of their product. For example, companies pay Satsuki Shibuya, a designer with more than a million followers, between $150 and $1200 per image. And because of Pinterest's authentic feel, it's almost impossible to tell the difference between paid pins and unpaid pins—something that can't be said of other sites.

It's little wonder, then, that so many other social media sites have taken note of Pinterest. Numerous copycat sites (such as Fancy and Polyvore) have mimicked Pinterest's look and feel, right down to the font selections.

The influence of Pinterest's design is also notable on sites such as Lady Gaga's social network LittleMonsters.com and the question-and-answer site Quora. Even Facebook's move to Timeline was notably Pinterest-like.

Despite all the ways that Pinterest has departed from the typical path of dot-com development, it has largely stayed the course in terms of making money. In other words, as of yet, Pinterest isn't generating any revenue, instead focusing on building its base and honing its site before it tries to do so. Still, Silbermann and friends are tossing lots of ideas around. For example, Pinterest could sell advertising, as so many other social media do. In fact, analysts estimate that Pinterest could generate $500 million in advertising revenue in 2016 when it adopts its new ad sales platform. It could also adopt a referral fee model, retaining a percentage of the sale price of every item sold as the result of a pin. And there are other possibilities as well. Pinterest has had no trouble raising all the venture capital that it needs and has been valued at $2.5 billion, despite the fact that it is yet to earn a nickel. "There was never a doubt in our minds that we could make a s#★%load of money," says a former Pinterest employee. Apparently, investors feel the same way.

QUESTIONS FOR DISCUSSION

1. Analyze the forces in the marketing environment that have contributed to Pinterest's explosion in popularity.

2. Why has Pinterest demonstrated such a high influence on consumers' decision to purchase products?

3. Discuss ways that companies can use Pinterest to build their own brands and generate sales.

4. What are some threats that Pinterest faces in the future? Give recommendations for dealing with those threats.

Sources: Based on information from Max Chafkin, "Can Ben Silbermann Turn Pinterest into the World's Greatest Shopfront?" *Fast Company*, October 2012, pp. 90–96+; Ekaterina Walter, "What the Pinterest Redesign Means for Brands," *Fast Company*, April 16, 2013, www.fastcompany.com/3008342/what-pinterest-redesign-means-brands; and J. J. Colao, "Why Is Pinterest a $2.5 Billion Company? An Early Investor Explains . . . ," *Forbes*, May 8, 2013, www.forbes.com/sites/jjcolao/2013/05/08/why-is-pinterest-a-2-5-billion-company-an-early-investor-explains.

Northern Lights projection mapping, courtesy Capital Celebrations and Christie®

AFTER STUDYING THIS CHAPTER, YOU SHOULD BE ABLE TO

1 explain company-wide strategic planning and its four steps

2 discuss how to design business portfolios and develop growth strategies

3 explain marketing's role in strategic planning and how marketing works with its partners to create and deliver customer value

4 describe the elements of a customer-driven marketing strategy and mix, and the forces that influence it

5 list the marketing management functions, including the elements of a marketing plan, and discuss the importance of measuring and managing return on marketing investment

Company and Marketing Strategy: Partnering to Build Customer Relationships

PREVIEWING THE CONCEPTS

In Chapter 1, we explored the marketing process by which companies create value for customers in order to capture value from them in return. In this chapter, we dig deeper into steps two and three of the marketing process—designing customer-driven marketing strategies and constructing marketing programs. First, we look at the organization's overall strategic planning, which guides marketing strategy and planning. Next, we discuss how, guided by the strategic plan, marketers partner closely with others inside and outside the firm to create value for customers. We then examine marketing strategy and planning—how marketers choose target markets, position their market offerings, develop a marketing mix, and manage their marketing programs. Finally, we look at the important step of measuring and managing return on marketing investment (marketing ROI).

Let's look at an example of a Canadian company whose careful strategic planning has helped it capitalize on a revolutionary new market—the need for ultra-high-tech visual display systems used in business, government, entertainment, and even advertising.

ORGANIZING AND PLANNING FOR SUCCESS AT CANADA'S CHRISTIE DIGITAL SYSTEMS

Christie Digital Systems Canada is a global visual technology company and a leader in Canada's ICT (information and communications technology) industry. The company designs and manufactures a variety of display technologies and solutions for cinema, large audience environments, control rooms, business presentations, training facilities, 3-D and virtual reality, simulation, education, media, and government. Its flagship line has been its digital cinema solutions—Christie is the only single-source provider of cinema projectors in all of North America, and one of only a handful in the world. The firm's design and engineering facility and main manufacturing facility are located in Kitchener, Ontario.

Christie Digital Systems Canada was formed in 1999, when Christie—a California-based film projector manufacturer—merged with Electrohome Visual Displays, at the time Canada's largest consumer electronics manufacturer, based in Kitchener. Over the past decade the company has experienced rapid growth. However, success didn't come overnight for Christie. When the company took its present form in late 1999, the first year's revenue for the new organization was about $100 million, and the Kitchener facility employed only 200 people. Today, annual revenues top $800 million and the employees number more than 1400 worldwide, with 700 in Kitchener.

And it was more than just the corporate letterhead that changed after the acquisition. The company had to change its business strategy as well as its marketing strategy. Christie Digital Systems Canada president Gerry Remers explains: "We went from being a company that was focused on its traditional dealer channels to a company whose product strategy was focused on the entertainment and film industries—a market that changes rapidly." This flexibility and commitment to innovation has led to an evolving mission for the company, which is to help its customers create and share the world's best visual experiences. Remers says that Christie has expanded beyond the entertainment industry to encompass the "unlimited opportunity in the area of visual communication, so we are going to continue to develop new products and new solutions to meet the needs of the market. The fact of the matter is we're going to see pixels everywhere."

The products that Christie designs, manufactures, and markets are not sold to consumers, though most consumers are probably familiar with the results. For example, Christie's projection or image-mapping projectors and software are used by scores of amusement parks, public festivals, and advertising agencies to deliver compelling visual content to all manner of outdoor and indoor surfaces. The company's technologies are also used by the post-production facilities of such filmmakers as James Cameron to produce high-resolution and immersive 3-D movie-going experiences. Christie signed a five-year agreement with Cameron's Lightstorm Entertainment to exchange research, testing, development, and technical support on the industry's most exciting new technology—high frame rate (HFR) movies that end the eye strain and nausea often associated with 3-D film viewing. Cameron said that he selected Christie for this "journey of discovery" because the company is fully committed to his vision and shares his dedication to continually push the boundary of digital cinema. The full potential of 3-D and HFR technology to fully immerse audiences in the world of the movie before them is the holy grail of cinematography. Peter Jackson's Park Road Post Production group also uses Christie technology, and Christie projectors were chosen for the world premiere of the first-ever HFR 3-D feature-length movie, *The Hobbit: An Unexpected Journey*.

For several summers, Christie's projection mapping technology has turned Ottawa's Parliament Hill into a virtual storybook with the production of a sound and light show. First there was "Mosaika—Canada through the Eyes of Its People;" later, a new show called Northern Lights. These shows are accompanied by a surround sound system and an audio track, and the digital lights "paint" a video canvas onto the six-story-high Parliament Building Centre Block, including the iconic Peace Tower in the middle. And those are just a few examples of where people might encounter Christie's technology. The company has installed more than 100 000 projection solutions worldwide and is recognized as one of the most innovative visual technology companies in the world, boasting 12 major patents, two Academy Awards, and countless industry awards.

In terms of top-level corporate organization, Christie Digital Systems Canada is a subsidiary of Christie Digital Systems, which in turn is a wholly owned subsidiary of Ushio Inc. of Japan. Its sister subsidiary is Christie Digital Systems USA, and both Christie Canada and Christie USA have their own presidents, reporting to the CEO and president of Christie Digital Systems, Inc. Christie has four major strategic business units (or SBUs): entertainment solutions, business products, visual environments, and managed services. Within these business units there are groups tasked with developing solutions for the following segmented markets: entertainment (both cinema and staging venues), visualization, business products, control room solutions, digital signage, managed (professional) services, medical imaging, and simulation solutions. Christie also has three subsidiary companies: Christie Medical (Memphis, Tennessee), Vista Systems (Phoenix, Arizona), and Nationwide (equipment leasing).

Christie's vice-president of global and corporate marketing, Kathryn Cress, is responsible for strategic planning and for reaching Christie's strategic marketing objectives: worldwide brand recognition and market leadership. She oversees brand equity management to ensure the delivery of tightly integrated global marketing strategies and communications. She is also responsible for outbound marketing programs, including the promotion of product launches, public relations, trade shows, events, partner marketing, advertising, Web marketing, and messaging platforms. Under her supervision, Christie's marketing function has been organized into six main departments: experiential marketing, digital marketing, marketing programs, communications and branding, publicity and promotions, and media and public relations.

Outside the organization, Christie's key suppliers and distributors compose part of its value delivery network—the chain of partner organizations that supply the raw materials to the manufacturing plant and the partner organizations that help move the finished products into the hands of end-user customers. The company has a mission statement for working with supplier partners: "Our mission is to drive world class value from our supply chain to meet Christie's business goals through proactive supplier and Christie stakeholder engagement, timely responsiveness, and the relentless pursuit of continuous improvement."

As for distribution, Christie sells its products through both a direct sales force and a multichannel system, including distributors who sign a contract committing them to purchase a minimum dollar amount of product, which they then resell to dealer/integrators; VIP partners, who are dealer/integrators that purchase more than six figures annually, then sell to end-user customers. There are also rental and staging companies that buy Christie products to run their productions, but that don't necessarily resell those products. And you might recognize the names of some of Christie's largest customers: Starbucks, Cineplex Entertainment, the London Stock Exchange, Boeing, Paramount, Cinépolis, IBM, University of Waterloo, Harrods, Industrial Light & Magic, Loews, the Montreal Police Service, Shell, and Deutsche Telekom.

In keeping with the company's leading-edge technology philosophy, Christie is fully engaged with social media. After each trade show appearance, the company's marketing managers produce an internal report on the show's effect on social media. For example, they count the number of mentions on Twitter and YouTube before and after the show. They also track the postings of industry bloggers and discover new bloggers who write about projection technology. On Facebook, they track the number of views of content related to the show; for example, the press releases and photo albums. In summarizing the social media findings after one trade show, the marketing managers noted that, in the future, Christie should explore using bloggers as a way of telling stories about Christie's presence at future trade shows and to develop these stories into content marketing.

As the global need for increased security and mission-critical public and private services expands, Christie is pouring more research into delivering solutions for the most complex control room environments. What sets Christie apart from—and ahead of—its global competitors? A spirit of teamwork and a welcoming attitude toward change are the building blocks upon which Christie has become number one in its customers' estimation, by delivering quality customer service, reliable products, and innovative solutions.[1]

LIKE Christie, outstanding marketing organizations employ strongly customer-driven marketing strategies and programs that create customer value and relationships. These marketing strategies and programs, however, are guided by broader company-wide strategic plans, which must also be customer focused. Thus, to understand the role of marketing, we must first understand the organization's overall strategic planning process.

Company-Wide Strategic Planning: Defining Marketing's Role [LO1]

Strategic planning
The process of developing and maintaining a strategic fit between the organization's goals and capabilities and its changing marketing opportunities.

Each company must find the game plan for long-run survival and growth that makes the most sense given its specific situation, opportunities, objectives, and resources. This is the focus of **strategic planning**—the process of developing and maintaining a strategic fit between the organization's goals and capabilities and its changing marketing opportunities.

Strategic planning sets the stage for the rest of the planning in the firm. Companies usually prepare annual plans, long-range plans, and strategic plans. The annual and long-range plans deal with the company's current businesses and how to keep them going. In contrast, the strategic plan involves adapting the firm to take advantage of opportunities in its constantly changing environment.

At the corporate level, the company starts the strategic planning process by defining its overall purpose and mission (see Figure 2.1). This mission is then turned into detailed supporting objectives that guide the whole company. Next, senior managers at the corporate level decide what portfolio of businesses and products is best for the company and how much support to give each one. In turn, each business and product develops detailed marketing and other departmental plans that support the company-wide plan. Thus, marketing planning occurs at the business-unit, product, and market levels. It supports company strategic planning with more detailed plans for specific marketing opportunities.

Defining a Market-Oriented Mission

An organization exists to accomplish something, and this purpose should be clearly stated. Forging a sound mission begins with the following questions: What is our business? Who is the customer? What do consumers value? What *should* our business be? These simple-sounding questions are among the most difficult the company will ever have to answer. Successful companies continually raise these questions and answer them carefully and completely.

Mission statement
A statement of the organization's purpose—what it wants to accomplish in the larger environment.

Many organizations develop formal mission statements that answer these questions. A **mission statement** is a statement of the organization's purpose—what it wants to accomplish in the larger environment. A clear mission statement acts as an "invisible hand" that guides people in the organization.

FIGURE 2.1 Steps in Strategic Planning

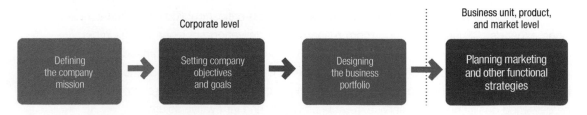

Some companies define their missions in product or technology terms ("We make and sell furniture" or "We are a chemical-processing firm"), and then run into problems when the nature of the market changes. Marketing guru Theodore Levitt calls this problem "marketing myopia," and suggests that mission statements should be *market oriented* and defined in terms of satisfying basic customer needs. Products and technologies eventually become outdated, but basic market needs may last forever. Indigo Books & Music's mission isn't simply to sell books and music. Its mission is "to inspire our customers and those they care about with life-enriching products and experiences." Likewise, Under Armour's mission isn't just to make performance sports apparel, it's "to make all athletes better through passion, design, and the relentless pursuit of innovation." Table 2.1 provides several other examples of product-oriented versus market-oriented business definitions.[2]

Mission statements should be meaningful and specific, and yet motivating at the same time. They should emphasize the company's strengths in the marketplace. Too often, mission statements are written for public relations purposes and lack specific, workable guidelines. Instead, they should emphasize the company's strengths and forcefully declare how it intends to win in the marketplace. For example, Google's mission isn't to be the world's best search engine; it's to organize the world's information and make it universally accessible and useful.

Finally, a company's mission should not be stated as making more sales or profits—profits are only a reward for creating value for customers. Instead, the mission should focus on customers and the customer experience the company seeks to create. Take Buffalo Wild Wings, for example. This sports bar chain started in Ohio in 1982 and now has more than 1000 locations in the U.S., Canada, and Mexico—but doesn't even mention wings in its mission statement:

Exhibit 2.1 Indigo Books & Music's mission is "to inspire our customers and those they care about with life-enriching products and experiences."

Indigo

Customers do, in fact, come to Buffalo Wild Wings to eat wings and drink beer, but also to watch sports, trash talk, cheer on their sports teams, and meet old friends and make new ones—that is, a total eating and social experience. "We realize that we're not just in the business of selling wings," says the company. "We're something much bigger. We're in the business of fueling the sports fan experience." True to that broader mission, Buffalo Wild Wings creates in-store and online promotions that inspire camaraderie. "It's about giving them tools to not just be spectators but advocates of the brand," says the chain. For example, the brand's very active website draws 1.4 million visitors per month, and its Facebook page has more than 10 million fans. Pursuing a customer-focused mission has paid big dividends for Buffalo Wild Wings. The wing joint's sales have quadrupled in the past eight years and the company brags that it's the number one brand in its industry for fan engagement.[3]

Setting Company Objectives and Goals

The company needs to turn its mission into detailed supporting objectives for each level of management. Each manager should have objectives and be responsible for reaching them. For example, most consumers recognize the name Heinz for its ketchup—the company, H.J. Heinz, sells more than 650 billion

From www.buffalowildwings.com. ©2013 by Buffalo Wild Wings, Inc. Reprinted by permission of Buffalo Wild Wings, Inc. Buffalo Wild Wings® is a registered trademark of Buffalo Wild Wings, Inc.

Exhibit 2.2 Customer-focused mission: The fast-growing Buffalo Wild Wings chain's mission is to provide a total eating and social environment that "fuels the sports fan experience." As a result, it creates in-store and online experiences that promote brand fan engagement.

TABLE 2.1   Market-Oriented Business Definitions

Company	Product-Oriented Definition	Market-Oriented Definition
Facebook	We are an online social network.	We connect people around the world and help them share important moments in their lives.
Google	We operate an online search engine.	We help you organize the world's information and make it universally accessible and useful.
Home Depot	We sell tools and home repair and improvement items.	We empower consumers to achieve the homes of their dreams.
Revlon	We make cosmetics.	We sell lifestyle and self-expression; success and status; memories, hopes, and dreams.
Ritz-Carlton Hotels & Resorts	We rent rooms.	We create the Ritz-Carlton experience—one that enlivens the senses, instills well-being, and fulfills even the unexpressed wishes and needs of our guests.

bottles of ketchup each year. But Heinz owns a breadth of other food products under a variety of brands, marketed in different countries around the world. For example, Heinz's most popular Canadian brands are Heinz Ketchup, Heinz 57, and Alpha-Getti. In New Zealand, Heinz markets food products such as condensed tomato soup under the brand Watties; and Plasmon, a Heinz-owned brand, is the leading brand of infant/nutrition products in Italy. Globally, Heinz ties this diverse product portfolio together under what it calls a vision statement rather than a mission statement: "To be the best food company, growing a better world."

This broad mission leads to a hierarchy of objectives, including business objectives and marketing objectives. Heinz's main business objective is to be the best food company. It does this by investing heavily in research. However, research is expensive and must be funded through improved profit, so improving profits becomes another major objective for Heinz. Profits can be improved by increasing sales or reducing costs. Sales can be increased by improving the company's share of domestic and international markets. These goals then become the company's current marketing objectives.

Marketing strategies and programs must be developed to support these marketing objectives. To increase its market share, Heinz is constantly broadening its product lines and expanding into new markets. For example, in the last few years Heinz added breakfast products to its Weight Watchers Smart Ones brand, a new line of potatoes called Grillers to its Ore Ida brand, and Balsamic Ketchup to its ketchup line in Canada. The company works at expanding its ability to create and manufacture new products, for example by purchasing an 80 percent stake in Quero (a Brazilian brand of tomato-based sauces, ketchup, condiments, and vegetables) and, more recently, by partnering with the Chinese government to build the largest infant cereal production plant in the world in Foshan City, Guangdong province.[4]

These are Heinz's broad marketing strategies. Each broad marketing strategy must then be defined in greater detail. For example, increasing the product's promotion may require more advertising and public relations efforts; if so, both requirements will need to be spelled out. In this way, the firm's mission is translated into a set of objectives for the current period.

Exhibit 2.3 Company objectives: Heinz's overall objective is "to be the best food company, growing a better world."

Designing the Business Portfolio LO2

Guided by the company's mission statement and objectives, management must now plan its **business portfolio**—the collection of businesses and products that make up the company. The best business portfolio is the one that best fits the company's strengths and weaknesses to opportunities in the environment.

Business portfolio
The collection of businesses and products that make up the company.

Most large companies have complex portfolios of businesses and brands. Strategic and marketing planning for such business portfolios can be a daunting but critical task. Consider the size and scope of Rogers Communications Inc., for example. Rogers is a large and diversified communications and media company that operates a number of businesses. The company operates in four main areas: it is Canada's largest provider of wireless communications services and runs a chain of retail stores; it provides cable television and high-speed Internet services; it offers business telecom, data networking, and IP solutions to small, medium, and large enterprises and government customers; and it owns large-scale media assets, including television stations, radio stations, the Toronto Blue Jays and Rogers Centre, the Shopping Channel, and dozens of publications in English and French, including *Chatelaine, Maclean's, Flare, Marketing, Canadian Business, Today's Parent,* and *Sportsnet*, in both print and digital formats. Managing this vast business portfolio profitably requires a combination of diligence, skill, and talent.

Whether the company's business portfolio consists of only one or two operations or dozens, the strategic planning process is the same: First, the company must analyze its *current* business portfolio and determine which businesses should receive more, less, or no investment. Second, it must shape the *future* portfolio by developing strategies for growth and downsizing.

Analyzing the Current Business Portfolio

The major activity in strategic planning is business **portfolio analysis**, whereby management evaluates the products and businesses that make up the company. The company will want to put strong resources into its more profitable businesses and phase down or drop its weaker ones.

Portfolio analysis
The process by which management evaluates the products and businesses that make up the company.

Management's first step is to identify the key businesses that make up the company, called *strategic business units* (SBUs). An SBU can be a company division, a product line within a division, or sometimes a single product or brand. The company next assesses the attractiveness of its various SBUs and decides how much support each deserves. When designing a business portfolio, it's a good idea to add and support products and businesses that fit closely with the firm's core philosophy and competencies.

The purpose of strategic planning is to find ways in which the company can best use its strengths to take advantage of attractive opportunities in the environment. So most standard portfolio analysis methods evaluate SBUs on two important dimensions—the attractiveness of the SBU's market or industry, and the strength of the SBU's position in

Exhibit 2.4 Managing the business portfolio: Many people think of Rogers as just the cable company, but in reality it is a collection of media and entertainment businesses.

© Rogers Communications Inc.

FIGURE 2.2 The BCG Growth–Share Matrix

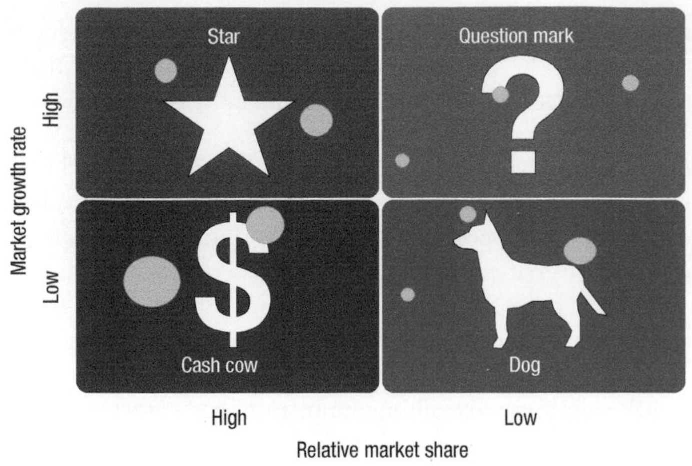

that market or industry. The best-known portfolio-planning method was developed by the Boston Consulting Group, a leading management consulting firm.[5]

Growth–share matrix

A portfolio-planning method that evaluates a company's strategic business units (SBUs) in terms of its market growth rate and relative market share. SBUs are classified as stars, cash cows, question marks, or dogs.

The Boston Consulting Group Approach Using the now-classic Boston Consulting Group (BCG) approach, a company classifies all its SBUs according to the **growth–share matrix**, as shown in Figure 2.2. On the vertical axis, *market growth rate* provides a measure of market attractiveness. On the horizontal axis, *relative market share* serves as a measure of company strength in the market. The growth–share matrix defines four types of SBUs:

Stars. Stars are high-growth, high-share businesses or products. They often need heavy investments to finance their rapid growth. Eventually their growth will slow down, and they will turn into cash cows.

Cash Cows. Cash cows are low-growth, high-share businesses or products. These established and successful SBUs need less investment to hold their market share. Thus, they produce a lot of cash that the company uses to pay its bills and support other SBUs that need investment.

Question Marks. Question marks are low-share business units in high-growth markets. They require a lot of cash to hold their share, let alone increase it. Management has to think hard about which question marks it should try to build into stars and which should be phased out.

Dogs. Dogs are low-growth, low-share businesses and products. They may generate enough cash to maintain themselves but do not promise to be large sources of cash.

The 10 circles in the growth–share matrix represent a company's 10 current SBUs. The company has two stars, two cash cows, three question marks, and three dogs. The areas of the circles are proportional to the SBU's dollar sales. This company is in fair shape, although not in good shape. It wants to invest in the more promising question marks to make them stars and to maintain the stars so that they will become cash cows as their markets mature. Fortunately, it has two good-sized cash cows. Income from these cash cows will help finance the company's question marks, stars, and dogs. The company should take some decisive action concerning its dogs and its question marks.

Once it has classified its SBUs, the company must determine what role each will play in the future. One of four strategies can be pursued for each SBU. The company can invest more in the business unit to *build* its share. Or it can invest just enough to *hold* the SBU's share at the current level. It can *harvest* the SBU, milking its short-term cash flow regardless of the long-term effect. Finally, the company can *divest* the SBU by selling it or phasing it out and using the resources elsewhere.

As time passes, SBUs change their positions in the growth–share matrix. Many SBUs start out as question marks and move into the star category if they succeed. They later become cash cows as market growth falls, then finally die off or turn into dogs toward the end of their life cycles. The company needs to continually add new products and units so that some of them will become stars and, eventually, cash cows that will help finance other SBUs.

Problems with Matrix Approaches The BCG and other formal methods revolutionized strategic planning. However, such centralized approaches have limitations: They can be difficult, time-consuming, and costly to implement. Management may find it difficult to define SBUs and measure market share and growth. In addition, these approaches focus on classifying *current* businesses but provide little advice for *future* planning.

Exhibit 2.5 **Strategic planning through cross-functional teams:** One of the reasons why Disney is a top media conglomerate is that it disabled its centralized strategic planning group and replaced it with division managers.

Martin Beddall/Alamy

Because of such problems, many companies have dropped formal matrix methods in favour of more customized approaches that better suit their specific situations. Moreover, unlike former strategic-planning efforts that rested mostly in the hands of senior managers at company headquarters, today's strategic planning has been decentralized. Increasingly, companies are placing responsibility for strategic planning in the hands of cross-functional teams of divisional managers who are close to their markets.

For example, consider The Walt Disney Company. Most people think of Disney as theme parks and wholesome family entertainment. But in the mid-1980s, Disney set up a powerful, centralized strategic planning group to guide the company's direction and growth. Over the next two decades, the strategic planning group turned The Walt Disney Company into a huge and diverse collection of media and entertainment businesses. The sprawling Walt Disney Company grew to include everything from theme resorts and film studios (Walt Disney Pictures, Touchstone Pictures, Pixar, and others) to media networks (ABC Television plus Disney Channel, ESPN, A&E, History Channel, and a half-dozen others), consumer products, and a cruise line.

The newly transformed Disney proved hard to manage and performed unevenly. To improve performance, Disney disbanded the centralized strategic planning unit, decentralizing its functions to Disney division managers. As a result, Disney retains its position at the head of the world's media conglomerates. Disney's sound strategic management of its broad mix of businesses has helped it fare better than rival media companies.[6]

Developing Strategies for Growth and Downsizing Beyond evaluating current businesses, designing the business portfolio involves finding businesses and products the company should consider in the future. Companies need growth if they are to compete more effectively, satisfy their stakeholders, and attract top talent. At the same time, a firm must be careful not to make growth itself an objective. The company's objective must be to manage *profitable* growth.

Marketing has the main responsibility for achieving profitable growth for the company. Marketing needs to identify, evaluate, and select market opportunities and establish strategies

FIGURE 2.3 The Product–Market Expansion Grid

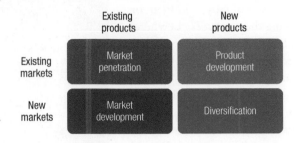

Product–market expansion grid

A portfolio-planning tool for identifying company growth opportunities through market penetration, market development, product development, or diversification.

for capturing them. One useful device for identifying growth opportunities is the **product–market expansion grid**, shown in Figure 2.3.[7] We apply it here to Starbucks.

> In only three decades, Starbucks has grown at an astonishing pace, from a small Seattle coffee shop to a nearly $13.3 billion powerhouse with more than 18 000 retail stores in 62 countries. In the United States alone, Starbucks serves more than 70 million espresso-dependent customers each week. Starbucks gives customers what it calls a "third place"—away from home and away from work. Growth is the engine that keeps Starbucks perking. However, in recent years, the company's remarkable success has drawn a full litter of copycats, ranging from direct competitors such as Caribou Coffee to fast-food merchants such as McDonald's McCafé. Almost every eatery, it seems, now serves its own special premium brew. To maintain its incredible growth in an increasingly overcaffeinated marketplace, Starbucks must brew up an ambitious, multipronged growth strategy.[8]

Market penetration

A strategy for company growth by increasing sales of current products to current market segments without changing the product.

First, Starbucks' management might consider whether the company can achieve deeper **market penetration**—making more sales to current customers without changing its original products. It might add new stores in current market areas to make it easier for customers to visit. In fact, Starbucks plans to add 3000 new stores over the next few years. Improvements in advertising, prices, service, menu selection, or store design might encourage customers to stop by more often, stay longer, or buy more during each visit. For example, Starbucks is remodelling many of its stores to give them more of a neighbourhood feel—with earth tones, wood counters, and handwritten menu boards. And to boost business beyond the breakfast rush, which still constitutes the bulk of the company's revenue, the chain has added an evening menu in some markets featuring wine, beer, and tapas such as "Warmed Rosemary and Brown Sugar Cashews" and "Bacon Wrapped Dates with Balsamic Glaze."

Market development

A strategy for company growth by identifying and developing new market segments for current company products.

Second, Starbucks might consider possibilities for **market development**—identifying and developing new markets for its current products. For instance, managers could review new demographic markets. Perhaps new groups—such as seniors—could be encouraged to visit Starbucks coffee shops for the first time or to buy more from them. Managers could also review new geographic markets. Starbucks is now expanding swiftly in non-U.S. markets, especially Asia. The company has 1000 stores in Japan, more than 1500 stores in China, and approximately 700 in South Korea.

Product development

A strategy for company growth by offering modified or new products to current market segments.

Third, Starbucks could consider **product development**—offering modified or new products to current markets. For example, to capture a piece of the $2 billion single-serve market, Starbucks developed Via instant coffee, and sells its coffees and Tazo teas in K-Cup packs that fit Keurig at-home brewers. Starbucks has also introduced a lighter-roast coffee called Blonde, developed to meet the tastes of the 40 percent of U.S. coffee drinkers who prefer lighter, milder roasts. As well, Starbucks is forging ahead into new product categories. For instance, it has entered the US$8 billion energy drink market with Starbucks Refreshers, a beverage that combines fruit juice and green coffee extract.

Diversification

A strategy for company growth through starting up or acquiring businesses outside the company's current products and markets.

Finally, Starbucks might consider **diversification**—starting up or buying businesses beyond its current products and markets. For example, the company acquired Evolution Fresh, a boutique provider of super-premium fresh-squeezed juices. Starbucks intends to use Evolution as its entry into the "health and wellness" category, including stand-alone stores called Evolution By Starbucks.

Companies must not only develop strategies for *growing* their business portfolios but also strategies for **downsizing** them. There are many reasons why a firm might want to abandon products or markets. The firm may have grown too fast or entered areas where it lacks experience. The market environment might change, making some of the company's products or markets less profitable. For example, in difficult economic times, many firms prune out weaker, less-profitable products and markets to focus their more limited resources on the strongest ones. Finally, some products or business units simply age and die.

Exhibit 2.6 Strategies for growth: To maintain its incredible growth, Starbucks has brewed up an ambitious, multipronged growth strategy.

Downsizing
Reducing the business portfolio by eliminating products or business units that are not profitable or that no longer fit the company's overall strategy.

When a firm finds brands or businesses that are unprofitable or that no longer fit its overall strategy, it must carefully prune, harvest, or divest them. For example, P&G sold off the last of its food brands, Pringles, to Kellogg, allowing the company to focus on household care and beauty and grooming products. And in recent years, GM has pruned several underperforming brands from its portfolio, including Oldsmobile, Pontiac, Saturn, Hummer, and Saab. Weak businesses usually require a disproportionate amount of management attention. Managers should focus on promising growth opportunities instead of frittering away energy trying to salvage fading ones.

Planning Marketing: Partnering to Build Customer Relationships LO3

The company's strategic plan establishes what kinds of businesses the company will operate and its objectives for each. Then, within each business unit, more detailed planning takes place. The major functional departments in each unit—marketing, finance, accounting, purchasing, operations, information systems, human resources, and others—must work together to accomplish strategic objectives.

Marketing plays a key role in the company's strategic planning in several ways. First, marketing provides a guiding *philosophy*—the marketing concept—that suggests that company strategy should revolve around building profitable relationships with important consumer groups. Second, marketing provides *inputs* to strategic planners by helping to identify attractive market opportunities and by assessing the firm's potential to take advantage of them. Finally, within individual business units, marketing designs *strategies* for reaching the unit's objectives. Once the unit's objectives are set, marketing's task is to help carry them out profitably.

Customer value is the key ingredient in the marketer's formula for success. However, as we noted in Chapter 1, marketers alone cannot produce superior value for customers. Although marketing plays a leading role, it can be only a partner in attracting, keeping, and growing customers. In addition to *customer relationship management*, marketers must practise *partner relationship management*. They must work closely with partners in other company departments to form an effective internal *value chain* that serves the customer. Moreover, they must partner effectively with other companies in the marketing system to form a competitively superior external *value delivery network*. One company that epitomizes the concept of providing value for its customers by developing relationships with them is Nike. (See Marketing@Work 2.1.)

MARKETING@WORK   2.1

Nike's Customer-Driven Marketing: Building Brand Engagement and Community

The Nike "swoosh"—it's everywhere! Just for fun, try counting the swooshes whenever you pick up the sports pages or watch a basketball game or tune into a televised soccer match. Over the past nearly 50 years, through innovative marketing, Nike has built the ever-present swoosh into one of the best-known brand symbols on the planet.

Early on, a brash, young Nike revolutionized sports marketing. To build image and market share, the brand lavishly outspent competitors on big-name endorsements, splashy promotional events, and big-budget, in-your-face "Just Do It" ads. Whereas competitors stressed technical performance, Nike built customer relationships. Beyond shoes, apparel, and equipment, Nike marketed a way of life, a genuine passion for sports, a "just do it" attitude. Customers didn't just wear their Nikes, they *experienced* them. As the company stated on its site, "Nike has always known the truth—it's not so much the shoes but where they take you."

Nike powered its way through the early years, aggressively adding products in a dozen new sports, including baseball, golf, skateboarding, wall climbing, bicycling, and hiking. It seemed that things just couldn't be going any better. In the late 1990s, however, Nike stumbled and its sales slipped. As the company grew larger, its creative juices seemed to run a bit dry and buyers seeking a new look switched to competing brands. Looking back, Nike's biggest obstacle may have been its own incredible success. As sales grew, the swoosh may have become too common to be cool. Instead of being *anti*-establishment, Nike *was* the establishment, and its hip, once-hot relationship with customers cooled. Nike needed to rekindle the brand's meaning to consumers.

To turn things around, Nike returned to its roots: new product innovation and a focus on customer relationships. But it set out to forge a new kind of brand–customer connection—a deeper, more personal, more engaging one. This time around, rather than simply outspending competitors on big media ads and celebrity endorsers who talk *at* customers, Nike shifted toward cutting-edge digital and social media marketing tools that interact *with* customers to build brand connections and community.

According to one industry analyst, "The legendary brand blew up its single-slogan approach and drafted a whole new playbook for the digital era."

Nike still invests heavily in traditional advertising. But its spending on TV and print media has dropped by a whopping 30 percent in only three years, even as its global marketing budget has increased steadily. Traditional media now account for only about 20 percent of the brand's $1 billion U.S. promotion budget. Instead, Nike spends the lion's share of its marketing budget on nontraditional media. Using community-oriented, digital-based social networking tools, Nike is now building communities of customers who talk not just with the company about the brand, but with each other as well.

Nike has mastered social networking, both online and off. Whether customers come to know Nike through ads, in-person events at Niketown stores, a local Nike running club, or at one of the company's profusion of community Web and social media sites, more and more people are bonding closely with the Nike brand.

Nike has raced ahead of its industry in the use of today's new social networking tools. In a ranking of 42 sportswear companies, digital consultancy L2 crowned Nike "top genius" in "digital IQ" for its innovative use of online, mobile, and social media. L2 also placed Nike first in creating brand "tribes"—large groups of highly engaged users—with the help of social media platforms such as Facebook, Twitter, Instagram, and Pinterest. For example, the main Nike Facebook page has more than 23 million Likes. The Nike Basketball page adds another 8 million, NIKEiD 2.5 million more, and Nike Running another 5.6 million. More than just numbers, Nike's social media presence engages customers at a high level and gets them talking with each other about the brand.

Nike excels at cross-media campaigns that integrate the new media with traditional tools to build brand community. For example, Nike's "Find Your

Stefano Dal Pozzolo/Newscom

Exhibit 2.7   Nike has mastered social networking, both online and off, creating deep engagement and community among customers. Its Nike+ and FuelBand apps and technologies have made Nike a part of the daily fitness routines of millions of customers around the world.

Greatness" campaign for the 2012 Olympics launched two days before the opening ceremonies—not with splashy media ads but with a video posted on YouTube, Nike websites, and other digital platforms. The compelling video featured people getting in touch with their inner athlete. Then, on opening day, Nike followed up with big-budget TV ads in 25 countries based on the video. But rather than just running the ads in isolation, the campaign urged customers to share their feelings about the "Find Your Greatness" message via Twitter and other digital media using a "#findgreatness" hashtag. Within a month, the video had been viewed more than 5 million times on Nike's YouTube channel alone.

Nike has also built brand community through groundbreaking mobile apps and technologies. For example, its Nike+ apps have helped Nike become a part of the daily fitness routines of millions of customers around the world. The Nike+ FuelBand, for instance, is an ergonomic work of art. Worn on the wrist, FuelBand converts just about every imaginable physical movement into NikeFuel, Nike's own universal activity metric. According to a Nike video called "Counts," whether your activity is running, jumping, baseball, skating, dancing, stacking sports cups, or chasing chickens, it counts for

Nike Fuel points. "Life is a sport," the video concludes. "Make it count." Everyday athletes can use NikeFuel to track their personal performance, then share and compare it across sports and geographic locations with others in the global Nike community. The Nike+ FuelBand mobile app lets users watch their progress, get extra motivation on the go, and stay connected with friends.

Nike+ has engaged a huge global brand community. The tickers on nikeplus.com update continually with numbers in the billions: 35 566 409 830 steps taken, 50 841 842 647 calories burned, and 14 364 639 579 NikeFuel points earned. The site also tracks personal achievements earned and daily goals hit by individuals in the Nike+ community. To date, the millions of Nike+ users worldwide have logged 844 265 265 miles. That's 33 740 trips around the world, or 1759 journeys to the moon and back.

Thus, Nike has built a new kinship and sense of community with and between the brand and its customers. Nike's marketing strategy is no longer only about big-budget ads at arm's length and aloof celebrity endorsers. Instead, the brand is connecting directly with customers, whether it's through local running clubs, a performance-tracking wristband, a 30-storey billboard that posts fan

headlines from Twitter, or videos that debut on YouTube rather than on prime-time TV. More than just something to buy, the Nike brand has once again become a part of customers' lives and times.

As a result, Nike remains the world's largest sports apparel company, an impressive 25 percent larger than closest rival Adidas. During the past several years, even as the faltering economy left most sports apparel and footwear competitors gasping for breath, Nike's global sales and income sprinted ahead nearly 60 percent.

As in sports competition, the strongest and best-prepared brand has the best chance of winning. With deep brand–customer relationships comes powerful competitive advantage. And Nike is once again very close to its customers. Notes Nike CEO Mark Parker, "Connecting used to be, 'Here's some product, and here's some advertising. We hope you like it.' Connecting today is a dialogue."

Sources: Austin Carr, "Nike: The No. 1 Most Innovative Company of 2013," *Fast Company*, March 2013, pp. 89–93+; Mary Lisbeth D'Amico, "Report Sends Nike and Adidas to Head of Digital Marketing Class," *Clickz*, September 25, 2012, www.clickz.com/clickz/news/2208172/report-sends-nike-and-adidas-to-head-of-digital-marketing-class; Brian Morrissey, "Nike Plus Starts to Open Up to Web," *Adweek*, July 20–July 27, 2009, p. 8; and Sebastian Joseph, "Nike Takes Social Media In-House," *Marketing Week*, January 3, 2013.

Partnering with Other Company Departments

Each company department can be thought of as a link in the company's internal **value chain**.[9] That is, each department carries out value-creating activities to design, produce, market, deliver, and support the firm's products. The firm's success depends not only on how well each department performs its work, but also on how well the various departments coordinate their activities.

For example, Walmart's goal is to create customer value and satisfaction by providing shoppers with the products they want at the lowest possible prices. Marketers at Walmart play an important role. They learn what customers need and stock the stores' shelves with the desired products at unbeatable low prices. They prepare advertising and merchandising programs and assist shoppers with customer service. Through these and other activities, Walmart's marketers help deliver value to customers.

However, the marketing department needs help from the company's other departments. Walmart's ability to help you "Save Money. Live Better" depends on the purchasing department's skill in developing the needed suppliers and buying from them at low cost. Walmart's information technology (IT) department must provide fast and accurate information about which products are selling in each store. And its operations people must provide effective, low-cost merchandise handling.

Value chain
The series of internal departments that carry out value-creating activities to design, produce, market, deliver, and support a firm's products.

Geoffrey Robinson/Alamy

Exhibit 2.8 The value chain:
Walmart's ability to help you "Save money. Live Better" by offering the right products at lower prices depends on the contributions of people in all of the company's departments.

A company's value chain is only as strong as its weakest link. Success depends on how well each department performs its work of adding customer value and on how well the activities of various departments are coordinated. At Walmart, if purchasing can't obtain the lowest prices from suppliers, or if operations can't distribute merchandise at the lowest costs, then marketing can't deliver on its promise of unbeatable low prices.

Ideally, then, a company's different functions should work in harmony to produce value for its customers. But, in practice, departmental relations are full of conflicts and misunderstandings. The marketing department strives to always understand the customer's point of view, but sometimes marketing's focus on customer satisfaction can cause other departments to do a poorer job *in their terms*. Marketing department actions can increase purchasing costs, disrupt production schedules, increase inventories, and create budget headaches. Sometimes, the other departments may resist the marketing department's efforts.

Yet marketers must find ways to get all departments to "think customer" and to develop a smoothly functioning value chain. One marketing expert puts it this way: "True market orientation . . . means that the entire company obsesses over creating value for the customer and views itself as a bundle of processes that profitably define, create, communicate, and deliver value to its target customers. . . . Everyone must do marketing regardless of function or department." Says another, "Engaging customers today requires commitment from the entire company. We're all marketers now."[10] This means that whether you're an accountant, operations manager, financial analyst, IT specialist, or human resources manager, you need to understand marketing and your role in creating customer value.

Partnering with Others in the Marketing System

In its quest to create customer value, the firm needs to look beyond its own internal value chain and into the value chains of its suppliers, distributors, and, ultimately, its customers. Consider McDonald's. People do not swarm to McDonald's because they love the chain's hamburgers—they flock to the McDonald's *system*, for everything it comprises and represents: a familiar restaurant, breakfast sandwiches, late-night snacks, fun products and services for kids, a drive-through, and a consistent level of service and value for the money. Throughout the world, McDonald's finely tuned value delivery system delivers a high standard of QSCV—quality, service, cleanliness, and value. McDonald's is effective only to the extent that it successfully partners with its franchisees, suppliers, and others to jointly create and consistently reinforce this positioning.

More companies today are partnering with other members of the supply chain—suppliers, distributors, and, ultimately, customers—to improve the performance of the customer **value delivery network**. For example, cosmetics maker L'Oréal knows the importance of building close relationships with its extensive network of suppliers, who supply everything from polymers and fats to spray cans and packaging to production equipment and office supplies.

Value delivery network
The network made up of the company, suppliers, distributors, and, ultimately, customers who partner with each other to improve the performance of the entire system.

L'Oréal is the world's largest cosmetics manufacturer, with 25 brands ranging from L'Oréal Paris and Maybelline New York to Kiehl's, Lancôme, and Redken. The company's supplier network is crucial to its success. As a result, L'Oréal treats suppliers as respected partners. On the one hand, it expects a lot from suppliers in terms of design innovation, quality, and socially responsible actions. The company carefully screens new suppliers and regularly assesses the performance of current suppliers. On the other hand, L'Oréal works closely with suppliers to help them meet its exacting standards. Whereas some companies make unreasonable demands of their suppliers and "squeeze" them for short-term gains, L'Oréal builds long-term supplier relationships based on mutual benefit and growth. According to the company's supplier website, it treats suppliers with "fundamental respect for their business, their culture, their growth, and the individuals who work there. Each relationship is based on . . . shared efforts aimed at promoting growth and mutual profits that make it possible for suppliers to invest, innovate, and compete." As a result, more than 75 percent of L'Oréal's supplier-partners have been working with the company for 10 years or more, and the majority of them for several decades. Says the company's head of purchasing, "The CEO wants to make L'Oréal a top performer and one of the world's most respected companies. Being respected also means being respected by our suppliers."[11]

INTS KALNINS/Reuters/Corbis

Exhibit 2.9 The value delivery system: L'Oréal builds long-term supplier relationships based on mutual benefit and growth. It "wants to make L'Oréal a top performer and one of the world's most respected companies. Being respected also means being respected by our suppliers."

Increasingly in today's marketplace, competition no longer takes place between individual competitors. Rather, it takes place between the entire value delivery networks created by these competitors. L'Oréal's performance against, say, Estée Lauder depends on the quality of L'Oréal's overall value delivery network versus Estée Lauder's. Even if L'Oréal makes the best products, it might lose in the marketplace if Estée Lauder's distribution network provides more customer-satisfying sales and service.

Marketing Strategy and the Marketing Mix LO4

Simulate on MyMarketingLab

Marketing Mix

The strategic plan defines the company's overall mission and objectives. Marketing's role and activities are shown in Figure 2.4, which summarizes the major activities involved in managing a customer-driven marketing strategy and the marketing mix.

Customers are at the centre of every organization's business, and the organization's goal is to create value for those customers and to build profitable relationships with them. Next comes **marketing strategy**—the marketing logic by which the company hopes to create this customer value and achieve these profitable relationships. The company decides which customers it will serve (segmentation and targeting) and how (differentiation and positioning). It identifies the total market, then divides it into smaller segments, selects the most promising segments, and focuses on serving and satisfying the customers in these segments.

Guided by marketing strategy, the company designs an integrated *marketing mix* made up of factors under its control—product, price, place, and promotion (the four *P*s). To find the best marketing strategy and mix, the company engages in marketing analysis, planning, implementation, and control. Through these activities, the company watches and adapts to the actors and forces in the marketing environment. We will now look briefly at each activity. Then, in later chapters, we will discuss each one in more depth.

Marketing strategy
The marketing logic by which the company hopes to create customer value and achieve profitable customer relationships.

FIGURE 2.4 Managing Marketing Strategies and the Marketing Mix

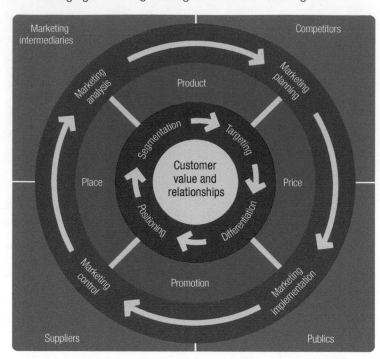

Customer-Driven Marketing Strategy

As we emphasized throughout Chapter 1, to succeed in today's competitive marketplace, companies need to be customer centred. They must win customers from competitors, and then keep and grow them by delivering greater value. But before it can satisfy customers, a company must first understand their needs and wants. Effective marketing begins with careful customer analysis.

Companies know that they cannot profitably serve all customers in all markets—at least, not in the same way. There are too many different kinds of customers—both individual consumers and business customers—with too many different kinds of needs. And most companies are in a position to serve some segments better than others. Thus, each company must divide up the total market, choose the best segments, and design strategies for profitably serving chosen segments. This process involves *market segmentation*, *market targeting*, *differentiation*, and *positioning*.

Market Segmentation The market consists of many types of customers, products, and needs. The marketer has to determine which segments offer the best opportunities. Consumers can be grouped and served in various ways based on geographic, demographic, psychographic, and behavioural factors. The process of dividing a market into distinct groups of buyers who have different needs, characteristics, or behaviours and who might require separate products or marketing programs is called **market segmentation**.

Every market has segments, but not all ways of segmenting a market are equally useful. For example, Tylenol would gain little by distinguishing between low-income and high-income pain-reliever users if both respond the same way to marketing efforts. A **market segment** consists of customers who have similar needs and requirements, and who therefore respond in a similar way to a given set of marketing efforts. In the car market, for example, consumers who want the biggest, most comfortable car regardless of price make up one market segment, while those who care mainly about price make up another segment. Plus, there are many other market segments for automobiles, including

Market segmentation
Dividing a market into distinct groups of buyers who have different needs, characteristics, or behaviours and who might require separate products or marketing programs.

Market segment
A group of customers who respond in a similar way to a given set of marketing efforts.

corporations that purchase company cars, taxi companies, and car rental companies, not to mention the different consumer segments such as families with small children, college and university students, sports car enthusiasts, and retirees. And that's just for cars—what about the different market segments for trucks? It would be impossible to make one car (or truck) model that would be favoured by customers in all these segments. That's why marketers must focus their efforts on understanding the needs of the people and organizations that make up the various market segments—and focus on meeting the needs of those market segments the company chooses to serve.

Market Targeting   After a company has defined market segments, it can enter one or many of these segments. **Market targeting** involves evaluating each market segment's attractiveness and selecting one or more segments to enter. A company should target segments in which it can profitably generate the greatest customer value and sustain it over time.

> **Market targeting**
> The process of evaluating each market segment's attractiveness and selecting one or more segments to enter.

A company with limited resources might decide to serve only one or a few special segments or "market niches." Such "nichers" specialize in serving customer segments that major competitors overlook or ignore. For example, Ferrari sells only 1500 of its very high-performance cars in the United States each year, but at very high prices—such as its Ferrari 458 Italia at $255 000, or the 740-horsepower F-12 Berlinetta at an eye-popping $400 000. Most nichers aren't quite so exotic. Profitable low-cost airline Allegiant Air avoids direct competition with larger major airline rivals by targeting smaller, neglected markets and new flyers. Nicher Allegiant "goes where they ain't." And Red Bull dominates its energy drink niche in the beverage industry so well that even giant competitors such as Coca-Cola and PepsiCo can't crack it (see Marketing@Work 2.2).

Alternatively, a company might choose to serve several related segments—perhaps those with different kinds of customers but with the same basic wants. Abercrombie & Fitch, for example, targets college and university students, teens, and kids with the same upscale, casual clothes and accessories in three different outlets: the original Abercrombie & Fitch, Hollister, and Abercrombie. Or a large company (like Honda and Ford) might decide to offer a complete range of products to serve all market segments.

Most companies enter a new market by serving a single segment, and if this proves successful, they add more segments. For example, Nike started with innovative running shoes for serious runners. Large companies eventually seek full market coverage. Nike now makes and sells a broad range of sports products for just about anyone and everyone, with the goal of "helping athletes at every level of ability reach their potential."[12] It has different products designed to meet the special needs of each segment it serves.

Market Differentiation and Positioning   After a company has decided which market segments to enter, it must decide how it will differentiate its market offering for each targeted segment and what positions it wants to occupy in those segments. A product's *position* is the place the product occupies relative to competitors' products in consumers' minds. Marketers must develop a positioning strategy that makes it clear to the market what differentiates their brand from the competition.

Positioning involves arranging for a product to occupy a clear, distinctive, and desirable place relative to competing products in the minds of consumers. This topic will be discussed in more detail in Chapters 7 and 8.

> **Positioning**
> Arranging for a product to occupy a clear, distinctive, and desirable place relative to competing products in the minds of consumers.

Marketers develop positioning strategies for their brands and products for the purpose of distinguishing them from competing brands. A positioning strategy is designed to make the consumer "think" a certain way about a brand, and, when done well, to create an emotional bond between the consumer and the brand. For example, when most Canadians think of Scotiabank they also think of hockey, because Scotiabank sponsors many hockey events and programs. When they think of BMO, they think of investments;

MARKETING@WORK 2.2

Red Bull: This Nicher "Gives You Wings"

There's no question: Coca-Cola and PepsiCo dominate the global beverage industry. Each boasts leading brands in almost every category, from carbonated soft drinks to enhanced juice drinks to bottled waters. Coca-Cola sells more than $48 billion worth of beverages worldwide, and PepsiCo isn't far behind, at approximately $32 billion. Both companies spend hundreds of millions of dollars annually on sophisticated marketing and advertising programs, and few competitors can match their distribution prowess. So how does a small company breaking into the beverage business compete with such global powerhouses? The best answer: It doesn't—at least not directly. Instead, it finds a unique market niche and runs where the big dogs don't.

That's what Red Bull does. When Red Bull first introduced its energy drink in 1987, few imagined that it would become the $5 billion-a-year success that it is today. Red Bull has succeeded by avoiding head-to-head battles with giants like Coca-Cola and Pepsi. Instead, it found a new beverage niche—energy drinks—that the market leaders had overlooked. Then it energized this niche with a unique product, brand personality, and marketing approach.

Back in 1987, energy drinks simply didn't exist. If you wanted a quick pick-me-up, about the only options were caffeinated soft drinks or a good old cup of coffee. But Red Bull founder Dietrich Mateschitz saw an unfilled customer need. He formulated a new beverage containing a hefty dose of caffeine, along with little-known ingredients such as taurine and glucuronolactone. It tasted terrible. But it packed the right punch, producing unique physical-energy and mental-clarity benefits. To make the new beverage even more distinctive, Mateschitz gave it a unique name—Red Bull, packaged it in a slim 245-millilitre blue-and-silver can with a distinct red-and-yellow logo, and tagged it with a $2-per-can price. With that unlikely combination, a whole new energy drink

category was born, with Red Bull as its only player.

The unique Red Bull product demanded equally unique brand positioning and personality, a declaration that this was no ordinary beverage. Red Bull's early marketing didn't disappoint. The brand's first and still only slogan—"Red Bull Gives You Wings"—communicated the product's energy-inducing benefits. More important, it tapped into the forces that moved the brand's narrow target niche—customers seeking to live life in the adrenalin-stoked fast lane.

To reinforce the "Gives You Wings" brand promise, and in line with the new brand's meagre early finances, Red Bull shunned the big-budget mass-media advertising common in the beverage industry at the time. Instead, it relied on grassroots, high-octane sports and event marketing. It sponsored extreme sports events (such as snowboarding and free-style motocross) and athletes who were overlooked by big beverage competitors but were spiking in popularity with Red Bull's target customers (such as Shawn White and Travis Pastrana).

In the years since, Red Bull has turned event marketing into a science. Today, the brand holds hundreds of events each year in dozens of sports around the

world. Each event features off-the-grid experiences designed to bring the high-octane world of Red Bull to its narrow but impassioned community of enthusiasts. Red Bull owns Formula 1 car racing teams and soccer clubs. Its name is plastered all over events such as the Red Bull Crashed Ice World Championship, the Red Bull Cliff Diving World Series, and the annual Red Bull Rampage free ride mountain bike competition. But it's not just about the events. It's about creating tactile engagements where people can feel, touch, taste, and live the brand face to face rather than simply reading about or watching it. Red Bull doesn't just sponsor an event—it *is* the event. The brand experience is often as much the story as the event itself.

Just one example of Red Bull's niche marketing genius is the Red Bull Stratos project, in which extreme skydiver Felix Baumgartner jumped from a helium balloon almost 40 kilometres above the Earth, breaking the sound barrier and numerous other records in the process. The jump also set records for consumer brand engagement. Baumgartner diving into space fit perfectly with Red Bull's "Gives You Wings" brand message. And both Baumgartner's capsule and his space-age jumpsuit were emblazoned

Stratos/ZUMA Press/Newscom

Exhibit 2.10 Niche marketing: Red Bull uses grassroots, high-octane event marketing to engage and energize its focused customer core, building an impassioned brand community that even resourceful competitors such as Coca-Cola and PepsiCo can't crack.

with the Red Bull name and logo. More than 8 million people watched the event live on 40 TV stations and 130 digital channels. For months before and after the event, you couldn't see or hear anything about Baumgartner without thinking about Red Bull.

Red Bull's niche marketing engages customers in a way that big-budget traditional marketing by competitors like Coca-Cola or Pepsi can't. According to one sports marketing executive, "When you're in the Super Bowl, you're one of 70 ads or so. When you go around the NASCAR track, you're one of 44 teams. This is about owning something that will leave an impression." For example, within 40 minutes of posting photos of Baumgartner's jump, Red Bull's Facebook page gained almost 216 000 Likes, 10 000 comments, and over 29 000 shares. On Twitter, literally half of the worldwide trending topics were related to Red Bull Stratos. And by one estimate, 90 million people worldwide followed the campaign on social media, creating 60 million trusted brand impressions. You just can't buy that kind of consumer engagement in traditional media. "Red Bull Stratos was a priceless brand experience," concludes one social marketing analyst. "No company has ever triggered brand advocacy at this scale."

More than just a niche beverage company, Red Bull today has become a close-knit brand community that engages customers with both products and absorbing brand content. Beyond its products, Red Bull produces a steady stream of event and social media content that engages and entertains brand fans in relevant ways. During the last few years, for example, Red Bull's Media House unit has filmed movies, signed a deal with NBC for a show called *Red Bull Signature Series*, developed reality-TV ideas with big-name producers, become one of YouTube's biggest partners in publishing original content, and loaded its own Web and mobile sites with unique content features. "Whenever we [have done] any event, or signed an athlete or executed a project, everything has been put on film or photographed. Stories have been told," says the head of the Red Bull Media House unit. "It's part of the DNA of the brand."

Red Bull can't compete directly across the board with the Coca-Colas and PepsiCos of the beverage industry—it doesn't even try. Then again, given the depth of consumer engagement and loyalty that Red Bull engenders in its own small corner of the beverage world, Coke and Pepsi have found it even more difficult to compete with Red Bull in the energy drink niche. Red Bull still owns 44 percent of the energy drink category it created, with other independents Monster and Rockstar holding strong second- and third-place positions. By contrast, despite hefty investments, Coca-Cola and PepsiCo have yet to put much of a dent in the category. Coca-Cola's NOS and Full Throttle brands capture only about a 5 percent combined market share; Pepsi's Amp and Kickstart brands have suffered the same dismal fate.

That's what niche marketing is all about—a well-defined brand engaging a focused customer community with meaningful brand relationships that even large and resourceful competitors can't crack. Through smart niching, Red Bull has given its customers—and itself—new wings and a whole new shot of energy.

Sources: Travis Hoium, "Coke and Pepsi Up Against a Young Monster—and Losing," *Daily Finance*, March 26, 2013; Janean Chun, "Bull Stratos May Change Future of Marketing," *Huffington Post*, October 15, 2012; Brian Kotlyar, "7 Social Campaign Insights from Red Bull Stratos," *DG Blog*, October 23, 2012; Teressa Iezzi, "Red Bull Media House," *Fast Company*, March, 2013; and Redbull's website (redbull.com), accessed March 2015.

and when they think of RBC, they think of Arbie, the character with the bowler hat who is featured in most of the bank's marketing communications materials.

In positioning a product or brand, the company first identifies possible customer value differences that provide competitive advantages upon which to build the position. In other words, the company must identify what it is about its product that offers greater value, and that would motivate a customer to choose it over the competition's offering. Of course, if the company *promises* greater value, it must then *deliver* that greater value. Effective positioning begins with **differentiation**—actually *differentiating* the company's market offering so that it gives consumers more value. Once the company has chosen a desired position, it must take strong steps to deliver and communicate that position to target consumers. The company's entire marketing program should support the chosen positioning strategy.

A company's differentiation and positioning strategy is usually a decision that's made once and then reinforced through all its marketing and communications activities for many years. However, sometimes a brand must be repositioned, and doing so requires just as much careful strategic planning as the original positioning did. Take Kentucky Fried Chicken, for example—or, rather, KFC, as it prefers to be known today. The name was changed in the early 1990s when the company began a carefully planned repositioning of its famous brand, placing less emphasis on fried foods and more emphasis on healthier options in an effort to change the way consumers thought about it. Although the Original Recipe fried chicken in a bucket is still available, today's KFC customers can

Differentiation
Actually differentiating the market offering to create superior customer value.

choose grilled chicken instead of fried, and can choose from a variety of sandwiches, wraps, and chicken-related snacks. This repositioning changed the perception of KFC from "greasy fried chicken" to "healthy chicken choices."

Developing an Integrated Marketing Mix

After deciding on its overall marketing strategy, the company is ready to begin planning the details of the marketing mix, one of the major concepts in modern marketing. The **marketing mix** is the set of controllable, tactical marketing tools that the firm blends to produce the response it wants in the target market. The marketing mix consists of everything the firm can do to influence the demand for its product. The many possibilities can be collected into four groups of variables known as "the four Ps": *product*, *price*, *place*, and *promotion*. Figure 2.5 shows the marketing tools under each *P*.

Marketing mix
The set of controllable, tactical marketing tools—product, price, place, and promotion—that the firm blends to produce the response it wants in the target market.

- *Product* refers to the market offering—whether it's a tangible product, a service, or a combination of goods and services. For example, a Ford Escape is a product that comes in different colours and different model variations. It also has optional features that a consumer may choose to purchase. The car comes fully serviced and with a comprehensive warranty, which is also part of the product. And many Ford dealerships also include service centres to keep the Escape running smoothly.

- *Price* is the amount of money customers must pay to obtain the product. Ford calculates suggested retail prices that its dealers might charge for each Escape. But Ford dealers rarely charge the full sticker price. Instead, they negotiate the price with each customer, offering discounts, trade-in allowances, and credit terms. These actions adjust prices for the current competitive and economic situations and bring them into line with the buyer's perception of the car's value.

- *Place* refers to the distribution of the product and the availability of the service. Ford partners with a large body of independently owned dealerships that sell the company's many different models. Ford selects its dealers carefully and supports them strongly. The dealers keep an inventory of Ford automobiles, demonstrate them to potential buyers, negotiate prices, close sales, and service the cars after the sale.

FIGURE 2.5 The Four *P*s of the Marketing Mix

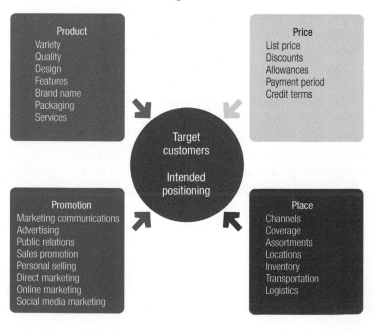

FIGURE 2.6 Transforming the Four *P*s into the Four *C*s

Four *P*s	Four *C*s
Product	Customer solution
Price	Customer cost
Place	Convenience
Promotion	Communication

- *Promotion* means activities that communicate the merits of the product and persuade customers to buy it. Ford spends more than $2.1 billion each year on advertising to communicate the benefits of its products to consumers.[13] Dealership salespeople assist potential buyers and persuade them that Ford is the best car for them. Ford and its dealers offer special promotions—sales, cash rebates, and low financing rates—as added purchase incentives. And Ford's Facebook, Twitter, YouTube, and other social media platforms engage consumers with the brand as well as with other brand fans.

An effective marketing program blends all of the marketing mix elements into an integrated marketing program designed to achieve the company's marketing objectives by delivering value to customers. The marketing mix constitutes the company's tactical tool kit for establishing strong positioning in target markets.

Some critics think that the four *P*s may omit or underemphasize certain important activities. For example, they ask, "Where are services? Just because they don't start with a *P* doesn't justify omitting them." The answer is that services, such as banking, airline, and retailing services, are products too. We might call them *service products*. "Where is packaging?" the critics might ask. Marketers would answer that they include packaging as one of many product decisions. All said, as Figure 2.5 suggests, many marketing activities that might appear to be left out of the marketing mix are included under one of the four *P*s. The issue is not whether there should be 4, 6, or 10 *P*s so much as what framework is most helpful in designing integrated marketing programs.

There is another concern, however, that is valid. It holds that the four *P*s concept takes the seller's view of the market, not the buyer's view. From the buyer's viewpoint, in this age of customer value and relationships, the four *P*s might be better described as the four *C*s:[14]

Customer solution: Whereas marketers see themselves as selling products, customers see themselves as buying value or solutions to their problems.

Customer cost: Marketers set prices, but customers are interested in the total costs to them of obtaining, using, and disposing of a product.

Convenience: Customers want the product and service to be conveniently available.

Communication: Of course, today's consumer demands communication from marketers.

It's a matter of perspective—the consumer views the market differently from the marketer. So marketers would do well to think through the four *C*s first and then build the four *P*s on that platform.

Managing the Marketing Effort LO5

In addition to being good at the *marketing* in marketing management, companies need to pay attention to the *management*. Managing the marketing process requires the four marketing management functions shown in Figure 2.7—*analysis*, *planning*, *implementation*, and *control*. The company first develops company-wide strategic plans and then translates them into marketing and other plans for each division, product, and brand. Through

FIGURE 2.7   Managing Marketing: Analysis, Planning, Implementation, and Control

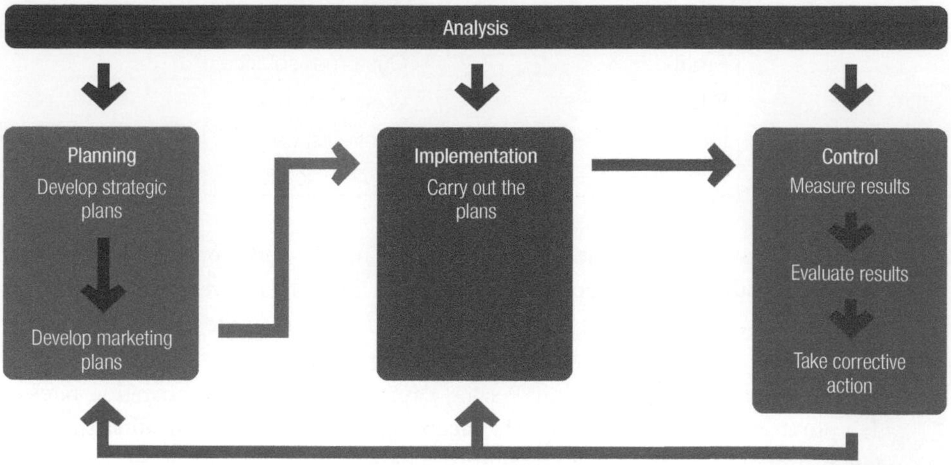

Analysis

Planning
Develop strategic plans

Develop marketing plans

Implementation
Carry out the plans

Control
Measure results

Evaluate results

Take corrective action

implementation, the company turns the plans into actions. Control consists of measuring and evaluating the results of marketing activities and taking corrective action where needed. Finally, marketing analysis provides information and evaluations needed for all of the other marketing activities.

Marketing Analysis

SWOT analysis

An overall evaluation of the company's strengths (S), weaknesses (W), opportunities (O), and threats (T).

Managing the marketing function begins with a complete analysis of the company's situation. The marketer should conduct a **SWOT analysis**, by which it evaluates the company's overall strengths (S), weaknesses (W), opportunities (O), and threats (T) (see Figure 2.8). Strengths include internal capabilities, resources, and positive situational factors that may help the company serve its customers and achieve its objectives. Weaknesses include internal limitations and negative situational factors that may interfere with the company's performance. Opportunities are favourable factors or trends in the external environment that the company may be able to exploit to its advantage. And threats are unfavourable external factors or trends that may present challenges to performance.

The company should analyze its markets and marketing environment to find attractive opportunities and identify environmental threats. It should analyze company strengths and weaknesses as well as current and possible marketing actions to determine which opportunities it can best pursue. The goal is to match the company's strengths to attractive

FIGURE 2.8   SWOT Analysis: Strengths (S), Weaknesses (W), Opportunities (O), and Threats (T)

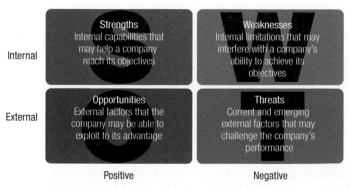

Source: Roland T. Rust, Katherine N. Lemon, and Valerie A. Zeithaml, "Return on Marketing: Using Consumer Equity to Focus Marketing Strategy," *Journal of Marketing*, January 2004, p. 112.

opportunities in the environment, while eliminating or overcoming the weaknesses and minimizing the threats. Marketing analysis provides inputs to each of the other marketing management functions. We discuss marketing analysis more fully in Chapter 4.

Marketing Planning

Through strategic planning, the company decides what it wants to do with each business unit. Marketing planning involves deciding on marketing strategies that will help the company attain its overall strategic objectives. A detailed marketing plan is needed for each business, product, or brand. What does a marketing plan look like? Our discussion focuses on product or brand marketing plans.

Table 2.2 outlines the major sections of a typical product or brand marketing plan. (See Appendix 2 for a sample marketing plan.) The plan begins with an executive summary that quickly reviews major assessments, goals, and recommendations. The main section of the plan presents a detailed SWOT analysis of the current marketing situation

TABLE 2.2	Contents of a Marketing Plan
Section	**Purpose**
Executive summary	Presents a brief summary of the main goals and recommendations of the plan for management review, helping top management find the plan's major points quickly. A table of contents should follow the executive summary.
Current marketing situation	Describes the target market and company's position in it, including information about the market, product performance, competition, and distribution. This section includes the following: ■ A *market description* that defines the market and major segments, and then reviews customer needs and factors in the marketing environment that may affect customer purchasing. ■ A *product review* that shows sales, prices, and gross margins of the major products in the product line. ■ A review of *competition* that identifies major competitors and assesses their market positions and strategies for product quality, pricing, distribution, and promotion. ■ A review of *distribution* that evaluates recent sales trends and other developments in major distribution channels.
Threats and opportunities analysis	Assesses major threats and opportunities that the product might face, helping management anticipate important positive or negative developments that might have an impact on the firm and its strategies.
Objectives and issues	States the marketing objectives that the company would like to attain during the plan's term and discusses key issues that will affect their attainment. For example, if the goal is to achieve 15 percent market share, this section looks at how this goal might be achieved.
Marketing strategy	Outlines the broad marketing logic by which the business unit hopes to create customer value and relationships as well as the specifics of target markets, positioning, and marketing expenditure levels. How will the company create value for customers in order to capture value from customers in return? This section also outlines specific strategies for each marketing mix element and explains how each responds to the threats, opportunities, and critical issues spelled out earlier in the plan.
Action programs	Spells out how marketing strategies will be turned into specific action programs that answer the following questions: *What* will be done? *When* will it be done? *Who* will do it? *How* much will it cost?
Budgets	Details a supporting marketing budget that is essentially a projected profit-and-loss statement. It shows expected revenues (forecasted number of units sold and the average net price) and expected costs of production, distribution, and marketing. The difference is the projected profit. Once approved by higher management, the budget becomes the basis for materials buying, production scheduling, personnel planning, and marketing operations.
Controls	Outlines the control that will be used to monitor progress and allow higher management to review implementation results and spot products that are not meeting their goals. It includes measures of return on marketing investment.

Exhibit 2.11 Marketing implementation: At Michelin, marketing implementation requires that thousands of people inside and outside the company work together to convince customers that "the right tire changes everything."

Marketing implementation
The process that turns marketing strategies and plans into marketing actions to accomplish strategic marketing objectives.

as well as potential threats and opportunities. The plan next states major objectives for the brand and outlines the specifics of a marketing strategy for achieving them.

A *marketing strategy* consists of specific strategies for target markets, positioning, the marketing mix, and marketing expenditure levels. It outlines how the company intends to create value for target customers in order to capture value in return. In this section, the planner explains how each strategy responds to the threats, opportunities, and critical issues spelled out earlier in the plan. Additional sections of the marketing plan lay out an action program for implementing the marketing strategy, along with the details of a supporting *marketing budget*. The last section outlines the controls that will be used to monitor progress, measure return on marketing investment, and take corrective action.

Marketing Implementation

Planning good strategies is only a start toward successful marketing. A brilliant marketing strategy counts for little if the company fails to implement it properly. **Marketing implementation** is the process that turns marketing *plans* into marketing *actions* to accomplish strategic marketing objectives. Whereas marketing planning addresses the *what* and *why* of marketing activities, implementation addresses the *who*, *where*, *when*, and *how*.

Many managers think that "doing things right" (implementation) is as important as, or even more important than, "doing the right things" (strategy). The fact is that both are critical to success, and companies can gain competitive advantages through effective implementation. One firm can have essentially the same strategy as another, yet win in the marketplace through faster or better execution. Still, implementation is difficult—it's often easier to think up good marketing strategies than it is to carry them out.

In an increasingly connected world, people at all levels of the marketing system must work together to implement marketing strategies and plans. At Michelin, for example, marketing implementation for the company's original equipment, replacement, industrial, and commercial tires requires day-to-day decisions and actions by thousands of people both inside and outside the organization. Marketing managers make decisions about target segments, branding, product development, pricing, promotion, and distribution. They talk with engineering about product designs, with manufacturing about production and inventory levels, and with finance about funding and cash flows. They also connect with outside people, such as advertising agencies to plan ad campaigns and the news media to obtain publicity support. The sales force works closely with automobile manufacturers and supports independent Michelin dealers and large retailers like Walmart in their efforts to convince buyers of all types and sizes of tires that "the right tire changes everything."

Marketing Department Organization

The company must design a marketing organization that can carry out marketing strategies and plans. If the company is very small, one person might do all of the research, selling, advertising, customer service, and other marketing work. As the company expands, a marketing department emerges to plan and carry out marketing activities. In large companies, this department contains many specialists. They have product and market managers, sales managers and salespeople, market researchers, advertising experts, and many other specialists.

To head up such large marketing organizations, many companies have now created a *chief marketing officer* (or CMO) position. The CMO is the newest member of the team of senior executives at major corporations, sometimes referred to as the "C-suite." They include the chief executive officer (CEO) or chief operating officer (COO), the chief financial officer (CFO), the chief communications officer (CCO), and the chief technology officer (CTO). The chief marketing officer is responsible for all top-level marketing functions, including sales management, product development, distribution and channel management, pricing strategy, and market research; all marketing communications activities, including advertising, sales promotions, direct marketing, and online marketing; and the management of outside advertising and media agencies. In most organizations, the CMO is even responsible for customer service. It's no wonder that the director of McKinsey & Company once said, "The job of CMO is not for the faint of heart."[15] Consider, for example, Duncan Fulton.

Duncan Fulton is not your typical CMO. With a background in public relations and an all-in commitment to social and digital media, he's in charge of all marketing activities at the Mark's and FGL Sports divisions of Canadian Tire Corporation. As a member of the executive team, he works across all the company's business areas— including Canadian Tire Retail, Automotive, Part Source, Petroleum, and Financial Services—and is closely involved with Jumpstart, the company's charity. That's a lot of marketing for one person to oversee!

But Fulton is up for the challenge. That's because his background is primarily in PR, consumer research, and digital—disciplines historically undervalued in the CMO role. Fulton is an out-of-the-box thinker and creative marketing strategist. Since he joined the corporation in 2009, he's been the brains behind some very successful and innovative marketing programs— including Canadian Tire's Christmas in July event, for which the company rented a three-floor penthouse at the SoHo Metropolitan in downtown Toronto, decked it out with seven different Debbie Travis themes, and had staff make cookies and apple cider so that by the time media walked in it even smelled like Christmas.

Fulton was also behind the rebranding of Sport Chek and the launch of the new flagship store on Yonge Street in Toronto. He applied the lessons learned rallying people around causes and ideas to rallying consumers around Canadian Tire and its associated retailers. Says Fulton, "We see a general inability of sporting goods retailers to inspire their customers, but when you inspire someone, you're connecting at a more emotional level than by just completing a transaction with them."[16]

John Hryniuk

Exhibit 2.12 Not your typical CMO: Duncan Fulton, chief marketing officer for Mark's and FGL Sports at Canadian Tire Corporation, strives to rally all the company's marketing activities and personnel around the idea of inspiring consumers through sports.

Modern marketing departments can be arranged in several ways. The most common form of marketing organization is the *functional organization*. Under this organization, different marketing activities are headed by a functional specialist—a sales manager, advertising manager, marketing research manager, customer-service manager, or new-product manager.

A company that sells across the country or internationally often uses a *geographic organization*. Its sales and marketing people are assigned to specific countries, regions, and districts. Geographic organization allows salespeople to settle into a territory, get to know their customers, and work with a minimum of travel time and cost. Companies with many very different products or brands often create a *product management organization*. Using this approach, a product manager develops and implements a complete strategy and marketing program for a specific product or brand.

For companies that sell one product line to many different types of markets and customers that have different needs and preferences, a *market* or *customer management organization* might be best. A market management organization is similar to the product management organization. Market managers are responsible for developing marketing strategies and plans for their specific markets or customers. This system's main advantage is that the company is organized around the needs of specific customer segments. Many companies develop special organizations to manage their relationships with large customers. For example, companies such as Procter & Gamble and Black & Decker have large teams, or even whole divisions, set up to serve large customers such as Walmart, Safeway, or Home Depot.

Large companies that produce many different products flowing into many different geographic and customer markets usually employ some *combination* of the functional, geographic, product, and market organization forms.

Marketing organization has become an increasingly important issue in recent years. More and more, companies are shifting their brand management focus toward *customer management*—moving away from managing only product or brand profitability and toward managing customer profitability and customer equity. They think of themselves not as managing portfolios of brands but as managing portfolios of customers. And rather than managing the fortunes of a brand, they see themselves as managing customer–brand engagement, experiences, and relationships.

Marketing Control

Marketing control
The process of measuring and
evaluating the results of marketing
strategies and plans and taking
corrective action to ensure that
objectives are achieved.

Because many surprises occur during the implementation of marketing plans, marketers must practise constant **marketing control**—the process of measuring and evaluating the results of marketing strategies and plans and taking corrective action to ensure that objectives are attained. Marketing control involves four steps. Management first sets specific marketing goals. It then measures its performance in the marketplace and evaluates the causes of any differences between expected and actual performance. Finally, management takes corrective action to close the gaps between its goals and its performance. This may require changing the action programs or even changing the goals.

Operating control involves checking ongoing performance against the annual plan and taking corrective action when necessary. Its purpose is to ensure that the company achieves the sales, profits, and other goals set out in its annual plan. It also involves determining the profitability of different products, territories, markets, and channels. *Strategic control* involves looking at whether the company's basic strategies are well matched to its opportunities. Marketing strategies and programs can quickly become outdated, and each company should periodically reassess its overall approach to the marketplace.

Measuring and Managing Return on Marketing Investment

Marketing managers must ensure that their marketing dollars are being well spent. For every planned marketing activity—whether it's creating a new product, changing the packaging, opening a new store, or developing and running an advertising campaign—there must be clearly stated objectives and a method for measuring the success of the activity after it's been completed. Marketers are being increasingly called upon to justify their activities through **return on marketing investment, or marketing ROI**—the net return from a marketing investment divided by the costs of the marketing investment. It measures the profits generated by investments in marketing activities.

A company can assess return on marketing in terms of standard marketing performance measures, such as brand awareness, sales, or market share. Marketing performance measurements are called *metrics*, and are measured and calculated using software tools, a process that has become much easier since the advent of the Internet and online advertising.

Some of the most frequently used marketing metrics include measurements of customer satisfaction, customer retention, market share, marketing spending, revenue, website traffic, and profits. The challenge facing today's marketers, however, is that not everything can be reduced to numbers: Many qualitative marketing results, including enhanced brand recognition, reputation, and customer loyalty, are difficult to measure. Moreover, although marketing executives are under increasing pressure to show a return on investment for their programs, many say that they lack the technological resources needed to measure these programs. When asked to identify the internal barriers to implementing marketing ROI programs, nearly half of the marketing managers surveyed reported problems with data availability or integrity, and more than half said that lack of technology and infrastructure was a problem. They also reported that their organizations lacked the know-how to implement marketing metrics.[17]

With the rise of social media, most companies today have a Facebook and Twitter presence for their brand, and are experimenting with Instagram and other forms of social and mobile marketing tools. There are two major challenges facing marketers, however. The first is how to use these tools in a way that achieves marketing goals. The second is how to measure the effects of social media programs. One expert suggests that marketers measure social media effects through engagement, retention, and awareness levels rather than in monetary terms. The key is to clearly define business, marketing, and consumer objectives; however, this is often harder than it seems. "Often marketers will say, 'I want to be on Facebook. I want to be on Twitter.' These aren't objectives as much as they are tactics—objectives need to be measurable and achievable. For example, a marketing objective would be to improve the usability of the homepage to ultimately increase [sales] conversion."[18]

There are many tools available to assist marketers with measuring and analyzing their marketing activities. Google Analytics, for example, is a free software tool that helps marketers and website owners understand who is coming to their website, what they are doing there, and how they can use that information to optimize their online activities. It tracks details such as which pages on the website visitors land on, how much time they spend on each page, and which links they click on—and collects all that data as sets of numbers, or metrics. But numbers and metrics by themselves have no meaning; they become usable marketing information only through analysis—and that's where tools such as Google Analytics come in.

Exhibit 2.13 Marketing metrics: Google Analytics is used by major marketers such as Dolby, Adobe, and many other Fortune 500 companies. It's also used by the White House and the FBI to analyze the activity on their websites.

Return on marketing investment (or marketing ROI)
The net return from a marketing investment divided by the costs of the marketing investment.

FIGURE 2.9 Return on Marketing Investment

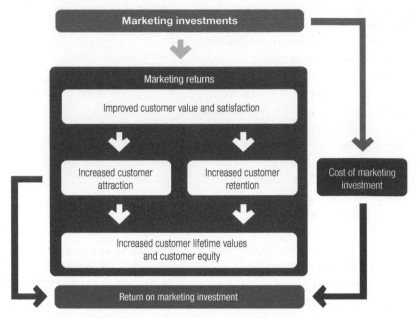

Source: Adapted from Roland T. Rust, Katherine N. Lemon, and Valerie A. Zeithaml, "Return on Marketing: Using Consumer Equity to Focus Marketing Strategy," *Journal of Marketing*, January 2004, p. 112.

Increasingly, however, beyond standard performance measures, marketers are using customer-centred measures of marketing impact, such as customer acquisition, customer retention, customer lifetime value, and customer equity. These measures capture not just current marketing performance but also future performance resulting from stronger customer relationships. Figure 2.9 illustrates marketing expenditures as investments that produce returns in the form of more profitable customer relationships.[19] Marketing investments result in improved customer value and satisfaction, which increase customer attraction and retention. This in turn increases individual customer lifetime values and the firm's overall customer equity. Increased customer equity, in relation to the cost of the marketing investments, determines return on marketing investment.

Regardless of how it's defined or measured, marketing ROI is here to stay, and the modern marketing manager must learn how to use marketing metrics and analytics. In today's super-connected world, with seemingly limitless amounts of data available to marketers, the ability to measure marketing activities and analyze marketing information is the key to understanding customer behaviour and being able to predict how target customers will react to the company's marketing offerings. As one marketer puts it, marketers "have got to know how to count."[20]

The Four Pillars Strategy

A look at the familiar storefront of any Boston Pizza location across Canada suggests a simplified way to dine out with your family or friends. It would make sense, then, that the general philosophy directing the brand is similarly simple. So simple, in fact, that the driver for all decision making is based on what BP calls the four pillars:

1. A Commitment to Continually Improving the Guest Experience
2. A Commitment to Building the Boston Pizza Brand
3. A Commitment to Franchisee Profitability
4. A Commitment to Being Involved in Our Communities
   (Boston Pizza Royalties Income Trust Fund, Annual Report, 2014)

Such commitments are more than just fancy corporate-speak; president and CEO Mark Pacinda credited these four pillars with BP's record-breaking success in 2014. That was the year Boston Pizza celebrated its 50th anniversary, not only by selling more than 85 000 pizzas from coast to coast in a single day (to mark the milestone), but also by ringing up over $1 billion in sales. "While bigger isn't always better," Pacinda noted, "we view this record sales level as further evidence that Boston Pizza is strengthening its position as Canada's number one casual dining brand by focusing on our four pillars strategy."

But while the four pillars seem to have served Boston Pizza well, making it into Canada's premier full-service restaurant with over 370 stores nationwide and expanding at a rapid clip, "there's still more to accomplish," said Pacinda. As BP entered into its 51st year, he introduced the brand's new "We'll Make You a Fan" campaign as more than just a tagline. "It's a promise to our guests that we'll do what it takes to provide them with exceptional service, delicious and craveable food, and the perfect guest experience in our restaurants from coast to coast."

QUESTIONS

1. Do you think there is a priority system to Boston Pizza's four pillar strategy? If not, do you think there should be? Why?
2. Is it practical (or even possible) to make all corporate decisions while ensuring that all four decision criteria (aka the four pillars strategy) are met?
3. Visit bostonpizza.com. Find and state BP's mission statement. Does it appear to be consistent with the brand's four pillar strategy?

REVIEWING THE CONCEPTS

 Explain company-wide strategic planning and its four steps.

Strategic planning sets the stage for the rest of the company's planning. Marketing contributes to strategic planning, and the overall plan defines marketing's role in the company.

Strategic planning involves developing a strategy for long-run survival and growth. It consists of four steps: (1) defining the company's mission, (2) setting objectives and goals, (3) designing a business portfolio, and (4) developing functional plans. The company's mission should be market oriented, realistic, specific, motivating, and consistent with the market environment. The mission is then transformed into detailed *supporting goals and objectives*, which in turn guide decisions about the *business portfolio*. Then each business and product unit must develop *detailed marketing plans* in line with the company-wide plan.

 Discuss how to design business portfolios and develop growth strategies.

Guided by the company's mission statement and objectives, management plans its *business portfolio*, or the collection of businesses and products that make up the company. The firm wants to produce a business portfolio that best fits its strengths and weaknesses to opportunities in the environment. To do this, it must analyze and adjust its *current* business portfolio and develop growth and downsizing strategies for adjusting the *future* portfolio. The company might use a formal portfolio-planning method. But many companies are now designing more-customized portfolio-planning approaches that better suit their unique situations.

LO3 **Explain marketing's role in strategic planning and how marketing works with its partners to create and deliver customer value.**

Under the strategic plan, the major functional departments—marketing, finance, accounting, purchasing, operations, information systems, human resources, and others—must work together to accomplish strategic objectives. Marketing plays a key role in the company's strategic planning by providing a *marketing concept philosophy* and *inputs* regarding attractive market opportunities. Within individual business units, marketing designs *strategies* for reaching the unit's objectives and helps carry them out profitably.

Marketers alone cannot produce superior value for customers. Marketers must practise *partner relationship management*, working closely with partners in other departments to form an effective *value chain* that serves the customer. And they must partner effectively with other companies in the marketing system to form a competitively superior *value delivery network*.

 Describe the elements of a customer-driven marketing strategy and mix, and the forces that influence it.

Consumer value and relationships are at the centre of marketing strategy and programs. Through market segmentation, targeting, differentiation, and positioning, the company divides the total market into smaller segments, selects segments it can best serve, and decides how it wants to bring value to target consumers in the selected segments. It then designs an *integrated marketing* mix to produce the response it wants in the target market. The marketing mix consists of product, price, place, and promotion decisions (the four Ps).

 List the marketing management functions, including the elements of a marketing plan, and discuss the importance of measuring and managing return on marketing investment.

To find the best strategy and mix and put them into action, the company engages in marketing analysis, planning, implementation, and control. The main components of a *marketing plan* are the executive summary, current marketing situation, threats and opportunities, objectives and issues, marketing strategies, action programs, budgets, and controls. To plan good strategies is often easier than to carry them out. To be successful, companies must also be effective at *implementation*—turning marketing strategies into marketing actions.

Marketing departments can be organized in one or a combination of ways: *functional marketing organization, geographic organization, product management organization,* or *market management organization*. In this age of customer relationships, more and more companies are now changing their organizational focus from product or territory management to customer relationship management. Marketing organizations carry out *marketing control*, both operating control and strategic control.

Marketing managers must ensure that their marketing dollars are being well spent. In a tighter economy, today's marketers face growing pressures to show that they are adding value in line with their costs. In response, marketers are developing better measures of *return on marketing investment*. Increasingly, they are using customer-centred measures of marketing impact as a key input into their strategic decision making.

MyMarketingLab

Study, practise, and explore real marketing situations with these helpful resources:

- **Interactive Lesson Presentations:** Work through interactive presentations and assessments to test your knowledge of marketing concepts.
- **Study Plan:** Check your understanding of chapter concepts with self-study quizzes.
- **Dynamic Study Modules:** Work through adaptive study modules on your computer, tablet, or mobile device.
- **Simulations:** Practise decision-making in simulated marketing environments.

DISCUSSION QUESTIONS

1. Explain why it is important for all departments of an organization—marketing, accounting, finance, operations management, human resources, and so on—to "think customer." Why is it important that even people who are not in marketing understand it?

2. Imagine you are a team of marketing managers at a large consumer packaged-goods company, and you're planning the launch of a new line of shampoo. With which departments in your company will you need to work to plan the launch, and what role will each department play?

3. Discuss how TELUS, the Canadian telecommunications company, might use the processes of market segmentation, market targeting, and market positioning. How is TELUS differentiated from its competitors?

4. In a small group, develop a SWOT analysis for a business in your community. From that analysis, recommend a marketing strategy and marketing mix for this business.

5. Go to www.pg.com to learn about the brands offered by P&G. Select one product category in which P&G offers multiple brands. What is P&G's positioning for each brand in that product category? Then, visit a store and record the prices of each brand, using a common basis such as price per millilitre. Write a brief report on what you learn. Are there meaningful positioning differences between the brands? Are any price differences you find justified?

CRITICAL THINKING EXERCISES

1. In a small group, research a company and construct a growth–share matrix of the company's products, brands, or strategic business units. Recommend a strategy for each unit in the matrix.

2. Find the mission statements of two for-profit and two not-for-profit organizations. Evaluate these mission statements with respect to their market orientations.

ONLINE, MOBILE, AND SOCIAL MEDIA MARKETING

In 2011, Hewlett-Packard CEO Leo Apothekar made the strategic decision to exit the personal computer (PC) business, but he got fired and incoming CEO Meg Wittman reversed that decision. However, sales of PCs have plummeted since the introduction of post-PC devices such as tablets, e-readers, and smartphones. Some people are now referring to PCs as "PC-osauruses." In the first quarter of 2013 alone, total PC shipments fell almost 14 percent, and no one felt that more than leading PC-maker HP. The company's PC sales fell 23.7 percent that quarter. Now, PC-makers are dropping prices—some more than 50 percent—on laptops and some are offering touchscreens to compete with tablets and mobile devices in an attempt to gain back market share. HP's former CEO wanted to shift strategic focus more toward offering software to business markets. Maybe he had read the future correctly and was on the right strategic path. With the game-changing introduction of tablets, mobile technology, and social media, the future is not what it used to be.

QUESTIONS

1. Explain which product–market expansion grid strategy PC-makers are currently pursuing to deal with the threat of post-PC devices.

2. Research the current market information about PC sales as compared with "post-PC devices" for HP and its competitors. Do you think these companies' product–market expansion strategy needs to change?

THINK LIKE A MARKETING MANAGER

Apple markets several lines of personal electronic devices, including computers, smartphones, and tablets. Spend some time on Apple's website and learn more about its products, and then think like a marketing manager to answer the following questions.

QUESTIONS

1. Which of Apple's products are its stars, cash cows, question marks, and dogs?

2. Which of the four market growth strategies in the product–market expansion grid have you observed Apple using?

3. How does Apple employ the elements of the marketing mix—product, price, place (distribution), and promotion?

4. The iPhone was available in the United States in June 2007 but was not available in Canada until a year later. Similarly, although Apple released the iPad in the United States in April 2010, international consumers, who were able to "pre-order" the product in May, were told that availability in their country had not yet been determined. Research what happened with the Apple Watch, and any other new Apple products. What can you infer about Apple's international growth strategy?

MARKETING ETHICS

More than half of the world's population lives under autocratic regimes, limiting access to the Internet. But that is changing, opening new market opportunities for companies specializing in digital monitoring technologies. Everything an oppressive regime needs to build a digital police state is commercially available and is being implemented. For example, filtering devices manufactured by Blue Coat Systems, a Silicon Valley–based company, are used in Syria to suppress civil unrest. Although Blue Coat Systems acknowledges this, it claims that it did not sell the product to the Syrian government. North Korea, China, Libya, and other oppressive states demand data mining software and surveillance cameras as well as cutting-edge technologies that collect, store, and analyze biometric information. As social media proliferates in these countries, off-the-shelf facial recognition software and cloud computing can identify people in a matter of seconds, enabling these states to quash dissent. Although the United States may have sanctions against U.S.-based companies selling products to these governments, others may not, resulting in those countries' products as well as U.S.-based products getting into the hands of oppressive regimes.

QUESTIONS

1. In most cases, it is not illegal to sell such products to governments, oppressive or otherwise. But is it moral? Should companies be allowed to pursue a market development strategy wherever they find demand?

2. Research the Blue Coat Systems incident and write a report on your findings. Did the company illegally sell surveillance products to Syria? Which element of the marketing mix is most related to this issue?

MARKETING BY THE NUMBERS

Appendix 3, Marketing by the Numbers, discusses other marketing profitability metrics beyond the return on marketing investment (marketing ROI) measure described in this chapter. The text on the right is a profit-and-loss statement for a business. Review Appendix 3 and answer the questions below.

QUESTIONS

1. Calculate the net marketing contribution (NMC) for this company.

2. Calculate both marketing return on sales (or marketing ROS) and marketing return on investment (or marketing ROI) as described in Appendix 3. Is this company doing well?

Net sales		$800 000 000
Cost of goods sold		(375 000 000)
Gross margin		$425 000 000
Marketing expenses		
Sales expenses	$70 000 000	
Promotion expenses	30 000 000	
		(100 000 000)
General and administrative expenses		
Marketing salaries and expenses	$10 000 000	
Indirect overhead	60 000 000	70 000 000
Net profit before income tax		$255 000 000

DYSON: SOLVING CUSTOMER PROBLEMS IN WAYS THEY NEVER IMAGINED

From a head-on perspective, it has a sleek, stunning stainless-steel design. With wings that extend downward at a 15-degree angle from its centre, it appears ready for take-off. The latest aeronautic design from Boeing? No. It's the most innovative sink faucet to hit the market in decades. Dyson—the company famous for vacuum cleaners, hand dryers, and fans unlike anything else on the market—is about to revolutionize the traditional sink faucet.

The Airblade Tap—a faucet that washes *and* dries hands with a completely touch-free operation—is the latest in a line of revolutionary Dyson products that have reinvented their categories. In fact, Dyson was founded on a few very simple principles. First, every Dyson product must provide real consumer benefits that make life easier. Second, each product must take a totally unique approach to accomplishing common, everyday tasks. Finally, each Dyson product must infuse excitement into products so mundane that most people never think much about them.

THE MAN BEHIND THE NAME

James Dyson was born and raised in the United Kingdom. After studying design at the Royal College of Art, he had initially planned to design and build geodesic structures for use as commercial space. But with no money to get his venture started, he took a job working for an acquaintance, who handed him a blow torch and challenged him to create a prototype for an amphibious landing craft. With no welding experience, he figured things out on his own. Before long, the company was selling 200 boats a year based on his design.

That trial-and-error approach came naturally to Dyson, who applied it to create Dyson Inc.'s first product. In 1979, he had purchased what was claimed to be the most powerful vacuum cleaner on the market. He found it to be anything but. Instead, it seemed simply to move dirt around the room. This left Dyson wondering why no one had yet invented a decent vacuum cleaner. At that point, he remembered something he'd seen in an industrial sawmill—a cyclonic separator that removed dust from the air. Why wouldn't that approach work well in vacuum cleaners? "I thought no one was bothering to use technology in vacuum cleaners," said Dyson. Indeed, the core technology of vacuum motors at the time was more than 150 years old. "I saw a great opportunity to improve."

Dyson then did something that very few people would have the patience or the vision to do. He spent 15 years and made 5127 vacuum prototypes—all based on a bag-less cyclonic separator—before he had the one that went to market. In his own words, "There were 5126 failures. But I learned from each one. That's how I came up with a solution."

Dyson's all-new vacuum was far more than techno-gadgetry. Dyson had developed a completely new motor that ran at 110 000 revolutions per minute—three times faster than any other vacuum on the market. It provided tremendous suction that other brands simply couldn't match. The bag-less design was very effective at removing dirt and particles from the air, and the machine was much easier to clean out than vacuums requiring the messy process of changing bags. The vacuum also manoeuvred more easily and could reach places other vacuums could not. Dyson's vacuum really worked.

With a finished product in hand, Dyson pitched it to all the appliance makers. None of them wanted it. So Dyson borrowed $900 000 and began manufacturing the vacuum himself. He then convinced a mail-order catalogue to carry the Dyson instead of Hoover or Electrolux, "Because your catalogue is boring." Dyson vacuums were soon picked up by other mail-order catalogues, then by small appliance chains, and then by large department stores. By the late 1990s, Dyson's full line of vacuums was being distributed in multiple global markets. At that point, Dyson, the company that had quickly become known for vacuum cleaners, was already on to its next big thing.

THE DYSON METHOD

During the development of Dyson's vacuums, a development model began to take shape. Take everyday products, focus on their shortcomings, and improve them to the point of reinvention. "I like going for unglamorous products and making them a pleasure to use," Dyson told *Fortune* magazine. By taking this route, the company finds solutions to the problems it's trying to solve. At the same time, it sometimes finds solutions for other problems.

For example, the vacuum motor Dyson developed sucked air with unprecedented strength. But the flipside of vacuum suction is exhaust. Why couldn't such a motor blow air at wet hands so fast that the water would be pressed off in a squeegee-like manner rather than the slow, evaporative approach employed by commercial hand dryers?

With that realization, Dyson created and launched the Airblade, a hand dryer that blows air through a .2-millimetre slot at 675 kilometres per hour. It dries hands in 12 seconds rather than the more typical 40 seconds required by other hand dryers. It also uses cold air—a huge departure from the standard warm-air approach of existing commercial dryers. This not only reduced energy consumption by 75 percent—a major bonus for commercial enterprises that pay the electric bills—but customers were much more likely to use a product that worked fast and did the job right.

With very observable benefits, the Airblade was rapidly adopted by commercial customers. For example, as part of a comprehensive plan to improve its environmental impact, Los Angeles International Airport (LAX) was looking for a solution to the financial and environmental costs of manufacturing, distributing, and servicing the paper towel dispensers in more than 100 restrooms throughout its terminals. Switching to recycled paper towels helped, but only minimally. The energy used by conventional hand dryers made them an unattractive alternative. But when LAX management saw a demonstration of the Dyson Airblade, it was a no-brainer. With Airblades installed throughout its terminals, LAX was able to significantly reduce landfill waste as well as costs. The overwhelmingly positive feedback from travellers was icing on the cake.

Today's Airblades have evolved, guided by Dyson's customer-centric approach to developing products. With the first Airblade, it was apparent that all that high-powered air is noisy. So Dyson spent seven years and a staggering US$42 million to develop the V4 motor, one of the smallest and quietest commercial motors available. The new Airblade is quieter and almost three kilograms lighter than the original. But even more advanced is Dyson's new Blade V, a sleeker design that is 60 percent thinner than the Airblade, protruding only 10 centimetres from the wall.

ASSESSING REAL CUSTOMER NEEDS

Although Dyson sees itself as a technology-driven company, it develops products with the end user in mind. But rather than using traditional market research methods, Dyson takes a different approach. "Dyson avoids the kind of focus group techniques that are, frankly, completely averaging," says Adam Rostrom, group marketing director for Dyson. "Most companies start with the consumer and say, 'Hey Mr. or Mrs. X, what do you want from your toothbrush tomorrow or what do you want from your shampoo tomorrow?' The depressing reality is that often you won't get many inspiring answers."

Rather, Dyson's uses an approach it calls "interrogating products" to develop new products that produce real solutions to customer problems. After identifying the most obvious shortcomings in everyday products, it finds ways to improve them. It then tests prototypes with real consumers under heavy nondisclosure agreements. In this manner, Dyson can observe consumer reactions in the context of real people using products in their real lives.

This approach enables Dyson to develop revolutionary products like the Air Multiplier, a fan that moves large volumes of air around a room with no blades. In fact, the Air Multiplier looks nothing like a fan. By using technology similar to that found in turbochargers and jet engines, the Air Multiplier draws air in, amplifies it 18 times, and spits it back out in an uninterrupted stream that eliminates the buffeting and direct air pressure of conventional fans. Referring to the standard methods of assessing customer needs and wants, Rostrom explains, "If you . . . asked people what they wanted from their fan tomorrow, they wouldn't say 'get rid of the blades.' Our approach is about product breakthroughs rather than the approach of just running a focus group and testing a concept."

NO-NONSENSE PROMOTION

In yet another departure from conventional marketing, Dyson claims to shun one of the core concepts of marketing. "There is only one word that's banned in our company: brand," Mr. Dyson proclaimed at *Wired* magazine's Disruption By Design conference. What Dyson seems to mean is that the company is not about creating images and associations that do not originate with the quality and function of the product itself. "We're only as good as our latest product."

With its rigid focus on product quality and its innovative approaches to common problems, Dyson's approach to brand building centres on simply letting its products speak for themselves. Indeed, from the mid-1990s when it started promoting its bag-less vacuums, Dyson invested heavily in television advertising. But unlike most creative approaches, Dyson's ads are simple and straightforward, explaining to viewers immediately what the product is, what it does, and why they need one.

"It's a really rational subject matter that we work on, so we don't need to use white horses on beaches or anything like that," Rostrom says, referring to Dyson's no-nonsense approach to advertising. "We need only to explain the products. One thing we're careful to avoid is resorting to industry-standard ways of communicating—fluffy dogs and sleeping babies and so on. We don't want to blend in that way."

Today, Dyson complements traditional advertising with digital efforts. Like its TV advertising, such methods are simple, straightforward, and right to the point. For example, email communications are used sparingly, targeted to existing customers, and timed for maximum impact. And beyond the media it buys, Dyson considers public relations as the promotional medium that carries most of the weight. From product reviews in the mainstream media to online reviews and tweets about its products, word of its Dyson's products gets around fast.

The Airblade Tap sink faucet, Dyson's most recent new product, is a microcosm of Dyson's marketing strategy. It took 125 engineers three years and 3300 prototypes to develop the final product. The Airblade Tap provides clearly communicated solutions to everyday problems—solutions that make life easier. It solves those problems in ways that no other product has ever attempted, claiming to "reinvent the way we wash our hands." And it injects style into an otherwise boring product. Dyson sums it up this way: "Washing and drying your hands tends not to be a very pleasant experience. Water splashes, paper is wasted, and germs are passed along. The Tap is a totally different experience. You have your own sink, your own dryer." And at $1500, it illustrates another element of the Dyson marketing mix—a high price point that communicates quality and benefits that are worth it.

If the Airblade Tap is a hit, it will serve to forward Dyson's goal of doubling its annual revenues of $1.5 billion "quite quickly." The company is not only continuing to demonstrate that it can come up with winning products again and again; it's expanding throughout the world at a rapid pace. Dyson products are sold in over 50 global markets, selling well in emerging economies as well as developed first-world nations. Dyson does well in both economic good times and recessionary periods. Dyson also sees another big move in its future—a chain of company stores (as many as 20 000 stores in the United States alone) carved in the image of Apple's beloved hangouts. From a single vacuum cleaner to what Dyson is today in less than 20 years—that's quite an evolution.

Sources: Omar Akhtar, "Three Questions for Design Genius Mr. Dyson," *Fortune,* February 5, 2013, www.tech.fortune.cnn.com/2013/02/05/3-questions-for-design-genius-Mr.-dyson; Matt Warman, "Sir Mr. Dyson: Master of Invention Has the Wind Behind Him," *The Telegraph,* February 9, 2013, www.telegraph.co.uk/technology/news/9858568/Sir-Mr.-Dyson-master-of-invention-has-the-wind-behind-him.html; Jonathan Bacon, "Cleaning Up All Over the World," *Marketing Week,* November 22, 2012, www.marketingweek.co.uk/trends/cleaning-up-all-over-the-world/4004751.article; Matthew Creamer, "Mr. Dyson: 'I Don't Believe in Brand,'" *Advertising Age,* May 2, 2012, http://adage.com/print/234494; Kelsey Campbell-Dollaghan, "Dyson's Latest Coup: A $1,500 Sink Faucet That Dries Hands, Too," *Fastco Design,* February 5, 2013, www.fastcodesign.com/1671788/dyson-s-latest-coup-a-1500-sink-faucet-that-dries-hands-too; Burt Helm, "Dyson Marketing: So Simple, It's Brilliant," *The Marketing Robot,* April 16, 2012, www.themarketingrobot.com/dyson-marketing-so-simple-its-brilliant; Burt Helm, "How I Did It: Mr. Dyson," *Inc.,* February 28, 2012, www.inc.com/magazine/201203/burt-helm/how-i-did-it-Mr.-dyson.html; and information found at www.dyson.com, accessed June 2013.

QUESTIONS FOR DISCUSSION

1. Write a market-oriented mission statement for Dyson.

2. What are Dyson's goals and objectives?

3. Does Dyson have a business portfolio? Explain.

4. Discuss Dyson's marketing mix techniques and how they fit within the context of its business and marketing strategy.

5. Is Dyson a customer-centred company? Explain.

INSPIRING SUSTAINABLE LIVING

A Summary of Unilever's Five Levers for Change

make it a HABIT

This Lever is about reinforcing and reminding.
- Once people have made a change, what can we do to help them keep doing it?

make it UNDERSTOOD

This Lever raises awareness and encourages acceptance.
- Do people know about the behaviour?
- Do they believe it's relevant to them?

make it REWARDING

This Lever demonstrates the proof and payoff.
- Do people know when they're doing the behaviour 'right'?
- Do they get some sort of reward for doing it?

make it EASY

This Lever establishes convenience & confidence.
- Do people know what to do & feel confident doing it?
- Can they see it fitting into their lives?

make it DESIRABLE

This Lever is about understanding people's perceptions of themselves and their relationship with broader society.
- Will doing this new behaviour fit with their actual or aspirational self-image?
- Does it fit with how they relate to others or want to?

AFTER STUDYING THIS CHAPTER, YOU SHOULD BE ABLE TO

1 define *sustainable marketing* and discuss its importance

2 identify the major social criticisms of marketing

3 define *consumer activism* and *environmentalism*, and explain how they affect marketing strategies

4 describe the principles of sustainable marketing

5 explain the role of ethics in marketing

Sustainable Marketing, Social Responsibility, and Ethics

PREVIEWING THE CONCEPTS

In this chapter, we'll examine the concepts of sustainable marketing, meeting the needs of consumers, businesses, and society—now and in the future—through socially and environmentally responsible marketing actions. We'll start by defining sustainable marketing and then look at some common criticisms of marketing as it impacts individual consumers and public actions that promote sustainable marketing. Finally, we'll see how companies themselves can benefit from proactively pursuing sustainable marketing practices that bring value not just to individual customers but also to society as a whole. You'll see that sustainable marketing actions are more than just the right thing to do; they're also good for business.

First, let's look at an example of sustainable marketing in action at Unilever, the world's third-largest consumer products company. For 14 years running, Unilever has been named sustainability leader in the food and beverage industry by the Dow Jones Sustainability Indexes. And with the company's Sustainable Living Plan, it intends to double its size by 2020 while at the same time reducing its impact on the planet and increasing the social benefits arising from its activities. That's an ambitious goal.

SUSTAINABILITY AT UNILEVER: CREATING A BETTER FUTURE EVERY DAY

When Paul Polman took over as CEO of Unilever, the foods, home, and personal care products company was a slumbering giant. Despite its stable of star-studded brands—including the likes of Dove, Axe, Noxema, Sunsilk, VO5, Hellmann's, Lipton, and Ben & Jerry's—Unilever had experienced a decade of stagnant sales and profits. The company needed renewed energy and purpose. "To drag the world back to sanity, we need to know why we are here," said Polman.

To answer the "why are we here" question and find a more energizing mission, Polman looked beyond the usual corporate goals of growing sales, profits, and shareholder value. Instead, he asserted, growth results from accomplishing a broader social and environmental mission. Unilever exists "for consumers, not shareholders," he said. "If we are in sync with consumer needs and the environment in which we operate, and take responsibility for our [societal impact], then the shareholder will also be rewarded."

Evaluating and working on societal and environmental impact is nothing new at Unilever. Prior to Polman taking the reins, the company already had multiple programs in place to manage the impact of its products and operations. But the existing programs and results—while good—simply didn't go far enough for Polman. So in late 2010 Unilever launched its Sustainable Living Plan—an aggressive long-term plan that takes capitalism to the next level. Under the plan, the company has set out to "create a better future every day for people around the world: the people who work for us, those we do business with, the billions of people who use our products, and future generations whose quality of life depends on the way we protect the environment today." According to Polman, Unilever's long-run *commercial* success depends on how well it manages the *social* and *environmental* impact of its actions.

The Sustainable Living Plan sets out three major social and environmental objectives to be accomplished by 2020: "(1) To help more than one billion people take action to improve their health and well-being; (2) to halve the environmental footprint of the making and use of our products; and (3) to source 100 percent of our agricultural raw materials sustainably."

The Sustainable Living Plan pulls together all the work Unilever had already been doing and sets ambitious new sustainability goals. These goals span the entire value chain, from how the company sources raw materials to how consumers use and dispose of its products. "Our aim is to make our activities more sustainable and also encourage our customers, suppliers, and others to do the same," says the company.

On the "upstream supply side," more than half of Unilever's raw materials come from agriculture, so the company is helping suppliers develop sustainable farming practices that meet its own high expectations for environmental and social impact. Unilever assesses suppliers against two sets of standards. The first is the Unilever Supplier Code, which calls for socially responsible actions regarding human rights, labour practices, product safety, and care for the environment. Second, specifically for agricultural suppliers, the Unilever Sustainable Agriculture Code details Unilever's expectations for sustainable agriculture practices, so that it and its suppliers "can commit to the sustainability journey together."

But Unilever's Sustainable Living Plan goes far beyond simply creating more responsible supply and distribution chains. Approximately 68 percent of the total greenhouse gas footprint of Unilever's products, and 50 percent of the water footprint, occur during consumer use. So Unilever is also working with its consumers to improve the social and environmental impact of its products in use. Around 2 billion people in 190 markets worldwide use a Unilever product on any given day. Unilever sums up the effect with this equation: "Unilever brands × small everyday actions × billions of consumers = big difference."

For example, almost one-third of households worldwide use Unilever laundry products to do their washing—approximately 125 billion washes every year. Therefore, under its Sustainable Living Plan, Unilever is both creating more eco-friendly laundry products and motivating consumers to improve their laundry habits.

Around the world, for instance, Unilever is encouraging consumers to wash clothes at lower temperatures and use the correct dosage of detergent. Unilever products such as OMO and Persil Small & Mighty concentrated laundry detergents use less packaging, making them cheaper and less polluting to transport. More important, they wash efficiently at lower temperatures and use less energy. Another Unilever product, Comfort One Rinse fabric conditioner, was created for hand-washing clothes in developing and emerging markets where water is often in short supply. The innovative product requires only one bucket of water for rinsing rather than three, saving consumers time, effort, and 30 litres of water per wash.

Such energy and water savings don't show up on Unilever's income statement, but they will be extremely important to the people and the planet. Similarly, small changes in product nutrition and customer eating habits can have a surprisingly big impact on human health. "Ultimately," says the company, "we will only succeed if we inspire people around the world to take small, everyday actions that can add up to a big difference for the world." To meet this objective, Unilever has identified "Five Levers for Change"—things that its marketers can do to inspire people to adopt specific sustainable behaviours. The model helps marketers identify the barriers and triggers for change. The levers for change include the following: make it understood, make it easy, make it desirable, make it rewarding, and make it a habit.

Will Unilever's Sustainable Living Plan produce results for the company? So far, so good. The firm's revenues in the second year of the plan grew 12.7 percent, a solid figure considering global market volatility. Perhaps more important, at the same time that it improves its top-line performance, Unilever is progressing toward its aggressive Sustainable Living Plan goals. The company is right on target with 54 of its 59 specific targets involving improved health and well-being, reducing its environmental footprint, and enhancing livelihoods. And it's making good progress on the other five.

The sustainability plan is not just the right thing to do for people and the environment, claims Polman; it's also right for Unilever. The quest for sustainability saves money by reducing energy use and minimizing waste. It fuels innovation, resulting in new products and new consumer benefits. And it creates new market opportunities: More than half of Unilever's sales are from developing countries, the very places that face the greatest sustainability challenges.

In all, Polman predicts, the sustainability plan will help Unilever double in size, while also creating a better future for billions of people without increasing the environmental footprint. "We do not believe there is a conflict between sustainability and profitable growth," he concludes. "The daily act of making and selling consumer goods drives economic and social progress. There are billions of people around the world who deserve the better quality of life that everyday products like soap, shampoo, and tea can provide. Sustainable living is not a pipedream. It can be done, and there is very little downside."[1]

RESPONSIBLE marketers such as Unilever discover what consumers want and respond with market offerings that create value for buyers in order to capture value in return. The *marketing concept* is a philosophy of customer value and mutual gain. Not all marketers follow the marketing concept, however. In fact, some companies use questionable marketing practices that serve their own rather than consumers' or society's interests. Responsible marketers must consider whether their actions are *sustainable* in the longer run.

Consider sport-utility vehicles (SUVs). These large vehicles meet the immediate needs of many drivers in terms of capacity, power, and utility; however, they raise larger questions of consumer safety and environmental responsibility. For example, in accidents, SUVs are more likely to kill both their own occupants and the occupants of other vehicles. Moreover, SUVs are gas guzzlers. According to Sierra Club, a well-known environmental activist group, switching from an average car to an SUV wastes more energy per year than if you left your refrigerator door open for 6 years or left your bathroom light burning for 30 years![2]

This chapter examines *sustainable* marketing and the social and environmental effects of private marketing practices. First, we address this question: What is sustainable marketing and why is it important?

FIGURE 3.1 Sustainable Marketing

Sustainable Marketing LO1

Sustainable marketing

Socially and environmentally responsible marketing that meets the present needs of consumers and businesses while also preserving or enhancing the ability of future generations to meet their needs.

Sustainable marketing calls for socially and environmentally responsible actions that meet the present needs of consumers and businesses while also preserving or enhancing the ability of future generations to meet their needs. Figure 3.1 compares the sustainable marketing concept with other marketing concepts we studied in Chapters 1 and 2.

The *marketing concept* recognizes that organizations thrive from day to day by determining the current needs and wants of target-group customers and fulfilling those needs and wants more effectively and efficiently than competitors do. It focuses on meeting the company's short-term sales, growth, and profit needs by giving customers what they want now. However, satisfying consumers' immediate needs and desires doesn't always serve the future best interests of either customers or the business.

Whereas the *societal marketing concept* identified in Figure 3.1 considers the future welfare of consumers and the *strategic planning concept* considers future company needs, the *sustainable marketing concept* considers both. Sustainable marketing calls for socially and environmentally responsible actions that meet both the immediate and future needs of customers and the company.

Consider McDonald's. The company's early decisions to market tasty but fat- and salt-laden fast foods created immediate satisfaction for customers and sales and profits for the company, but in the 1990s critics and activists began to blame fast food chains for contributing to the obesity problem, burdening the health system, and causing unnecessary pollution and waste on a global scale. It was not a sustainable strategy, but in recent years, all that's changed.

McDonald's has responded to these challenges in recent years with a more sustainable "Plan to Win" strategy of diversifying into salads, fruits, grilled chicken, low-fat milk, and other healthy fare. The company also launched a major multifaceted education campaign—called "it's what i eat and what i do . . . i'm lovin' it"—to help consumers better understand the keys to living balanced, active lifestyles. And recently, McDonald's began a "favourites under 400 calories" campaign in which 400-and-fewer-calorie items are featured in its advertising and on menu boards in its restaurant. The chain points out that 80 percent of its

© Michael Neelon(misc)/Alamy

Exhibit 3.1 Sustainable marketing: Under its "Plan to Win" strategy, McDonald's has created sustainable value for both customers and the company. Now, 80 percent of the chain's menu is under 400 calories, including this Egg White Delight McMuffin, which weighs in with 8 grams of whole grain against only 250 calories and 5 grams of fat.

national menu is under 400 calories and that it wants to help customers feel better about the items they're choosing.

The McDonald's "Plan to Win" strategy also addresses environmental issues. For example, it calls for food-supply sustainability, reduced and environmentally sustainable packaging, reuse and recycling, and more responsible store designs. McDonald's has even developed an environmental scorecard that rates its suppliers' performance in areas such as water use, energy use, and solid waste management.

McDonald's more sustainable strategy is benefiting the company as well as its customers. Since announcing its "Plan to Win" strategy, McDonald's sales have increased by almost 60 percent, and profits have more than tripled. Thus, McDonald's is well positioned for a sustainably profitable future.[3]

Truly sustainable marketing requires a smooth-functioning marketing system in which consumers, companies, public policy makers, and others work together to ensure socially and environmentally responsible marketing actions. Unfortunately, however, the marketing system doesn't always work smoothly. The following sections examine several sustainability questions: What are the most frequent social criticisms of marketing? What steps have private citizens taken to curb marketing ills? What steps have legislators and government agencies taken to promote sustainable marketing? What steps have enlightened companies taken to carry out socially responsible and ethical marketing that creates sustainable value for both individual customers and society as a whole?

Social Criticisms of Marketing LO2

←⊙ **Simulate** on MyMarketingLab

Ethics

Marketing receives much criticism. Some of this criticism is justified; much is not. Social critics claim that certain marketing practices hurt individual consumers, society as a whole, and other business firms, but to be fair, it is not the practice of marketing itself that is bad or harmful—it's the way companies choose to implement it that matters. In most ways, we all benefit greatly from marketing activities. However, like most other human endeavours, marketing has its flaws.

Marketing's Impact on Consumers

Consumers have many concerns about how well the marketing system serves their interests. Surveys usually show that consumers hold mixed or even slightly unfavourable attitudes toward marketing practices. Consumer advocates, government agencies, and other critics have accused marketing of harming consumers through high prices, deceptive practices, high-pressure selling, shoddy or unsafe products, planned obsolescence, and poor service to disadvantaged consumers. Such questionable marketing practices are not sustainable in terms of long-term consumer or business welfare.

High Prices Many critics charge that the marketing system causes prices to be higher than they would be under more "sensible" systems. Critics point to three factors—*high costs of distribution*, *high advertising and promotion costs*, and *excessive markups*.

HIGH COSTS OF DISTRIBUTION A long-standing charge is that channel intermediaries mark up prices beyond the value of their services. Critics say that there are too many "middlemen," and that they are inefficient, or that they provide unnecessary or duplicate services. As a result, distribution costs too much, and consumers pay for these excessive costs in the form of higher prices.

As we'll discuss in Chapter 11, marketing intermediaries provide a variety of services in the chain of distribution—the movement of products from their source of production to the hands of the final customer. The planning, organization, and ongoing management of these channels is an expensive proposition for any firm, and since all firms are

Mira/Alamy

Exhibit 3.2 Criticisms of marketing: A heavily promoted brand of Aspirin sells for much more than a virtually identical nonbranded or store-branded product. Critics charge that promotion adds only psychological value to the product rather than functional value.

concerned about their bottom line, any channel partners or intermediaries who were not adding value would quickly be cut from the process.

HIGH ADVERTISING AND PROMOTION COSTS Modern marketing is also accused of pushing up prices to finance heavy advertising and sales promotion. For example, a few dozen tablets of a heavily promoted brand of pain reliever sell for the same price as 100 tablets of less-promoted brands. Differentiated products—cosmetics, detergents, toiletries—include promotion and packaging costs that can amount to 40 percent or more of the manufacturer's price to the retailer. Critics charge that much of the packaging and promotion adds only psychological value to the product rather than functional value.

Marketers respond that although advertising is expensive, it also adds value by informing potential buyers of the availability and merits of a product. Brand-name products may cost more, but branding gives buyers assurances of consistent quality. Moreover, consumers can usually buy functional versions of products at lower prices. However, they *want* and are willing to pay more for products that also provide psychological benefits—that make them feel wealthy, attractive, or special. Also, advertising and promotion are sometimes necessary, especially for marketers of products such as consumer electronics, cars, and personal care products—product categories in which there exist many brands and many competitors. Otherwise, the firm would not be able to compete.

Though it may seem logical that advertising is expensive and therefore if firms did no advertising the price of their products would go down, this is in fact a fallacy. Without advertising, sales would decrease, therefore production would decrease. When fewer products are manufactured, the price to manufacture each product goes up—and prices would go up correspondingly. When consumer activists in the U.K. called for more regulation in the advertising of children's toys, arguing that all toy advertising should be banned, economics researcher and journalist Chris Snowdon argued that the prohibition of advertising would lead to monopolistic markets and result in higher prices for consumers.[4]

EXCESSIVE MARKUPS Critics also charge that some companies mark up goods excessively. They point to the drug industry as an example of the worst offenders, where a pill costing five cents to make may cost the consumer $2 to buy. Marketers sometimes respond that consumers often don't understand the reasons for high markups. For example, pharmaceutical markups must cover the costs of purchasing, promoting, and distributing existing medicines, plus the high research and development costs of *formulating and testing* new medicines—all of which is very expensive. The simple fact is that all companies are in business to offer something of value to the market, and producing that market offering involves much more than just the costs of the manufacturing process.

Most businesses try to deal fairly with their customers because they want to build relationships and repeat business—it's simply not in their own best interests to cheat or mislead those customers. There are, of course, exceptions to the rule, and when consumers perceive any abuse of marketing, whether it's false advertising or unfair pricing, they should report those abuses to their local Better Business Bureaus or to the provincial Consumer Affairs office.

Deceptive Practices Marketers are sometimes accused of deceptive practices that lead consumers to believe they will get more value than they actually do. Deceptive practices fall into three groups: pricing, promotion, and packaging. *Deceptive pricing* includes practices such as falsely advertising "factory" or "wholesale" prices or a large price reduction from a phony high retail list price. *Deceptive promotion* includes practices such as misrepresenting the product's features or performance or luring customers to the store for a bargain that is out of stock. *Deceptive packaging* includes exaggerating package contents through subtle design, using misleading labelling, or describing size in misleading terms.

In Canada, the Competition Bureau acts as a watchdog to prevent such practices. They are alerted to instances of deceptive marketing through consumer complaints, and they *do* take action. For example, they took Rogers Communications to court and charged the telecommunications giant with violating Canada's false advertising rules when it claimed that its Chatr cellphone service had "fewer dropped calls" than the competition. The Bureau charged that Rogers produced "false and misleading" ads and failed to back up its claims about dropped calls with "adequate and proper tests"—and sought to impose a $10 million fine.[5] The federal watchdog also forced Bell Canada to stop making what the Bureau had concluded were misleading representations about the prices offered for its services—and required it to pay a penalty of $10 million, the maximum amount allowed under the Competition Act.[6]

Exhibit 3.3 Deceptive practices: Ferrero settled a class action suit claiming that ads for its popular, gooey-good Nutella chocolate hazelnut spread made deceptive claims that the product was "healthy" and "part of a balanced meal."

Stefano Rellandini/REUTERS

And it's not just in Canada that measures are taken to protect consumers from false advertising. In the U.S., the Federal Trade Commission (FTC) upheld charges that POM Wonderful made false and unsupported health claims for its pomegranate juice and supplements. Skechers was forced to pay $55 million to resolve allegations by the FTC and attorneys general in 44 U.S. states that it made false advertising claims that its rocker-bottom Shape-ups and other toning shoes would help customers tone muscles and lose weight.[7] And confections and candy maker Ferrero paid out $3 million to settle a class action suit claiming that ads for its popular Nutella chocolate hazelnut spread made deceptive claims that the product was "healthy" and "part of a balanced meal."[8]

In addition to the long-standing rules enforced by the Competition Bureau, new federal, provincial, and municipal guidelines and regulations are created as they become necessary. For example, in 2008, as a result of claims of "greenwashing"—companies that claim to be environmentally friendly in some way but that aren't really doing what they claim to be doing—the Competition Bureau in collaboration with the Canadian Standards Association issued guidelines to provide the business community with tools to ensure that green marketing claims are not misleading.[9]

Companies who greenwash should take note: Consumers everywhere are paying attention and crying foul when they perceive they've been greenwashed. In a survey taken in the U.K., four out of five residents said they suspect companies of trying to get away with false claims of green marketing. That country's watchdog organization, the Advertising Standards Authority (ASA), received 93 complaints about 40 different ads in one month alone. Among the offenders were Lexus, which ran an ad with the headline "High Performance. Low Emissions. Zero Guilt," deemed to give the misleading impression that the car caused little or no harm to the environment. Likewise, Volkswagen ran an ad promising that its car was "better for the planet"—an ad that was banned by the ASA because the claims were "too general."[10] And in today's always online and socially connected universe, offenders not only get caught, but information about their offences is quickly spread through social media.

The toughest problem is defining what is "deceptive." One noted marketing thinker, Theodore Levitt, once claimed that advertising puffery and alluring imagery are bound to occur—and that they may even be desirable: "There is hardly a company that would not go down in ruin if it refused to provide fluff, because nobody will buy pure functionality. . . . Worse, it denies people's honest needs and values. Without distortion, embellishment, and elaboration, life would be drab, dull, anguished, and at its existential worst."[11]

In today's world of marketing, the term *puffery* actually has meaning in a legal sense. The law in Canada and the United States recognizes that some statements made in advertising are not intended to be taken literally, and are therefore not illegal. A famous example that's often cited is the Barnum & Bailey Circus promoting itself as "the greatest show on earth." Puffery and hyperbole—extreme exaggeration for effect—are the staples of advertising.

Although it is sometimes debatable what constitutes deception, Ontario's Consumer Protection Act lays down some pretty clear definitions of false, misleading, and deceptive marketing practices:

1. A representation that the goods or services have sponsorship, approval, performance characteristics, accessories, uses, ingredients, benefits, or qualities they do not have.

2. A representation that the person who is to supply the goods or services has sponsorship, approval, status, affiliation, or connection the person does not have.

3. A representation that the goods or services are of a particular standard, quality, grade, style, or model, if they are not.

4. A representation that the goods are new, or unused, if they are not or are reconditioned or reclaimed, provided that the reasonable use of goods to enable the person to service, prepare, test, and deliver the goods for the purpose of sale shall not be deemed to make the goods used for the purposes of this paragraph.

5. A representation that the goods have been used to an extent that is materially different from the fact.

6. A representation that the goods or services are available for a reason that does not exist.

7. A representation that the goods or services have been supplied in accordance with a previous representation, if they have not.

8. A representation that the goods or services or any part of them are available or can be delivered or performed when the person making the representation knows or ought to know they are not available or cannot be delivered or performed.

9. A representation that the goods or services or any part of them will be available or can be delivered or performed by a specified time when the person making the representation knows or ought to know they will not be available or cannot be delivered or performed by the specified time.

10. A representation that a service, part, replacement, or repair is needed or advisable, if it is not.

11. A representation that a specific price advantage exists, if it does not.

12. A representation that misrepresents the authority of a salesperson, representative, employee, or agent to negotiate the final terms of the agreement.

13. A representation that the transaction involves or does not involve rights, remedies, or obligations if the representation is false, misleading, or deceptive.

14. A representation using exaggeration, innuendo, or ambiguity as to a material fact or failing to state a material fact if such use or failure deceives or tends to deceive.

15. A representation that misrepresents the purpose or intent of any solicitation of or any communication with a consumer.

16. A representation that misrepresents the purpose of any charge or proposed charge.

17. A representation that misrepresents or exaggerates the benefits that are likely to flow to a consumer if the consumer helps a person obtain new or potential customers.

High-Pressure Selling Salespeople are sometimes accused of high-pressure selling that persuades people to buy goods they had no thought of buying. It is often said that insurance, real estate, and used cars are *sold*, not *bought*. Salespeople are trained to be persuasive, and their companies reward them for reaching and exceeding their sales quotas.

In Canada, there are laws that protect consumers from the dangers of being pressured into making a purchase. Ontario's Consumer Protection Act, for example, states that it is an "unconscionable representation" if "the consumer is being subjected to undue pressure to enter into a consumer transaction." In addition, the Act makes several provisions for "cooling-off periods"; that is, a period of time during which consumers may change their mind about what they've purchased, and return it or get out of the deal with no penalty. And throughout Canada there are many similar laws protecting consumers against high-pressure sales tactics.

Shoddy, Harmful, or Unsafe Products Another criticism concerns poor product quality or function. One complaint is that, too often, products are not made well and services are not performed well. A second complaint is that many products deliver little benefit, or that they might even be harmful.

The Canada Consumer Product Safety Act (CCPSA), introduced in 2011, set new requirements for the industry so as to help protect Canadians from unsafe consumer products. Manufacturers are now required to report to Health Canada any incident related to health and safety caused by a consumer product, and retailers are required to keep records that provide enough details about suppliers to be able to recall products if it becomes necessary. The CCPSA website, part of Health Canada's website, provides detailed information for both businesses and consumers, including how to report an unsafe product, and a search engine for finding information about products that have been recalled.

Product problems are not usually caused by a company's indifference or other improper behaviour—most manufacturers *want* to produce quality goods. But problems with product quality and safety do happen, and the way a company deals with them can damage or help its reputation. Companies selling poor-quality or unsafe products risk damaging their reputation, engendering product liability suits, and having to pay large awards for damages. Also, with the ubiquity of social media, once a problem is discovered it is quickly made public; if a company doesn't take steps to respond, its reputation is at stake. Today's marketers know that good quality results in customer value and satisfaction, which in turn create sustainable customer relationships.

Planned Obsolescence Critics have also charged that some companies practise *planned obsolescence*, causing their products to become obsolete before they should actually need replacement. They accuse some producers of using materials and components that will break, wear, rust, or rot sooner than they should. And if the products themselves don't wear out fast enough, other companies are charged with *perceived obsolescence*—continually changing consumer

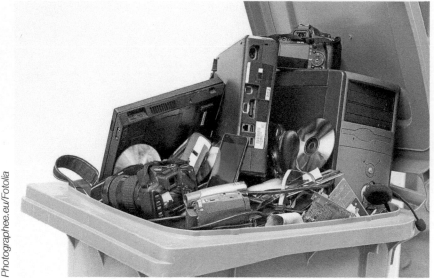

Exhibit 3.4 **Planned obsolescence:** Almost everyone, it seems, has a "drawer filled with the detritus of yesterday's hottest product, now reduced to the status of fossils."

concepts of acceptable styles to encourage more and earlier buying. An obvious example is constantly changing clothing fashions.

Still others are accused of introducing planned streams of new products that make older models obsolete, turning consumers into "serial replacers." Critics claim that this occurs in the consumer electronics industries. If you're like most people, you probably have a drawer full of yesterday's hottest technological gadgets—from mobile phones and cameras to iPods and flash drives—now reduced to the status of fossils.[12] It seems that anything more than a year or two old is hopelessly out of date. For example, early iPods had non-removable batteries that failed in about 18 months, so that they had to be replaced. It wasn't until unhappy owners filed a class action suit that Apple started offering replacement batteries. Also, rapid new product launches—as many as three in one 18-month period—made older iPod models obsolete.[13]

Marketers respond that consumers *like* style changes; they get tired of the old goods and want a new look in fashion. Or they *want* the latest high-tech innovations, even if older models still work. No one has to buy a new product, and if too few people like it, it will simply fail. Finally, most companies do not design their products to break down earlier, since they don't want to lose customers to other brands. Instead, they seek constant improvement to ensure that products will consistently meet or exceed customer expectations.

Much of the so-called planned obsolescence is the working of the competitive and technological forces in a free society—forces that lead to ever-improving goods and services. For example, if Apple produced a new iPhone or iPad that would last 10 years, few consumers would want it. Instead, buyers want the latest technological innovations. "Obsolescence isn't something companies are forcing on us," confirms one analyst. "It's progress, and it's something we pretty much demand. As usual, the market gives us exactly what we want."[14]

Marketing's Impact on Society as a Whole

The marketing system has been accused of adding to several "evils" in society at large. Advertising has been a special target of many of these accusations.

False Wants and Too Much Materialism Critics have charged that the marketing system urges too much interest in material possessions, and that North Americans' love affair with worldly possessions is not sustainable. Too often, people are judged by what they *own* rather than by who they *are*. The critics view this "rampant consumerism" as the fault of marketing. Marketers, they claim, stimulate people's desires for goods and create false wants and materialistic models of the good life—a distorted interpretation of the "American Dream."

One such social critic group is Adbusters, which began in Vancouver in the mid-1980s and has evolved into a highly effective social-activist movement that spans the globe. The organization's magazine now reaches over 120 000 people in 40 countries around the world, and its anti-consumption campaigns and spoof ads are getting noticed. For example, consider Buy Nothing Day, an Adbusters-sponsored campaign that began in 1992. This global event draws attention to the harmful effects of overconsumption and not only asks consumers to stop shopping for 24 hours, but also asks them to think about such questions as where their products originate from, why they're making purchases, and what they do with their products after purchase. Usually held the Friday after American Thanksgiving, the day has been praised for drawing attention to issues such as how many resources consumers use in developed versus developing countries.[15]

Another anti-consumerist activist is Annie Leonard, who founded "The Story of Stuff" project with a 20-minute online video about the social and environmental consequences of America's love affair with stuff—"How our obsession with stuff is trashing the planet, our communities, and our health." The video has been viewed more than 11.7 million times online and in thousands of schools and community centres around the world.[16]

Exhibit 3.5 False wants and too much materialism: Consumer activist Annie Leonard's "The Story of Stuff" video about the social and environmental consequences of America's love affair with stuff has been viewed more than 11.7 million times online and in thousands of schools and community centres around the world.

Marketers respond that such criticisms overstate the power of business to create needs. People have strong defences against advertising and other marketing tools. Marketers are most effective when they appeal to existing wants rather than when they attempt to create new ones. Furthermore, people seek information when making important purchases and often do not rely on single sources. Even minor purchases that may be affected by advertising messages lead to repeat purchases only if the product delivers the promised customer value. Finally, the high failure rate of new products shows that companies are not able to control demand.

On a deeper level, our wants and values are influenced not only by marketers but also by family, peer groups, religion, cultural background, and education. If Canadians and Americans are highly materialistic, these values arose out of basic socialization processes that go much deeper than what business and mass media could produce alone.

Moreover, consumption patterns and attitudes are also subject to larger forces, such as the economy. The 2008–2009 recession put a damper on materialism and conspicuous spending, and caused consumers to re-evaluate their spending habits. Many observers predict a new age of more sensible consumption. As a result, instead of encouraging today's more sensible consumers to overspend their means, most marketers are working to help them find greater value with less.

Too Few Social Goods Business has been accused of overselling private goods at the expense of public goods. As private goods increase, they require more public services that are usually not forthcoming. For example, an increase in automobile ownership (private good) requires more highways, traffic control, parking spaces, and police services (public goods). The overselling of private goods results in "social costs." For cars, some of the social costs include traffic congestion, gasoline shortages, and air pollution. Millions of litres of fuel and hours of time are wasted in traffic jams.

A way must be found to restore a balance between private and public goods. One option is to make producers bear the full social costs of their operations. For example, the government is requiring automobile manufacturers to build cars with more efficient engines and better pollution-control systems. Automakers will then raise their prices to cover the extra costs. If buyers find the price of some cars too high, however, the producers of these cars will disappear. Demand will then move to those producers that can support the sum of the private and social costs.

A second option is to make consumers pay the social costs. For example, many cities around the world are now charging "congestion tolls" in an effort to reduce traffic

Exhibit 3.6 Balancing private and public goods: In response to lane-clogging traffic congestion, London now levies a congestion charge. The charge has reduced congestion by 21 percent and raised money to shore up the city's public transportation system.

congestion. To unclog its streets, the city of London levies a congestion charge of £8 per day per car to drive in an eight-square-mile area downtown. The charge has not only reduced traffic congestion within the zone by 21 percent (70 000 fewer vehicles per day) and increased bicycling by 43 percent, but has also raised money to shore up London's public transportation system.[17]

Cultural Pollution Critics charge the marketing system with creating *cultural pollution*. Our senses are being constantly assaulted by marketing and advertising. Commercials interrupt television programs; pages of ads obscure magazines; billboards mar beautiful scenery; junk email fills our inboxes. Some feel that these interruptions continually pollute people's minds with messages of materialism, sex, power, or status.

And in the age of social media and mass electronic communications, consumer concerns about too many commercial messages have increased. Marketers must proceed with caution when devising strategies for advertising and promotion campaigns, because when consumers perceive that they are being bombarded with commercial messages, they become resentful. One study revealed that 75 percent of respondents reported they would resent a brand after being bombarded by emails. Although consumers are used to TV commercials and billboards, they are not yet used to advertising on their personal electronic devices, which they perceive as more intimate than mass media.[18]

Marketers respond to charges of "pollution" by attempting to target their communications as much as possible, so that only those consumers who are likely to be interested in the products or services will see the communications about them. People who buy fashion magazines, for example, rarely complain about the ads for fashion brands contained in them, nor do avid golfers complain about ads for the latest equipment in their golf magazines. "Junk mail" is only junk when we're not interested in it—that is, when it's not well targeted; but when coupons appear in our mailbox for stores or products we like (i.e., that are well targeted), we don't think of them as junk!

Another approach, especially in online marketing, is the trend toward blurring the distinction between advertising and the surrounding content, using techniques such as *branded entertainment* (which we'll discuss in Chapter 9) and *native advertising*, which is defined as the "uninterrupted delivery of content produced by or in collaboration with a brand."[19]

Marketing's Impact on Other Businesses

Critics also charge that a company's marketing practices can harm other companies and reduce competition. Three problems are involved: acquisitions of competitors, marketing practices that create barriers to entry, and unfair competitive marketing practices.

Critics claim that firms are harmed and competition reduced when companies expand by acquiring competitors rather than by developing their own new products. The large number of acquisitions and the rapid pace of industry consolidation over the past several decades have caused concern that vigorous young competitors will be absorbed and that competition will be reduced. In virtually every major industry—retailing, entertainment, financial services, utilities, transportation, automobiles, telecommunications, healthcare—the number of major competitors is shrinking.

Acquisition is a complex subject. Acquisitions can sometimes be good for society. The acquiring company may gain economies of scale that lead to lower costs and lower prices. A well-managed company may take over a poorly managed company and improve its efficiency. An industry that was not very competitive might become more competitive after the acquisition. But acquisitions can also be harmful and, therefore, are closely regulated by the government.

Critics have also charged that marketing practices bar new companies from entering an industry. Large marketing companies can use patents and heavy promotion spending or tie up suppliers or dealers to keep out or drive out competitors. Those concerned with antitrust regulation recognize that some barriers are the natural result of the economic advantages of doing business on a large scale. Other barriers could be challenged by existing and new laws. For example, some critics have proposed a progressive tax on advertising spending to reduce the role of selling costs as a major barrier to entry.

Finally, some firms have in fact used unfair competitive marketing practices with the intention of hurting or destroying other firms. They may set their prices below costs, threaten to cut off business with suppliers, or discourage the buying of a competitor's products. Various laws work to prevent such predatory competition. It is difficult, however, to prove that the intent or action was really predatory.

Consumer Actions to Promote Sustainable Marketing LO3

Sustainable marketing is a philosophy that has been increasingly at the forefront of Canadian society, and while many companies are taking steps toward sustainability, there are also consumer and grassroots organizations that exist to keep businesses in line. The two major movements have been *consumer activism* and *environmentalism*.

Consumer Activism

The rise of *consumerism*—economic and social policies that encourage consumer spending—in Canada and the United States began in the early 1900s, and although it shows no signs of slowing down, many consumer activist organizations have risen up and attempted to do just that. The first consumer movement took place in the early 1900s. It was fuelled by rising prices, by Upton Sinclair's writings on conditions in the meat industry, and by scandals in the drug industry. The second consumer movement, in the mid-1930s, was sparked by an upturn in consumer prices during the Great Depression and another drug scandal.

The third movement began in the 1960s. Consumers had become better educated, products had become more complex and potentially hazardous, and people were unhappy with institutions. Ralph Nader appeared on the scene to force many issues, and other well-known writers accused big business of wasteful and unethical practices. President John F. Kennedy declared that consumers had the right to safety and to be informed, to choose, and to be heard. Since then, many consumer groups have been organized; and in Canada, many federal and provincial laws protecting consumers have been put in place. The consumer movement has spread internationally and has become very strong in Europe.

But what *is* the consumer movement? **Consumer activism** is an organized movement of citizens and government agencies to improve the rights and power of buyers in relation to sellers.

Consumer activism
An organized movement of citizens and government agencies to improve the rights and power of buyers in relation to sellers.

Traditional *sellers' rights* include the following:

- The right to introduce any product in any size and style, provided it is not hazardous to personal health or safety; or, if it is, to include proper warnings and controls
- The right to charge any price for the product, provided no discrimination exists among similar kinds of buyers
- The right to spend any amount to promote the product, provided it is not defined as unfair competition
- The right to use any product message, provided it is not misleading or dishonest in content or execution
- The right to use any buying incentive programs, provided they are not unfair or misleading

Traditional *buyers' rights* include the following:

- The right not to buy a product that is offered for sale
- The right to expect the product to be safe
- The right to expect the product to perform as claimed

Comparing these rights, many believe that the balance of power lies on the seller's side. True, the buyer can refuse to buy. But critics feel that the buyer has too little information, education, and protection to make wise decisions when facing sophisticated sellers. Consumer advocates call for the following additional consumer rights:

- The right to be well informed about important aspects of the product
- The right to be protected against questionable products and marketing practices
- The right to influence products and marketing practices in ways that will improve the "quality of life"
- The right to consume now in a way that will preserve the world for future generations of consumers

Each proposed right has led to more specific proposals by activists. The right to be informed includes the right to know the true interest on a loan (truth in lending), the true cost per unit of a product (unit pricing), the ingredients in a product (ingredient labelling), the nutritional value of foods (nutritional labelling), product freshness (open dating), and the true benefits of a product (truth in advertising). Proposals related to consumer protection include strengthening consumer rights in cases of business fraud, requiring greater product safety, ensuring information privacy, and giving more power to government agencies. Proposals relating to quality of life include controlling the ingredients that go into certain products and packaging and reducing the level of advertising "noise." Proposals for preserving the world for future consumption include promoting the use of sustainable ingredients, recycling and reducing solid wastes, and managing energy consumption.

Marketing is a global societal reality, and serves an important function in promoting economic development around the world. When harnessed responsibly, marketing can encourage us as consumers to recycle, reuse, buy fair trade, eat healthily, drink sensibly, save energy, and support good causes. And if marketers adopt practices that sustain, rather than consume or destroy, natural resources, these practices will not only be good for consumers, but also good for business, and good for the world. For example, several years ago, Loblaw, the largest grocery chain in Canada, launched its sustainable seafood program, and removed products such as Chilean Sea Bass and Orange Roughy from its stores. The goal of the program is to educate consumers on what constitutes sustainable seafood, which species are at risk, and what the company is doing to improve the state of the world's oceans.[20]

A Boston Consulting Group study of 9000 consumers in nine countries concluded that green and ethical issues were a significant factor influencing what they chose to buy. If sustainability were to become a central component of all marketing thought and practice, consumers would undoubtedly react favourably.[21] It's a principle that seems to be working for Canada's Bullfrog Power:

> Bullfrog Power is Canada's leading green energy provider. The Toronto-based company was founded in 2005. Today it stands out as the only company providing 100 percent green energy to homes and businesses across Canada. When homes and businesses sign on for Bullfrog Power, Bullfrog's generators put renewable electricity or green natural gas onto the respective energy system to match the amount of electricity or natural gas the home or business uses; the electricity or natural gas is not injected directly into the facility. Across Canada, Bullfrog's electricity comes exclusively from wind and hydro facilities that have been certified as low impact by Environment Canada—instead of from polluting sources such as coal, oil, natural gas, and nuclear. Sourced from a unique, ground-breaking methane-capture project situated on one of Canada's thousands of landfill sites, Bullfrog's green natural gas is a climate-friendly alternative to conventional, polluting natural gas. Through this innovative technology, biogas is captured, cleaned up, and injected onto the national natural gas pipeline, displacing fossil-fuel-based gas and reducing CO_2 emissions into the atmosphere.
>
> Bullfrog is working hard to build its customer base of both end consumers and businesses. Its business and organizational clients include such firms as Unilever Canada, Walmart Canada, BMO Financial Group, Mountain Equipment Co-op, and Staples Canada.
>
> Bullfrog has excelled by living by strong brand values. Its mission is to provide Canadians with easy and practical 100 percent renewable energy solutions for their homes, businesses, and transportation. The organization believes that businesses can serve a vital function as community leaders in promoting and fostering responsible environmental action. It is a "double bottom line" company that maintains a dual focus on environmental responsibility and profitability. The company has pledged to donate 10 percent of profits to organizations that support sustainability. Bullfrog not only provides green energy for its customers; it empowers them to be change agents in the world. Bullfrog and its customers hope to demonstrate that change can come through collective action. The more people who sign up with Bullfrog, the more demand grows for renewable energy.[22]

Environmentalism
An organized movement of concerned citizens, businesses, and government agencies to protect and improve people's current and future living environment.

Environmentalism

Whereas consumer activists consider whether the marketing system is efficiently serving consumer wants, environmentalists are concerned with marketing's effects on the environment and with the environmental costs of serving consumer needs and wants. **Environmentalism** is an organized movement of concerned citizens, businesses, and government agencies to protect and improve people's current and future living environment.

Environmentalists are not against marketing and consumption; they simply want people and organizations to operate with more care for the environment.

Exhibit 3.7 Sustainable marketing: Bullfrog Power is Canada's leading green energy provider. The company provides energy solutions to end consumers and businesses.

Bullfrog Power Inc. Used with permission

They call for doing away with what sustainability advocate and Unilever CEO Paul Polman calls "mindless consumption." According to Polman, "the road to well-being doesn't go via reduced consumption. It has to be done via more responsible consumption."[23]

Environmentalism is concerned with damage to the ecosystem caused by global warming, resource depletion, toxic and solid wastes, litter, the availability of fresh water, and other problems. Other issues include the loss of recreational areas and the increase in health problems caused by bad air, polluted water, and chemically treated food.

Over the past several decades, such concerns have resulted in laws and regulations governing industrial commercial practices impacting the environment. Some companies have strongly resented and resisted such environmental regulations, claiming that they are too costly and have made their industries less competitive. These companies responded to consumer environmental concerns by doing only what was required to avert new regulations or keep environmentalists quiet.

In recent years, however, most companies have accepted responsibility for doing no harm to the environment. They are shifting from protest to prevention and from regulation to responsibility. More and more companies are now adopting policies of **environmental sustainability**. Simply put, environmental sustainability is about generating profits while helping to save the planet. Today's enlightened companies are taking action not because someone is forcing them to or to reap short-run profits but because it's the right thing to do—because it's for their customers' well-being, the company's well-being, and the planet's environmental future. For example, fast-food chain Chipotle has successfully built its core mission around environmental sustainability (see Marketing@Work 3.1).

Figure 3.2 shows a grid that companies can use to gauge their progress toward environmental sustainability. It includes both internal and external "greening" activities that will pay off for the firm and the environment in the short run and "beyond greening" activities that will pay off in the longer term. At the most basic level, a company can practise pollution prevention. This involves more than pollution control—cleaning up waste after it has been created. Pollution prevention means eliminating or minimizing waste before it is created. Companies emphasizing prevention have responded with internal "green marketing" programs—designing and developing ecologically safer products, recyclable and biodegradable packaging, better pollution controls, and more energy-efficient operations.

For example, SC Johnson—maker of familiar household brands ranging from Windex, Pledge, Shout, and Scrubbing Bubbles to Ziploc, OFF!, and Raid—sells concentrated versions of most of its household cleaners in recyclable bottles, helping to reduce the number of empty trigger bottles from entering landfills. Using renewable energy sources, the company's largest facility (the size of 36 football fields) is now able to generate most of its electrical energy onsite. And SC Johnson's Greenlist process developed lighter weight Windex bottles that reduced consumer waste by 1 million pounds annually; and

Environmental sustainability
A management approach that involves developing strategies that both sustain the environment and produce profits for the company.

FIGURE 3.2 The Environmental Sustainability Portfolio

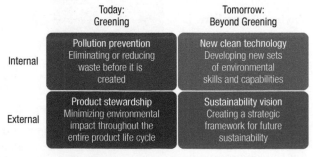

Source: Stuart L. Hart, "Innovation, Creative Destruction, and Sustainability," *Research Technology Management*, September–October 2005, pp. 21–27.

Exhibit 3.8 Environmental sustainability: SC Johnson's Greenlist process is an ongoing initiative that finds ways to both minimize the company's greenhouse gas emissions and make its products more environmentally friendly.

Pledge aerosol cans propelled by compressed air which reduced volatile organic compounds (VOCs). SC Johnson lives by its motto to "make life better with innovative products, great workplaces, and a commitment to people and the planet."[24]

For years, the auto giant Honda has been on a search-and-destroy mission to eliminate waste. A majority of its huge North American manufacturing plants now send no waste at all to landfills; the remaining few dump only small amounts of plastic and paper trash from their cafeterias. To ferret out sources of waste, Honda even sends teams of employees to comb through plant dumpsters and refuse piles. Such teams have initiated hundreds of waste-reduction and recycling efforts. Whether it's by reducing metal scrap in manufacturing processes or replacing cafeteria paper and plastic with washable dishware, in the space of 10 years, Honda's garbage-picking employees eliminated 4.4 billion pounds of potential landfill waste. Whereas the company sent 62.8 pounds of waste per car to landfills in 2001, in 2011 it sent only 1.8 pounds per car.[25]

At the next level, companies can practise *product stewardship*—minimizing not just pollution from production and product design but all environmental impacts throughout the full product life cycle, all the while reducing costs. Many companies are adopting *design for environment (DFE)* and *cradle-to-cradle* practices. These involve thinking ahead to design products that are easier to recover, reuse, recycle, or safely return to nature after usage, becoming part of the ecological cycle. Design for environment and cradle-to-cradle practices not only help sustain the environment but can also be highly profitable for the company.

For example, more than a decade ago, IBM started a business—IBM Global Asset Recovery Services—designed to reuse and recycle parts from returned mainframe computers and other equipment. Last year, IBM processed more than 37 900 metric tons of

MARKETING@WORK 3.1

Chipotle's Environmental Sustainability Mission: Food with Integrity

Envision this. You're sitting in a restaurant where the people—from the CEO on down to the kitchen crew—obsess over using only the finest ingredients. They come to work each morning inspired by all the "fresh produce and meats they have to marinate, rice they have to cook, and fresh herbs they have to chop," says the CEO. The restaurant prefers to use sustainable, naturally raised ingredients sourced from local family farms. This restaurant is on a mission not just to serve its customers good food but to change the way its entire industry produces food. This sounds like one of those high-falutin', gourmet specialty restaurants, right? Wrong. It's your neighbourhood Chipotle Mexican Grill. That's right, it's a fast-food restaurant.

In an age when many fast-feeders seem to be finding ever-cheaper ingredients and centralizing much of their food preparation to cut costs and keep prices low, Chipotle is doing just the opposite. The chain's core sustainable mission is to serve "Food with Integrity." What does that mean? The company explains it this way:

> Chipotle is committed to finding the very best ingredients raised with respect for animals, the environment, and farmers. It means serving the very best sustainably raised food possible with an eye to great taste, great nutrition, and great value. It means that we support and sustain family farmers who respect the land and the animals in their care. It means that whenever possible we use meat from animals raised without the use of antibiotics or added hormones. And it means that we source organic and local produce when practical, and that we use dairy from cows raised without the use of synthetic hormones. In other words, "integrity" is kind of a funny word for "good."

When founder and CEO Steve Ells opened the first Chipotle in Denver in 1993, his primary goal was to make the best gourmet burrito around. However, as the chain grew, Ells found that he didn't like the way the ingredients Chipotle used were raised and processed. So in 2000, Chipotle began developing a supply chain with the goal of producing and using naturally raised, organic, hormone-free, non–genetically modified ingredients. Pursuing this healthy-food mission was no easy task. As the fast-food industry increasingly moved toward low-cost, efficient food processing, factory farms were booming, whereas independent farms producing naturally raised and organic foods were in decline.

To obtain the ingredients it needed, Chipotle had to develop many new sources. To help that cause, the company founded the Chipotle Cultivate Foundation, which supports family farming and encourages sustainable farming methods. Such efforts have paid off. For example, when Chipotle first started serving naturally raised pork in 2000, there were only 60 to 70 farms producing meat for the Niman Ranch pork cooperative, an important Chipotle supplier. Now, there are over 700.

Sourcing such natural and organic ingredients not only serves Chipotle's sustainability mission; it also results in one of the most nutritious, best-tasting fast-food burritos on the market—something the company can brag about to customers. "Typically, fast-food marketing is a game of trying to obscure the truth," says Chipotle's chief marketing officer. "The more people know about most fast-food companies, the less likely they'd want to be a customer." But Chipotle doesn't play that game. Instead, it commits fast-food heresy by proudly telling customers what's really inside its burritos.

Chipotle chose the "Food with Integrity" slogan because it sends the right message in an appetizing way. "Saying that we don't buy dairy from cows that are given the hormone rBGH is not an appetizing message," says Ells. So the company is building its marketing campaign around the more positive message that food production should be healthier and more ethical. Chipotle communicates this positioning via an integrated mix of traditional and digital promotion venues, ranging from its Farm Team invitation-only loyalty program—by which customers earn rewards based not on frequent buying but on knowledge about food and how it is produced—to its Pasture Pandemonium smartphone app, where players try to get their pig across a pasture without getting trapped in pens or pricked by antibiotic needles.

© Chipotle Mexican Grill Inc.

Exhibit 3.9 Fast-food chain: Chipotle has successfully built its core mission around an environmental sustainability theme: "Food with Integrity."

In 2010, Chipotle made a big splash during the broadcast for the Grammy Awards with its first-ever national television ad—a two-and-a-half-minute stop-motion animation film showing a family hog farm converting to an efficient, industrialized farm. Then, when the farmer realizes that it's not the right thing to do, he tears down his factory farm and reverts to raising hogs sustainably in open pastures. Willie Nelson provides the soundtrack with a cover of Coldplay's "The Scientist," giving the ad its name, "Back to the Start." Before it ever aired as a TV ad, the video played in 10 000 movie theatres and online, where it became a viral hit on YouTube. Viewers were urged to download the Willie Nelson tune via iTunes, with the proceeds going to the Chipotle Cultivate Foundation.

Companies with a socially responsible business model often struggle to grow and make profits. But Chipotle is proving that a company can do both. Last year, its 37 000 employees chopped, sliced, diced, and grilled their way to $2.7 billion in revenues and $278 million in profits at Chipotle's 1410 restaurants in 41 states. And the chain is growing fast, opening a new restaurant almost every two days. In 2010–2012, Chipotle's stock price tripled, suggesting that the company's investors were as pleased as its fast-growing corps of customers.

Founder and CEO Ells wants Chipotle to grow and make money. But ultimately, on a larger stage, he wants to change the way fast food is produced and sold—not just by Chipotle but by the entire industry. "We think the more people understand where their food comes from and the impact that has on independent family farmers [and] animal welfare, the more they're going to ask for better ingredients," says Ells. Whether customers stop by Chipotle's restaurants to support the cause, gobble down the tasty food, or both, it all suits Ells just fine. Chipotle's sustainability mission isn't an add-on, created just to position the company as "socially responsible." Doing good "is the company's ethos and ingrained in everything we do," says Chipotle's director of communications. "Chipotle is a very different kind of company where the deeper you dig into what's happening, the more there is to like and feel good about."

Sources: Based on information and quotes from Danielle Sacks, "Chipotle: For Exploding All the Rules of Fast Food," *Fast Company*, March 2012, pp. 125–126; John Trybus, "Chipotle's Chris Arnold and the Food with Integrity Approach to Corporate Social Responsibility," *The Social Strategist*, March 22, 2012, https://blogs.commons.georgetown.edu/socialimpact/2012/03/22/the-social-strategist-part-xvi-chipotle's-chris-arnold-and-the-food-with-integrity-approach-to-corporate-social-responsibility; Emily Bryson York, "Chipotle Ups the Ante on Its Marketing," *Chicago Tribune*, September 30, 2011; Elizabeth Olson, "An Animated Ad with a Plot Line and a Moral," *New York Times*, February 10, 2012, p. B2; Ed Sealover, "Chipotle Rolls Out Expansion, Marketing Plans for 2013," *Denver Business Journal*, February 5, 2013; and information from www.chipotle.com, accessed June 2015.

end-of-life products and product waste worldwide, stripping down old equipment to recover chips and valuable metals. The cumulative weight processed by IBM's remanufacturing and de-manufacturing operations would fill 4480 rail cars stretching 49 miles. IBM Global Asset Recovery Services finds uses for more than 99 percent of what it takes in, sending less than 1 percent to landfills and incineration facilities. What started out as an environmental effort has now grown into a multibillion-dollar IBM business that profitably recycles electronic equipment at 22 sites worldwide.[26]

Today's "greening" activities focus on improving what companies already do to protect the environment. The "beyond greening" activities identified in Figure 3.2 look to the future. First, internally, companies can plan for *new clean technology*. Many organizations that have made good sustainability headway are still limited by existing technologies. To create fully sustainable strategies, they will need to develop innovative new technologies.

For example, by 2020, Coca-Cola has committed to reclaiming and recycling the equivalent of all the packaging it uses around the world. It has also pledged to dramatically reduce its overall environmental footprint. To accomplish these goals, the company invests heavily in new clean technologies that address a host of environmental issues, such as recycling, resource usage, and distribution:

> First, to attack the solid waste problem caused by its plastic bottles, Coca-Cola invested heavily to build the world's largest state-of-the-art plastic-bottle-to-bottle recycling plant. As a more permanent solution, Coke is researching and testing new bottles made from aluminum, corn, or bioplastics. It has been steadily replacing its PET plastic bottles with PlantBottle packaging, which incorporates 30 percent plant-based materials. The company is also designing more eco-friendly distribution alternatives. Currently, some 10 million vending machines and refrigerated coolers gobble up energy and use potent greenhouse gases called hydrofluorocarbons (HFCs) to keep Cokes cold. To eliminate them, the company invested $40 million in research and recently began installing sleek new HFC-free coolers that use 30 to 40 percent less energy. Coca-Cola also aims to become "water neutral" by researching ways to help its bottlers add back all the fresh water they extract during the production of Coca-Cola beverages.[27]

Exhibit 3.10 **Sustainability vision:** For Walmart, sustainability is about more than just doing the right thing. Above all, its strategy for sustainability makes good business sense—"driving out hidden costs, conserving our natural resources for future generations, and providing sustainable and affordable products for our customers so they can save money and live better."

Finally, companies can develop a *sustainability vision*, which serves as a guide to the future. It shows how the company's products and services, processes, and policies must evolve and what new technologies must be developed to get there. This vision of sustainability provides a framework for pollution control, product stewardship, and new environmental technology for the company and others to follow.

Most companies today focus on the upper-left quadrant of the grid in Figure 3.2, investing most heavily in pollution prevention. Some forward-looking companies practise product stewardship and are developing new environmental technologies. Few companies have well-defined sustainability visions. However, emphasizing only one or a few quadrants in the environmental sustainability grid can be short-sighted. Investing only in the left half of the grid puts a company in a good position today but leaves it vulnerable in the future. In contrast, a heavy emphasis on the right half suggests that a company has good environmental vision but lacks the skills needed to implement it. Thus, companies should work at developing all four dimensions of environmental sustainability.

Walmart, for example, is doing just that. Through its own environmental sustainability actions and its impact on the actions of suppliers, Walmart has emerged in recent years as the world's super "eco-nanny."

> When it comes to sustainability, perhaps no company in the world is doing more good these days than Walmart. That's right—big, bad Walmart. The giant retailer is now one of the world's biggest crusaders for the cause of saving the world for future generations. For starters, Walmart is rolling out new high-efficiency stores, each one saving more energy than the last. These stores use wind turbines to generate energy, high-output linear fluorescent lighting to reduce what energy stores do use, and native landscaping to cut down on watering and fertilizer. Store heating systems burn recovered cooking oil from the deli fryers and motor oil from the Tire and Lube Express centres. All organic waste, including produce, meats, and paper, is hauled off to a company that turns it into mulch for the garden.
>
> Walmart is not only greening up its own operations but also laying down the eco-law to its vast network of 100 000 suppliers to get them to do the same. It plans to cut some 20 million metric tons of greenhouse gas emissions from its supply chain—equivalent to removing more than 3.8 million cars from the road for a year. To get this done, Walmart is asking its huge corps of suppliers to examine the carbon life cycles of their products and rethink how they source, manufacture, package, and transport these goods. With its immense buying power, Walmart can humble even the mightiest supplier. When imposing its environmental demands on suppliers, Walmart has even more clout than government regulators. Whereas the EPA can only level nominal fines, Walmart can threaten a substantial chunk of a supplier's business.[28]

For Walmart, leading the eco-charge is about more than just doing the right thing. Above all, it also makes good business sense. More efficient operations and less wasteful products are not only good for the environment but also save Walmart money. Lower costs, in turn, let Walmart do more of what it has always done best—save customers money.

Environmental policies still vary widely from country to country. Countries such as Denmark, Germany, Japan, and the United States have fully developed environmental policies and high public expectations. But major countries such as China, India, Brazil, and Russia are in only the early stages of developing such policies. Moreover, environmental factors that motivate consumers in one country may have no impact on consumers in another. For example, PVC soft-drink bottles cannot be used in Switzerland or Germany. However, they are preferred in France, which has an extensive recycling process for them. Thus, international companies have found it difficult to develop standard environmental practices that work around the world. Instead, they are creating general policies and then translating these policies into tailored programs that meet local regulations and expectations.

Public Actions to Regulate Marketing

Citizen concerns about marketing practices will usually lead to public attention and legislative proposals. New bills will be debated—many will be defeated, others will be modified, and a few will become workable laws.

Many of the laws that affect marketing are listed in Chapter 4. The task is to translate these laws into the language marketing executives understand as they make decisions about competitive relations, products, price, promotion, and channels of distribution.

Business Actions Toward Sustainable Marketing LO4

At first, many companies opposed the idea of social and sustainable marketing. They thought the criticisms from consumer and environmental activists were either unfair or unimportant. But by now, most companies have grown to embrace the new consumer rights, at least in principle. They might oppose certain pieces of legislation as inappropriate ways to solve specific consumer problems, but they recognize the consumer's right to information and protection. Many of these companies have responded positively to sustainable marketing as a way to create greater immediate and future customer value and to strengthen customer relationships.

Sustainable Marketing Principles

Under the sustainable marketing concept, a company's marketing should support the best long-run performance of the marketing system. It should be guided by five sustainable marketing principles: *consumer-oriented marketing, customer-value marketing, innovative marketing, sense-of-mission marketing,* and *societal marketing.*

Consumer-Oriented Marketing
Consumer-oriented marketing means that the company should view and organize its marketing activities from the consumer's point of view. It should work hard to sense, serve, and satisfy the needs of a defined group of customers, both now and in the future. All the good marketing companies we've discussed in this text have had this in common: an all-consuming passion for delivering superior value to carefully chosen customers. Only by seeing the world through its customers' eyes can the company build lasting and profitable customer relationships.

Consumer-oriented marketing
The philosophy of sustainable marketing that holds that the company should view and organize its marketing activities from the consumer's point of view.

Customer-Value Marketing
According to the principle of **customer-value marketing**, the company should put most of its resources into customer-value-building marketing investments. Many things marketers do—one-shot sales promotions, cosmetic packaging changes, direct-response advertising—may raise sales in the short run but add less *value* than would actual improvements in the product's quality, features, or convenience. Enlightened marketing calls for building long-run customer loyalty and relationships by continually improving the value customers receive from the firm's market offering. By creating value *for* customers, the company can capture value *from* customers in return.

Customer-value marketing
A principle of sustainable marketing that holds that a company should put most of its resources into customer-value-building marketing investments.

Rodrigo Reyes Marin/AFLO/Newscom

Exhibit 3.11 Innovative marketing: New products, such as the Nike FuelBand and Flyknit Racer, along with its innovative social media marketing efforts, recently earned Nike the title of *Fast Company's* number one most innovative marketer.

Innovative marketing
A principle of sustainable marketing that requires that a company seek real product and marketing improvements.

Sense-of-mission marketing
A principle of sustainable marketing that holds that a company should define its mission in broad social terms rather than narrow product terms.

Innovative Marketing The principle of **innovative marketing** requires that the company continually seek real product and marketing improvements. The company that overlooks new and better ways to do things will eventually lose customers to another company that has found a better way. Nike is an excellent example of an innovative marketer:

> For nearly 50 years, through innovative marketing, Nike has built the ever-present swoosh into one of the world's best-known brand symbols. When sales languished in the late 1990s and new competitors made gains, Nike knew it had to reinvent itself via product and marketing innovation. "One of my fears is being this big, slow, constipated, bureaucratic company that's happy with its success," says Nike CEO Mark Parker. Instead, over the past few years, a hungry Nike has unleashed a number of highly successful new products. For example, the collaborative Apple Nike+ iPod sensor and the Nike FuelBand have

created strong Nike brand communities. And with the new Nike Flyknit Racer, Nike has now reinvented the very way that shoes are manufactured. The featherweight Flyknit feels more like a sock with a sole. Woven, not sewn, the Flyknit is super comfortable and durable, more affordable to make, and more environmentally friendly than traditional sneakers. Top off Nike's new products with a heavy investment in social media content, and Nike remains the world's largest sports apparel company, an impressive 25 percent larger than closest rival Adidas. In 2013, *Fast Company* anointed Nike as the world's number one most innovative company.[29]

Sense-of-Mission Marketing **Sense-of-mission marketing** means that the company should define its mission in broad *social* terms rather than narrow *product* terms. When a company defines a social mission, employees feel better about their work and have a clearer sense of direction. Brands linked with broader missions can serve the best long-run interests of both the brand and the consumers. For example, outdoor apparel and equipment maker Patagonia even goes so far as to urge customers to buy *less* of its merchandise. More than just sales and profits, Patagonia wants to "reimagine a world where we take only what nature can replace" (see Marketing@Work 3.2).

As another example of sense-of-mission marketing, the PEDIGREE brand makes good dog food, but that's not what the brand is really all about. Instead, six years ago, the brand came up with the manifesto, "We're for dogs." That statement is a perfect encapsulation of everything PEDIGREE stands for. "Everything that we do is because we love dogs," says a PEDIGREE marketer. "It's just so simple." This mission-focused positioning drives everything the brand does—internally and externally. One look at a PEDIGREE ad or a visit to the pedigree.com website confirms that the people behind the PEDIGREE brand really do believe the "We're for dogs" mission. Associates are even encouraged to take their dogs to work. To further fulfill the "We're for dogs" brand promise, the company created the PEDIGREE Foundation, which, along with the PEDIGREE Adoption Drive campaign, has raised millions of dollars for helping "shelter dogs" find good homes. Sense-of-mission marketing has made PEDIGREE the world's number-one dog food brand.[30]

Some companies define their overall corporate missions in broad societal terms. For example, in narrow product terms, the mission of sports footwear and apparel maker PUMA might be "to sell sports shoes, clothing, and accessories." However, PUMA states

MARKETING@WORK 3.2

Patagonia's "Conscious Consumption" Mission: Telling Consumers to Buy *Less*

Patagonia—the high-end outdoor clothing and gear company—was founded on a mission of using business to help save the planet. More than 40 years ago, mountain-climber entrepreneur Yvon Chouinard started the company with this enduring mission: "Build the best product, cause no unnecessary harm, use business to inspire and implement solutions to the environmental crisis." Chouinard and Patagonia have since taken that mission to new extremes. They're actually telling consumers "don't buy our products."

It started with a full-page *New York Times* ad on Black Friday, the day after U.S. Thanksgiving and heaviest shopping day of the year, showing Patagonia's best-selling R2 jacket and pronouncing "Don't Buy This Jacket." Patagonia backed the ad with messaging in its retail stores, on its website, and with additional ads at NYTimes.com. To top things off, Patagonia customers received a follow-up email prior to Cyber Monday—the season's major online shopping day—reasserting the brand's buy less message. Here's part of what it said:

> Because Patagonia wants to be in business for a good long time—and leave a world inhabitable for our kids—we want to do the opposite of every other business today. We ask you to buy less and to reflect before you spend a dime on this jacket or anything else.
>
> The environmental cost of everything we make is astonishing. Consider the R2 Jacket shown, one of our best sellers. To make it required 135 liters of water, enough to meet the daily needs (three glasses a day) of 45 people. Its journey from its origin as 60% recycled polyester to our Reno warehouse generated nearly 20 pounds of carbon dioxide, 24 times the weight of the finished product. This jacket left behind, on its way to Reno, two-thirds its weight in waste. And this is a 60% recycled polyester jacket, knit and sewn to a high standard. But, as is true of all the

things we can make and you can buy, this jacket comes with an environmental cost higher than its price.

> There is much to be done and plenty for us all to do. Don't buy what you don't need. Think twice before you buy anything. [Work with us] to reimagine a world where we take only what nature can replace.

A for-profit firm telling its customers to buy *less*? It sounds crazy. But that message is right on target with Patagonia's reason for being. Founder Chouinard contends that capitalism is on an unsustainable path. Today's companies and customers are wasting the world's resources by making and buying low-quality goods that they buy mindlessly and throw away too quickly. Instead, Chouinard and his company are calling for *conscious consumption*, asking customers to think before they buy and to stop consuming for consumption's sake.

Coming from Patagonia, a company that spends almost nothing on traditional advertising, the paradoxical "Don't Buy This Jacket" ad had tremendous impact. The Internet was soon ablaze with comments from online journalists, bloggers, and customers regarding the meaning and motivation behind Patagonia's message. Analysts speculated about whether the ad would help or harm sales—whether it would engage customers and build loyalty or be perceived as little more than a cheap marketing gimmick.

But to Patagonia, far from a marketing gimmick, the campaign expressed the brand's deeply held philosophy of sustainability. The purpose was to increase awareness of and participation in the Patagonia Common Threads Initiative, which urges customers to take a pledge to work together with the company to consume more responsibly.

Common Threads rests on five Rs of joint action toward sustainability:

Reduce: **WE** make useful gear that lasts a long time. **YOU** don't buy what you don't need.

Repair: **WE** help you repair your Patagonia gear. **YOU** pledge to fix what's broken.

Reuse: **WE** help find a home for Patagonia gear you no longer need. **YOU** sell or pass it on.

Recycle: **WE** take back your Patagonia gear that is worn out. **YOU** pledge

DON'T BUY THIS JACKET

Exhibit 3.12 Sense-of-mission marketing: A for-profit company telling consumers to buy less sounds crazy. But it's right on target with Patagonia's conscious consumption mission.

to keep your stuff out of the landfill and incinerator.

Reimagine: **TOGETHER** we reimagine a world where we take only what nature can replace.

So Patagonia's conscious consumption solution seems pretty simple. Making, buying, repairing, and reusing higher-quality goods results in less consumption, which in turn uses fewer resources and lowers costs for everyone. "Have a Patagonia ski parka with a rip in the arm?" asks one reporter. "Don't throw it away and buy a new one. Send it back, and the company will sew it up. Is your tent beyond repair? Send it back, and Patagonia will recycle the material." Patagonia has always been committed to the idea of quality as a cure for overconsumption. To that end, it makes durable products with timeless designs, products that customers can keep and use for a long time.

So on that Black Friday weekend, while other companies were inundating customers with promotions that encouraged them to "buy, buy, buy," Patagonia stood on its founding principles. It said, "Hey, look: Only purchase what

you need," explains Rob BonDurant, vice president of marketing and communications at Patagonia. "The message, 'Don't buy this jacket,' is obviously super counterintuitive to what a for-profit company would say, especially on a day like Black Friday, but honestly [it] is what we really were after, [communicating] this idea of evolving capitalism and conscious consumption that we wanted to effect."

Not just any company can pull off something like this—such a message can only work if it's real. Patagonia didn't just suddenly stick an ad in the *New York Times* on Black Friday. It had been sending—and living—this message for decades. Can other companies follow Patagonia's lead? "If it is [just] a marketing campaign, no," says BonDurant. "If it is a way they live their lives and do their business, absolutely. . . . The key to the whole effort [is]: Put your money where your mouth is," he says. "You can't just apply it to your messaging or to a particular window of time. It has to be done 24 hours a day, 365 days a year."

Pushing conscious consumption doesn't mean that Patagonia wants

customers to stop buying its products. To the contrary; like other for-profit brands, Patagonia really does care about doing well on Black Friday and the rest of the holiday season. As a company that sells products mostly for cold-weather activities, Patagonia reaps a whopping 40 percent of its revenues during the final two months of the year. But to Patagonia, business is about more than making money. And according to BonDurant, the "Don't Buy This Jacket" campaign has more than paid for itself with the interest and involvement it created for the Common Threads Initiative. If the campaign also boosts sales, that's a nice bonus.

"It is not enough just to make good products anymore," says BonDurant. "There also has to be a message that people can buy into, that people feel they are a part of, that they can be solutions-based. That is what [Patagonia's "buy only what you need"] communication efforts are really all about."

Sources: Based on information from Katherine Ling, "Walking the Talk," *Marketing News*, March 15, 2012, p. 24; Brian Dumaine, "Built to Last," *Fortune*, August 13, 2012, p. 16; and information from Patagonia.com.

its mission more broadly, as one of producing customer-satisfying products while also contributing to a sustainable future.

> At PUMA, we believe that our position as the creative leader in sport lifestyles gives us the opportunity and the responsibility to contribute to a better world for the generations to come. A better world in our vision—PUMA Vision—would be safer, more peaceful, and more creative than the world we know today. We believe that by staying true to our values, inspiring the passion and talent of our people, working in sustainable, innovative ways, and doing our best to be Fair, Honest, Positive, and Creative, we will keep on making the products our customers love, and at the same time bring that vision of a better world a little closer every day. Through our programs of puma.safe (focusing on environmental and social issues), puma.peace (supporting global peace) and puma.creative (supporting artists and creative organizations), we are providing real and practical expressions of this vision and building for ourselves and our stakeholders, among other things, a more sustainable future.[31]

Under its PUMA Vision mission, the company has made substantial progress in developing more sustainable products, packaging, operations, and supply chains. It has also sponsored many innovative initiatives to carry forward its puma.peace and puma.creative missions. For example, it sponsored a series of "peace starts with me" videos aimed at "fostering a more peaceful world than the one we live in today." Although such efforts may not produce immediate sales, PUMA sees them as an important part of "who we are."

However, having a *double bottom line* of values and profits isn't easy. Over the years, companies such as Patagonia, Ben & Jerry's, The Body Shop, and Burt's Bees—all known and respected for putting "principles before profits"—have at times struggled with less-than-

FIGURE 3.3 Societal Classification of Products

Immediate satisfaction

	Low	High
High (Long-run consumer benefit)	Salutary products	Desirable products
Low	Deficient products	Pleasing products

stellar financial returns. In recent years, however, a new generation of social entrepreneurs has emerged, well-trained business managers who know that to *do good*, they must first *do well* in terms of profitable business operations. Moreover, today, socially responsible business is no longer the sole province of small, socially conscious entrepreneurs. Many large, established companies and brands—from Walmart and Nike to Starbucks and PepsiCo—have adopted substantial social and environmental responsibility missions.

Societal Marketing Following the principle of **societal marketing**, a company makes marketing decisions by considering consumers' wants and interests, the company's requirements, and society's long-run interests. The company is aware that neglecting consumer and societal long-run interests is a disservice to consumers and society. Alert companies view societal problems as opportunities.

Sustainable marketing calls for products that are not only pleasing but also beneficial. The difference is shown in Figure 3.3. Products can be classified according to their degree of immediate consumer satisfaction and long-run consumer benefit.

Deficient products, such as bad-tasting and ineffective medicine, have neither immediate appeal nor long-run benefits. **Pleasing products** give high immediate satisfaction but may hurt consumers in the long run. Examples include cigarettes and junk food.

Salutary products have low immediate appeal but may benefit consumers in the long run; for instance, bicycle helmets or some insurance products. **Desirable products** give both high immediate satisfaction and high long-run benefits, such as a tasty *and* nutritious breakfast food.

Examples of desirable products abound. Philips AmbientLED light bulbs provide good lighting at the same time that they give long life and energy savings. Envirosax reusable shopping bags are stylish and affordable while also eliminating the need for less-eco-friendly disposable paper and plastic store bags. And Nau's durable, sustainable urban outdoor apparel fits the "modern mobile lifestyle." Nau clothing is environmentally sustainable—using only materials such as natural and renewable fibres produced in a sustainable manner and synthetic fibres that contain high recycled content. It's also aesthetically sustainable—versatile and designed for lasting beauty. And Nau clothing is socially sustainable, too— the company donates 2 percent of every sale to

Societal marketing
A principle of sustainable marketing that holds that a company should make marketing decisions by considering consumers' wants, the company's requirements, consumers' long-run interests, and society's long-run interests.

Deficient products
Products that have neither immediate appeal nor long-run benefits.

Pleasing products
Products that give high immediate satisfaction but may hurt consumers in the long run.

Salutary products
Products that have low appeal but may benefit consumers in the long run.

Desirable products
Products that give both high immediate satisfaction and high long-run benefits.

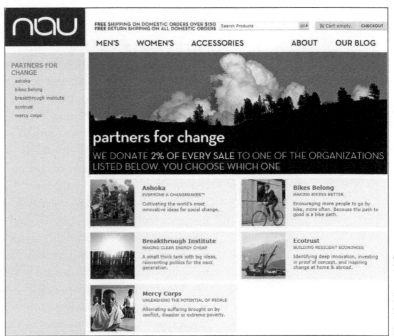

Exhibit 3.13 Desirable products: Nau's urban outdoor apparel products are environmentally, aesthetically, and socially sustainable. The company donates 2 percent of every sale to Partners for Change organizations chosen by customers.

Nau Holdings, LLC.

Partners for Change organizations and ensures that its factories adhere to its own strict code of conduct.[32]

Companies should try to turn all their products into desirable products. The challenge posed by pleasing products is that they sell very well but may end up hurting the consumer. The product opportunity, therefore, is to add long-run benefits without reducing the product's pleasing qualities. The challenge posed by salutary products is to add some pleasing qualities so that they will become more desirable in consumers' minds.

 Simulate on MyMarketingLab

Management and Ethics

Marketing Ethics LO5

Good ethics are a cornerstone of sustainable marketing. In the long run, unethical marketing harms customers and society as a whole. Further, it eventually damages a company's reputation and effectiveness, jeopardizing the company's very survival. Thus, the sustainable marketing goals of long-term consumer and business welfare can be achieved only through ethical marketing conduct.

Conscientious marketers face many moral dilemmas. The best thing to do is often unclear. Because not all managers have fine moral sensitivity, companies need to develop *corporate marketing ethics policies*—broad guidelines that everyone in the organization must follow. These policies should cover distributor relations, advertising standards, customer service, pricing, product development, and general ethical standards.

The finest guidelines cannot resolve all the difficult ethical situations the marketer faces. In many cases, it comes down to personal choice—what kind of marketing manager do you want to be? Managers need a set of principles that will help them figure out the moral importance of each situation and decide how far they can go in good conscience. Table 3.1 lists some difficult ethical issues that today's marketing managers might face during their careers.

But *what* principle should guide companies and marketing managers on issues of ethics and social responsibility? One philosophy is that such issues are decided by the free-market and legal system. Under this principle, companies and their managers are not responsible for making moral judgments. Companies can in good conscience do whatever the market and legal systems allow.

A second philosophy puts responsibility not on the system but in the hands of individual companies and managers. This more enlightened philosophy suggests that a company should have a "social conscience." Companies and managers should apply high standards of ethics and morality when making corporate decisions, regardless of "what the system allows." History provides an endless list of examples of company actions that were legal but highly irresponsible.

Each company and marketing manager must work out a philosophy of socially responsible and ethical behaviour. Under the societal marketing concept, each manager must look beyond what is legal and allowed and develop standards based on personal integrity, corporate conscience, and long-run consumer welfare. Dealing with issues of ethics and social responsibility in an open and forthright way helps to build strong customer relationships based on honesty and trust. In fact, many companies now routinely include consumers in the social responsibility process.

For example, Graco—maker of strollers, car seats, and other children's products—relies heavily on parental trust to keep customers loyal. In January 2010, after receiving seven reports of severe injuries to children's fingers caused by its strollers, Graco quickly recalled some 1.5 million units, making it the biggest stroller recall in history. But the company didn't stop with the official recall. Instead, it swiftly launched a proactive campaign to alert parents of the problem, answer their questions, and give them detailed advice on what steps to take. Graco went live and interactive with specific information

TABLE 3.1 Examples of Difficult Ethical Marketing Questions

1. Your R&D department has changed one of your products slightly. Legally speaking, if a product has changed, even only slightly, it can be called "new and improved." But you know the product is not really new and improved. Would you use that phrase in advertising the product?

2. You are a product manager at a company that designs and manufactures televisions. The engineers have developed a component that, if used in the development of your next model, would make the TV last for ten years instead of five years (the industry standard). Would you use it? Think about how your decision would affect the pricing strategy for the new model.

3. You work for a small company that manufactures a line of cosmetics that meets all the highest standards of ethical treatment of animals, yet sales are minuscule compared with similar products from larger manufacturers. You have researched the market and learned that the problem is not so much that consumers aren't aware of your product, but that they aren't aware that the big brands' products are *not* manufactured with ethical practices. You could develop a promotional campaign that, without making any untrue statements, would paint the competition as unethical. Would you do it?

4. You work in the marketing department at an automobile company whose most popular product is a gas-guzzling SUV. There is independent data showing that your company's SUV has a slightly better km/100 litre gas consumption rating than some of its competitors—it ranks fifth in a field of 12. The company wants you to develop marketing materials that position the SUV as eco-friendly in the minds of consumers. What would you do?

5. You work for a pharmaceutical company that markets an over-the-counter antacid product. Advertising for this type of product typically shows someone over-indulging in spicy or fatty foods, then taking the antacid as a remedy for the resulting stomach upset. The product developers are working on a variation of the product designed to be taken *before* consuming foods. The company naturally wants to market the benefits of this product; however, you believe that to do so means communicating the message that consumers should eat whatever they want—promoting unhealthy and unsafe behaviour. How would you proceed?

on the Graco Blog, YouTube, Twitter, Facebook, and a dedicated webpage. For example, customers who messaged Graco's Twitter account received prompt responses from Graco's tweeters about whether their strollers were part of the recall as well as useful, one-on-one information about how to order and install repair kits. Graco's swift and responsible actions drew praise from both public policy advocates and customers. "I will ALWAYS continue to use Graco products," tweeted one customer, "thanks to the way this was handled."[33]

As with environmentalism, the issue of ethics presents special challenges for international marketers. Business standards and practices vary a great deal from one country to the next. For example, bribes and kickbacks are illegal for Canadian firms, and a variety of treaties against bribery and corruption have been signed and ratified by more than 60 countries. Yet these are still standard business practices in many countries. The World Bank estimates that more than US$1 trillion per year worth of bribes are paid out worldwide. One study showed that the most flagrant bribe-paying firms were from Indonesia, Mexico, China, and Russia. Other countries where corruption is common include Somalia, Myanmar, and Haiti. The least corrupt were companies from Belgium, Switzerland, and the Netherlands.[34]

The question arises as to whether a company must lower its ethical standards to compete effectively in countries with lower standards. The answer is no. Many industrial and professional associations have suggested codes of ethics, and many companies are now adopting their own codes. For example, the Canadian Marketing Association developed the code of ethics shown in Table 3.2. Companies are also developing programs to teach managers about important ethics issues and to help them find the proper responses. They hold ethics workshops and seminars and set up ethics committees. Furthermore, most

TABLE 3.2 Excerpts from Code of Ethics and Standards of Practice of the Canadian Marketing Association (CMA)
Mission of the CMA To create an environment which fosters the responsible growth of marketing in Canada by: 1. Representing the interests of our members on key issues; 2. Taking a leadership role in identifying, planning for, and reacting to issues affecting marketing in Canada, and 3. Influencing and shaping policy initiatives which impact marketing, through education of government, media, special interest groups, and the public; 4. Establishing and promoting ethical standards of practice for marketing and taking an active role in ensuring compliance; 5. Promoting integrity and high standards of business conduct among our members in the interests of consumers and each other; 6. Being a major source of knowledge, marketing intelligence, and professional development; and 7. Providing opportunities for members to meet, network, exchange information, and do business together.
Purpose of the CMA Code of Ethics and Standards of Practice Marketers acknowledge that the establishment and maintenance of high standards of practice are a fundamental responsibility to the public, essential to winning and holding consumer confidence, and the foundation of a successful and independent marketing industry in Canada.
Definition of Marketing Marketing is a set of business practices designed to plan for and present an organization's products or services in ways that build effective customer relationships.
Personal Information Practices Marketers must promote responsible and transparent personal information management practices in a manner consistent with the provisions of the Personal Information Protection and Electronic Documents Act (Canada).
Truthfulness Marketing communications must be clear and truthful. Marketers must not knowingly make a representation to a consumer or business that is false or misleading.
Campaign Limitations Marketers must not participate in any campaign involving the disparagement or exploitation of any person or group on the grounds of race, colour, ethnicity, religion, national origin, gender, sexual orientation, marital status, or age. Marketers must not knowingly exploit the credulity, lack of knowledge, or inexperience of any consumer, taking particular care when dealing with vulnerable consumers. The term "vulnerable consumer" includes, but is not limited to, children, teenagers, people with disabilities, the elderly, and those for whom English or French is not their first language.
Accuracy of Representation Marketers must not misrepresent a product, service, or marketing program and must not mislead by statement or manner of demonstration or comparison.

TABLE 3.2 *(Continued)*

Support for Claims

Test or survey data referred to in any marketing communication must be reliable, accurate, and current and must support the specific claim being made. Marketers must be able to substantiate the basis for any performance claim or comparison and must not imply a scientific, factual, or statistical basis where none exists.

Disguise

Marketers must not engage in marketing communications in the guise of one purpose when the intent is a different purpose.

Marketers must not claim to be carrying out a survey or research when their real purpose is to sell a product or service, or to raise funds.

Marketers must not mislead or deceive consumers or businesses into believing that a marketing communication is news, information, public service, or entertainment programming when its purpose is to sell products or services or to seek donations to causes or charities.

Disparagement

Marketers must not use inaccurate information to attack, degrade, discredit, or damage the reputation of competitors' products, services, advertisements, or organizations.

Protection of Personal Privacy

All consumer marketers must abide by the Personal Information Protection and Electronic Documents Act (PIPEDA), and/or applicable provincial privacy laws and the following ten Privacy Principles from the National Standard of Canada and five additional requirements as outlined in this section.

Ten Privacy Principles:
1. **Accountability:** An organization is responsible for personal information under its control and shall designate an individual or individuals who are accountable for the organization's compliance with the following principles.
2. **Identifying Purposes:** The purposes for which personal information is collected shall be identified by the organization at or before the time the information is collected.
3. **Consent:** The knowledge and consent of the individual are required for the collection, use, or disclosure of personal information, except where inappropriate.
4. **Limiting Collection:** The collection of personal information shall be limited to that which is necessary for the purposes identified by the organization. Information shall be collected by fair and lawful means.
5. **Limiting Use, Disclosure, and Retention:** Personal information shall not be used or disclosed for purposes other than those for which it was collected, except with the consent of the individual or as required by law. Personal information shall be retained only as long as necessary for the fulfillment of those purposes.
6. **Accuracy:** Personal information shall be as accurate, complete, and up-to-date as is necessary for the purposes for which it is being used.
7. **Safeguards:** Personal information shall be protected by security safeguards appropriate to the sensitivity of the information.
8. **Openness:** An organization shall make readily available to individuals specific information about its policies and practices relating to the management of personal information.
9. **Individual Access:** Upon request, an individual shall be informed of the existence, use and disclosure of his or her personal information and shall be given access to that information. An individual shall be able to challenge the accuracy and completeness of the information and have it amended as appropriate.
10. **Challenging Compliance:** An individual shall be able to address a challenge concerning compliance with the above principles to the designated individual or individuals accountable for the organization's compliance.

Source: Excerpts from Code of Ethics and Standards of Practice of the Canadian Marketing Association (CMA). Used with permission.

Exhibit 3.14 **Marketing ethics:** Canadian marketers are required by federal law to comply with the National Do Not Call List maintained by the CRTC. Consumers may also use this website to complain about marketers who break the rules.

CRTC/Government of Canada

major Canadian and American companies have appointed high-level ethics officers to champion ethics issues and help resolve ethics problems and concerns facing employees.

Do Not Contact Service and Do Not Call List In Canada, marketers have always been required by law to use the CMA's Do Not Contact Service when conducting a telemarketing or direct mail campaign. In recent years, in addition to the CMA's DNC list, the CRTC created the National Do Not Call List (in French, Liste Nationale de Numéros de Télécommunication Exclus)—and marketers are required to abide by this list as well. Consumers can register their telephone numbers at www.lnnte-dncl.gc.ca, and can also use the website to register complaints against offending telemarketers.

Even more recently, the federal government passed a law called the Personal Information Protection and Electronic Documents Act. These and other federal guidelines and regulations governing the use of contact lists by Canadian marketers are available on Industry Canada's website (www.ic.gc.ca).

The Sustainable Company

At the foundation of marketing is the belief that companies that fulfill the needs and wants of customers will thrive. Companies that fail to meet customer needs or that intentionally or unintentionally harm customers, others in society, or future generations will decline.

Says one observer, "Sustainability is an emerging business megatrend, like electrification and mass production, that will profoundly affect companies' competitiveness and even their survival." Says another, "Increasingly, companies and leaders will be assessed not only on immediate results but also on . . . the ultimate effects their actions have on societal wellbeing. This trend has been coming in small ways for years but now is surging. So pick up your recycled cup of fair-trade coffee, and get ready."[35]

Sustainable companies are those that create value for customers through socially, environmentally, and ethically responsible actions. Sustainable marketing goes beyond caring for the needs and wants of today's customers. It means having concern for tomorrow's customers in ensuring the survival and success of the business, shareholders, employees, and the broader world in which they all live. It means pursuing the mission of a triple bottom line: "people, planet, profits."[36] Sustainable marketing provides the context in which companies can build profitable customer relationships by creating value *for* customers in order to capture value *from* customers in return—now and in the future.

The Boston Pizza Foundation

Boston Pizza's four pillar strategy includes a commitment to the community, and the Boston Pizza Foundation is ample proof that that pillar is rock solid. Having raised and donated more than $20 million since its inception in 1990, the foundation also stands as a direct reflection of the men who started the company and the brand it has become. But George Melville, co-owner and co-chairman of Boston Pizza International (BPI), is quick to point out that this history of giving started long before the creation of the foundation. "For over 50 years, Boston Pizza has been involved with causes that are important to us as an organization as well as to our people," he says.

So what are the important causes supported by Boston Pizza? The kinds of things one might expect from Canada's leading casual dining chain—families and kids. Mentorship in particular is a key theme. "We see the impact and benefit of strong mentorship in our restaurants every day as more than 23 000 young people are employed at Boston Pizza Restaurants from coast to coast," states an emphatic Melville.

The focus on guidance for Canada's youth was consolidated in 2014 with the launch of a program called Future Prospects. "Boston Pizza believes that strong role models inspire kids to be great," said Cheryl Treliving, the foundation's executive director. "With the launch of BPF Future Prospects we are committed to working with our franchisees from coast to coast to address the growing need to provide kids with access to mentors and role models that inspire them to thrive, succeed, and realize their individual goals."

While the program supports a number of youth-oriented charitable organizations, Big Brothers Big Sisters and the Rick Hansen Foundation are two immediate beneficiaries, as Future Prospects has committed to raising an annual $1.5 million and $1 million, respectively, to help these organizations achieve their goals.

QUESTIONS

1. Research Big Brothers Big Sisters. Identify and describe the goals of this organization in Canada. How will money raised from BP's Future Prospects help this organization achieve its goals?

2. Research the Rick Hansen Foundation's School Program. Identify and describe the goals of this organization in Canada. How will money raised from BP's Future Prospects help this organization achieve its goals?

REVIEWING THE CONCEPTS

 Define *sustainable marketing* and discuss its importance.

Sustainable marketing calls for meeting the present needs of consumers and businesses while still preserving or enhancing the ability of future generations to meet their needs. Whereas the marketing concept recognizes that companies thrive by fulfilling the day-to-day needs of customers, sustainable marketing calls for socially and environmentally responsible actions that meet both the immediate and future needs of customers and the company. Truly sustainable marketing requires a smooth-functioning marketing system in which consumers, companies, public policy makers, and others work together to ensure responsible marketing actions.

 Identify the major social criticisms of marketing.

Marketing's *impact on individual consumer welfare* has been criticized for its high prices, deceptive practices, high-pressure selling, shoddy or unsafe products, planned obsolescence, and poor service to disadvantaged consumers. Marketing's *impact on society* has been criticized for creating false wants and too much materialism, too few social goods, and cultural pollution. Critics have also criticized marketing's *impact on other businesses* for harming competitors and reducing competition through acquisitions, practices that create barriers to entry, and unfair competitive marketing practices. Some of these concerns are justified; some are not.

 Define *consumer activism* and *environmentalism*, and explain how they affect marketing strategies.

Concerns about the marketing system have led to *citizen action movements*. *Consumer activism* is an organized social movement intended to strengthen the rights and power of consumers relative to sellers. Alert marketers view it as an opportunity to serve consumers better by providing more consumer information, education, and protection. *Environmentalism* is an organized social movement seeking to minimize the harm done to the environment and quality of life by marketing practices.

The first wave of modern environmentalism was driven by environmental groups and concerned consumers whereas the second wave was driven by government, which passed laws and regulations governing industrial practices impacting the environment. The first two environmentalism waves are now merging into a third and stronger wave in which companies are accepting responsibility for doing no environmental harm. Companies now are adopting policies of *environmental sustainability*—developing strategies that both sustain the environment and produce profits for the company.

LO4 Describe the principles of sustainable marketing.

Many companies originally opposed these social movements and laws, but most of them now recognize a need for positive consumer information, education, and protection. Under the sustainable marketing concept, a company's marketing should support the best long-run performance of the marketing system. It should be guided by five sustainable marketing principles: *consumer-oriented marketing, customer-value marketing, innovative marketing, sense-of-mission marketing,* and *societal marketing*.

LO5 Explain the role of ethics in marketing.

Increasingly, companies are responding to the need to provide company policies and guidelines to help their managers deal with questions of *marketing ethics*. Of course, even the best guidelines cannot resolve all the difficult ethical decisions that individuals and firms must make. But there are some principles that marketers can choose among. One principle holds that such issues should be decided by the free market and legal system. A second, and more enlightened, principle puts responsibility not on the system but in the hands of individual companies and managers. Each firm and marketing manager must work out a philosophy of socially responsible and ethical behaviour. Under the sustainable marketing concept, managers must look beyond what is legal and allowable and develop standards based on personal integrity, corporate conscience, and long-term consumer welfare.

MyMarketingLab

Study, practise, and explore real marketing situations with these helpful resources:

- **Interactive Lesson Presentations:** Work through interactive presentations and assessments to test your knowledge of marketing concepts.
- **Study Plan:** Check your understanding of chapter concepts with self-study quizzes.
- **Dynamic Study Modules:** Work through adaptive study modules on your computer, tablet, or mobile device.
- **Simulations:** Practise decision-making in simulated marketing environments.

DISCUSSION QUESTIONS

1. A bottle of Asacol, a drug for controlling intestinal inflammation, is more expensive than a bottle of the same drug as a generic product. Consumers accuse pharmaceutical manufacturers of unfair markups when the brand price is compared with the lower price of the generic product. As a marketer at a pharmaceutical company, how would you defend the higher prices for your company's branded products?

2. The Consumers' Association of Canada (http://consumer.ca) represents and informs consumers about issues affecting their quality of life. Visit the organization's website to learn about this association. Select one of the issues or activities listed on its home page. Discuss how the information helped you become a more informed consumer.

3. Imagine that you work for a large consumer products company that makes soaps, detergents, and other products, such as shampoos, that ultimately end up being washed down the drain. How would you go about making sure that these products are not harming the environment?

4. Choose a company that you admire, shop at, or buy from—a company that you personally believe is a responsible social marketer. Investigate its website and find out what it does that you would consider "good" social marketing. What could it improve on?

5. If Kellogg's stops advertising to children, how should it change its marketing of products such as Froot Loops and Eggo waffles?

6. Consumer activist groups are beginning to raise awareness of the horrible wastefulness of bottled water. In Canada, no cities have unsafe drinking water, and since it was recently revealed that some branded bottled waters, such as Dasani, come from public sources (i.e., they are nothing more than bottled tap water), there is, logically, no reason for anyone to buy bottled water. What can consumer groups do to discourage or ban the sale of bottled water in Canada? Or should they?

CRITICAL THINKING EXERCISES

1. Some cultures are more accepting than others of corrupt practices such as bribery. Corruption is not tolerated in Canada or by Canadian firms operating abroad. However, in some countries, it's the price of entry for many foreign firms. Visit www.transparency.org and look at the Corruption Perception Index (CPI) report. The CPI can range from 0 to 100, where a low index score means that a country is perceived as highly corrupt and a higher score means highly ethical. Choose three countries that are rated as least corrupt and three that are highly corrupt, and explain why you think they may be that way.

2. Many consumers want to recycle, but rules vary among localities, making it difficult for consumers to know whether something is recyclable. In the United States, voluntary "How2Recycle" labels are starting to appear on products to help consumers. Visit www.how2recycle.info to learn about these voluntary labels and the types of products that will be carrying them. Do you think these labels will make it easier for consumers to recycle?

3. Discuss an example of a company committing an unethical marketing practice. What was the violation? How was the unethical behavior dealt with?

ONLINE, MOBILE, AND SOCIAL MEDIA MARKETING

With the explosion of mobile devices and apps, it's not surprising that medical apps are taking off. There are apps to identify pills, track pregnancy, check for melanoma skin cancer, and even teach medical professionals how to read electrocardiograms. Some apps are replacing devices used by healthcare professionals in hospitals and doctors' offices. There are more than 40 000 medical applications currently available, and the market is still in its infancy. In the United States, this has caught the attention of the Food and Drug Administration (FDA), the agency regulating medical devices. So far, medical apps have been unregulated, but that is about to change. The FDA released guidelines requiring app developers to apply for FDA approval, which could take years. According to the Government Accountability Office, it takes the FDA six months to approve a device that is similar to an existing one and up to 20 months for new devices. According to another report, approval costs $24 million to $75 million. Not all apps would require FDA approval—only ones making medical claims. Although many developers think regulation is necessary to protect the public, most believe that the current process is too slow and a new regulatory framework is necessary.

QUESTIONS

1. Find and describe two examples of mobile apps for healthcare providers. Are these only for U.S. providers, or would Canadian providers be able to use them as well?

2. Do you think regulatory approval of medical mobile apps is necessary in the United States? What about in Canada?

3. Do you think the FDA's requirement for approval constrains innovation?

4. Find out whether the market for these apps exists in Canada, and, if so, which government body, if any, is regulating it.

THINK LIKE A MARKETING MANAGER

A forest full of trees has been spared thanks to a new paperless wine list being used at Aureole restaurants in Las Vegas and New York. The wine selection boasts an awe-inspiring 4000 different wine labels that would be impractical to print onto paper in the form of a manageable wine list. Instead of a paper wine list, customers are presented with a lightweight, wireless computer tablet. Pages are turned and selections are made by customers using either a stylus or their fingers. Aside from the positive environmental impact, there are other marketing applications for the electronic wine list. For example, the tablet can be used to display wine reviews and narratives about the winery, customers are allowed to bookmark favourite wine selections, and the tablet has the ability to let customers request that wine selection information and special offers be emailed to them at home.

QUESTIONS

1. What other businesses could benefit from using this sort of electronic device?

2. What sort of resistance do you think consumers may have to accessing printed material in an electronic format? How could such resistance be overcome?

3. What other typical paper documents do you commonly see when you go shopping, eat out, or purchase services that could be replaced with electronic devices?

4. List all the environmental benefits of such a system.

MARKETING ETHICS

K.G.O.Y. stands for "kids getting older younger," and marketers are getting much of the blame. Kids today see all types of messages, especially on the Internet, that they would never have seen in the past. Whereas boys may give up their G.I. Joes at an earlier age to play war games on their Xbox 360s, the greater controversy seems to surround claims of how girls have changed, or rather, how marketers have changed girls. Critics describe clothing designed for young girls aged 8 to 11 as "floozy" and sexual, with department stores selling thongs for youngsters and T-shirts that say "Naughty Girl!" Although Barbie's sexuality has never been subtle, she was originally targeted to girls 9 to 12 years old. Now, Barbie dolls target primarily 3- to 7-year-old girls.

QUESTIONS

1. Are marketers to blame for kids getting older younger? Give some examples other than those listed above.

2. Give an example of a company that is countering this trend by offering age-appropriate products for children.

MARKETING BY THE NUMBERS

"High-low" pricing is popular with retailers but considered deceptive by some. Using this practice, retailers set initial prices very high for a short period and then discount the merchandise for the majority of the selling season. Critics complain that the supposed discounted price is in reality the regular price. For example, Canadian retailers such as Suzy Shier and Hudson's Bay were accused of double tagging—placing sale tags on goods right in the factory, so that the sale price was in fact the regular price.

QUESTIONS

1. Refer to Appendix 3, Marketing by the Numbers, to answer the following questions. If The Bay's cost for a piece of jewellery is $50 and it was marked up five times the cost, what is the "high" retail price? What is the "low" sales price if the price is reduced to 60 percent off the "regular" price? What is Hudson's Bay's markup percentage on cost at this price? What is its markup percentage on the "low" selling price?

2. Judgments of some cases of high-low pricing have ruled that the retailer did not violate any laws and that one retailer cannot be singled out because most jewellery competitors promote sales prices in a similar way. Is it ethical for retailers to use this pricing tactic?

BELL CANADA'S CLEAN CAPITALISM: COMBINING PLANET AND PROFIT

When you think of the most sustainable corporations in the world, Bell Canada may not jump to mind. Nonetheless, *Corporate Knights* listed Bell as one of only eight Canadian companies to make the Global 100 list of sustainable companies for 2011. Bell Canada Enterprises (BCE) was also named by *Maclean's*/Jantzi-Sustainalytics as one of Canada's Top 50 Socially Responsible Corporations. It also made the prestigious FTSE4Good Global Index. It is not surprising that it is an active member of the United Nations Global Compact and that it adheres to the Compact's principles on human rights, labour, the environment, and anticorruption.

Bell is Canada's largest communications company, providing consumers and businesses with solutions to all their communications needs. Bell is wholly owned by BCE Inc. It has a number of divisions, including Bell Mobility and Bell Media (Canada's premier multimedia company with assets in television, radio, and digital media, including CTV, Canada's number-one television network, and the country's most-watched specialty channels).

Bell takes social responsibility and sustainability seriously. It has no doubt that acting responsibly is central to achieving the sustainable business success that is essential to achieving its corporate goal of being recognized by customers as Canada's leading communications company. "Corporate responsibility is not a program at Bell. It is a way of life," said Michael Sabia, Bell's former CEO. "Our success as a company—and as a country—will be defined by the sustainability of the communities in which we live and work."

In achieving sustainability, the company stresses that each employee has a part to play in accomplishing this agenda. George Cope, Bell's president and CEO, adds that Bell operates "according to the highest ethical principles and remain[s] committed to the highest standards of corporate responsibility" in all of its interactions with customers, shareholders, suppliers, and team members as well as with the broader communities in which people work and live.

Bell's sustainability vision is one of contributing to the well-being of society by enabling responsible economic growth, connecting communities, and safeguarding the natural environment. As Canada's largest communications company, Bell believes that it has a responsibility to make its services accessible to all members of society, including those with disabilities or living in remote areas. The company takes pride in the fact that its founder, Alexander Graham

Bell, was driven by the conviction that he could help deaf people hear and communicate better. "That same spirit—of innovation, of altruism, of service"—remains at Bell today, more than 130 years later. Not only does it still help those with disabilities to communicate easily and more efficiently, it also provides telemedicine, telepsychiatry services, and e-learning services to remote communities.

Bell has a multifaceted sustainability program. It begins with the workplace, where it strives not only to have a safe and healthy working environment, but also to have fully engaged employees. It invested almost $15 million in training and development, and was honoured in 2011 for its excellence in workplace diversity and inclusiveness. Bell conducts trend analysis and benchmark studies, monitors stakeholder feedback, and undertakes surveys to ensure that it is responding to issues relevant to Canadian consumers. Its 2010 survey revealed that privacy and data security, responsible marketing practices, protection of children in the online world, reduction of energy consumption and emissions, and the use of responsible suppliers were among the issues of greatest importance to its customers.

The company also has a wide range of responsible marketing programs. First, protecting privacy and the use of customer information is never taken lightly at Bell. In addition to having all its team members review and sign its code of ethics on an annual basis, its representatives undergo privacy training so that customer rights are carefully protected. It has developed an easier-to-read privacy statement and has posted answers to privacy questions its customers frequently ask on its website.

Bell has been working to improve telemarketing practices and has been working with the Canadian Radio-television and Telecommunications Commission (CRTC) to encourage companies to respect the National Do Not Call List. It also works with the CRTC to investigate complaints.

Bell knows that customers want clear price information, so it works to ensure that it provides clear descriptions of rates and charges for its products and service plans. Bell seeks out suppliers who have a commitment to sustainable development, environmental protection, health, safety, ethics, and fair labour practices. All suppliers have to conform to Bell's Supplier Code of Conduct. Rare minerals are critical inputs to many telecommunication products, but many of these come from conflict-torn countries. Many know the story of conflict diamonds, but other rare minerals may also be mined in conditions that abuse human rights or result in the support of armed conflict. Bell works with the manufacturers of its products to avoid the use of such minerals.

Life cycle issues and product disposal are growing in importance. Bell was the first company to establish a Canada-wide collection program for reusing and recycling mobile phones. Customers can drop off their old mobile devices, batteries, and accessories at Bell's authorized retailers and at participating Caisse Desjardins, or they can ship them back to Bell free of charge via Canada Post. Since 2003, Bell has recovered more than 879 000 phones. In 2010 alone, it also collected for reuse or recycling 4.7 tonnes of batteries and accessories that would have otherwise ended up in landfills.

Protecting children from exploitation in a complex communication environment is another of Bell's priorities. The company founded the Canadian Coalition Against Internet Child Exploitation. As part of this initiative, Bell developed Cleanfeed Canada, which reduces accidental access to images of child sexual abuse and discourages those trying to access or distribute child pornography. Bell is also a lead partner in www.cybertip.ca, Canada's tip line for reporting the online exploitation of children. As well, it is the founding sponsor of Media Awareness Network's Be Web Aware website, which promotes the safe use of the Internet for children and their parents.

Bell plays a leadership role in the telecommunications industry, and it takes environmental protection into account in all aspects of its operations, including the deployment and maintenance of its networks and the efficient use of energy and resources. As its 2010 Sustainability report notes, "Using energy efficiently not only helps the environment—it also saves money and supports our strategic imperative of achieving a competitive cost structure."

Bell is continually working to reduce its carbon footprint. Since 2003, it has reduced its greenhouse gas emissions by 22 percent. It recycled 89.8 percent of its waste materials. By using more electronic billing, it saved the paper equivalent of 33 000 trees, and by using teleconferencing instead of travelling to distant meetings, it further lowered its contribution to harmful emissions. Bell has a large fleet of service vehicles. By equipping 6000 vehicles with telematics (integrated use of telecommunications and informatics), Bell was able to reduce fuel consumption in 2010 by 2.8 million litres and reduce greenhouse gas emissions by 7777 tonnes (the equivalent of taking 1900 mid-sized cars off the road for a year).

When building new facilities (called *campuses* at Bell), it strives to make them as environmentally friendly as possible through the use of natural light, energy recovery cooling systems, water saving devices, and landscaping that does not require irrigation. Its new Montreal campus was LEED-certified by the Canadian Green Building Council, and its Mississauga, Ontario, campus received a waste minimization award from the Recycling Council of Ontario.

Bell also supports the communities in which it operates, including northern communities. Its employees logged more than 256 000 hours as community volunteers. Bell targeted improved mental health, Canada's most pressing health concern, as its primary cause. In 2010 alone, it contributed $15.8 million to mental health and centres for addiction across the country. In a 2011 program called Bell let's Talk Day, an anti-stigma initiative, Bell contributed 5 cents for each of its customers' 66 million text messages and long distance calls, raising an additional $3.3 million for mental health programs.

As well, Bell is one of the chief supporters of the Kids Help Phone. The annual Walk for Kids raised $2.5 million for the cause in 2010 and drew 15 000 participants, including 2000 Bell team members.

Bell Canada is a company that certainly demonstrates that you can do well by doing good. It has been consistently profitable, and it does all of these things while sustaining the world for future generations. Indeed, Bell proves that good business and good corporate citizenship can go hand in hand.

Sources: Extracts and other case information are from Bell Canada 2010 Corporate Responsibility Report, "Let's Talk About Sustainability" (available on the Bell Canada website, BCE.ca), and Bell News Release, "Bell Recognized Nationally and Internationally for Leadership in Corporate Social Responsibility," July 2007, both accessed January 2012.

QUESTIONS FOR DISCUSSION

1. Give as many examples as you can for how Bell Canada defies the common social criticisms of marketing.

2. Why is Bell successful in applying concepts of sustainability?

3. Analyze Bell according to the environmental sustainability portfolio in Figure 3.2.

4. Does Bell practise enlightened marketing? Support your answer with as many examples as possible.

5. Would Bell be more financially successful if it were not so focused on social responsibility? Explain.

Justin Sullivan/Getty Images

AFTER STUDYING THIS CHAPTER, YOU SHOULD BE ABLE TO

1 describe the environmental forces that affect the company's ability to serve its customers

2 explain how changes in the demographic and economic environments affect marketing decisions

3 identify the major trends in the firm's natural and technological environments

4 explain the key changes in the political and cultural environments

5 discuss how companies can react to the marketing environment

Analyzing the Marketing Environment

PREVIEWING THE CONCEPTS

So far, you've learned about the basic concepts of marketing and the steps in the marketing process for engaging and building profitable relationships with targeted consumers. Next, we'll begin digging deeper into the first step of the marketing process—understanding the marketplace and customer needs and wants. In this chapter, you'll see that marketing operates in a complex and changing environment. Other actors in this environment, including suppliers, intermediaries, customers, competitors, and publics, may work with or against the company. Major environmental forces—demographic, economic, natural, technological, political, and cultural—shape marketing opportunities, pose threats, and affect the company's ability to build customer relationships. To develop effective marketing strategies, then, a company must first understand the environment in which marketing operates.

To start, let's look at Microsoft, the technology giant that dominated the computer software world throughout the 1990s and much of the 2000s. With the recent decline in stand-alone personal computers and the surge in digitally connected devices—everything from smartphones and tablets to Internet-connected TVs—mighty Microsoft has struggled a bit to find its place in a fast-changing digital marketing environment. Now, however, the tech giant is making fresh moves to re-establish itself as a relevant brand that consumers can't live without in the post-PC world.

MICROSOFT: ADAPTING TO THE FAST-CHANGING DIGITAL MARKETING ENVIRONMENT

Just a dozen years ago, talking high-tech meant talking about the almighty personal computer. Intel provided the PC microprocessors, and manufacturers such as Dell and HP built and marketed the machines. But it was Microsoft that really drove the PC industry—it made the operating systems that made most PCs go. As the dominant software developer, Microsoft put its Windows operating system and Office productivity suite on almost every computer sold.

The huge success of Windows drove Microsoft's revenues, profits, and stock price to dizzying heights. By the start of 2000, the total value of Microsoft's stock had hit a record US$618.9 billion, making it the most valuable company in history. In those heady days, no company was more relevant than Microsoft.

But moving into the new millennium, the high-tech marketing environment took a turn. PC sales growth flattened as the world fell in love with a rush of alluring new digital devices and technologies. It started with iPods and smartphones, and evolved rapidly into a full complement of digital devices—from e-readers, tablets, and sleek new laptops to Internet-connected TVs and game consoles. These devices are connected and mobile, not stationary stand-alones like the PC. They link users to an ever-on, head-spinning new world of information, entertainment, and socialization options. And, for the most part, these new devices don't use the old Microsoft products. Increasingly, even the trusty old PC has become a digital-connection device—a gateway to the Web, social media, and cloud computing. And these days, much of that can be done without once-indispensable Microsoft software.

In this new digitally connected world, Microsoft found itself lagging behind more-glamorous competitors such as Google, Apple, Samsung, and even Amazon and Face-book, which seemed to provide all things digital—the smart devices, the connecting technologies, and even the digital destinations. Over the past decade, although still finan-cially strong and still the world's dominant PC software provider with 1.3 billion Windows users around the world, Microsoft has lost some of its lustre. In the year 2000—due largely to the collapse of the stock market technology bubble—Microsoft's value plummeted by 60 percent. And whereas other tech stocks recovered, Microsoft's share price and profits have languished at 2000's levels for the past years.

But recently, Microsoft has begun a dramatic transformation in its vision and direction to better align itself with the new digital world order. Today, rather than just creating the software that makes PCs run, Microsoft wants to be a full-line digital devices and services company that delivers "delightful, seamless technology experiences" that connect people to communication, productivity, entertainment, and one another. Its mission is to help peo-ple and businesses realize their full professional and personal potential.

To make this mission a reality, during the past few years, Microsoft has unleashed a flurry of new, improved, or acquired digital products and services. Over one short span, it introduced a new version of Windows that serves not just computers but also tablets and smartphones; a next-generation Xbox console; a music and movie service to rival iTunes and Google Play; an upgraded version of Skype (acquired in 2011); a SkyDrive cloud stor-age solution; and even an innovative new tablet—the Microsoft Surface—that will give it a firmer footing in digital devices. Also rumoured to be in the works is an Xbox TV device for TV streaming. And the company recently acquired Yammer, a Web-services provider and hip maker of business social networking tools—a sort of Facebook for businesses. In its boldest expansion move yet, Microsoft recently paid more than US$7 billion dollars to acquire Nokia's smartphone business.

More important than the individual new devices, software, and services is the way they all work together to deliver a full digital experience. It all started with Windows 8, a dramatic digital-age metamorphosis from previous Windows versions, and has continued with the release of Windows 10 in 2015. Windows 8 was the first version to employ large, colourful, interactive tiles and touchscreen navigation, making it feel lively and interactive. It works seamlessly across desktops and laptops, tablets, phones, and even Xbox, providing the cloud-based connectivity that today's users crave.

Using Windows 8 software and apps with Windows-based devices and cloud com-puting services, you can select a movie from a tablet, start playing it on the TV, and finish watching it on your phone, pausing to call or text a friend using Skype. What you do on one

Windows device is automatically updated on other devices. Playlists created or songs and TV programs purchased from a mobile device will be waiting for you on your home PC. And Windows 8 is a social creature; for example, it updates contacts automatically with tweets and photos from friends.

The latest version of Office has also been transformed for the connected age. Using touchscreen interfaces, you can use an Office app and share files across PCs, Windows tablets, Windows phones, and even Macs via the SkyDrive cloud. Or you can tap into a continually updated, online-only version of Office from almost any device. In fact, Microsoft views Office as a service, not software. "It embraces the notion of social," says Microsoft CEO Steve Ballmer. "You stay connected and share information with the people you care about."

Perhaps Microsoft's biggest about-face is the development of its own hardware devices. In the past, the company relied on partners like Dell, HP, and Nokia to develop the PCs, tablets, and phones that run its software. But to gain better control in today's super-heated digital and mobile markets, Microsoft is now doing its own hardware development. For starters, it developed the cutting-edge Surface tablet. The Surface not only employs the Windows 8 interface and connectivity, it sports a nifty kickstand and thin detachable keyboard that also serves as a cover, making the Surface a unique combination of tablet and mini-laptop. The Surface, plus Xbox and the Nokia smartphone acquisition, gives Microsoft better control of access to three important new digital screens beyond the PC—tablets, TVs, and phones.

Thus, Microsoft's sweeping transformation is well underway. The company is putting a whopping US$1.5 billion of marketing support behind its revamped mission and all its new software, hardware, and services. Still, Microsoft has a long way to go. The Windows 8 system encountered mixed reviews, while the Surface tablet and other initiatives appear to be off to a decent start. However, many tentative customers are playing wait-and-see, despite very positive reviews for the Windows 10 system released in 2015. Many still see Microsoft as mostly a PC software company; it will take a sustained effort to change both customer and company thinking. Some skeptics think Microsoft may still be too tightly wedded to the old ways. "Just having the Windows name still around captures the problems of this company," says one technology forecaster. "In their heads, they know the personal computer revolution is over and that they have to move on, but in their hearts they can't do it. If Microsoft is around in 100 years, they will try and sell us a Windows teleporter."

But Microsoft seems to be making all the right moves to stay with or ahead of the times. Microsoft's sales have trended upward over the past few years, and the company is confident that it's now on the right track. "It truly is a new era at Microsoft—an era of incredible opportunity for us . . . and for the people and businesses using our products to reach their full potential," says CEO Balmer. "Although we still have a lot of hard work ahead, our products are generating excitement. And when I pause to reflect on how far we've come over the past few years and how much further we'll go in the next [few], I couldn't be more excited and optimistic."[1]

A COMPANY'S marketing environment consists of the actors and forces outside marketing that affect marketing management's ability to build and maintain successful relationships with target customers. Like Microsoft, companies constantly watch and adapt to the changing environment—or, in many cases, lead those changes.

Marketing environment
The actors and forces outside marketing that affect marketing management's ability to build and maintain successful relationships with target customers.

More than any other group in the company, marketers must be environmental trend trackers and opportunity seekers. Although every manager in an organization should watch the outside environment, marketers have two special aptitudes. They have disciplined methods—marketing research and marketing intelligence—for collecting information about the marketing environment. They also spend more time in customer and competitor environments. By carefully studying the environment, marketers can adapt their strategies to meet new marketplace challenges and opportunities.

The marketing environment consists of a *microenvironment* and a *macroenvironment*. The **microenvironment** consists of the actors close to the company that affect its ability to serve its customers—the company, suppliers, marketing intermediaries, customer markets, competitors, and publics. The **macroenvironment** consists of the larger societal forces that affect the microenvironment—demographic, economic, natural, technological, political, and cultural forces. We look first at the company's microenvironment.

Microenvironment

The actors close to the company that affect its ability to serve its customers—the company, suppliers, marketing intermediaries, customer markets, competitors, and publics.

Macroenvironment

The larger societal forces that affect the microenvironment—demographic, economic, natural, technological, political, and cultural forces.

◀◉ **Simulate** on MyMarketingLab

The Marketing Environment

The Microenvironment [LO1]

Marketing management's job is to build relationships with customers by creating customer value and satisfaction. However, marketing managers cannot do this alone. Figure 4.1 shows the major actors in the marketer's microenvironment. Marketing success requires building relationships with other company departments, suppliers, marketing intermediaries, competitors, various publics, and customers, which combine to make up the company's value delivery network.

The Company

In designing marketing plans, marketing management takes other company groups into account—groups such as top management, finance, research and development (R&D), purchasing, operations, and accounting. All of these interrelated groups form the internal environment. Top management sets the company's mission, objectives, broad strategies, and policies. Marketing managers make decisions within these broader strategies and plans. Then, as we discussed in Chapter 2, marketing managers must work closely with other company departments. With marketing taking the lead, all departments—from manufacturing and finance to legal and human resources—share the responsibility for understanding customer needs and creating customer value.

Suppliers

Suppliers form an important link in the company's overall customer value delivery network. They provide the resources needed by the company to produce its goods and

FIGURE 4.1 Actors in the Microenvironment

services. Supplier problems can seriously affect marketing. Marketing managers must watch supply availability and costs. Supply shortages or delays, labour strikes, natural disasters, and other events can cost sales in the short run and damage customer satisfaction in the long run. Rising supply costs may force price increases that can harm the company's sales volume.

Most marketers today treat their suppliers as partners in creating and delivering customer value. For example, giant Swedish furniture retailer IKEA doesn't just buy from its suppliers. It involves them deeply in the process of delivering a stylish and affordable lifestyle to IKEA's customers:

> IKEA, the world's largest furniture retailer, is the quintessential global cult brand. Each year, customers from Beijing to Moscow to Middletown, Ohio, flock to the Scandinavian retailer's more than 300 huge stores in 40 countries, snapping up more than US$28 billion worth of IKEA's trendy but simple and practical furniture at affordable prices. But IKEA's biggest obstacle to growth isn't opening new stores and attracting customers. Rather, it's finding enough of the right kinds of suppliers to help design and make all the products that customers will carry out of its stores. IKEA currently relies on more than 2000 suppliers in 50 countries to stock its shelves. IKEA can't just hope to find spot suppliers who might be available when needed. Instead, it must systematically develop a robust network of supplier-partners that reliably provide the more than 12 000 items it stocks. IKEA's designers start with a basic customer value proposition. Then they find and work closely with key suppliers to bring that proposition to market. Thus, IKEA does more than just buy from suppliers. It involves them deeply in questions of quality, design, and price to create the kinds of products that keep customers coming back.[2]

Used with the permission of Inter IKEA Systems B.V.

Exhibit 4.1 Giant Swedish furniture manufacturer IKEA doesn't just buy from suppliers. It involves them deeply in the process of delivering a stylish and affordable lifestyle to its customers worldwide.

Marketing Intermediaries

Marketing intermediaries help the company promote, sell, and distribute its products to final buyers. They include resellers, physical distribution firms, marketing services agencies, and financial intermediaries. *Resellers* are distribution-channel firms that help the company find customers or make sales to them. These include wholesalers and retailers that buy and resell merchandise. Selecting and partnering with resellers is not easy. No longer do manufacturers have many small, independent resellers from which to choose. They now face large and growing reseller organizations, such as Walmart, Target, Home Depot, and Costco. These organizations frequently have enough power to dictate terms or even shut smaller manufacturers out of large markets.

Physical distribution firms help the company stock and move goods from their points of origin to their destinations. *Marketing services agencies* are the marketing research firms, advertising agencies, media firms, and marketing consulting firms that help the company target and promote its products to the right markets. *Financial intermediaries* include banks, credit companies, insurance companies, and other businesses that help finance transactions or insure against the risks associated with the buying and selling of goods.

Like suppliers, marketing intermediaries form an important component of the company's overall value delivery network. In its quest to create satisfying customer relationships, the company must do more than just optimize its own performance. It must partner effectively with marketing intermediaries to optimize the performance of the entire system.

Thus, today's marketers recognize the importance of working with their intermediaries as partners rather than simply as channels through which they sell their products.

Marketing intermediaries
Firms that help the company to promote, sell, and distribute its goods to final buyers.

For example, when Coca-Cola signs on as the exclusive beverage provider for a fast-food chain, such as McDonald's, Wendy's, or Subway, it provides much more than just soft drinks. It also pledges powerful marketing support:

> Coca-Cola assigns cross-functional teams dedicated to understanding the finer points of each retail partner's business. It conducts a staggering amount of research on beverage consumers and shares these insights with its partners. It analyzes the demographics of U.S. zip code areas and helps partners determine which Coke brands are preferred in their areas. Coca-Cola has even studied the design of drive-through menu boards to better understand which layouts, fonts, letter sizes, colours, and visuals induce consumers to order more food and drink. Based on such insights, the Coca-Cola Food Service group develops marketing programs and merchandising tools that help its retail partners improve their beverage sales and profits. Its website, www.CokeSolutions.com, provides retailers with a wealth of information, business solutions, merchandising tips, and techniques on how to go green. "We know that you're passionate about delighting guests and enhancing their real experiences on every level," says Coca-Cola to its retail partners. "As your partner, we want to help in any way we can." Such intense partnering has made Coca-Cola a runaway leader in the fountain-soft-drink market.[3]

Competitors

The marketing concept holds that, to be successful, a company must provide greater customer value and satisfaction than its competitors do. Thus, marketers must do more than simply adapt to the needs of target consumers. They must also gain strategic advantage by positioning their offerings strongly against competitors' offerings in the minds of consumers.

No single competitive marketing strategy is best for all companies. Each firm should consider its own size and industry position compared with those of its competitors. Large firms with dominant positions in an industry can use certain strategies that smaller firms cannot afford. But being large is not enough. There are winning strategies for large firms, but there are also losing ones. And small firms can develop strategies that give them better rates of return than what large firms enjoy.

Publics

Public
Any group that has an actual or potential interest in or impact on an organization's ability to achieve its objectives.

The company's marketing environment also includes various publics. A **public** is any group that has an actual or potential interest in or impact on an organization's ability to achieve its objectives. We can identify seven types of publics:

- *Financial publics:* This group influences the company's ability to obtain funds. Banks, investment analysts, and stockholders are the major financial publics.

- *Media publics:* This group carries news, features, editorial opinions, and other content. It includes television stations, newspapers, magazines, and blogs and other social media.

- *Government publics:* Management must take government developments into account. Marketers must often consult the company's lawyers on issues of product safety, truth in advertising, and other matters.

- *Citizen-action publics:* A company's marketing decisions may be questioned by consumer organizations, environmental groups, minority groups, and others. Its public relations department can help it stay in touch with consumer and citizen groups.

- *Local publics:* This group includes neighbourhood residents and community organizations. Large companies usually create departments and programs that deal with local community issues and provide community support. For example, Life is good, Inc. recognizes the importance of community publics in helping accomplish the brand's "spread optimism" mission (remember the Chapter 1 Life is good, Inc.

story in Marketing@Work 1.2?). Its Life is good Playmakers program promotes the philosophy that "Life can hurt, play can heal." It provides training and support for child-care professionals to use the power of play to help children overcome challenges ranging from violence and illness to extreme poverty in cities around the world, from Danbury, Connecticut, to Port-au-Prince, Haiti. So far, the organization has raised more than US$9 million to benefit children.[4]

■ *General public:* A company needs to be concerned about the general public's attitude toward its products and activities. The public's image of the company affects its buying behaviour.

■ *Internal publics:* This group includes workers, managers, volunteers, and the board of directors. Large companies use newsletters and other means to inform and motivate their internal publics. When employees feel good about the companies they work for, this positive attitude spills over to the external publics.

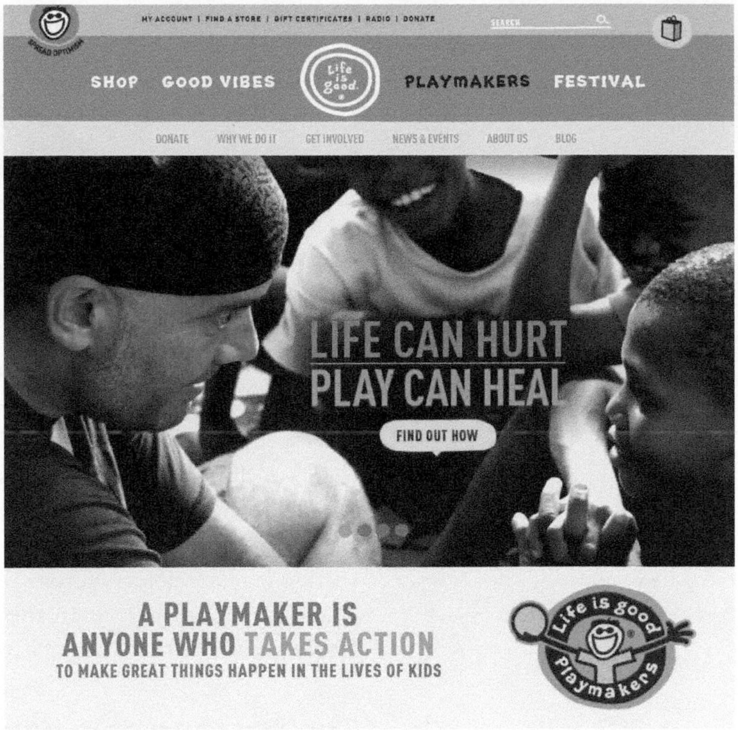

A company can prepare marketing plans for these major publics as well as for its customer markets. Suppose the company wants a specific response from a particular public, such as goodwill, favourable word of mouth and social sharing, or donations of time or money. The company would have to design an offer to this public that is attractive enough to produce the desired response.

The Life is Good Company

Exhibit 4.2 Publics: The Life is good Company recognizes the importance of community publics. Its Life is good Playmakers program provides training and support for child-care professionals in cities around the world to use the power of play to help children overcome challenges ranging from violence and illness to extreme poverty.

Customers

Customers are the most important actors in the company's microenvironment. The aim of the entire value delivery network is to serve target customers and create strong relationships with them. The company might target any or all of five types of customer markets. *Consumer markets* consist of individuals and households that buy goods and services for personal consumption. *Business markets* buy goods and services for further processing or use in their production processes, whereas *reseller markets* buy goods and services to resell at a profit. *Government markets* consist of government agencies that buy goods and services to produce public services or transfer the goods and services to others who need them. Finally, *international markets* consist of these buyers in other countries, including consumers, producers, resellers, and governments. Each market type has special characteristics that call for careful study by the seller.

The Macroenvironment LO2

◀●─**Simulate** on MyMarketingLab

Human Resources and Diversity

The company and all the other actors operate in a larger macroenvironment of forces that shape opportunities and pose threats to the company. Figure 4.2 shows the six major forces in the company's macroenvironment. Even the most dominant companies can be vulnerable to the often turbulent and changing forces in the marketing environment.

FIGURE 4.2 Major Forces in the Company's Macroenvironment

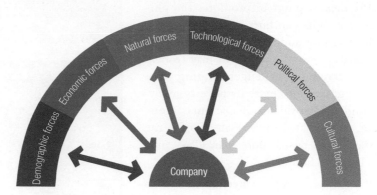

Some of these forces are unforeseeable and uncontrollable. Others can be predicted and handled through skilful management. Companies that understand and adapt well to their environments can thrive. Those that don't can face difficult times. One-time dominant market leaders such as Xerox, Sears, and Sony have learned this lesson the hard way (see Marketing@Work 4.1). In the remaining sections of this chapter, we examine these forces and show how they affect marketing plans.

The Demographic Environment

Demography
The study of human populations in terms of size, density, location, age, gender, race, occupation, and other statistics.

Demography is the study of human populations in terms of size, density, location, age, gender, race, occupation, and other statistics. The demographic environment is of major interest to marketers because it involves people, and people make up markets. The world population is growing at an explosive rate. It now exceeds 7 billion people and is expected to grow to more than 8 billion by the year 2030.[5] The world's large and highly diverse population poses both opportunities and challenges.

Changes in the world demographic environment have major implications for business. Thus, marketers keep a close eye on demographic trends and developments in their markets. They analyze changing age and family structures, geographic population shifts, educational characteristics, and population diversity. Here, we discuss the most important demographic trends in Canada.

The Changing Age Structure of the Population The Canadian population exceeded 35.7 million in 2015 and is expected to reach between 40.1 and 47.7 million by 2036.[6] The single most important demographic trend in Canada is the changing age structure of the population. The Canadian population contains several generational groups. Here, we discuss four groups—the baby boomers, Generation X, the Millennials, and Generation Z—and their impact on today's marketing strategies.

Baby boomers
The 9.8 million Canadians born during the baby boom following World War II and lasting until the mid-1960s.

THE BABY BOOMERS The post–World War II baby boom, which began in 1947 and ran through 1966, produced 9.8 million **baby boomers** in Canada. Although there was a baby boom in both Canada and the United States, Canadian marketers have to recognize that our baby boom was unique. It started later than the American version (1947 versus 1946) and lasted longer (the American boom ended in 1964; the Canadian boom continued until 1966). While the American baby boom resulted in 3.5 children per family, the Canadian boom produced an average of 4 children. Furthermore, the baby boom was not a worldwide phenomenon. Among the other developed countries, only Australia and New Zealand experienced the same expansion in the birth rate. In Europe, there was no baby boom, and in Japan, the birth rate declined during our baby boom years, which explains why these countries have a higher proportion of older people in their societies.[7]

MARKETING@WORK   4.1

Sony: Battling the Marketing Environment's "Perfect Storm"

After a decade of struggle, the year 2011 was supposed to be a comeback year for Sony. The consumer electronics and entertainment giant had one of its best batches of new products ever heading for store shelves. Even more important, Sony was heading back into the digital big leagues with the launch of an iTunes-like global digital network that would combine Sony's strengths in movies, music, and video games for all its televisions, PCs, phones, game consoles, and tablets. Analysts forecasted a US$2 billion profit. "I really and truly believed that I was going to have a year to remember," says Sony's chairman Sir Howard Stringer. "And I did, but in the wrong way."

Instead of a banner year, 2011 produced a near-perfect storm of environmental calamities for Sony. For starters, in March 2011, eastern Japan was devastated by a mammoth earthquake and tsunami. The disaster forced Sony to shutter 10 plants, disrupting operations and the flow of Sony products worldwide. In April, a hacking attack on the company's Internet entertainment services—the second-largest online data breach in U.S. history—forced the company to shut down its PlayStation Network. Only four months later, fires set by rioters in London destroyed a Sony warehouse and an estimated 25 million CDs and DVDs, gutting an inventory of 150 independent labels. To round out the year, floods in Thailand shut down component plants there.

When the rubble was cleared, Sony's projected US$2 billion profit ended up as a US$6.4 billion loss—the company's largest ever. That loss marked a three-year streak of losses that had begun with yet another environmental upheaval—the Great Recession and global financial meltdown of 2008–2009. By mid-2013, a shell-shocked Sony was still looking for a return to profitability.

There's no doubt that environmental unforeseeables have dealt Sony some heavy blows. But not all the blame for Sony's woes goes to uncontrollable

environmental forces. Sony's difficulties began long before the 2011 string of events. More to blame than any natural disaster has been Sony's longer-term inability to adapt to one of the most powerful environmental forces of our time—dramatic changes in digital technology.

Interestingly, it was Sony's magical touch with technology that first built the company into a global powerhouse. Only 15 years ago, Sony was a high-tech rock star, a veritable merchant of cool. Not only was it the world's largest consumer electronics company, its history of innovative products—such as Trinitron TVs, Walkman portable music players, Handycam video recorders, and PlayStation video-game consoles—had revolutionized entire industries. Sony's innovations drove pop culture, earned the adoration of the masses, and made money for the company. The Sony brand stood for innovation, style, and high quality.

Today, however, although still a US$78 billion company, Sony is more a relic than a rock star, lost in the shadows of high-fliers such as Apple, Samsung, and Microsoft. Samsung overtook Sony

as the world's largest consumer electronics maker over a decade ago. Samsung's sales recently more than tripled Sony's, and Samsung's profits surged as Sony's losses still mounted. Likewise, Apple has pounded Sony with one new product after another. "When I was young, I had to have a Sony product," summarizes one analyst, "but for the younger generation today it's Apple."

How did Sony fall so hard so fast? It fell behind in technology. Sony built its once-mighty empire based on the innovative engineering and design of stand-alone electronics—TVs, CD players, and video-game consoles. As the Internet and digital technologies surged, however, creating a more connected and mobile world, stand-alone hardware was rapidly replaced by new connecting technologies, media, and content. As our entertainment lives swirled toward digital downloads and shared content accessed through PCs, iPods, smartphones, tablets, and Internet-ready TVs, Sony was late to adapt.

Behaving as though its market leadership could never be challenged, an

Bloomberg via Getty Images

Exhibit 4.3 **The marketing environment:** Environmental unforeseeables have dealt Sony some heavy blows. But the company's inability to adapt to the changing technological environment has turned Sony's "Make. Believe" brand promise into more of a "make-believe" one.

arrogant Sony clung to successful old technologies rather than embracing new ones. For example, prior to the launch of Apple's first iPod in 2001, Sony had already developed devices that would download and play digital music files. Sony had everything it needed to create an iPod/iTunes-type world, including its own recording company. But it passed on that idea in favour of continued emphasis on its then-highly successful CD business. "[Apple's] Steve Jobs figured it out, we figured it out, we didn't execute," says Sony chairman Stringer. "The music guys didn't want to see the CD go away."

Similarly, as the world's largest TV producer, Sony clung to its cherished Trinitron cathode-ray-tube technology. Meanwhile, Samsung, LG, and other competitors were moving rapidly ahead with flat screens. Sony eventually responded. But today, both Samsung and LG sell more TVs than Sony. Sony's TV business, once its main profit centre, has suffered losses for the past 10 years in excess of US$7 billion, but finally posted a slim profit margin in 2014.

It was a similar story for Sony's PlayStation consoles, once the undisputed market leader and accounting for one-third of Sony's profits. Sony yawned when Nintendo introduced its innovative motion-sensing Nintendo Wii, dismissing it as a "niche game device." Instead, Sony engineers loaded up the PS3 with pricey technology that produced a loss of US$300 per unit sold. Wii became a smash hit and the best-selling game console; the PS3 lost billions for Sony, dropping it from first place to third.

Even as a money loser, the PlayStation system, with its elegant blending of hardware and software, had all the right ingredients to make Sony a leader in the new world of digital entertainment distribution and social networking. Executives inside Sony even recognized the PlayStation platform as the "epitome of convergence," with the potential to create "a fusion of computers and entertainment." But that vision never materialized, and Sony has lagged in the burgeoning business of connecting people to digital entertainment.

To his credit, CEO Stringer made a credible effort to reignite Sony. After taking over in 2005, he drew up a turnaround plan aimed at changing the Sony mindset and moving the company into the new connected and mobile digital age. Under his early leadership, the consumer electronics giant began to show renewed life as revenues and profits rose. Then came the Great Recession, once again knocking the bottom out of profits.

And just as Sony began digging out from that disaster, it was struck by the string of 2011 environmental calamities.

Thus, environmental forces—whether unforeseeable natural and economic events or more predictable turns in technology—can heavily impact company strategy. Sony's difficult times provide a cautionary tale of what can happen when a company—even a dominant market leader—fails to adapt to its changing marketing environment. Despite the setbacks, however, giant Sony still has a lot going for it. For example, although it was a money loser, the PS3 was a hit with consumers, and when the much anticipated PS4 was released for the 2014 holiday season, it became an instant success for Sony. With over 22 million units sold by March 2015, the PS4 has helped Sony return to profitability. Now, if Sony can just get the economy and Mother Nature to cooperate. . . .

Sources: Bryan Gruley and Cliff Edwards, "Sony Needs a Hit," *Bloomberg Businessweek*, November 21, 2011, pp. 72–77; Hiroko Tabuchi, "Sony Revises Expected Loss to $6.40 Billion," *New York Times*, April 11, 2012, p. B3; Daisuke Wakabayashi, "Sony Posts Loss, Curbing Stock's Rally," WallStreetJournal.com, February 7, 2013, http://online.wsj.com/article/SB10001424127887324590904578289103990967408.html; Cliff Edwards and Mariko Yasu, "Sony's Search for Cool. The Old-Fashioned Way," *Bloomberg Businessweek*, February 24, 2013, pp. 20–21; and information from www.sony.net/SonyInfo/IR, accessed November 2013.

After years of prosperity, free spending, and not much saving, many baby boomers were hit hard by the Great Recession. A sharp decline in stock prices and home values ate into their nest eggs and retirement prospects. As a result, many boomers are now spending more carefully and are rethinking the purpose and value of their work, responsibilities, and relationships.

However, although some might still be feeling the post-recession pinch, the baby boomers are still the wealthiest generation in Canadian history. Today's boomers account for about one-third of Canada's population and control over 50 percent of the nation's disposable income. The 50-plus consumer segment now buys more than 55 percent of all consumer goods.[8] As they reach their peak earning and spending years, the boomers will continue to constitute a lucrative market for financial services, new housing and home remodelling, new cars, travel and entertainment, eating out, health and fitness products, and just about everything else.

It would be a mistake to think of the older boomers as phasing out or slowing down; many of these boomers see themselves as entering new life phases. The more active boomers—sometimes called zoomers—have no intention of abandoning their youthful lifestyles as they age. For example, one study found that whereas 9 percent of baby boomers attended the symphony or opera during the previous 12 months, 12 percent attended a rock concert. As one expert noted, baby boomers "are showing the nation that their heyday is far from over by taking pleasure in life's adventures."[9]

For example, many travel companies—such as ElderTreks, 50PlusExpeditions, and Row Adventures—now design adventure travel expeditions for active baby boomers. ElderTreks, for instance, offers small-group, off-the-beaten-path tours designed exclusively for people 50 and over. Whether it's for wildlife and tribal African safaris, active hiking in the Himalayas or Andes, or an expedition by icebreaker to the Arctic or Antarctic, ElderTreks targets active boomers who have the time, resources, and passion for high-adventure travel but prefer to do it with others their own age—no young'uns allowed.[10]

GENERATION X The baby boom was followed by a "birth dearth," creating another generation of 7 million Canadians born between 1967 and 1976. Author Douglas Coupland famously dubbed them **Generation X** because they lie in the shadow of the boomers and lack obvious distinguishing characteristics.

Generation X
The 7 million Canadians born between 1967 and 1976 in the "birth dearth" following the baby boom.

Considerably smaller than the boomer generation that precedes them and the Millennials who follow, the Generation Xers are a sometimes overlooked consumer group. Although they seek success, they are less materialistic than the other groups; they prize experience, not acquisition. For many of the Gen Xers who are parents, family comes first—both children and their aging parents—and career second. From a marketing standpoint, the Gen Xers are a more skeptical bunch. They tend to research products before they consider a purchase, prefer quality to quantity, and tend to be less receptive to overt marketing pitches. They are more likely to be receptive to irreverent ad pitches that make fun of convention and tradition.

The first to grow up in the Internet era, Generation X is a connected generation that embraces the benefits of new technology. Some 49 percent own smartphones and 11 percent own tablets. Of the Xers on the Internet, 74 percent use the Internet for banking, 72 percent use it for researching companies or products, and 81 percent have made purchases online. Ninety-five percent have an active Facebook page.

The Gen Xers have now grown up and are taking over. They are increasingly displacing the lifestyles, culture, and values of the baby boomers. They are moving up in their careers, and many are proud homeowners with growing families. They are the most educated generation to date, and they possess hefty annual purchasing power. However, like the baby boomers, the Gen Xers now face growing economic pressures. Like almost everyone else these days, they are spending more carefully.[11]

Still, with so much potential, many brands and organizations are focusing on Gen Xers as a prime target segment. For example, Dairy Queen targets this segment directly, with a marketing campaign that fits the Gen Xer family situation and sense of humour:

Exhibit 4.4 Targeting Gen Xers: Dairy Queen's "So Good It's RiDQulous" campaign targets Gen Xers with irreverent humour and online ad placements.

Generation X is Dairy Queen's new sweet spot. Its primary target market—parents roughly 34 to 44 years old with young children—falls squarely within the Gen X cohort. So what does that mean for DQ's marketing? A "So Good It's RiDQulous" advertising campaign loaded with irreverent Gen X humour—as in old-fashioned shaving bunnies, a guitar that sounds like a dolphin, fencing ninjas, and kittens in bubbles. In one ad, DQ's new pitchman—a mustachioed 30-something—touts Dairy Queen birthday cakes, then says, "And we don't just blow bubbles, we blow bubbles with kittens inside them [which he then does], because at Dairy Queen, good isn't good enough." To reach Gen X consumers better, DQ has shifted a batch of its ads from TV to social

American Dairy Queen Corporation

media and online sites such as Hulu. "We're going where our Gen X customers' eyeballs are," says DQ's chief brand officer. An independent study in 2012 found the "So Good It's RiDQulous" ads to be the most effective in the quick service restaurant segment.[12]

Millennials (or Generation Y)
The 10.4 million children of the baby boomers born between 1977 and 2000.

MILLENNIALS Both the baby boomers and Gen Xers will one day be passing the reins to the **Millennials** (also called **Generation Y** or the echo boomers). Born between 1977 and 2000, these children of the baby boomers number 10.4 million or more, dwarfing the Gen Xers and becoming larger even than the baby boomer segment. In the post-recession era, the Millennials are the most financially strapped generation. Facing higher unemployment and saddled with more debt, many of these young consumers have near-empty piggy banks. Still, because of their numbers, the Millennials make up a huge and attractive market, both now and in the future.

One thing that all Millennials have in common is their comfort with digital technology. They don't just embrace technology; it's a way of life. The Millennials were the first generation to grow up in a world filled with computers, mobile phones, satellite TV, iPods and iPads, and online social media. As a result, they engage with brands in an entirely new way, such as with mobile or social media. "They tend to expect one-to-one communication with brands," says one analyst, "and embrace the ability to share the good and bad about products and services with friends and strangers."[13]

Many brands are now fielding specific products and marketing campaigns aimed at Millennial needs and lifestyles. For example, the Kia Soul targets young Millennial consumers. It's a funky but practical entry-level vehicle with an affordable price to match. Kia Soul "Hamstar" ads have a distinctly youthful appeal, featuring a trio of hamsters hip-hopping their way through scenes ranging from an apocalyptic landscape to an eighteenth-century opera house, accompanied by infectious soundtracks such as LMFAO's "Party Rock Anthem." The campaign—featuring everything from Super Bowl ads to online, mobile, and social media platforms—is built around what Kia's U.S. chief marketing officer calls "the four pillars of Millennials' lifestyles: music, sports, pop culture, and the 'connected life.'" Both the car and the marketing campaign have been a smash hit with targeted buyers.[14]

Generation Z
People born after 2000 (although many analysts include people born after 1995) who make up the kid, tween, and teen markets.

GENERATION Z Hard on the heels of the Millennials is **Generation Z**, young people born after 2000 (although many analysts include people born after 1995 in this group). The Gen Zers make up important kid, tween, and teen markets. For example, by themselves, U.S. tweens (ages 8–12) number 20 million girls and boys who spend an estimated $30 billion annually of their own money and influence another $150 billion of their parents' spending. In Canada, the 0–14-year-old demographic has declined to 16.7 percent of the population, but still represents approximately 5.6 million individuals.[15] These young consumers also represent tomorrow's markets—they are now forming brand relationships that will affect their buying well into the future.

Even more than the Millennials, the defining characteristic of Gen Zers is their utter fluency and comfort with digital technologies. Generation Z

KIA Motors America

Exhibit 4.5 Targeting Millennials: The Kia Soul and its Hamster ads have been a smash hit with Millennials, helping to make the Kia one of the nation's fastest-growing car brands.

take smartphones, tablets, iPods, Internet-connected game consoles, wireless Internet, and digital and social media for granted—they've always had them—making this group highly mobile, connected, and social. "If they're awake, they're online," quips one analyst. They have "digital in their DNA," says another.[16]

Gen Zers blend the online and offline worlds seamlessly as they socialize and shop. According to recent studies, despite their youth, more than half of all Generation Z tweens and teens do product research before buying a product, or having their parents buy it for them. Of those who shop online, more than half *prefer* shopping online in categories ranging from electronics, books, music, sports equipment, and beauty products to clothes, shoes, and fashion accessories.[17]

Companies in almost all industries market products and services aimed at Generation Z. For example, many retailers have created special lines or even entire stores appealing to Gen Z buyers and their parents—consider Abercrombie Kids, Gap Kids, Old Navy Kids, and Pottery Barn Kids. The Justice chain targets tween girls, with apparel and accessories laser-focused on their special preferences and lifestyles. Although these young buyers often have their mothers in tow, "the *last* thing a 10- or 12-year-old girl wants is to look like her mom," says Justice's CEO. Justice's stores, website, and social media pages are designed with tweens in mind. "You have to appeal to their senses," says the CEO. "They love sensory overload—bright colours, music videos, a variety of merchandise, the tumult of all of that." Fast-growing Justice now outsells even Walmart and Target in girls' apparel (which is impressive, considering that Walmart has almost 4000 U.S. stores compared with Justice's 920).[18]

Media companies and publishers are also targeting today's connected, tech-savvy Gen Zers and their parents. For example, Netflix has created a "Just for Kids" portal and app, by which children can experience Netflix on any or all of their screens—TVs, computers, and tablets or other mobile devices. "Just for Kids" is filled with movies and TV shows appropriate for children 12 and under, organized in a kid-friendly way with large images of their favourite characters and content categories.[19]

Marketing to Gen Zers and their parents presents special challenges. Traditional media are still important to this group. Magazines such as *J-14* and *Twist* are popular with some Gen Z segments, as are TV channels such as Nickelodeon and the Disney Channel. But marketers know they must meet Gen Zers where they hang out and shop. Increasingly, that's in the digital, online, and mobile worlds. Although the under-13 set remains barred from social media such as Facebook and Instagram, at least officially (half of all tweens say they use Facebook), the social media will play a crucial marketing role as the kids and tweens grow into teens.

Today's kids are notoriously hard to pin down, and they have short attention spans. Gen Zers "don't want to be hit over the head with ad messages," says one kid-marketing expert. They "don't want *products*, they want *experiences*. You want to engage them." Says another expert, "Today's tweens demand a more personal, more tactile, truly up-close-and-in-person connection to their favourite brands."[20]

Another Generation Z concern involves children's privacy and their vulnerability to marketing pitches. Companies marketing to this group must do so responsibly or risk the wrath of parents and public policy makers.

Photo courtesy of Gary Armstrong

Exhibit 4.6 Targeting Generation Z: Justice targets only tween girls, with apparel and accessories laser-focused on their special preferences and lifestyles. Its rapid expansion now includes 45 outlets in Canada.

GENERATIONAL MARKETING Do marketers need to create separate products and marketing programs for each generation? Some experts warn that marketers need to be careful about turning off one generation each time they craft a product or message that appeals effectively to another. Others caution that each generation spans decades of time and many socioeconomic levels. For example, marketers often split the baby boomers into three smaller groups—leading-edge boomers, core boomers, and trailing-edge boomers—each with its own beliefs and behaviours. Similarly, they split the Generation Z into kids, tweens, and teens.

Thus, marketers need to form more precise age-specific segments within each group. More important, defining people by their birth date may be less effective than segmenting them by lifestyle, life stage, or the common values they seek in the products they buy. We will discuss many other ways to segment markets in Chapter 7.

The Changing Canadian Household When one uses the term *household*, a stereotype of the typical family living in the suburbs with its two children may leap to mind. However, this stereotype is far from accurate. The 2011 census (the latest one completed) reveals some interesting trends. For example, there is a growing "crowded nest" syndrome. About 42 percent of young Canadians aged 20 to 29 now live with their parents. There are almost 9.4 million families in Canada, but fewer are having children. In fact, the 2006 census marked the first time there were more census families without children than with children during the past 20 years, and this trend continued in 2011. The 2011 census counted more one-person households than couple households with children for the first time, and the average size of the Canadian family now stands at 2.9 persons. Canada also experienced growth in diverse family structures, including common-law marriages, same-sex couples, and blended families.[21] Given these trends, marketers must increasingly consider the distinctive needs and buying habits of these nontraditional households, because they are now growing more rapidly than traditional ones.

Responsibility for household tasks and the care of children is also changing. There are now more dual-income families as more and more women enter the workforce. Today women account for more than 50 percent of the Canadian workforce. The employment rate of women with children has grown particularly sharply in the past two decades, especially for those with preschool-aged children. In 2009, 72.9 percent of women with children under the age of 16 living at home were employed, more than double the 1976 figure.[22]

The significant number of women in the workforce has spawned the child daycare business and increased the consumption of career-oriented women's clothing, convenience foods, financial services, and time-saving services. Royal Caribbean targets time-crunched working moms with budget-friendly family vacations that are easy to plan and certain to wow the family. Royal Caribbean estimates that, although vacations are a joint decision, 80 percent of all trips are planned and booked by women—moms who are pressed for time, whether they work or not. "We want to make sure that you're the hero, that when your family comes on our ship, it's going to be a great experience for all of them," says a senior marketer at Royal Caribbean, "and that you, Mom, who has done all the planning and scheduling, get to enjoy that vacation."[23]

Geographic Shifts in Population The population of Canada grew by approximately 4.5 percent between 2010 and 2014. As Table 4.1 shows, however, growth rates across all provinces and territories are not uniform. The Prairie provinces (Alberta, Saskatchewan, and Manitoba) and two of our three territories (Yukon and Nunavut) experienced growth rates higher than the national average. However, growth was below the national average for the remainder of the country.

Interprovincial migration is driven by differences in unemployment rates and wages, and the oil boom in Alberta has lured many Canadians westward. However, while Alberta

TABLE 4.1 Canada's Population			
	2010 (thousands)	**2014 (thousands)**	**Change (%)**
Canada	34 005.3	35 540.4	4.5
Newfoundland and Labrador	522.0	527.0	1.0
Prince Edward Island	141.7	146.3	3.2
Nova Scotia	942.1	942.7	0.0
New Brunswick	753.0	753.9	0.0
Quebec	7929.4	8214.7	3.6
Ontario	13 135.1	13 678.7	4.1
Manitoba	1220.9	1282.0	5.0
Saskatchewan	1051.4	1125.4	7.0
Alberta	3732.6	4121.7	10.4
British Columbia	4465.9	4631.3	3.7
Yukon	34.6	36.5	5.5
Northwest Territories	43.3	43.6	0.7
Nunavut	33.4	36.6	9.6

Source: "Population by Year, by Province and Territory," www.statcan.gc.ca/tables-tableaux/sum-som/l01/cst01/demo02a-eng.htm. Statistics Canada, 2015. Reproduced with the permission of the Minister of Public Works and Government Services Canada, 2015.

has seen a bump in interprovincial migration in recent years, flows between provinces remain lower than they were in the 1970s and 1980s. A study by Ipsos Reid found that only 20 percent of Canadians were willing to relocate to another city for a few years, even with a pay hike of at least 10 percent and all moving expenses covered. Moving costs are often cited as the single biggest reason preventing Canadians from moving. In addition, however, some professional qualifications aren't transferable between provinces, meaning that people would have to get recertified when they move. As well, many Canadians are now caring for aging parents or younger children, making moving to another province more difficult.[24]

Canada's cities are changing as well. Canadian cities are often surrounded by large suburban areas; Statistics Canada calls these combinations of urban and suburban populations Census Metropolitan Areas (CMAs). Census data for 2011 showed that 23 123 441 people, or 69.1 percent of the total population, lived in one of Canada's 33 CMAs. The three largest CMAs—Toronto, Montreal, and Vancouver—accounted for 35.0 percent of the total Canadian population. The two fastest growing CMAs were both in Alberta: Calgary, where the population rose 12.6 percent, and Edmonton, where it increased 12.1 percent.[25] The shift in where people live has also caused a shift in where they work. For example, the migration toward metropolitan and suburban areas has resulted in a rapid increase in the number of people who telecommute—that is, work at home or in a remote office, and conduct their business by phone, fax, or the Internet. This trend, in turn, has created a booming SOHO (small office/home office) market. An increasing number of people are working from home with the help of PCs, smartphones, and broadband Internet access. One study estimates that 24 percent of employed individuals do some or all of their work at home.[26]

Many marketers are actively courting the lucrative telecommuting market. For example, WebEx, the Web-conferencing division of Cisco, helps connect people who telecommute or work remotely. With WebEx, people can meet and collaborate online via computer or smartphone, no matter what their work location. And companies ranging

Exhibit 4.7 Serving the telecommuter market: Companies such as Grind rent out shared office space by the day or month to telecommuters and others who work away from the main office.

from Salesforce.com to Google and IBM offer cloud computing applications that let people collaborate anywhere and everywhere through the Internet and mobile devices. Additionally, companies such as Regus or Grind rent out fully equipped shared office space by the day or month for telecommuters and others who work away from the main office.[27]

A Better-Educated, More White-Collar, More Professional Population The Canadian population is becoming better educated. Statistics Canada reported that in 2011, 89 percent of Canadians had completed high school and 64 percent of Canadians aged 25 to 64 had completed post-secondary education (university, college, or trade school).[28] The rising number of educated people will increase the demand for quality products, books, travel, computers, and Internet services.

Higher education is a must to maintain a skilled labour force in Canada. It is estimated that roughly two-thirds of all job openings between 2007 and 2017 will be in occupations requiring postsecondary education (university, college, or apprenticeship training) or in management occupations. These jobs will cover a wide range of diverse options, from nursing to construction. In fact, the Canadian Chamber of Commerce predicted that over the next decade there will be labour shortfalls of 163 000 in construction, 130 000 in oil and gas, 60 000 in nursing, 37 000 in trucking, 22 000 in the hotel industry, and 10 000 in the steel trades. The Chamber also lists the skilled labour shortage as the number one barrier to increasing the country's international competitiveness.[29]

Increasing Diversity Countries vary in their ethnic and racial makeup. At one extreme is Japan, where almost everyone is Japanese. At the other extreme are countries such as Canada and the United States, with people from virtually all nations who have mixed together, but have maintained their diversity by retaining and valuing important ethnic and cultural differences. Anyone who has walked the streets of Vancouver, Montreal, Calgary, or Toronto will immediately understand that visible minorities in Canada are a force to be reckoned with. More than 6.2 million Canadians (19.1 percent) identified themselves as visible minorities in the 2011 census and more than 200 ethnic origins were reported. Toronto is the most ethnically diverse, with 47 percent of the city's population identified as a visible minority. According to Statistics Canada's population projections, members of visible minority groups could account for over 30 percent of the total population by 2031.[30]

Most large companies, from P&G and Walmart, to McDonald's and Levi Strauss, now target specially designed products, ads, and promotions to one or more of these groups. For example, Procter & Gamble has long been the leader in African American advertising, spending nearly 50 percent more than the second-place spender in Hispanic media. P&G also tailors products to the specific needs of black consumers. For instance, its CoverGirl Queen Collection is specially formulated "to celebrate the beauty of women of colour." In addition to traditional product marketing efforts, P&G supports a broader "My Black Is Beautiful" movement:

> Created by a group of African American women at P&G, the movement aims "to ignite and support a sustained national conversation by, for, and about black women" and how they are reflected in popular culture. P&G discovered that black women spend three times more than the general market on beauty products, yet they feel they're portrayed in a worse manner than

other women in media and advertising. Supported by brands such as Crest, Pantene, Always, Secret, the CoverGirl Queen Collection, and Olay Definity, the My Black Is Beautiful movement's goal is to empower African American women to embrace their beauty, health, and wellness and, of course, to forge a closer relationship between P&G brands and African American consumers in the process. My Black Is Beautiful includes a rich website, national media platforms, a TV series in its third season on BET, and a full slate of major social media such as Twitter, Facebook, and Pinterest. It maintains a presence at key events that allow women to interact with brands and the My Black Is Beautiful movement in trusted and relevant environments.[31]

Diversity goes beyond ethnic heritage. For example, many major companies explicitly target gay and lesbian consumers. According to one estimate, the 6 to 7 percent of U.S. adults who identify themselves as lesbian, gay, bisexual, or transgender (LGBT) have buying power of more than US$790 billion.[32] While the exact percentage of Canadians who identify themselves as LGBT is unknown, Statistics Canada now identifies same-sex couples in the census. The 2011 census enumerated 64 575 same-sex couples in Canada, up 42.4 percent from 45 300 in 2006.[33] As a result of TV shows such as *Modern Family* and *Glee*, movies like *Brokeback Mountain* and *The Perks of Being a Wallflower*, and openly gay celebrities and public figures such as Neil Patrick Harris, Ellen DeGeneres, and David Sedaris, the LGBT community has increasingly emerged in the public eye.

Numerous media now provide companies with access to this market. For example, Planet Out Inc., a leading global media and entertainment company that exclusively serves the LGBT community, offers several successful magazines (*Out, The Advocate, Out Traveler*) and websites (Gay.com and PlanetOut.com). Canada's only digital television channel specifically targeted at the gay and lesbian community, OUTtv, was launched nationally in 2001. By 2011, it became Canada's fastest-growing digital cable channel and had 1 million subscribers.

Companies in a wide range of industries are now targeting the LGBT community with gay-specific ads and marketing efforts—from Amazon and Apple to household goods retailer Crate & Barrel. American Airlines has a dedicated LGBT sales team, sponsors gay community events, and offers a special gay-oriented site (www.aa.com/rainbow) that features travel deals, an e-newsletter, podcasts, and a gay events calendar. The airline's focus on gay consumers has earned it double-digit revenue growth from the LGBT community each year for more than a decade.[34]

Another attractive diversity segment is the 14.3 percent of the Canadian population (4.4 million) who have some form of disability. This group has considerable spending power as well as a great need for tailored products and services. Not only do they value services that make daily life easier, but they're also a growing market for travel, sports, and other leisure-oriented products. The Canadian Abilities Foundation provides a wealth of information, ranging from products and services to housing and travel advice on its website (www.abilities.ca).

Exhibit 4.8 Targeting consumers with disabilities: Samsung features people with disabilities in its mainstream advertising and signs endorsement deals with Paralympic athletes.

How are companies trying to reach consumers with disabilities? Many marketers now recognize that the worlds of people with disabilities and those without disabilities are one and the same. Marketers such as McDonald's, Nike, Samsung, and Honda have featured people with disabilities in their mainstream marketing. For instance, Samsung and Nike sign endorsement deals with Paralympic athletes and feature them in advertising.

As the population in Canada grows more diverse, successful marketers will continue to diversify their marketing programs to take advantage of opportunities in fast-growing segments.

GEPA/Imago/Icon SMI 429/GEPA/Imago/Icon SMI/Newscom

The Economic Environment

Economic environment
Economic factors that affect consumer purchasing power and spending patterns.

Markets require buying power as well as people. The **economic environment** consists of economic factors that affect consumer purchasing power and spending patterns. Marketers must pay close attention to major trends and consumer spending patterns both across and within their world markets.

Nations vary greatly in their levels and distribution of income. Some countries have *industrial economies*, which constitute rich markets for many different kinds of goods. At the other extreme are *subsistence economies*; they consume most of their own agricultural and industrial output and offer few market opportunities. In between are *developing economies* that can offer outstanding marketing opportunities for the right kinds of products.

Consider Brazil, with its population of more than 196 million people. Until recently, only well-heeled Brazilians could afford to travel by air. Azul Brazilian Airlines has changed that:

> For decades, Brazilians with lesser means travelled the sprawling country—which is about the size of the continental United States but with less-well-developed roads—mostly by bus. However, David Neeleman, founder and former CEO of JetBlue and himself a native Brazilian, saw a real opportunity in serving Brazil's fast-growing middle class of more than 100 million people. He founded Azul Brazilian Airlines, a low-fare airline modelled after JetBlue ("azul" is Portuguese for "blue"). Azul provides a good-quality but affordable alternative to long bus rides—a trip that used to take 34 hours by bus now takes only 2 via Azul. And with many Azul flights costing the same or less than a bus trip, the thrifty airline has converted millions of Brazilians to air travel. Azul even provides free buses to the airport for its many passengers who don't have cars or access to public transportation. Customers with no or low credit can pay for tickets with bank withdrawals or by installment. After only five years, Azul has grown rapidly to become Brazil's third-largest air carrier, with a more than 14 percent domestic travel market share.[35]

Changes in Consumer Spending Economic factors can have a dramatic effect on consumer spending and buying behaviour. For example, until relatively recently, Canadian consumers spent freely, fuelled by income growth, a boom in the stock market, rapid increases in housing values, and other economic good fortunes. They bought and bought, seemingly without caution, amassing record levels of debt. However, the free spending and high expectations of those days were dashed by the Great Recession of 2008–2009.

As a result, as discussed in Chapter 1, consumers have now adopted a back-to-basics sensibility in their lifestyles and spending patterns that will likely persist for years to come. They are buying less and looking for greater value in the things that they do buy. In turn, *value marketing* has become the watchword for many marketers. Marketers in all industries are looking for ways to offer today's more financially frugal buyers greater value—just the right combination of product quality and good service at a fair price.

Agencia Estado/AP Images

Exhibit 4.9 Economic environment: To tap Brazil's large and fast-growing middle class, former JetBlue founder David Neeleman, shown here, started low-fare Azul Brazilian Airlines, which provides a good-quality but affordable alternative to long bus rides across the sprawling country.

Income Distribution Marketers should pay attention to income distribution as well as income levels. Canadians in the top 5 percent of wage earners account for approximately 25 percent of the total income earned. According to the 2006 census, the median earnings among the top 20 percent of full-time workers increased over 16 percent, while the median earnings among those in the bottom one-fifth of the distribution fell by over 20 percent. In Canada, the rich are getting richer, the poor are getting poorer, and the earnings of the middle class are stagnating. Canadians are definitely feeling the effects of the past recession. From 2009 to 2010, only 52.8 percent of Canadians saw an increase in their after-tax household income, compared with 62.4 percent from 2006 to 2007, despite the fact that the cost of living continues to rise. Furthermore, roughly 3 million Canadians (including 546 000 children) lived below the poverty line in 2010.[36]

This distribution of income has created a tiered market. Many companies—such as Holt Renfrew and La Maison Simons department stores—aggressively target the affluent. Others—such as Giant Tiger and Dollarama stores—target those with more modest means. Still other companies tailor their marketing offers across a range of markets, from the affluent to the less affluent. For example, Ford offers cars ranging from the low-priced Ford Fiesta, starting at $11 200, to the luxury Lincoln Navigator SUV, starting at $70 300.

Changes in major economic variables, such as income, cost of living, interest rates, and savings and borrowing patterns, have a large impact on the marketplace. Companies watch these variables by using economic forecasting. Businesses do not have to be wiped out by an economic downturn or caught short in a boom. With adequate warning, they can take advantage of changes in the economic environment.

The Natural Environment LO3

The **natural environment** involves the physical environment and the natural resources that are needed as inputs by marketers or that are affected by marketing activities. At the most basic level, unexpected happenings in the physical environment—anything from weather to natural disasters—can affect companies and their marketing strategies. For example, an unexpectedly warm winter put the chill on sales of products ranging from cold-weather apparel to facial tissues and Campbell's soups. In contrast, warmer weather can boost demand for products such as hiking and running shoes, house paint, and gardening supplies. Similarly, the damage caused by the earthquake and tsunami in Japan had a devastating effect on the ability of Japanese companies such as Sony and Toyota to meet worldwide demand for their products. Although companies can't prevent such natural occurrences, they should prepare contingency plans for dealing with them.[37]

At a broader level, environmental sustainability concerns have grown steadily over the past three decades. In many cities around the world, air and water pollution have reached dangerous levels. World concern continues to mount about global warming, and many environmentalists fear that we'll soon be buried in our own trash.

Marketers should be aware of several trends in the natural environment. The first involves *growing shortages of raw materials*. Air and water may seem to be infinite resources, but some groups see long-run dangers. Air pollution chokes many of the world's large cities, and water shortages are already a big problem in some parts of the world. It's estimated that by 2030, more than one in three people in the world will not have enough water to drink.[38] Renewable resources, such as forests and food, also have to be used wisely. Nonrenewable resources, such as oil, coal, and various minerals, pose a serious problem. Firms making products that require these scarce resources face large cost increases, even if the materials remain available.

A second environmental trend is *increased pollution*. Industry will almost always damage the quality of the natural environment. Consider the disposal of chemical and nuclear wastes, the dangerous mercury levels in the ocean, the quantity of chemical pollutants in

Natural environment
The physical environment and the natural resources that are needed as inputs by marketers or that are affected by marketing activities.

the soil and food supply, and the littering of the environment with nonbiodegradable bottles, plastics, and other packaging materials.

A third trend is *increased government intervention* in natural resource management. The governments of different countries vary in their concern and efforts to promote a clean environment. Some, such as the German government, vigorously pursue environmental quality. Others, especially many poorer nations, do little about pollution, largely because they lack the needed funds or political will. Even richer nations lack the vast funds and political accord needed to mount a worldwide environmental effort. The general hope is that companies around the world will accept more social responsibility and that less expensive devices can be found to control and reduce pollution.

The Canadian government passed the Environmental Protection Act in 1989. This act established stringent pollution-control measures as well as the means for their enforcement, including fines as high as $1 million if regulations are violated. In the United States, the Environmental Protection Agency (EPA) was created in 1970 to set and enforce pollution standards and to conduct pollution research. In the future, companies doing business in Canada and the United States can expect continued strong controls from government and pressure groups. Instead of opposing regulation, marketers should help develop solutions to the material and energy problems facing the world.

Concern for the natural environment has spawned the so-called green movement. Today, enlightened companies go beyond what government regulations dictate. They are developing strategies and practices that support **environmental sustainability**—an effort to create a world economy that the planet can support indefinitely. Environmental sustainability means meeting present needs without compromising the ability of future generations to meet their needs.

Many companies are responding to consumer demands with more environmentally responsible products. Others are developing recyclable or biodegradable packaging, recycled materials and components, better pollution controls, and more energy-efficient operations. For example, Timberland's mission is about more than just making rugged, high-quality boots, shoes, clothes, and other outdoor gear. The brand is about doing everything it can to reduce the environmental footprint of its products and processes:

> Timberland is on a mission to develop processes and products that cause less harm to the environment and to enlist consumers in the cause. For example, it has a solar-powered distribution centre in California and a wind-powered factory in the Dominican Republic. It has installed energy-efficient lighting and equipment retrofits in its facilities and is educating workers about production efficiency. Timberland is constantly looking for and inventing innovative materials that allow it to reduce its impact on the planet while at the same time making better gear. Its Earthkeepers line of boots is made from recycled and organic materials, and the brand has launched footwear collections featuring outsoles made from recycled car tires. Plastic from recycled soda bottles goes into its breathable linings and durable shoe laces. Coffee grounds find a place in its odour-resistant jackets. Organic cotton without toxins makes it into its rugged canvas. To inspire consumers to make more sustainable decisions, Timberland puts Green Index tags on its products that rate each item's ecological footprint in terms of climate impact, chemicals used, and resources consumed. To pull it all together, Timberland launched an Earthkeeper's campaign, an online social networking effort that seeks to inspire people to take actions to lighten their environmental footprints.[39]

Environmental sustainability
Developing strategies and practices that create a world economy that the planet can support indefinitely.

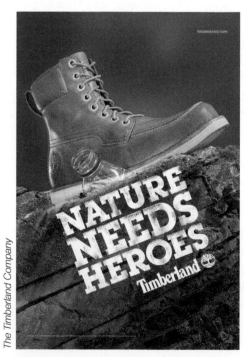

The Timberland Company

Exhibit 4.10 Environmental sustainability:
Timberland is on a mission to do everything it can to reduce its impact on the planet while at the same time making better outdoor gear.

Companies today are looking to do more than just good deeds. More and more, they are recognizing the link between a healthy ecology and a healthy economy. They are learning that environmentally responsible actions can also be good business.

The Technological Environment

The **technological environment** is perhaps the most dramatic force now shaping our destiny. Technology has released such wonders as antibiotics, robotic surgery, miniaturized electronics, smartphones, and the Internet. It has also released such horrors as nuclear missiles, chemical weapons, and assault rifles. It has released such mixed blessings as the automobile, television, and credit cards. Our attitude toward technology depends on whether we are more impressed with its wonders or its blunders.

New technologies can offer exciting opportunities for marketers. For example, what would you think about having tiny little transmitters implanted in all the products you buy, which would allow tracking of the products from their point of production through use and disposal? Or how about a bracelet with a chip inserted that would let you make and pay for purchases, receive personalized specials at retail locations, or even track your whereabouts or those of friends? On the one hand, such technology would provide many advantages to both buyers and sellers. On the other hand, it could be a bit scary. Either way, with the advent of radio-frequency identification (RFID) transmitters, it's already happening.

Many firms are already using RFID technology to track products through various points in the distribution channel. For example, Walmart has strongly encouraged suppliers shipping products to its distribution centres to apply RFID tags to their pallets. So far, more than 600 Walmart suppliers are doing so. And retailers such as American Apparel, Macy's, and Bloomingdales are now installing item-level RFID systems in their stores. Fashion and accessories maker Burberry even uses chips embedded in items and linked to smartphones to provide personalized, interactive experiences for customers in its stores and at runway shows.[40] Disney has taken RFID technology to new levels with its cool MagicBand RFID wristband:

> Wearing a MagicBand at The Walt Disney World Resort opens up a whole new level of Disney's famed magic. After registering for cloud-based MyMagic+ services, with the flick of your wrist you can enter a park or attraction, buy dinner or souvenirs, or even unlock your hotel room. But Disney has only begun to tap the MagicBand's potential for personalizing guest experiences. Future applications could be truly magical. Imagine, for example, the wonder of a child who receives a warm hug from Mickey Mouse, or a bow from Prince Charming, who then greets the child by name and wishes her a happy birthday. Imagine animatronics that interact with nearby guests based on personal information supplied in advance. You get separated from family or friends? No problem. A quick scan of your MagicBand at a nearby directory could pinpoint the locations of your entire party. Linked to your Disney phone app, the MagicBand could trigger in-depth information about park features, ride wait times, Fast-Pass check-in alerts, and your reservations schedule. Of course, the MagicBand also offers Disney a potential motherlode of digital data on guest activities and movements in minute detail, helping to improve guest logistics, services, and sales. If all this seems too big-brotherish, there are privacy options—for example, letting parents opt out of things like characters knowing children's names. In all, such digital technologies promise to enrich the Disney experience for both guests and the company.[41]

The technological environment changes rapidly. Think of all of today's common products that weren't available 100 years ago—or even 30 years ago. John A. Macdonald didn't know about automobiles, airplanes, radios, or the electric light. William Lyon Mackenzie King didn't know about xerography, synthetic detergents, tape recorders, birth control pills, jet engines, or Earth satellites. John Diefenbaker didn't know about personal computers, cellphones, the Internet, or Google.

Technological environment
Forces that create new technologies, creating new product and market opportunities.

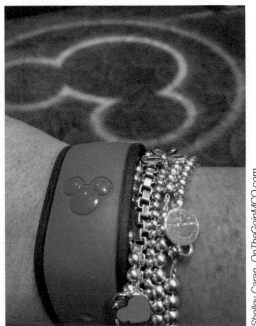

Exhibit 4.11 Marketing technology: Disney has taken RFID technology to new levels with its cool MagicBand RFID wristband.

Shelley Caran, OnTheGoinMCO.com

New technologies create new markets and opportunities. However, every new technology replaces an older technology. Transistors hurt the vacuum-tube industry, digital photography hurt the film business, and MP3 players and digital downloads are hurting the CD business. When old industries fought or ignored new technologies, their businesses declined. Thus, marketers should watch the technological environment closely. Companies that do not keep up will soon find their products outdated. If that happens, they will miss new product and market opportunities.

As products and technology become more complex, the public needs to know that these are safe. Canada has a complex web of departments and regulations devoted to issues associated with product safety. For example, Agriculture and Agri-Food Canada and the Canadian Food Inspection Agency monitor the safety of food products. The Department of Justice Canada oversees the Consumer Packaging and Labelling Act, the Food and Drug Act, and the Hazardous Products Act. Health Canada also has a food safety and product safety division. Transport Canada governs vehicle recalls. Such regulations have resulted in much higher research costs and in longer times between new-product ideas and their introduction. Marketers should be aware of these regulations when applying new technologies and developing new products.

The Political and Social Environment LO4

Marketing decisions are strongly affected by developments in the political environment. The **political environment** consists of laws, government agencies, and pressure groups that influence or limit various organizations and individuals in a given society.

Political environment
Laws, government agencies, and pressure groups that influence and limit various organizations and individuals in a given society.

Legislation Regulating Business Even the strongest advocates of free-market economies agree that the system works best with at least some regulation. Well-conceived regulation can encourage competition and ensure fair markets for goods and services. Thus, governments develop *public policy* to guide commerce—sets of laws and regulations that limit business for the good of society as a whole. Almost every marketing activity is subject to a wide range of laws and regulations.

Legislation affecting business around the world has increased steadily over the years. Canada has many laws covering issues such as competition, fair trade practices, environmental protection, product safety, truth in advertising, consumer privacy, packaging and labelling, pricing, and other important areas (see Table 4.2). The European Commission has been active in establishing a new framework of laws covering competitive behaviour, product standards, product liability, and commercial transactions for the nations of the European Union.

Understanding the public policy implications of a particular marketing activity is not a simple matter. For example, in Canada, many laws are created at the federal, provincial/territorial, and municipal levels, and these regulations often overlap. Moreover, regulations are constantly changing—what was allowed last year may now be prohibited, and what was prohibited may now be allowed. Marketers must work hard to keep up with changes in regulations and their interpretations.

Business legislation has been enacted for a number of reasons. The first is to *protect companies* from each other. Although business executives may praise competition, they sometimes try to neutralize it when it threatens them. Therefore, laws are passed to define and prevent unfair competition.

The second purpose of government regulation is to *protect consumers* from unfair business practices. Some firms, if left alone, would make shoddy products, invade consumer privacy, mislead consumers in their advertising, and deceive consumers through their packaging and pricing. Rules defining and regulating unfair business practices are enforced by various agencies.

TABLE 4.2 Major Federal Legislation Affecting Marketing

The Competition Act is a major legislative act affecting the marketing activities of companies in Canada. Specific sections and the relevant areas are as follows:

- Section 34: Pricing—Forbids suppliers from charging different prices to competitors purchasing like quantities of goods (price discrimination). Forbids price-cutting that lessens competition (predatory pricing).

- Section 36: Pricing and Advertising—Forbids advertising prices that misrepresent the "usual" selling price (misleading price advertising).

- Section 38: Pricing—Forbids suppliers from requiring subsequent resellers to offer products at a stipulated price (resale price maintenance).

- Section 33: Mergers—Forbids mergers by which competition is, or is likely to be, lessened to the detriment of the interests of the public.

- Other selected acts that have an impact on marketing activities are the following:

- National Trade Mark and True Labelling Act—Established the term *Canada Standard*, or *CS*, as a national trademark; requires certain commodities to be properly labelled or described in advertising for the purpose of indicating material content or quality.

- Consumer Packaging and Labelling Act—Provides a set of rules to ensure that full information is disclosed by the manufacturer, packer, or distributor. Requires that all prepackaged products bear the quantity in French and English in metric as well as traditional Canadian standard units of weight, volume, or measure.

- Motor Vehicle Safety Act—Establishes mandatory safety standards for motor vehicles.

- Food and Drug Act—Prohibits the advertisement and sale of adulterated or misbranded foods, cosmetics, and drugs.

- Personal Information Protection and Electronic Documents Act—Establishes rules to govern the collection, use, and disclosure of personal information that recognize the right of privacy of individuals. The law recognizes the needs of organizations to collect, use, or disclose personal information for appropriate purposes. (For full details of the act, see http://laws.justice.gc.ca/en/P-8.6.)

The third purpose of government regulation is to *protect the interests of society* against unrestrained business behaviour. Profitable business activity does not always create a better quality of life. Regulation arises to ensure that firms take responsibility for the social costs of their production or products.

International marketers will encounter dozens, or even hundreds, of agencies set up to enforce trade policies and regulations. In Canada, several federal agencies, such as Health Canada, the Canadian Food Inspection Agency, Industry Canada, and the Canadian Environmental Assessment Agency, have been established. Because such government agencies have some discretion in enforcing the laws, they can have a major impact on a company's marketing performance.

New laws and their enforcement will continue to increase. Business executives must watch these developments when planning their products and marketing programs. Marketers need to know about the major laws protecting competition, consumers, and society. They need to understand these laws at the local, provincial/territorial, national, and international levels.

Increased Emphasis on Ethics and Socially Responsible Actions Written regulations cannot possibly cover all potential marketing abuses, and existing laws are often difficult to enforce. However, beyond written laws and regulations, business is also governed by social codes and rules of professional ethics.

SOCIALLY RESPONSIBLE BEHAVIOUR Enlightened companies encourage their managers to look beyond what the regulatory system allows and simply "do the right thing." These socially responsible firms actively seek out ways to protect the long-run interests of their consumers and the environment.

Almost every aspect of marketing involves ethics and social responsibility issues. Unfortunately, because these issues usually involve conflicting interests, well-meaning people can honestly disagree about the right course of action in a given situation. Thus, many industrial and professional trade associations have suggested codes of ethics. And more companies are now developing policies, guidelines, and other responses to complex social responsibility issues.

The boom in online, mobile, and social media marketing has created a new set of social and ethical issues. Critics worry most about online privacy issues. There has been an explosion in the amount of personal digital data available. Users themselves supply some of it. They voluntarily place highly private information on social media sites, such as Facebook or LinkedIn, or on genealogy sites that are easily searched by anyone with a computer or a smartphone.

However, much of the information is systematically developed by businesses seeking to learn more about their customers, often without consumers realizing that they are under the microscope. Legitimate businesses track consumers' Internet browsing and buying behaviour and collect, analyze, and share digital data from every move consumers make at their online sites. Critics worry that these companies may now know *too* much and might use digital data to take unfair advantage of consumers. Although most companies fully disclose their Internet privacy policies and most try to use data to benefit their customers, abuses do occur. As a result, consumer advocates and policy makers are taking action to protect consumer privacy.

CAUSE-RELATED MARKETING To exercise their social responsibility and build more positive images, many companies are now linking themselves to worthwhile causes. These days, every product seems to be tied to some cause. For example, the P&G Tide Loads of Hope program provides mobile laundromats and loads of clean laundry to families in disaster-stricken areas—P&G washes, dries, and folds clothes for these families for free. Down the street, needy people will probably find the P&G Duracell Power Relief Trailer, which provides free batteries and flashlights as well as charging stations for phones and laptops. Walgreens sponsors a "Walk with Walgreens" program—do simple things like walk and log your steps, hit your goals, or just comment on other walkers' posts at the site, and you'll be rewarded with coupons and exclusive offers from Bayer, Vaseline, Degree, Slimfast, Dr. Scholls, or another program partner.

Some companies are founded on cause-related missions. Under the concept of "values-led business" or "caring capitalism," their mission is to use business to make the world a better place. For example, Warby Parker—the online marketer of low-priced prescription eyewear—was founded with the hope of bringing affordable eyewear to the masses. The company sells "eyewear with a purpose." For every pair of glasses Warby Parker sells, it distributes a free pair to someone in need. The company also works with not-for-profit organizations that train low-income entrepreneurs to sell affordable glasses. "We believe that everyone has the right to see," says the company.[42]

Warby Parker; photographer: Esther Havens

Exhibit 4.12 Cause-related marketing: Eyewear company Warby Parker offers designer glasses at a revolutionary low price while also leading the way for socially conscious businesses. For every pair of glasses sold, Warby Parker distributes a pair to someone in need.

Cause-related marketing has become a primary form of corporate giving. It lets companies "do well by doing good" by linking purchases of the company's products or services with benefiting worthwhile causes or charitable organizations. Beyond being socially admirable, Warby Parker's Buy a Pair, Give a Pair program also makes good economic sense, for both the company and its customers. "Companies can do good in the world while still being profitable," says Warby Parker co-founder Neil Blumenthal. "A single pair of reading glasses causes, on average, a 20 percent increase in income. Glasses are one of the most effective poverty alleviation tools in the world."[43]

Cause-related marketing has stirred some controversy. Critics worry that it's more a strategy for selling than a strategy for giving—that "cause-related" marketing is really "cause-exploitative" marketing. Thus, companies using cause-related marketing might find themselves walking a fine line between increased sales and an improved image and facing charges of exploitation. However, if handled well, cause-related marketing can greatly benefit both the company and the cause. The company gains an effective marketing tool while building a more positive public image. The charitable organization or cause gains greater visibility and important new sources of funding and support. Spending on cause-related marketing in the United States skyrocketed from only $120 million in 1990 to $1.78 billion in 2013.[44]

The Cultural Environment

The **cultural environment** consists of institutions and other forces that affect a society's basic values, perceptions, preferences, and behaviours. People grow up in a particular society that shapes their basic beliefs and values. They absorb a worldview that defines their relationships with others. The following cultural characteristics can affect marketing decision making.

Cultural environment
Institutions and other forces that affect society's basic values, perceptions, preferences, and behaviours.

The Persistence of Cultural Values People in a given society hold many beliefs and values. Their core beliefs and values have a high degree of persistence. For example, many Canadians believe in cultural diversity (versus assimilation), democracy, gender equality, sustainable development, universal healthcare, a love of nature, hard work, and being honest. These beliefs shape more specific attitudes and behaviours found in everyday life. *Core* beliefs and values are passed on from parents to children and are reinforced by schools, businesses, religious institutions, and government.

Secondary beliefs and values are more open to change. Believing in marriage is a core belief; believing that people should get married early in life is a secondary belief. Marketers have some chance of changing secondary values but little chance of changing core values. For example, family-planning marketers could argue more effectively that people should get married later than not get married at all.

Shifts in Secondary Cultural Values Although core values are fairly persistent, cultural swings do take place. Consider the impact of popular music groups, movie personalities, and other celebrities on young people's hairstyle and clothing norms. Marketers want to predict cultural shifts to spot new opportunities or threats. The major cultural values of a society are expressed in people's views of themselves and others, as well as in their views of organizations, society, nature, and the universe.

PEOPLE'S VIEWS OF THEMSELVES People vary in their emphasis on serving themselves versus serving others. Some people seek personal pleasure, wanting fun, change, and escape. Others seek self-realization through religion, recreation, or the avid pursuit of careers or other life goals. Some people see themselves as sharers and joiners; others see themselves as individualists. People use products, brands, and services as a means of self-expression, and they buy products and services that match their views of themselves.

Courtesy of Benjamin Moore Paints

Exhibit 4.13 People's self-views: In its ads, Benjamin Moore appeals to people who view themselves as outgoing fashion individualists.

For example, ads for Sherwin Williams paint—headlined "Make the most for your color with the very best paint"—seem to appeal to older, more practical do-it-yourselfers. By contrast, Benjamin Moore's ads, along with its several social media pitches, appeal to younger, more outgoing fashion individualists. One Benjamin Moore print ad—consisting of a single long line of text in a crazy quilt of fonts—describes Benjamin Moore's Hot Lips paint colour this way: "It's somewhere between the color of your lips when you go outside in December with your hair still wet and the color of a puddle left by a melted grape popsicle mixed with the color of that cough syrup that used to make me gag a little. Hot lips. Perfect."

PEOPLE'S VIEWS OF OTHERS People's attitudes toward and interactions with others shift over time. In recent years, some analysts have voiced concerns that the Internet age would result in diminished human interaction, as people buried themselves in social media pages or emailed and texted rather than interacting personally. Instead, today's digital technologies seem to have launched an era of what one trend watcher calls "mass mingling." Rather than interacting less, people are using online social media and mobile communications to connect more than ever. Basically, the more people meet, network, tweet, and socialize online, the more likely they are to eventually meet up with friends and followers in the real world.[45]

However, these days, even when people are together, they are often "alone together." Groups of people sit or walk in their own little bubbles, intensely connected to tiny screens and keyboards. One expert describes the latest communication skill—"maintaining eye contact with someone while you text someone else; it's hard but it can be done," she says. "Technology-enabled, we are able to be with one another, and also elsewhere, connected to wherever we want to be."[46] Whether the new technology-driven communication is a blessing or a curse is a matter of much debate.

This new way of interacting strongly affects how companies market their brands and communicate with customers. "Consumers are increasingly tapping into their networks of friends, fans, and followers to discover, discuss, and purchase goods and services in ever-more sophisticated ways," says one analyst. "As a result, it's never been more important for brands to make sure they [tap into these networks] too."[47]

PEOPLE'S VIEWS OF ORGANIZATIONS People vary in their attitudes toward corporations, government agencies, trade unions, universities, and other organizations. By and large, people are willing to work for major organizations and expect them, in turn, to carry out society's work.

The past two decades have seen a sharp decrease in confidence in and loyalty toward business and political organizations and institutions. In the workplace, there has been an overall decline in organizational loyalty. Waves of company downsizings bred cynicism and distrust. In just the last decade, major corporate scandals, rounds of layoffs resulting from the recession, the financial meltdown triggered by Wall Street bankers' greed and incompetence, and other unsettling activities have resulted in a further loss of confidence in big business. Many people today see work not as a source of satisfaction but as a required chore to earn money to enjoy their nonwork hours. This trend suggests that organizations need to find new ways to win consumer and employee confidence.

PEOPLE'S VIEWS OF SOCIETY People vary in their attitudes toward their society—nationalists defend it, reformers want to change it, and malcontents want to leave it. People's orientation to their society influences their consumption patterns and attitudes toward the marketplace. National pride in Canada has been increasing gradually for the past two decades, and many Canadian companies are responding to this trend with Canadian themes and promotions. From the famous Molson "I am Canadian" rant to the more recent Tide commercial that claimed "No self-respecting Canadian says let's wait for a warmer day!," companies are jumping on the patriotic bandwagon. In fact, since the Vancouver Olympics in 2010, national pride has soared. According to a survey conducted by Ipsos Reid, 80 percent of Canadians agree that they are Canadian nationalists, up from 72 percent polled one year before the Olympics.[48]

Marketers respond with patriotic products and promotions, offering everything from beer to clothing with patriotic themes. Although most of these marketing efforts are tasteful and well received, waving the flag can prove tricky. Except in cases where companies tie product sales to charitable contributions, such flag-waving promotions can be viewed as exploitative. Marketers must take care when responding to such strong national emotions.

PEOPLE'S VIEWS OF NATURE People vary in their attitudes toward the natural world—some feel ruled by it, others feel in harmony with it, and still others seek to master it. A long-term trend has been people's growing mastery over nature through technology and the belief that nature is bountiful. More recently, however, people have recognized that nature is finite and fragile; it can be destroyed or spoiled by human activities.

This renewed love of things natural has created a 41-million-person "lifestyles of health and sustainability" (LOHAS) market, consumers who seek out everything from natural, organic, and nutritional products to fuel-efficient cars and alternative medicine. This segment spends an estimated US$290 billion annually on such products.[49]

Headquartered in Montreal, GoGo Quinoa caters to such consumers by creating an ethical business promoting organic food and fair trade practices. The company product line includes over 30 gluten-free, vegan and organic products made from quinoa and amaranth, which are distributed across Canada. The company's mission "to contribute to the nutritional well-being of all by offering nutritious, innovative and flavourful products."[50]

Food producers have also found fast-growing markets for natural and organic products. In total, the U.S. organic food market recently generated $31 billion in sales, more than doubling over the previous five years. Niche marketers, such as Whole Foods Market, have sprung up to serve this market, and traditional food chains, such as Loblaw and Safeway, have added separate natural and organic food sections. Even pet owners are joining the movement as they become more aware of what goes into Fido's food. Almost every major pet food brand now offers several types of natural foods.[51]

PEOPLE'S VIEWS OF THE UNIVERSE Finally, people vary in their beliefs about the origin of the universe and their place in it. Although many Canadians practise religion, religious conviction and practice have been gradually declining through the years. Statistics Canada surveys show Canadians' continuing slide out the doors of the country's churches, temples, and synagogues. In 1946, 67 percent of adult Canadians regularly attended religious services, but by 2001 the figure had dropped to 20 percent. In fact, 23.9 percent of adult Canadians were reported to have no religious affiliation in 2011.[52]

Exhibit 4.14 Riding the trend toward all things natural: GoGo Quinoa "contributes to the nutritional well-being of all by offering nutritious, innovative, and flavourful products."

Courtesy GoGo Quinoa

However, the fact that people are dropping out of organized religion doesn't mean that they are abandoning their faith. Some futurists have noted a renewed interest in spirituality, perhaps as a part of a broader search for a new inner purpose. People have been moving away from materialism and dog-eat-dog ambition to seek more permanent values—family, community, earth, faith—and a more certain grasp of right and wrong. Rather than calling it "religion," they call it "spirituality."[53] This changing spiritualism affects consumers in everything from the television shows they watch and the books they read to the products and services they buy.

Responding to the Marketing Environment LO5

Someone once observed, "There are three kinds of companies: those who make things happen, those who watch things happen, and those who wonder what's happened." Many companies view the marketing environment as an uncontrollable element to which they must react and adapt. These companies passively accept the environment and don't try to change it. Instead, they analyze environmental forces and design strategies that will help the company avoid the threats and take advantage of the opportunities the environment provides.

Other companies take a *proactive* stance toward the marketing environment. Rather than assuming that strategic options are bounded by the current environment, these firms develop strategies to change the environment. Companies and their products—such as Ford's Model T car, Apple's iPod and iPhone, and Google's search engine—often create and shape new industries and their structures.

Even more, rather than simply watching and reacting to environmental events, proactive firms take aggressive actions to affect the publics and forces in their marketing environment. Such companies hire lobbyists to influence legislation affecting their industries and stage media events to gain favourable press coverage. They run "advertorials" (ads expressing editorial points of view) and blogs to shape public opinion. They press lawsuits and file complaints with regulators to keep competitors in line, and they form contractual agreements to better control their distribution channels.

By taking action, companies can often overcome seemingly uncontrollable environmental events. For example, whereas some companies try to hush up negative talk about their products, others proactively counter false information. Taco Bell did this when its brand fell victim to potentially damaging claims about the quality of the beef filling in its tacos:

> When a California woman's class-action suit questioned whether Taco Bell's meat filling could accurately be labelled "beef," the company's reaction was swift and decisive. The suit claimed that Taco Bell's beef filling is 65 percent binders, extenders, preservatives, additives, and other agents. It wanted Taco Bell to stop calling it "beef." But Taco Bell fought back quickly with a major counterattack campaign, in print and on YouTube and Facebook. In full-page ads in the *Wall Street Journal*, the *New York Times*, and *USA Today*, the company boldly thanked those behind the lawsuit for giving it the opportunity to tell the "truth" about its "seasoned beef," which it claimed contains only quality beef with other ingredients added to maintain the product's flavour and quality. Taco Bell further announced that it would take legal action against those making the false statements. The company's proactive counter-campaign quickly squelched the false information in the lawsuit, which was voluntarily withdrawn only a few months later.[54]

Marketing management cannot always control environmental forces. In many cases, it must settle for simply watching and reacting to the environment. For example, a company would have little success trying to influence geographic population shifts, the economic environment, or major cultural values. But whenever possible, smart marketing managers take a *proactive* rather than *reactive* approach to the marketing environment (see Marketing@Work 4.2).

In the Social Media Age: When the Dialogue Gets Nasty

Marketers have hailed the Internet and social media as the great new way to nurture customer relationships. Brands use social media to engage customers, gain insights into their needs, and create customer community. In turn, today's more-empowered consumers use the now digital media to share their brand experiences with companies and with each other. All of this back-and-forth helps both the company and its customers. But sometimes, the dialogue can get nasty. Consider the following examples:

- Upon receiving a severely damaged computer monitor via FedEx, YouTube user goobie55 posts footage from his security camera. The video clearly shows a FedEx delivery man hoisting the monitor package over his head and tossing it over goobie55's front gate, without ever attempting to ring the bell, open the gate, or walk the package to the door. The video—with FedEx's familiar purple and orange logo prominently displayed on everything from the driver's shirt to the package and the truck—goes viral, with 5 million hits in just five days. TV news and talk shows go crazy discussing the clip.
- A young creative team at Ford's ad agency in India produces a Ford Figo print ad and releases it to the Internet without approval. The ad features three women—bound, gagged, and scantily clad—in the hatch of a Figo, with a caricature of a grinning Silvio Berlusconi (Italy's sex-scandal-plagued ex–prime minister) at the wheel. The ads tagline: "Leave your worries behind with Figo's extra-large boot (trunk)." Ford quickly pulls the ad, but not before it goes viral. Within days, millions of people around the world have viewed the ad, causing an online uproar and giving Ford a global black eye.
- When eight-year-old Harry Winsor sends a crayon drawing of an

airplane he's designed to Boeing with a suggestion that the company might want to manufacture it, the company responds with a stern, legal-form letter. "We do not accept unsolicited ideas," the letter states. "We regret to inform you that we have disposed of your message and retain no copies." The embarrassing blunder would probably go unnoticed were it not for the fact that Harry's father—John Winsor, a prominent ad exec—blogs and tweets about the incident, making it instant national news.

Extreme events? Not anymore. The Internet and social media have turned the traditional power relationship between businesses and consumers upside down. In the good old days, disgruntled consumers could do little more than bellow at a company service rep or shout out their complaints from a street corner. Now, armed with only a laptop or smartphone, they can take it public, airing their gripes to millions on blogs,

social media sites, or even hate sites devoted exclusively to their least favourite corporations.

"I hate" and "sucks" sites are almost commonplace. These sites target some highly respected companies with some highly disrespectful labels: Walmartblows.com, PayPalSucks.com (aka NoPayPal), IHateStarbucks.com, DeltaREALLYsucks.com, and UnitedPackageSmashers.com (UPS), to name only a few. "Sucks" videos on YouTube and other video sites also abound. For example, a search of "Apple sucks" on YouTube turns up more than 600 000 videos; a similar search for Microsoft finds 143 000. An "Apple sucks" search on Facebook links to hundreds of groups. If you don't find one you like, try "Apple suks" or "Apple sux" for hundreds more.

Some of these sites, videos, and other online attacks air legitimate complaints that should be addressed. Others, however, are little more than anonymous, vindictive slurs that unfairly ransack brands and corporate reputations. Some

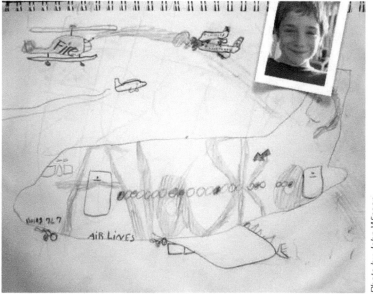

Photo by John Winsor

Exhibit 4.15 Today's empowered consumers: Boeing's embarrassing blunder over young Harry Winsor's airplane design made instant national news. However, Boeing quickly took responsibility and turned the potential public relations disaster into a positive.

of the attacks are only a passing nuisance; others can draw serious attention and create real headaches.

How should companies react to online attacks? The real quandary for targeted companies is figuring out how far they can go to protect their images without fuelling the already raging fire. One point on which all experts seem to agree: Don't try to retaliate in kind. "It's rarely a good idea to lob bombs at the fire starters," says one analyst. "Pre-emption, engagement, and diplomacy are saner tools." Such criticisms are often based on real consumer concerns and unresolved anger. Hence, the best strategy might be to proactively monitor these sites and respond to the concerns they express.

For example, Boeing quickly took responsibility for mishandling aspiring Harry Winsor's designs, turning a potential PR disaster into a positive. It called and invited young Harry to visit Boeing's facilities. On its corporate Twitter site, it confessed "We're experts at airplanes but novices in social media. We're learning as we go." In response to its Figo ad fiasco, Ford's chief marketing officer issued a deep public apology, citing that Ford had not approved the ads and that it had modified its ad review process. Ford's ad agency promptly fired the guilty creatives. Similarly, FedEx drew praise by immediately posting its own YouTube video addressing the monitor-smashing incident. In the video, Matthew Thornton, senior vice-president of operations, stated that he'd personally met with the aggrieved customer, who had accepted the company's apology. "This goes directly against all FedEx values," declared Thornton. The FedEx video struck a responsive chord. Numerous journalists and bloggers responded with stories about FedEx's outstanding package handling and delivering record.

Many companies have now created teams of specialists that monitor online conversations and engage unhappy consumers. For example, the social media team at Southwest Airlines includes a chief Twitter officer who tracks Twitter comments and monitors Facebook groups, an online representative who checks facts and interacts with bloggers, and another person who takes charge of the company's presence on sites such as YouTube, Instagram, Flickr, and LinkedIn. So if someone posts an online comment, the company can respond promptly in a personal way.

Not long ago, Southwest's team averted what could have been a major PR catastrophe when a hole popped open in a plane's fuselage on a flight from Phoenix to Sacramento. The flight had Wi-Fi, and the first passenger tweet about the incident, complete with a photo, was online in only 9 minutes—11 minutes before Southwest's official dispatch channel report. But Southwest's monitoring team picked up the social media chatter and was able to craft a blog post and other social media responses shortly after the plane made an emergency landing in Yuma, Arizona. By the time the story hit the major media, the passenger who had tweeted initially was back on Twitter praising the Southwest crew for its professional handling of the situation.

Thus, by monitoring and proactively responding to seemingly uncontrollable events in the environment, companies can prevent the negatives from spiralling out of control or even turn them into positives. Who knows? With the right responses, Walmartblows.com might even become Walmartrules.com. Then again, probably not.

Sources: Quotes, excerpts, and other information based on Matt Wilson, "How Southwest Airlines Wrangled Four Social Media Crises," Ragan.com, February 20, 2013, www.ragan.com/Main/Articles/How_Southwest_Airlines_wrangled_four_social_media_46254.aspx#; Vanessa Ko, "FedEx Apologizes after Video of Driver Throwing Fragile Package Goes Viral," *Time*, December 23, 2011, http://newsfeed.time.com/2011/12/23/fedex-apologizes-after-video-of-driver-throwing-fragile-package-goes-viral; Michelle Conlin, "Web Attack," *BusinessWeek*, April 16, 2007, pp. 54–56; "Boeing's Social Media Lesson," May 3, 2010, http://mediadecoder.blogs.nytimes.com/2010/05/03/boeings-social-media-lesson; Brent Snavely, "Ford Marketing Chief Apologizes for Ads," *USA Today*, March 27, 2013; and www.youtube.com/watch?v=C5ulH0VTg_o, accessed November 2013.

GlutenWise, or Gluten-Free

Boston Pizza's main menu items have historically been made using wheat flour, which is off-limits to gluten-free dieters. But while gluten was once thought to negatively impact only a small percentage of the general public—those with celiac disease—it has more recently been linked to number of allergies and intolerances, which has driven a wedge into wheat-based food consumption and turned gluten-free alternatives into a burgeoning food industry.

The growing demand for gluten-free foods presented BP with both a threat and an opportunity. While up to 10 percent of its market was suddenly abstaining from items on its menu, that same market was in need of healthy alternatives. The magnitude of the market had also jumpstarted research and development into gluten-free alternatives—a technological opportunity that was embraced by Boston Pizza, which introduced gluten-free to its menu in 2010.

The only problem was that the gluten-free dishes were prepared in same kitchens as everything else, raising the possibility of cross-contamination, which BP was legally obligated to disclose. But rather than view this political-legal threat as a barrier, BP again turned it into a competitive opportunity. The company branded its gluten-free products as "GlutenWise," a trademark that not only showed BP's commitment to respecting dietary sensitivities, but also positioned the company ahead of competitors who were struggling with the same dilemma.

The move was a total win, generating positive feedback even from the most demanding critics. "Everyone has the right to safe food," said Anne Wraggett, president of the Canadian Celiac Association, "and we are excited that Boston Pizza is taking steps to provide for the gluten-free community. Having safe gluten-free choices when dining out enhances our quality of life."

QUESTIONS

1. Factors in the marketing environment are broken into categories. Identify the opportunities and threats that emerged in BP's path toward introducing its GlutenWise menu, and sort them into their appropriate categories.
2. Why is cross-contamination of gluten-free dishes with non-gluten-free dishes categorized as a political-legal threat?
3. The microenvironment comprises internal forces that are controlled by the organization and that reveal a firm's strengths and weaknesses. Is Boston Pizza's introduction of GlutenWise a strength, weakness, opportunity, or threat? Why?

REVIEWING THE CONCEPTS

 Describe the environmental forces that affect the company's ability to serve its customers.

The company's *microenvironment* consists of actors close to the company that combine to form its value delivery network or that affect its ability to serve its customers. It includes the company's *internal environment*—its several departments and management levels—as it influences marketing decision making. *Marketing channel firms*—suppliers, marketing intermediaries, physical distribution firms, marketing services agencies, and financial intermediaries—cooperate to create customer value. *Competitors* vie with the company in an effort to serve customers better. Various *publics* have an actual or potential interest in or impact on the company's ability to meet its objectives. Finally, five types of customer *markets* exist: consumer, business, reseller, government, and international markets.

The *macroenvironment* consists of larger societal forces that affect the entire microenvironment. The six forces making up the company's macroenvironment are demographic, economic, natural, technological, political/social, and cultural. These forces shape opportunities and pose threats to the company.

 Explain how changes in the demographic and economic environments affect marketing decisions.

Demography is the study of the characteristics of human populations. Today's *demographic environment* shows a changing age structure, shifting family profiles, geographic population shifts, a better-educated and more white-collar population, and increasing diversity. The *economic environment* consists of factors that affect buying power and patterns. The economic environment is characterized by more frugal consumers who are seeking greater value—the right combination of good quality and service at a fair price. The distribution of income is also shifting. The rich have grown richer, the middle class has shrunk, and the poor have remained poor, leading to a two-tiered market.

 Identify the major trends in the firm's natural and technological environments.

The *natural environment* shows three major trends: shortages of certain raw materials, higher pollution levels, and more government intervention in natural resource management. Environmental concerns create marketing opportunities for alert companies. The *technological environment* creates both opportunities and challenges. Companies that fail to keep up with technological change will miss out on new product and marketing opportunities.

 Explain the key changes in the political and cultural environments.

The *political environment* consists of laws, agencies, and groups that influence or limit marketing actions. The political environment has undergone changes that affect marketing worldwide: increasing legislation regulating business, strong government agency enforcement, and greater emphasis on ethics and socially responsible actions. The *cultural environment* consists of institutions and forces that affect a society's values, perceptions, preferences, and behaviours. The environment shows trends toward new technology-enabled communication, a lessening trust of institutions, increasing patriotism, greater appreciation for nature, a changing spiritualism, and the search for more meaningful and enduring values.

LO5 Discuss how companies can react to the marketing environment.

Companies can passively accept the marketing environment as an uncontrollable element to which they must adapt, avoiding threats and taking advantage of opportunities as they arise. Or they can take a *proactive* stance, working to change the environment rather than simply reacting to it. Whenever possible, companies should try to be proactive rather than reactive.

DISCUSSION QUESTIONS

1. Name and briefly describe the elements of an organization's microenvironment and discuss how they affect marketing.

2. What is demography, and why is it so important for marketers?

3. Who are the Millennials, and why are they of so much interest to marketers?

4. Discuss trends in the natural environment of which marketers must be aware, and provide examples of companies' responses to them.

5. Compare and contrast core beliefs/values and secondary beliefs/values. Provide an example of each and discuss the potential impact marketers have on each.

6. How should marketers respond to the changing environment?

CRITICAL THINKING EXERCISES

1. Research a current or emerging change in the legal or regulatory environment affecting marketing. Explain its impact on marketing and how companies are reacting to the law or regulation.

2. Cause-related marketing has grown considerably over the past 10 years. Visit www.causemarketingforum.com to learn about companies that have won Halo Awards for outstanding cause-related marketing programs. Present an award-winning case study to your class.

ONLINE, MOBILE, AND SOCIAL MEDIA MARKETING

If you have a great product idea but no money, never fear: There's Kickstarter, an online crowdfunding site. Founded in 2008, Kickstarter enables companies to raise money from multiple individuals; since its founding, it has helped launch more than 91 000 projects. For example, when Pebble Technology Corporation created a "smart" wristwatch called Pebble, which works with iPhones or Android phones, it didn't have the funding to produce and market the device. So young CEO Eric Migicovsky turned to Kickstarter for crowdfunding. His modest goal was to raise US$100 000—but the company raised US$1 million in only one day and a total of US$10.27 million in just over one month! Nearly 70 000 people pre-ordered the $115 watch, and Pebble had to deliver on the promise. Kickstarter takes a 5 percent fee on the total funds raised, with Amazon Payments handling the processing of the funds. Kickstarter charges pledgers' credit cards, and the project creator receives the funds within only a few weeks.

The JOBS Act legislation in the United States, signed into law in 2012, provides a legal framework for this type of financing, which is expected grow even faster as a result. (Canadian legislators have been slow to regulate the crowdfunding industry, although a few provinces have proposed guidelines to do so.) However, Kickstarter and similar sites don't guarantee that the projects will be delivered as promised, and some people are concerned that crowd*funding* will beget crowd*frauding*.

QUESTIONS

1. Find another crowdfunding site and describe two projects featured on that site.

2. Learn more about the JOBS Act and how it impacts crowdfunding for start-up businesses. What protections are in place for investors with regard to crowdfrauding? What types of regulation exists in Canada for Canadian start-ups?

THINK LIKE A MARKETING MANAGER

Customer loyalty for online travel companies is low because the average consumer checks several different travel sites for the best prices on air travel, hotels, and rental cars before booking. With consumers highly motivated to make their selections based on price, online travel companies are trying to figure out other ways to differentiate themselves from the competition.

QUESTIONS

1. What macroenvironmental forces do you think are having the greatest positive and negative impact on online travel companies?

2. What do you think will be the most significant environmental issues facing the online travel industry in the next five years?

MARKETING ETHICS

The roughly 25 percent of the North American population under 18 years old wields billions of dollars in purchasing power. Companies such as eBay and Facebook want to capitalize on those dollars—legitimately, that is. eBay is exploring ways to allow consumers under 18 years old to set up legitimate accounts to both buy and sell goods. Children already trade on the site, either through their parents' accounts or through accounts set up after they lie about their ages. Similarly, even though children under 13 are not allowed to set up Facebook accounts, about 7.5 million of them have accounts, and nearly 5 million account holders are under 10 years old. That translates to almost 20 percent of U.S. 10-year-olds and 70 percent of 13-year-olds active on Facebook. Many of these accounts were set up with parental knowledge and assistance. Both eBay and Facebook say that protections will be put in place on children's accounts and that parents will be able to monitor their children's accounts.

QUESTIONS

1. Debate the pros and cons of allowing these companies to target children. Are these efforts socially responsible behaviour?

2. Review the Children's Online Privacy Protection Act at www.coppa.org. Explain how eBay and Facebook can target this market and still comply with this act.

MARKETING BY THE NUMBERS

Do you know of Danica from the Philippines, Peter from London, Nargis from India, Marina from Russia, Chieko from Japan, or Miran from the United States? These are some of the babies whose parents claimed they were the 7th billion human born into the world. The world population continues to grow, even though women are having fewer children than ever before. Markets are made up of people, and to stay competitive, marketers must know where populations are located and where they are going. The fertility rate in North America is declining and the population is aging, creating opportunities as well as threats for marketers. That is why tracking and predicting demographic trends are so important in marketing. Marketers must plan to capitalize on opportunities and deal with the threats before it is too late.

QUESTIONS

1. Develop a presentation on a specific demographic trend in Canada. Explain the reasons behind this trend and discuss the implications for marketers.

2. Discuss global demographic trends. What are the implications of those trends, and how should marketers respond to them?

XEROX: ADAPTING TO THE TURBULENT MARKETING ENVIRONMENT

Xerox introduced the first plain-paper office copier more than 50 years ago. In the decades that followed, the company that invented photocopying flat-out dominated the industry it had created. The name Xerox became almost generic for copying (as in "I'll Xerox this for you"). Through the years, Xerox fought off round after round of rivals to stay atop the fiercely competitive copier industry. Through the late 1990s, Xerox's profits and stock price were soaring.

Then things went terribly wrong for Xerox. The legendary company's stock and fortunes took a stomach-churning dive. In only 18 months, Xerox lost some US$38 billion in market value. Its stock price plunged from almost US$70 in 1999 to under US$5 by mid-2001. The once-dominant market leader found itself on the brink of bankruptcy. What happened? Blame it on change—or, rather, on Xerox's failure to adapt to its rapidly changing marketing environment. The world was quickly going digital, but Xerox hadn't kept up.

In the new digital environment, Xerox customers no longer relied on the company's flagship products—stand-alone copiers—to share information and documents. Instead of pumping out and distributing stacks of black-and-white copies, they created digital documents and shared them electronically. Or they printed out multiple copies on their nearby networked printer. On a broader level, while Xerox was busy perfecting copy machines, customers were looking for more sophisticated "document management solutions." They wanted systems that would let them scan documents in Frankfurt, weave them into colourful, customized showpieces in Toronto, and print them on demand in London—even altering for Canadian spelling.

This left Xerox on the edge of financial disaster. "We didn't have any cash and few prospects for making any," says CEO Ursula Burns. "The one thing you wanted was good and strong leaders that were aligned and could get us through things and we didn't have that." Burns didn't realize it back then, but she would one day lead the company she began working for as a summer intern in 1981. In fact, Burns almost left the company in 2000, but her colleague and friend Anne Mulcahy became CEO and convinced her to stay. Burns was named a senior vice-president and was then charged with cleaning house.

THE TURNAROUND BEGINS

Task number one: Outsource Xerox's manufacturing. An often criticized and unpopular move, outsourcing was critical to Xerox's cost-saving efforts. Burns oversaw the process in a way that preserved quality while achieving the desired cost benefits. And she did so with the blessing of Xerox's employee union by convincing the union that it was either lose some jobs or have no jobs at all. With the restructuring of manufacturing, in only four years, Xerox's workforce dropped from 100 000 employees to 55 000. Although this and other efforts returned Xerox to profitability within a few years, the bigger question still remained: What business is Xerox really in?

To answer this question, Xerox renewed its focus on the customer. The company had always focused on copier hardware. But "we were being dragged by our customers into managing large, complex business processes for them," says Burns. Before developing new products, Xerox researchers held seemingly endless customer focus groups. Sophie Vandebroek, the company's chief technology officer, called this "dreaming with the customer." The goal, she argued, was "involving [Xerox] experts who know the technology with customers who know the pain points... . Ultimately innovation is about delighting the customer." In the process, Xerox discovered that understanding customers is just as important as understanding technology.

What Xerox learned is that customers didn't want just copiers; they wanted easier, faster, and less costly ways to share documents and information. As a result, the company had to rethink, redefine, and reinvent itself. Xerox underwent a remarkable transformation. It stopped defining itself as a "copier company." In fact, it even stopped making stand-alone copiers. Instead, Xerox began billing itself as the world's leading document-management technology and services enterprise. The company's newly minted mission was to help companies "be smarter about their documents."

This shift in emphasis created new customer relationships, as well as new competitors. Instead of selling copiers to equipment purchasing managers, Xerox found itself developing and selling document-management systems to high-level information technology managers. And instead of competing head-on with copy machine competitors like Sharp, Canon, and Ricoh, Xerox was now squaring off against information technology companies like HP and IBM. Although it encountered many potholes along the way, the company once known as the iconic "copier company" became increasingly comfortable with its new identity as a document-management company.

BUILDING NEW STRENGTHS

Xerox's revenue, profits, and stock price began to show signs of recovery. But before it could declare its troubles over, yet another challenging environmental force arose—the Great Recession. The recession severely depressed Xerox's core printing and copying equipment and services business, and the company's sales and stock price tumbled once again. So in a major move to maintain its transition momentum, Xerox acquired Affiliated Computer Services (ACS), a US$6.4 billion information technology (IT) services powerhouse with a foot in the door of seemingly every back office in the world. The expertise, capabilities, and established channels of ACS were just what Xerox needed to take its new business plan to fruition.

The synergy between Xerox, ACS, and other acquired companies has resulted in a broad portfolio of customer-focused products, software, and services that help Xerox's customers manage documents and information. In fact, Xerox has introduced more than 130 innovative new products in the past few years. It now offers digital products and systems ranging from network printers and multifunction devices to colour printing and publishing systems, digital presses, and "book factories." It also offers an impressive array of print-management consulting and outsourcing services that help businesses develop online document archives, operate in-house print shops or mailrooms, analyze how employees can most efficiently share documents and knowledge, and build Internet-based processes for personalizing direct mail, invoices, and brochures.

These new products have allowed Xerox to supply solutions to clients, not just hardware. For example, Xerox has a new device for insurance company customers—a compact computer with scanning, printing, and Internet capabilities. Instead of relying on the postal service to transport hard copies of claims, these and related documents are scanned on-site, sorted, routed, and put immediately into a workflow system. This isn't just a fancy new gadget for the insurance companies. They are seeing real benefits. Error rates have plummeted along with processing times, and that means increases in revenues and customer satisfaction.

DREAMING BEYOND ITS BOUNDARIES

Riding the combination of Xerox's former strengths and its new acquisitions, Burns and the Xerox team now have a utopian image of what lies ahead. They believe that the tools and services they offer clients are getting smarter. "It's not just processing Medicaid payments," says Stephen Hoover, director of Xerox's research facilities. "It's using our social cognition research to add wellness support that helps people better manage conditions like diabetes." Hoover adds that the future may see a new generation of Xerox devices, such as those that can analyze real-time parking and traffic data for municipal customers, allowing them to help citizens locate parking spots or automatically ticket them when they are going too fast. Already, Xerox is market testing parking meters that are capable of calling 911 or taking photos when a button is pushed. Not all products such as these will hit the market, but Xerox now has a model that allows it to dream beyond its known boundaries.

In another example of smarter tools for clients, in 2014 Xerox rolled out Ignite, a software and Web-based service that turns its copiers/scanners/printers already in service at schools around the world into paper-grading machines. Previous automated grading technologies (such as Scantron) worked only on multiple-choice responses filled out on special forms. But Ignite grades work where answers are written in by students—even numeric math problems. The real revolutionary potential of Ignite, however, is not just in automated grading, but in taking the results and turning them into Web-accessible data that allow teachers to identify problem areas and make improvements to their techniques.

Throughout this corporate metamorphosis, Xerox isn't focused on trying to make better copiers. Rather, it's focused on improving any process that a business or government customer needs to perform and performing it more efficiently. Xerox's new machines have learned to read and understand the documents they scan, reducing complex tasks that once took weeks down to minutes or even seconds. From now on, Xerox wants to be a leading global document-management and business-process technology and services provider.

With all the dazzling technologies emerging today, Burns acknowledges that the business services industry in which Xerox now operates is decidedly unsexy. But she also points out that "These are processes that companies need to run their businesses. They do it as a sideline; it's not their main thing." But running these seemingly mundane business processes *is* now Xerox's main thing. Xerox provides these basic document and IT services to customers so that customers can focus on what matters most—their real businesses.

Xerox's transition is still a work in progress. Revenues were down in 2014, and in the first two quarters of 2015 as well. Part of the reason is that Xerox still relies to some extent on its copier and printer products for its success, even with its recent diversification strategy. And just as email and desktop software killed photocopying, smartphones and tablets are killing inkjet and photo printers. But Xerox depends much less on such products than competitors such as Hewlett-Packard and Lexmark International do. Thus, experts predict, Xerox will rebound much more quickly than its rivals. Burns and crew are also confident that as Xerox continues its transition to solutions provider, the seeds it has planted over the past few years will soon bear fruit.

Xerox knows that change and renewal are ongoing and never-ending. "The one thing that's predictable about business is that it's fundamentally unpredictable," says the company's annual report. "Macro forces such as globalization, emerging technologies, and, most recently, depressed financial markets bring new challenges every day to businesses of all sizes." The message is clear. Even the most dominant companies can be vulnerable to the often turbulent and changing marketing environment. Companies that understand and adapt well to their environments can thrive. Those that don't risk their very survival.

Sources: Quotes and other information from or based on Mia Lamar, "Xerox's Net Rises 10%, but Revenue Falls Short," *Wall Street Journal*, April 23, 2013, http://online.wsj.com/article/SB100014241278873 248742045784404442381235524.html; Muneeza Iqbal, "The Makers: Xerox CEO Ursula Burns Tells Her Story," *Daily Finance*, February 27, 2013, www.dailyfinance.com/2013/02/25/ursula-burns-makers-pbs-xerox; Ellen McGirt, "Fresh Copy: How Ursula Burns Reinvented Xerox," *Fast Company*, November 29, 2011, www. fastcompany.com/magazine/161/ursula-burns-xerox; Scott Gamm, "Xerox Works to Duplicate Copier Glory in Digital Services Model," *Forbes*, July 19, 2012, www.forbes.com/sites/scottgamm/2012/07/19/xerox-works-to-duplicate-copier-glory-in-digital-services-model; Geoff Colvin, "Ursula Burns Launches Xerox into the Future," *Fortune*, May 3, 2010, p. 5; Matthew Daneman, "Xerox Stepping into Grading School Papers," *USA Today*, May 7, 2013, www.usatoday.com/story/tech/2013/05/07/xerox-school-grades/2140749; and annual reports and other information at www.xerox.com, accessed May 2013.

QUESTIONS FOR DISCUSSION

1. What microenvironmental factors have affected Xerox's performance since the late 1990s?

2. What macroenvironmental factors have affected Xerox's performance during that period?

3. By focusing on the business services industry, has Xerox pursued the best strategy? Why or why not?

4. What alternative strategy might Xerox have pursued following the first signs of declining revenues and profits?

5. Given Xerox's current situation, what recommendations would you make to Burns for the future of Xerox?

PepsiCo Canada ULC

AFTER STUDYING THIS CHAPTER, YOU SHOULD BE ABLE TO

1 explain the importance of information in gaining insights about the marketplace and customers

2 define the marketing information system and discuss its parts

3 outline the steps in the marketing research process

4 explain how companies analyze and use marketing information

5 discuss the special issues some marketing researchers face, including public policy and ethics issues

5

Managing Marketing Information to Gain Customer Insights

PREVIEWING THE CONCEPTS

In this chapter, we continue our exploration of how marketers gain insights into consumers and the marketplace. We look at how companies develop and manage information about important marketplace elements: customers, competitors, products, and marketing programs. To succeed in today's marketplace, companies must know how to turn mountains of marketing information into fresh customer insights that will help them deliver greater value to customers.

Let's start with a good story about marketing research and customer insights in action. When Pepsi's market share and sales took an embarrassing dip, putting the iconic brand in third place behind archrival Coca-Cola's Coke and Diet Coke brands, Pepsi turned to consumer research for answers. It launched an exhaustive nine-month global search for fresh consumer insights about just what it is that makes Pepsi different from Coke. The answer: Whereas Coke is *timeless*, Pepsi is *timely*. This simple but powerful consumer insight resulted in Pepsi's global "Live for Now" marketing campaign.

PEPSI'S MARKETING INSIGHT: PEPSI DRINKERS "LIVE FOR NOW"

Pepsi has long pitched itself to a now-generation of youthful cola drinkers, those young in mind and spirit. About 50 years ago, the brand invited consumers to "Come Alive! You're the Pepsi Generation!" Pepsi was different from Coca-Cola. "You've got a lot to live," went the jingle, "and Pepsi's got a lot to give."

But PepsiCo's flagship cola brand has begun losing some of its youthful fizz. Partly to blame is the fact that soft drink consumption has been declining for the past several years. But even harder for PepsiCo to swallow was that the Pepsi brand was losing ground in its century-long battle with archrival Coca-Cola, dropping from its perennial number two position to number three, behind both Coca-Cola and Diet Coke. The embarrassing market-share slip sent a strong signal: The brand's positioning needed a pick-me-up.

To diagnose the issues behind the slide and find answers, PepsiCo launched an intense global consumer research effort. It set out to rediscover just what it is that makes Pepsi different from Coke. The company created a secretive, high-level research task force, located in an unmarked building in upstate New York. Charged with charting a new course for the Pepsi brand, the group embarked on an exhaustive nine-month worldwide search for new consumer insights.

Practice on MyMarketingLab
Web Analytics Mini Case: Evaluating a Sponsored Search Campaign

Practice on MyMarketingLab
Share of Customer at the "Hopping Handbag Hut"

Practice on MyMarketingLab
Estimating if a Customer is Active

The Pepsi task force left no stone unturned. It poured through reels of past Pepsi advertising. It fielded traditional focus groups, in-depth personal interviews, and lengthy quantitative surveys. Researchers and top executives participated in ethnographic studies, "moving in" with customers, observing them as they went about their daily lives, and immersing themselves in cultures throughout North and South America, Asia, Europe, Africa, and Australia.

The Pepsi research team discovered that the longtime iconic brand had lost sight of what it stands for and the role it plays in customers' lives. Top brands such as Nike, Disney, Starbucks, and Coca-Cola have a clear sense of their meaning. But Pepsi no longer had clear positioning that defined the essence of the brand, drove marketing and innovation, and fuelled consumer engagement. In only the past few years, for example, Pepsi's positioning had jumped around from "Every Pepsi Refreshes the World" to "Summer Time Is Pepsi Time" to "Where There's Pepsi, There's Music."

So what does Pepsi mean to consumers? How does it differ from rival Coca-Cola in terms of consumer perceptions and feelings? The research task force boiled its extensive findings down to two simple but powerful customer insights. Whereas Coke is *timeless*, Pepsi is *timely*. Whereas Coca-Cola drinkers seek *happiness*, Pepsi drinkers seek *excitement*. According to Brad Jakeman, Pepsi's president of global enjoyment and chief creative officer, Coca-Cola stands for moments of joy and happiness, and for protecting the culture and status quo. In contrast, Pepsi stands for creating culture rather than preserving it, and Pepsi customers would rather lead an exciting life than a happy one. Whereas Coca-Cola means belonging, Pepsi embraces individuality. "Brands that are timeless want to have museums," says Jakeman. "Pepsi is not a brand that belongs in a museum."

Interestingly, such insights harken back to the old, youthful "choice of a new generation" positioning that built the Pepsi brand so powerfully decades ago. And despite its recent slide, Pepsi remains a formidable brand. Although it has never been the leading cola, Pepsi has always acted as if it were. According to Jakeman, Pepsi has done best when projecting the confidence and swagger of a leader, and Pepsi drinkers have always identified with that boldness. Looking forward, the key will be to regain that boldness and swagger. "This brand does not need to be reinvented," he asserts. "It needs to be reignited."

The "timely" versus "timeless" research insights—the idea of "capturing the excitement of now"—opened new creative doors for Pepsi. The result was a global marketing campaign called "Live for Now," which began with the 2013 Super Bowl and wrapped up in 2015. Giving a kind of modern twist to the brand's classic "Pepsi Generation" positioning, the campaign provided a new rallying cry for the next generation of Pepsi drinkers. "Live for Now" was designed to shape culture, capture the excitement of the moment, and re-establish Pepsi's connection with entertainment and pop culture. To back the new campaign, PepsiCo increased its marketing budget by 50 percent, which put Pepsi's promotional spending at levels close to those of Coca-Cola.

"Live for Now" burst onto the scene with an abundance of traditional and digital media. The campaign partnered with a full roster of music and sports stars, linking the brand with some of today's most exciting celebrities. For example, the first ads featured singer/rapper Nicki Minaj, whose hit "Moment 4 Life" contained lyrics made in heaven for Pepsi "Live for Now" commercials and videos ("I wish that I could have this moment for life. 'Cuz in this moment I just feel so alive"). Next, Pepsi inked a deal with Beyoncé that had her pitching

Pepsi's new message on everything from commercials and social media videos to Pepsi cans and a Super Bowl halftime extravaganza.

At the heart of the campaign, the interactive "Pepsi Pulse" site—what one analyst calls "a company-curated dashboard of pop culture"—served as a portal to Pepsi's world of entertainment, featuring pop-culture information, entertainment news, and original content. Pepsi forged a music-related partnership with Twitter; as well, its Mi Pepsi site and Facebook page catered to Latino lifestyles and culture, urging customers to "Vive Hoy." Every aspect of the "Live for Now" campaign put customers in the middle of the action. For example, during Super Bowl XLVII, Pepsi commercials and the Pepsi-sponsored halftime show featured youthful consumers as participants. "It really begins with the insight that Pepsi consumers want to be active participants, not observers of life," said a Pepsi marketer.

Pepsi's extensive research also showed that Pepsi drinkers around the globe are remarkably similar, which gave the "Live for Now" positioning worldwide appeal. For example, in India, Pepsi's consumer research revealed that the country's young people are among the most optimistic in the world but are impatient for the future to happen sooner. So Pepsi TV ads in India featured brand endorsers such as cricket captain MS Dhoni, actress-turned-pop-singer Priyanka Chopra, and Bollywood star Ranbir Kapoor overcoming moments of impatience, interspersed with images of young people doing exciting spur-of-the-moment things. The "Live for Now" campaign told young consumers that "there's nothing wrong with wanting something now," said a senior PepsiCo India marketer.

The campaign may have done little to reverse Pepsi's fortunes, as the overall consumer demand for soft drinks continues to decline. But it's clear that the folks at Pepsi did their homework. Based on what Pepsi's Jakeman described as the "most exhaustive and consumer-insights-led process" he'd ever witnessed, the swagger was back at Pepsi. Backed by months and months of intensive consumer research, "Live for Now" re-energized the Pepsi brand, those who worked on it, and those who drink it. According to one Pepsi bottler who cut his teeth in the industry back when the original "Pepsi Generation" campaign was in full stride, "Live for Now" "[brought] back the roots of what Pepsi is all about."[1]

AS THE Pepsi story highlights, good products and marketing programs begin with good customer information. Companies also need an abundance of information on competitors, resellers, and other actors and marketplace forces. But more than just gathering information, marketers must *use* the information to gain powerful *customer and market insights*.

Marketing Information and Customer Insights LO1

To create value for customers and build meaningful relationships with them, marketers must first gain fresh, deep insights into what customers need and want. Such customer insights come from good marketing information. Companies use these customer insights to develop a competitive advantage.

For example, Apple wasn't the first company to develop a digital music player. However, Apple's research uncovered two key insights: People wanted personal music players that let them take all their music with them, and they wanted to be able to listen to it unobtrusively. Based on these insights, Apple applied its design and usability magic to

Beck Diefenback/Reuters

Exhibit 5.1 Key customer insights, plus a dash of Apple's design and usability magic, have made the iPod a blockbuster. It now captures a more than 78 percent market share and has spawned other Apple blockbusters such as the iPhone and iPad.

create the phenomenally successful iPod. The iPod now captures more than a 78 percent share of the global MP3 player market. Apple has sold more than 350 million iPods, and "to put that in context," says Apple CEO Tim Cook, "it took Sony 30 years to sell just 230 000 Walkman cassette players."[2]

Despite its huge success, iPod sales have been steadily decreasing as the market for MP3 players declines. However, Apple's initial success with the iPod has meant an easier transition for consumers, who now listen to music on their iPhone instead.

Although customer and market insights are important for building customer value and relationships, these insights can be very difficult to obtain. Customer needs and buying motives are often anything but obvious—consumers themselves usually can't tell you exactly what they need and why they buy. To gain good customer insights, marketers must effectively manage marketing information from a wide range of sources.

With the recent explosion of information technologies, companies can now generate marketing information in great quantities. Moreover, consumers themselves are now generating tons of marketing information. Through email, text messaging, blogging, Facebook, Twitter, and other grassroots digital channels, consumers are now volunteering a tidal wave of bottom-up information to companies and to each other. Companies that tap into such information can gain rich, timely customer insights at lower cost.

Far from lacking information, most marketing managers are overloaded with data and often overwhelmed by it. For example, when a company such as Pepsi monitors online discussions about its brands by searching key words in tweets, blogs, posts, and other sources, its servers take in a stunning 6 million public conversations a day, more than 2 billion a year. That's far more information than any manager can digest. And for every Pepsi manager, a ton more information is only a Google search away. According to IBM, 90 percent of the data that companies collect from social media and other real-time sources isn't being used effectively.[3] Thus, marketers don't need *more* information; they need *better* information. And they need to make better *use* of the information they already have.

Customer insights

Fresh understandings of customers and the marketplace derived from marketing information that become the basis for creating customer value and relationships.

The real value of marketing research and marketing information lies in how it is used—in the **customer insights** that it provides. Based on such thinking, many companies are now restructuring their marketing research and information functions. They are creating *customer insights teams*, headed by a vice-president of customer insights and composed of representatives from all of the firm's functional areas. For example, Coca-Cola's vice-president of marketing strategy and insights heads up a team of 25 strategists who develop strategy based on marketing research insights. This executive believes that marketing researchers need to do more than just provide data. They need to "tell the stories behind the data" and provide "now what" answers based on the insights gained.[4]

Customer insights groups collect customer and market information from a wide variety of sources, ranging from traditional marketing research studies to mingling with and observing consumers to monitoring social media conversations about the company and its products. Then they *use* this information to develop important customer insights from which the company can create more value for its customers.

LO2

Thus, companies must design effective marketing information systems that give managers the right information, in the right form, at the right time and help them to use this information to create customer value and stronger customer relationships.

FIGURE 5.1 The Marketing Information System

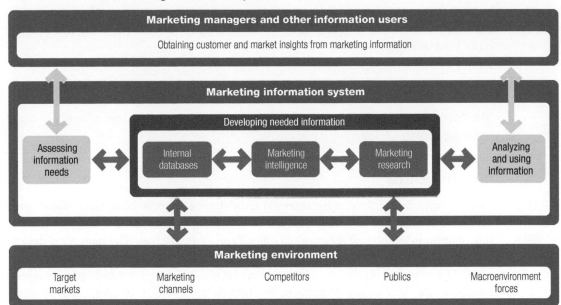

A **marketing information system (MIS)** consists of people and procedures dedicated to assessing information needs, developing the needed information, and helping decision makers use the information to generate and validate actionable customer and market insights.

Figure 5.1 shows that the MIS begins and ends with information users—marketing managers, internal and external partners, and others who need marketing information. First, it interacts with these information users to assess information needs. Next, it interacts with the marketing environment to develop needed information through internal company databases, marketing intelligence activities, and marketing research. Finally, the MIS helps users analyze and use the information to develop customer insights, make marketing decisions, and manage customer relationships.

Marketing information system (MIS)
People and procedures dedicated to assessing information needs, developing the needed information, and helping decision makers use the information to generate and validate actionable customer and market insights.

Assessing Marketing Information Needs

The marketing information system primarily serves the company's marketing and other managers. However, it may also provide information to external partners, such as suppliers, resellers, or marketing services agencies. For example, Walmart's Retail Link system gives key suppliers access to information on everything from customers' buying patterns and store inventory levels to how many items they've sold in which stores in the past 24 hours.[5]

A good MIS balances the information users would *like* to have against what they really *need* and what is *feasible* to offer. Some managers will ask for whatever information they can get without thinking carefully about what they really need. Too much information can be as harmful as too little. Other managers may omit things they ought to know, or they may not know to ask for some types of information they should have. For example, managers might need to know about surges in favourable or unfavourable consumer discussions about their brands on blogs or online social media. But because they don't know about these discussions, they don't think to ask about them. The MIS must monitor the marketing environment to provide decision makers with information they should have to better understand customers and make key marketing decisions.

Finally, the costs of obtaining, analyzing, storing, and delivering information can quickly mount. The company must decide whether the value of insights gained from additional information is worth the costs of providing it, and both value and cost are often hard to assess.

Developing Marketing Information

Marketers can obtain the needed information from *internal data*, *marketing intelligence*, and *marketing research*.

Internal Data

Internal databases

Electronic collections of consumer and market information obtained from data sources within the company network.

Many companies build extensive **internal databases**, electronic collections of consumer and market information obtained from data sources within the company's network. Information in an internal database can come from many sources. The marketing department furnishes information on customer characteristics, sales transactions, and website visits. The customer service department keeps records of customer satisfaction or service problems. The accounting department provides detailed records of sales, costs, and cash flows. Operations reports on production, shipments, and inventories. The sales force reports on reseller reactions and competitor activities, and marketing channel partners provide data on point-of-sale transactions. Harnessing such information can provide powerful customer insights and competitive advantage.

For example, consider Canada's Indigo Books & Music:

Indigo Books & Music is the largest book retailer in Canada, operating bookstores in all 10 provinces. After its acquisition of Chapters in 2001, the company faced a huge problem with its customer databases. Customers had to be tracked through multiple retail and online records, resulting in frequent processing delays, customer dissatisfaction, and an inability to effectively analyze sales, marketing, and retail data. The company turned to Infusion, a firm specializing in customer database design, to help overhaul its systems. Infusion created a single customer database containing all retail, Internet, and prospective customer information, which was also able to track data relating to Indigo's "irewards" loyalty program.

The results for Indigo included an increase from 40 to 80 percent of new signups who provided a working email address and the re-engagement via email with more than 100 000 existing Indigo customers. Says Sumit Oberai, chief information officer at Indigo, "We've stopped talking about online customers and retail store customers and loyalty customers and just talk about customers." In 2011, Indigo launched the Plum Rewards program, after getting feedback from customers that they wanted a free loyalty program that would enable them to earn and redeem points on both book and nonbook purchases. "Customization is critical" with rewards programs, says Heather Reisman, founder and CEO of Indigo Books & Music. "It's essential to make a loyalty program meaningful to customers." A large part of the success of the Indigo rewards program is a function of how personalized customer communications are; relevant messages help increase member engagement.[6]

Exhibit 5.2 Internal data: Indigo Books & Music has found a wealth of actionable customer insights by analyzing internal databases.

© Helen Sessions/Alamy

Internal databases can usually be accessed more quickly and cheaply than other information sources, but they also present some problems. Because internal information is often collected for other purposes, it may be incomplete or in the wrong form for making marketing decisions. Data also age quickly; keeping the database current requires a major effort. Finally, managing the mountains of information that a large company produces requires highly sophisticated equipment and techniques.

Competitive Marketing Intelligence

Competitive marketing intelligence involves the systematic collection and analysis of publicly available information about consumers, competitors, and developments in the marketplace. The goal of competitive marketing intelligence is to improve strategic decision making by understanding the consumer environment, assessing and tracking competitors' actions, and providing early warnings of opportunities and threats. Marketing intelligence techniques range from observing consumers firsthand to quizzing the company's own employees, benchmarking competitors' products, researching on the Internet, and monitoring social media buzz.

Competitive marketing intelligence
The systematic collection and analysis of publicly available information about consumers, competitors, and developments in the marketing environment.

Good marketing intelligence can help marketers gain insights into how consumers talk about and connect with their brands. Many companies send out teams of trained observers to mix and mingle personally with customers as they use and talk about the company's products. Other companies routinely monitor consumers' online chatter. For example, PepsiCo's Gatorade brand has created an extensive control centre to monitor real-time brand-related social media activity.[7] Whenever someone mentions anything related to Gatorade (including competitors, Gatorade athletes, and sports nutrition–related topics) on Twitter, Facebook, a blog, or in other social media, it pops up in various visualizations and dashboards on one of six big screens at Gatorade's Mission Control. Staffers also monitor online-ad and website traffic, producing a consolidated picture of the brand's Internet image. Gatorade uses what it sees and learns at Mission Control to improve its products, marketing, and interactions with customers.

Samsung used intelligence gained from real-time monitoring of the social media activity surrounding the introduction of competitor Apple's iPhone 5 to capture record-breaking sales of its own signature Galaxy S smartphone:

At the same time that Apple CEO Tim Cook was on stage in San Francisco unveiling the much-anticipated iPhone 5, Samsung marketing and ad agency executives were huddled around their computers and TV screens in a Los Angeles war room hundreds of miles away watching events unfold. The Samsung strategists carefully monitored not only each iPhone 5 feature as it was presented, but also the gush of online consumer commentary flooding blogs and social media channels. Even as the real-time consumer and competitive data surged in, the Samsung team began shaping a marketing response. By the time Cook had finished his iPhone 5 presentation two hours later, the Samsung team was already drafting a series of TV, print, and social media ads. The following week, just as the iPhone 5 was hitting store shelves, Samsung aired a 90-second

The Gatorade Company

Exhibit 5.3 Competitive marketing intelligence: PepsiCo's Gatorade brand has created an extensive control centre to monitor real-time brand-related social media activity.

"Fanboys" TV commercial. The ad mocked iPhone fans lined up outside Apple stores buzzing about the features of the new iPhone, only to be upstaged by two passersby and their Samsung Galaxy smartphones ("The next big thing is already here!"). Lines in the ad were based on thousands upon thousands of actual tweets and other social media interactions poking fun at or complaining about specific iPhone 5 features. The real-time, insights-based ad became the tech-ad sensation of the year (grabbing more than 70 million online views), allowing Samsung to rechannel excitement surrounding the iPhone 5 debut to sell a record number of its own Galaxy S phones.[8]

Many companies have even appointed *chief listening officers*, who are charged with sifting through online customer conversations and passing along key insights to marketing decision makers. As a Dell marketing executive puts it, "Our chief listener is critical to making sure that the right people in the organization are aware of what the conversations on the Web are saying about us, so the relevant people in the business can connect with customers."[9]

Companies also need to actively monitor competitors' activities. Firms use competitive marketing intelligence to gain early warnings of competitor moves and strategies, new product launches, new or changing markets, and potential competitive strengths and weaknesses. Much competitor intelligence can be collected from people inside the company—executives, engineers and scientists, purchasing agents, and the sales force. The company can also obtain important intelligence information from suppliers, resellers, and key customers. It can monitor competitors' sites and use the Internet to search specific competitor names, events, or trends and see what turns up. And tracking consumer conversations about competing brands is often as revealing as tracking conversations about the company's own brands.

Intelligence seekers can also pour through any of the thousands of online databases. Some are free. For example, you can search the System for Electronic Document Analysis and Retrieval (SEDAR) database for documents and information filed by public companies and for investment funds with the Canadian Securities Administrators. For a fee, companies can also subscribe to any of the more than 3000 online databases and information search services, such as Hoover's, LexisNexis, and Dun & Bradstreet. Today's marketers have an almost overwhelming amount of competitor information only a few keystrokes away.

The intelligence game goes both ways. Facing determined competitive marketing intelligence efforts by competitors, most companies are now taking steps to protect their own information. For example, Apple is obsessed with secrecy, and it passes that obsession along to its employees. "At Apple everything is a secret," says an insider. "Apple wants new products to remain in stealth mode until their release dates." Information leaks about new products before they are introduced gives the competition time to respond, raises customer expectations, and can steal thunder and sales from current products. So Apple employees are taught a "loose-lips-sink-ships" mentality: A T-shirt for sale in the company store reads, "I visited the Apple campus, but that's all I'm allowed to say."[10]

One self-admitted corporate spy advises that companies should try conducting marketing intelligence investigations of themselves, looking for potentially damaging information leaks. They should start by "vacuuming up" everything they can find in the public record, including job postings, court records, company advertisements and blogs, webpages, press releases, online business reports, social media postings by customers and employees, and other information available to inquisitive competitors.[11]

The growing use of marketing intelligence also raises ethical issues. Some intelligence-gathering techniques may involve questionable ethics. Clearly, companies should take advantage of publicly available information. However, they should not stoop to snoop. With all the legitimate intelligence sources now available, a company does not need to break the law or accepted codes of ethics to get good intelligence.

Marketing Research LO3

◄⊙⊢**Simulate** on MyMarketingLab

Market Research

In addition to marketing intelligence information about general consumer, competitor, and marketplace happenings, marketers often need formal studies that provide customer and market insights for specific marketing situations and decisions. For example, Budweiser wants to know what appeals will be most effective in its Super Bowl advertising. Yahoo! wants to know how Web searchers will react to a proposed redesign of its site. Or Samsung wants to know how many and what kinds of people will buy its next-generation, ultrathin televisions. In such situations, managers will need marketing research.

Marketing research is the systematic design, collection, analysis, and reporting of data relevant to a specific marketing situation facing an organization. Companies use marketing research in a wide variety of situations. For example, marketing research gives marketers insights into customer motivations, purchase behaviour, and satisfaction. It can help them assess market potential and market share or measure the effectiveness of pricing, product, distribution, and promotion activities.

Some large companies have their own research departments that work with marketing managers on marketing research projects. In addition, these companies—like their smaller counterparts—frequently hire outside research specialists to consult with management on specific marketing problems and to conduct marketing research studies. Sometimes firms simply purchase data collected by outside firms to aid in their decision making.

The marketing research process has four steps (see Figure 5.2): defining the problem and research objectives, developing the research plan, implementing the research plan, and interpreting and reporting the findings.

Marketing research
The systematic design, collection, analysis, and reporting of data relevant to a specific marketing situation facing an organization.

Defining the Problem and Research Objectives

Marketing managers and researchers must work closely together to define the problem and agree on research objectives. The manager best understands the decision for which information is needed, whereas the researcher best understands marketing research and how to obtain the information. Defining the problem and research objectives is often the hardest step in the research process. The manager may know that something is wrong, without knowing the specific causes.

After the problem has been defined carefully, the manager and the researcher must set the research objectives. A marketing research project might have one of three types of objectives. The objective of **exploratory research** is to gather preliminary information that will help define the problem and suggest hypotheses. The objective of **descriptive research** is to describe things, such as the market potential for a product or the demographics and attitudes of consumers who buy the product. The objective of **causal research** is to test hypotheses about cause-and-effect relationships. For example, would a 10 percent decrease in tuition at a university result in an enrollment increase sufficient to offset the reduced tuition? Managers often start with exploratory research and later follow with descriptive or causal research.

The statement of the problem and research objectives guides the entire research process. The manager and the researcher should put the statement in writing to be certain that they agree on the purpose and expected results of the research.

Exploratory research
Marketing research to gather preliminary information that will help define problems and suggest hypotheses.

Descriptive research
Marketing research to better describe marketing problems, situations, or markets, such as the market potential for a product or the demographics and attitudes of consumers.

Causal research
Marketing research to test hypotheses about cause-and-effect relationships.

FIGURE 5.2 The Marketing Research Process

Jarrold Weaton/Weaton Digital, Inc.

Exhibit 5.4 A decision by Red Bull to add a line of enhanced waters to its already successful mix of energy drinks would call for marketing research that provides lots of specific information.

Developing the Research Plan

Once researchers have defined the research problem and objectives, they must determine the exact information needed, develop a plan for gathering it efficiently, and present the plan to management. The research plan outlines sources of existing data and spells out the specific research approaches, contact methods, sampling plans, and instruments that researchers will use to gather new data.

Research objectives must be translated into specific information needs. For example, suppose that Red Bull wants to know how consumers would react to a proposed new vitamin-enhanced water drink that would be available in several flavours and sold under the Red Bull name. Red Bull currently dominates the worldwide energy drink market with a more than 40 percent market share worldwide—it sold more than 5.6 billion cans in 2014 alone and earned revenues of approximately US$5.74 billion. The brand also introduced Red Bull Total Zero, an energy drink for calorie-averse consumers.[12] A new line of enhanced, fizzless waters—akin to Glacéau's vitaminwater—might help Red Bull leverage its strong brand position even further. The proposed research might call for the following specific information:

- The demographic, economic, and lifestyle characteristics of current Red Bull customers: Do current customers also consume enhanced-water products? Are such products consistent with their lifestyles? Or would Red Bull need to target a new segment of consumers?

- The characteristics and usage patterns of the broader population of enhanced-water users: What do they need and expect from such products, where do they buy them, when and how do they use them, and what existing brands and price points are most popular? (The new Red Bull product would need strong, relevant positioning in the crowded enhanced-water market.)

- Retailer reactions to the proposed new product line: Would they stock and support it? Where would they display it? (Failure to get retailer support would hurt sales of the new drink.)

- Forecasts of sales of both the new and current Red Bull products: Will the new enhanced waters create new sales or simply take sales away from current Red Bull products? Will the new product increase Red Bull's overall profits?

Red Bull's marketers will need these and many other types of information to decide whether or not to introduce the new product and, if so, the best way to do it.

The research plan should be presented in a *written proposal*. A written proposal is especially important when the research project is large and complex or when an outside firm carries it out. The proposal should cover the management problems addressed, the research objectives, the information to be obtained, and how the results will help management's decision making. The proposal also should include estimated research costs.

To meet the manager's information needs, the research plan can call for gathering secondary data, primary data, or both. **Secondary data** consist of information that already exists somewhere, having been collected for another purpose. **Primary data** consist of information collected for the specific purpose at hand.

Gathering Secondary Data

Researchers usually start by gathering secondary data. The company's internal database provides a good starting point. However, the company can also tap into a wide assortment of external information sources.

Companies can buy secondary data from outside suppliers. For example, Nielsen sells shopper insight data from a consumer panel of more than 250 000 households in 25 countries worldwide, with measures of trial and repeat purchasing, brand loyalty, and buyer demographics. Experian Simmons carries out a full spectrum of consumer studies that provide a comprehensive view of the consumer. The U.S. Yankelovich MONITOR service by The Futures Company sells information on important social and lifestyle trends. These and other firms supply high-quality data to suit a wide variety of marketing information needs.[13]

Using *commercial online databases*, marketing researchers can conduct their own searches of secondary data sources. General database services such as Dialog, ProQuest, and LexisNexis put an incredible wealth of information at the fingertips of marketing decision makers. Beyond commercial sites offering information for a fee, almost every industry association, government agency, business publication, and news medium offers free information to those tenacious enough to find their websites or apps.

Internet search engines can also be a big help in locating relevant secondary information sources. However, they can be very frustrating and inefficient. For example, a Red Bull marketer Googling "enhanced-water products" would come up with about 3700 hits. Still, well-structured, well-designed online searches can be a good starting point for any marketing research project.

Secondary data
Information that already exists somewhere, having been collected for another purpose.

Primary data
Information collected for the specific purpose at hand.

Exhibit 5.5 Consumer database services such as LexisNexis put an incredible wealth of information at the fingertips of marketing decision makers.

Secondary data can usually be obtained more quickly and at a lower cost than primary data. Also, secondary sources can sometimes provide data that an individual company cannot collect on its own—information that either is not directly available or would be too expensive to collect. For example, it would be too expensive for Red Bull's marketers to conduct a continuing retail store audit to find out about the market shares, prices, and displays of competitors' brands. But those marketers can buy the InfoScan service from SymphonyIRI Group, which provides this information based on scanner and other data from 34 000 retail stores.[14]

Secondary data can also present problems. Researchers can rarely obtain all the data they need from secondary sources. For example, Red Bull will not find existing information about consumer reactions to a new enhanced-water line that it has not yet placed on the market. Even when data can be found, the information might not be very usable. The researcher must evaluate secondary information carefully to make certain that it's *relevant* (fits the research project's needs), *accurate* (reliably collected and reported), *current* (up to date enough for current decisions), and *impartial* (objectively collected and reported).

Primary Data Collection

Secondary data provide a good starting point for research and often help to define research problems and objectives. In most cases, however, the company must also collect primary data. Table 5.1 shows that designing a plan for primary data collection calls for a number of decisions on *research approaches*, *contact methods*, the *sampling plan*, and *research instruments*.

Research Approaches Research approaches for gathering primary data include observation, surveys, and experiments. We discuss each one in turn.

Observational research

Gathering primary data by observing relevant people, actions, and situations.

OBSERVATIONAL RESEARCH Observational research involves gathering primary data by observing relevant people, actions, and situations. For example, a bank might evaluate possible new branch locations by checking traffic patterns, neighbourhood conditions, and the locations of competing branches.

Researchers often observe consumer behaviour to glean customer insights they can't obtain by simply asking customers questions. For instance, Fisher-Price has established an observation lab in which it can observe the reactions little tots have to new toys. The Fisher-Price Play Lab is a sunny, toy-strewn space where lucky kids get to test Fisher-Price prototypes, under the watchful eyes of designers who hope to learn what will get them worked up into a new-toy frenzy.

Marketers not only observe what consumers do but also observe what consumers are saying. As discussed earlier, marketers now routinely listen in on consumer conversations on blogs, social networks, and websites. Observing such naturally occurring feedback

TABLE 5.1	Planning Primary Data Collection		
Research Approaches	**Contact Methods**	**Sampling Plan**	**Research Instruments**
Observation	Mail	Sampling unit	Questionnaire
Survey	Telephone	Sample size	Mechanical instruments
Experiment	Personal Online	Sampling procedure	

can provide inputs that simply can't be gained through more structured and formal research approaches.

A wide range of companies now use **ethnographic research**. Ethnographic research involves sending observers to watch and interact with consumers in their "natural environments." The observers might be trained anthropologists and psychologists or company researchers and managers. For example, P&G uses extensive ethnographic research to gain deep insights into serving the world's poor. In 2009, P&G launched the "$2-a-Day Project," named for the average income of the people it targets worldwide. The project sends ethnographic researchers trekking through the jungles of Brazil, the slums of India, and farming villages in rural China seeking insights into the needs of very-low-income consumers. As an example, P&G researchers spent time with poor Chinese potato farmer Wei Xiao Yan, observing in detail as she washed her long black hair using only three cups of water. Her family's water supply is a precious commodity— it comes from storing rainwater. P&G must find affordable and practical solutions that work in Wei's harsh environment while also supporting her needs to feel attractive.[15]

Ethnographic research
A form of observational research that involves sending trained observers to watch and interact with consumers in their "natural environments."

Insights from P&G's $2-a-Day Project have already produced some successful new products for emerging markets—such as a skin-sensitive detergent for women who wash clothing by hand. In the works is a body cleanser formulated to clean without much water—it generates foam, which can be easily wiped away, instead of lather. Another product is a leave-in hair conditioner that requires no water at all. For underserved customers like Wei Xiao Yan, P&G has learned, it must develop products that are not just effective and affordable but also aspirational.

Beyond conducting ethnographic research in physical consumer environments, many companies now routinely conduct *Netnography* research—observing consumers in a natural context on the Internet. Observing people as they interact and move about online can provide useful insights into both online and offline buying motives and behaviour.[16]

Observational and ethnographic research often yield the kinds of details that just don't emerge from traditional research questionnaires or focus groups. Whereas traditional quantitative research approaches seek to test known hypotheses and obtain answers to well-defined product or strategy questions, observational research can generate fresh customer and market insights that people are unwilling or unable to provide. It offers a window into customers' unconscious actions and unexpressed needs and feelings.

In contrast, however, some things simply cannot be observed, such as attitudes, motives, or private behaviour. Long-term or infrequent behaviour is also difficult to observe. Finally, observations can be very difficult to

Benjamin Lowy/Getty Images

Exhibit 5.6 Ethnographic research: To better understand the needs of the world's poor, P&G sends researchers trekking through the jungles of Brazil, the slums of India, and farming villages in rural China to observe consumers in their "natural environments." Here, they watch Chinese potato farmer Wei Xiao Yan wash her long black hair with great care using only three cups of water.

interpret. Because of these limitations, researchers often use observation along with other data collection methods.

SURVEY RESEARCH **Survey research**, the most widely used method for primary data collection, is the approach best suited for gathering descriptive information. A company that wants to know about people's knowledge, attitudes, preferences, or buying behaviour can often find out by asking them directly.

The major advantage of survey research is its flexibility; it can be used to obtain many different kinds of information in many different situations. Surveys addressing almost any marketing question or decision can be conducted by phone or mail, in person, or online.

However, survey research also presents some problems. Sometimes people are unable to answer survey questions because they can't remember or have never thought about what they do and why they do it. People may be unwilling to respond to unknown interviewers or about things they consider private. Respondents may answer survey questions even when they don't know the answer just to appear smarter or more informed. Or they may try to help the interviewer by giving pleasing answers. Finally, busy people may not take the time, or they might resent the intrusion into their privacy.

EXPERIMENTAL RESEARCH Whereas observation is best suited for exploratory research and surveys for descriptive research, **experimental research** is best suited for gathering causal information. Experiments involve selecting matched groups of subjects, giving them different treatments, controlling unrelated factors, and checking for differences in group responses. Thus, experimental research tries to explain cause-and-effect relationships.

For example, before adding a new sandwich to its menu, McDonald's might use experiments to test the effects on sales of two different prices it might charge. It could introduce the new sandwich at one price in one city and at another price in another city. If the cities are similar, and if all other marketing efforts for the sandwich are the same, then differences in sales in the two cities could be related to the price charged.

Contact Methods Information can be collected by mail, telephone, personal interview, or online. Table 5.2 shows the strengths and weaknesses of each contact method.

MAIL, TELEPHONE, AND PERSONAL INTERVIEWING *Mail questionnaires* can be used to collect large amounts of information at a low cost per respondent. Respondents may give more honest answers to more personal questions on a mail questionnaire than to an

Survey research
Gathering primary data by asking people questions about their knowledge, attitudes, preferences, and buying behaviour.

Experimental research
Gathering primary data by selecting matched groups of subjects, giving them different treatments, controlling related factors, and checking for differences in group responses.

TABLE 5.2 Strengths and Weaknesses of Contact Methods

	Mail	Telephone	Personal	Online
Flexibility	Poor	Good	Excellent	Good
Quantity of data that can be collected	Good	Fair	Excellent	Good
Control of interviewer effects	Excellent	Fair	Poor	Fair
Control of sample	Fair	Excellent	Good	Excellent
Speed of data collection	Poor	Excellent	Good	Excellent
Response rate	Poor	Poor	Good	Good
Cost	Good	Fair	Poor	Excellent

Source: Based on Donald S. Tull and Del I. Hawkins, *Marketing Research: Measurement and Method*, 7th ed. (New York: Macmillan Publishing Company, 1993). Adapted with permission of the authors.

unknown interviewer in person or over the phone. Also, no interviewer is involved to bias respondents' answers.

However, mail questionnaires are not very flexible; all respondents answer the same questions in a fixed order. Mail surveys usually take longer to complete, and the response rate—the number of people returning completed questionnaires—is often very low. Finally, the researcher often has little control over the mail questionnaire sample. Even with a good mailing list, it's hard to control *who* at a particular address fills out the questionnaire. As a result of the shortcomings, more and more marketers are now shifting to faster, more flexible, and lower-cost email and online surveys.

Telephone interviewing is one of the best methods for gathering information quickly, and it provides greater flexibility than mail questionnaires. Interviewers can explain difficult questions and, depending on the answers they receive, skip some questions or probe on others. Response rates tend to be higher than with mail questionnaires, and interviewers can ask to speak to respondents with the desired characteristics or even by name.

However, with telephone interviewing, the cost per respondent is higher than with mail or online questionnaires. Also, people may not want to discuss personal questions with an interviewer. The method introduces interviewer bias—the way interviewers talk, how they ask questions, and other differences that may affect respondents' answers. Finally, in this age of do-not-call lists and promotion-harassed consumers, potential survey respondents are increasingly hanging up on telephone interviewers rather than talking with them.

Personal interviewing takes two forms: individual interviewing and group interviewing. *Individual interviewing* involves talking with people in their homes or offices, on the street, or in shopping malls. Such interviewing is flexible. Trained interviewers can guide interviews, explain difficult questions, and explore issues as the situation requires. They can show subjects actual products, advertisements, or packages and observe reactions and behaviour. However, individual personal interviews may cost three to four times as much as telephone interviews.

Group interviewing consists of inviting 6 to 10 people to meet with a trained moderator to talk about a product, service, or organization. Participants are normally paid a small sum for attending. A moderator encourages free and easy discussion, hoping that group interactions will bring out actual feelings and thoughts. At the same time, the moderator "focuses" the discussion—hence the name **focus group interviewing**.

In traditional focus groups, researchers and marketers watch the focus group discussions from behind a one-way mirror and record comments in writing or on video for later study. Focus group researchers often use videoconferencing and Internet technology to connect marketers in distant locations with live focus group action. Using cameras and two-way sound systems, marketing executives in a far-off boardroom can look in and listen, using remote controls to zoom in on faces and pan the focus group at will.

Along with observational research, focus group interviewing has become one of the major qualitative marketing research tools for gaining fresh insights into consumer thoughts and feelings. In focus group settings, researchers not only hear consumer ideas and opinions; they can also observe facial expressions, body movements, group interplay, and conversational flows. However, focus group studies present some challenges. They usually employ small samples to keep time and costs down, and it may be hard to generalize from the results. Moreover, consumers in focus groups are not always open and honest about their real feelings, behaviour, and intentions in front of other people.

To overcome these problems, many researchers are tinkering with the focus group design. Some companies use *immersion groups*—small groups of consumers who interact directly and informally with product designers without a focus group moderator present. Other researchers are changing the environments in which they conduct focus groups to

Focus group interviewing
Personal interviewing that involves inviting 6 to 10 people to gather for a few hours with a trained interviewer to talk about a product, service, or organization. The interviewer "focuses" the group discussion on important issues.

Exhibit 5.7 **New focus group environments:** Lexus USA general manager Mark Templin hosts "An Evening with Lexus" dinners with luxury car buyers to figure out why they did or didn't become Lexus owners.

help consumers relax and elicit more authentic responses. For example, Lexus hosted a series of "An Evening with Lexus" dinners with groups of customers in customers' homes:

> According to Lexus group vice-president and general manager Mark Templin, the best way to find out why luxury car buyers did or didn't become Lexus owners is to dine with them—up close and personal in their homes. At the first dinner, 16 owners of Lexus, Mercedes, BMW, Audi, Land Rover, and other high-end cars traded their perceptions of the Lexus brand over a sumptuous meal prepared by a famous chef at a home in Beverly Hills. Templin gained many actionable insights. For example, some owners viewed Lexus vehicles as unexciting. "Everyone had driven a Lexus at some point and had a great experience," he says. "But the Lexus they [had] wasn't as fun to drive as the car they have now. It's our challenge to show that Lexus is more fun to drive today than it was 15 years ago." Templin was also surprised to learn the extent to which the grown children of luxury car buyers influence what car they purchase. Now, Templin says, future Lexus marketing will also target young adults who may not buy luxury cars but who influence their parents' decisions.[17]

Individual and focus group interviews can add a personal touch as opposed to more numbers-oriented research. "We get lots of research, and it tells us what we need to run our business, but I get more out of talking one-on-one," confirms Lexus's Templin. "It really comes to life when I hear people say it."

ONLINE MARKETING RESEARCH The growth of the Internet has had a dramatic impact on how marketing research is conducted. Increasingly, researchers are collecting primary data through **online marketing research**: Internet surveys, online panels, experiments, and online focus groups and brand communities.

Online marketing research
Collecting primary data online through Internet surveys, online focus groups, Web-based experiments, or tracking consumers' online behaviour.

Online research can take many forms. A company can use the Internet as a survey medium: It can include a questionnaire on its Web or social media sites or use email to invite people to answer questions. It can create online panels that provide regular feedback or conduct live discussions or online focus groups. Researchers can also conduct online experiments. They can experiment with different prices, headlines, or product features on different Web or mobile sites or at different times to learn the relative effectiveness of their offers. They can set up virtual shopping environments and use them to test new products and marketing programs. Or a company can learn about the behaviour of online customers by following their click streams as they visit the site and move to other sites.

The Internet is especially well suited to *quantitative* research—for example, conducting marketing surveys and collecting data. Almost 95 percent of Canadians now use the Internet, making it a fertile channel for reaching a broad cross-section of consumers.[18] As response rates for traditional survey approaches decline and costs increase, the Internet is quickly replacing mail and the telephone as the dominant data collection methodology.

Internet-based survey research offers many advantages over traditional phone, mail, and personal interviewing approaches. The most obvious advantages are speed and low costs. By going online, researchers can quickly and easily distribute Internet surveys to thousands of respondents simultaneously via email or by posting them on selected sites. Responses can be almost instantaneous, and because respondents themselves enter the information, researchers can tabulate, review, and share research data as the information arrives.

Online research also usually costs much less than research conducted through mail, phone, or personal interviews. Using the Internet eliminates most of the postage, phone, interviewer, and data-handling costs associated with the other approaches. Moreover, sample size has little impact on costs. Once the questionnaire is set up, there's little difference in cost between 10 respondents and 10 000 respondents on the Internet.

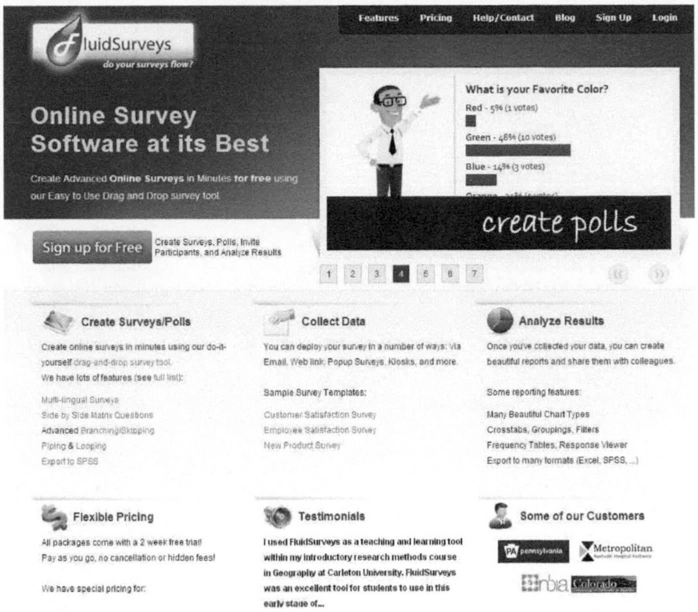

Its low cost puts online research well within the reach of almost any business, large or small. In fact, with the Internet, what was once the domain of research experts is now available to almost any would-be researcher. Even smaller, less sophisticated researchers can use online survey services such as Snap Surveys (www.snapsurveys.com) and SurveyMonkey (www.surveymonkey.com) to create, publish, and distribute their own custom online or mobile surveys in minutes.

Exhibit 5.8 Online research: Thanks to survey services such as FluidSurveys, almost any business, large or small, can create, publish, and distribute its own custom surveys in minutes.

courtesy FluidSurveys/SurveyMonkey

However, tighter privacy legislation in several provinces, implemented in response to the U.S. Patriot Act, now requires Canadian companies to store their customer data in Canada. As a result, Canadian-based survey tools, such as FluidSurveys (fluidsurveys.com), offer similar survey tools while storing consumer data on Canadian servers.

Internet-based surveys also tend to be more interactive and engaging, easier to complete, and less intrusive than traditional phone or mail surveys. As a result, they usually garner higher response rates. The Internet is an excellent medium for reaching the hard-to-reach consumer—for example, the often-elusive teen, single, affluent, and well-educated audiences. It's also good for reaching people who lead busy lives, from working mothers to on-the-go executives. Such people are well represented online, and they can respond in their own space and at their own convenience.

Just as marketing researchers have rushed to use the Internet for quantitative surveys and data collection, they are now also adopting *qualitative* Internet-based research approaches, such as online focus groups, blogs, and social networks. The Internet can provide a fast, low-cost way to gain qualitative customer insights.

A primary qualitative Internet-based research approach is **online focus groups**. For example, online research firm FocusVision offers its InterVu service, which harnesses the power of Web conferencing to conduct focus groups with participants at remote locations, anywhere in the world, at any time. Using their own Webcams, InterVu participants can log on to focus sessions from their homes or offices and see, hear, and react to each other in real-time, face-to-face discussions.[19] Such focus groups can be conducted in any language and viewed with simultaneous translation. They work well for bringing together people from different parts of the country or world at low cost. Researchers can view the sessions in real time from just about anywhere, eliminating travel, lodging, and facility costs. Finally, although online focus groups require some advance scheduling, results are almost immediate.

Online focus groups
Gathering a small group of people online with a trained moderator to chat about a product, service, or organization and gain qualitative insights about consumer attitudes and behaviour.

Although growing rapidly, both quantitative and qualitative Internet-based research have some drawbacks. One major problem is controlling who's in the online sample.

FocusVision Worldwide, Inc.

Exhibit 5.9 Online focus groups: FocusVision's InterVu service lets focus group participants at remote locations see, hear, and react to each other in real-time, face-to-face discussions.

Without seeing respondents, it's difficult to know who they really are. To overcome such sample and context problems, many online research firms use opt-in communities and respondent panels. Alternatively, many companies are now developing their own custom social networks and using them to gain customer inputs and insights. For example, in addition to picking customers' brains in face-to-face events such as "An Evening with Lexus" dinners in customers' homes, Lexus has built an extensive online research community called the Lexus Advisory Board, which consists of 20 000 invitation-only Lexus owners representing a wide range of demographics, psychographics, and model ownership. Lexus regularly surveys the group to obtain input on everything from perceptions of the brand to customer relationships with dealers.[20]

ONLINE BEHAVIOURAL AND SOCIAL TRACKING AND TARGETING In recent years, the Internet has become an important tool for conducting research and developing customer insights. But today's marketing researchers are going even further—well beyond structured online surveys, focus groups, and Internet communities. Increasingly, they are listening to and watching consumers by actively mining the rich veins of unsolicited, unstructured, "bottom-up" customer information already coursing around the Internet. Whereas traditional marketing research provides more logical consumer responses to structured and intrusive research questions, online listening provides the passion and spontaneity of unsolicited consumer opinions.

Tracking consumers online might be as simple as scanning customer reviews and comments on the company's brand site or on shopping sites such as Amazon.com or BestBuy.com. Or it might mean using sophisticated online-analysis tools to deeply analyze the mountains of consumer brand-related comments and messages found in blogs or on social media sites, such as Facebook, Yelp, YouTube, or Twitter. Listening to and engaging customers online can provide valuable insights into what consumers are saying or feeling about a brand. It can also provide opportunities for building positive brand experiences and relationships. Companies like Dell excel at listening online and responding quickly and appropriately. (See Marketing@Work 5.1.)

Information about what consumers do while trolling the vast expanse of the Internet—what searches they make, the sites they visit, what music and programming they consume, how they shop, and what they buy—is pure gold to marketers. And today's marketers are busy mining that gold. Then, in a practice called **behavioural targeting**, marketers use the online data to target ads and offers to specific consumers. For example, if you place a mobile phone in your Amazon.com shopping cart but don't buy it, you might expect to see some ads for that very type of phone the next time you visit your favourite ESPN site to catch up on the latest sports scores.

The newest wave of Web analytics and targeting takes online eavesdropping even further—from *behavioural* targeting to *social* targeting. Whereas behavioural targeting tracks consumer movements across sites, social targeting also mines individual social

Behavioural targeting
Using online consumer tracking data to target advertisements and marketing offers to specific consumers.

Dell Goes Social: Listening to and Engaging Customers Online

When it comes to listening, engaging, and responding to customers through online social media, Dell really gets it. The company has learned that good listening is an important part of building customer relationships. Similarly, not being a part of the social conversation can lead to serious missteps. It's not about controlling the online conversation; it's about making certain that the company knows what's being said about the brand and participates in the dialogue. Today, Dell has become a poster child for using social media to listen to and connect with customers.

But Dell learned its social media lessons through hard experience. It all started more than 10 years ago with a painful online incident—dubbed "Dell Hell"—that dramatically demonstrated the power of social media in giving voice to consumer opinions and concerns, often to a company's detriment. It began with a brief but scathing blog entry by well-known tech blogger Jeff Jarvis of BuzzMachine about the many failings of his Dell computer and his struggles with Dell's customer support. "I just got a new Dell laptop and paid a fortune for the four-year, in-home service," raged Jarvis. "The machine is a lemon and the service is a lie." After detailing his problems with the PC and the shortcomings of Dell's support, Jarvis signed off "DELL SUCKS. DELL LIES. Put that in your Google and smoke it, Dell."

In the old days, Jarvis's complaint, perhaps in the form of a letter to the editor in a local newspaper or a short commentary in an obscure technical journal, probably wouldn't have attracted much of an audience. But in today's superheated social media environment, Jarvis's blog post immediately went viral, becoming the third-most-linked-to post in the blogosphere the day it appeared. The ensuing online dialogue unleashed a firestorm of complaints from customers who shared Jarvis's displeasure with Dell. Jarvis's headline—Dell Hell—became shorthand for the ability of a lone consumer using digital and social media to deliver a body blow to an unsuspecting business.

The Dell Hell incident opened Dell's eyes to the importance of social media in shaping brand conversations and opinions. If consumers are talking about your brand online, you need to be there, too. Beyond monitoring social media to catch and deal with the rants of disgruntled consumers, Dell saw opportunities to use social media to proactively engage consumers, learn from them, and build positive brand experiences. Even before "Dell Hell," Michael Dell had seen social media as a perfect fit for a company with a deep heritage of working directly with customers. "Our customers have the best ideas and insights," says the company. So why not tap these insights and ideas as they fly around social media?

In the aftermath of Dell Hell, Dell began to build an organization that actively and systematically listens to and interacts with customers online. At the heart of the effort is Dell's Social Media Listening Command Center, a state-of-the-art social media hub focused on monitoring, engaging, and responding to all things Dell online. The command center aggregates and analyzes 25 000 English-language conversations about Dell (and thousands more in 10 other languages) every day, looking for opportunities to reinforce the Dell brand. The Command Center isn't interested only in customer service or marketing matters. It sorts through oceans of online interactions that are important to all areas of Dell's business—from customer complaints, compliments, and support requests to product feedback and intelligence on an array of technology topics.

But as well as just listening in on and responding to social media conversations, Dell has created its own social media empire for engaging customers and other stakeholders. For example, the company now sponsors nine blogs, such as Direct2Dell.com, designed to provide "a direct exchange with Dell customers about the technology that connects us all." Dell's IdeaStorm site provides a forum where everyone from information technology professionals to regular folks can evaluate Dell's products and services and offer suggestions on how to improve them. Dell maintains an active presence on major public social media, ranging from Facebook, Twitter, LinkedIn, Google+, YouTube, Flickr, and Pinterest to Brazil's Orkut, Germany's Xing, and China's Renren and YouKu social communities. Dell's participation in such social media goes well beyond the typical brand pages. All of Dell's social media efforts are designed to create and monitor consumer exchanges, gather feedback, provide customer service and support, and build customer relationships. Dell urges consumers to "get connected to Dell and let your voice be heard."

Dell's online listening and response culture pervades every aspect of its operations. At the top, Dell created the position of Listening Czar, an executive charged with making certain that social media are woven into the very fabric the organization. It established a Social Outreach Services group, comprising scores of dedicated social media

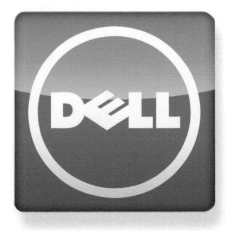

© PSL Images/Alamy

Exhibit 5.10 When it comes to listening, engaging, and responding to customers through online social media, Dell really gets it.

support people who form a frontline response team that is ready to pounce on any hot topic or customer need, turning online rants into raves. Dell even has a social media governance team that helps promote a company-wide social media mindset. And in an effort to turn every employee into an online brand advocate, Dell set up a social media certification program that trains employees on how to get social in their jobs, technical support, and customer care. More than 7500 Dell employees worldwide have become Dell Certified Social Media and Community Professionals.

Finally, to engage online influencers in an offline, in-person way, Dell now holds annual Consumer Advisory Panel (CAP) Days. During the two-day events, Dell invites 30 people active in social media to its headquarters to interact with Dell executives and discuss firsthand their thoughts about Dell's brand, products, website, and customer service. Dell teams take the feedback seriously—they know that the success of CAP Days depends on what happens after the customer advisers leave.

Thus, Dell has come a long way from its Dell Hell days. It now uses the social media skilfully to listen to, learn from, and engage its customers. Dell has become so good at social listening that it has formed a social media services group that helps clients such as Caterpillar, Aetna, Kraft Foods, the American Red Cross, and others to develop their own social media strategies. Dell understands that conversations in social media can shape customer attitudes and experiences as powerfully as a big-budget advertising campaign or a high-powered customer service or sales force. "Social media is far more than a tool," agrees Karen Quintos, Dell's chief marketing officer. "It's an extension of our brand. If your [customers] are in the social space, they are talking about your brand—so either engage and be part of the conversation or be left behind."

Sources: Based on information from Jennifer Rooney, "In Dell Social-Media Journey, Lessons for Marketers about the Power of Listening," *Forbes,* September 25, 2012, www.forbes.com/sites/jenniferrooney/2012/09/25/in-dell-social-media-journey-lessons-for-marketers-about-the-power-of-listening/2; Jason Falls, "Why Dell Is Still a Great Case Study," *Social Media Explorer,* December 13, 2011, www.socialmediaexplorer.com/social-media-marketing/why-dell-is-a-great-case-study; Jeff Jarvis, "Dell Lies. Dell Sucks," *BuzzMachine,* June 21, 2005, http://buzzmachine.com/2005/06/21/dell-lies-dell-sucks; "Dell Launches New Unit to Provide Social-Media Strategy to Brands," *Advertising Age,* December 4, 2012, http://adage.com/print/238594; "Dell Social Media," www.slideshare.net/dellsocialmedia, accessed March 2013; and http://content.dell.com/us/en/corp/about-dell-social-media.aspx and http://en.community.dell.com/dell-blogs/direct2dell/b/direct2dell/default.aspx, accessed October 2013.

connections and conversations from social networking sites. Research shows that consumers shop a lot like their friends and are much more likely to respond to ads from brands friends use. So, instead of just having a Sportchek.ca ad for running shoes pop up because you've recently searched online for running shoes (behavioural targeting), an ad for a specific pair of running shoes pops up because a friend you're connected to via Twitter just bought those shoes from Sportchek.ca last week (social targeting).

Online listening, behavioural targeting, and social targeting can help marketers harness the massive amounts of consumer information swirling around the Internet. However, as marketers get more adept at trolling blogs, social networks, and other Internet domains, many critics worry about consumer privacy. At what point does sophisticated online research cross the line into consumer stalking? Proponents claim that behavioural and social targeting benefit more than abuse consumers by feeding back ads and products that are more relevant to their interests. But to many consumers and public advocates, following consumers online and stalking them with ads feels more than just a little creepy. Regulators and others are stepping in. The U.S. Federal Trade Commission (FTC) has recommended the creation of a "Do Not Track" system (the Internet equivalent of the "Do Not Call" registry), which would let people opt out of having their actions monitored online. Meanwhile, the major Internet browsers have heeded the concerns by adding "Do Not Track" features.[21]

Sample

A segment of the population selected for marketing research to represent the population as a whole.

Andresr/Shutterstock

Exhibit 5.11 Behavioural targeting: Marketers watch what consumers say and do online, then use the resulting insights to personalize online shopping experiences. Is it sophisticated Web research or "more than just a little creepy"?

Sampling Plan Marketing researchers usually draw conclusions about large groups of consumers by studying a small sample of the total consumer population. A **sample** is a segment of the population selected for marketing research to represent the population as a whole. Ideally, the sample should be representative so that the researcher can make accurate estimates of the thoughts and behaviours of the larger population.

TABLE 5.3 Types of Samples

Probability Sample

Simple random sample	Every member of the population has a known and equal chance of selection.
Stratified random sample	The population is divided into mutually exclusive groups (such as age groups), and random samples are drawn from each group.
Cluster (area) sample	The population is divided into mutually exclusive groups (such as blocks), and the researcher draws a sample of the groups to interview.

Nonprobability Sample

Convenience sample	The researcher selects the easiest population members from whom to obtain information.
Judgment sample	The researcher uses his or her judgment to select population members who are good prospects for accurate information.
Quota sample	The researcher finds and interviews a prescribed number of people in each of several categories.

Designing the sample requires three decisions. First, *who* is to be studied (what *sampling unit*)? The answer to this question is not always obvious. For example, to learn about the decision-making process for a family automobile purchase, should the subject be the husband, the wife, other family members, dealership salespeople, or all of these? Second, *how many* people should be included (what *sample size*)? Large samples give more reliable results than small samples. However, larger samples usually cost more, and it is not necessary to sample the entire target market or even a large portion to get reliable results.

Finally, *how* should the people in the sample be chosen (what *sampling procedure*)? Table 5.3 describes different kinds of samples. Using *probability samples*, each population member has a known chance of being included in the sample, and researchers can calculate confidence limits for sampling error. But when probability sampling costs too much or takes too much time, marketing researchers often take *nonprobability samples*, even though their sampling error cannot be measured. These varied ways of drawing samples have different costs and time limitations as well as different accuracy and statistical properties. Which method is best depends on the needs of the research project.

Research Instruments In collecting primary data, marketing researchers have a choice of two main research instruments: *questionnaires* and *mechanical instruments*.

QUESTIONNAIRES The questionnaire is by far the most common instrument, whether administered in person, by phone, by email, or online. Questionnaires are very flexible—there are many ways to ask questions. Closed-ended questions include all the possible answers, and subjects make choices among them. Examples include multiple-choice questions and scale questions. Open-ended questions allow respondents to answer in their own words. In a survey of airline users, WestJet might simply ask, "What is your opinion of WestJet Airlines?" Or it might ask people to complete a sentence: "When I choose an airline, the most important consideration is . . ." These and other kinds of open-ended questions often reveal more than closed-ended questions because they do not limit respondents' answers.

Open-ended questions are especially useful in exploratory research, when the researcher is trying to find out *what* people think but is not measuring *how many* people

Exhibit 5.12 Time Warner's MediaLab uses high-tech observation to capture the changing ways that today's viewers are using and reacting to television and Web content.

think in a certain way. Closed-ended questions, on the other hand, provide answers that are easier to interpret and tabulate.

Researchers should also use care in the *wording* and *ordering* of questions. They should use simple, direct, and unbiased wording. Questions should be arranged in a logical order. The first question should create interest if possible, and difficult or personal questions should be asked last so that respondents do not become defensive.

MECHANICAL INSTRUMENTS Although questionnaires are the most common research instrument, researchers also use mechanical instruments to monitor consumer behaviour. Nielsen Media Research attaches people meters to television sets, cable boxes, and satellite systems in selected homes to record who watches which programs. Retailers likewise use checkout scanners to record shoppers' purchases. Other mechanical devices measure subjects' physical responses to marketing offerings. Consider this example:

> Time Warner's MediaLab at its New York headquarters looks more like a chic consumer electronics store than a research lab. But the lab employs a nifty collection of high-tech observation techniques to capture the changing ways that today's viewers are using and reacting to television and Web content. The MediaLab uses biometric measures to analyze every show subjects watch, every site they visit, and every commercial they skip. Meanwhile, mechanical devices assess viewer engagement via physiological measures of skin temperature, heart rate, sweat level, leaning in, and facial and eye movements. Observers behind two-way mirrors or using cameras that peer over each subject's shoulder make real-time assessments of Web browsing behaviour. In all, the deep consumer insights gained from MediaLab observations are helping Time Warner prepare for marketing in today's rapidly changing digital media landscape.[22]

Still other researchers are applying *neuromarketing*, measuring brain activity to learn how consumers feel and respond. Marketing scientists using MRI scans and EEG devices have learned that tracking brain electrical activity and blood flow can provide companies with insights into what turns consumers on and off regarding their brands and marketing. "Companies have always aimed for the customer's heart, but the head may make a better target," suggests one neuromarketer. "Neuromarketing is reaching consumers where the action is: the brain."[23]

Companies ranging from PepsiCo and Disney to Google and Microsoft now hire neuromarketing research companies such as Sands Research, NeuroFocus, and EmSense to help figure out what people are really thinking. For example, PepsiCo's Frito-Lay worked with Nielsen's NeuroFocus to assess consumer motivations underlying the success of its Cheetos snack brand. After scanning the brains of carefully chosen consumers, NeuroFocus learned that part of what makes Cheetos a junk-food staple is the messy orange cheese dust—that's right, the neon stuff that gloms onto your fingers and then smears on your shirt or the couch cushions. As it turns out, the icky coating triggers a powerful brain response: a sense of "giddy subversion" that makes the messiness more than worth the trouble it causes. Using this finding, Frito-Lay successfully framed an entire advertising campaign around the mess Cheetos make. For its part, NeuroFocus won an award for outstanding advertising research.[24]

Although neuromarketing techniques can measure consumer involvement and emotional responses second by second, such brain responses can be difficult to interpret. Thus, neuromarketing is usually used in combination with other research approaches to gain a more complete picture of what goes on inside consumers' heads.

Implementing the Research Plan

The researcher next puts the marketing research plan into action. This involves collecting, processing, and analyzing the information. Data collection can be carried out by the company's marketing research staff or outside firms. Researchers should watch closely to make sure that the plan is implemented correctly. They must guard against problems of interacting with respondents, with the quality of participants' responses, and with interviewers who make mistakes or take shortcuts.

Researchers must also process and analyze the collected data to isolate important information and insight. They need to check data for accuracy and completeness and code it for analysis. The researchers then tabulate the results and compute statistical measures.

Interpreting and Reporting the Findings

The market researcher must now interpret the findings, draw conclusions, and report them to management. The researcher should not try to overwhelm managers with numbers and fancy statistical techniques. Rather, the researcher should present important findings and insights that are useful in the major decisions faced by management.

However, interpretation should not be left only to researchers. Although they are often experts in research design and statistics, the marketing manager knows more about the problem and the decisions that must be made. The best research means little if the manager blindly accepts faulty interpretations from the researcher. Similarly, managers may be biased. They might tend to accept research results that show what they expected and reject those that they did not expect or hope for. In many cases, findings can be interpreted in different ways, and discussions between researchers and managers will help point to the best interpretations. Thus, managers and researchers must work together closely when interpreting research results, and both must share responsibility for the research process and resulting decisions.

Analyzing and Using Marketing Information LO4

Information gathered in internal databases and through competitive marketing intelligence and marketing research usually requires additional analysis. Managers may need help applying the information to gain customer and market insights that will improve their marketing decisions. This help may include advanced statistical analysis to learn more about the relationships within a set of data. Information analysis might also involve the application of analytical models that will help marketers make better decisions.

Once the information has been processed and analyzed, it must be made available to the right decision makers at the right time. In the following sections, we look deeper into analyzing and using marketing information.

Customer Relationship Management

The question of how best to analyze and use individual customer data presents special problems. Most companies are awash in information about their customers. In fact, smart companies capture information at every possible customer *touch point*. These touch points include customer purchases, sales force contacts, service and support calls, online site visits, satisfaction surveys, credit and payment interactions, market research studies—every contact between a customer and a company.

Unfortunately, this information is usually scattered widely across the organization. It is buried deep in the separate databases and records of different company departments. To overcome such problems, many companies are now turning to **customer relationship management (CRM)** to manage detailed information about individual customers and carefully manage customer touch points to maximize customer loyalty.

Customer relationship management (CRM)
Managing detailed information about individual customers and carefully managing customer touch points to maximize customer loyalty.

CRM consists of sophisticated software and analytical tools from companies such as Salesforce.com, Oracle, Microsoft, and SAS that integrate customer information from all sources, analyze it in depth, and apply the results to build stronger customer relationships. CRM integrates everything that a company's sales, service, and marketing teams know about individual customers, providing a 360-degree view of the customer relationship.

CRM analysts develop *data warehouses* and use sophisticated *data mining* techniques to unearth the riches hidden in customer data. A data warehouse is a company-wide electronic database of finely detailed customer information. Its purpose is not only to gather information but also to pull it together into a central, accessible location. Then, once the data warehouse brings the data together, the company uses high-powered data mining techniques to sift through the mounds of data and dig out interesting findings about customers.

These findings often lead to marketing opportunities. Sobeys, for example, uses CRM to provide its customers with coupons relevant to their individual needs:

> Sobeys, the second largest grocery chain in Canada, operates over 1500 stores in 10 provinces under different banners, including IGA, Thrifty Foods, Foodland and FreshCo. The company has invested heavily in CRM by leveraging the data from its various loyalty programs, which include Air Miles in Atlantic Canada and Quebec, Club Sobeys in Ontario and the West, and Club Thrifty Foods in British Columbia. Toronto-based Exchange Solutions, the company's CRM provider, developed an offer-targeting capability for Sobeys to ensure that consumers receive coupons they'll actually want to use. By using data from their loyalty program database, Sobeys developed six segmentation models that group consumers by a number of factors, such as how often they shop, how price conscious they are, and their lifestyles. When coupon offers are entered into the system, Sobeys' offer-matching engine uses additional logic (for instance, whether you've bought the product or a similar one before) to determine the best recipients. The system ensures that you won't receive a diaper coupon if you don't have a baby, and won't tempt you to buy a name brand if you're already buying the private-label equivalent. The Club Sobeys quarterly statement is sent to over 2 million members, containing 1.4 million unique combinations of offers. CMO Belinda Youngs says that this system results in coupon redemptions that are well above the industry average.[25]

Exhibit 5.13 Sobeys digs deeply into data obtained from its various loyalty programs, such as Club Sobeys.

© Kathy deWitt/Alamy

By using CRM to understand customers better, companies can provide higher levels of customer service and develop deeper customer relationships. They can use CRM to pinpoint high-value customers, target them more effectively, cross-sell the company's products, and create offers tailored to specific customer requirements. For example, Caesars Entertainment, the world's largest casino operator, maintains a vast customer database and uses its CRM system to manage day-to-day relationships with important customers at its 52 casino properties around the world (see Marketing@Work 5.2).

MARKETING@WORK 5.2

Netflix Streams Success with Big Data and CRM

North Americans now watch more movies and TV programs streamed via the Internet than they watch on DVDs and Blu-ray disks. And with its library of more than 60 000 titles, Netflix streams more movie and program content by far than any other video service. Netflix's 48 million paid subscribers watch more than 1.4 billion hours of movies and TV programs every month. During peak hours on any given day, a remarkable one-third of all downloads on the Internet are devoted to streamed programming from Netflix.

All of this comes as little surprise to avid Netflixers. But members might be startled to learn that while they're busy watching Netflix videos, Netflix is busy watching them—watching them very, very closely. Netflix tracks and analyzes heaps of customer data in excruciating detail. Then it uses the big-data insights to give customers exactly what they want. Netflix knows in depth what its audience wants to watch, and it uses this knowledge to fuel recommendations to subscribers, decide what programming to offer, and even develop its own exclusive content.

No company knows its customers better than Netflix. The company has mind-boggling access to real-time data on member viewing behaviour and sentiments. Every day, Netflix tracks and parses member data on 3 million searches, 4 million ratings, and 30 million "plays." Netflix's bulging database contains every viewing detail for each and every individual subscriber—what shows they watch, at what time of day, on what devices, at what locations, and even when they hit the pause, rewind, or fast-forward buttons during programs.

Netflix supplements this already massive database with consumer information purchased from Nielsen, Facebook, Twitter, and other sources. Finally, the company employs experts to classify each video based on hundreds of characteristics, such as talent, action, tone, genre, colour, volume, scenery, and many, many others. Using this rich data-base, Netflix builds detailed subscriber profiles based on individual viewing habits and preferences. It then uses these profiles to personalize each customer's viewing experience. According to Netflix, there are 40 million different versions of Netflix, one for each individual subscriber worldwide.

For example, Netflix uses data on viewing history to make personalized recommendations. Wading through 60 000 titles to decide what to watch can be overwhelming. So when new customers sign up, Netflix asks them to rate their interest in movie and TV genres and to rate specific titles they've already seen. It then cross-references what people like with other similar titles to predict additional movies or programs customers will enjoy.

But that's just the beginning. As customers watch and rate more and more video content, and as Netflix studies the details of their viewing behaviour, the predictions become more and more accurate. Netflix often comes to know individual customer viewing preferences better than customers themselves do. How accurate are Netflix's recommendations? Seventy-five percent of viewing activity results from these suggestions. That's important. The more subscribers watch, the more likely they are to stay with Netflix—viewers who watch at least 15 hours of content each month are 75 percent less likely to cancel. Accurate recommendations increase average viewing time, keeping subscribers in the fold.

Increased viewing also depends on offering the right content in the first place. But adding new programming is expensive—content licensing fees constitute the lion's share of Netflix's cost of goods sold. With so many new and existing movies and TV programs on the market, Netflix must be very selective in what it

© OJO Images Ltd/Alamy (photo)

© PSL Images/Alamy (logo)

Exhibit 5.14 Netflix, big data, and CRM: While members are busy watching Netflix videos, Netflix is busy watching *them*—watching them very, very closely. Then it uses the big-data insights to give customers exactly what they want.

adds to its content inventory. Once again, it's big data to the rescue. Just as Netflix analyzes its database to come up with subscriber recommendations, it uses the data to assess what additional titles customers might enjoy and how much each is worth. The goal is to maximize subscriber "happiness-per-dollar-spent" on new titles. "We always use our in-depth knowledge about what our members love to watch to decide what's available on Netflix," says a Netflix marketer. "If you keep watching, we'll keep adding more of what you love."

To get even more viewers watching even more hours, Netflix is now using its extensive big-data insights to add its own exclusive video content—things you can see only on Netflix. In its own words, Netflix wants "to become HBO faster than HBO can become Netflix." For example, Netflix stunned the media industry when it outbid both HBO and AMC by paying US$100 million for exclusive rights to air the first two seasons of *House of Cards*, the U.S. version of the hit British political drama produced by Hollywood bigwigs David Fincher and Kevin Spacey.

To outsiders, the huge investment in *House of Cards* seemed highly risky. However, using its powerful database, Netflix was able to predict accurately which and how many existing members would watch the new *House of Cards* regularly, and how many new members would sign up because of the show.

Netflix also used its viewer knowledge to pinpoint and personalize promotion of the exclusive new series. Rather than spending millions of dollars to promote the show broadly, Netflix tailored pitches to just the right members using viewer profiles and the recommendation feature. Before *House of Cards* premiered, selected subscribers (based on their profiles) saw 1 of 10 different trailers of the show aimed at their specific likes and interests.

Thanks to Netflix's big data and its CRM prowess, *House of Cards* was a smash hit. It brought in 3 million new subscribers in only the first three months. These new subscribers alone covered almost all of the US$100 million investment. More important, a Netflix survey revealed that for the average *House of Cards* viewer, 86 percent were less likely to cancel because of the new program. Such success came as no surprise to Netflix. Its data had predicted that the program would be a hit before the director ever shouted "action."

Based on its success with *House of Cards*, Netflix developed a number of other original series, including *Hemlock Grove*, *Arrested Development*, and *Orange Is the New Black*, its most successful release to date. For traditional broadcast networks, the average success rate for new television shows is 35 percent. In contrast, Netflix is batting almost 70 percent. To continue the momentum, the company

has committed US$300 million a year to developing new original content. It plans to add at least five original titles annually, including drama series, comedy specials, movies, and documentaries.

As more and more high-quality video streams out of Netflix, more success streams in. Netflix's sales spurted 60 percent in 2012–2013. In 2013 alone, membership grew by 25 percent, and Netflix's stock price quadrupled. Netflix thrives on using big data and CRM to know and serve its customers. The company excels at helping customers figure out just what they want to watch and to offer just the right content profitably. Says Netflix's chief communications officer, "Because we have a direct relationship with consumers, we know what people like to watch, and that helps us [immeasurably]."

Sources: David Carr, "Giving Viewers What They Want," *New York Times*, February 25, 2013, p. B1; Zach Bulygo, "How Netflix Uses Analytics to Select Movies, Create Content, and Make Multimillion Dollar Decisions," *Kissmetrics*, September 6, 2013, blog.kissmetrics.com/how-netflix-uses-analytics; Rip Empson, "Netflix Tops HBO in Paid U.S. Subscribers as Members Stream 5 Billion Hours of Content in Q3," *Tech Crunch*, October 21, 2013, http://techcrunch.com/2013/10/21/netflix-tops-hbo-in-paid-u-s-subscribers-as-members-stream-5-billion-hoursof-content-in-q3; Mark Rogowsky, "Hulu's Billion-Dollar Milestone: A Sign of Just How Far Behind Netflix It Has Fallen," *Forbes*, December 19, 2013, www.forbes.com/sites/markrogowsky/2013/12/19/hulus-billion-dollar-milestone-a-sign-of-just-how-far-behind-netflix-it-has-fallen; Mike Snider, "Netflix, Adding Customers and Profits, Will Raise Prices," *USA Today*, April 22, 2014, www.usatoday.com/story/tech/2014/04/21/netflix-results/7965613; and www.netflix.com, accessed July 2014.

CRM benefits don't come without costs or risk, either in collecting the original customer data or in maintaining and mining it. The most common CRM mistake is to view CRM as a technology and software process only. Yet technology alone cannot build profitable customer relationships. Companies can't improve customer relationships by simply installing some new software. Instead, marketers should start with the fundamentals of managing customer relationships and *then* employ high-tech solutions. They should focus first on the R—it's the *relationship* that CRM is all about.

Distributing and Using Marketing Information

Marketing information has no value until it is used to gain customer insights and make better marketing decisions. Thus, the marketing information system must make the information readily available to managers and others who need it, when they need it. In some cases, this means providing managers with regular performance reports, intelligence updates, and reports on the results of research studies.

But marketing managers may also need nonroutine information for special situations and on-the-spot decisions. For example, a sales manager having trouble with a large customer may want a summary of the account's sales and profitability over the past year. Or a brand manager may want to get a sense of the amount of social media buzz surrounding the launch of a recent advertising campaign. These days, therefore, information distribution involves making information available in a timely, user-friendly way.

Many firms use internal CRM systems to facilitate this process. These systems provide ready access to research and intelligence information, customer contact information, reports, shared work documents, and more. For example, the CRM system at phone and online gift retailer 1-800-Flowers.com gives customer-facing employees real-time access to customer information. When a repeat customer calls, the system immediately pulls up data on previous transactions and other contacts, helping reps make the customer's experience easier and more relevant. For instance, if a customer usually buys tulips for his wife, the rep can talk about the best tulip selections and related gifts. Such connections result in greater customer satisfaction and loyalty and greater sales for the company. "We can do it in real time," says a 1-800-Flowers.com executive, "and it enhances the customer experience."[26]

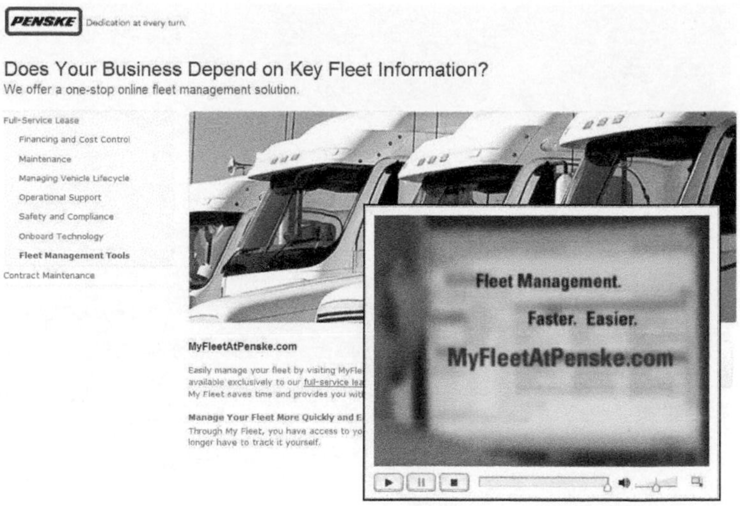

In addition, companies are increasingly allowing key customers and value-network members to access account, product, and other data on demand. Suppliers, customers, resellers, and select other network members may access information to update their accounts, arrange purchases, and check orders against inventories to improve customer service. For example, Penske Truck Leasing's site, MyFleetAtPenske.com, lets Penske business customers access all the data about their fleets in one spot and provides an array of tools and applications designed to help fleet managers manage their Penske accounts and maximize efficiency.[27]

Today's marketing managers can gain direct access to a company's information system at any time and from virtually anywhere. They can tap into the system from a home office, hotel room, or the local Starbucks—anyplace they can connect on a laptop, tablet, or smartphone. Such systems allow managers to get the information they need directly and quickly and tailor it to their own needs.

Penske Truck Leasing

Exhibit 5.15 Penske Truck Leasing's site, MyFleetAtPenske.com, lets Penske customers access all the data about their fleets in one spot and provides tools to help fleet managers manage their Penske accounts and maximize efficiency.

Other Marketing Information Considerations LO5

This section discusses marketing information in two special contexts: marketing research in small businesses and nonprofit organizations and international marketing research. Then, we look at public policy and ethics issues in marketing research.

Marketing Research in Small Businesses and Nonprofit Organizations

Just like larger firms, small organizations need market information and the customer insights it can provide. Managers of small businesses and not-for-profit organizations often think that marketing research can be done only by experts in large companies with big research budgets. True, large-scale research studies are beyond the budgets of most small organizations. However, many of the marketing research techniques discussed in this chapter can also be used by smaller organizations in a less formal manner and at little or no expense. Consider how one small-business owner conducted market research on a shoestring before even opening his doors:

After a string of bad experiences with his local dry cleaner, Robert Byerley decided to open his own dry-cleaning business. But before jumping in, he conducted plenty of market research. He

Bibbentuckers

Exhibit 5.16 Before opening Bibbentuckers dry cleaner, owner Robert Byerly conducted research to gain insights into what customers wanted. First on the list: quality.

needed a key customer insight: How would he make his business stand out from the others? To start, Byerley spent an entire week in the library and online, researching the dry-cleaning industry. To get input from potential customers, using a marketing firm, Byerley held focus groups on the store's name, look, and brochure. He also took clothes to the 15 best competing cleaners in town and had focus group members critique their work. Based on his research, he made a list of features for his new business. First on his list: quality. His business would stand behind everything it did. Not on the list: cheap prices. Creating the perfect dry-cleaning establishment simply didn't fit with a discount operation.

With his research complete, Byerley opened Bibbentuckers, a high-end dry cleaner positioned on high-quality service and convenience. It featured a bank-like drive-through area with curbside delivery. A computerized bar code system read customer cleaning preferences and tracked clothes all the way through the cleaning process. Byerley added other differentiators, such as decorative awnings, TV screens, and refreshments (even "candy for the kids and a doggy treat for your best friend"). "I wanted a place . . . that paired five-star service and quality with an establishment that didn't look like a dry cleaner," he says. The market research yielded results. Today, Bibbentuckers is a thriving eight-store operation.[28]

Thus, small businesses and not-for-profit organizations can obtain good marketing insights through observation or informal surveys using small convenience samples. Also, many associations, local media, and government agencies provide special help to small organizations. For example, the Conference Board of Canada and the Canadian Council for Small Business and Entrepreneurship offer dozens of free publications that give advice on topics ranging from preparing a business plan to ordering business signs. Other excellent Web resources for small businesses include Statistics Canada (www.statscan.gc.ca) and Industry Canada (www.ic.gc.ca). Finally, small businesses can collect a considerable amount of information at very little cost online. They can scour competitor and customer websites and use Internet search engines to research specific companies and issues.

In summary, secondary data collection, observation, surveys, and experiments can all be used effectively by small organizations with small budgets. However, although these informal research methods are less complex and less costly, they must still be conducted with care. Managers must think carefully about the objectives of the research, formulate questions in advance, recognize the biases introduced by smaller samples and less skilled researchers, and conduct the research systematically.[29]

International Marketing Research

International marketing research has grown tremendously over the past decade. International researchers follow the same steps as domestic researchers, from defining the research problem and developing a research plan to interpreting and reporting the results. However, these researchers often face more and different problems. Whereas domestic researchers deal with fairly homogeneous markets within a single country, international researchers deal with diverse markets in many different countries. These markets often vary greatly in their levels of economic development, cultures and customs, and buying patterns.

In many foreign markets, the international researcher may have a difficult time finding good secondary data. Whereas Canadian and U.S. marketing researchers can obtain reliable secondary data from dozens of domestic research services, many countries have almost no research services at all. Some of the largest international research services operate in many countries. For example, The Nielsen Company (the world's largest marketing research company) has offices in more than 100 countries, from Schaumburg, Illinois, to Hong Kong to Nicosia, Cyprus. However, most research firms operate in only a relative handful of countries.[30] Thus, even when secondary information is available, it must usually be obtained from many different sources on a country-by-country basis, making the information difficult to combine or compare.

Because of the scarcity of good secondary data, international researchers must often collect their own primary data. And yet obtaining primary data may be no easy task. For example, it can be difficult simply to develop good samples. Canadian researchers can use current telephone directories, email lists, census tract data, and any of several sources of socioeconomic data to construct samples. However, such information is largely lacking in many countries.

Once the sample is drawn, the researcher can usually reach most respondents easily by telephone, by mail, online, or in person. However, reaching respondents is often not so easy in other parts of the world. Researchers in Mexico cannot rely on telephone, Internet, and mail data collection—most data collection is conducted door to door and concentrated in three or four of the largest cities. In some countries, few people have computers, let alone Internet access. For example, whereas there are 94 Internet users per 100 people in Canada, there are only 49 Internet users per 100 people in Mexico. In Ethiopia, the number drops to fewer than 2 Internet users per 100 people. Moreover, in some countries, the postal system is notoriously unreliable. In Brazil, for instance, an estimated 30 percent of the mail is never delivered; in Russia, mail delivery can take several weeks. And in many developing countries, poor roads and transportation systems make certain areas hard to reach, making personal interviews difficult and expensive.[31]

Cultural differences from country to country cause additional problems for international researchers. Language is the most obvious obstacle. For example, questionnaires must be prepared in one language and then translated into the languages of each country researched. Responses must then be translated back into the original language for analysis and interpretation. This adds to research costs and increases the risk of error. Even within a given country, language can be a problem. For example, in India, English is the language of business, but consumers may use any of 14 "first languages," with many additional dialects.

Translating a questionnaire from one language to another is anything but easy. Many idioms, phrases, and statements mean different things in different cultures. For example, a Danish executive noted, "Check this out by having a different translator put back into English what you've translated from English. You'll get the shock of your life. I remember [an example in which] 'out of sight, out of mind' had become 'invisible things are insane.'"[32]

Consumers in different countries also vary in their attitudes toward marketing research. People in one country may be very willing to respond; in other countries, nonresponse can be a major problem. Customs in some countries may prohibit people from talking with strangers. In certain cultures, research questions are often considered too personal. For example, in many Muslim countries, mixed-gender focus groups are taboo, as is videotaping female-only focus groups. And even when respondents are *willing* to respond, they may not be *able* to because of high functional-illiteracy rates.

Exhibit 5.17 Some of the most successful research services firms have large international departments. Nielsen has offices in more than 100 countries.

Despite these problems, as global marketing grows, global companies have little choice but to conduct these types of international marketing research. Although the costs and problems associated with international research may be high, the costs of not doing it—in terms of missed opportunities and mistakes—might be even higher. Once recognized, many of the problems associated with international marketing research can be overcome or avoided.

Public Policy and Ethics in Marketing Research

Most marketing research benefits both the sponsoring company and its consumers. Through marketing research, companies gain insights into consumers' needs, resulting in more satisfying products and services and stronger customer relationships. However, the misuse of marketing research can also harm or annoy consumers. Two major public policy and ethics issues in marketing research are intrusions on consumer privacy and the misuse of research findings.

Intrusions on Consumer Privacy Many consumers feel positive about marketing research and believe that it serves a useful purpose. Some actually enjoy being interviewed and giving their opinions. However, others strongly resent or even mistrust marketing research. They don't like being interrupted by researchers. They worry that marketers are building huge databases full of personal information about customers. Or they fear that researchers might use sophisticated techniques to probe our deepest feelings, peek over our shoulders as we shop, or track us as we browse and interact on the Internet and then use this knowledge to manipulate our buying.

There are no easy answers when it comes to marketing research and privacy. For example, is it a good or bad thing that marketers track and analyze consumers' online clicks and target ads to individuals based on their browsing and social networking behaviour? Should we worry when marketers track consumer locations via their mobile phones to issue location-based ads and offers? Should we care that some retailers use mannequins with cameras hidden in one eye to record customer demographics and shopping behaviour? Similarly, should we applaud or resent companies that monitor consumer discussions on YouTube, Facebook, Twitter, or other social media in an effort to be more responsive?[33]

For example, Dunkin' Donuts regularly eavesdrops on consumer online conversations as an important input to its customer relationship–building efforts. Take the case of customer Jeff Lerner, who recently tweeted about a loose lid that popped off his Dunkin' Donuts drive-through coffee and soaked his white shirt and new car. Within minutes, Dunkin' picked up Lerner's tweet, sent him a direct message asking for his phone number, called him to apologize, and sent him a $10 gift card. Lerner found Dunkin's actions laudable. "*This* is social media. This is listening. This is engagement," he stated in a later blog post. However, some disconcerted consumers might see Dunkin's Twitter monitoring as an invasion of their privacy.[34]

Increasing consumer privacy concerns have become a major problem for the marketing research industry. Companies face the challenge of unearthing valuable but potentially sensitive consumer data while also maintaining consumer trust. At the same time, consumers wrestle with the trade-offs between personalization and privacy. "The debate over online [privacy] stems from a marketing paradox," says a privacy expert. "Internet shoppers want to receive personalized, timely offers based on their wants and needs but they resent that companies track their online purchase and browsing histories."[35] The key question: When does a company cross the line in gathering and using customer data? One study shows that nearly half of adults worry that they have little or no control over the personal information that companies gather about them online.[36]

Failure to address privacy issues could result in angry, less cooperative consumers and increased government intervention. As a result, the marketing research industry is considering several options for responding to intrusion and privacy issues. One example is the Marketing Research Association's "Your Opinion Counts" and "Respondent Bill of Rights" initiatives to educate consumers about the benefits of marketing research and distinguish it from telephone selling and database building. The industry has also considered adopting broad standards, perhaps based on the International Chamber of Commerce's International Code of Marketing and Social Research Practice. This code outlines researchers' responsibilities to respondents and the general public. For example, it urges that researchers make their names and addresses available to participants and be open about the data they are collecting.[37]

Most major companies—including Facebook, Microsoft, IBM, Citigroup, and American Express—have now appointed a chief privacy officer (CPO), whose job is to safeguard the privacy of consumers who do business with the company. In the end, however, if researchers provide value in exchange for information, customers will gladly provide it. For example, Amazon.com's customers don't mind if the firm builds a database of products they buy as a way to provide future product recommendations. This saves time and provides value. The best approach is for researchers to ask only for the information they need, use it responsibly to provide customer value, and avoid sharing information without the customer's permission.

Misuse of Research Findings Research studies can be powerful persuasion tools; companies often use study results as claims in their advertising and promotion. Today, however, many research studies appear to be little more than vehicles for pitching the sponsor's products. In fact, in some cases, research surveys appear to have been designed just to produce the intended effect. For example, a Black Flag survey once asked: "A roach disk . . . poisons a roach slowly. The dying roach returns to the nest and after it dies is eaten by other roaches. In turn these roaches become poisoned and die. How effective do you think this type of product would be in killing roaches?" Not surprisingly, 79 percent said effective.

However, few advertisers openly rig their research designs or blatantly misrepresent the findings—most abuses tend to be more subtle "stretches." Or disputes arise over the validity and use of research findings. Consider this example:

> The U.S. Federal Trade Commission charged POM Wonderful—the pomegranate juice sold in the distinctive curvy bottle—and its parent company with making false and unsubstantiated health claims in its advertising. The disputed ads suggest that POM Wonderful Pomegranate Juice can prevent or treat heart disease, prostate cancer, and even erectile dysfunction. For instance, one ad boasted that POM has "Super Health Powers!" while another proclaimed "I'm off to save prostates!" POM has stood behind its ad claims, asserting that they are backed by $35 million worth of company research showing that antioxidant-rich pomegranate products are good for you. The brand even retaliated during two years of legal wrangling with ads disputing the FTC and its allegations. But the FTC isn't buying the research behind POM's claims—it issued a final ruling ordering the brand to refrain from making claims that its products could improve a user's health unless backed by more stringent research. "When a company touts scientific research in its advertising, the research must squarely support the claims made," says the agency. "Contrary to POM Wonderful's advertising, the available scientific information does not prove that POM Juice . . . effectively treats or prevents these illnesses." POM Wonderful appealed the FTC ruling, but it was upheld early in 2015.[38]

Exhibit 5.18 Use of research findings: The U.S. Federal Trade Commission ruled against POM Wonderful's research-based advertising claims that the brand could improve a user's health.

Recognizing that surveys can be abused, several associations—including the Canadian Marketing Association, the American Marketing Association, and the Marketing Research Association—have developed codes of research ethics and standards of conduct. In the end, however, unethical or inappropriate actions cannot simply be regulated away. Each company must accept responsibility for policing the conduct and reporting of its own marketing research to protect consumers' best interests and its own.

BP Location—A Market-Driven Decision

With more than 365 restaurants (and counting) from Victoria to St. John's, it's not surprising to learn that Canada's leading casual dining chain knows a thing or two about geography and demographics. And when it comes to selecting where to place a new restaurant, the mantra is not dissimilar to that of your local real estate agent—location, location, location.

"It applies to our business as well," explains Jim Treliving, co-founder of the chain, current co-owner, and co-chairman of Boston Pizza International, not to mention one-time co-owner of 18 of his own BP franchises. "The nice thing about demonstrating stable growth, a well-established brand, and regional drawing power is that Boston Pizza is a preferred tenant, so when we see lease opportunities for a new location, the property owner welcomes us."

Exactly what does location, location, location need to be for a new Boston Pizza location? All the traditional criteria apply, such as high-profile and high-traffic centres. However, as consumer patterns have evolved, it has become equally important to be near office and entertainment centres as well as big-box retail clusters.

Location decisions therefore need to be based on marketing intelligence supplied by thorough secondary research of the marketing environment, but also through BP's own primary research initiatives. In 2012, for instance, BP entered into the growing "fast casual" dining category by opening a location in the food court at SAIT Polytechnic in Calgary. "This concept is something we're developing for university and college campuses, hospitals, airports, leisure and sports complexes, and even select high-profile mall food courts," declared Alan Howie, BPI's executive vice-president of operations. "While we continue to open traditional Boston Pizza locations across the country, we're also excited about new concepts like SAIT, our urban-concept location in downtown Toronto, and our new smaller-store concept."

QUESTIONS

1. Differentiate between primary and secondary research. Provide an example of each that Boston Pizza might have used in determining that the SAIT Polytechnic campus in Calgary would be a logical choice for a new "fast casual" location.
2. What research objective would BP need to establish before conducting marketing research on optimal new restaurant locations? Explain your answer.

REVIEWING THE CONCEPTS

 LO1 Explain the importance of information in gaining insights about the marketplace and customers.

The marketing process starts with a complete understanding of the marketplace and consumer needs and wants. Thus, the company needs sound information to produce superior value and satisfaction for its customers. The company also requires information on competitors, resellers, and other actors and forces in the marketplace. Increasingly, marketers are viewing information not only as an input for making better decisions but also as an important strategic asset and marketing tool.

 LO2 Define the marketing information system and discuss its parts.

The *marketing information system* (*MIS*) consists of people and procedures for assessing information needs, developing the needed information, and helping decision makers use the information to generate and validate actionable customer and market insights. A well-designed information system begins and ends with users.

The MIS first *assesses information needs.* The MIS primarily serves the company's marketing and other managers, but it may also provide information to external partners. Then the MIS *develops information* from internal databases, marketing intelligence activities, and marketing research. *Internal databases* provide information on the company's own operations and departments. Such data can be obtained quickly and cheaply but often need to be adapted for marketing decisions. *Marketing intelligence* activities supply everyday information about developments in the external marketing environment. *Market research* consists of collecting information relevant to a specific marketing problem faced by the company. Last, the MIS helps users analyze and use the information to develop customer insights, make marketing decisions, and manage customer relationships.

LO3 Outline the steps in the marketing research process.

The first step in the marketing research process involves *defining the problem and setting the research objectives*, which may be exploratory, descriptive, or causal research. The second step consists of *developing a research plan* for collecting data from primary and secondary sources. The third step calls for *implementing the marketing research plan* by gathering, processing, and analyzing the information. The fourth step consists of *interpreting and reporting the findings.* Additional information analysis helps marketing managers apply the information and provides them with sophisticated statistical procedures and models from which to develop more rigorous findings.

Both *internal* and *external* secondary data sources often provide information more quickly and at a lower cost than primary data sources, and they can sometimes yield information that a company cannot collect by itself. However, needed information might not exist in secondary sources. Researchers must also evaluate secondary information to ensure that it is *relevant, accurate, current,* and *impartial.*

Primary research must also be evaluated for these features. Each primary data collection method—*observational, survey,* and *experimental*—has its own advantages and disadvantages. Similarly, each of the various research contact methods—mail, telephone, personal interview, and online—has its own advantages and drawbacks.

 LO4 Explain how companies analyze and use marketing information.

Information gathered in internal databases and through marketing intelligence and marketing research usually requires more analysis. To analyze individual customer data, many companies have now acquired or developed special software and analysis techniques—called *customer relationship management* (*CRM*)—that integrate, analyze, and apply the mountains of individual customer data contained in their databases.

Marketing information has no value until it is used to make better marketing decisions. Thus, the MIS must make the information available to managers and others who make marketing decisions or deal with customers. In some cases, this means providing regular reports and updates; in other cases, it means making nonroutine information available for special situations and on-the-spot decisions. Today's marketing managers can gain direct access to marketing information at any time and from virtually any location.

LO5 Discuss the special issues some marketing researchers face, including public policy and ethics issues.

Some marketers face special marketing research situations, such as those conducting research in small business, not-for-profit, or international situations. Marketing research can be conducted effectively by small businesses and non-profit organizations with limited budgets. International marketing researchers follow the same steps as domestic researchers do but often face more and different problems.

All organizations need to act responsibly concerning major public policy and ethical issues surrounding marketing research, including issues of intrusions on consumer privacy and misuse of research findings.

MyMarketingLab

Study, practise, and explore real marketing situations with these helpful resources:

- **Interactive Lesson Presentations:** Work through interactive presentations and assessments to test your knowledge of marketing concepts.
- **Study Plan:** Check your understanding of chapter concepts with self-study quizzes.
- **Dynamic Study Modules:** Work through adaptive study modules on your computer, tablet, or mobile device.
- **Simulations:** Practise decision-making in simulated marketing environments.

DISCUSSION QUESTIONS

1. What is a marketing information system, and how is it used to create customer insights?

2. Explain how marketing intelligence differs from marketing research.

3. What is ethnographic research, and how is it conducted online?

4. How are marketers using customer relationship management (CRM) to reveal customer insights from the vast amounts of data gathered?

5. What is neuromarketing, and how is it useful in marketing research? Why is this research approach usually combined with other approaches?

6. What are the similarities and differences between conducting research in the domestic market and in another country?

CRITICAL THINKING EXERCISES

1. In a small group, identify a problem faced by a local business or charitable organization and propose a research project addressing that problem. Develop a research proposal that implements each step of the marketing research process. Discuss how the research results will help the business or organization.

2. Focus groups are commonly used during exploratory research. A focus group interview entails gathering a group of people to discuss a specific topic. In a small group, research how to conduct a focus group interview and then conduct one with 6 to 10 other students to learn what services your university could offer to better meet student needs. Assign one person in your group to be the moderator while the others observe and interpret the responses from the focus group participants. Present a report of what you learned from this research.

3. Search "social media monitoring" on a search engine to find companies that specialize in monitoring social media. Discuss two of these companies. Next, find two more sites that allow free monitoring and describe how marketers can use these to monitor their brands. Write a brief report on your findings.

ONLINE, MOBILE, AND SOCIAL MEDIA MARKETING

Marketers have always been interested in buyers' personality traits and how they influence behaviours, but it's difficult to measure personality. Until now, that is. Online, mobile, and social media technologies are now providing researchers with new tools to predict someone's personality traits and lifestyle activities. Microsoft and researchers from the University of Cambridge analyzed over 58 000 Facebook users' Likes and developed an algorithm that matched them with demographic information and personality profiles. The resulting personality profiles determined, with over 80 percent accuracy, factors such as users' gender, ethnicity, religion, sexual orientation, alcohol and drug use, and even whether their parents had separated before they turned 21 years old. Researchers even predicted IQ and found that users with higher IQs like curly fries and those with lower IQs like Harley-Davidson. All that and more can be predicted just from users' Like-clicking behaviour on websites, social media, and mobile apps. This research gives marketers another tool that will help them customize their offerings and communications with greater accuracy.

QUESTIONS

1. Visit applymagicsauce.com to see what your Likes say about you. You will have to log on to Facebook to see the results. What characteristics are shown? Does the profile describe you accurately?

2. Look up information related to targeted advertising. How does this concept relate to the measures of personality described above?

THINK LIKE A MARKETING MANAGER

Jack Astor's Bar and Grill currently operates 39 restaurants in five provinces across Canada. Jack Astor's marketing department is working on a strategic plan to expand to other provinces. They have come to you, the head of the marketing research department, for information that will help them decide which markets would be likely candidates.

QUESTIONS

1. Make a list of three questions you can find the answers to in secondary sources. Which secondary sources will you use to find the answers to these questions? Can you find the answers to all three questions just by using free Internet sources and your university's library databases?

2. You're going to have to prepare a research plan to conduct some primary research. Which type or types of research will you use: observational, experimental, or causal? Think this through and make notes. What would you observe, and for what purpose? What kind of experiment might you conduct? What cause-and-effect relationships would you want to understand?

3. What type of research would you conduct to determine which markets in Canada are likely to respond most favourably to Jack Astor's menu?

MARKETING ETHICS

As the Pepsi, P&G, and Lexus examples in this chapter illustrate, companies are increasingly using qualitative research methods such as observation, ethnography, and in-depth interviews to gain customer insights. However, qualitative research brings up ethical issues. Unlike quantitative data collection methods that use surveys or mechanical means, qualitative research puts researchers in close physical proximity to consumers—even in their homes—where the researchers may see or hear private and confidential things. Most research extends confidentiality to research subjects so that they'll be open in responding to questions, but what if a researcher learns something troublesome? For example, marketing research is advancing into more sensitive consumer behaviours related to product abuse and deviant behaviours, and consumers may reveal harmful or illegal behaviour to the researcher. Alternatively, like all experiments, marketing research experiments, such as a researcher pretending to shoplift in a store to observe other customers' reactions, necessarily involve some type of deception. Such experiments can be conducted without customer knowledge, or customers may even be induced to participate in the deception. They may be told later and feel uncomfortable with their actions. These are just a few of the ethical issues related to qualitative marketing research.

QUESTIONS

1. What should marketing researchers do in situations such as those just described? Visit www.iccindiaonline.org/policy_state/esomar.pdf and discuss whether the International Code of Marketing and Social Research Practice provides guidance in dealing with such issues.

2. Do these issues relate only to qualitative methods, or might quantitative methods of data collection result in similar ethical concerns? Support your answer.

MARKETING BY THE NUMBERS

Have you ever been disappointed when a television network cancelled one of your favourite television shows because of "low ratings"? The network didn't ask your opinion, did it? It probably didn't ask any of your friends, either. That's because estimates of television audience sizes are based on research done by The Nielsen Company, which uses a sample of only 9000 households out of the more than 116 million TV households in the United States to determine national ratings for television programs. That doesn't seem like enough. But as it turns out, statistically, it's many more than enough.

QUESTIONS

1. Go to www.surveysystem.com/sscalc.htm to determine the appropriate sample size for a population of 113 million households. Briefly explain what is meant by *confidence interval* and *confidence level*. Assuming a confidence interval of 5, how large should the sample of households be when desiring a 95 percent confidence level? How large for a 99 percent confidence level?

2. What sample sizes are necessary at population sizes of 1 billion, 10 000, and 100 with a confidence interval of 5 and a 95 percent confidence level? Explain the effect that population size has on required sample size.

ORACLE: GETTING A GRIP ON BIG DATA

Earlier in this chapter, in our discussion of Netflix, we used the term *big data*. But in the broader sense, what exactly does this term mean? Consider this: Every day, the people and systems of the world generate 11 quintillion bytes of new data (that's 11 billion gigabytes). In 2014, that added up to about 4 zettabytes of information. A zettabyte is a trillion gigabytes. If you can't wrap your head around these numbers, let's just say that they're huge. If you were to put all that data on good old CD-ROMs, every person in the world would have 773 of them annually. If you stacked all 5.4 trillion CDs on top of one another, it would create a stack tall enough to go to the moon and back eight times (and you thought you had storage problems). This is big data.

The amount of data that we humans and our beloved machines generate has been growing exponentially. Consider that if every word uttered by every human being who ever lived were written down and digitized, it would equal only two days' worth of the data that is being generated at today's rate. Of all the information that was stored in 2012, 90 percent of it was created in the previous two years alone. And of course, the data explosion isn't slowing down.

Just where does all that data come from? Consider that every Google search, Facebook status update, YouTube video, text message, and purchase transaction generates data. There are about 15 billion devices connected to the Internet; by the end of the decade, there will be 75 billion. Beyond just mobile devices and laptops, the number of smart machines that are talking to other smart machines is rapidly adding to the mass of connected devices. Utility meters, vending machines, appliances, automobiles, surgical devices, heavy industrial equipment, and even pets and shoes are now stuffed with technology that allows them to automatically collect consumption data and relay that information to the manufacturers, to the companies that own the systems that connect the machines, or to any company that is willing to pay for such data.

BIG DATA: A BLESSING AND A CURSE

This tsunami of data surging over corporations of all shapes and sizes is widely considered to be the most important issue in corporate strategy today. Ginni Rometty, CEO of IBM, predicted that big data will be the primary basis of competitive advantage in the future, calling it "the next natural resource." She thinks it will change how decisions are made, how value is created, and how

value is delivered. Angela Ahrendts, CEO of Burberry, agrees. "Consumer data will be the biggest differentiator in the next two to three years. Whoever unlocks the reams of data and uses it strategically will win."

But harnessing and making sense of all this data is easier said than done. For decades, companies have made decisions based on data they've gathered from their own transactions and stored in relational databases. When a company designs its own databases, the information is organized and structured. However, the flood of data from new sources, many of which are external, is much less structured and often incompatible with a given company's own data systems. For example, how do you store a photo, a sound bite, a video clip, or a Facebook status update in a way that it can be combined with other data and mined for useful insights?

Most companies are simply overwhelmed by big data. It's challenging enough to get up to speed with data as it exists today, much less prepare for the increases in tomorrow's data flows. Companies need guidance from experts who can do most of the heavy lifting in gathering and making sense of all that information. They desperately need help in gleaning big-data insights that will put them ahead of the competition in making decisions that will win with consumers, vendors, and partners.

ORACLE TO THE RESCUE

That's where Oracle comes in. Oracle has specialized in computer hardware and software products since 1977. Now the third-largest software maker (behind Microsoft and IBM), Oracle builds database management, resource planning, customer relationship management, and supply chain management systems. All this expertise, plus the visionary leadership of founder and CEO Larry Ellison, has moved Oracle to the forefront of gathering, organizing, and analyzing big data. Oracle claims that it "offers the broadest and most integrated portfolio of products to help you acquire and organize these diverse data sources and analyze them alongside your existing data to find new insights and capitalize on hidden relationships."

Oracle's portfolio includes software, platform (the architecture that connects software to hardware), and hardware products. According to Bob Evans, Oracle's chief communications officer, "Oracle is the only tech company on Earth that has a full line at [each of these] levels." Oracle's portfolio of products is immense, and includes database products that allow databases to collect, connect, integrate, and analyze. Its hardware systems include server products as well as big-data appliances that are engineered to optimize all of Oracle's software products, as well as products from external sources.

With its completely integrated systems, Oracle can provide unique benefits to companies that other big-data companies simply can't match. In the oil, gas, and mining industries, new machine-to-machine devices are being used to track exactly what's going into and coming out of each mine, reducing losses and maximizing profits. In the transportation industry, devices in shipping containers can monitor a shipment throughout its journey, keeping track of things like temperature, humidity, and even whether or not the container has been opened. And in the mobile services industry, virtual wallet services that let people pay for transactions with their phones are expanding rapidly and putting the capability in smartphones as well as in traditional-feature phones. Oracle is at work in each of these situations, with expertise that lets clients gather and transmit data from enabled devices to systems that analyze the data in ways that provide better customer outcomes and maximize profits.

As an indication of Oracle's big-data leadership and innovation, many of the products the company is now introducing to handle big data were designed well before terms such as *cloud computing* or even *big data* were being used. For example, the design of Oracle's Fusion applications—software suites designed to handle data management across corporate areas ranging from supply chain to human resources to customer relationship management—began in 2004. And Oracle began developing its database product in 2007. Yet both of these products lines are optimized for the cloud, and both can be used on-site or over the Internet.

As another example of visionary development, Oracle's software-based enterprise applications have built-in social media capabilities. According to Abhay Parasnis, senior vice-president of Oracle Public Cloud, "Oracle's social relationship management capabilities bring social into everything and can light up our core large object applications with social capabilities." No other company even attempted to do this, and it puts Oracle on the leading edge of pushing the industry to deliver the customer value benefits of social media.

FIGHTING FOR A PIECE OF THE PIE

The recent developments in big data have sparked a frenzy of competitive activity. Massive competitors such as Microsoft, IBM, and Dell are all grabbing for a piece of the big data pie, and a deluge of start-ups such as Hadapt,

Precog, and Platfora are joining the fray. Oracle threw fuel on the fire with the release of its Sparc T5 server series. Oracle CEO Larry Ellison framed the advantages of the Sparc line this way: "You can go faster, but only if you're willing to pay 80 percent less than what IBM charges."

Facing Oracle's line of faster and cheaper products, Colin Parris, general manager for IBM's Power systems, quickly downplayed the advantages of faster machines. He suggested that the race for faster processors is a thing of the past. Instead, today's companies are much more concerned about reliability, security, and cost effectiveness. But considering how fast the big-data world is moving, the speed advantage has real-world applications for executives who want to accelerate internal operations, make better decisions, and engage customers more intimately. When processes that formerly took weeks can be accomplished in just days, it provides competitive advantage in numerous ways.

Despite Oracle's apparent sizable lead in the race to dominate big data, the data giant faces challenges. For starters, many companies large and small are finding that they can fulfill their big-data needs more efficiently by using cheap hardware and open-source software. For example, years ago when Google faced the problem of indexing the Internet for its search engine, it built a huge database system comprising cheap hardware and internally developed software that got the job done. And Google isn't alone.

Additionally, Oracle has missed its financial goals a few times. That's hard for Wall Street to swallow. Although big data represents only a portion of Oracle's overall business, analysts have observed that many of the big innovations are happening at smaller, more nimble companies. Thus, many talented employees are jumping ship from the big developers, leaving the likes of Oracle with high turnover and less innovative minds.

So although Oracle has the expertise and products to tackle today's big-data needs, it also has its work cut out for it. However, even as the young and nimble start-ups nip at Oracle's heals and the other big dogs fight for positions on the big-data porch, there is little question that no other single company is better poised to help companies use big data to optimize marketing opportunities.

Sources: Andrew Gill, "IBM CEO Ginni Rometty Believes Big Data and Social Will Change Everything," *London Calling*, March 11, 2013, http://londoncalling.co/2013/03/ibm-ceo-ginni-rometty-believes-big-data-and-social-will-change-everything-how-about-other-ceos; Bob Evans, "You Can Get a Chip Slower Than the New Sparc T5, You Just Have to Pay More," *Forbes*, April 2, 2013, www.forbes.com/sites/oracle/2013/04/02/big-data-performance-speed-cost; "Billions of Reasons to Get Ready for Big

Data," *Forbes*, December 12, 2013, www.forbes.com/sites/oracle/2012/12/13/billions-of-reasons-to-get-ready-for-big-data; Bob Evans, "Larry Ellison Doesn't Get the Cloud," *Forbes*, October 9, 2012, www.forbes.com/sites/oracle/2013/04/02/big-data-performance-speed-cost; Rolfe Winkler, "Oracle's Little Issue with Big Data," *Wall Street Journal*, April 9, 2012, http://online.wsj.com/article/SB10001424052702304587704577333823771344922.html; Ron Bodkin, "Cracks in the Oracle Empire," *Thinkbiganalytics*, March 25, 2013, http://thinkbiganalytics.com/big_data_affects_database_oracle; and www.oracle.com/us/technologies/big-data/index.html, accessed May 2013.

QUESTIONS FOR DISCUSSION

1. Discuss ways that Oracle could provide clients with the ability to form better relationships with customers.

2. Discuss the similarities and differences between big data and the more traditional marketing research concepts discussed in this chapter.

3. Does competition from small start-ups really pose a big competitive threat to Oracle? Explain why or why not.

4. From a consumer point of view, what are some of the downsides to the developments in big data?

5. In the future, will consumers be more concerned about these downsides or less?

GoPro

AFTER STUDYING THIS CHAPTER, YOU SHOULD BE ABLE TO

1 understand the consumer market and the major factors that influence consumer buyer behaviour

2 identify and discuss the stages in the buyer decision process

3 describe the adoption and diffusion process for new products

4 define the business market and identify the major factors that influence business buyer behaviour

5 list and define the steps in the business buying decision process

Understanding Consumer and Business Buyer Behaviour

PREVIEWING THE CONCEPTS

We've examined how marketers obtain, analyze, and use information to develop customer insights and assess marketing programs. In this chapter, we take a closer look at the most important element of the marketplace—customers. The aim of marketing is to affect how customers think and act. To affect the *whats*, *whens*, and *hows* of buyer behaviour, marketers must first understand the *whys*. We first look at *final consumer* buying influences and processes and then at the buyer behaviour of *business customers*. You'll see that understanding buyer behaviour is an essential but very difficult task.

To get a better sense of the importance of understanding consumer behaviour, we begin by looking at GoPro. You may have never heard of GoPro, the small but fast-growing company that makes tiny, wearable HD video cameras. Yet few brands can match the avid enthusiasm and intense loyalty that GoPro has created in the hearts and minds of its customers.

GoPro: BE A HERO

A growing army of GoPro customers—many of them extreme sports enthusiasts—are now strapping amazing little GoPro cameras to their bodies, or mounting them on anything from the front bumpers of race cars to the heels of skydiving boots, in order to capture the extreme moments of their lives and lifestyles. Then, they can't wait to share those emotion-packed GoPro moments with friends. In fact, the chances are good that you've seen many GoPro-created videos on YouTube or Facebook, or even on TV.

Maybe it's the one shot by the skier who sets off an avalanche in the Swiss Alps and escapes by parachuting off a cliff—that amateur video received 2.6 million YouTube views in nine months. Or maybe you saw the one where a seagull picks up a tourist's camera and makes off with it, capturing a bird's-eye view of a castle in Cannes, France (3 million views in seven months). Or what about the video of the mountain biker in Africa who is ambushed by a full-grown gazelle (more than 13 million views in four months)? A promotional video featuring five minutes of clips captured by fans with the latest GoPro HERO4 model snared more than 20 million YouTube views in only four months.

GoPro's avid customers have become evangelists for the brand. On average, they upload a new video to YouTube about every minute. The videos inspire new GoPro customers in turn, and even more video sharing. As a result, GoPro is growing explosively.

✓• **Practice** on MyMarketingLab

Evaluating Segments Across the Buying Process

✓• **Practice** on MyMarketingLab

Evaluating Awareness, Knowledge, and Attitude Across Geographic Markets

✓• **Practice** on MyMarketingLab

Evaluating the Prospect Lifetime Value of new Customers in a B2B Setting

In 2014 the company sold a cool 5.2 million cameras, generating revenues of US$1.4 billion—a 41 percent increase from 2013—and an estimated 90 percent share of the wearable-camera market.

What makes GoPro so successful? Part of the formula is the cameras themselves: GoPro cameras are marvels of modern technology, especially given their affordable starting price of US$200 to US$400. Only about five centimetres wide, a GoPro HD video camera looks like little more than a small grey box. But the lightweight, wearable or mountable GoPro is extremely versatile, and it packs amazing power for capturing stunning HD-quality video. A removable housing makes GoPro cameras waterproof to depths of 55 metres. And GoPro cameras are drop-proof from 900 metres (so claims one skydiver).

But GoPro knows that consumer behaviour is driven by much more than just high-quality products with innovative features. The brand is all about what its cameras let customers *do*. GoPro users don't just want to take videos. More than that, they want to tell the stories and share the adrenalin-pumped emotions of the extreme moments in their lifestyles. "Enabling you to share your life through incredible photos and video is what we do," says GoPro. We "help people capture and share their lives' most meaningful experiences with others—to celebrate them together."

When people view a stunning GoPro video clip—like the one of New Zealand's Jed Mildon landing the first-ever BMX triple backflip captured by his helmet camera—they experience to some degree what the subject experiences. They feel the passion and adrenalin. And when that happens, GoPro creates an emotional connection between the GoPro storyteller and the audience.

Thus, making good cameras is only the start of GoPro's success. GoPro founder Nick Woodman, himself an extreme sports junkie, talks about helping customers through four essential steps in their storytelling and emotion-sharing journeys: capture, creation, broadcast, and recognition. *Capture* is what the cameras do—shooting pictures and videos. *Creation* is the editing and production process that turns raw footage into compelling videos. *Broadcast* involves distributing the video content to an audience. *Recognition* is the payoff for the content creator. Recognition might come in the form of YouTube views or Likes and Shares on Facebook. More probably, it's the enthusiastic oohs and ahs that their videos evoke from friends and family. The company's slogan sums up pretty well the consumer's deeper motivations: GoPro—Be a HERO.

So far, the company has focused primarily on the capture step of the overall customer storytelling experience. GoPro bills itself as the "World's Most Versatile Camera. Wear It. Mount It. Love It." It offers a seemingly endless supply of rigs, mounts, harnesses, straps, and other accessories that make GoPro cameras wearable or mountable just about anywhere. Users can strap the little cameras to their wrists or mount them on helmets. They can attach them to the tip of a snow ski, the bottom of a skateboard, or the underside of an RC helicopter. The handy little GoPro lets even the rankest video amateur capture some pretty incredible footage.

But Woodman knows that to keep growing, GoPro must broaden its offer to address the full range of customer needs and motivations—not just capture, but also creation, broadcast, and recognition. For example, on the creation side, GoPro acquired a digital-video software company, CineForm, and now provides free software for creating 3-D videos from footage shot by GoPro cameras rigged side by side and calibrated to shoot simultaneously. On the broadcast side, GoPro has partnered with YouTube to create a

GoPro YouTube network offering a Wi-Fi plug-in that lets GoPro customers upload video directly from their cameras or using a mobile app. GoPro's YouTube channel long ago passed 200 million video views. As for recognition, GoPro now airs TV commercials created from the best videos submitted by customers at its website. GoPro's future lies in enabling and integrating the full user experience, from capturing video to sharing stories and life's emotions with others.

GoPro's rich understanding of what makes its customers tick is serving the young company well. Its enthusiastic customers are among the most loyal and engaged of any brand. For example, GoPro's Facebook fan base is more than 8.9 million and growing fast. Beyond uploading approximately one video per minute to YouTube, GoPro fans interact heavily across a broad range of social media. "I think we have the most socially engaged online audience of any consumer brand in the world," claims Woodman.

All that customer engagement and enthusiasm has made GoPro the fastest-growing camera company in the world. Today GoPro cameras are available in more than 35 000 stores in 100 or more countries, from small sports-enthusiast shops to REI, Best Buy, and Amazon.com. GoPro's remarkable little cameras have also spread beyond amateurs. They have become standard equipment for many professional filmmakers—whether it's the Discovery Channel or a news show team filming rescues, wildlife, and storms or the production crew of hit reality-TV shows such as *Deadliest Catch* taking pictures of underwater crab pots or the sides of ships in heavy seas. And GoPro teamed with ESPN to capture unprecedented angles and perspectives in its global X Games broadcasts. The use of GoPro equipment by professionals lends credibility that fuels even greater consumer demand.

The moral of this story: Success begins with understanding customer needs and motivations. GoPro knows that it doesn't just make cameras. More than that, it enables customers to share important moments and emotions. According to one industry expert, GoPro understands "how to wrap technology beautifully around human needs so that it matters to people." Says Woodman: "We spent a lot of time recently thinking about, What are we really doing here? We know that our cameras are arguably the most socially networked consumer devices of our time, so it's clear we're not just building hardware." GoPro customers know the truth, he asserts. "A GoPro really is that good for capturing and sharing their lives."[1]

THE GoPro example shows that factors at many levels affect consumer buying behaviour. Buying behaviour is never simple, yet understanding it is an essential task of marketing management. First we explore the dynamics of the consumer market and consumer buyer behaviour. We then examine business markets and the business buyer process.

Consumer Markets and Consumer Buyer Behaviour LO1

Consumer buyer behaviour refers to the buying behaviour of final consumers—individuals and households that buy goods and services for personal consumption. All of these final consumers combine to make up the **consumer market**. The North American consumer market consists of more than 345 million people in Canada and the United States who consume more than US$15 trillion worth of goods and services each year, making it one of the most attractive consumer markets in the world.[2]

Consumer buyer behaviour
The buying behaviour of final consumers—individuals and households that buy goods and services for personal consumption.

Consumer market
All the individuals and households that buy or acquire goods and services for personal consumption.

◄◉⊢Simulate on MyMarketingLab

Consumer Behaviour

Consumers around the world vary tremendously in age, income, education level, and tastes. They also buy an incredible variety of goods and services. How these diverse consumers relate with each other and with other elements of the world around them impacts their choices among various products, services, and companies. Here we examine the fascinating array of factors that affect consumer behaviour.

What Is Consumer Behaviour?

Consumers make many purchase decisions, and some of these are more complex than others. For example, a consumer buying a cup of coffee would go through a very different decision-making process from one buying his or her first house. Most large companies research consumer buying decisions in great detail to answer questions about what consumers buy, where they buy, how and how much they buy, when they buy, and why they buy. Marketers can study actual consumer purchases to find out what they buy, where, and how much. But learning about the *whys* of consumer buying behaviour is not so easy—the answers are often locked deep within the consumer's mind.

The central question for marketers, then, is this: Given all the characteristics (cultural, social, personal, and psychological) affecting consumer behaviour, how do we best design our marketing efforts to reach our consumers most effectively? Thus, the study of consumer behaviour begins and ends with the individual. In the past, the field was often referred to as *buyer behaviour*, reflecting an emphasis on the actual exchange of goods for money. Marketers now recognize that the study of consumer behaviour is an ongoing process that starts long before the consumer purchases a product or service, and continues long after he or she consumes it. This extended definition of consumer behaviour means that, in order to build brand loyalty and lasting relationships with their customers, marketers must be aware of a number of issues before, during, and after purchase. Figure 6.1 illustrates some issues that arise during each stage of the consumption process, but there are many more.

FIGURE 6.1 Some Issues That Arise During Stages in the Consumption Process

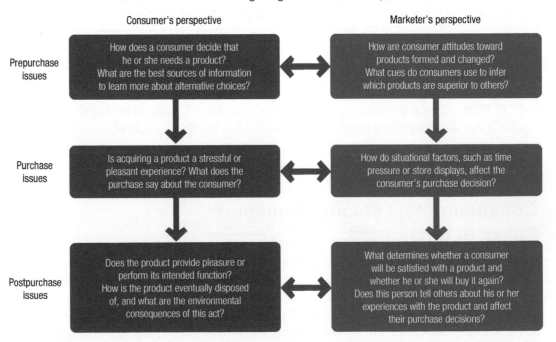

Source: Michael R. Solomon, Judith L. Zaichkowsky, and Rosemary Polegato (2011), *Consumer Behaviour: Buying, Having, and Being*, 5th Canadian Edition (Toronto: Pearson Education Canada).

Consumers' responses, which can range from actual purchase to merely engaging in word-of-mouth communications about the product, is the ultimate test of whether or not a marketing strategy is successful. In the next section, we will examine each of the characteristics affecting consumer behaviour in more detail.

Characteristics Affecting Consumer Behaviour

Consumer purchases are influenced strongly by cultural, social, personal, and psychological characteristics, as shown in Figure 6.2. For the most part, marketers cannot control such factors, but they must take them into account.

Cultural Factors Cultural factors exert a broad and deep influence on consumer behaviour. Marketers need to understand the role played by the buyer's *culture*, *subculture*, and *social class*.

CULTURE Culture is the most basic cause of a person's wants and behaviour. Human behaviour is largely learned. Growing up in a society, a child learns basic values, perceptions, wants, and behaviours from his or her family and other important institutions. A child in the United States normally learns or is exposed to the following values: achievement and success, individualism, freedom, hard work, activity and involvement, efficiency and practicality, material comfort, youthfulness, and fitness and health. In contrast, Canadians value freedom; the beauty of our natural landscape; our belief in respect, equality, and fair treatment; family life; and being Canadian. In fact, one public opinion poll found that 86 percent of Canadians agreed with the statement that their country was "the greatest in the world."[3] Despite our differences, both the United States and Canada are consumer cultures, and marketing practices reinforce this as a way of life. Every group or society has a culture, and cultural influences on buying behaviour may vary greatly from country to country.

Marketers are always trying to spot *cultural shifts* so as to discover new products that might be wanted. For example, the cultural shift toward greater concern about health and fitness has created a huge industry for health-and-fitness services, exercise equipment and clothing, organic foods, and a variety of diets.

SUBCULTURE Each culture contains smaller **subcultures**, or groups of people with shared value systems based on common life experiences and situations. Subcultures include nationalities, religions, racial groups, and geographic regions. Many subcultures make up important market segments, and marketers often design products and marketing programs tailored to their needs. Examples of three such important subculture groups in Canada include regional subcultures, founding nations, and ethnic subcultures.

Culture
The set of basic values, perceptions, wants, and behaviours learned by a member of society from family and other important institutions.

Subculture
A group of people with shared value systems based on common life experiences and situations.

FIGURE 6.2 Factors Influencing Consumer Behaviour

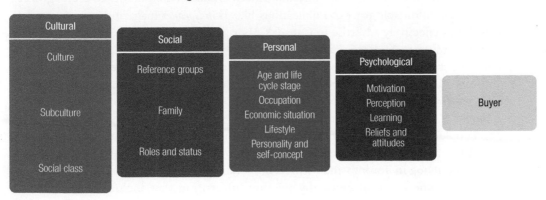

Exhibit 6.1 *Windspeaker* magazine is one tool promoted by the Aboriginal Multi-Media Society (AMMSA) to assist marketers who want to communicate with Canada's Aboriginal peoples effectively and efficiently.

Canada is a regional country, so marketers may develop distinctive programs for the Atlantic provinces, Quebec, Central Canada, the Prairies, and British Columbia. The sheer size of the country and its varied geographic features and climate have certainly shaped regional character and personality. For example, Atlantic Canada is largely defined by its proximity to and historical relationship with the sea. Equally, the isolation imposed by the mountain barrier, along with the abundance and grandeur of British Columbia's natural environment, shaped the outlook of that region's residents. Immigration has also had a differential effect on the various regions within Canada. The economy of each region furthers these differences. The fate of regions linked to the rise and fall of commodities, such as fish, timber, wheat, minerals, or oil, has affected regional mindsets as well as economies. Perceived disparities in political power have also increased regionalism, especially in Quebec, Newfoundland and Labrador, and Alberta.[4]

Canada had three founding nations: the English, French, and Aboriginal peoples. The unique history and language of each of these nations has driven many of the cultural differences that result in different buying behaviours across Canada. The most recent census results (2011) reported that people noting their English-language roots (anglophones) accounted for approximately 58 percent of the population, and people whose mother tongue is French (francophones) made up approximately 22 percent of the population. In total, approximately 213 500 Canadians reported an Aboriginal language as their mother tongue.

Aboriginal Canadians are making their voices heard both in the political arena and in the marketplace. There are more than 1.17 million Aboriginal Canadians, including Métis and Inuit, and this number is expected to double by 2031.[5] Among Canada's Aboriginal population, Cree is reported as the most common mother tongue. Not only do Aboriginal Canadians have distinct cultures that influence their values and purchasing behaviour, but they have also profoundly influenced the rest of Canada through their art, love of nature, and concern for the environment.

While the banking industry has been particularly responsive to the unique needs of Aboriginal Canadians, other firms are now following suit. For example, Quality Market, a grocery store in Thunder Bay, Ontario, launched an online ordering and delivery service that will allow residents of isolated northern Ontario communities to access groceries at more affordable prices.[6] Publications like *Windspeaker* magazine are also used as vehicles to effectively advertise to Canada's Aboriginal peoples.

According to Statistics Canada, roughly one out of every five people in Canada could be a member of a visible minority by 2017, when Canada celebrates its 150th anniversary. Approximately, 250 000 new immigrants come to Canada each year.[7] Thus, being sensitive to their cultural values is important, because 70 percent of the visible minority population were born outside Canada.

People with a Chinese background are still the largest group among visible minorities in Canada. Almost 4 percent of Canada's population is Chinese, with 40 percent of this group living in Toronto and 31 percent in Vancouver. Canadian companies are realizing the importance of culturally relevant advertising that includes a multimedia approach to reach the Chinese-Canadian market. A 2008 poll conducted by Solutions Research Group revealed that Internet use among Chinese Canadians exceeds time spent listening to radio and watching TV combined. Media outlets such as 51.ca and singtao.ca, which serve as free markets for information for Canada's Chinese community, have captured the attention of many Canadian advertisers. Chinese Canadians appreciate advertising delivered in their native tongue. "There's a certain emotional connection a person makes when somebody speaks their own language," said Solutions Research Group president Kaan Yigit. "It speaks to the issue of showing respect or feeling like you're being acknowledged."[8]

People who identified themselves as "black" in the 2006 census are Canada's third largest visible minority.[9] While some members of this group trace their ancestry back to Africa, many others have more recently emigrated from the Caribbean. In recent years, many companies have developed special products, appeals, and marketing programs for this subculture. While the data from the 2011 census is limited, it does show that the three largest visible minority groups in Canada—South Asians, Chinese, and blacks—accounted for 61.3 percent of the visible minority population.

Beyond targeting segments such as Aboriginals, Asian Canadians, and African Canadians with specially tailored efforts, many marketers now embrace **cross-cultural marketing**—the practice of including ethnic

Exhibit 6.2 Since its launch in 1978, *Sing Tao Daily* (singtao.ca) has developed into one of the most influential media for Chinese Canadians, and now publishes in Toronto, Vancouver, and Calgary.

© picturelibrary/Alamy

themes and cross-cultural perspectives within their mainstream marketing. Cross-cultural marketing appeals to consumer similarities across subcultures rather than differences. Many marketers are finding that insights gleaned from ethnic consumers can influence their broader markets.

For example, in the United States, today's youth-oriented lifestyle is influenced heavily by Hispanic and African-American entertainers. So it follows that consumers expect to see many different cultures and ethnicities represented in the advertising and products they consume. For instance, McDonald's takes cues from African Americans, Hispanics, and Asians to develop menus and advertising in hopes of encouraging mainstream consumers to buy smoothies, mocha drinks, and snack wraps as avidly as they consume hip-hop and rock 'n' roll. "The ethnic consumer tends to set trends," says McDonald's chief marketing officer. "So they help set the tone for how we enter the marketplace." Thus, McDonald's might take an ad primarily geared toward African Americans and run it in general-market media. "The reality is that the new mainstream is multicultural," concludes one cross-cultural marketing expert.[10]

SOCIAL CLASS Almost every society has some form of social class structure. **Social classes** are society's relatively permanent and ordered divisions whose members share similar values, interests, and behaviours. Social class is not determined by a single factor, such as income, but instead measured as a combination of occupation, income, education, wealth, and other variables. In some social systems, members of different classes are reared for certain roles and cannot change their social positions. In North America,

Cross-cultural marketing
Including ethnic themes and cross-cultural perspectives within a brand's mainstream marketing, appealing to consumer similarities across subcultures rather than differences.

Social class
Relatively permanent and ordered divisions in a society whose members share similar values, interests, and behaviours.

however, the lines between social classes are not fixed and rigid; people can move to a higher social class or drop into a lower one.

Most Canadians see themselves as middle class, and we are less likely or willing to think of ourselves in terms of social class than our neighbours south of the border. It is for this reason that the New Democratic Party no longer tries to appeal to "the working class" but to "ordinary Canadians." Marketers are interested in social class because people within a given social class tend to exhibit similar buying behaviour. Social classes show distinct product and brand preferences in areas such as clothing, home furnishings, leisure activity, and automobiles.

Social Factors   A consumer's behaviour is also influenced by social factors, such as the consumer's *small groups*, *social networks*, *family*, and *social roles and status*.

Group

Two or more people who interact to accomplish individual or mutual goals.

GROUPS AND SOCIAL NETWORKS   Many small **groups** influence a person's behaviour. Groups that have a direct influence and to which a person belongs are called *membership groups*. In contrast, *reference groups* serve as direct (face-to-face interactions) or indirect points of comparison or reference in forming a person's attitudes or behaviour. People are often influenced by reference groups to which they do not belong. For example, an *aspirational group* is one to which the individual wishes to belong, as when a young hockey player hopes to someday emulate Sidney Crosby and play in the NHL.

Marketers try to identify the reference groups of their target markets. Reference groups expose a person to new behaviours and lifestyles, influence the person's attitudes and self-concept, and create pressures to conform that may affect the person's product and brand choices. The importance of group influence varies across products and brands. It tends to be strongest when the product is visible to others whom the buyer respects.

Word-of-mouth influence

The impact of the personal words and recommendations of trusted friends, associates, and other consumers on buying behaviour.

Word-of-mouth influence can have a powerful impact on consumer buying behaviour. The personal words and recommendations of trusted friends, associates, and other consumers tend to be more credible than those coming from commercial sources, such as advertisements or salespeople. One study showed that 92 percent of consumers trust recommendations from friends and family above any form of advertising.[11] Most word-of-mouth influence happens naturally: Consumers start chatting about a brand they use or feel strongly about one way or the other. Often, however, rather than leaving it to chance, marketers can help to create positive conversations about their brands.

Opinion leader

A person within a reference group who, because of special skills, knowledge, personality, or other characteristics, exerts social influence on others.

Marketers of brands subjected to strong group influence must figure out how to reach **opinion leaders**—people within a reference group who, because of special skills, knowledge, personality, or other characteristics, exert social influence on others. Some experts call this group the *influentials* or *leading adopters*.

Can we help people wake up in a town where the sun doesn't rise?

Longyearbyen. Arctic Circle.

Follow the Wake-up Light experiment
www.philips.com/wakeup

PHILIPS
sense and simplicity

Philips

Exhibit 6.3 Creating word of mouth: Philips's award-winning "Wake up the Town" word-of-mouth campaign created knowledgeable consumers who helped explain the benefits of its complex Wake-up Light bedside lighting system to others.

When these influentials talk, consumers listen. Marketers try to identify opinion leaders for their products and direct marketing efforts toward them.

Buzz marketing involves enlisting or even creating opinion leaders to serve as "brand ambassadors" who spread the word about a company's products. For example, Nike created a lot of buzz worldwide during the 2012 London Olympics when it shod 400 of its Nike-sponsored athletes in can't-miss incandescent green/yellow Volt Flyknit shoes. The shoes became the talk of the Olympics.

Many companies turn everyday customers into brand evangelists. For instance, Philips turned users into brand ambassadors for its novel Wake-up Light lighting system:

> In 2006, Philips launched the first Wake-up Light—a bedside lighting system that simulated a natural sunrise, helping people wake up more naturally and happily. At first, however, Philips had difficulty explaining the complex benefits of the wake-up concept to skeptical consumers. The solution: Create knowledgeable consumer advocates who could explain the product to others. Philips did this through an award-winning integrated media campaign called "Wake up the Town," in which it supplied the Wake-up Light to 200 residents in Longyearbyen, Norway—the northernmost town in the Arctic Circle. The town's 2000 residents experience complete darkness 24 hours a day for 11 straight weeks each year. As you might imagine, waking up and starting the day in total darkness can be physically and mentally challenging. As the social experiment progressed, Philips asked consumers who used the Wake-up Light to honestly share their experiences on an interactive website, in blog posts, and on Facebook. Philips also arranged media interviews and posted video mini-documentaries on the site. The three-month word-of-mouth campaign paid off handsomely as potential buyers followed the stories of those using the light. Of the 200 participants in "Wake up the Town," 87 percent reported that they were waking up feeling more refreshed, alert, and ready for the day; 98 percent reported that they would continue to use the Wake-up Light. During the campaign, purchase consideration in target markets in Sweden and the Netherlands grew by 17 percent and 45 percent, respectively. Unit demand grew by 29 percent.[12]

More broadly, over the past several years, a new type of social interaction has exploded onto the scene—online social networking. **Online social networks** are online communities where people socialize or exchange information and opinions. Social networking media range from blogs (Consumerist, Gizmodo, Zenhabits) and message boards (Craigslist) to social media sites (Facebook, Twitter, Pinterest, and Foursquare) and virtual worlds (Second Life and Everquest). This form of consumer-to-consumer and business-to-consumer dialogue has big implications for marketers.

Online social networks
Online social communities—blogs, social networking websites, and other online communities—where people socialize or exchange information and opinions.

Marketers are working to harness the power of these new social networks and other "word-of-Web" opportunities to promote their products and build closer customer relationships. Instead of throwing more one-way commercial messages at consumers, they hope to use the Internet and social networks to *interact* with consumers and become a part of their conversations and lives.

For example, Red Bull has almost 44 million Likes on Facebook; Twitter and Facebook are the primary ways it communicates with university students. Dell sponsors nine blogs designed to provide "a direct exchange with Dell customers about the technology that connects us all." Even the Mayo Clinic uses social media extensively. It maintains Facebook, Flickr, and Twitter pages; a YouTube channel; smartphone patient apps that "put Mayo in your pocket wherever you are"; and a Sharing Mayo Clinic blog on which patients share their Mayo Clinic experiences and employees offer a behind-the-scenes view.

Most brands have built a comprehensive social media presence. Eco-conscious outdoor shoe and gear maker Timberland, for instance, has created an online community (http://community.timberland.com) that connects like-minded "Earthkeepers" with each other and the brand through a network that includes several websites, a

Facebook page, a YouTube channel, a Bootmakers Blog, an email newsletter, and several Twitter feeds. We will dig deeper into online social networks as a marketing tool in Chapter 14.

However, although much of the current talk about tapping social influence focuses on the Internet and social media, some 90 percent of brand conversations still take place the old-fashioned way—face to face. So most effective word-of-mouth marketing programs begin with generating person-to-person brand conversations and integrating both offline and online social influence strategies. The goal is to create opportunities for customers to get involved with brands and then help them share their brand passions and experiences with others in both their real world and virtual social networks (see Marketing@Work 6.1).

FAMILY Family members can strongly influence buyer behaviour. The family is the most important consumer buying organization in society, and it has been researched extensively. Marketers are interested in the roles and influence of the husband, wife, and children on the purchase of different products and services.

Husband–wife involvement varies widely by product category and by stage in the buying process. Buying roles change with evolving consumer lifestyles. For example, in Canada and the United States, the wife has traditionally been considered the main purchasing agent for the family in the areas of food, household products, and clothing. But with more women working outside the home and the willingness of husbands to do more of the family's purchasing, all this is changing. A survey of men aged 18 to 64 found that 52 percent identify themselves as primary grocery shoppers in their households, and 39 percent handle most of their household's laundry. At the same time, today women outspend men by three to two on new technology purchases and influence two-thirds of all new car purchases.[13]

Such shifting roles signal a new marketing reality. Marketers in industries that have traditionally sold their products to only women or only men—from groceries and personal care products to cars and consumer electronics—are now carefully targeting the opposite sex. For example, P&G's "My Tide" campaign has a commercial featuring a stay-at-home dad who does the household laundry using Tide Boost. A General Mills ad shows a father packing Go-Gurt yogurt in his son's lunch as the child heads off to school in the morning, with the slogan "Dads who get it, get Go-Gurt."

Children may also have a strong influence on family buying decisions. Canadian kids influence over $20 million in household spending each year and have memorized between 300 and 400 brand names by the age of 10. They also influence how much their families spend on them in areas such as food, clothing, entertainment, and personal care items. One study found that kids significantly influence family decisions about everything from what cars they buy to where they eat out and take vacations.[14]

ROLES AND STATUS A person belongs to many groups—family, clubs, organizations, online communities. The person's position in each group can be defined in terms of both role and status. A role consists of the activities people are expected to perform according to the people around them. Each role carries a status reflecting the general esteem given to it by society.

People usually choose products appropriate to their roles and status. Consider the various roles a working mother plays. In her company, she may play the role of a brand manager; in her family, she plays the role of wife and mother; at her favourite sporting events, she plays the role of avid fan. As a brand manager, she will buy the kind of clothing that reflects her role and status in her company. At the game, she may wear clothing supporting her favourite team.

MARKETING@WORK 6.1

Word-of-Mouth Marketing: Sparking Brand Conversations and Helping Them Catch Fire

People love talking with others about things that make them happy—including their favourite products and brands. Say you really like WestJet—it flies with flair and gets you there at an affordable price. Or you just plain love your new little GoPro HERO4 Black Edition video camera—it's too cool to keep to yourself. So you spread the good word about your favourite brands to anyone who will listen. In the old days, you'd have chatted up these brands with a few friends and family members. But these days, thanks to the Internet, social media, and mobile technology, anyone can share brand experiences with thousands, even millions, of other consumers digitally.

In response, marketers are now feverishly working to harness today's newfound technologies and get people interacting with each other about their brands, both online and offline. The aim is inspire, nurture, and amplify brand conversations. Whether it entails seeding a product among high-potential consumers to get them talking, creating brand ambassadors, tapping into existing influentials and social media, or developing conversation-provoking events and videos, the idea is to get people involved with and talking about the brand.

Generating successful word of mouth might be as simple as prompting Facebook Likes, Twitter streams, online reviews, blog commentaries, or YouTube videos. Even companies with small budgets can earn global exposure in the social media. For example, little-known start-up DollarShave-Club.com—which ships quality razors directly to customers for as little as one dollar a month—became an overnight sensation thanks largely to a single YouTube video. Founder Michael Dubin scraped together $4500 to produce a clever video featuring himself, some corny props, a guy in a bear suit, and very salty language to pitch the new service. "Are the blades any good?" Dubin asks in the video. "No. Our blades are f***ing great," he answers. "So stop forgetting where you're going to buy your blades every month and start deciding where you're going to stack all those dollar bills I'm saving you." The edgy video went viral, and the word-of-mouth firestorm quickly earned DollarShave-Club.com more than 12 million YouTube views, 60 000 Twitter followers, 197 000 Likes on Facebook, dozens of response videos, and US$10 million in venture capital funding.

But most successful social influence campaigns go well beyond a YouTube video or Facebook Likes. For example, many companies start by creating their own brand evangelists. That's what Ford did to introduce its Fiesta subcompact model in the United States. Under its now classic Fiesta Movement campaign, it handed out Fiestas to 100 young Millennial drivers—the target audience for the car—selected from 4000 applicants. These "Fiesta Agents" lived with their cars for six months, all the while sharing their experiences via blogs, tweets, Facebook updates, and YouTube and Flickr posts. The highly successful Fiesta Movement campaign generated 58 percent pre-launch brand awareness among Fiesta's under-30 target consumers. The Fiesta ambassadors posted 50 000 items, generating 28 million social media views, 52 000 test drives, and 10 000 online vehicle reservations.

Ford Motor Company

Exhibit 6.4 Creating brand buzz: Ford's highly successful Fiesta Movement campaign turned customers into brand evangelists, who shared their experiences via blogs, tweets, Facebook updates, and YouTube and Flickr posts.

Five years later, the Fiesta Movement was still rolling. Ford recruited 100 new Fiesta agents to create a year's worth of advertising for the 2014 Fiesta, including video clips to be used as commercials, digital ads, ads for social media such as Facebook and YouTube, and even magazine and newspaper ads. The Fiesta Movement has been so successful that Ford created similar social media evangelist campaigns for the Ford Escape ("Escape Routes") and its latest generation Ford Fusion ("Random Acts of Fusion").

Beyond creating their own ambassadors, companies looking to harness influence can work with the army of self-made influencers already plying the Internet—independent bloggers. Believe it or not, there are now almost as many people making a living as bloggers as there are lawyers. No matter what the interest area, there are probably hundreds of bloggers covering it. Moreover, research shows that 90 percent of bloggers post about their favourite and least favourite brands.

As a result, most companies try to form relationships with influential bloggers and online personalities. The key is to find bloggers who have strong networks of relevant readers, a credible voice, and a good fit with the brand. For example, companies ranging from P&G and McDonald's to Walmart work closely with influential "mommy bloggers." And you'll no doubt cross paths with the likes of climbers and skiers blogging for Patagonia, bikers blogging for Harley-Davidson, and foodies blogging for Whole Foods Market or Trader Joe's. Sometimes, bloggers and other social media mavens focus exclusively on a given brand. For example, StarbucksMelody.com is "an unofficial fan site for any and all Starbucks enthusiasts everywhere." Thanks to their independence, such blogs often generate more trustworthy buzz than a company's own blogs or online sites can.

Much of the word-of-mouth marketing frenzy today seems to centre on creating online buzz. However, the majority of brand conversations still take place offline. According to one expert, some 90 percent of brand conversations still happen in the real world rather than the virtual one. So many marketers work first to create good old face-to-face brand conversations.

For example, Kraft enlisted the help of word-of-mouth agency House Party to launch its Philadelphia Cooking Crème line of flavoured cream cheeses. Kraft and House Party selected 10 000 cooking hobbyists from House Party's army of advocates to host Cooking Crème parties in their homes, where invited guests sampled recipes jazzed up with the flavourful new product. Kraft supplied kits filled with samples, recipes, coupons, and other incentives to help stage the parties and encourage invited guests to spread the good news afterward. The Philadelphia Cooking Crème word-of-mouth campaign was an overwhelming success. More than 138 000 people attended the dinner parties. And, of course, participants shared their in-person experiences on their social media channels. As a result, brand familiarity for the new product increased 39 percent while purchase intention rose 60 percent. Partygoers generated more than 22 million brand impressions, leading to 1 million product trials and a 175 percent return on campaign investment.

Whether offline, online, or both, effective word-of-mouth marketing isn't something that just happens. And it's more than just building a following on Facebook. Marketers must build comprehensive programs that spark person-to-person brand conversations and then help them catch fire. The goal of word-of-mouth marketing is to "find and nurture true brand advocates [and to] encourage and amplify the narrative that naturally occurs," says one expert. It's about finding the company's best customers, giving them opportunities to become more involved, and helping them spread their brand passion and enthusiasm within their in-person and online social networks. "That's good advice to share with all your marketing friends and associates," advises another marketer.

Sources: Jack Neff, "Dollar Shave Club's Dubin Offers Tips for a Truly Viral Video," *Advertising Age*, July 18, 2012, http://adage.com/print/236099; Stuart Feil, "Gift for Gab: What Marketers Are Doing to Encourage and Amplify Word-of-Mouth," *Adweek*, December 10, 2012, pp. W1–W2; Giselle Abramovich, "Why Ford Credits Social Media in Turnaround," *Digiday*, October 10, 2012, www.digiday.com/brands/why-ford-credits-social-media-in-turnaround; Stuart Elliott, "Ford Turns to the Crowd for New Fiesta Ads," *New York Times*, February 19, 2013, http://mediadecoder.blogs.nytimes.com/2013/02/19/ford-turns-to-the-crowd-for-new-fiesta-ads; and www.escaperoutes.com, www.randomactsoffusion.com, and www.fiestamovement.com, accessed October 2013.

Personal Factors   A buyer's decisions are also influenced by personal characteristics such as the buyer's *age and life-cycle stage, occupation, economic situation, lifestyle,* and *personality and self-concept.*

AGE AND LIFE-CYCLE STAGE   People change the goods and services they buy over their lifetimes. Tastes in food, clothes, furniture, and recreation are often age related. Buying is also shaped by the stage of the family life cycle—the stages through which families might pass as they mature over time. Life-stage changes usually result from demographics and life-changing events—marriage, having children, purchasing a home, divorce, children going to university, changes in personal income, moving out of the house, and retirement. Marketers often define their target markets in terms of life-cycle stage and develop appropriate products and marketing plans for each stage.

For example, consumer information giant Acxiom's Personicx life-stage segmentation system places households into one of 70 consumer segments and 21 life-stage groups, based on specific consumer behaviour and demographic characteristics. Personicx includes life-stage groups with names such as *Beginnings, Taking Hold, Cash & Careers, Jumbo Families, Transition Time, Our Turn, Golden Years*, and *Active Elders*. The *Taking Hold* group consists of young, energetic, well-funded couples and young families who are busy with their careers, social lives, and interests, especially fitness and active recreation. *Transition Time* are blue-collar, less-educated, mid-income consumers who are transitioning to stable lives and talking about marriage and children.

"Consumers experience many life-stage changes during their lifetimes," says Acxiom. "As their life stages change, so do their behaviours and purchasing preferences." Armed with data about the timing and makeup of life-stage changes, marketers can create targeted, personalized campaigns.[15]

OCCUPATION A person's occupation affects the goods and services bought. Blue-collar workers tend to buy more rugged work clothes, whereas executives buy more business suits. Marketers try to identify the occupational groups that have an above-average interest in their products and services. A company can even specialize in making products needed by a given occupational group. For example, Moores Clothing for Men has grown to become Canada's leading national retailer of men's business attire. In 30 years, the company has grown to more than 100 stores across Canada, including stores in virtually every major city. The company's founders attribute their success to their commitment to offer Canada's largest selection of quality menswear at the lowest possible everyday prices, and to customer satisfaction. The company guarantees its customers that "if for any reason you are not satisfied with any Moores purchase, simply bring it back for a full refund or exchange." The company strives "to provide customers with everything they want: high quality, outstanding selection, superior customer service, and everyday low prices."[16]

ECONOMIC SITUATION A person's economic situation will affect his or her store and product choices. Marketers watch trends in personal income, savings, and interest rates. In the more frugal times following the Great Recession, most companies have taken steps to redesign, reposition, and reprice their products and services. For example, upscale discounter Target has replaced some of its "chic" with "cheap." It is putting more emphasis on the "Pay less" side of its "Expect more. Pay less" positioning promise.

As mentioned in the opening story in Chapter 1, Canadian brand Joe Fresh signed a deal with major U.S. retailer JCPenney to bring "stylish, fresh and affordable fashion" to nearly 700 locations in the U.S. market. This was one aspect of JCPenney's sweeping changes in its marketing, which included an everyday-low-price strategy featuring simpler pricing and an end to seemingly endless deals and sales. "Enough. Is. Enough" said the retailer's commercials that introduced the new strategy. Ads depicted shoppers screaming in frustration at having to clip coupons, rush to take advantage of sales, and stand in line for blowout promotions.[17]

PERSONICX

HOUSEHOLD SEGMENTATION
REACHES A NEW LEVEL OF ACCURACY

People aren't just a parent or only a doctor or simply a scuba diver. They can be all of these things – and more. Acxiom's 70 segments and 21 Life Stage groupings will let you know your customers and target them with unmatched precision. And Personicx® is the only household-level segmentation product that uses our industry-leading InfoBase® data. You'll now see your prospects as they really are.

www.acxiom.com • 1.888.3ACXIOM   ACXIOM

Acxion Corporation

Exhibit 6.5 Life-stage segmentation: Personicx's 21 life-stage groupings let marketers see customers as they really are and target them precisely. "People aren't just a parent or only a doctor or simply a scuba diver. They are all of these things."

Lifestyle
A person's pattern of living as expressed in his or her activities, interests, and opinions.

LIFESTYLE People coming from the same subculture, social class, and occupation may have quite different lifestyles. **Lifestyle** is a person's pattern of living as expressed in his or her psychographics. It involves measuring consumers' major AIO dimensions—activities (work, hobbies, shopping, sports, social events), interests (food, fashion, family, recreation), and opinions (about themselves, social issues, businesses, products). Lifestyle captures something more than the person's social class or personality. It profiles a person's whole pattern of acting and interacting in the world.

When used carefully, the lifestyle concept can help marketers understand changing consumer values and how they affect buyer behaviour. Consumers don't just buy products; they buy the values and lifestyles those products represent. For example, outdoor outfitter REI sells a lot more than just outdoor gear and clothing. It sells an entire outdoor lifestyle for active people who "love to get outside and play."[18] One REI ad shows a woman biking in the wide-open spaces, proclaiming "REI prefer hitting the trails over the snooze button, whatever that is." At the REI website, outdoor enthusiasts can swap outdoors stories, enroll in REI Outdoor School classes at local locations, or even sign up for any of dozens of REI-sponsored outdoor travel adventures around the world.

Marketers look for lifestyle segments with needs that can be served through special products or marketing approaches. Such segments might be defined by anything from family characteristics or outdoor interests to pet ownership. In fact, today's involved pet ownership lifestyles have created a huge and growing lifestyle segment of indulgent "pet parents":

Personality
The unique psychological characteristics that distinguish a person or group.

> For many devoted pet parents, having a pet affects just about every buying decision they make, from what car they buy or where they stay on vacation to even what TV channels they watch. For example, The Benjamin Hotel in New York takes "pet friendly" to a whole new level. Its "Dream Dog" program offers "everything a pampered pet needs to enjoy travel in tail-wagging style." The program provides orthopedic dog beds, plush doggie bathrobes, canine room service, and DVDs for dogs, as well as access to pet spa treatments and a pet psychic. "We will ensure your furry friend never has to lift a paw," says the hotel.
>
> The list goes on and on. For owners of overweight dogs (40 percent of them are), there's the PetZen doggie treadmill (US$500 to US$900). For those who must leave their dogs behind while they work or play, there's DogTV, a cable channel "designed to keep your dog happy and contained while you're away." For owners who don't want their male pets to suffer the blow to their self-esteem that comes from being neutered, there are Neuticles, patented testicular implants for pets. Some 500 000 dogs, cats, monkeys, rats, and even a water buffalo sport a pair. And for a growing number of people who find it just too hard to part with their deceased pets, you can have them freeze-dried, stuffed, and preserved in a natural pose so that they'll always be around. Now that's the pet owner lifestyle.[19]

The Benjamin Hotel

Exhibit 6.6 Catering to pet-owner lifestyles: The Benjamin Hotel's Dream Dog program "offers everything a pampered pooch needs to enjoy traveling in tail-wagging style, from grooming services to a lush bathrobe to a consultation with a pet psychic."

PERSONALITY AND SELF-CONCEPT Each person's distinct personality influences his or her buying behaviour. **Personality** refers to the unique psychological characteristics that distinguish a person or group. Personality is usually described in terms of traits such as self-confidence, dominance, sociability, autonomy, defensiveness, adaptability, and aggressiveness. Personality can be useful in analyzing consumer behaviour for certain product or brand choices.

The idea is that brands also have personalities, and consumers are likely to choose brands with personalities that match their own. A *brand personality* is the specific mix of human traits that may be attributed to a particular brand. One researcher identified five brand personality traits: *sincerity* (down-to-earth, honest, wholesome, and cheerful), *excitement* (daring, spirited, imaginative, and up to date), *competence* (reliable, intelligent, and successful), *sophistication* (glamorous, upper class, charming), and *ruggedness* (outdoorsy and tough). "Your personality determines what you consume, what TV shows you watch, what products you buy, and [most] other decisions you make," says one consumer behaviour expert.[20]

Most well-known brands are strongly associated with one particular trait: the Ford F150 with "ruggedness," Apple with "excitement," the *Washington Post* with "competence," Method with "sincerity," and Gucci with "class" and "sophistication." Hence, these brands will attract persons who are high on the same personality traits.

Skullcandy, the performance headphone and audio accessory maker, projects a young, active, trendsetting, rebellious personality. The brand's leading-edge designs, vibrant colours, and unique styles provide "instant gratification for your ears." Skullcandy enhances its stylish, trend-setting persona through associations with a host of high-profile endorsers ranging from rappers Jay-Z, Snoop Dogg, and Wale to supermodels Kate Upton and Chanel Iman to NBA stars Kevin Durant and Derrick Rose to surfer Dane Reynolds and a whole team of skateboarders, including legend Eric Koston. Like-minded fans can keep track of their adventures, opinions, and interests on Skullcandy's website and blog.[21]

Associated Press

Exhibit 6.7 Brand personality: Consumers are likely to choose brands with personalities that match their own. The Gucci brand is associated with "class" and "sophistication."

Many marketers use a concept related to personality—a person's *self-concept* (also called *self-image*). The idea is that people's possessions contribute to and reflect their identities—that is, "we are what we consume." Thus, to understand consumer behaviour, marketers must first understand the relationship between consumer self-concept and possessions.

Psychological Factors A person's buying choices are further influenced by four major psychological factors: *motivation*, *perception*, *learning*, and *beliefs and attitudes*.

MOTIVATION A person has many needs at any given time. Some are biological, arising from states of tension such as hunger, thirst, or discomfort. Others are psychological, arising from the need for recognition, esteem, or belonging. A need becomes a motive when it is aroused to a sufficient level of intensity. A **motive** (or **drive**) is a need that is sufficiently pressing to direct the person to seek satisfaction. Psychologists have developed theories of human motivation. Two of the most popular—the theories of Sigmund Freud and Abraham Maslow—carry quite different meanings for consumer analysis and marketing.

Motive (drive)
A need that is sufficiently pressing to direct the person to seek satisfaction of the need.

Sigmund Freud assumed that people are largely unconscious about the real psychological forces shaping their behaviour. His theory suggests that a person's buying decisions are affected by subconscious motives that even the buyer may not fully understand. Thus, an aging baby boomer who buys a sporty BMW convertible might explain that he simply likes the feel of the wind in his thinning hair. At a deeper level, he may be trying to impress others with his success. At a still deeper level, he may be buying the car to feel young and independent again.

The term *motivation research* refers to qualitative research designed to probe consumers' hidden, subconscious motivations. Consumers often don't know or can't describe why they act as they do. Thus, motivation researchers use a variety of probing techniques to uncover underlying emotions and attitudes toward brands and buying situations.

Many companies employ teams of psychologists, anthropologists, and other social scientists to carry out motivation research. One ad agency routinely conducts one-on-one, therapy-like interviews to delve into the inner workings of consumers. Another company asks consumers to describe their favourite brands as animals or cars (say, a Mercedes versus a Chevy) to assess the prestige associated with various brands. Still others rely on hypnosis, dream therapy, or soft lights and mood music to plumb the murky depths of consumer psyches.

FIGURE 6.3 Maslow's Hierarchy of Needs

Such projective techniques seem pretty goofy, and some marketers dismiss such motivation research as mumbo jumbo. But many marketers use such touchy-feely approaches, now sometimes called *interpretive consumer research*, to dig deeper into consumer psyches and develop better marketing strategies.

Abraham Maslow sought to explain why people are driven by particular needs at particular times. Why does one person spend a lot of time and energy on personal safety and another on gaining the esteem of others? Maslow's answer is that human needs are arranged in a hierarchy, as shown in Figure 6.3, from the most pressing at the bottom to the least pressing at the top.[22] They include *physiological* needs, *safety* needs, *social* needs, *esteem* needs, and *self-actualization* needs.

A person tries to satisfy the most important need first. When that need is satisfied, it will stop being a motivator, and the person will then try to satisfy the next most important need. For example, starving people (physiological need) will not take an interest in the latest happenings in the art world (self-actualization needs), nor in how they are seen or esteemed by others (social or esteem needs), nor even in whether they are breathing clean air (safety needs). But as each important need is satisfied, the next most important need will come into play. Critics of Maslow's Hierarchy argue that human motivation does not always follow this hierarchical structure. For example, consumers may often seek to satisfy esteem needs by purchasing a $400 pair of designer jeans while ignoring lower-order safety needs by not paying the rent!

PERCEPTION A motivated person is ready to act. How the person acts is influenced by his or her own perception of the situation. All of us learn by the flow of information through our five senses: sight, hearing, smell, touch, and taste. However, each of us receives, organizes, and interprets this sensory information in an individual way. **Perception** is the process by which people select, organize, and interpret information to form a meaningful picture of the world.

Perception
The process by which people select, organize, and interpret information to form a meaningful picture of the world.

People can form different perceptions of the same stimulus because of three perceptual processes: selective attention, selective distortion, and selective retention. People are exposed to a great amount of stimuli every day—including an estimated 3000 to 5000 ad messages.[23] It is impossible for a person to pay attention to all these stimuli. *Selective attention*—the tendency for people to screen out most of the information to which they are exposed—means that marketers must work especially hard to attract the consumer's attention.

Even noticed stimuli do not always come across in the intended way. Each person fits incoming information into an existing mindset. *Selective distortion* describes the tendency of people to interpret information in a way that will support what they already believe. People also will forget much of what they learn. They tend to retain information that supports their attitudes and beliefs. *Selective retention* means that consumers are likely to remember good points made about a brand they favour and forget good points made about competing brands. Because of selective attention, distortion, and retention, marketers must work hard to get their messages through.

Interestingly, although most marketers worry about whether their offers will be perceived at all, some consumers worry that they will be affected by marketing messages without even knowing it—through *subliminal advertising*. More than 50 years ago, a researcher announced that he had flashed the phrases "Eat popcorn" and "Drink Coca-Cola" on a screen in a New Jersey movie theater every five seconds for 1/300th of a second. He reported that although viewers did not consciously recognize these messages, they absorbed them subconsciously and bought 58 percent more popcorn and 18 percent more Coke. Suddenly advertisers and consumer-protection groups became intensely interested in subliminal perception. Although the researcher later admitted to making up the data, the issue has not died. Some consumers still fear that they are being manipulated by subliminal messages.

Numerous studies by psychologists and consumer researchers have found little or no link between subliminal messages and consumer behaviour. Recent brain-wave studies have found that in certain circumstances, our brains may register subliminal messages. However, it appears that subliminal advertising simply doesn't have the power attributed to it by its critics. One classic ad from the American Marketing Association pokes fun at subliminal advertising. "So-called 'subliminal advertising' simply doesn't exist," says the ad. "Overactive imaginations, however, most certainly do."[24]

LEARNING When people act, they learn. **Learning** describes changes in an individual's behaviour arising from experience. Learning theorists say that most human behaviour is learned. Learning occurs through the interplay of drives, stimuli, cues, responses, and reinforcement.

A *drive* is a strong internal stimulus that calls for action. A drive becomes a motive when it is directed toward a particular *stimulus object*. For example, a person's drive for self-actualization might motivate him or her to look into buying a camera. The consumer's response to the idea of buying a camera is conditioned by the surrounding cues. *Cues* are minor stimuli that determine when, where, and how the person responds. For example, the person might spot several camera brands in a shop window, hear of a special sale price, or discuss cameras with a friend. These are all cues that might influence a consumer's *response* to his or her interest in buying the product.

Suppose the consumer buys a Nikon camera. If the experience is rewarding, the consumer will probably use the camera more and more, and his or her response will be *reinforced*. Then the next time he or she shops for a camera, or for binoculars or some similar product, the probability is greater that he or she will buy a Nikon product. The practical significance of learning theory for marketers is that they can build up

Learning
Changes in an individual's behaviour arising from experience.

PEOPLE HAVE BEEN TRYING TO FIND THE BREASTS IN THESE ICE CUBES SINCE 1957.

The advertising industry is sometimes charged with sneaking seductive little pictures into ads.
    Supposedly, these pictures can get you to buy a product without your even seeing them.
    Consider the photograph above. According to some people, there's a pair of female breasts

hidden in the patterns of light refracted by the ice cubes.
    Well, if you really searched you probably *could* see the breasts. For that matter, you could also see Millard Fillmore, a stuffed pork chop and a 1946 Dodge.
    The point is that so-called "subliminal advertising" simply

doesn't exist. Overactive imaginations, however, most certainly do.
    So if anyone claims to see breasts in that drink up there, they aren't in the ice cubes.
    They're in the eye of the beholder.

ADVERTISING
ANOTHER WORD FOR FREEDOM OF CHOICE.
American Association of Advertising Agencies

American Association of Advertising Agencies, Inc.

Exhibit 6.8 This classic ad from the American Association of Advertising Agencies pokes fun at subliminal advertising. "So-called 'subliminal advertising' simply doesn't exist," says the ad. "Overactive imaginations, however, most certainly do."

demand for a product by associating it with strong drives, using motivating cues, and providing positive reinforcement.

BELIEFS AND ATTITUDES Through doing and learning, people acquire beliefs and attitudes. These, in turn, influence their buying behaviour. A **belief** is a descriptive thought that a person holds about something. Beliefs may be based on real knowledge, opinion, or faith and may or may not carry an emotional charge. Marketers are interested in the beliefs that people formulate about specific products and services because these beliefs make up product and brand images that affect buying behaviour. If some of the beliefs are wrong and prevent purchase, the marketer will want to launch a campaign to correct them.

People have attitudes regarding religion, politics, clothes, music, food, and almost everything else. **Attitude** describes a person's relatively consistent evaluations, feelings, and tendencies toward an object or idea. Attitudes put people into a frame of mind of liking or disliking things, of moving toward or away from them. Our camera buyer may hold attitudes such as "Buy the best," "The Japanese make the best electronics products in the world," and "Creativity and self-expression are among the most important things in life." If so, the Nikon camera would fit well into the consumer's existing attitudes.

Attitudes are difficult to change. A person's attitudes fit into a pattern; changing one attitude may require difficult adjustments in many others. Thus, a company should usually try to fit its products into existing attitudes rather than attempt to change attitudes. Of course, there are exceptions. For example, trying to convince parents that their children would actually like onions—that's right, onions—seems like an uphill battle against prevailing attitudes. Convincing the children themselves seems like an even bigger challenge. However, in the United States, the Vidalia Onion Committee (VOC), formed to promote one of Georgia state's most important agricultural products, managed to do just that:

> It can be hard selling children on the idea of eating onions. Onions have a strong smell, they can make you cry, and many kids simply refuse to eat them. So to help change these attitudes, the VOC developed a unique plan. It employed Shrek, the famous ogre from the hugely popular animated films. The inspiration came from a scene in the first Shrek film, in which Shrek explains ogres to his friend, Donkey. "Onions have layers, ogres have layers," says Shrek. "Ogres are like onions. End of story."
>
> The result was a national "Ogres and Onions" marketing campaign, launched to coincide with both the onion harvest and the premier of the latest Shrek film. The campaign featured giant Shrek placards in grocery store aisles alongside bags of Vidalia onions on which Shrek asked, "What do ogres and onions have in common?" At the Vidalia Onion site, Shrek offered kid-friendly Vidalia onion recipes. The award-winning campaign soon had kids clamouring for onions, and surprised and delighted parents responded. Sales of bagged Vidalia onions increased almost 30 percent for the season.[25]

We can now appreciate the many forces acting on consumer behaviour. The consumer's choice results from the complex interplay of cultural, social, personal, and psychological factors.

The Buyer Decision Process LO2

Now that we've looked at the influences that affect buyers, we are ready to look at how consumers make buying decisions. Figure 6.4 shows that the buyer decision process consists of five stages: *need recognition, information search, evaluation of alternatives, purchase decision,* and *postpurchase behaviour.* Clearly, the buying process starts long before the actual purchase and continues long after. Marketers need to focus on the entire buying process rather than on the purchase decision only.

Figure 6.4 suggests that consumers pass through all five stages with every purchase in a considered way. But buyers may pass quickly or slowly through the buying decision process. And in more routine purchases, consumers often skip or reverse some of the

Belief
A descriptive thought that a person holds about something.

Attitude
A person's consistently favourable or unfavourable evaluations, feelings, and tendencies toward an object or idea.

The Vidalia Onion Committee

Exhibit 6.9 Attitudes and beliefs are difficult to change: The Vidalia Onion Committee's award-winning Ogres and Onions campaign made children believers and delighted their parents. Sales of bagged Vidalia onions shot up 30 percent.

FIGURE 6.4 Buyer Decision Process

| Need recognition | → | Information search | → | Evaluation of alternatives | → | Purchase decision | → | Postpurchase behaviour |

stages. Much depends on the nature of the buyer, the product, and the buying situation. A woman buying her regular brand of toothpaste would recognize the need and go right to the purchase decision, skipping information search and evaluation. However, we use the model in Figure 6.4 because it shows all the considerations that arise when a consumer faces a new and complex purchase situation.

Need Recognition The buying process starts with *need recognition*—the buyer recognizes a problem or need. The need can be triggered by *internal stimuli* when one of the person's normal needs—for example, hunger or thirst—rises to a level high enough to become a drive. A need can also be triggered by *external stimuli*. For example, an advertisement or a discussion with a friend might get you thinking about buying a new car. At this stage, the marketer should research consumers to find out what kinds of needs or problems arise, what brought them about, and how they led the consumer to this particular product.

Information Search An interested consumer may or may not search for more information. If the consumer's drive is strong and a satisfying product is near at hand, he or she is likely to buy it then. If not, the consumer may store the need in memory or undertake an *information search* related to the need. For example, once you've decided you need a new car, at the least, you will probably pay more attention to car ads, cars owned by friends, and car conversations. Or you may actively search the Web, talk with friends, and gather information in other ways.

Consumers can obtain information from any of several sources. These include *personal sources* (family, friends, neighbours, acquaintances), *commercial sources* (advertising, salespeople, dealer websites, packaging, displays), *public sources* (mass media, consumer rating organizations, social media, online searches, and peer reviews), and *experiential sources* (examining and using the product). The relative influence of these information sources varies with the product and the buyer.

Traditionally, consumers have received the most information about a product from commercial sources—those controlled by the marketer. The most effective sources, however, tend to be personal. Commercial sources normally *inform* the buyer, but personal sources *legitimize* or *evaluate* products for the buyer. Few advertising campaigns can be as effective as a next-door neighbour leaning over the fence and raving about a wonderful experience with a product you are considering.

Increasingly, that "neighbour's fence" is a digital one. Today, consumers share product opinions, images, and experiences freely across social media. And buyers can find an abundance of user-generated reviews alongside the products they are considering at sites ranging from Amazon.com or BestBuy.com to Yelp, TripAdvisor, Epinions, and Epicurious. Although individual user

Exhibit 6.10 Need recognition can be triggered by advertising: Time for a snack?

MARS CHOCOLATE NORTH AMERICA

reviews vary widely in quality, an entire body of reviews often provides a reliable product assessment—straight from the fingertips of people like you who've actually purchased and experienced the product.

As more information is obtained, the consumer's awareness and knowledge of the available brands and features increase. In your car information search, you may learn about several brands that are available. The information might also help you to drop certain brands from consideration. A company must design its marketing mix to make prospects aware of and knowledgeable about its brand. It should carefully identify consumers' sources of information and the importance of each source.

Evaluation of Alternatives We have seen how consumers use information to arrive at a set of final brand choices. Next, marketers need to know about *alternative evaluation*, that is, how consumers process information to choose among alternative brands. Unfortunately, consumers do not use a simple and single evaluation process in all buying situations. Instead, several evaluation processes are at work.

How consumers go about evaluating purchase alternatives depends on the individual consumer and the specific buying situation. In some cases, consumers use careful calculations and logical thinking. At other times, the same consumers do little or no evaluating. Instead they buy on impulse and rely on intuition. Sometimes consumers make buying decisions on their own; sometimes they turn to friends, online reviews, or salespeople for buying advice.

Suppose you've narrowed your car choices to three brands. And suppose that you are primarily interested in four attributes—price, style, operating economy, and warranty. By this time, you've probably formed beliefs about how each brand rates on each attribute. Clearly, if one car rated best on all the attributes, the marketer could predict that you would choose it. However, the brands will no doubt vary in appeal. You might base your buying decision mostly on one attribute, and your choice would be easy to predict. If you wanted style above everything else, you would buy the car that you think has the most style. But most buyers consider several attributes, each with a different importance. By knowing the importance that you assigned to each attribute, the marketer could predict your car choice more reliably.

Marketers should study buyers to find out how they actually evaluate brand alternatives. If marketers know what evaluative processes go on, they can take steps to influence the buyer's decision.

Purchase Decision In the evaluation stage, the consumer ranks brands and forms purchase intentions. Generally, the consumer's *purchase decision* will be to buy the most preferred brand, but two factors can come between the purchase *intention* and the purchase *decision*. The first factor is the *attitudes of others*. If someone important to you thinks that you should buy the lowest-priced car, then the chances of your buying a more expensive car are reduced.

The second factor is *unexpected situational factors*. The consumer may form a purchase intention based on factors such as expected income, expected price, and expected product benefits. However, unexpected events may change the purchase intention. For example, the economy might take a turn for the worse, a close competitor might drop its price, or a friend might report being disappointed in your preferred car. Thus, preferences and even purchase intentions do not always result in an actual purchase choice.

Postpurchase Behaviour The marketer's job does not end when the product is bought. After purchasing the product, the consumer will be either satisfied or dissatisfied and will engage in *postpurchase behaviour* of interest to the marketer. What determines whether the buyer is satisfied or dissatisfied with a purchase? The answer lies in the relationship between the *consumer's expectations* and the product's *perceived performance*. If the product falls short of expectations, the consumer is disappointed; if it meets expectations, the consumer is satisfied; if it exceeds expectations, the consumer is delighted. The larger the gap between expectations and performance, the greater the consumer's dissatisfaction. This suggests that sellers should promise only what their brands can deliver so that buyers are satisfied.

Almost all major purchases, however, result in **cognitive dissonance**, or discomfort caused by postpurchase conflict. After the purchase, consumers are satisfied with the benefits of the chosen brand and are glad to avoid the drawbacks of the brands not bought. However, every purchase involves compromise. So consumers feel uneasy about acquiring the drawbacks of the chosen brand and about losing the benefits of the brands not purchased. Thus, consumers feel at least some postpurchase dissonance for every purchase.[26]

Stephane Bidouze/Shutterstock.com

Exhibit 6.11 Postpurchase cognitive dissonance: No matter what choice they make, consumers feel at least some postpurchase dissonance for every decision.

Why is it so important to satisfy the customer? Customer satisfaction is a key to building profitable relationships with consumers—to keeping and growing consumers and reaping their customer lifetime value. Satisfied customers buy a product again, talk favourably to others about the product, pay less attention to competing brands and advertising, and buy other products from the company. Many marketers go beyond merely *meeting* the expectations of customers—they aim to *delight* customers.

A dissatisfied consumer responds differently. Bad word of mouth often travels farther and faster than good word of mouth. It can quickly damage consumer attitudes about a company and its products. But companies cannot simply wait for dissatisfied customers to volunteer their complaints. Most unhappy customers never tell the company about their problems. Therefore, a company should measure customer satisfaction regularly. It should set up systems that *encourage* customers to complain. In this way, the company can learn how well it is doing and how it can improve.

By studying the overall buyer decision process, marketers may be able to find ways to help consumers move through it. For example, if consumers are not buying a new product because they do not perceive a need for it, marketing might launch advertising messages that trigger the need and show how the product solves customers' problems. If customers know about the product but are not buying because they hold unfavourable attitudes toward it, marketers must find ways to change either the product or consumer perceptions.

Cognitive dissonance
Buyer discomfort caused by postpurchase conflict.

The Buyer Decision Process for New Products LO3

We now look at how buyers approach the purchase of new products. A **new product** is a good, service, or idea that is perceived by some potential customers as new. It may have been around for a while, but our interest is in how consumers learn about products for the first time and make decisions on whether to adopt them. We define the **adoption process** as the mental process through which an individual passes from first learning about an innovation to final adoption. *Adoption* is the decision by an individual to become a regular user of the product.[27]

New product
A good, service, or idea that is perceived by some potential customers as new.

Adoption process
The mental process through which an individual passes from first hearing about an innovation to final adoption.

CHEVY'S
LOVE IT OR RETURN IT
GUARANTEE*

Go to chevyconfidence.com for details.

Exhibit 6.12 **The adoption process:** To help buyers past the car-buying decision hurdle in a still-tight economy, Chevrolet offered a "Love It or Return It" guarantee giving uncertain buyers up to 60 days to reverse the buying decision.

Stages in the Adoption Process Consumers go through five stages in the process of adopting a new product:

Awareness: The consumer becomes aware of the new product but lacks information about it.

Interest: The consumer seeks information about the new product.

Evaluation: The consumer considers whether trying the new product makes sense.

Trial: The consumer tries the new product on a small scale to improve his or her estimate of its value.

Adoption: The consumer decides to make full and regular use of the new product.

This model suggests that marketers should think about how to help consumers move through these stages. For example, to help customers past the car-purchase decision hurdle in a still-tight economy, in 2012, Chevrolet launched a "Love It or Return It" guarantee at U.S. dealerships. The program promised uncertain buyers of 2013 models up to 60 days to return cars that had been driven fewer than 4000 miles and had no damage. Car maker Hyundai had offered a similar but even greater incentive program to help reduce purchasing barriers following the economic meltdown in 2008. Its Hyundai Assurance Plan promised to let buyers who financed or leased their new Hyundais to return them at no cost and with no harm to their credit rating if they lost their jobs or incomes within a year. Sales of the Hyundai Sonata surged 85 percent in the month following the start of the campaign.[28]

Individual Differences in Innovativeness People differ greatly in their readiness to try new products. In each product area, there are "consumption pioneers" and early adopters. Other individuals adopt new products much later. People can be classified according to the adopter categories shown in Figure 6.5.[29] As shown by the curve, after a slow start, an increasing number of people adopt the new product. As successive groups of consumers adopt the innovation, it eventually reaches its cumulative saturation level. Innovators are defined as the first 2.5 percent of buyers to adopt a new idea (those beyond two standard deviations from mean adoption time); the early adopters are the next 13.5 percent (between one and two standard deviations); and then come early mainstream, late mainstream, and lagging adopters.

The five adopter groups have differing values. *Innovators* are venturesome—they try new ideas at some risk. *Early adopters* are guided by respect—they are opinion leaders in their communities and adopt new ideas early but carefully. *Early mainstream* adopters are deliberate—although they are rarely leaders, they adopt new ideas before the average person. *Late mainstream* adopters are skeptical—they adopt an innovation only after a majority of people have tried it. Finally, *lagging adopters* are tradition bound—they are suspicious of changes and adopt the innovation only when it has become something of a tradition itself.

This adopter classification suggests that an innovating firm should research the characteristics of innovators and early adopters in their product categories and direct initial marketing efforts toward them.

FIGURE 6.5 Adopter Categories Based on Relative Time of Innovation Adoption

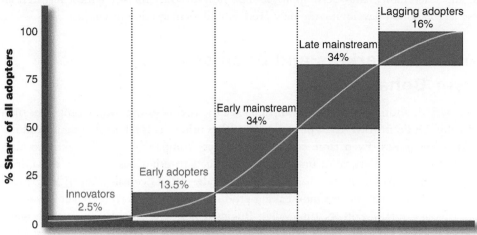

Influence of Product Characteristics on Rate of Adoption The characteristics of the new product affect its rate of adoption. Some products catch on almost overnight. For example, Apple's iPod, iPhone, and iPad flew off retailers' shelves at an astounding rate from the day they were first introduced. Others take a longer time to gain acceptance. For example, the first HDTVs were introduced in North America in the 1990s, but the proportion of households owning a high-definition set stood at only 12 percent by 2007. By the end of 2012, HDTV penetration was more than 75 percent.[30]

Five characteristics are especially important in influencing an innovation's rate of adoption. For example, consider the characteristics of HDTV in relation to the rate of adoption:

Relative advantage: The degree to which the innovation appears superior to existing products. HDTV offers substantially improved picture quality. This accelerated its rate of adoption.

Compatibility: The degree to which the innovation fits the values and experiences of potential consumers. HDTV, for example, is highly compatible with the lifestyles of the TV-watching public. However, in the early years, HDTV was not yet compatible with programming and broadcasting systems, which slowed adoption. Now, as high-definition programs and channels have become the norm, the rate of HDTV adoption has increased rapidly.

Complexity: The degree to which the innovation is difficult to understand or use. HDTVs are not very complex. Therefore, as more programming has become available and prices have fallen, the rate of HDTV adoption has increased faster than that of more complex innovations.

Divisibility: The degree to which the innovation may be tried on a limited basis. Early HDTVs and HD cable and satellite systems were very expensive, which slowed the rate of adoption. As prices have fallen, adoption rates have increased.

Communicability: The degree to which the results of using the innovation can be observed or described to others. Because HDTV lends itself to demonstration and description, its use spread faster among consumers.

Other characteristics influence the rate of adoption, such as initial and ongoing costs, risk and uncertainty, and social approval. The new-product marketer must research all these factors when developing the new product and its marketing program.

◄⊙ Simulate on MyMarketingLab

B2B

Business Markets and Business Buyer Behaviour LO4

In one way or another, most large companies sell to other organizations. Companies such as Boeing, DuPont, IBM, Caterpillar, and countless other firms sell *most* of their products to other businesses. Even large consumer-products companies, which make products used by final consumers, must first sell their products to other businesses. For example, General Mills makes many familiar consumer brands—Big G cereals (Cheerios, Wheaties, Trix, Chex, Total, Fiber One), baking products (Pillsbury, Betty Crocker, Bisquick, Gold Medal flour), snacks (Nature Valley, Bugles, Chex Mix), Yoplait yogurt, Häagen-Dazs ice cream, and many others. But to sell these products to consumers, General Mills must first sell them to its wholesaler and retailer customers, who in turn serve the consumer market.

Business buyer behaviour refers to the buying behaviour of the organizations that buy goods and services for use in the production of other products and services that are sold, rented, or supplied to others. It also includes the behaviour of retailing and wholesaling firms that acquire goods to resell or rent them to others at a profit. In the **business buying process**, business buyers determine which products and services their organizations need to purchase and then find, evaluate, and choose among alternative suppliers and brands. *Business-to-business (B-to-B) marketers* must do their best to understand business markets and business buyer behaviour. Then, like businesses that sell to final buyers, they must build profitable relationships with business customers by creating superior customer value.

Business buyer behaviour
The buying behaviour of organizations that buy goods and services for use in the production of other products and services that are sold, rented, or supplied to others.

Business buying process
The decision process by which business buyers determine which products and services their organizations need to purchase and then find, evaluate, and choose among alternative suppliers and brands.

Business Markets

The business market is *huge*. In fact, business markets involve far more dollars and items than do consumer markets. For example, think about the large number of business transactions involved in the production and sale of a single set of Goodyear tires. Various suppliers sell Goodyear the rubber, steel, equipment, and other goods that it needs to produce tires. Goodyear then sells the finished tires to retailers, which in turn sell them to consumers. Thus, many sets of *business* purchases were made for only one set of *consumer* purchases. In addition, Goodyear sells tires as original equipment to manufacturers that install them on new vehicles and as replacement tires to companies that maintain their own fleets of company cars, trucks, or other vehicles.

In some ways, business markets are similar to consumer markets. Both involve people who assume buying roles and make purchase decisions to satisfy needs. However, business markets differ in many ways from consumer markets. The main differences are in *market structure and demand*, the *nature of the buying unit*, and the *types of decisions and the decision process* involved.

Market Structure and Demand   The business marketer normally deals with *far fewer but far larger buyers* than the consumer marketer does. Even in large business markets, a few buyers often account for most of the purchasing. For example, when Goodyear sells replacement tires to final consumers, its potential market includes millions of car owners around the world. But its fate in business markets depends on getting orders from only a handful of large automakers.

Further, business demand is **derived demand**—it ultimately derives from the demand for consumer goods. For example, W. L. Gore & Associates sells its Gore-Tex brand to manufacturers who make and sell outdoor apparel brands made from Gore-Tex fabrics. If demand for these brands increases, so does demand for Gore-Tex fabrics. So to boost demand for Gore-Tex, Gore advertises to final consumers to educate them on the benefits of Gore-Tex fabrics in the brands they buy. It also directly markets brands containing Gore-Tex—from Arc'teryx, Marmot, and The North Face to Burton and L.L.Bean—on its own website (www.gore-tex.com).

To further deepen its direct relationship with outdoor enthusiasts, Gore even sponsors an "Experience More" online community in which members can share experiences and videos, connect with outdoor experts, and catch exclusive gear offers from partner brands. As a result, consumers around the world have learned to look for the familiar Gore-Tex brand label, and both Gore and its partner brands win. No matter what brand of apparel or footwear you buy, says the label, if it's made with Gore-Tex fabric, it's "guaranteed to keep you dry."

Finally, many business markets have *inelastic and more fluctuating demand*. The total demand for many business products is not much affected by price changes, especially in the short run. A drop in the price of leather will not cause shoe manufacturers to buy much more leather unless it results in lower shoe prices that, in turn, increase consumer demand for shoes. And the demand for many business goods and services tends to change more—and more quickly—than does the demand for consumer goods and services. A small percentage increase in consumer demand can cause large increases in business demand.

Exhibit 6.13 Derived demand: You can't buy anything directly from Gore, but to increase demand for Gore-Tex fabrics, the company markets directly to the buyers of outdoor apparel and other brands made from its fabrics. Both Gore and its partner brands—here, The North Face—win.

W. L. Gore & Associates

Derived demand
Business demand that ultimately comes from (derives from) the demand for consumer goods.

Nature of the Buying Unit Compared with consumer purchases, a business purchase usually involves *more decision participants* and a *more professional purchasing effort*. Often, business buying is done by trained purchasing agents who spend their working lives learning how to buy better. The more complex the purchase, the more likely it is that several people will participate in the decision-making process. Buying committees composed of technical experts and top management are common in the buying of major goods. Beyond this, B-to-B marketers now face a new breed of higher-level, better-trained supply managers. Therefore, companies must have well-trained marketers and salespeople to deal with these well-trained buyers.

Types of Decisions and the Decision Process Business buyers usually face *more complex* buying decisions than do consumer buyers. Business purchases often involve large sums of money, complex technical and economic considerations, and interactions among people at many levels of the buyer's organization. The business buying process also tends to be *longer* and *more formalized*. Large business purchases usually call for detailed product specifications, written purchase orders, careful supplier searches, and formal approval.

Finally, in the business buying process, the buyer and seller are often much *more dependent* on each other. B-to-B marketers may roll up their sleeves and work closely with their customers during all stages of the buying process—from helping customers define problems, to finding solutions, to supporting after-sale operation. They often

Exhibit 6.14 Dow Performance Plastics isn't just selling commodity plastics—it's helping the businesses that buy its plastics to be heroes with their own customers. "We believe in a simple concept . . . if you win, we win."

customize their offerings to individual customer needs. In the short run, sales go to suppliers who meet buyers' immediate product and service needs. In the long run, however, business-to-business marketers keep customers by meeting current needs *and* by partnering with them to help solve their problems.

For example, Dow Performance Plastics doesn't just sell commodity plastics *to* its industrial customers—it works *with* these customers to help them succeed in their own markets. "Whether they're using Dow's plastics to make bags for Safeway or for complex [automotive] applications, we have to help them succeed in their markets," says a Dow spokesperson. "Think of Dow as the team behind your team," says Dow at its website. "We believe in a simple concept . . . if you win, we win."[31]

As in Dow's case, in recent years, relationships between most customers and suppliers have been changing from downright adversarial to close and chummy. In fact, many customer companies are now practising **supplier development**, systematically developing networks of supplier-partners to ensure a dependable supply of the products and materials they use in making their own products or reselling to others. For example, Walmart doesn't have a "Purchasing Department"; it has a "Supplier Development Department." The giant retailer knows that it can't just rely on spot suppliers who might be available when needed. Instead, Walmart manages a huge network of supplier-partners that help provide the hundreds of billions of dollars of goods that it sells to its customers each year.

Supplier development
Systematic development of networks of supplier-partners to ensure an appropriate and dependable supply of products and materials for use in making products or reselling them to others.

Business Buyer Behaviour

At the most basic level, marketers want to know how business buyers will respond to various marketing stimuli. Figure 6.6 shows a model of business buyer behaviour. In this model, marketing and other stimuli affect the buying organization and produce certain buyer responses. To design good marketing strategies, marketers must understand what happens within the organization to turn stimuli into purchase responses.

FIGURE 6.6 Business Buyer Behaviour Model

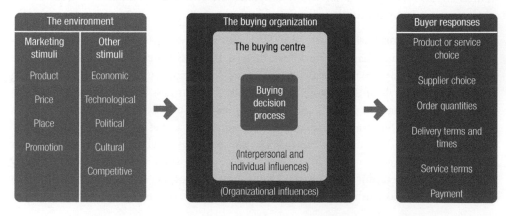

Within the organization, buying activity consists of two major parts: the *buying centre*, composed of all the people involved in the buying decision, and the *buying decision process*. The model shows that the buying centre and the buying decision process are influenced by internal organizational, interpersonal, and individual factors as well as external environmental factors.

The model in Figure 6.6 suggests four questions about business buyer behaviour: What buying decisions do business buyers make? Who participates in the business buying process? What are the major influences on buyers? How do business buyers make their buying decisions?

Major Types of Buying Situations There are three major types of buying situations.[32] In a **straight rebuy**, the buyer reorders something without any modifications. It is usually handled on a routine basis by the purchasing department. To keep the business, "in" suppliers try to maintain product and service quality. "Out" suppliers try to find new ways to add value or exploit dissatisfaction so that the buyer will consider them.

In a **modified rebuy**, the buyer wants to modify product specifications, prices, terms, or suppliers. The "in" suppliers may become nervous and feel pressured to put their best foot forward to protect an account. "Out" suppliers may see the modified rebuy situation as an opportunity to make a better offer and gain new business.

A company buying a product or service for the first time faces a **new task** situation. In such cases, the greater the cost or risk, the larger the number of decision participants and the greater the company's efforts to collect information. The new task situation is the marketer's greatest opportunity and challenge. The marketer not only tries to reach as many key buying influences as possible, but also provides help and information. As you would expect, the buyer makes the fewest decisions in a straight rebuy and the most decisions in a new task situation.

Many business buyers prefer to buy a complete solution to a problem from a single seller rather than buying separate products and services from several suppliers and putting them together. The sale often goes to the firm that provides the most complete *system* for meeting the customer's needs and solving its problems. Such **systems selling** (or **solutions selling**) is often a key business marketing strategy for winning and holding accounts. Consider IBM and its customer Six Flags Entertainment Corporation:

Six Flags operates 19 regional theme parks across the United States, Mexico, and Canada, featuring exciting rides and water attractions, world-class roller coasters, and special shows and concerts. To deliver a fun and safe experience for guests, Six Flags must carefully and effectively manage thousands of park assets—from rides and equipment to buildings and other facilities. Six Flags needed a tool for managing all those assets efficiently and effectively across its far-flung collection of parks. So it turned to IBM, which has software—called Maximo Asset Management software—that handles that very problem well.

But IBM didn't just hand the software over to Six Flags with best wishes for a happy implementation. Instead, IBM's Maximo Professional Services group is combining the software with an entire set of services designed to get and keep the software up and running. IBM is working hand-in-hand with Six Flags to customize the application and strategically implement it across Six Flags' far-flung facilities, along with on-site immersion training and planning workshops. "We've implemented the solution at five parks to date, and as the implementation team completes

Straight rebuy
A business buying situation in which the buyer routinely reorders something without any modifications.

Modified rebuy
A business buying situation in which the buyer wants to modify product specifications, prices, terms, or suppliers.

New task
A business buying situation in which the buyer purchases a product or service for the first time.

Systems selling (or solutions selling)
Buying a packaged solution to a problem from a single seller, thus avoiding all the separate decisions involved in a complex buying situation.

Photo by Mathew Imaging/WireImage/Getty Images

Exhibit 6.15 Solutions selling: Delivering a fun and safe experience for Six Flags guests requires careful and effective management of thousands of park assets across its 19 regional theme parks. IBM works hand-in-hand with Six Flags to provide not just software, but a complete solution.

each deployment, they move to the next property," says Six Flags' director of corporate project management. "We have one implementation team to make sure that all the deployments across our parks are consistent." IBM will work with Six Flags throughout the process. Thus, IBM isn't just selling the software, it's selling a complete solution to Six Flags' complex asset management problem.[33]

Participants in the Business Buying Process Who does the buying of the trillions of dollars' worth of goods and services needed by business organizations? The decision-making unit of a buying organization is called its **buying centre**. It consists of all the individuals and units that play a role in the business purchase decision-making process. This group includes the actual users of the product or service, those who make the buying decision, those who influence the buying decision, those who do the actual buying, and those who control buying information.

Buying centre

All the individuals and units that play a role in the purchase decision-making process.

The buying centre is not a fixed and formally identified unit within the buying organization. It is a set of buying roles assumed by different people for different purchases. Within the organization, the size and makeup of the buying centre will vary for different products and for different buying situations. For some routine purchases, one person—say, a purchasing agent—may assume all the buying centre roles and serve as the only person involved in the buying decision. For more complex purchases, the buying centre may include 20 or 30 people from different levels and departments in the organization.

The buying centre concept presents a major marketing challenge. The business marketer must learn who participates in the decision, each participant's relative influence, and what evaluation criteria each decision participant uses. This can be difficult.

The buying centre usually includes some obvious participants who are involved formally in the buying decision. For example, the decision to buy a corporate jet will probably involve the company's CEO, the chief pilot, a purchasing agent, some legal staff, a member of top management, and others formally charged with the buying decision. It may also involve less obvious, informal participants, some of whom may actually make or strongly affect the buying decision. Sometimes, even the people in the buying centre are not aware of all the buying participants. For example, the decision about which corporate jet to buy may actually be made by a corporate board member who has an interest in flying and who knows a lot about airplanes. This board member may work behind the scenes to sway the decision. Many business buying decisions result from the complex interactions of ever-changing buying centre participants.

Major Influences on Business Buyers Business buyers are subject to many influences when they make their buying decisions. Some marketers assume that the major influences are economic. They think buyers will favour the supplier who offers the lowest price or the best product or the most service. They concentrate on offering strong economic benefits to buyers. Such economic factors are very important to most buyers, especially in a tough economy. However, business buyers actually respond to both economic and personal factors. Far from being cold, calculating, and impersonal, business buyers are human and social as well. They react to both reason and emotion.

Today, most B-to-B marketers recognize that emotion plays

Great Little Box Company

Exhibit 6.16 Emotions play an important role in business buying: Great Little Box Company has succeeded by becoming known to its customers as "great people to deal with."

FIGURE 6.7 Major Influences on Business Buyer Behaviour

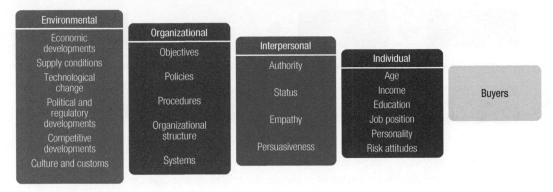

an important role in business buying decisions. For example, you might expect that a company selling corrugated boxes, protective packaging, and point-of-purchase displays would stress objective factors such as price, quality, and delivery. However, Great Little Box Company of British Columbia has built a reputation on the strength of its people. Its tagline "Great people to deal with" sums up the company's philosophy. Owner Robert Meggy attributes the company's success to his employees, who are committed to providing the company's customers with good service, quick turnaround, and on-time delivery. "If you keep your staff happy, they will keep your customers happy," says James Palmer, vice-president of sales and marketing. The company's focus on people resulted in its being selected as one of Canada's top 100 employers and one of B.C.'s top employers in 2015.[34]

Figure 6.7 lists various groups of influences on business buyers—environmental, organizational, interpersonal, and individual. Business buyers are heavily influenced by factors in the current and expected *economic environment*, such as the level of primary demand, the economic outlook, and the cost of money. Another environmental factor is the *supply* of key materials. Many companies are now more willing to buy and hold larger inventories of scarce materials to ensure adequate supply. Business buyers also are affected by *technological*, *political*, and *competitive* developments in the environment. Finally, *culture and customs* can strongly influence business buyer reactions to the marketer's behaviour and strategies, especially in the international marketing environment. The business buyer must watch these factors, determine how they will affect the buyer, and try to turn these challenges into opportunities.

Organizational factors are also important. Each buying organization has its own objectives, strategies, structure, systems, and procedures, and the business marketer must understand these factors well. Questions such as these arise: How many people are involved in the buying decision? Who are they? What are their evaluative criteria? What are the company's policies and limits on its buyers?

The buying centre usually includes many participants who influence each other, so *interpersonal factors* also influence the business buying process. However, it is often difficult to assess such interpersonal factors and group dynamics. Buying centre participants do not wear tags that label them as "key decision maker" or "not influential." Nor do buying centre participants with the highest rank always have the most influence. Participants may influence the buying decision because they control rewards and punishments, are well liked, have special expertise, or have a special relationship with other important participants. Interpersonal factors are often very subtle. Whenever possible, business marketers must try to understand these factors and design strategies that take them into account.

Each participant in the business buying decision process brings in personal motives, perceptions, and preferences. These *individual factors* are affected by personal characteristics such as age, income, education, professional identification, personality, and attitudes toward risk. Also, buyers have different buying styles. Some may be technical types who make

FIGURE 6.8 Stages of the Business Buying Process

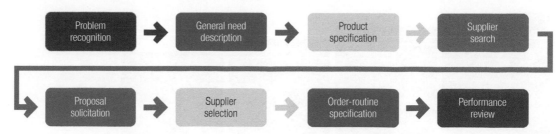

| Problem recognition | → | General need description | → | Product specification | → | Supplier search |

| Proposal solicitation | → | Supplier selection | → | Order-routine specification | → | Performance review |

in-depth analyses of competitive proposals before choosing a supplier. Other buyers may be intuitive negotiators who are adept at pitting the sellers against one another for the best deal.

LO5

Simulate on MyMarketingLab

B2B

Product value analysis

Carefully analyzing a product's or service's components to determine whether they can be redesigned and made more effectively and efficiently to provide greater value.

The Business Buying Process Figure 6.8 lists the eight stages of the business buying process.[35] Buyers who face a new-task buying situation usually go through all stages of the buying process. Buyers making modified or straight rebuys, in contrast, may skip some of the stages. We will examine these steps for the typical new-task buying situation.

The buying process begins with *problem recognition*—when someone in the company recognizes a problem or need that can be met by acquiring a specific product or service. Problem recognition can result from internal or external stimuli. Business marketers use their sales forces or advertising to alert customers to potential problems and then show how their products provide solutions. For example, an award-winning ad from Quill.com, an online office products supplier that strives for strong customer service, highlights an important customer problem: what to do when your printer runs out of toner. The visual in the ad—which shows the headline fading then reappearing—effectively suggests both the problem and the solution. "If you run out of toner," says the ad, "we will replace it this quickly. At Quill.com, we are here whenever you need us."

Having recognized a need, the buyer next prepares a *general need description* that describes the characteristics and quantity of the needed items or solutions. For standard purchases, this process presents few problems. For complex items, however, the buyer may need to work with others—engineers, users, consultants—to define what's needed.

Once the buying organization has defined the need, it develops the item's technical *product specifications*, often with the help of a value analysis engineering team. **Product value analysis** is an approach to cost reduction in which the company carefully analyzes a product's or service's components to determine whether they can be redesigned and made more effectively and efficiently to provide greater value. The team decides on the best product or service characteristics and specifies them accordingly. Sellers, too, can use value analysis as a tool to help secure new accounts and keep old ones. Improving customer value and helping customers find more cost-effective solutions gives the business marketer an important edge in keeping current customers loyal and winning new business.

In the next buying process step, the buyer conducts a *supplier search* to find the best vendors. The buyer can locate qualified suppliers through trade directories, computer searches, or recommendations from others. Today, more and more companies are turning to the Internet to find suppliers. For marketers, this has levelled the playing field—the Internet gives smaller suppliers

Quill.com agency—Euro RSCG Chicago, Creative Director, Blake Ebel

Exhibit 6.17 Problem recognition: Quill.com uses this award-winning ad to alert customers to both an important problem and the solution. "At Quill.com, we're here whenever you need us."

many of the same advantages as larger competitors. The task of suppliers is to understand the search process and make certain that their firms are considered.

In the *proposal solicitation* stage of the business buying process, the buyer invites qualified suppliers to submit proposals. When the purchase is complex or expensive, the buyer will usually require detailed written proposals or formal presentations from each potential supplier. In response, business marketers must be skilled in researching, writing, and presenting proposals. The proposals should be marketing documents, not just technical documents. They should spell out how the seller's solution creates greater value for the customer than competing solutions.

The buyer next reviews the proposals and selects a supplier or suppliers. During *supplier selection*, the buyer will consider many supplier attributes and their relative importance. Such attributes include product and service quality, reputation, on-time delivery, ethical corporate behaviour, honest communication, and competitive prices. In the end, buyers may select a single supplier or a few suppliers. Today's supplier development managers often want to develop a full network of supplier-partners that can help the company bring more value to its customers.

The buyer now prepares an *order-routine specification*. It includes the final order with the chosen supplier or suppliers and lists items such as technical specifications, quantity needed, expected time of delivery, return policies, and warranties. Many large buyers now practise *vendor-managed inventory*, in which they turn over ordering and inventory responsibilities to their suppliers. Under such systems, buyers share sales and inventory information directly with key suppliers. The suppliers then monitor inventories and replenish stock automatically as needed. For example, most major suppliers to large retailers such as Walmart, Target, Home Depot, and Lowe's assume vendor-managed inventory responsibilities.

The final stage of the business buying process is the supplier *performance review*, in which the buyer assesses the supplier's performance and provides feedback. For example, Home Depot has issued a set of supplier guidelines and policies and regularly evaluates each supplier in terms of quality, delivery, and other performance variables. It gives suppliers online performance scorecards that provide ongoing feedback that helps them improve their performance.[36] The supplier performance review may lead the buyer to continue, modify, or drop the arrangement. The seller's job is to monitor the same factors used by the buyer to make sure that the seller is giving the expected satisfaction.

The eight-stage buying process model provides a simple view of business buying as it might occur in a new-task buying situation. The actual process is usually much more complex. In the modified rebuy or straight rebuy situation, some of these stages would be compressed or bypassed. Each organization buys in its own way, and each buying situation has unique requirements.

Different buying centre participants may be involved at different stages of the process. Although certain buying process steps usually do occur, buyers do not always follow them in the same order, and they may add other steps. Often, buyers will repeat certain stages of the process. Finally, a customer relationship might involve many different types of purchases ongoing at a given time, all in different stages of the buying process. The seller must manage the total customer relationship, not just individual purchases.

E-Procurement and Online Purchasing Advances in information technology have changed the face of the B-to-B marketing process. Online purchasing, often called **e-procurement**, has grown rapidly in recent years. Virtually unknown 20 years ago, online purchasing is standard procedure for most companies today. E-procurement gives buyers access to new suppliers, lowers purchasing costs, and hastens order processing and delivery. In turn, business marketers can connect with customers online to share marketing information, sell products and services, provide customer support services, and maintain ongoing customer relationships.

E-procurement
Purchasing through electronic connections between buyers and sellers—usually online.

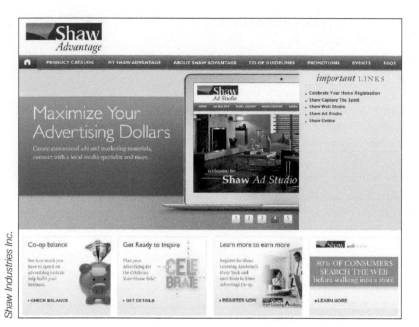

Shaw Industries Inc.

Exhibit 6.18 B-to-B websites: This Shaw Floors site builds strong links with Shaw's retailers. It provides marketing ideas and tools that make retailers more effective in selling Shaw's products to final customers.

Companies can do e-procurement in any of several ways. They can conduct *reverse auctions*, in which they put their purchasing requests online and invite suppliers to bid for the business. Or they can engage in online *trading exchanges*, through which companies work collectively to facilitate the trading process. Companies also can conduct e-procurement by setting up their own *company buying sites*. For example, GE operates a company trading site on which it posts its buying needs and invites bids, negotiates terms, and places orders. Or companies can create *extranet links* with key suppliers. For instance, they can create direct procurement accounts with suppliers such as Dell or Staples, through which company buyers can purchase equipment, materials, and supplies directly. Staples operates a business-to-business procurement division called Staples Advantage, which serves the office supplies and services buying needs of businesses of any size, from 20 employees to the Fortune 1000.

B-to-B marketers can help customers online and build stronger customer relationships by creating well-designed, easy-to-use websites. For example, *BtoB* magazine rated the site of Shaw Floors—a market leader in flooring products—as one of its "10 great B-to-B websites." The site helps Shaw build strong links with its business and trade customers:

> At one time, flooring manufacturer Shaw Floors' website was nothing more than "brochure-ware." Today, however, the site is a true interactive experience. At the site, design and construction professionals as well as customers can "see"—virtually—the company's many product lines. At the popular "Try on a Floor" area, designers or retailers can even work with final buyers to upload digital images of an actual floor and put any of the company's many carpets on it to see how they look. They can select various lines and colours immediately without digging through samples. And the extremely detailed images can be rotated and manipulated so that a designer, for example, can show a client what the pile of the carpet looks like and how deep it is.
>
> The Shaw Floors site also provides a rich set of easy-to-navigate resources for Shaw retailers. The "For Retailers" area lets retail-partners search the company's products, make inventory checks, track order status, or order brochures for their stores. At the Shaw AdSource area, retailers can find resources to create their own ads. The Shaw Web Studio lets retailers—many of which are mom-and-pop stores—download the photography, catalogue engines, and other tools they need to build their own websites. "So many retailers don't have the time or money to build their own online presence," says Shaw's interactive marketing manager, "so this really helps them."[37]

More generally, today's business-to-business marketers are using a wide range of digital and social marketing approaches—from websites, blogs, and smartphone apps to mainstream social media such as Facebook, LinkedIn, YouTube, and Twitter—to reach business customers and manage customer relationships anywhere, at any time. Digital and social media marketing has rapidly become *the* new space for engaging business customers (see Marketing@Work 6.2).

Business-to-business e-procurement yields many benefits. First, it shaves transaction costs and results in more efficient purchasing for both buyers and suppliers. E-procurement reduces the time between order and delivery. Moreover, an online-powered purchasing program eliminates the paperwork associated with traditional requisition and ordering

MARKETING@WORK 6.2

B-to-B Social Marketing: The Space to Engage Business Customers

A video featured at the Makino Machine Tools YouTube channel shows Makino's D500 five-axis vertical machining centre in action, with metal chips flying as the machinery mills a new industrial part. Sound exciting? Probably not to you. But to the right industrial customer, the video is downright spellbinding. "Wow," says one viewer, "that's a new concept to have the saddle ride in Y rather than X. Is that a rigidity enhancement?" In all, the video has been viewed more than 40 000 times, mostly by current or prospective Makino customers. For B-to-B marketer Makino, that's great exposure.

When you think of digital marketing and social media, you most likely think of marketing to final consumers. But today, most business-to-business marketers, like Makino, have also upped their use of these new approaches to reach and engage business customers. The use of digital and social media channels in business marketing isn't just growing, it's exploding. Even as most major B-to-B marketers are cutting back on traditional media and event marketing, they are ramping up their use of everything from websites, blogs, mobile apps, and proprietary online networks to mainstream social media such as Facebook, LinkedIn, Google+, You-Tube, and Twitter. Research shows that 92 percent of B-to-B companies now use social media, 83 percent send out e-newsletters, 81 percent post articles on their company website, 80 percent blog, 76 percent post videos online, and 64 percent conduct webinars.

Digital and social media have become *the* space in which to engage B-to-B customers and strengthen customer relationships. Again, consider Makino, a leading manufacturer of metal cutting and machining technology:

Makino employs a wide variety of social media initiatives that inform customers and enhance customer relationships. For example, it hosts an ongoing series of industry-specific webinars that position the company as an industry thought leader. Makino produces about three webinars each month and offers a library of more than 100 on topics ranging from optimizing machine tool performance to discovering new metal-cutting processes. Webinar content is tailored to specific industries, such as aerospace or medical, and is promoted through carefully targeted banner ads and emails. The webinars help to build Makino's customer database, generate leads, build customer relationships, and prepare the way for salespeople by providing relevant information and educating customers online.

Makino even uses Twitter, Facebook, and YouTube to inform customers and prospects about the latest Makino innovations and events and to vividly demonstrate the company's machines in action. The results have been gratifying. "We've shifted dramatically into the electronic marketing area," says Makino's marketing manager. "It speeds up the sales cycle and makes it more efficient—for both the company and the customer. The results have been outstanding."

Compared with traditional media and sales approaches, digital and social media approaches can create greater customer engagement and interaction. B-to-B marketers know that they aren't really targeting *businesses*, they're targeting *individuals* in those businesses who affect buying decisions. "We are selling business-to-people," notes one B-to-B marketer. And today's business buyers are always connected. They have their digital devices—whether PCs, tablets, or smartphones—hardwired to their brains. As one B-to-B marketer puts it, "Being at work is no longer a place; it is a state of mind."

Digital and social media can play an important role in engaging today's always-connected business buyers in a way that personal selling alone cannot. Instead of the old model of sales reps calling on business customers at work or maybe meeting up with them at trade shows, the new digital approaches

Courtesy of Makino, Inc.; Facebook is a trademark of Facebook, Inc

Exhibit 6.19 B-to-B social media: Machining tool manufacturer Makino engages its business customers through extensive digital and social marketing—everything from proprietary online communities and webinars to Facebook, YouTube, and Twitter.

facilitate any time, anywhere connections between a wide range of people in the selling and customer organizations. It gives both sellers and buyers more control of and access to important information. B-to-B marketing has always been social network marketing, but today's digital environment offers an exciting array of new networking tools and applications.

No company seems to grasp the new digital and social media opportunities more fully than one of the oldest companies around—IBM. With 435 000 employees in 170 countries, Big Blue is as fresh and relevant—and profitable—as ever when it comes to social media. It uses a decentralized approach: "We represent our brand online the way it always has been," says an IBM social media executive. "Our brand is largely shaped by the interactions that [IBMers] have with customers."

From that perspective, IBM encourages employees to talk publicly on social media—to each other and to customers—and lets them go about it with no intervention or oversight. And go about it they do. Thousands of IBMers are the voice of the company. There are 100 000 IBMers using 17 000 internal blogs and 53 000 members on Social-Blue (IBM's own internal Facebook-like network). "Run an online search for 'IBM blog' and you'll find countless IBMers

posting publicly on everything from service-oriented architecture to sales to parenthood," says one analyst. "If you want to blog at IBM, you simply start." IBM employees by the tens of thousands or even hundreds of thousands are also actively involved on Twitter, LinkedIn, Facebook, YouTube, and many other public social media.

All this IBMer-led social networking drives an incredible amount of interaction among IBM employees, customers, and suppliers. For example, an IBM "innovation jam" can include a diverse group of as many as 500 000 people inside and outside the company. Such online interactions helped spawn what is now a major IBM movement, Smarter Planet—an initiative that puts the collective minds and tools at IBM and outside the company toward solving issues ranging from rush-hour traffic to natural disaster response.

Whether it's IBM's decentralized approach to digital and social media or Makino's more focused and deliberate strategy, B-to-B marketers are discovering just how effective these new networking channels can be for engaging and interacting with business customers. Digital and social marketing aren't passing B-to-B fads; they signal a new way of doing business. Gone are the days when B-to-B marketers can just push out infor-

mation about their products and services in a sales call or at a marketing event. Instead, marketers need to engage customers in meaningful and relevant ways, whenever and wherever customers demand it, 24 hours a day, 7 days a week. As one B-to-B social media director states, "Customer expectations have changed. Customers want, on demand, to have a say in how they interact with you as a company." Says another social media expert, "Social media is how the current and next generation of B-to-B customers is choosing to learn about new solutions and stay current on brands."

Sources: Kate Maddox, "Online Marketing Summit Focuses on Social, Search, Content," btobonline.com, February 13, 2012; Elizabeth Sullivan, "One to One," *Marketing News*, May 15, 2009, pp. 10–13; Sean Callahan, "Is B2B Marketing Really Obsolete?" btobonline.com, January 17, 2011; Casey Hibbard, "How IBM Uses Social Media to Spur Employee Innovation," Socialmediaexaminer.com, February 2, 2010; Joe Pulizzi, "2012 B2B Content Marketing Benchmarks, Budgets, and Trends," contentmarketinginstitute.com, December 5, 2011; "Analytics, Content, and Apps Are Hot Topics at 'BtoB's SF NetMarketing Breakfast," *BtoB*, February 17, 2012, www.btobonline.com/article/20120217/EVENT02/302179995/analytics-content-and-apps-are-hot-topics-at-btobs-sf-netmarketing; Louis Columbus, "B2B Marketers Need to Get Real About Social Media and Customer Engagement," *Forbes*, January 17, 2013, www.forbes.com/sites/louiscolumbus/2013/01/17/b2b-marketers-need-to-get-real-about-social-media-and-customer-engagement/print; Kate Maddox, "Study: 86% of B-to-B Marketers Now Use Content Marketing," *Advertising Age*, October 1, 2014, http://adage.com/article/digitalnext/study-86-b-b-marketers-content-marketing/295230; and www.youtube.com/user/MakinoMachineTools, accessed October 2013.

procedures and helps an organization keep better track of all purchases. Finally, beyond the cost and time savings, e-procurement frees purchasing people from a lot of drudgery and paperwork. In turn, it frees them to focus on more-strategic issues, such as finding better supply sources and working with suppliers to reduce costs and develop new products.

The rapidly expanding use of e-procurement, however, also presents some problems. For example, at the same time that the Internet makes it possible for suppliers and customers to share business data and even collaborate on product design, it can also erode decades-old customer–supplier relationships. Many buyers now use the power of the Internet to pit suppliers against one another and search out better deals, products, and turnaround times on a purchase-by-purchase basis.

E-procurement can also create potential security concerns. Although home shopping transactions can be protected through basic encryption, the secure environment that businesses need to carry out confidential interactions is sometimes still lacking. Companies are spending millions for research on defensive strategies to keep hackers at bay. Cisco Systems, for example, specifies the types of routers, firewalls, and security procedures that its partners must use to safeguard connections. In fact, the company goes even further; it sends its own security engineers to examine a partner's defences and holds the partner liable for any security breach that originates from its computers.

The Wings Two-Four

Consumer behaviour is one of the most important concepts in marketing, and it focuses squarely on the importance of knowing your market—right down to personal habits, traits, and preferences. Successful Canadian consumer brands such as Tim Hortons, Canadian Tire, and Boston Pizza have stood the test of time because, above all else, they were built by Canadians for Canadians. And that identity has never been forgotten.

In early 2015, as Boston Pizza began the second half of its first century, it launched a brand-new promotional campaign called "We'll Make You a Fan." More than just a catchy tagline coined by an ad agency, the statement deliberately lends itself to multiple interpretations. While one intent was to emphasize BP's commitment to earn consumers' business, another was to reinforce BP's position in the sports bar category. And what better way to resonate with the quintessential Canadian sports fan than with a quintessential and uniquely Canadian icon—the two-four?

"If there's one thing Canadians know and love, it's the two-four. It's a part of our culture, especially during playoffs and summer weekends. But, until now, Canadians have never been able to eat one," said Steve Silverstone, Boston Pizza International's executive vice-president of marketing. "Unlike other two-fours, Canadians can crack open a Wings Two-Four virtually anywhere, any time they want. It really is the perfect union of BP's famous wings and the ubiquitous two-four." BP cleverly tied in the chicken wing two-four with a hockey-glove-shaped pitcher to serve Molson Canadian beer during the 2015 Stanley Cup Playoffs.

Consumers have a lot of choices in where to eat out, and what to eat once they get there. Understanding the psychological triggers, such as the Canadian hockey fan's emotional tie to the social aspect of watching the playoffs, helps develop product and promotional ideas, and ultimately assists fans and foodies in their purchase decision.

QUESTIONS

1. Using the steps in the consumer purchase decision process, describe the thought process that a guest at Boston Pizza's Sports Bar might go through before deciding on the Wings Two-Four.
2. While the purchase decision has five known steps, a variety of decision influencers come into play as well. List these categories and provide an example as it pertains to a diner at Boston Pizza.

REVIEWING THE CONCEPTS

 LO1 Understand the consumer market and the major factors that influence consumer buyer behaviour.

The *consumer market* consists of all the individuals and households that buy or acquire goods and services for personal consumption. Consumer behaviour should be viewed as an ongoing process that starts long before the consumer purchases a product or service and continues long after he or she consumes it. This extended definition of consumer behaviour means that marketers must be aware of a number of issues before, during, and after purchase in order to build brand loyalty and lasting relationships with their customers.

Consumer buyer behaviour is influenced by four key sets of buyer characteristics: cultural, social, personal, and psychological. Understanding these factors can help marketers identify interested buyers and shape products and appeals to serve consumer needs better. *Culture* is the most basic determinant of a person's wants and behaviour. People in different cultural, subcultural, and social class groups have different product and brand preferences. *Social factors*—such as small group, social network, and family influences—strongly affect product and brand choices, as do *personal characteristics*, such as age, life-cycle stage, occupation, economic circumstances, lifestyle, and personality. Finally, consumer buying behaviour is influenced by four major sets of *psychological factors*—motivation, perception, learning, and beliefs and attitudes. Each of these factors provides a different perspective for understanding the workings of the buyer's black box.

LO2 Identify and discuss the stages in the buyer decision process.

When making a purchase, the buyer goes through a decision process consisting of need recognition, information search, evaluation of alternatives, purchase decision, and postpurchase behaviour. During *need recognition*, the consumer recognizes a problem or need that could be satisfied by a product or service. Once the need is recognized, the consumer moves into the *information search* stage. With information in hand, the consumer proceeds to *alternative evaluation* and assesses brands in the choice set. From there, the consumer makes a *purchase decision* and actually buys the product. In the final stage of the buyer decision process, *postpurchase behaviour*, the consumer takes action based on satisfaction or dissatisfaction. The marketer's job is to understand the buyer's behaviour at each stage and the influences that are operating.

 LO3 Describe the adoption and diffusion process for new products.

The product *adoption process* is made up of five stages: awareness, interest, evaluation, trial, and adoption. New-product marketers must think about how to help consumers move through these stages. With regard to the *diffusion process* for new products, consumers respond at different rates depending on consumer and product characteristics. Consumers may be innovators, early adopters, early majority, late majority, or laggards. Each group may require different marketing approaches. Marketers often try to bring their new products to the attention of potential early adopters, especially those who are opinion leaders.

 LO4 Define the business market and identify the major factors that influence business buyer behaviour.

The *business market* comprises all organizations that buy goods and services for use in the production of other products and services or for the purpose of reselling or renting them to others at a profit. As compared with consumer markets, business markets usually have fewer, larger buyers who are more geographically concentrated. Business demand is derived demand, and the business buying decision usually involves more, and more professional, buyers.

Business buyers make decisions that vary with the three types of *buying situations*: straight rebuys, modified rebuys, and new tasks. The decision-making unit of a buying organization—the *buying centre*—can consist of many different persons playing many different roles. The business marketer needs to know the following: Who are the major buying centre participants? In what decisions do they exercise influence and to what degree? What evaluation criteria does each decision participant use? The business marketer also needs to understand the major environmental, organizational, interpersonal, and individual influences on the buying process.

 LO5 List and define the steps in the business buying decision process.

The *business buying decision process* itself can be quite involved, with eight basic stages: problem recognition, general need description, product specification, supplier search, proposal solicitation, supplier selection, order-routine specification, and performance review. Buyers who face a new-task buying situation usually go through all stages of the buying process. Buyers making modified or straight rebuys may skip some of the stages. Companies must manage the overall customer relationship, which often includes many different buying decisions in various stages of the buying decision process. Advances in information technology have given birth to e-procurement, by which business buyers are purchasing all kinds of products and services online. Business marketers are increasingly connecting with customers online and through social media to share marketing information, sell products and services, provide customer support services, and maintain ongoing customer relationships.

MyMarketingLab

Study, practise, and explore real marketing situations with these helpful resources:

- **Interactive Lesson Presentations:** Work through interactive presentations and assessments to test your knowledge of marketing concepts.
- **Study Plan:** Check your understanding of chapter concepts with self-study quizzes.
- **Dynamic Study Modules:** Work through adaptive study modules on your computer, tablet, or mobile device.
- **Simulations:** Practise decision-making in simulated marketing environments.

DISCUSSION QUESTIONS

1. Discuss the elements of culture that influence buyer behaviour and give a personal example of how each has influenced a purchase decision you or your family made.

2. What is an opinion leader? Describe how marketers attempt to use opinion leaders to help sell their products.

3. How does the market structure and demand faced by business marketers differ from that faced by consumer marketers?

4. Explain what is meant by systems selling and discuss why it is a preferred approach to buying for many organizations.

5. Describe how online purchasing has changed the business-to-business marketing process and discuss the advantages and disadvantages of electronic purchasing.

CRITICAL THINKING EXERCISES

1. Form a small group of four or five students. Have each group member interview 10 consumers about if and when they purchased their first smartphone. Research when smartphones were first introduced, and based on each respondent's answer, identify which adopter category best describes that consumer. Create a chart similar to Figure 6.6 to present your results for all group members' interviews. How far along are smartphones in their adoption cycle?

2. In Malcolm Gladwell's *The Tipping Point*, he describes the Law of the Few, Stickiness, and the Law of

Context. Research these concepts and describe how understanding them helps marketers better understand and target consumers.

3. Business buying occurs worldwide, so marketers need to be aware of cultural factors influencing business customers. In a small group, select a country and develop a multimedia presentation on proper business etiquette and manners, including appropriate appearance, behaviour, and communication. Include a map showing the location of the country as well as a description of the country in terms of its demographics, culture, and economic history.

ONLINE, MOBILE, AND SOCIAL MEDIA MARKETING

Every culture has rituals for mourning the dead, but technology is now changing many of our long-held cultural norms. The conservative funeral industry is slowly embracing new digital and social media technologies, resulting in new mourning behaviours. High-definition video screens play video homage to the deceased, live-streamed funerals reach all corners of the globe, digital guest books remain permanently active, emails remind the bereaved of the anniversary of a loved one's death, and digital candles remain perpetually "lit" on memorial pages. The deceased can now live on in cyberspace and friends can visit them on Facebook long after they have passed on. Quick-response code chips ("QR codes") affixed to tombstones can bring a person virtually "back to life" on a smartphone. With a large number of consumers owning smartphones and tablets and visiting social media sites, the time is now right for the funeral industry to capitalize on these digital trends. And with the still-sluggish economy and new competitors squeezing profit margins (for example, Costco now sell caskets online), the funeral industry is more open than ever to ways to satisfy consumers' mourning needs digitally.

QUESTIONS

1. Describe the characteristics of a new product that affect its rate of adoption. Which characteristics will impact how quickly the new digital services described above will be accepted by mourners in Canada?

2. With new technologies, our digital lives can last much longer than our physical lives. Discuss how marketers might use social media such as Twitter, Facebook, YouTube, and Instagram to create social sharing and remembrance among mourners long after a loved one passes on.

THINK LIKE A MARKETING MANAGER

Would you like to sell to a customer that spends millions of dollars per year on contractors? If so, you need to learn how to crack the federal government market. The federal government purchases goods ranging from toilet paper to aircraft carriers and services from janitorial supplies to high-tech information technology (IT). This is a lucrative market—especially during economic downturns. Many companies focus their marketing solely on this market. How do businesses—big and small—find out about opportunities in this market? One way is to search the government's website for opportunities. A great deal of the government's buying is now done online.

QUESTIONS

1. Go to the Public Works and Government Services Canada website (www.tpsgc-pwgsc.gc.ca/comm/index-eng.html) and review the information for businesses. Search for Tenders on buyandsell.gc.ca, the government's electronic tendering services. Are there many opportunities in your province?

2. What types of products and services are most frequently listed?

3. Write a brief report describing the usefulness of this website for businesses desiring to sell to the government market.

MARKETING ETHICS

In the early 1990s, Eldon Roth figured out a way to profit from slaughterhouse meat trimmings, by-products that were once used only in pet food and cooking oil. This cheap and safe beef product is called "lean, finely textured beef" (LFTB). The fatty bits of beef are heated and treated with a puff of ammonium hydroxide gas to kill bacteria. LFTB use isn't permitted in Canada, but if you've travelled to the U.S., you may have eaten hamburgers that included it. LFTB makes ground beef leaner and cheaper. Shortly after it was developed, a health safety inspector dubbed LFTB "pink slime," but the name didn't become public until the major "pink slime" media brouhaha erupted in 2012. Consumers were repulsed to learn that they were eating unappealing beef parts that were "soaked in ammonia." Sales of ground beef fell 11 percent in one month. Ground beef producer AFA Foods sought bankruptcy protection and Cargill lost 80 percent of its customers. The industry's leading LFTB manufacturer, Beef

Products, Inc., shuttered 75 percent of its processing plants and laid off 650 workers. McDonald's and other fast food restaurants, supermarkets, and institutional buyers such as schools and hospitals discontinued using beef products containing LFTB, even though the safe and inexpensive product has been around for many years.

QUESTIONS

1. Was the uproar over LFTB warranted, given the fact that it is a product deemed safe for consumption by the U.S. Food and Drug Administration? Research other types of products that are included in consumer products that could face a similar fate if consumers were aware of them.

2. Explain the type of buying situation faced by the companies that dropped the use of LFTB. Describe the buying decision process they likely went through to find a replacement product.

MARKETING BY THE NUMBERS

One way consumers can evaluate alternatives is to identify important attributes and assess how purchase alternatives perform on those attributes. Consider the purchase of an automobile. Each attribute, such as gas mileage, is given a weight to reflect its level of importance to that consumer. Then the consumer evaluates each alternative on each attribute. For example, in the following table, gas mileage (weighted at 0.5) is the most important attribute for this consumer. The consumer believes that Brand C performs best on gas mileage, rating it 7 (higher ratings indicate higher performance). Brand B is perceived as performing the worst on this attribute (rating of 3). Styling and price are the consumer's next most important attributes. Warranty is least important.

Attributes	Importance Weight	Alternative Brands		
		A	B	C
Styling	0.2	4	6	2
Gas mileage	0.5	6	3	7
Warranty	0.1	5	5	4
Price	0.2	4	6	7

A score can be calculated for each brand by multiplying the importance weight for each attribute by the brand's score on that attribute. These weighted scores are then summed to determine the score for that brand. For example, $Score_{Brand\ A}$ = $(0.2 \times 4) + (0.5 \times 6) + (0.1 \times 5) + (0.2 \times 4)$ = $0.8 + 3.0 + 0.5 + 0.8 = 5.1$. This consumer will select the brand with the highest score.

QUESTIONS

1. Calculate the scores for Brands B and C. Which brand would this consumer likely choose?

2. Which brand is this consumer least likely to purchase? Discuss two ways the marketer of this brand can enhance consumer attitudes toward purchasing its brand.

DOVE: BUILDING CUSTOMER RELATIONSHIPS EVERYWHERE, ONE GENDER AT A TIME

When it comes to consumer packaged goods, Unilever is about as big as they come. One of the leading suppliers of food, home, and personal care products, Unilever products can be found in a whopping 7 out of 10 homes globally, are available in over 190 countries, and are used by more than 2 billion people on a daily basis. Having this kind of global scope is rare, and with revenues of more than US$64 billion per year, you'd think that Unilever would be content to slow down a bit and tend to the businesses at hand. Instead, Unilever has set a goal to double its revenues by the year 2020.

How does Unilever do it? By continually creating and developing brands that form strong relationships with consumers in multiple consumer product market segments. If Unilever's portfolio of brands overlooks certain types of customers, then the company creates or acquires a new brand. This "house of brands" approach has made Unilever the proud owner of powerhouse brands such as Noxzema, Ragu, Axe, Ben & Jerry's, Slim-Fast, Hellmann's, Q-tips, Vaseline, Wish-Bone, and Dove, to name just a few.

DOVE: MADE FOR WOMEN?

Take Dove, for example. Dove is the number-one brand of personal cleansing products in the United States, with a product portfolio that includes beauty bars, body washes, face care treatments, deodorants, body mists, hair care products, and styling aids. All by itself, the Dove brand pulls in over US$2 billion a year for Unilever. But coming off its very successful long-term "Campaign for Real Beauty," Dove was starting to experience the stagnation that many mature brands face. Dove found that it was reaching the limits of expansion and the types of extensions it could support. After stumbling in its efforts to penetrate the hair care market, Unilever managers knew that Dove needed to discover a new way to grow.

Dove had always been an undeniably feminine brand. Everything about Dove's brand image—its name, logo, color palette, and communications—was created with women in mind. Although this laser-focused targeting had been a primary factor in the brand's decades-long success, ironically, it had become the brand's greatest limiting factor, especially given the rapid growth in the men's personal care products category. Could Dove sell its products to men? This question left Unilever managers conflicted. Success would provide the much-needed expansion for the brand. However, attempting to get men to perceive Dove as a manly brand risked damaging the brand's successful image among women. Additionally, Unilever already had a wildly successful men's personal care brand in Axe. However, with Dove, Unilever would be targeting men not interested in Axe's edgy—at times even risqué—and youthful image. Positioning Dove for men would require great care.

BREAKING OUT OF THE BOX

Dove supported its decision to enter the men's care market with a comprehensive strategy and genuine consumer insight. Rather than simply releasing products designed for men under the standard Dove brand, Unilever created a brand within the brand—Dove Men+Care. This sub-brand provides a masculine foundation and much-needed separation from the core Dove brand. But just as important, Men+Care was extendable into virtually any type of men's personal care product. Dove also appealed to men through packaging design. With a base colour of dark grey and a masculine palette of accent colours, the very appearance of Dove Men+Care products left no question as to the intended target customer.

Unilever's highly successful Axe personal care line targets single men aged 24 and under who have an active interest in socializing and dating. So, by contrast, Dove Men+Care took aim at men age 25 to 54. Research revealed that men in this distinctive demographic were evolving. Typically married, they were taking on more household duties like cleaning and shopping than similarly aged men in prior decades. More than half of men in this category were buying their own personal care products, and most of the rest were influencing those purchases.

The first products in the Dove Men+Care portfolio were skin care items. The line included three body washes, two bar soaps, and a shower scrub, products strategically designed to complement each other. The idea was to appeal to "men who are comfortable in their own skin," but who were receptive to the proven moisturizing power of Dove products. Dove is one of the few personal care brands that most men had in their homes growing up. So there was an established level of brand recognition and brand knowledge.

Shortly after introducing the initial products, Dove added an antiperspirant to the Men+Care line. More recently, Dove Men+Care has become a more full-spectrum brand that includes facial care and hair care products. With its line of facial care products, Dove urges men to

"Take better care of your face," whereas its hair care products promise "3X stronger hair." These new product lines extend Dove's heritage in cleansing, moisturizing, and providing the ultimate care.

The Dove Men+Care facial care products are designed to complement each other by helping men care for their skin in three easy steps: facial cleansing (a cleanser that fights dryness), shaving (a shaving gel that prevents irritation), and face care (a post-shave balm soothes skin and a moisturizer that hydrates and protects). Dove's research revealed that 48 percent of men in the United States never use face wash and 46 percent never use a face moisturizer, even though most men admit they know they should. Rob Candelino, vice president of Unilever Skincare, explains the insight behind the facial care products and their positioning:

> Men today have a great deal to care about, from their families to their careers, but they don't always give their personal care the same level of attention. Neglecting to properly cleanse and moisturize their skin, or doing so but using harsh products like regular soap, all contribute to a man's face looking tired and feeling worn. New Dove Men+Care Face products seek to help men eliminate needless torture from their grooming routine and help put their best face forward when it matters most.

Unilever has taken great care to craft promotional messages consistent with the brand image of Dove Men+Care. The launch of its facial care products was accompanied by an ad showing the abuse a man's face takes. Snowballs, motor oil, pokes from a child, windburn from a roller coaster, and "deserved" slaps provided illustration for the tagline "End the face torture." A series of follow-up ads showed real men describing their typical face care routine (soap, no moisturizer, stinging aftershave) followed by the results they experience ("It feels tight," "It doesn't feel good at all," and "Definitely stings").

Most recently, Dove has taken its advertising for Men+Care to a new level. According to Candelino, "We hear from 73 percent of men that they're falsely or inaccurately depicted in advertising." Specifically, says Candelino, the common depictions of men in advertising can be boiled down to three categories: guys obsessed with winning the affections of women, he-men who are into stereotypical manly activities such as body building or fast cars, and dads who are seen more as buffoons than respected parents. So Dove Men+Care launched a campaign to combat these caricatures as much as build its own brand. Called "Real Moments," the campaign promotes real-life fatherhood tales from father figures like *Miami Heat* star Dwyane Wade. Having just written a book entitled *A Father First: How My Life Became Bigger Than Basketball*, Wade was the perfect celebrity to give his endorsement.

"When fans learn that playing 'defence' for Dwyane Wade means teaching his sons how to guard a mini-hoop in his living room instead of a fellow player during a professional game," says Candelino, "it hits home where men today place priority—caring for their family comes first."

AN INSTANT SUCCESS

In a short period of time, Dove has accomplished a great deal. It successfully stepped outside the established boundaries of a brand created to target a specific market segment—women. In breaking beyond segment, the brand has become an authority on men's personal grooming. And Dove has done this without alienating its core segment of women.

Unilever's investment in Dove as a men's care brand seems to have paid off. Shortly after the new Dove Men+Care line debuted, SymphonyIRI put the new brand on its list of top 10 new products. In an annual study of most desirable brands, Dove ranked fourth among both women *and* men. Best of all for Unilever, Dove's previously flat overall sales rose 9.8 percent in Men+Care's first year on the market. It seems that Dove's stated objective for Dove Men+Care, to "allow men to better care for themselves so they can care for what matters most to them," is right on target.

Sources: Based on information from John Miziolek, "How Dove Reinvented Its Brand for Men," *Fast Company*, March, 14, 2012, www.fastcompany.com/1824772/how-dove-reinvented-its-brand-men; Jack Neff, "Dove Gives Guys a Break in Men+Care Push," *Advertising Age*, March 12, 2013, http://adage.com/print/240257; "New NCAA Campaign Shares Real Moments Off-the-Court That Highlight How Men Care for What Matters," *Multivu*, March 13, 2013, www.multivu.com/mnr/60739-dove-men-care-real-moments; Ellen Byron, "Marketing Decoder—Dove Men+Care," *Wall Street Journal*, February 13, 2013, p. D2; Jacquelyn Smith, "The Best New Products," *Forbes*, March 29, 2011, www.forbes.com/sites/jacquelynsmith/2011/03/29/best-new-products; and "Dove Men+Care Launches New Skin Care Range to Help Men Finally Care for Their Faces," *Reuters*, February 5, 2013.

QUESTIONS FOR DISCUSSION

1. How do personal factors, discussed in the chapter, influence Dove's ability to build strong customer relationships?

2. How does Dove effectively guide each consumer segment through the five stages of the buyer decision process?

3. As a new product, how can Dove ensure the success of Dove Men+Care?

4. Can Dove and Dove Men+Care continue to succeed as side-by-side brands? Why or why not?

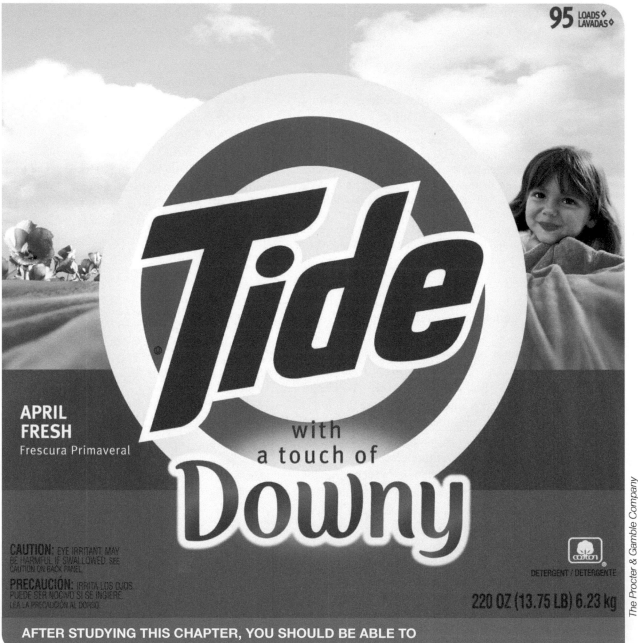

The Procter & Gamble Company

AFTER STUDYING THIS CHAPTER, YOU SHOULD BE ABLE TO

1 define the major steps in designing a customer-driven marketing strategy: market segmentation, targeting, differentiation, and positioning

2 list and discuss the major bases for segmenting consumer and business markets

3 explain how companies identify attractive market segments and choose a market-targeting strategy

4 discuss how companies differentiate and position their products for maximum competitive advantage

Segmentation, Targeting, and Positioning

PREVIEWING THE CONCEPTS

So far, you've learned what marketing is, and about the importance of understanding consumers and the marketplace environment. With that as background, you're now ready to delve deeper into marketing strategy and tactics. This chapter looks further into key customer-driven marketing strategy decisions—how to divide up markets into meaningful customer groups (*segmentation*), choose which customer groups to serve (*targeting*), create market offerings that best serve targeted customers (*differentiation*), and position the offerings in the minds of consumers (*positioning*). Then, the chapters that follow explore the tactical marketing tools—the four *P*s—by which marketers bring these strategies to life.

At their most basic, target markets are simply groups of people with similar characteristics, and while those characteristics may have always been around for the targeting, it sometimes takes a new kind of thinking to decide to serve a particular group with a line of products that's new to them—in other words, to define a new market segment.

To open our discussion of segmentation, targeting, differentiation, and positioning, let's look at master marketer Procter & Gamble (P&G). For more than 175 years, P&G has led the way in brand management and marketing.

P&G: COMPETING WITH ITSELF—AND WINNING

Procter & Gamble is the world's premier consumer products company. P&G invented brand management, and few companies do it better. The company markets more than 100 brands—most of them household names—to customers in over 180 countries around the world. An estimated 99 percent of all U.S. households use at least one P&G brand. And according to P&G, its brands now serve 4.6 billion of the planet's nearly 7 billion people.

P&G builds *big* brands. Just 50 of its brands account for 90 percent of the company's $84 billion in annual sales. Twenty-five of P&G's brands generate more than $1 billion annually, three times more billion-dollar brands than its nearest competitor and more than the total of the remaining competitors combined.

P&G brands flat-out dominate in many household and personal care categories. For example, the company sells a laundry room full of bestselling detergent and laundry care brands (including Tide, Gain, Cheer, Era, Dreft, Bold, Bounce, and Downy), alongside multiple brands of familiar household cleaning and homecare products (Mr. Clean, Swiffer,

✓• **Practice** on MyMarketingLab

Growing the Category or Fighting for Competitors' Customers?

✓• **Practice** on MyMarketingLab

Interpreting Market Segment Information from a Secondary Database

✓• **Practice** on MyMarketingLab

Interpreting Perceptual Maps

Febreze), dishwashing detergents (Dawn, Gain, Joy, and Cascade), and hand soaps and sanitizers (Safeguard, Olay, Ivory, and Camay). P&G markets more than a half-dozen each of shampoo and hair care brands (Head & Shoulders, Pantene, Herbal Essences, Pert, Vidal Sassoon, Wella, and Clairol) and fragrance brands (Old Spice, Gucci Fragrances, Hugo Boss, Lacoste, Puma, Dolce&Gabbana, and Escada). The list of iconic brands goes on and on, with megabrands in oral care (Crest, Oral-B, Scope), deodorants (Secret, Old Spice), shaving and grooming (Gillette, Braun), skin care (Olay, SK-II), cosmetics (Cover Girl, Max Factor), disposable diapers and baby care (Luvs, Pampers), and tissues and towels (Bounty, Charmin, Puffs).

Interestingly, many of these P&G brands compete directly with one another on the same supermarket shelves. But why would P&G introduce several brands in one category instead of concentrating its resources on a single leading brand? The answer lies in the concepts of segmentation and positioning, which are based on the fact that different people want different sets of benefits from the products they buy.

Take laundry detergents, for example. People use laundry detergents to get their clothes clean. But they also seek other benefits from their detergents—such as strength or mildness, stain removing, fabric softening, fresh scent, economy, and convenience. We all want *some* of every one of these detergent benefits, but we may have different *priorities* for each benefit. To some people, cleaning and bleaching power are most important; to others, fabric softening matters most. Still others want a mild, fresh-scented detergent. In other words, each segment of laundry detergent buyers seeks a special combination of benefits.

P&G has identified several important laundry detergent segments, along with numerous sub-segments, and has developed distinct brands with value propositions to meet the needs of each. P&G's major detergent brands are positioned for different segments as follows:

- *Tide* is the original all-purpose, heavy-duty family detergent that gets out grime and tough stains.
- *Gain* leaves clothes smelling "irresistibly fresh."
- *Cheer* is specially formulated to protect bright and dark coloured clothing.
- *Era* is the economical, concentrated liquid detergent brand.
- *Dreft* is specially formulated to be gentle on babies' skin.

Each brand is positioned to communicate with, and be attractive to, a distinct segment of the market—families; people who want their clothes to have a strong, fresh smell; people who like brightly coloured clothing; people who want the most economical detergent; and mothers with new babies.

Within each segment, P&G has identified sub-segments. For example, you can buy Tide in any of more than 40 different formulations. Here's just a sampling:

- *Tide Original* comes in powder and liquid form, and in regular original scent or special scents such as Clean Breeze and Mountain Spring.
- *Tide Coldwater* is specially formulated to work in cold water, and appeals to those who want to save energy and money by washing in cold water.
- *Ultra Tide* is a concentrated formula, so you can use one-third less.
- *Tide HE* is specially formulated for use in high-efficiency washers.
- *Tide Free & Gentle* is dye- and perfume-free.
- *Tide Vivid White + Bright* is formulated to clean whites without bleaching them.

- *Tide plus Downy* combines Tide laundry detergent with Downy fabric softener.
- *Tide plus Febreze* combines Tide laundry detergent with Febreze fabric freshener.
- *Tide plus Febreze Sport* is specially designed to eliminate sports apparel odours.
- *TidePods* are a new form of Tide laundry detergent. Instead of the usual powder or liquid form, they combine detergent, stain remover, and brightener in a small, convenient, single-use packet.

And there are more new forms and products, all under the Tide master brand: Tide To Go stain removal pens and pads, Tide Boost in-wash stain booster, and Tide Washing Machine Cleaner, to name just a few. As we'll learn in Chapter 8, marketers are constantly developing new products, new versions of their products, and brand extensions—especially when they have a strong, recognizable brand to work with.

P&G's brands and sub-brands do compete head to head in the crowded detergents market. But thanks to careful market segmentation and positioning, P&G has something special to offer consumers in each preference group or "segment." Combined, its many detergent brands capture much more market share than any single brand could achieve on its own. As a result, P&G is really cleaning up in the $7 billion U.S. laundry detergent market. Incredibly, by itself, the Tide family of brands captures about one-third of all U.S. detergent sales; the Gain brand pulls in another 15 percent. Even more incredible, all P&G detergent brands combined capture an almost 70 percent market share. P&G's dominance has forced major competitors such as Unilever and Colgate to throw in the towel and sell off their U.S. laundry detergent brands. So by competing with itself, P&G wins.[1]

COMPANIES today recognize that they cannot appeal to all buyers in the marketplace, or at least not to all buyers in the same way. Buyers are too numerous, too widely scattered, and too varied in their needs and buying practices. Moreover, the companies themselves vary widely in their abilities to serve different segments of the market. Instead, a company must identify the parts of the market that it can serve best and most profitably. It must design customer-driven marketing strategies that build the *right* relationships with the *right* customers.

Companies are being choosier about the customers with whom they connect. Most have moved away from mass marketing and toward market segmentation and targeting—identifying market segments, selecting one or more of them as the most appropriate to serve, and developing products and marketing programs tailored to each.

Figure 7.1 shows the four major steps in designing a customer-driven marketing strategy. In the first two steps, the company selects the customers that it will serve. Market **segmentation** involves dividing a market into smaller groups of buyers with distinct needs, characteristics, or behaviours that might require separate marketing strategies or

LO1

Simulate on MyMarketingLab

Segmentation, Targeting, Positioning

Segmentation

Dividing a market into distinct groups with distinct needs, characteristics, or behaviours that might require separate marketing strategies or mixes.

FIGURE 7.1 Designing a Customer-Driven Marketing Strategy

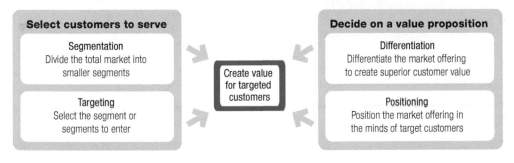

Targeting
The process of evaluating each market segment's attractiveness and selecting one or more segments to enter.

Differentiation
Actually differentiating the market offering to create superior customer value.

Positioning
Arranging for a market offering to occupy a clear, distinctive, and desirable place relative to competing products in the minds of target consumers.

←●—**Simulate** on MyMarketingLab

Segmentation, Targeting, Positioning

Geographic segmentation
Dividing a market into different geographical units, such as global regions, countries, regions within a country, provinces, cities, or even neighbourhoods.

mixes. The company identifies different ways to segment the market and develops profiles of the resulting market segments. Market **targeting** consists of evaluating each market segment's attractiveness and selecting one or more market segments to enter. Next, the company decides on a value proposition—on how it will create value for target customers, and how it can stand out from its competition, or **differentiate** itself. When all these decisions have been made, the company positions its brand, or product, in the market. **Positioning** consists of arranging for a market offering to occupy a clear, distinctive, and desirable place relative to competing products in the minds of consumers. In this chapter, we'll look in detail at each of these four concepts.

Market Segmentation `LO2`

Buyers in any market differ in their wants, resources, locations, buying attitudes, and buying practices. Through market segmentation, companies divide large, heterogeneous markets into smaller segments that can be reached more efficiently and effectively with products and services that match their unique needs. In this section, we discuss four important segmentation topics: segmenting consumer markets, segmenting business markets, segmenting international markets, and requirements for effective segmentation.

Segmenting Consumer Markets

There is no single way to segment a market. A marketer has to try different segmentation variables, alone and in combination, to find the best way to view the market structure. Table 7.1 outlines the major variables that might be used in segmenting consumer markets. Here we look at the major *geographic, demographic, psychographic,* and *behavioural* variables.

Geographic Segmentation Geographic segmentation calls for dividing a market into different geographical units, such as global regions, countries, regions within a country, provinces, cities, or even neighbourhoods. A company may decide to operate in one or a few geographical areas or to operate in all areas but pay attention to geographical differences in needs and wants.

Many companies today are localizing their products, advertising, promotion, and sales efforts to fit the needs of individual regions, cities, and even neighbourhoods. For example, Yukon Brewing produces products made especially for residents of the Yukon Territory:

When Alan Hansen and Bob Baxter opened their craft brewery in Whitehorse, their mission was to service the north with quality beer while keeping jobs and money in the territory. It didn't hurt that Yukoners consume 132 litres of beer per capita each year, more than anyone else in the country. It wasn't easy being the first craft brewery in the region, however. After years of drinking Canadian and Blue, Yukoners didn't trust the new brand, and, it seemed, they didn't like the flavourful, full-bodied brews.

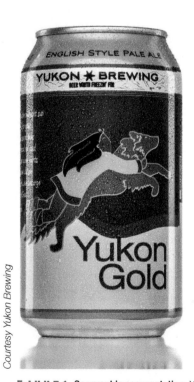

Courtesy Yukon Brewing

Exhibit 7.1 Geographic segmentation: Yukon Brewing produces colourfully named products like Yukon Gold and Yukon Red, made especially for Yukoners who prefer to drink their beer from a can.

TABLE 7.1 Major Segmentation Variables for Consumer Markets

Geographic Segmentation

World region	North America, South America, Western Europe, Eastern Europe, the British Isles, the Middle East, the Pacific Rim, Asia, Southeast Asia, Africa, Australia
Country	Canada, the United States, Brazil, England, China, and so on
Region of the country	The Maritimes, the Prairie provinces, Southern Ontario, Victoria and the Gulf Islands, Quebec
Population size	Under 5000; 5000–250 000; 250 000–500 000; 500 000–1 000 000; over 1 000 000, and so on
Type of region	Urban, suburban, rural, mountainous, far north, ocean/beaches, and so on

Demographic Segmentation

Age	Under 6, 6–12, 13–19, 20–34, 35–49, 50–64, 65 ı; or children, teens, young adults, middle-aged, seniors
Gender	Male, female
Family size	2, 3, 4, 5, more than 5
Life cycle	Young couple, young couple with children, single-parent family, older couple with grown children, divorced, and so on
Household income (HHI)	Under $20 000; $20 000–$50 000; $50 000–$100 000; over $100 000, and so on
Occupation	Professional, union worker, academic, small business owner, sales, farming/fishing, student, retired, homemaker, unemployed
Education	High school, college or trade school, university undergraduate, post-graduate
Ethnic or cultural group	African, Canadian, American, Chinese, Japanese, Korean, Caribbean/West Indies, East Indian, Filipino, Greek, Italian, German, Portuguese, Muslim, Jewish, Inuit, Métis, North American Indian
Generation	Baby boomer, Generation X, Millennial

Psychographic Segmentation

Social class	Lower lowers, upper lowers, working class, middle class, upper middles, lower uppers, upper uppers
Lifestyle	Athletic/outdoors type, active suburban family, student, single urban professional, and so on
Personality	Highly organized and detail oriented; outgoing and adventurous; creative or artistic; quiet and solitary; ambitious, and so on

Behavioural Segmentation

Occasions	Regular occasion, special occasion, holiday, seasonal
Benefits	Quality, service, economy, convenience, speed
User status	Non-user, ex-user, potential user, first-time user, regular user
User rates	Light user, medium user, heavy user
Loyalty status	None, medium, strong, absolute
Readiness stage	Unaware, aware, informed, interested, desirous, intending to buy
Attitude toward product	Enthusiastic, positive, indifferent, negative, hostile

Success came after the company discovered that the reason their beer wasn't selling wasn't the taste, it was that Yukoners were used to drinking beer from a can, and Yukon Brewing was available only in bottles. So in 2000 they changed their packaging to cans, and the product took off. Today, Yukon Brewing sells more draft in the territory than giants Molson-Coors and Labatt combined; and in stores, Yukon Brewing enjoys a market share most microbreweries only dream of, with colourfully named brews: Chilkoot Lager, Deadman Creek Cranberry Wheat, Ice Fog India Pale Ale, Midnight Sun Espresso Stout, and Lead Dog Olde English Ale, and Bonanza Brown Ale. Yukon beer can be found across the territory, as well as in the Northwest Territories, Alberta, Saskatchewan, and British Columbia.[2]

Other companies are seeking to cultivate as-yet-untapped geographic territory. For example, Four Points by Sheraton hotels has opened a chain of smaller-format hotels in places such as Kingston, Ontario, and Canmore, Alberta, that are too small for its standard-size, more upscale hotels. Small businesses such as hair salons and dentists' offices typically focus their marketing efforts on a local region within a few kilometres of their location, while destination-type businesses, such as restaurants and sporting facilities, might market to a larger region.

Demographic segmentation

Dividing the market into segments based on variables such as age, gender, family size, life cycle, household income (HHI), occupation, education, ethnic or cultural group, and generation.

Demographic Segmentation **Demographic segmentation** divides the market into segments based on variables such as age, gender, family size, life cycle, household income (HHI), occupation, education, ethnic or cultural group, and generation. Demographic factors are the most popular bases for segmenting customer groups. One reason is that consumer needs, wants, and usage rates often vary closely with demographic variables. Another is that demographic variables are easier to measure than most other types of variables. Even when marketers first define segments by using other bases, such as benefits sought or behaviour, they must know segment demographic characteristics to assess the size of the target market and to reach it efficiently.

Age and life-cycle segmentation

Dividing a market into different age and life-cycle groups.

Gender segmentation

Dividing a market into different segments based on gender.

AGE AND LIFE-CYCLE SEGMENTATION   Consumer needs and wants change with age. Some companies segment the market based on age or, more specifically, family status, offering different products or using different marketing approaches for different groups. For example, for kids, Oscar Mayer offers Lunchables, full-of-fun, kid-appealing finger food. For older generations, it markets Deli Creations, everything these consumers need to create a microwaveable sandwich.

Other companies focus on marketing to groups that are in the same life-cycle stage. Some people get married and have children in their early 20s, some wait until they are 40; some people retire at age 50, some at 75, but retirement is a life-cycle stage. Companies that divide their markets by either age or life-cycle stage are using **age and life-cycle segmentation**. Disney Cruise Lines targets families with children, so most of its destinations and shipboard activities are designed with this life-cycle stage in mind. On board, Disney provides trained counsellors who help younger kids join in hands-on activities, teen-only spaces for older children, and family-time or individual-time options for parents and other adults. It's difficult to find a Disney Cruise Line advertisement or webpage that doesn't feature a family full of smiling faces. In contrast, Viking River Cruises, the deluxe smaller-boat cruise line that offers tours along the world's great rivers, primarily targets older adults, couples and singles. You won't find a single child in a Viking ad or webpage.

GENDER **Gender segmentation** has long been used in clothing, cosmetics, toiletries, and magazines. For example, P&G was among the first with Secret antiperspirant, a brand specially formulated for a woman's chemistry, packaged and advertised to reinforce the female image. Since women make 70 percent of shopping decisions, big-box stores such as home-improvement chain RONA are courting women consumers with trendy "paint cafés" and

Rona

Exhibit 7.2 Gender segmentation: Hardware stores were once the domain of men, who shopped for tools and construction materials, but modern hardware stores like RONA target women with beautiful kitchen displays.

luxurious display kitchens. Owens Corning aimed a major advertising campaign for home insulation at women, after a study showed that two-thirds of all women were involved in materials installation, with 13 percent doing it themselves.

On the other side of the gender coin, male grooming is a booming market, and developing and marketing new products that cater to this new segment has been a top trend for the last several years. There has been a huge increase not only in the level of acceptance of men's skin-care products but also in usage rates. As a result, Holt Renfrew stores in Montreal, Toronto, and Vancouver now have a large men's cosmetics area, designed with manly details such as dark hardwood floors. And many companies that traditionally marketed only to women, such as Dove, Clinique, Nivea, Lancôme, and L'Oréal, have launched complete lines of skin-care products for men. Catering to this new market segment requires developing new terminology, because men don't buy "cosmetics" or "makeup":

> L'Oréal's Men's Expert line includes a host of products with decidedly unmanly names such as Men's Expert Vita Lift SPF 15 Anti-Wrinkle & Firming Moisturizer and Men's Expert Hydra-Energetic Ice Cold Eye Roller (for diminishing under-eye dark circles). Other brands, however, try to craft more masculine positions. For example, Mënaji promises "Skincare for the Confident Man." Manly men such as Tim McGraw, Kevin Bacon, and Kid Rock use it. Mënaji products come in discreet packaging such as old cigar boxes, and the line's "undetect-able" foundation and concealer (or rather "Camo") come in easy-to-apply Chap Stick–style containers. Mënaji founder Michele Probst doesn't call any of it makeup. "The M word is cancer to us," she says. "We are skin care that looks good." Whatever you call it, Mënaji sales have been up 70 percent annually in recent years as the U.S. men's grooming market has grown to $3 billion.
>
> Similarly, Unilever's testosterone-heavy male body spray brand, Axe, is now waking up to new gender segments—it released a new scent, Anarchy, marketed in different versions to both men and women. Nearly one-quarter of Axe's four million Facebook and Twitter fans are women, and Unilever's research suggested that these women have been wanting an Axe scent of their very own. Past Axe commercials have featured young men spraying the brand on themselves to gain an edge in the mating game. "Now women also have something to spray on themselves," notes an Axe marketer, creating "more of an equilibrium between the sexes."[3]

Finally, a neglected gender segment can offer new opportunities in markets ranging from consumer electronics to motorcycles. For example, Harley-Davidson has traditionally targeted its product design and marketing to a bread-and-butter demographic of 35- to 55-year-old males, but since launching an advertising campaign targeting women, the number of female Harley-Davidson owners has tripled in the past 25 years, and female buyers now account for over 13 percent of new Harley-Davidson purchases. Today, Harley-Davidson is reaching a more diverse customer pool—young adults aged

Mënaji Skincare

Exhibit 7.3 Gender segmentation: Many cosmetics makers now successfully market men's lines. Mënaji tells men to "Put your best face forward."

18–34, women, African Americans, and Hispanics—while still maintaining sales to its core customer segment, Caucasian men aged 35 plus. And Harley-Davidson has become the number one seller of new motorcycles to each of these segments.[4]

Household Income (HHI) segmentation
Dividing a market into different income segments.

HOUSEHOLD INCOME (HHI) The marketers of products and services such as automobiles, clothing, cosmetics, financial services, and travel have long used **household income (HHI) segmentation**. Household income refers to the total income for the family that lives in the household, whether that consists of a single person, a couple, or a family with children. Many companies target affluent consumers (families with an HHI of over $100k per year) with luxury goods and convenience services such as pet-friendly hotels with doggie daycare and doggie spas.

Take Seadream Yacht Club, for example. The small-ship luxury cruise line calls select guests after every cruise and offers to have the CEO fly out to their home and host, at Seadream's expense, a brunch or reception for a dozen of the couple's best friends. The cruisers tell the story of their cruise. Seadream offers a great rate to their guests and sells several cruises at $1000 per person per night to the friends (and even friends of friends). Such highly personal marketing creates a community of "brand evangelists" who tell the story to affluent prospective buyers and friends—precisely the right target group. This has been so successful for Seadream that it has abandoned most traditional advertising.[5]

Income segmentation doesn't only mean targeting the wealthy with luxury goods. Many retailers such as No Frills, Giant Tiger, and the many dollar-store chains successfully target low- and middle-income groups. The core market for such stores is families with household incomes under $30 000.

Segmenting the market according to household income is one of the main ways car marketers divide the market, as each brand offers an economy car for the first-time buyer—the Toyota Yaris, for example—and a luxury model—like the much more expensive Lexus sedans and SUVs, which can reach nearly $100 000. A family that has a household income of $40 000 a year is not likely to purchase a car that costs twice as much as their income. Consumers at all income levels, including affluent consumers, primarily seek value from their purchases—however they personally define value.

ETHNIC OR CULTURAL GROUP Given Canada's multicultural makeup and two national languages (not to mention all the other languages spoken in our country), marketers often segment markets based on easy-to-define criteria such as race, ethnicity, and language. Statistics Canada, as we discussed in Chapter 4, compiles census data about Canadians, and makes it available to marketers. It's not difficult, for example, to identify markets in Canada with high numbers of Chinese-speaking consumers, and place your advertising accordingly. Coast Capital Savings identifies a market segment of Cantonese- and Mandarin-speaking customers who have recently arrived in Canada. To promote its free chequing account to this segment, it created ads featuring Jan Walls, a well-known retired Asian studies professor from Simon Fraser University.[6]

Quebec is a large market segment of its own, defined by geography, but more importantly by ethnicity and language. Hyundai created a French-only advertising campaign featuring Quebec actor Guillaume Lemay-Thivierge, who was chosen because the marketers felt his personality was similar to the brand personality of Hyundai— dynamic and exciting. The spots show Lemay-Thivierge bungee jumping and engaging in other thrilling pastimes, after which he yawns because those activities are boring compared with his Hyundai.[7]

Psychographic segmentation
Dividing a market into different segments based on social class, lifestyle, or personality characteristics.

Psychographic Segmentation **Psychographic segmentation** divides buyers into different segments based on social class, lifestyle, or personality characteristics. People in the same demographic group can have very different psychographic makeups.

In Chapter 6 we discussed how the products people buy reflect their *lifestyles.* As a result, marketers often segment their markets by consumer lifestyles and base their marketing strategies on lifestyle appeals. For example, retailer Anthropologie, with its whimsical "French flea market" store atmosphere, sells a bohemian-chic lifestyle to which its young women customers aspire. And although W Hotels books out hotel rooms by the night, just like any other hotel chain, it doesn't see itself as a hotel company. Instead, it positions itself as "an iconic lifestyle brand," inviting guests to "step inside the worlds of design, music, and fashion." (See Marketing@Work 7.1.)

VF Corporation offers a closet full of more than 30 premium lifestyle brands that "fit the lives of consumers the world over, from commuters to cowboys, surfers to soccer moms, sports fans to rock bands":

Exhibit 7.4 Lifestyle segmentation: VF Corporation offers a closet full of over 30 premium lifestyle brands, each of which taps into consumer aspirations to fashion, status, and well-being in a well-defined segment.

VF Corporation

> You may have never heard of VF corporation, but you're probably familiar with many of their brands. They make Lee, Riders, Rustler, and Wrangler jeans; Jansport and Eastpak bags and knapsacks; and Vans and Timberland footwear. But the company's brands don't target markets by type of clothing—rather, they target by lifestyle segments, which they define as Jeanswear, Imagewear, Outdoor and Action Sports, Sportswear, and Contemporary. The North Face and Timberland brands, both part of the Outdoor segment, offer top-of-the-line gear and apparel for outdoor enthusiasts. From the Sportswear segment, Nautica focuses on people who enjoy high-end casual apparel inspired by sailing and the sea. Vans began as a skate shoe-maker, and Reef features surf-inspired footwear and apparel. In the Contemporary segment, Lucy features upscale active-wear, whereas 7 for All Mankind supplies premium denim and accessories sold in boutiques and high-end department stores such as Saks and Nordstrom. At the other end of the spectrum, Horace Small, part of the Imagewear segment, markets uniforms for police and fire departments and other first responders. No matter who you are, says the company, "We fit your life."[8]

Marketers also use *personality* variables to segment markets. For example, different soft drinks target different personalities. On the one hand, Mountain Dew projects a youthful, rebellious, adventurous, go-your-own-way personality. Its ads remind customers that "It's different on the Mountain." By contrast, Coca-Cola Zero appears to target more mature, practical, and cerebral but good-humoured personality types. Its subtly humorous ads promise "Real Coca-Cola taste and zero calories."

Behavioural Segmentation Behavioural segmentation divides buyers into segments based on their knowledge, attitudes, uses, or responses to a product. Many marketers believe that behaviour variables are the best starting point for building market segments.

OCCASIONS Buyers can be grouped according to occasions when they get the idea to buy, actually make their purchase, or use the purchased item. **Occasion segmentation** can help firms build up product usage. For example, most consumers drink orange juice in the morning, but orange growers have promoted drinking orange juice as a cool, healthful refresher at other times of the day. Occasion segmentation also applies to Christmas, Halloween, and other holiday decorations; food products associated with certain occasions; greeting cards; red and white products and products adorned with maple leaves around Canada Day; flowers for Mother's Day; and tools and ties for Father's Day.

Behavioural segmentation

Dividing a market into segments based on consumer knowledge, attitudes, uses, or responses to a product.

Occasion segmentation

Dividing the market into segments according to occasions when buyers get the idea to buy, actually make their purchase, or use the purchased item.

MARKETING@WORK   7.1

W Hotels: It's Not Just a Room, It's a Trendsetter Lifestyle

In London, U.K., you approach the glitzy, contemporary 10-storey structure encased in a translucent glass veil. Cameras mounted on the roof capture the surrounding skyline and project it onto the building's surface, creating a seamless blend of structure and setting. Inside, you're greeted by thumping hip-hop music, large mirrored glitter balls, open fires, and a huge sofa that snakes around the lounge bar. You're in a nightclub perhaps, or the latest trendy restaurant. No, you're in the W London, a hotel that offers much more than just rooms for the night.

Starwood Hotels and Resorts operates nine different hotel chains—something for everyone, you might say. But its W Hotels brand stands out from all the rest. In fact, W Hotels doesn't really think of itself as just a hotel chain. Instead, it positions itself as "an iconic lifestyle brand." More than just rooms, W Hotels prides itself on "offering guests unprecedented insider access to a world of 'Wow' through contemporary cool design, fashion, music, nightlife, and entertainment." W Hotels exudes a youthful, outgoing, jet-setting lifestyle that fits its ultra-hip, trendsetter clientele—mostly from the media, music, fashion, entertainment, and consulting industries. For these patrons, W provides an unmatched sense of belonging.

W Hotels' lifestyle positioning starts with unique design. Whereas most hotel chains churn out cookie-cutter locations in search of a consistent brand image, W Hotels' 54 properties worldwide look nothing alike. W's patrons view themselves as unique, so they demand the same from the hotels they choose. Every W Hotel projects a common "energetic, vibrant, forward-thinking attitude," and an appreciation for fashion, art, and music befitting its lifestyle image. But in terms of design, each W Hotel is uniquely inspired by its destination, mixing cutting-edge design with local influences.

The W Hotel in Montreal, for example, is located in the historic Banque du Canada building, and suites include oversized windows opening onto Square Victoria Park, goose-down comforters and pillows, community-sized furniture, illuminated side tables, and "voyeur" rainforest showers. And the W Taipei in Taiwan, located near Taipei 101, the city's tallest skyscraper, is designed around the theme of nature electrified, blending soft wooden walls; geometric, box-shaped shelves; and lighting inspired by Chinese lanterns. With each unique design, however, W maintains a consistent ambiance that leaves no question in guests' minds that they're living the W lifestyle. The W Paris, for example, blends the facade of its historic and elegant 1870s building with the theme of Paris as the "City of Light," all wrapped in W's signature contemporary energy:

> The hotel design revolves around an oversized backlit digital undulating wall that defines the central core of the building and weaves through the public and private spaces. "Our design feeds off the elegance, richness, and radiance of Paris . . . and W's DNA for infusing a sense of energy" says the head of the hotel's design group. In true W fashion, it brings the historic building to life with a glowing vibrancy.

But unique design is only part of W Hotels' lifestyle formula. The brand also bridges connections with the worlds of fashion, music, and art. For example, the chain acquired a fashion director, Jenné Lombardo, who has been hosting cutting-edge fashion events in New York for years. Lombardo heads up W's ongoing Fashion Next program, which forges relationships with up-and-coming designers. W sponsors the young design talent by paying for fees and space at major runway events, supplying a W DJ to help with music and providing hair and makeup, catering, and other services. In return, the designers participate in shows, art exhibitions, luncheons, and other events that attract fashion-conscious guests at W hotels around the world. Such events provide "insider access" for W's patrons, contributing further to the hotel's lifestyle appeal.

W Hotels works with music in the same way that it works with fashion. Under the direction of a global music director, W's long-running Symmetry Live concert series offers guests access to exclusive performances by some of the world's hottest, just-discovered acts, such as Cee Lo Green, Janelle Monae, Ellie Goulding, and Theophilus London. W has sponsored an exclusive travelling exhibition of the photography of Madonna, curated by Rock Paper Photo and sponsored by vitaminwater. The exclusive exhibit featured never-before-seen photos of pop star Madonna from the 1980s and celebrated music and fashion, two of the W brand's core passions.

Beyond its passion for art, fashion, and entertainment, as you might expect, another constant at W Hotels is first-class service—what W calls

Courtesy W Hotels

Exhibit 7.5 Lifestyle segmentation and positioning: Montreal's W Hotel, in the historic Banque du Canada building, is an excellent example of the look and feel of this lifestyle brand, which invites guests to step inside a world of design, music, and fashion.

"Whatever-Whenever" service. "We aim to provide whatever, whenever, as long as it is legal—something that is very much consistent throughout the W brand," explains one W Hotel manager. W Hotels don't have concierges; instead, they have "W Insiders." The Insiders go a step beyond. Rather than waiting to be asked for advice, they proactively seek out things they can do to enhance the stay of each guest. In keeping with the brand's lifestyle positioning, insiders stay in tune with special need-to-know happenings and advise guests on all the latest places to see and be seen.

Adding even more lustre to W's lifestyle allure, the chain's hotels attract a star-studded list of celebrities. The W South Beach in Miami, for example, in addition to its modern art collection, is known for guests like Sean Penn, Leonardo DiCaprio, LeBron James, and Italian soccer sensation Alessandro Nesta.

Staying at a W Hotel isn't cheap. The basic W room runs about $450 a night, with top suites running up to five figures. But a W Hotel isn't just a place where you rent a room and get a good night's sleep. It's the design of the place, the contemporary ambiance, what's hanging

on the walls, the music that's playing, the other guests who stay there—all of these things contribute mightily to the W's lifestyle positioning and the allure it holds for its young, hip, upscale clientele. It's not just a room—it's part of an entire trendsetter lifestyle.

Sources: Janet Harmer, "W London—A Hotel That Dares to Be Different," *Caterer & Hotelkeeper*, March 4–10, 2011, pp. 26–28; Nancy Keates, "The Home Front: His Hotel, His Hangout," *Wall Street Journal*, June 3, 2011, p. D6; Christina Binkley, "Putting the Hot Back in Hotel," *Wall Street Journal*, August 18, 2011; "W Hotels Unveils Innovative Design Concept of the Soon-to-Open W Paris-Opéra by Acclaimed Rockwell Group Europe," Starwood press release, December 14, 2011; and information from StarwoodHotels.com and WMontrealHotel.com, accessed July 2015.

BENEFITS SOUGHT A powerful form of segmentation is to group buyers according to the different *benefits* they seek from the product. **Benefit segmentation** requires finding the major benefits people look for in the product class, the kinds of people who look for each benefit, and the major brands that deliver each benefit.

For example, people buying bikes are looking for any of numerous benefits, from competitive racing and sports performance to recreation, fitness, touring, transportation, and just plain fun. Trek Bicycle Corporation, for example, makes bikes in three major benefit groups: road bikes, mountain bikes, and town bikes. Road bikes are fast bikes designed to fly over pavement—for racing, recreating, or both. Trek further divides the road bike segment into six benefit sub-segments, such as race performance and touring. Trek's mountain bikes are for people seeking rugged competition or recreational trail bikes. And Trek's town bikes are for people seeking recreation, fitness, and urban utility. In all, Trek makes some 40 different families of bikes, each designed for a specific benefit segment. And these bicycles are marketed under seven different brand names, in 90 countries worldwide.[9]

USER STATUS Markets can be segmented into non-users, ex-users, potential users, first-time users, and regular users of a product. Marketers want to reinforce and retain regular users, attract non-users, and reinvigorate relationships with ex-users.

Included in the potential user group are consumers facing life-stage changes—such as newlyweds and new parents—who can be turned into heavy users. For example, to get new parents off to the right start, P&G makes certain that its Pampers Swaddlers are the diaper most U.S. hospitals provide for newborns. And to capture newly engaged couples who will soon be equipping their new kitchens, upscale kitchen and cookware retailer Williams-Sonoma takes the usual bridal registry a step further. Through a program called "The Store Is Yours," it opens its stores after hours, by appointment, exclusively for

St Petersburg Times/ZUMAPRESS/Newscom

Exhibit 7.6 Occasion **segmentation:** Targeting consumers with products based on an occasion, like Halloween.

Benefit segmentation
Dividing the market into segments according to the different benefits that consumers seek from the product.

individual couples to visit and make their wish lists. About half the people who register are new to the Williams-Sonoma brand.

USAGE RATE Markets can also be segmented into light, medium, and heavy product users. Heavy users are often a small percentage of the market but account for a high percentage of total consumption. For example, Burger King targets what it calls "Super Fans," people aged 18 to 34 who make up 18 percent of the chain's customers but account for almost half of all customer visits, and who eat at Burger King an average of 16 times a month.

Segmenting the marketing in this way is sometimes referred to by marketers as the "heavy half" concept, or the "80/20 rule"—the idea that 80 percent of the volume of a product is consumed by 20 percent of its consumers. Figuring out how to identify the members of the heavy user segment, however, can be challenging to marketers. Some even call it the Holy Grail of target marketing! Marketing researchers say that psychographic characteristics are much more valuable than demographic characteristics in describing the segment of heavy users of any product. For example, one study on users of various packaged foods found that heavy users were differentiated by six lifestyle factors (active lifestyle, family spirited, homebody, intellectually stimulating pastimes, TV lover, and pet lover) and five personality characteristics (mentally alert, social, athletic, carefree, and stubborn).[10]

LOYALTY STATUS A market can also be segmented by consumer loyalty. Consumers can be loyal to brands, such as Apple or Adidas; to retailers, such as Forever 21 or H&M; and to companies, such as Honda or Tim Hortons. Buyers can be divided into groups according to their degree of loyalty.

Some consumers are completely loyal—they buy one brand all the time. For example, Apple has an almost cult-like following of loyal users. Other consumers are somewhat loyal—they are loyal to two or three brands of a given product or favour one brand while sometimes buying others. Still other buyers show no loyalty to any brand. They either want something different each time they buy or they buy whatever's on sale.

A company can learn a lot by analyzing loyalty patterns in its market. It should start by studying its own loyal customers. For example, by studying Mac fanatics, Apple can better pinpoint its target market and develop marketing appeals. By studying its less-loyal buyers, the company can detect which brands are most competitive with its own. By looking at customers who are shifting away from its brand, the company can learn about its marketing weaknesses.

Using Multiple Segmentation Bases Marketers rarely limit their segmentation analysis to only one or a few variables. Rather, they often use multiple segmentation bases in an effort to identify smaller, better-defined target groups.

There are several business information services that provide multi-variable segmentation systems that merge geographic, demographic, lifestyle, and behavioural data to help companies segment their markets down to neighbourhoods, and even households. One of the leading segmentation systems, The Nielsen Company's PRIZM, classifies households based on a host of demographic factors—such as age, educational level, income, occupation, family composition, ethnicity, and housing—and behavioural and lifestyle factors—such as purchases, free-time activities, and media preferences. It then classifies and names each segment. For example, one of PRIZM's newest segments is called Mobile Wallet Users—consumers who use "tap and go" and other forms of mobile payment. Nielsen found that 29 percent of Mobile Wallet Users are aged 35 to 44, and 20 percent are aged 25 to 34. These users skew toward the more affluent; they tend to have many banking products, including investment accounts, and so represent excellent opportunities for marketers.[11]

Another example of how geographic, demographic, and psychographic characteristics can all be brought to bear in describing a market segment is the LGBT (lesbian, gay, bisexual, and transgender) market:

The LGBT community in Canada is an identifiable niche market that has a higher than average spending power and that tends to be hyper loyal to brands and companies they like. This makes them a very desirable market segment to target with all sorts of products and services. One Toronto marketing strategist points out that it's possible to gain a competitive advantage in certain categories—the travel industry, for example. Travel is a category that can be isolated and contextualized in terms of marketing to a straight or gay couple, whereas there are no real differences in marketing, say, a car to either group.

The sheer size of this market segment is another reason why it's coveted by marketers. The LGBT sector is larger than any other identifiable market segment in Canada—conservative estimates are between 6 and 9 percent of the population, or 3.7 million people. It's also a very valuable sector—their total before-tax income is roughly $98 billion, or 7.2 percent of the GDP. But it's not really one homogenous market segment; rather, it contains many sub-segments. "If you really want to be successful, you need to really target and segment," says Darrell Shuurman, president of Travel Gay Canada. "Too often we group the LGBT market into one market, but you wouldn't go after the straight market without segmenting."

TD Canada Trust is one marketer that openly targets gays and lesbians by featuring them in its mainstream advertising. The company bases its advertising decisions on its own research, and by gathering insights from employees. "They tell us what we should and shouldn't do," says one branch manager. "We consult people from the community to make sure that we're not crossing any lines and that we're being respectful. We ensure that our communications are reflective of the TD brand, respectful, and true to their lifestyle."[12]

Exhibit 7.7 Multiple segmentation bases: The LGBT market is a large segment containing many sub-segments, each targeted by a combination of demographic and psychographic factors. TD directly targets this market segment in its advertising.

Such segmentation provides a powerful tool for marketers of all kinds. It can help companies identify and better understand key customer segments, target them more efficiently, and tailor market offerings and messages to their specific needs.

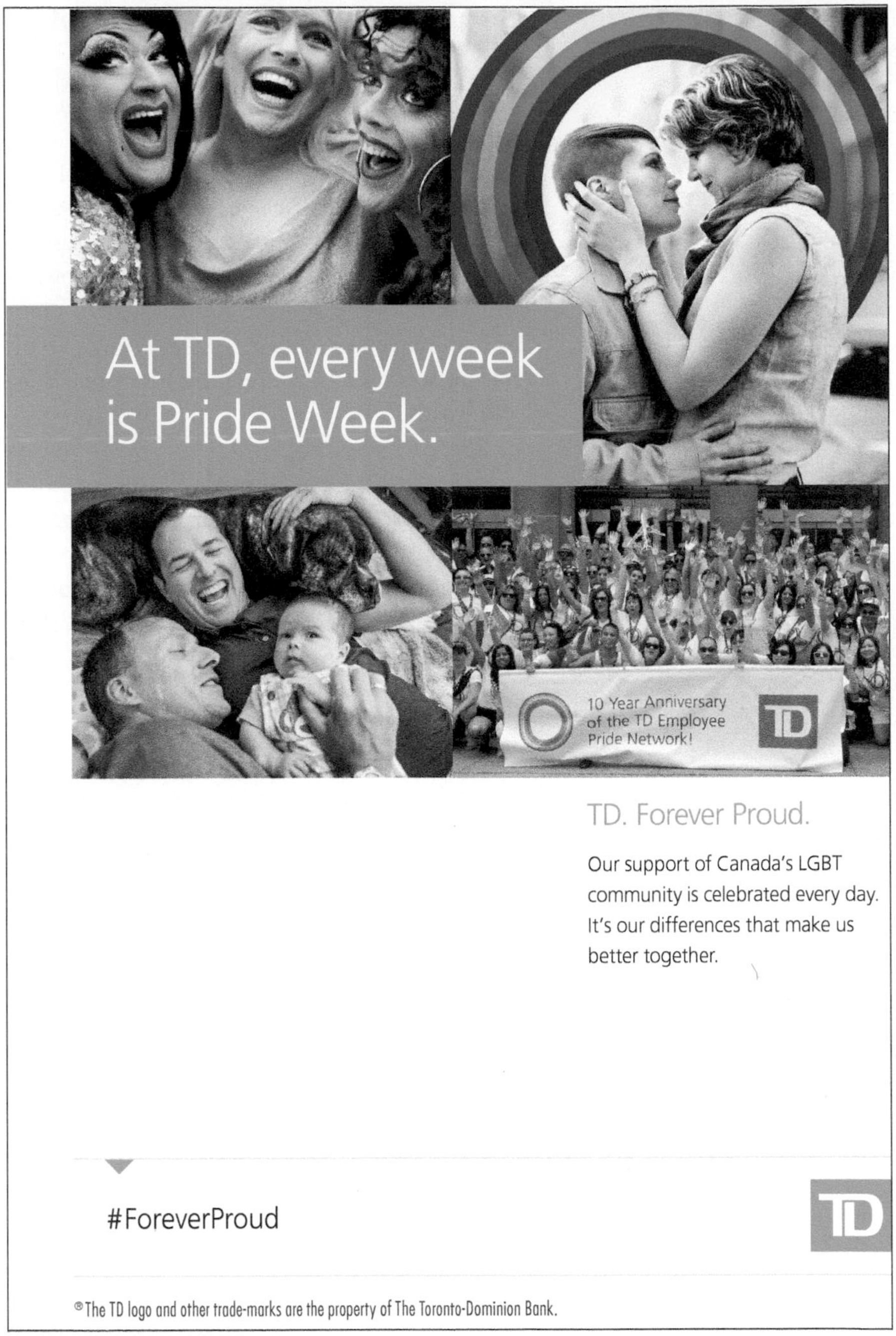

Segmenting Business Markets

Consumer and business marketers use many of the same variables to segment their markets. Business buyers can be segmented geographically, demographically (industry, company size), or by benefits sought, user status, usage rate, and loyalty status. Yet business marketers also use some additional variables, such as customer *operating characteristics*, *purchasing approaches*, *situational factors*, and *personal characteristics*.

Almost every company serves at least some business markets. For example, Starbucks has developed distinct marketing programs for each of its two business segments: the office coffee and the food service segments. In the office coffee and vending segment, Starbucks Office Coffee Solutions markets a variety of workplace services to businesses of any size, helping them make Starbucks coffee and related products available to their employees in their workplaces. Starbucks helps these business customers design the best office solutions involving its coffees (the Starbucks or Seattle's Best brands), teas (Tazo), syrups, and branded paper products and its methods of serving them—portion packs, single cups, or vending. The Starbucks Foodservice division teams up with businesses and other organizations—ranging from airlines, restaurants, colleges, and hospitals to baseball stadiums—to help them serve the well-known Starbucks brand to their own customers. Starbucks provides not only the coffee, tea, and paper products to its food-service partners, but also equipment, training, and marketing and merchandising support.[13]

Many companies set up separate systems for dealing with larger or multiple-location customers. For example, Steelcase, a major producer of office furniture, first segments customers into seven industries, including banking, biosciences, healthcare, and higher education. Next, company salespeople work with independent Steelcase dealers to handle smaller, local, or regional Steelcase customers in each segment. But many national, multiple-location customers, such as ExxonMobil or IBM, have special needs that may reach beyond the scope of individual dealers. So Steelcase uses national account managers to help its dealer networks handle its national accounts.

Within a given target industry and customer size, the company can segment by purchase approaches and criteria. As in consumer segmentation, many marketers believe that *buying behaviour* and *benefits* provide the best basis for segmenting business markets.

Segmenting International Markets

Few companies have either the resources or the will to operate in all, or even most, of the countries that dot the globe. Although some large companies, such as Coca-Cola and Sony, sell products in more than 200 countries, most international firms focus on a smaller set. Operating in many countries presents new challenges. Different countries, even those that are close together, can vary greatly in their economic, cultural, and political makeup. Thus, just as they do within their domestic markets, international firms need to group their world markets into segments with distinct buying needs and behaviours.

Companies can segment international markets by using one or a combination of several variables. They can segment by *geographic location*, grouping countries by regions such as Western Europe, the Pacific Rim, the Middle East, or Africa. Geographic segmentation assumes that nations close to one another will have many common traits and behaviours. Although this is often the case, there are many exceptions. For example, some U.S. marketers lump all Central and South American countries together, and assume they all speak Spanish, even though Brazilians speak Portuguese, and millions in other countries speak a variety of Indian dialects. And although North America consists of three countries, Mexico is usually ignored when marketers consider the North American market. Even Canada and the United States, though they have much in common, differ culturally, socially, and economically, and cannot be assumed to respond the same way to marketing offers.

World markets can also be segmented on the basis of *economic factors*. Countries might be grouped by their population's income levels or their overall level of economic development. A country's economic structure shapes its population's product and service needs and, therefore, the marketing opportunities it offers. For example, many companies are now targeting fast-growing developing economies like India and China, whose populations have increasing buying power.

Countries can be segmented by *political and legal factors* such as the type and stability of government, receptivity to foreign firms, monetary regulations, and amount of bureaucracy. *Cultural factors* can also be used, grouping markets according to common languages, religions, values and attitudes, customs, and behavioural patterns.

Segmenting international markets based on geographic, economic, political, cultural, and other factors presumes that segments should consist of clusters of countries. However, as new communications technologies, such as satellite TV and the Internet, connect consumers around the world, marketers can define and reach segments of like-minded consumers no matter where in the world they are. Using **intermarket segmentation** (also called **cross-market segmentation**), they form segments of consumers who have similar needs and buying behaviours even though they are located in different countries.

Intermarket (cross-market) segmentation
Forming segments of consumers who have similar needs and buying behaviours even though they are located in different countries.

For example, retailer H&M targets fashion-conscious but frugal shoppers in 43 countries with its low-priced, trendy apparel and accessories. And Coca-Cola creates special programs to target teens, core consumers of its soft drinks the world over. By 2020, one-third of the world's population—some 2.5 billion people—will be under 18 years of age. Coca-Cola reaches this important market through the universal language of music:

Coca-Cola launched a Coca-Cola Music campaign to engage the world's teens in more than 100 global markets. The brand extended these efforts with a highly successful "Move to the Beat" teen-focused campaign centred on the London 2012 Olympics, inspired by the sounds, spirit, and culture of the host city. Coca-Cola Music has also joined forces with Spotify to provide a global music network that helps teens discover new music, connect with other music-loving teens, and share their experiences with friends worldwide both online and offline. "The number one passion point for teens is music," says a Coca-Cola global marketing executive. Coca-Cola's CEO agrees: "Our success . . . today depends on our ability to grow and connect with teens, the generation of tomorrow."[14]

Requirements for Effective Segmentation

Clearly, there are many ways to segment a market, but not all segmentation methods are effective. For example, buyers of table salt could be divided into blond and brunette customers, but hair colour is obviously not a relevant criterion because it doesn't influence a consumer's choice of salt brand. Furthermore, if all salt buyers bought the same amount of salt each month, believed that all salt is the same, and wanted to pay the same price, the company would not benefit from segmenting this market.

Exhibit 7.8 Intermarket segmentation: Retailer H&M targets fashion-conscious but frugal shoppers in 43 countries with its low-priced, trendy apparel and accessories.

REUTERS/Toru Hanai

To be useful, market segments must be the following:

- *Measurable:* The size, purchasing power, and profiles of the segments can be measured. Certain segmentation variables are difficult to measure. For example, although approximately 7 to 10 percent of adults are left-handed, there is no way to identify and target them. Perhaps this is why so few products are targeted toward this market segment.

- *Accessible:* The market segments can be effectively reached and served. Suppose a fragrance company finds that heavy users of its brand are single men and women who stay out late and socialize a lot. Unless this group lives or shops at certain places and is exposed to certain media, its members will be difficult to reach.

- *Substantial:* The market segments are large or profitable enough to serve. A segment should be the largest possible homogeneous group worth pursuing with a tailored marketing program. It would not pay, for example, for an automobile manufacturer to develop cars especially for people who are more than seven feet tall.

- *Differentiable:* The segments are conceptually distinguishable and respond differently to different marketing-mix elements and programs. If married and unmarried women respond similarly to a sale on perfume, they do not constitute separate segments.

- *Actionable:* Effective programs can be designed for attracting and serving the segments. For example, although one small airline identified seven market segments, its staff was too small to develop separate marketing programs for each segment.

Market Targeting LO3

Market segmentation is essentially an exercise in which marketers theoretically divide up the market into opportunities—groups of people with shared characteristics that the marketers believe will make them attracted to their products. Think of the market as a pie, and each segment as a slice.

Once that's done, the marketers must decide which segment or segments (or slices) to target with their products, services, and communications.

← ⊙ Simulate on MyMarketingLab

Segmentation, Targeting, Positioning

Evaluating Market Segments

In evaluating different market segments, marketers must look at three factors: segment size and growth, segment structural attractiveness, and company objectives and resources. They do this by collecting and analyzing data on current segment sales, growth rates, and expected profitability for various segments. They choose their target market segments by figuring out which ones have the "right" size and growth characteristics.

But "right size and growth" is a relative matter. The largest, fastest-growing segments are not always the most attractive ones for every company. Smaller companies may lack the skills and resources needed to serve the larger segments. Or they may find these segments to be too competitive. Such companies may target segments that are smaller and less attractive, in an absolute sense, but that are potentially more profitable for them. And if a company identifies a segment as being unprofitable, it might even take steps to encourage that group to shop at the competition instead.

Marketers also need to examine major structural factors that affect long-run segment attractiveness. This is where marketing strategy meets corporate strategy, and executives analyze the "five forces" that most affect and influence a company's ability to compete in a particular area. These five forces are *competitors* (How many, and are they direct or indirect competition for business in this segment?); *new entrants* (How easy or difficult is it for an existing company to start serving this segment, or for a new company to start up and start doing it?); *substitute products* (If we don't serve this segment, what else can they buy that will serve the same purpose?); relative *power of buyers* (When it comes to this segment, do buyers have strong bargaining power relative to sellers? If so, will they try to force prices down, demand more services, and set competitors against one another?); and relative *power of suppliers* (If suppliers have control over us, that can affect our prices and reduce the quality or quantity of products we can produce).[15]

Even if a segment has the right size and growth and is structurally attractive, the company must consider its own objectives and resources. Some attractive segments can be dismissed quickly because they do not mesh with the company's long-run objectives. Or the company may lack the skills and resources needed to succeed in an attractive segment. For example, given current economic conditions, the economy segment of the automobile market is large and growing. And so, given its objectives and resources, it would make little sense for luxury-performance carmaker BMW to enter this segment. A company should enter only those segments in which it can create superior customer value and gain advantages over competitors.

Selecting Target Market Segments

After evaluating different segments, the company must decide which and how many segments it will target. A **target market** consists of a set of buyers who share common needs or characteristics that the company decides to serve. Market targeting can be carried out at several different levels. Figure 7.2 shows that companies can target very broadly (*undifferentiated marketing*), very narrowly (*micromarketing*), or somewhere in between (*differentiated or concentrated marketing*).

By using an **undifferentiated marketing** (or **mass marketing**) strategy, a firm might decide to ignore market segment differences and target the whole market with one offer. This mass-marketing strategy focuses on what is *common* in the needs of consumers rather than on what is *different*. The company designs a product and a marketing program that will appeal to the largest number of buyers.

As noted earlier in the chapter, most modern marketers have strong doubts about this strategy. Difficulties arise in developing a product or brand that will satisfy all consumers. Moreover, mass marketers often have trouble competing with more-focused firms that do a better job of satisfying the needs of specific segments and niches.

Differentiated Marketing By using a **differentiated marketing** (or **segmented marketing**) strategy, a firm decides to target several market segments and designs separate offers for each. Toyota, for example, produces many different brands of cars, from Yaris to Lexus, each targeting a different group of car buyers—a different market segment. Procter & Gamble markets six different laundry detergent brands, which compete with each other on supermarket shelves. But perhaps no brand practises differentiated marketing quite like Hallmark Cards:

> Hallmark vigorously segments the greeting card market. In addition to its broad Hallmark card line and popular sub-branded lines such as the humorous Shoebox Greetings, Hallmark has introduced lines targeting a dozen or more specific segments. Fresh Ink targets 18- to

Target market
A set of buyers sharing common needs or characteristics that the company decides to serve.

Undifferentiated (mass) marketing
A market-coverage strategy in which a firm decides to ignore market segment differences and go after the whole market with one offer.

Differentiated (segmented) marketing
A market-coverage strategy in which a firm decides to target several market segments and designs separate offers for each.

FIGURE 7.2 Market Targeting Strategies

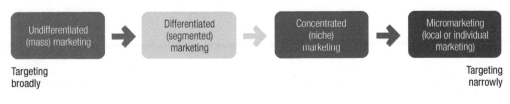

Targeting broadly   Targeting narrowly

Gary Armstrong

Exhibit 7.9 Differentiated (segmented) marketing: Hallmark vigorously segments the greeting card market using characteristics such as age, stage of life, family status, lifestyle, personality, occasion, and geography.

39-year-old women. Hallmark Warm Wishes offers hundreds of affordable 99-cent cards. Hallmark's three ethnic lines—Mahogany, Sinceramente Hallmark, and Tree of Life—target African-American, Hispanic, and Jewish consumers, respectively. Hallmark's newer Journeys line of encouragement cards focuses on such challenges as fighting cancer, coming out, and battling depression. The brand has created new market segments for interactive and online greeting "cards," with musical greeting cards incorporating sound clips from popular movies, TV shows, and songs. Recordable storybooks let people record each page of a book and have it played back as the recipient turns the pages. Online, Hallmark offers e-cards as well as personalized printed greeting cards that it mails for consumers. The company also targets the business segment with Hallmark Business Expressions. And of course it segments the market by geography, offering cards for sale in 100 countries around the world.[16]

But differentiated marketing also increases the costs of doing business. A firm usually finds it more expensive to develop and produce, say, 10 units of 10 different products than 100 units of one product. Developing separate marketing plans for the separate segments requires extra marketing research, forecasting, sales analysis, promotion planning, and channel management. And trying to reach different market segments with different advertising campaigns increases promotion costs. Marketers must take all these factors into consideration when deciding on a differentiated marketing strategy.

Concentrated (niche) marketing
A market-coverage strategy in which a firm goes after a large share of one or a few segments or niches.

Concentrated Marketing By using a **concentrated marketing** (or **niche marketing**) strategy, instead of going after a small share of a large market, the firm goes after a large share of one or a few smaller segments or niches. Through concentrated marketing, the firm achieves a strong market position because of its greater knowledge of consumer needs in the niches it serves and the special reputation it acquires. It can market more *effectively* by fine-tuning its products, prices, and programs to the needs of carefully defined segments. It can also market more *efficiently*, targeting its products or services, channels, and communications programs toward only those consumers that it can serve best and most profitably. Consider Sabian, the second largest cymbal manufacturer in the world:

> The village of Meductic, New Brunswick, has a population of only a few hundred people, and you've likely never heard of it—unless you're a musician. More specifically, a drummer. Neil Peart and Phil Collins, two of the most respected drummers in the world, have visited Meductic because it's home to Sabian, a world-renowned cymbal maker. Sabian employs 130 people, sells its cymbals in 120 countries, and holds about half the market share.
>
> How big is the worldwide market for cymbals? In dollar terms, it's less than $100 million per year, which definitely qualifies it as a niche market. Sabian's only competitor to speak of is the company that holds the other half of this small market segment, the Avedis Zildjian Company of Boston. Sabian differentiates itself from Zildjian by projecting the idea that it is a creative, innovative company, whereas Zildjian is more traditional. Sabian cymbals are used by Red Hot Chili Peppers drummer Chad Smith, Nickelback's Daniel Adair, and Peter Gabriel's drummer Felix Sabal-Lecco, to name just a few.
>
> The Sabian factory in New Brunswick has become something of a mecca for the world's best drummers. Sabian invites them to visit and to invent new cymbal sounds, which the

company then markets as a signature line. One of these lines, called Paragon, was designed in collaboration with legendary Rush drummer Neil Peart. Sabian recently added several new products to the Paragon line in celebration of Rush's fortieth anniversary, including the larger 17-, 19-, and 22-inch crash cymbals that are so popular with drummers today.[17]

Whereas most market segments are fairly large and normally attract several competitors, niche markets are smaller and may attract only one or two competitors. Niche marketing lets smaller companies focus their limited resources on serving very small groups of customers that may be unimportant to or overlooked by larger competitors. Many companies start as niche marketers to get a foothold against larger, more-resourceful competitors and then grow into broader competitors. For example, rather than competing with Hertz and Avis in airport locations, Enterprise Rent-A-Car began by building a network of neighbourhood offices that served the niche market of city dwellers who don't own a car. Fancy Feather (FancyFeather.com) sells items such as feather boas, fans, and masks made of ostrich feathers; and Edmonton's Kinnikinnick Foods reaches a worldwide market of consumers online with its gluten-free baked goods.

Micromarketing Differentiated and concentrated marketers tailor their offers and marketing programs to meet the needs of market segments consisting of groups of people; however, they do not go so far as to customize their offers to each individual customer. **Micromarketing** is the practice of tailoring products and marketing programs to suit the tastes of specific individuals and locations. Micromarketing is an extreme form of market segmentation, where the market segment is so small that it's contained within a small geographic area—*local marketing*—or so small that it consists of only one person—*individual marketing*.

Craig Renwick/Sabian

Exhibit 7.10 Niche marketing: Though the worldwide market for cymbals is small, New Brunswick's Sabian has captured half of it, owing in part to their brand partnerships with famous drummers, like Neil Peart.

Micromarketing
The practice of tailoring products and marketing programs to the needs and wants of specific individuals and local customer segments—includes *local marketing and individual marketing.*

Local marketing
A small group of people who live in the same city or neighbourhood or who shop at the same store.

LOCAL MARKETING **Local marketing** involves tailoring brands and promotions to the needs and wants of a small group of people who live in the same city or neighbourhood or who shop at the same store. Most convenience stores practise local marketing, stocking their shelves with the items they know the people in their neighbourhood are likely to want.

Advances in communications technology have given rise to a new high-tech version of location-based marketing. Using location-based social networks such as Foursquare, and local marketing deal-of-the-day services such as Groupon, local retailers can target consumers based on where they are right now:

Location-based apps such as Shopkick, CheckPoints, and Swarm are all check-in services that offer users some kind of rewards, whether real or virtual. Shoppers using Shopkick collect

Exhibit 7.11 Location-based marketing: Groupon provides local marketers with a way to advertise deals to consumers in their city.

Individual marketing (mass customization)

Tailoring products and marketing programs to the needs and preferences of individual customers.

points called "kicks" just by walking into stores, and CheckPoints users collect points by checking into locations or checking out (i.e., looking at) certain products within a store. Foursquare split off its check-in feature as a separate app called Swarm. And Groupon partners with local businesses to offer local shopping deals to subscribers based on where they live and what they like.

Location-based apps provide users with a way to locate deals in their neighbourhood and share information with friends. For marketers, though, check-in services provide attractive targeting opportunities. According to the Internet Advertising Bureau, from 2012 to 2014 mobile advertising campaigns using mobile location data grew from $1.2 billion to an estimated $3.9 billion. Retailers seem to be most interested in the possibilities of location-based marketing—Apple's recent launch of iBeacon technology prompted marketers at Lord & Taylor and Hudson's Bay to install location-sensitive devices that send out push notifications to shoppers who have downloaded their mobile app. The rise of mobile has helped marketers stay alert to trends and consumer habits, and to offer content and promotions that are highly targeted—and therefore more likely to catch and hold the consumer's attention.[18]

Local marketing has some drawbacks. It can drive up manufacturing and marketing costs by reducing economies of scale. It can also create logistics problems as companies try to meet the varied requirements of different regional and local markets. Still, as companies face increasingly fragmented markets, and as new supporting technologies develop, the advantages of local marketing often outweigh the drawbacks. Local marketing helps a company market more effectively in the face of pronounced regional and local differences in demographics and lifestyles. It also meets the needs of the company's first-line customers—retailers—who prefer more finely tuned product assortments for their neighbourhoods.

INDIVIDUAL MARKETING In the extreme, micromarketing becomes **individual marketing**—tailoring products and marketing programs to the needs and preferences of individual customers. Individual marketing is also known as **mass customization**.

The modern custom of mass marketing has obscured the fact that for centuries consumers *were* served as individuals: The tailor custom-made a suit, the cobbler designed shoes for an individual, the cabinet-maker made furniture to order. So, in a sense we are returning to a time-honoured tradition, but employing contemporary technology to improve upon it. Computer databases, robotic production, flexible manufacturing, and interactive

Exhibit 7.12 Individual marketing: Nike's NikeID program lets users choose shoe materials, personalize colours, imprint text on the heels, and even size the left and right shoes differently.

communication media have combined to foster mass customization. Today's marketers have the tools to interact on a one-to-one basis with masses of customers to produce products that are in some way customized to the individual.

Companies these days are hyper-customizing everything from food to artwork, earphones, sneakers, and motorcycles. At mymms.com, candy lovers can buy M&M's embossed with images of their kids or pets. JH Audio in Orlando makes music earphones based on moulds of customers' ears to provide optimized fit and better and safer sound. The company even laser-prints designs on the tiny ear buds—some people request a kid for each ear; others prefer a dog. Nike's NikeID program lets users choose materials for their shoes' tread (say, for trail or street) and upper (Gore-Tex, mesh, or other), pick the colour of the swoosh symbol and stitching, and even imprint text on the heels. Different-sized right and left feet? That, too, can be retooled. On a much larger scale, Harley-Davidson's H-D1 factory customization program lets customers go online, design their own Harley, and get it in as little as four weeks. It invites customers to explore some 8000 ways to create their own masterpiece. "You dream it. We build it," says the company.[19]

Business-to-business marketers are also finding new ways to customize their offerings. For example, John Deere manufactures seeding equipment that can be configured in more than 2 million versions to individual customer specifications. The seeders are produced one at a time, in any sequence, on a single production line. Mass customization provides a way to stand out against competitors.

Unlike mass production, which eliminates the need for human interaction, mass customization has made relationships with customers more important than ever. Just as mass production was the marketing principle of the twentieth century, mass customization is becoming a marketing principle for the twenty-first. The world appears to be coming full circle—from the good old days when customers were treated as individuals, to mass marketing when nobody knew your name, and back again.

Choosing a Targeting Strategy Companies need to consider many factors when choosing a market-targeting strategy. Which strategy is best depends on *company resources*. When the firm's resources are limited, concentrated marketing makes the most sense. The best strategy also depends on the degree of *product variability*. Undifferentiated marketing is more suited for uniform products such as grapefruit or steel. Products that can vary in design, such as cameras and cars, are more suited to differentiation or concentration. The *product's life-cycle stage* must also be considered. (More about this in Chapter 8.) When a firm introduces a new product, it may be practical to launch only one version, and undifferentiated marketing or concentrated marketing may make the most sense. In the mature stage of the product life cycle, however, differentiated marketing often makes more sense.

Another factor is *market variability*. If most buyers have the same tastes, buy the same amounts, and react the same way to marketing efforts, undifferentiated marketing is appropriate. Finally, *competitors' marketing strategies* are important. When competitors use differentiated or concentrated marketing, undifferentiated marketing can be suicidal. Conversely, when competitors use undifferentiated marketing, a firm can gain an advantage by using differentiated or concentrated marketing, focusing on the needs of buyers in specific segments.

Socially Responsible Target Marketing

Smart targeting helps companies become more efficient and effective by focusing on the segments they can satisfy best and most profitably. Targeting also benefits consumers—

Jarrod Weaton/Weaton Digital, Inc.

Exhibit 7.13 Socially responsible marketing: Critics worry that marketers of everything from lingerie and cosmetics to Barbie dolls are targeting young girls with provocative products.

companies serve specific groups of consumers with offers carefully tailored to their needs. However, target marketing sometimes generates controversy and concern. The biggest issues usually involve the targeting of vulnerable or disadvantaged consumers with controversial or potentially harmful products.

For example, over the years marketers in a wide range of industries—from cereal, soft drinks, and fast food to toys and fashion—have been heavily criticized for their marketing efforts directed toward children. Critics worry that premium offers and high-powered advertising appeals presented through the mouths of lovable animated characters will overwhelm children's defences.

Other problems arise when the marketing of adult products spills over into the children's segment—intentionally or unintentionally. For example, Victoria's Secret targets its highly successful Pink line of young, hip, and sexy clothing to young women from 18 to 30 years old. However, critics charge that Pink is now all the rage among girls as young as 11 years old. Responding to Victoria's Secret's designs and marketing messages, tweens are flocking into stores and buying Pink, with or without their mothers. More broadly, critics worry that marketers of everything from lingerie and cosmetics to Barbie dolls are, directly or indirectly, targeting young girls with provocative products, promoting a premature focus on sex and appearance.

The digital era may make children even more vulnerable to targeted marketing messages. Traditional child-directed TV and print ads usually contain obvious pitches that are easily detected and controlled by parents. However, marketing in digital media may be subtly embedded within the content and viewed by children on personal, small-screen devices that are beyond even the most watchful parent's eye. Such marketing might take the form of immersive "advergames"—video games specifically designed to engage children with products. Or they might consist of embedded ads, quizzes, or product placements that let marketers cross-promote branded products, TV shows, popular characters, or other marketable entities.

In Canada, advertising to children is strictly controlled by several organizations, including Advertising Standards Canada, which publishes the Canadian Code of Advertising Standards; the Canadian Association of Broadcasters, which has its own code for television advertising aimed at children; and Concerned Children's Advertisers, an advocacy group dedicated to promoting media literacy, ethics, and responsibility in advertising to children. Still, many consumers feel that more should be done to protect vulnerable groups from being targeted.

Most market targeting, however, draws no criticism because it benefits consumers. For example, all shampoo marketers target multiple market segments defined by various demographic characteristics by offering products for different colours of hair, for hair that is colour treated, for grey hair, and special products for men's hair. Samsung markets the Jitterbug, an easy-to-use phone, directly to seniors who need a simpler cellphone with bigger buttons, large screen text, and a louder speaker. And Colgate makes a large selection of toothbrush shapes and toothpaste flavours for children—from Colgate SpongeBob SquarePants Mild Bubble Fruit toothpaste to Colgate Dora the Explorer character toothbrushes. Such products help make tooth brushing more fun and get children to brush longer and more often.

Therefore, in target marketing, the issue is not really who is targeted but rather how and for what. Controversies arise only when unscrupulous marketers attempt to profit by unfairly targeting vulnerable segments with questionable products or tactics. Socially responsible marketing calls for segmentation and targeting that serve not just the interests of the company but also the interests of those targeted.

Differentiation and Positioning LO4

Beyond deciding which segments of the market it will target, the company must decide on a *value proposition*—how it will create differentiated value for targeted segments, and what positions it wants to occupy in those segments. A **product position** is the way the product is *defined by consumers* on important attributes—the place the product occupies in consumers' minds relative to competing products. More often, positioning is based not just on the product, but on the product's brand name. Branding experts say that products are created in the factory, but brands are created in the mind.

Product position
The way the product is defined by consumers on important attributes—the place the product occupies in consumers' minds relative to competing products.

Consumers are overloaded with information about products and services. They cannot re-evaluate products every time they make a buying decision. To simplify the buying process, consumers organize products, services, and companies into categories and "position" them in their minds. A product's position is the complex set of perceptions, impressions, and feelings that consumers have for the product compared with competing products.

The less differentiated the product actually is, the more important positioning becomes. Think of personal care products, for example. Old Spice is positioned as being the choice for manly men, Axe is the brand for young men who want to score with the opposite sex, and Dove is for the regular, everyday family man. Subway restaurants positioned themselves with spectacular success as the healthy fast food. Beer is a relatively undifferentiated product, so beer brands position themselves on the basis of lifestyle: Corona is for when you're on vacation (or want to feel like you are); Molson Canadian is the hockey fan's beer, and Kokanee is for the outdoorsy type. And most mobile devices and telecommunications services have similar features, so marketers attempt to position their smartphone's brand in the mind of the consumer by using emotional appeals. TELUS has been doing this for years with their colourful and quirky animals.

Even when many products within the category *do* have significant differences, positioning is very important. Think of what happens every time a new soft drink is introduced. (See Marketing@Work 7.2.)

Consumers position products in their minds with or without the help of marketers. But marketers do not want to leave their products' positions to chance. They must *plan* positions that will give their products the greatest advantage in selected target markets, and they must design marketing mixes to create these planned positions.

Positioning Maps

In planning their differentiation and positioning strategies, marketers often prepare *perceptual positioning maps*, which show consumer perceptions of their brands versus competing products on important buying dimensions. Figure 7.3 shows a positioning map for the large luxury sport-utility-vehicle market in the United States. The position of each circle on the map indicates the brand's perceived positioning on two dimensions—price and orientation (luxury versus performance). The size of each circle indicates the brand's relative market share.

MARKETING@WORK 7.2

Positioning New Soft Drinks in an Overcrowded Market

Carbonated soft drinks such as Coke and Pepsi were once the only choices consumers had when it came to convenient on-the-go drinks, but those days are long gone. For the last two decades sales of carbonated soft drinks have been sliding as consumers increasingly turn to juices, cold teas, flavoured water, and new offerings such as energy drinks, coconut milk, almond milk, soy beverages, and coconut water.

With soda consumption at a multi-decade low with no signs of rebounding, the prospects for Coca-Cola and other carbonated beverage makers seem pretty bleak. Good thing that the Atlanta-based soda giant has discovered the high-protein beverage market. The company dipped its toe in the market in 2012 when it announced it was forming Fair Oaks Farms Brands L.L.C. with Select Milk Processors, a group of dairy firms. Their plan was to develop what they called an "innovative portfolio of brands and products that feature the value-added nutrition of dairy."

Fair Oaks has recently begun selling Fairlife, which has 50 percent more natural protein and less sugar than regular milk. Fairlife is also lactose-free and has 30 percent more calcium than regular milk. The product is being offered in the U.S. in whole milk, fat-free, chocolate, and reduced-fat options, with prices ranging from $3.98 to $4.20.

The timing couldn't be better. Consumers are becoming more health conscious and are increasingly attracted to protein-fortified products — even though nutritionists argue that most people don't need them. Industry trade publications say the high-protein drink market is up for grabs, and Coca-Cola is hoping to snag a big part of it by investing in a $30 million advertising campaign to promote the new Fairlife brand.

"I hope it's Coke's next billion-dollar brand," said Fairlife CEO Steve Jones.

Positioning the new brand is turning out to be a challenge for marketers, though. It seems that consumers have started referring to Fairlife as Coke Milk.

"Coke is not making any milk here," says Mike McCloskey, co-founder of Fairlife and CEO of the dairy farm co-op Select Milk Producers. He believes that just as consumers are willing to pay big for premium coffees, they will pay big for premium milk.

Perhaps the marketers of new milk beverages should look at how coconut water entered the highly fragmented soft drink market with great success a few years ago. A major advertising campaign featuring Rihanna saying, "Hydrate naturally, from a tree, not a lab," positioned coconut water in the minds of consumers as being natural, and therefore superior, to other types of soft drinks. It even made consumers believe that it was "better" than juice, even though juice is also natural. Up until then, most consumers thought of coconut water, if they thought of it at all, as

something you would sip while on a tropical vacation.

The most important trend in the refreshment business—going on for more than a decade—is the flight away from sugary, carbonated soft drinks like Coke and Pepsi toward drinks perceived as healthier, more natural choices. The decline of the soda stems in part from the aging of the baby boomers, the original target market for those drinks. But there is also a general movement toward something the trend spotters call "wellness." The wellness trend has inspired several profitable beverage launches—inspiring massive bottled water brands like Dasani and Aquafina, alternative sports drink concoctions like Vitamin Water, and single-ingredient juices like Pom Wonderful. The launch of coconut water, and now protein-fortified milk drinks, are just the latest marketing efforts to ride the trend.

It seems the biggest competition for Fairlife premium milk is, well, milk. Fairlife is a chilled product, with a shelf life of 90 days in the cooler. That's longer than the 15 days conventional

Exhibit 7.14 Positioning a new brand: Coca-Cola's new Fairlife brand is positioned as something different from and better than "traditional" milk.

milk lasts, but is that difference something consumers care about? And if the positioning of Fairlife is that it's fortified (i.e., it has things added to it), how does that jive with the wellness trend, where consumers seek natural products?

The experts can't agree on whether fortified milk is a good idea or a bad one. One beverage industry expert says it's a smart move. "I think getting into beverages which supply protein makes sense for the big beverage companies," says John Sicher, editor and publisher of the trade magazine *Beverage Digest.*

But one nutritionist is unimpressed. "Milk is already an excellent nutritious beverage that does not require any engineering," says Rebecca Solomon, director of clinical nutrition at Mount Sinai Beth Israel in New York City. "I fail to see why milk needs to be improved upon by the soda industry."

Will "Coke Milk" be the next Gatorade, or the next New Coke? Only time will tell.

Sources: John Kell, "U.S. Soda Sales Dropped for the 10th Straight Year in 2014," *Fortune* online, March 26, 2015; Jonathan Berr, "Coca-Cola's Bet on Premium Milk Could Be a Winner for KO Stock," InvestorPlace.com, March 16, 2015; Sabrina Toppa, "Coca-Cola Is About to Start Selling a New Protein-Packed Milk," *Time* online, February 4, 2015; Bruce Horovitz, "Coke Gets into Moo Juice with Premium-Price Milk," *USA Today,* February 3, 2015; and Seth Stevenson, "Gatorade Is the Antichrist," Slate.com, November 7, 2011.

Consumers view the market-leading Cadillac Escalade as a large, moderately priced SUV with a balance of luxury and performance. The Escalade is positioned on urban luxury, and, in its case, performance probably means power and safety. You'll find no mention of off-road adventuring in an Escalade ad. By contrast, Range Rover and Land Cruiser are positioned on luxury with nuances of off-road performance.

Choosing a Differentiation and Positioning Strategy

Some marketers find it easy to choose a differentiation and positioning strategy for their products and brands. For example, a brand well known for its high quality and style in its existing market segments will continue to position its new products in a similar manner. But when two or more brands go after the same position, each will have to find other ways to set itself apart. Marketers must differentiate their product offerings by building a unique bundle of benefits that appeals to a substantial group within the segment. Above all else, a brand's positioning must serve the needs and preferences of well-defined target markets.

The differentiation and positioning task consists of three steps: identifying a set of differentiating competitive advantages upon which to build a position, choosing the right

FIGURE 7.3 Positioning Map for Large Luxury SUVs

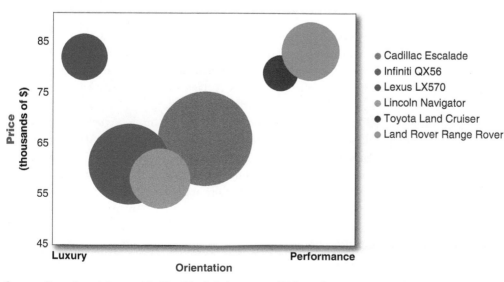

Source: Based on data provided by WardsAuto.com and Edmunds.com.

competitive advantages, and selecting an overall positioning strategy. The company must then effectively communicate and deliver the chosen position to the market.

Identifying Possible Value Differences and Competitive Advantages To build profitable relationships with target customers, marketers must understand customer needs better than competitors do and deliver more customer value. To the extent that a company can differentiate and position itself as providing superior customer value, it gains **competitive advantage**.

But solid positions cannot be built on empty promises. If a company positions its product as *offering* the best quality and service, it must actually differentiate the product so that it *delivers* the promised quality and service. Companies must do much more than simply shout out their positions in ad slogans and taglines. They must first *live* the slogan. For example, when Staples set out to differentiate itself on the basis of an easier shopping experience, it worked for a year to remodel its stores, retrain employees, and simplify customer communications. Only when everything was in place did it begin its advertising campaign with the tagline, "Staples: that was easy."[20]

To find points of differentiation, marketers must think through the customer's entire experience with the company's product or service. An alert company can find ways to differentiate itself at every customer contact point. In what specific ways can a company differentiate itself or its market offer? It can differentiate along the lines of *product*, *services*, *channels*, *people*, or *image*.

Through *product differentiation* brands can be differentiated on features, performance, or style and design. For example, Maple Leaf Foods claims that its Maple Leaf Prime Naturally–branded chicken is fresher and more tender—and gets a price premium based on this differentiation. Whirlpool promotes its dishwashers on performance—they run more quietly—and Bose positions its speakers on their striking design characteristics. Similarly, companies can differentiate their products on attributes such as consistency, durability, reliability, or repairability.

Beyond differentiating its physical product, a firm can differentiate the services that accompany the product. Some companies gain *services differentiation* through speedy, convenient, or careful delivery. For example, TD Canada Trust positions itself as the bank that makes banking "comfortable," and differentiates itself by offering services other banks don't, such as branches that are open on Sundays. Others differentiate their service based on high-quality customer care. Lexus makes fine cars but is perhaps even better known for the quality service that creates outstanding ownership experiences for Lexus owners.

Firms that practise *channel differentiation* gain competitive advantage through the way they design their channel's coverage, expertise, and performance. Caterpillar's success in the heavy equipment industry is based on its superior marketing channels starring local Caterpillar dealers. Online marketers such as Amazon and Dell similarly distinguish themselves by their high-quality direct channels.

Companies can also gain a strong competitive advantage through *people differentiation*—hiring and training better people than their competitors do. Singapore Airlines enjoys an excellent reputation, largely because of the beauty and grace of its flight attendants, and WestJet staffers are known for their sense of humour. People differentiation requires that a company select its customer-contact people carefully and train them well.

Even when competing offers look the same, buyers may perceive a difference based on company or brand *image differentiation*. A company or brand image should convey a product's distinctive benefits and positioning. Developing a strong and distinctive image calls for creativity and hard work. A company cannot develop an image in the public's mind overnight by using only a few ads. If Ritz-Carlton means quality, this image must

Competitive advantage
An advantage over competitors gained by offering greater customer value, either through lower prices or by providing more benefits that justify higher prices.

be supported by everything the company says and does. We will look more closely at developing and managing a brand image in Chapter 9.

Choosing the Right Competitive Advantages Suppose a company is fortunate enough to discover several potential differentiations that provide competitive advantages. It must now choose the ones on which it will build its positioning strategy. It must decide *how many* differences to promote and *which ones*.

HOW MANY DIFFERENCES TO PROMOTE Some marketers believe that the best approach is to aggressively promote only one benefit to the target market; in other words, to focus on the product or brand's *unique selling proposition (USP)*. If a product has a clear USP, all marketing communications in support of it then focus on saying, "Buy this product, and you will receive this benefit." For example, Head & Shoulders shampoo's USP is that it gets rid of dandruff, and FedEx's USP is overnight delivery.

Other marketers choose to position their brands on more than one differentiator. This may be necessary if two or more companies or products are claiming to be best on the same attribute, especially today, when what was once a mass market is fragmenting into many small market segments.

For example, SC Johnson introduced Pledge multi-surface cleaner, an extension of its well-known furniture polish brand. The new Pledge product was positioned as a cleaner that works on wood, electronics, glass, marble, stainless steel, and other surfaces. The benefit it provides is the ability to use only one product to clean everything in a room. Consumers almost certainly want these multiple benefits; however, it can be a challenge to convince them that one product can do it all. As companies increase the number of claims for their brands, they risk disbelief and a loss of clear positioning.

WHICH DIFFERENCES TO PROMOTE Not all brand differences are meaningful or worthwhile; not every difference makes a good differentiator. Each difference has the potential to create company costs as well as customer benefits. A difference is worth establishing to the extent that it satisfies the following criteria:

- *Important:* The difference delivers a highly valued benefit to target buyers.
- *Distinctive:* Competitors do not offer the difference, or the company can offer it in a more distinctive way.
- *Superior:* The difference is superior to other ways customers might obtain the same benefit.
- *Communicable:* The difference is communicable and visible to buyers.
- *Pre-emptive:* Competitors cannot easily copy the difference.
- *Affordable:* Buyers can afford to pay for the difference.
- *Profitable:* The company can introduce the difference profitably.

Many companies have introduced differentiations that failed one or more of these tests. When the Westin Stamford Hotel in Singapore once advertised itself as the world's tallest hotel, it was a distinction that wasn't important to most tourists—in fact, it turned many off. Polaroid's Polarvision, a unique product (for its time) that produced instantly developed home movies, turned out to offer a benefit no one wanted.

Choosing competitive advantages upon which to position a product or service can be difficult, yet such choices may be crucial to success. Choosing the right differentiators can help a brand stand out from the pack of competitors.

Selecting an Overall Positioning Strategy The full positioning of a brand is called the brand's **value proposition**—the full mix of benefits upon which the brand is

Value proposition
The full positioning of a brand—the full mix of benefits upon which it is positioned.

FIGURE 7.4 Possible Value Propositions

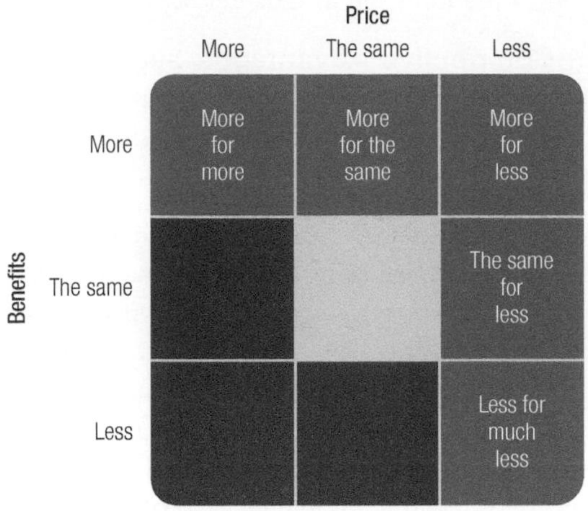

differentiated and positioned. It is the answer to the customer's question "Why should I buy your brand?" Volvo's value proposition hinges on safety but also includes reliability, roominess, and styling, all for a price that is higher than average but seems fair for this mix of benefits.

Figure 7.4 shows possible value propositions upon which a company might position its products. In the figure, the five green cells represent winning value propositions—differentiation and positioning that give the company competitive advantage. The red cells, however, represent losing value propositions. The centre cell represents at best a marginal proposition. In the following sections, we discuss the five winning value propositions upon which companies can position their products: more for more, more for the same, the same for less, less for much less, and more for less.

MORE FOR MORE "More-for-more" positioning involves providing the most upscale product or service and charging a higher price to cover the higher costs. Four Seasons hotels, Montblanc writing instruments, Mercedes automobiles, LG electronics and appliances—each claims superior quality, craftsmanship, durability, performance, or style and charges a price to match. Not only is the market offering high in quality, it also gives prestige to the buyer. It symbolizes status and a loftier lifestyle. Often, the price difference exceeds the actual increment in quality.

MORE FOR THE SAME Companies can attack a competitor's more-for-more positioning by introducing a brand offering comparable quality but at a lower price. For example, Toyota introduced its Lexus line with a "more-for-the-same" value proposition versus Mercedes and BMW. Its first advertisements read "Perhaps the first time in history that trading a $72,000 car for a $36,000 car could be considered trading up."

THE SAME FOR LESS Offering "the same for less" can be a powerful value proposition—everyone likes a good deal. Discount stores such as Walmart and "category killers" such as Best Buy, PetSmart, and Payless Shoes use this positioning. They don't claim to offer different or better products. Instead, they offer many of the same brands as department stores and specialty stores but at deep discounts based on superior purchasing power and lower-cost operations.

LESS FOR MUCH LESS A market almost always exists for products that offer less and therefore cost less. Few people need, want, or can afford "the very best" in everything they buy. In many cases, consumers will gladly settle for less than optimal performance or give up some of the bells and whistles in exchange for a lower price. For example, many travellers seeking lodgings prefer not to pay for what they consider unnecessary extras, such as a pool, attached restaurant, or mints on the pillow. Hotel chains such as Ramada Limited suspend some of these amenities and charge less accordingly.

MORE FOR LESS Of course, the winning value proposition would be to offer "more for less." Many companies claim to do this. And, in the short run, some companies can actually achieve such lofty positions. For example, when it first opened for business, Home Depot had arguably the best product selection, the best service, *and* the lowest prices compared with local hardware stores and other home improvement chains, but today Home Depot is positioned more on selection than on price.

All said, each brand must adopt a positioning strategy designed to serve the needs and wants of its target markets. "More for more" will draw one target market, "less for much less" will draw another, and so on. Thus, in any market, there is usually room for many different companies, each successfully occupying different positions. The important thing is that each company must develop its own winning positioning strategy, one that makes it special to its target market.

Developing a Positioning Statement Company and brand positioning should be summed up in a **positioning statement**. The statement should follow the form: To (target segment and need) our (brand) is (concept) that (point of difference).[21] For example, "To always online, socially connected Millennials, the Apple iWatch is a whole new kind of conversation that not only helps you send and receive messages, but lets you express yourself in new, fun, and more personal ways."

Positioning statement
A statement that summarizes company or brand positioning—it takes this form: To (target segment and need) our (brand) is (concept) that (point of difference).

Note that the positioning first states the product's membership in a category (wireless connectivity solution) and then shows its point of difference from other members of the category (easier, more reliable connections to data, people, and resources). Placing a brand in a specific category suggests similarities that it might share with other products in the category. But the case for the brand's superiority is made on its points of difference.

Sometimes marketers put a brand in a surprisingly different category before indicating the points of difference. For example, Delissio frozen pizza is positioned in the delivered pizza category. Advertising for Delissio features the tagline "It's not delivery. It's Delissio!" and television commercials feature characters trying to trick each other into believing that they ordered takeout pizza when they really made Delissio at home.

Communicating and Delivering the Chosen Position

Once it has chosen a position, the company must take strong steps to deliver and communicate the desired position to target consumers. All the company's marketing-mix efforts must support the positioning strategy.

Pizza this delicious definitely calls for a replay.

It's not delivery. It's Delissio.

Courtesy of Nestle

Exhibit 7.15 Positioning by points of difference: Delissio positions its frozen pizza brand by suggesting that it belongs in a different category altogether—home-delivered pizza.

As we noted earlier, positioning the company calls for concrete action, not just talk. Designing the marketing mix—product, price, place, and promotion—involves working out the tactical details of the positioning strategy. Thus, a firm that seizes on a more-for-more position knows that it must produce high-quality products, charge a high price, distribute through high-quality dealers, and advertise in high-quality media. It must hire and train more service people, find retailers who have a good reputation for service, and develop sales and advertising messages that broadcast its superior service. This is the only way to build a consistent and believable more-for-more position.

Companies often find it easier to come up with a good positioning strategy than to implement it. Establishing a position or changing one usually takes a long time. In contrast, positions that have taken years to build can quickly be lost. Once a company has built the desired position, it must take care to maintain the position through consistent performance and communication. It must closely monitor and adapt the position over time to match changes in consumer needs and competitors' strategies. However, the company should avoid abrupt changes that might confuse consumers. Instead, a product's position should evolve gradually as it adapts to the ever-changing marketing environment.

Two Markets Under One Roof

Depending on the time of year (and whether the home team is playing on television), the emotional outcry from embattled fans on the "sports bar" side of a Boston Pizza restaurant can sometimes be heard penetrating the walls into the "family dining" side. Such is the harmonious conjoining of two distinctly different target markets under the familiar Boston Pizza roof.

It may have been an unheard of concept when Boston Pizza founder Gus Agioritis opened the first BP restaurant in Edmonton in 1964, but today the dual restaurant–sports bar product is as much a part of BP's brand as its signature gourmet pizza. Even outsiders agree that it's a match made in heaven. "Boston Pizza seems to have a formula that works extremely well," said Leslie Lundquist, a portfolio analyst speaking to investors. "It appeals to two separate demographics, and they know how to open new markets profitably." What's more, the voracious sports fan and the hungry family together shore up three distinct and profitable "dayparts" in a restaurant's business day: lunch, dinner, and late night.

However, recent research conducted by BP and its media agency would suggest a significant overlap between the sporties and the foodie families. It turns out that 85 percent of Canadians watch sports, while 71 percent of Canadian children play sports. So while much of BP's marketing efforts have been aimed at solidifying its position as the leader in Canadian family dining, the 2015 campaign, "We'll Make You a Fan," was about connecting all Canadians with a passion for sports—whether it's pro sports, recreational sports, watching sports, or participating as a coach.

"Sports goes right back to 50 years ago, when the brand was founded," said Steve Silverstone, executive vice-president of marketing. "We've had a deep connection to sports and to community throughout our history. [The campaign] leverages what we think is core to our DNA and something that no other brand in our space in Canada can stand for."

QUESTIONS

1. Use the bases of segmentation to describe Boston Pizza's sports bar target market.
2. Use the bases of segmentation to describe Boston Pizza's family dining target market.
3. Why has Boston Pizza shifted emphasis toward the sports bar segment?

REVIEWING THE CONCEPTS

 Define the major steps in designing a customer-driven marketing strategy: market segmentation, targeting, differentiation, and positioning.

Customer-driven marketing strategy begins with selecting which customers to serve and deciding on a value proposition that best serves the targeted customers. It consists of four steps. *Market segmentation* is the act of dividing a market into distinct segments of buyers with different needs, characteristics, or behaviours who might require separate products or marketing mixes. Once the groups have been identified, *market targeting* evaluates each market segment's attractiveness and selects one or more segments to serve. Market targeting consists of designing strategies to build the *right relationships* with the *right customers*. *Differentiation* involves actually differentiating the market offering to create superior customer value. *Positioning* consists of positioning the market offering in the minds of target customers.

 List and discuss the major bases for segmenting consumer and business markets.

There is no single way to segment a market. Therefore, the marketer tries different variables to see which give the best segmentation opportunities. For consumer marketing, the major segmentation variables are geographic, demographic, psychographic, and behavioural. In *geographic segmentation*, the market is divided into different geographical units, such as nations, regions, provinces, municipalities, cities, or neighbourhoods. In *demographic segmentation*, the market is divided into groups based on demographic variables, including age, gender, family size, family life cycle, income, occupation, education, religion, race, generation, and nationality. In *psychographic segmentation*, the market is divided into different groups based on social class, lifestyle, or personality characteristics. In *behavioural segmentation*, the market is divided into groups based on consumers' knowledge, attitudes, uses, or responses to a product. Business marketers use many of the same variables to segment their markets. But business markets can also be segmented by business consumer *demographics* (industry, company size), *operating characteristics*, *purchasing approaches*, *situational factors*, and *personal characteristics*. The effectiveness of segmentation analysis depends on finding segments that are *measurable*, *accessible*, *substantial*, *differentiable*, and *actionable*.

 Explain how companies identify attractive market segments and choose a market-targeting strategy.

To target the best market segments, the company first evaluates each segment's size and growth characteristics, structural attractiveness, and compatibility with company objectives and resources. It then chooses one of four market-targeting strategies—ranging from very broad to very narrow targeting. The seller can ignore segment differences and target broadly by using *undifferentiated (or mass) marketing*. This method involves mass producing, mass distributing, and mass promoting the same product in about the same way to all consumers. Or the seller can adopt *differentiated marketing*—developing different market offers for several segments. *Concentrated marketing (or niche marketing)* involves focusing on only one or a few market segments. Finally, *micromarketing* is the practice of tailoring products and marketing programs to suit the tastes of specific individuals and locations. *Local marketing* refers to customizing marketing offers to a small group of people living in the same city or neighbourhood or shopping at the same store, and *individual marketing*, better known as *mass customization*, is the practice of customizing a marketing offer to an individual.

 Discuss how companies differentiate and position their products for maximum competitive advantage.

Once a company has decided which segments to enter, it must decide on its *differentiation and positioning strategy*. The differentiation and positioning task consists of three steps: identifying a set of possible differentiations that create competitive advantage, choosing advantages upon which to build a position, and selecting an overall positioning strategy. The brand's full positioning is called its *value proposition*—the full mix of benefits upon which the brand is positioned. In general, companies can choose from one of five winning value propositions upon which to position their products: more for more, more for the same, the same for less, less for much less, or more for less. Company and brand positioning are summarized in positioning statements that state the target segment and need, positioning concept, and specific points of difference. The company must then effectively communicate and deliver the chosen position to the market.

MyMarketingLab

Study, practise, and explore real marketing situations with these helpful resources:

- **Interactive Lesson Presentations:** Work through interactive presentations and assessments to test your knowledge of marketing concepts.
- **Study Plan:** Check your understanding of chapter concepts with self-study quizzes.
- **Dynamic Study Modules:** Work through adaptive study modules on your computer, tablet, or mobile device.
- **Simulations:** Practise decision-making in simulated marketing environments.

DISCUSSION QUESTIONS

1. Think of a product or a brand you're familiar with that caters to a niche market. Describe the shared characteristics of consumers in that market in terms of the four main bases of segmentation: geography, demographics, psychographics, and behaviour.

2. As a basis of market segmentation, *geography* can refer to a country, region of a country, or region that is defined by its climate or its terrain, such as coastal areas, the far north, the prairies, or the Rockies. Describe three distinct geographic market segments in Canada. Then think of a product that could be successfully marketed to each of those segments but might not be as successful in another geographic market segment.

3. The George Foreman Grill is a compact cooking appliance with a double-sided cooking surface that is angled to allow fat to drip off the food and out of the grill. Describe a likely target market for this product in terms of

its geographic, demographic, psychographic, and behavioural characteristics. How does this target market rate with respect to size, growth, and structural attractiveness?

4. Find out what is the bestselling beer in Quebec and one other province. Describe each province as a market segment. Why do you think those particular beers have the most appeal in those provinces?

5. Think of an example of a hotel chain that falls into each of the five general value propositions. What does each hotel you selected do on the benefits dimension to offer more, the same, or less than competitors?

6. When A&W celebrated its fiftieth anniversary, it invited customers to write in about their favourite memories. Many customers, most of them baby boomers, reminisced about carhop service. Do you think A&W should target baby boomers by reinstating carhops?

CRITICAL THINKING EXERCISES

1. Advertisers use market segmentation when promoting products to consumers. For each major consumer segmentation variable, find an example of a print ad that appears to be based on that variable. For each ad, identify the target market and explain why you think the advertiser is using the segmentation variable you identified for that ad.

2. Perceptual positioning maps are useful for showing consumer perceptions of brands in a product category.

Search the Internet for guides on creating perceptual maps and create a map of your perceptions of brands in a product category of your choice. How can the brand you perceived least favourably improve?

3. In a small group, create an idea for a new product or service. Describe your business strategy (i.e., how you'll make money), and write a one-paragraph positioning statement for your product or service.

ONLINE, MOBILE, AND SOCIAL MEDIA

Consumers enjoy having Google's search power at their fingertips, but if things go as planned, they'll have that Google power right before their very eyes, no fingers necessary. Augmented reality—the ability to project information in front of our eyes—is now being used in commercial and military operations. For example, the U.S. Air Force

uses it to display weapons information in fighter pilot helmets. However, the technology has yet to take off in the consumer market. That's because the required headgear has been uncomfortable, unattractive, and expensive. But Google is peering into the future and has tentative plans to sell its Google Glass device to consumers soon. The sleek wraparound glasses place a single lens above a person's right eye that displays digital information that can be voice and gesture controlled. Connecting the device to a smartphone opens up a world of possibilities. The only product close to Google Glass currently on the consumer market is a GPS device that skiers and snowboarders insert into goggles and that displays speed information.

QUESTIONS

1. Research the definition of augmented reality, and find examples of other companies that are developing augmented-reality products. Are any competitors developing something similar to Google Glass?

2. Discuss the most appropriate variables for segmenting the consumer market for products like Google Glass.

THINK LIKE A MARKETING MANAGER

A trend that has been growing in recent years is small groups of same-sex friends going on vacation together. Some call these "mancations," when that group of friends is male. This is an example of creating a new market segment by virtue of behaviour, something marketers refer to as behavioural segmentation. The size of this market indicates that it's a worthwhile one for marketers to target: According to one online survey, 34 percent of American male respondents said they had taken at least one trip with guy friends in the past year.

QUESTIONS

1. Imagine you are the marketing director at a hotel in Banff. What services could you offer that would appeal to this market segment? What forms of marketing communications would you use to reach this target market?

2. What tourist destinations in Canada, specifically, would appeal to this market? (For example, could Canada's Wonderland appeal to this group effectively?)

3. There are cruises that cater to families, cruises that cater to singles, and cruises that cater to gays and lesbians. Do you think it would be worthwhile for a cruise line to create a special cruise to cater to the mancationer market segment? How would you go about evaluating the potential value? Do you consider this a niche market? What ports of call would such a cruise visit, and what sorts of activities could the cruise company offer?

4. What's the female equivalent of mancations? What local marketing could be done to attract groups of female friends who want to travel together?

MARKETING ETHICS

K.G.O.Y. stands for "kids getting older younger," and marketers are getting much of the blame. Kids today see all types of messages, especially on the Internet, that they would never have seen in the past. Whereas boys may give up their G.I. Joe's at an earlier age to play war games on their Xbox 360s, the greater controversy seems to surround claims of how girls have changed, or rather, how marketers have changed girls. Critics describe clothing designed for young girls aged 8 to 11 as "floozy" and sexual, with department stores selling youngsters thongs and T-shirts that say "Naughty Girl!" Although Barbie's sexuality has never been subtle, she was originally targeted to girls 9 to 12 years old. Now, Barbie dolls target primarily 3- to 7-year-old girls! And Barbie's competitor, Bratz dolls, has an "in-your-face" attitude that has some parents complaining that they are too sexual.

QUESTIONS

1. Do you think marketers are to blame for kids getting older younger? Give some other examples that could support marketing's responsibility in K.G.O.Y.

2. Give an example of a company that is countering this trend by offering age-appropriate products for children.

MARKETING BY THE NUMBERS

Tesla Motors is a publicly traded company based in California that produces fully electric sports cars. To date, Tesla has delivered more than 10 000 electric vehicles to customers in 31 countries. Tesla has confirmed that its all-electric Model 3, which is expected to have a 200-mile range between charges, will begin production in 2017. The company needs to estimate the market potential for the Tesla Model 3 before doing a full scale market launch in Canada.

QUESTIONS

1. Discuss variables Tesla should consider when estimating the potential number of buyers for the Tesla 3.

2. Using the chain ratio method described in Appendix 3, Marketing by the Numbers, estimate the market potential for the Tesla 3. Search the Internet for reasonable numbers to represent the factors you identified in the previous question. Assume that each buyer will purchase only one automobile and that the average purchase price is $40 000.

ZIPCAR: IT'S NOT ABOUT CARS—IT'S ABOUT URBAN LIFE

Imagine a world in which no one owns a car. Cars would still exist, but rather than owning cars, people would just share them. Sounds crazy, right? But Scott Griffith, CEO of Zipcar, the world's largest car-share company, paints a picture of just such an imaginary world. And he has nearly 800 000 passionate customers—or Zipsters, as they're called—who will back him up.

Zipcar specializes in renting out cars by the hour or day. Although this may sound like a minor variation on the established rental car agency business, it's actually an entirely different concept.

A CAR RENTAL COMPANY THAT ISN'T ABOUT CARS

As Griffith considered what Zipcar had to offer, it was apparent that it couldn't be all things to all people. The market for car rentals would have to be carefully segmented, and Zipcar would have to choose just the right segment to target. Griffith identified a segment of the market that was not being served by traditional car rental companies: Not travellers visiting another city, but people who sometimes need a car for a few hours, or a day, in the city they live in. People who live in big cities like New York, Boston, and San Francisco, who don't own a car of their own. And students who don't have cars, and occasionally need one.

In Canada, Zipcar has locations in Kitchener-Waterloo, London, Ottawa, Toronto, Vancouver, and Victoria—all of which are university towns. The Zipcar concept is also particularly well suited to people who live or work in densely populated neighbourhoods in cities, where owning a car is difficult, costly, and environmentally irresponsible. Interestingly, Zipcar doesn't see itself as a car-rental company. Instead, it's selling a lifestyle. "It's not about cars," says CEO Griffith, "it's about urban life. We're creating a lifestyle brand that happens to have a lot of cars."

So Griffith segmented the market, identified a market that was underserved, and decided to target it. The next step was to position Zipcar in the minds and hearts of consumers.

Initially, the Zipcar brand was positioned exclusively round a value system. As an urban lifestyle brand, Zipcar focused on traits that city dwellers have in common. For starters, the lifestyle is rooted in environmental consciousness. At first, Zipcar focused on green-minded customers with promotional pitches such as "We ♥ Earth" and "Imagine a world with a million fewer cars on the road." Zipcar's vibrant green logo reflects this save-the-Earth philosophy. And Zipcar really does deliver on its environmental promises. Studies show that every shared Zipcar takes up to 20 cars off the road and cuts carbon emissions by up to 50 percent per user. On average, Zipsters travel 44 percent fewer miles than when they owned a car, leaving an average of 219 gallons of crude oil in the ground. Multiply all this out by 11 000 cars in Zipcar's fleet, and that's a pretty substantial impact on the environment.

But it wasn't long before Griffith realized that if Zipcar was going to grow, it needed to move beyond just being green. So the brand has broadened its positioning to include other urban lifestyle benefits, based on the most common needs consumers have: I don't want the hassle of owning a car; I want to save money; I take public transit, but need a car sometimes; Once in a while I need a second car; I need a big car for a big job; and I want to impress my boss.

Another important benefit Zipcar offers its target market is convenience. Owning a car in a densely populated urban area can be a real hassle. Zipcar lets customers focus on driving, not on the complexities of car ownership.

FULFILLING CONSUMER NEEDS

Zipcar operates on a membership plan. To join, you pay around $60 for an annual membership and receive your personal Zipcard, which unlocks any Zipcar vehicle located in urban areas around the world. Then, when you need a car, reserve one—minutes or months in advance—online, by phone, or using a smartphone app. You can choose the car you want, when and where you want it, and drive it for as little as $7.50 an hour, including gas, insurance, and free miles. When you're ready, walk to the car, hold your Zipcard to the windshield to unlock the doors, and you're good to go. When you're done, you drop the car off at the same parking spot—Zipcar worries about the maintenance and cleaning.

Zipcar not only eliminates the hassle of urban car ownership, it also saves money. By living with less, the average Zipster saves $600 a month on car payments, insurance, gas, maintenance, and other car ownership expenses. That's like getting a $10 000 a year raise after taxes. In an era when consumers have become more frugal, this is a big plus, especially for those looking to live more minimally.

Zipcar isn't for everyone—it doesn't try to be. Instead, it zeros in on a narrowly defined urban lifestyle positioning. For starters, Zipcar "pods" (a dozen or so vehicles located in a given neighbourhood) are stocked from a portfolio of over 50 different models that trendy urbanites love. The vehicles are both hip and fuel efficient: Toyota Priuses, Honda CRVs, MINIs, Volvo S60s, BMW 328s, Toyota Tacomas, Toyota Siennas, Subaru Outbacks, and others. And Zipcar now has plug-in hybrids, fully electric vehicles, and full-size vans for big jobs. Each car has its own personality—a name and profile created by a Zipster. For example, Prius Ping "jogs in the morning; doesn't say much," whereas Civic Carlos "teaches yoga; loves to kayak." Such personal touches make it feel as if you're borrowing the car from a friend rather than being assigned whatever piece of metal happens to be available.

To further eliminate hassles and make Zipcar as convenient as possible, company promotional tactics are designed to appeal to city dwellers. The company's goal is for Zipsters to not have to walk more than seven minutes to get to one of its car pods—no easy task. "Even with today's highly targeted Web and mobile technologies, it's hard to target at that hyper-local level," says Griffith. "So our street teams do it block by block, zip code by zip code." Thus, in addition to local ads and transit advertising, Zipcar reps are beating the streets in true guerilla fashion.

With its eye sharply focused on maintaining the Zipcar image, the company is consistently developing new features that appeal to tech-savvy urbanites. Recently, the company has shifted its focus a bit from being a Web-based business to being an overwhelmingly mobile concern. Soon, Zipcars will have in-car device holders for smartphones that will allow for easy plug-in and hands-free navigation. The interface between the cars and the users will allow playlists stored on the phone to be played through the car's audio system. Users will be provided with information specific to the vehicle they are in, a personalized deal recommendation service, and a real-time feedback loop where users can report on vehicle cleanliness, damage, and fuel levels.

FOSTERING BRAND COMMUNITY

Zipcar's orientation around the urban, environmentally conscious lifestyle fosters a tight-knit sense of customer community. Zipsters are as fanatically loyal as the hardcore fans of Harley-Davidson or Apple, brands that have been nurturing customer relationships for decades. Loyal Zipsters serve as neighbourhood brand ambassadors; 30 percent of new members join up at the recommendation of existing customers. "When I meet another Zipcar member at a party or something, I feel like we have something in common," says one Brooklyn Zipster. "It's like we're both making intelligent choices about our lives." And just as Harley owners get together on weekends to ride, the Internet is littered with announcements for Zipster parties at bars, restaurants, and comedy clubs, among other places.

As Zipcar has taken off, it has broadened the appeal of its brand to include a different type of urban dweller—businesses and other organizations. Companies such as Google now encourage employees to be environmentally conscious by commuting via a company shuttle and then using Zipcars for both business and personal use during the day. Other companies are using Zipcar as an alternative to black sedans, long taxi rides, and congested parking lots. Government agencies are getting into the game as well. The city of Chicago recently partnered with Zipcar to provide a more efficient and sustainable transportation alternative for city agencies. And Washington, D.C., now saves more than $1 million a year using Zipcar. Fleet manager Ralph Burns says that he has departments lining up. "Agencies putting their budgets together for next year are calling me up and saying, 'Ralph, I've got 25 cars I want to get rid of!'"

How is Zipcar's strategy of positioning itself as an urban lifestyle brand working? By all accounts, the young car-sharing nicher has the pedal to the metal and its tires are smoking. In just the past five years, Zipcar's annual revenues have rocketed nearly five-fold, to more than $270 million. Zipcar has also reached the milestone of being profitable. And with 10 million people now within walking distance of a Zipcar, there's plenty of room to grow. As more cars are added, Zipcar's reach will only increase.

Zipcar's rapid growth has sounded alarms at the traditional car-rental giants. Enterprise, Hertz, Thrifty, and even U-Haul now have their own car-sharing operations. Avis also had one, but decided to shut down its own service and buy Zipcar for nearly $500 million. The Zipcar brand will now benefit from cost savings that the large-scale rental service enjoys.

As for the others, Zipcar has a big head start in terms of size and experience, cozy relationships in targeted neighbourhoods, and an urban hipster cred that corporate giants like Hertz will have trouble matching. To Zipsters, Hertz rents cars, but Zipcar is a part of their hectic urban lives.

Sources: Based on information from Mark Clothier, "Zipcar Soars After Profit Topped Analysts' Estimates," Bloomberg.com, November 9, 2012; Darrell Etherington, "Zipcar CEO Details In-Car Assistant, Personalized Deals and Member Onboarding for Mobile

App," *Techcrunch*, October 9, 2012; Jerry Hirsch, "Zipcar CEO Talks About Car Sharing as Lifestyle Choice," *Seattle Times*, May 13, 2012; Paul Keegan, "Zipcar: The Best New Idea in Business," *Fortune*, August 27, 2009; and Stephanie Clifford, "How Fast Can This Thing Go, Anyway?" *Inc.*, March 1, 2008; and Zipcar.ca.

QUESTIONS FOR DISCUSSION

1. Briefly describe the process of segmentation, targeting, and positioning that the marketers at Zipcar followed.

2. Describe typical (target) Zipcar customers in terms of their demographic, psychographic, geographic, and behavioural characteristics.

3. Which of the four value propositions for positioning is Zipcar following? Explain your answer.

4. Zipcar was acquired by Avis in 2013, and since then several other traditional car rental companies have tried to replicate Zipcar's short-term rental programs. Research the top five car rental companies, and find out what they are doing to compete in this market segment. If you were on the marketing team at Zipcar, how would you defend against this new competition?

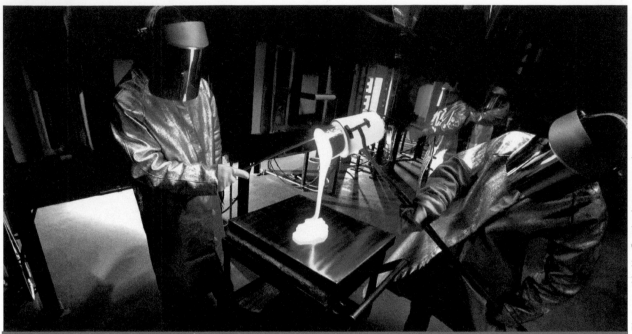

Photo provided by Corning Incorporated

AFTER STUDYING THIS CHAPTER, YOU SHOULD BE ABLE TO

1 define *product* and describe and classify different types of product offerings

2 list and define the steps in the new-product development process and the major considerations in managing this process, and explain why new products fail

3 describe the stages of the product life cycle and how marketing strategies change during the product's life cycle

4 describe the decisions companies make regarding their individual products and services, product lines, and product mixes

5 identify the four characteristics that affect the marketing of services and the additional marketing considerations that services require

Developing and Managing Products and Services

PREVIEWING THE CONCEPTS

Now that you've had a good look at customer-driven marketing strategy, we'll take a deeper look at the marketing mix—the tactical tools that marketers use to implement their strategies and deliver superior customer value. In this chapter, we'll study how a product is defined, how companies develop new products, and how marketers manage products over time. You'll see that every product passes through several life-cycle stages and that each stage poses new challenges requiring different marketing strategies and tactics. We'll also consider the special challenges of marketing services—which are actually a type of product. But first, let's look at the story of how a company you probably thought only made dishes is actually an innovated, highly technical R&D firm that's been collaborating with customers to solve technology challenges with products that have transformed people's lives.

CORNING: NEW PRODUCT INNOVATION FOR MORE THAN 160 YEARS

Sometime around 1960, scientists at Corning made a significant advance while experimenting with ways to strengthen glass. Using a recently developed method that involved dipping glass in a hot potassium salt bath, they discovered that adding aluminum oxide to the glass before dipping produced a product with never-before-seen strength and durability. The scientists hurtled everything they could think of at this new super glass, including frozen chickens at high speeds, and even dropped it from the top of their nine-storey building. They found that the new glass could withstand 100 000 pounds of pressure per square inch (normal glass can only handle about 7000).

This super glass, Corning assumed, would surely be embraced by manufacturers of products ranging from eyeglasses to phone booths, prison windows, and automobile windshields. Corning named the glass Chemcor and put it on the market. But most potential customer companies did not deem the strength benefits of Chemcor worth the premium price mandated by its high cost of production. Making matters worse, when it did break, Chemcor had the potential to explode, leading the few companies that had placed orders to recall their products. When it realized that it had created an expensive upgrade nobody wanted, Corning shelved Chemcor in 1971.

When Amory Houghton, Sr., founded Corning in 1851, not even he could have foreseen the vast array of products his company would develop—products that would revolutionize the

Practice on MyMarketingLab

Using Conjoint Experiments to Tailor New Product Offerings

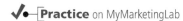
Practice on MyMarketingLab

Assessing the New Product Development Process of Strategic Business Units

Practice on MyMarketingLab

Assessing Market share after the Entrant of a New Product

twenty-first century. Most people in the 1850s thought of glass as, well, just glass. But Corning thought differently. It went on to develop innovative products that would change the way people live, including light bulbs, television tubes, cookware, ceramic substrates, optical fibre, active-liquid crystal displays, and even missile nose cones. Corning achieved these feats because Houghton established research and development as the company's foundation.

From its origins, Corning has relied upon sound relationships with suppliers and customers to keep the innovation machine churning. On the supply side, producing the quantities of glass that pour off the Corning production lines requires massive amounts of sand (silicon dioxide). But because sand has such a high melting point, other chemicals—such as sodium oxide—are used to lower the melting point, making glass easier and cheaper to produce. Corning also relies on many elements and chemicals to give different types of glass their useful qualities. For example, Chemcor contains not only silicon dioxide, but also aluminum, magnesium, and sodium.

To keep the right kinds of chemicals and other raw materials flowing, price and quality are only baseline criteria at Corning. To maximize long-term success for itself and for its suppliers, Corning has also established a Supplier Code of Conduct. The Code ensures that all supplier operations are conducted within the laws, customs, and cultural norms of the regions where Corning does business. It also ensures that they comply with the company's own corporate values. Corning invests considerable energy in selecting suppliers. The Code of Conduct includes specific criteria regarding ethics, labour, health and safety, and environmental concerns. On the surface, such criteria seem to have little to do with making glass. But Corning knows that such factors can ultimately affect the quality, price, and availability of the raw materials the company needs for making its products.

Some of Corning's products are consumer products. For example, take CorningWare. Corning scientist Don Stookey found that product by accident when a faulty temperature controller allowed a sample of photosensitive glass to reach 1600 degrees Fahrenheit rather than the intended 1100 degrees. He thought the result would be a blob of melted glass and a ruined furnace. On closer inspection, however, Stookey discovered that he had a milky white plate that was lighter than aluminum, harder than high-carbon steel, and far stronger than regular soda-lime glass. When he dropped it on the floor, instead of shattering, it bounced. When CorningWare hit the market in 1959, it was a space-age wonder.

But most of Corning's products are supplied to manufacturers as components or raw materials in other products such as televisions and automobiles. That's where successful outcomes depend most on good supplier relationships. In this case, however, Corning is the supplier. Always on the lookout for ways to forge new relationships with manufacturing customers, Corning came up with an idea in 2005 when Motorola released the Razr V3, a mobile flip phone that featured a glass screen instead of the usual high-impact plastic. Maybe Chemcor—the super strong glass that Corning had shelved in 1971—would make a good glass for mobile phones. The company quickly formed a team to explore the possibilities and code-named the project Gorilla Glass. Its team's main goal was to reduce the thickness of the glass from its current 4 millimetres to something that could be used in a phone.

Within a few years, as the team was making progress on the thickness issue, Corning CEO Wendell Weeks received a phone call that would give Gorilla Glass its big chance. The call came from late Apple founder Steve Jobs. Jobs and Weeks had collaborated previously; in fact, Weeks had pitched to Jobs the idea of using laser-based microprojection technologies—something Corning scientists were toying with—to provide larger screens for increasingly smaller phones. Jobs said the idea was dumb and that he was working on something better—a device whose entire surface was a display. The world would soon know that product as the iPhone.

Jobs was relentless in getting the iPhone's design just right. So he put in the call to Wendell Weeks and explained what he needed: smooth, clear glass that would resist scratches and breaking and act as a conductor for touchscreen technology. And it had to be 1.3 millimetres thick. Jobs gave Weeks a seemingly impossible mandate—make millions of square feet of Gorilla Glass, make it ultra-thin, and have it ready in six months, because the iPhone would be on store shelves in seven months.

The mandate posed many unknowns for Gorilla Glass. The product had never been mass produced, and it was unclear whether a process could be developed to produce the quantity of glass that Apple needed. Weeks was also uncertain whether Gorilla Glass could be made so thin and still retain its strength. And even if these issues could be ironed out, how long would it take? So in responding to Jobs, Weeks did what any risk-taking CEO would do. He said yes. Then he formed a team to make it happen.

With such a tight deadline, Corning had no time to develop a new manufacturing process. Instead, the team adapted a process the company was already using—called fusion draw. To maintain the desired toughness characteristics, the team tweaked the existing Gorilla Glass recipe, changing the levels of several of the glass's seven individual components and adding one new secret ingredient. But there was still one hitch: Corning had only one factory—in Harrodsburg, Kentucky—capable of producing glass by means of fusion draw, and that plant's seven production lines were already going full blast to meet demand for sold-out LCD glass for TV panels. However, the factory was somehow able to squeeze Apple's initial Gorilla Glass order into one of its production lines. Incredibly, and ahead of schedule, Corning produced enough 1.3-millimetre Gorilla Glass to cover seven football fields.

The rest, as they say, is history. Every iPhone and iPad that Apple has ever sold features Gorilla Glass. Today, Corning has more than 40 customers for Gorilla Glass, the newest of which is Meizu Technology of China. These manufacturers build more than 1400 different products such as smartphones, tablets, notebooks, and TVs. Globally, more than 3 billion products feature Gorilla Glass.

How has Corning been able to continually invent and reinvent new products? The product marketers at the company believe that "there are no accidents." Instead, Corning believes in "patient capital," the idea of investing in unproven technologies even if there's no quick profit. The firm is rife with stories of inventions that sat on the shelves for decades until the right opportunity came along. The weather-resistant borosilicate glass designed for railroad signal lanterns gave rise to Pyrex cookware. The glass-ceramics technology the company invented, called Pyroceram, was used to make CorningWare casserole dishes and missile nose cones. It's certainly the story of Gorilla Glass, originally intended for car windshields and prison windows.

"We invent all sorts of stuff for weird reasons that then becomes something else," says Adam Ellison, a Corning corporate research fellow and scientist who helped lead the Gorilla Glass project. Corning is all about "unique materials going through a unique process. That's our future. That's how we're going to be around for another 162 years."

Today, Corning's partnerships with customers like Apple and Samsung are more important than ever. For starters, Gorilla Glass isn't entirely unbreakable. Manufacturers round up broken devices that get returned and send them back to Corning, where a team tries to replicate activities that caused the breaks. The research provides vital information for developing new glass. If Corning learns how Gorilla Glass typically breaks, it can try to prevent those breaks in future products by altering the composition of the glass or tweaking the chemicals that strengthen it. Corning relies on help from its customers to develop new versions of Gorilla Glass—making it thinner, stronger, and more scratch resistant.

A culture of innovation, strong partnerships with its customers, and a hard-working team of scientists and engineers are what have kept Corning on the cutting edge for more than 160 years. In only a handful of years, a simple thing like a glass display has gone from a component to an aesthetic. When a user touches the outer layer of Gorilla Glass, the body closes the circuit between an electrode beneath the screen and the glass itself, transforming motion into data. It's a seamless partition that connects people's physical selves with the infinite digital world—so seamless, in fact, that most people have a hard time determining exactly where that partition exists.[1]

AS THE CORNING story suggests, companies that excel at developing and managing new products reap big rewards. Product is the first *P* of marketing, and is usually the first and most basic marketing consideration. It's also the subject of this chapter. We'll start with a seemingly simple question: What is a product? As it turns out, however, the answer is not so simple.

What Is a Product? LO1

Product
Anything that can be offered to a market for attention, acquisition, use, or consumption that might satisfy a want or need.

We define a **product** as anything that can be offered to a market for attention, acquisition, use, or consumption that might satisfy a want or need. Products include more than just tangible objects, such as cars, computers, or cellphones. Broadly defined, "products" also include services, events, persons, places, organizations, ideas, or mixes of these. Throughout this text, we use the term *product* broadly to include any or all of these entities—so an Apple iPad, a Toyota Camry, and a box of Timbits are products, but so are Air Canada flights and BMO investments.

Because of their importance in the world economy, we give special attention to services. **Services** are a form of product that consists of activities, benefits, or satisfactions offered for sale that are essentially intangible and do not result in the ownership of anything; for example, a day at an amusement park or a night in a hotel. We will look at services more closely later in this chapter.

Service
An activity, benefit, or satisfaction offered for sale that is essentially intangible and does not result in the ownership of anything.

Products, Services, and Experiences

Product is a key element in the overall *market offering*. Marketing-mix planning begins with building an offering that brings value to target customers. This offering becomes the basis upon which the company builds profitable customer relationships.

A company's market offering often includes both tangible goods and services. At one extreme, the offer may consist of a *pure tangible good*, such as soap, toothpaste, or salt—no services accompany the product. At the other extreme are *pure services*, for which the offer consists primarily, or solely, of a service; credit cards are one example. Between these two extremes, however, many goods-and-services combinations are possible.

Today, as products and services become more commoditized, many companies are moving to a new level in creating value for their customers. To differentiate their offers, beyond simply making products and delivering services, they are creating and managing customer *experiences* with their brands or their company.

Experiences have always been an important part of marketing for some companies. Disney has long manufactured dreams and memories through its movies and theme parks. Today, however, all kinds of firms are recasting their traditional goods and services to create experiences. You might think of Starbucks as a place to buy coffee, but Starbucks thinks of itself as providing a "third place" for consumers—a place that's neither their home nor their workplace, but is just as familiar and comfortable. The Starbucks experience includes the smells, the sounds of hissing steam, the comfy chairs, and the sense of community.

Organizations, Persons, Places, and Ideas

In addition to tangible products and services, marketers have broadened the concept of a product to include other market offerings—organizations, persons, places, and ideas. Organization marketing consists of activities undertaken to create, maintain, or change the attitudes and behaviour of customers and the general public toward an organization. Both profit and not-for-profit organizations practise organization marketing.

People can also be thought of as products. Person marketing consists of activities undertaken to create, maintain, or change attitudes or behaviour toward particular people. People ranging from politicians, entertainers, and sports figures to professionals such as real estate agents, lawyers, and architects use person marketing to build their reputations.

Place marketing involves activities undertaken to create, maintain, or change attitudes or behaviour toward particular places. Cities and countries compete to attract tourists, new residents, conventions, and company offices and factories. For example, Canada is marketed around the world by the Canadian Tourism Commission (CTC), a federal Crown corporation. And many foreign countries are marketed to Canadians as travel destinations; for example, the government of China operates the China National Tourist Office (CNTO), with 15 overseas offices, including one in Toronto, for the purpose of promoting travel to China, which has been booming since the Beijing Olympics.

Canadian Tourism Commission

Exhibit 8.1 Marketing a place as a product: The Canadian Tourism Commission develops and pays for advertising campaigns in Europe and the United States that promote Canada as a tourism destination.

Ideas can also be marketed. For example, Molson runs ads warning of the dangers of drunk driving, and various Canadian health services promote the idea of getting a flu shot when flu season rolls around. In one sense, all marketing is the marketing of an idea, whether it's the general idea of brushing your teeth or the specific idea that Crest toothpastes create "healthy, beautiful smiles for life." So we see that the line between hard products and pure services is not clear cut, but rather is a continuum—and that today's marketing managers think about products and services in terms of levels.

Levels of Products and Services

Product marketers need to think about the product they manage as consisting of three levels (see Figure 8.1). Each level adds more customer value. The most basic level is the *core customer value*, which addresses the question "What is the buyer really buying?" When designing products, marketers must first define the core problem-solving benefits or services that consumers seek. For example, the core product of all beauty products is the feeling of being beautiful, and the core product of all smartphones is constant connectivity.

At the second level, product marketers must turn the core benefit into an *actual product*—the physical device with all its features and associated brand name and packaging. Finally, marketers must consider the *augmented product*—the additional services and

FIGURE 8.1 Three Levels of Product: Core, Actual, and Augmented

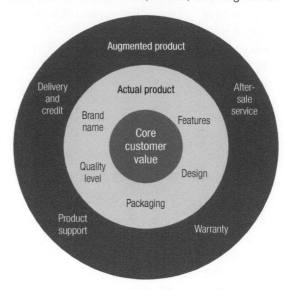

benefits that go with it. So, for example, if the core product of a smartphone is constant connectivity, and the actual product is an iPhone, then the augmented product is the iPhone plus a calling plan and data plan.

Consumers see products as complex bundles of benefits that satisfy their needs. When developing products, marketers first must identify the *core customer value* that consumers seek from the product. They must then design the *actual* product and find ways to *augment* it to create this customer value and the most satisfying customer experience.

Product and Service Classifications

Products and services fall into two broad classes: consumer products and industrial products. **Consumer products** are purchased by consumers for their personal (i.e., nonbusiness) use. Marketers usually classify these products and services further based on how consumers go about buying them. Consumer products include *convenience products*, *shopping products*, *specialty products*, and *unsought products*. These products differ in the ways consumers buy them and, therefore, in how they are marketed (see Table 8.1).

Convenience products are consumer products and services that customers usually buy frequently, immediately, and with a minimum of comparison and buying effort. Convenience products are distributed through drugstores, grocery stores, and, of course, convenience stores, and include such things as laundry detergent, candy, magazines, and fast food. Convenience products are usually low priced, and marketers place them in many locations to make them readily available when customers need them.

Shopping products are less frequently purchased consumer products and services that shoppers compare carefully on suitability, quality, price, and style. When buying shopping products and services, consumers spend much time and effort in gathering information and making comparisons. Examples include furniture, clothing, used cars, major appliances, and hotel and airline services. Shopping-products marketers usually distribute their products through fewer outlets but provide deeper sales support to help customers in their comparison efforts.

Specialty products are consumer products and services with unique characteristics or brand identification for which a significant group of buyers is willing to make a special purchase effort. Examples include specific brands of cars, high-priced photographic

Consumer products
Products purchased by consumers for their personal (i.e., nonbusiness) use.

Convenience product
A consumer product that customers usually buy frequently, immediately, and with a minimum of comparison and buying effort.

Shopping product
Less frequently purchased consumer products and services that shoppers compare carefully on suitability, quality, price, and style.

Specialty product
A consumer product with unique characteristics or brand identification for which a significant group of buyers is willing to make a special purchase effort.

TABLE 8.1	Marketing Considerations for Consumer Products			
	Type of Consumer Product			
Marketing Considerations	**Convenience**	**Shopping**	**Specialty**	**Unsought**
Customer buying behaviour	Frequent purchase, little planning, little comparison or shopping effort, low customer involvement	Less frequent purchase, much planning and shopping effort, comparison of brands on price, quality, style	Strong brand preference and loyalty, special purchase effort, little comparison of brands, low price sensitivity	Little product awareness, knowledge (or, if aware, little or even negative interest)
Price	Low price	Higher price	High price	Varies
Distribution	Widespread distribution, convenient locations	Selective distribution in fewer outlets	Exclusive distribution in only one or a few outlets per market area	Varies
Promotion	Mass promotion by the producer	Advertising and personal selling by both producer and resellers	More carefully targeted promotion by both producer and resellers	Aggressive advertising and personal selling by producer and resellers
Examples	Toothpaste, magazines, laundry detergent	Major appliances, televisions, furniture, clothing	Luxury goods, such as Rolex watches or fine crystal	Life insurance, donations to Canadian Blood Services

equipment, designer clothes, and the services of medical or legal specialists. A Lamborghini automobile, for example, is a specialty product because buyers are usually willing to travel great distances to buy one. Buyers normally do not compare specialty products. They invest only the time needed to reach dealers carrying the wanted products.

Unsought products are consumer products that the consumer either does not know about or knows about but does not normally think of buying. Most major new innovations are unsought until the consumer becomes aware of them through advertising. Classic examples of known but unsought products and services are life insurance, preplanned funeral services, and blood donations. By their very nature, unsought products require a lot of advertising, personal selling, and other marketing efforts.

Marketing unsought products requires a different approach from typical product marketing. For example, consider the challenges of marketing funeral services and cemetery plots. Montreal's Mount Royal Commemorative Services has one of the nicer products to offer in that category: The cemetery is located on the mountain in the middle of the city, and is designated as a national historic site by the federal government. It has a certain celebrity cachet by virtue of the former prime ministers, hockey stars, and *Titanic* victims who rest there. But it's still not easy to promote this product to customers who would rather not think about it. When market research revealed that the single biggest thing consumers want from the funeral industry is information,

Unsought product
A consumer product that the consumer either does not know about or knows about but does not normally think of buying.

© Rubens Abboud/Alamy

Exhibit 8.2 Unsought products: Even with a beautiful product, like the Mount Royal Cemetery in Montreal, marketers have a difficult time promoting services that people would rather not think about.

Mount Royal decided to focus its market efforts on educating Montrealers. It purchased easy-to-remember toll-free phone numbers, then launched a radio advertising campaign with a "Did you know . . . ?" theme. At the end of each spot, consumers were encouraged to call to request a no-obligation information kit.[2]

Industrial product
A product bought by individuals and organizations for further processing or for use in conducting a business.

Industrial Products Industrial products are those purchased for further processing or for use in conducting a business. The distinction between a consumer product and an industrial product is based on the *purpose* for which the product is bought. If a consumer buys a lawn mower for use around home, the lawn mower is a consumer product. If the same consumer buys the same lawn mower for use in a landscaping business, the lawn mower is an industrial product.

The three groups of industrial products and services are materials and parts, capital items, and supplies and services. *Materials and parts* include raw materials and manufactured materials and parts. Raw materials consist of farm products (wheat, cotton, livestock, fruits, vegetables) and natural products (fish, lumber, crude petroleum, iron ore). Manufactured materials and parts consist of component materials (iron, yarn, cement, wires) and component parts (small motors, tires, castings). Most manufactured materials and parts are sold directly to industrial users. Price and service are the major marketing factors; branding and advertising tend to be less important.

Capital items are industrial products that aid in the buyer's production or operations, including installations and accessory equipment. Installations consist of major purchases such as buildings (factories, offices) and fixed equipment (generators, drill presses, large computer systems, elevators). Accessory equipment includes portable factory equipment and tools (hand tools, lift trucks) and office equipment (computers, scanners, desks). They have a shorter life than installations and simply aid in the production process.

The final group of industrial products is *supplies and services*. Supplies include operating supplies (lubricants, coal, paper, pencils) and repair and maintenance items (paint, nails, brooms). Supplies are the convenience products of the industrial field because they are usually purchased with a minimum of effort or comparison. Business services include maintenance and repair services (window cleaning, computer repair) and business advisory services (legal, management consulting, advertising). Such services are usually supplied under contract.

◄◉┤Simulate on MyMarketingLab
New Product Development

New Product Development [LO2]

Now that we've learned that there's more to the first *P* of marketing, the product, than just hard goods, let's look at how new products are developed and managed.

Whether it's a new type of credit card from the Bank of Montreal or a new snowmobile from Bombardier, Canadians have a long history as inventors of new products. McIntosh apples, Pablum, frozen fish, and instant mashed potatoes are food products that all originated in Canada. Canadians are also responsible for developing such sports and leisure activities as basketball, five-pin bowling, table hockey, and Trivial Pursuit. Many Canadian inventions spawned entire industries. Reginald Fessenden, born near Sherbrooke, Quebec, was known as the father of radio after he invented amplitude modulation (AM) radio and transmitted his first broadcast in 1900. In 1844, Nova Scotia's Charles Fenerty developed the product we now call newsprint, which is made from wood pulp. Modern air travel was made possible by another Canadian, Wallace Rupert Turnbull, who developed the variable-pitch propeller. Canadian marketers are leaders in technology, e-commerce, and especially telecommunications: from Bell Canada to Nortel to BlackBerry.

Let's look at the formal process for developing, managing, and marketing new products.

New Product Development Strategy

A firm can obtain new products in two ways. One is through *acquisition*—by buying a whole company, a patent, or a licence to produce someone else's product. The other is through the firm's own **new-product development** efforts. By *new products*, we mean original or "new to the world" products, product improvements, product modifications, and new brands that companies like Corning develop through their own research and development (R&D) efforts.

New products are typically new to the world only once, as when the first mouse and keyboard were invented. But product marketers are continually improving on those products, making them new in a different way. Take for example the new waterproof and washable keyboard developed by Logitech. It resists spills and can actually be immersed in water, washed, and set on its edge to dry. Water runs out of small drainage holes, and the letters are laser printed and UV coated to ensure that they won't fade in the wash.

New products are important to both customers and the marketers who serve them. For customers, they bring new solutions and variety to their lives. For companies, new products are a key source of growth. Yet innovation can be very expensive and very risky, because a surprisingly high percentage—some say as high as 80 percent—of new products fail.

Exhibit 8.3 New products: Sometimes new products are completely new inventions, but more frequently they are improvements to existing products, like the Logitech K310 Washable Keyboard.

Raina & Wilson Photography

Why New Products Fail

No one knows exactly how many new products fail each year, but all marketing managers are aware that the number is very high, and it's a frightening thought. Still, companies are in the business of continually offering new products to the market, and so, every year, consumers see a parade of new products on the shelves.

Many new beers are launched on the market every year, most of which fail, and for reasons that have nothing to do with taste. The major soft drink companies also launch many new products every year, most of which are destined for failure for various reasons. Pepsi Blue, a too-sweet blue drink, lasted less than six months on store shelves because people didn't want to drink something that looked like window cleaner. When Coke and Nestlé partnered to produce Enviga, a drink that claimed to have "negative calories," production ceased after several lawsuits challenged claims made by the beverage makers. Even brilliant, forward-thinking marketer Richard Branson has had his share of failures:

> You're probably familiar with some of the products offered by Britain's Virgin Group, a British multinational conglomerate created by Richard Branson in 1970. You're likely also familiar with its flamboyant founder, who has built his own rocket ship for space travel and was knighted by the Queen, among other notable achievements. It may seem as if everything Sir Richard does is successful, but that's far from the truth. Virgin Group has experienced its fair share of failures.

New-product development
The development of original or "new to the world" products, product improvements, product modifications, and new brands through the firm's own product development efforts.

YOSHIKAZU TSUNO/AFP/Getty Images

Exhibit 8.4 Failed products: Tycoon Richard Branson dressed in a Virgin Cola costume to hand out free samples. Despite heavy promotion and a well-known brand, the product failed in the marketplace.

Back in the 1990s, Virgin introduced Virgin Cola to the market. At the time, Virgin's brand was soaring, and Branson was tempted to think that he could put his company's name on any new product and it would be an instant success. The mere rumours of Virgin Cola sent the executives at Coca-Cola into a tailspin. Virgin Cola was initially available only on Virgin planes and in Virgin cinemas before Branson sought wider distribution. "It tasted better than Coke. For one wonderful year we had the dream of Virgin Cola being the brand on everyone's lips." Instead, Branson claimed, "swat teams and bagfuls of money" sent from Coke's Atlanta headquarters gobbled up his drink, whose market share peaked at 0.5 percent in the three years it was on sale in the United States. In 2012, the U.K. producer went bust and no one else acquired the licence.

Other notable product failures from the Virgin Group include Virgin Vodka, Virgin Clothing, and cosmetics venture Virgin Vie. And Virgin Brides, a proposed chain of bridal stores, never really took off. Says Branson, "I think because there aren't many virgin brides." Either that, or the publicity photo of Branson in a wedding dress put consumers off![3]

Not every electronic device is a hit, either. Just ask Apple about its Newton, or Microsoft about Zune, the music player that was supposed to rival the iPod. Even marketers of well-established brands can fail with product line extensions that somehow hit a wrong note with consumers: Ben-Gay Aspirin, Smith and Wesson Mountain Bikes, Cosmopolitan (the magazine) Yogurt, and Colgate Kitchen Entrees.

One study of 128 senior marketers from some of the world's leading consumer packaged-goods companies suggests that the biggest problem with most new products is that they lack differentiation. In fact, of the marketing managers surveyed, only 12 percent felt that their own recently launched products were sufficiently differentiated. At the same time, these marketers reported operating in highly competitive categories, which suggests an explanation for the problem: If everyone is exploiting similar technology within a given category, the market is sure to be flooded with products too similar in design, features, and benefits.[4]

Diffusion of innovations theory
A social sciences theory that divides members of a social group into segments according to how likely they are to adopt a new idea.

Another reason why new products fail can be explained by the **diffusion of innovations theory**, a social sciences theory that divides members of a social group into segments according to how likely they are to adopt a new idea. (We first discussed this division in Chapter 6.) The theory suggests that the new idea must be diffused through the group via various forms of communications, and that because each group has very different motivations and beliefs, that diffusion is much more difficult than it might seem. Marketers have adopted this theory to explain why it is difficult to get a new product adopted, even when it has obvious advantages. While there are always a few early adopters of any new idea, product, or technology, most people tend to wait until the idea is proven before they are willing to try it.[5]

Technology Adoption Life Cycle
A marketing theory that proposes that when marketing a technology product, marketers must cross a chasm, or significant gap, between members of the early adopters segment and members of the early majority segment before a new product will become successful.

In the marketing of high-tech products, marketers believe there is a "chasm" that must be crossed before mainstream consumers will accept the product—that is, before the product can become a success. Figure 8.2 illustrates where the chasm occurs in the **Technology Adoption Life Cycle**, a model created by Geoffrey Moore, the author of *Crossing the Chasm*, which is based on the diffusions of innovations theory. (Note that Figure 6.5 illustrates another version of the cycle.) This theory proposes that when marketing a technology product, marketers must cross a chasm, or significant gap, between members of the early adopters segment and members of the early majority segment before a new product will become successful.

FIGURE 8.2 Developed by Geoffrey Moore, the Technology Adoption Life Cycle shows five different market segments, each separated by a gap. The "chasm," or most significant gap, occurs between members of the early adopters and members of the early majority segments.

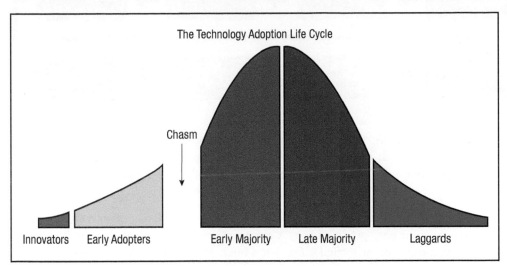

Each of the groups in Moore's model can be viewed as a different market segment, each with its own characteristics. Moore suggests that *innovators* pursue new technology for its own sake—they are the kind of people who line up overnight to be among the first to purchase the new iPhone or iPad. *Early adopters* will purchase new technology soon after it is released, but only if they have a use or purpose for it. The *early majority* are the more practical market segment. While they might want the new gadget, they wait until they have a real need for it, or until the price becomes more affordable. Members of the *late majority* are those who wait until the new technology has been proven and has more or less become a standard. Once "everyone" is using it, so will they. And finally, *laggards* are people who are not comfortable with technology or have no interest in it, and so are not a valuable market to pursue.

High-tech marketing requires marketers to understand the psychographics of the target market; that is, the lifestyle and behaviours that will make it more likely for a consumer to fall into the innovator or early adopter category—the first market segments that must be targeted. Notice that in Figure 8.2 there are gaps between each of the groups. These gaps symbolize the dissociation between the two groups—that is, the difficulty any group will have in accepting a new product if it is presented in the same way as it was to the group to its immediate left. For example, a message designed to persuade an innovator to try a new product will not be effective with a member of the early or late majority. Marketers, therefore, must choose a different approach in their positioning strategy and marketing communications if they decide to target more than one of these market segments.

Finally, consumers in the two groups on each side of the chasm make their purchase decision about the new technology largely on the basis of benefits sought. Early adopters are seeking in the new technology a change agent—they want something radically different, which they believe will be better, and will therefore give them some sort of advantage over the competition. By contrast, the early majority are seeking a productivity improvement in the new technology. They want evolution, not revolution.

The New-Product Development Process

Companies face a problem—they must develop new products, but the odds weigh heavily against success. In all, to create successful new products, a company must understand

FIGURE 8.3 Major Stages in New-Product Development

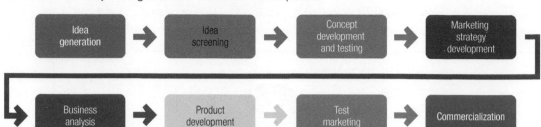

its consumers, markets, and competitors and develop products that deliver superior value to customers. It must carry out strong new-product planning and set up a systematic, customer-driven *new-product development process* for finding and growing new products. This process consists of eight major stages (see Figure 8.3).

Idea generation
The systematic search for new product ideas.

Idea Generation New-product development starts with **idea generation**—the systematic search for new-product ideas. A company typically generates hundreds of ideas, even thousands, in order to find a few good ones. Major sources of new-product ideas include internal sources and external sources such as customers, competitors, distributors and suppliers, and others.

Companies can also obtain good new-product ideas from any of a number of external sources. For example, *distributors and suppliers* can contribute ideas. Distributors are close to the market and can pass along information about consumer problems and new-product possibilities. Suppliers can tell the company about new concepts, techniques, and materials that can be used to develop new products. *Competitors* are another important source. Companies watch competitors' ads to get clues about their new products. They buy competing new products, take them apart to see how they work, analyze their sales, and decide whether they should bring out a new product of their own. Other idea sources include trade magazines, shows, and seminars; government agencies; advertising agencies; marketing research firms; university and commercial laboratories; and inventors.

Perhaps the most important source of new product ideas is *customers* themselves. The company can analyze customer questions and complaints to find new products that better

THE LIGHTWEIGHT COLLECTION

Courtesy of Canada Goose

LODGE VEST   LODGE HOODY   LODGE JACKET

Exhibit 8.5 Idea generation: Suggestions and requests from customers led to Canada Goose's new product line of lightweight down outerwear.

solve consumer problems. Their questions, complaints, and comments on social media provide insights into what new products the market wants. For example, Canada Goose's customers said they wanted a jacket they could wear when a parka was too warm; something that was more than a non-insulated coat but less than a full parka. This generated an idea for a new line of lightweight down outerwear products. Canada Goose developed the new line, incorporating a new technology called Thermal Mapping (which takes into consideration unique male and female heat-conservation needs), while still retaining the traditional Canada Goose soft-shell lightness and flexibility.

Customers have always found new uses for products beyond what the company originally envisioned, and sometimes those new uses can lead to the development of new products. For example, the makers of Arm & Hammer baking soda learned that customers used baking soda as a deodorant for their cat litter boxes, and for other purposes such as brushing their teeth. This led to the development of many new products, including Arm & Hammer cat litter, Arm & Hammer laundry detergent, Arm & Hammer deodorant, and Arm & Hammer toothpaste.

Exhibit 8.6 Internal product ideas: Twitter hosts an annual "Hack Week: Let's Hack Together" event, which actively promotes internal innovation through experimentation around the company.

Twitter, Inc.

Several companies, including Eli Lilly, SAP, Fujitsu, and the World Bank, have implemented an "idea market" within the company, where any employee can submit suggestions for solving a problem, or for a new product, in return for a reward. And Twitter hosts a quarterly Hack Week: Let's Hack Together event, which actively promotes internal innovation through experimentation around the company:

> During Hack Week, a wide range of Twitter folks take time away from their day-to-day work to collaborate and see what crazy cool new things they can develop. Says one employee, "No meetings for a week. No releases for a week. And almost no rules. Go Hack Week!" At one Hack Week some 100 teams worked on wide-ranging projects, from developing new Twitter products and features to improving the Twitter user experience. "Some projects were technical and strategic; some were simply fun and off the wall, giving people a chance to stretch their creative muscles," says Twitter. Some of the ideas developed during Hack Week will become blockbuster additions; others will fall quietly by the wayside. It's still too soon to tell. "We can't wait to find out," says Twitter. But "one thing we do know: We'll have a bunch of awesome new products, features, and ideas."[6]

A relatively new approach to idea generation that some companies are employing today is **crowdsourcing**—inviting broad communities of people such as customers, employees, independent scientists and researchers, and even the public at large into the new-product innovation process. For example, rather than relying only on its own R&D labs to produce all the new-product innovations needed to support growth, Procter & Gamble developed its Connect + Develop crowdsourcing process. Through Connect + Develop, the company uncovers promising innovations from entrepreneurs, scientists, engineers, and other researchers—even consumers themselves—that will help it meet its goal of improving consumers' lives (see Marketing@Work 8.1).

Rather than creating and managing their own crowdsourcing platforms, companies can use third-party crowdsourcing networks, such as InnoCentive, TopCoder, Hypios, and jovoto. For example, organizations ranging from Facebook and PayPal to ESPN,

Crowdsourcing
Inviting broad communities of people such as customers, employees, independent scientists and researchers, and even the public at large into the new-product innovation process.

MARKETING@WORK 8.1

Crowdsourcing at Procter & Gamble

Since its founding more than 175 years ago, Procter & Gamble has set the gold standard for breakthrough innovation and new-product development in its industry. P&G's Tide detergent, introduced in the late 1940s, was the first synthetic laundry detergent for automatic washing machines. Its Pampers brand was the first successful disposable diaper, and Crest was the first fluoride toothpaste that really did prevent cavities. And until recently, most of the company's innovations came from within P&G's own R&D labs.

P&G invests $2 billion a year in R&D, and employs more than 8000 researchers in 26 facilities around the globe, some of the best research talent in the world. Then, about 10 years ago, P&G shook up its research process. It transitioned from an internal R&D model that relied on P&G's own labs to produce needed innovation to an open-innovation model that invites outside partners to help develop new products and technologies that will delight customers.

P&G doesn't want to replace its 8000 researchers; it wants to leverage them better. The company realized that much of today's important innovation is happening at entrepreneurial companies, universities, and government labs all around the world. For every researcher working at P&G, there are hundreds of scientists and engineers working elsewhere—millions in all. Moreover, thanks to the Internet, the world's talent markets are increasingly linked. P&G had to shift from its old "not invented here" culture (one that discounted solutions coming from outside the company) to one that embraced ideas found elsewhere. "We needed to change how we defined, and perceived, our R&D organization," says P&G's vice-president for innovation and knowledge.

With this objective in mind, P&G launched Connect + Develop and invited entrepreneurs, scientists, engineers, and other researchers—even consumers themselves—to submit ideas for new technologies, product design, packaging, marketing models, research methods, engineering, or promotion—anything that has the potential to create better products and services that will help P&G meet its goal of improving more consumers' lives. Today, P&G collaborates with a truly global innovation network—more than 50 percent of its innovations involve some kind of external partner. So far, Connect + Develop has resulted in more than 2000 successful agreements. The long list of successful new products brought to market through Connect + Develop includes, among many others, Tide Pods, Tide Total Care, Olay Regenerist, Swiffer Dusters, Glad ForceFlex Bags, Clairol Perfect 10, CoverGirl Eyewear, the Oral B Pulsonic toothbrush, Febreze Candles, and Mr. Clean Magic Eraser.

Under Connect + Develop, innovative ideas and technologies roll in from a wide diversity of sources: The new peptide for P&G's blockbuster Olay Regenerist, a $2 billion brand, came from a small French company. The Oral B Pulsonic sonic toothbrush came from a partnership with a Japanese firm—it was in the market less than a year after the first meeting. Connect + Develop was the source of the idea behind Febreze Candles. P&G provided the Febreze odour-care technology but worked with an external candle company to develop the candles. And Mr. Clean Magic Eraser got its start when an independent technology entrepreneur discovered a stain-removing sponge already on the market in Osaka, Japan, and alerted P&G via Connect + Develop. The product's magic ingredient was a packing foam made by German chemical company BASF, which happened to already be a major P&G supplier!

The Connect + Develop crowdsourcing program has produced big benefits for P&G. Connect + Develop "opened our minds and doors to external

Exhibit 8.7 P&G's highly successful Connect + Develop crowdsourcing program invites outside innovation partners to help develop new technologies and products that will delight customers.

Procter & Gamble

collaboration," says Bruce Brown, P&G's chief technology officer. "It changed our culture from 'invented here' to 'partnering for greater value.'" As a result of the program, P&G's R&D productivity has increased 60 percent, and its innovation success rate has more than doubled, even as the cost of innovation has fallen. "Connect + Develop has created a culture of open innovation that has already generated sustainable growth," says P&G CEO Bob McDonald, "but we know we can do more. We want the best minds in the world to work with us to create big ideas that can touch and improve the lives of more consumers, in more parts of the world, more completely."

Sources: Based on quotes and other information in "P&G Connect + Develop Launches New Open Innovation Website," a

press release published on PG.com February 7, 2013; "P&G Adapts R&D Model," *warc*, January 31, 2012; Larry Huston and Nabil Sakkab, "Connect and Develop: Inside Procter & Gamble's New Model for Innovation," *Harvard Business Review*, March 2006, pp. 2–9; Bruce Brown, "Why Innovation Matters," *Technology Management*, November–December 2010, pp. 18–23; "P&G Sets Two New Goals for Open Innovation Partnerships," *PR Newswire*, October 28, 2010; Issie Lapowsky, "Why Every Company Is Now an Incubator," *Inc.*, December 21, 2012; and the P&G Connect + Develop site at www.pgconnectdevelop.com.

NASA, and the Salk Institute tap into TopCoder's network of nearly 400 000 mathematicians, engineers, software developers, and designers for ideas and solutions, offering prizes of $100 to $100 000. PayPal posted a challenge to the TopCoder community seeking the development of an innovative Android or iPhone app that would successfully and securely run its checkout process, awarding the winners $5000 each. After only four weeks of competition and two weeks of review, PayPal had its solutions. The Android app came from a programmer in the United States; the iPhone app from a programmer in Colombia.[7]

Idea Screening The purpose of idea generation is to create a large number of ideas. The purpose of the succeeding stages is to *reduce* that number. The first idea-reducing stage is **idea screening**, which helps spot good ideas and drop poor ones as soon as possible. Product development costs rise greatly in later stages, so the company wants to go ahead only with the product ideas that will turn into profitable products.

Idea screening
Screening new-product ideas to spot good ideas and drop poor ones as soon as possible.

This more detailed consideration of the new-product idea may be reviewed by a committee, who will consider such things as the proposed customer value proposition, the target market, and the competition. They will make rough estimates of market size, product price, development time and costs, manufacturing costs, and rate of return, then recommend which ideas should go forward into the concept development and testing stage.

Concept Development and Testing Once the company has generated, and then screened, new-product ideas, the next step is to develop those ideas into a product concept. Whereas a product idea is an idea for a possible product that the company can potentially offer to the market, a **product concept** is a detailed description, drawing, or prototype of that idea that can be shown to potential customers. That product concept must then be developed and tested; that is, the new product idea is developed in various alternative forms, and tested with a group of potential customers.

Product concept
A detailed version of the new-product idea stated in meaningful consumer terms.

Exhibit 8.8 Concept development and testing: The latest concept car from Volvo is positioned as a family friendly sedan—it has a built-in car seat for children.

Every year automobile marketers promote their latest "concept cars" at auto shows. Concept cars are real cars that can be driven; however, they are not yet in production, which means they are not yet available to the public. Concept cars are displayed at auto shows so that the automobile marketers can gauge the market's response to their product concept. Automobile marketers may also let journalists from magazines like *Motor Trend* and *Car and Driver* drive and review their concept cars in hopes that a good review will result in enough market interest to justify a full-scale development and release of the new car.

Marketing Strategy Development After the product concept has been tested with members of the target market, and their opinions about the

Volvo

Marketing strategy development
Designing an initial marketing strategy for a new product based on the product concept.

concept have been collected, the next step in the product development process is to design the marketing strategy. **Marketing strategy development** involves designing an initial marketing strategy for a new product based on the product concept. The strategy must answer questions about how, when, where, and to whom the product will be introduced.

The marketing strategy begins with a detailed description of the target market for the new product. It outlines the value proposition of the new product, and describes its positioning with respect to existing product. The strategy must describe where and how the product will be made available to customers. It also proposes a target launch date, and the details of advertising and other promotional activities that must accompany the release of the new product. Finally, the marketing strategy must state sales goals, market share goals, and profit goals. Typically, this initial marketing strategy encompasses plans for the first year of the product.

Business analysis
A review of the sales, costs, and profit projections for a new product to find out whether these factors satisfy the company's objectives.

Business Analysis Once management has decided on its product concept and marketing strategy, it can evaluate the business attractiveness of the proposal. **Business analysis** involves a review of the sales, costs, and profit projections for a new product to find out whether they satisfy the company's objectives. If they do, the product can move to the product development stage.

To estimate sales, the company might look at the sales history of similar products and conduct market surveys. It can then estimate minimum and maximum sales to assess the range of risk. After preparing the sales forecast, management can estimate the expected costs and profits for the product, including marketing, R&D, operations, accounting, and finance costs. The company then uses the sales and costs figures to analyze the new product's financial attractiveness.

Product development
Developing the product concept into a physical product to ensure that the product idea can be turned into a workable market offering.

Test marketing
The stage of new-product development in which the product and marketing program are tested in realistic market settings.

Product Development So far, for many new-product concepts, the product may have existed only as a word description, a drawing, or perhaps a crude mock-up. If the product concept passes the business test, it moves into **product development**. Here, R&D or engineering develops the product concept into a physical product. The product development step, however, now calls for a large jump in investment. It will show whether the product idea can be turned into a workable product.

Developing the new product—that is, turning the new product idea into a workable, mass-produced market offering—takes months, even years. During the development process the new product will undergo rigorous testing to make sure that it works the way it is supposed to work, and that customers will be able to use it safely and effectively.

Marketers often involve actual customers in product testing. For example, Patagonia selects tried-and-true customers—called Patagonia Ambassadors—to work closely with its design department to field-test and refine its products under harsh conditions. Patagonia even created a website for the ambassadors to showcase their feats!

Exhibit 8.9 Product testing: Patagonia uses tried-and-true customers—its Patagonia Ambassadors—to help field-test its products under harsh conditions and help designers refine them.

Test Marketing If the product passes concept and product tests, the next step is **test marketing**, the stage at which the product and marketing program are introduced into realistic market settings. Test marketing gives the marketer experience with marketing the product before going to the great expense of full introduction. It lets the company test the product and its entire marketing program—targeting and positioning strategy, advertising, distribution, pricing, branding and packaging, and budget levels.

Commercialization The final step in the new-product development process is **commercialization**, or the full-scale introduction of the product into the market. If the company goes ahead with this stage, it will invest heavily in advertising and promotion.

Now that we've learned about the process that brings new products to market, let's look at what happens during the lifespan of a product in marketing terms.

The Product Life Cycle _{LO3}

The new-product development process gets the new product to market, and marks the beginning of the product's life. Every company wants its new products to enjoy a long, happy, and profitable life, but realistically, it understands that the new product won't sell forever. Marketing managers must accept that each product launched in the market will have a life cycle. The **product life cycle**, or PLC, is the course that a product's sales and profits take over its lifetime. Figure 8.4 shows a typical progression of a new product over the course of its life.

The typical product life cycle sees the product move through five stages: *product development, introduction, growth, maturity,* and *decline.* In theory, all products follow the PLC—eventually—though some well-established and mature products such as Coca-Cola and Tide laundry detergent may stay in the mature stage indefinitely, and never decline. The many products that are introduced to the market and then fail can be viewed as having skipped their growth and maturity stages and gone directly to decline. And some products that enter the decline stage are saved by revitalizing them or somehow making them "new and improved"—which sends them back to the introduction stage.

Stages of the Product Life Cycle

We looked at the product development stage of the product life cycle earlier in this chapter. We now look at strategies for each of the other life-cycle stages.

Introduction Stage The **introduction stage** starts when the new product is first launched. There's no formula for guaranteed success with any new product introduction—

Commercialization
The full-scale introduction of the new product into the market.

◀●▌ **Simulate** on MyMarketingLab
Product Life Cycle

Product life cycle
The course of a product's sales and profits over its lifetime. It involves five stages: product development, introduction, growth, maturity, and decline.

Introduction stage
The product life-cycle stage in which the new product is first distributed and made available for purchase.

FIGURE 8.4 Representation of Sales and Profits Over a Typical New Product's Life Cycle

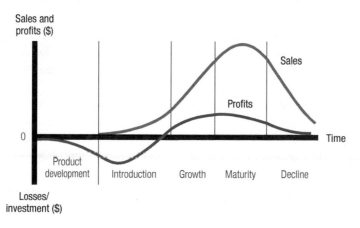

as we've already learned, many new products fail during this stage. Some products take off very quickly, as Apple's iPod did; others, like HDTV, can linger for years in this stage before experiencing growth. Today, the Fitbit is in the introduction stage. By the time you read this it may have entered the growth stage, or it may have failed and been withdrawn from the market. And perhaps 10 years from now it will be viewed in retrospect as a fad.

Growth stage
The product life-cycle stage in which a product's sales start climbing quickly.

Growth Stage If the new product satisfies the market, it will enter a **growth stage**, in which sales will start climbing quickly. The early adopters will continue to buy, and later buyers will start following their lead, especially if they hear favourable word of mouth. Competitors will release their versions of the new product, and the first marketer will need to make improvements or lower prices in order to compete. Profits increase during the growth stage as promotion costs are spread over a larger volume and unit manufacturing costs fall. During this stage, the marketing strategy is to sustain the growth for as long as possible, perhaps by adding new features or new models, or by targeting new market segments, or adding new distribution channels. Tablets are currently in the growth stage, while their predecessors, desktop and laptop computers, are in decline.

Maturity stage
The product life-cycle stage in which sales growth slows or levels off.

Maturity Stage At some point, a product's sales growth will slow down, and the product will enter a **maturity stage**. This maturity stage normally lasts longer than the previous stages, and it poses strong challenges to marketing management. Most products are in the maturity stage of the life cycle, and therefore most of marketing management deals with the mature product.

The main marketing goal when a product is in the mature stage is to prevent it from declining. Marketers who handle mature products must be constantly developing strategies and managing marketing programs to keep their product consistently profitable. One way to do this is by *modifying the market*, or trying to increase consumption by finding new market segments. Another way is by *modifying the product*—changing characteristics such as quality, features, style, or packaging to attract new users and inspire more usage. Or marketers can try *modifying the marketing mix*—improving sales by changing one or more marketing mix elements, such as improving services, adjusting prices, or running a sales promotion.

Some products become classics; as we've seen, they seem to be able to stay in the maturity stage indefinitely. Take Coca-Cola, for example. It's been in the mature stage for over 50 years. Or 10 000, depending on whom you ask. (See Marketing@ Work 8.2.)

Decline stage
The product life-cycle stage in which a product's sales decline.

Decline Stage Many mature products that continue to be useful, such as brands of laundry detergent and shampoo, can stay in the maturity stage indefinitely, but other products such as computers, televisions, and telephones will eventually decline, die, and be replaced by different new products. Some products that are currently in the **decline stage** are small digital cameras, which have become unnecessary due to the growth of smartphones. Home or "landline" telephones are also on the decline, as many consumers use only a cellphone.

Marketing product managers need not despair because their product is in decline, however. Some marketers decide to maintain their declining products without change in the hope that competitors will leave the industry. For example, P&G made good profits by remaining in the declining liquid soap business as others withdrew. Another strategy for managing products as they decline is to reposition them and try to appeal to a new market segment. For example, TAB, the original diet soda, had practically disappeared from the market before being repositioned as an energy drink for women; and Old Spice,

MARKETING@WORK 8.2

The Myth of Innovation: New Products Typically Take Years, If Not Decades, to Develop

There's a myth about creativity: that only people who are geniuses can create and invent, and that their creations come to them as inspirations. The famous letter in which Mozart claimed to have written his symphonies in one sitting after spending a short time "imagining" them was proven to have been a forgery—yet it's still a widely held belief. The truth is, the creation of art and new products is always a result of hard work and trial and error; many of our most common products represent years, if not decades, of cumulative invention by many different people. Take, for example, the lowly yet ubiquitous can of Coke. There was a time, of course, when it didn't exist, but it didn't spring into existence overnight, either. Cans of Coca-Cola are the end result of 10 000 years of new product development.

That last can of Coke you purchased originated in a town called Pinjarra in Western Australia, the site of the world's largest bauxite mine. Bauxite is aluminum ore, and aluminum is what, eventually, will hold that can of Coke. But first the bauxite must be scraped and dug from the ground, then crushed and washed, then cooled, then heated to over a thousand degrees to turn it into aluminum oxide, which is then dissolved into a molten substance called cryolite, a rare mineral first discovered in Greenland. Cryolite can be turned into aluminum using a process called electrolysis, which was invented by Michael Farraday.

But back up—who discovered aluminum? Although aluminum is an element, and the most abundant metal in the earth's crust, it is never found free in nature. A Danish chemist, Hans Christian Oersted, figured out a process to produce pure aluminum in 1825, but he could make only tiny amounts. Twenty years later, Friedrich Wöhler, a German chemist, developed a way to produce samples large enough to determine some of aluminum's basic properties. Wöhler's method was improved in 1854 by Henri Étienne Sainte-Claire Deville, a French chemist, and it was Deville's process that allowed for the commercial production of aluminum. Then, in 1886, Charles Martin Hall, an American chemist, and Paul L. T. Héroult, a French chemist, figured out the process of obtaining aluminum from aluminum oxide. The two scientists didn't work together and didn't even know each other, and yet they both "discovered" this process in the same year, an ocean apart. Finally, in 1888, an Austrian chemist, Karl Joseph Bayer, "invented" the process of extracting aluminum from bauxite—the process that's still used today to produce the aluminum for that can of Coke.

So now we know how aluminum was invented, but aluminum cans are a different product altogether. Today, the production of aluminum cans is such big business that a monthly trade magazine, called *The Canmaker*, exists just to provide information about can making to packaging professionals. According to *The Canmaker*, Coca-Cola uses 300 000 tonnes of aluminum sheet per year just to produce its cans in the United States, and while that's not all the aluminum in the world, North America is the biggest market for cans, and the U.S. uses 20 percent of all the aluminum produced in the world just to make them. The good news is that, because aluminum is an element, it's infinitely recyclable. But how does aluminum get transformed into cans?

The refined aluminum is formed into bars at the bauxite mine in Australia, then those bars are transported to a port and loaded onto a container ship to begin a month-long journey to the United States. Corpus Christi, Texas, is one of the ports that unloads the containers of aluminum bars, transfers them to trucks, and sends them to a rolling mill, where the bars are rolled flat and turned into enormous thin sheets. The sheets are punched into circles and shaped into a cup by a mechanical process called drawing and ironing, a process that takes about a fifth of a

George Frey/Bloomberg/Getty Images

Exhibit 8.10 Ten thousand years of innovation: The product we know as a can of Coca-Cola begins its existence at a bauxite mine in Australia, and what's inside the can evolved over thousands of years.

second. The outside of the can is decorated with the Coca-Cola colours and symbols using a base layer of urethane, then seven layers of coloured acrylic paint and varnish. The inside of the can is painted with a chemical, called a comestible polymeric coating, to prevent the aluminum from getting into the soda.

And that's just the production of the *sides* of the can. The tops and bottoms are engineered differently, because they need to be thicker and stronger than the rest of the can to withstand the pressure of the carbon dioxide gas. So the aluminum for the tops and bottoms must be processed into an alloy with magnesium. The lids are produced in a separate process, then punched and scored, and then the tab (which is made of aluminum) must be installed. The finished lid is put on top of the filled can, and the edges of the can are folded over it and welded shut. Twelve of these cans are packaged into a paperboard box called a fridge pack, using a machine capable of producing 300 such packs a minute.

But the Coca-Cola Company didn't invent the soft drink can. The idea to preserve food in cans evolved from glass jars used to preserve foods for Napoleon's troops in the early nineteenth century. An Englishman, Peter Durand, patented a process using a can made of tinplate. The first cans used solder to seal the seams, and the process, though useful and practical, wasn't entirely sanitary. It took another 100 years of product developers improving on the process before it became automated and safe.

Then there was the problem of how to get the food or liquids *out* of the cans. The first cans required a can opener to remove the lid entirely. Then an invention called the church key, a small, portable tool, let the consumer pierce a triangular hole in the lid to drink from. As early as 1922, inventors were applying for patents for tab tops—a mechanism to open the can without a tool. Mikola Kondakow of Thunder Bay, Ontario, invented the pull tab for bottles in 1956. Then, in 1962, Ermal Cleon

Fraze of Dayton, Ohio, invented the pull tab for cans—a ring attached by a rivet that would come off completely and be discarded.

But this new product development caused an unforeseen problem: Consumers tended to either throw those tabs on the ground or put them inside the can, causing problems for both the environment and personal safety. So the inventors went back to the drawing board and came up with the push tab, a raised circular scored area that could be pushed down into the can, with a small unscored piece that kept the tab connected after being pushed inside. Push tabs never gained wide popularity, however, because although they'd solved the litter problem of the pull tab, they'd created a safety hazard: Upon pushing the tab into the can, the person's finger was immediately exposed to the sharp edges of the opening. It took an untold number of product developers until 1975 to develop the stay-on tab, the kind we still find on our Coca-Cola cans today.

Interestingly, none of these inventions was created by Coca-Cola, the largest user of the final product. Coca-Cola's first production can was made in 1955 for exclusive export to U.S. troops stationed overseas. Executives at the company worried that the taste was affected by the tin in the cans, so they didn't want to use these cans in the domestic market for fear that the company's reputation would suffer. It wasn't until 1967 that cans were made of aluminum and production of Coca-Cola in cans became widespread in the U.S. and Canada.

Now, what about what's *inside* the can? Surely Coca-Cola itself was invented by the Coca-Cola Company? Not really. Swedish chemists in the late 1700s were the first to develop medicinal beverages made of effervescent spring water and various herbs, although around the same time Johann Jacob Schweppe patented the process and started the Schweppes Company. The minerals in the spring water could be replicated using phosphate—and since carbonation was a

straightforward process, the production of bubbly soft drinks was simply a matter of creating recipes with herbs and flavourings.

Because both the producers and consumers of these early soft drinks considered them to have medicinal properties, exotic ingredients such as vanilla, cinnamon, the fruit of the African baobab tree, roots supposedly extracted from swamps, opium, and cocaine were used. One of these medicines, invented by chemist John Pemberton in Georgia in 1865, was made from ingredients including cola nut and coca leaf, as well as alcohol. Twenty years later, when parts of Georgia banned alcohol consumption, Pemberton made a non-alcoholic version, which he called "Coca-Cola," and in 1887 he sold the formula to a drugstore clerk named Asa Candler.

For the next hundred years or so, Coca-Cola syrup was mixed with carbonated water in drugstores and sold as a beverage. Its medicinal claims eventually fell to the wayside, and the drink was promoted as being "refreshing" and "invigorating." Today, Coca-Cola is made from syrup produced by the Coca-Cola Company of Atlanta, Georgia. The syrup is the only thing the Coca-Cola Company provides; the bottling operation belongs to a separate, independent corporation called the Coca-Cola Bottling Company.

Today the Coca-Cola Company is 130 years old and worth nearly $50 billion, and while it's true that the exact recipe for the liquid inside the can is a secret, almost nothing about the product itself is the result of innovation by the company that owns the brand. Despite how things may appear to us as consumers, new products never spring into existence overnight. Sometimes they're the culmination of thousands of years of invention and creation by thousands of people.

Sources: Based on Kevin Ashton, *How to Fly a Horse*, Doubleday, 2015. Additional sources: John Nutting, Frequently Asked Questions, *The Canmaker* (www.canmaker.com), January 18, 2011; CollectibleSodaCans.com; the website of Jefferson Lab, a subsidiary of the U.S. Department of Energy.

TABLE 8.2 Summary of Product Life-Cycle Characteristics, Objectives, and Strategies

	Introduction	Growth	Maturity	Decline
Characteristics				
Sales	Low sales	Rapidly rising sales	Peak sales	Declining sales
Costs	High cost per customer	Average cost per customer	Low cost per customer	Low cost per customer
Profits	Negative	Rising profits	High profits	Declining profits
Customers	Innovators	Early adopters	Middle majority	Laggards
Competitors	Few	Growing number	Stable number beginning to decline	Declining number
Marketing Objectives				
	Create product awareness and trial	Maximize market share	Maximize profit while defending market share	Reduce expenditure and milk the brand
Strategies				
Product	Offer a basic product	Offer product extensions, service, warranty	Diversify brand and models	Phase out weak items
Price	Use cost-plus	Price to penetrate market	Price to match or beat competitors	Cut price
Distribution	Build selective distribution	Build intensive distribution	Build more intensive distribution	Go selective: phase out unprofitable outlets
Advertising	Build product awareness among early adopters and dealers	Build awareness and interest in the mass market	Stress brand differences and benefits	Reduce to level needed to retain hard-core loyalists
Sales Promotion	Use heavy sales promotion to entice trial	Reduce to take advantage of heavy consumer demand	Increase to encourage brand switching	Reduce to minimal level

Source: Philip Kotler and Kevin Lane Keller, *Marketing Management*, 14th ed. (Upper Saddle River, NJ: Prentice Hall, 2012), p. 317. © 2012. Printed and electronically reproduced by permission of Pearson Education, Inc., Upper Saddle River, New Jersey.

known for years as your father's aftershave, repositioned itself to appeal to a younger generation of men.

If decline is unpreventable, marketers may decide to *harvest* the product, which means reducing various costs (plant and equipment, maintenance, R&D, advertising, sales force) and hoping that sales hold up. If successful, harvesting will increase the company's profits in the short run. Sometimes declining products can be sold to another firm or simply liquidated at salvage value. In recent years, P&G has sold off a number of lesser or declining brands such as Crisco oil, Comet cleanser, Sure deodorant, and Duncan Hines cake mixes.

Table 8.2 summarizes the key characteristics of each stage of the product life cycle. The table also lists the marketing objectives and strategies for each stage.[8]

Styles, Fashions, and Fads

The PLC concept also can be applied to *styles, fashions,* and *fads* (see Figure 8.5). A **style** is a basic and distinctive mode of expression. For example, styles appear in homes (colonial, ranch, transitional), clothing (formal, casual), and art (realist, surrealist, abstract). Once a

Style
A basic and distinctive mode of expression.

FIGURE 8.5 Styles, Fashions, and Fads

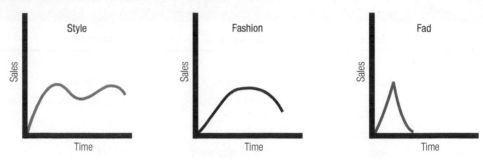

Fashion

A currently accepted or popular style of design, colour, or theme.

Fad

A temporary period of unusually high sales driven by consumer enthusiasm and immediate product or brand popularity.

style is invented, it may last for generations, passing in and out of vogue. A style has a cycle with several periods of renewed interest. A **fashion** is a currently accepted or popular style of design, colour, or theme. There are fashions in clothing, of course, but also in cars, furniture, music, and even sports. Punk was a fashion in music, clothing, and hairstyles in the 1970s. Playing handball was fashionable in the 1980s, golf was a fashion in the 1990s but is now declining, and snowboarding is a relatively new fashion, still on the rise. Fashions tend to grow slowly, remain popular for a while, and then decline slowly.

Fads are new products that are extremely popular for a very short period of time, then disappear almost completely. Every decade has its memorable fads, but they're not usually identified as fads until years later. For example, in 2005 the upside-down Christmas tree was a fad—luxury gadget catalogue marketer Hammacher Schlemmer even offered a $599.95 version that came pre-strung with 800 clear commercial-grade lights. Other products, as razor scooters, Crocs, and the Tamagotchi, have also been viewed in retrospect as fads.

Just because something is a fashion or a fad doesn't mean it wasn't successful as a new product. Take Guitar Hero, for example:

> Guitar Hero, the hugely popular video game with the guitar-shaped controller, was in production for only six years, from 2005 to 2011. The first version of Guitar Hero sold 1.5 million copies and generated US$45 million in revenue, prompting Activison Blizzard Inc., the makers of World of Warcraft, to purchase the company. It launched Guitar Hero II, which improved the product by doubling the song selection and adding stage effects, and made US$200 million in profit.
>
> Competitors such as Rock Band soon appeared on the market, and Guitar Hero released a stream of new products such as Guitar Hero: Aerosmith, Guitar Hero: Metallica, and Guitar Hero World Tour. At the height of its popularity, an entire episode of *South Park* was dedicated to Guitar Hero. Rick Mercer played Guitar Hero with Rush guitarist Alex Lifeson on an episode of *The Rick Mercer Report*, musicians like Dave Navarro and Matt Sorum helped promote the latest edition of the game in live events, and endless Hollywood celebrities were photographed enthusiastically playing the game.
>
> Sadly, the game's stratospheric growth didn't last long. By 2009 sales had declined, and in 2010 only one new title was released (Guitar Hero: Warrior of Rock). Finally, in 2011, Activision shut down Guitar Hero operations for good.[9]

Exhibit 8.11 Was it a fad, or a wildly successful new product? Hollywood celebrities Adam Gregory, Brandon Michael Vayda, and Matt Prokop play Guitar Hero during the Guitar Hero World Tour VIP Launch Event in 2008 at Best Buy in Los Angeles.

Tony D iPhoto Inc./Newscom

How long does a new product's life cycle have to last? As the example of Guitar Hero shows, there are no hard and fast rules. Some might say Guitar Hero was a wildly successful new product that simply followed the PLC: It grew quickly, generated millions in sales, matured three years after it was introduced, and declined three years later. But one day, marketing historians may look back on Guitar Hero as "just a fad."

Product and Service Decisions LO4

Marketers make product and service decisions at three levels. At the first level, they make individual product decisions, which include decisions about product attributes such as quality, features, and style and design, as well as decisions about packaging, labelling, and product support services for each product. At the next level are decisions about product lines, or groups of products. Finally, marketers make decisions about the company's overall product portfolio, or product mix.

Individual Product and Service Decisions

The important decisions in the development and marketing of individual products and services include decisions about *product attributes*, *packaging*, *labelling*, and *product support* services.

Product and Service Attributes Developing a product or service involves defining the benefits that it will offer. These benefits are communicated and delivered by product attributes such as *quality*, *features*, and *style and design*.

PRODUCT QUALITY **Product quality** is one of the marketer's major positioning tools. Quality has a direct impact on product or service performance; thus, it is closely linked to customer value and satisfaction. In the narrowest sense, quality can be defined as "freedom from defects." But most customer-centred companies go beyond this narrow definition. Instead, they define quality in terms of creating customer value and satisfaction. Product quality is a serious matter for marketers, many of whom belong to the Society of Quality Assurance (SQA), an international professional membership organization that provides a forum for organizations to exchange information about research and regulations that govern quality assurance practices.

> **Product quality**
> The characteristics of a product or a service that bear on its ability to satisfy stated or implied customer needs.

The level of quality a product has determines the type of marketing programs that will be created to promote it. For example, Rolex watches are the highest quality watch available on the market, and all point-of-sale materials and advertising tend to mention the craftsmanship and length of time that goes into building one. Similarly, marketers of high-end sports cars focus on promoting the quality of their vehicles, while smaller, less expensive cars focus on price promotions.

PRODUCT FEATURES A product can be offered with varying features. Features are a competitive tool for differentiating the company's product from competitors' products. Being the first producer to introduce a valued new feature is one of the most effective ways to compete. Automobile marketers are always developing new features to add to their cars, from keyless doors to rearview cameras, to cars that actually drive themselves:

> They've already come up with a name for them. They're called AVs, for autonomous vehicles, or cars that drive themselves. Not all the time, and not in all weather conditions—that would be impossible. Futurists predict that most AVs will instead boast capabilities such as lane-departure warnings and collision-avoidance braking, and that more

Volvo

Exhibit 8.12 Marketing that focuses on features: Volvo is testing a fleet of self-driving cars on the roads of Sweden.

sophisticated systems in luxury models will enable the car to make its own decisions three-quarters of the time. Imagine a car that can drive you to the door of your destination, then leave to find its own parking space!

Most automakers have R&D projects devoted to autonomous capabilities. Nissan and Mercedes-Benz have given themselves a deadline of 2020 to put AVs on the market. But Volvo is more ambitious: The company is currently deploying a test fleet of 100 largely autonomous cars on the roads of Sweden, and in 2017 it plans to put its AVs in the hands of 100 customers and turn them loose on public roads.

According to technology consultancy Lux Research, the business of making cars drive themselves will be worth US$87 billion by 2030, and the opportunities for software developers to create the programs that make them run will be worth US$25 billion a year.[10]

STYLE AND DESIGN Another way to add customer value is through distinctive *style and design*. Design is a larger concept than style. *Style* simply describes the appearance of a product. Styles can be eye-catching or yawn producing. A sensational style may grab attention and produce pleasing aesthetics, but it does not necessarily make the product *perform* better. Unlike style, *design* is more than skin deep—it goes to the very heart of a product. Good design contributes to a product's usefulness as well as to its looks.

The way a product is *designed*—what features it has, where they are located, and how they are used—and the way a product looks—*its style*—are important factors that influence consumers in choosing one company's product over another. Good design begins with observing customers and developing a deep understanding of their needs. More than simply creating product or service attributes, it involves shaping the customer's product-use experience. The Nest thermostat is an excellent example of how marketers can transform a boring old product into something new and beautiful:

Packaging

The activities of designing and producing the container or wrapper for a product.

> The Nest learning thermostat looks great—its sleek, clean, curved design and neutral brushed-silver finish create a chameleon effect that grounds Nest within its environment. But Nest's beauty is more than just skin deep. Before Nest, programmable thermostats developed in the 1970s were supposed to both improve comfort and conserve energy. But research showed that 89 percent of owners rarely or never programmed them because they were just too complicated.
>
> So Nest Labs assembled a corps of Silicon Valley designers who reinvented the thermostat to fit the needs of today's smartphone generation. The result is Nest, a "learning thermostat" that—all by itself—learns from your preferences, behaviours, and surroundings and then optimizes your heating and cooling schedule to keep you comfortable while you're at home while saving energy while you're away. Nest remembers the temperatures you like and builds a schedule for you. Users can also control the device simply via Wi-Fi, at home or away using a laptop, tablet, or smartphone app. Good design has transformed the lowly home thermostat into a beautiful device that you're proud to hang on your wall and also a cool, connected device that's fun to use.[11]

Handout/MCT/Newscom

Exhibit 8.13 Good design: Nest Labs transformed the lowly home thermostat into a beautiful device that's fun to use.

Packaging and Labelling

Packaging is much more than just the container to hold the product—it's an important marketing tool as well. It protects the product from breakage, tampering, and theft; it provides information about the product; and it can be used as a promotional tool to describe the benefits of the product and identify the brand. How important is packaging? One study showed that 20 percent of shoppers will buy products they had no intention of buying before entering the store—all based on the packaging they see while shopping.[12]

Sometimes, the package is the most important marketing tool of all. "The fundamental truth about packaging is that it's the only marketing vehicle that 100 percent of the shoppers who buy your product actually see," points out Jason Dubroy, vice-president of shopper marketing at DDB Canada. Pet food marketer Petcurean took this advice to heart and spent a year redesigning its packaging:

Petcurean

Exhibit 8.14 Packaging: Petcurean spent a year redesigning the packaging for its GO! and NOW FRESH lines of premium pet food because the company's director of marketing believes there is nothing more vital to the brand than its package.

When Vancouver's Subplot Design was hired by Petcurean to redesign the packaging for its GO! and NOW FRESH lines of premium dog and cat food, the first thing creative director Matthew Clark thought of was packaging in Europe—it's more minimalist, more frugal, and usually has some level of higher engagement through fun, wit, or whimsy. His package design philosophy is to be simpler and quieter, to free up space, and to say one thing clearly, not 12 things in a cluttered way.

The redesigned packaging for the NOW FRESH product line brings to life the tagline "It could only be fresher if you made it from scratch." The packaging expresses this through "Fresh Market" signage, burlap textures, and soft, warm, natural colours. The project took a full year, which explains why some marketers shy away from major redesigns of their packaging, but Petcurean's director of marketing, Jaimie Turkington, had a different vision: "There is nothing more vital to this brand than packaging, because in the absence of everything else, it's the entire consumer experience. So why wouldn't we invest significant time and resources into creating an outstanding end product?"[13]

Sustainable Packaging In today's marketing environment, consumers are increasingly aware of which products are environmentally responsible and sustainable, and which are not. Whether or not a particular product's packaging is excessive or recyclable can make the difference between whether a consumer purchases that product or not. Today, many marketers are exploring options for **sustainable packaging**—packaging that meets the requirements of the product while minimizing the environmental, economic, and social impacts of the product and its package.

The Sustainable Packaging Coalition, an organization of retailers, manufacturers, designers, educational institutions, and government agencies, promotes the idea of using sustainable packaging made from materials that are sourced, manufactured, transported, and recycled using renewable energy. Sustainable packaging optimizes the use of renewable or recycled source materials, and is manufactured using clean production technologies. It should also be itself recyclable, thus creating a closed loop system for all packaging materials.[14]

This closed loop system is also being called "circular thinking": the idea that packaging can be recycled and thereby reused over and over again. For example, Carlsberg joined forces with six key suppliers to create a "circular community" to review how it could optimize packaging for recycling and reuse, and importantly, retain or improve product quality. With 42 percent of Carlsberg's CO_2 emissions derived from packaging, innovations of this kind stand to help the company make big leaps forward in cutting its

Sustainable packaging
Packaging that meets the requirements of the product while minimizing the environmental, economic, and social impacts of the product and its package.

environmental footprint. Its next project is the world's first biodegradable wood-fibre beer bottle.[15]

Labelling Labels range from simple tags attached to products to complex graphics that are part of the package. They perform several functions. At the very least, the label *identifies* the product or brand, such as the name Sunkist stamped on oranges. The label might also *describe* several things about the product—who made it, where it was made, when it was made, its contents, how it is to be used, and how to use it safely. For many companies, labels have become an important element in broader marketing campaigns. In Canada, labelling decisions play a very important role in product marketing, because what must be, and what can be, included on a label is strictly regulated. Health Canada, a federal department responsible for helping Canadians maintain and improve their health, regulates labelling for all food products. To that end, nutrition labelling of all prepackaged foods became mandatory in Canada in 2007. Regulations governing the packaging of nonfood items are outlined in the Consumer Packaging and Labelling Act. Some forward-thinking packaged-food marketers have benefited from these regulations by promoting the nutritious features of their products long before it became trendy to do so.

Product Support Services Customer service is another element of product strategy. A company's offer usually includes some support services, which augment actual products. Many companies use the Internet to provide support services, but sometimes the human touch is necessary, for example Apple's Genius service provided in Apple retail stores.

Product Line Decisions

Beyond decisions about individual products and services, product strategy calls for building a product line. A **product line** is a group of products that are closely related because they function in a similar manner, are sold to the same customer groups, are marketed through the same types of outlets, or fall within given price ranges. For example, Nike produces several lines of athletic shoes and apparel, and Marriott offers several lines of hotels.

The major product line decision involves *product line length*—the number of items in the product line. The line is too short if the manager can increase profits by adding items; the line is too long if the manager can increase profits by dropping items.

Product line length is influenced by company objectives and resources. For example, one objective might be to allow for up-selling. Thus, BMW wants to move customers up from its 3-series models to 5- and 7-series models. Another objective might be to allow cross-selling: Hewlett-Packard sells printers as well as cartridges. Still another objective might be to protect against economic swings: Gap runs several clothing-store chains (Gap, Old Navy, and Banana Republic), covering different price points.

A company can expand its product line in two ways: by *line filling* or *line stretching*. *Product line filling* involves adding more items within the present range of the line. There are several reasons for product line filling: reaching for extra profits, satisfying dealers, using excess capacity, being the leading full-line company, and plugging holes to keep out competitors. However, line filling is overdone if it results in cannibalization and customer confusion. The company should ensure that new items are noticeably different from existing ones.

Product line stretching occurs when a company lengthens its product line beyond its current range. Companies located at the upper end of the market can stretch their lines

Product line
A group of products that are closely related because they function in a similar manner, are sold to the same customer groups, are marketed through the same types of outlets, or fall within given price ranges.

downward to plug a market hole that would otherwise attract a new competitor or to respond to a competitor's attack on the upper end. Companies can also stretch their product lines *upward* to add prestige to their current products. For example, some years ago, each of the leading Japanese auto companies introduced an upmarket automobile: Honda launched Acura; Toyota launched Lexus; and Nissan launched Infiniti. They used entirely new names rather than their own names.

Product Mix Decisions

An organization with several product lines has a product mix. A **product mix (or product portfolio)** consists of all the product lines and items that a company markets. Some companies manage very complex product portfolios. For example, the Campbell Soup Company's product mix consists of three product lines: healthy beverages, baked snacks, and simple meals. Each product line consists of several sub-lines. For example, the simple meals line consists of soups, sauces, and pastas, and each of these has many individual items. Altogether, Campbell's product mix includes hundreds of items.

> **Product mix (or product portfolio)**
> The set of all product lines and items that a company markets.

A company's product mix has four important dimensions: width, length, depth, and consistency.

Product mix *depth* refers to the number of versions offered of each product in the line. Campbell's has a very deep product mix. For example, it makes and markets many kinds of soups, sauces, and other food products. Finally, the *consistency* of the product mix refers to how closely related the various product lines are in end use, production requirements, distribution channels, or some other way. Within each of their three major product lines, Campbell's products are fairly consistent in that they perform similar functions for buyers and go through the same distribution channels.

International Product Marketing Decisions

Product managers must make strategic decisions about marketing their products not only at home but also in international markets, where product strategy must be adapted to suit local markets. For example, Kraft Foods adapted its Oreos product and marketing strategies for the large Chinese market with great success:

> Kraft Foods had a problem—the Chinese weren't buying Oreos. The company's most popular cookie controlled a mere 3 percent of the Chinese cookie market. What could possibly be the problem?
>
> The first problem the marketers discovered was that Oreo wasn't competing in the right market segments. The billion-dollar Chinese biscuit market is segmented into sandwich biscuits, plain sweet biscuits, wafers, plain savoury cookies, soda crackers, and egg-roll biscuits— but Oreos were competing only in the sandwich biscuit category. The company needed to develop new product forms to compete in more categories.
>
> Then there was flavour. Kraft discovered that Chinese consumers thought our version of the Oreo was too sweet. The company also learned that the Chinese have what they call "heaty" foods and cooling foods for different times of the year. Cookies were considered a "heaty" food, so to boost summer sales Oreo developed a crème that had a cooling sensation when licked to create both a vanilla and a green-tea ice-cream-flavoured cookie. Fruits are also cooling foods, so after researching what fruit flavours Chinese consumers would like best, the company launched Oreo double fruits that put combinations like orange-mango and blueberry-raspberry between the familiar biscuits.
>
> The packaging needed adaptation, too. When Kraft found that its traditional package size was too big and expensive for the average Chinese consumer, it introduced smaller sizes so that the packages could get into smaller grocery stores and mom-and-pop stores. Finally, new advertising featuring Chinese celebrities like Yao Ming was created.

ChinaFotoPress/Getty Images

Exhibit 8.15 International product marketing decisions: Oreos weren't selling well in China until the marketers at Kraft adapted the product and its advertising to appeal to the Chinese.

The result? Oreo has increased its sandwich biscuit take to 46 percent and launched an Oreo wafer cookie that's nabbed 30 percent of the wafer market, boosting its overall share in China to almost 15 percent. That's the highest market share for Oreo anywhere in the world, including Canada and the United States.[16]

Listening to stories of international marketing blunders is part of the training process for junior marketers. Some of these stories have become legends—they may or may not be true, but there are lessons to be learned from them. There's the curling iron called the Mist Stick that didn't do well in Germany, where the word *mist* means "manure." Electrolux runs ads in Europe with the slogan "Nothing sucks like an Electrolux," which for obvious reasons don't work in Canada and the United States. Kentucky Fried Chicken's famous tagline, "Finger lickin' good," was translated in China to read "Eat your fingers off." (Not only that, but in China licking one's fingers is considered improper behaviour, and children get their hands slapped if they do it.) And Pampers diapers didn't sell well in Japan because the packaging had an image of a stork delivering a baby. In Japan, giant floating peaches bring babies to their parents.[17]

The only way to avoid these blunders is to have someone "on the ground" who understands the local culture. Marketing is about much more than just translating the words in an advertisement!

Services Marketing LO5

Services are considered a type of product because they are a marketing offer—but marketing offers that are not tangible hard goods require special considerations.

The *service sector*, as it's called, is the single most important industry in Canada's economy, accounting for nearly 70 percent of total gross domestic product. Whereas only about 4 million Canadians work in the goods-producing sector, about 14 million are employed in the service sector.[18] This sector includes all government services, hospitals, the military, police and fire departments, Canada Post, schools, colleges, and universities. It also includes not-for-profit organizations such as museums, charities, and churches. But the largest part of the service industry is the business services segment: for-profit companies that market and sell services to either consumers or businesses, and that develop and maintain profitable customer relationships. Business services include airlines, banks, hotels, insurance companies, consulting firms, law and accounting firms, entertainment companies, real estate firms, and advertising agencies.

Services also make up 15 percent of Canada's exports, and over the past decade services have accounted for three of Canada's fastest-growing exports: financial and insurance services, management services, and IT services. Jobs of the future, then, will be found at companies like Stantec:

> One of Canada's most international engineering firms is Edmonton-based Stantec. The company now employs 15 000 people, triple the number from a decade ago, in its operations worldwide. Launched in 1954, Stantec started off by supplying engineering services to Alberta's oil and gas industry; however, in the wake of a particularly severe downturn in the early 1980s, management made the decision to diversify into other sectors and countries, and it's been growing steadily ever since. Nearly half of Stantec's revenues are now generated outside Canada, with the lion's share of that coming from the United States, where a resurgent economy and rising demand for infrastructure such as municipal transit are expected to drive growth. In Asia and the Middle East, Stantec is eyeing what it believes is a significant opportunity created by soaring economic growth and an emerging middle class. Many developing countries are building, for the first time, everything from road systems and power grids to airports, and Stantec is betting it can show them how. For the past three years, revenue and net profit have risen at double-digit rates, and the company expects continued strong performance.

Exhibit 8.16 **The service sector:** Edmonton's Stantec is a services firm, consulting on engineering, architecture, interior design, and environmental sciences. Here, structural engineer Bruce Hopper of Stantec inspects the environmental systems at a school in Anchorage, Alaska.

Erik Hill/The Alaska Dispatch News/AP

> Yet, despite the impressive track record, the company rarely shows up in the media. Even more surprising, Stantec's business model would have been extremely difficult to implement just 20 years ago, when the Internet was only just becoming widely available. According to the Conference Board of Canada, "We didn't have the ability to communicate the data. Now, we're much more able to sell services in global markets; we can coordinate activities more easily, and we can communicate more quickly."[19]

Service intangibility means that services cannot be seen, tasted, felt, heard, or smelled before they are bought. For example, people undergoing cosmetic surgery cannot see the result before the purchase. Airline passengers have nothing but a ticket and the promise that they and their luggage will arrive safely at the intended destination, ideally at the same time. To reduce uncertainty, buyers look for "signals" of service quality. They draw conclusions about quality from the place, people, price, equipment, and communications that they can see.

Service intangibility
A major characteristic of services—they cannot be seen, tasted, felt, heard, or smelled before they are bought.

FIGURE 8.6 Special Characteristics of Services

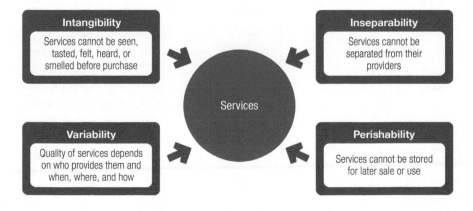

Intangibility: Services cannot be seen, tasted, felt, heard, or smelled before purchase

Inseparability: Services cannot be separated from their providers

Services

Variability: Quality of services depends on who provides them and when, where, and how

Perishability: Services cannot be stored for later sale or use

Therefore, the service provider's task is to make the service tangible in one or more ways and to send the right signals about quality. One analyst calls this *evidence management*, in which the service organization presents its customers with organized, honest evidence of its capabilities.

Physical goods are produced, then stored, later sold, and still later consumed. In contrast, services are first sold, then produced and consumed at the same time. In services marketing, the service provider is the product. **Service inseparability** means that services cannot be separated from their providers, whether the providers are people or machines. If a service employee provides the service, then the employee becomes a part of the service. Because the customer is also present as the service is produced, *provider–customer interaction* is a special feature of services marketing. Both the provider and the customer affect the service outcome.

Service variability means that the quality of services depends on who provides them as well as when, where, and how they are provided. For example, some hotels—say, Marriott—have reputations for providing better service than others. Still, within a given Marriott hotel, one registration-counter employee may be cheerful and efficient, whereas another standing just a metre away may be unpleasant and slow. Even the quality of a single Marriott employee's service varies according to his or her energy and frame of mind at the time of each customer encounter.

Service perishability means that services cannot be stored for later sale or use. Some salons charge customers for missed appointments because the service value existed only at that point and disappeared when the customer did not show up. The perishability of services is not a problem when demand is steady. However, when demand fluctuates, service firms often have difficult problems. For example, because of rush-hour demand, public transportation companies have to own much more equipment than they would if demand were even throughout the day. Service firms must therefore design strategies for producing a better match between demand and supply. Hotels and resorts charge lower prices in the off-season to attract more guests. And restaurants hire part-time employees to serve during peak periods.

Marketing Strategies for Service Firms

As we've seen, differentiation is very important for new products. But it's perhaps even more important for services because they are intangible. So, without having a physical product, service firms position themselves based on associations and advertising messages. Take banks, for example. RBC uses a brand icon named Arbie—a cartoon gentleman in a blue suit and a bowler hat—in all its advertising and signage. Arbie is seen interacting with bank offerings, and projects an affable personality. RBC also associates

Service inseparability
A major characteristic of services—they are produced and consumed at the same time and cannot be separated from their providers.

Service variability
A major characteristic of services—their quality may vary greatly, depending on who provides them and when, where, and how.

Service perishability
A major characteristic of services—they cannot be stored for later sale or use.

Courtesy Scotiabank

Exhibit 8.17 Positioning of service firms: Scotiabank's positioning as the bank that helps regular people do more with their money is reinforced with its slogan "You're richer than you think," which appears in all the bank's marketing communications.

itself with TIFF, the Toronto International Film Festival, and positions itself as being dedicated to culture. Scotiabank, on the other hand, uses "real people" in authentic situations to demonstrate that there is more to life than money. And RBC's association with hockey, through numerous sponsorships, extends its "enabling richer lives" value proposition through community support.

Because services differ from tangible products, they often require additional marketing approaches. These include understanding and managing the *service-profit chain*, and *internal marketing*.

The Service-Profit Chain In a service business, the customer and the frontline service employee *interact* to create the service. Effective interaction, in turn, depends on the skills of frontline service employees and on the support processes backing these employees. Because of this, successful service companies must focus their attention on *both* their customers and their employees. They understand the **service-profit chain**, which links service firm profits with employee and customer satisfaction. This chain consists of five links (see Figure 8.7):[20]

Service-profit chain
The chain that links service firm profits with employee and customer satisfaction.

- *Internal service quality:* superior employee selection and training, a quality work environment, and strong support for those dealing with customers, which results in . . .
- *Satisfied and productive service employees:* more satisfied, loyal, and hard-working employees, which results in . . .
- *Greater service value:* more effective and efficient customer value creation and service delivery, which results in . . .
- *Satisfied and loyal customers:* satisfied customers who remain loyal, repeat purchase, and refer other customers, which results in . . .
- *Healthy service profits and growth:* superior service firm performance.

An important aspect of the service-profit chain is **internal marketing**, or orienting and motivating customer-contact employees and supporting service people to work as a team to provide customer satisfaction. Part of the job for marketing managers in a service firm is to get everyone in the organization to be customer centred. In fact, internal marketing should precede external marketing.

Internal marketing
Orienting and motivating customer-contact employees and supporting service people to work as a team to provide customer satisfaction.

Today, as competition and costs increase, and as productivity and quality decrease, more service marketing sophistication is needed. Service companies face three major

FIGURE 8.7 The Service-Profit Chain

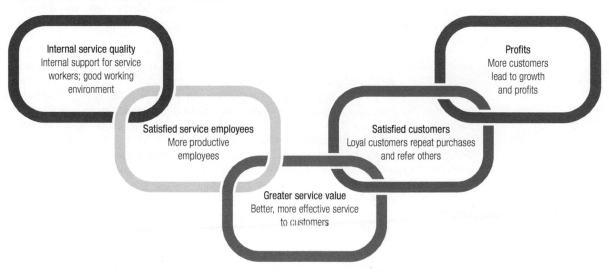

marketing tasks: They want to increase their *service differentiation*, *service quality*, and *service productivity*.

Managing Service Differentiation

In these days of intense price competition, service marketers often complain about the difficulty of differentiating their services from those of competitors. To the extent that customers view the services of different providers as similar, they care less about the provider than the price.

The solution to price competition is to develop a differentiated offer, delivery, and image—in other words, to establish a clear *positioning*. The offer can include innovative features that set one company's offer apart from competitors' offers. For example, in the last few years, banks, telecom companies, and other service providers have been rethinking the purpose of their storefronts, and have been redesigning them to not only attract customers, but to encourage them to stay longer. Many such stores now have comfortable chairs and sofas, free coffee, and play areas to keep children occupied while adults shop. At Rogers stores, one-on-one stations have warm, incandescent lights that give a feeling of home. BMO redesigned its teller counters—they're smaller and more comfortable, and the customer now has a bar stool to sit on—to reduce the confrontational nature of sales and the psychological distance between seller and customer. And some banks have hired greeters to welcome customers and answer basic questions.[21]

Managing Service Quality

A service firm can differentiate itself by delivering consistently higher quality than its competitors provide. Like manufacturers before them, most service industries have now joined the customer-driven quality movement. And like product marketers, service providers need to identify what target customers expect with regard to service quality.

Unfortunately, service quality is harder to define and judge than product quality. For instance, it is harder to agree on the quality of a haircut than on the quality of a hair dryer. Customer retention is perhaps the best measure of quality—a service firm's ability to hang on to its customers depends on how consistently it delivers value to them.

Top service companies set high service-quality standards. They watch service performance closely, both their own and that of competitors. They do not settle for merely good service; they strive for 100 percent defect-free service. These days, social media such as Facebook and Twitter can help companies root out and remedy customer dissatisfaction with service. Consider Marriott International:

> John Wolf, Marriott Hotel's director of public relations, heads a team of Marriott people who work full-time monitoring the company's Twitter feed and other social media. The team seeks out people who are complaining about problems they've had at Marriott. "We'd rather know that there's an issue than not know it, and we'd rather be given the opportunity to solve the problem," Wolf says. This strategy helps Marriott solve customer problems as they arise and recover previously dissatisfied customers. For example, when the team discovered an unhappy Marriott regular tweeting and blogging about an experience at a Marriott hotel that resulted in a ruined pair of shoes and big dry cleaning bill, they contacted him directly via Twitter, asking for his contact information. The next day, the disgruntled customer received a personal call from Marriott offering an explanation, a sincere apology, and a generous amount of reward points added to his account to be applied to future stays at Marriott. The result: a once-again happy and loyal customer who now blogged and tweeted to others about his positive experience.[22]

Managing Service Productivity

With their costs rising rapidly, service firms are under great pressure to increase service productivity. They can do so in several ways. They can train current employees better or hire new ones who will work harder or more skilfully. Or they can increase the quantity of their service by giving up some quality. The provider can "industrialize the service" by adding equipment and standardizing production, as in McDonald's assembly-line approach to fast-food retailing. Finally, the service provider can harness the power of technology. Although we often think of technology's power to save time and costs in manufacturing companies, it also has great—and often untapped—potential to make service workers more productive.

However, companies must avoid pushing productivity so hard that doing so reduces quality. Attempts to industrialize a service or cut costs can make a service company more efficient in the short run. But they can also reduce its longer-run ability to innovate, maintain service quality, or respond to consumer needs and desires. For example, some airlines have learned this lesson the hard way as they attempt to economize in the face of rising costs. They stopped offering even the little things for free—such as in-flight snacks—and began charging extra for everything from luggage check-in to aisle seats. The result is a plane full of resentful customers who avoid the airline whenever they can. In their attempts to improve productivity, these airlines mangled customer service.

In attempting to improve service productivity, companies must be mindful of how they create and deliver customer value. In short, they should be careful not to take the "service" out of service.

Pizza Burgers, Boneless Wings, and Other Foodie Game Changers

Conventional marketing wisdom, and theory, would suggest that you don't create products just to create products. Everything must be calculated; there must be demand from a known and defined market; and, most importantly, that demand must be convertible into profit. But if you're Boston Pizza and you're competing for market in the casual dining space, you sometimes have to think—and act—outside the box.

Of course, when your core product lends itself so well to fun-food creativity, it tends to take some of the risk out of the equation. In 2014, after paving the way with such innovative menu offerings as the Pizza Burger, BP took the concept of pizza and turned it inside out. With its cleverly named "Pizza Game Changers" campaign, Canada's leading family dining chain introduced its own new plays on pizza—like the Pizza Taco, Pizza Burger Sliders, and the, wait for it, Candied Bacon Carrot Cake—and then turned product development over to its customers.

As Joanne Forrester, vice-president of marketing, declared at the launch, "The Pizza Game Changers campaign allows Canadians to not only explore our limit-pushing new menu items and pizza innovations, but to have the opportunity to take the reins and tell us what pizza innovation they'd like to see next."

The campaign was a customer engagement and media hit, with global news coverage and viral social media attention doing more to enhance the "family fun" part of BP's brand than to increase sales. The winning game-changing idea? The pizza cake—an over-the-top multilayered round "cake" made entirely of pizza. Although the pizza cake never made it to BP's menu, it was made and served as a prize in a later Boston Pizza contest.

So while marketing theory and practical business process do require research and due diligence in order to minimize risk and maximize success, particularly with new product launches, sometimes unconventional thinking is required to reinforce what the brand stands for.

QUESTIONS

1. What was the goal of BP's "Pizza Game Changers" campaign: to sell pizzas or to build brand reputation? Support your response.
2. Despite the suggestion that the decision to add, say, Pizza Tacos to the BP menu was made spontaneously, in the name of "fun," it's probably more realistic to assume that there was some adherence to the new-product development process. At what stage in the process do you think the Pizza Taco was found to have potential where other ideas did not?

REVIEWING THE CONCEPTS

 LO1 Define *product* and describe and classify different types of product offerings.

Broadly defined, a *product* is anything that can be offered to a market for attention, acquisition, use, or consumption that might satisfy a want or need. Products include physical objects but also services, events, persons, places, organizations, ideas, or mixes of these entities. *Services* are products that consist of activities, benefits, or satisfactions offered for sale that are essentially intangible, such as banking, hotel, tax preparation, and home-repair services.

A product is more than a simple set of tangible features. Each product or service offered to customers can be viewed on three levels. The *core customer value* consists of the core problem-solving benefits that consumers seek when they buy a product. The *actual product* exists around the core and includes the quality level, features, design, brand name, and packaging. The *augmented product* is the actual product plus the various services and benefits offered with it, such as a warranty, free delivery, installation, and maintenance.

Products and services fall into two broad classes based on the types of consumers who use them. *Consumer products*—those bought by final consumers—are usually classified according to consumer shopping habits (convenience products, shopping products, specialty products, and unsought products). *Industrial products*—purchased for further processing or for use in conducting a business—include materials and parts, capital items, and supplies and services. Other marketable entities—such as organizations, persons, places, and ideas—can also be thought of as products.

 LO2 List and define the steps in the new-product development process and the major considerations in managing this process, and explain why new products fail.

The new-product development process consists of eight stages, starting with *idea generation*. A relatively new approach to idea generation that some companies are employing today is *crowdsourcing*—inviting broad communities of people, such as customers, employees, independent scientists and researchers, and even the public at large, into the new product innovation process. Next comes *idea screening*, which reduces the number of ideas based on the company's own criteria. Ideas that pass the screening stage continue through *product concept development*, in which a detailed version of the new-product idea is stated in meaningful consumer terms. In the next stage, *concept testing*, new-product concepts are tested with a group of target consumers to determine whether the concepts have strong consumer appeal. Strong concepts proceed to *marketing strategy development*, in which an initial marketing strategy for the new product is developed from the product concept. In the *business-analysis* stage, a review of the sales, costs, and profit projections for a new product is conducted to determine whether the new product is likely to satisfy the company's objectives. With positive results here, the ideas become more concrete through *product development* and *test marketing* and are finally launched during *commercialization*.

Despite this careful process, many new products fail, sometimes because they lack differentiation, and sometimes because they were not positioned properly, or the wrong market segment was targeted. The diffusion of innovations theory suggests that new products sometimes fail because they are unable to cross the gaps between the different market segments of innovators, early adopters, early majority, and late majority. The Technology Adoption Life Cycle suggests that, in the marketing of high-tech products, a chasm exists between the early adopters and the early majority, and that only new technology products that are able to cross that gap will be successful.

 LO3 Describe the stages of the product life cycle and how marketing strategies change during the product's life cycle.

Each product has a *life cycle* marked by a changing set of problems and opportunities. The sales of the typical product follow an S-shaped curve made up of five stages. The cycle begins with the *product development stage* in which the company finds and develops a new-product idea. The *introduction stage* is marked by slow growth and low profits as the product is distributed to the market. If successful, the product enters a *growth stage*, which offers rapid sales growth and increasing profits. Next comes a *maturity stage* in which sales growth slows down and profits stabilize. Finally, the product enters a *decline stage* in which sales and profits dwindle. The company's task during this stage is to recognize the decline and to decide whether it should maintain, harvest, or drop the product.

In the *introduction stage*, the company must choose a launch strategy consistent with its intended product positioning. Much money is needed to attract distributors, build inventories, and inform consumers of the new product to achieve the trial phase. In the *growth stage*, companies continue to educate potential consumers and distributors. In addition, the company works to stay ahead of the competition and sustain rapid market growth by improving product quality, adding new product features and models, entering new market segments and distribution channels, shifting advertising from building product awareness to building product conviction and purchase, and lowering prices at the right time to attract new buyers.

In the *maturity stage*, companies continue to invest in maturing products and consider modifying the market, the product, and the marketing mix. When *modifying the market*, the company attempts to increase the consumption of the current product. When *modifying the product*, the company changes some of the product's characteristics—such as quality, features, or style—to attract new users or inspire more usage. When *modifying the marketing mix*, the company works to improve sales by changing one or more of the marketing-mix elements. Once the company recognizes that a product has entered the *decline stage*, management must decide whether to *maintain* the brand without change, hoping that competitors will drop out of the market; *harvest* the product, reducing costs and trying to maintain sales; or *drop* the product, selling it to another firm or liquidating it at salvage value.

LO4   Describe the decisions companies make regarding their individual products and services, product lines, and product mixes.

Individual product decisions involve product attributes, packaging, labelling, and product support services. *Product attribute* decisions involve product quality, features, and style and design. *Packaging* provides many key benefits, such as protection, economy, convenience, and promotion. Today, many marketers are exploring options for *sustainable packaging*—packaging that meets the requirements of the product while minimizing the environmental,

economic, and social impacts of the product and its package. Package decisions often include designing *labels*, which identify, describe, and possibly promote the product. Companies also develop *product support services* that enhance customer service and satisfaction and safeguard against competitors.

Most companies produce a product line rather than a single product. A *product line* is a group of products that are related in function, customer-purchase needs, or distribution channels. *Line stretching* involves extending a line downward, upward, or in both directions to occupy a gap that might otherwise be filled by a competitor. In contrast, *line filling* involves adding items within the present range of the line. All product lines and items offered to customers by a particular seller make up the *product mix*. The mix can be described by four dimensions: width, length, depth, and consistency. These dimensions are the tools for developing the company's product strategy.

When making international product marketing decisions, managers must make strategic decisions about how to adapt their product strategy to suit local markets.

LO5   Identify the four characteristics that affect the marketing of services and the additional marketing considerations that services require.

Services are characterized by four key characteristics: they are *intangible*, *inseparable*, *variable*, and *perishable*. Each characteristic poses problems and marketing requirements. Marketers work to find ways to make the service more tangible, to increase the productivity of providers who are inseparable from their products, to standardize the quality in the face of variability, and to improve demand movements and supply capacities in the face of service perishability.

Good service companies focus attention on *both* customers and employees. They understand the *service-profit chain*, which links service firm profits with employee and customer satisfaction. Services marketing strategy calls not only for external marketing but also for *internal marketing* to motivate employees. To succeed, service marketers must create *competitive differentiation*, offer high *service quality*, and find ways to increase *service productivity*.

MyMarketingLab

Study, practise, and explore real marketing situations with these helpful resources:

- **Interactive Lesson Presentations:** Work through interactive presentations and assessments to test your knowledge of marketing concepts.
- **Study Plan:** Check your understanding of chapter concepts with self-study quizzes.
- **Dynamic Study Modules:** Work through adaptive study modules on your computer, tablet, or mobile device.
- **Simulations:** Practise decision-making in simulated marketing environments.

DISCUSSION QUESTIONS

1. Choose a company whose products you are familiar with. If you were a marketing manager at that company, what specific sources might you turn to for new product ideas? How might the company's website be used to interact with the market to generate new product ideas? Brainstorm your own new product ideas for this company.

2. Yoplait markets a line of products called GoGurt, and Danone has a line called Danino. Both of these product lines are targeted to children. Visit the companies' websites to find the newest children's product. Now, assume the role of the product manager responsible for that product. You have been asked to modify the market to make the products appeal to adults—without changing either the product itself or the packaging. Come up with a plan for testing the product with 25- to 45-year-olds. What factors would be critical to your test? What questions would you ask the testers?

3. If you were a marketing manager at Tim Hortons' head office, what sort of internal and interactive marketing programs would you develop?

4. Discuss how the four characteristics of services—intangibility, inseparability, variability, and perishability—affect Air Canada. What marketing initiatives could Air Canada employ to try to mitigate the negative effects of these characteristics as much as possible?

CRITICAL THINKING EXERCISES

1. Choose three of the products mentioned in this chapter. Which stage of the product life cycle is each of these products in? Explain how you were able to identify the stage. How long do you think it will be before each product enters the next stage of the life cycle?

2. Think of a product that you believe is an example of a fad. What evidence can you find that supports your theory? Explain why you believe that the product won't last in the market.

3. Visit the Product Development and Management Association's site (www.pdma.org) to learn about this organization. Click on "OCI Award" in the "About PDMA" dropdown menu. Describe this award and the criteria used when granting it, and discuss one company that has received the OCI Award.

4. Find an example of a recent (within the last few years) new-to-the-world consumer product. Explain how the company implemented the four Ps in launching the product and report on the product's success since the launch.

ONLINE, MOBILE, AND SOCIAL MEDIA MARKETING

You've heard of mobile Wi-Fi hotspots, but one truly is mobile—your car. Automobile manufacturers Audi, Ford, Nissan, and General Motors are equipping cars with 10-inch screens and Internet access. Cadillac's XTS includes an iPad-like touchscreen and voice commands so that you can keep in touch with your friends on Facebook. General Motors offers 4G mobile broadband technology. In short, cars are being transformed into virtual smartphones. There are, of course, concerns that these new features will cause a spike in accidents owing to increased driver distraction. Some have proposed that the devices be programmed to work only when the car is in park. Such guidelines are only suggestions, however, leaving car manufacturers to include whatever they think customers want in their vehicles. The industry's argument is that these new gadgets are safer than the handheld ones drivers are already using in their cars. Automakers claim that there will be even fewer buttons than currently found in cars, possibly resulting in greater safety for drivers and passengers.

QUESTIONS

1. Describe the core, actual, and augmented levels of product associated with an automobile. What level does the mobile Wi-Fi system represent? Explain.

2. Research your favourite car brand and find out what it offers in terms of in-car technology. Have any modifications been made to the actual product in order to comply with safety concerns?

THINK LIKE A MARKETING MANAGER

Dell revolutionized the personal computer industry in the 1990s by giving consumers what they wanted at the time: commodity components they needed without having to buy the ones they didn't need. The focus was on functionality, not on style. Now that all personal computers are functional, and prices have come down, computer makers compete on the basis of features and design. A few years ago Dell offered a line of notebooks with colourful shells. Then came the Ultrabook, a slim-design laptop that converts to a tablet. Next was the Inspiron 2-in-1 series. The core product, computing and connectivity, has never changed; it's only been improved upon. Dell also offers many options to augment its products.

QUESTIONS

1. As a consumer, what do you value most in your personal computing devices? Do you own a laptop, or a tablet, or both? Talk to your friends and find out whether they value the same thing, or whether they name other features or benefits as most important. How could the marketers at Dell use this information to develop its next new personal computing device?

2. Dell once marketed a line of Inspiron laptops in colours that ranged from pink to "spring green." Apple did the same with Mac desktops and laptops. Do you think device colour is a feature consumers value? Were coloured computers a fashion, a fad, or a style? (Your answer depends on whether you think they'll come back.)

3. Other computer manufacturers offer similar two-in-one products. Find out what similar products are available. What is Dell's point of differentiation?

4. What else could Dell do to make its computers more stylish?

MARKETING ETHICS

You may be using a book you purchased or borrowed from another student. People sell or share books all the time, but not e-books! With the growth of electronic readers, such as Amazon's Kindle, buying electronic books is easy and growing in popularity. But purchasers of e-books don't have the same rights as those purchasing physical books. Some consumers found out that it's just as easy for sellers to take them back as it is for buyers to get them. For instance, Amazon.com realized that it didn't have the proper rights to sell certain books—such as George Orwell's *1984*—and used its wireless technology to delete them from its customers' Kindle e-readers. While purchases were refunded, some called the company an Orwellian "Big Brother" because the deletion was done without their knowledge. Imagine if you purchased *1984* and tried to read it right before the test, only to learn that it had disappeared from your Kindle. Owning an e-book is much like licensing software, with digital rights management software embedded within it in order to prevent sharing and selling. And yet such software confuses consumers and limits the number of devices that can play a single e-book.

QUESTIONS

1. How would you classify e-books—as a tangible good, an experience, or a service? Explain your choice.

2. What new developments have there been in e-books since the Amazon recall incident?

3. Do you think consumers should be able to do whatever they want with an e-book once they purchase it, just as they can with a tangible book?

MARKETING BY THE NUMBERS

When introducing a new product, it's usually not easy to determine at what price it should be offered. At the very least, however, a marketer must understand the costs associated with producing the product and set the price at some level above those costs. For example, suppose that a manufacturer of lawn mowers incurs a cost of $75 for each mower it produces, and that it produces a total of 1 million mowers each year. Fixed costs for this company are $5 million.

QUESTIONS

1. What is the unit cost for each mower this company produces?

2. If the manufacturer desires a markup of 60 percent on sales, at what price should this product be sold to a reseller such as a wholesaler or a distributor?

BRINGING A NEW PRODUCT TO MARKET: THE STORY OF THE NISSAN LEAF

In August 2009, the Nissan Motor Company unveiled the Nissan LEAF, the world's first affordable, zero-emission car powered by a lithium-ion battery. Three years later the LEAF became the best-selling electric vehicle of all time. How did this revolutionary new car become so successful so quickly? The secret lies in the years of careful planning that went into bringing the LEAF to market.

The name itself makes a significant statement about the car. Just as leaves purify the air in nature, so the Nissan LEAF purifies mobility by taking emissions out of the driving experience. This medium-sized hatchback has ample cargo space and seating for five adults. Its battery, which generates 107 horsepower and 207 lb-ft of torque, can be fully charged in seven hours with a 240-volt home charging dock—although with a quick charger, it can achieve 80 percent capacity in only 26 minutes. And when fully charged, the LEAF has a range of 160 kilometres.

Let's start with the story of how this new product was built.

PRODUCTION BEGINS

Production of the Nissan LEAF began in October 2010 at a vehicle assembly plant in Oppama, Japan. The LEAF's lithium-ion battery modules are manufactured at the Automotive Energy Supply Corporation (AESC) operation in Zama, Japan—a joint venture of Nissan Motor Co., Ltd. and NEC Corporation. The battery modules, which contain four battery cells, are assembled at Zama and then shipped to the Oppama facility, where 48 of them are assembled into the electric car's battery pack. The LEAF's batteries are also produced in Portugal, France, the U.K., and the U.S. Nissan began construction of a manufacturing facility in Smyrna, Tennessee, in early 2010. It is now one of the largest vehicle battery manufacturing plants in North America, capable of producing 200 000 advanced-technology batteries annually.

The battery plant is located adjacent to Nissan's existing vehicle assembly plant in Tennessee, which was retooled to accommodate production of the LEAF. Part of the assembly line had to be modified to mount battery modules at the stage of production where fuel tanks are traditionally installed; motors and inverters, meanwhile, are mounted at the point where engines are installed in gasoline-powered vehicles. The Tennessee vehicle assembly plant builds LEAFs for North America, and has the ability to produce 150 000 electric cars each year.

The electric motor that powers the Nissan LEAF has more than one mile of copper wiring inside. It takes more time to assemble an electric motor than it does a gas engine, and Nissan says it takes about 25 people per shift to ensure that an electric motor is made properly. At first the motors were assembled only in Japan, but today they're also produced in Decherd, Tennessee, about 100 kilometres from Smyrna. Adam Reed, Nissan's globally certified trainer for eMotor production, spent two three-month stints at Nissan's global headquarters in Japan learning how to sculpt these motors. He now supports the team in Decherd that began building the motors for the 2013 Nissan LEAF, which was assembled in Smyrna.

Another key requirement of bringing the Nissan LEAF to market was to develop charging systems—and to continually improve on them. A year after production on the LEAF began, Nissan and 4R Energy Corporation (itself a joint venture established by Nissan and Sumitomo Corporation) began testing a new charging system that combines a solar power generation system with high-capacity lithium-ion batteries. With the new charging system, electricity is generated through solar cells installed at Nissan's global headquarters, and is stored in lithium-ion batteries. With seven charging stations (three quick charge, four normal charge) located on headquarter grounds, the total electricity that can be generated and stored is equivalent to fully charging about 1800 Nissan LEAFs annually. This new system will enable electric vehicles, which don't emit any CO_2 when driven, to be charged through a completely renewable energy source, resulting in a cycle whose total CO_2 emissions is zero.

A quick charger is also available for sale at Nissan parts companies throughout Japan. The quick-charging unit retains the high performance of the current quick charger manufactured by Nissan, but its smaller size takes up less space and enables easier installation. The quick charger costs less than 1 million yen (about $11 000), which is actually less than the "regular" charging unit. The charging units are marketed both to individual customers and to buildings and other public facilities, such as rental car operations.

Because there's no traditional engine, the LEAF is ultra-quiet (for safety reasons, a sound had to be added so that pedestrians could hear the car coming). The car is also ultra–high tech. The instrument panel provides the driver with regular updates on range and driving efficiency, and using a system called CARWINGS, the driver can communicate with the car via smartphone and the LEAF app. With the app, drivers can check the state of the battery charge, begin charging, and check when the battery charge is complete. They can also see the estimated driving range and turn the climate control system on or off. The car includes an IT system complete with an onboard remote-controlled timer that can be programmed to recharge batteries. Nissan views the IT system as a partner for the driver and an enhancement for the passengers. It's also an important aspect of the new product's positioning.

MARKET POSITIONING

The LEAF is positioned in the Canadian market as the first mass market, affordable, fully electric car that offers environmentally conscious drivers a zero-emission option for real environmental impact. It provides 90 percent of Canadians with the range needed for their daily commutes, and at the same time it offers plenty of room, comfort, and style, and an uncompromising driving experience. The environmentally friendly theme is communicated through the car's name, the "Aqua Globe" body colour of the introductory model, and the interior blue dashboard highlights and instrument illumination.

While the product developers in Japan worked on producing the LEAF, the marketing team at Nissan Canada focused on preparing the Canadian market for its first fully electric car. The first step was to establish relationships with energy producers such as Hydro-Québec and governments such as the City of Toronto and the Government of Manitoba, so that all could work together to plan for the necessary charging infrastructure and otherwise pave the way for the arrival of electric vehicles on Canada's streets. Nissan Canada lobbied governments to put incentives in place to promote the adoption of electric cars. A year before the first LEAF was sold in Canada, Kathleen Wynne, at the time Ontario's transportation minister, announced provincial incentives between $5000 and $8500 (depending on battery size) to promote electric vehicles in Ontario. In all, Nissan formed partnerships with approximately 100 governments, cities, and other organizations to advance the deployment of electric vehicles worldwide.

Then there was the task of getting Nissan dealers ready to sell and service the LEAF. The project began with the certification of 27 selected retailers located in regions where Nissan had established partnerships with local governments. In order to be certified, these dealers had to pass a rigorous training process and complete modifications to their sales and service departments. Special lifts and pallets to handle the battery, along with EV-skilled technicians, are required to service the car. Still, with no engine, no oil, and very few moving parts, the Nissan LEAF requires much less maintenance and service than a vehicle with an internal combustion engine. Eventually, all Nissan dealers across Canada will be EV-certified.

One of the most important marketing programs for the LEAF in Canada is the online reservation system. Electric cars aren't for everyone—they're just for most people—but until charging systems are as common as gas stations, consumers who want a Nissan LEAF must live in the vicinity of a certified dealer, and in a municipality whose government and utilities are making preparations for electric vehicles. Interested prospective customers must register online at nissan.ca/leaf and answer a few basic questions to make sure they're eligible to own a LEAF. Once qualified, these customers are given a "reservation" to purchase the car. Nissan prepared to release around 600 Nissan LEAFs on the Canadian market through several waves of such reservations.

THE LEAF DEBUTS

In October 2009 the LEAF made its North American debut in Los Angeles. Nissan announced a 22-city promotional tour that included a stop in Vancouver, and so that December, the first Nissan LEAF rolled into Canada for a brief visit. Nissan Canada executives and representatives from the Province of British Columbia, the City of Vancouver, and BC Hydro were all present to commemorate the occasion—and to establish a partnership agreement that would see British Columbia as the initial launch point for the Nissan LEAF in Canada when it was rolled out to the market two years later.

The finished, market-ready LEAF was first viewed at the Montreal Auto Show in January 2011. Shortly afterward, details about Canadian pricing, models, and trim availability were announced. In Canada, the 2011 LEAF started at $38 395 and was available in two trim levels: the SV base model with a cold-weather package, 16-inch alloy wheels, LED headlights, Bluetooth, XM Satellite radio, and USB ports; and the upgraded SL model, priced about $2000 higher, with a rear spoiler, solar panel charger, and fog lights. That April, at the Green Living Show in Toronto, Canadians were allowed to test-drive the car for the first time. Throughout the fall of 2011 Nissan Canada orchestrated a cross-Canada tour, allowing Canadians to test-drive and learn more about the LEAF at certified dealer locations. The Drive Electric Tour began in Montreal and ended in Vancouver in late October, stopping at all 27 LEAF certified dealers across the country for one or two days each.

The first Canadian sales happened in the summer of 2011, when PowerStream, an electricity distribution company in Ontario, purchased two of the vehicles for its fleet. Two months later the first Canadian consumer took possession of a LEAF. Ricardo Borba of Ottawa, a 44-year old electric engineer and software developer with IBM, was the first person in Canada to place a Nissan LEAF order. "My family and I were starting to look for a new car last year when the Deepwater Horizon oil spill occurred and prompted us to think about alternatives to gas-powered vehicles," said Borba. "We considered several options, and the Nissan LEAF was the one that best fits our needs. It's all-electric and looks and drives just like a regular car with five seats, ample cargo space, and loaded with high-tech features. It's smooth, quiet, and has incredible acceleration. In other words, it's fun to drive!"

The promotions didn't end with the first sales, however. In 2012 Nissan Canada sponsored the second annual National Tree Day, awarding a 2012 Nissan LEAF SL as the grand prize for a new "Tree Canada" contest that asked Canadians to "Get Treemotional" by submitting an image of their favourite tree and explaining what makes that tree special in 50 words or less. Nissan Canada participated in the kick-off ceremonies, tree-planting events across the country, and Nissan LEAF test drives. And that fall, Toronto International Film Festival attendees were offered free rides in two Nissan LEAF taxis based in the Entertainment District. The taxis were driven by professional drivers, and winners of free rides were chosen at random from tweets sent with the hashtag #LEAFTAXI.

Social media played a role as well. Nissan Canada had launched its LEAF consumer website in April 2010, promoting it with a 60-second commercial that aired in movie theatres across Canada. A year later, the Canadian LEAF Facebook page opened with a promotion that saw 40 lucky fans invited to a ride-and-drive event held at Nissan Canada's head office in Mississauga. Around the same time, the LEAF Twitter account (@NissanLEAF_CAN) began to share up-to-date news and information on all things related to the LEAF's arrival in Canada. A dedicated moderator from Nissan was assigned to manage the Facebook and Twitter accounts and to engage in conversation with and answer questions from fans across Canada.

Perhaps the largest social media promotion was 2012's "The Big Turn On," Nissan's ambitious online campaign designed to get 1 million people worldwide "turned on" to electric vehicles. The initial plan was to reach the 1 million mark in 100 days, but the campaign so captured the imagination of the public that the milestone was reached 15 days ahead of schedule. As well as encouraging car drivers from France, Germany, the Netherlands, and the U.K. to consider the benefits of zero-emission driving, the campaign demonstrated that the Nissan LEAF is safe, environmentally friendly, and economical to run, with the range between charges being easily sufficient for the vast majority of daily trips. At the end of the campaign, the city with the most drivers turned on to electric vehicles was given 30 Nissan quick chargers, while the individual who encouraged the most people to turn on won a Nissan LEAF.

Many promotional events were held in Europe in conjunction with The Big Turn On. In theory, the LEAF goes just as fast backward as it does forward because of the direct drive from the electric motor to its wheels. That theory was tested and proven at the U.K.'s Goodwood Festival of Speed, where professional stunt driver Terry Grant raced the LEAF backward up the famous Hill Climb course, covering the distance in 1 minute and 37.02 seconds at an average speed of 88.5 kilometres per hour, and setting a new Guinness World Record for the fastest time over a distance of one mile in reverse.

CUSTOMER SATISFACTION

By February 2013, 50 000 cars had been sold worldwide. Within a year the LEAF was available in 17 European countries, with more than 7000 cars on the road. In the U.S., after Hurricane Sandy devastated the east coast and made gasoline a rare commodity, LEAF owners were able to charge their cars and keep moving. A LEAF owner in Spain clocked up over 43 000 kilometres in one year, far beyond an average annual mileage and a testament to the car's reliability. The LEAF has an extraordinary customer satisfaction rating of over 95 percent, the highest of any Nissan vehicle. And it's quiet: Portuguese criminals need to take extra care if they want to avoid being caught red-handed— because Portugal's PSP (Polícia de Segurança Pública), the security force responsible for policing the large urban areas of the country, has a fleet of LEAFs that will allow them to arrive at the scene of a crime in near silence.

Not only do consumers worldwide seem to be loving their LEAFs, but the car has also won numerous awards and accolades. The LEAF was recognized as the most fuel-efficient vehicle in the mid-size class for 2012, 2013, 2014, and 2015 by Natural Resources Canada. It was named 2011 European Car of the Year and World Car of the Year. Also in 2011, the European New Car Assessment Programme (Euro NCAP) awarded the LEAF the highest level of car safety following its performance in the independent organization's stringent crash tests. The zero-emission vehicle received a five-star rating, the first electric vehicle ever to earn this distinction. Similarly, in the U.S., the LEAF earned a five-star overall vehicle rating for safety as part of the National Highway Traffic Safety Administration's New Car Assessment Program (NCAP)—the first electric vehicle to earn this distinction from the program—

and was also awarded a "Top Safety Pick" rating from the Insurance Institute for Highway Safety. All of this allows marketers to add a new element to the car's positioning: The LEAF isn't just the most innovative car on the planet; it's also one of the safest.

Source: All information provided by Nissan Canada.

QUESTIONS FOR DISCUSSION

1. Research the latest news about the Nissan LEAF in the Canadian market. Have any new features been added since the car was launched as a new product? Has the style changed? Find out what colours the car is available in. How do you think automobile marketers decide which colours to offer?

2. Describe the core, actual, and augmented product.

3. Which stage of the product life cycle is the Nissan LEAF in right now? Explain.

4. Make a list of all the countries where the Nissan LEAF is available. How have marketers adapted the product to suit these markets?

5. When the LEAF first came to market it was promoted as the world's first affordable zero-emission car. Is this still the product's point of differentiation today?

Steve Russell/Toronto Star /Newscom

AFTER STUDYING THIS CHAPTER, YOU SHOULD BE ABLE TO

1. define and describe the concept of a brand

2. explain the roles of logos, brand personality, brand status, and brand equity in building brands

3. list and describe the major strategic and ongoing management decisions marketers must make about brands

4. summarize the ways marketers can engage consumers through brand communications

5. describe the roles of storytelling, branded content, branded entertainment, social media, and brand advocates in brand communications

Brand Strategy and Management

PREVIEWING THE CONCEPTS

In this chapter, we'll study how companies create, develop, and manage brands—but what, exactly, is a brand? Many people think that a brand is just a logo, but it is so much more than that. A strong brand gives meaning to a name; it stands for something in the mind of the consumer. Some marketers say that a brand is the sum total of what the company stands for.

The first step in creating a brand is giving it a name. Once the brand is named, marketers can begin positioning the brand, developing the brand's personality, and telling the brand story—a process that, if you're lucky, never ends. Even after 30 years, the marketers responsible for the President's Choice brand have new stories to tell, using traditional marketing communications and new channels, like social media, about the meaning of President's Choice:

PRESIDENT'S CHOICE: REINVENTING A 30-YEAR-OLD BRAND

The TV commercial opens with a shot of a dense tropical forest, and a hand pulling back the leaves to reveal a pineapple. The voiceover says, "Who thought to bite *this*?" If you think you recognize the voice, you probably do—it's Galen Weston, executive chairman and president of Loblaw Companies Limited. After posing further questions—"Who discovered you could eat *these*?" (mushrooms); "Who thought, I bet *that* would taste great?" (lobsters); and "Who figured *this* out? (popcorn)—the spot concludes with Weston on camera encapsulating the company's vision: "If you don't search for more, you'll never find it."

Loblaw's new "Crave More" campaign was designed to modernize the brand for increasingly food-savvy Canadians. The company describes Crave More as "the most ambitious and comprehensive campaign in [our] history: a modified brand position, an innovative television and print campaign, and a reimagined digital and social media presence."

With more than 2300 corporate, franchised, and associate-owned locations, Loblaw Companies Limited is Canada's largest food and pharmacy retailer. And with approximately 192 000 full- and part-time employees, it's also one of the country's largest private sector employers.

Loblaw owns the President's Choice brand, born in 1984. It was conceived by then president Dave Nichol, who was constantly on the lookout for new additions to the company's lineup of No Name generic store-brand products. Legend has it that, when Loblaw's

✔●―**Practice** on MyMarketingLab

Assessing the Cannibalization Risk

✔●―**Practice** on MyMarketingLab

Understanding Market Share by Volume and by Sales

✔●―**Practice** on MyMarketingLab

Calculating Brand Equity

buyers were working on a new high-grade coffee product, they suggested it shouldn't be offered in the traditional No Name yellow packaging, which had come to connote lower quality. They decided to call the coffee President's Blend, which later evolved into President's Choice—the logo for which is Nichol's own handwriting.

For more than 30 years, the President's Choice brand has stood for discovering new tastes. The trailblazing Insider's Report first invited Canadians to discover and celebrate food; The Decadent line introduced a higher standard of richness to elevate what a chocolate experience could be; Memories Of products brought global flavours to Canadian kitchens; PC G.R.E.E.N. (now a quarter-century old) was Canada's first eco label; PC Organics offers Canada's widest selection of fresh and grocery organic products; the PC Blue Menu brand combines healthier formulations with great taste; and PC Free From meats are free of antibiotics and hormones. And those are just some of the trademarks and registered trademarks owned by the corporation.

"At a time of bologna sandwiches, Dave Nichol travelled the world and brought these foods to Canadians," says Uwe Stueckmann, Loblaw's senior vice-president of marketing. But consumers have changed: After three decades, they've become adept at discovering their own new foods. So what do you do next? Why, encourage them to crave more, of course.

The strategy behind the Crave More campaign is to strengthen the positioning of the President's Choice brand as innovative, appealing to food-savvy Canadians. And it's more than just an advertising campaign; it's a philosophy. It even applied to the company's agencies and media vendors—Loblaw issued an RFP (request for proposal) to Canada's largest media companies and invited them to its Brampton, Ontario, headquarters to present ideas on how to bring to fruition the company's internal mantra: "The new, the next, the never been done."

The Crave More launch was orchestrated by ZenithOptimedia, after a five-month competitive process with agencies vying for Loblaw's business based on the brief, which said, "The time has come to evolve or even reinvent the PC brand."

The media winner was Rogers, and the reward was a major piece of the largest marketing campaign in Loblaw's history. The campaign launched with a national social media effort—Canada's ultimate Twitter party. The Twitter handles of various Rogers media properties all tweeted about food using the hashtag #PCdiscoveries (sample tweet from @BTEdmonton: "Along with @PresChoice we're asking 'Fill in the blank, I can't go without_____in the AM?"). #PCdiscoveries was a trending topic in Canada that day.

Next was a three-and-a-half-minute version of the first Crave More commercial, a longer version of which aired during the season premiere of *Modern Family* on City TV. That long spot (preceded by "snipes," or graphic overlays, on the lower third of the screen during the show's first segment) took over the entire first commercial break with a mixture of traditional brand-sell spots and a 60-second content piece. The piece told the story of PC's New World EVOO Extra Virgin Olive Oil, which comes from South America, and connected it to the new brand mantra: If you don't search for more, you'll never find it. During the episode there was a live cutaway to a *Modern Family* viewing party being held at the Loblaw store in Toronto's Maple Leaf Gardens.

Future media executions will include everything from Rogers' radio stations to its various consumer magazines. The PC chefs, for example, are working with the *Chatelaine* test kitchen to create recipes that will be featured in future issues of the magazine, while a series of special-edition covers are also in the works. Other Rogers-owned consumer titles, including *Today's Parent* and *Maclean's*, will also feature President's Choice–related content. The campaign includes billboards and banners that pose questions such as, "What if organic was a commitment, not just a trend?" and "Why can't Wednesday night taste like Saturday night?"

The creative production of the Crave More TV commercials was done by Toronto ad agency John St. The ads capture the passion for finding the new and the next, and help communicate the new positioning to foodies and foodie wannabes. They convey the idea that anyone can be a foodie if you're curious and willing to try new things. And it's on trend with today's consumer behaviour: "There's just this discussion and fascination about food that is going on across every demographic," said Angus Tucker, partner and executive creative director at John St. "It's almost what people talk about instead of the weather. Everybody is yakking about food."

Anchoring the new brand positioning is a revamped President's Choice website (PC.ca). Instead of just providing information about PC products, the site has become a social network of sorts for home chefs and food lovers across the country. Created by SapientNitro, based in Boston, the new Crave More site is based around one idea—that Canadians should expect more from their food.

Loblaw also created a new internal team dedicated entirely to content marketing. Their job is to focus on storytelling through articles and videos: Instead of telling consumers about the latest food trends, the stories will speak to the trends shoppers are already discussing. Website editorial is constantly updated, and users can share via Twitter and Instagram and on the PC Pinterest page. "Discoveries" is a community forum feature where food enthusiasts can engage in conversations. The first eight weeks after launch, the communities and Discoveries platforms had more than 60 000 views. Product views were up 45 percent and recipe views were up 174 percent over the previous year. And, just three days after introduction, the #pcdiscoveries hashtag had a potential reach of over 101 000 000.

"It's a very different approach to marketing. It's no longer about 'We've invented this new product and you can try it,'" Stueckmann says. "It's about engaging in a real conversation about food with consumers." The content on the site and on Loblaw's social media channels will be determined by what people are talking about. If beets are a hot topic, for example, the retailer will serve up images, recipes, polls, and information about the root vegetable. If people are wondering about gluten-free Thanksgiving meals, Loblaw will respond.

Loblaw also partnered with Google Canada to build a Food Pulse Index, which tracks online conversations about food across Canada. It will publish the results on a regularly updated map on the corporate website, which will show food trends by region. Information gathered from the Google trends will influence not just marketing but also product development at the retail giant. This new social strategy puts President's Choice squarely in the middle of the discussion, not only at the supermarket or around the dinner table, but online. The Food Pulse Index is the first of its kind to utilize Google Canada search insights to track trends in food nationally and by province.

"You have an environment where food is so important nowadays," says Stueckmann. "The conversation about food is louder than ever, so the time is right for us to take a leadership role."

Overall, Loblaw's new approach to marketing the PC brand focuses on its appeal to a certain lifestyle—and to those who aspire to that lifestyle. In the past, PC was marketed as a product-focused brand. A year after the launch of the Crave More campaign, Loblaw was named one of the top 10 marketers of the year by *Marketing* magazine for having staked new ground in media integration and custom executions. The company says the approach they took with Crave More will influence its entire media buying model going forward. The PC.ca website traffic has increased more than threefold, and sales have increased every quarter. Said Galen Weston, "This is an exciting beginning for what we expect to be a sustained campaign."[1]

IN CHAPTER 8 we learned that when developing a new product, marketers must make many important decisions about features, style, and design; level of quality; packaging; and labelling. In addition to these important decisions about how the product looks, feels, and works, marketers must make decisions about branding—which has more to do with how customers *perceive* the product. Brands have personality, brands have value, brands position the product in the mind of the consumer and perform many other important functions in product marketing—and yet a brand is not the same as a product. In this chapter, we'll look more closely at the abstract concepts of brands and branding, and how they are applied in marketing.

What Is a Brand? LO1

Brand
A name, symbol, icon, design, or a combination of these, that identifies the maker or marketer of a product.

Perhaps the most distinctive skill of professional marketers is their ability to build and manage brands. The basic definition of a **brand** is a name, symbol, icon, design, or a combination of these, that identifies the maker or marketer of a product. But truly understanding what a brand is, and the important role it plays in marketing, is far from simple. Says one advertising expert, "What's a brand? You realize that no two people, let alone two marketers, agree on the answer. It's a word, a metaphor, an analogy, a concept, or some sort of thing with an existence and personality."[2]

A brand is not a logo, not a corporate identity system, and not a product. Branding expert Marty Neumeier, author of two books on the subject, says, "Marketing people often talk about managing their brands, but what they usually mean is managing their products. To manage a brand is to manage something much less tangible—an aura, an invisible layer of meaning that surrounds the product."[3] That said, a brand name may identify a company, one of its products, or a product line. If used for the firm as a whole, the preferred term is *trade name*—but a brand is much more than just a trade name. Brands are powerful. Brands have status and value. Brands have personality, and so they involve our emotions as consumers, and as human beings. But for all that, a brand is not real. It can't be touched, or pointed at. A brand is nothing more than an idea—and for the biggest brands in the world, it is precisely that idea that generates most of the company's revenue.

Even though the idea of a brand has been around for thousands of years, in today's information-rich modern society, where each purchase requirement offers a multitude of choices, we no longer have time to make comparisons based on features and benefits. We base our choices on more symbolic attributes, like what kind of people buy it, and what other people are saying about it. In other words, we make our purchase decisions based on what we know, feel, or believe about the brand.

Branding has become so strong that, today, hardly anything goes unbranded. Commodities

Exhibit 9.1 Anything can be branded: Salt is salt, but Windsor is a brand name for salt products made by the Canadian Salt Factory, which differentiates it from other manufacturers' salt products.

like salt can be branded. Common nuts and bolts are packaged with a distributor's label, and automobile parts—spark plugs, tires, filters—bear brand names that differ from those of the automakers. Even fruits, vegetables, dairy products, and poultry are branded— Sunkist oranges, BC apples, Neilson Dairy Oh! milk, and Maple Leaf Prime chickens.

Branding helps buyers in many ways. Brand names help consumers identify products that might benefit them. Brands also say something about product quality and consistency—people who always buy the same brand know that they'll get the same level of quality each time they buy. As well, branding gives the marketer several advantages. The brand name becomes the basis on which a whole story can be built about a product's special qualities. The brand name and trademark provide legal protection for unique product features that otherwise might be copied by competitors. And branding helps the marketer segment markets. For example, instead of offering just one general product for all consumers, Toyota Motor Corporation can offer the major Lexus, Toyota, and Scion brands, each with numerous sub-brands such as the Camry, Corolla, Prius, Matrix, Yaris, Tundra, Land Cruiser, and others.

Brand Meaning

In the beginning, products were just products, and they stayed that way for a long time. Then, someone came up with the idea of trademarks. Consumers came to trust trademarks, because they reassured them that the product they were getting had the attributes they wanted and expected from that maker. One of the first makers of products to learn the value of trademarking was Louis Vuitton. In 1986 the company designed and patented its signature quatrefoil and flowers pattern, along with its LV monogram, to protect itself from counterfeit luggage makers. Today the Louis Vuitton brand is one of the most valuable luxury brands in the world.

Trademarks can be names, symbols, characters (like the Pillsbury Doughboy), and even shapes, such as the Coca-Cola bottle, whose design was registered as a trademark in 1960. Trademark names have monetary value, and therefore must be protected, and distinguished from regular or generic words with a similar meaning. Trademarked names are indicated with a superscript TM, and after the company has gone through a lengthy legal process of registering its trademark, it indicates it with this symbol: ®.

The name Kleenex, for example, is a registered trademark belonging to Kimberly-Clark Worldwide, which means it should always be spelled with a capital and used to refer to the name-brand tissue. This is an important issue, important enough for Kimberly-Clark to take out ads to explain it (see Exhibit 9.2). Companies can lose their trademarks if their name becomes a generic word; for example, Aspirin was originally a trademarked name for acetylsalicylic acid, owned by Bayer. It's still a trademark in Canada and in many countries in Europe, but in the United States it has become a generic term. Other trademarks that have been lost for this reason are lanolin, kerosene, thermos, zipper, and escalator.

Marketers also keep a close eye on competitors who use names or symbols that might be infringing on their trademark rights, which can often result in lawsuits. For example, Nestlé challenged a trademark that protected the colour purple used on Kraft's Cadbury Dairy Milk, claiming that a colour shouldn't be protected under such laws. But the

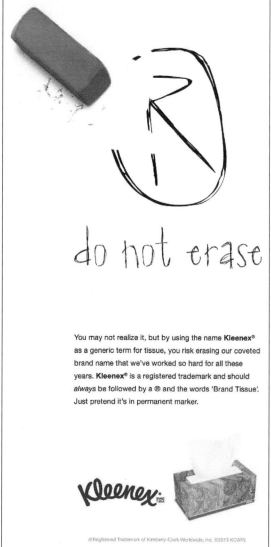

You may not realize it, but by using the name **Kleenex**® as a generic term for tissue, you risk erasing our coveted brand name that we've worked so hard for all these years. **Kleenex**® is a registered trademark and should *always* be followed by a ® and the words 'Brand Tissue'. Just pretend it's in permanent marker.

Exhibit 9.2 Trademarks: The name Kleenex is a registered trademark, which means it should always be spelled with a capital and used to refer to the name brand tissue.

Clement Allard/CP

Exhibit 9.3 Brand meaning: Red Bull is synonymous with the word *extreme* due to its sponsorship of extreme activities, such as Red Bull Crashed Ice.

judge ruled in Cadbury's favour, and prohibited Nestlé from using the colour purple to wrap its milk chocolate products. Interestingly, since the trademark applies only to milk chocolate, that means Nestlé is free to produce white- or dark-chocolate candy bars wrapped in purple.[4]

Trademarks and logos often represent brands, yet the *meaning* of a brand encompasses much more than just a name and a logo. Customers attach meanings to brands and develop brand relationships that go well beyond a product's physical attributes. For example, a Stanford University study offered children two identical samples of french fries, one in McDonald's packaging and the other in plain, unmarked packaging. When the children were then asked which tasted better, 77 percent chose the french fries in the McDonald's packaging.[5]

Branding expert Al Reis says that the key to communicating brand meaning is to get consumers to associate your brand with just one word, so that your brand "owns" that word in terms of brand positioning. Volvo, for example, owns the word *safety*, and Coors Light owns the word *cold*. Another example is Red Bull, which owns the word *extreme*. The energy drink brand has built its reputation by associating itself with, and sponsoring, extreme sports and activities around the world. Red Bull Racing is a Formula One racing team that drives cars built by Infiniti and competes in Formula One races around the world; the Red Bull Storm Chase is a windsurfing competition that takes place in cold water and storm-force winds. The brand is associated with every extreme cycling, aerial, and water sport, some of which they create themselves, like Red Bull Crashed Ice, the annual tournament where skaters race down and around a half-kilometre-long ice track in the middle of Quebec City. Perhaps the most extreme activity this extreme brand has ever sponsored was daredevil Felix Baumgartner's jump to Earth from the stratosphere in 2012, during which he became the first human to break the sound barrier without vehicular power.

Brand Relationships

Brands are more than just names and symbols. They are a key element in the company's relationships with consumers. Brands represent consumers' perceptions and feelings about a product and its performance—everything that the product or service means to them. In the final analysis, brands exist in the heads of consumers. As one well-respected marketer once said, "Products are created in the factory, but brands are created in the mind."[6]

A key factor in consumers' relationships with brands is what they *believe* about them. Human beliefs can be very strong, and since beliefs are not based on facts but only on emotion, once formed they are nearly unbreakable. Here's an example of what Jean (not her real name), an American woman of Italian heritage, believes about her favourite brands:

> Jean's brand relationships are close, enduring, and deeply held commitments, many of which have survived for decades, and many of which are connected to her identity as an Italian wife and mother. She is loyal to Pastene tomatoes, Hunt's tomato sauce, Bertolli olive oil, and

Contadina tomato paste—all of which she uses to make her "trademark" sauce. Jean believes that "Pastene whole tomatoes in the can are the best. They use the good tomatoes, the ones that are perfect and nice and ripe. The other brands use the tomatoes that can't pass inspection."

Some other beliefs Jean has about brands include "Tide detergent is better because of the way they make their powders. They do something so the powder dissolves in the washer. The other ones are made different and they don't dissolve"; and "Other shampoos have chemicals that interact with the water in my house so they don't work right. They make my hair flat. This one (Aussie Miracle) doesn't have that"; and "Bounty paper towels, they are the best . . . Maytag, they say that is the best . . . Frigidaire makes the best fridge . . . Krups makes the best coffee . . . Electrolux is the best vacuum. It's expensive, yeah, but . . ."[7]

Exhibit 9.4 Brand relationships: With so many brands to choose from on every grocery store shelf, how do consumers make their decisions? For many products, the choice is based on what the consumer believes about the brand.

Of course, marketers can't force people to enter into relationships with their brands, any more than you can force someone to enter into a relationship with another person. Still, when marketers are able to create brands with good, memorable names, personalities, and stories to tell, consumers sometimes fall in love with them. Branding expert Kevin Roberts, the author of *Lovemarks: The Future Beyond Brands*, points out that human beings are powered by emotion, not by reason, and that brand marketers must strive to inspire among consumers a loyalty "beyond reason" for their brands.[8]

People as Brands

People become brands when, just as with products, their name takes on meanings that transcend the person. The true mark of any brand is the ability to apply it to products in other categories and have the same meaning and positioning transfer with it—the way Red Bull has done with extreme sports and events. A true brand has life beyond its original product, and in the case of people as brands, the brand must have life and meaning outside the person. For example, Gianni Versace, Coco Chanel, Louis Vuitton, and Levi Strauss are all people who became brands that live on today, even though the people themselves are all dead. Some of today's larger-than-life people who have become brands are Donald Trump, Rachael Ray, and Kim Kardashian. And then there's Quebec's own celebrity chef Chuck Hughes, who catapulted to fame by beating Bobby Flay on *Iron Chef America*, and has turned that fame into a brand:

Exhibit 9.5 People as brands: Celebrities like Chuck Hughes become brands when their names can be applied to products and carry meaning with them.

> Chuck Hughes is the chef and co-owner of Garde Manger and Le Bremner in Montreal, and has hosted many TV shows, including *Chuck's Day Off* and *Chuck's Eat the Street*. He has his own website at Chuck-Hughes.ca, and he's partnered with the Montreal Canadiens to produce a series of videos called "Tattoos and Tailgates with Chuck Hughes" (in French, "Manger les Bandes avec Chuck Hughes"). He's appeared in ads for Le Crueset cookware and Vans shoes, and has written cookbooks in both English and French. But what really launched him to stardom and changed the meaning of his name from "chef" to "celebrity" was beating Bobby Flay in battle lobster on *Iron Chef America*.
>
> Hughes says his luck may have been in the shellfish. He is such a fan of lobster that he has a tattoo of one on his arm, alongside shrimp, lemon meringue pie, and bacon—his favourite foods. His winning menu on the competition TV show included lobster roll with a

bloody caesar cocktail, and lobster poutine. His tattoos, his bilingualism, and his love for the Habs are all part of what makes up the Chuck Hughes brand.

So is the team behind the man, which includes a manager and a publicist, not to mention his sous chefs and business partners at his restaurants. Plans may be in the works to launch a Chuck Hughes line of food products. Says Hughes, "At this point, I'm not saying yes or no to anything, but we've built our brand and our business around being honest and authentic and real, so for me, as long as we can find those things within that world, then yes we can make it happen."[9]

Some of these names may still be living as brands 10 or even 100 years from now; others may not. Developing, growing, and managing a person as a brand requires the same amount of dedication to marketing as marketers apply to products. Today's athletes who aspire to become brands must begin their marketing efforts before their playing days are over. For example, retired Canadian basketball star Steve Nash appeared in Nike commercials during his days as a player, and today keeps his brand top of mind by organizing charity games and, in 2015, participating in the opening ceremonies of the Pan Am Games in Toronto.

Brand Characteristics LO2

Most established brands are represented by a powerful name or icon; however, these symbols are only part of what makes up the brand. Brands ultimately exist in the minds and hearts of consumers, but it is the job of brand managers to create representations of the brand, such as *logos*. Brands also have *personality*, *status*, and value (*brand equity*).

Logos

Logos are designs that represent the brand, and that may or may not incorporate the brand name. The Nike swoosh, for example, originally appeared in conjunction with the word *Nike*, but once the market had been "trained" to recognize the swoosh as a representation of the Nike brand, the name was removed from the logo.

Sometimes brand managers feel that their logo needs an update. The Royal Bank, for example, updates its lion every 10 years or so to make it more modern looking. Pepsi updated its red, white, and blue swirl logo a few years ago to make it look more like a smile. And the Hudson's Bay Company rebranded its stores from "The Bay" to "Hudson's Bay," unveiling a redesigned logo to communicate the change. Usually, though, a new logo isn't simply an exercise in design; it's part of a larger strategic business plan to make changes to the company's image or positioning. Such was the case with the recent makeover of Second Cup:

Marketers at Second Cup were hearing from their customers and franchisees that the brand was tired and in need of a refresh, so president and CEO Alix Box decided it was time to make some changes. Second Cup Coffee Co. is Canada's largest specialty coffee retailer, but the market for specialty coffee had dramatically changed since the chain was established in 1975. "It's a competitive space," Box says, "and we needed to be revolutionary and do something fresh and unexpected."

So just before Christmas 2014, Second Cup Coffee Co. unveiled its "café of the future" at one

Second Cup Coffee Co. ™

Exhibit 9.6   Changing a brand's logo, as Second Cup did, is not a decision that marketers make lightly.

of its oldest locations, the corner of King and John streets in Toronto. The new café represents an important component in the company's transformation and a first step in its three-year strategic plan—and showcases Second Cup's obsession with bringing the ultimate coffee experience to Canadians. It features a Slow Bar where customers can interact with baristas and hone their coffee-tasting skills; a Healthy Granola and Hearty Oatmeal bar; new artistic cups, created in collaboration with Canadian artists; a community wall mural; built-in charging pads for customers to use, free of charge; a custom music program featuring predominantly Canadian content; and a stylish new employee dress code.

The brand's new logo was designed by Jackknife, a Toronto design firm. The old brown and yellow logo, which featured a steaming cup of coffee, has been replaced by a streamlined, modern-looking white-on-black logo that reads SECOND CUP COFFEE CO. It's meant to express a premium brand experience and a commitment to coffee quality. Says Box, "It's been a year of huge change. It's also been a year of learning and listening. There's been a lot of activity—fixing the foundation so we can go forward in transforming what I believe is an iconic Canadian brand."[10]

Brand Personality

Many of the most successful brands are those that have a distinctive *personality*. A **brand personality** is the sum total of all the attributes of a brand, and the emotions it inspires in the minds of consumers. Brand managers describe their brands by using the same kinds of adjectives we might use to describe people, and they use those attributes to establish the brand's positioning. For example, Coca-Cola is traditional, while Pepsi is youthful; Apple is stylish and hip. Starbucks is sophisticated, and Ford is reliable. IBM is conservative and practical, while Google is quirky and fun-loving.

But where do brand's personalities come from? They are created by marketers, of course, deliberately and strategically. And sometimes, when the marketers aren't happy with their first creation, they start from scratch and create a whole new brand with a completely different personality. (That's what Flying Monkeys did; see Marketing@Work 9.1.)

Another aspect of a brand's personality is its *status*. Brands occupy a level of social regard with respect to one another. Rolls-Royce and Bentley are higher-status car brands than Ford and Toyota; and Hyundai and Kia are lower-status brands. Within just about every product category there are high-status and low-status brands; however, status should not be confused with value or popularity. Many high-status brands, such as Chanel and Rolex, tend to be exclusive rather than popular, while lower-status brands, such as Canadian Tire and Keds, can still be highly popular.

Brand personality
The sum total of all the attributes of a brand, and the emotions it inspires in the minds of consumers.

Brand Equity

A powerful brand has monetary value and equity. **Brand equity** is the dollar amount attributed to the value of the brand, based on all the intangible qualities that create that value. Brand equity is difficult to calculate, but one indicator is the extent to which people are willing to pay more for the brand.

Brand equity is also a measure of the brand's ability to capture consumer preference and loyalty. A brand has positive brand equity when consumers react more favourably to it than to a generic or unbranded version of the same product. It has negative brand equity if consumers react less favourably than to an unbranded version.

Ad agency Young & Rubicam's BrandAsset Valuator measures brand strength along four consumer perception dimensions: *differentiation* (what makes the brand stand out), *relevance* (how consumers feel it meets their needs), *knowledge* (how much consumers know about the brand), and *esteem* (how highly consumers regard and respect the brand). Brands with strong brand equity rate high on all four dimensions. The brand must be distinct, or consumers will have no reason to choose it over other brands. However, the

Brand equity
The dollar amount attributed to the value of the brand, based on all the intangible qualities that create that value.

MARKETING@WORK   9.1

Creating a Brand with Personality from the Ground Up—Twice

When it comes to branding beer—a product that isn't highly differentiated—creating a memorable brand may be the most important part of the company's marketing strategy. An unusual name sometimes doesn't hurt. Ask Andrea Chiodo, who created the brand at Flying Monkeys Craft Brewery in Barrie, Ontario. "If you had told me 20 years ago that I'd be creating a company called Flying Monkeys Craft Brewery," she remarks, "I would have said it sounds like something spit out by a random word generator."

Flying Monkeys means craft beer that isn't afraid to be different. And in the craft beer business, being successful requires building a strong, memorable brand that's able to establish a clear position in the mind of the beer-drinking consumer. The Flying Monkeys brand is rich, colourful, and quirky. It's brought to life in their crazy packaging, their slogan, "Normal is weird," and their pun (and fun)-filled product names: Antigravity Light Ale, Hoptical Illusion Almost Pale Ale, Netherworld Cascadian Dark Ale, and Smashbomb Atomic IPA. Every illustration, every communication, and every

product that comes out of Flying Monkeys headquarters represents this brand personality, right down to the bottle caps with their offbeat, fortune cookie-esque sayings. And it's a brand personality that grew and developed from the personalities of Andrea and Peter Chiodo.

Peter had grown up helping his grandfather brew beer in his basement, an introduction to a passion he'd continue for life. In grad school Peter and his friends started brewing concoctions in a spare closet of his student house, and on weekends Peter and Andrea would explore and sample all the interesting, flavourful craft beer they could find. Hooked on the beer bug, they bought some recipe books and better home-brewing supplies, sought out advice, and while Peter worked on beer recipes, Andrea thought about the brand. What should they call their brewery? What names should they give to their beers? What would their story be?

At the time, the city of Barrie was gearing up for its sesquicentennial, and Andrea, being a history buff, loved the story of Robert Simpson, the first reeve and mayor of Barrie and renowned

brewmaster—so she named their brewery the Simcoe Steam Brewing Company. It was a brand that fit with the trend, as most Ontario breweries seemed to be named after historically significant people and geographical regions—Great Lakes, Wellington County, Mill Street, Muskoka. But that was the problem. "We had our brand, and it fit right in with all the other beer brands," says Andrea. "We were in the middle of the pack. We took our place in the tradition. Our brand was nationalistic yet local, catchy yet still classy. We thought of ourselves as the Creemore of Barrie."

Then one fateful night the phone rang and the Chiodos were told that the San Francisco Bay Brewing Company, brewers of Anchor Steam, had a trademark on the word *steam* as it applies to steam beer and brewing. Anyone using the word *steam* in the name of a brewery or a beer was subject to a trademark infringement lawsuit. Says Andrea, "After the shock subsided we started thinking, Maybe this was our chance to change our brand. Maybe we should forget about Ontario history and create a brand with a name like Dogfish Head—something that was truly our own." But instead of recreating the brand they simply changed the name to Robert Simpson Brewing Company, and continued what they had been doing.

Says Andrea, "We chickened out. But later we thought about it again. We realized that even though we *owned* a microbrewery, we looked forward to trips to the States where we would stock up on the beers we *wanted* to drink!" So, for the second time, the Chiodos took a good hard look at their brand and no longer liked what they saw. There they were, brewing their "inoffensive" beer, which they sold to consumers but preferred not to drink themselves. "We asked ourselves, Why weren't we brewing the kinds of beers we want to drink?"

They decided to get funky, be true to their off-centred nature, and craft the kind of brews they wanted to drink

Courtesy Flying Monkeys Craft Brewery

Exhibit 9.7 Creating a brand personality: The personality of the Flying Monkeys brand is exhibited through the names of their products, their packaging and labelling, and their website.

themselves. They realized that it was "weird to be normal." So they threw out what Andrea later referred to as the "dead white guy" branding, and went back to the drawing board. They brainstormed crazy new brand names that just got weirder and weirder: BioEngibeer, Hopzilla, Hopnotic Suggestion, Moon Radio, Genius of Suburbia, Dark Succubus, Braincube, Time Warp, Polar Bomb, Borealis Lamp . . . and finally settled on Flying Monkeys Craft Brewery because, says Andrea, "There's a sign in

the mudroom of our house that reads, 'Don't make me get my Flying Monkeys!' It's a joke and a threat telling our kids to put their crap away, or else."

No longer an inoffensive brand surrounded by similar brews, Flying Monkeys is now the leader of the pack—well ahead of the trend that has recently seen major breweries scrambling to create their own "craft-like" beers. Each Flying Monkey brew has a story, a personality, an ethos. "We name our beers to reflect flavour and the spirit of the brew," says

Andrea. "What we discovered in both the brewing of Hoptical Illusion and the package design was that our competitive advantage was our creativity. Our packaging has become synonymous with our name, and, really, all we have is our brand to convey our brewery's mission, and explain our mantra: *Normal is weird*."

Source: From information provided by Andrea and Peter Chiodo.

fact that a brand is highly differentiated doesn't necessarily mean that consumers will buy it. The brand must stand out in ways that are relevant to consumers' needs. Even a differentiated, relevant brand is far from a shoo-in. Before consumers will respond to the brand, they must first know about and understand it. And that familiarity must lead to a strong, positive consumer–brand connection.[11]

Every two years, consulting firm Interbrand evaluates and ranks the best global brands and the best Canadian brands in terms of their value, or brand. It's a complex formula, but here are some of the most recent results: The top two Canadian brands are TD, valued at $10 795 million, and RBC, valued at $10 531 million. Remember, that's not the value of the company; it's *just the value of the brand*. Also on the list of best Canadian brands are Tim Hortons, Bell, lululemon, Molson, WestJet, IMAX, La Senza, and Dollarama. Apple tops the most valuable global brands list, valued at US$188 million. Not far behind are Google (US$107 million), Coca-Cola (US$82 million), IBM (US$72 million), and Microsoft (US$61 million). And Interbrand considers Facebook, Volkswagen, Nissan, Amazon, and Audi to be "top risers."[12]

A powerful brand forms the basis for building strong and profitable customer relationships. The fundamental asset underlying brand equity is *customer equity*—the value of the customer relationships that the brand creates. A powerful brand is important, but what it really represents is a profitable set of loyal customers. The proper focus of marketing is building customer equity, with brand management serving as a major marketing tool.

Branding Strategy and Management LO3

Marketing managers responsible for brands must make high-level strategic decisions that govern the management of the brand and guide the public and market perceptions about the brand. The main branding strategy decisions are *brand name selection*, *brand positioning*, and *brand sponsorship*. In addition, because brands are valuable corporate assets, they must be carefully developed, either by creating *line extensions* or *brand extensions*, pursuing a *multibrand* strategy, or creating entirely *new brands*. Finally, it is the job of the brand manager to manage and protect the brand on an ongoing basis.

Brand Name Selection

A good name can add greatly to a product's success. However, finding the best brand name is a difficult task. It begins with a careful review of the product and its benefits, the target market, and proposed marketing strategies. After that, naming a brand becomes part science, part art, and a measure of instinct. According to brand experts, here are the things to consider when coming up with a new brand name:

- It should suggest something about the type of products it will brand, such as Beautyrest, Craftsman, Facebook.
- It should be easy to pronounce, recognize, and remember, such as Tide, Crest, Ziploc.
- It should be distinctive, such as Google, Lexus, BlackBerry.
- It should be extendable; that is, not tied too closely to one product. Good names that illustrate this example are Apple, Amazon, and Nike.
- It should be pronounceable in many languages, such as Kodak.
- It should be capable of registration and protection as a trademark. A brand name cannot be registered if it infringes on existing brand names. Unique, "made up" names work best for this: Yahoo!, Novartis, Ugg.

A great brand absolutely requires a good, strong, memorable name. When Google burst onto the scene in 1998, no one had to say the name twice. It was instantly memorable, and, only a few short years later, it had become synonymous with "Internet search." Sometimes companies resurrect brand names from the past and give them a new life, for example when Nike bought the Converse brand (see Marketing@Work 9.2).

Brand Positioning

In Chapter 7 we learned about the importance of segmenting the market and positioning a product in the marketplace—and positioning is even more important for brands, because they are intangible. Canadian branding expert Ted Matthews says, "To stand out in our over-communicated world, brands must establish and own a unique, honest, meaningful, and clear position."[13]

Brands can be positioned based on *product attributes.* For example, P&G invented the disposable diaper category with its Pampers brand. Early Pampers marketing focused on attributes such as fluid absorption, fit, and disposability. In general, however, attributes are the least desirable quality for brand positioning, because competitors can easily copy them.

Consumers are more interested in what the products will do for them, so a better positioning strategy is to associate the brand with a particular *benefit.* Pampers' later marketing communications focused on the benefits of dry baby bottoms. Other successful brands positioned on benefits are Volvo (safety), FedEx (guaranteed on-time delivery), Nike (performance), and Staples (easy).

The strongest brands go beyond attribute or benefit positioning. They are positioned on strong *beliefs and values,* and as such they engage consumers on a deep, emotional level. Brands such as Godiva, Starbucks, Apple, and Victoria's Secret rely less on a product's tangible attributes and more on creating surprise, passion, and excitement.

Brand Sponsorship

Brand sponsorship is an important branding strategy decision, and begins with the question, "To brand or not to brand?" Not all products are branded, but those that are may be *national brands* or *private brands.* Marketers may choose *licensing* as a method of branding a new product, or they may partner with another firm to *co-brand* a product.

National brand (or manufacturer's brand)
A brand created and owned by the manufacturer of the product.

National Brands A new product may be launched as a **national brand (or manufacturer's brand)**, as when Samsung and Kellogg sell their output under their own brand names (Samsung Galaxy or Kellogg's Frosted Flakes). National brands are so

Converse: An Old Brand with a New Beginning

The Converse brand officially reached 100 years of age in 2008, and didn't celebrate its birthday until seven years later—but what a celebration it was! A major advertising and promotional campaign called "Made By You" featured real people and celebrities who turn their Chucks into a personal artistic canvas. Art installations and murals were set up around the world in cities like New York, London, and Shanghai. And custom Chucks were featured in video ads across social media, some created by the brand's marketers, and some created by consumers themselves.

The Converse brand began as the name of a company that invented high top basketball shoes. In 1923 it introduced the first pair of Chuck Taylor All Stars—known around the world as Cons, Connies, Convics, Verses, or just plain Chucks. Throughout the '30s, '40s, '50s, and '60s, Chucks were *the* shoes to have. The first U.S. Olympic basketball team wore them, and they dominated basketball courts—amateur and professional—for more than 50 years. By the mid-1970s, 70 to 80 percent of basketball players still wore Converse, and so did every little kid who aspired to be like them.

But then tastes changed, and Nike, Reebok, and Adidas—all large companies that managed brands by the same names—rose to popularity. By 2001, Converse's market share had dwindled to only 1 percent and the company behind the once dominant brand declared bankruptcy. The Converse brand story would likely have ended right there if not for the foresight of an unlikely suitor. In 2003, market leader Nike stepped in and quietly bought Converse for US$305 million. Nike still saw promise in the venerable-though-depleted old brand. However, it faced a perplexing product life-cycle question: How does a megabrand like Nike bring a fading icon like Converse back to life? To find answers, Nike assigned a new management team to Converse, gave it a fresh

infusion of cash, and left the brand alone to shape its own strategy outside the shadow of the swoosh.

The new team discovered that, despite its dwindling market share, the Converse brand had acquired a small but fiercely loyal following. During the 1990s, street kids had begun wearing affordable Converse shoes as an expression of individuality. Soon to follow were emerging artists, designers, and musicians, who wore Chucks because of their simplicity and classic looks. Converse became a favourite of the anti-establishment, anti-corporate crowd, those tired of trendy fashions. Individualistic Converse fans would take a pair of cheap but comfy All Stars, trash them, scribble on them, and customize them as a canvas for personal expression. This small but loyal following provided a lifeline for rejuvenating the aging brand.

Today, clever marketing of brand extensions with new designs and new channels has grown the brand in market segments where Converse can shine (and where Nike, Reebok, and Adidas don't venture). Converse One Star is a low priced line available at lower end retail stores, while higher-priced versions of All Stars, created by fashion designers, are now sold through upscale retailers like Saks and Bloomingdales. And the brand has been extended to offer everything from kids' shoes, work shoes, sandals, and boots to Converse-branded eyewear and watches.

At the heart of the rekindled Converse brand is the philosophy that customers control brands, not companies. In the eyes of consumers, Converse today is less about the shoes and more about self-expression and the Converse experience. According to Converse's chief marketing officer Geoff Cottrill, largely on their own, consumers have come to define the Converse brand around five ideas: "American, sneaker, youthful, rebellious, and a blank canvas."

Naturally, Converse has also embraced social media, an ideal forum

for engaging young consumers and letting them help define the brand. Converse now spends more than 90 percent of its marketing dollars on emerging media, and it is now the most popular sneaker brand on Facebook!

In recent years, Converse has focused its brand identity on one of the ultimate forms of youthful self-expression—rock 'n' roll music. For example, the company has released several popular lines of All Stars designed by legendary rock artists. It has even built its own music studio—Converse Rubber Tracks—where undiscovered artists can have free access to high-end equipment and lay down tracks that might land them record deals elsewhere. More than 300 artists, signed and unsigned, used the studio in the first 12 months. Converse's focus on self-expression and music has helped it create real and

Moxie Productions /Blend Images/Getty

Exhibit 9.8 The value of a brand name: Nike purchased the Converse brand in 2003 for US$305 million—that's what almost 100 years of building brand equity is worth.

relevant brand conversations with and among people who might wear its sneakers.

Today, Converse is thriving as a lifestyle brand with a distinct name and personality. Converse is creative, disruptive, optimistic, and courageous.

It symbolizes how anyone can evolve from being what they were, to what they are, to what they will become.

Sources: Eric Blattberg, "'Made By You': Converse Celebrates 100 Years of Chucks," Digiday Retail Newsletter (Digiday.com), March 2, 2015; Jeffrey Summers, "Why Converse Has 42

Million Facebook Fans," *Forbes* video interview, February 22, 2012, accessed at www.youtube.com/watch?v=BV1ilkKoy1o; Todd Wasserman, "How Converse Became the Biggest Little Sneaker Brand on Facebook," *Mashable*, May 4, 2011; Doug Schumacher, "TopTen: On Converse's Facebook Page, the Fans Do the Selling," *iMedia Connection*, March 13, 2012; Robert Klara, "Chuck's Big Comeback," *Adweek*, October 4, 2012; and information from Converse.com.

called because they are well-known and well-established throughout the country, or even internationally.

Private brand

(store brand, private label)

Brand names applied by the marketer to products manufactured for them under contract.

Private Brands **Private brands**, also called **store brands** and **private labels**, are brand names applied by the marketer to products manufactured for them under contract. Shoppers Drug Mart's Life Brand is a private label; so is Walmart's Great Value brand. Perhaps the most well known private brand of all is President's Choice, which has reached the status of a national brand and has spawned many brand extensions.

Private-label products account for approximately 25 percent of Canadian grocery stores' and drugstores' revenues. As consumers, we are not usually familiar with the manufacturer of the private brand, only with the name of the brand. For example, Best Buy Canada uses Desjardins Group, a major financial services company, to manage its store-brand credit cards.[14] And one of the largest manufacturers of private-label soft drinks around the world is Canada's own Cott Corporation:

> Cott is one of the world's largest producers of beverages on behalf of retailers, brand owners, and distributors. The company produces multiple types of beverages, including carbonated soft drinks; juice products; clear, still, and sparkling flavoured waters; energy products; and ready-to-drink teas. The company was created by Polish immigrant Harry Pencer, who began importing Cott sodas into Canada and, three years later, established Cott Beverages Ltd. to bottle beverages in Quebec. Later that decade, Cott became the first company in the world to launch a diet soft drink, developing a formula by request for diabetic patients at the Royal Victoria Hospital in Montreal.
>
> Today, Cott employs approximately 4000 people; supplies over 500 retailer, licensed, and company-owned brands; and operates manufacturing facilities in Canada, the United States, the United Kingdom, and Mexico. Cott also develops and manufactures beverage concentrates, which it exports to over 50 countries around the world. Its single largest customer is Walmart, which accounts for 26 percent of the company's $10 million annual revenues. The company owns dozens of trademarks in over 120 countries, which it vigorously monitors and protects. Recently, Cott acquired U.S. water and coffee supplier DDS Group to expand into the business of supplying corporate water and coffee products, both of which are growing markets.[15]

In the so-called battle of the brands between national and private brands, retailers have many advantages. They control what products they stock, where they go on the shelf, what prices they charge, and which ones they will feature in local circulars. Retailers often price their store brands lower than comparable national brands, thereby appealing to the budget-conscious shopper in all of us. Although store brands can be hard to establish and costly to stock and promote, they also yield higher profit margins for the reseller. And they give resellers exclusive products that cannot be bought from competitors, resulting in greater store traffic and loyalty.

Licensing

The buying and selling of the rights to use a brand name, logo, character, icon, or image.

Licensing While some manufacturers take years and spend millions to create their own brand names, others *license* the right to use a brand name, then focus on marketing and selling their products under that name. **Licensing** is the buying and selling of the rights to use a brand name, logo, character, icon, or image.

Many makers of clothing and other soft goods license the rights to use the names of well-known celebrities or characters from popular movies and books. If you've ever bought an NHL team jersey or any other item bearing the logo of a professional sports team, you own an item made by a company that licensed the right to make that item. The value of a brand can be determined, in part, by the willingness of other companies to purchase the rights to use it.

Licensing is such big business that each year the Licensing Expo brings together hundreds of exhibitors representing thousands of brands, with 15 000 decision makers at retailers, manufacturers, and advertising agencies. It is "the" meeting place for the global licensing industry. One of the hottest offerings at a recent Licensing Expo was 3DPlusMe's mobile 3-D face scanning and 3-D printing device, which delivers personalized merchandise through its licensing agreements with such brands as Marvel and Hasbro. It literally turns consumers into their favourite superheroes in action-figure form![16]

Exhibit 9.9 **Licensing:** Super Awesome Me is an action figure that can be customized to look like a child. It is manufactured by 3DPlusMe under license from Marvel, which owns the rights to superheroes like Spiderman and Captain America.

Courtesy 3DplusMe

Co-Branding One branding strategy that's growing in popularity is to partner with another company, take the strongest elements of your each of your products, and combine them to produce a *co-branded* offering. **Co-branding** occurs when two established brand names of different companies are used on the same product. For example, financial services firms often partner with other companies to create co-branded credit cards, such as when CIBC and Air Canada joined forces to create the Aeroplan Visa card. Similarly, Costco teamed up with mattress maker Stearns & Foster to market a line of Kirkland Signature by Stearns & Foster mattress sets.

In order for co-branding to work, the two brands must be complementary; for example, *Elle Canada* (the fashion magazine) recently partnered with Sally Hansen (a marketer of nail polish) to promote the Sally Hansen Complete Salon Manicure collection through a co-branded "Fall Fashion Trend Report" that appeared in the magazine. The promotion included a custom inside front cover ad with a half-page bookmark, complemented by three consecutive one-third-page vertical ads integrated with each fall trend and colour palette within the trend report. The ads drove readers to ElleCanada.com/falltrends, where they could view custom videos featuring the magazine's beauty vlogger Marisa Roy sharing her favourite Sally Hansen colours.[17]

Co-branding
The practice of using the established brand names of two different companies on the same product.

Co-branding offers many advantages. Because each brand dominates in a different category, the combined brands create broader consumer appeal and greater brand equity. Co-branding also allows a company to expand its existing brand into a category it might otherwise have difficulty entering alone.

Brand Development

Brands are powerful, valuable assets that must be carefully developed. In general, a company has four options when it comes to developing brands (see Figure 9.1). It can create *line extensions* or *brand extensions*, pursue a *multibrand* strategy, or create entirely *new brands*.

Line Extensions **Line extensions** occur when a company extends existing brand names to new forms, colours, sizes, ingredients, or flavours of an existing product category; for

Line extensions
Extending an existing brand name to new forms, colours, sizes, ingredients, or flavours of an existing product category.

FIGURE 9.1 Brand Development Strategies

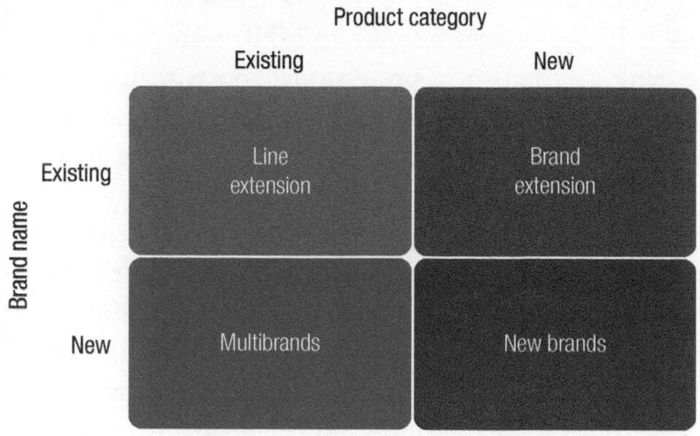

example, Honey Nut Cheerios and MultiGrain Cheerios are extensions of the Cheerios product line.

A company might use line extensions as a low-cost, low-risk way to introduce new products. Or it might want to meet consumer desires for variety, to use excess capacity, or simply to command more shelf space from resellers. However, line extensions involve some risks. An overextended brand name might lose its specific meaning. Another risk is that sales of an extension may come at the expense of other items in the line. For example, the original Doritos Tortilla Chips have now morphed into a full line of 20 different types and flavours of chips, including such high-decibel flavours as Jalapeno & Cheddar, Sweet Chili Heat, Spicy Nacho, and Scream Cheese. Although the line seems to be doing well, the original Doritos chips seem like just another flavour. A line extension works best when it takes sales away from competing brands, not when it "cannibalizes" the company's other items.

Brand extensions

Extending an existing brand name to new product categories.

Brand Extensions **Brand extensions** extend a current brand name to new or modified products in a new category. For example, Campbell Soup extended its V8 juice brand to a line of soups, and Ritz extended its brand to mini Ritz Bits Sandwiches; the Mr. Clean brand was extended to Mr. Clean Magic Erasers; KitKat has done many brand extensions, including KitKat Chunky, KitKat Chunky Peanut Butter, and KitKat Chunky Caramel. And finally, in what some have called the most overdue brand extension in history, Kraft extended its Planters peanut brand to—peanut butter, of course!

> The Planters brand, owned by Kraft, is more than 100 years old—and it took nearly all that time for marketers to extend the Planters name to something other than peanuts. But finally the brand and its mascot, Mr. Peanut, were extended to a new product: peanut butter. But this is not your kids' peanut butter. Kraft is targeting adults, who consume two-thirds of the $2 billion worth of peanut butter sold each year in Canada and the United States.
>
> Planters Peanut Butter was introduced first to the U.S. market, then, a year later, to Canada. Promotions featured celebrity chef Marcus Samuelsson, who showcased adult recipes like peanut butter yogurt and even peanut butter soup. In keeping with the adult theme, Kraft created an advertising campaign (aired only in the U.S.) around the idea that Mr. Peanut (an animated character voiced by Robert Downey, Jr.) needed a stunt double—or, rather, stunt peanut. In a series of TV commercials, Mr. Peanut's stunt double, Doug (voiced by actor Kevin Dillon, who played Johnny Drama on *Entourage*), performed death-defying feats deemed too dangerous for the venerable peanut pitchman. Unfortunately, Doug's exploits always end the same way: with him getting crushed and turned into peanut butter. Doug gets flattened by a statue, charged by an insect-bull, and crushed by a lighting rig. Each time, all

that remains of Doug is a jar of peanut butter—as he flashes a thumbs-up through the top to let us know he's fine.

Sadly, Planters Peanut Butter was not successful in the U.S., despite all that brand equity, and Kraft pulled it from the market. It continues to be available in Canada, however.[18]

A brand extension gives a new product instant recognition and faster acceptance. It also saves the high advertising costs usually required to build a new brand name. At the same time, a brand extension strategy involves some risk. Brand extensions such as Cheetos lip balm, Heinz pet food, and Life Savers gum met early deaths. The extension may confuse the image of the main brand. And if a brand extension fails, it may harm consumer attitudes toward the other products carrying the same brand name.

Courtesy Johnvince Foods (Planters Canada)

Exhibit 9.10 Brand extensions: It's been called the most overdue brand extension in history, but now you can buy Planters Peanut Butter in Canada.

Multibrands **Multibranding** is a brand development strategy in which the same manufacturer produces many different brands in a given product category. For example, the Whirlpool Corporation markets appliances under its corporate brand, Whirlpool, but also under the brand names Maytag, KitchenAid, Jenn-Air, Amana, and Inglis—all of which the corporation manufactures.

A major drawback of multibranding is that each brand might obtain only a small market share, and none may be very profitable. The company may end up spreading its resources over many brands instead of building a few brands to a highly profitable level. This happened to General Motors, which was forced to cut several unprofitable brands from its portfolio, including Saturn, Oldsmobile, Pontiac, Hummer, and Saab.

Multibranding
A brand development strategy in which the same manufacturer produces many different brands in the same product category.

New Brands Sometimes a company that has a long-established name and has been in business for many years decides to adopt a new strategy—to brand itself and its products. This is what Montreal's Gildan did:

> Gildan Activewear Inc., with its headquarters in Montreal, has been in business since 1984; it's traded on the TSX and the NYSE, has 30 000 employees worldwide, and has registered the trademark of its name: Gildan®. The company sells T-shirts, sport shirts, and fleece as undecorated "blanks," which are subsequently decorated by screenprinters with designs and logos (which they license). It's also one of the world's largest wholesale suppliers of men's socks, which are sold under many different brand names, including Under Armour and New Balance. The company sells millions of T-shirts every year, but the problem is, the consumers who have those T-shirts in their closets have no idea they are made by Gildan.
>
> So Gildan decided to pursue a strategy to grow its sales of branded underwear and activewear products in the American retail market. As part of its $25 million branding campaign, the company bought a spot during the Super Bowl. Gildan launched its men's underwear line that same year, and quickly managed to acquire 7 percent of the market share from long-time frontrunners Hanes and Fruit of the Loom. Next, Gildan chose Blake Shelton, whose popularity as a country music star had earned him notoriety among both men and women, to star in two TV commercials promoting the brand's socks.
>
> What's next for this new old brand? Women's underwear. Gildan is also planning to raise awareness of its sustainability efforts in order to attract the segment of the market that cares about where their clothes come from.[19]

More frequently, an established company creates a new brand when it develops a new product or product line. For example, Toyota created the Scion brand to appeal to Millennials, and Grocery chain Sobeys redesigned some of its suburban stores under the banner of a new brand name, FreshCo.

Ongoing Brand Management

One of the most important marketing management roles is that of the brand manager. The brand manager's job, day in and day out, is to be responsible for, and to manage, a brand. Brand managers need to continually audit their brands' strengths and weaknesses, and ask (and answer) questions such as the following: Does our brand excel at delivering benefits that consumers truly value? Is the brand properly positioned? Do all of our consumer touchpoints support the brand's positioning? Do the brand's managers understand what the brand means to consumers? Does the brand receive proper, sustained support? The brand manager makes decisions about which brands need more support, which brands need to be dropped, and which brands should be rebranded or repositioned because of changing customer preferences or new competitors.

Another of the brand manager's ongoing tasks is to carefully manage the marketing communications and advertising that communicates the brand's attributes and positioning to the market. Brands must be maintained, not just by advertising but by the overall brand experience, points of purchase, word of mouth, websites, and, increasingly, social media.

Why is it so important to manage brands? Does it really matter whether Rachael Ray says "olive oil" or "EVOO," or whether Mickey Mouse has two buttons or five on his pants? To brand managers, it's everything. Brand images and logos must be consistent and exact to be recognizable, so the way Mickey Mouse looks—his white gloves, the two buttons on his pants, and the proportional size of his ears—must be carefully controlled and managed. In fact, it is illegal for a manufacturer to print Mickey Mouse T-shirts without Disney's permission. Disney actually polices the use of its brand images and goes after offenders with all its legal guns. If that seems harsh, consider what would happen if a company didn't carefully manage its brands. It wouldn't be long before Mickey would start to look different, and we wouldn't recognize him anymore.

Brand Communications LO4

Brand communications is a specialized form of marketing communications and advertising that focuses on communicating brand positioning, or image, rather than on product features. In addition to advertising, brand messages are communicated through *brand experiences, touchpoints, brand icons* and *characters, brand ambassadors, brand stories, branded content,* and *branded entertainment.* Furthermore, with the increasing use and popularity of *social media,* consumers become a part of the brand communications, and can serve as *brand advocates.*

Brand Experiences and Touchpoints

Advertising campaigns can help create name recognition, brand knowledge, and maybe even some brand preference. However, the fact is that brands are not maintained by advertising but by people's brand experiences. Today, customers come to know a brand through a wide range of contacts and **touchpoints**. These include advertising and other forms of marketing communications, but also personal experience with the brand, word of mouth, social media, company and brand websites, store displays, and many others. The company must put as much care into managing these touchpoints as it does into producing its ads. Some branding experts believe that managing each customer's experiences with a brand is the most important ingredient in building brand loyalty.

Brand experience is composed of four dimensions: sensory, affective, behavioural, and intellectual. These responses are evoked in consumers when they come into contact

Touchpoints

Advertising, marketing communications, personal experience with the brand, word of mouth, social media, company and brand websites, store displays, and anything else that brings a consumer into contact with a brand.

with brand-related stimuli (i.e., touchpoints) like brand design, communications, and environments. Researchers have found that affective brand experiences affect brand trust and brand commitment positively, and that a behavioural brand experience positively affects brand commitment. All in all, brand experiences are crucial for building a brand relationship and brand loyalty.[20]

For example, when people are considering buying a new car, their consideration set—the brands they will consider—is created almost entirely based on their experiences with various car brands. According to a study by Starcom MediaVest Group, people in the United States talk about their auto purchases 30 000 times a day on social media, and that if a brand is not part of the social conversation during consideration phase, it rarely gets purchased. Social media has dramatically altered the purchase decision "journey" for automobiles. The journey now includes an expanded "purchase" phase that reflects the rise of social check-ins and status updates via mobile devices, and a new "post-purchase satisfaction and dissatisfaction" stage. For automobile marketers, that means brand experiences need to be created, and brand ambassadors assigned to watch and respond to post-purchase dissatisfaction in social media.[21]

Brand Icons and Characters

Brands with well-established histories and personalities often develop **brand icons** or characters (sometimes called *brand mascots*) to aid with brand communications. Brand icons are objects associated with the brand, such as the unique shape of the Volkswagen Beetle and a Corvette Stingray, Coca-Cola's red and white swoosh, NBC's peacock, and Disney's castle. **Brand characters**, also called mascots, are also icons but they move, speak, interact, and have personality traits.

Brand icons
Objects with distinct shapes, colours, or patterns that are associated with the brand.

The Pillsbury Doughboy, Tony the Tiger, and the Michelin Man are all examples of brand characters which have been used by brand managers for decades to help establish and communicate the meaning of the brand. In fact the Michelin Man, whose name is actually Bibendum, has been demonstrating the safety features of Michelin tires for more than 120 years!

Brand characters
Lifelike brand icons, or mascots, that can move speak, and interact, and that have personality traits.

Brand characters can also be human, like Betty Crocker, who was created by Gold Medal Flour in 1921. Her name was the signature on letters responding to customer questions, and her voice was on the radio in the 1920s as host of *The Betty Crocker School of the Air*, the first radio cooking show in the United States. According to *Fortune* magazine, Betty Crocker was the second most famous American woman, after Eleanor Roosevelt. In 1936 the company created the visual representation of Betty Crocker; since then, her look has been updated approximately every 10 years so that she always appears modern. And she has always embodied the brand's attributes: she's resourceful, committed to family, community-minded, and likes to bake.[22]

Brand icons and characters help establish the brand personality, and because they can move, speak, and interact, they're also an important tool for **brand engagement**. Brand engagement is the interaction between consumers and brands that's based on the emotional connection consumers feel toward the brand.

Brand engagement
The interaction between consumers and brands, based on the emotional connection consumers feel toward the brand.

Marketers and brand managers work to develop marketing programs, especially through the use of social media, that serve to engage consumers with their brand. For example, consumer health and hygiene company RB promoted its new brand, AMOPÉ, in Canada by engaging consumers—with free pedicures:

AMOPÉ PediPerfect Electronic Foot File is a new product: a battery-operated handheld device designed to gently buff away hard, tough skin on one's feet, with no soaking required. The roller head is removable and can be rinsed to clear away built-up residue. It sounds like a great product, targeted to women (and men) who'd like to save money

Ryan Emberley

Exhibit 9.11 Brand engagement:
When new footcare brand AMOPÉ
launched the company organized a
live event to engage consumers with
the brand.

Brand ambassador

A real person who, under contract with
the brand's marketing organization,
acts as a spokesperson for the brand.

by doing their own pedicures at home. The problem is, AMOPÉ is a new brand, so consumers don't know what or how to think about it. They have no information to be able to position the brand AMOPÉ in their minds relative to other similar products and brands.

So the brand marketers responsible for AMOPÉ decided to do something big and memorable to get the attention of the target market: They transformed Toronto's Yonge-Dundas Square into "AMOPÉ Pedi Park," promoted the event using Facebook and Twitter, and in the process set a new Guinness World Records title for most pedicures given in eight hours. The day was kicked off by Sarah Rafferty, a star of the TV show *Suits*. Yonge-Dundas Square was decorated with Muskoka chairs, picnic blankets, umbrellas, and a variety of summer games. By the end of the day, 1083 people had received pedicures using the electronic foot file, surpassing the goal of 1000 pedicures. There were lineups throughout the day, with people waiting an average 30 to 45 minutes, and about 25 to 30 percent of those who received pedicures were men.[23]

Brand Ambassadors Brand ambassadors are real people who, under contract with the brand's marketing organization, act as spokespersons for the brand. For example, popular Quebec actress Sonia Vachon is a brand ambassador for plus-size clothing brand Pennington's, and Canadian tennis star Milos Raonic is a brand ambassador for Canada Goose.

Unlike political ambassadors or traditional marketing spokespeople, brand ambassadors are typically selected for their looks, and may be used for a limited time. For example, alternative clothing brand Benetton, known for its provocative print ads, ran an advertising campaign that featured a cast of brand ambassadors selected for their unusual characteristics, none of which are obvious in the photos: Mario Galla, a disabled model from Germany; Lea T, a transsexual Brazilian model; Kiera Chaplin, granddaughter of Charlie Chaplin and an active supporter of UNESCO; Dudley O'Shaughnessy, British former national welterweight boxing champion; Matias Perdomo, an Uruguayan chef; and Californian Charlotte Free, who is known for her pink hair. Benetton describes the campaign as "an effort to confront prejudice."[24]

Brand Stories

Every brand has a history, and smart brand managers use elements of a company's history, as well as elements of fiction, to create stories for their brands. Branding expert Kevin Roberts says that stories are what bring brands to life and keep them interesting. Stories are how we explain the world to ourselves; they give value to the things we love. And so those businesses with a good story that involves the listeners—that is, consumers—will succeed in capturing their attention and cultivating favourable feelings toward the brand. A great story can never be told too often, and that's why the really good ones become classics, even legends. This is the kind of storytelling brand managers should aspire to. "Ask your friends if they can tell you a story about your brand. If they haven't got one, you have work to do," Roberts says.[25]

Today's brand managers think of their brands as a form of storytelling. When brand managers tell stories about brands, the rich details of character, place, and action embellish the basic "information maps" we all keep in our heads. Psychologists refer to these information maps as *schemas*: the structures of information about products and objects upon which we "hang" new information that we learn. While new products provide us with new information—this is what it's called, this is what it looks like, and this is what it does—brands enrich this information with details that give the new information *meaning*.

A good story has characters we care about interacting in a world or a situation in which something happens or changes. We all love stories *because* we care about the characters, and as we watch or hear about what happens to them, we experience strong emotions. In brand storytelling, the goal is to elicit those feelings, and transfer them to the brand.

"What's your story?" It's common slang for "What are you doing?" or "What's happening?," but when branding experts ask that question, they mean something very different. They mean, What is the story of your brand? Stories are "one of the primary ways we make sense of our world and our place in it," says one expert. And the same is true of brands: "Brands are the stories that unite us all in a common purpose within an enterprise, and connect us with the people we serve on the outside . . . brand stories give meaning to who we are and what we do . . . they're strategic."[26]

Brand stories are an excellent strategy for inspiring loyalty among consumers for a brand that might otherwise go unnoticed. Take potatoes, for example. They are ubiquitous, inexpensive, and popular, but rarely inspire emotion. Cavendish Farms changed all that by creating a rich story for its From the Farm brand of frozen potato products:

> At Cavendish Farms, marketers are telling the story of their From the Farm brand using the voices of their key suppliers—PEI potato farmers. These farmers love what they do, and they don't just *talk* about their passion for potatoes in the commercials; they literally sing their praises. The commercial shows the farmers in their fields, on their trucks (with their potatoes), and at a large picnic table, enjoying Cavendish Farms' From the Farm potatoes with their families. Oh, and singing, "There's nothing like a PEI potato."
>
> Halfway through the commercial, titles appear on the screen: "Actual PEI farmers." Pause, then, "Actually singing." It's hard not to feel a wide range of favourable emotions toward these lovable characters, and to admire their bravery in singing, slightly off key, on national television. It just goes to prove how much they really love and believe in their product. Cavendish Farms senior brand manager Suzanne Milner explains: "We wanted to make a connection between the pride our farmers take in growing the potatoes and the product that's delivered to consumers' homes."
>
> Chris Torbay, of Toronto-based Yield Branding, the creative talent behind the TV commercial, said, "Throughout the day of the shoot, the farmers "loosened up ... and by the end of the day, we started to have some fun. We tried a bunch of [friendly jabs] that fit in with their personalities after their personalities started to come out. That really plays to the honesty of the spot, that these aren't actors, they're real guys."[27]

J.D. Irving, Limited

Exhibit 9.12 Brand stories: Cavendish Farms tells the story of its From the Farm brand by having real PEI potato farmers literally singing its praises in a television commercial.

Branded content (content marketing)
Any form of information or story written and produced by a brand marketer, with the brand clearly and prominently featured.

Branded Content   In addition to advertising and other traditional marketing communications channels, brand stories can also be communicated through *branded content* or *content marketing*. **Branded content** is any form of information or story written and produced by a brand marketer, with the brand clearly and prominently featured. Branded content is also referred to as **content marketing**, and defined by some Canadian marketers as "telling real stories that help and entertain" and "using the power of storytelling to move consumers into action."[28]

The word *content* was traditionally applied to the editorial content of a newspaper or magazine: the stories written by journalists, managed by editors, and for the purpose of engaging readers. But in today's brand-driven world, some content is now being written for the purpose of promoting brands—and it's created a new opportunity for traditional content providers, like the *Globe and Mail*, which now operates a Custom Content Group that writes and produces content for marketers like Toronto's Sunnybrook Health Sciences Centre.

Branded Entertainment   Another vehicle through which brands can tell stories is to partner with filmmakers, musicians, and other artists to create *branded entertainment*. **Branded entertainment** is a form of entertainment, usually video, that is created with the cooperation or financial support of a marketer.

Branded entertainment
A form of entertainment, usually video, that is created with the cooperation or financial support of a marketer.

The first brand to create branded entertainment was BMW, with its series of short films called BMW Films. Each was written, acted, directed, and produced with the flair of a Hollywood movie, but the star of each film was a BMW car. The success of BMW Films led many marketers to produce their own films and music videos. Since then, many marketers have created branded entertainment. Labatt's Kokanee even went so far as to create a feature-length motion picture titled *The Movie Out Here*, produced by Alliance Films and Grip, Labatt's advertising agency, with help from professional screenwriters and Canadian beer fans.

In recent years, branded content and branded entertainment have become so widely used as marketing tools that the Cannes International Festival of Creativity now awards Lions in a new category: Branded Content & Entertainment. And Canadian advertising agencies are cleaning up in the category: Leo Burnett won a Silver Lion for P&G's "#LikeAGirl" campaign, and BBDO Toronto won for its Skittles "Struck by a Rainbow" fake documentary. Toronto agency John St. was awarded a Bronze Lion for Canadian Safe School Network's "Kids Read Mean Tweets," and LG2 won for "Reviveaphone."

Brands and Social Media

Social media and other emerging technologies are radically changing how consumers think, act, and relate to others, which is in turn forcing brand managers to rethink their marketing strategies and tactics. "Your brand is more than what you say it is; it's also what you produce and the experiences you create," advises a senior brand analyst.[29] Today's brand managers must create social groups and fan pages, host dialogues with consumers, and solicit feedback from them. In other words, they must *engage* them.

"In the era of the social web, we are all brand advocates and managers," says Brian Solis, author of the book *Engage!* He advises brand managers to use social media to define the face, voice, and personality of the brand.[30] Good advice, but not so easy to accomplish because of the challenges posed by how, exactly, to display and present a long-established brand across the social web. This challenge is further complicated by the addition of consumer voices and personalities into the mix. But for brand marketers willing to develop well-planned social media campaigns, there are rewards to be had. The Four Seasons hotel brand, for example, has successfully engaged professionals online through LinkedIn by creating a presence with videos, content, and even job listings.

Brand Advocates Today's consumers are telling stories about brands and spreading them through social media. Although it isn't possible for brand managers to control what consumers say about their brands, it *is* possible to encourage feedback and story-telling from those consumers who love the brand, and to create **brand advocates—** customers, employees, and others who willingly and voluntarily promote their favourite brands.

Brand advocates
Customers, employees, and others who willingly and voluntarily promote their favourite brands.

Brand advocates differ from brand ambassadors in that they're not being paid to talk about the brand; therefore, marketers must tread carefully in how they approach, create, and cultivate these people. Here are some principles to keep in mind:

- *Advocacy begins with trust:* Word of mouth, good or bad, has always influenced perceptions of brands. Online consumer opinions have also gained importance as new communications channels have emerged. Build trust with potential advocates by nurturing their recommendations and opinions.

- *Advocacy starts close to home:* A brand must first build a strong base of brand supporters—people who simply love the brand, and want to talk about it. If you gain the passionate support of customers and employees, their enthusiasm for the brand will spill over into words and actions.

- *Make customers and employees part of the brand story:* Transforming customers and employees into advocates puts them at the heart of the brand. Zappos, the online clothing and shoe retailer, has employees who are valued and empowered partners in creating and delivering the customer experience. Real customer-service calls have been featured in television commercials; "I hear Zappos" stories are posted online; and CEO Tony Hsieh tells brand stories on his numerous speaking tours.

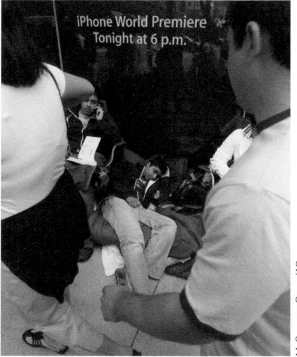
iPhone World Premiere
Tonight at 6 p.m.

M. Spencer Green/AP

- *Deliver an experience that gets them talking:* Creating brand advocates requires persistence and effort. Loyalty is not enough, because loyalists can be quiet and passive, like Microsoft's customers. On the other hand, Apple's advocates go beyond loyalty to actively promote the brand.

- *Outperform where they care the most:* The secret to creating advocates is to outperform for brand participants when they most need it. Understanding and solving problems is universally one of the most effective ways to create brand advocates.

Social media campaigns engage consumers, and now there's proof that engagement works. According to a study of over 100 social gaming campaigns commissioned by MediaBrix, a company that develops and produces in-app and in-game social and mobile advertising solutions for Fortune 500 brands, social and mobile gaming ads give advertisers 20 percent engagement rates. The study also showed that gaming ads outperformed mobile banner ads, Facebook ads, and standard banner ads in average click-through rates. "It comes as no surprise that social and mobile gaming advertising sees results 30 to 100 times better than standard online

Exhibit 9.13 Brand advocates: Truly devoted fans of a brand, like these consumers willing to sleep on the sidewalk to be first in line to get the newest Apple product, can be cultivated by marketers to act as brand advocates.

advertising campaigns," says Ari Brandt, CEO and co-founder of MediaBrix. "This is largely due to the fact that people are driven by a deep well of positive emotions—such as joy, excitement, and brand affinity—when playing social and mobile games."[31]

To sum up, brand management and brand marketing are all about building brands that connect deeply with customers. In the era of social media, marketers must rethink their processes, broaden the channels of communication available to consumers who seek information about their products and services, and engage consumers in conversations about brands.

From Family Favourite to Category Killer

Set one foot inside a Boston Pizza restaurant and the nuances are like a familiar reminder of a comforting place where you've been before. There's that one-of-a-kind aroma that can only be produced by real pizza made of real ingredients in real pizza ovens. Tables are buzzing with chatter and laughter among families and friends as energetic young employees welcome incoming guests, busily prep tables, and of course deliver heaping trays brimming with steaming hot dishes from the kitchen. It is an ambience that has become familiar to 40 million guests every year across North America, but mostly in Canada, where its 370 locations have made it more than just the country's number one casual dining brand, but quite possibly a category killer.

To be fair, the term *category killer* here is not to be confused with the big box, where the aggressive tactics of the more dominant retailers have leveraged their sheer brute force against the competitive landscape. Nope, in Boston Pizza's case, the meaning of the term suggests a firm so efficient, so dominant that it's almost synonymous with the category. As president and CEO Mark Pacinda indicates, "The BP concept and model is now so scalable that a stringent screening process is required to ensure that each new franchisee is going to be a strong brand ambassador."

The creation of the wholesome family brand and the overwhelming corporate success are not coincidental. They are interdependent. The business concept, established in 1964 in Edmonton, evolved into a number of same-style, same-values franchises scattered around Alberta and B.C. over the next three decades. The expansion through the remainder of Canada in the late 1990s gave way to a natural penetration into the United States and then Mexico in the early 2000s.

The Boston Pizza Royalty Income Trust Fund, launched in July 2002, has provided extraordinarily consistent positive returns to investors while maintaining the cash reserves required to seize opportunities and maintain an aggressively frequent store-renovation cycle. "Our focus on our four pillars strategy has formed the decision-making process that has led to the success of the organization," says Pacinda, referring to BP's long-held policy of improving the guest experience, continually building the brand, committing to franchise profitability, and doing good work in the community. With a checklist like that, the "Canada's favourite family restaurant" brand is well supported by a sound overarching strategy.

QUESTIONS

1. What is more important to BP's brand: its reputation for family-friendly dining or its commitment to sound business philosophy? Support your answer.

2. Research BP's competitors in Canada's casual dining category. List the names of other restaurant chains with properties across most of the country, and provide any available data about them, such as number of restaurants, history, financial results, and any other performance metrics. Compare and analyze your findings with Boston Pizza, using information found at www.bpincomefund.com.

REVIEWING THE CONCEPTS

 Define and describe the concept of a brand.

The basic definition of a *brand* is a name, symbol, icon, design, or a combination of these, that identifies the maker or marketer of a product. A brand may identify a company, one of its products, or a product line, but a brand is much more than just a *trade name*. Brands are powerful, and appeal to our emotions. They have status, personality, and monetary value. However, brands are intangible. A brand is an abstract concept or an idea—and for the biggest brands in the world, it is precisely that idea that generates most of the company's revenue.

Today, hardly anything goes unbranded. Branding helps consumers identify products that might benefit them. For marketers, the brand name becomes the basis on which a whole story can be built about a product's special qualities. The brand name and *trademark* provide legal protection for unique product features that might otherwise be copied by competitors. Trademarked names are indicated with a superscript TM, and registered trademarks are indicated with the symbol ®.

Consumers attach meanings to brands and develop *brand relationships* that go well beyond a product's physical attributes. The most powerful brands are those that consumers associate with just one word. Finally, people can become brands when, just as with products, their name takes on meanings that transcend the person.

 Explain the role of logos, brand personality, brand status, and brand equity in building brands.

While brands ultimately exist only as an abstract concept in the minds and hearts of consumers, it is the job of brand managers to create representations of the brand, such as *logos*. Logos are designs that represent the brand, and that may or may not incorporate the brand name. Logos may be redesigned from time to time, but these updates must be done without changing the meaning of the brand.

The most successful brands are those that have a distinctive personality. A *brand personality* is the sum total of all the attributes of a brand, and the emotions it inspires in the minds of consumers. Brand personalities are described in the same manner as human personalities, using words such as fun-loving, conservative, colourful, shy, and friendly. Another aspect of a brand's personality is its *status*, or level of social regard. Within every product category there are high-status and low-status brands; however, status should not be confused with value or popularity.

Many high-status brands tend to be exclusive rather than popular, while lower-status brands can still be highly popular. A brand's personality and status are key to establishing the positioning of that brand.

A powerful brand has monetary value and equity. *Brand equity* is the dollar amount attributed to the value of the brand, based on all the intangible qualities that create that value. Brand equity is difficult to calculate, but one indicator is the extent to which people are willing to pay more for the brand.

LO3 **List and describe the major strategic and ongoing management decisions marketers must make about brands.**

Marketing managers responsible for brands must make high-level strategic decisions that govern the management of the brand, and that guide the public and market perceptions about the brand. The first is *brand name selection*. A great brand requires a good, strong, memorable name. Brand experts advise that a new brand name should suggest something about the type of products it will brand; be easy to pronounce, recognize, and remember; be distinctive, extendable, pronounceable in many languages, and capable of registration and protection as a trademark.

To stand out in our overcommunicated world, brands must establish and own a unique, honest, meaningful, and clear position. Brand *positioning* is based on product attributes, benefits, or beliefs and values. The strongest brands are those that engage consumers on a deep, emotional level.

Brand sponsorship is an important branding strategy decision, and begins with the question, "To brand or not to brand?" Not all products are branded, but those that are may be *national brands* or *private brands* (also called *store brands* and *private labels*). Private brands are brand names applied by marketers to products manufactured for them under contract. While some manufacturers take years and spend millions to create their own brand names, others *license* the right to use a brand name, then focus on marketing and selling their products under that name. Finally, marketers may partner with another company, take the strongest elements of each company's products, and combine them to produce a *co-branded* offering.

In addition, because brands are valuable corporate assets, they must be carefully developed, either by creating *line extensions* or *brand extensions*, pursuing a *multibrand* strategy, or creating entirely *new brands*. Finally, it is the job of the brand manager to manage and protect the brand on an ongoing basis, by carefully managing the marketing communications and advertising that communicates the brand's attributes and positioning to the market. Brands must be maintained, not just by advertising, but by the overall brand experience, points of purchase, word of mouth, websites, and, increasingly, social media.

LO4 **Summarize the ways marketers can engage consumers through brand communications.**

Brand communications is a specialized form of marketing communications and advertising that focuses on communicating brand positioning, or image, rather than on product features. Advertising campaigns can help create name recognition and product knowledge, but consumers "get to know" a brand through their own *brand experiences* and through a wide range of *touchpoints* such as other forms of marketing communications, word of mouth, social media, company and brand websites, store displays, and many others. Brand experiences are evoked in consumers when they come into contact with brand touchpoints.

Brand communications efforts may employ *brand icons* or *characters* (sometimes called *brand mascots*). Brand icons are objects associated with the brand, while *brand characters*, also called *mascots*, are icons that move, speak, interact, and have personality traits. Brand icons and characters are also an important tool for *brand engagement*, the interaction between consumers and brands based on the emotional connection consumers feel toward the brand. Marketers and brand managers work to develop marketing programs, especially through the use of social media, that serve to

engage consumers with their brand. Brand communications tactics may also include *brand ambassadors*, real people who, under contract with the brand's marketing organization, act as spokespersons for the brand.

LO5 **Describe the role of storytelling, branded content, branded entertainment, social media, and brand advocates in brand communications.**

Today's brand managers use elements of a company's history, as well as elements of fiction, to create stories for their brands. In fact, brands themselves can be thought of as a form of storytelling. While new products provide us with new information, brand stories enrich this information with details that give the facts *meaning*.

In addition to advertising and other traditional marketing communications channels, brand stories can be communicated through *branded content* or *content marketing*, the brand marketer's production of any form of information or story in which the brand is clearly and prominently featured. A similar form of storytelling is *branded entertainment*, which is any form of entertainment, usually video, that is created with the cooperation or financial support of a marketer.

Brand managers can use social media to tell brand stories. In addition, they can cultivate consumers who are telling stories about their brands and turn them into *brand advocates*. Brand advocates are people who care about, or are interested in, the brand, and who willingly and voluntarily promote it. In the era of social media, marketers must engage consumers in conversations about brands.

MyMarketingLab

Study, practise, and explore real marketing situations with these helpful resources:

- **Interactive Lesson Presentations:** Work through interactive presentations and assessments to test your knowledge of marketing concepts.
- **Study Plan:** Check your understanding of chapter concepts with self-study quizzes.
- **Dynamic Study Modules:** Work through adaptive study modules on your computer, tablet, or mobile device.
- **Simulations:** Practise decision-making in simulated marketing environments.

DISCUSSION QUESTIONS

1. What is a brand? How would you explain the concept to someone who has never heard the term before? How would you explain what a brand is to a CEO who believes a brand is just a logo?

2. How does branding help both buyers and sellers?

3. Choose a car manufacturer and brand that you are familiar with. How would you describe the brand's attributes, personality, and positioning? How do you feel about the brand? In other words, describe your emotions and beliefs about it.

4. Find an example of a brand extension and a line extension. Why do you think the marketers made these brand decisions for the products you've chosen? In other words, why do you think they decided on a brand extension instead of a line extension, and vice versa?

CRITICAL THINKING EXERCISES

1. Spend some time browsing the TELUS website, and, if you are a TELUS customer, think about how you feel about the brand. How would you describe TELUS's brand personality? What role does packaging play in TELUS's brand communications strategy?

2. Think of a specialty product you purchased in the past. How important was brand to your purchase decision? What other aspects of the product played important roles in your decision to purchase that brand of that particular product?

3. Find or describe three TV commercials you remember seeing recently. Are these examples of brand communications? Explain why or why not.

4. NextPhase Strategy is a branding and marketing agency in Vancouver. Visit its website, and examine some of the work it has done for clients. How does it help clients manage brands?

ONLINE, MOBILE, AND SOCIAL MEDIA MARKETING

What does the future of brand advertising via social media channels hold? According to Peter Kim, chief digital officer at Cheil Worldwide, both consumers and brands must become less self-absorbed if they are to thrive in the next decade of social media. Kim was speaking at the Cannes International Festival of Creativity, a 60-year-old event that used to be about honouring the best in advertising creativity, but in recent years has become more about figuring out what to do with the latest advertising technology. Kim believes that social media is narcissistic, and that popular culture fuels this behaviour, reinforcing the idea that being social is actually about self-promotion. Brand marketers need to focus on the power of social media for genuine empowerment as opposed to self-aggrandizement. Consumers aren't looking to "join the conversation," says Kim. Rather, they want the ability to engage brands in direct action.[32]

QUESTIONS

1. Investigate everything that your favourite brand is currently doing in social media. Explain, in marketing terms, the strategy behind its social media marketing.

2. As a consumer, do you feel that what your brand is doing to engage you is successful? In other words, are they engaging you? If not, what do you *wish* they would do to engage you with the brand?

THINK LIKE A MARKETING MANAGER

General Mills owns, markets, and manages over 300 brands. On the company's website (www.generalmills.com), these brands are organized by food category: baking, breads, cereals, pasta, and so on. Visit the company's site, choose one of the food categories to examine, and then answer the following questions about the brands in that category.

QUESTIONS

1. How many brands are in your food category? Are they line extensions, brand extensions, or new brand names? Briefly describe the positioning and brand personality for each.

2. Let's say General Mills wants to launch a new brand in your category. Would you recommend a line extension, brand extension, or new brand name? Briefly describe how the new brand should be positioned; for example, should it be a new flavour or colour, and if so, which one? Come up with a new brand name for your product.

MARKETING ETHICS

There are hundreds of different beer brands available to Canadian consumers, most of which are marketed to different segments based on lifestyle, and with advertising campaigns based on communicating brand personality. Yet alcohol is a controlled substance and cannot legally be promoted to underage drinkers. Visit the "Our Brands" section of Labatt Breweries of Canada website, and consider the following ethical questions.

QUESTIONS

1. Labatt has a Facebook page, and there is also a Facebook page for each of its beer brands. For marketers, the main reason for having a Facebook page is to get as many people as possible to "like" it—yet there are no controls for keeping underage children from liking a beer page on Facebook. Visit the Facebook pages of three of Labatt's beer brands and compare the fans on both. How many are there? Do most of them seem to be of legal drinking age? If you were a marketing manager at Labatt, what additional steps would you recommend to attempt to prevent children from becoming fans of the beers on Facebook?

2. Look closely at the website of your favourite Labatt beer brand. Does it offer any communications that associate the brand with responsible drinking? Do you think the marketers are making any attempt to position the brand as "responsible?"

MARKETING BY THE NUMBERS

Special K is the number one brand in the diet food category, and the Kellogg Company is planning to turn it into a megabrand. Since brand extensions must be consistent with the brand's positioning as a weight-management food, the company planned to roll out Special K–branded protein waters and protein bars. The worldwide market for bottled water is worth approximately $75 billion. In Canada, retail sales in the snack food category—which includes candy, gum, snacks, and bars—have totalled about $500 million; the natural snacks and bars segment makes up about 10 percent of this category. Sales of Special K–branded cereals are more than $500 million worldwide, and its advertising budget is $45 million.

QUESTIONS

1. Kellogg hoped to capture 3 percent of the market with its new Special K protein water products. How much should the company spend on advertising in Canada to support this new product line?

2. How much should the company spend to advertise the new Special K protein bars in Canada? What percentage of the snack food market do you think it will be able to capture in the first year, and what is the value of that market?

SLEEMAN'S NOTORIOUS BRAND POSITIONING

Brand managers strive to associate their brands with powerful emotions that bring the brand to life in the mind of the consumer and establish a clear and unique positioning. That's particularly difficult to do for a product like beer, which, let's face it, is not highly differentiated. Coors associates its brand with the feeling of "cold"—it wants to own that space in the beer consumer's mind. Molson is all about hockey and rock music. Corona is the beer for relaxing and feeling as if you're on vacation. And Sleeman is, well, notorious.

As a brand positioning strategy, hanging your image on a word such as "notorious" is risky. *Notorious* means widely and publicly known, usually for a particular trait, but it has connotations of being dangerous. That's okay with John Sleeman, though, because he's an important part of the Sleeman brand story—and somewhat notorious himself. In the 1970s, he opened a pub in Oakville, Ontario, and started a company to import and distribute beers from abroad in Canada. In 1984, his aunt thought that, since John was in the beer business anyway, it was time he found out about his family heritage. There had been a family brewery, she told him, which had closed in 1933; she encouraged him to restart the business. "They were told no one with the name Sleeman would get a liquor licence for 50 years," said Sleeman's aunt. "Now it's 51. Here you go." Then she handed him an old bottle and a leather-bound book filled with his grandfather's beer recipes, and the rest is history.

Sleeman traced the ownership of the dormant company to Nabisco, purchased the rights for just a few dollars, and opened the new brewery in Guelph, Ontario. Like any good notorious character, he's had his ups and downs. "There are few things that motivate me as much as somebody telling me I'm wrong or I'm going to fail," he said. But fail he did. When the bank called in a loan a year after the brewery relaunched, John Sleeman lost his family home. He didn't stay down for long, though. He sought refinancing from a U.S. bank and rose from the ashes to build Canada's largest microbrewery and create a brand based on the family's history. His grandfather's brewery had been called The Sleeman Brewing and Malting Company, but it went out of business after suffering the consequences of selling contraband liquor to the United States during Prohibition. "We haven't hidden the fact that my grandfather's brothers got caught smuggling," says Sleeman, though he adds that the family is not particularly proud of it.

Sleeman's beer bottles are notorious, too. The first product developed by the newly reopened brewery was a cream ale, painstakingly recreated from his grandfather's recipe and bottled in a recreation of the original clear glass bottle, a move unique among beer brands in the 1980s. Unfortunately, that doubled packaging costs and increased quality control expenses, because clear bottles make the beer more susceptible to light. "We felt we needed to stay as close to the original as possible, and went over budget to get everything right," says Sleeman. In the days before the company could afford to advertise, the bottles got the beer noticed. Consumers liked the bottles so much that they kept them instead of returning them to the beer store. There was even a time in the 1990s when the company put out a call to consumers to please return them, as they were running out.

Beer sales in Canada have held steady for more than a decade, and many Canadian brands have made inroads into the much larger U.S. market. It's likely no surprise to any Canadian that we consume, by far, more beer than any other alcoholic beverage. According to Statistics Canada, the beer industry provides approximately 200 000 jobs and contributes $2 billion per year to the country's economy. Despite this, however, a decade ago Sleeman began experiencing intense competition from premium imports and discount brews, and again found itself struggling financially. In 2006, Sapporo Breweries purchased Sleeman, a match that seems to be built in brand heaven. Sapporo is one of Japan's oldest beers, dating back to 1876. It has a firmly established brand image and its own unique packaging in the form of an asymmetric, top-heavy silver can.

Sapporo recognized the unique talent of John Sleeman, who'd managed to build the country's largest craft brewery in a market dominated by two very large players, and invited him to stay on and run the company's operations in Canada. Sleeman agreed. "I explained to [Sapporo] that as consumers, Canadians are very proud of our beer and our heritage. . . . We still talk about the things that got us here: heritage, quality, caring about our customers, and putting money back into the community."

With this new financial support, Sleeman hired advertising agency Dentsu Canada for a brand positioning project, and after two years of working on it, the "Notorious" strategy was born. The creative genius behind the campaign was Glen Hunt, who is notorious himself in advertising circles as the writer behind the famous Molson Canadian "I Am Canadian" commercial, featuring a plaid-shirted "Joe" proclaiming his pride in being Canadian. "We went out and spoke to consumers who said, 'Where are you? [We] haven't heard from you in a while and we'd like to,'" said Hunt of Sleeman's return to TV. About the new campaign, Hunt joked, "'Notoriously Good' targets individuals 25 and older who are looking for a 'notoriously good evening.'"

The campaign featured a 60-second spot that introduces viewers to a cast of real-life characters who inspired the brewery's beginnings, while the shorter ads focused on individual characters. Other marketing communications efforts included print ads, posters, and in-bar elements such as specially designed pint glasses, tap handles, and coasters with a character on one side and a little history of the individual on the other.

The five TV commercials were all done in the style of a vaudeville-era theatre. The first ad begins with a red velvet curtain under the title "Our History." The curtain opens to reveal a Sleeman beer case on the stage floor. The top opens, and the colourful, historical characters climb out: a pirate, a beer wench holding frosty mugs, dancing girls, a smuggler, and a philanderer. They gather on the stage in the manner of a cast assembling for their curtain call at the end of a play. Finally, a tuxedo-clad John Sleeman emerges from the box, holding the signature Sleeman clear bottle in one hand and the famous black leather book in the other, as the announcer proclaims, "Five generations of infamous family brewing heritage. Sleeman: Notoriously good since 1834."

Subsequent executions told stories about the brand: "Some of John Sleeman's early ancestors were pirates, philanderers, bootleggers, and smugglers," says one. Another shows a pirate climbing slyly out of the Sleeman beer case on the stage as the announcer tells us, "Our ancestors were pirates. The name was Slyman. On land they opened taverns. The name became Sleeman. Born of pirates. Brewed in Guelph." In another, we learn, "Prohibitionists wanted to run George Sleeman out of town. But George Sleeman ran for mayor, and ran *them* out of town." And finally, we are told of a particularly famous notorious character: "Sleeman beer was enjoyed by Al Capone. A man who did what he did, and took what he wanted."

The brand has always traded on its history. In 2005, the company announced the John Sleeman Presents series of beers, featuring an India Pale Ale designed "to recapture a piece of history of the British Empire" and described by John Sleeman as "inspired by page 46 in my grandfather's recipe book. [It] has an abundance of hops, a distinctive

flavour, and a fascinating history." And behind each beer there's a story: India Pale Ale was originally developed in the 1700s, when breweries would send ale from England to British troops and expatriates in India. Because the voyage took months, the brewers came up with the idea of improving the beer's shelf life by adding extra hops, which acted as a natural preservative.

More than a decade after the merger with Sapporo, the Sleeman brand name is still going strong. Says John Sleeman, "I restarted a 100-and-something-year-old business thinking I was going to be this generation's custodian, and that someone in my family might be interested in taking over when I ended up in my pine box." With nearly two centuries of notorious history behind it, there seems to be no end to the potential for telling stories about this brand, even long after its founder is no longer part of the story.

Sources: Kristin Laird, "Dentsu Launches Sapporo's First National Canadian Campaign, *Marketing,* June 7, 2010, marketingmag.ca; Kristin Laird, "Sleeman Puts Its Notorious History on TV," *Marketing,* May 7, 2010, marketingmag.ca; "Sleeman Brews Up a Crafty Takeover of Established Quebec-Based Beermaker," *Canadian Packaging, 57*(5), May 2004, p. 7; Andy Holloway, "John Sleeman," *Canadian Business,* 77(10), Summer 2004, pp. 204–205; "Sleeman Swallows Up Maritime Beer Producer," *Canadian Packaging, 53*(10), October 2000, p. 7; Interview with John Sleeman in "Ask the Legends," *Profit,* November 2008, pp. 112–113; Colin Campbell, "Our Beer Sure Goes Down Smooth," *Maclean's,* September 4, 2006, pp. 38–39; Alicia Clegg, "Old Brands in New Bottles," *Financial Times,* June 1, 2006, p. 12; and "Sleeman Brews Up Another Holiday Treat with Historic Recipe and Classy Packaging," *Canadian Packaging,* November 2005, p. 7.

QUESTIONS

1. The original "Notorious" advertising campaign is no longer running, but Sleeman has continued to position its brand based on this word and its associations. Find the latest Sleeman advertising and explain how it functions as brand communication to convey to consumers the idea that Sleeman is notorious.

2. How is the idea that Sleeman is notorious being communicated on the brand's website?

3. How is the idea that Sleeman is notorious being communicated through social media?

4. Do you think Sleeman's brand communications and positioning strategy is a good one? Do you think it should keep using it indefinitely, or should it change the positioning of the brand? Explain why or why not.

Claudio Papapietro

AFTER STUDYING THIS CHAPTER, YOU SHOULD BE ABLE TO

1. identify the three major pricing strategies and discuss the importance of understanding customer-value perceptions, company costs, and competitor strategies when setting prices

2. identify and define the other important external and internal factors affecting a firm's pricing decisions

3. describe the major strategies for pricing new products

4. explain how companies find a set of prices that maximizes the profits from the total product mix

5. discuss how companies adjust their prices to take into account different types of customers and situations

6. discuss the key issues related to initiating and responding to price changes

7. list and briefly describe the major legislation in Canada that affects marketers' pricing decisions

Pricing: Understanding and Capturing Customer Value

PREVIEWING THE CONCEPTS

We continue your marketing journey with a look at another major marketing mix tool—pricing. If effective product development, promotion, and distribution sow the seeds of business success, effective pricing is the harvest. Firms successful at *creating* customer value with the other marketing mix activities must *capture* some of this value in the prices they set. In this chapter, we begin with the following question: What is a price? Next, we look at three major pricing strategies—customer value-based, cost-based, and competition-based pricing—and at other factors that affect pricing decisions. Finally, we examine strategies for new-product pricing, product-mix pricing, price adjustments, and dealing with price changes. But first, let's look at a new company with a catchy name you might be familiar with—Warby Parker—and see how a new company determines its pricing strategy.

WARBY PARKER: TRANSFORMING THE EXPERIENCE OF BUYING EYEGLASSES

As young brothers in rural India, Toti and Omprakash Tewtia did everything together. They started a farming business together, and raised their families together. But as they grew old together, their vision began to decline, and it was taking a toll on their business as well. For years, they had cultivated the land in their village, but the last crop had been lost. How on earth could career farmers, who had been working the land since childhood, have allowed this to happen? They couldn't see the insects that were ravaging their fields. Without proper glasses, their livelihood was put in jeopardy.

All that changed when the folks from Warby Parker showed up. Now proudly sporting his new glasses, Toti looks in the mirror and sees a much younger man. "These glasses have taken me back to my young time!" Story time is again a nightly tradition for the Tewtias' grandkids, and the crops on their farm are again healthy and ready to harvest.

Warby Parker is a lifestyle brand based in New York City with a lofty objective: to offer designer eyewear at a revolutionary price, while leading the way for socially conscious businesses. The company was formed in 2010 by four classmates at the Wharton School of the University of Pennsylvania: Neil Blumenthal, Dave Gilboa, Andy Hunt, and Jeff Raider. The idea for Warby Parker was formed when Dave Gilboa lost his glasses on a

✓● Practice on MyMarketingLab
Maximizing total revenue for bubble tea sales

✓● Practice on MyMarketingLab
Mobile App Pricing Strategy

✓● Practice on MyMarketingLab
Calculating Profits

backpacking trip. The cost of replacing them was so high that he spent the first semester of grad school without them. All four friends were amazed at how hard it was to find a pair of great frames that didn't leave wallets bare.

"We each had [the same] experience: Walking to an optical shop, getting super excited about a pair of glasses, and walking out feeling like we got punched in the stomach," relates Neil Blumenthal, one of the four co-founders of Warby Parker. "We thought, There's got to be a better way here."

That's when the four business school students started doing some research to answer a simple question: Why are prescription eyeglasses so expensive? They discovered a few key reasons. For starters, although there are many eyeglass retailers, the majority of the industry is owned and controlled by one company. The Luxottica Group of Italy owns brands such as Oakley and Ray-Ban and retail chains such as LensCrafters, Pearle Vision, and Sunglass Hut. Luxottica's stranglehold on the eyeglass industry keeps prices high. The team also discovered that all those fancy fashion brands (e.g., Armani, Ralph Lauren, Gucci) emblazoned on eyewear frames don't actually make the glasses. The brands are licensed to manufacturers (most of them owned by Luxottica) and get a fat cut just for lending their brand names.

They chose a unique name for their new company, and new brand: Warby Parker—a combination of two characters created by Jack Kerouac. Next, they set out to create a business plan that would bypass the standard manufacturers and channels and reinvent how you buy eyewear. Their strategy was to remove the middlemen to sell fashionable eyewear at a fair price. "The mark-ups in this industry are insane," notes Blumenthal, pointing out that most glasses are sold for at least three times their wholesale price.

To come in at a low price, Warby Parker developed its own line of fashionable frames in-house, contracted its own manufacturing, and opened up an online storefront to sell it all directly to customers. The price point: $95, including anti-scratch and anti-glare polycarbonate lenses. That's one-third to one-sixth the price charged by major retailers. And Warby Parker sports some of the most fashionable designs around, all made from the same high-quality materials that the market leaders use.

Warby Parker opened its online shop in 2010. With almost no competitors selling glasses online, Warby Parker had a chance to really stand out. It made buying easy for customers with its Home Try-On program, which allows customers to try on up to five frames for five days. After some features in *GQ* and *Vogue*, the young start-up was inundated with purchases and requests for home try-ons. In fact, it had so many requests that it ran out of inventory and had a waitlist of 20 000 customers.

The company didn't have a retail space, but co-founder Neil Blumenthal had an idea. "We said, well, the store's my apartment. Come on over." So Blumenthal and his buddies were soon hosting people from all over in Blumenthal's New York apartment. With glasses laid out on the dining room table, customers flowed in by the dozens, even hundreds.

Although the company's founders started with the objective of selling affordable designer eyewear, they quickly realized that they wanted to do more. They wanted to make a difference in people's lives on a more fundamental level. They learned that almost 1 billion people worldwide lack access to glasses. And without good vision, people like the Tewtia brothers are not able to work or learn to their full potential. So, with demand established, Warby Parker looked into feasibility of providing the supply. Although in business for only a short time, the company was not only breaking even at the $95 price point, it was making a nice margin. In fact, there were more than enough profits to cover the cost of donating a pair of glasses for every pair sold. By partnering with nonprofit organizations such as VisionSpring, Warby Parker ensures that for every pair of glasses sold, a pair is distributed to someone in need.

What started as an afterthought quickly became Warby Parker's brand story, point of differentiation, and brand positioning. The company calls it their Buy a Pair, Give a Pair program. "We believe that everyone has the right to see," the Warby Parker site states, adding that getting the correct glasses can add 20 percent to someone's income by increasing productivity and performance.

Today, Warby Parker has distributed more than 1 million pairs of glasses to people in need worldwide. Its business model is built around a snowball concept—helping one person has an impact on other people, who help even more people, and so on. Take the case of Juana, a 30-year-old mother who lives in Sololá, a mountainside village in Guatemala. Having been on her own from an early age, she learned how to work hard and take care of herself. Recently, Juana received training from Community Enterprise Solutions, a nonprofit organization (and Warby Parker partner) that helps distribute eyewear to people whose livelihoods have been compromised by poor vision. Now, in her tiny but clean and well-organized space, she offers free eye exams and sells eyeglasses, right alongside efficient wood stoves and water filters.

On the home front, Warby Parker is making it easier for customers. The firm has started rolling out its own Warby Parker stores, so not only can shoppers try out glasses online or at home, they can do so in person at a growing number of brick-and-mortar locations. Given the company's quick early success, it has no shortage of investors willing to provide the funds needed for expansion.

Warby Parker is a great example of a company that does well by doing good, and it's setting the bar high for companies that want to do the same. It not only distributes a pair of glasses for every one purchased, its products are also *much* less expensive than competing goods, the opposite of most one-for-one operations. And Warby Parker's one-for-one model is setting a standard for genuinely empowering people to help themselves while helping others do the same. Warby Parker has transformed what was an essentially physical, often colourless, sometimes stressful shopping experience into a highly engaging one. Warby Parker is now a beloved brand valued at an estimated $1.2 billion.[1]

Exhibit 10.1 Pricing: No matter what the state of the economy, companies should sell value, not price.

Little Whale/Shutterstock

COMPANIES TODAY face a fierce and fast-changing pricing environment. As a result of increased information and online price comparison tools, plus the increasing number of low price and discount retailers, today's value-seeking shoppers have put increased pricing pressure on many companies. It would seem that all companies should respond by tightening their belts and reducing their prices, yet cutting prices is often not the best answer.

Reducing prices unnecessarily can lead to lost profits and damaging price wars. It can cheapen a brand by signalling to customers that the price is more important than the value the brand delivers. Instead, companies should sell value, not price. In some cases, that means selling lesser products at rock-bottom prices. But in most cases, it means persuading customers that paying a higher price for the company's brand is justified by the greater value they gain.

What Is a Price?

Price
The amount of money charged for a product or a service, or the sum of the values that customers exchange for the benefits of having or using the product or service.

In the narrowest sense, **price** is the amount of money charged for a product or a service. More broadly, price is the sum of all the values that customers give up to gain the benefits of having or using a product or service. Historically, price has been the major factor affecting buyer choice. In recent decades, nonprice factors have gained increasing importance. However, price still remains one of the most important elements determining a firm's market share and profitability.

Price is the only element in the marketing mix that produces revenue; all other elements represent costs. Price is also one of the most flexible marketing mix elements. Unlike product features and channel commitments, prices can be changed quickly. At the same time, pricing is the number one problem facing many marketing executives, and many companies do not handle pricing well. Some managers view pricing as a big headache, preferring instead to focus on the other marketing mix elements. However, smart managers treat pricing as a key strategic tool for creating and capturing customer value.

Prices have a direct impact on a firm's bottom line. A small percentage improvement in price can generate a large percentage in profitability. More importantly, as a part of a company's overall value proposition, price plays a key role in creating customer value and building customer relationships. So, instead of shying away from pricing, smart marketers are embracing it as an important competitive asset.[2]

◄◉│**Simulate** on MyMarketingLab

Pricing Strategies

◄◉│**Simulate** on MyMarketingLab

Pricing

Major Pricing Strategies [LO1]

The price the company charges will fall somewhere between one that is too high to produce any demand and one that is too low to produce a profit. Figure 10.1 summarizes the major considerations in setting price. Customer perceptions of the product's value set the *ceiling* for prices. If customers perceive that the price is greater than the product's value, they will not buy the product. Product costs set the *floor* for prices. If the company prices the product below its costs, company profits will suffer. In setting its price between these two extremes, the company must consider a number of other internal and external factors, including competitors' strategies and prices, the company's overall marketing strategy and mix, and the nature of the market and the demand.

The figure suggests three major pricing strategies: customer value-based pricing, cost-based pricing, and competition-based pricing.

Customer Value-Based Pricing

In the end, the customer will decide whether a product's price is right. Pricing decisions, like other marketing mix decisions, must start with customer value. When customers buy a product, they exchange something of value (the price) to get something of value (the benefits of having or using the product). Effective, customer-oriented pricing involves

FIGURE 10.1 Considerations in Setting Price

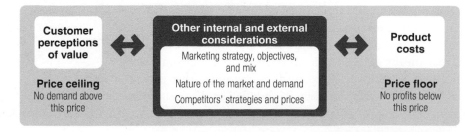

FIGURE 10.2 Value-Based Pricing versus Cost-Based Pricing

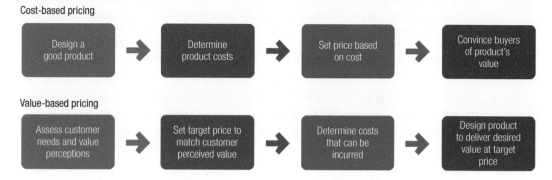

Cost-based pricing

Design a good product → Determine product costs → Set price based on cost → Convince buyers of product's value

Value-based pricing

Assess customer needs and value perceptions → Set target price to match customer perceived value → Determine costs that can be incurred → Design product to deliver desired value at target price

understanding how much value consumers place on the benefits they receive from the product and setting a price that captures this value.

Customer value-based pricing uses buyers' perceptions of value, not the seller's cost, as the key to pricing. Value-based pricing means that the marketer cannot design a product and marketing program and then set the price. Price is considered along with the other marketing mix variables *before* the marketing program is set.

Figure 10.2 compares value-based pricing with cost-based pricing. Although costs are an important consideration in setting prices, cost-based pricing is often product driven. The company designs what it considers to be a good product, adds up the costs of making the product, and sets a price that covers costs plus a target profit. Marketing must then convince buyers that the product's value at that price justifies its purchase. If the price turns out to be too high, the company must settle for lower mark-ups or lower sales, both resulting in disappointing profits.

Value-based pricing reverses this process. The company first assesses customer needs and value perceptions. It then sets its target price based on customer perceptions of value. The targeted value and price drive decisions about what costs can be incurred and the resulting product design. As a result, pricing begins with analyzing consumer needs and value perceptions, and price is set to match consumers' perceived value.

It's important to remember that "good value" is not the same as "low price." For example, a Steinway piano—any Steinway piano—costs a lot. But to those who own one, a Steinway is a great value.

> At the Steinway Piano Gallery Toronto you can purchase a custom-made Crown Jewel Edition Steinway piano, encased in your choice of magnificent woods, with the grain meticulously matched from one end of the piano to the other. It's not just a piano, it's an original, handmade work of art, unique in the world—and it will cost you about $800 000. For the less extravagant buyer, a Steinway piano can be had for $26 000. But ask anyone who owns one and they'll tell you that, when it comes to Steinway, price is nothing; the Steinway experience is everything. Steinway makes very high quality pianos—handcrafting each Steinway requires up to one full year. But more important, owners get the Steinway mystique. The Steinway name evokes images of classical concert stages and the celebrities and performers who've owned and played Steinway pianos across more than 155 years.

Customer value-based pricing
Setting price based on buyers' perceptions of value rather than on the seller's cost.

Corbis

Exhibit 10.2 Perceived value: Glenn Gould's Steinway CD 318 now belongs to the National Arts Centre in Ottawa. Its value is in the fame of its owner, but for many aficionados the value is in the brand name, Steinway.

World-renowned Canadian classical pianist Glenn Gould owned one—in fact, his favourite Steinway is on permanent display at the National Arts Centre in Ottawa. But Steinways aren't just for world-class pianists and the wealthy. Ninety-nine percent of all Steinway buyers are amateurs who perform only in their dens. To such customers, whatever a Steinway costs, it's a small price to pay for the value of owning one. As one Steinway owner puts it, "My friendship with the Steinway piano is one of the most important and beautiful things in my life." Who can put a price on such feelings?[3]

Companies often find it hard to measure the value customers will attach to its product. For example, calculating the cost of ingredients in a meal at a fancy restaurant is relatively easy. But assigning a value to other satisfactions such as taste, environment, relaxation, conversation, and status is very hard. These values are subjective—they vary for both different consumers and different situations.

Still, consumers will use these perceived values to evaluate a product's price, so the company must work to measure them. Sometimes, companies ask consumers how much they would pay for a basic product and for each benefit added to the offer. Or a company might conduct experiments to test the perceived value of different product offers. According to an old Russian proverb, there are two fools in every market—one who asks too much and one who asks too little. If the seller charges more than the buyers' perceived value, the company's sales will suffer. If the seller charges less, its products will sell very well but will produce less revenue than they would if they were priced at the level of perceived value.

We now examine two types of value-based pricing: *good-value pricing* and *value-added pricing*.

Good-value pricing

Offering just the right combination of quality and good service at a fair price.

Good-Value Pricing More and more, marketers are adopting **good-value pricing** strategies—offering just the right combination of quality and good service at a fair price.

In many cases, this has involved introducing less expensive versions of established, brand-name products. For example, fast-food restaurants such as Taco Bell and McDonald's offer value meals and dollar menu items. Armani offers the less-expensive, more-casual Armani Exchange fashion line, and Donna Karan has DKNY. Alberto-Culver's TRESemmé hair care line is marketed as a salon look and feel at a fraction of the price.

It's difficult to define the word *value*, because what any consumer deems valuable or "worth the price" is entirely subjective. There are many, however, who define value as being able to get brand-name or high-quality products at lower prices than "normal"—and so a retailer with a pricing strategy that caters to that need is likely to be a winner. (See Marketing@Work 10.1.)

In other cases, good-value pricing has involved redesigning existing brands to offer more quality for a given price or the same quality for less. Some companies even succeed by offering less value but at rock-bottom prices. For example, passengers flying low-cost European airline Ryanair won't get much in the way of free amenities, but they'll like the airline's unbelievably low prices. Ireland's Ryanair bills itself as Europe's only ultra-low-cost carrier, and it seems that no other EU airline can match Ryanair's fares—because they are nearly free! There is a catch,

Markus Scholz/dpa/picture-alliance/Newscom

Exhibit 10.3 Good-value pricing: People who choose Ryanair do so because the prices for the flights are low, even though they have to pay extra for everything else. Consumers feel that they're getting good value for their money at these prices.

MARKETING@WORK 10.1

Off-Price Retailing at Winners: Find Fabulous for Less

"Find fabulous for less!" is the slogan—and the positioning—of Winners, an off-price apparel and home goods chain with 239 stores across Canada. Winners is owned by TJX Companies Inc., a global retailer that, in addition to Winners, operates Marshalls and HomeSense in Canada; T.J. Maxx and Marshalls in the U.S.; T.K. Maxx in the U.K. and Ireland, and many other chain stores in Europe. What these stores all have in common is their pricing strategy, known as off-price retailing.

Off-price retail is not the same as a discount store. Whereas items for sale at a discount retailer such as Giant Tiger and Dollarama were made to sell for those very low prices, merchandise at Winners was originally made to sell for more than what Winners prices it at. TJX describes itself this way: "We see ourselves as a global, value retailer, and our off-price mission is to deliver great value to customers through the combination of brand, fashion, price, and quality. We offer a rapidly changing assortment of brand name and designer merchandise at prices generally 20 to 60 percent below department and specialty store regular prices on comparable merchandise, every day."

Quality and value are the biggest differences between off-price retailing and discounting. If you've ever shopped at Winners, you know that you'll find brand name items at prices much lower than what you'd pay in a department store. TJX's buyers source merchandise from around the globe, dealing with more than 17 000 vendors in more than 100 countries. They look for purchasing opportunities such as a department or specialty store cancelling a large order; a manufacturer making up too much product, or a close-out deal when a vendor wants to clear merchandise at the end of a season.

The clothing and home goods you'll find at Winners, Marshalls, and HomeSense might be well-known designer brands, or they might be artisan creations, some of which are manufactured for TJX Companies, and some of which are designed by the company's own style experts. The buyers at TJX search for exactly the right combination of fashion, brand, quality, and price. For example, they buy beautiful blown glass from Poland, ceramics from Italy, and quality furniture from right here in Canada. The buyers are "opportunistic and entrepreneurial," and are always seeking great quality and value all over the world.

Since the 2008–2009 financial crisis, off-price chains have been one of the fastest growing segments, as shoppers gravitate toward designer brands at big discounts. Outlets and off-price chains first emerged years ago. They helped clear out unsold merchandise from earlier in the season or products with defects. But now, much of what is sold is no longer as a result of close-outs; instead, it's made to order for off-price and outlet stores.

Today, TJX operates a total of 3441 stores in seven countries—Canada, the United States, the United Kingdom, Ireland, Germany, Poland, and Austria—and three e-commerce sites. These include 1126 T.J. Maxx, 987 Marshalls, 498 HomeGoods, and 6 Sierra Trading Post stores, as well as tjmaxx.com and sierratradingpost.com in the United States; 239 Winners, 97 HomeSense, and 39 Marshalls stores in Canada; and 416 T.K. Maxx and 33 HomeSense stores, as well as tkmaxx.com, in Europe. The company is already the largest off-price retailer in Canada and the United States, and with an ever-growing market demand for low-priced, high-value goods, TJX seems destined to become the world's largest off-price retailer.

Sources: Phil Wahba, "Macy's CEO Admits He Was an Obstacle to Launching New Discount Chain," Fortune.com, June 29, 2015; Lauren Gensler, "TJX Profit Rises, Says It Will Boost Worker Pay," Forbes.com, February 25, 2015; The TJX Companies, Inc. 2014 Annual Report; and information from TJX.com, Investor.TJX.com, Winners.ca, and HomeSense.ca.

Exhibit 10.4 Off-price retailing: Winners is the largest off-price retailer in Canada. Its pricing strategy is to sell everything for 20 to 60 percent less than original retail prices.

however. The airline charges for virtually everything except the seat itself, from baggage check-in to seat-back advertising space. Once in the air, flight attendants hawk everything from scratch-card games to perfume and digital cameras to their captive audience. Lately, Ryanair's controversial Michael O'Leary has taken aim at price-comparison websites, claiming they "make no sense" and "shouldn't exist," and has been encouraging other European airlines to post competitors' prices on their own websites.[4]

An important type of good-value pricing at the retail level is *everyday low pricing (EDLP)*. EDLP involves charging a constant, everyday low price with few or no temporary price discounts. Retailers such as Costco and furniture seller Leon's, with its Integrity Pricing guarantee, practise EDLP. The king of EDLP is Walmart, which practically defined the concept. Except for a few sale items every month, Walmart promises everyday low prices on everything it sells. In contrast, *high-low pricing* involves charging higher prices on an everyday basis but running frequent promotions to lower prices temporarily on selected items. Department stores such as Sears and Hudson's Bay practise high-low pricing by having frequent sales days, early-bird savings, and bonus earnings for store credit-card holders.

Value-Added Pricing   Value-based pricing doesn't mean simply charging what customers want to pay or setting low prices to meet the competition. Instead, many companies adopt **value-added pricing** strategies. Rather than cutting prices to match competitors, they attach value-added features and services to differentiate their offers and justify higher prices. Similarly, some movie theatre chains are *adding* amenities and charging *more* rather than cutting services to maintain lower admission prices.

> Cineplex is turning some of its multiplexes into smaller, roomier viewing rooms with luxurious features such as high-backed leather seats, food service, and even alcohol. Cineplex Entertainment, for example, offers a premium theatre experience called VIP Cinemas. When purchasing tickets, guests choose exactly where they would like to sit in the auditorium, and all seats are reserved. Each VIP Cinema auditorium features stadium seating with extra leg room and luxurious high-back leather seats fitted with movable tray tables. When guests take their seat they're presented with a menu, and their order is taken and delivered in the same manner as in a restaurant. There's also a licensed lounge for the exclusive use of VIP Cinema guests.
>
> Cineplex operates 12 VIP Cinemas across Canada, and given their incredible popularity with guests, the company plans to open several more in the coming years. The VIP Cinemas experience takes in-theatre dining to a new level, offering all the traditional movie snacks as well as VIP menu items: calamari, flatbread pizza, wraps, salads, and much more. VIP Cinemas also offer a special drink menu, including a wide selection of beer, wine, cocktails, and martinis. The strategy is designed to appeal to adults, and only those of legal drinking age are allowed in.[5]

The Cineplex example illustrates that people are motivated not by price, but by what they get for what they pay. It's clear that how consumers define value is a personal decision—if the "best deal" was simply a question of dollar amount, we'd all be shopping in one big discount store—and that they are willing to pay accordingly.

Cost-Based Pricing

Whereas customer-value perceptions set the price ceiling, costs set the floor for what price the company can charge. **Cost-based pricing** involves

Value-added pricing
Attaching value-added features and services to differentiate a company's offers and charging higher prices.

Cost-based pricing
Setting prices based on the costs for producing, distributing, and selling the product plus a fair rate of return for effort and risk.

Jean Levac/ Ottawa Citizen. Reprinted by permission.

Exhibit 10.5 Value-added pricing: Some Cineplex theatres are adding value to movie tickets by providing luxurious seating, tray tables, and food and beverage service.

setting prices based on the costs for producing, distributing, and selling the product plus a fair rate of return for its effort and risk. A company's costs may be an important element in its pricing strategy.

Some companies, such as Ryanair, Walmart, and Dell, work to become the "low-cost producers" in their industries. Companies with lower costs can set lower prices that result in smaller margins but greater sales and profits. Other companies, however, intentionally pay higher costs so that they can claim higher prices and margins. For example, it costs more to make a handcrafted Steinway piano than a Yamaha production model, but the higher costs result in higher quality, justifying the much higher price. The key is to manage the spread between costs and prices—how much the company makes for the customer value it delivers.

Types of Costs A company's costs take two forms, fixed and variable. **Fixed costs** (also known as **overhead**) are costs that do not vary with production or sales level. For example, a company must pay each month's bills for rent, heat, interest, and executive salaries, whatever the company's output. **Variable costs** vary directly with the level of production. For example, each tablet produced by Apple or Microsoft involves the cost of computer chips, wires, plastic, packaging, and other inputs. These costs tend to be the same for each unit produced. They are called variable because their total varies with the number of units produced. **Total costs** are the sum of the fixed and variable costs for any given level of production. When deciding on a wholesale and suggested retail price, marketers must charge a price that will at least cover the total production costs at a given level of production.

> **Fixed costs (overhead)**
> Costs that do not vary with production or sales level.

> **Variable costs**
> Costs that vary directly with the level of production.

> **Total costs**
> The sum of the fixed and variable costs for any given level of production.

The company must watch its costs carefully. If it costs the company more than competitors to produce and sell a similar product, the company will need to charge a higher price or make less profit, putting it at a competitive disadvantage.

Cost-Plus Pricing The simplest pricing method is **cost-plus pricing (or mark-up pricing)**—adding a standard mark-up to the cost of the product. For example, an electronics retailer might pay a manufacturer $20 for an HDMI cable and mark it up to sell at $30, a 50 percent mark-up on cost. The retailer's gross margin is $10. If the store's operating costs amount to $8 per HDMI cable sold, the retailer's profit margin will be $2. The manufacturer that made the HDMI cable probably used cost-plus pricing, too. If the manufacturer's standard cost of producing the HDMI cable was $16, it might have added a 25 percent mark-up, setting the price to retailers at $20.

> **Cost-plus pricing (or mark-up pricing)**
> Adding a standard mark-up to the cost of the product.

Does using standard mark-ups to set prices make sense? Generally, no. Any pricing method that ignores consumer demand and competitor prices is not likely to lead to the best price. Still, mark-up pricing remains popular for many reasons. First, sellers are more certain about costs than about demand. By tying the price to cost, sellers simplify pricing. Second, when all firms in the industry use this pricing method, prices tend to be similar, minimizing price competition.

Another cost-oriented pricing approach is **break-even pricing**, or a variation called **target return pricing**. The firm tries to determine the price at which it will break even or make the target return it is seeking. Target return pricing uses the concept of a *break-even chart*, which shows the total cost and total revenue expected at different sales volume levels. Figure 10.3 shows a break-even chart for the HDMI cable manufacturer discussed previously. Fixed costs are $6 million regardless of sales volume, and variable costs are $5 per unit. Variable costs are added to fixed costs to form total costs, which rise with volume. The slope of the total revenue curve reflects the price. Here, the price is $15 (for example, the company's revenue is $12 million on 800 000 units, or $15 per unit).

> **Break-even pricing (or target return pricing)**
> Setting price to break even on the costs of making and marketing a product, or setting price to make a target return.

At the $15 price, the manufacturer must sell at least 600 000 units to *break even* (break-even volume = fixed costs ÷ (price − variable costs) = $6 000 000 ÷ ($15 − $5) = 600 000).

FIGURE 10.3 Break-Even Chart for Determining Target Return Price and Break-Even Volume

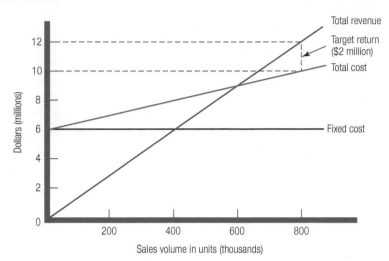

That is, at this level, total revenues will equal total costs of $9 million, producing no profit. If the manufacturer wants a target return of $2 million, it must sell at least 800 000 units to obtain the $12 million of total revenue needed to cover the costs of $10 million plus the $2 million of target profits. In contrast, if the company charges a higher price, say $20, it will not need to sell as many units to break even or to achieve its target profit. In fact, the higher the price, the lower the manufacturer's break-even point will be.

The major problem with this analysis, however, is that it fails to consider customer value and the relationship between price and demand. As the *price* increases, *demand* decreases, and the market may not buy even the lower volume needed to break even at the higher price. For example, suppose the HDMI cable manufacturer calculates that, given its current fixed and variable costs, it must charge a price of $30 for the product in order to earn its desired target profit. But marketing research shows that few consumers will pay more than $25. In this case, the company must trim its costs to lower the break-even point so that it can charge the lower price consumers expect.

Thus, although break-even analysis and target return pricing can help the company determine minimum prices needed to cover expected costs and profits, they do not take the price–demand relationship into account. When using this method, the company must also consider the impact of price on sales volume needed to realize target profits and the likelihood that the needed volume will be achieved at each possible price.

Competition-Based Pricing

Competition-based pricing
Setting prices based on competitors' strategies, prices, costs, and market offerings.

Competition-based pricing involves setting prices based on competitors' strategies, costs, prices, and market offerings. Consumers will base their judgments of a product's value on the prices that competitors charge for similar products.

In assessing competitors' pricing strategies, the company should ask several questions. First, how does the company's market offering compare with competitors' offerings in terms of customer value? If consumers perceive that the company's product or service provides greater value, the company can charge a higher price. If consumers perceive less value relative to competing products, the company must either charge a lower price or change customer perceptions to justify a higher price.

Next, how strong are current competitors and what are their current pricing strategies? If the company faces a host of smaller competitors charging high prices relative to the value they deliver, it might charge lower prices to drive weaker competitors out of the market. If the market is dominated by larger, low-price competitors, the company may decide to target unserved market niches with value-added products at higher prices.

Sometimes, changes in technology force marketers to rethink their product offerings and their pricing strategies. This was the case with streaming video services.

In 1999 Netflix began its subscription video service—mailing DVDs to subscribers, who mailed them back when they were finished watching them. Ten years later, consumers had stopped buying DVDs and Netflix evolved into the first subscription-based digital video streaming service, delivering unlimited movie and TV entertainment to consumers in their homes, via their Internet connections, for about $10 per month.

The cable companies saw their share of the entertainment market shrinking. As well, their customers were paying for Netflix but using it over their connections without their benefiting—and they had to do something about it. So in late 2014 Rogers launched its own streaming service called Shomi. Shomi was initially available only to Rogers and Shaw customers, via their Rogers or Shaw Internet or TV connection, for $8.99 per month. That was in addition to whatever those customers were already paying for "regular" cable and Internet services. Not to be outdone, Bell launched a similar service called CraveTV, available only to Bell TV and Internet customers, for an additional $4.00 per month.

Both services can be streamed on tablet, mobile, and online platforms. They can also be streamed to televisions via the customer's cable box. Pricing the services, however, continues to be a challenge: unless customers are paying for expensive unlimited Internet, they can easily find themselves going over their monthly data limits, given that streaming a movie with the best quality stream consumes approximately 2 gigabytes per hour. Customers who choose to access the service through their set-top box avoid paying exorbitant data fees, but may find themselves wondering why they are paying for a cable service on top of their existing cable service.

A year after launch, both Shomi and CraveTV were available to anyone with an Internet connection, for about the same price as Netflix. So now, regardless of who your Internet provider is, you have three video streaming services to choose from, all of which cost about the same. It's too early to tell whether price will be the deciding factor for consumers, or whether the services will evolve again into differentiated offerings, but eventually the market will decide.[6]

What principle should guide marketers' decisions about what price to charge relative to those of competitors? The answer is simple in concept but often difficult in practice: No matter what price marketers charge—high, low, or in between—they must be certain to give customers superior value for that price.

Other Internal and External Considerations Affecting Pricing Decisions LO2

Beyond customer value perceptions, costs, and competitor strategies, the company must consider several additional internal and external factors. Internal factors affecting pricing include the company's overall marketing strategy, objectives, and marketing mix, as well as other organizational considerations. External factors include the nature of the market and the demand and other environmental factors.

Overall Marketing Strategy, Objectives, and Mix

Price is only one element of the company's broader marketing strategy. Before setting price, the company must decide on its overall marketing strategy for the product or the service. If the company has selected its target market and positioning carefully, then its marketing mix strategy, including price, will be fairly straightforward. For example, when Honda developed its Acura brand to compete with European luxury-performance cars, it needed to set prices in line with luxury performance cars. In contrast, when it introduced the Honda Fit subcompact, it needed to set a price in line with subcompacts. Thus, pricing strategy is largely determined by decisions on brand positioning. Burt's Bees positioned its brand right from the beginning as natural and eco-friendly, and set a correspondingly high price for its products. (See Marketing@Work 10.2.)

Pricing may play an important role in helping to accomplish company objectives at many levels. A firm can set prices to attract new customers or to profitably retain existing ones. It can set prices low to prevent competition from entering the market, or set prices at competitors' levels to stabilize the market. It can price to keep the loyalty and support of resellers or to avoid government intervention. Prices can be reduced temporarily to create excitement for a brand. Or one product may be priced to help the sales of other products in the company's line.

Price is only one of the marketing mix tools that a company uses to achieve its marketing objectives. Pricing decisions must be coordinated with product design, distribution, and promotion decisions to form a consistent and effective integrated marketing program. Decisions made for other marketing mix variables may affect pricing decisions. For example, a decision to position the product on high-performance quality will mean that the seller must charge a higher price to cover higher costs. And producers whose resellers are expected to support and promote their products may have to build larger reseller margins into their prices.

Companies often position their products on price and then tailor other marketing mix decisions to the prices they want to charge. Here, price is a crucial product-positioning factor that defines the product's market, competition, and design. Many firms support such price-positioning strategies with a technique called **target costing**. Target costing reverses the usual process of first designing a new product, determining its cost, and then asking, "Can we sell it for that?" Instead, it starts with an ideal selling price based on customer-value considerations, and then targets costs that will ensure that the price is met. For example, when Honda set out to design the Fit, it began with a US$13 950 starting price point and 33-miles-per-gallon operating efficiency firmly in mind. It then designed a stylish, peppy little car with costs that allowed it to give target customers those values.

Target costing
Pricing that starts with an ideal selling price, and then targets costs that will ensure that the price is met.

Other companies de-emphasize price and use other marketing mix tools to create *non-price* positions. Often, the best strategy is not to charge the lowest price but rather to differentiate the marketing offer to make it worth a higher price. For example, Bang & Olufsen—known for its cutting-edge consumer electronics—builds more value into its products and charges sky-high prices. There are only five B&O retailers in Canada, all of which are located in extremely high end shopping districts—like Bang & Olufsen Custom Home in Calgary, which specializes in working with the customer's designer to create a custom built-in home entertainment system. If you have to ask how much it costs, you probably can't afford it, but for those customers who can, Bang & Olufsen's very high quality is worth the price.

Some marketers even position their products on *high* prices, featuring high prices as part of their product's allure. For example, Grand Marnier offers a US$225 bottle of Cuvée du Cent Cinquantenaire that's marketed with the tagline "Hard to find, impossible to pronounce, and prohibitively expensive." And Titus Cycles, a premium bicycle manufacturer, features its high prices in its advertising. Ads humorously show people working unusual second jobs to earn the money to afford a Titus. Suggested retail price for a Titus Solera: US$7750. But "It's worth a second job," the ads confirm.

MARKETING@WORK 10.2

Burt's Bees: Wilfully Overpriced

How much are you willing to pay for a standard-sized tube of lip balm? The market leader charges just a bit more than $1. But would you pay $2 for a comparable product? How about $3? When it comes to price, your first thought might be, "The lower the better." Many companies follow this reasoning and try to outdo each other by providing the cheapest option, but such a strategy can lead to razor-thin margins and even losses. Although low price might seem to be the most attractive way to lure customers into purchasing goods and services, when it comes to actually creating value for customers, that's not always the case.

Burt's Bees understands that sometimes it pays to charge more. When the company first started out, the popular maker of natural personal care products was a niche brand, distributed only in boutiques and natural-food stores. But Burt's Bees' sales exploded when major supermarket and discount retail chains started carrying the small company's line. Although Walmart and other national chains are known for pressuring manufacturers to cut costs and lower prices, Burt's Bees achieved its distribution victory through a strategy that has been called "wilful overpricing." In Burt's Bees' case, that means charging price premiums of 80 percent or more over comparable non-natural brands. Burt's Bees lip balm, the brand's best-selling product, sells for $4.89 a tube in Canada, while market-leading ChapStick can be had for about a third of that price. A 300 ml bottle of Burt's Bees shampoo costs $10, and a bar of soap (or, in Burt's Bees terms, an energizing or replenishing body bar) costs $8. A pricing strategy like this can only succeed if there's something about the brand that makes it special.

Burt's Bees started like many entrepreneurial ventures, with founders who had a good idea but not a penny to their names. In the late 1980s, Burt Shavitz was a beekeeper in northern Maine selling honey out of his pickup truck and living in a modified turkey coop. Roxanne Quimby, a wife and mother looking for a way to supplement the family income, had the idea to buy Burt's surplus beeswax to make and sell candles. Later, Roxanne happened upon a nineteenth-century book of homemade personal care recipes and acquired a second-hand industrial mixer from a university cafeteria. That's when the Burt's Bees brand began to take shape. The main product line of natural beeswax candles was slowly replaced by personal care products, including the brand's famous lip balm made with beeswax, coconut and sunflower oils, and other ingredients that you could just as easily eat as put on your lips.

As Burt's Bees grew, it automated its manufacturing processes, yet the products that rolled off those automated lines maintained the quality and feel of natural homemade goods. Right from the start, the Burt's Bees brand stood for natural ingredients, and today that continues to be the brand's main point of differentiation, as is clear from its "about us" statement on its website: "Your well-being is affected every single day by the personal care products you use. Our goal is to create and educate people on truly natural products that have a positive effect on both you and the world you live in for the good of your well-being, for the good of the environment and for The Greater Good. Simply put, we strive to make people's lives better every day—naturally."

It seems that part of the reason for Burt's Bees success is its prestige pricing strategy. Higher prices serve as an indicator of quality level and, in the case of Burt's Bees, higher prices also served to peak customer curiosity. When people compare brands, a moderately higher-priced option causes them to take notice and look a little deeper to understand why a certain brand is more expensive. They may learn that the product contains features that justify the higher price—features they may not have even considered before. Customers then ask themselves, "Do I need this benefit or not?" Some studies show that in such situations, customers recall nearly twice as much product information and can cite more arguments in favour of buying the products. If the price premium

Exhibit 10.6 Burt's Bees prides itself on its products made from natural ingredients, its eco-friendly and socially responsible attitude, and its pricing strategy.

charged is too high or too low, however, shoppers ignore the option.

Fortunately for Burt's Bees, its strategy of wilful overpricing coincided with a trend of growing consumer preference toward natural products and environmentally friendly goods. Burt's Bees' natural ingredients and company values were enough to justify the brand's higher prices for many. But can a pricing strategy that relies on trends in consumer preferences work forever?

Burt's Bees is now owned by Clorox, and is part of the company's comprehensive strategy to become more

environmentally friendly. Advertisements in magazines compare natural ingredients in Burt's Bees to chemical ingredients found in other products. For all intents and purposes, Clorox allows Burt's Bees to operate as an independent division, remaining true to its original mission and values. The Burt's Bees brand remains a very solid contributor to Clorox's results, with sales growth and profit margins above the company average, and it's the fastest growing business unit in the company. Clorox CEO Benno Dorer says that Burt's Bees is a "standout example" of the

company's strategic plan to drive growth. It seems that Burt's Bees' pricing strategy is proof that, by leveraging a brand's strengths, customers will continue to buy on value, not just on price.

Sources: Lauren K. Ohnesorge, "Clorox to Seek 'New Categories' for Durham's Burt's Bees," *Triangle Business Journal* online, August 4, 2015; Tess Stynes and Paul Ziobro, "Clorox Forecasts Profit, Sales Below Expectations," *Wall Street Journal*, January 3, 2011; Tim Donnelly, "How to Sell on Value Rather Than Price," *Inc.*, July 20, 2011; Marco Bertini and Luc Wathieu, "How to Stop Customers from Fixating on Price," *Harvard Business Review*, May 2010, pp. 85–91; Mitch Maranowski, "The Triple Value Proposition: Why Inauthentic Green Brands Are Doomed to Fail," *Fast Company*, May 18, 2011; and information from BurtsBees.ca.

Marketers must consider the total marketing strategy and mix when setting prices, but even when featuring price, marketers need to remember that customers rarely buy on price alone. Instead, they seek products that give them the best value in terms of benefits received for the prices paid.

Organizational Considerations

Management must decide who within the organization should set prices. Companies handle pricing in a variety of ways. In small companies, prices are often set by top management rather than by the marketing or sales departments. In large companies, pricing is typically handled by divisional or product line managers. In industrial markets, salespeople may be allowed to negotiate with customers within certain price ranges. Even so, top management sets the pricing objectives and policies, and it often approves the prices proposed by lower-level management or salespeople.

In industries in which pricing is a key factor (airlines, aerospace, steel, railroads, oil companies), companies often have pricing departments to set the best prices or help others in setting them. These departments report to the marketing department or top management. Others who have an influence on pricing include sales managers, production managers, finance managers, and accountants.

The Market and Demand

As noted earlier, good pricing starts with an understanding of how customers' perceptions of value affect the prices they are willing to pay. Both consumer and industrial buyers balance the price of a product or a service against the benefits of owning it. Thus, before setting prices, the marketer must understand the relationship

The India Today Group/Getty Images

Exhibit 10.7 Positioning on high price: Some brands, like Bang & Olufsen, deliberately charge prices that are significantly higher than competitors' products. If you have to ask how much it is, you probably can't afford it.

between price and demand for the company's product. In this section, we take a deeper look at the price–demand relationship and how it varies for different types of markets. We then discuss methods for analyzing the price–demand relationship.

Pricing in Different Types of Markets The seller's pricing freedom varies with different types of markets. Economists recognize four types of markets, each presenting a different pricing challenge.

Under *pure competition*, the market consists of many buyers and sellers trading in a uniform commodity such as wheat, copper, or financial securities. No single buyer or seller has much effect on the going market price. In a purely competitive market, marketing research, product development, pricing, advertising, and sales promotion play little or no role. Thus, sellers in these markets do not spend much time on marketing strategy.

Under *monopolistic competition*, the market consists of many buyers and sellers who trade over a range of prices rather than a single market price. A range of prices occurs because sellers can differentiate their offers to buyers. Sellers try to develop differentiated offers for different customer segments and, in addition to price, freely use branding, advertising, and personal selling to set their offers apart. For example, although the Nissan LEAF isn't the first electric car, nor the only electric car currently available on the market, it's differentiated as the first mass-market fully electric car. As such, the LEAF is positioned against the Tesla, which, though electric, is a much more expensive sports car. Because there are many competitors in such markets, each firm is less affected by competitors' pricing strategies than in oligopolistic markets.

Under *oligopolistic competition*, the market consists of a few sellers who are highly sensitive to each other's pricing and marketing strategies. Because there are few sellers, each seller is alert and responsive to competitors' pricing strategies and moves.

In a *pure monopoly*, the market consists of one seller. The seller may be a government monopoly (Canada Post), a private regulated monopoly (a power company), or a private

Exhibit 10.8 Pricing in monopolistic competition: Branding and positioning—such as the Nissan LEAF's claim that it's the first mass-market electric car—are more important, strategically, than price.

FIGURE10.4 Demand Curve

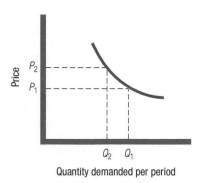

nonregulated monopoly (DuPont when it introduced nylon). Pricing is handled differently in each case.

Demand curve
A curve that shows the number of units the market will buy in a given time period, at different prices that might be charged.

Analyzing the Price–Demand Relationship Each price the company might charge will lead to a different level of demand. The relationship between the price charged and the resulting demand level is shown in the **demand curve** in Figure 10.4. The demand curve shows the number of units the market will buy in a given time period at different prices that might be charged. In the normal case, demand and price are inversely related; that is, the higher the price, the lower the demand. Thus, the company would sell less if it raised its price from P_1 to P_2. In short, consumers with limited budgets will probably buy less of something if its price is too high.

Understanding a brand's price–demand curve is crucial to good pricing decisions. ConAgra Foods learned this lesson when pricing its Banquet frozen dinners:

> ConAgra Foods, the company behind popular food brands such as Hunt's, Reddi-wip, PAM, and Orville Redenbacher, found out the hard way about the perils of pushing up the price of a Banquet frozen dinner. When ConAgra tried to cover higher commodity costs by raising the list price of Banquet dinners from $1 to $1.25, consumers turned up their noses to the higher price. Sales dropped, forcing ConAgra to sell off excess dinners at discount prices. It turns out that "the key component for Banquet dinners—the key attribute—is you've got to be at $1," says ConAgra's CEO Gary Rodkin. "Everything else pales in comparison to that." Banquet dinner prices are now back to a buck a dinner. To make money at that price, ConAgra is doing a better job of managing costs by shrinking portions and substituting less expensive ingredients for costlier ones. More than just Banquet dinners, ConAgra prices all of its frozen and canned products at under $1 per serving. Consumers are responding well to the brand's efforts to keep prices down. After all, where else can you find dinner for $1?[7]

Most companies try to measure their demand curves by estimating demand at different prices. The type of market makes a difference. In a monopoly, the demand curve shows the total market demand resulting from different prices. If the company faces competition, its demand at different prices will depend on whether competitors' prices stay constant or change with the company's own prices.

Price elasticity
A measure of the sensitivity of demand to changes in price.

Price Elasticity of Demand Marketers also need to know **price elasticity**—how responsive demand will be to a change in price. If demand hardly changes with a small change in price, we say demand is *inelastic*. If demand changes greatly, we say the demand is *elastic*.

If demand is elastic rather than inelastic, sellers will consider lowering their prices. A lower price will produce more total revenue. This practice makes sense as long as the extra costs of producing and selling more do not exceed the extra revenue. At the same time, most firms want to avoid pricing that turns their products into commodities. The ease of finding pricing information on the Internet has increased consumer price sensitivity, turning products ranging from cellphones and televisions to new automobiles into commodities in some consumers' eyes.

The Economy

Economic conditions can have a strong impact on the firm's pricing strategies. Economic factors such as a boom or a recession, inflation, and interest rates affect pricing decisions because they affect consumer spending, consumer perceptions of the product's price and value, and the company's costs of producing and selling a product.

In the aftermath of the 2008–2009 recession in the United States and the resulting downturn in Canada, consumers began to rethink the price–value equation. Many consumers tightened their belts and became more value conscious, and marketers expect that trend to continue. As a result, many marketers have increased their emphasis on value-for-the-money pricing strategies.

The most obvious response to a slow economy is to cut prices and offer deep discounts. And thousands of companies did just that. Lower prices make products more affordable and help spur short-term sales. However, such price cuts can have undesirable long-term consequences. Consider upscale brands such as Starbucks, Tiffany's, or Whole Foods Market, which position themselves as providing premium products at premium prices—the "more for more" strategy. When consumer spending rates decrease, companies like these face the difficult task of realigning their value propositions with their positioning.

Rather than cut prices, marketers can instead shift their focus to more affordable items in their product mixes. Another approach is to hold steady on price but redefine the "value" in value propositions. For instance, Unilever repositioned its higher-end Bertolli frozen meals as an eat-at-home brand that's more affordable than eating out, and Kraft's advertising for Velveeta cheese communicates the value of a package of Velveeta being twice the size of a package of cheddar.

Remember, no matter what state the economy is in, people continue to make purchases, and their purchase decisions are not based on prices alone. They balance the price they pay against the value they receive. For example, despite selling its shoes for as much as $150 a pair, Nike continues to command a high degree of customer loyalty, because consumers perceive the value of Nike's products and the Nike ownership experience to be well worth the price. The marketing lesson? No matter what price they charge—low or high—companies need to offer great *value for the money*.

Other External Factors

When setting prices, beyond the market and the economy, the company must consider a number of other factors in its external environment. It must know what impact its prices will have on other parties in its environment. How will *resellers* react to various prices? The company should set prices that give resellers a fair profit, encourage their support, and help them sell the product effectively. The *government* is another important external influence on pricing decisions. Finally, *social concerns* may need to be taken into account. In setting prices, a company's short-term sales, market share, and profit goals may need to be tempered by broader societal considerations. We will examine public policy issues in pricing later in the chapter.

We've seen that pricing decisions are subject to a complex array of customer, company, competitive, and environmental forces. To make things even more complex, a company sets not a single price but rather a *pricing structure* that changes over time as products move through their life cycles. The company adjusts its prices to reflect changes in costs and demand, and to account for variations in buyers and situations. As the competitive environment changes, the company considers when to initiate price changes and when to respond to them.

We now examine additional pricing approaches used in special pricing situations, or to adjust prices to meet changing situations. We look in turn at *new-product pricing* for products in the introductory stage of the product life cycle, *product mix pricing* for related products in the product mix, *price adjustment tactics* that account for customer differences and changing situations, and strategies for initiating and responding to *price changes*.

◄●–**Simulate** on MyMarketingLab

Pricing

New-Product Pricing [LO3]

Pricing strategies usually change as the product passes through its life cycle. The introductory stage is especially challenging. Companies bringing out a new product face the challenge of setting prices for the first time. They can choose between two broad strategies: *market-skimming pricing* and *market-penetration pricing*.

Market-Skimming Pricing

Market-skimming pricing (or price skimming)
Setting a high price for a new product to skim maximum revenues layer by layer from the segments willing to pay the high price; the company makes fewer but more profitable sales.

Many companies that invent new products set high initial prices to "skim" revenues layer by layer from the market. Sony frequently uses this strategy, called **market-skimming pricing (or price skimming)**. For example, every time Apple introduces a new iPhone or iPad model, the initial price is very high, because for the type of customer who anxiously awaits the newest gadget, price is no object. After about six months the prices come down slightly; after a year they are lowered even more; and after two years, when rumours of the next version appear, the prices drop again. Finally, when the latest model is released, the prices of the last generation model are drastically discounted. During that period, carriers such as Bell and Rogers typically offer the older models as free upgrades in exchange for a renewed three-year contract. There is a segment of the market that waits for that to happen, and then buys the older model for the lowest possible price.

Market skimming makes sense only under certain conditions. First, the product's quality and image must support its higher price and enough buyers must want the product at that price. Second, the costs of producing a smaller volume cannot be so high that they cancel the advantage of charging more. Finally, competitors should not be able to enter the market easily and undercut the high price.

Market-Penetration Pricing

Market-penetration pricing
Setting a low initial price for a new product in order to attract a large number of buyers and a large market share.

Rather than setting a high initial price to skim off small but profitable market segments, some companies use **market-penetration pricing**. They set a low initial price in order to *penetrate* the market quickly and deeply—to attract a large number of buyers quickly and win a large market share. The high sales volume results in falling costs, allowing the companies to cut their prices even further. For example, giant Swedish retailer IKEA used penetration pricing to boost its success in the Chinese market:

> When IKEA first opened stores in China in 2002, people crowded in, but not to buy home furnishings. Instead, they came to take advantage of the freebies—air conditioning, clean toilets, and even decorating ideas. Chinese consumers are famously frugal. When it came time to actually buy, they shopped instead at local stores just down the street that offered

knockoffs of IKEA's designs at a fraction of the price. So to lure the finicky Chinese customers, IKEA slashed its prices in China to the lowest in the world, the opposite approach of many Western retailers there. By increasingly stocking its Chinese stores with China-made products, the retailer pushed prices on some items as low as 70 percent below prices in IKEA's outlets outside China. The penetration pricing strategy worked. IKEA now captures a 43 percent market share of China's fast-growing homewares market.[8]

For a low-price strategy like IKEA's to work, the market must be highly price sensitive so that a low price produces more market growth. In order to maintain the strategy long term, production and distribution costs must fall as sales volume increases. And to keep out the competition, the low-price positioning must be sustainable.

Product Mix Pricing LO4

The strategy for setting a product's price often has to be changed when the product is part of a product mix. In this case, the firm looks for a set of prices that maximizes the profits on the total product mix. Pricing is difficult because the various products have related demand and costs, and face different degrees of competition. We now take a closer look at the five product mix pricing situations summarized in Table 10.1: *product line pricing*, *optional-product pricing*, *captive-product pricing*, *by-product pricing*, and *product bundle pricing*.

Exhibit 10.9 Penetration pricing: To lure frugal Chinese customers and gain penetration into the market, IKEA slashed its prices in China to the lowest in the world.

Wang Jiaowen/Color China Photos/ZUMAPRESS/Newscom

Product Line Pricing

Companies usually develop product lines rather than single products. For example, Samsonite offers some 20 different collections of bags, from its Aramon NXT line of laptop bags that range in price from $20 to $35 to its high-end Cosmolite luggage line, where a small suitcase retails for more than $500. In **product line pricing**, management must decide on the price steps to set between the various products in a line.

The price steps should take into account cost differences between the products in the line. More importantly, they should account for differences in customer perceptions of the value of different features—in other words, the positioning of the brand.

Product line pricing

Setting the price steps between various products in a product line based on cost differences between the products, customer evaluations of different features, and competitors' prices.

TABLE 10.1	Product Mix Pricing
Pricing Situation	**Description**
Product line pricing	Setting prices across an entire product line
Optional-product pricing	Pricing optional or accessory products sold with the main product
Captive-product pricing	Pricing products that must be used with the main product
By-product pricing	Pricing low-value by-products to get rid of them
Product bundle pricing	Pricing bundles of products sold together

Courtesy Samsonite Canada

Exhibit 10.10 Product line pricing: Samsonite's Aramon NXT is a line of laptop sleeves and shuttles constructed of lightweight neoprene with protective rubber corners for added security.

Optional-product pricing
The pricing of optional or accessory products along with a main product.

Captive-product pricing
Setting a price for products that must be used along with a main product, such as blades for a razor and games for a video-game console.

By-product pricing
Setting a price for by-products to make the main product's price more competitive.

Optional-Product Pricing

Optional-product pricing is a pricing strategy in which the main product is sold at a low margin or near cost price, and marketers focus on promoting the extras and upgrades—the optional products. For example, new cars offer sound systems, Bluetooth, GPS systems, and many other options; new computers and phones can come with hardware and software extras, and service plans.

Captive-Product Pricing

Companies that make products that must be used along with a main product are using **captive-product pricing**. Examples of captive products are razor blade cartridges, video games, and ink cartridges for printers. Producers of the main products (razors, video-game consoles, and printers) often price them low and set high mark-ups on the supplies.

In the case of services, this captive-product pricing is called *two-part pricing*. The price of the service is broken into a *fixed fee* plus a *variable usage rate*. For example, at amusement parks you pay a daily-ticket or season-pass charge just to get in, but once inside there are many other fees that must be paid, depending on your usage.

By-Product Pricing

Producing products and services often generates by-products. If the by-products have no value and if getting rid of them is costly, this will affect the pricing of the main product. Using **by-product pricing**, the company seeks a market for these by-products to help offset the costs of disposing of them and to help make the price of the main product more competitive. The by-products themselves can even turn out to be profitable—turning trash into cash.

For example, Gildale Farms in St. Mary's, Ontario, sources wood biomass from various by-product processes to create fuel pellets and animal bedding pellets, which are then marketed to farmers. The company produces hardwood pellets from sawdust—a by-product of timber mills' lumber production. Lower-grade pellets are made from damaged or unwanted wood skids and other "leftover" wood. Animal bedding pellets are made from furniture manufacturers' wood by-products. In fact, everything the company produces is made from leftover or "diverted" wood, not from cutting down trees. In another example, animal manure is being used at the Toronto Zoo to create power for the Ontario grid. ZooShare is a "zoo-based biogas plant" that, when operational, will recycle 3000 tonnes of zoo poo into renewable power, reducing greenhouse gas emissions and returning valuable nutrients to the soil.

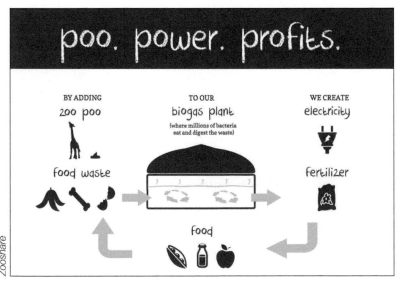

Zooshare

Exhibit 10.11 By-product pricing: ZooShare is a zoo-based biogas plant created in partnership with the Toronto Zoo. The plant is not yet operational. You can find out more at Zooshare.ca.

Product Bundle Pricing

By using **product bundle pricing**, sellers often combine several of their products and offer the bundle at a reduced price. For example, fast-food restaurants bundle a burger, fries, and a soft drink at a "combo" price. Bath & Body Works offers "three-fer" deals on its soaps and lotions (such as three antibacterial soaps for $10). And Rogers Communications bundles TV, Internet, and phone services at a low combined price. Price bundling can promote the sale of products that consumers might not otherwise buy, but the combined price must be low enough to get them to buy the bundle.

Product bundle pricing
Combining several products and offering the bundle at a reduced price.

Price Adjustment Strategies LO5

Companies usually adjust their basic prices to account for various customer differences and changing situations. Here we examine the seven price adjustment strategies summarized in Table 10.2: *discount and allowance pricing*, *segmented pricing*, *psychological pricing*, *promotional pricing*, *geographical pricing*, *dynamic pricing*, and *international pricing*.

Discount and Allowance Pricing

Most companies adjust their basic price to reward customers for certain responses, such as early payment of bills, volume purchases, and off-season buying. These price adjustments—called *discounts* and *allowances*—can take many forms.

The many forms of **discounts** include a *cash discount*, a price reduction to buyers who pay their bills promptly. A typical example is "2/10, net 30," which means that although payment is due within 30 days, the buyer can deduct 2 percent if the bill is paid within 10 days. A *quantity discount* is a price reduction to buyers who buy large volumes. Under the provisions of the Competition Act, quantity discounts must be offered equally to all customers and must not exceed the seller's cost savings associated with selling large quantities. A *seasonal discount* is a price reduction to buyers who buy merchandise or services out of season.

Allowances are another type of reduction from the list price. For example, *trade-in allowances* are price reductions given for turning in an old item when buying a new one. Trade-in allowances are most common in the automobile industry but are also given for

Discount
A straight reduction in price on purchases during a stated period of time or on larger quantities.

Allowance
Promotional money paid by manufacturers to retailers in return for an agreement to feature the manufacturer's products in some way.

TABLE 10.2 Price Adjustments

Strategy	Description
Discount and allowance pricing	Reducing prices to reward customer responses such as paying early or promoting the product
Segmented pricing	Adjusting prices to allow for differences in customers, products, or locations
Psychological pricing	Adjusting prices for psychological effect
Promotional pricing	Temporarily reducing prices to increase short-run sales
Geographical pricing	Adjusting prices to account for the geographic location of customers
Dynamic pricing	Adjusting prices continually to meet the characteristics and needs of individual customers and situations
International pricing	Adjusting prices for international markets

other durable goods. *Promotional allowances* are payments or price reductions to reward dealers for participating in advertising and sales support programs.

Segmented Pricing

Segmented pricing
Selling a product or service at two or more prices, where the difference in prices is not based on differences in costs.

Companies will often adjust their basic prices to allow for differences in customers, products, and locations. In **segmented pricing**, the company sells a product or service at two or more prices, even though the difference in prices is not based on differences in costs.

Segmented pricing takes several forms. Under *customer-segment pricing*, different customers pay different prices for the same product or service. Museums, for example, may charge a lower admission for students and senior citizens. Under *product-form pricing*, different versions of the product are priced differently but not according to differences in their costs. For example, a round-trip economy seat on a flight from Toronto to London might cost $1200, whereas a business-class seat on the same flight might cost $5000 or more. Although business-class customers receive roomier, more comfortable seats and higher quality food and service, the differences in costs to the airlines are much less than the additional prices to passengers. However, to passengers who can afford it, the additional comfort and services are worth the extra charge.

By using *location-based pricing*, a company charges different prices for different locations, even though the cost of offering each location is the same. For instance, sports arenas and theatres vary their seat prices because of audience preferences for certain locations. Finally, by using *time-based pricing*, a firm varies its price by the season, the month, the day, and even the hour. Movie theatres charge matinee pricing during the daytime. Resorts give weekend and seasonal discounts.

For segmented pricing to be an effective strategy, certain conditions must exist. The market must be segmentable, and the segments must show different degrees of demand. The costs of segmenting and watching the market cannot exceed the extra revenue obtained from the price difference. Of course, the segmented pricing must also be legal.

Most importantly, segmented prices should reflect real differences in customers' perceived value. Consumers in higher price tiers must feel that they're getting their extra money's worth for the higher prices paid. By the same token, companies must be careful not to treat customers in lower price tiers as second-class citizens. Otherwise, in the long run, the practice will lead to customer resentment and ill will. For example, in recent years, the airlines have incurred the wrath of frustrated customers at both ends of the airplane. Passengers paying full fare for business or executive seats often feel that they're being gouged. At the same time, passengers in lower-priced economy seats feel that they're being ignored or treated poorly.

ROBYN BECK/AFP/Getty Images

Exhibit 10.12 Segmented pricing: There is a segment of the market that is willing and able to pay for luxurious airplane seats.

Psychological Pricing

Price says something about the product. For example, many consumers use price to judge quality. A $100 bottle of perfume may contain only $3 worth of materials, but consumers are willing to pay the $100 because this price indicates something special.

In using **psychological pricing**, sellers consider the psychology of prices and not simply the economics. For example, consumers usually perceive higher-priced products as having higher quality. When they can judge the quality of a product by examining it or calling on past experience with it, they use price less to judge quality. But when they cannot judge quality because they lack the information or skill, price becomes an important quality signal. For example, who's the better lawyer, one who charges $50 per hour or one who charges $500 per hour? You'd have to do a lot of digging into the respective lawyers' credentials to answer this question objectively, and even then, you might not be able to judge accurately. Most of us would simply assume that the higher-priced lawyer is better.

The Image Gate/Getty Images

Exhibit 10.13 Psychological pricing: All Patek Philippe watches are expensive. Some are deliberately made to be collectors' items. One owned by Eric Clapton fetched $3.6 million at auction. The other 40 000 watches the company makes each year are sold to the "merely well off."

Another aspect of psychological pricing is **reference prices**—prices that buyers carry in their minds and refer to when looking at a given product. The reference price might be formed by noting current prices, remembering past prices, or assessing the buying situation. Sellers can influence or use these consumers' reference prices when setting price. For example, a company could display its product next to more expensive ones to imply that it belongs in the same class, as when a grocery retailer shelves its store brand of bran-flakes-and-raisins cereal priced at $3.99 next to Kellogg's Raisin Bran priced at $5.29.

For most purchases, consumers don't have all the skill or information they need to figure out whether they are paying a good price. They don't have the time, ability, or inclination to research different brands or stores, compare prices, and get the best deals. Instead, they may rely on certain cues that signal whether a price is high or low. Interestingly, such pricing cues are often provided by sellers, in the form of sales signs, price-matching guarantees, loss-leader pricing, and other helpful hints.

Even small differences in price can signal product differences. Consider a flat screen TV priced at $500 compared with one priced at $499.99. The actual price difference is only one cent, but the psychological difference can be much greater. For example, some consumers will see the $499.99 as a price in the $400 range rather than in the $500 range. The $499.99 will more likely be seen as a bargain price, whereas the $500 price suggests more quality. Some psychologists argue that each digit has symbolic and visual qualities that should be considered in pricing. Thus, eight is round and even and creates a soothing effect, whereas seven is angular and creates a jarring effect.

Promotional Pricing

With **promotional pricing**, companies will temporarily price their products below list price and sometimes even below cost to create buying excitement and urgency. Promotional pricing takes several forms. A seller may simply offer *discounts* from normal prices to increase sales and reduce inventories. Sellers also use *special-event pricing* in certain seasons to draw more customers. For example, electronics retailers such as Best Buy typically offer promotional pricing (i.e., discounts) in November and December to attract Christmas shoppers into stores.

Psychological pricing
Pricing that considers the psychology of prices and not simply the economics; the price is used to say something about the product.

Reference prices
Prices that buyers carry in their minds and refer to when they look at a given product.

Promotional pricing
Temporarily pricing products below the list price and sometimes even below cost to increase short-run sales.

Manufacturers sometimes offer *cash rebates* to consumers who buy the product from dealers within a specified time; the manufacturer sends the rebate directly to the customer. Rebates have been popular with automakers and producers of cellphones and small appliances, but they are also used with consumer packaged goods. Some manufacturers offer *low-interest financing*, *longer warranties*, or *free maintenance* to reduce the consumer's "price." This practice has become another favourite of the auto industry.

Promotional pricing, however, can have adverse effects. Used too frequently and copied by competitors, price promotions can create "deal-prone" customers who wait until brands go on sale before buying them. Or, constantly reduced prices can erode a brand's value in the eyes of customers.

Geographical Pricing

Geographical pricing

Setting prices for customers located in different parts of the country or the world.

Marketers must also make decisions about how to price their products for customers located in different parts of the country or the world. Should the company risk losing the business of more-distant customers by charging them higher prices to cover the higher shipping costs? Or should the company charge all customers the same prices regardless of location?

Let's look at three **geographical pricing** strategies for a hypothetical situation.

The Peerless Paper Company is located in Vancouver and sells paper products to customers all over Canada. The cost of freight is high and affects the companies from whom customers buy their paper. Peerless wants to establish a geographical pricing policy. It is trying to determine how to price a $10 000 order to three specific customers: Customer A (Vancouver), Customer B (Winnipeg), and Customer C (Halifax).

One option is for Peerless to ask each customer to pay the shipping cost from the Vancouver factory to the customer's location. All three customers would pay the same factory price of $10 000, with Customer A paying, say, $100 for shipping; Customer B, $150; and Customer C, $250. Called *FOB-origin pricing*, this practice means that the goods are placed *free on board* (hence, *FOB*) a carrier. At that point the title and responsibility pass to the customer, who pays the freight from the factory to the destination. Because each customer picks up its own cost, supporters of FOB pricing feel that this is the fairest way to assess freight charges. The disadvantage, however, is that Peerless will be a high-cost firm to distant customers.

Another option is *uniform-delivered pricing*, where the company charges the same price plus freight to all customers, regardless of their location. The freight charge is set at the average freight cost. Suppose this is $150. Uniform-delivered pricing therefore results in a higher charge to the Vancouver customer (who pays $150 freight instead of $100) and a lower charge to the Halifax customer (who pays $150 instead of $250). Although the Vancouver customer would prefer to buy paper from another local paper company that uses FOB-origin pricing, Peerless has a better chance of winning over the Halifax customer.

The third option is *zone pricing*, where all customers within a given zone pay a single total price, and the more distant the zone, the higher the price. Peerless might set up a West Zone and charge $100 freight to all customers in this zone, a Central Zone in which it charges $150, and an East Zone in which it charges $250. In this way, the customers within a given price zone receive no price advantage from the company. For example, customers in Vancouver and Calgary pay the same total price to Peerless. The complaint, however, is that the Vancouver customer is paying part of the Calgary customer's freight cost.

Dynamic Pricing

Throughout most of history, prices were set by negotiation between buyers and sellers. *Fixed price* policies—setting one price for all buyers—is a relatively modern idea that arose with the development of large-scale retailing at the end of the nineteenth century. Today, most prices are set this way. However, some companies are now reversing the fixed pricing trend. They are using **dynamic pricing**—adjusting prices continually to meet the characteristics and needs of individual customers and situations.

Dynamic pricing
Adjusting prices continually to meet the characteristics and needs of individual customers and situations.

For example, think about how the Internet has affected pricing. From the mostly fixed pricing practices of the past century, the Web seems now to be taking us back—into a new age of fluid pricing. The flexibility of the Internet allows online sellers to instantly and constantly adjust prices on a wide range of goods based on demand dynamics (sometimes called *real-time* pricing). In other cases, customers control pricing by bidding on auction sites such as eBay, or negotiating on sites such as Priceline. Still other companies customize their offers based on the characteristics and behaviours of specific customers.

Dynamic pricing offers many advantages for marketers. For example, online retailers such as Amazon can mine their databases to gauge a specific shopper's desires, measure his or her means, instantaneously tailor products to fit that shopper's behaviour, and price products accordingly. Catalogue retailers such as L.L.Bean or Tilley Endurables can adjust prices on the fly according to changes in demand or costs, altering prices for specific items on a day-by-day or even hour-by-hour basis. And many direct marketers monitor inventories, costs, and demand at any given moment and adjust prices instantly.

Consumers also benefit from the Web and dynamic pricing. Price comparison sites—such as Shopbot.ca, RedFlagDeals.com, and PriceGrabber.ca—offer instant product and price comparisons from thousands of vendors. Shopbot.ca, for instance, lets shoppers browse by category or search for specific products and brands in either English or French. It lists only products available from reliable Canadian retailers, allows users to compare prices from various sellers, and enables shoppers to order them right on the site.

In addition, consumers can negotiate prices at online auction sites and exchanges. Suddenly the centuries-old art of haggling is back in vogue. Want to sell that antique pickle jar that's been collecting dust for generations? Post it on eBay or Kijiji. Want to name your own price for a hotel room or a rental car? Visit Priceline.com or another reverse auction site. Want to bid on a ticket to a Coldplay show? Check out Ticketmaster.com, which now offers an online auction service for concert tickets.

Dynamic pricing makes sense in many contexts—it adjusts prices according to market forces, and it usually works to the benefit of the customer.

International Pricing

Companies that market their products internationally must decide what prices to charge in the different countries in which they operate. In some cases, a company can set a uniform worldwide price. For example, Bombardier sells its jetliners at about the same price everywhere, whether Canada, Europe, or a developing country. However, most companies adjust their prices to reflect local market conditions and cost considerations.

The price that a company should charge in a specific country depends on many factors, including economic conditions, competitive situations, laws and regulations, and development of the wholesaling and retailing system. Consumer perceptions and preferences also may vary from country to country, calling for different prices. Or the company may have different marketing objectives in various world markets, which require changes in pricing strategy. For example, Samsung might introduce a new product into mature markets in highly developed countries with the goal of quickly gaining mass-market share—this would call for a penetration-pricing strategy. In contrast, it might enter a less-developed market by targeting smaller, less price-sensitive segments; in this case, market-skimming pricing makes sense.

Costs play an important role in setting international prices. Travellers abroad are often surprised to find that goods that are relatively inexpensive at home may carry outrageously higher price tags in other countries. A pair of Levi's selling for $50 in Canada might go for $150 in Tokyo and $100 in Paris. A McDonald's Big Mac selling for a modest $3.50 here might cost $7.50 in Reykjavik, Iceland, and an Oral-B toothbrush selling for $2.49 at home may cost $10 in China. Conversely, a Gucci handbag going for only $140 in Milan, Italy, might fetch $240 in Canada.

In some cases, such *price escalation* may result from differences in selling strategies or market conditions. In most instances, however, it is simply a result of the higher costs of selling in another country—the additional costs of product modifications, shipping and insurance, import tariffs and taxes, exchange-rate fluctuations, and physical distribution.

Pricing has become a key element in the international marketing strategies of companies attempting to enter emerging markets, such as China, India, and Brazil. Not long ago, the preferred way for many Western companies to market their products in developing markets such as India or Indonesia was to paste new labels on them and sell them at premium prices to the privileged few who could afford them. However, when Unilever—the maker of such brands as Dove, Sunsilk, Lipton, and Vaseline—realized that such pricing put its products out of the reach of tens of millions of consumers in emerging markets, it forged a different approach. It shrunk its packaging and set low prices that even the world's poorest consumers could afford. By developing single-use packages of its shampoo, laundry detergent, face cream, and other products, Unilever can make a profit while selling its brands for just pennies a pack. As a result, today, more than 55 percent of Unilever's revenues come from emerging economies.[9]

Although this strategy has been successful for Unilever, most companies are learning that selling profitably to the bottom of the pyramid requires more than just repackaging or stripping down existing products and selling them at low prices. Just like more well-to-do consumers, low-income buyers want products that are both functional *and* aspirational.

Price Changes LO6

After developing their pricing structures and strategies, companies often face situations in which they must initiate price changes or respond to price changes by competitors.

Initiating Price Changes

In some cases, the company may find it desirable to initiate either a *price cut* or a *price increase*. In both cases, it must anticipate possible buyer and competitor reactions.

Initiating Price Cuts One situation that may lead a firm to consider cutting its price is excess capacity. Another is falling demand. In such cases, marketers may slash prices to boost sales and share, but cutting prices in an industry loaded with excess capacity may lead to price wars. A company may also cut prices in a drive to dominate the market through lower costs. Costco, for example, used this strategy to become the world's largest warehouse retailer.

Initiating Price Increases A successful price increase can greatly improve profits. For example, if the company's profit margin is 3 percent of sales, a 1 percent price increase will boost profits by 33 percent if sales volume is unaffected. A major factor in price increases is cost inflation. Rising costs squeeze profit margins and lead companies to pass cost increases along to customers. If possible, the company should try to find ways to cut costs instead of raising prices.

When they do raise prices, the company must avoid being perceived as a *price gouger*. For example, when gasoline prices rise rapidly, angry customers often accuse the major oil companies of enriching themselves at the expense of consumers. Customers have long memories, and they will eventually turn away from companies or even whole industries that they perceive as charging excessive prices. In the extreme, claims of price gouging may even bring about increased government regulation.

Buyer Reactions to Price Changes Customers do not always interpret price changes in a straightforward way. A price *increase*, which would normally lower sales, may have some positive meanings for buyers. For example, what would you think if Rolex *raised* the price of its latest watch model? On the one hand, you might think that the watch is even more exclusive or better made. On the other hand, you might think that Rolex is simply being greedy by charging what the market will bear.

Similarly, consumers may view a price *cut* in several ways. For example, what would you think if Rolex were to suddenly cut its prices? You might think you're getting a better deal on an exclusive product. More likely, however, you'd think quality had been reduced, and the brand's luxury image might be tarnished. A brand's price and its image are closely linked, and any price change can adversely affect how consumers view the brand.

Competitor Reactions to Price Changes A firm considering a price change must worry about the reactions of its competitors as well as those of its customers. Competitors are most likely to react when the number of firms involved is small, when the product is uniform, and when the buyers are well informed about products and prices.

How can marketers anticipate the likely reactions of competitors? The problem is complex because, like the customer, the competitor can interpret a company price cut in many ways. It might think that the company is trying to grab a larger market share, or that it's doing poorly and trying to boost its sales. Or it might think that the company wants the whole industry to cut prices in order to increase total demand.

The company must guess each competitor's likely reaction. If all competitors behave alike, this amounts to analyzing only a typical competitor. In contrast, if the competitors do not behave alike—perhaps because of differences in size, market shares, or policies—then separate analyses are necessary. However, if some competitors will match the price change, there is good reason to expect that the rest will also match it.

Responding to Price Changes

Here we reverse the question and ask how a company should respond to a price change by a competitor. The company must consider several issues: Why did the competitor change the price? Is the price change temporary or permanent? What will happen to the company's market share and profits if it does not respond? Are other competitors going to respond? Besides these issues, the company must also consider its own situation and strategy and possible customer reactions to price changes.

Figure 10.5 shows the ways a company might assess and respond to a competitor's price cut. Suppose the company learns that a competitor has cut its price and decides that this price cut is likely to harm company sales and profits. It might simply decide to hold its current price and profit margin. The company might believe that it will not lose too much market share, or that it would lose too much profit if it reduced its own price. Or it might decide that it should wait and respond when it has more information on the effects of the competitor's price change. However, waiting too long to act might let the competitor get stronger and more confident as its sales increase.

If the company decides that effective action can and should be taken, it might make any of four responses. First, it could *reduce its price* to match the competitor's

FIGURE 10.5 Assessing and Responding to Competitor Price Changes

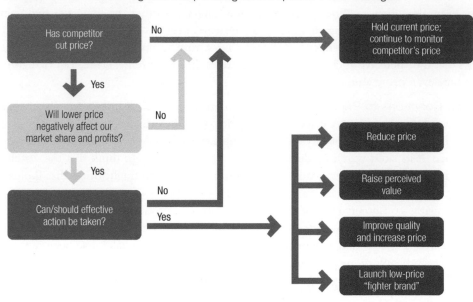

price. It may decide that the market is price sensitive and that it would lose too much market share to the lower-priced competitor. Cutting the price will reduce the company's profits in the short run. Some companies might also reduce their product quality, services, and marketing communications to retain profit margins, but this will ultimately hurt long-run market share. The company should try to maintain its quality as it cuts prices.

Alternatively, the company might maintain its price but *raise the perceived value* of its offer. It could improve its communications, stressing the relative value of its product over that of the lower-price competitor. The firm may find it cheaper to maintain price and spend money to improve its perceived value than to cut price and operate at a lower margin. Or, the company might *improve quality and increase price*, moving its brand into a higher price–value position. The higher quality creates greater customer value, which justifies the higher price. In turn, the higher price preserves the company's higher margins.

Finally, the company might *launch a low-price "fighter brand"*—adding a lower-price item to the line or creating a separate lower-price brand. This is necessary if the particular market segment being lost is price sensitive and will not respond to arguments of higher quality. For example, to fight against market share being lost to low-cost carriers, TELUS created Koodo, a telecommunications brand whose pricing structure is very different from its TELUS-branded services. Fighter brands are created explicitly to win back customers who have switched to a lower-priced rival; however, they sometimes result in customers switching from the company's own premium offering to its fighter brand. "Positioning a fighter brand

Exhibit 10.14 Fighter brands: TELUS markets its lower-priced mobile phone services under the brand Koodo.

presents a manager with a dual challenge," says one marketing expert. "You must ensure that it appeals to the price-conscious segment you want to attract while guaranteeing that it falls short for current customers of your premium brand."[10]

Public Policy and Pricing LO7

Price competition is a core element of our free-market economy. In setting prices, then, companies are usually free to charge whatever prices they wish. However, several laws restrict pricing practices. As well, companies must consider broader societal pricing concerns.

In Canada, the main law governing business practices, including pricing, is the Competition Act. Its purpose is "to maintain and encourage competition in Canada in order to promote the efficiency and adaptability of the Canadian economy, in order to expand opportunities for Canadian participation in world markets while at the same time recognizing the role of foreign competition in Canada, in order to ensure that small and medium-sized enterprises have an equitable opportunity to participate in the Canadian economy and in order to provide consumers with competitive prices and product choices."[11]

The sections of the Competition Act that regulate pricing are Part VI: Offences in Relation to Competition and Part VII.1: Deceptive Marketing Practices. The Act prohibits *price fixing*, meaning that sellers must set prices without talking to competitors. Otherwise, price collusion is suspected. Price fixing is illegal—that is, the government does not accept any excuses for it. Under the Competition Act, the legal charge for offences of this nature is *conspiracy*. Companies found guilty of such practices can receive heavy fines. In fact, 2009 changes to the Competition Act increased potential fines by as much as $25 million and increased jail sentences for breaching new conspiracy provisions to 14 years.[12]

Section 47 of the Act also identifies *bid rigging*—where one party agrees not to submit a bid or tender in response to a call, or agrees to withdraw a bid or tender submitted at the request of another party—as another indictable offence pertaining to price fixing. And under Section 78 (abuse of dominant position), sellers are prohibited from using *predatory pricing*—selling below cost with the intention of punishing a competitor, or gaining higher long-run profits by putting competitors out of business. This protects small sellers from larger ones who might sell items below cost temporarily or in a specific locale to drive them out of business. The biggest problem is determining just what constitutes predatory pricing behaviour. Selling below cost to unload excess inventory is not considered predatory; selling below cost to drive out competitors is. For example, in 2001 the short-lived Roots Air accused Air Canada of predatory pricing designed to drive it out of business. The Competition Bureau ordered Air Canada to stop offering deeply discounted fares on some of its routes; however, that didn't save Roots Air from going out of business. Thus, the same action may or may not be predatory depending on intent, and intent can be very difficult to determine or prove.

The Competition Act seeks to prevent unfair *price discrimination* by ensuring that sellers offer the same price terms to customers at a given level of trade. For example, every retailer is entitled to the same price terms from a given manufacturer, whether the retailer is Sears or your local bicycle shop. And yet price discrimination is allowed if the seller can prove that its costs are different when selling to different retailers—for example, that it costs less per unit to sell a large volume of bicycles to Sears than to sell a few bicycles to the local dealer. In other words, quantity or volume discounts are not prohibited. However, discriminatory promotional allowances (those not offered on proportional terms to all other competing customers) are illegal. Thus, large competitors cannot negotiate special discounts, rebates, and price concessions that are not made proportionally available to smaller competitors. For example, a small customer purchasing one-third as much as a larger competitor must receive a promotional allowance equal to one-third of what the large competitor was offered.

Although *functional discounts* (offering a larger discount to wholesalers than to retailers) are legal in the United States, they are illegal in Canada. In Canada, retailers and wholesalers are considered competing customers who must receive proportionally equal promotional allowances. Often, Canadian marketers who work for multinational firms must explain the differences in the law to their U.S. counterparts. Canadian marketers must also keep in mind that it is illegal for a buyer to knowingly benefit from any form of price discrimination. Price differentials may be used to "match competition" in "good faith," provided that the firm is trying to meet competitors at its own level of competition and that the price discrimination is temporary, localized, and defensive rather than offensive. Canadian marketers are allowed to offer price breaks for one-shot deals, such as store-opening specials, anniversary specials, and stock clearance sales. However, regional price differentials that limit competition are illegal. Canadian firms cannot price products unreasonably low in one part of the country with the intent of driving out the competition.

Laws also prohibit *retail (or resale) price maintenance*—a manufacturer cannot require dealers to charge a specified retail price for its product. Although the seller can propose a manufacturer's *suggested* retail price to dealers, it cannot refuse to sell to a dealer who takes independent pricing action, nor can it punish the dealer by shipping late or denying advertising allowances.

Deceptive pricing practices are outlined in Section 74 of the Competition Act. Deceptive pricing occurs when a seller states prices or price savings that are not actually available to consumers. For example, firms cannot advertise a product at a low price, carry very limited stock, and then tell consumers that they're out of the product so that they can entice them to switch to a higher-priced item. This "bait and switch" advertising is illegal in Canada. Firms must offer their customers "rain cheques" to avoid legal sanctions if advertised items are not stocked in sufficient quantities to cover expected demand. However, some deceptions are difficult for consumers to discern, such as when an airline advertises a low one-way fare that is available only with the purchase of a round-trip ticket, or when a retailer sets artificially high "regular" prices, and then announces "sale" prices close to its previous everyday prices.

Other deceptive pricing issues include *scanner fraud* and price confusion. The widespread use of scanner-based computer checkouts has led to increasing complaints of retailers overcharging their customers. Most of these overcharges result from poor management—from a failure to enter current or sale prices into the system. Other cases, however, involve intentional overcharges. Price confusion results when firms employ pricing methods that make it difficult for consumers to understand just what price they are really paying. Canadian law requires firms to charge consumers the lesser price in cases where more than one price is supplied by the seller either through its advertising, packaging, or in-store display.

Cost of Foods Sold

A funny thing happens when you decide to eat healthier—the food is sometimes not quite as tasty, yet usually more expensive. When Boston Pizza decided to address the emerging healthy eating trend with its Smart Eats menu, the challenge was threefold. First, the food had to be up to the delicious standards held by the brand for 50 years. Second, the meals had to have evident health benefits. Third, despite the cost of providing healthy ingredients, the prices had to be congruent with family casual dining.

The same three challenges existed to an even greater extent with BP's GlutenWise line of products catering to the growing gluten-intolerant market. Although in this situation, a fourth challenge—developing a pizza dough that would adequately adhere to the "hand-kneaded" texture BP's customers are accustomed to—introduced a direct and significant variable cost to the mix. Anyone on a gluten-free diet will tell you that any gluten-free baking with any quality of flavour and texture is going to cost more.

While Boston Pizza offsets the costs of making gluten-free pizza by marginally increasing its price, that product line, along with Smart Eats—and the entire menu, for that matter—are exposed to the ups and downs of economic cycles as well. Since the nature of healthy eating is often defined by fresh versus processed food, the cost of goods sold is very difficult to predict, given that it's more prone to fluctuations in global supply and demand and, in Canada's case, often volatile swings in the exchange rate.

As president and CEO Mark Pacinda says, "A lot of our vegetables come from California, so a) we're dealing with the exchange rate, which creates an uptick in costs, and b) yes, there has been an increase in the price of vegetables over the years." He adds, "We monitor our costs, so we tend to know what's going up and we work with our suppliers and try to lock that [price] in."

The other silver lining for BP is that 50 percent of its business is either pizza or pasta, "so we've been able to hold pricing across our chain," claims Pacinda. The cash-cow nature of BP's biggest sellers also allows the brand to provide the healthier, costlier menu items at prices that are consistent with standard BP fare.

QUESTIONS

1. If Boston Pizza's profit margin is less on its Smart Eats and GlutenWise menu offerings, why doesn't it just increase the price of these items more significantly to create greater profit margins?
2. Based on the theory outlined in this chapter, how would you classify Boston Pizza's overall pricing strategy? Support your response.
3. How does demand affect the price of Boston Pizza's products?

REVIEWING THE CONCEPTS

 Identify the three major pricing strategies and discuss the importance of understanding customer-value perceptions, company costs, and competitor strategies when setting prices.

A price is the sum of all the values that customers give up to gain the benefits of having or using a product or service. The three major pricing strategies are customer value-based pricing, cost-based pricing, and competition-based pricing. Good pricing begins with a complete understanding of the value that a product or service creates for customers and setting a price that captures that value. The price the company charges will fall somewhere between one that is too high to produce any demand and one that is too low to produce a profit.

Customer perceptions of the product's value set the ceiling for prices. If customers perceive that the price is greater than the product's value, they will not buy the product. At the other extreme, company and product costs set the floor for prices. If the company prices the product below its costs, its profits will suffer. Between these two extremes, consumers will base their judgments of a product's value on the prices that competitors charge for similar products. Thus, in setting prices, companies need to consider all three factors: customer-perceived value, costs, and competitor's pricing strategies.

 Identify and define the other important external and internal factors affecting a firm's pricing decisions.

Other *internal* factors that influence pricing decisions include the company's overall marketing strategy, objectives, and marketing mix, as well as organizational considerations. Price is only one element of the company's broader marketing strategy. If the company has selected its target market and positioning carefully, then its marketing mix strategy, including price, will be fairly straightforward. Some companies position their products on price and then tailor other marketing mix decisions to the prices they want to charge. Other companies de-emphasize price and use other marketing mix tools to create *nonprice* positions.

Other *external* pricing considerations include the nature of the market and the demand and environmental factors such as the economy, reseller needs, and government actions. The seller's pricing freedom varies with different types of markets. Ultimately, the customer decides whether the company has set the right price. The customer weighs the price against the perceived values of using the product—and if the price exceeds the sum of the values, consumers will not buy.

So the company must understand concepts such as demand curves (the price–demand relationship) and price elasticity (consumer sensitivity to prices).

Economic conditions can also have a major impact on pricing decisions. The recent economic downturn caused consumers to rethink the price–value equation. Marketers have responded by increasing their emphasis on value-for-the-money pricing strategies. Even in tough economic times, however, consumers do not buy based on prices alone. Thus, no matter what price they charge—low or high—companies need to offer superior value for the money.

 Describe the major strategies for pricing new products.

Pricing is a dynamic process. Companies design a *pricing structure* that covers all their products. They change this structure over time and adjust it to account for different customers and situations. Pricing strategies usually change as a product passes through its life cycle. The company can decide on one of several price–quality strategies for introducing an imitative product, including premium pricing, economy pricing, good value, or overcharging. In pricing innovative new products, it can use *market-skimming pricing* by initially setting high prices to "skim" the maximum amount of revenue from various segments of the market. Or it can use *market-penetrating pricing* by setting a low initial price to penetrate the market deeply and win a large market share.

Explain how companies find a set of prices that maximizes the profits from the total product mix.

When the product is part of a product mix, the firm searches for a set of prices that will maximize the profits from the total mix. In *product line pricing*, the company decides on price steps for the entire set of products it offers. In addition, the company must set prices for *optional products* (optional or accessory products included with the main product), *captive products* (products that are required for use of the main product), *by-products* (waste or residual products produced when making the main product), and *product bundles* (combinations of products at a reduced price).

 Discuss how companies adjust their prices to take into account different types of customers and situations.

Companies apply a variety of *price adjustment strategies* to account for differences in consumer segments and situations. One is *discount and allowance pricing*, whereby the company establishes cash, quantity, functional, or seasonal discounts, or varying types of allowances. A second strategy is *segmented pricing*, where the company sells a product at two or more prices to accommodate different customers, product forms, locations, or times. Sometimes companies consider more than economics in their pricing decisions, using *psychological pricing* to better communicate a product's intended position. In *promotional* pricing, a company offers discounts or temporarily sells a product below list price as a special event, sometimes even selling below cost as a loss leader. Another approach is *geographical pricing*, whereby the company decides how to price to distant customers, choosing from such alternatives as FOB-origin pricing, uniform-delivered pricing, and zone pricing. Finally, *international pricing* means that the company adjusts its price to meet different conditions and expectations in different world markets.

LO6 Discuss the key issues related to initiating and responding to price changes.

When a firm considers initiating a *price change*, it must consider customers' and competitors' reactions. There are different implications to *initiating price cuts* and *initiating price increases*. Buyer reactions to price changes are influenced by the meaning customers see in the price change. Competitors' reactions flow from a set reaction policy or a fresh analysis of each situation.

There are also many factors to consider in responding to a competitor's price changes. The company that faces a price change initiated by a competitor must try to understand the competitor's intent as well as the likely duration and impact of the change. If a swift reaction is desirable, the firm should preplan its reactions to different possible price actions by competitors. When facing a competitor's price change, the company might sit tight, reduce its own price, raise perceived quality, improve quality and raise price, or launch a fighting brand.

LO7 List and briefly describe the major legislation in Canada that affects marketers' pricing decisions.

In Canada, the main law governing business practices, including pricing, is the Competition Act. Its purpose is to maintain and encourage competition in Canada, and to ensure that small and medium-sized enterprises have an equitable opportunity to compete. The Act prohibits *price-fixing*, meaning that sellers must set prices without talking to competitors. Sellers are also prohibited from using *predatory pricing*—selling below cost with the intention of punishing a competitor, or gaining higher long-run profits by putting competitors out of business. The Competition Act seeks to prevent unfair *price discrimination* by ensuring that sellers offer the same price terms to customers at a given level of trade. Thus, large competitors cannot negotiate special discounts, rebates, and price concessions that are not made proportionally available to smaller competitors.

Although functional discounts (offering a larger discount to wholesalers than to retailers) are legal in the United States, they are illegal in Canada. In Canada, retailers and wholesalers are considered competing customers who must receive proportionally equal promotional allowances. Laws also prohibit *retail (or resale) price maintenance*—a manufacturer cannot require dealers to charge a specified retail price for its product. *Deceptive pricing* occurs when a seller states prices or price savings that are not actually available to consumers, and is against the Competition Act. *Bait-and-switch* advertising (advertising a product at a low price, carrying very limited stock, and then telling consumers that the seller is out of the product so that it can entice them to switch to a higher-priced item) is also illegal in Canada. Other deceptive pricing issues include *scanner fraud* and price confusion. Canadian law requires firms to charge consumers the lesser price in cases where more than one price is supplied by the seller through its advertising, packaging, or in-store displays.

MyMarketingLab

Study, practise, and explore real marketing situations with these helpful resources:

- **Interactive Lesson Presentations:** Work through interactive presentations and assessments to test your knowledge of marketing concepts.
- **Study Plan:** Check your understanding of chapter concepts with self-study quizzes.
- **Dynamic Study Modules:** Work through adaptive study modules on your computer, tablet, or mobile device.
- **Simulations:** Practise decision-making in simulated marketing environments.

DISCUSSION QUESTIONS

1. Why do marketers charge customers different prices for the same product or service? Explain how this type of pricing is implemented and the conditions under which it is effective.

2. Explain market-skimming and market-penetration pricing strategies. Why would a marketer of innovative high-tech products choose market-skimming pricing rather than market-penetration pricing when launching a new product?

3. What is price elasticity? Why is it important for marketers to consider price elasticity when making pricing decisions?

4. What does the following positioning statement suggest about the firm's marketing objectives, marketing-mix strategy, and costs? "No one beats our prices. We crush the competition."

5. Retailers often use psychological pricing as a price-adjustment strategy. Explain this pricing strategy. How do reference prices affect psychological pricing decisions?

CRITICAL THINKING EXERCISES

1. Identify three price-comparison shopping websites, and shop for a tablet of your choice. Compare the price ranges given at these three websites.

2. You are an owner of a small independent chain of coffeehouses competing head-to-head with Starbucks. The retail price your customers pay for coffee is exactly the same as at Starbucks. The wholesale price you pay for roasted coffee beans has increased by 25 percent. You know that you cannot absorb this increase and that you must pass it on to your customers. However, you are concerned about the consequences of an open price increase. Describe three alternative price-increase strategies that address these concerns. Which would you choose, and why?

3. Find the Canadian Consumer Price Index. Select one of the reports and create a presentation on price changes over the past two years. Discuss the reasons for those changes.

ONLINE, MOBILE, AND SOCIAL MEDIA

If you've travelled in a big city, you know how congested traffic can get. Many major cities now have HOV (high-occupancy vehicle) lanes that allow vehicles with two or more occupants to sail past all the other vehicles in single-occupancy lanes. The lanes are usually barricaded off between the opposing-direction lanes and switch directions from morning to evening to cater to the flow of heavy traffic. Mobile technology has resulted in a new opportunity for communities by converting these lanes to HOT (high-occupancy toll) lanes. For example, while travellers in Houston can drive in these lanes for free if more than two people are in the car, single riders can jump in these lanes as well for a toll. But the toll varies depending on the volume of traffic. The "dynamic pricing" lanes now appear in about a dozen cities in the U.S., with digital signs indicating the fluctuating prices. Tolls range from 25 cents to $1.40 per mile, depending on the speed of traffic.

QUESTIONS

1. Suggest another example of how dynamic pricing can be applied based on information obtained from consumers' digital behaviour on the Internet, use of social media, or through mobile technology usage.

2. In your opinion, is dynamic pricing ethical? Explain why or why not.

THINK LIKE A MARKETING MANAGER

The printer industry is intensively competitive with respect to pricing. The first home printers, marketed by companies such as Epson and Hewlett-Packard, were almost as expensive as computers themselves. But like most technology products, as technology improves and features are added, the price is forced down. Today, consumers can choose from a wide range of desktop printers for home use. Printers come with a variety of features and can be purchased from many different vendors.

QUESTIONS

1. What role does price play in a consumer's selection of a home printer? What about a business buyer making a purchase decision about an office printer? What about a business person selecting a portable printer to take on business trips?

2. List all the different features a printer can have. Which of these do you think are most important to consumers, and how much extra are they willing to pay for them? Which do you think are most important to business buyers?

3. Do some online research and find three different marketers that sell printers suitable for home use. Are the prices of the three brands the same or very different? If they are different, what accounts for the difference? What pricing strategy do you think each marketer is using?

4. Today, many printers designed for home use are "all in one" devices that print, scan, and fax. Explain the pricing strategy used by marketers of all-in-one printers.

MARKETING ETHICS

Businesses often charge different prices to different customers. For example, movie theatres charge less to students and senior citizens, and prices vary across times of the day. Women are charged more for dry cleaning and haircuts. Business flyers pay more than leisure travellers. And that person sitting next to you on the airplane may have paid more or less than you did—the same goes for hotel rooms. Consumers with arthritis pay more per milligram of pain relief when they buy the Tylenol Arthritis product than when they buy regular Tylenol, even though the active ingredient, acetaminophen, and dosage over an eight-hour period are identical. Technology offers marketers the ability to price-discriminate in various ways. For example, Coca-Cola once experimented with vending machines that raised prices as outdoor temperatures went higher. Electronic shelf labels allow retailers to change prices based on supply and demand. Moreover, the Internet provides the capability for businesses to charge different prices on their websites to different customers of the same product.

QUESTIONS

1. Is it fair for businesses to charge different prices to different customers?

2. Go to Wikipedia and research the "three degrees of price discrimination." Does this discussion impact your opinion stated in question 1 regarding the fairness of this practice? Explain.

MARKETING BY THE NUMBERS

When introducing new products, some manufacturers use a price-skimming strategy by setting a high initial price and then reducing the price later. However, reducing the price also reduces contribution margins, which in turn impacts profitability. To be profitable, the reduced price must sufficiently increase sales. For example, a company with a contribution margin of 30 percent on sales of $60 million realizes a total contribution to fixed costs and profits of $18 million ($60 million 0.30 = $18 million). If this company decreases price, the contribution margin will also decrease. So to maintain or increase profitability, the price reduction must increase sales considerably.

QUESTIONS

1. Refer to Appendix 3, Marketing by the Numbers, and calculate the new contribution margin for the company discussed above if it reduces price by 10 percent. Assume that unit variable costs are $70 and the original price was $100.

2. What total sales must the company capture at the new price to maintain the same level of total contribution (that is, total contribution = $18 million)?

FUZION WINES CATCHES THE ATTENTION OF ONTARIO WINE DRINKERS

Case prepared by David Rose, Conrad Business, Entrepreneurship & Technology Centre, University of Waterloo

The Liquor Control Board of Ontario (LCBO) is one of the world's largest buyers and retailers of beverage alcohol. With more than 630 retail stores throughout the province, it offers nearly 19 000 products directly to consumers and to licensed establishments. The LCBO's sales are over $4 billion per year, with spirit sales making up about 43 percent, wine 36 percent, and beer 21 percent of the total. As an Ontario government enterprise, the LCBO pays dividends to the province that help pay for healthcare, education, and other important services. Moreover, since 1990, LCBO has won more than 200 awards in customer service, innovative retailing, social responsibility, staff training, store design, marketing, and corporate communications.

In setting retail prices for the products it sells, the LCBO strives to balance several key elements of its mandate, including promoting social responsibility in the sale and consumption of beverage alcohol; providing excellent customer service, including offering customers a broad product selection and value at all price points; and generating maximum profit to fund government programs and priorities. The LCBO also ensures that it meets the legislated requirements under the Liquor Control Act concerning minimum price and uniform price. (Minimum prices are the lowest prices that products can be sold for, and uniform price requires that the price for a particular product be the same throughout the province.)

To achieve this necessary balance among the key elements of its mandate, and to meet public sector standards of openness, fairness, and transparency when it buys products for resale, the LCBO uses a standard mark-up pricing structure. Mark-ups vary by product category (among beer, wine, fortified wine, spirits, and liqueurs, for example), and a charge is added to imports to cover supplementary costs associated with those products, but otherwise the mark-up is consistent for all products. This standard mark-up pricing structure, established by the LCBO in consultation with the Ministry of Finance many years ago, allows suppliers to be confident that the LCBO provides fair and equitable treatment to its business partners.

As a result of this fixed mark-up structure, when LCBO buyers and suppliers discuss possible purchases they focus on the product's final retail price. The payment to the supplier for the products follows automatically from the application of the fixed mark-ups and other elements of the pricing structure (for example, freight costs and currency exchange rates if the purchase is in a foreign currency). As part of the agreement to purchase, the supplier must provide the final quote or cost to the LCBO, usually per case.

LCBO buyers make every effort to get the best products in each price band, whether for sub-$8 wines or super-premium spirits. They review more than 50 000 submissions annually and negotiate with suppliers to make the best of these products available at good prices. The LCBO is an attractive customer for manufacturers, and there is fierce competition for listings. As a result, suppliers frequently submit products to the LCBO at prices lower than those charged to other jurisdictions.

One of the newer additions to the LCBO's lineup is Fuzion, a line of affordable wines from Argentina's Familia Zuccardi, one of that country's largest and most famous wineries. Making wine in the South American country of Argentina is not new—they've been doing it for 400 years—but sometimes a tiny push in the right direction is all a region needs to put it on the map, and that push came in the form of Fuzion. When Fuzion's Shiraz-Malbec blend was first launched in Ontario it caused near riots in the aisles of LCBO stores, as the fruity, soft sensation—at the time $7.45 per bottle—was snapped up at an alarming rate after receiving favourable reviews and being compared to wines at twice and three times the cost. Such was the frenzy over the new wine that LCBO instituted a waiting list and reported jammed phone lines as customers called to add their names to the list. Customers spent so much time searching for Fuzion that when they did find a supply they bought it by the case, prompting the LCBO to stack cases near checkout counters rather than trying to keep up with restocking of shelves.

Fuzion did for Argentina what Yellow Tail did for Australia—sending exports soaring and other wineries scrambling to catch the wave of excitement. At one time, Fuzion was not only the hottest selling wine in Ontario, it was also the fourth best selling product at the LCBO behind only Heineken, Smirnoff, and Corona. While sales have since cooled, the company has added to the portfolio with a wide range of new wines, including a Blanc de Blancs Chardonnay that lists for $24.95, an Organic Malbec Cabernet at $12.95, Fuzion Alta Reserve Malbec at $9.95, and a couple of easy-drinking white wines in the under-$10 category.

While the Fuzion hysteria has subsided, there is no denying that consumers have come to love the bold fruity flavours and soft tannins of Malbec, the main ingredient in the red wines of Argentina. The country's profile has been elevated and the door opened to so many other interesting wines, many of them attractive for their low price, but also because the wines are so consumer friendly. Perfect growing conditions in the regions near the Andes and Colorado River have allowed varieties such as Cabernet Sauvignon, Malbec, Pinot Noir, Semillon, Merlot, and Chardonnay to grow successfully. Today, over 230 000 hectares of vineyards are planted in Argentina—almost half of those to red varieties and a quarter each to "pink" and white varieties. The most popular grapes are Malbec, Chardonnay, Cabernet Sauvignon, and various indigenous varieties.

While Argentina is currently the world's fifth largest wine producer by volume—after France, Italy, Spain, and the United States—it is only in recent years that it has emerged as a major player in the wine world. The most important aspect of Argentina's wine boom is what people usually call the price–quality ratio. Argentina's grape-growing regions are warm and dry, which means there are few problems with pests and moulds and so little need to buy pesticides, fungal treatments, and so on. Argentina's other production costs (labour, grapes) are also generally low by international standards. Together, these low costs mean that Argentine wineries can offer the same quality product for less money than other producers.

However, Argentine wines aren't the only value-priced wines available in Ontario. The LCBO lists more than 500 wines for under $10, with products from all of the world's major wine-producing regions. How was the launch of one wine—Fuzion's original Shiraz-Malbec—able to create such a sensation in this very crowded market? The situation was different in 2008, and the timing was perfect for Fuzion's entry. At the time, the LCBO was being challenged for moving away from wines selling below $10 and not searching out suppliers in the low-price category. In response to this criticism, it began looking for added-value brands for its product lineup and picked Fuzion, thinking it would be perfect to address consumer demands for better, cheaper wines. And the LCBO was right: Fuzion found the magical boundary between the affordable and the highly enjoyable, and the rest is history.

Meanwhile, value-seeking wine lovers in the United States are lamenting the end of the "Two-Buck Chuck" era. For more than a decade, shoppers at Trader Joe's stores in California paid just $1.99 for a bottle of Charles Shaw Shiraz or Cabernet Sauvignon, making it Trader Joe's best-selling wine. While the price has been higher in other parts of the United States for years, the increase to $2.49 in California created quite a stir. According to Bronco Wine, the company that produces the Charles Shaw brand, it was able to maintain such low prices for so long in part because it owns 45 000 acres of vineyard land, which helps the company ride out wild fluctuations in grape prices like those the industry has seen in recent years. However, bad crops in 2010 and 2011 spelled the end of "Two-Buck Chuck."

Sources: Information from LCBO website, www.lcbo.com; Gord Stimmell, "Fuzion Frenzy Uncorked," *Toronto Star*, January 24, 2009; "Plonk for the Privileged: Fuzion Malbec," *Choosy-Beggars* (Choosy-Beggars.com), June 10, 2009; Rick VanSickle, "Argentina Wines," *Traveling Golfer*, February 1, 2011; "Canada Signs Up for the Cult of Fuzion," *Ontario Wine Review*, October 8, 2008; and Cathy Bussewitz, "Price Hiked for 'Two-Buck Chuck,'" *The Press Democrat*, January 23, 2013.

QUESTIONS FOR DISCUSSION

1. Which of the major pricing strategies does the LCBO employ when introducing new products?

2. What other factors does the LCBO consider when setting prices for its products?

3. By pricing the first Shiraz–Malbec blend below the value perceived by most of the wine drinkers who tried it, Fuzion created a sensation in the Ontario wine market. Are there any risks involved when selling a product for less than other products of similar quality?

IanDagnall Computing/Alamy

AFTER STUDYING THIS CHAPTER, YOU SHOULD BE ABLE TO

1 explain what channels are, and why marketers need channel partners

2 list and describe the major types of channel partners

3 describe the process of organizing and managing channels, and explain how channel conflict can occur

4 explain the strategy behind intensive, selective, and exclusive distribution

5 list and describe the major channel design decisions marketers must make

6 explain the role of supply chain management and logistics management, and why companies often choose third parties to handle these tasks

Marketing Channels

PREVIEWING THE CONCEPTS

Marketing channels, or channels of distribution, collectively comprise the third *P* or third marketing mix tool—place. Marketers in every organization must design, develop, and manage the channels through which their products and services move from their point of production to the hands of the final customer. Some products, like software, move electronically while others, like clothing, furniture, and cars, move physically. Sometimes a firm's overall success can depend on how well it designs its channels or how well it manages them compared with its competitors. This chapter describes marketing channels and channel partners (also known as intermediaries), and explores some of the issues in designing and managing effective marketing channels. It also looks at the supply chain—the back end of the distribution channel—and considers the challenges of inventory movement and logistics management. Because retail is such an important (and visible) marketing channel, we'll take a closer look at the business of retail in Canada in Chapter 12. But first, let's start by considering how Netflix, the world's largest video subscription service, handles the challenges of distribution.

NETFLIX'S CHANNEL INNOVATION: FINDING THE FUTURE BY ABANDONING THE PAST

Time and again, Netflix has innovated its way to the top in the distribution of video entertainment. In the early 2000s, Netflix's revolutionary DVD-by-mail service put all but the most powerful movie-rental stores out of business. In 2007, Netflix's then ground-breaking move into digital streaming once again revolutionized how people accessed movies and other video content. Now, with Netflix leading the pack, video distribution has become a boiling, roiling pot of emerging technologies and high-tech competitors, one that offers both mind-bending opportunities and stomach-churning risks.

Just ask Blockbuster. The giant bricks-and-mortar movie-rental chain once flat-out owned the industry. Then along came Netflix, the fledgling DVD-by-mail service. First thousands then millions of subscribers were drawn to Netflix's innovative distribution model—no more trips to the video store, no more late fees, and a selection of more than 100 000 titles that dwarfed anything Blockbuster could offer. Even better, Netflix's $5-a-month subscription rate (in the U.S.) cost little more than renting a single video from Blockbuster. In 2010, as Netflix surged, once-mighty Blockbuster fell into bankruptcy.

 **Practice** on MyMarketingLab
Assessing Inventory of Retail Partners

 **Practice** on MyMarketingLab
Assessing Delivery Performance to Buyers

 **Practice** on MyMarketingLab
Assessing Performance of Product Displays in Store

The Blockbuster riches-to-rags story underscores the turmoil that typifies today's video distribution business. In only the past few years, a glut of video access options has materialized. At the same time that Netflix ascended and Blockbuster plunged, Redbox came out of nowhere to build a novel network of $1-a-day DVD-rental kiosks. Then Hulu launched in the U.S., with its high-quality, ad-supported free access to movies and current TV shows.

All along the way, Netflix has acted boldly to stay ahead of the competition. For example, in 2007, rather than sitting on the success of its still-hot DVD-by-mail business, Netflix and its CEO, Reed Hastings, set their sights on a then-revolutionary new video distribution model: Deliver the Netflix service to every Internet-connected screen, from laptops to Internet-ready TVs to mobile phones and other Wi-Fi-enabled devices. Netflix began by launching its Watch Instantly service, which let Netflix members stream movies instantly to their computers as part of their monthly membership fee, even if it came at the expense of Netflix's still-booming DVD business.

Although Netflix didn't pioneer digital streaming, it poured resources into improving the technology and building the largest streaming library. It built a customer base of nearly 25 million subscribers, and sales and profits soared. With its massive physical DVD library and a streaming library of more than 20 000 high-definition movies accessible via 200 different Internet-ready devices, it seemed that nothing could stop Netflix.

But Netflix's stunning success drew a slew of resourceful competitors. In 2010, video giants such as Google's YouTube and Apple's iTunes began renting movie downloads, and Hulu introduced subscription-based Hulu Plus. A few years later, Canadian cable companies Rogers and Bell got into the business, launching their video streaming services, Shomi and CraveTV. To stay ahead, even to survive, Netflix needed to keep the innovation pedal to the metal. So in the summer of 2011, in an ambitious but risky move, CEO Hastings made an all-in bet on digital streaming. He split off Netflix's still-thriving DVD-by-mail service into a separate business named Qwikster and required separate subscriptions for DVD rentals and streaming (at a startling 60 percent price increase for customers using both). The Netflix name would now stand for nothing but digital streaming, which would be the primary focus of the company's future growth.

Although perhaps visionary, Netflix's abrupt changes didn't sit well with customers. Some 800 000 subscribers dropped the service and Netflix's stock price plummeted by almost two-thirds. To repair the damage, Netflix quickly admitted its blunder and reversed its decision to set up a separate Qwikster operation. However, despite the setback, Netflix retained its separate, higher pricing for DVDs by mail. Netflix rebounded quickly, replacing all of its lost subscribers and then some. What's more, with a 60 percent higher price, revenues and profits rose as well. Netflix's stock price was once again skyrocketing.

With the quick recovery, now more than ever, Hastings seems bent on speeding up the company's leap from success in DVDs to success in streaming. Although customers can still access Netflix's world's-biggest DVD library, the company's promotions and website barely mention that option. The focus is now squarely on streaming video.

Despite its continuing success, Netflix knows that it can't rest its innovation machine. Competition continues to move at a blurring rate. For example, Amazon's Prime Instant Video offers instant streaming of thousands of movies and TV shows to Amazon Prime members at no extra cost. Google has moved beyond its YouTube rental service with Google Play, an all-media entertainment portal for movies, music, e-books, and apps. Comcast offers Xfinity Streampix, which lets subscribers stream older movies and television programs via their TVs, laptops, tablets, or smartphones. Coinstar and Verizon have now joined forces to form Redbox Instant by Verizon, which offers subscription-based streaming of older movies and newer pay-per-view content. And Apple and Samsung are creating smoother integration with streaming content via smart TVs.

Moving ahead, as the industry settles into streaming as the main delivery model, content—not just delivery—will be a key to distancing Netflix from the rest of pack. Given its head start, Netflix remains well ahead in the content race. However, Amazon, Hulu Plus, and other competitors are working feverishly to sign contracts with big movie and TV content providers. But so is Netflix. It scored a big win with a Disney exclusive—and it's now the only place where viewers can stream Disney's deep catalogue and new releases from Walt Disney Animation, Marvel, Pixar, and Lucasfilm.

But as content-licensing deals with movie and television studios become harder to get, in yet another innovative video distribution twist, Netflix and its competitors are now developing their own original content. Once again, Netflix appears to have the upper hand with *House of Cards*, a series produced by Hollywood bigwigs David Fincher and Kevin Spacey. The Netflix series has received rave reviews and set a number of industry "firsts." *House of Cards* is the first major TV show to completely bypass the traditional broadcast and cable networks. With its $100 million price tag, it's by far the most expensive series to air on a streaming network. And it marks the first time a series has released an entire season all at once. With *House of Cards*, Netflix has left the rest of the video industry scrambling to keep up.

Thus, from DVDs by mail, to Watch Instantly, to video streaming on almost any device, to developing original content, Netflix has stayed ahead of the howling pack by doing what it does best—innovate and revolutionize distribution. What's next? No one really knows. But one thing seems certain: Whatever's coming, if Netflix doesn't lead the change, it risks being left behind—and quickly. In this fast-changing business, new tricks grow old in a hurry. To stay ahead, as one headline suggests, Netflix must "find its future by abandoning its past."[1]

AS THE NETFLIX STORY SHOWS, marketing channel decisions such as when and how to enter a new market take careful planning, but if done well can result in superior customer value and competitive advantage—both for the firm and for its channel partners. Companies like Netflix—in other words, all companies that offer a product or service to the market—cannot bring value to customers by themselves, but must work closely with other firms in a larger value delivery network. In this chapter, we consider marketing channels, or channels of distribution; why they are important; and the major marketing decisions companies make in managing their channels. We then look at the task of supply chain management, or the "back end" of the distribution channel.

Distribution Channels:
The Value Delivery Network LO1

Producing a product or service and making it available to buyers requires building relationships not just with customers, but also with key suppliers "upstream" in the company's *supply chain*, and distributors and resellers that act as intermediaries to help move the product "downstream." Upstream from the company is the set of firms that supply the raw materials, components, parts, information, finances, and expertise needed to create a product or service. Marketers, however, have traditionally focused on the "downstream" side—the *marketing channels* (or *distribution channels*) that look toward the customer. Downstream marketing channel partners, such as wholesalers and retailers, form a vital connection between the firm and its customers.

Consider the many suppliers and distributors involved in the process of building and selling a car: from the makers of the tires, the engines, the windows, and every other part to the movement of the finished vehicles on trucks and trains and to the neighbourhood car dealership that displays, markets, and sells the vehicle to a consumer. Viewed from beginning to end, these chains and channels comprise a continually evolving *value delivery network*. A firm's **value delivery network** is made up of the company, suppliers, distributors, and ultimately customers who partner with each other to improve the performance of the entire system.

The term *supply chain* may be too limited, as it takes a *make-and-sell* view of the business. It suggests that raw materials, productive inputs, and factory capacity should serve as the starting point for market planning. A better term would be *demand chain* because it suggests a *sense-and-respond* view of the market. Under this view, planning starts by identifying the needs of target customers, to which the company responds by organizing a chain of resources and activities with the goal of creating customer value.

This chapter focuses on marketing channels—on the downstream side of the value delivery network. We examine four major questions concerning marketing channels: What is the nature of marketing channels and why are they important? How do channel firms interact and organize to do the work of the channel? What problems do companies face in designing and managing their channels? What role do physical distribution and supply chain management play in attracting and satisfying customers? In Chapter 12, we'll look at marketing channel issues from the viewpoints of retailers and wholesalers.

Value delivery network
The network made up of the company, suppliers, distributors, and ultimately customers who partner with each other to improve the performance of the entire system in delivering customer value.

What Is a Channel?

Few producers, whether they are tire manufacturers or farmers, sell their goods directly to the final users of their products. Instead, most use intermediaries to bring their products to market. They forge a **marketing channel (or distribution channel)**—a set of interdependent organizations that help make a product or service available for use or consumption by the consumer or business customer.

A company's channel decisions directly affect every other marketing decision. Pricing depends on whether the company works with national discount chains, uses high-quality specialty stores, or sells directly to consumers online. The firm's sales force and communications decisions depend on how much persuasion, training, motivation, and support its channel partners need. Whether a company develops or acquires certain new products may depend on how well those products fit the capabilities of its channel members.

Designing channels and choosing channel partners are strategic marketing decisions, made only after carefully studying the market and considering its opportunities. For example, Enterprise Rent-A-Car looked at the market and decided to take a different approach to distribution strategy. Instead of establishing locations in airports as all the other companies did, Enterprise opened off-airport, neighbourhood locations that provided short-term car-replacement rentals for people whose cars were wrecked, stolen, or being serviced, or for people who simply wanted a different car for a short trip or a special occasion. Today, although Enterprise also serves airports, it has a virtual lock on the home city market, and is well known for its point of differentiation in a crowded market: It picks you up.

Sometimes developing a marketing channel, especially in a new country, requires changing the brand name. For example, the Coastal Forest and Lumber Association, marketers of B.C. hemlock, a hardwood grown in abundance in that province, renamed its product Canada Tsunga for the Japanese market, and created a multimillion-dollar marketing campaign to

**Marketing channel
(or distribution channel)**
A set of interdependent organizations that help make a product or service available for use or consumption by the consumer or business customer.

support the channel partners in that country. Marketers designed a new logo and created an advertising campaign to communicate the fact that Canada Tsunga was stronger than other hardwoods. The ads featured a well-known but comparatively lightweight Sumo wrestler named Mai-no-umi, and compared his qualities to that of the lumber.[2]

Distribution channel decisions often involve long-term commitments to other firms. For example, companies such as Ford, McDonald's, or Nike can easily change their advertising, pricing, or promotion programs. They can scrap old products and introduce new ones as market tastes demand. But when they set up distribution channels through contracts with franchisees, independent dealers, or large retailers, they cannot readily replace these channels with company-owned stores or websites if the conditions change. Therefore, marketing managers must design channels carefully, with an eye on today's likely selling environment and tomorrow's as well.

How Channel Partners Add Value

Why do producers give some of the selling job to channel partners? After all, doing so means giving up some control over how and to whom they sell their products. Producers use intermediaries because they create greater efficiency in making goods available to target markets. Through their contacts, experience, specialization, and scale of operation, intermediaries usually offer the firm more than it can achieve on its own.

Figure 11.1 shows how using intermediaries can provide economies. Figure 11.1A shows three manufacturers, each using direct marketing to reach three customers. This system requires nine different contacts. Figure 11.1B shows the three manufacturers working through one distributor, which contacts the three customers. This system requires only six contacts. In this way, intermediaries reduce the amount of work that must be done by both producers and consumers.

From the economic system's point of view, the role of marketing intermediaries is to transform the assortments of products made by producers into the assortments wanted by consumers. Producers make narrow assortments of products in large quantities, but consumers want broad assortments of products in small quantities. Marketing channel members buy large quantities from many producers and break them down into the smaller quantities and broader assortments wanted by consumers.

For example, Unilever makes millions of bars of Lever 2000 hand soap each week. However, you most likely want to buy only a few bars at a time. Therefore, big food,

FIGURE 11.1 How Adding a Distributor Reduces the Number of Channel Transactions

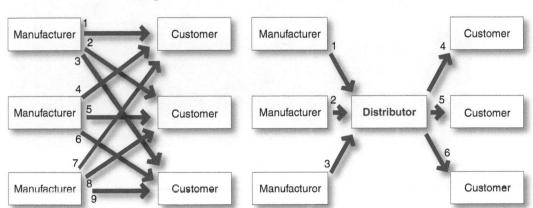

A. Number of contacts without a distributor
M × C = 3 × 3 = 9

B. Number of contacts with a distributor
M + C = 3 + 3 = 6

drug, and discount retailers, such as Safeway, Walmart, and Shoppers Drug Mart, buy Lever 2000 by the truckload and stock it on their stores' shelves. In turn, you can buy a single bar of Lever 2000, along with a shopping cart full of small quantities of toothpaste, shampoo, and other related products, as you need them. In this way, intermediaries play an important role in matching supply and demand.

In general, channel members add value by bridging the major time, place, and possession gaps that separate goods and services from those who would use them. These are some of the specific functions channel partners can perform:

- *Information gathering and distribution:* Channel partners, such as retailers that are closer to the final customer, have access to information the manufacturer might not have. Channel partners can collect market intelligence and communicate it back to the original producer.

- *Promotion at point of purchase:* National brand advertising is typically handled by the manufacturer, but promotions at point of purchase, such as locally advertised sales, are handled by distributors and retailers.

- *Contact:* Channel members, such as sales agents operating in the field and in local markets, can find new customers.

- *Matching and arranging:* Channel partners often play a role in adapting the product to fit the buyer's needs, such as customizing the installation of kitchen cabinets. Channel members such as specialty retailers also display and arrange products to offer customers a choice.

- *Negotiation:* Channel partners such as brokers and agents negotiate price and terms of delivery so that the product can move from one channel member to another.

- *Physical distribution:* Trucking and other transportation companies act as channel members by transporting and storing products as they move through the channel.

Exhibit 11.1 Functions served by channel members: Caterpillar's local dealers are the main point of contact with the customer and perform many other channel functions, including matching the customer with the right product, negotiating terms, and communicating information about Caterpillar to the customer (and collecting intelligence from the customers to report back to Caterpillar). They also handle the last leg of the physical distribution of the product, and they take care of all the after-sales support.

© Horizon International Images Limited/Alamy

- *Financing:* Companies such as Canadian Tire that offer store credit cards, and companies that sell large products such as cars, may have finance organizations as channel partners.

- *Risk taking:* Depending on the partner arrangement, channel members may assume the risk of handling, transporting, and storing the product as it moves through the channel.

- *After-sales support:* Some products, such as electronics and automobiles, require after-sales support and servicing. These functions are typically performed by channel partners.

The question is not *whether* these functions need to be performed—they must be—but rather *who* will perform them. Consider the many valuable functions served by the channel partners of heavy-equipment manufacturer Caterpillar, for example:

> Caterpillar is the world's leading manufacturer of construction and mining equipment, diesel and natural gas engines, industrial gas turbines and diesel-electric locomotives. Time and time again, the company has said that one of the keys reasons for its success is its value delivery network of outstanding independent dealers worldwide. Caterpillar's distribution strategy is part of the company's strategic vision: "Our distribution system is a competitive advantage; our supply chain is world class."
>
> There are 21 Caterpillar factories around the world, and after the finished product leaves the door, Caterpillar dealers take over. They are the ones on the front line; the ones the customers interact with, and trust. When a big piece of Caterpillar equipment breaks down, customers know that they can count on Caterpillar and its outstanding dealer network for support. Dealers play a vital role in almost every aspect of Caterpillar's operations, from product design and delivery to product service and support. As Stu Levenick, group president of the company's customer and dealer support division, says, "For our customers, combining the world's leading manufacturer with a local dealer relationship in their own language and culture is unbeatable. I think our designers and manufacturers are the best in the industry, but what really sets us apart is the dealer organization."
>
> The company recently celebrated 90 years in business, and with annual sales topping $55 billion worldwide, it looks like Caterpillar's channel partnership strategy is working very well![3]

We've learned about one type of channel partner, the independent dealer, so now let's look at what other types of businesses and organizations can act as channel partners in a company's supply chain and distribution channels.

Types of Channel Partners `LO2`

Channel partners are businesses that are owned and operated independently from the manufacturer, and that are contracted by the manufacturer to perform a specific function in the movement of the product. The major types of channel partners are *retailers*, *wholesalers*, *drop shippers*, *rack jobbers*, *brokers*, and *agents*.

Retailers **Retailing** is the business of selling products and services directly to consumers for their personal use. It includes all the activities involved in running the business, such as operating and managing a bricks-and-mortar location and/or a website; selecting, purchasing, and displaying merchandise; and marketing and sales. Although some wholesalers and manufacturers engage in some retailing, either by having a storefront at their location or by opening their doors to the public on occasion, **retailers** are businesses whose sales come primarily from retailing.

Retail is one of the most important, and certainly the most visible, of marketing channels. Every store that is open to the public, from your corner convenience store to that big box store in the suburbs, is a retailer, but so is your local bank branch, your regular gas station, and your favourite restaurant or bar. Because retail is such an important and complex marketing channel, we'll look at it in more detail in Chapter 12.

Wholesalers **Wholesaling** includes all activities involved in selling goods and services to those buying for resale or business use. **Wholesalers** are companies that buy from

Retailing
The business of selling goods or services to consumers for their personal use.

Retailer
A business that primarily sells products and services to consumers.

Wholesaling
All activities involved in selling goods and services to those buying for resale or business use.

Wholesalers
Companies whose primary business is wholesaling.

producers and sell to retailers, business customers, and other wholesalers. According to Statistics Canada, wholesaling contributes nearly $60 billion to the economy every year. Because wholesalers do not sell directly to consumers, you may have never heard of some of the largest and most important wholesalers like Grainger and Sysco. Companies like Apple and Samsung, and those that produce automobiles and even most clothing brands, are also wholesalers in that they sell their products to retailers, which in turn make them available to consumers.

Some wholesalers are also the manufacturers of the products, but typically wholesalers are companies that purchase goods from the manufacturers, then resell them either to retailers or through other channels. Wholesalers like these are also referred to as *merchant wholesalers* and *distributors* because they purchase and take possession of the products, then physically distribute them to their customers. A wholesaler that takes possession of inventory also assumes the risk (of theft, damage, spoilage) that goes with it.

Drop Shippers and Rack Jobbers   There are other types of intermediaries that do not take possession of merchandise and that instead perform very specific functions in the distribution channel.

Drop shipping refers to a process in which the intermediary takes the order from the customer and passes it to a manufacturer or wholesaler, which then ships the item directly to the customer. Some retailers engage in drop shipping at times, especially for large items that are not kept in stock at each store location. For example, if a consumer orders a mattress set from Sears (whether online, over the phone, or in the store), the Sears employee takes the payment and delivery information, then passes it to the Sears distribution centre. From there it is drop-shipped to the customer. Smaller retailers might also engage in drop shipping if they receive a large order from a customer that exceeds the stock they have on hand.

There are also businesses that never keep inventory or handle the product, and so are full-time **drop shippers**. Examples of this type of business are companies that sell customized clothing and other small items like key chains and mouse pads to groups such as minor-league sports teams and small businesses. Many of these vendors do not have physical storefronts but operate only online; they do not manufacture the goods they sell, but rather they choose from a network of suppliers to produce the customer's order. When Amazon.com began operations, it only drop-shipped books from the publisher to the consumer. Today, it still drop-ships certain titles, but maintains warehouses to handle more popular and frequently ordered books. Because drop shippers take payment from the customer (i.e., sell) and later pay the supplier for the order (i.e., buy), they are considered wholesalers.

Another type of wholesaler is the **rack jobber**. Rack jobbers buy merchandise and then set up "rack" displays inside retail stores, where the merchandise is sold to customers. Rack jobbers typically serve grocery and drug retailers, mostly in nonfood items. They set up point-of-purchase displays, keep inventory records, and retain ownership of the goods until they are sold. The consumer who purchases an item from the display pays at the retailer's checkout, and later, the rack jobber bills the retailer for the items that were sold.

Brokers   Brokers differ from merchant wholesalers in two ways: They do not take title to goods, and they perform only a few functions. Like merchant wholesalers, they generally specialize by product line or customer type. A **broker** brings buyers and sellers together and assists in negotiation, but does not carry inventory, get involved in financing, or assume risk. Think of a stockbroker, who buys stocks on behalf of a client and earns a commission.

Agents   Agents are similar to brokers in that they perform only a few functions and do not take title to goods, but while a broker makes deals with many different buyers and sellers, an **agent** typically has a more permanent relationship representing either one or the other. A real estate agent, for example, typically represents the seller of a home, and performs functions

Drop shipper
An intermediary that takes orders and payment from the customer, then arranges to have the merchandise shipped to the customer directly from the supplier.

Rack jobber
A wholesaler that buys merchandise and resells it on "racks" inside a retail store, in partnership with the retailer.

Broker
A wholesaler that does not take title to goods and whose function is to bring buyers and sellers together and assist in negotiation.

Agent
A representative, either of a buyer or a seller, who performs only a few functions and does not take title to goods.

such as taking pictures, listing it on the MLS, producing marketing support materials, and advising the seller about how best to attract a buyer.

Manufacturers' agents are a common type of agent, typically contracted by smaller manufacturers that don't have their own sales staff. The agent sells the manufacturer's goods to buyers and receives a commission from the manufacturer.

Advertising agencies are another type of agent, and valuable members of the marketing channel. They provide marketing communications services such as designing and producing advertisements and buying the media (television, radio, magazines, Internet) in which to run them.

Traditionally, advertising agencies refer to their upstream channel partners as clients, but that may be changing. Some agencies are now referring to their clients as partners:

Exhibit 11.2 Advertising agencies as channel partners: Sun Life is a household name in Canada, but when it moved into the United States it needed a marketing communications partner that understood the American market. Today, the company's name is on the Miami stadium that is home to the Dolphins.

Having an advertising agency as marketing channel partner can help open doors when entering a new market, as Sun Life Financial learned. While Sun Life is a household name in Canada, it was virtually unknown in the United States, and so it knew it would need a strong marketing channel partner to help it gain recognition and respect in that fiercely competitive market. The company had already established a channel of distribution in the U.S., but had been hearing that the job of those sales representatives was very difficult. "It's one thing to explain very complex financial products and services to consumers," they said. "It's quite another to have to explain who Sun Life is."

So Sun Life went shopping for an agency partner, and ultimately chose The Martin Agency, the creative minds behind the Geico gecko and the great advertising slogan, "Virginia Is for Lovers." The agency is based in Richmond, Virginia, and that's part of the reason why Sun Life chose it. Many large agencies are located in New York or Chicago, which gives them something of a skewed view of what the average American consumer is really like. As Martin's senior vice-president of marketing communications explains, "I remember that when we were in a review for Saab, we were the only agency whose employees drove to work every day. When we were in the review for Walmart, we were the only agency with Walmarts in our town. There are no Walmarts in Manhattan."

Martin's understanding of the average American helped it create a successful advertising campaign that "taught" Americans who Sun Life was by using Canadian images that Americans recognize. In one television commercial, for example, representatives of Sun Life try to persuade Cirque de Soleil to change its name to Cirque de Sun Life. Today, Sun Life Financial is a leading provider of employee benefits in the U.S., and its name is on the Miami stadium that is home to the Dolphins.[4]

We've seen how some of the major types of channel members provide valuable services in the movement of goods and associated services from producers to final customers, but there are many other companies and organizations that can play a role in a well-designed channel. We'll look at the "back end" or "upstream" members, the channel partners in the supply chain, later in this chapter.

Organization and Management of Channels LO3

Marketing channels don't happen by themselves; rather, they must be built to meet strategic business goals, then continually managed. Marketers must first *select* their channel partners. They must then decide how many *channel levels* to create (i.e., how many intermediaries or channel partners to have), whether to set up *direct marketing channels* or *indirect marketing channels*, or both, and whether to create a *vertical marketing system*, a *horizontal marketing system*, or to *franchise*. Then, on an ongoing basis, they must *manage and motivate channel partners* and work to avoid *channel conflict*.

Selecting Channel Partners

Producers vary in their ability to attract qualified marketing intermediaries. Some producers have no trouble signing up channel members. For example, when Toyota first introduced its Lexus line in the United States, it had no trouble attracting new dealers. In fact, it had to turn down many would-be resellers.

At the other extreme are producers that have to work hard to line up enough qualified intermediaries. For example, when Timex first tried to sell its inexpensive watches through regular jewellery stores, most jewellery stores refused to carry them. The company then managed to get its watches into department stores and mass merchandise retail outlets like Walmart.

Even established brands may have difficulty gaining and keeping their desired distribution, especially when dealing with powerful resellers. For example, you won't find P&G's Pampers diapers in a Costco store. After P&G declined to manufacture Costco's Kirkland store-brand diapers a few years ago, Costco gave Pampers the boot and now carries only Huggies and its own Kirkland brand (manufactured by Huggies maker Kimberly-Clark). The removal by Costco, the number two diaper retailer after Walmart, has cost P&G an estimated $150 million to $200 million in annual sales. In a similar dispute, Costco temporarily stopped carrying Coca-Cola products, and it swapped out Coke for Pepsi in the beloved hot dog and soft drink combo sold in its food courts. That was a big loss for Coca-Cola: Costco serves up 100 million hot dog combos a year, more than four times the combined hot dog sales at all Major League Baseball parks.[5]

When considering which channel partners to work with, marketers evaluate each potential partner's years in business, other lines carried, location, growth and profit record, cooperativeness, and reputation.

How Many Channel Levels?

Companies can design their distribution channels to make products and services available to customers in different ways. Each layer of marketing intermediaries that performs some work in bringing the product and its ownership closer to the final buyer is a **channel level**. Because both the producer and the final consumer perform some work, they are part of every channel.

Direct versus Indirect Channels The number of levels of the channel, or number of channel members that function as intermediaries between the producer and the consumer, constitutes the *length* of a channel. The shortest possible channel is a channel with no intermediaries—this is referred to as a *direct marketing channel*, where the producer of the goods sells directly to the final customer. Most channels, however, have one or more intermediaries, and are therefore *indirect marketing channels*.

Figure 11.2 shows both consumer and business channels of different lengths. Figure 11.2A shows several common consumer distribution channels. Channel 1, called a **direct marketing channel**, has no intermediary levels—the company sells directly to consumers. Most businesses, however, use one or more intermediaries to reach their final customers, and these are referred to as **indirect marketing channels** (Figure 11.2B).

Figure 11.2 also illustrates the difference between business-to-consumer (B-to-C) and business-to-business (B-to-B) distribution channels. B-to-B companies often market and sell their products directly to their customers through their own sales force, and they

Channel level
A layer of intermediaries that performs some work in bringing the product and its ownership closer to the final buyer.

Direct marketing channel
A marketing channel that has no intermediary levels.

Indirect marketing channel
A marketing channel containing one or more intermediary levels.

FIGURE 11.2 Direct and Indirect Marketing Channels, for Both Business-to-Consumer and Business-to-Business

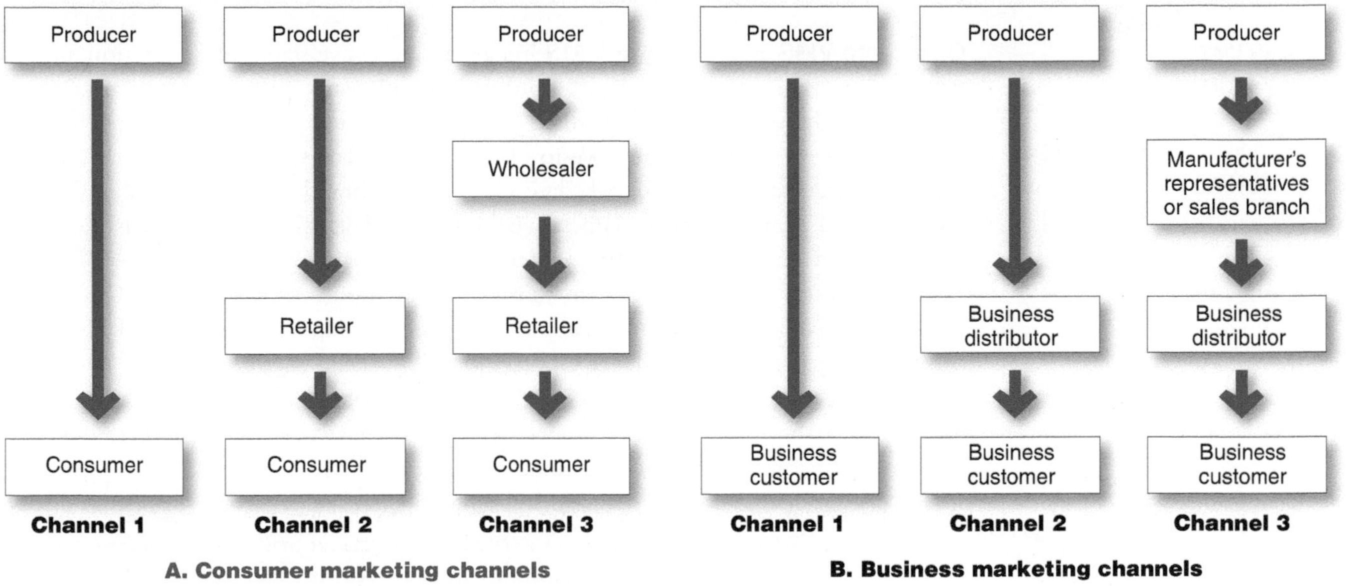

A. Consumer marketing channels

Channel 1	Channel 2	Channel 3
Producer	Producer	Producer
		Wholesaler
	Retailer	Retailer
Consumer	Consumer	Consumer

B. Business marketing channels

Channel 1	Channel 2	Channel 3
Producer	Producer	Producer
		Manufacturer's representatives or sales branch
	Business distributor	Business distributor
Business customer	Business customer	Business customer

can also market, sell, and physically distribute their product using channel partners such as distributors, wholesalers, and retailers. (More about this in Chapter 12.) From the producer's point of view, a greater number of levels means less control and greater channel complexity. Moreover, all the institutions in the channel are connected by several types of *flows*. These include the *physical flow* of products, the *flow of ownership*, the *payment flow*, the *information flow*, and the *promotion flow*. These flows can make even channels with only one or a few levels very complex.

While it may seem at first glance that companies like Mary Kay, Avon, and The Pampered Chef are direct marketing channels, they are, in fact, more complex than that. Mary Kay and The Pampered Chef sell their products through home parties, which are organized by independent representatives acting as an agent. Avon and other marketers sell products in a similar manner, or door to door, but also offer online sales that truly are a direct channel—unless, of course, the products are drop-shipped. Insurance companies, banks, and other service providers often sell their services via the telephone, and that means either an inside sales staff or, more likely, a third-party telephone-marketing company—another channel partner.

In reality, there are very few companies that sell directly to customers without the assistance of any intermediaries or channel partners.

Vertical Marketing Systems

In traditional, or conventional, distribution systems, one producer distributes products through one wholesaler or distributor, and from there to several or many retailers. Each of the businesses in the process is independently owned and is seeking to maximize its own profits, perhaps even at the expense of the others. No channel member has much control over the other members, and no formal means exists for assigning roles and resolving channel conflict.

In contrast, a **vertical marketing system (VMS)** consists of producers, wholesalers, and retailers acting as a unified system. One channel member owns the others, has contracts with them, or wields so much power that they must all cooperate. The VMS

Vertical marketing system (VMS)
A distribution channel structure in which producers, wholesalers, and retailers act as a unified system. One channel member owns the others, has contracts with them, or has so much power that they all cooperate.

can be dominated by the producer, wholesaler, or retailer. Three types of VMSs are *corporate*, *administered*, and *contractual*.

Corporate VMS

A vertical marketing system that combines successive stages of production and distribution under single ownership; channel leadership is established through common ownership.

Corporate VMS A **corporate VMS** integrates successive stages of production and distribution under single ownership. Coordination and conflict management are attained through regular organizational channels. For example, George Weston Limited is a corporation that owns and operates Weston Foods and Loblaw Companies Limited. Weston Foods produces and distributes baked goods under the brands Weston, Wonder, Colonial Cookies, and ACE Bakery. Its largest retail customer is Loblaw, which owns more than 1000 retail grocery stores operating under 22 different banners, including Real Canadian Superstore, No Frills, Fortinos, Zehrs, Provigo, Extra Foods, and Wholesale Club. It also owns many well-known food brands that it produces under contract and distributes through its retail stores: President's Choice, Joe Fresh, Blue Menu, and The Decadent.

Another example of a vertical marketing system is popular fashion brand Zara, a prototype "fast fashion" house that owes its success to the fact that it controls every member of its marketing and distribution channel:

> Fashion retailer Zara is known for cheap chic—designs that resemble those of big-name fashion houses but at moderate prices. It's a new breed of retailer that responds to the latest fashion trends quickly and nimbly, thanks to its cutting-edge distribution system and its vertical marketing strategy. Zara controls all phases of its supply chain, marketing channel, and distribution channel, and that allows the company to take a new fashion concept through design, manufacturing, and store-shelf placement in as little as two weeks.
>
> How can it move so quickly? One reason is the value of timely information provided by Zara's store managers, who use handheld computers to report in real time what's selling and what's not. They talk with customers to learn what they're looking for but not yet finding. At the same time, Zara trend-seekers roam fashion shows in Paris and concerts in Tokyo, looking for young people who might be wearing something new or different. When they find something, they notify company headquarters in tiny La Coruña, Spain, and the company's team of 300 designers conjures up a version of the new item.
>
> Once the designers have done their work, production begins. But rather than relying on a hodgepodge of slow-moving suppliers in Asia, as most competitors do, Zara makes 40 percent of its own fabrics and produces more than half of its own clothes. Even farmed-out manufacturing goes primarily to local contractors. Almost all clothes sold in Zara's stores worldwide are made quickly and efficiently at or near company headquarters in the remote northwest corner of Spain. Finished goods then feed into Zara's modern, highly automated distribution centres, which can sort, pack, label, and allocate up to 80 000 items an hour, readying them for direct shipment to Zara stores around the world. Now that's fast![6]

Administered VMS

A vertical marketing system that coordinates successive stages of production and distribution, not through common ownership or contractual ties, but through the size and power of one of the parties.

There are many such corporate VMSs, though the names of the overseeing corporations may not be ones we recognize. You may not be familiar with an Italian company called Luxottica, for example, but you're likely familiar with its well-known sunglasses brands, Ray-Ban and Oakley. Luxottica also produces eyewear under licence for brands such as Polo Ralph Lauren, Dolce & Gabbana, Prada, Versace, and Bulgari. It then sells these brands through two of the world's largest optical chains, LensCrafters and Sunglass Hut, which it also owns.

Exhibit 11.3 Corporate vertical marketing system: Zara either owns or controls most of its distribution system, from manufacturing through to retailing.

© Caro/Alamy

Administered VMS In an **administered VMS**, leadership is assumed not through common ownership or contractual ties, but through the size and power of one or a few dominant channel members. Manufacturers of a top brand can obtain strong trade cooperation and support from resellers. For example, General Electric, Procter & Gamble, and Kraft can command unusual cooperation from retailers regarding displays, shelf space, promotions, and price policies. In turn, large retailers can exert strong influence on the many manufacturers that supply the products they sell.

Contractual VMS The third type of vertical marketing system is the **contractual VMS**, which consists of independent firms at different levels of production and distribution that work together under contract. The companies that band together in such a system do so in order to achieve economies of scale and other efficiencies that are greater than if each business were to operate on its own. The most common type of contractual vertical marketing system is the franchise organization.

Franchise Organizations A franchise organization is a special type of contractual vertical marketing system, and perhaps the one most familiar to us as consumers. A *franchise* is a retailer or service provider that operates under licence using another firm's proven, successful business model. McDonald's, for example, began as one restaurant in 1940, but was the first restaurant to serve what we now call fast food. It was a new business model, and it became successful, and therefore franchisable. In terms of marketing and distribution, the *franchisor* is the corporation that owns the rights to the brand and the business model, and that allows independent business owners, called *franchisees*, to use its trademark. The franchisor dictates and controls the look and feel of the franchisee's operation, and also typically supplies the franchisee with the necessary ingredients to run the franchise. Together the franchisor and franchisees comprise the **franchise organization**, a marketing system that links several stages in the production and distribution process, and controls operations from a central head office.

There are three types of franchises. The first type is the *manufacturer-sponsored retailer franchise system*—for example, Ford and its network of independent franchised dealers. The second type is the *manufacturer-sponsored wholesaler franchise system*—Coca-Cola licenses bottlers (wholesalers) in various markets that buy Coca-Cola syrup concentrate and then bottle and sell the finished product to retailers in local markets.

The third type is the *service firm–sponsored retailer franchise system*—for example, Boston Pizza has over 370 locations from coast to coast, most of which are franchises. Boston Pizza franchise owners run their own local restaurant and pay a royalty of 7 percent on gross food sales to the corporation. Once a franchisee's application is approved, decisions must be made, and agreements entered into, between the parties; for example, the specific location of the new franchise must be selected, and the land or building lease secured. There are also contractual agreements governing the design of the interior, the use of the Boston Pizza logo, and a co-op fund to pay for national advertising.[7]

For people who want to run their own businesses, franchising is a common way to do so. In Canada, franchise owners have formed a trade association, called the Canadian Franchise Association (CFA), to assist franchisees. They offer events, programs, and publications to help educate Canadians about how to get into franchising, how to choose a franchise, and what franchise opportunities are available. The CFA publishes *Franchise-Canada* magazine, a bi-monthly consumer publication for entrepreneurs interested in acquiring a franchise.

Horizontal Marketing Systems

Another type of cooperative marketing system is the **horizontal marketing system**, in which two or more companies that operate at the same channel level join together to follow a new marketing opportunity. By working together, companies can combine their

Contractual VMS
A vertical marketing system in which independent firms at different levels of production and distribution work together under contract.

Franchise organization
A marketing system that links several stages in the production and distribution process, and controls operations from a central head office.

Horizontal marketing system
An arrangement in which two or more companies that operate at the same channel level join together to follow a new marketing opportunity.

Exhibit 11.4 Horizontal marketing system: Many Esso gas stations now include an On the Run convenience store and a Tim Hortons, creating a horizontal marketing system. On the Run stores are owned by Alimentation Couch-Tard, and are themselves franchises.

financial, production, or marketing resources to accomplish more than any one company could alone.

Companies in a horizontal marketing system might join forces with competitors or noncompetitors. They might work with each other on a temporary or permanent basis, or they may create a separate company. For example, Tim Hortons set up express versions of its stores at Esso gas stations so that commuters can fill up and get a coffee on the way to work without making two stops. Similarly, many Home Depot stores in Canada have a self-contained Subway restaurant. Each business is run by its own corporate management, but the companies join forces to reach the same market—hungry shoppers.

The Star Alliance is an example of companies that compete in the same industry, in this case air travel, and cooperate in a (horizontal) marketing system that allows frequent fliers of one of the member airlines to book travel on another member's planes. More than 25 airlines, including Air Canada, Lufthansa, and United, are members of the Star Alliance.

Multichannel (Hybrid) Distribution Systems

We've seen that there are many different types of distribution systems a company can use to move its products from their point of origin to the hands of the consumer or business customer, but companies are not restricted to choosing one or the other. With so many channel opportunities available, both online and offline, many companies opt for a **multichannel or hybrid distribution system**. This form of multichannel marketing occurs when a single firm sets up two or more marketing channels to reach one or more market segments.

Some of the examples we've already looked at are, in fact, multichannel distribution systems. Many fashion brands and retailers such as Zara sell their merchandise online as well as through their traditional retail distribution channel. A business-to-business marketer may operate a channel that includes wholesalers and distributors, but may also sell directly through its own sales force.

These days, almost every large company and many small ones distribute through multiple channels. For example, John Deere sells its familiar green and yellow lawn and garden tractors, mowers, and outdoor power products to consumers and commercial users through several channels, including John Deere retailers, Lowe's home improvement stores, independent equipment retailers in its smaller markets (such as Green Diamond Equipment Ltd. in Nova Scotia), and online. It sells and services its tractors, combines, planters, and other agricultural equipment through its premium John Deere dealer network. And it sells large construction and forestry equipment through selected large, full-service John Deer dealers and their sales forces.

Multichannel distribution systems offer many advantages to companies facing large and complex markets. With each new channel, the company expands its sales and market coverage and gains opportunities to tailor its products and services to the specific needs of diverse customer segments. But such multichannel systems are harder to control, and they can generate conflict as more channels compete for customers and sales.

Multichannel (hybrid) distribution system
A distribution system in which a single firm sets up two or more marketing channels to reach one or more market segments.

Ongoing Management of Channel Partners

Once selected, channel members must be continually managed and motivated to do their best. The company must sell not only *through* the intermediaries but also *to* and *with* them. Most companies see their intermediaries as first-line customers and partners. They practise strong partner relationship management to forge long-term partnerships with channel members. This creates a value delivery system that meets the needs of both the company and its marketing partners.

In managing its channels, a company must convince suppliers and distributors that they can succeed better by working together as a part of a cohesive value delivery system. Toyota, for example, has long known the importance of building close relationships with suppliers. In fact, it even includes the phrase "achieve supplier satisfaction" in its mission statement. Toyota truly partners with its channel members to help them meet its very high expectations. It learns about their businesses, conducts joint improvement activities, helps train supplier employees, gives daily performance feedback, and actively seeks out supplier concerns. It even recognizes top suppliers with annual performance awards. Such high supplier satisfaction means that Toyota can rely on suppliers to help it improve its own quality, reduce costs, and develop new products quickly.[8]

L'Oréal is another company that treats its suppliers with a fundamental respect for their business, their culture, their growth, and the individuals who work there. On the one hand, it expects a lot from suppliers in terms of design innovation, quality, and socially responsible actions. The company carefully screens new suppliers and regularly assesses the performance of current suppliers. On the other hand, L'Oréal works closely with suppliers to help them meet its exacting standards. Whereas some companies make unreasonable demands on their suppliers and "squeeze" them for short-term gains, L'Oréal builds long-term supplier relationships based on mutual benefit and growth.

Many companies are now installing integrated high-tech partnership relationship management (PRM) systems to coordinate their whole-channel marketing efforts. Just as they use customer relationship management (CRM) software systems to help manage relationships with important customers, companies can now use PRM and supply chain management (SCM) software to help recruit, train, organize, manage, motivate, and evaluate relationships with channel partners.

Channel Conflict Each channel member plays an important role in the marketing channel, but sometimes disagreements over goals, roles, and rewards among channel members can create what is known as **channel conflict**. Take the distribution and marketing of cellphones, for example. A mobile phone manufacturer like Samsung wants its product distributed as widely as possible, so as to end up in the hands of as many consumers as possible. However, its distributors—telecommunications companies such as Rogers, Bell, and TELUS—see things a little differently: They want to distribute as many new devices as possible to their customers, but they don't favour one manufacturer over another, which can lead to channel conflict among those manufacturers.

Horizontal conflict occurs among firms that perform the same function at the same level of the channel. For example, it can happen when a Toyota dealer in Burnaby feels that the Toyota dealer in Vancouver is stealing business by pricing too low or advertising outside its assigned territories; or when a Holiday Inn franchise owner feels that another Holiday Inn franchise is giving poor service, hurting the brand image.

Vertical conflict, conflict between different levels of the same channel, is even more common. For example, KFC and its franchisees came into conflict over the company's

Channel conflict
Disagreement among marketing channel members over goals, roles, and rewards.

Joshua Lutz/Redux

Exhibit 11.5 Channel conflict: KFC came into conflict with its franchisees over the brand's "Unthink KFC" repositioning, which emphasized grilled chicken over its traditional Kentucky fried.

decision to emphasize grilled chicken and sandwiches over the brand's traditional fried chicken:

> Several years ago Kentucky Fried Chicken changed its name to KFC and repositioned its brand around grilled rather than fried chicken in order to reach increasingly health-conscious consumers. However, a sizable group of the company's more than 4000 U.S. franchisees cried "foul" when the chain introduced grilled chicken, supported by a major marketing campaign with the slogan "Unthink KFC." The franchisees were concerned that abandoning the brand's Southern fried chicken legacy would confuse consumers and hurt sales. It "tells our customers not to think of us as a fried chicken chain," complained one franchisee who operates 60 franchises in five states. Soon after the "Unthink" campaign began, the KFC National Council & Advertising Cooperative, which represents all U.S. KFC franchisees, sued KFC to halt it. And the Association of Kentucky Fried Chicken Franchises, which represents two-thirds of U.S. franchisees, developed its own local marketing campaign emphasizing good old Kentucky fried. KFC eventually dropped "Unthink KFC." However, that and others have left a bad aftertaste in mouths on both sides. "We ought to be walking arm in arm to figure out a way out of [the current] sales decline. We ought to be shooting the competition," said one franchisee. "Instead, we're shooting one another."[9]

Companies that market and sell their products through bricks-and-mortar and online channels are especially susceptible to channel conflict. Toy marketer Mattel, for example, sells through thousands of retailers and also online at Shop.Mattel.com, Fisher-Price.com, MattyCollector.com, BarbieCollector.com, and HotWheelsCollectors.com. The sites target different segments of the toy-buying population, and cater to serious aficionados of those brands, many of whom subscribe to receive certain new Mattel toys the day they become available. But according to Mike Young, director of ecommerce for Mattel, the main goal of the sites isn't necessarily to generate revenue. Mattel avoids channel conflict with retailers by not competing online on the basis of price.[10]

Some conflict in the channel takes the form of healthy competition. Such competition can be good for the channel, since without it, the channel could become passive and susceptible to competition. KFC's conflict with its franchisees could be considered normal give-and-take over the respective rights of the channel partners; however, severe or prolonged conflict can disrupt channel effectiveness and cause lasting harm to channel relationships. It's for this reason that marketing managers must carefully manage their channels.

Evaluating Channel Members Finally, the company producing the goods to be delivered via the channel must continually evaluate the performance of its channel partners. Standards or quotas must be met for sales, inventory levels, delivery times, treatment of damaged and lost goods, cooperation in company promotion and training programs, and customer service. The company should recognize and reward partners that are performing well, and assist or possibly replace those that are performing poorly.

Above all, marketers must be sensitive to the needs of their channel partners. Those that treat their partners poorly risk not only losing their support but also causing some legal problems.

Changing Channel Organization

Disintermediation
The cutting out of marketing channel intermediaries by product or service producers or the displacement of traditional resellers by radical new types of intermediaries.

Changes in technology and the explosive growth of direct and online marketing are having a profound impact on the nature and design of marketing channels. One major trend is toward **disintermediation**—a big word with a clear message and important consequences. Disintermediation occurs when an established intermediary becomes unnecessary, and is cut out of the channel.

Disintermediation is an economics term that became popular with the advent of the Internet and the new types of online businesses that came with it. As the Internet developed as a channel of distribution, some traditional businesses that had once held an important role in the channel became, unfortunately, unnecessary. A classic example of disintermediation occurred when online travel sites, such as Travelocity, were introduced. Since they allowed consumers to book their own travel arrangements, the traditional travel agent was rendered redundant. Indeed, in today's ever-online and connected world, the business of offering travel services requires marketers to stay on top of every new development—just as WestJet has done. (See Marketing@ Work 11.1.)

Perhaps the most well known example of an online-only business that successfully changed a traditional distribution model is Netflix. As we saw at the beginning of this chapter, Netflix created a subscription business that distributed movies and TV series on DVD to consumers via the mail; later, it evolved into online-only distribution via streaming video. Netflix disintermediated bricks-and-mortar movie rental retailers such as Blockbuster—retailers that could once be found in every neighbourhood and have now virtually disappeared.

Sometimes new intermediaries provide competition to established providers of services, but do not necessarily render them obsolete. For example, ZipCar operates without the need for retail outlets that most other car rental companies have, but that doesn't mean those other car rental companies will cease to exist. And Uber, the ride-sharing app, provides consumers with an alternative to taxis, and although the taxi companies aren't happy about it, it is unlikely that Uber will disintermediate them.

The phenomenon of disintermediation presents both opportunities and problems for marketers and their channel partners. Channel innovators that find new ways to add value in the channel can displace traditional resellers and reap the rewards. In turn, traditional intermediaries must continue to innovate to avoid being swept aside. For example, superstore booksellers Chapters and Indigo pioneered huge book selections and low prices, sending most small independent bookstores into ruin. Then, along came Amazon.com, which threatened even the largest bricks-and-mortar bookstores through online book sales. Now, both offline and online sellers of physical books are being threatened by digital book downloads and e-readers. Rather than being threatened by these digital developments, however, Amazon.com developed its highly successful Kindle e-readers, and other companies, like Kobo, have followed suit.

Marketers at every company in the channel—from manufacturers to retailers—must continually work to develop new channel opportunities. However, developing these new channels may result in conflict. To ease this problem, marketers must always take their channel partners into consideration, and look for ways to grow that will benefit all members of the channel. For example, guitar and amp maker Fender knows that many customers would prefer to buy its guitars, amps, and accessories online, but selling directly through its website would create conflict with its retail partners. So the marketers at Fender decided to use their website for marketing purposes only, and not for sales. Consumers can read all about the company's products online, but they can't buy a new Fender Stratocaster that way. The Fender website also refers consumers to their nearest retailer—helping both the company and its channel partners.

Rakuten Kobo Inc

Exhibit 11.6 Disintermediation: To combat the threat of disintermediation by electronic books, booksellers developed e-book readers like Kindle and Kobo.

MARKETING@WORK   11.1

WestJet's Continually Expanding Channels

WestJet Airlines, based in Calgary, began operations in 1996 with a fleet of three 737-200s flying between five cities in western Canada. In 2002 the company moved into the business travel market, introducing flights to Toronto and London. A few years later it expanded into the winter vacation market, flying to California and Florida. Next, it added new service divisions, WestJet Vacations and WestJet Encore. WestJet even partnered with Disney to create the "Magic Plane," custom painted with a *Walt Disney World* theme featuring Mickey Mouse in his role as the Sorcerer's Apprentice. You might not think of a service like air travel as having distribution channels—there's no physical product to move. But airlines *do* have channel partners: aircraft manufacturers, airports,

and of course suppliers of everything from jet fuel to onboard food and beverages, all of which help WestJet deliver its product to the market.

Channel decisions for an airline also mean deciding which locations to serve (that is, fly to)—after all, the fourth *P* of marketing means "place." For example, when Edmonton was the fastest growing city in Canada, WestJet increased the number of flights it offered out of Edmonton, adding 60 additional flights per week to Kelowna, Regina, Saskatoon, Grande Prairie, and Calgary. Most recently, WestJet has expanded its service to offer flights to international destinations, including Europe, Hawaii, and the Caribbean.

Another area in which WestJet works with channel partners is through what air-

lines call "code sharing." Code sharing allows customers to book a flight through WestJet to destinations where WestJet doesn't fly itself, but where its code share partners (American Airlines, British Airways, Delta, KLM, and Qantas, just to name a few) *do*. By sharing customers with its channel partners, WestJet is able to greatly expand its service offerings, allowing travellers to book with WestJet and fly to many more destinations.

Services provided in flight are also done with the help of channel partners such as food service companies and entertainment suppliers. Recently, WestJet decided to get rid of seatback screens and live TV, and instead offer an in-flight Wi-Fi entertainment system that relies on customers using their own phones, tablets, or laptops to access it.

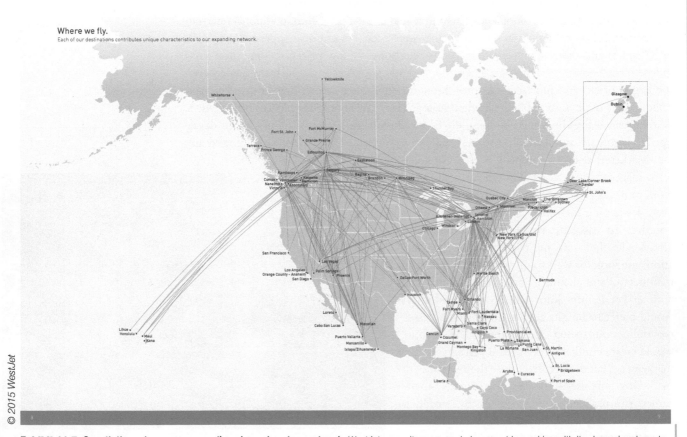

Where we fly.
Each of our destinations contributes unique characteristics to our expanding network.

Exhibit 11.7 **Growth through an ever-expanding channel partner network:** WestJet grows its company in large part by working with its channel partners to expand its reach.

The new service, called Connect, includes recorded content like movies and TV shows for free, and allows customers to connect to the Internet for an additional charge. The airline will also offer tablets, for a fee, to those who don't have one. While partnerships with content providers remain more or less the same, WestJet had to source new partners to provide and maintain the Wi-Fi service. On the other hand, it no longer has to buy and maintain hundreds of screens to outfit every plane.

Up until the advent of e-commerce, the intermediary of the commercial travel sector was the bricks-and-mortar travel agency. Today, of course, that space is reliant on e-tailers led by Expedia, Travelocity, and more recently unique blind auction sites such as Hotwire. "These services are partners for WestJet," says Manoj Jasra, WestJet's digital director, "but my mandate is to gain as much channel share as possible, which means making the guests' online experience as positive as possible."

In 2013, WestJet invested $40 million in a system upgrade to assist Jasra and his team. "We replaced our Internet booking engine with a system that allowed us greater merchandising capabilities … things like cross-selling flights with cars, having a shopping cart, and a better booking management system for customers who may want or need to change their flights." These and other features allowed WestJet to compete with substitutes like Expedia and rivals like Air Canada.

That said, an online guest experience is predicated first upon guests visiting a site. Jasra explains the two key components in driving that traffic: "Analytics measures everything about the number and nature of visits to our website: where they came from, how long they stayed, where they dropped off, and so on. Optimization attempts to maximize traffic to our website by knowing where people search and what they search with. We know that 25 percent of our customers begin their search on Google, so it's easy to ensure that we show up number one in Google searches using the word 'WestJet.' It becomes more challenging, although not impossible, to earn a high ranking on searches like 'cheap flights to Vegas.'"

WestJet's customers' online expectations are continually changing, however. In fact, every company relying on online shopping has found itself painted into a corner, since everything that was once done on a 21-inch screen must now be doable on a smartphone device. Admitting that WestJet was late in launching an app, Jasra says that overcoming that issue is made more challenging by today's customer expectations. "If you're late to the party, you better come up with something really strong. What is that set of functionality features that will really resonate with our guests? My vision is one that encompasses the different parts of a guest's journey. So what if you can book a flight? Our app needs to do more."

Mission accomplished: WestJet travellers must download the WestJet app in order to be able to access WestJet's Connect service in flight—the first of its kind in Canada.

Sources: Howard Slutsken, "WestJet Gets a New Logo. Kind of …," AirlineReporter.com, August 10, 2015; Kyle Bakx, "What's Behind WestJet's New Connect Wi-Fi System," CBC News online (CBC.ca), August 7, 2015; Slav Kornik, "WestJet Expanding Edmonton Regional Services," Global News online (GlobalNews.ca), July 27, 2015; and information from WestJet and WestJet.com.

Channel Strategy and Design LO4

As we've seen, many marketing management decisions are involved in creating channels of distribution and in their ongoing organization and management. We now consider the decisions a marketer must make not just about *where* and *how* to distribute its products, but *in how many places*. Next we examine *channel design decisions* such as analyzing customer needs, setting channel objectives, determining which type of channel members are required, and what their responsibilities should be. Finally, we consider international channel strategy.

Distribution (Channel) Strategy

At first glance it may seem as if all marketers would wish to distribute their products in as many locations as possible—*intensive* distribution—but that's not always the best strategy. Sometimes it's better to choose *selective* or even *exclusive* distribution.

Intensive Distribution Marketers of everyday convenience products such as soft drinks and snack foods typically choose **intensive distribution**, a strategy in which they stock their products in as many outlets as possible. The types of products found in convenience stores are often impulse purchases, and so the marketing strategy is to make them available where and when consumers want them. Other necessities such as toothpaste and toilet paper are often purchased hastily when the consumer has just run out of them, and so marketers like Kimberly-Clark choose intensive distribution to make their products available at just about every store the consumer might run to in a shopping emergency.

Intensive distribution
A marketing strategy in which the product is stocked in as many outlets as possible.

Courtesy of STIHL, Inc.

Why is the world's number one selling brand of chain saw not sold at Lowe's or The Home Depot®?

We can give you 8,000 reasons, our legion of independent STIHL dealers nationwide. We count on them every day and so can you. To give you a product demonstration, straight talk and genuine advice about STIHL products. To offer fast and expert on-site service. And to stand behind every product they carry, always fully assembled. You see, we won't sell you a chain saw in a box, not even in a big one. **Are you ready for a STIHL?**

To find a dealer: stihlusa.com or call 1-800 GO STIHL.

This Home Depot and Lowe's are registered trademarks of their respective companies.

STIHL®

Exhibit 11.8 Selective distribution: Stihl distributes its products selectively, through a dealer network that does *not* include big box hardware stores.

Selective distribution

A distribution strategy in which the marketer selects a set of retailers that specialize in their product category.

Selective Distribution Selective distribution is a marketing strategy typically chosen by makers of brand name appliances, furniture, and electronics. In **selective distribution**, the marketer selects a set of retailers that specialize in their product category. For example, Whirlpool and General Electric sell their major appliances at Sears and other large department stores, and Le Creuset sells its cookware through specialty stores such as Williams-Sonoma, William Ashley, and independent retailers of fine cookware.

Often, the selection of which retailers to use as channel partners is made so as to reflect the status of the brand. For example, midmarket mattress brands such as Sealy and Serta are distributed through Leon's (a furniture retailer) and Sleep Country (a mattress specialty store), but more upscale mattress brands such as Hypnos (found in the homes of royalty and celebrities) are available only in very high-end specialty stores, such as The Bedroom Shoppe in Calgary. Similarly, high-quality brands like Sony, Denon, and Bose and are distributed at high-end electronics retailers but would not be found at discount retailers; and designer clothing labels such as Stella McCartney and Burberry are available at retailers such as Holt Renfrew but would never be found in a store like Giant Tiger. And then there's Stihl (pronounced "steel"), the German marketer of high-quality chain saws and other power tools that doesn't sell its products through Home Depot or any big box stores:

In 1926, Andreas Stihl, a Swiss-born engineer, set up shop in Stuttgart, Germany, and started making washing machines as well as one of the world's first chain saws—a two-person model with an inch-wide chain that ran on electricity. Today, Stihl products are sold worldwide, but only at small retailers like Speed's Power Equipment in Salt Lake City. Speed Power's owner, Sam Wilson, was worried when a Home Depot opened eight blocks away, so he decided to change his business strategy. He stopped carrying almost every brand of machinery that could be found in a big box home-improvement store, which left him primarily with a bunch of chain saws, blowers, and hedge trimmers made by Stihl. "I'm not going to lie; I was nervous," says Wilson. "But my sales went crazy. It was just awesome."

Stihl has become the world's top chain saw seller and a manufacturing powerhouse by actively positioning itself against two of the most powerful forces in commerce: big box retail and the Internet. Stihl built its business model around retailers such as Speed's—mom-and-pop hardware stores, lawn mower repair shops, and thousands of other small outfits with creaky signs out front and piles of greasy spare parts in back. The company's strategy is to selectively distribute its products through scrappy underdogs, like Wilson. And it's paid off in spades: Stihl has cultivated a fiercely dedicated sales force in these independent dealers. Small shops also give Stihl a chance to demonstrate how well its machines work. When Stihl's sales representatives visit these dealers, they can go out to the woodpile and try out the new models. "It's a very old sales tactic," says the company.

Of course the big box retailers weren't happy about Stihl's refusal to sell them product, and their buyers continually hounded the manufacturer. So Stihl decided to take out full-page ads in the *Wall Street Journal* that read, "Why is the world's number one selling brand of chain saw not sold at Lowe's or Home Depot? We can give you 8,000 reasons, our legion of independent Stihl dealers nationwide."[11]

Exclusive Distribution Exclusive distribution is a deliberate marketing strategy chosen by brands that wish to associate themselves with an air of, well, exclusivity. It is usually associated with luxury brands such as Rolex and Tiffany, which give exclusive rights to carry their products in a particular region to one retailer, but it is also the distribution strategy employed by IKEA. In **exclusive distribution**, the marketer gives the rights to distribute its products to only one retailer, or to only one retailer in a particular geographic territory. Sleep Number beds, for example, are available exclusively at Radisson Hotels and Resorts; Breville designer toasters are available exclusively at Hudson's Bay; and the Cindy Crawford line of home furnishings is available exclusively at The Brick.

Another form of exclusive distribution occurs when the manufacturer of a line of products makes those products available only through its own retail channels, whether they be in stores, online, or through catalogues. (It's also a vertical marketing system.) For example, Veritas Tools of Ottawa is a world leader in woodworking and gardening tool design, and it's also the manufacturing arm of retailer Lee Valley Tools, which distributes approximately 1000 products exclusively through its own outlets:

> Lee Valley Tools is a family owned and operated business founded in Ottawa in 1978 by Leonard Lee. It manufactures many of its high-quality woodworking and gardening tools through its own manufacturing arm, Veritas Tools. It prides itself on its high level of customer satisfaction, and customers can return any product for a full refund within three months of purchase. To ensure that its customers are served by people with a high level of knowledge about its products, and given good advice about products and their uses, the company sells through its 16 retail stores located across Canada and through its catalogues and website. Such exclusive distribution enables it to promise to "treat every customer like a friend." Close customer relationships have helped the company better understand customer needs and get ideas about how to improve its tools or design new tools. In fact, it developed a line of surgical tools for doctors after it discovered that one plastic surgeon, Dr. Michael Bell, had been using tools from Lee Valley in his practice.[12]

Lee Valley Tools Ltd.

Exhibit 11.9 Exclusive distribution: Lee Valley retail stores are the exclusive distributor of Veritas Tools.

Exclusive distribution
A distribution strategy in which the marketer gives the rights to distribute its products to only one retailer, or to only one retailer in a particular geographic territory.

Channel Design Decisions LO5

In designing marketing channels, manufacturers struggle between what is ideal and what is practical. A new firm with limited capital usually starts by selling in a limited market area. In this case, deciding on the best channels might not be a problem: The problem might simply be how to convince one or a few good intermediaries to handle the line.

If successful, the new firm can branch out to new markets through existing intermediaries. In smaller markets, the firm might sell directly to retailers; in larger markets, it might sell through distributors. In one part of the country, it might grant exclusive franchises; in another, it might sell through all available outlets. Then it might set up an online store that sells directly to hard-to-reach customers. In this way, channel systems often evolve to meet market opportunities and conditions.

For maximum effectiveness, however, channel analysis and decision making should be more purposeful. **Marketing channel design** calls for analyzing customer needs,

Marketing channel design
Designing effective marketing channels by analyzing customer needs, setting channel objectives, determining the types and responsibilities of channel members, and making decisions about international distribution channels.

setting channel objectives, determining the types and responsibilities of channel members, and making decisions about international distribution channels.

Analyzing Customer Needs Remember, marketing channels are part of the overall *customer value delivery network*. Each channel member and level adds value for the customer. And since all marketing activities are about figuring out what customers want and then delivering value to them, designing the marketing channel starts with finding out what customers want from that channel.

No matter what product is being marketed, marketers must ask and answer questions like these: Do consumers want to buy in person from nearby locations or are they willing to travel to more distant and centralized locations? Would business customers rather buy in person, by phone, or online? Do they want to deal with an agent or broker, or would they prefer to deal directly with the producer/manufacturer? Do consumers who use our product value breadth of assortment or do they prefer specialization? Do they want many add-on services (delivery, installation, repairs), or will they obtain these services elsewhere?

Providing customer service is also part of marketing, so in making channel design decisions, marketers must reflect on what kinds of services the customer will require. The faster the delivery, the greater the assortment provided, and the more add-on services supplied, the greater the channel's service level. Service may be provided by the producer/manufacturer but more likely by a channel member, such as a retailer. And higher levels of service result in higher costs for the channel and higher prices for consumers. For example, your local independent hardware store probably provides more personalized service, a more convenient location, and less shopping hassle than the nearest huge Home Depot or Lowe's store. But it may also charge higher prices. The company must balance consumer needs not only against the feasibility and costs of meeting these needs but also against customer price preferences. The success of discount retailing shows that consumers will often accept lower service levels in exchange for lower prices.

Setting Channel Objectives Companies should state their marketing channel objectives in terms of targeted levels of customer service. Usually, a company can identify several segments wanting different levels of service. The company should decide which segments to serve and the best channels to use in each case. In each segment, the company wants to minimize the total channel cost of meeting customer service requirements.

The company's channel objectives are also influenced by the nature of the company, its products, its marketing intermediaries, its competitors, and the environment. For example, the company's size and financial situation determine which marketing functions it can handle itself and which it must give to intermediaries. Companies selling perishable products, for example, may require more direct marketing to avoid delays and too much handling.

In some cases, a company may want to compete in or near the same outlets that carry competitors' products. For example, Maytag and other appliance makers want their products displayed alongside competing brands to facilitate comparison shopping. In other cases, companies may avoid the channels used by competitors. Mary Kay Cosmetics, for example, sells directly to consumers

DAVID WALTER BANKS/The New York Times/Redux Pictures

Exhibit 11.10 Meeting customers' channel service needs: Your local hardware store probably provides more personalized service, a more convenient location, and less shopping hassle than a huge Home Depot or Lowe's store. But it may also charge higher prices.

through its corps of more than 2.4 million independent beauty consultants in more than 35 markets worldwide rather than going head-to-head with other cosmetics makers for scarce positions in retail stores.

Finally, environmental factors such as economic conditions and legal constraints must be taken into consideration when setting channel objectives.

Types and Responsibilities of Channel Members A firm should identify the types of channel members available to carry out its channel work. Most companies face many channel member choices. For example, until recently, Dell sold directly to final consumers and business buyers only through its sophisticated phone and Internet marketing channel. It also sold directly to large corporate, institutional, and government buyers using its direct sales force. However, to reach more consumers and match competitors such as Samsung and Apple, Dell now sells indirectly through retailers such as Best Buy, Staples, and Walmart. It also sells indirectly through value-added resellers—independent distributors and dealers that develop computer systems and applications tailored to the special needs of small- and medium-sized business customers.

Using many types of resellers in a channel provides both benefits and drawbacks. For example, by selling through retailers and value-added resellers in addition to its own direct channels, Dell can reach more and different kinds of buyers. However, the new channels will be more difficult to manage and control. In addition, the direct and indirect channels will compete with each other for many of the same customers, causing potential conflict. In fact, Dell often finds itself "stuck in the middle," with its direct sales reps complaining about competition from retail stores while its value-added resellers complain that the direct sales reps are undercutting their business.

The producer and the intermediaries need to agree on the terms and responsibilities of each channel member. They should agree on price policies, conditions of sale, territory rights, and the specific services to be performed by each party. The producer should establish a list price and a fair set of discounts for the intermediaries. It must define each channel member's territory, and it should be careful about where it places new resellers.

Mutual services and duties need to be spelled out carefully, especially in franchise and exclusive distribution channels. For example, McDonald's provides franchisees with promotional support, a record-keeping system, training at Hamburger University, and general management assistance. In turn, franchisees must meet company standards for physical facilities and food quality, cooperate with new promotion programs, provide requested information, and buy specified food products.

Suppose a company has identified several channel alternatives and wants to select the one that will best satisfy its long-run objectives. Each alternative should be evaluated against economic, control, and adaptability criteria.

Using *economic criteria*, a company compares the likely sales, costs, and profitability of different channel alternatives. What will be the investment required by each channel alternative, and what returns will result? The company must also consider *control issues*. Using intermediaries usually means giving them some control over the marketing of the product, and some intermediaries take more control than others. Other things being equal, the company prefers to keep as much control as possible. Finally, the company must apply *adaptability criteria*. Channels often involve long-term commitments, yet the company wants to keep the channel flexible so that it can adapt to environmental changes. Therefore, to be considered, a channel involving long-term commitments should be greatly superior on economic and control grounds.

International Distribution Channels International marketers face many additional complexities in designing their channels. Each country has its own unique distribution system that has evolved over time and changes very slowly—so rather than change the channel, international marketers usually adapt their channel strategies to the existing structures within each country.

In some markets, the distribution system is complex and hard to penetrate, consisting of many layers and large numbers of intermediaries. For example, many Western companies find Japan's distribution system difficult to navigate. It's steeped in tradition and very complex, with many distributors touching the product before it arrives on the store shelf.

At the other extreme, distribution systems in developing countries may be scattered, inefficient, or altogether lacking. For example, China and India are huge markets—each with a population well over 1 billion people. However, because of inadequate distribution systems, most companies can profitably access only a small portion of the population located in each country's most affluent cities. Rural markets in both countries are highly decentralized and comprise many distinct submarkets, each with its own subculture. China's distribution system is so fragmented that logistics costs to wrap, bundle, load, unload, sort, reload, and transport goods amount to 18 percent of the nation's GDP, far higher than in most other countries. (In comparison, U.S. logistics costs account for about 8.5 percent of the nation's GDP.) After years of effort, even Walmart executives admit that they have been unable to assemble an efficient supply chain in China.[13]

Sometimes local conditions can greatly influence how a company distributes products in global markets. For example, in low-income neighbourhoods in Brazil where consumers have limited access to supermarkets, Nestlé supplements its distribution with thousands of self-employed salespeople who sell Nestlé products from refrigerated carts door to door. And in crowded cities in Asia and Africa, fast-food restaurants such as McDonald's and KFC offer delivery:

> When we want a quick meal delivered to our homes we might order Chinese, but people in China are now ordering in from McDonald's and KFC! In big cities such as Beijing, Cairo, and Tokyo, where crowded streets and high real estate costs make drive-throughs impractical, delivery is becoming an important part of fast food strategy. In these markets, McDonald's and KFC now dispatch legions of motorbike delivery drivers in colourful uniforms to dispense Big Macs and buckets of chicken to customers who call in. In McDonald's Asia/Pacific, Middle East, and Africa division, more than 1500 of its 8800 restaurants now offer "McDelivery." "We've used the slogan, 'If you can't come to us, we'll come to you,'" says the division's president. More than 30 percent of McDonald's total sales in Egypt and 12 percent of its Singapore sales come from delivery. Similarly, for KFC, delivery accounts for nearly half of all sales in Kuwait and a third of sales in Egypt.[14]

Exhibit 11.11 International distribution channels: In cities like Beijing, Seoul, and Cairo, armies of motorbike delivery drivers outfitted in colourful uniforms and bearing food in specially designed boxes strapped to their backs make their way through bustling traffic to deliver Big Macs.

We've learned what marketing channels are, how they are organized and managed, and why marketers need intermediaries to help get their products to market. In the days before computers were commonly used, marketers used to call this plain old "physical distribution." But with the advent of the Internet and the ease of use of computer systems, the complex task of moving products has become more sophisticated, and more players have entered the game to aid companies with their supply chain management and logistics operations. In the next section we look at these in more detail.

Supply Chain Management and Logistics LO6

◄●▫Simulate on MyMarketingLab
Supply Chain

At the beginning of this chapter, we learned that the supply chain is the "upstream" part of any channel of distribution. The supply chain supplies the manufacturer with the parts and supplies it needs to be able to create products that it then sells "downstream" through its marketing channels to, eventually, its customers. The task of coordinating and controlling the physical flow of all those supplies and products—the logistics—is called *logistics management* or *supply chain management.*

Modern logistics is much more than just trucks and warehouses. **Logistics management** requires planning, implementing, and controlling the physical flow of goods, services, and related information from points of origin to points of consumption to meet customer requirements at a profit. In short, it involves getting the right product to the right customer in the right place at the right time.

In the days before technology, distribution managers (as they were called then) typically started with products at the plant and then tried to find the least expensive method to get them to their customers. Today, logistics managers use sophisticated computer systems that allow them to see the bigger picture—and to plan the movement of supplies by starting with the customer and the marketplace and working backward to the factory, or even to sources of supply. Logistics involves not only *outbound distribution* (moving products from the factory to resellers and ultimately to customers) but also *inbound distribution* (moving products and materials from suppliers to the factory) and *reverse distribution* (moving broken, unwanted, or excess products returned by consumers or resellers). That is, it involves management of the entire supply chain—upstream and downstream value-added flows of materials, final goods, and related information among suppliers, the company, resellers, and customers.

Logistics management is also concerned with the management of inventory—the delicate balance between carrying too little inventory and carrying too much (which is very expensive). Many companies have greatly reduced their inventories and related costs through **just-in-time logistics systems**. With such systems, producers and retailers carry only small inventories of parts or merchandise, often only enough for a few days of operations. New stock arrives exactly when needed rather than being stored in inventory until being used. Just-in-time systems require accurate forecasting and can result in substantial savings in inventory-carrying and handling costs.

Logistics management (supply chain management)
Planning, implementing, and controlling the physical flow of materials, final goods, and related information from points of origin to points of consumption to meet customer requirements at a profit.

Just-in-time logistics systems
A type of inventory management system in which only small inventories of parts or merchandise are held, and new stock arrives "just in time" when it is needed.

The Nature and Importance of Logistics Management in the Marketing System

The logistics manager's task is to coordinate the activities of suppliers, purchasing agents, marketers, channel members, and customers. These activities include forecasting, information systems, purchasing, production planning, order processing, inventory, warehousing, and transportation planning.

Companies today are placing greater emphasis on logistics for several reasons. First, companies can gain a powerful competitive advantage by using improved logistics to give customers better service or lower prices. Second, improved logistics can yield tremendous cost savings to both the company and its customers. As much as 20 percent of an average product's price is accounted for by shipping and transport alone. This far exceeds the cost of advertising and many other marketing costs.

Exhibit 11.12   **Logistics management:** Every day, logistics managers control the movement of physical goods through Port Metro Vancouver—which, as the third largest port in North America, is home to 27 major marine cargo terminals and three Class 1 railroads.

For example, in the United States, companies spent $1.45 trillion in 2014 to wrap, bundle, load, unload, sort, reload, and transport goods. "Today's market-leading companies use their supply chains to drive innovation and competitive advantage," says a logistics industry expert. "This in-turn drives demand for logistics providers. While demand for logistics is increasing, the industry faces a talent shortage and needs more logistics engineers, technology professionals, warehouse workers, and truck drivers to meet the needs of current and evolving freight fulfillment models that businesses and consumers rely on for their goods and services." In Canada, the largest association for supply chain management professionals, the Supply Chain Management Association (SCMA), reports that approximately $130 billion is spent each year moving products through the supply chain. This professional organization includes nearly 8000 members working in the private and public sectors in marketing-related activities such as purchasing/procurement, strategic sourcing, contract management, materials/inventory management, and logistics and transportation.[15]

Shaving off even a small fraction of logistics costs can mean substantial savings. For example, Walmart implemented a program of logistics improvements through more efficient sourcing, better inventory management, and greater supply chain productivity that was estimated to reduce supply chain costs by 5 to 15 percent over five years—that's a whopping $4 billion to $12 billion.[16]

The growth of logistics management in modern marketing is largely a result of the explosion in product variety over the last century. In the early 1900s, a local grocery store might have carried 500 to 600 different products. Today, a Walmart store carries more than 30 000 grocery products, and has approximately 100 000 different products available. As you can imagine, ordering, shipping, stocking, and controlling such a variety of products presents a sizable logistics challenge.

Improvements in information technology have created opportunities for major gains in distribution efficiency. Today's companies are using sophisticated supply chain management software, Internet-based logistics systems, point-of-sale scanners, RFID tags, satellite tracking, and electronic transfer of order and payment data. Such technology lets them quickly and efficiently manage the flow of goods, information, and finances through the supply chain.

Environmental Impact of Logistics

More than almost any other business activity, logistics affects the environment and a firm's environmental sustainability efforts. Transportation, warehousing, and packaging are typically the biggest supply chain contributors to the company's environmental footprint. At the same time, they also provide one of the most fertile areas for cost savings. So developing a green supply chain is not only environmentally responsible, it can also be profitable (see Marketing@Work 11.2).

One way logistics managers can reduce the environmental impact of their activities is by adopting slow shipping, the simple practice of slowing the speed at which ships travel so as to save fuel and reduce pollution. International shipping contributes nearly

MARKETING@WORK   **11.2**

Greening the Supply Chain: It's the Right Thing to Do—and It's Profitable, Too

You may remember the old song in which Kermit the Frog laments, "It's not easy bein' green." That's often as true for a company's supply chains as it is for the Muppet. Greening up a company's channels often takes substantial commitment, ingenuity, and investment. However, although it's challenging, today's supply channels are getting ever greener.

Companies have many reasons for reducing the environmental impact of their supply chains. For one thing, in the not-too-distant future, if companies don't green up voluntarily, a host of "green laws" and sustainability regulations enacted around the world will require them to do so. For another, many large customers are demanding it. Environmental sustainability has become an important factor in supplier selection and performance evaluation, so suppliers need to think green or put their relationships with prime customers at risk. And perhaps even more important than *having* to do it, designing more environmentally responsible supply chains is simply the *right* thing to do. It's one more way that companies can contribute to saving our world for future generations.

But that's all pretty heady stuff. As it turns out, companies have a more immediate and practical reason for turning their supply chains green. Not only are green channels good for the world, they're also good for a company's bottom line. Companies green their supply chains through greater efficiency, and greater efficiency means lower costs and higher profits. This cost-savings side of environmental responsibility makes good sense. The very logistics activities that create the biggest environmental footprint—such as transportation, warehousing, and packaging—are also the ones that account for a lion's share of logistics costs, especially in an age of scarce resources and soaring energy prices. Although it may require an upfront investment, in the long run, greening up channels usually costs less.

Here are just a few examples of how creating greener supply chains can benefit both the environment and a company's bottom line:

Stonyfield Farm. As the world's largest yogurt maker grew over the years, inefficiencies crept into its distribution system. So Stonyfield worked with Ryder Systems, the large transportation and logistics services firm, to design a new logistics system that cut distribution costs at the same time as it improved customer service levels and dramatically reduced the company's carbon footprint. After evaluating the Stonyfield network, Ryder helped the company set up a small, dedicated truck fleet, including fuel-efficient hybrid vehicles, to make regional deliveries in New England. It then replaced Stonyfield's national less-than-truckload distribution network with a regional multistop truckload system. As a result, Stonyfield now moves more product in fewer but fuller trucks, cutting in half the number of miles travelled. In all, the changes produced a 40 percent reduction in transportation-related carbon dioxide emissions while knocking an eye-popping 14 percent off Stonyfield's transportation costs. Says Stonyfield's director of logistics, "We're surprised. We understand that environmental responsibility can be profitable. We expected some savings, but not really in this range."

Nike. The iconic sports shoe and apparel company has developed a sweeping strategy for greening every phase of its supply chain. For example, Nike teamed with Levi's, REI, Target, and other members of the Sustainable Apparel Coalition to develop the Higg Index—a tool that measures how a single apparel product impacts the environment across the entire supply chain. Based in part on Nike's years-old Materials Sustainability Index, the Higg Index lets Nike work with suppliers and distributors to reduce the supply chain's environmental footprint. For instance, in just three years, the more than 900 contract factories that make Nike footwear worldwide reduced their carbon emissions by 6 percent, despite production increases of 20 percent. That's equivalent to an

The Higg Index
Sustainable Apparel Coalition

Sergio Zaenha/Alamy

Exhibit 11.13 Green supply chains: Nike has developed a sweeping strategy for greening its supply chain. The Higg Index lets Nike work with suppliers and distributors to reduce the supply chain's environmental footprint.

emissions savings equal to more than 1 billion car-miles.

Nike has found that even seemingly simple supply chain adjustments can produce big benefits. For example, Nike sources its shoes in Asia, but most are sold in North America. Until over a decade ago, the shoes were shipped from factory to store by air freight. After analyzing distribution costs more carefully, Nike shifted a sizable portion of its cargo to ocean freight. That simple shoes-to-ships shift reduced emissions per product by 4 percent, making environmentalists smile. But it also put a smile on the faces of Nike's accountants by saving the company some $8 million a year in shipping costs.

Walmart. The world's largest retailer is often criticized for its huge carbon footprint. But it turns out that Walmart is perhaps the world's biggest green-channels champion. Among dozens of other major greening initiatives, the giant retailer has worked diligently to reduce the environmental impact of its huge fleet of more than 7000 trucks. It has installed more efficient tires and hybrid engines, adopted alternative fuels, and developed more effective load-management and routing systems. As a result, in five years, Walmart's fleet delivered 361 million more cases of product in 287 million fewer miles, reducing carbon emissions by 25 percent and cutting a big chunk out of distribution costs.

Walmart also works with its throng of suppliers to help them clean up their environmental acts. For example, it set a goal to reduce overall supplier packaging by 5 percent. Given Walmart's size, even small changes make a substantial impact. For instance, a slight change in the design of one supplier's shoeboxes resulted in a 43 percent reduction in the amount of paper required to make them. In only 10 months, that Walmart-led design improvement cut out 692 tons of paper from shoeboxes crossing Walmart's checkout scanners. That equates to saving 2500 trees, 400 000 pounds of solid waste, 2.4 million gallons of water, and 14.5 billion BTUs. The change also resulted in a 28 percent reduction in supply chain costs.

So when it comes to supply chains, Kermit might be right—it's not easy bein' green. But it's now more necessary than ever, and it can pay big returns. It's a challenging area, says one supply chain expert, "but if you look at it from a pure profit-and-loss perspective, it's also a rich one." Another expert concludes, "It's now easier than ever to build a green supply chain without going into the red, while actually saving cash along the way."

Sources: Based on information from Ryan Boccelli and Mark Swenson, "Improving Transportation and Supply Chain Efficiency while Reducing Your Carbon Footprint," http://investors.ryder.com/files/doc_downloads/stonyfield_ryder_carbon.pdf, accessed August 2015; Jessica Stillman, "Green Cred: Sustainability a Cost-Cutting Move for Suppliers," *Forbes*, December 11, 2012; William Hoffman, "Supplying Sustainability," *Traffic World*, April 7, 2008; "Supply Chain Standard: Going Green Without Going into the Red," *Logistics Manager*, March 2009, p. 22; Amy Westervelt, "Target, Nike, Levi's Join Forces on Sustainable Clothing," *Forbes*, July 26, 2012; and information from NikeResponsibility.com and Walmart.com.

3 percent to global greenhouse gas emissions, compared with the 1.5 percent generated by airplanes. An environmental group called Seas at Risk commissioned a study and found that companies can reduce emissions by as much as 30 percent just by slowing the ships.[17] And consumer packaged goods marketer SC Johnson reduced its greenhouse gas emissions by making a seemingly simple but smart—and profitable—change in the way it packs its trucks:

> Under the old system, a load of SC Johnson's Ziploc products filled a truck trailer before reaching the maximum weight limit. In contrast, a load of Windex glass cleaner hit the maximum weight before the trailer was full. By strategically mixing the two products, SC Johnson found that it could send the same amount of products with 2098 fewer shipments, while burning 168 000 fewer gallons of diesel fuel and eliminating 1882 tons of greenhouse gases. Thus, smart supply chain thinking not only helped the environment; it also saved the company money. Says the company's director of environmental issues, "Loading a truck may seem simple, but making sure that a truck is truly full is a science. Consistently hitting a trailer's maximum weight provided a huge opportunity to reduce our energy consumption, cut our greenhouse gas emissions, and save money [into the bargain]." Green supply chains aren't just something companies have to do; they make good business sense as well. "Sustainability shouldn't be about [government] jamming green stuff down your throat," concludes one supply chain expert. "This is a lot about money, about reducing costs."[18]

Goals of the Logistics System

Some companies state their logistics objective as providing maximum customer service at the least cost. Unfortunately, as nice as this sounds, no logistics system can *both* maximize customer service *and* minimize distribution costs. Maximum customer service implies rapid delivery, large inventories, flexible assortments, liberal returns policies, and other services—all of which raise distribution costs. In contrast, minimum distribution costs imply slower delivery, smaller inventories, and larger shipping lots—which represent a lower level of overall customer service.

The goal of marketing logistics should be to provide a targeted level of customer service at the least cost. A company must first research the importance of various distribution services to customers and then set desired service levels for each segment of the market they serve. The objective is to maximize *profits*, not sales. Therefore, the company must weigh the benefits of providing higher levels of service against the costs. Some companies offer less service than their competitors and charge a lower price. Other companies offer more service and charge higher prices to cover higher costs.

Warehousing and Distribution Centres

Production and consumption cycles rarely match, so most companies must store their goods while they wait to be sold. For example, Snapper, Toro, and other lawn mower manufacturers run their factories all year long and store up products for the heavy spring and summer buying seasons. The storage function overcomes differences in needed quantities and timing, ensuring that products are available when customers are ready to buy them.

Warehouses may or may not also function as distribution centres. Distribution centres are designed to move goods in and out, and to store them for as little time as possible. Today's warehouses and distribution centres could not function without technology such as computers, scanners, and robots. For example, in the United States, Home Depot operates 18 giant Rapid Deployment Centers (RDCs)—huge, highly mechanized distribution centres that supply almost all the daily needs of Home Depot's more than 2200 stores around the country. The RDC in Westfield, Massachusetts, covers 60 000 square metres (or 13 football fields) under a single roof and serves some 115 Home Depot stores throughout New England. Nothing is stored at the RDCs. Instead, they are "pass-through" centres at which product shipments are received from suppliers, processed, and efficiently redistributed to individual Home Depot stores. The RDCs provide a maximum 72-hour turnaround from the time products reach the centre until their delivery to stores, where 80 percent go directly to the sales floor. With such rapid and accurate delivery, individual Home Depot stores can improve merchandise availability to customers while at the same time carrying less in-store stock and reducing inventory costs.[19]

Like almost everything else these days, warehousing has been dramatically improved as a result of new technologies. Outdated materials-handling methods are steadily being replaced by newer, computer-controlled systems requiring few employees. Computers and scanners read orders and direct lift trucks, electric hoists, or robots to gather goods, move them to loading docks, and issue invoices. For example, office supplies retailer Staples now employs teams of Day-Glo orange robots in its warehouses around the country. The robots work tirelessly 16 hours a day, seven days a week, carrying racks of pens, paper clips, pads of paper, and other items to packing stations, where

Brent Humphreys/Redux

Exhibit 11.14 High-tech distribution centres: Staples employs a team of super-retrievers—robots—to move inventory through its distribution centres as efficiently as possible.

humans fill and pack customer orders. The super-efficient robots, which never complain about the workload or ask for pay raises, are pretty much maintenance free. "When they run low on power, they head to battery-charging terminals," notes one observer, "or, as warehouse personnel say, 'They get themselves a drink of water.'" At Staples' huge Chambersburg, Pennsylvania, distribution centre, some 150 robots have helped improve average daily output by 60 percent.[20]

Inventory Management

One of the most important technologies that has improved the ability to manage inventory is RFID, or radio frequency ID tags: tiny computer chips embedded in products or product containers that allow scanners to track their movement without touching them. The use of RFID tags by manufacturers is increasing, and the latest technology allows an RFID software system to be used at every stage of the supply chain, from producing the tags, tagging the goods, and recording the movement of items from the warehouse to the sales floor to tracking in-store inventory and recording items that have left the system at the retailer's checkout process. The information provided to the logistics system by the RFID tags is then stored and can be analyzed later to improve the efficiency of the distribution channel.

Collecting information about the movement of goods is important, and that information must be shared between the parties involved in the transactions. Most information sharing takes place through electronic data interchange, or EDI: computer systems that allow members of the supply chain to communicate and share information. A retailer the size of Walmart, for example, has thousands of suppliers, so keeping track of all that inventory, along with knowing where it is and where it's headed, requires that a great deal of data be shared in real time or near real time.

Some retailers and suppliers even set up vendor-managed inventory systems, sometimes called *continuous inventory replenishment systems*. These systems allow the supplier to keep track of what the retailer needs, and to generate orders and arrange deliveries.

Inventory management greatly affects customer satisfaction, so it's important for marketing managers to maintain the delicate balance between carrying too little inventory and carrying too much. With too little stock, products are not on the shelves when customers want to buy, and having to remedy this by making emergency shipments or ordering emergency production is usually cost-prohibitive. On the other hand, carrying too much inventory results in higher-than-necessary inventory-carrying costs and stock obsolescence. Managing inventory is one of the most important aspects of logistics and supply chain management, because it can greatly affect the firm's profitability.

Transportation

The choice of transportation carriers affects the pricing of products, delivery performance, and the condition of goods when they arrive—all of which will affect customer satisfaction. In shipping goods to its warehouses, dealers, and customers, the company can choose among five main transportation modes: truck, rail, water, pipeline, and air, along with an alternative mode for digital products—the Internet.

Trucks are one of the oldest forms of transportation of hard goods, and account for approximately 40 percent of cargo moved in North America. Many communities, especially in remote regions, can be reached only by trucks. Trucks are highly flexible in their routing and time schedules, and they can usually offer faster service than railroads. They are efficient for short hauls of high-value merchandise. Trucking firms have evolved to become full-service providers of global transportation services, and offer everything from satellite tracking, Internet-based shipment management, and logistics planning software to cross-border shipping operations.

Railroads account for another 40 percent of the total cargo ton-miles moved. They are one of the most cost-effective modes for shipping large amounts of bulk products—coal, sand, minerals, and farm and forest products—over long distances. Railroad companies have also used modern technology to increase their levels of service—by designing new equipment to handle special categories of goods, providing flatcars for carrying truck trailers by rail (piggyback), and providing in-transit services such as the diversion of shipped goods to other destinations en route and the processing of goods en route.

Water carriers (ships and barges) are used mainly for shipping goods across the oceans. Once the shipping containers have arrived, for example at the Port of Vancouver, they are offloaded and transferred either to trucks or to railroad cars. Although the cost of water transportation is very low for shipping bulky, low-value, nonperishable products such as sand, coal, grain, oil, and metallic ores, water transportation is the slowest mode and may be affected by the weather.

Pipelines are a specialized means of shipping petroleum, natural gas, and chemicals from sources to markets. Most pipelines are used by their owners to ship their own products.

Air carriers transport less than 1 percent of cargo ton-miles of goods because the cost to ship by air is much higher than by rail or truck. Air freight is typically used only when speed of delivery is more important than cost, or in special circumstances such as the shipment of perishables (such as fresh fish, cut flowers) and high-value, low-bulk items (technical instruments, jewellery).

The *Internet* carries digital products from producer to customer via satellite, cable, phone wire, or wireless signal. Software firms, the media, music and video companies, and education all make use of the Internet to transport digital products. The Internet holds the potential for lower product distribution costs. Whereas planes, trucks, and trains move freight and packages, digital technology moves information bits.

Multimodal (or intermodal) transportation
Combining two or more modes of transportation.

Third-party logistics (3PL) provider
An independent logistics provider that performs any or all of the functions required to get its client's product to market.

Shippers also use **multimodal (or intermodal) transportation**—combining two or more modes of transportation. Regardless of their main line of activity, most logistics carriers now recognize the importance of multimodal transportation. For example, you probably know Canadian Pacific as the railway company, but it's much more than that. CP has direct links to eight major ports in the U.S. and Canada, where it partners with ocean liners to export Canadian goods around the world. It also offers "ramp to ramp" direct shipping services via truck and rail—which CP refers to as its intermodal transportation services. In addition, CP offers third-party logistics management and supply chain services to any company that needs to move its products across and around the country.

Third-Party Logistics

Logistics management is a complex activity, and one that is critically important to many businesses. It is not, however, usually a business's "core competency." As such, some companies choose to outsource their logistics management to firms that specialize in just that. These companies are called **third-party logistics (3PL) providers**. For

Exhibit 11.15 Intermodal transportation: Kuehne+Nagel is a global logistics company that operates intermodal terminals, where freight is transferred from one mode of transportation to another.

courtesy Kuehne + Nagel

example, Whirlpool uses third-party logistics supplier Ryder to provide order fulfillment and worldwide distribution of Whirlpool's service parts across six continents to hundreds of customers, which include (in addition to consumers) the Sears service network, authorized repair centres, and independent parts distributors that in turn ship parts out to a network of service companies and technicians. There are many other 3PLs, among them Canadian Pacific, Penske Logistics, BAX Global, DHL Logistics, and UPS:

> UPS knows that, for many companies, logistics can be a real nightmare. But logistics is exactly what UPS does best. To UPS, logistics is today's most powerful force for creating competitive advantage. "We ❤ logistics," proclaims UPS. "It makes running your business easier. It can make your customers happier. It's a whole new way of thinking." As one UPS ad concludes: "We love logistics. Put UPS to work for you and you'll love logistics too." Consumer electronics maker Toshiba lets UPS handle its entire laptop PC repair process—lock, stock, and barrel.
>
> UPS's logistics prowess was the answer to one of Toshiba's biggest challenges—turnaround time on laptop repairs. Toshiba once used UPS only to ship its finished PCs from the factory to customers. But when the two companies worked together to examine the entire supply chain, including parts management and the PC repair process, they forged a much broader logistics relationship. Now, customers ship laptops needing repair to a special UPS facility in Louisville, Kentucky. There, UPS employees receive the units, run diagnostics to assess the repairs needed, pick the necessary parts, quickly complete the service, and return the laptops to their owners. UPS can now fix and ship a laptop in a single day, shortening a door-to-door repair process that once took two to three weeks down to four or fewer days. Together, UPS and Toshiba greatly improved the customer repair experience while at the same time reducing Toshiba's costs. More than just delivering packages for Toshiba, UPS has become a strategic logistics partner. Says Toshiba America's CEO, "They really understand the overall experience we're trying to create for the customers."[21]

Managing the supply chain (the "chain" of businesses that supply a manufacturer or producer) as well as the downstream distribution of products from the producer to the consumer is a complex task. Logistics managers plan and coordinate the movement of all these goods and supplies, and sometimes use third parties to do the job. Companies use 3PL providers because getting the product to market is their main focus, and these providers can often do it more efficiently and at lower cost. Finally, whether logistics management is handled in-house or by a third party, managers must constantly strive to find lower cost and more environmentally friendly solutions.

BP Franchising

Throughout these chapter-end cases, you've no doubt come to appreciate how much emphasis Boston Pizza has placed on its "four pillars strategy," which it treats as the litmus test for decision making. One of those pillars is "commitment to franchisee profitability," which is further explained as follows:

> The best way to ensure the success of the Boston Pizza Royalties Income Fund, Boston Pizza International Inc., and the Boston Pizza brand is to ensure the success of Boston Pizza franchisees.

A number of key elements go into franchisee profitability. Primary among them is an inviting guest experience—in everything from the food to the design and layout of tables across the restaurant floor. "Boston Pizza continues to innovate, grow, and thrive both in Alberta and across the country, due in large part to our commitment to continually evolve our brand, menu, and design of our store," said Alan Howie, Boston Pizza International's executive vice-president of operations. The 100th location in Alberta also became the first to introduce BP's new design concept, which features enhanced lighting, more intimate use of space and materials, and improved sightlines in the sports bar component of every restaurant.

These innovations weren't made overnight. "We took a collaborative approach to our new store design. Working with a cross-functional team of architects, design firms, and internal stakeholders in marketing, operations, and our franchisee community, we've taken the Boston Pizza experience to a whole new level," said Howie.

But beyond the milestone makeover that marked BP's 50th anniversary in 2014, the company has a rigidly executed store-renovation schedule. "BPI's franchise agreement requires that each Boston Pizza restaurant undergo a complete store renovation every seven years," claims CEO Mark Pacinda. "Restaurants typically close for two to three weeks to complete the renovation and experience an incremental sales increase in the year following the reopening."

QUESTIONS

1. Boston Pizza franchisees must pay royalties on all sales, and they must commit to renovating their stores every seven years, not to mention all the other costs that go into operating a BP franchise. Given these sacrifices, which must be made by the individual franchisee, why do you think BP franchising is so popular?

2. Go to http://bostonpizza.com/en/franchising/success-stories and view the videos shown. Do you think these videos are effective in attracting new and potential franchisees to Boston Pizza? Why or why not?

REVIEWING THE CONCEPTS

 Explain what channels are, and why marketers need channel partners.

Producing a product or service and making it available to buyers requires building relationships with both key suppliers "upstream" in the company's *supply chain* and distributors and resellers that act as intermediaries to help move the product "downstream." Downstream marketing channel partners, such as wholesalers and retailers, form a vital connection between the firm and its customers. A firm's *value delivery network* is made up of the company, suppliers, distributors, and ultimately customers who partner with each other to improve the performance of the entire system.

Few producers sell their goods directly to the final users of their products. Instead, most use intermediaries to bring their products to market via *marketing channels* (or *distribution channels*)—a set of interdependent organizations that help make a product or service available for use or consumption by the consumer or business customer.

A company's channel decisions directly affect every other marketing decision; therefore, designing channels and choosing channel partners are strategic marketing decisions, made only after carefully studying the market and considering its opportunities. Distribution channel decisions typically involve long-term commitments to other firms, called *channel partners*. Through their contacts, experience, specialization, and scale of operation, channel partners help the producer achieve more than it could on its own. As intermediaries, they add value by bridging the major time, place, and possession gaps that separate goods and services from those who would use them.

 List and describe the major types of channel partners.

Channel partners are businesses that are owned and operated independently from the manufacturer, which contracts them to perform a specific function in the movement of the product. The major types of channel partners are *retailers*, which purchase products from manufacturers and distributors and offer them to consumers through a bricks-and-mortar location or an online store; *wholesalers* that buy from producers and sell to retailers, business customers, and other wholesalers; *drop shippers*, intermediaries that take the order from the customer and pass it to a manufacturer or wholesaler, which then ships the item directly to the customer; *rack jobbers*, intermediaries that buy merchandise and then set up "rack" displays inside retail stores, where the merchandise is sold to customers; *brokers*, which bring buyers and sellers together and assist in negotiation, but do not carry inventory, get involved in financing, or assume risk; and *agents*, which are similar to brokers in that they perform only a few functions and do not take title to goods, but while a broker makes deals with many different buyers and sellers, an agent typically has a more permanent relationship representing either one or the other.

Manufacturers' agents are a common type of agent, typically contracted by smaller manufacturers that don't have their own sales staff. The agent sells the manufacturer's goods to buyers and receives a commission from the manufacturer. *Advertising agencies* are another type of agent, and valuable members of the marketing channel. They provide marketing communications services such as designing and producing advertisements, and buying the media (television, radio, magazines, Internet) in which to run them.

 Describe the process of organizing and managing channels, and explain how channel conflict can occur.

Marketing channels must be built to meet strategic business goals, then continually managed. Marketers must first *select* their channel partners. When considering which channel partners to work with, marketers evaluate each potential partner's years in business, other lines carried, location, growth and profit record, cooperativeness, and reputation. Next, they must decide how many *channel levels* to create (i.e., how many intermediaries or channel partners to have), and whether to set up *direct marketing channels* or *indirect marketing channels*, or both. Each layer of marketing intermediaries that performs some work in bringing the product and its ownership closer to the final buyer is a *channel level*. Because both the producer and the final customer perform some work, they are part of every channel. All the institutions in the channel are connected by several types of *flows*. These include the *physical flow* of products, the *flow of ownership*, the *payment flow*, the *information flow*, and the *promotion flow*.

A *vertical marketing system (VMS)* consists of producers, wholesalers, and retailers acting as a unified system. One channel member owns the others, has contracts with them, or wields so much power that they must all cooperate. The VMS can be dominated by the producer, wholesaler, or retailer. Three types of VMSs are *corporate*, *administered*, and *contractual*. A *franchise* organization is a special type of contractual vertical marketing system in which a retailer or service provider operates under licence using another firm's proven, successful business model. There are three types of franchises: the *manufacturer-sponsored retailer franchise system*, the *manufacturer-sponsored wholesaler franchise system*, and the *service firm–sponsored retailer franchise system*. Another type of cooperative marketing system is the *horizontal marketing system*, in which two or more companies that operate at the same channel level join together to follow a marketing opportunity. Companies may opt for a *multichannel or hybrid distribution system*, in which a single firm sets up two or more marketing channels to reach one or more market segments.

Once selected, channel members must be continually managed and motivated to do their best. The company must sell not only *through* the intermediaries but also *to* and *with* them. Each channel member plays an important role in the marketing channel, but sometimes disagreements over goals, roles, and rewards among channel members can create what is known as *channel conflict*. The company producing the goods to be delivered via the channel must continually evaluate the performance of its channel partners. Above all, marketers must be sensitive to the needs of their channel partners.

Finally, marketers must stay on top of changes in technology, which can have a profound impact on the nature and design of marketing channels. *Disintermediation* occurs when an established intermediary becomes unnecessary and is cut out of the channel. Sometimes new intermediaries provide competition to established providers of services, but do not necessarily render them obsolete. Channel partners must be innovative, and look for new ways to add value in the channel.

 LO4 **Explain the strategy behind intensive, selective, and exclusive distribution.**

Marketers must make strategic decisions not just about *where* and *how* to distribute their products, but also *in how many places*. At first glance it may seem as if all marketers would wish to distribute their products in as many locations as possible, but that's not always the best strategy. Marketers of everyday convenience products such as soft drinks and snack foods typically choose *intensive distribution*, a strategy in which they stock their products in as many outlets as possible. *Selective distribution* is a marketing strategy typically chosen by makers of brand name appliances, furniture, and electronics. In selective distribution the marketer selects a set of retailers that specialize in their product category. *Exclusive distribution* is a deliberate marketing strategy chosen by brands that wish to associate themselves with an air of exclusivity. In exclusive distribution the marketer gives the rights to distribute its products to only one retailer, or to only one retailer in a particular geographic territory. It's usually associated with luxury brands such as Rolex and Tiffany, which give exclusive rights to carry their products in a particular region to one retailer, but it's also the distribution strategy employed by IKEA, which exclusively distributes its products in its own stores.

 LO5 **List and describe the major channel design decisions marketers must make.**

Marketing channel design calls for analyzing customer needs, setting channel objectives, determining the types and responsibilities of channel members, and making decisions about international distribution channels. Designing the marketing channel starts with finding out what customers want from the channel. Providing customer service is also part of marketing, so in making channel design decisions, marketers must reflect on what kinds of services the customer will require. Companies should state their *marketing channel objectives* in terms of targeted levels of customer service. The company's channel objectives are also influenced by the nature of the company, its products, its marketing intermediaries, its competitors, and the environment.

The company must identify the *types of channel members* available to carry out its channel work, and both the producer and the intermediaries need to agree on the terms and responsibilities of each channel member. They should agree on price policies, conditions of sale, territory rights, and the specific services to be performed by each party. Mutual services and duties need to be spelled out carefully, especially in franchise and exclusive distribution channels. Each alternative should be evaluated against economic, control, and adaptability criteria.

Marketers must also decide whether to distribute their product to international markets. International marketers face many complexities in designing their channels; rather than change the channel, they usually adapt their channel strategies to the existing structures within each country.

LO6 **Explain the role of supply chain management and logistics management, and why companies often choose third parties to handle these tasks.**

The task of coordinating and controlling the physical flow of all the supplies and products through the supply chain is called *logistics management* or *supply chain management*. Logistics managers use sophisticated computer systems that allow them to plan the movement of supplies by starting with the customer and the marketplace and working backward to the factory, or even to sources of supply.

Logistics involves not only *outbound distribution* (moving products from the factory to resellers and ultimately to customers) but also *inbound distribution* (moving products and materials from suppliers to the factory) and *reverse distribution* (moving broken, unwanted, or excess products returned by consumers or resellers).

Logistics management is also concerned with the management of inventory. Many companies have greatly reduced their inventories and related costs through *just-in-time* logistics systems. Shaving off even a small fraction of logistics costs can mean substantial savings for the company. Improvements in information technology have created opportunities for major gains in distribution efficiency. Today's companies are using sophisticated supply chain management software, Internet-based logistics systems, point-of-sale scanners, RFID tags, satellite tracking, and electronic transfer of order and payment data. Logistics also affects the environment and a firm's environmental sustainability efforts. Transportation, warehousing, and packaging are typically the biggest supply chain contributors to the company's environmental footprint. Many companies today are making efforts to "green" their supply chain.

Most companies must store their goods in *warehouses*, which may also function as *distribution centres*, where computers and scanners read orders and direct lift trucks, electric hoists, or robots to gather goods, move them to loading docks, and issue invoices. RFID tags allow scanners to track inventory, recording its movement from the warehouse to the sales floor and to checkout by the consumer. The information provided to the logistics system by the RFID tags is then stored and can be analyzed later to improve the efficiency of the distribution channel. EDI systems allow members of the supply chain to communicate and share information. In shipping goods to its warehouses, dealers, and customers, the company can choose from truck, rail, water, pipeline, and air, or a combination of any of these, which is referred to as *multimodal or intermodal transportation*. Digital products are usually transported via the Internet.

Finally, because logistics management is a complex activity, critically important to most businesses, and not usually a business's core competency, many companies choose to outsource their logistics management to firms that specialize in it. These companies are called *third-party logistics (3PL) providers*.

MyMarketingLab

Study, practise, and explore real marketing situations with these helpful resources:

- **Interactive Lesson Presentations:** Work through interactive presentations and assessments to test your knowledge of marketing concepts.
- **Study Plan:** Check your understanding of chapter concepts with self-study quizzes.
- **Dynamic Study Modules:** Work through adaptive study modules on your computer, tablet, or mobile device.
- **Simulations:** Practise decision-making in simulated marketing environments.

DISCUSSION QUESTIONS

1. Describe the marketing channel, and all the intermediaries, that would be involved in moving apples produced in British Columbia's Okanagan Valley to a grocery store in Kingston, Ontario, and for moving T-shirts manufactured in Montreal to an independent clothing retailer in Saskatoon.

2. Which distribution strategy—intensive, selective, or exclusive—is used for the following products and why? (a) Piaget watches, (b) Acura automobiles, and (c) Snickers chocolate bars.

3. Why do you think a company would choose to use an intermediary to distribute its products rather than handling the distribution itself? What are the benefits and risks of using a channel partner for this function?

4. Coca-Cola markets an astonishing 2800 different beverages. Not all these beverages are available for sale in all areas, and certainly there is no retailer that offers all 2800. What marketing decisions does the retailer need to make when deciding which of those 2800 to stock on its shelves? How can the distributor (the bottler) help the retailer with this decision?

CRITICAL THINKING EXERCISES

1. What is *disintermediation*? Think of an example (other than those given in the chapter) of a company that has been disintermediated and one that has disintermediated another type of company. Do you think bricks-and-mortar retailers will ever be completely disintermediated?

2. The most common type of contractual vertical marketing system is the franchise organization. Visit the International Franchise Association at www.franchise.org and find a franchise that interests you. Write a report describing the franchise. Identify what type of franchise it represents, and research the market opportunities for that product or service in Canada.

3. In a small group, research the distribution challenges faced by a company that has expanded into an emerging international market such as China, Africa, or India. Develop a multimedia presentation on how the company overcame these challenges.

4. List all the services you can think of that can be delivered from the producer to the customer via the Internet (that is, with no physical distribution required). What products, other than software, can be distributed electronically? Can you think of any other levels of the marketing channel that could be conducted online or electronically rather than physically?

ONLINE, MOBILE, AND SOCIAL MEDIA MARKETING

Movie and television program distribution technology is changing fast. Consumers can now watch movies and TV shows on demand on TVs, computers, tablets, and smartphones. While this has caused a surge in demand for online video-streaming services such as Netflix, it's causing problems for traditional subscription TV service providers such as Rogers and Bell. Interestingly, however, these service providers also provide a channel of distribution for the video-streaming services. The fact that Rogers, for example, has control over its competitors' distribution channel causes uncomfortable conflicts. Rogers has invested millions building its scheduled programming network, and it doesn't want to become a mere conduit as its subscribers drop cable in favour of streamed programming from one of the competing services. And because it controls the Internet channel, it can cause problems for those competitors. Now Rogers has created Shomi, a video-on-demand service available to anyone with an Internet connection—not only Rogers Internet customers.

QUESTIONS

1. What types of channel conflicts are present in this channel of distribution? Explain.

2. What do you think will happen in the next few years that will change the way video is distributed? Some experts are predicting that cable and satellite television will become obsolete. Do you think that will happen?

THINK LIKE A MARKETING MANAGER

A group of 50 Coca-Cola bottlers in the United States sued the Coca-Cola Company when it announced a plan to ship its Powerade sports drink directly to Walmart warehouses, thus upsetting the established chain of distribution. Coca-Cola uses a distribution system called "direct-to-store delivery" that relies on the licensed bottlers to package and deliver Coca-Cola products to retailers. Bottlers also set up retail displays and stock the shelves. Rival Pepsi-Cola, which markets Gatorade, the competitor to Powerade, ships its products directly to retailers' warehouses. Coca-Cola says that forcing it to distribute its products through bottlers will make the company less competitive. From Walmart's perspective, cutting the bottlers out of the channel of distribution could reduce its operating costs and therefore increase its profits. Walmart's margin on Gatorade is 30 percent, but on Powerade it's only 20 percent.

QUESTIONS

1. Not all retailers have warehouses; convenience stores and smaller independent grocery stores, for example, don't have them. Assuming that the Coca-Cola bottlers deliver to these stores as well as to Walmart, why were they so upset about the possibility of losing just one customer?

2. Walmart makes more profit on each bottle of Gatorade it sells than on a bottle of Powerade. List all the things a Walmart store manager could do to encourage consumers to choose Gatorade over Powerade.

3. If it wants to be more competitive with Pepsi, why doesn't Coca-Cola simply increase Walmart's margin on Powerade?

4. If Pepsi has been shipping direct to Walmart's warehouse all along, why aren't its bottlers upset?

MARKETING ETHICS

Fast-fashion retailers such as Zara and H&M demand short lead times and quick changes from suppliers to feed consumers' demand for changing fashions. Retailers used to place orders almost a year in advance, and suppliers produced high volumes cheaply. But fast-fashion retailers now offer new inventory in their stores almost weekly to get customers coming back. Additionally, many retailers are placing small initial orders, and if styles take off with consumers, they quickly reorder—a tactic known as "chasing." Appropriate inventory levels in the apparel industry have always been difficult to predict, but it appears that retailers are pushing this worry back onto suppliers. Bangladesh is the second-largest apparel producer for North American and European brands and retailers. However, recent fires and building collapses due to lax safety concerns have killed thousands of workers and even some factory executives. Unlike in more developed countries, the industry is loosely regulated in Bangladesh. That, coupled with the demands to feed the fast-fashion industry, is alleged to be the cause of these tragedies. As a result, brands and retailers are coming under greater scrutiny concerning supplier issues. IndustriALL, a Geneva-based international union, organized a proposal to enhance supplier safety in Bangladesh that many, but not all, Western retailers/brands accepted.

QUESTIONS

1. Discuss the concerns of suppliers and retailers in the apparel channel of distribution. Is it fair that retailers should expect suppliers to respond so quickly? Is it fair that suppliers should demand long lead times?

2. Write a brief report on the Bangladesh Accord on Fire and Building Safety proposed by IndustriALL. Which retailers signed the agreement, and why have some retailers refused to sign the pact?

MARKETING BY THE NUMBERS

One external factor that manufacturers must consider when setting prices is reseller margins. Manufacturers do not have the final say concerning the price to consumers— retailers do. So, manufacturers must start with their suggested retail prices and work back, subtracting out the mark-ups required by resellers that sell the product to consumers. Once that is considered, manufacturers know at what price to sell their products to resellers, and they can determine what volume they must sell to break even at that price and cost combination. To answer the following questions, refer to Appendix 3, Marketing by the Numbers.

QUESTIONS

1. A consumer purchases a flat iron to straighten her hair for $150 from a salon at which she gets her hair cut. If the salon's mark-up is 40 percent and the wholesaler's mark-up is 15 percent, both based on their selling prices, for what price does the manufacturer sell the product to the wholesaler?

2. If the unit variable costs for each flat iron are $40 and the manufacturer has fixed costs totalling $200 000, how many flat irons must this manufacturer sell to break even? How many must it sell to realize a profit of $800 000?

UPS LOVES LOGISTICS!

Mention UPS and most people envision one of those familiar brown trucks with a friendly driver, rumbling around their neighbourhood dropping off parcels. For most of us, seeing a brown UPS truck evokes fond memories of past package deliveries. However, most of UPS's revenue comes not from the residential customers who receive the packages, but from the business customers who send them. For most businesses, physical package delivery is just part of a much more complex logistics process that involves purchase orders, inventories, order status checks, invoices, payments, returned merchandise, fleets of delivery vehicles, and even cross-border dealings. Companies need timely information about their inbound and outbound packages—what's in them, where they're currently located, to whom they are going, when they'll get there, and how much is owed. UPS knows that, for many companies, logistics can be a real nightmare.

UPS is much more than a delivery service; they are a third-party logistics (3PL) company—and logistics is what it does best. Over the years, UPS has grown to become much more than a neighbourhood package delivery service. It is now a $65 billion corporate giant providing a broad range of global logistics solutions. Whereas many customers hate dealing with the logistics process, UPS proclaims, "We ♥ logistics!" To UPS's thinking, the new logistics is today's most powerful force for creating competitive advantage. Today's logistics offers a lot more than just getting products efficiently where they need to be. It contributes broadly to better business practice. Says UPS: "It makes running your business easier. It lets you serve your customers better. And it can help you grow. It's a whole new way of thinking. It's the new logistics."

If it has to do with logistics anywhere in the world, UPS can probably do it better than any other company. UPS offers customers efficient multi-modal package, mail, and freight distribution services. It can also help customers streamline sourcing, maintain leaner inventories, manage and fulfill orders, warehouse goods, assemble and customize products, and manage post-sales warranty repair and returns services. And it does all this on a global scale. Here are three case studies of small businesses that grew their revenues by letting UPS handle their logistics:

K2 MOTORS

K2 Motors is in the business of selling motor and car parts to customers all over Canada and the United States. While business was good, what really accelerated the company's growth was the launch of its e-commerce website, which increased sales nearly tenfold in just seven years. "E-commerce means opportunity, if you learn how to capture it," says Jacky Lau, K2 Motors' executive director. He certainly makes sure that K2 Motors captures its share. K2 grew annual online sales from $2.4 million to $20 million, partly attributable to leveraging the logistics of UPS and the online marketing opportunities of eBay.

Lau credits much of K2's success to his fulfillment capabilities. "UPS is one of the biggest advantages we have over other companies," he says. "UPS smart logistics allows us to fully focus on the growth of our business." UPS designed solutions for e-commerce early, creating shipping functionality within eBay and PayPal. The tool allows sellers anywhere in Canada and the U.S. to easily calculate shipping rates and display them with product listings.

K2 uses a technology called ChannelAdvisor to pull in orders from other websites (such as eBay, and wherever else K2 has ads). K2's internal systems then bring together orders, inventory, and shipping transactions. It's integrated with UPS's WorldShip service, which features easy-to-integrate UPS technology connected to K2's internal system to pull out shipping information and eliminate the need to manually key-enter orders. Plus, it prints labels and sends tracking information back to eBay. To say that this improved K2's productivity is an understatement: "We went from a dozen people processing 200 orders a day to a dozen people processing 800 orders a day," Lau says.

As K2's channel partner, UPS added even more value by re-engineering the K2 warehouse. First, UPS's Customer Solutions team helped Lau better understand warehousing through an overview of inventory methodologies and metrics. "We don't have the vision or the experience that UPS has," Lau says. "UPS deals with millions of packages every day, so many of the things they show us are eye-popping."

UPS showed K2 new ways to organize inventory, reducing time spent in searches or fulfilling frantic orders. Specifically, UPS helped K2 design an optimal "pick path," positioning items in the warehouse so that they could be selected and shipped much more efficiently. Also UPS designed an automated shipping station, a single point where all outbound goods could be neatly scanned, packed, labelled, and sealed. Says Lau, "UPS packaging experts showed us ways to pack our shipments that saved us 30 percent in packaging costs."

Finally, UPS introduced new ways to measure productivity, such as numbers of product lines picked per hour and numbers of product lines put away per hour. These standards allow K2 to measure the effectiveness of its warehouse operations against industry and peer warehouse processes, apples to apples.

TICKETPRINTING.COM

TicketPrinting.com needed reliable, high-tech help to deliver from deep in the mountains of Montana. Harlowton, called "Harlo" by its 931 (or thereabouts) proud Montana citizens, sits two hours from the nearest settlement big enough to appear on most maps. It's a lonely spot where the wild prairie meets the Crazy Mountains. To Mike Yinger, it was the perfect place to launch a business. Yinger founded TicketPrinting.com after a career as a jet-setting IBM software architect. He loved Montana, but he found some things lacking: printing capabilities, for instance, for tickets to shows at the local playhouse. So he built a desktop PC solution that allowed users to print tickets at home.

Customers soon wanted actual physical tickets that could be shipped overnight, and the little start-up morphed into TicketPrinting.com, now the largest employer in Harlo. It has operations on three continents, with UKTicketPrinting.co.uk in the U.K. and TicketRiver.com.au in Australia. And UPS is the little company's global logistics partner. "People should understand," says CEO Lance Trebesch, "that you can create a successful business anywhere today if you have great people, a good idea, a broadband network, and a robust, reliable distribution network like the one we have with UPS."

UPS saw in TicketPrinting.com something that other shippers didn't—the potential of a custom manufacturing venture in the electronic age. "The world is changing from a 'push' to a 'pull' set of business practices," says Elizabeth Richardson, UPS account manager. "The new logistics of UPS can support companies like this with e-commerce solutions and with reliable, flexible shipping options that bring growth … no matter where they are."

Part of that new logistics was offering special operating practices to serve the start-up. Because overnight delivery is key to getting tickets to waiting customers quickly and reliably, UPS introduced UPS Next Day Air service to this remote area of Montana. UPS also integrated technology tools into the TicketPrinting.com site, improving access to transit times, order entry, and accounting. The company's customer service managers can track ticket shipments by using the free Quantum View Manage service. On the back end, TicketPrinting.com reconciles UPS invoices electronically with the UPS billing centre.

Another success factor is the UPS team, which has been known to take extraordinary measures to make the tickets run on time, braving bad weather, working longer hours than required, and helping make sure that connections happen. "We fight so hard to keep every customer," Trebesch says. "UPS always does what it takes to get the tickets to the plane. That kind of commitment is why we expect UPS to be with us in more countries as we expand, to be our partner for the long run." Adds Richardson, "Our relationship proves that UPS really wants to be a business partner in all aspects. A partner, not a vendor. We'll truly go above and beyond for customers, wherever they want to do business."

HAYDEL'S BAKERY

There's an orchestrated beauty to the chaos that is Mardi Gras in New Orleans. Colourful beads rain down from second-storey balconies, blaring brass bands float down Bourbon Street, and masses of body-painted parade-goers cheer and dance throughout the French Quarter. A year's worth of celebration is packed into the long weekend leading up to "Fat Tuesday," the final day before Lent begins. The Haydel family knows the energy of that intense pace well. In the two months before Fat Tuesday, Haydel's Bakery ships 60 000 freshly baked and sweetly iced Mardi Gras "king cakes" all over the world. It's the business's greatest moneymaker, but distributing its delicious product is no piece of cake.

"Mardi Gras season would be a *heapa* mess without UPS," says Dave Haydel Jr., whose grandfather founded the bakery in 1959. "We've tried everyone, and we found UPS's on-time overnight delivery light years ahead of everyone else. I can call UPS and get any problem solved. With a company as big as UPS, that's almost unheard of."

"Our competitors offer some of the technical solutions we bring to Haydel's Bakery," says Philip Ehrhardt, UPS senior account manager. "How we help this customer, especially in their peak season, and even for special projects—that's what makes the difference."

It certainly makes a difference for Haydel's Bakery. Up to 80 percent of the company's annual revenue comes at Mardi Gras. King cakes—made of Danish dough that's braided with cinnamon and sugar and adorned with Mardi Gras–coloured icing of purple, green, and gold—must go out and arrive on time. From a custom manifest system to its own call centre for taking orders, innovation has spearheaded growth at Haydel's. It's less a traditional warehouse than a modern assembly line, with cakes popped from ovens, conveyed through icing and sprinkling, rolled into packaging, then loaded directly onto a dedicated UPS delivery truck called a package car.

Leading up to Mardi Gras, a UPS driver parks his personal vehicle in Haydel's lot every afternoon at five and takes a package car filled with king cakes to the UPS shipping centre. After his sorting shift, the driver returns an empty package car at midnight to Haydel's loading dock for the bakery to fill the next day. At peak demand, UPS replaces the package car with an even larger truck. UPS has seamlessly integrated its technology into existing processes at Haydel's, allowing operators to send a king cake almost anywhere in North America, and to more than 220 countries and territories, using just a keystroke or two.

"Haydel's is growing, and we have a great relationship to grow with them," says Ehrhardt. "Our centre in Metairie is less than a mile from the bakery, so visits are easy. It sometimes gets really crazy, but our operating team always does a good job." Dave Haydel agrees. "From Thanksgiving to Mardi Gras, our business is pedal to the metal, and we're limited only by the constraints of the human body," he says. "Now we've started talking about the rest of the year. We're out to invent demand, to find another niche. And whatever we end up doing, UPS will be our partner."

As one UPS ad concludes: "We love logistics. Put UPS to work for you and you'll love logistics too."

Sources: "Revving up Business: K2 Motor Sales Mount Through UPS and eBay ecommerce," UPS's magazine, *Compass*, May, 2011; "Winning Ticket," *Compass*, Spring 2011; "A Baker Says: 'Long Live the Cake,'" *Compass*, Spring 2011; "How to Level a Playing Field: Why Even the Smallest Companies Should Embrace Logistics," special advertising feature, *Inc.*, June 2011, p. 94; Brian Shactman, "How UPS, Fedex Grow by Tapping Adjacent Business," *USA Today*, February 5, 2012; and information from UPS.com.

QUESTIONS

1. Visit the UPS website and make a list of all the third-party supply chain and logistics services UPS offers, and briefly describe each service.

2. Why are companies like K2, TicketPrinting.com, and Haydel's willing to pay UPS to manage their shipments rather than doing it themselves?

3. Why doesn't K2 use a UPS package car, as Haydel's does?

4. UPS recently purchased a company called Coyote Logistics for $1.8 billion. Research the acquisition and explain why one logistics company would buy another—in other words, what did UPS get out of the deal?

Courtesy Walmart

AFTER STUDYING THIS CHAPTER, YOU SHOULD BE ABLE TO

1 explain the role of retailers in the distribution channel, and describe the major types of retailers

2 list and describe the major marketing decisions made by retailers

3 identify and discuss the major trends and developments in contemporary retailing

4 explain the role of wholesalers in the distribution channel, and describe the major types of wholesalers

5 list and describe the major marketing decisions made by wholesalers

Retailing and Wholesaling

PREVIEWING THE CONCEPTS

We now look more deeply into the two major intermediary marketing channel functions: retailing and wholesaling. You already know something about retailing—retailers of all shapes and sizes serve you every day. However, you probably know much less about the horde of wholesalers working behind the scenes. In this chapter, we examine the characteristics of different kinds of retailers and wholesalers, the marketing decisions they make, and trends for the future.

When it comes to retailers, you have to start with Walmart, the world's megaretailer. Each week, more than 245 million customers visit nearly 11 000 Walmart stores under 71 banners in 27 countries. Day in and day out, Walmart lives up to its promise: "Save money. Live better." Yet, despite its huge success, Walmart still faces plenty of fresh opportunities and daunting challenges.

WALMART: THE WORLD'S LARGEST RETAILER, AND THE WORLD'S SECOND-LARGEST COMPANY

Walmart is almost unimaginably big. It's the world's largest retailer—the world's second-largest company. It employs 2.2 million people, and has rung up an incredible US$482 billion in annual worldwide sales—almost double the volume of its next six competitors combined. In the United States, Walmart is the number one seller in many categories of consumer products, including groceries, clothing, toys, DVDs, and pet care products. It sells nearly 2.5 times as many groceries as Kroger, the leading grocery-only food retailer, and its clothing and shoe sales alone exceed the total revenues of Macy's.

In Canada, Walmart has long been the country's biggest mass merchandiser, but it began selling groceries only in 2006. Its share of that $88 billion market has been increasing steadily, and reached approximately 12 percent at the end of 2014. Walmart Canada operates 394 stores nationwide and serves more than 1.2 million customers each day. With more than 95 000 associates, Walmart Canada is one of the country's largest employers and has been ranked one of Canada's top 10 most influential brands four years in a row.

But in the United States, Walmart is *the* largest employer—one out of every 225 men, women, and children in the U.S. is a Walmart associate. It's hard to fathom Walmart's impact on the U.S. economy. Its average *daily* sales of $1.32 billion exceed the *annual*

 **Practice** on MyMarketingLab
Using a CRM System to Assess Marketing Impact

 **Practice** on MyMarketingLab
Shopping Cart Analysis of a ecommerce Website

 **Practice** on MyMarketingLab
Basic Shopping Basket Analysis

GDPs of 22 countries. By one estimate, through its own low prices and impact on competitors' prices, Walmart saves the average American household $2500 each year, equivalent to more than six months' worth of groceries for the average family.

What's behind this spectacular success? First and foremost, Walmart is passionately dedicated to its long-time, low-price value proposition and what its low prices mean to customers: "Save money. Live better." To accomplish this mission, Walmart offers a broad selection of goods at "unbeatable low prices," day in and day out. No other retailer has come nearly so close to mastering the concepts of everyday low prices and one-stop shopping. Sam Walton himself summed up Walmart's mission best when he said, "If we work together, we'll lower the cost of living for everyone . . . we'll give the world an opportunity to see what it's like to save and have a better life."

How does Walmart make money with such low prices? Walmart is a lean, mean distribution machine—it has the lowest cost structure in the industry. Low costs let the giant retailer charge lower prices while remaining profitable. Lower prices attract more shoppers, producing more sales, making the company more efficient, and enabling it to lower prices even more.

Walmart's low costs result from superior operations management, sophisticated information technology, and good-old "tough buying." Its huge, fully automated distribution centres supply stores efficiently. It employs an information technology system that gives managers around the world instant access to sales and operating information. And Walmart is known for using its massive scale to wring low prices from suppliers. "Don't expect a greeter and don't expect friendly," said one supplier's sales executive after a visit to Walmart's buying offices. "Once you are ushered into one of the spartan little buyers' rooms, expect a steely eye across the table and be prepared to cut your price. They are very, very focused people, and they use their buying power more forcefully than anyone else in America."

Despite its incredible success over the past five decades, mighty Walmart faces some weighty challenges ahead. Having grown so big, the maturing giant is having difficulty maintaining the rapid growth rates of its youth. Think about this: To grow just 7 percent, Walmart would have to add nearly $34 billion in new sales. That's a sales *increase* greater than the *total* sales of all but the top 92 companies on the Fortune 500, including companies such as American Express, Allstate, Macy's, McDonald's, 3M, and Nike. The bigger Walmart gets, the harder it is to maintain a high rate of growth.

To keep growing, Walmart has pushed into new, faster-growing product and service lines, including organic foods, store brands, in-store health clinics, and consumer financial services. To combat trendier competitors such as Target, Walmart even gave itself a modest image face-lift. It spruced up its stores with a cleaner, brighter, more open look and less clutter to make them more shopper friendly. In search of broader appeal, it has added new, higher-quality products. Many Walmart stores now carry a selection of higher-end consumer electronics products, from Samsung ultra-thin televisions to Dell and Toshiba laptops to Apple iPhones and iPads. The retailer has also dressed up its apparel racks with more-stylish fashion lines.

Despite its massive presence, Walmart still has room to expand geographically. Believe it or not, there are plenty of places in Canada and the United States that still don't have a Walmart. And the giant retailer is expanding rapidly in other international markets. Walmart also faces substantial growth opportunities—and challenges—in e-commerce. Its online sales of an estimated $9 billion account for less than 2 percent of total sales, making it a distant online also-ran next to Amazon.com, which has annual sales of approximately $60 billion. Walmart lists "winning in global e-commerce" as one of its top priorities for the future.

As Walmart continues to adapt and grow, however, one thing seems certain. The giant retailer may add new products lines and services. It might go digital and global. It might brush up its look and image. But Walmart has no intention of ever giving up its core low-price value proposition. After all, Walmart is and always will be a discounter. "I don't think Walmart's . . . ever going to be edgy," says a Walmart marketer. "I don't think that fits our brand. Our brand is about saving people money" so that they can live better.[1]

THE WALMART story sets the stage for examining the fast-changing world of today's resellers. This chapter looks at *retailing* and *wholesaling.* In the first section, we look at the nature and importance of retailing, the major types of store and nonstore retailers, the decisions retailers make, and the future of retailing. In the second section, we discuss these same topics as they apply to wholesalers.

Retailing LO1

Simulate on MyMarketingLab

Retailing/Wholesaling

What is retailing? We all know that Sobeys, Home Depot, and Hudson's Bay are retailers, but so are Amazon.com and other online retailers; hotels, gas stations, and restaurants; and service providers with "storefront" locations—like banks, hair salons, and dentists. **Retailing** includes all the activities involved in selling products or services directly to final consumers for their personal, nonbusiness use. Many institutions—manufacturers, wholesalers, and retailers—do retailing. But most retailing is done by **retailers**, businesses whose sales come *primarily* from retailing.

Retailing plays a very important role in marketing channels—perhaps the most important role of all. In Canada, jobs in retail account for the largest labour force segment in the country and in most of the provinces. There are approximately 2.7 million retail outlets in Canada, and retailing provides more than 2.1 million jobs, representing 11.5 percent of the total labour force. All together, Canadian retailers generate more than $450 billion in sales each year. The largest sector is food and beverage retailers, contributing more than $104 billion to our economy. The automotive sector, which includes new car dealerships, used car dealerships, and retailers that sell parts, supplies, and tires, is almost as large ($100 billion). Next is supermarkets and other grocery (except convenience) stores ($74 billion), followed by gasoline stations ($58 billion), general merchandise stores ($56 billion), health and personal care ($33 billion), and building and gardening supplies ($27 billion).[2]

Each year the Retail Council of Canada compiles monthly retail sales across all sectors, and produces a pie chart that shows at a glance the breakdown of retail in Canada (see Figure 12.1).

Because retailing is such a large industry, employs so many people, and is therefore so important to our economy, Statistics Canada publishes detailed monthly reports on the state of retail in Canada. It measures the volume of retail trade sales in each province using information from the Consumer Price Index (CPI) the Retail Commodity Survey (RCS), and the Monthly Retail Trade Survey (MRTS).

Despite the availability of online shopping, most retailing today (and most consumer purchasing) is still done in some type of traditional bricks-and-mortar retail locations. There are many new trends and technologies that are changing the face of retailing as we once knew it. These will be discussed later in the chapter; for now, we will focus on traditional storefront retailing.

Retailing
All the activities involved in selling goods or services directly to final consumers for their personal, nonbusiness use.

Retailer
A business whose sales come *primarily* from retailing.

FIGURE 12.1 Annual Summary of Retail Sales in Canada

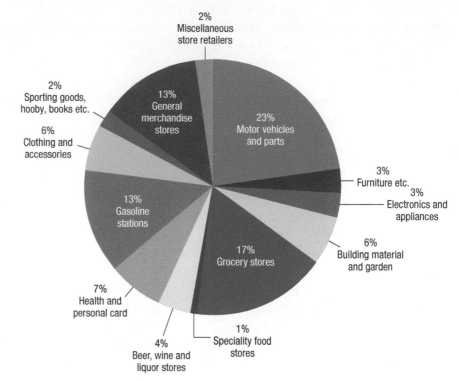

Source: Retail Council of Canada.

Convenience store

A small store, located near a residential area, that is open long hours or seven days a week and carries a limited line of high-turnover convenience goods.

Discount store

A retail operation that sells standard merchandise at lower prices by accepting lower margins and selling at higher volume.

Specialty store

A retail store that carries a narrow product line with a deep assortment within that line.

Department store

A retail store that carries a wide variety of product lines, each operated as a separate department managed by specialist buyers or merchandisers.

Exhibit 12.1 **Types of retailers:** Sometimes full-service retailers, like Tim Hortons, partner with self-service retailers, like Irving.

Types of Retailers

Retail stores come in all shapes and sizes—from your local hairstyling salon or family-owned restaurant to national chains such as Hudson's Bay and Loblaw, specialty retailers like PetSmart and Structube, and of course service retailers like Esso and Shell. Retail outlets can be classified in terms of the *amount of service* they offer, the breadth and depth of their *product lines*, the *relative prices* they charge, and how they are *organized*.

Amount of Service Different types of customers and products require different amounts of service. To meet these varying service needs, retailers may offer one of three service levels: self-service, limited service, and full service.

For example, **convenience stores** and **discount stores** are typically *self-serve retailers*, which allow customers to perform their own locate-compare-select process to save time or money. Today most gas stations are self-serve, though some still offer limited service. *Limited-service retailers*, such as Home Depot, Canadian Tire, and Best Buy, provide some sales assistance because they carry products that often require the customer to seek expert advice and information. In *full-service retailers*, salespeople assist customers in every phase of the shopping process.

Full-service retailers typically serve a higher-end market (Holt Renfrew), or sell luxury goods (jewellery stores) or specialty items such as expensive cookware or wedding dresses.

Product Line Another way to define retailers is by the breadth and depth of their product lines. **Specialty stores**, for example, carry narrow product lines with deep assortments within those lines. Shoe stores, women's clothing stores, toy stores, and electronics stores are all specialty stores. In contrast, **department stores** carry a wide variety of product lines, organized into shoe, clothing, toy, and electronics departments. **Supermarkets** carry a wide assortment of food and grocery products. **General merchandise stores** such as Walmart also sell food, but offer a much narrower selection. General merchandise stores evolved from the "general store" that used to exist on the main street of every town and in rural communities. They are stores that sell a broad selection of merchandise where people can purchase all their general goods.

A new trend in retailing in Canada is the combination of specialty retailing with department store retailing to create luxury retailers, like Nordstrom:

In 1887, 16-year-old John W. Nordstrom left his home in Sweden for the promise of New York City. Lured by the Alaska gold rush, he ventured west, and in 1901 settled in Seattle and opened a shoe repair shop. By 1929 Nordstrom was a small chain of shoe stores, run now by Nordstrom's sons. In the 1960s women's apparel was added, and over the next 50 years Nordstrom grew into the "fashion specialty retailer" we know today, with 304 stores in Canada and the United States.

The first Nordstrom in Canada opened in 2015 in the Rideau Centre in Ottawa, where hundreds of shoppers lined up hours before the pre-opening beauty bash that started at 7:30 a.m. Elegant beauty stations were set up in the middle of the party on the mall's first floor, where stylists pampered the crowd with consultations and makeovers using luxury fragrance and cosmetic brands like La Mer, Chanel, Diptyque, and Tom Ford.

The energy was palpable, with DJs pumping out music while dozens of well-manicured Nordstrom employees fawned over guests—and whether it was handing out free totes and samples or serving complimentary coffee, juice, and croissants, customers were happy with the effort put into the glitzy launch.

Some describe the luxury retailer as providing "gob-smackingly extraordinary service" that goes above and beyond in a way that customers never forget. Nordstrom lore is full of stories about security guards and housekeeping staff stepping in to help customers—even racing to the airport to deliver shopping bags to women before they board flights. Retail expert Robert Kozinets, of Toronto's Schulich School of Business, says that Canadian retailers should take note: The customer service bar has been raised.[3]

Exhibit 12.2 Specialty stores: Specialty stores carry a narrow product line, like wedding dresses, with a deep assortment of those products.

Semjonow Juri/Shutterstock

Supermarket
A large, low-cost, low-margin, high-volume, self-service store that carries a wide variety of grocery and household products.

General merchandise store
A store that sells a broad selection of merchandise where people can purchase all their general goods.

Exhibit 12.3 A new breed of retailer: Experts describe Nordstrom as providing "gob-smackingly extraordinary service" that goes above and beyond in a way that customers never forget.

Jean Levac/Ottawa Citizen. Reprinted by permission.

Superstore

A store much larger than a regular supermarket that offers a large assortment of routinely purchased food products, nonfood items, and services.

Category killer (or big box store)

A giant specialty store that carries a very deep assortment of a particular line.

Service retailer

A retailer whose product line is actually a service; examples include hotels, airlines, banks, restaurants, and many others.

Discount store

A retail operation that sells standard merchandise at lower prices by accepting lower margins and selling at higher volume.

Off-price retailer

A retailer that buys at less-than-regular wholesale prices and sells at less than retail.

Independent off-price retailer

An off-price retailer that is either independently owned and run or a division of a larger retail corporation.

Whereas convenience stores carry a small selection of high-turnover convenience goods, **superstores** are much larger than regular supermarkets and offer a large assortment of routinely purchased food products, nonfood items, and services. Very large specialty stores that carry thousands of products in a particular category, such as Home Depot and Best Buy, are sometimes referred to as **category killers or big box stores**.

Finally, for many retailers, the product line is actually a service. **Service retailers** include hotels and motels, banks, airlines, restaurants, movie theatres, tennis clubs, bowling alleys, repair services, hair salons, and dry cleaners.

Relative Prices Retailers can also be classified according to the prices they charge. Most retailers charge regular prices and offer normal-quality goods and customer service. Others offer higher-quality goods and service at higher prices. Two types of retailers that position themselves on low prices are discount stores and off-price retailers. **Discount stores** such as Dollarama and Giant Tiger are retail operations that sell standard merchandise at lower prices on a daily basis; that is, without "sales." They typically make lower margins than department stores, and make up for it by selling at higher volume. **Off-price retailers** are stores that buy at less-than-regular wholesale prices and charge consumers less than retail. Winners is the largest off-price retail chain in Canada.

The three main types of off-price retailers are *independents*, *factory outlets*, and *warehouse clubs*. **Independent off-price retailers** are either independently owned and run or divisions of larger retail corporations. Although many off-price operations are run by smaller independents, most large off-price retailer operations are owned by bigger retail chains such as TJX Companies, which owns Winners and Marshalls.

Factory outlets—manufacturer-owned and operated stores by firms such as J. Crew, Gap, Levi Strauss, and others—sometimes group together in *factory outlet malls* and *value-retail centres*. At these centres, dozens of outlet stores offer prices as much as 50 percent below retail on a wide range of mostly surplus, discontinued, or irregular goods. Whereas outlet malls consist primarily of manufacturers' outlets, value-retail centres combine manufacturers' outlets with off-price retail stores and department store clearance outlets.

These malls in general are now moving upscale—and even dropping *factory* from their descriptions. A growing number of outlet malls now feature luxury brands such as Coach, Polo Ralph Lauren, Dolce & Gabbana, Giorgio Armani, Burberry, and Versace. Many companies now regard outlets not simply as a way of disposing of problem merchandise but as an additional way of gaining business for fresh merchandise. The combination of highbrow brands and lowbrow prices found at outlets provides powerful shopper appeal, since every shopper loves a good deal.

Warehouse clubs (also known as *wholesale clubs* or *membership warehouses*), such as Costco, operate in huge, drafty, warehouse-like facilities and offer few frills. However, they offer ultra-low prices and surprise deals on selected branded

Kathy deWitt/Alamy

Exhibit 12.4 Discount and off-price retailers: Giant Tiger is both a discount retailer and a franchise organization, with more than 200 stores across Canada.

TABLE 12.1 Major Types of Retail Organizations

Type	Description	Examples
Corporate chain	Two or more outlets that are commonly owned and controlled. Corporate chains appear in all types of retailing but are strongest in department stores, discount stores, food stores, drugstores, and restaurants.	SaveOnFoods, Shoppers Drug Mart, Hudson's Bay, Sobeys
Voluntary chain	Wholesaler-sponsored group of independent retailers engaged in group buying and merchandising.	Independent Grocers Alliance (IGA)
Retailer cooperative	Group of independent retailers who jointly establish a central buying organization and conduct joint promotion efforts.	Home Hardware, Best Western
Franchise organization	Contractual association between a franchisor (a manufacturer, wholesaler, or service organization) and franchisees (independent businesspeople who buy the right to own and operate one or more units in the franchise system).	Boston Pizza, Subway, Mr. Lube, Giant Tiger, 7-Eleven

merchandise. Warehouse clubs have grown rapidly in recent years. These retailers appeal not only to low-income consumers seeking bargains on bare-bones products but also to all kinds of customers shopping for a wide range of goods, from necessities to extravagances.

Organizational Approach Although many retail stores are independently owned, others band together under some form of corporate or contractual organization. Table 12.1 describes four major types of retail organizations—*corporate chains, voluntary chains, retailer cooperatives,* and *franchise organizations.*

Corporate chains are two or more outlets that are commonly owned and controlled. They have many advantages over independents. Their size allows them to buy in large quantities at lower prices and gain promotional economies. They can hire specialists to deal with areas such as pricing, promotion, merchandising, inventory control, and sales forecasting.

The great success of corporate chains caused many independents to band together in one of two forms of contractual associations. One is the *voluntary chain*—a wholesaler-sponsored group of independent retailers that engages in group buying and common merchandising. IGA stores are independent retailers that are part of a voluntary chain. The other type of contractual association is the *retailer cooperative*—a group of independent retailers that bands together to set up a jointly owned, central wholesale operation and conduct joint merchandising and promotion efforts. Examples are Home Hardware and Best Western. These organizations give independents the buying and promotion economies they need to meet the prices of corporate chains.

Another form of contractual retail organization is the **franchise**, which we examined in Chapter 11. The main difference between franchise organizations and other contractual systems (voluntary chains and retail cooperatives) is that franchise systems are normally based on some unique product or service; a method of doing business; or the trade name, goodwill, or patent that the franchisor has developed. Franchising has been prominent in fast food restaurants, motels, health and fitness centres, auto sales and service dealerships, and real estate agencies.

Some of the best known Canadian franchises are Boston Pizza, Second Cup, Subway, Pizza Pizza, Harvey's, Tim Hortons, and Cold Stone Creamery; H&R Block, Shoppers

Factory outlet
An off-price retailing operation that is owned and operated by a manufacturer and normally carries the manufacturer's surplus, discontinued, or irregular goods.

Warehouse club
An off-price retailer that sells a limited selection of brand name grocery items, appliances, clothing, and other goods at deep discounts to members who pay annual membership fees.

Corporate chains
Two or more outlets that are commonly owned and controlled.

Franchise
A contractual association between a manufacturer, wholesaler, or service organization (a franchisor) and independent businesspeople (franchisees) who buy the right to own and operate one or more units in the franchise system.

Exhibit 12.5 Franchise: Pet Valu franchise owner Brent Bannis (and furry friend) at the opening of his store in Binbrook, Ontario.

Drug Mart, Sports Experts, Midas, and Mister Transmission; Canadian Tire, Days Inn, Travelodge, and Holiday Inn Express; and Molly Maid, Two Men and a Truck, AMJ Campbell Van Lines, and Sylvan Learning Centres. Pet Valu is also a Canadian franchise. This specialty retailer of pet food and pet-related supplies has close to 400 stores located throughout Canada and the United States. One of the most recent franchises opened in Binbrook, Ontario, a community just outside of Hamilton:

> Brent Banis is proud to be the owner of a Pet Valu retail store, but it's not an easy job. Franchisees are required to take a course through the University of California, and all the store's employees need to train in dog and cat nutrition. "Pet Valu is the only pet retailer that has that kind of mandatory training," said Banis.
>
> The store carries pet food brands ranging from raw, wheat-free, and organic foods to the

store's own grain-free brand, Ultra Performance. But they do much more than just sell pet food. They carry pet toys and holistic treats and cater to non-furry pets like birds, fish, and reptiles. "We also have a self-serve dog wash station that people seem to really enjoy," adds Banis, "and it's pretty entertaining to watch. We have all the shampoo, towels, and blow dryers that people can use and we take care of the clean-up."

Banis has also linked up with the Hamilton SPCA and a local cat rescue to connect people with animals in need of adoption. The store has been very well received in Binbrook, which Banis attributes to the community feel of the franchise's brand. "Pet Valus actually do better in smaller communities because I think that they [residents] respect the fact that the business owner is usually part of the community, and they like to shop local," said Banis.[4]

◄⊙┤**Simulate** on MyMarketingLab

Planning

◄⊙┤**Simulate** on MyMarketingLab

Plans and Planning Tools

Retailer Marketing Decisions LO2

Retailers are always searching for new marketing strategies to attract and hold customers. In the past, retailers attracted customers with unique product assortments and more or better services. Today, though, retailers' assortments and services are looking more and more alike. You can find most consumer brands not only in department stores but also in mass-merchandise discount stores, off-price discount stores, and all over the Internet—so it's now more difficult for any one retailer to offer exclusive merchandise.

Service differentiation among retailers has also eroded. Many department stores have trimmed their services, whereas discounters have increased theirs. In addition, customers have become smarter and more price sensitive. They see no reason to pay more for identical brands, especially when service differences are shrinking. For all these reasons, many retailers today are rethinking their marketing strategies.

As shown in Figure 12.2, retailers face major marketing decisions about *segmentation and targeting, store differentiation and positioning,* and the *retail marketing mix.*

Segmentation, Targeting, Differentiation, and Positioning Decisions
Retailers must first segment and define their target markets and then decide how they will differentiate and position themselves in these markets—just as product marketers do. Should the store focus on upscale, midscale, or downscale shoppers? Should the store target shoppers wanting variety, depth of assortment, convenience, or low prices? Until they define and profile their markets, retailers cannot make consistent decisions about product assortment, services, pricing, advertising, store decor, or any of the other decisions that must support their positions.

Too many retailers, even big ones, fail to clearly define their target markets and positions. For example, what market does Sears target? For what is the department store

FIGURE 12.2 Retailer Marketing Strategies

known? What is its value proposition versus, say, Walmart on one hand and Hudson's Bay or Nordstrom on the other? If you're having trouble answering those questions, you're not alone—so is Sears's management (see Marketing@Work 12.1).

By contrast, successful retailers define their target markets well and position themselves strongly. For example, fine food retailers like Pusateri's in Toronto are positioned as upscale, and target shoppers who have no desire to shop around for the best price. Walmart, on the other hand, is strongly positioned on low prices and what those always-low prices mean to its customers. And highly successful retailer Mountain Equipment Co-op positions itself as catering to those who live their lives outdoors.

With solid targeting and positioning, a retailer can compete effectively against even the largest and strongest competitors. For example, compare little Five Guys Burger and Fries to giant McDonald's. Five Guys has only about 1000 stores and $1 billion in sales; McDonald's has more than 34 000 stores worldwide and system-wide sales of $95 billion. McDonald's has 27.7 million Facebook Likes; Five Guys has only 834 000. How does this smaller burger chain compete with Big Mac? It doesn't—at least not directly. Five Guys succeeds by carefully positioning itself *away* from McDonald's:

Five Guys' menu is limited—really limited. Aside from hamburgers, the chain has only hot dogs and grilled cheese or veggie sandwiches (which hardly anyone buys). You won't find salads or breakfasts or Chicken McBites at Five Guys, or even a chocolate milkshake. But what you *can* get at Five Guys you simply *can't* get at McDonald's—such as a mouth-watering Five Guys cheeseburger consisting of two patties and 840 gluttonous calories, piled high with cheese, lettuce, tomatoes, pickles, jalapenos, grilled mushrooms, or any of 11 free toppings, made to order with all-fresh ingredients and buried under an absurdly large serving of just-cooked hand-cut fries. The chain claims that there are more than 250 000 ways to order a Five Guys burger, crowned Zagat's "Best Burger." What's more, it's all very fresh—there are no freezers in any Five Guys locations, just coolers. The small burger joint's unique offerings and generous portions set it apart, allowing it to charge more than regular fast-food places.[5]

Radharc Images/Alamy

Exhibit 12.6 Retail targeting and positioning: Five Guys Burger and Fries succeeds by positioning itself strongly away from McDonald's and other large fast food giants. The menu is very limited, but what you can get at Five Guys you simply can't get at McDonald's.

MARKETING@WORK   12.1

Positioning Sears: Why Should You Shop There?

Most Americans don't shop much at Sears, and when they do, it's usually to catch a sale on appliances or tools, or maybe to browse the selection of Lands' End apparel, a brand owned by Sears since 2002. Even then, the merchandise and brands probably seem a bit stale, and the store itself feels a little old and run down. Shopping at Sears just doesn't provide the modern, feel-good shopping experience that Americans get at competing retailers such as Macy's or Nordstrom, or even Target or Walmart. Sears Canada is 51 percent owned by Sears Holdings, and the state of the Sears brand in both countries is pretty much the same. Sears is in need of a new positioning.

Today's successful retailers position themselves strongly—customers know what the store stands for and how it delivers value. Mention Walmart and people think "Save money. Live better." Bring up Target, and they know to "Expect more. Pay less." Successful discounter Kohl's tells customers to "Expect great things." At Macy's you get "the magic of Macy's," and Nordstrom promises to "take care of customers no matter what it takes." But mention Sears and people are stumped. They are left wondering, "Why should I shop at Sears?"

Founded in 1886, over the next century, Sears grew to become America's iconic retailer. It began as a mail-order catalogue company in the 1880s, expanded into a national chain of urban department stores during the early to mid 1900s, and became an important anchor store in the fast-growing suburban malls of the 1960s and 1970s. Through the 1980s, Sears was the nation's largest retail chain—the Walmart of its time. Its then-well-known slogan, "Where America Shops," was more than just an advertising tagline—it was a meaningful positioning statement. Almost every American relied on Sears for everything from basic apparel and home goods to appliances and tools.

But during the past two decades, as the retail landscape has shifted, once-mighty Sears has lost its way. Squeezed between lower-priced big box discount stores on the one hand and trendier, more targeted upscale department and specialty stores on the other, Sears has gotten lost in the murky middle. Its old "Where America shops" positioning has little meaning these days for a store with only about one-twelfth the sales of competitor Walmart. And Sears has failed to refresh its positioning to make itself relevant in today's marketplace.

A look at Sears advertising or a visit to the Sears website testifies to the retailer's almost complete lack of current positioning. Headlines scream "Buy more, save more on appliances," "50% off your favourite apparel brands," "Lowest prices on Craftsman lawn and garden," and "Big brand sale: great values, top brands." It seems that about the only thing Sears has going for it these days is that everything it sells is always on sale. However, price is not a convincing value proposition for Sears, which has trouble matching the low prices of competitors such as Walmart, Target, or Kohl's.

In 2005, a struggling Sears merged with an even more distressed Kmart to become Sears Holding Corporation. The merger of the two failing retailers left analysts scratching their heads and customers even more confused about the value propositions of the respective chains. Following the merger, the corporation jumped from one questionable tactic to another. For example, Kmart stores began carrying well-known Sears brands such as Craftsman tools, Kenmore appliances, and Diehard batteries, diluting one of Sears's only remaining differentiating assets.

Sears Holding has also tried a variety of store formats. For instance, it converted 400 Kmart stores to Sears Essentials stores, which it later changed to Sears Grand stores—Walmart-like outlets that carry regular Sears merchandise plus everything from health and beauty brands, toys, and baby products to party supplies and groceries. It has also dabbled with a confusing assortment of other formats carrying the Sears name, such as Sears Hometown stores (a franchised smaller version of full-sized Sears stores), Sears Hardware stores, Sears Home Appliance Showrooms, Sears Outlet stores, and Sears Auto Centres.

Despite all the new store formats, Sears has done little to refresh its positioning. "A lot of traditional department stores have reinvigorated themselves through merchandising. You haven't seen that from Sears," says one analyst. To make matters worse, whereas most competing retailers have invested heavily to spruce up their stores, Sears has spent

Exhibit 12.7 To once again position Sears as the place "Where America Shops," the retailer must first answer the question, "Why should people shop at Sears?"

less than one-quarter of the industry average on store maintenance and renovation, leaving many of its outlets looking old and shabby. "There's no reason to shop at Sears," concludes a retailing expert. "It offers a depressing shopping experience and uncompetitive prices."

Many critics place the blame for Sears's lack of sound marketing and positioning on Sears Holding Company chairman Edward Lampert, a hedge fund manager and the driving force behind the Sears/Kmart merger. Lampert and his funds own about 60 percent of Sears Holding's stock. Critics claim that since the 2005 merger, Lampert has run the company more as a portfolio of financial assets than as a retail chain. Indeed, Lampert has hired four CEOs since the merger, not a single one with any retailing experience. Most recently, he assumed CEO responsibilities himself. "Being a successful hedge fund manager doesn't make you a good retailer," says one Sears watcher.

Sears's lack of customer and marketing thinking has taken a big toll. Sears Holding Corporation revenues have fallen every year since the Sears/Kmart merger;

in a recent year they ended down 4.1 percent at $39.8 billion, with losses of $930 million. Sears's stock price has fallen 70 percent since 2007. With no cogent marketing plan and seemingly no way out of its financial tailspin, some analysts even predict that once-dominant Sears will soon disappear entirely. "They are letting . . . Sears die on the vine," says one doubter. "As strong as a brand is, and it has huge familiarity and favourability over the years, you can't continue to have a lack of focus without causing long-term damage."

Sears does have some strengths. One bright spot is online sales, which account for nearly 10 percent of Sears's total revenues, compared with only the 1 to 2 percent of sales that Walmart and Target have struggled to achieve online. Another positive is Sears's enduring store brands. Craftsman tools and Kenmore appliances still lead their categories, and the DieHard brand of automotive batteries remains strong. And the company has announced that it will license its brands to makers of related products. Thus, we might soon see Craftsman work apparel, Kenmore

kitchenware, and DieHard flashlights and household batteries.

However, creating more online business and renting out its store brands will not overcome what one industry expert characterizes as "the horror show that is the . . . Sears stores themselves." Restoring Sears's relevance and lustre will require nothing short of a complete strategic turnaround that positions Sears and its brands on differentiated customer value. To once again position Sears as the place "Where America Shops," the retailer must first answer the question, "Why should people shop at Sears?"

Sources: Based on quotes and other information from Lauren Coleman-Lochner and Carol Hymowitz, "A Money Man's Trials in Retailing," *Businessweek*, January 5, 2012, pp. 24–25; "Prediction: These Famous Brands Will Disappear in 2012," *The Business Insider*, January 5, 2012, http://finance.yahoo.com/blogs/daily-ticker/prediction-famous-brands-disappear-2012-010414512.html; Phil Wahba, "Sears Closing More Stores as Holiday Sales Slide," *Reuters*, December 27, 2011; Jeff Macke, "Sears Done Pretending It's a Retailer," *Yahoo! Finance*, August 16, 2012; Karen Talley, "Sears to License Names of Kenmore, Craftsman Brands," *Wall Street Journal*, April 5, 2012; Karen Talley and Saabira Chaudhuri, "Sears Loss Narrows; Kohl's Net Falls," *Wall Street Journal*, March 1, 2013, p. B3; and Sears.com and Sears.ca, accessed May 2015.

Five Guys can't match McDonald's massive economies of scale, incredible volume purchasing power, ultra-efficient logistics, diverse menu, and low prices. But then again, it doesn't even try. By positioning itself away from McDonald's and other large competitors, Five Guys has become one of the fastest-growing fast-casual restaurant chains.

Product Assortment and Services Decisions Retailers must decide on three major product variables: product assortment, services mix, and store atmosphere.

The retailer's *product assortment* should differentiate it while matching target shoppers' expectations. One strategy is to offer merchandise that no other competitor carries, such as store brands or national brands on which it holds exclusive rights. For example, Hudson's Bay recently acquired Saks, and so gets exclusive rights to carry some well-known designer labels. Alternatively, a retailer can differentiate itself by offering a highly targeted product assortment: Addition Elle carries plus-size clothing, Aldo focuses on shoes and accessories, and La Senza has a deep assortment of lingerie targeting women.

The *services mix* can also help set one retailer apart from another. For example, some retailers invite customers to ask questions or consult service representatives in person or via phone or keyboard. Home Depot offers a diverse mix of services to do-it-yourselfers, from "how-to" classes and "do-it-herself" and kid workshops to a proprietary credit card. Nordstrom delivers top-notch service and promises to "take care of the customer, no matter what it takes."

The *store's atmosphere* is another important element in the reseller's product arsenal. Retailers want to create a unique store experience, one that suits the target market and

Courtesy of FGL Sports Ltd.

Exhibit 12.8 Experiential retailing: Sport Chek's 12 000-square-foot "retail lab" store in Toronto demonstrates the latest in experiential retail combined with the high-energy environment of a sports stadium.

moves customers to buy. Many retailers practise *experiential retailing*. For example, Canadian retailer Sport Chek has combined the latest trends in concept stores and experiential retailing into its 12 000-square-foot "retail lab" store in downtown Toronto:

> The Sport Chek "retail lab" incorporates the latest digital technology to enable interaction between customers and the brand in every corner of the store. Samsung installed 140 digital screens with ultra-thin borders, touch technology, and near-field communication (NFC) capabilities, which allow customers to interact with the merchandise. There are smaller-format screens such as digital tiles built into display tables, tablets that have been incorporated into the top of clothing racks, and loads of digital displays to showcase videos and still images. The Yonge Street exterior of the store features a 5-by-32-foot digital projection screen that displays high-definition video, still images, and may eventually show live feeds of sporting events. Next to the store's escalator is a wall of 19 screens. When consumers approach, an Xbox Kinect activates and displays promotions or a simulated chairlift on the screens. An electronic community board on the second floor provides customers with schedules of fitness classes as well as updates and statistics for local sports teams, and visitors to the store can log on to the Sport Chek Facebook page to submit photos for the board. All the digital content is controlled from a facility in Calgary, which can produce and send material to specific screens within 12 minutes. The store is believed to be the most advanced digital retail space of any category in North America.[6]

Today's successful retailers carefully orchestrate virtually every aspect of the consumer's in-store experience. The next time you step into a retail store—whether it sells consumer electronics, hardware, or high fashion—stop and carefully consider your surroundings. Think about the store's layout and displays. Listen to the background music. Check out the colours. Smell the smells. Chances are good that everything in the store, from the layout and lighting to the music and even the colours and smells, has been carefully orchestrated to help shape the customers' shopping experiences—and open their wallets.

Price Decisions A retailer's price policy must fit its target market and positioning, product and service assortment, the competition, and economic factors. All retailers would like to charge high mark-ups and achieve high volume, but the two seldom go together. Most retailers seek either high mark-ups on lower volume (most specialty stores) *or* low mark-ups on higher volume (mass merchandisers and discount stores). Retailers like Holt Renfrew, which cater to the upper crust with designer brands and bespoke formal wear and pamper their customers with personal service, rarely have "sales." By contrast, Winners, which targets middle-class Canadians, offers everything at a reduced price. Other retailers—such as Walmart, Costco, and Dollarama—practise *everyday low pricing (EDLP)*, charging constant, everyday low prices with few sales or discounts.

Still other retailers practise *high-low pricing*—charging higher prices on an everyday basis, coupled with frequent sales and other price promotions, to increase store traffic, create a low-price image, or attract customers who will buy other goods at full prices.

Which pricing strategy is best depends on the retailer's overall marketing strategy, the pricing approaches of its competitors, and the economic environment.

Promotion Decisions Retailers use any or all of the five promotion tools—advertising, personal selling, sales promotion, public relations (PR), and direct marketing—to reach consumers. They advertise in newspapers and magazines and on radio and television. Advertising may be supported by newspaper inserts and catalogues. Store salespeople greet customers, meet their needs, and build relationships. Sales promotions may include in-store demonstrations, displays, sales, and loyalty programs. PR activities, such as new store openings, special events, newsletters and blogs, store magazines, and public service activities, are also available to retailers.

Many retailers also interact with customers via websites, online catalogues, online advertising, YouTube videos, email, Facebook, Twitter, and Instagram. Today almost every retailer, large or small, maintains a full social media presence.

Place (Distribution) Decisions Retailers often point to three critical factors in retailing success: location, location, and location. It's very important that retailers select locations that are accessible to the target market in areas that are consistent with the retailer's positioning. For example, Apple locates its stores in high-end malls and trendy shopping districts, such as the Pacific Centre in Vancouver. You'll never find an Apple store in a low-rent strip mall on the edge of town.

Most stores today cluster together to increase their customer pulling power and give consumers the convenience of one-stop shopping. Central business districts were the main form of retail cluster until the 1950s. Every large city and town had a central business district with department stores, specialty stores, banks, and movie theatres. When people began moving to the suburbs, however, many of these central business districts began to lose business, and the retailers moved to the shopping centres.

A **shopping centre** is a group of retail businesses built on a site that is planned, developed, owned, and managed as a unit. A *regional shopping centre*, or *regional shopping mall*, the largest and most dramatic shopping centre, has from 50 to more than 100 stores, including two or more full-line department stores. It's like a covered mini-downtown and attracts customers from a wide area. A *community shopping centre* contains between 15 and 50 retail stores. It normally contains a branch of a department store or variety store, a supermarket, specialty stores, professional offices, and sometimes a bank. Most shopping centres are *neighbourhood shopping centres* or *strip malls* that generally contain between 5 and 15 stores. These centres, which are close and convenient for consumers, usually contain a supermarket, perhaps a discount store, and several service stores—dry cleaner, drugstore, hardware store, local restaurant, or other stores.

A newer form of shopping centre is the so-called power centre. *Power centres* are huge unenclosed shopping centres consisting of a long strip or clusters of retail stores, including large, freestanding anchors such as Walmart, Home Depot, Costco, Best Buy, Michaels, and PetSmart. Each store has its own entrance with parking directly in front for shoppers who wish to visit only one store. In contrast, *lifestyle centres* are smaller open-air malls with upscale stores, convenient locations, and nonretail activities, such as a playground, skating rink, hotel, dining establishments, and a movie theatre. "Think of lifestyle centres as part Main Street and part Fifth Avenue," comments an industry observer. In fact, the original power centre and lifestyle centre concepts are now morphing into hybrid lifestyle-power centres that combine the convenience and community feel of a neighbourhood centre with the brute force of a power centre. In all, today's centres are more places to hang out than just places to shop.[7]

Shopping centre
A group of retail businesses built on a site that is planned, developed, owned, and managed as a unit.

◄●─ Simulate on MyMarketingLab
Retailing/Wholesaling

Retailing Trends and Developments LO3

Retailers operate in a harsh and fast-changing environment, which offers threats as well as opportunities. New retail forms continue to emerge to meet new situations and consumer needs, but the life cycle of new retail forms is getting shorter. Department stores took about 100 years to reach the mature stage of the life cycle; more recent forms, such as warehouse stores, reached maturity in about 10 years. To remain successful, retailers must continually monitor the new trends and new technology available to them, and keep evolving.

And keeping pace in retail is about more than just changing technology. Some experts say that it's really the customers who are driving changes in retail. Today's always-online consumers know what they want, and they know how to find it, so retailers need to focus less on their products and more on their shoppers. *Canadian Retailer* magazine conducted a Global Total Retail study to analyze "disruptors" from the consumers' perspective. They found that while 78 percent of Canadians have been shopping online for more than three years, 66 percent have never used their mobile phone to make a purchase. They do, however, use their smartphones to check prices, locate stores, use coupons, and access loyalty programs.[8]

Experiential Retail

One marketer who is adapting well to the changing retail environment is BMW—it's not just renovating, but entirely rethinking what its dealerships look like. The first BMW "concept store" opened in Paris, and it looks nothing like a traditional Canadian or American dealership. For one thing, there are no giant signs, which makes it difficult to find but also gives it an air of exclusivity. Once found, the dealer showroom looks and feels as if you're entering a really posh department store. The sleek, high-ceilinged space is mostly white and equipped with giant flat screens and other digital technology. BMW refers to its new store as "future retail" and says that it offers a whole range of initiatives and tools designed to enhance the customer experience and set new standards for retail in the automotive industry and beyond.[9]

BMW's new concept store, like Sport Chek's "retail lab," are variations of what marketers have come to call experiential retailing—the idea that the retail environment shouldn't be simply a display of products for sale, but rather an experience that engages the customer. The concept was pioneered by Rainforest Café and the Hard Rock Café, but today retailers like IKEA and even Home Depot are running with experiential retail.

In-Store, Mobile, and Wearable Technology

Sport Chek has gone all-out with digital in its new store, but it's not the only retailer to be embracing in-store technology. Walmart is testing Scan and Go, a checkout system that would allow shoppers to skip checkout lines by using their mobile phone to scan items and pay at self-serve kiosks. L.L.Bean uses RFID tags to launch product-related video when a consumer picks up a shoe from a display. And Major League Baseball teams are

Exhibit 12.9 Experiential retail: BMW's concept store in Paris looks more like a posh retailer than a car dealership.

Bloomberg/Getty Images

starting to use location-aware transmitters (called *beacons*) that send low-power Bluetooth signals to mobile devices as they pass close by. The teams hope to create a better visitor experience by automatically checking people in at the gates and sending them fun facts about points of interest around the stadium as they walk past them.[10]

Perhaps the next big thing in retail technology is wearable devices—like the Nymi Band, which identifies the individual wearing it, and presents new opportunities for retailers to offer personalized service to customers:

Exhibit 12.10 Wearable retail technology: At DX3 in Toronto, people wearing a Nymi Band with the "changeRoom" application could order an item, pick it up, and use their MasterCard to pay for it—all without lifting a finger.

Nymi Band™

> Nordstrom and other retailers have been experimenting with Wi-Fi sensors that sniff out the unique (though anonymous) signals emitted by shoppers' smartphones. Although this technology doesn't allow retailers to identify the individual shopper, it does let them collect information about how often people come back to the store, which aisles they visit, and how long they spend there. But now there's the Nymi Band—an electronic wristband that emits a wireless signal identifying the wearer and vouching for his or her identity. Wearing it makes you instantly recognizable to other wireless devices.
>
> At DX3, Canada's largest conference and trade show dedicated to digital marketing, advertising, and retail, Nymi partnered with MasterCard and a company called Trideit to create a one-of-a-kind retail experience. People wearing a Nymi Band with Trideit's "changeRoom" application could reserve a clothing item from a tablet to pick up in store. When users walk into the store, they're greeted with a personalized welcome message that recognizes them via their Nymi Band. The changeRoom app uses the Nymi Band to authenticate the users' identity, and uses MasterCard's MasterPass so that customers can seamlessly pay for the clothing item without a transaction.
>
> Marketers at both Nymi and MasterCard refer to this new technology as "persistent identity," and say that it will change the relationship between consumers and retailers. Since consumers won't opt in and share their data with a retailer if they don't receive sufficient value in return (whether that comes in the form of a new experience or a discount), it's very much up to the retailer to work with emerging technology to create exciting new experiences to surprise and delight shoppers.[11]

The latest buzzword in retail marketing is *shoppable media*, meaning video or print vehicles that encourage customers to immediately purchase products using various technologies, especially their personal mobile devices. For example, Target produced a video called "Falling for You," a three-part romantic comedy featuring Kristen Bell and 110 Target products. Consumers, while viewing the video, could click on a product and order it from Target right then and there. And an advertising campaign for fashion retailer H&M, featuring David Beckham, allowed consumers with a Samsung smart TV to use their remote control to purchase Beckham's latest designs.[12]

There's even new technology that brings the consumer's sense of smell into play. Retailers have long understood that scents can lead to more lingering and ultimately more spending, and now they can create digital interactive installations that include scent. Intel, HP, and 5thScreen Digital Services worked together to create five interactive scent-based games at The McCormick World of Flavors, in the McCormick spice company's flagship store in Baltimore. Games include "Guess That Spice" and "FlavorPrint," which allows consumers to find spices to match their taste preferences.[13]

Retailers must evolve because their customers are evolving. When Canadians were asked what they would like to see from retailers of the future, 38 percent said they would like to have the ability to check store inventory online; 33 percent said they wanted self-checkouts; and 26 percent wanted free, easy-access Wi-Fi while in the store. And the

Evan Agostini/Invision/AP

Exhibit 12.11 Shoppable Media:
An advertising campaign for fashion retailer H&M, featuring David Beckham, allowed consumers with a Samsung smart TV to use their remote control to purchase Beckham's latest designs.

Shopper marketing
Using point-of-sale promotions and advertising to extend brand equity to "the last mile" and encourage favourable in-store purchase decisions.

more consumers are exposed to what's possible, the more these demands will increase. What this means for Canadian retailers is that they need to start adopting new technologies now—after all, change takes time, and no retailer wants to be left behind.[14]

Increasing Use of Gift Cards

Gift cards are a billion-dollar industry in Canada and one of the fastest growing areas of retail—and it's not just the big retailers who are offering them. Today, many restaurants, salons, and even gas stations have their own gift cards, and retailers are developing new ways to incorporate them into their marketing efforts. The attraction for retailers goes beyond generating sales. Gift cards attract new customers and build brand awareness.

One of the reasons gift cards are so popular with retailers is that they're profitable, because many cards go unused—by some estimates, one in four gift cards remains unused a year after it was received. To help solve that problem for consumers, two Canadian entrepreneurs founded a business called CardSwap.ca, and successfully pitched their idea on *Dragons' Den*. Their online service allows consumers to buy, sell, and swap unwanted gift cards for cash. If you buy a gift card you pay the face value of the card, and if you sell a card you receive between 75 and 90 percent of its value. Alternatively, when you sell a gift card you can opt to have CardSwap turn it into a donation to a charitable organization; the charity will provide the donor with a tax receipt.

Shopper Marketing

Many retail marketers are now embracing the concept of **shopper marketing**, using point-of-purchase promotions and advertising to extend brand equity to "the last mile" and encouraging favourable point-of-purchase decisions. Shopper marketing involves focusing the entire marketing process—from product and brand development to logistics, promotion, and merchandising—toward turning shoppers into buyers at the point of sale.

Retail marketing used to be about guiding the consumer along the last few steps on the path to purchase, but the shopping experience and consumer behaviour are no longer that clear cut. The typical path to purchase began with awareness, then moved through investigation and selection, and finally to purchase—a straight line, or linear process. Today that process is anything but linear, and retailers are looking beyond traditional in-store marketing tactics to digital, mobile, and social media to create ongoing bonds with consumers—hence, shopper marketing. It's more of a circular process.

In order to be competitive, retailers are paying closer attention to the three elements of shopper marketing—pre-shopping, shopping, and post-shopping—and are using methods such as social media and search engine marketing to reach consumers at every stage in the process. For example, because 80 percent of consumers research their purchases online before going into a store, retailers can reach consumers in this pre-shopping stage by purchasing relevant keywords on Google. During stage two, the actual shopping process, retailers use digital technologies to provide a more personalized shopping experience. For example, Indigo suggests specific books to members of its Plum Rewards loyalty program through direct email, online, and at its in-store kiosks. In the post-shopping stage, retailers continue to engage with customers through social media. For example, Best Buy makes sure that any questions it receives through its social channels are always followed by a response from an appropriate employee. Technical questions are answered by a "Geek Agent," and in Best Buy's online community forum, "Plug In," customers can converse with one another and get answers to questions from Best Buy experts. In shopper marketing, this type of consumer-plus-expert forum exemplifies shopper marketing, which is all about sharing and conversing.

Marketing experts say that a successful shopper marketing campaign must use social media to drive other marketing initiatives; it must focus on engaging the consumer; it must tell a story; and, above all, it must be targeted to the right audience.[15]

Online Retail

Canadians have always been leaders in communications technologies, Internet usage, and e-commerce, and today, regular home use of the Internet is commonplace. Statistics Canada reports that more than 80 percent of Canadian households have access to the Internet, and half of those use more than one device to go online. The rates of access are highest in British Columbia (87 percent), followed closely by Alberta (85 percent) and Ontario (84 percent). As for online shopping, 7 percent of Canadians say they use the Internet for "window shopping"—browsing for goods or services but not placing an order—and 56 percent use it to order personal goods or services, spending a total of $19 billion.[16]

Online retail in Canada continues to grow at astonishing rates—in the double digits every year for the last several years, reaching $22.3 billion in 2014. That amount is expected to reach $40 billion by 2019. Some of the most popular online shopping sites are Chapters-Indigo and Best Buy, and recently a new online shopping destination, Shoptiques.com, opened its virtual doors to Canadians. Shoptiques lets consumers around the globe purchase clothing, accessories, and home decor items from Canadian boutiques in Toronto, Vancouver, and Montreal.[17]

A report from the NPD Group, a leading market research firm, revealed that consumers between the ages of 25 and 44 are the "sweet spot" for online retailers, because they are the generation that feels most at home online. Says Rick Brown, director of analytic solutions at NPD Group, "The online super buyers that exist in this age bracket are drawn to how easy it is to research and compare the products they're interested in buying, but their dexterity in hunting for discounts means that they expect to find better deals on the Web." The report also includes the surprising finding that men tend to spend more online than women: Men spend an average of $371 shopping online, whereas women spend $266. Men seem to prefer online shopping over manual shopping because they find better deals online, and are able to compare popular products in real time. On the other hand, women seem to shop online for products that are not easily available in retail stores across Canada. Further, they seem to enjoy the convenience of online shopping, which is more hassle-free than manual shopping.[18]

The influence of retailers' websites on traditional retailing has led to a new phenomenon called *showrooming*—and it has many retailers worried (see Marketing@Work 12.2). The term refers to consumers' increasing tendency to treat bricks-and-mortar retailers as showrooms, where they view and test products before leaving to buy them elsewhere or online for a lower price. Showroomers tend to be young female shoppers who frequently purchase online, have a lower household income, and are therefore motivated almost exclusively by price. One study found that locating a mere 2.5 percent discount on an in-store item online is enough to entice 5 percent of customers to leave a store; 60 percent would leave for a 5 percent discount; and 87 percent would leave if they found the same product online for 20 percent less.[19]

MARKETING@WORK 12.2

Showrooming: Shopping in Stores but Buying Online

At the local Best Buy, a helpful sales associate in the familiar blue shirt patiently assists a customer who's itching to buy a new computer monitor. After 20 minutes, the customer settles on a beautiful new 27-inch Samsung LED monitor, priced at $399. Everyone seems happy, and it looks like the associate has earned a well-deserved sale.

However, instead of reaching for his credit card, the customer whips out his smartphone. With the salesperson looking on, he uses an app called TheFind to scan the Samsung's barcode. The app spouts out a list of eight online retailers who sell the same model, along with their prices. Amazon.com has the best price—only $349, and with his Amazon Prime membership, says the customer, he can have it delivered to his doorstep in two days, with no shipping fee and no sales tax. Best Buy doesn't price-match online competitors. So with apologies to the helpful sales associate, the customer taps the Amazon.com "Buy Now" button and walks out of the store empty-handed.

This now-common shopping practice of going into stores to scope out merchandise and prices and then buying them from an online-only rival—that is, showrooming—has become the bane of many store retailers. According to one recent survey, half of shoppers who buy products online now check them out first in a traditional store. Another survey shows that about 40 percent of shoppers have used an in-store shopping app—such as TheFind, eBay's RedLaser, or Amazon's Price Check—to find better prices online and purchase from an online retailer while still in the store.

Showrooming has wreaked damage to many store retailers, especially those selling consumer electronics, which are easy to order online and expensive enough to make price comparisons worthwhile. For example, Target's sales in the U.S. during the holiday season fell short of expectations, with the greatest fallout in electronics, movies, books, music, and toys—products experiencing the biggest shift in sales to e-tailers. It's no surprise, then, that Best Buy—still the largest consumer electronics retailer—has been posting losses, closing stores, and laying off workers. But store retailers in all categories—from electronics retailers such as Best Buy to general discounters such as Walmart to specialty stores such as Toys "R" Us—are now looking for ways to keep smartphone-wielding shoppers from defecting. Says one store retailing executive, who refers to Amazon.com as "the A-word," comparison shopping in the smartphone and tablet era has "amped up to a whole 'nother level."

Price-matching is one way to thwart showrooming, but it's often not a realistic option. Online sellers have significant cost advantages—they don't bear the expense of running physical store locations and they aren't always subject to the same sales taxes. Most major bricks-and-mortar retailers aggressively track online competitor pricing and do their best to match it, but store retailers have already trimmed costs and are running on paper-thin margins. So, in most cases, they simply can't match online prices and remain profitable.

With so little room to manoeuvre on price, store retailers are exploring nonprice tactics to combat showrooming. One tactic is to shift toward exclusive products and store-branded merchandise that don't allow direct comparisons. For example, 56 percent of the products offered by health-and-wellness retailer GNC are either exclusives or GNC-branded items. At specialty retailer Brookstone, many best sellers, such as a $229 smartphone projector, are developed internally. Similarly, Target sent an urgent letter to suppliers requesting that they create exclusive Target-only lines and models that would shield it from showrooming price comparisons. It suggested that such exclusives could include all-new products or modifications in packaging and model numbers that would make direct comparisons difficult.

However, rather than just side-stepping the issue of showrooming—or online shopping more generally—many store retailers are trying to ride the trend by boosting their own online and digital options as an alternative or enhancement to shopping in their stores. For example, Target upgraded its website and quadrupled the number of items it sells online. Walmart has upped its emphasis on in-store pickups for online orders. It tells customers that they can order from its Walmart.com site, sometimes pick up items on the same day, avoid shipping fees, and easily return items to the store if not satisfied. Customers now pick up half of all Walmart.com purchases in stores, often buying additional merchandise during the visit.

ZUMA Press/Newscom

Exhibit 12.12 Showrooming: The now-common shopping practice of viewing products in stores but buying them elsewhere or online has become the bane of store retailers. But what can they do about it?

Both Walmart and Target are also testing digital apps that pull customers to both their websites and stores, let them prepare shopping lists, and, in Target's case, receive personalized daily-alert deals and exclusive discounts sent to their mobile phones. To help keep customers in the store once they arrive, Walmart has adopted a strategy that it calls the "endless aisle," by which in-store clerks help customers order immediately from Walmart.com when they can't find particular items in the store. Both retailers are working feverishly to provide multichannel strategies that merge the advantages of digital shopping with the unique advantages of in-store shopping, such as instant buying gratification, easy returns, and personal sales assistance.

Best Buy is looking for additional ways to make in-store buying more attractive. In a strategy patterned after the "Genius Bars" at Apple stores, Best Buy has tested what it calls "Connected Stores," which feature tech support, wireless connections, and a large customer-assistance hub at the centre, as well as new areas and checkout lanes to speed pickup on items purchased online. The hope is that additional in-store services will make higher shelf prices more palatable.

Despite such tactics to combat showrooming and digital buying, many experts remain skeptical about the future of store retailers such as Best Buy. Online retailers like Amazon have transformed how people buy, and when it comes to online commerce, traditional retailers have a lot of catching up to do. Online sales account for only 1 to 2 percent of Target's and Walmart's total sales. And although online sales currently represent only about 8 percent of total retail buying, they are growing at a breathtaking rate. For example, Amazon.com, with sales of $61 billion, is growing at an average annual rate of 34 percent. The world's leading online retailer has surged past Best Buy, whose sales have stagnated at about $50 billion.

For now, although it's a clear and present danger to Best Buy and certain other specialty retailers, showrooming is little more than a nuisance to the Targets and Walmarts of the world. But showrooming sales have more than doubled in just the past year, and as more and more shoppers are leaving stores empty-handed, bricks-and-mortar retailers are rising to meet the threat. Target laid out the challenge in its petition to suppliers: "What we aren't willing to do is let online-only retailers use our brick-and-mortar stores as a showroom for their products and undercut our prices without making investments, as we do, to proudly display your brands." The key question for Target, however, is this: "What are you going to do about it?"

Sources: Based on information from "Consumers Visit Retailers, Then Go Online for Cheaper Sources," *Adweek*, March 14, 2013; Ann Zimmerman, "Can Retailers Halt 'Showrooming'?" *Wall Street Journal*, April 11, 2012, p. B1; Dana Mattioli, "Retailers Try to Thwart Price Apps," *Wall Street Journal*, December 23, 2011; Ann Zimmerman, "Showdown over 'Showrooming,'" *Wall Street Journal*, January 23, 2012, p. B1; Laurie Sullivan, "Online Content Discovery Heightens Traditional Shopping," *MediaPost News*, November 15, 2012; and Bob Ankosko, "Retailers Embrace Showrooming," *Dealerscope*, January 2013.

Social Media and Mobile

We know that shoppers are using social media on their mobile devices, but how do retailers use social media? Many retailers have rushed to create Facebook pages and Twitter accounts, but fewer have figured out how to use them effectively. While 90 percent of the top 50 retailers (in the United States) have a presence on Twitter, a mere 29 percent use it to actively engage with consumers. One expert says that the number one mistake retailers make is to create a Twitter account and then ignore it: "More often than not they assign either an already overworked marketer or young, inexperienced, entry-level person to man the Twitter account. This person will do the obligatory tweets during the course of a day without any thought to content or more importantly, engagement." The solution, suggests a public relations expert, is that brands should view Twitter just as they do customer call centres—as a customer service communication tool that everyone sees.[20]

According to *Canadian Retailer* magazine, 47 percent of Canadians regularly use Facebook as part of their shopping experience, while 29 percent use Google, 23 percent use YouTube, and 13 percent use Twitter. Overall, 60 percent of Canadian consumers say they have used some form of social media while shopping, and 46 percent of those say their social media interactions have led them to make purchases. All this means that retailers who use social media for strategic marketing communications are having the desired effect—influencing consumer behaviour at point of purchase. Says Carol Deacon, senior vice-president of digital and loyalty marketing at Canadian Tire, "We're using social media as a marketing platform, a customer service tool, and a direct communication channel with our customers. Gaining customer feedback, loyalty, and engagement is a top priority, and social media plays a key role."[21]

David Cooper / GetStock.com

Exhibit 12.13 Pop-up stores: HBO opened a pop-up store in Toronto's trendy Queen West shopping district, where customers could purchase *Game of Thrones* merchandise and take pictures on a replica Iron Throne.

New Retail Forms and Retail Convergence

Forms of retail are continually evolving and changing, from the small town general store to catalogues, to suburban shopping malls, to big box stores, to e-commerce. One of the newest forms of retail is the *pop-up store*—a temporary retail outlet sometimes set up in a vacant building, sometimes in a tent, that allows retailers to showcase their products and create a buzz. Fashion retailer H&M set up a pop-up store in a large wooden crate on a beach in the Hague's coastal suburb of Scheveningen. And to capitalize on the success of the hit TV show *Game of Thrones*, HBO launched a pop-up store on Queen Street in Toronto, where customers could purchase *Thrones*-themed T-shirts, figurines, pint glasses, and puzzles, and take selfies sitting on a replica Iron Throne.[22]

Today's retail forms also appear to be converging. Increasingly, different types of retailers now sell the same products at the same prices to the same consumers. For example, you can buy brand name home appliances at department stores, discount stores, home-improvement stores, off-price retailers, electronics superstores, and a slew of online sites that all compete for the same customers. If you can't find the microwave oven you want at Sears, you can step across the street and find one for a better price at Lowe's or Best Buy—or just order one online from Amazon.com. This merging of consumers, products, prices, and retailers is called *retail convergence*. Such convergence means greater competition for retailers and greater difficulty in differentiating the product assortments of different types of retailers.

Green Retailing

Today's retailers are increasingly adopting environmentally sustainable practices. They are "greening up" their stores and operations, promoting more environmentally responsible products, launching programs to help customers be more responsible, and working with channel partners to reduce their environmental impact.

Retailers can get help with their green programs from a Canadian organization called Greening Retail, which conducts research, develops resources and programs, and facilitates demonstrations to help retailers implement environmental best practices. For example, they advise grocery stores, restaurants, and hotels on how they can reduce food waste. They also help retailers reduce their carbon footprint by developing partnerships with renewable energy providers. For example, they worked with Kohl's, an American department store with 1097 locations, to help them become the largest single retail host of solar electricity in North America.[23]

Other retailers have launched programs that help consumers make more environmentally responsible decisions. Staples' Easy on the Planet program "makes it easier to make a difference" by helping customers to identify green products sold in its stores and to recycle printer cartridges, mobile phones, computers, and other office technology products. Staples recycles some 30 million printer cartridges and 10 million pounds of old technology each year.[24]

Finally, as we learned in Chapter 11, many retailer channel partners are working to create more sustainable products, packaging, and distribution systems. For example,

Amazon.com works closely with the producers of many of the products it sells to reduce and simplify their packaging. And beyond its own substantial sustainability initiatives, Walmart wields its huge buying power to urge its army of suppliers to improve their environmental impact and practices. The retailer has even developed a worldwide Sustainable Product Index, by which it rates suppliers. It plans to translate the index into a simple rating for consumers to help them make more sustainable buying choices.

Green retailing yields both top- and bottom-line benefits. Sustainable practices lift a retailer's top line by attracting consumers looking to support environmentally friendly sellers and products. They also help the bottom line by reducing costs. For example, Amazon.com's reduced-packaging efforts increase customer convenience and eliminate "wrap rage" while at the same time saving packaging costs. And Kohl's earth-friendly and environmentally friendly buildings not only appeal to customers and help save the planet but also cost less to operate.

International Retailing

According to the National Retail Federation (an American trade association), the top 10 global retailers in terms of annual revenue are Walmart (U.S.), Costco (U.S.), Carrefour S.A. (France), Schwarz Unternehmens Treuhand (Germany), Tesco (U.K.), Kroger (U.S.), Metro Ag (Germany), Aldi Einkauf (Germany), The Home Depot, and Target. Canada's Loblaw Companies Limited ranks globally at number 31, and Empire Company Limited, the owner of Sobeys, comes in at number 48. Of the top 10 fastest growing global retailers, only one, Southeastern Grocers, is American. Three of the top five are Chinese retailers: JD.com Inc., Yonghui Superstores, and Chongqing Department Store Co.

Retailers with unique formats and strong brand positions are increasingly moving into other countries. Swedish retailer H&M operates over 3500 stores in 57 countries. British grocery and general merchandise retailer Tesco has stores in 12 countries across Asia and Europe. Starbucks and McDonald's can be found in nearly every country in the world, and mega-retailer Walmart now operates more than 6100 stores outside the United States. Of course, there are many American retailers that operate in Canada—including Staples, Victoria's Secret, The Gap, PetSmart, and Home Depot, just to name a few. And there are also many Canadian retailers that operate in the U.S.: Tim Hortons, Boston Pizza, Best Buy, Aldo, Roots, Fluevog Shoes, and Vancouver's Aritzia:

Exhibit 12.14 International retailing: Vancouver's Aritzia is expanding into the U.S., carefully choosing just the right locations for its unique stores.

Aritzia is a high-end women's fashion retailer founded in 1984 by CEO Brian Hill in Vancouver. Aritzia positions itself on unparalleled customer service both in-store and online, and "curates" a collection of fashion brands catering to shoppers who want beautiful, high-quality clothes that are on trend for every season. Aritzia's bricks-and-mortar stores feature natural materials and ambient lighting, creating a lounge-like atmosphere, and no two stores are the same. Its bilingual website, Aritzia.com, won Canada Post's e-commerce innovation award for best e-commerce shopping experience.

Aritzia's flagship U.S. store opened inside the famed Rockefeller Center at the corner of Fifth Avenue and 49th Street, the dividing point between "Lower Fifth," where the fast fashion retailers are, and "Upper Fifth," where you'll find high-end retailers like Saks. The location was carefully and strategically selected, and the interior was designed to mesmerize jaded New York shoppers. The store's interior features "verdant murals of fruits and nymph-like creatures . . . a central glass staircase . . . and a canopy of a fantastical, 30-foot-tall mushroom forest carved from cherrywood."

Natan Dvir/Polaris/Newscom

The store targets young women in their 20s and 30s, but their prices are well above chains like Forever 21, Zara, and H&M. Aritzia is after the style-savvy set who can't quite afford a closet full of luxury garments, but who aren't satisfied with a closet full of disposable fast fashion, either. "Aritzia is the bridge between upscale boutique shopping and fast fashion," says one retail expert.[25]

International retailing presents challenges as well as opportunities. Retailers can face dramatically different retail environments when crossing countries, continents, and cultures. Simply adapting the operations that work well in the home country is usually not enough to create success abroad. Just look at Target, which opened 120 stores across Canada in 2013, only to close all of them a year and a half later. Many U.S. retailers assume that expanding into Canada is like expanding into another state. And yet without understanding the Canadian market and the Canadian consumer, that strategy—or, rather, lack of it—is doomed to fail. The minimum wage is higher in Canada, so the cost of doing business is higher. Real estate is more limited than in the U.S., and its costs are higher. And moving goods across the border and around our very large country means dealing with customs and managing inventory. U.S. shoe retailer Zappos closed down its Canadian e-commerce operations as a result of the logistical challenges of shipping across the border.[26]

Wholesaling LO4

Wholesaling includes all the activities involved in selling goods and services to those buying them for resale or business use. Firms engaged *primarily* in wholesaling activities are called **wholesalers**. In Canada, national revenues from wholesale operations total approximately $865 billion per year. The industry is divided into nine major sub-sectors, including motor vehicles and parts; petroleum; and machinery, equipment, and supplies.[27]

Wholesalers buy mostly from producers and sell mostly to retailers, industrial consumers, and other wholesalers. As a result, many of the nation's largest and most important wholesalers are largely unknown to final consumers. Grainger, for example, is very well known and much valued by its more than 2 million business and institutional customers in 157 countries:

Grainger may be the biggest market leader you've never heard of. It's a $9 billion business that offers more than 1 million maintenance, repair, and operating (MRO) products from 3500 manufacturers in 30 countries to 2 million active customers. Through its branch network, service centres, sales reps, catalogue, and online and social media sites, Grainger links customers with the supplies they need to keep their facilities running smoothly—everything from light bulbs, cleaners, and display cases to nuts and bolts, motors, valves, power tools, test equipment, and safety supplies. Grainger's 711 branches, 28 strategically located distribution centres, nearly 21 500 employees, and innovative websites handle more than 115 000 transactions a day. Its customers include organizations ranging from factories, garages, and grocers to schools and military bases.

Grainger operates on a simple value proposition: to make it easier and less costly for customers to find and buy MRO supplies. It starts by acting as a one-stop shop for products needed to maintain facilities. On a broader level, it builds lasting relationships with customers by helping them find *solutions* to their overall MRO problems. Acting as consultants, Grainger sales reps help buyers with everything from improving their supply chain management to reducing inventories and streamlining warehousing operations.[28]

So, how come you've never heard of Grainger? Perhaps it's because the company operates in the not-so-glamorous world of MRO supplies, which are important to every business but not so

(sidebar)

Wholesaling
All the activities involved in selling goods and services to those buying for resale or business use.

Wholesaler
A firm engaged *primarily* in wholesaling activities.

Exhibit 12.15 Wholesaling: Many of the largest and most important wholesalers—like Grainger—are largely unknown to consumers. But they are very well known and much valued by the business customers they serve.

W. W. Grainger, Inc.

important to consumers. More likely, it's because Grainger is a wholesaler. And like most wholesalers, it operates behind the scenes, selling mostly to other businesses.

Why are wholesalers important to sellers? For example, why would a producer use wholesalers rather than selling directly to retailers or consumers? Simply put, wholesalers add value by performing one or more of the following channel functions:

- *Selling and promoting:* Wholesalers' sales forces help manufacturers reach many small customers at a low cost. The wholesaler has more contacts and is often more trusted by the buyer than the distant manufacturer.
- *Buying and assortment building:* Wholesalers can select items and build assortments needed by their customers, thereby saving much work.
- *Bulk breaking:* Wholesalers save their customers money by buying in carload lots and breaking bulk (breaking large lots into small quantities).
- *Warehousing:* Wholesalers hold inventories, thereby reducing the inventory costs and risks of suppliers and customers.
- *Transportation:* Wholesalers can provide quicker delivery to buyers because they are closer to buyers than are producers.
- *Financing:* Wholesalers finance their customers by giving credit, and they finance their suppliers by ordering early and paying bills on time.
- *Risk bearing:* Wholesalers absorb risk by taking title and bearing the cost of theft, damage, spoilage, and obsolescence.
- *Market information:* Wholesalers give information to suppliers and customers about competitors, new products, and price developments.
- *Management services and advice:* Wholesalers often help retailers train their salesclerks, improve store layouts and displays, and set up accounting and inventory control systems.

Types of Wholesalers

Wholesalers fall into three major groups: *merchant wholesalers, full-service wholesalers,* and *limited-service wholesalers*. Some of these we have already examined in Chapter 11, because all wholesalers are channel partners (though not all channel partners are wholesalers). The different types of wholesalers and the functions they perform are explained in Table 12.2.

Wholesaler Marketing Decisions LO5

Wholesalers now face growing competitive pressures, more-demanding customers, new technologies, and more direct-buying programs on the part of large industrial, institutional, and retail buyers. As a result, they have taken a fresh look at their marketing strategies. As with retailers, their marketing decisions include choices of segmentation and targeting, differentiation and positioning, and the marketing mix—product and service assortments, price, promotion, and distribution (see Figure 12.3).

Segmentation, Targeting, Differentiation, and Positioning Decisions Like retailers, wholesalers must segment and define their target markets and differentiate and position themselves effectively—they cannot serve everyone. They can choose a target group by size of customer (for example, large retailers only), type of customer (convenience stores only), the need for service (customers who need credit), or other factors. Within the target group, they can identify the more profitable customers, design stronger offers, and build better relationships with them. They can propose automatic reordering systems, establish management-training and advisory systems, or even sponsor a voluntary chain. They can discourage less-profitable customers by requiring larger orders or adding service charges to smaller ones.

TABLE 12.2 Major Types of Wholesalers

Type	Description
Merchant Wholesalers	Independently owned businesses that take title to all merchandise handled. There are full-service wholesalers and limited-service wholesalers.
Full-Service Wholesalers	Provide a full line of services: carrying stock, maintaining a sales force, offering credit, making deliveries, and providing management assistance. Full-service wholesalers include wholesale merchants and industrial distributors.
Wholesale merchants	Sell primarily to retailers and provide a full range of services. General merchandise wholesalers carry several merchandise lines, whereas general line wholesalers carry one or two lines in great depth. Specialty wholesalers specialize in carrying only part of a line.
Industrial distributors	Sell to manufacturers rather than to retailers. Provide several services, such as carrying stock, offering credit, and providing delivery. May carry a broad range of merchandise, a general line, or a specialty line.
Limited-Service Wholesalers	Offer fewer services than full-service wholesalers. Limited-service wholesalers are of several types:
Cash-and-carry wholesalers	Carry a limited line of fast-moving goods and sell to small retailers for cash. Normally do not deliver.
Truck wholesalers (or truck jobbers)	Perform primarily a selling and delivery function. Carry a limited line of semiperishable merchandise (such as milk, bread, snack foods), which is sold for cash as deliveries are made to supermarkets, small groceries, hospitals, restaurants, factory cafeterias, and hotels.
Producers' cooperatives	Farmer-owned members that assemble farm produce for sale in local markets. Producers' cooperatives often attempt to improve product quality and promote a co-op brand name, such as Sun-Maid raisins, Sunkist oranges, or Diamond nuts.
Mail-order or Web wholesalers	Send catalogues to or maintain websites for retail, industrial, and institutional customers featuring jewellery, cosmetics, specialty foods, and other small items. Their primary customers are businesses in small outlying areas.
Manufacturers' agents	Represent two or more manufacturers of complementary lines. Often used in such lines as apparel, furniture, and electrical goods. A manufacturer's agent is hired by small manufacturers who cannot afford their own field sales forces and by large manufacturers who use agents to open new territories or cover territories that cannot support full-time salespeople.
Selling agents	Have contractual authority to sell a manufacturer's entire output. The selling agent serves as a sales department and has significant influence over prices, terms, and conditions of sale. Found in product areas such as textiles, industrial machinery and equipment, coal and coke, chemicals, and metals.
Purchasing agents	Generally have a long-term relationship with buyers and make purchases for them, often receiving, inspecting, warehousing, and shipping the merchandise to buyers. Purchasing agents help clients obtain the best goods and prices available.
Commission merchants	Take physical possession of products and negotiate sales. Used most often in agricultural marketing by farmers who do not want to sell their own output. Take a truckload of commodities to a central market, sell it for the best price, deduct a commission and expenses, and remit the balance to the producers.
Manufacturers' and Retailers' Branches and Offices	Wholesaling operations conducted by sellers or buyers themselves rather than operating through independent wholesalers. Separate branches and offices can be dedicated to either sales or purchasing.
Sales Branches and Offices	Set up by manufacturers to improve inventory control, selling, and promotion. Sales branches carry inventory and are found in industries such as lumber and automotive equipment and parts. Sales offices do not carry inventory and are most prominent in the dry goods and notions industries.
Purchasing Offices	Perform a role similar to that of brokers or agents but are part of the buyer's organization. Many retailers set up purchasing offices in major market centres, such as Toronto and Vancouver.

FIGURE 12.3 Wholesaler Marketing Strategies

Marketing Mix Decisions Like retailers, wholesalers must decide on product and service assortments, prices, promotion, and place. Wholesalers add customer value though the *products and services* they offer. They are often under great pressure to carry a full line and stock enough for immediate delivery. But this practice can damage profits. Wholesalers today are cutting down on the number of lines they carry, choosing to carry only the more profitable ones. They are also rethinking which services count most in building strong customer relationships and which should be dropped or paid for by the customer. The key for companies is to find the mix of services most valued by their target customers.

Price is also an important wholesaler decision. Wholesalers usually mark up the cost of goods by a standard percentage—say, 20 percent. Expenses may run 17 percent of the gross margin, leaving a profit margin of 3 percent. In grocery wholesaling, the average profit margin is often less than 2 percent. And in times of economic downturn when retail and industrial customers face sales and margin declines, these customers turn to wholesalers, looking for lower prices. Wholesalers may, in turn, cut their margins on some lines to keep important customers. They may also ask suppliers for special price breaks in cases where they can turn them into an increase in the suppliers' sales.

Although *promotion* can be critical to wholesaler success, most wholesalers are not promotion minded. They use largely scattered and unplanned trade advertising, sales promotion, personal selling, and public relations. Many are behind the times in personal selling; they still see selling as a single salesperson talking to a single customer instead of as a team effort to sell, build, and service major accounts. Wholesalers also need to adopt some of the nonpersonal promotion techniques used by retailers. They need to develop an overall promotion strategy and make greater use of supplier promotion materials and programs. Digital and social media are playing an increasingly important role. For example, Grainger maintains an active presence on Facebook, YouTube, Twitter, LinkedIn, and Google+. It also provides a feature-rich mobile app. On its YouTube channel, Grainger lists more than 500 videos on topics ranging from the company and its products and services to keeping down inventory costs.

Finally, *distribution* (location) is important. Wholesalers must choose their locations, facilities, and Web locations carefully. There was a time when wholesalers could locate in low-rent, low-tax areas and invest little money in their buildings, equipment, and systems. Today, however, as technology zooms forward, such behaviour results in outdated systems for material handling, order processing, and delivery.

Instead, today's large and progressive wholesalers have reacted to rising costs by investing in automated warehouses and IT systems. Orders are fed from the retailer's information system directly into the wholesaler's, and the items are picked up by mechanical devices and automatically taken to a shipping platform where they are assembled. Most large wholesalers use technology to carry out accounting, billing, inventory control, and forecasting. Modern wholesalers are adapting their services to the needs of target customers and finding cost-reducingmethods of doing business. They are also transacting more business online. For example, e-commerce is Grainger's fastest growing sales channel, making Grainger the 15th largest e-tailer in the United States and Canada. Online purchasing now accounts for more than 30 percent of the wholesaler's total sales.

Trends in Wholesaling

Today's wholesalers face considerable challenges. The industry remains vulnerable to its most enduring trends—the need for ever-greater efficiency and the demands for lower prices. Progressive wholesalers constantly watch for better ways to meet the changing needs of their suppliers and customers. They recognize that their only reason for existence comes from adding value, which occurs by increasing the efficiency and effectiveness of the entire marketing channel.

As with other types of marketers, the goal is to build value-adding customer relationships. McKesson provides an example of progressive, value-adding wholesaling. The company is a wholesaler of pharmaceuticals, health and beauty care, home healthcare, and medical supply and equipment products. To survive, especially in a tight economic environment, McKesson has to be more cost effective than manufacturers' sales branches. Thus, the company has built efficient automated warehouses, established direct computer links with drug manufacturers, and created extensive online supply management and accounts receivable systems for customers. It offers retail pharmacists a wide range of online resources, including supply management assistance, catalogue searches, real-time order tracking, and an account management system. It has also created solutions such as automated pharmaceutical-dispensing machines that assist pharmacists by reducing costs and improving accuracy. Retailers can even use the McKesson systems to maintain prescription histories and medical profiles on their customers.

McKesson's medical-surgical supply and equipment customers receive a rich assortment of online solutions and supply management tools, including an online order management system and real-time information on products and pricing, inventory availability, and order status. According to McKesson, it adds value in the channel by providing "supply, information, and healthcare management products and services designed to reduce costs and improve quality across healthcare."[29]

The distinction between large retailers and large wholesalers continues to blur. Many retailers now operate formats such as wholesale clubs and supercentres that perform many wholesale functions. For example, Loblaw is both a retailer—operating stores under the banners Loblaws, Zehr's, Great Canadian Superstore, and No Frills—and a wholesaler, selling and distributing products to its retail stores.

Wholesalers will continue to increase the services they provide to retailers—retail pricing, cooperative advertising, marketing and management information services, accounting services, online transactions, and others. However, both the tight economy and the demand for increased services have put the squeeze on wholesaler profits. Wholesalers that do not find efficient ways to deliver value to their customers will soon drop by the wayside. Fortunately, the increased use of computerized, automated, and Internet-based systems will help wholesalers contain the costs of ordering, shipping, and inventory holding, thus boosting their productivity.

The Perfect Server

Technology has changed a lot of marketing functions, processes, and procedures, and maybe none more so than the actual transaction. And while some view online purchasing as the death of retail, others simply embrace it as its extension. After all, the exchange of value between buyer and seller still takes place—it just doesn't happen in person all the time as it did pre-dotcom.

Boston Pizza is a restaurant that has not only embraced online purchasing but is actually benefiting from it. "The real benefit is found by our customers," claims president and CEO Mark Pacinda. "Our online orders are 15 percent higher than those phoned in," he adds. This spells a significant shift in trend, particularly when you consider that the traditional pizza delivery model was entirely reliant on telephone. "Online is great for us because it's the perfect server. It knows who you are, it knows what you've ordered . . . [and] if there's something you haven't ordered, it prompts you."

That said, Boston Pizza's in-store experience isn't lagging. "If you want to go out and have a great time with your friends, we're a great place for that," says Pacinda. "But when you're compressed for time, and you have friends over and you can't all agree on where to go, we're a great option for that. Stay in and basically have the same meal you'd have at Boston Pizza, but have it delivered to your home."

"Takeout and delivery are our fastest growing segments," he continues. "I think it's because Canadians are just so challenged for time." Certainly the convenience factor is the chief driver of the shift in purchasing from offline (in-store) to online. This trend is what has driven the success of companies like Amazon and forever changed the retail landscape. But make no mistake: It's still retail, as it still completes the final step of the marketing channel from producer to intermediary to consumer.

QUESTIONS

1. Why was it important for Boston Pizza to invest in an online ordering system?
2. Why do you think online ordering has surpassed telephone ordering at Boston Pizza?
3. Why does Mark Pacinda call online ordering the "perfect server"?

REVIEWING THE CONCEPTS

 Explain the role of retailers in the distribution channel, and describe the major types of retailers.

Retailing includes all the activities involved in selling products or services directly to final consumers for their personal, nonbusiness use. Many institutions—manufacturers, wholesalers, and retailers—do retailing. But most retailing is done by *retailers*, businesses whose sales come primarily from retailing. In Canada, jobs in retail account for the largest labour force segment in the country. Despite the availability of online shopping, most retailing today (and most consumer purchasing) is still done in some type of traditional bricks-and-mortar retail locations.

Retail outlets can be classified in terms of the *amount of service* they offer, the breadth and depth of their *product lines*, the *relative prices* they charge, and how they are *organized*. Retailers such as convenience stores and discount stores are typically *self-serve retailers*, which allow customers to perform their own locate-compare-select process. *Limited-service retailers*, such as Home Depot, Canadian Tire, and Best Buy, provide some sales assistance because they carry products that often require the customer to seek expert advice and information. In *full-service retailers*, salespeople assist customers in every phase of the shopping process. Full-service retailers typically serve a higher-end market, or sell luxury goods. Retailers may carry narrow product lines with deep assortments within those lines, like shoe stores, or they may carry a wide product line, like department stores. *Service retailers* primarily sell services, and include hotels, banks, airlines, restaurants, and movie theatres.

Retailers can also be classified according to the prices they charge. Most retailers charge regular prices and offer normal-quality goods and customer service. Others offer higher-quality goods and service at higher prices. *Discount stores* such as Dollarama and Giant Tiger sell standard merchandise at lower prices on a daily basis, that is, without "sales." And *off-price retailers* are stores that buy at less-than-regular wholesale prices and charge consumers less than retail. *Factory outlets* and *warehouse clubs* are also off-price retailers. Finally, although many retail stores are independently owned, others band together in organizations: *corporate chains*, *voluntary chains*, *retailer cooperatives*, or *franchise organizations*.

 List and describe the major marketing decisions made by retailers.

Just as with product marketers, retailers must make marketing decisions about *segmentation and targeting*, *store dif-* *ferentiation and positioning*, and the *retail marketing mix*. Retailers must first segment and define their target markets and then decide how they will differentiate and position themselves in these markets. Until they define and profile their markets, retailers cannot make consistent decisions about product assortment, services, pricing, advertising, store decor, or any of the other decisions that must support their positions. Retailers must also make decisions about their *product assortment*, *services mix*, and *store atmosphere*. Today's successful retailers carefully orchestrate virtually every aspect of the consumer's in-store experience.

A retailer's *price decisions* must fit its target market and positioning, product and service assortment, the competition, and economic factors. *EDLP (everyday low pricing)* is a pricing strategy practised by retailers such as Walmart and Dollarama. Other retailers practise *high-low pricing*—charging higher prices on an everyday basis, coupled with frequent sales and other price promotions, to increase store traffic, create a low-price image, or attract customers who will buy other goods at full prices. Retailers also use any or all of the five promotion tools—advertising, personal selling, sales promotion, public relations (PR), and direct marketing—to reach consumers, and many retailers interact with customers online and through social media. *Place* (or distribution) decisions for retailers mean selecting locations that are accessible to the target market in areas that are consistent with the retailer's positioning.

LO3 **Identify and discuss the major trends and developments in contemporary retailing.**

New retail forms continue to emerge to meet new situations and consumer needs, but the life cycle of new retail forms is getting shorter. To remain successful, retailers must continually monitor the new trends and new technology available to them, and keep evolving. A trend that began with retailers like the Hard Rock Café is *experiential retailing*—the idea that the retail environment should not be simply a display of products for sale, but rather an experience that engages the customer. Retailers must keep up with the latest in *technology*, such as automated checkout systems, RFID tags, Bluetooth, mobile devices, and even wearable devices that interact with the retailer's wireless networks. The latest buzzword in retail marketing is *shoppable media*, meaning video or print vehicles that encourage customers to immediately purchase products using various technologies, especially their personal mobile devices.

The *increasing use of gift cards* is influencing the retail landscape. More than just generating sales, gift cards attract new customers and build brand awareness. With *shopper marketing*, retailers use point-of-purchase promotions and in-store advertising to encourage favourable in-store purchase decisions. *Online retail* continues to grow, with more than half of Canadians buying online to the tune of $19 billion per year. The influence of retailers' websites on traditional retailing has led to a new phenomenon called *showrooming*, in which consumers are increasingly treating bricks-and-mortar retailers as showrooms, where they view and test products before leaving to buy them elsewhere or online for a lower price. While over 60 percent of Canadians use *social media* in some manner to enhance their shopping experience, retailers are still struggling with how to use it effectively to engage with consumers.

New forms of retail include the *pop-up store*, a temporary retail outlet sometimes set up in a vacant building, sometimes in a tent, that allows retailers to showcase their products and create a buzz. And retail forms also appear to be converging. Increasingly, different types of retailers now sell the same products at the same prices to the same consumers. Today's retailers are increasingly adopting environmentally sustainable practices, or *green retailing*, by developing programs to help customers be more environmentally responsible and working with channel partners to reduce their environmental impact. Finally, retailers with unique formats and strong brand positions are increasingly moving into other countries. *International retailing* presents challenges as well as opportunities. Retailers can face dramatically different retail environments when crossing countries, continents, and cultures. Simply adapting the operations that work well in the home country is usually not enough to create success abroad.

 Explain the role of wholesalers in the distribution channel, and describe the major types of wholesalers.

Wholesaling includes all the activities involved in selling goods and services to those buying them for resale or business use. Firms engaged primarily in wholesaling activities are called *wholesalers*. In Canada, national revenues from wholesale operations total approximately $865 billion per year. The industry is divided into nine major sub-sectors, including motor vehicles and parts; petroleum; and machinery, equipment, and supplies. Wholesalers buy mostly from producers and sell mostly to retailers, industrial consumers, and other wholesalers. As a result, many of the nation's largest and most important wholesalers are largely unknown to final consumers.

Wholesalers add value by performing one or more of the following channel functions: selling and promoting, buying and assortment building, bulk breaking, warehousing, transportation, financing, risk bearing, providing market information, and providing management services and advice. The major types of wholesalers are *merchant wholesalers* (independently owned businesses that take title to merchandise), *full-service wholesalers* (which provide a full line of services, carry stock, and maintain a sales force), and *limited-service wholesalers* (which offer fewer services than full-service wholesalers). Limited-service wholesalers include cash-and-carry wholesalers, truck jobbers, producers' cooperatives, mail-order or Web wholesalers, manufacturers' agents, selling agents, purchasing agents, and commission merchants.

LO5 **List and describe the major marketing decisions made by wholesalers.**

As with retailers, wholesalers' marketing decisions include choices of segmentation and targeting, differentiation and positioning, and the marketing mix—product and service assortments, price, promotion, and distribution. Wholesalers must segment and define their target markets and differentiate and position themselves effectively; they cannot serve everyone. They can choose a target group by size of customer (for example, large retailers only), type of customer (convenience stores only), the need for service (customers who need credit), or other factors. Wholesalers must decide how to add customer value through the *products and services* they offer.

Price is also an important wholesaler decision. Wholesalers typically operate with standard margins, but in times of economic downturn when retail and industrial customers face sales and margin declines, these customers turn to wholesalers for lower prices. Although *promotion* can be critical to wholesaler success, most wholesalers are not promotion minded. They use largely scattered and unplanned trade advertising, sales promotion, personal selling, and public relations. Many are behind the times in personal selling; they still see selling as a single salesperson talking to a single customer rather than as a team effort to sell, build, and service major accounts. Of course, *distribution* (location) is important. Wholesalers must choose their locations, facilities, and Web locations carefully. As with other types of marketers, the goal of wholesalers is to build value-adding customer relationships. They recognize that their only reason for existence comes from adding value, which occurs by increasing the efficiency and effectiveness of the entire marketing channel.

MyMarketingLab

Study, practise, and explore real marketing situations with these helpful resources:

- **Interactive Lesson Presentations:** Work through interactive presentations and assessments to test your knowledge of marketing concepts.
- **Study Plan:** Check your understanding of chapter concepts with self-study quizzes.
- **Dynamic Study Modules:** Work through adaptive study modules on your computer, tablet, or mobile device.
- **Simulations:** Practise decision-making in simulated marketing environments.

DISCUSSION QUESTIONS

1. Choose a retailer you are familiar with, and explain what type of retailer it is and how you would classify it in terms of its product lines, amount of service, and relative prices.

2. Define corporate chain, voluntary chain, retailer cooperative, and franchise, and give an example of each.

3. Explain how retailers must make decisions about the four *P*s of marketing.

4. What are the major trends in retailing today? How do you think retailing will evolve and change in the next five years?

5. Explain how wholesalers add value in the channel of distribution.

6. Name and describe the three major groups of wholesalers.

CRITICAL THINKING EXERCISES

1. Explain the phenomenon of showrooming. If you were a marketing manager at an independent electronics retailer, what would you do to combat this phenomenon?

2. Retailers that accept credit cards pay a "swipe fee" to credit-card issuers such as Visa and MasterCard ranging from 1 to 3 percent of the purchase. Retailers typically absorb that cost, but some want to pass the fee on to consumers. Look up the Code of Conduct for the Credit and Debit Card Industry in Canada. Is there a law or rule that prohibits retailers from adding a surcharge to credit purchases?

3. Think of an example of a retailer that recently went out of business, or that is currently in financial trouble.

Research what the media have reported about the reasons for the retailer's troubles. In your opinion, what could the retailer have done, or what should it do, to remain successful?

4. Study the Grainger website and research Grainger through other sources. Prepare a brief report or presentation that answers the following questions: What is the extent of Grainger's operations in Canada? Who are its major customers? What products does Grainger supply to those customers? Are there any other channel members in the supply chain between Grainger and its customers? Who are Grainger's competitors?

ONLINE, MOBILE, AND SOCIAL MEDIA

According to Nielsen, more than 50 percent of mobile phone consumers own smartphones. Many of them use free Wi-Fi when available for faster connections and to reduce data usage charges. But even when they don't log on to the Wi-Fi, the device continues to search, giving information on users' locations. By using the signals emitted by shoppers' smartphones, retailers can keep tabs on shoppers, knowing where they are and what they're searching for on their phones' browsers. Retailers can learn in which aisles shoppers are most likely to check online prices at retailers such as Amazon.com and can send an alert to a sales representative. "Heat mapping" identifies traffic patterns and locations attracting the greatest number of shoppers checking the Internet. This gives retailers an idea of which products are most vulnerable to showrooming—the practice of shoppers visiting stores to learn about and try products and later purchasing them for less online.

QUESTIONS

1. What is *shopper marketing*, and how might retailers use Wi-Fi technology to implement it?

2. What will be the likely response as more shoppers learn that retailers gather information about their movements without their knowledge?

THINK LIKE A MARKETING MANAGER

When Target entered the Canadian market in 2013 it hired Canadians to act as buyers, marketing managers, and customer service representatives—and yet despite the company's best efforts, Target was not successful in Canada. Now Nordstrom is entering the Canadian market, although it's taking a very different approach.

QUESTIONS

1. Research what the experts say were the reasons for Target's failure in Canada. Make a list of the major problems and what, in retrospect, it should have done differently.

2. Find out how many Nordstrom stores are currently open in Canada, where they are located, and what the plans are for opening new locations. Assuming Nordstrom is still successful in Canada, what did it do differently from Target that accounts for this success?

3. If you were a marketing manager at one of the Nordstrom locations in Canada, responsible only for that store, which retailer marketing decisions would you have control over, and which would come from the head office? What would you do at your store to help ensure its success?

MARKETING ETHICS

In order for retailers to take advantage of social media, wearable, and other technologies, consumers have to be willing to allow retailers to access their devices. And so in order to get the data that will help them customize offers, retailers must first gain the trust of their customers. The challenge is this: There's a lot of distrust going around. Consumers are skeptical of what will happen to their information should they enter it into an online form, or put it in an app, or even give it to a sales associate in a retail store. In fact, 63 percent of Canadians in a recent survey said they're concerned about having their personal information hacked while using a smartphone. And 51 percent said they were *not* okay with retailers knowing their location through their mobile devices. Without the trust of consumers, location-based apps, beacons, and other devices are useless to retailers.

QUESTIONS

1. Find and read the CMA's code of ethics, especially the guidelines for the collection and use of personal information. If consumers walk into a store with their mobile devices turned on and location information enabled, is the retailer obligated to inform them that their movements in the store might be tracked?

2. If the answer to question 1 is yes, how can, or how should, the retailer do so? As a consumer, what would you expect or want them to do?

MARKETING BY THE NUMBERS

Retailers need merchandise to make sales. In fact, a retailer's inventory is its biggest asset. Not stocking enough merchandise can result in lost sales, but carrying too much inventory increases costs and lowers margins. Both circumstances reduce profits. One measure of a reseller's inventory management effectiveness is its *stockturn rate* (also called *inventory turnover rate* for manufacturers). The key to success in retailing is realizing a large volume of sales on as little inventory as possible while maintaining enough stock to meet customer demands.

QUESTIONS

1. Refer to Appendix 3, Marketing by the Numbers, and determine the stockturn rate of a retailer carrying an average inventory at a cost of $350 000, with a cost of goods sold of $800 000.

2. If this company's stockturn rate was 3.5 last year, is the stockturn rate calculated in question 1 better or worse?

MABEL'S LABELS: MOVING FROM ONLINE TO WALMART

Case prepared by David Rose, Conrad Business, Entrepreneurship & Technology Centre, University of Waterloo

While many bricks-and-mortar retailers are developing multichannel marketing systems by adding online options to their distribution strategies, one Canadian online retailer is moving in the other direction. Mabel's Labels, a Hamilton, Ontario, company that manufactures and markets personalized labels for children's clothing, lunch boxes, and other items, has started selling its products through Walmart Canada.

Mabel's Labels began when four moms—Julie Cole, Julie Ellis, Tricia Mumby, and Cynthia Esp—grew tired of their kids coming home from daycare, school, or camp without all their belongings and decided to come up with a solution to the problem. They created a line of personalized labels that can be affixed to clothes, lunch boxes, backpacks, water bottles, and anything else kids tote around and often leave behind. Ten years later, the business had sold more than 50 million labels in 97 countries through its website, and they have registered the trademark for the slogan, "Labels for the stuff kids lose!" They have mastered social media, hired public relations companies to generate attention in mom-oriented media, won plenty of business awards, and built an incredibly loyal customer base. Many celebrity moms have used Mabel's Labels, including Jennifer Garner, Rachel Weisz, Reese Witherspoon, Gwyneth Paltrow, and Victoria Beckham.

Despite the devoted online following, the move to sell products through retailers was in response to the needs of the market, particularly the calls from customers needing labels quickly. As Julie Cole explains, "We all know that feeling—you've procrastinated ordering and your child leaves for camp TOMORROW. Now when you're having a last-minute panic, you'll have the convenience of being able to pick something up in a nearby retail location."

The move to Walmart also provides a convenient way for parents to experience and access the products. The labels are now more widely available to busy moms on the go, who can grab the labels along with other essentials ahead of sending kids off to camp or back to school. People who don't feel comfortable shopping online can now get their hands on Mabel's Labels, too. The partners worried about cannibalizing their own online business by going the retail route, but after conducting market research and focus groups they determined that the two channels served different markets.

A NEW PRODUCT FOR A NEW CHANNEL

Mabel's Labels come in a variety of styles, including sticky labels, clothing labels, shoe tags, and bag tags. All labels can be personalized by choosing the label style and a colourful design and adding the child's name. This highly individualized approach works well in an online environment but created a major challenge when the partners decided to make their labels available in a retail setting. One approach they considered was to stock the most popular names in spinning racks at the stores, the way some other personalized products are displayed, but they were concerned about the potential challenges of managing that system. Cole says, "How do you keep track? Oh, the Jennifers are sold out there and the Alexes are all gone there. It was too overwhelming."

Mabel's Labels' solution was to create a new line of products for the retail channel. After two years of development, they created Write Away!, a new line of peel-and-stick labels that are written on with marker and a clear overlay that is pressed over top as a lamination, making the labels dishwasher and microwave proof. They sell at Walmart for $10.47 for a package of 30.

WORKING WITH WALMART

The partners were intimidated at the thought of approaching such a big retailer, but they had an incredible experience. From the outset, Walmart Canada was extremely open to learning about an offering from a small Canadian manufacturer, especially one with a strong online presence but no retail presence. The partners discovered that, for Walmart buyers, it's important to stay in touch with what Canadian moms are buying online and what brands they care about. Businesses owned by women are also a big focus for Walmart. Cole describes their reception by Walmart: "Here's little Mabel and big, old Walmart. But they responded really warmly to us. They recognized the value of the product and knew their customers would love it."

DEVELOPING NEW CAPABILITIES

Retail was a whole new territory for the partners, and so it was hard for them to even know where to start. Walmart could move vast quantities of their Write Away! Labels, but what they didn't realize at first was how thoroughly a

Walmart listing would transform their business—and how quickly. From establishing a new supply chain from China to decoding the world of third-party logistics, Mabel's Labels had just four months to reinvent the way it did business to meet Walmart's deadline for the 2012 back-to-school season. "It was as if we were starting a second company," says Cole.

The firm approached this task systematically, doing intensive preparations under the guidance of a key adviser with experience dealing with Walmart and carefully executing the sweeping changes needed to become a Walmart supplier. The Mabel's Labels team's copious preparations helped it overcome the "be careful what you wish for" moment many Walmart suppliers experience when they realize how much they'll have to do to meet the retailer's exacting standards. They first needed to develop realistic sales projections. From there, they determined the production volumes and capital they'd need and mapped out how they'd pick an overseas manufacturer to produce enough labels for 275 Walmart Canada stores. A month after the pitch meeting with Walmart, the two parties struck a deal that met Walmart's two key requests. One request was that Mabel's Labels charge $12 a pack for the labels on its website, 15 percent more than the $10.47 Walmart would sell them for. ("They need their everyday low prices," says Cole.) The other was that Walmart would have exclusivity on the Write Away! line among big box stores for one year.

With the deal done, two of the Mabel's Labels partners flew to China to tour three factories recommended by manufacturers they respected. The partners had each plant manufacture a limited run of the labels and then went through a round of quality testing before making a selection. Next, they hired a China-based company recommended by the Canadian consulate in Hong Kong to conduct continuous quality control. As well, they hired a third-party firm in Canada to handle electronic data interchange, the paperless system that Walmart uses to issue purchase orders, receive invoices, process credit memos, and handle other administrative tasks. Finally, they hired a third-party logistics firm to manage shipping the labels from China, taking them through customs, unloading the container, packing smaller shipments, and trucking them to Walmart warehouses across Canada.

They also had to come up with the financing to make all of this happen months before the products hit Walmart's shelves and long before the label maker saw a cent. Cole says that the upfront preparatory work they'd done for the Walmart pitch prepared the partners for how much credit their firm would need. They were careful to have this financing in place before even pitching to Walmart.

Cole says that the Walmart deal is a huge step for the company, and will mean some hiring. "I can hardly believe it. The labels are on the shelves as of last week. I have never been to Walmart so many times in my life," she jokes. "It was a huge investment, but the outlay of time and money is already paying off."

The strong performance of the Write Away! line in the first few months of sales in Canada helped persuade Walmart to carry the labels in some of its U.S. stores for the 2013 back-to-school season. Plans are also underway for Mabel's Labels products to soon be available in Target.

Sources: Company website, www.mabelslabels.com; Mabel's Labels press releases published on *Market Wire*, December 8, 2009, and June 25, 2012; Eleanor Beaton, "Wowing Wal-Mart (W100 Profile)," PROFITGuide.com, October 1, 2012; Francine Kopun, "Mabel's Labels at Wal-Mart Canada," Moneyville.ca, June 25, 2012; Julie Cole, "Big News for Mabel's Labels and Other Local Mompreneurs," YummyMummyClub.ca, June 20, 2012; Meredith MacLeod, "Mabel Sticking to Walmart," HamiltonBusiness.com, June 26, 2012; and Julie Cole, "The Mabel's Labels Story," RaiseTheHammer.org, June 6, 2012.

QUESTIONS FOR DISCUSSION

1. Why has Mabel's Labels been so successful selling exclusively online?

2. Can Mabel's Labels maintain its competitive advantage when selling through retail stores? How can it reduce the threat of other competitors entering the write-on label market?

3. Should Mabel's Labels be concerned about Write Away! labels cannibalizing its online products? Should it continue to sell a different product in stores and online?

4. Channel conflict does not appear to be an issue yet, provided Walmart is able to sell at a retail price lower than Mabel's online prices. What steps does Mabel's Labels need to take to prevent channel conflict once it starts to sell through other retail chains?

5. Mabel's Labels' website was very focused on moms, its target market. Now that products are available in retail stores, should it consider targeting other segments that might have different uses for write-on labels?

AFTER STUDYING THIS CHAPTER, YOU SHOULD BE ABLE TO

1 define the five promotion mix tools for communicating customer value

2 discuss the changing communications landscape and the need for integrated marketing communications

3 describe how advertising objectives are set and how advertising strategy is developed

4 explain how advertising effectiveness is evaluated and the role of the advertising agency

5 explain how companies use public relations to communicate with their publics

Communicating Customer Value: Advertising and Public Relations

PREVIEWING THE CONCEPTS

We'll forge ahead now into the last of the marketing mix tools—promotion. Companies must do more than just create customer value. They must also use promotion to clearly and persuasively communicate that value. You'll find that promotion is not a single tool but rather a mix of several tools. Ideally, under the concept of *integrated marketing communications*, the company will carefully coordinate these promotion elements to deliver a clear, consistent, and compelling message about the organization and its products. We'll begin by introducing you to the various promotion mix tools. Next, we'll examine the rapidly changing communications environment and the need for integrated marketing communications. Finally, we'll look more closely at two of the promotion tools—advertising and public relations. In Chapter 14, we'll visit two other promotion mix tools—sales promotion and personal selling. Then, in Chapter 15, we'll explore direct and online marketing.

Let's start by looking at a good integrated marketing communications campaign—autoTRADER.ca's "The Most Cars in One Place" campaign. From TV and radio to engaging websites and a unique Facebook app, the campaign employed a rich mix of promotional elements.

autoTRADER.ca: THE MOST CARS IN ONE PLACE

Looking to buy or sell a car? Your first inclination might be to check out listings on Craigslist or Kijiji. But before the world went digital, for over 25 years autoTRADER magazine was the go-to-source for Canadians in the market to buy or sell vehicles. The magazine dominated the marketplace—that is, it did until the Internet came along. Then things changed rapidly for the company. More and more consumers were finding information online, and new websites such as Craigslist and Kijiji provided consumers with thousands of vehicles for them to view. Gradually, autoTRADER's dominance eroded as consumers chose digital information over print. So the company made the tough decision to go 100 percent digital to capture a larger slice of the dealer market, boost customer traffic, and work toward recapturing the number one position as the resource for consumers looking to buy and sell automobiles.

However, autoTRADER.ca began its move to digital with a shaky start. In 2011, its traffic performance was in a downward spiral, declining on average 4 percent per month. In just seven months, the site experienced a decline of over 1.7 million visitors, which represented

Practice on MyMarketingLab
Attribution Modeling Advertising Effectiveness

Practice on MyMarketingLab
Price Waterfall Analysis

Practice on MyMarketingLab
Assessing Salesforce Effectiveness

a 31 percent decrease in traffic. The company desperately needed to reinvigorate the brand and breathe life into a struggling digital endeavour.

In order to deal with stiff competition from Craigslist and Kijiji, the company enlisted the help of advertising agency DDB Canada, which identified a number of core business objectives. First, the ad agency wanted to attract at least 500 000 visitors per month in 2012. They also wanted to increase private seller listings to the site by 25 percent and dealer listings by 10 percent during the new ad campaign. Finally, the new ad campaign was intended to drive traffic growth by at least 5 percent, especially in western Canada, where site traffic levels were the lowest.

The overall communication objective of this new campaign was to make autoTRADER.ca not only relevant in the minds of Canadian car buyers and sellers, but also the number one digital automotive destination in the country. When examining autoTRADER.ca's strengths, DDB Canada quickly realized that it had the largest car inventory of any digital site in the country. This factor became a major selling feature in the new ad campaign. To ensure that it was a valuable feature to consumers, the advertising agency conducted a qualitative research study, which concluded that a large inventory was a very strong motivator for consumers because it made them feel as if they had "left no stone unturned" in their quest to find the perfect car.

The new tagline, "The Most Cars in One Place," quickly became the driving force behind the new ad campaign. No matter where or how the brand was going to be communicated, it would always be clear: autoTRADER.ca was the online destination with "The Most Cars in One Place." The new campaign incorporated a number of different media, including TV, radio, online, social media, public relations, and business-to-business communications. The campaign launched across the country in both French and English and used humour to get the message across to consumers. For example, one TV ad shows a young couple enjoying a dinner date. All is going well, and then the conversation turns to "children" and "the future." The man realizes he has a potential relationship with an attractive woman and quickly agrees that children are part of his future. As he glances outside at his obviously impractical-for-a-family Hummer, he quickly lists it on autoTRADER.ca. The next shot shows a huge bodybuilder looking at his perfect new automobile, the Hummer, on a laptop. The goal: to convince consumers that no matter what the reason for selling or buying, autoTRADER.ca is where to shop for or sell a vehicle online.

Other forms of media soon followed the TV campaign. The firm used radio ads specific to Calgary and Edmonton, where the online adoption of autoTRADER.ca lagged behind the rest of the country. Standard online banner ads reinforced the "most cars" message and reminded consumers that autoTRADER.ca specialized in vehicles only, not the wide variety of listings found on Craigslist or Kijiji. The campaign also used geotargeted homepage takeovers on YouTube and MSN.ca to show potential consumers the breadth of vehicle selection on autoTRADER.ca. As a consumer scrolled over the vehicles, they were provided with a real-time count of how many of a certain vehicle type were available within a 100-kilometre radius of their current location.

The company also created a unique Facebook application labelled "the auto-LYZER." This app was designed to help Canadians discover three automobiles for sale on autoTRADER.ca that best suited their personality and social life. The app analyzed real-time Facebook data by looking at an individual's lifestyle, interests, social activities, and Facebook friends' opinions via existing posts. This information was then compiled and used to recommend cars currently for sale that would best match the customer's personality.

autoTRADER.ca's promotional activities were equally aggressive toward auto dealers. The site's landing page was developed to introduce dealers to the new message and strategy and to convince them that the company was investing in their current and future business success.

This new marketing campaign rolled out in February 2012 with a national TV campaign coupled with the B2B initiative targeting dealers. autoTRADER.ca simultaneously engaged in heavy public relations to bring media attention to the new campaign. The company followed up a month later with the online banner ads, then a social media push and the introduction of the autoLYZER app in May.

The results of this campaign were astounding. Since the launch of this integrated marketing campaign (IMC), website traffic increased over 18 percent, with a 27 percent increase in growth in monthly unique visitors. From February to July, the site logged 3.6 million unique visits. Not only were consumers visiting the site, but the results proved that they were interested in what the company had to offer, as page views were up over 76 percent from the previous year.

Unaided awareness of the autoTRADER.ca brand also increased post-campaign. The launch of the autoLYZER app and the publicity it generated resulted in substantial interest in the brand. Dealer listings on the site increased over 18 percent and private listings skyrocketed, up 169 percent since the launch of the campaign. Even in Edmonton and Calgary, where Web traffic was the lowest, autoTRADER.ca saw an immediate spike in Web traffic of close to 15 percent. The company now has over 34 000 Likes on Facebook and over 7700 followers on Twitter.

The national campaign for autoTRADER.ca was an overwhelming success for the company and the ad agency responsible for it. In fact, DDB Canada was the Grand Prix winner at the 2013 CASSIES awards, which recognize the best business-building communication campaigns in Canada. This unique and highly creative campaign certainly repositioned autoTRADER.ca as the number one destination for car buyers and sellers and also generated triple-digit growth in consumer traffic for the website.

However, autoTRADER.ca did not rest on a single successful ad campaign. In 2014, it added a News and Features section to the site to target car buyers earlier on in the decision-making process. The company also partnered with Yahoo to start placing ads across Yahoo's pages and apps, resulting in an average click-through rate of 2.4 percent and nearly 400 000 impressions for one of its top-performing ads. This ad campaign continued to drive visitors to the site, resulting in 250 000 unique visitors in only two months. Then, in 2015, autoTRADER.ca hired a new advertising firm, CO-OP Advertising, to create a fresh campaign to be rolled out in that year in the hopes of building on its market position as "Canada's #1 automotive marketplace."[1]

BUILDING good customer relationships calls for more than just developing a good product, pricing it attractively, and making it available to target customers. Companies must also *communicate* their value propositions to customers, and what they communicate should not be left to chance. All communications must be planned and blended into carefully integrated programs. Just as good communication is important in building and maintaining any other kind of relationship, it is a crucial element in a company's efforts to engage customers and build profitable customer relationships.

The Promotion Mix LO1

Promotion mix (or marketing communications mix)
The specific blend of promotion tools that the company uses to engage consumers, persuasively communicate customer value, and build customer relationships.

Advertising
Any paid form of nonpersonal presentation and promotion of ideas, goods, or services by an identified sponsor.

Sales promotion
Short-term incentives to encourage the purchase or sale of a product or service.

Personal selling
Personal customer interactions by the firm's sales force for the purpose of making sales and building customer relationships.

Public relations (PR)
Building good relations with the company's various publics by obtaining favourable publicity, building up a good corporate image, and handling or heading off unfavourable rumours, stories, and events.

Direct and digital marketing
Engaging and interacting directly with carefully targeted individual consumers and consumer communities to both obtain an immediate response and cultivate lasting customer relationships.

←◉—**Simulate** on MyMarketingLab
IMC

A company's total **promotion mix**—also called its **marketing communications mix**—consists of the specific blend of advertising, public relations, personal selling, sales promotion, and direct marketing tools that the company uses to engage consumers, persuasively communicate customer value, and build customer relationships. The five major promotion tools are defined as follows:[2]

- **Advertising**: Any paid form of nonpersonal presentation and promotion of ideas, goods, or services by an identified sponsor.
- **Sales promotion**: Short-term incentives to encourage the purchase or sale of a product or service.
- **Personal selling**: Personal customer interactions by the firm's sales force for the purpose of making sales and building customer relationships.
- **Public relations**: Building good relations with the company's various publics by obtaining favourable publicity, building up a good corporate image, and handling or heading off unfavourable rumours, stories, and events.
- **Direct and digital marketing**: Engaging directly with carefully targeted individual consumers and customer communities to both obtain an immediate response and build lasting customer relationships.

Each category involves specific promotional tools that are used to communicate with customers. For example, *advertising* includes broadcast, print, Internet, mobile, outdoor, and other forms. *Sales promotion* includes discounts, coupons, displays, and demonstrations. *Personal selling* includes sales presentations, trade shows, and incentive programs. *Public relations (PR)* includes press releases, sponsorships, events, and webpages. And *direct and digital marketing* includes direct mail, catalogues, online and social media, mobile marketing, and more.

At the same time, marketing communication goes beyond these specific promotion tools. The product's design, its price, the shape and colour of its package, and the stores that sell it—*all* communicate something to buyers. Thus, although the promotion mix is the company's primary communications and engagement activity, the entire marketing mix—promotion *as well as* product, price, and place—must be coordinated for greatest impact.

Integrated Marketing Communications LO2

In past decades, marketers perfected the art of mass marketing: selling highly standardized products to masses of customers. In the process, they developed effective mass-media communications techniques to support these strategies. Large companies now routinely invest millions or even billions of dollars in television, magazine, or other mass-media advertising, reaching tens of millions of customers with a single ad. Today, however, marketing managers face some new marketing communications realities. Perhaps no other area of marketing is changing so profoundly as marketing communications, creating both exciting and anxious times for marketing communicators.

The New Marketing Communications Model

Several major factors are changing the face of today's marketing communications. First, *consumers* are changing. In this digital, wireless age, consumers are better informed and more communications empowered. Rather than relying on marketer-supplied information, they can use the Internet, social media, and other technologies to find information on their own. They can connect easily with other consumers to exchange brand-related information or even create their own brand messages.

Second, *marketing strategies* are changing. As mass markets have fragmented, marketers are shifting away from mass marketing. More and more, they are developing focused marketing programs designed to build closer relationships with customers in more narrowly defined micromarkets.

Finally, sweeping advances in *digital technology* are causing remarkable changes in the ways companies and customers communicate with each other. The digital age has spawned a host of new information and communication tools—from smartphones and tablets to satellite and cable television systems to the many faces of the Internet (brand sites, email, blogs, social media and online communities, the mobile Web, and so much more). These explosive developments have had a dramatic impact on marketing communications. Just as mass marketing once gave rise to a new generation of mass-media communications, the new digital and social media have given birth to a more targeted, social, and engaging marketing communications model.

Although network television, magazines, newspapers, and other traditional mass media remain very important, their dominance is declining. In their place, advertisers are now adding a broad selection of more-specialized and highly targeted media to engage smaller customer segments with more-personalized, interactive content. The new media range from specialty cable television channels and made-for-the-Web videos to online display ads, Internet catalogues, email and texting, blogs, mobile coupons and other content, and social media such as Twitter, Facebook, and Google+. Such new media have taken marketing by storm.

Some advertising industry experts even predict that the old mass-media communications model will eventually become obsolete. Mass-media costs are rising, audiences are shrinking, ad clutter is increasing, and viewers are gaining control of message exposure through technologies such as video streaming or DVRs that let them skip disruptive television commercials. As a result, the skeptics suggest, marketers are shifting ever-larger portions of their marketing budgets away from old-media mainstays and moving them to online, social, mobile, and other new-age media. In recent years, although TV leads as an advertising medium with a 31 percent share of global ad spending in 2013, its growth has stagnated. Spending in magazines, newspapers, and radio has lost considerable ground. Meanwhile, digital media have come from nowhere during the past few years to account for more than 25 percent of global advertising spending in 2013, second only to TV. By far the fastest-growing ad-spending category, digital's share is expected to grow to 33 percent by 2018, surpassing that of TV.[3]

In some cases, marketers are skipping traditional media altogether. For example, when Rovio Entertainment introduced the Angry Birds Space version of its popular game, it used only online video. It began by posting a 20-second video teaser containing only the game title and launch date—and that video landed 2.2 million views. Next, in an inspired move, Rovio

Exhibit 13.1 The new marketing communications model: Rovio Entertainment introduced the Angry Birds Space version of its popular game using only an online video campaign. The campaign reaped an astonishing 134 million views and 168 570 social shares.

Entertainment teamed with NASA and astronaut Don Pettit to do a video in outer space on the International Space Station, which demonstrated the actual physics of a stuffed Angry Bird in space—and that video went viral. Six million views and a few days later, Rovio Entertainment released a video trailer briefly introducing the game's characters, which grabbed another cool 1 million views in only two days. Finally, at launch time, Rovio Entertainment posted a two-minute video fully introducing the new game. In total, the award-winning video campaign reaped an astonishing 134 million views and 168 570 social shares.[4]

Similarly, eco-friendly household products maker Method recently employed a full but digital-only promotional campaign themed "Clean happy":

> Method is known for offbeat campaigns using slogans like "People against dirty" and "For the love of clean." But the most notable thing about the "Clean happy" campaign is that, unlike previous Method campaigns, it at first used zero ads in traditional media like TV or magazines. Instead, the centrepiece of the campaign was a two-minute brand video that could be watched only on YouTube and on the Method Facebook page. That video was followed at monthly intervals by four other clips that focused on individual Method products. The campaign also employed online media ads as well as a major presence in social media that included, in addition to YouTube and Facebook, the Method Twitter feed and blogs.
>
> The "Clean happy" campaign fit both Method's personality and its budget. "Method is the type of brand that benefits from word-of-mouth—from the moms in mom groups telling each other about it," says a Method ad agency executive. Moreover, "Clean happy" ran a first-year budget of only about US$3.5 million, compared with the whopping US$150 million or so that rival P&G might spend to bring out a new product, such as its Tide Pods detergent packets. "We're embracing this grass-roots movement," says the Method ad executive. "When you don't have 150 million bucks, that's what you have to do." Method ran the digital-only campaign for a full year before beginning to bring it to TV.[5]

In the new marketing communications world, rather than using old approaches that interrupt customers and force-feed them mass messages, new media formats let marketers reach smaller communities of consumers in more interactive, engaging ways. For example, think about television viewing these days. Consumers can now watch their favourite programs on just about anything with a screen—on televisions but also laptops, mobile phones, or tablets. And they can choose to watch programs whenever and wherever they wish, often without commercials. Increasingly, some programs, ads, and videos are being produced only for Internet viewing.

However, rather than the old-media model rapidly collapsing, most industry insiders see a more gradual blending of new and traditional media. The new marketing communications model will consist of a shifting mix of traditional mass media and a wide array of online, mobile, and social media that engage more-targeted consumer communities in a more-personalized, interactive way.

Many advertisers and ad agencies are still grappling with this transition. In the end, however, regardless of the communications channel, the key is to integrate all of these media in a way that best engages customers, communicates the brand message, and enhances the customer's brand experience. As the marketing communications environment shifts, so will the role of marketing communicators. Rather than just creating and placing "TV ads" or "print ads" or "Facebook display ads," many marketers now view themselves more broadly as **brand content managers**. As such, they create, inspire, and share brand messages and conversations with and among customers across a fluid mix of *paid, owned, earned, and shared* communications channels. These channels include media that are both traditional and new, and controlled and not controlled (see Marketing@Work 13.1).

Brand content management
Creating, inspiring, and sharing brand messages and conversations with and among consumers across a fluid mix of paid, owned, earned, and shared channels.

The Need for *Integrated* Marketing Communications

The shift toward a richer mix of media and communication approaches poses a problem for marketers. Consumers today are bombarded by commercial messages from a broad

MARKETING@WORK 13.1

Brand Content Management: Paid, Owned, Earned, and Shared

In the good old days, life seemed so simple for advertisers: Come up with a good creative idea, develop a media plan, produce and run a set of TV commercials and magazine ads, and maybe issue a press release to stir up some news. But today's marketing communications landscape seems more complex, characterized by a spate of new digital and social media and rapidly blurring lines within and between traditional and new channels. The old practice of placing "advertisements" in well-defined "media," within the tidy framework of a carefully managed promotional campaign, doesn't work as well as it once did.

Traditional message and media classifications just don't fit like they used to. For example, a TV ad isn't really just a TV ad anymore. Instead, it's "video content" that might be seen anywhere—on a consumer's TV screen but also on a PC, tablet, or phone. Other brand video content looks a lot like TV advertising but was never intended for TV, such as made-for-the-Web videos posted on YouTube, Facebook, or other social media. Video content about the brand may even be prepared by consumers and shared with others online.

Similarly, printed brand messages and pictures no longer appear only in carefully crafted ads placed in magazines, newspapers, or direct mail pieces. Instead, such content, created by a variety of sources, pops up in anything from formal advertisements and brand webpages to consumer posts on online social media and editorials by independent bloggers. In the hands of today's empowered consumers, the creation and distribution of brand messages can—and often does—take on a life of its own, beyond the design or control of the brand's marketers.

As a result, instead of creating "TV ads" or "print ads" or "PR press releases," many marketers now view themselves more broadly as creating, sharing, and managing "brand content" and leveraging it across a wealth of

integrated communications channels— both traditional and new, controlled and not controlled. This new thinking has led to a new marketing communications framework. Rather than classifying communications by traditional media breakdowns, the new framework builds on the broader concept of how and by whom brand content is created, controlled, and distributed. The new classification identifies four major types of media: paid, owned, earned, and shared (POES):

Paid media—includes promotional channels paid for by the sponsor, such as traditional media (TV, radio, print, or outdoor) and online and digital media (paid search ads, Web and social media display ads, mobile ads, or email marketing).

Owned media—includes promotional channels owned and controlled by the company, such as company websites, corporate blogs, owned social media pages, proprietary brand communities, sales forces, and events.

Earned media—includes PR media channels, such as television, newspapers, blogs, online video sites, and

other media not directly paid for or controlled by the marketer but that include the content because of viewer, reader, or user interest.

Shared media—includes media shared by consumers with other consumers, such as social media, blogs, mobile media, and viral channels, as well as traditional word of mouth.

In the past, marketers have focused on traditional paid (broadcast, print) or earned (public relations) media. Now, however, they are rapidly adding the new generation of owned (websites, blogs, brand communities) and shared (online social networks, mobile, email) media. Whereas a successful paid ad or PR piece used to be an end in itself, marketers are now asking "What else can I do with this content?" The marketer's goal is to leverage the combined power of all the POES channels. "The important thing is to be in all streams—paid, owned, earned, and shared—so the message is heard," says one expert.

Careful integration across the POES channels can produce striking communications results. A now-classic example is

© 2012 Jennie-O Turkey Store, LLC.

Exhibit 13.2 Hormel's JENNIE-O turkey brand successfully leveraged its imaginative "Make the Switch" campaign across paid, owned, earned, and shared media.

the highly successful Old Spice "The Man Your Man Could Smell Like" campaign, featuring football player Isaiah Mustafa. The campaign began with TV commercials (paid), which Old Spice then posted to its website and its YouTube and Facebook pages (owned). The campaign quickly went viral, as consumers by the millions buzzed about the ads through email, Facebook, and Twitter (shared). In turn, Old Spice received seemingly endless media coverage on everything from network TV to professional blog editorials (earned). In all, the campaign was viewed and discussed hundreds of millions of times across dozens of channels, all voicing the same integrated brand message.

Here's another example of a brand that successfully leveraged its campaign across paid, owned, earned, and shared media:

Hormel's wholly owned subsidiary JENNIE-O Turkey Store wanted to find a way to get consumers to appreciate how easy—and tasty—it was to substitute JENNIE-O ground turkey in recipes that called for ground beef. To get things cooking, it staged an imaginative "Make the Switch" marketing event (owned media). For five days, JENNIE-O took over the Bistro Truck, a popular Manhattan food truck, wrapping it with "Make the Switch" banners. Instead of ground beef, the truck's burgers were made from ground turkey. Each day, courtesy of JENNIE-O, the truck gave away 500 free gourmet turkey burgers at lunch. The truck's location and menu were previewed to local foodies and bloggers (earned media), and posted daily on Facebook, Twitter, Pinterest, and a special microsite (owned media). Then, the social media universe took over (shared media). About 450 000 tweets and retweets mentioned the "Make the Switch" promotion and locations. People lined up for thousands of free JENNIE-O burgers. Within five days the Facebook page had 23 000 Likes, and ground turkey sales rose 7 percent in New York. The "Make the Switch" takeover was so successful that it's been extended to other cities and has become the subject of JENNIE-O TV commercials (paid).

Thus, today's shifting and sometimes chaotic marketing communications environment calls for more than simply creating and placing some ads in well-defined and controlled media spaces. Rather, it calls for inspired brand content management, an integrated effort to create and share the right brand content, whatever the sources, and help it catch fire. Today's marketing communicators must be more than just advertising copywriters or media analysts. They must be brand content strategists, creators, connectors, and catalysts who manage brand conversations with and among customers across a fluid mix of message channels. That's a tall order, but with today's new communications thinking, anything is POES–ible!

Sources: Extract example and quotes from Julie Liesse, "The Big Idea," *Advertising Age*, November 28, 2011, pp. C4–C6; with additional information from Julie Liesse, "Top Trends for 2012," *Advertising Age*, November 28, 2011, p. C8; Peter Himler, "Paid, Earned & Owned: Revisited," Theflack.blogspot.com, June 21, 2011; Natalie Zmuda, "Solving the Content Creation Conundrum," *Advertising Age*, January 14, 2013, pp. 12–13; and www.hormelfoods.com/brands/jennieO, www.switchtoturkey.com, and www.facebook.com/jennieoturkey/app_175338739199041, accessed October 2013. JENNIE-O® and "Make the Switch®" are registered trademarks of JENNIE-O Turkey Store, LLC.

range of sources. But consumers don't distinguish between message sources the way marketers do. In the consumer's mind, messages from different sources and promotional approaches—whether it's a Super Bowl ad, store display, or a friend's social media post—all become part of a single message about the company. Conflicting messages from these different sources can result in confused company images, brand positions, and customer relationships.

All too often, companies fail to integrate their various communications channels. The result is a hodgepodge of communications to consumers. Mass-media ads say one thing, whereas an in-store promotion sends a different signal, and the company's website, emails, Facebook page, or videos posted on YouTube say something altogether different. The problem is that these communications often come from different parts of the company. Advertising messages are planned and implemented by the advertising department or an ad agency. Other company departments or agencies are responsible for public relations (PR), sales promotion events, and online or social media efforts. However, whereas companies may have separated their communications tools, customers don't. Mixed communications from these sources result in blurred brand perceptions by consumers.

The new world of online and social media marketing, tablet computers, smartphones, and apps presents tremendous opportunities but also big challenges. It can "give companies increased access to their customers, fresh insights into their preferences, and a broader creative palette to work with," says one marketing executive. But "the biggest

FIGURE 13.1 Integrated Marketing Communications

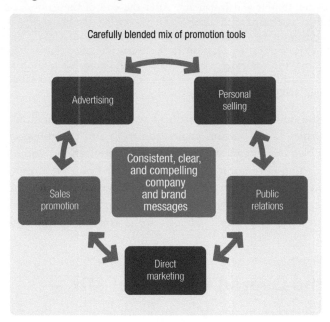

issue is complexity and fragmentation . . . the amount of choice out there," says another. The challenge is to "make it come together in an organized way."[6]

To that end, more companies today are adopting the concept of **integrated marketing communications (IMC)**. Under this concept, as illustrated in Figure 13.1, the company carefully integrates its many communications channels to deliver a clear, consistent, and compelling message about the organization and its brands.

Integrated marketing communications calls for recognizing all touch points where the customer may encounter the company and its brands. Each contact with the brand will deliver a message—whether good, bad, or indifferent. The company's goal should be to deliver a consistent and positive message at each contact. Integrated marketing communications ties together all of the company's messages and images. Its television and print ads have the same message, look, and feel as its email and personal selling communications. And its PR materials project the same image as its website, online social media, or mobile marketing efforts. Often, different media play unique roles in attracting, informing, and persuading consumers; these roles must be carefully coordinated under the overall marketing communications plan.

A great example of a well-integrated marketing communications effort is Coca-Cola's "Mirage" campaign. Built around two Super Bowl XLVII ads, the campaign integrated the clout of traditional big-budget TV advertising with the interactive power of social media to create real-time customer engagement with the Coke brand:

> Coca-Cola's "Mirage" tells the story of three bands of desert vagabonds—Cowboys, Show-girls, and *Mad Max*–inspired "Badlanders"—as they trek through the blazing hot desert pursuing the same elusive mirage—a frosty bottle of Coca-Cola. The Mirage campaign began two weeks before the Super Bowl with a 30-second teaser ad on *American Idol* as well as a posting on YouTube and other online destinations inviting fans to visit CokeChase. com to get to know the story and teams. Then, during the game, a 60-second Mirage ad set up the exciting chase, with a cliff-hanging close that urged viewers to visit CokeChase. com, where they could help decide the outcome by casting votes for their favourite team and throwing obstacles in front of rival teams. During the rest of the game, Coca-Cola listening teams monitored related activity on major social media, and put fans in the middle

Integrated marketing communications (IMC)
Carefully integrating and coordinating the company's many communications channels to deliver a clear, consistent, and compelling message about the organization and its products.

of the action by posting real-time chase updates on Facebook, YouTube, and Twitter and chase photos on Tumblr and Instagram. After the end of the game, a second Mirage ad announced the chase team with the most viewer votes—the Showgirls, in their glam pink and silver outfits, won the Coke. But the real winner was Coca-Cola. The Mirage campaign exceeded all expectations. In addition to the usual huge Super Bowl audience numbers, during the game, the campaign captured an eye-popping 8.2 million online and social-media interactions and 910 000 votes, far exceeding the brand's internal goals of 1.6 million interactions and 400 000 votes.[7]

In the past, no one person or department was responsible for thinking through the communication roles of the various promotion tools and coordinating the promotion mix. To help implement integrated marketing communications, some companies have appointed a marketing communications director who has overall responsibility for the company's communications efforts. This helps produce better communications consistency and greater sales impact. It places the responsibility in someone's hands—where none existed before—to unify the company's image as it is shaped by thousands of company activities.

Shaping the Overall Promotion Mix

The concept of integrated marketing communications suggests that the company must blend the promotion tools carefully into a coordinated *promotion mix*. But how does it determine what mix of promotion tools to use? Companies within the same industry differ greatly in the design of their promotion mixes. For example, cosmetics maker Mary Kay spends most of its promotion funds on personal selling and direct marketing, whereas competitor CoverGirl spends heavily on consumer advertising. We now look at factors that influence the marketer's choice of promotion tools.

The Nature of Each Promotion Tool

Each promotion tool has unique characteristics and costs. Marketers must understand these characteristics in shaping the promotion mix.

ADVERTISING Advertising can reach masses of geographically dispersed buyers at a low cost per exposure, and it enables the seller to repeat a message many times. For example, television advertising can reach huge audiences. More than 114 million people watched the 2015 Super Bowl, more than 36 million people watched at least part of the 2015 Academy Awards broadcast, and over 19 million avid fans tuned in each week for the 2014–2015 season of *The Big Bang Theory*. What's more, a popular TV ad's reach can be extended through online and social media. For example, as well as the 100+ plus million TV viewers of the 2015 Super Bowl, in the four months leading up to the big game, Dorito's popular "Crash the Super Bowl" competition generated an estimated 3.2 million impressions in the form of online and social media views, tweets, and posts. (For companies that want to reach a mass audience, TV is the place to be.)[8]

Beyond its reach, large-scale advertising says something positive about the seller's size, popularity, and success. Because of advertising's public nature, consumers tend to view advertised products as more legitimate. Advertising is also very expressive; it allows the company to dramatize its products through the artful use of visuals, print, sound, and colour. On the one hand, advertising can be used to build up a long-term image for a product (such as Coca-Cola ads). On the other hand, advertising can trigger quick sales (as when Sears advertises weekend specials).

Advertising also has some shortcomings. Although it reaches many people quickly, advertising is impersonal and lacks the direct persuasiveness of company salespeople. For the most part, advertising can carry on only a one-way communication with an audience, and the audience does not feel that it has to pay attention or respond. In addition, advertising can be very costly. Although some advertising forms, such as newspaper and radio advertising, can be done on smaller budgets, other forms, such as network TV advertising, require very large budgets.

PERSONAL SELLING Personal selling is the most effective tool at certain stages of the buying process, particularly in building up buyers' preferences, convictions, and actions. It involves personal interaction between two or more people, so each person can observe the other's needs and characteristics and make quick adjustments. Personal selling also allows all kinds of customer rela-

Exhibit 13.3 With personal selling, the customer feels a greater need to listen and respond, even if the response is a polite "No thank you."

tionships to spring up, ranging from matter-of-fact selling relationships to personal friendships. An effective salesperson keeps the customer's interests at heart in order to build a long-term relationship by solving a customer's problems. Finally, with personal selling, the buyer usually feels a greater need to listen and respond, even if the response is a polite "No thank you."

These unique qualities come at a cost, however. A sales force requires a longer-term commitment than does advertising—although advertising can be turned up or down, the size of a sales force is harder to change. Personal selling is also the company's most expensive promotion tool, costing companies on average $600 or more per sales call, depending on the industry.[9] Many firms spend up to three times as much on personal selling as they do on advertising.

SALES PROMOTION Sales promotion includes a wide assortment of tools—coupons, contests, discounts, premiums, and others—all of which have many unique qualities. They attract consumer attention, offer strong incentives to purchase, and can be used to dramatize product offers and boost sagging sales. Sales promotions invite and reward quick response. Whereas advertising says "Buy our product," sales promotion says "Buy it now." Sales promotion effects are often short-lived, however, and are often not as effective as advertising or personal selling in building long-run brand preference and customer relationships.

PUBLIC RELATIONS Public relations is very believable—news stories, features, sponsorships, and events seem more real and believable to readers than ads do. PR can also reach many prospects who avoid salespeople and advertisements—the message gets to buyers as "news" rather than as a sales-directed communication. And, as with advertising, public relations can dramatize a company or product. Marketers tend to underuse public relations or use it as an afterthought. Yet a well-thought-out public relations campaign used with other promotion mix elements can be very effective and economical.

DIRECT AND DIGITAL MARKETING The many forms of direct and digital marketing—from direct mail, catalogues, and telephone marketing to online, mobile, and social media—all share some distinctive characteristics. Direct marketing is more targeted: It's usually

FIGURE 13.2 Push versus Pull Promotion Strategy

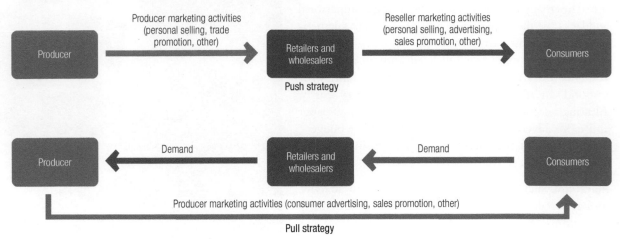

directed to a specific customer or customer community. It's also immediate and personalized: Messages can be prepared quickly—even in real time—and tailored to appeal to specific consumers or brand groups. Finally, direct marketing is interactive: It allows a dialogue between the marketing team and the consumer, and messages can be altered depending on the consumer's response. Thus, direct and digital marketing are well suited to highly targeted marketing efforts, creating customer engagement and building one-to-one customer relationships.

Promotion Mix Strategies

Marketers can choose from two basic promotion mix strategies: *push* promotion or *pull* promotion. Figure 13.2 contrasts the two strategies. The relative emphasis given to the specific promotion tools differs for push and pull strategies. A **push strategy** involves "pushing" the product through marketing channels to final consumers. The producer directs its marketing activities (primarily personal selling and trade promotion) toward channel members to induce them to carry the product and promote it to final consumers. For example, John Deere does very little promoting of its lawn mowers, garden tractors, and other residential consumer products to final consumers. Instead, John Deere's sales force works with Lowe's, Home Depot, independent dealers, and other channel members, who in turn push John Deere products to final consumers.

Using a **pull strategy**, the producer directs its marketing activities (primarily advertising, consumer promotion, and direct and digital media) toward final consumers to induce them to buy the product. For example, Unilever promotes its Axe grooming products directly to its young male target market using TV and print ads, a brand site, its YouTube channel and Facebook page, and other channels. If the pull strategy is effective, consumers will then demand the brand from such retailers as Shoppers Drug Mart, The Bay, or Walmart, which will in turn demand it from Unilever. Thus, under a pull strategy, consumer demand "pulls" the product through the channels.

Some industrial-goods companies use only push strategies, and some direct marketing companies use only pull strategies. However, most large companies use some combination of both. For example, Unilever spends more than US$8.5 billion worldwide each year on consumer marketing and sales promotions to create brand preference and pull customers into stores that carry its products.[10] At the same time, it uses its own and distributors' sales forces and trade promotions to push its brands through the channels, so that they will be available on store shelves when consumers come calling.

Push strategy
A promotion strategy that calls for using the sales force and trade promotion to push the product through channels. The producer promotes the product to channel members, which in turn promote it to final consumers.

Pull strategy
A promotion strategy that calls for spending a lot on consumer advertising and promotion to induce final consumers to buy the product, creating a demand vacuum that "pulls" the product through the channel.

Companies consider many factors when designing their promotion mix strategies, including the type of product and market. For example, the importance of different promotion tools varies between consumer and business markets. Business-to-consumer companies usually pull more, putting more of their funds into advertising, followed by sales promotion, personal selling, and then public relations. In contrast, business-to-business marketers tend to push more, putting more of their funds into personal selling, followed by sales promotion, advertising, and public relations.

Now that we've examined the concept of integrated marketing communications and the factors that firms consider when shaping their promotion mixes, let's look more closely at the specific marketing communications tools.

Advertising LO3

◄◉┤**Simulate** on MyMarketingLab

Advertising

Advertising can be traced back to the very beginnings of recorded history. Archaeologists working in countries around the Mediterranean Sea have dug up signs announcing various events and offers. The Romans painted walls to announce gladiator fights and the Phoenicians painted pictures on large rocks to promote their wares along parade routes. During the golden age in Greece, town criers announced the sale of cattle, crafted items, and even cosmetics. An early "singing commercial" went as follows: "For eyes that are shining, for cheeks like the dawn / For beauty that lasts after girlhood is gone / For prices in reason, the woman who knows / Will buy her cosmetics from Aesclyptos."

Modern advertising, however, is a far cry from these early efforts. Canadian ad spending reached US$13.2 billion in 2012 and is forecasted to reach US$15.5 billion by 2017. In contrast, U.S. advertisers surpassed US$171 billion in 2013 and are expected to exceed US$220 billion by 2017! Worldwide ad spending reached US$516 billion in 2013, with an estimated growth to US$668 billion by 2018.[11]

Although advertising is used mostly by business firms, a wide range of not-for-profit organizations, professionals, and social agencies also use advertising to promote their causes to various target publics. For example, the Canadian government boosted ad spending to more than $136 million in 2009–2010, up from only $41 million just four years earlier. In April and May of 2015, the Conservatives spent $13.5 million to advertise their pre-election budget.[12] Advertising is a good way to inform and persuade, whether the purpose is to sell Coca-Cola worldwide or educate people in developing nations on how to lead healthier lives.

Marketing management must make four important decisions when developing an advertising program (see Figure 13.3): *setting advertising objectives*, *setting the advertising budget*, *developing advertising strategy (message decisions and media decisions)*, and *evaluating advertising campaigns.*

FIGURE 13.3 Major Advertising Decisions

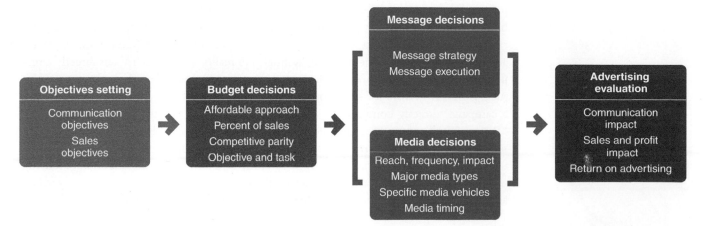

TABLE 13.1 Possible Advertising Objectives	
Informative Advertising	
Communicating customer value	Suggesting new uses for a product
Building a brand and company image	Informing the market of a price change
Telling the market about a new product	Describing available services and support
Explaining how a product works	Correcting false impressions
Persuasive Advertising	
Building brand preference	Persuading customers to purchase now
Encouraging switching to a brand	Creating customer engagement
Changing customer perceptions of product value	Building brand community
Reminder Advertising	
Maintaining customer relationships	Reminding consumers where to buy the product
Reminding consumers that the product may be needed in the near future	Keeping the brand in a customer's mind during off-seasons

Setting Advertising Objectives

The first step is to set *advertising objectives*. These objectives should be based on past decisions about the target market, positioning, and the marketing mix, which define the job that advertising must do in the total marketing program. The overall advertising objective is to help engage customers and build customer relationships by communicating customer value. Here, we discuss specific advertising objectives.

Advertising objective
A specific communication task to be accomplished with a specific target audience during a specific period of time.

An **advertising objective** is a specific communication *task* to be accomplished with a specific *target* audience during a specific period of *time*. Advertising objectives can be classified by their primary purpose—to *inform*, *persuade*, or *remind*. Table 13.1 lists examples of each of these specific objectives.

Informative advertising is used heavily when introducing a new product category. In this case, the objective is to build primary demand. Thus, early producers of HDTVs first had to inform consumers of the image quality and size benefits of the new product. *Persuasive advertising* becomes more important as competition increases. Here, the company's objective is to build selective demand. For example, once HDTVs became established, Samsung began trying to persuade consumers that *its* brand offered the best quality for their money. Such advertising wants to engage customers and create brand community.

Some persuasive advertising has become *comparative advertising* (or *attack advertising*), in which a company directly or indirectly compares its brand with one or more other brands. You see examples of comparative advertising in almost every product category, ranging from sports drinks and soup to car rentals, credit cards, wireless phone services, and even retail pricing. For example, Walmart ran reality-type local TV ads directly comparing its prices against those on shopper cash-register receipts from specific competitors such as Best Buy, Toys 'R' Us, Kroger, and other supermarket rivals.[13] And Microsoft ran a campaign directly comparing its Bing search engine to Google's search engine. The "Bing It On" campaign challenged consumers to make side-by-side comparisons of search results without knowing which results were from which search engine. According to Microsoft, to the surprise of many people, those making the comparison choose Bing over Google by a 2-to-1 margin. Microsoft backed the "Bing It On" challenge with an advertising campaign claiming that "people prefer Bing over Google 2–1."[14]

Advertisers should use comparative advertising with caution. All too often, such ads invite competitor responses, resulting in an advertising war that neither competitor can win. Upset competitors might also take more drastic action, such as filing complaints with the self-regulatory National Advertising Division of the Council of Better Business Bureaus or even filing false-advertising lawsuits. For example, Sara Lee's Ball Park brand hot dogs and Kraft's Oscar Mayer brand waged a nearly two-year "weiner war." It started when Sara Lee sued Kraft, challenging advertising claims that Oscar Mayer franks had won a national taste test over Ball Park and other brands and that they were "100% beef." Kraft, in turn, filed a countersuit, accusing Sara Lee of making similar advertising misstatements about its own "all-beef" Ball Park hot dogs, along with claims touting Ball Park as "America's best." By the time the lawsuits were settled, about all that the competitors had accomplished was to publicly call into question the taste and contents of both hot dog brands.[15]

Reminder advertising is important for mature products; it helps maintain customer relationships and keep consumers thinking about the product. Expensive Coca-Cola television ads primarily build and maintain the Coca-Cola brand relationship rather than inform consumers or persuade them to buy it in the short run.

Advertising's goal is to help move consumers through the buying process. Some advertising is designed to move people to immediate action. For example, a direct-response television ad by Weight Watchers urges consumers to go online and sign up right away, and a Best Buy newspaper insert for a weekend sale encourages immediate store visits. However, many ads focus on building or strengthening long-term customer relationships. For example, a Nike television ad in which well-known athletes work through extreme challenges in their Nike gear never directly asks for a sale. Instead, the goal is to somehow change the way the customers think or feel about the brand.

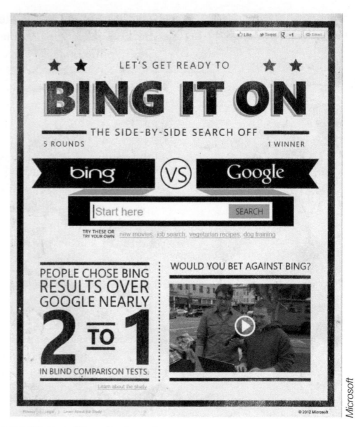

Exhibit 13.4 Microsoft's "Bing It On" campaign urged consumers to make side-by-side comparisons of the search results from its Bing search engine and Google's. It claimed that people making the comparison chose Bing by nearly 2 to 1.

Microsoft

Setting the Advertising Budget

After determining its advertising objectives, the company next sets its **advertising budget** for each product. Here, we look at four common methods used to set the total budget for advertising: the *affordable method*, the *percentage-of-sales method*, the *competitive-parity method*, and the *objective-and-task method*.[16]

Affordable Method Some companies use the **affordable method**: They set the promotion budget at the level they think the company can afford. Small businesses often use this method, reasoning that a company cannot spend more on advertising than it has. They start with total revenues, deduct operating expenses and capital outlays, and then devote some portion of the remaining funds to advertising.

Unfortunately, this method of setting budgets completely ignores the effects of promotion on sales. It tends to place promotion last among spending priorities, even in situations in which advertising is critical to the firm's success. It leads to an uncertain annual promotion budget, which makes long-range market planning difficult. Although the affordable method can result in overspending on advertising, it more often results in underspending.

Advertising budget
The dollars and other resources allocated to a product or a company advertising program.

Affordable method
Setting the promotion budget at the level management thinks the company can afford.

Percentage-of-sales method
Setting the promotion budget at a certain percentage of current or forecasted sales or as a percentage of the unit sales price.

Percentage-of-Sales Method Other companies use the **percentage-of-sales method**, setting their promotion budget at a certain percentage of current or forecasted sales. Or they budget a percentage of the unit sales price. The percentage-of-sales method has advantages. It is simple to use and helps management think about the relationships between promotion spending, selling price, and profit per unit.

Despite these claimed advantages, however, the percentage-of-sales method has little to justify it. It wrongly views sales as the *cause* of promotion rather than as the *result*. Although studies have found a positive correlation between promotional spending and brand strength, this relationship often turns out to be effect and cause, not cause and effect. Stronger brands with higher sales can afford the biggest ad budgets.

Thus, the percentage-of-sales budget is based on availability of funds rather than on opportunities. It may prevent the increased spending sometimes needed to turn around falling sales. And because the budget varies with year-to-year sales, long-range planning is difficult. Finally, the method does not provide any basis for choosing a *specific* percentage, except what has been done in the past or what competitors are doing.

Competitive-parity method
Setting the promotion budget to match competitors' outlays.

Competitive-Parity Method Still other companies use the **competitive-parity method**, setting their promotion budgets to match competitors' outlays. They monitor competitors' advertising or get industry promotion spending estimates from publications or trade associations, and then set their budgets based on the industry average.

Two arguments support this method. First, competitors' budgets represent the collective wisdom of the industry. Second, spending what competitors spend helps prevent promotion wars. Unfortunately, neither argument is valid. There are no grounds for believing that the competition has a better idea of what a company should be spending on promotion than does the company itself. Companies differ greatly, and each has its own special promotion needs. Finally, there is no evidence that budgets based on competitive parity prevent promotion wars.

Objective-and-task method
Developing the promotion budget by (1) defining specific objectives, (2) determining the tasks that must be performed to achieve these objectives, and (3) estimating the costs of performing these tasks. The sum of these costs is the proposed promotion budget.

Objective-and-Task Method The most logical budget-setting method is the **objective-and-task method**, whereby the company sets its promotion budget based on what it wants to accomplish with promotion. This budgeting method entails (1) defining specific promotion objectives, (2) determining the tasks needed to achieve these objectives, and (3) estimating the costs of performing these tasks. The sum of these costs is the proposed promotion budget.

The advantage of the objective-and-task method is that it forces management to spell out its assumptions about the relationship between dollars spent and promotion results. But it is also the most difficult method to use. Often, it is hard to figure out which specific tasks will achieve stated objectives. For example, suppose Microsoft wants 75 percent awareness for the latest version of its Surface tablet during the three-month introductory period. What specific advertising messages and media schedules should Microsoft use to attain this objective? How much would these messages and media schedules cost? Microsoft management must consider such questions, even though they are hard to answer.

No matter what method is used, setting the advertising budget is no easy task. John Wanamaker, the department store magnate, once said, "I know that half of my advertising is wasted, but I don't know which half. I spent $2 million for advertising, and I don't know if that is half enough or twice too much."

As a result of such thinking, advertising is one of the easiest budget items to cut when economic times get tough. Cuts in brand-building advertising appear to do little short-term harm to sales. For example, in the wake of the 2008 recession, U.S. advertising expenditures plummeted 12 percent over the previous year, while ad spending in Canada fell 8.4 percent. In the long run, however, slashing ad spending risks long-term damage to a brand's image and market share. In fact, companies that can maintain or even increase their advertising spending while competitors are decreasing theirs can gain competitive advantage. For example, during the recession, while competitors were cutting back, carmaker Audi actually increased its marketing and advertising spending. Audi "kept its foot on the pedal while everyone else is pulling back," said an Audi ad executive at the time. "Why would we go backwards now when the industry is generally locking the brakes and cutting spending?" As a result, Audi's brand awareness and buyer consideration reached record levels during the recession, outstripping those of BMW, Mercedes, and Lexus, and positioning Audi strongly for the post-recession era. In the post-recession economy, Audi is now one of the hottest auto brands on the market.[17]

Developing Advertising Strategy

Advertising strategy consists of two major elements: creating advertising *messages* and selecting advertising *media*. In the past, companies often viewed media planning as secondary to the message-creation process. After the creative department created good advertisements, the media department then selected and purchased the best media for carrying those ads to the desired target audiences. This often caused friction between creatives and media planners.

Today, however, soaring media costs, more-focused target marketing strategies, and the blizzard of new online, mobile, and social media have promoted the importance of the media-planning function. The decision about which media to use for an ad campaign—television, newspapers, magazines, a website or online social media, mobile devices, or email—is now sometimes more critical than the creative elements of the campaign. Also, brand content and messages are now often co-created through interactions with and among consumers. As a result, more and more advertisers are orchestrating a closer harmony between their messages and the media that deliver them. As discussed earlier, the goal is to create and manage brand content across a full range of media, whether they are paid, owned, earned, or shared.

Creating the Advertising Message No matter how big the budget, advertising can succeed only if it gains attention, engages consumers, and communicates well. Good advertising messages and content are especially important in today's costly and cluttered advertising environment. In 1950, the average household received only three network television channels and a handful of major national magazines. Today, the average household receives about 135 channels, and consumers have more than 20 000 magazines from which to choose.[18] Add in the countless radio stations and a continuous barrage of catalogues, direct mail, out-of-home media, email, and online, mobile, and social media exposures, and consumers are being bombarded with ads at home, work, and all points in between.

BREAKING THROUGH THE CLUTTER If all this advertising clutter bothers some consumers, it also causes huge headaches for advertisers. Take the situation facing American network television advertisers. They pay an average of US$354 000 to produce a single 30-second commercial. Then, each time they show it, they pay an average of US$122 000 for 30 seconds of advertising time during a popular primetime program. They pay even more if

Audi of America

Exhibit 13.5 Setting the promotion budget: Promotion spending is one of the easiest items to cut in tough economic times. But Audi gained competitive advantage by keeping its foot on the promotion pedal as competitors retrenched.

Advertising strategy
The strategy by which the company accomplishes its advertising objectives. It consists of two major elements: creating advertising messages and selecting advertising media.

it's an especially popular program, such as *American Idol* (US$355 000), *Sunday Night Football* (US$594 000), *The Big Bang Theory* (US$317 000), or a mega-event such as the Super Bowl (US$4.5 million in 2015, and expected to reach $5 million in 2016, per 30 seconds!).[19] Canadian advertising is a bargain in comparison, but the reach is smaller. For example, the number of TV households in Canada is only 14 million compared with the 116.4 million in the United States; and in 2013, advertisers in Canada spent about CAN$3.5 billion on TV advertising versus the US$62 billion spent south of the border.[20]

Network television ads are sandwiched in with a clutter of other commercials, announcements, and network promotions, totalling nearly 20 minutes of nonprogram material per primetime hour, with commercial breaks coming every six minutes on average. Such clutter in television and other ad media has created an increasingly hostile advertising environment. According to one study, more than 70 percent of viewers think there are too many ads on TV, and another study shows that 69 percent of advertisers themselves agree.[21]

Until recently, television viewers were pretty much a captive audience for advertisers. But today's digital wizardry has given consumers a rich new set of information and entertainment choices. With the growth in cable and satellite TV, the Internet, video streaming, tablets, and smartphones, today's viewers have many more options.

Digital technology has also armed consumers with an arsenal of weapons for choosing what they watch or don't watch. Increasingly, thanks to the growth of PVR systems, consumers are choosing *not* to watch ads. Fifty-four percent of Canadian (compared with 48 percent of U.S.) TV households had PVRs in 2014, triple the number reached only five years earlier. One ad agency executive calls these systems "electronic weedwhackers" when it comes to viewing commercials. It is estimated that PVR owners view only about 44 percent of the commercials during playback. At the same time, video downloads and streaming are exploding, letting viewers watch entertainment on their own time—with or without commercials.[22]

Thus, advertisers can no longer force-feed the same old cookie-cutter message content to captive consumers through traditional media. Just to gain and hold attention, today's content must be better planned, more imaginative, more entertaining, and more emotionally engaging. Simply interrupting or disrupting consumers no longer works. Unless ads provide information that is interesting, useful, or entertaining, many consumers will simply skip by them.

MERGING ADVERTISING AND ENTERTAINMENT To break through the clutter, many marketers have subscribed to a merging of advertising and entertainment, dubbed "**Madison & Vine**." You've probably heard of Madison Avenue, the New York City street that houses the headquarters of many of the nation's largest advertising agencies. You may also have heard of Hollywood & Vine, the intersection of Hollywood Avenue and Vine

Madison & Vine
A term that has come to represent the merging of advertising and entertainment in an effort to break through the clutter and create new avenues for reaching customers with more engaging messages.

Piotr Marcinski/Shutterstock

Exhibit 13.6 Advertising clutter: Today's consumers, armed with an arsenal of weapons, can choose what they watch and don't watch. Increasingly, they are choosing not to watch ads.

Street in Hollywood, California, long the symbolic heart of the U.S. entertainment industry. Now, Madison Avenue and Hollywood & Vine have come together to form a new intersection—Madison & Vine—that represents the merging of advertising and entertainment in an effort to create new avenues for reaching consumers with more engaging messages.

This merging of advertising and entertainment takes one of two forms: advertainment or branded entertainment. The aim of *advertainment* is to make ads themselves so entertaining, or so useful, that people *want* to watch them. There's no chance that you'd watch ads on purpose, you say? Think again. For example, the Super Bowl has become an annual advertainment showcase. Tens of millions of people tune in to the Super Bowl each year, as much to watch the entertaining ads as to see the game.

In fact, PVR systems can actually *improve* viewership of a really *good* ad. For example, most Super Bowl ads are typically viewed more in PVR households than non-PVR households. Rather than zipping past the ads, many people skip back to rewatch them during halftime and following the game.

These days, it's not unusual to see an entertaining ad or other brand message on You-Tube before you see it on TV. And you might well seek it out at a friend's suggestion rather than having it forced on you by the advertiser. Moreover, beyond making their regular ads more entertaining, advertisers are creating new advertising forms that look less like ads and more like short films or shows. A range of new brand messaging platforms—from webisodes and blogs to viral videos and apps—now blur the line between ads and entertainment. For example, T-Mobile created an entertaining two-minute video ad based on the royal wedding of Prince William and Kate Middleton, using impressive lookalikes of British royal family members dancing down the aisle to a funky pop song. The fun ad was never shown on TV but pulled down more than 26 million views on YouTube.

Branded entertainment (or *brand integrations*) involves making the brand an inseparable part of some other form of entertainment. The most common form of branded entertainment is product placements—embedding brands as props within other programming. It might be a brief glimpse of the latest LG phone on *Grey's Anatomy* or of Starbucks' coffee products on *Morning Joe* on MSNBC. Or the product placement might be scripted into an episode, as when *Big Bang Theory* character Sheldon Cooper uses Purell hand sanitizer after putting a live snake in his friend's desk drawer, spitting out the memorable line, "Oh dear. Oh dear. Purell, Purell, Purell, Purell...." An entire episode of *The Middle* centred on the show's Heck family coveting their neighbour's new VW Passat. Similarly, one memorable episode of *Modern Family* was built around the Dunphy family trying to find the recently released, hard-to-find Apple iPad their father, Phil, coveted as his special birthday present. Other episodes have featured brands ranging from Oreos to Target to Toyota Prius, all carefully integrated with the show's theme.

Originally created with TV in mind, branded entertainment has spread quickly into other sectors of the entertainment industry. For example, it is widely used in movies. The 35 movies that reached #1 at the box office in 2014 contained 464 identifiable placements—*Transformers: Age of Extinction* alone had 55 placements. And the 2015 release of *Entourage* had a whopping 65 placements![23] If you look carefully, you'll also see product placements in video games, comic books, Broadway musicals, and even pop music. For example, a Jeep Wrangler is prominently featured in the Call of Duty: Modern Warfare 3 video game—and Chrysler even sells a Call of Duty: MW3 limited-edition Jeep Wrangler.

Many companies are even producing their own branded entertainment. For example, Ford created "Random Acts of Fusion," a Web-only show that followed TV celebrities Joel McHale and Ryan Seacrest as they hosted video contests and free food festivals across America, letting people interact with the latest-model Ford Fusion as they went. The

Exhibit 13.7 Madison & Vine: IKEA produced its own branded entertainment in the form of the Web-only comedy "Easy to Assemble," set inside an IKEA store. In its four seasons, the show captured a cult following and millions of online and social media views and shares.

show increased traffic to the Ford Fusion site by 20 percent. Similarly, IKEA sponsored "Easy to Assemble," a tongue-in-cheek Web-only comedy series. The show followed the adventures of Illeana Douglas, who leaves Hollywood for a job at an IKEA store in Burbank, California. The IKEA store served as the show's set. IKEA's goal was to communicate the brand's fun, cheerful, and sophisticated image and values. The show achieved near cult status and has been shared more than 1.5 million times by social media users. "Our content resonates because it's produced by entertainers, not salespeople," says IKEA's media manager.[24]

So, Madison & Vine is now the meeting place for the advertising and entertainment industries. The goal is for brand messages to become a part of the entertainment rather than interrupting it. As advertising agency JWT puts it, "We believe advertising needs to stop *interrupting* what people are interested in and *be* what people are interested in." However, advertisers must be careful that the new intersection itself doesn't become too congested. With all the new ad formats and product placements, Madison & Vine threatens to create even more of the very clutter that it was designed to break through. At that point, consumers might decide to take yet a different route.

MESSAGE STRATEGY The first step in creating effective advertising messages is to plan a *message strategy*—the general message that will be communicated to consumers. The purpose of advertising is to get consumers to engage with or react to the product or company in a certain way. People will engage and react only if they believe they will benefit from doing so. Thus, developing an effective message strategy begins with identifying customer *benefits* that can be used as advertising appeals. Ideally, the message strategy will follow directly from the company's broader positioning and customer value–creation strategies.

Message strategy statements tend to be plain, straightforward outlines of benefits and positioning points that the advertiser wants to stress. The advertiser must next develop a compelling **creative concept**—or *big idea*—that will bring the message strategy to life in a distinctive and memorable way. At this stage, simple message ideas become great ad campaigns. Usually, a copywriter and an art director will team up to generate many creative concepts, hoping that one of these concepts will turn out to be the big idea. The creative concept may emerge as a visualization, a phrase, or a combination of the two.

The creative concept will guide the choice of specific appeals to be used in an advertising campaign. *Advertising appeals* should have three characteristics. First, they should be *meaningful*, pointing out benefits that make the product more desirable or interesting to consumers. Second, appeals must be *believable*. Consumers must believe that the product or service will deliver the promised benefits.

However, the most meaningful and believable benefits may not be the best ones to feature. Appeals should also be *distinctive*. They should tell how the product is better than competing brands. For example, the most meaningful benefit of using a body wash or fragrance is that it makes you feel cleaner or smell better. But Axe's Anarchy brand for men and women sets itself apart by the extreme nature of the "Axe Effect" it promises to create—Axe Anarchy for Him + for Her will "Unleash the Chaos." Similarly, the most meaningful benefit of owning a wristwatch is that it keeps accurate time, yet few watch ads feature this benefit. Instead, watch advertisers might select any of a number of advertising themes. For

Creative concept
The compelling "big idea" that will bring an advertising message strategy to life in a distinctive and memorable way.

years, Timex has been the affordable watch that "takes a licking and keeps on ticking." In contrast, Rolex ads talk about the brand's "obsession with perfection" and the fact that "Rolex has been the preeminent symbol of performance and prestige for more than a century."

MESSAGE EXECUTION The advertiser now must turn the big idea into an actual ad execution that will capture the target market's attention and interest. The creative team must find the best approach, style, tone, words, and format for executing the message. The message can be presented in various **execution styles**, such as the following:

- *Slice of life:* This style shows one or more "typical" people using the product in a normal setting. For example, a Silk Soymilk "Rise and Shine" ad shows a young professional starting the day with a healthier breakfast and high hopes.

- *Lifestyle:* This style shows how a product fits in with a particular lifestyle. For example, an ad for Athleta active wear shows a woman in a complex yoga pose and states: "If your body is your temple, build it one piece at a time."

- *Fantasy:* This style creates a fantasy around the product or its use. For example, IKEA ads show consumers creating fanciful room designs with IKEA furniture, such as "a bedroom for a queen made by Bree and her sister, designed by IKEA."

- *Mood or image:* This style builds a mood or image around the product or service, such as beauty, love, intrigue, or serenity. Few claims are made about the product or service except through suggestion. For example, a Nestlé Toll House ad shows a daughter hugging her mother after surprising her with an unexpected weekend home from college. The mother responds, "So I baked her the cookies she's loved since she was little."

Exhibit 13.8 Distinctive advertising appeals: Axe Anarchy For Him + For Her sets itself apart by the extreme nature of the "Axe Effect" it promises to create—Anarchy will "Unleash the Chaos."

- *Musical:* This style shows people or cartoon characters singing about the product. For example, M&Ms "Love Ballad" ad, part of the Better with M campaign, featured Red singing Meatloaf's "I would do anything for love," showcasing his commitment to actress Naya Rivera. Red has second thoughts, however, when Rivera can't resist adding Red to some of her favourite treats, including cookies, cake, and ice cream. To all of that, Red answers with the lyric "But I won't do that . . . or that . . . or that . . . or that."

- *Personality symbol:* This style creates a character that represents the product. The character might be animated (Mr. Clean, the GEICO Gecko, or the Michelin Man) or real (Flo, the perky Progressive Insurance spokeswoman; Wendy, the redheaded spokesperson for Wendy's Restaurant; Ronald McDonald).

- *Technical expertise:* This style shows the company's expertise in making the product. Thus, natural foods maker Kashi shows its buyers carefully selecting ingredients for its products, and Jim Koch of the Boston Beer Company tells about his many years of experience in brewing Samuel Adams beer.

Execution style
The approach, style, tone, words, and format used for executing an advertising message.

Walter McBride/Corbis

Exhibit 13.9 Message execution styles: Using celebrity endorsers to represent brands—Beyoncé speaks for Pepsi.

- *Scientific evidence:* This style presents survey or scientific evidence that the brand is better or better liked than one or more other brands. For years, Crest toothpaste has used scientific evidence to convince buyers that Crest is better than other brands at fighting cavities.

- *Testimonial evidence or endorsement:* This style features a highly believable or likable source endorsing the product. It could be ordinary people saying how much they like a given product. For example, Trivago's "sloppy but sexy pitchman" Tim Williams shows how the metasearch travel site can find the best hotel prices. *Rolling Stone* magazine touted him as the ideal pitchman, even suggesting that we "forget that Dos Equis dude, Trivago Guy is the Most Interesting Man in the World."[25] Or it might be a celebrity presenting the product, such as Beyoncé speaking for Pepsi.

The advertiser also must choose a *tone* for the ad. For example, P&G always uses a positive tone: Its ads say something very positive about its products. Other advertisers now use edgy humour to break through the commercial clutter. Bud Light commercials are famous for this.

The advertiser must use memorable and attention-getting *words* in the ad. For example, rather than claiming simply that its laundry detergent is "superconcentrated," Method asks customers, "Are you jug addicted?" The solution: "Our patent-pending formula that's so fricken' concentrated, 50 loads fits in a teeny bottle. . . . With our help, you can get off the jugs and get clean."

Finally, *format* elements make a difference in an ad's impact as well as in its cost. A small change in an ad's design can make a big difference in its effect. In a print ad, the *illustration* is the first thing the reader notices—it must be strong enough to draw attention. Next, the *headline* must effectively entice the right people to read the copy. Finally, the *copy*—the main block of text in the ad—must be simple but strong and convincing. Moreover, these three elements must effectively work *together* to persuasively present customer value. However, novel formats can help an ad stand out from the clutter. For example, striking Benjamin Moore paint ads consist mostly of a single long headline in mixed fonts balanced against a colour swatch and background that illustrate the colour discussed in the headline.

CONSUMER-GENERATED CONTENT Taking advantage of today's digital and social media technologies, many companies are now tapping consumers for marketing content, message ideas, or even actual ads. Sometimes the results are outstanding; sometimes they are forgettable. If done well, however, user-generated content can incorporate the voice of the customer into brand messages and generate greater customer engagement.

Many brands hold contests that invite consumers to submit ad message ideas and videos. For example, as we mentioned earlier in the chapter, PepsiCo's Doritos brand runs an annual "Crash the Super Bowl Challenge" contest that invites consumers to create their own 30-second video ads about the tasty triangular corn chips. A Doritos brand team whittles down the thousands of entries and posts the finalists on Facebook, where consumers vote for their favourites. The winners receive large cash awards and have their ads run during the Super Bowl.

Past "Crash the Super Bowl" campaigns have produced numerous top awards. For example, in Super Bowl XLVI, user-created Doritos ads earned two first-place finishes, one for the top ranking in the traditional *USA Today* AdMeter rankings and another for finishing first in a new *USA Today*/Facebook social media version of the AdMeter rankings.

Both ads earned their creators a cool $1 million cash award from Doritos. The favourite ad with online voters that year was one called "Sling Baby," created by 31-year-old Jonathan Friedman of Virginia Beach, Virginia, in which a grandmother slingshots a baby across the yard to nab a bag of Doritos chips from a taunting neighbour kid. For Doritos, "Crash the Super Bowl" has been an advertising and social media touchdown, triggering consumer involvement over several months before, during, and the Super Bowl.[26]

The Super Bowl is one thing, but many marketers employ consumer-generated content in a simpler way. For example, yogawear company lululemon's #TheSweatLife campaign invited customers to tweet or Instagram photos of themselves "getting their sweat on" in lululemon gear. "Your perspiration is our inspiration," said the brand at its website. "We want to see you living #thesweatlife." Within only a few months, the brand had received more than 7000 photos, which it featured in a #thesweatlife online gallery, quickly drawing more than 40 000 unique visitors. The user-generated content campaign created substantial customer engagement for lululemon. "We created the program as a way to connect with our guests and showcase how they're authentically sweating in our product offline," said a lululemon brand manager. "We see it as a unique way to bring their offline experiences into our online community."[27]

Frito-Lay, Inc.

Exhibit 13.10 Consumer-generated messages: In Super Bowl XLVI, two Doritos "Crash the Super Bowl" ads took first place in *USA Today*'s AdMeter/Facebook ratings, including this "Sling Baby" ad.

Not all consumer-generated advertising efforts, however, are so successful. As many big companies have learned, ads made by amateurs can be ... well, pretty amateurish. If done well, however, consumer-generated content efforts can produce new creative ideas and fresh perspectives on the brand from consumers who actually experience it. Such campaigns can boost consumer involvement and get customers talking and thinking about a brand and its value to them. "For those willing to give up control and trust the wisdom of the crowd," says one analyst, "collaboration on . . . marketing campaigns can bear amazing results."[28]

Selecting Advertising Media The major steps in **advertising media** selection are (1) determining *reach*, *frequency*, *impact*, and *engagement*; (2) choosing among major *media types*; (3) selecting specific *media vehicles*; and (4) choosing *media timing*.

Advertising media
The vehicles through which advertising messages are delivered to their intended audiences.

DETERMINING REACH, FREQUENCY, IMPACT, AND ENGAGEMENT To select media, the advertiser must determine the reach and frequency needed to achieve the advertising objectives. *Reach* is a measure of the *percentage* of people in the target market who are exposed to the ad campaign during a given period of time. For example, the advertiser might try to reach 70 percent of the target market during the first three months of the campaign. *Frequency* is a measure of how many *times* the average person in the target market is exposed to the message. For example, the advertiser might want an average exposure frequency of three.

But advertisers want to do more than just reach a given number of consumers a specific number of times. The advertiser also must determine the desired *media impact*—the *qualitative value* of message exposure through a given medium. For example, the same message in one magazine (say, *Maclean's*) may be more believable than in another (say, the *National*

Provided by The Weather Channel.

Exhibit 13.11 To engage consumers, Home Depot runs ads on Weather Channel's mobile app.

Enquirer). For products that need to be demonstrated, messages on television or in an online video may have more impact than messages on radio because they use sight, motion, *and* sound. Products for which consumers provide input on design or features might be better promoted at an interactive website or social media page than in a direct mailing.

More generally, the advertiser wants to choose media that will *engage* consumers rather than simply reach them. In any medium, the relevance of ad content for its audience is often much more important than how many people it reaches. Home Depot has learned that although it lacks the broad reach of local TV or print ads, a combination of mobile and online media can engage customers more deeply and personally. For example, it now runs ads on the Weather Channel's mobile app. When customers tap on the Home Depot banner ad, they're sent to the retailer's mobile site, which highlights products matching their local weather conditions and forecast. Expecting snow in your area? You'll likely see special deals on snow shovels and snow blowers. Such focused and engaging media placements nicely supplement Home Depot's broader advertising efforts.[29]

Although Nielsen is beginning to measure *media engagement* levels for some television, radio, and social media, such measures are still hard to find in most cases. Current media measures are things such as ratings, readership, listenership, and click-through rates. However, engagement happens inside the consumer. Notes one expert, "Just measuring the number of eyeballs in front of a television set is hard enough without trying to measure the intensity of those eyeballs doing the viewing."[30] Still, marketers need to know how customers connect with an ad and brand idea as a part of the broader brand relationship.

Engaged consumers are more likely to act upon brand messages and even share them with others. Thus, rather than simply tracking *consumer impressions* for a media placement—how many people see, hear, or read an ad—Coca-Cola now also tracks the *consumer expressions* that result, such as a comment, a Like, uploading a photo or video, or sharing brand content on social networks. Today's empowered consumers often generate more messages about a brand than a company can. Through engagement, "instead of having to always pay for their message to run somewhere, [marketers] can 'earn' media for free, via consumer spreading YouTube clips, Groupons, and tweets," says an advertising consultant.[31]

For example, Coca-Cola estimates that on YouTube there are about 146 million views of content related to Coca-Cola. However, only about 26 million of those are of content that Coca-Cola created. The other 120 million are of content created by engaged consumers. "We can't match the volume of our consumers' output," says Coca-Cola's chief marketing officer, "but we can spark it with the right type [and placement] of content."[32]

CHOOSING AMONG MAJOR MEDIA TYPES As summarized in Table 13.2, the major media types are television, digital and social media, newspapers, direct mail, magazines, radio, and outdoor. Each medium has its advantages and its limitations. Media planners want to choose media that will effectively and efficiently present the advertising message to target customers. Thus, they must consider each medium's impact, message effectiveness, and cost. As discussed earlier in the chapter, it's typically not a question of which one medium to use. Rather, the advertiser selects a mix of media and blends them into a fully integrated marketing communications campaign.

The mix of media must be re-examined regularly. For a long time, television and magazines dominated the media mixes of national advertisers, with other media often neglected. However, as mass-media costs rise, audiences shrink, and exciting new digital and social media emerge, many advertisers are finding new ways to reach consumers. They are supplementing the traditional mass media with more-specialized and highly targeted digital media that cost less, target more effectively, and engage consumers more fully.

As discussed earlier, today's marketers want to assemble a full mix of *paid, owned, earned,* and *shared media* that create and deliver involving brand content to target consumers.

TABLE 13.2	Profiles of Major Media Types	
Medium	**Advantages**	**Limitations**
Television	Good mass-marketing coverage; low cost per exposure; combines sight, sound, and motion; appealing to the senses	High absolute costs; high clutter; fleeting exposure; less audience selectivity
Online, mobile, and social media	Focus on individuals and customer communities; immediacy; personalization, interaction, and engagement capabilities; social sharing power; low cost	Potentially narrow impact; difficult to administer and control; the audience often controls content and exposure
Newspapers	Flexibility; timeliness; good local market coverage; broad acceptability; high believability	Short life; poor reproduction quality; small pass-along audience
Direct mail	High audience selectivity; flexibility; no ad competition within the same medium; allows personalization	Relatively high cost per exposure; "junk mail" image
Magazines	High geographic and demographic selectivity; credibility and prestige; high-quality reproduction; long life and good pass-along readership	Long ad purchase lead time; high cost; no guarantee of position
Radio	Good local acceptance; high geographic and demographic selectivity; low cost	Audio only; fleeting exposure; low attention ("the half-heard" medium); fragmented audiences
Outdoor	Flexibility; high repeat exposure; low cost; low message competition; good positional selectivity	Little audience selectivity; creative limitations

In addition to the explosion of online, mobile, and social media, cable and satellite television systems are thriving. Such systems allow narrow programming formats, such as all sports, all news, nutrition, arts, home improvement and gardening, cooking, travel, history, finance, and others that target select groups. Cable operators are even testing systems that will let them target specific types of ads to TVs in specific neighbourhoods or individually to specific types of customers. For example, ads for a French-language channel would run in only French neighbourhoods, or only pet owners would see ads from pet food companies. Advertisers can take advantage of such *narrowcasting* to "rifle in" on special market segments rather than use the "shotgun" approach offered by network broadcasting.

Finally, in their efforts to find less costly and more highly targeted ways to reach consumers, advertisers have discovered a dazzling collection of *alternative media*. These days, no matter where you go or what you do, you will probably run into some new form of advertising.

Tiny billboards attached to shopping carts urge you to buy JELL-O Pudding Pops or Pampers, while ads roll by on the store's checkout conveyor touting your local Chevy dealer. Step outside and there goes a city trash truck sporting an ad for Glad trash bags or a school bus displaying a Little Caesar's pizza ad. A nearby fire hydrant is emblazoned with advertising for KFC's "fiery" chicken wings. You escape to the ballpark, only to find billboard-size video screens running Budweiser ads while a blimp with an electronic message board circles lazily overhead. In mid-winter, you wait in a city bus shelter that looks like an oven—with heat coming from the coils—introducing Caribou Coffee's lineup of hot breakfast sandwiches.

Caribou Coffee.

Exhibit 13.12 Marketers have discovered a dazzling array of alternative media, like this heated Caribou Coffee bus shelter.

These days, you're likely to find ads—well—anywhere. Taxi cabs sport electronic messaging signs tied to GPS location sensors that can pitch local stores and restaurants wherever they roam. Ad space is being sold on DVD cases, parking-lot tickets, airline boarding passes, subway turnstiles, highway toll booth gates, golf scorecards, ATMs, municipal garbage cans, and even police cars, doctors' examining tables, and church bulletins. One company even sells space on toilet paper furnished free to restaurants, stadiums, and malls—the paper carries advertiser logos, coupons, and codes you can scan with your smartphone to download digital coupons or link to advertisers' social media pages. Now that's a captive audience.

Such alternative media seem a bit far-fetched, and they sometimes irritate consumers who resent it all as "ad nauseam." But for many marketers, these media can save money and provide a way to hit selected consumers where they live, shop, work, and play.

Another important trend affecting media selection is the rapid growth in the number of *media multitaskers*, people who absorb more than one medium at a time. For example, it's not uncommon to find someone watching TV with a smartphone in hand, tweeting, Snapchatting with friends, and chasing down product information on Google. One survey found that a whopping 88 percent of tablet owners and 86 percent of smartphone owners use the devices while watching TV. Although some of this multitasking is related to TV viewing—such as looking up related product and program information—most multitasking involves tasks unrelated to the shows being watched. Marketers need to take such media interactions into account when selecting the types of media they will use.[33]

SELECTING SPECIFIC MEDIA VEHICLES Media planners must also choose the best media vehicles—specific media within each general media type. For example, television vehicles include *Modern Family* and *Hockey Night in Canada*. Magazine vehicles include *Maclean's* and *Chatelaine*. Online and mobile vehicles include Twitter, Facebook, Pinterest, and YouTube.

Media planners must compute the cost per 1000 persons reached by a vehicle. For example, if a full-page, four-colour advertisement in the U.S. national edition of *Forbes* costs US$148 220 and *Forbes*'s readership is 900 000 people, the cost of reaching each group of 1000 persons is about $164. The same advertisement in *Bloomberg Businessweek*'s Northeast U.S. regional edition may cost only US$48 100 but reach only 155 000 people—at a cost per 1000 of about $310.[34] The media planner ranks each magazine by cost per 1000 and favours those magazines with the lower cost per 1000 for reaching target consumers. In the above case, if a marketer is targeting Northeast business managers, *BusinessWeek* might be the more cost-effective buy, even at a higher cost per thousand.

Media planners must also consider the costs of producing ads for different media. Whereas newspaper ads may cost very little to produce, flashy television ads can be very costly. Many online and social media ads cost little to produce, but costs can climb when producing made-for-the-Web videos and ad series.

In selecting specific media vehicles, media planners must balance media costs against several media effectiveness factors. First, the planner should evaluate the media vehicle's audience quality. For a Huggies disposable diapers advertisement, for example, *Parents* magazine would have a high exposure value; *Maxim* would have a low exposure value. Second, the media planner should consider audience engagement. Readers of *Vogue*, for example, typically pay more attention to ads than do *Canadian Business* readers. Third, the planner should assess the vehicle's editorial quality. The *Globe and Mail* and the *Wall Street Journal* are more believable and prestigious than the *National Enquirer*.

DECIDING ON MEDIA TIMING An advertiser must also decide how to schedule the advertising over the course of a year. Suppose sales of a product peak in December and drop in March (for winter outdoor gear, for instance). The firm can vary its advertising to follow the seasonal pattern, oppose the seasonal pattern, or be the same all year. Most firms do some seasonal advertising. For example, Mars currently runs M&M's special ads for almost every holiday and "season," from Easter and Halloween to the Super Bowl season and the Oscar season. Some marketers do *only* seasonal advertising: For instance, P&G advertises its Vicks NyQuil only during the cold and flu season.

Finally, the advertiser must choose the pattern of the ads. *Continuity* means scheduling ads evenly within a given period. *Pulsing* means scheduling ads unevenly over a given time period. Thus, 52 ads could either be scheduled at one per week during the year or pulsed in several bursts. The idea behind pulsing is to advertise heavily for a short period to build awareness that carries over to the next advertising period. Those who favour pulsing feel that it can be used to achieve the same impact as a steady schedule but at a much lower cost. However, some media planners believe that although pulsing achieves some awareness, it sacrifices depth of advertising communications.

Today's online and social media let advertisers create ads that respond to events in real time. For example, Lexus introduced a new model through live streaming from the North American International Auto Show via Facebook's News Feed. Some 100 000 people watched the introduction live in only the first 10 minutes; another 600 000 viewed it online within the next few days. As another example, Oreos reacted to a power outage during Super Bowl XLVII with an outage-related "You can still dunk in the dark" tweet. The fast-reaction ad was retweeted and favourited thousands of times in only 15 minutes. Similarly, drugstore retailer Walgreens tweeted "We do carry candles" and ". . . we also sell lights," messages that drew thousands of quick retweets and faves.[35]

FOR A **BETTER-LOOKING TOMORROW.**

Exhibit 13.13 Media timing: Vicks NyQuil runs ads like this only during the cold and flu season.

The Procter & Gamble Company

Evaluating Advertising Effectiveness and the Return on Advertising Investment LO4

Measuring advertising effectiveness and the **return on advertising investment** has become a hot issue for most companies, especially in a challenging economic environment. Even in a recovering economy with marketing budgets again on the rise, like consumers, advertisers are still pinching their pennies and spending conservatively. That leaves top management at many companies asking their marketing managers, "How do we know that we're spending the right amount on advertising?" and "What return are we getting on our advertising investment?"

Advertisers should regularly evaluate two types of advertising results: the communication effects and the sales and profit effects. Measuring the *communication effects* of an ad or ad campaign tells whether the ads and media are communicating the ad message well. Individual ads can be tested before or after they are run. Before an ad is placed, the advertiser can show it to consumers, ask how they like it, and measure message recall or attitude changes resulting from it. After an ad is run, the advertiser can measure how the ad affected consumer recall or product awareness, knowledge, and preference. Pre- and post-evaluations of communication effects can be made for entire advertising campaigns as well.

Advertisers have gotten pretty good at measuring the communication effects of their ads and ad campaigns. However, *sales and profit* effects of advertising are often much harder to measure. For example, what sales and profits are produced by an ad campaign that increases brand awareness by 20 percent and brand preference by 10 percent? Sales and profits are affected by many factors other than advertising—such as product features, price, and availability.

Return on advertising investment The net return on advertising investment divided by the costs of the advertising investment.

One way to measure the sales and profit effects of advertising is to compare past sales and profits with past advertising expenditures. Another way is through experiments. For example, to test the effects of different advertising spending levels, Coca-Cola could vary the amount it spends on advertising in different market areas and measure the differences in the resulting sales and profit levels. More complex experiments could be designed to include other variables, such as differences in the ads or media used.

However, because so many factors affect advertising effectiveness, some controllable and others not, measuring the results of advertising spending remains an inexact science. Managers must often rely on large doses of judgment along with quantitative analysis when assessing advertising performance.

Other Advertising Considerations

In developing advertising strategies and programs, the company must address two additional questions. First, how will the company organize its advertising function—who will perform which advertising tasks? Second, how will the company adapt its advertising strategies and programs to the complexities of international markets?

Organizing for Advertising Different companies organize in different ways to handle advertising. In small companies, advertising might be handled by someone in the sales department. Large companies have advertising departments whose job it is to set the advertising budget, work with the ad agency, and handle other advertising not done by the agency. However, most large companies use outside advertising agencies because they offer several advantages.

> **Advertising agency**
> A marketing services firm that assists companies in planning, preparing, implementing, and evaluating all or portions of their advertising programs.

How does an **advertising agency** work? Advertising agencies originated in the mid- to late 1800s from salespeople and brokers who worked for the media and received a commission for selling advertising space to companies. As time passed, the salespeople began to help customers prepare their ads. Eventually, they formed agencies and grew closer to the advertisers than to the media.

Today's agencies employ specialists who can often perform advertising tasks better than the company's own staff can. Agencies also bring an outside point of view to solving the company's problems, along with lots of experience from working with different clients and situations. So, today, even companies with strong advertising departments of their own use advertising agencies.

Some ad agencies are huge; the biggest U.S. agency, Y&R, has annual gross revenues of US$1.69 billion. In recent years, many agencies have grown by gobbling up other agencies, thus creating huge agency holding companies. The largest of these megagroups, WPP, includes several large advertising, PR, and promotion agencies, with combined worldwide revenues of more than US$17 billion.[36] Most big advertising agencies have the staff and resources to handle all phases of an advertising campaign for their clients, from creating a marketing plan to developing ad campaigns and preparing, placing, and evaluating ads and other brand content. Large brands commonly employ several agencies that handle everything from mass-media advertising campaigns to shopper marketing and social media content.

International Advertising Decisions International advertisers face many complexities not encountered by domestic advertisers. The most basic issue concerns the degree to which global advertising should be adapted to the unique characteristics of various country markets.

Some advertisers have attempted to support their global brands with highly standardized worldwide advertising, with campaigns that work as well in Bangkok as they do in Baltimore. For example, McDonald's unifies its creative elements and brand presentation under the familiar "i'm lovin' it" theme in all its 100-plus markets worldwide. Visa coordinates worldwide advertising for its debit and credit cards under the "more people go with Visa" creative platform, which works as well in Korea as it does in

MANOLO MORAN FOTOGRAFIA LTDA and ALPARGATAS S/A.

Exhibit 13.14 Ads from Brazilian flip-flops maker Havaianas make the same outrageously colourful splash worldwide, no matter what the country.

Canada or Brazil. And ads from Brazilian flip-flops maker Havaianas make the same outrageously colourful splash worldwide, no matter what the country.

In recent years, the increased popularity of online marketing and social media sharing has boosted the need for advertising standardization for global brands. Most big marketing and advertising campaigns include a large online presence. Connected consumers can now zip easily across borders via the Internet and social media, making it difficult for advertisers to roll out adapted campaigns in a controlled, orderly fashion. As a result, at the very least, most global consumer brands coordinate their websites internationally. For example, check out McDonald's sites from Germany to Jordan to China. You'll find the golden arches logo, the "i'm lovin' it" logo and jingle, a Big Mac equivalent, and maybe even Ronald McDonald himself.

Standardization produces many benefits—lower advertising costs, greater global advertising coordination, and a more consistent worldwide image. But it also has drawbacks. Most important, it ignores the fact that country markets differ greatly in their cultures, demographics, and economic conditions. Thus, most international advertisers "think globally but act locally." They develop global advertising *strategies* that make their worldwide efforts more efficient and consistent. Then they adapt their advertising *programs* to make them more responsive to consumer needs and expectations within local markets. For example, although Visa employs its "more people go with Visa" theme globally, ads in specific locales employ local language and inspiring local imagery that make the theme relevant to the local markets in which they appear.

Global advertisers face several special problems. For instance, advertising media costs and availability differ vastly from country to country. Countries also differ in the extent to which they regulate advertising practices. Many countries have extensive systems of laws restricting how much a company can spend on advertising, the media used, the nature of advertising claims, and other aspects of the advertising program. Such restrictions often require advertisers to adapt their campaigns from country to country.

Thus, although advertisers may develop global strategies to guide their overall advertising efforts, specific advertising programs must usually be adapted to meet local cultures and customs, media characteristics, and regulations.

Public Relations LO5

Another major mass-promotion tool, public relations, consists of activities designed to engage and build good relations with the company's various publics. PR departments may perform any or all of the following functions:[37]

- *Press relations or press agency:* Creating and placing newsworthy information in the news media to attract attention to a person, product, or service.
- *Product publicity:* Publicizing specific products.
- *Public affairs:* Building and maintaining national or local community relationships.
- *Lobbying:* Building and maintaining relationships with legislators and government officials to influence legislation and regulation.
- *Investor relations:* Maintaining relationships with shareholders and others in the financial community.
- *Development:* Working with donors or members of nonprofit organizations to gain financial or volunteer support.

Public relations is used to promote products, people, places, ideas, activities, organizations, and even nations. Companies use PR to build good relations with consumers, investors, the media, and their communities. Trade associations have used PR to rebuild interest in commodities, such as eggs, apples, potatoes, milk—and even chocolate milk. For example, the U.S. Milk Processor Education Program (MilkPEP), known for its successful "Got Milk?" campaign, and the Dairy Farmers of Canada have both created strong PR campaigns to promote the health benefits of chocolate milk and boost its consumption:

Dairy Farmers of Canada

Exhibit 13.15 The Dairy Farmers of Canada's "Recharge with Milk" campaign encourages physically active Canadians to drink chocolate milk as a post-workout recovery beverage.

In the U.S., MilkPEP launched an extensive, integrated PR campaign to reposition chocolate milk—the traditional children's favourite—as a post-workout, sports recovery beverage for adults. Backed by more than 20 research studies that support the refuelling benefits of chocolate milk, MilkPEP's "Built with Chocolate Milk" campaign enlists important influences—such as athletes, sports nutritionists, fitness bloggers, and health researchers—to help change perceptions of chocolate milk from just a kid's drink to a legitimate sports drink, one that's "Trusted by Athletes. Backed by Science." Ads and social media content featured both everyday and well-known athletes, such as the NHL's Zach Parise and NBA basketball star Carmelo Anthony. As well as working with professional athletes, MilkPEP participates in hundreds of local events across the U.S., passing out free chocolate milk. Similarly, the Dairy Farmers of Canada's "Recharge with Milk" campaign has been running in Ontario and Atlantic Canada since 2007. The 2015 campaign focused on the importance of training routines in order to reach athletes and encourage them to include chocolate milk as an excellent post-workout recovery beverage. In addition to an active website (rechargewithmilk. ca) and social media presence, the campaign sponsors several events, such as marathons, as well as various associations, including Rugby Ontario and the Greater Toronto Hockey League. The 2015 campaign has resulted in over 590 million online impressions.[38]

The Role and Impact of PR

Public relations can have a strong impact on public awareness at a much lower cost than advertising can. When using public relations, the company does not pay for the space or time in the media. Rather, it pays for a staff to develop and circulate information and manage events. If the company develops an interesting story or event, it could be picked up by several different media and have the same effect as advertising that would cost millions of dollars. What's more, public relations has the power to engage consumers and make them a part of the brand story and its telling (see Marketing@Work 13.2).

PR results can sometimes be spectacular. Consider the launches of Apple's iPad and iPad 2:

> Apple's iPad was one of the most successful new-product launches in history. The funny thing: Whereas most big product launches are accompanied by huge prelaunch advertising campaigns, Apple pulled this one off with no advertising. None at all. Instead, it simply fed the PR fire. It built buzz months in advance by distributing iPads for early reviews, feeding the offline and online press with tempting tidbits, and offering fans an early online peek at thousands of new iPad apps that would be available. At launch time, it fanned the flames with a cameo on the TV sitcom *Modern Family*, a flurry of launch-day appearances on TV talk shows, and other launch-day events. In the process, through PR alone, the iPad launch generated unbounded consumer excitement, a media frenzy, and long lines outside retail stores on launch day. Apple sold more than 300 000 of the sleek gadgets on the first day alone and more than 2 million in the first two months—even as demand outstripped supply. Apple repeated the feat a year later with the equally successful launch of iPad 2, which sold close to 1 million devices the weekend of its launch.[39]

Despite its potential strengths, public relations is occasionally described as a marketing stepchild because of its sometimes limited and scattered use. The PR department is often located at corporate headquarters or handled by a third-party agency. Its staff is so busy dealing with various publics—stockholders, employees, legislators, and the press—that PR programs to support product marketing objectives may be ignored. Moreover, marketing managers and PR practitioners do not always speak the same language. Whereas many PR practitioners see their jobs as simply communicating, marketing managers tend to be much more interested in how advertising and PR affect brand building, sales and profits, and customer engagement and relationships.

This situation is changing, however. Although public relations still captures only a small portion of the overall marketing budgets of most firms, PR can be a powerful brand-building tool. Especially in this digital age, the lines between advertising and PR are becoming more and more blurred. For example, are brand sites, blogs, viral brand videos, and social media activities advertising or PR efforts? All are both. And as the use of earned and shared digital content grows rapidly, PR may play a bigger role in marketing content management. More than any other department, PR has always been responsible for creating relevant marketing content that draws consumers to a brand rather than pushing messages out. "Knowing where influence and conversations are to be found is PR's stock in trade," says one expert. "PR pros are an organization's master storytellers. In a word, they *do* content."[40] The point is that PR should work hand in hand with advertising within an integrated marketing communications program to help build customer engagement and relationships.

Major Public Relations Tools

Public relations uses several tools. One of the major tools is *news*. PR professionals find or create favourable news about the company and its products or people. Sometimes news stories occur naturally; sometimes the PR person can suggest events or activities that would create news. Another common PR tool is *special events*, ranging from news conferences and speeches, brand tours, and grand openings to laser light shows, multimedia presentations, or educational programs designed to reach and interest target publics.

Public relations people also prepare *written materials* to reach and influence their target markets. These materials include annual reports, brochures, articles, and company newsletters and magazines. *Audiovisual materials*, such as DVDs and online videos, are being used

MARKETING@WORK   13.2

PR and Customer Engagement at Coca-Cola: From Impressions to Expressions to Transactions

Coca-Cola aims to do much more with public relations than just create passive "impressions." It's looking to create customer engagement and inspire customer "expressions." According to Coca-Cola's chief marketing officer, Joe Tripodi, the PR goal is to develop "strongly sharable pieces of communication information that generate huge numbers of impressions online—and then, crucially, lead to expressions from consumers, who join the story and extend it, and then finally to transactions." That is, Coca-Cola uses PR to engage consumers and start customer conversations that will inspire consumers themselves to extend the brand's theme of open happiness and optimism.

Consider Coca-Cola's "Hug Me" campaign, in which the company installed a "happiness" vending machine overnight at a university in Singapore. The machine had a solid red front and

trademark wavy white stripe, but it contained no Coca-Cola logo, no coin slot, and no soda selection buttons. Only the words "Hug Me" were visible in large white letters printed in Coca-Cola's famous script. With hidden cameras rolling, Coca-Cola captured the quizzical reactions of passersby as they first scratched their heads, then slowly approached the machine, and, finally, with smiles on their faces, gave it a big hug. Responding to that simple act of happiness, the machine magically dispensed a cold can of Coca-Cola, free of charge.

Coca-Cola's "Hug Me" video shows one person after another hugging the machine, receiving a Coke, and sharing their delight with others. Coca-Cola placed the video online, then stepped back and let the media and consumers carry the story forward. Within only one

week's time, the video generated 112 million impressions. Given the low costs of the free Cokes and producing the video, the "Hug Me" campaign resulted in an amazingly low cost per impression. But even more valuable were the extensive customer expressions that followed, such as "Liking" the video and forwarding it to others. "The Coca Cola Hug Machine is a simple idea to spread some happiness," said a Coca-Cola marketer. Our strategy is to deliver doses of happiness in an unexpected, innovative way . . . and happiness is contagious."

The "Hug Me" campaign was one instance in a long line of similar conversation-starting PR tactics by Coca-Cola. For example, on one Valentine's Day, the company placed a modified vending machine in the middle of a busy shopping mall that dispensed free Cokes to folks who confirmed their "couple" status with a hug or a kiss. A few years before that, another Coca-Cola Happiness machine placed at a university dispensed everything from free Cokes to popcorn, pizza, flowers, handshakes, and Polaroid photos. Making periodic "jackpot" sounds, the machine dispensed dozens of Cokes and a long plank layered with colourful cupcakes. These unexpected actions not only prompted smiles and cheers, but recipients could hardly wait to share their bounty and the story with anyone and everyone, extending Coke's happiness positioning.

Coca-Cola has fielded many other PR campaigns that employ its "impressions-expressions-transactions" model to inspire brand conversations. In its "Project Connect" campaign, the company printed 150 common first names on Coke bottles, an exploit that had consumers by the hundreds of thousands rifling through Coca-Cola displays in retail stores looking for their names. In its "Move to the Beat" project, Coca-Cola brought music, youth, and sports together for the London 2012 Olympics

Exhibit 13.16 The power of PR: Coca-Cola's "Hug Me" campaign created 112 million impressions in only one week. More important, it created countless customer expressions that extended the brand's theme of happiness and optimism.

through an original music track by British music producer Mark Ronson, which wrapped the live sounds of five different Olympic sports around the vocals of Katy B.

Coca-Cola's long-running Arctic Home campaign employs the power of publicity and shared media to create engagement by connecting the company's brands to a culturally relevant cause. In that campaign, Coca-Cola has partnered with the World Wildlife Fund (WWF) to protect the habitat of polar bears—a cause that fits perfectly with Coke's long-standing use of digitally produced polar bears as spokes-critters in its ads. The Arctic Home campaign goes well beyond clever seasonal ads by integrating PR efforts with virtually every aspect of promotion and marketing. The campaign includes a dedicated site, a smartphone app, a pledge of $3 million to the WWF, advertisements and online videos featuring footage from the IMAX film *To the Arctic 3D*, and attention-grabbing white Coke cans highlighting the plight of polar bears. In its first year, Arctic Home produced an astounding 1.3 billion impressions, which in turn inspired untold customer engagement and expressions.

Coca-Cola's "BHAG," or "big hairy audacious goal," is not just to hold its market share in the soft drink category, where sales have been flat for years, but to double its business by the end of the decade. Public relations and the social media will play a central role in achieving this goal by making customers a part of the brand story and turning them into an army of brand advocates who will carry the Coca-Cola Open Happiness message forward. "It's not just about pushing stuff out as we've historically done," says CMO Tripodi. "We have to create experiences that perhaps are had only by a few but are compelling enough to fuel conversations with many."

Sources: Tim Nudd, "Coca-Cola Joins the Revolution in a World Where the Mob Rules," *Adweek*, June 19, 2012, www.adweek.com/print/141217; Thomas Pardee, "Olympics Campaigns Go Big on the Viral Video Chart," *Advertising Age*, May 17, 2012, http://adage.com/print/234790; Natalie Zmuda, "Coca-Cola Gets Real with Polar Bears," *Advertising Age*, October 25, 2011, http://adage.com/print/230632; Emma Hall, "Coca-Cola Launches Global 2012 Olympics Campaign with Mark Ronson," *Advertising Age*, September 29, 2011, http://adage.com/print/230107; Anthony Wing Kosner, "Hug Me: Coca-Cola Introduces Gesture Based Marketing in Singapore," *Forbes*, April 11, 2012, www.forbes.com/sites/anthonykosner/2012/04/11/hug-me-coca-cola-introduces-gesture-based-marketing-in-singapore; "Cannes Lions 2012: Five Points to a Great Marketing Strategy," afaqs.com, June 20, 2012, www.afaqs.com/news/story/34444; and www.youtube.com/watch?feature=endscreen&NR=1&v= -A-7H4aOhq0, accessed November 2013.

increasingly as communication tools. *Corporate identity materials* can also help create a corporate identity that the public immediately recognizes. Logos, stationery, brochures, signs, business forms, business cards, buildings, uniforms, and company cars and trucks all become marketing tools when they are attractive, distinctive, and memorable. Finally, companies can improve public goodwill by contributing money and time to *public service activities*.

As previously discussed, the Web and social media are also important PR channels. Websites, blogs, and social media such as YouTube, Facebook, Pinterest, Storify, and Twitter are providing new ways to reach and engage people. As noted earlier, storytelling and engagement are core PR strengths, and that plays well into the use of online and social media. Consider the Wrangler NextBlue PR campaign:

> Wrangler wanted to reach out beyond its core consumers—to a young, metropolitan mindset. But rather than using ads or standard PR approaches, it created NextBlue, an online project giving consumers and fledgling designers a chance to create the next style of Wrangler jeans. Working with its PR agency, Wrangler created a microsite that asked consumers to create videos of themselves and their jeans designs. The campaign was promoted on Wrangler's website and Facebook page and in its emails to Wrangler subscribers. The brand also used a mix of traditional PR media, along with paid ads on Facebook and social media promotions on YouTube and Twitter, allowing the public to comment and vote on the submitted designs.
>
> The rich integration of paid, owned, earned, and shared PR media produced the desired results. Within just two weeks, Wrangler received 50 video submissions. The winning entry, created by Song Ahn Nguyen, was then sold on Wrangler.com as the first design in the NextBlue line. But in addition to the new design, Wrangler signed up 19 young designers to blog for its NextBlue site, garnered 5000 new subscribers to its email database, and counted more than 80 000 views of the finalist videos. "The heart of the NextBlue [PR] project was a brand collaboration with consumers," says a Wrangler marketing communications executive. "The social media are a natural fit for [that]."[41]

As with the other promotion tools, in considering when and how to use product public relations, management should set PR objectives, choose the PR messages and vehicles, implement the PR plan, and evaluate the results. The firm's PR should be blended smoothly with other promotion activities within the company's overall integrated marketing communications effort.

PR Meets Advertising: We'll Make You a Fan

According to the integrated marketing communications (IMC) approach, a firm can maximize the impact of its promotional tools only when they're all working together, bearing a similar message, carrying a similar theme, and generally "integrated."

Boston Pizza kicked off its 51st year by bringing forward an IMC program that was not only committed to delighting its customers but also celebrated its sports bar roots and the transcendent nature of sports in Canadian culture. The "We'll Make You a Fan" positioning "gets at the heart of what Boston Pizza is all about—a place for Canadians to connect over two things they love: sports and food," said Steve Silverstone, executive vice-president of marketing for Boston Pizza International. "Nearly every Canadian has some kind of connection to sports—whether as spectators, participants, players, coaches, managers, or parents who drive their kids to and from practice. Boston Pizza is the restaurant where you can show up with a group of 20 kids wearing soccer cleats or with a buddy after a game of pickup hockey to watch a game in the sports bar."

"We looked at our company and we asked, 'What makes people want to come into Boston Pizza unprompted?'" explains CEO Mark Pacinda. When the long-awaited Floyd Mayweather–Manny Pacquiao boxing title fight finally occurred in April 2015, Pacinda recalls going to a Boston Pizza location with his son to watch the fight. "It was packed. There were 120 people on the patio looking in to see the fight, and then 10 minutes before the fight, there were 150 people in the parking lot who couldn't get into the restaurant because we were at capacity." That anecdote says a thing or two about BP's clientele and culture: There's a pretty deep passion for sports. "We have a saying," Pacinda remarks. "We don't line up for the Academy Awards, but we'll line up for sports!"

True to the principle of IMC, the "We'll Make You a Fan" campaign crossed all forms of advertising, direct and social media, public relations, sales promotions, and personal selling. If today's best brands are also the best storytellers, BP etched its logo into that category with "We'll Make You a Fan."

QUESTIONS

1. Why is it important for marketing communications functions to be "integrated"?
2. Research Boston Pizza's "We'll Make You a Fan" campaign and list examples of the various IMC categories.
3. Did BP risk losing, or alienating, customers who weren't necessarily sports fans? Explain your response.

REVIEWING THE CONCEPTS

 Define the five promotion mix tools for communicating customer value.

A company's total *promotion mix*—also called its *marketing communications mix*—consists of the specific blend of *advertising*, *personal selling*, *sales promotion*, *public relations*, and *direct and digital marketing* tools that the company uses to persuasively communicate customer value and build customer relationships. Advertising includes any paid form of nonpersonal presentation and promotion of ideas, goods, or services by an identified sponsor. In contrast, public relations focuses on building good relations with the company's various publics. Personal selling is personal presentation by the firm's sales force for the purpose of making sales and building customer relationships. Firms use sales promotion to provide short-term incentives to encourage the purchase or sale of a product or service. Finally, firms seeking immediate response from targeted individual consumers and consumer communities use direct, digital, and social media marketing tools to engage consumers and cultivate relationships with them.

 Discuss the changing communications landscape and the need for integrated marketing communications.

The explosive developments in communications technology and changes in marketer and customer communication strategies have had a dramatic impact on marketing communications. The new digital and social media have given birth to a more targeted, social, and engaging marketing communications model. Along with traditional communications tools, advertisers are now adding a broad selection of more-specialized and highly targeted media to engage smaller customer segments with more-personalized, interactive content. As they adopt richer but more fragmented media and promotion mixes to reach their diverse markets, they risk creating a communications hodgepodge for consumers. To prevent this, companies are adopting the concept of *integrated marketing communications (IMC)*. Guided by an overall IMC strategy, the company works out the roles that the various promotional tools will play and the extent to which each will be used. It carefully coordinates the promotional activities and the timing of when major campaigns take place.

 Describe how advertising objectives are set and how advertising strategy is developed.

Advertising—the use of paid, owned, earned, and shared media by a seller to inform, persuade, and remind about its products or organization—is a strong promotion tool that takes many forms and has many uses. *Advertising decision making* involves decisions about the objectives, the budget, the message, the media, and, finally, the evaluation of results. Advertisers should set clear *objectives* as to whether the advertising is supposed to inform, persuade, or remind buyers. The advertising *budget* can be based on what is affordable, on sales, on competitors' spending, or on advertising objectives and tasks. The *message decision* calls for planning a "big idea" and message strategy and executing it effectively. The *media decision* involves defining reach, frequency, impact, and engagement goals; choosing major media types; selecting media vehicles; and deciding on media timing. Message and media decisions must be closely coordinated for maximum campaign effectiveness. Finally, *evaluation* calls for evaluating the communication and sales effects of advertising before, during, and after the advertising is placed and measuring advertising return on investment.

 Explain how advertising effectiveness is evaluated and the role of the advertising agency.

Evaluating advertising calls for evaluating the communication and sales effects of advertising before, during, and after the advertising is placed, and measuring advertising return on investment. Companies must measure the effectiveness of their advertising, and specifically try to measure the *return on advertising investment*. Advertising must be measured in terms of its *communication effects* as well as its sales and profit effects. Measuring return on advertising is difficult; however, most companies today recognize its importance and are constantly looking for new methods. Advertising *agencies* work with the company (i.e., the advertiser) to develop, produce, plan, and execute advertising campaigns. Most large companies use agencies, which employ specialists in design, production, and media planning.

LO5 **Explain how companies use public relations to communicate with their publics.**

Public relations involves building good relations with the company's various publics. Its functions include *press relations*, *product publicity*, *public affairs*, *lobbying*, *investor relations*, and *development*. Public relations can have a strong impact on public awareness at a much lower cost than advertising can, and PR results can sometimes be spectacular. Despite its potential strengths, however, PR sometimes sees only limited and scattered use. Public relations tools include *news*, *special events*, *written materials*, *audiovisual materials*, *corporate identity materials*, and *public service activities*. A company's website and online social media can be good PR vehicles. In considering when and how to use product

PR, management should set PR objectives, choose the PR messages and vehicles, implement the PR plan, and evaluate the results. Public relations should be blended smoothly with other promotion activities within the company's overall IMC effort.

MyMarketingLab

Study, practise, and explore real marketing situations with these helpful resources:

- **Interactive Lesson Presentations:** Work through interactive presentations and assessments to test your knowledge of marketing concepts.
- **Study Plan:** Check your understanding of chapter concepts with self-study quizzes.
- **Dynamic Study Modules:** Work through adaptive study modules on your computer, tablet, or mobile device.
- **Simulations:** Practise decision-making in simulated marketing environments.

DISCUSSION QUESTIONS

1. Discuss the factors changing the face of today's marketing communications.

2. What is integrated marketing communications (IMC), and how does a company go about implementing it?

3. How do marketers measure the effectiveness of advertising?

4. What are the role and functions of public relations within an organization?

5. Discuss the major public relations tools and the role played by the Internet and social media.

CRITICAL THINKING EXERCISES

1. Any message can be presented using different execution styles. Select a brand and target audience and design two advertisements, each using a different execution style to deliver the same message to the target audience but in a different way. Identify the types of execution styles you are using and present your advertisements.

2. The Public Relations Society of America (PRSA) awards the best public relations campaigns with Silver Anvil Awards. Visit www.prsa.org/Awards/Search and review several case reports of previous winners. What does the field of public relations encompass? Write a report on one of the award winners focusing on marketing-related activities.

ONLINE, MOBILE, AND SOCIAL MEDIA MARKETING

Visit any media outlet's site and you'll see the familiar Facebook and Twitter icons. Traditional news media have migrated to online versions and beyond through social media. But social media has become a major source of news for many people. Sixty percent of respondents in one study indicated Facebook as a source of news, and 20 percent used Twitter to learn what's happening in the world. Twitter might have a growing advantage because of the nature of short tweets and how quickly they spread.

Most news outlets have a presence on Twitter, promoting their content and directing audiences to their websites. But Twitter has found a way to make money through advertising and is hiring editorial personnel to produce and manage content. It appears that Twitter is moving away from being just a media platform to becoming a media entity, which is a concern for traditional media outlets. Twitter has been a partner with traditional media, but now it's becoming more of a competitor. Twitter's NASCAR and Olympics Hub editorial offerings were just the beginning. Part of Twitter's success stems from the relationships it has fostered with these outlets, but now Twitter is building a digital media business on content provided by its media partners as well as eyewitness input from people located where the news is happening.

QUESTIONS

1. Explain how Twitter makes money through advertising. Find examples of companies using Twitter as a promotional tool.

2. How does social media advertising spending compare with traditional mass-media advertising spending? How likely is it that Twitter can become a media entity rather than just a media platform, and what are the implications for advertisers?

THINK LIKE A MARKETING MANAGER

In Germany, it's "*Ich liebe es*"; in France, "*C'est tout ce que j'aime.*" In China, it translates into "I like it," because one doesn't say "love" lightly in that culture. The McDonald's "i'm lovin' it" campaign was launched simultaneously in more than 100 countries. It was unprecedented in McDonald's history because it was the first time an international campaign was consistent in flavour and brand message in every country McDonald's serves. "It's much more than just a new tagline or commercials—it's a new way of thinking about and expressing our worldwide brand appeal to the consumer," said Larry Light, McDonald's executive vice-president and global chief marketing officer, and the man behind the campaign. The McDonald's website at McDonalds.com features an international welcome page with a drop-down selection for each country's site. Here the online marketing is localized, the campaign adapted,

the words translated, but even while capturing the spirit, music, and flavour of each country, the brand message remains consistent.

QUESTIONS

1. Go to the McDonald's site, choose a country, and explore that country's site. How is the "i'm lovin' it" message translated and adapted? What are the signs that local culture, language, and customs have been incorporated into the campaign?

2. Find out what the most recent new menu item available at your local McDonald's is. Is it being promoted through advertising? What other forms of marketing communications are being used to promote it, and how are they integrated?

MARKETING ETHICS

On the eve of the biggest e-commerce shopping day of the year, Amazon's normally secretive founder and CEO, Jeff Bezos, scored a public relations home run by going on CBS's *60 Minutes* program to unveil the company's Prime Air unmanned aircraft project to deliver packages to consumers' doorsteps. Forget that it couldn't be implemented because the U.S. Federal Aviation Administration doesn't allow such use of drones and that it will likely be 2026 before drone delivery might even be possible. The interview set off the "Dronerama," as some have called it. The next morning—Cyber Monday—the media were abuzz about drone delivery, with news organizations and websites replaying the video of Amazon's cool drone delivering a package. The normally hard-hitting *60 Minutes* interview has been criticized because the interviewer, the famous Charlie Rose, seemed to gush all over Bezos and ignore other controversial issues, such as working conditions at Amazon. Rose further gushed over Amazon during

the *60 Minutes Overtime* digital supplement to the show. Critics believe that the normally unattainable Bezos called the shots in return for appearing on the show. The "Dronerama" not only got Amazon on every cyber shopper's lips on that all-important online shopping day; it also seemed to take some of the wind out of the sails of a recently released book about Bezos at a time when Amazon needed customers the most.

QUESTIONS

1. Watch the *60 Minutes* interview at www.cbsnews.com/news/amazons-jeff-bezos-looks-to-the-future. Is it ethical for companies to use the media this way to gain favourable exposure? Did Jeff Bezos acknowledge the fact that drones won't be feasible any time soon?

2. Create a presentation of the publicity Amazon received as a result of the *60 Minutes* interview. Would you judge this campaign a success or failure?

MARKETING BY THE NUMBERS

Nielsen ratings are very important to both advertisers and television programmers because the cost of television advertising time is based on these ratings. A show's *rating* is the number of households in Nielsen's sample that are tuned to that show divided by the number of television-owning households—115 million in the United States. One rating point represents 1 percent of the TV market, so one point equals 1.15 million households. Nielson's TV ratings, referred to as C3, measure viewers who watch commercials live or watch recorded commercials up to three days later. A common measure of advertising efficiency is cost per thousand (CPM), which is the ad cost per thousand potential audience contacts. Advertisers also assess the cost per rating point by dividing the ad cost by the rating. These numbers are used to assess the efficiency of a media buy. Use the following average price and rating information to answer the questions:

Program	Cost per 30-Second Spot	C3 Rating
Sunday Night Football	$425 000	11.8
American Idol	$475 000	9.0
Grey's Anatomy	$225 000	5.3
Two and a Half Men	$215 000	6.0
The Vampire Diaries	$75 000	1.2

QUESTIONS

1. How many households are expected to watch each program?

2. Calculate the cost per thousand (CPM) and cost per point (CPP) for each program. How should advertisers use these measures when planning a television media buy?

END-OF-CHAPTER CASE

THE SUPER BOWL: MORE THAN A SINGLE ADVERTISING EVENT—A SOCIAL-MEDIA FRENZY

Every year around Super Bowl season, a debate heats up among advertising professionals and media pundits. At the core is the big question: Is Super Bowl advertising worth the cost? In 2015, major advertisers spent over $330 million for Super Bowl advertising, with some paying a staggering $4.5 million per 30-second spot. And that's just for the airtime. Throw in ad production costs—which average US$2 to US$3 million per showcase commercial—and running even a single Super Bowl ad becomes a super-expensive proposition. Among other points, the naysayers assert that with costs so high, there is no reasonable hope for a decent return on the advertising investment.

But supporters of Super Bowl advertising have plenty of evidence on their side. For starters, the big game is always the most-watched television event of the year. In 2015, Super Bowl XLIX drew more than 114.4 million viewers, making it the largest TV event in history. In addition to sheer numbers of viewers, the Super Bowl stands alone as the TV program during which the ads draw as much or more viewership than the program itself. With that consideration, one recent study asserted that for consumer-packaged-goods firms, the return on investment (ROI) for one Super Bowl ad is equivalent to that of 250 regular TV ads.

Although there's no easy answer to the question of the value of the Super Bowl as an advertising venue, the debates of the past miss a key factor that has evolved over the last few years. These days, the Super Bowl is merely a gateway to something much bigger. Before the game begins and long after it's over, ad critics, media pundits, and consumers are previewing and reviewing, speculating, and rating the commercials. No longer do advertisers create an ad that will run for one 30-second time slot. They create a broader campaign that revolves around the Super Bowl ad, with strategies that include tactics for before, during, and after the game.

BEFORE THE GAME

For many years, advertisers have recognized the potential for water cooler buzz about ads following the Super Bowl. As online video became prevalent, the focus turned to creating an ad with the potential to go viral. But in the past few years, social media and mobile communications have changed the game once again. The previous rule of thumb was to build anticipation for ads by keeping them secret and unveiling them during the Super Bowl. But then some advertisers

decided to challenge this strategy by seeding information about their ads, releasing teaser ads, or even making the ad available for viewing online before the game—essentially starting the water cooler conversations early.

One of the most successful marketers to pioneer this strategy was Volkswagen, which had a stellar showing during the 2011 Super Bowl with its ad "The Force"—a 60-second spot featuring a pint-sized Darth Vader who surprises himself when he brings a Passat to life. After a heated internal debate over whether to release the spot early and ruin the surprise factor, Volkswagen decided to risk it. The decision paid off as "The Force" racked up more than 12 million views and became the most buzzed about commercial on Twitter before the kickoff of the Big Game. All that pregame buzz helped propel the ad to finish out the year as the most viral auto video, with over 63 million views. More important, Volkswagen reported its biggest increase in U.S. sales in nearly 40 years and was confident that its Super Bowl investment more than paid for itself.

Volkswagen's success fuelled a pregame media frenzy for the 2012 Super Bowl, with 34 out of 54 advertisers posting their ads online in some form in the weeks leading up to the game. Referring to this trend, one media buyer said, "This is the first Super Bowl where social media has been an integral part of marketers' plans," suggesting that this is happening because marketers realize "you can get more bang for your buck." Now almost all the ads that air during the Super Bowl are viewable online in one form or another prior to the date of the big game. "So many people are launching commercials early to feed the beast," says a media analyst.

For Super Bowl XLIX, ad previews were available for ads from all different types of companies and generated over 35 million views before the game. A newcomer to Super Bowl advertising, "Avocado's from Mexico" explained the origin of Mexican avocados: as a first-round draft pick. Released two days before the game, the ad generated over 1 million views on YouTube and has since generated more than 1.1 billion media impressions with its original and seven follow-up ads. It was also rated as the most loved Super Bowl ad as measured by positive Web sentiment.

But there's more than one way to measure ad success. Social media analytics company General Sentiment puts a dollar amount on this pregame ad screening. Its metric—called Impact Media Value—is a measure of consumer impact and awareness that identifies which Super Bowl advertisers are getting the most bang for their buck prior to the game. According to General Sentiment, numerous advertisers saw a powerful return on their investment in terms of both increased social media mentions and real revenue dollars generated before the game even aired. For example, Budweiser's "Lost Dog" ad released online before the big game had the highest impact media value of almost US$2.5 million, and it generated over 7 million views and 300 000 social actions in a single day! It went on to become the top-rated commercial of Super Bowl XLIX and is approaching 30 million views on YouTube.

DURING THE GAME

In addition to pregame festivities, companies are recognizing the potential to increase the effectiveness of their Super Bowl ads by engaging viewers during the game. The trend of "second screen viewing"—using a laptop or mobile device while watching TV—is exploding. One Nielsen survey revealed that 88 percent of tablet owners and 86 percent of smartphone owners had used their mobile devices while watching television in a 30-day period, numbers supported by social media activity during the 2013 Super Bowl. Across all social networks, game-related comments were three times higher than for the 2012 event. But more important, nearly 30 percent of the 20.9 million Super Bowl–related tweets sent during the game were about the ads. As a bonus, advertisers picked up thousands of new followers.

After the overwhelming success achieved from its animated "Polar Bowl" simulcast during the 2012 Super Bowl, Coca-Cola was more than ready to do battle in 2013. Nearly 40 executives from Coca-Cola and its advertising, social media, and PR agencies gathered at an office building in downtown Manhattan to manage the brand's second screen experience. "Mirage," an ad based on a desert race among showgirls, cowboys, a sheik, and some badlanders chasing a bottle of Coke, had been released online two weeks earlier. Consumers had been given the opportunity to vote for a team, determining which follow-up commercial would air right after the Super Bowl.

Coke's game-time activities included strategic retorts to Pepsi's digs at Coke. The team promoted photos being posted by previously identified Coke "super fans" who had been sent props from the filming of "Mirage." People live-streamed the game, called out plays, and tracked commercials as they aired. But the real activity began when "Mirage" aired. Coca-Cola listening teams for each of five social media platforms—Twitter, Facebook, Tumblr, Instagram, and YouTube—began executing routines they had practised during five trial runs prior to the game. They

gathered consumer comments into Google Docs while writers crafted responses and others pushed those responses back out through the social media outlets, complete with prepackaged content.

All the while, voting for the microsite for the ad, CokeChase.com, experienced a massive spike in traffic from 33 000 visitors to over 1.3 million in a matter of minutes, making it difficult for team members to access their own site. Working through technical and other issues to ensure that users could get through and vote paid off. As the polls closed, the showgirls were declared the winners. By then, the campaign's success was evident. During the period of the game following the airing of "Mirage," the Coca-Cola brand experienced 8.2 million interactions and 910 000 votes, far exceeding its internal goals of 1.6 million interactions and 400 000 votes. "The interactions were really critical, in terms of seeing how much people really engaged with the content, so that's probably the thing I'm most pleasantly surprised with," said Pio Schunker, senior vice-president of integrated marketing at Coca-Cola. "We struck out in a different direction, which was a risk, but it paid off."

THE AFTER PARTY

For Super Bowl advertisers, when the game is over, the advertising event is still in full swing. The traditional buzz factor results from the numerous "best and worst" lists generated by journalists and bloggers. And although "winners" and "losers" vary from list to list, it is clear that all ads that air on the Super Bowl achieve postgame buzz from all the online viewing and discussion.

Perhaps the greatest example of postgame buzz ever is Chrysler. The long-time number-three U.S. automaker kicked off its "Imported from Detroit" campaign during the 2011 Super Bowl with a two-minute epic featuring rapper Eminem and a resurgent Detroit as the backdrop. For 2012, Chrysler produced the two-minute sequel, "It's Half-Time in America," a patriotic tribute to the soul of America starring Clint Eastwood. Both ads came out at the top of the heap in terms of pregame buzz and postgame ratings, discussion, and views. The ads also served as anchors for a series of ads as part of an ongoing campaign. Sixteen months after the launch of the campaign, Chrysler won the Grand Effie—the top award granted at the advertising industry's Oscars. According to one jury member, "Imported from Detroit was the Grand Effie winner because they sold the product, the category, and the city."

But as the 2013 Super Bowl debuted, Chrysler revealed that it wasn't finished with its homage to rock-ribbed American values. Just prior to the second half of the game, the company aired "Whole Again," a two-minute tribute to the U.S. military and their loved ones narrated by Oprah Winfrey. In the form of a letter from the Jeep brand to the American people, Winfrey intoned, "Because when you're home, we're more than a family, we're a nation … that is whole again." If that wasn't enough to stand out as a tonic to the light-hearted, silly, and even confusing ads by other brands, Chrysler's ad during the second half topped off its Super Bowl patriotic three-peat. "Farmer," another two-minute epic, featured a voiceover of the tribute, "So God Made a Farmer," rendered by the late and legendary radio voice Paul Harvey. The spot served as a multimedia reminder of the role that perseverance and hard work played in making the United States a great nation. With more than 23 million views between the two ads in the few months following the Super Bowl, Chrysler showed for the third year in a row that it knows how to make ads that deliver long after they've stopped airing.

The efforts and successes by the most recent Super Bowl sponsors are far too numerous to mention here. And whether every tactic employed by every advertiser worked perfectly is not the point. The point is that now, more than ever, advertising during the Super Bowl isn't just about gaining huge exposure by running a single ad or group of ads in a television event with a huge audience. Instead, viewers watch, buzz, share, click, stream, and respond to Super Bowl ads before, during, and after the game. To get the most out of their investments, marketers must have a comprehensive program that takes advantage of the broad Super Bowl season.

Sources: Marketing Charts, "Super Bowl 2015 Data," www.marketingcharts.com/television/super-bowl-2015-advertising-viewer-attitudes-and-spending-trends-50857; "Super Bowl XLIX Posts the Largest Audience in TV History," *CNN Money*, http://money.cnn.com/2015/02/02/media/super-bowl-ratings; Andrew McMains, "The Story Behind Avocados from Mexico's Surprise Super Bowl Hit," *Adweek*, February 10, 2015, www.adweek.com/news/advertising-branding/story-behind-avocados-mexicos-surprise-super-bowl-hit-162864; Amy Gesenhues, "Top 10 2015 Super Bowl Commericials: Budweiser's "Lost Dog" in the Lead with 7 Million Views So Far," *Marketing Land*, January 29, 2015, http://marketingland.com/top-10-2015-super-bowl-commercials-budweisers-lost-dog-lead-7-million-views-far-116341; General Sentiment, "2015 Super Bowl Ads Recap," www.generalsentiment.com/2015-super-bowl-ads-recap; Brian Steinberg, "Think the Super Bowl Is Over? Fox Starts Early Haggling for 2014," *Advertising Age*, February 5, 2013, http://adage.com/print/239620; Michael Learmonth, "It's Official; Toyota Won the Super Bowl Pre-Game," *Advertising Age*, February 1, 2013, http://adage.com/print/239547; Rae Annfera, "4 Reasons Why Pre-Game Content Is a Winning Super Bowl Strategy," *Fast Company*, accessed May 2013, www.fastcocreate.com/1682308; Gavin O'Malley, "Super Bowl Ads Gain 'Impact Value' before Game," January 31, 2013, www.mediapost.com/appy-awards/article/ 192480; Natalie Zmuda, "Watching the Super Bowl from Coca-Cola's War Room(s)," *Advertising Age*, February 4, 2013, http://adage.com/print/239582; and Dale Buss, "Chrysler Scores Big—Twice—with Surprise Super Bowl Ads," *Forbes*, February 4, 2013, www.forbes.com/sites/dalebuss/2013/02/04/chrysler-scores-big-twice-with-surprise-super-bowl-ads.

QUESTIONS FOR DISCUSSION

1. What factors have played the biggest role in changing the dynamics of Super Bowl advertising in recent years?

2. Discuss the concepts of reach, frequency, and impact as they relate to Super Bowl advertising. How does consideration and planning for these concepts differ between the Super Bowl and other television events?

3. When assessing return on investment, what objectives must Super Bowl advertisers consider?

4. Choose a brand that has not recently run a Super Bowl ad. Design an effective campaign with promotional tactics for before, during, and after the game.

© AnayMann.com. Courtesy Vivek Gupta

AFTER STUDYING THIS CHAPTER, YOU SHOULD BE ABLE TO

1 discuss the role of a company's salespeople in creating value for customers and building customer relationships

2 identify and explain the six major sales force management steps

3 discuss the personal selling process, distinguishing between transaction-oriented marketing and relationship marketing

4 explain how sales promotion campaigns are developed and implemented

Personal Selling and Sales Promotion

14

PREVIEWING THE CONCEPTS

In Chapter 13, you learned about communicating customer value through integrated marketing communications (IMC) and two elements of the promotion mix: advertising and public relations. In this chapter, we examine two integrated marketing communications (IMC) elements: personal selling and sales promotion. Personal selling is the interpersonal arm of marketing communications, in which the sales force engages customers and prospects to build relationships and make sales. Sales promotion consists of short-term incentives to encourage the purchase or sale of a product or service. As you read, remember that although this chapter presents personal selling and sales promotion as separate tools, they must be carefully integrated with the other elements of the promotion mix.

To start, what is your first reaction when you think of a salesperson or a sales force? Perhaps you think of pushy retail sales clerks, "yell-and-sell" TV pitchmen, or the stereotypical glad-handing "used-car salesman." In reality, such stereotypes simply don't fit most of today's salespeople. Instead, today's sales professionals succeed not by taking advantage of customers but by listening to their needs and helping them forge solutions. Consider IBM, whose customer-focused sales force has been the model for modern personal selling for nearly a century.

IBM: A CLASSIC MODEL FOR MODERN CUSTOMER-FOCUSED SELLING

When Thomas J. Watson Sr. became president of the young Computing Tabulating Recording Corporation—as IBM was known in 1915—sales was considered by many to be a barely reputable profession. Back then, in the minds of most folks, salespeople were slick, fast-talking men who employed hard-sell tactics and fast-and-loose claims to peddle whatever they thought would make them a buck. Watson was a salesman at heart—he'd cut his teeth selling pianos off the back of a horse-drawn wagon to farmers in upstate New York. But he had a different vision for selling. By the time his company was renamed IBM in 1924, he had already put in place a sales force template that would forever change the face of professional sales.

At IBM, Watson hired only top-performing graduates from Ivy League universities, and he insisted that they wear conservative suits and white dress shirts. He demanded the highest ethical standards. IBM provided intensive sales training that focused on developing

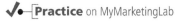

✔•─ **Practice** on MyMarketingLab

Assessing the Performance of PR Activities

a deep knowledge of the company and its customers. Above all, Watson stressed, "be a good listener, observe, study through observation." This advice became the foundation of what the company later came to call "solutions selling." By the time Watson handed over the reins of IBM to his son in the 1950s, his forward-looking sales principles were firmly ingrained in the company's culture, and IBM had become the model for modern customer-centred selling.

Now a US$105 billion company, IBM has survived and prospered for nearly 100 years—something no other Fortune top-25 company can claim. During that time, *what* IBM sells has changed dramatically, from cash registers to typewriters to mainframe computers and PCs to its current complex mix of information technology hardware, software, and services. What hasn't changed is *how* IBM sells. IBM salespeople have always been customer relationship developers and solutions providers.

Consider Vivek Gupta, who became IBM's top salesperson in its fastest-growing industry (telecommunications) and fastest-growing market (India). When Gupta first joined IBM in 2003, his sales strengths and philosophies were a perfect fit for the company. IBM was a newcomer in India, struggling to gain a foothold in a market where more than 70 percent of corporations are family controlled, where relationships, trust, and family ties trump almost everything else. In addition to his formal IBM training, Gupta launched his own extensive investigative effort, getting to know people, learning about IBM and its customers, and developing a rock-solid knowledge of how the company's products and services fit customer needs.

When Gupta first approached potential customer Vodafone—the dominant firm in India's exploding mobile phone market—the managing director there told him, "I don't do any business with IBM and I don't intend to." But the quietly determined Gupta kept at it, getting to know Vodafone's key decision makers and patiently listening, observing, and identifying how IBM might be able to help Vodafone succeed in its volatile and competitive markets. Gupta came to know more about Vodafone than many people who worked there. It took him nearly four years, but Gupta finally sold Vodafone—the same people who vowed never to do business with IBM—on a gigantic five-year, US$600 million turn-key contract to handle everything from Vodafone's customer service to its finances. Gupta became such a well-known figure at Vodafone's offices in Mumbai that many people there were surprised that his badge said "IBM" and not "Vodafone."

Gupta thrives on rooting out customer problems to solve. "You have to understand [customers'] pain points," he explains. "And they are not going to spell them out." For example, when another big prospect told him "Thanks, but we don't need anything," Gupta asked for permission to study the potential customer's business anyway, no strings attached. When chatting with the company's engineers, he learned that the microwave radio technology they were using in their mobile phone towers was crashing their network six or seven times each week, a very costly problem that greatly annoyed mobile customers. Returning to make a second sales call on the decision maker who'd snubbed him initially, Gupta explained that he understood the network reliability problem and that IBM had a relatively inexpensive fix. That call resulted in a small contract for new microwave radios—not much to brag about. But within a year, the small foothold had led to additional business worth more than US$100 million.

Flush with success, Gupta set his sights on still bigger targets. He realized that many big Indian telecoms were so busy simply hammering out their basic back-office operating systems that they had little money and brainpower left for strategy, branding, and marketing.

However, IBM had all the technology and expertise required to build and maintain such systems. What if IBM were to take over managing the system innards, freeing the customer to attend to strategy and marketing? Gupta proposed just such a novel solution to Bharti Airtel, then a relative newcomer to India's wireless industry. The result: IBM now runs the bulk of Bharti Airtel's back-office operations, while Bharti Airtel focuses on taking care of its own customers. In the first five years, the deal produced an incredible US$1 billion for IBM. Bharti Airtel is now India's wireless industry leader, and the deal is a staple "how-to" case study in IBM's emerging-markets sales training.

IBM's culture has always dictated that its salespeople be "part teacher, part psychologist, and part glad-hander," observes one IBM watcher. But Vivek Gupta's success demonstrates that, to be really good in sales today, they must also be "part diplomat, part entrepreneur, and part inventor"—complete customer problem solvers. Gupta doesn't just sell IBM computer hardware and software—he sells the people and systems that will make the hardware and software come to life. He sells the essential concepts behind the entire system of IBM people and products that will deliver results for the customer. "It's at once radically simple and just plain radical," says the analyst. "He wants to convince you that IBM can run your business—your entire business, save for strategy and marketing— better than you can."

Thus, over the past 100 years, many things have changed as IBM has adapted to the turbulent technological environment. But one thing has remained constant—IBM salespeople are still inspired by Watson's founding principles of selling. Today, IBM still asks aspiring prospective sales candidates, "Can you sell a solution? Can you sell change? Can you create value through industry knowledge?" Vivek Gupta is all about solutions. That's what made him a sales superstar at Big Blue. "I don't remember a single deal in my career which I pursued and I lost," he says. "It's just a question of time. If I play very smart, I can crack the nuts very quickly. If I don't play smart, it might take some time."[1]

LET'S BEGIN by looking at personal selling—those interactions that enable salespeople to not only make sales but also to maintain customer relationships. We'll follow that discussion with a look at sales promotion, with its use of short-term incentives to encourage customer purchasing, reseller support, and sales force efforts.

Personal Selling [LO1]

 ◄●┤**Simulate** on MyMarketingLab

Personal Selling

Robert Louis Stevenson once noted, "Everyone lives by selling something." Companies around the world use sales forces to sell products and services to business customers and final consumers. But sales forces are also found in many other kinds of organizations. For example, universities use recruiters to attract new students, and churches use membership committees to attract new members. Museums and fine arts organizations use fundraisers to contact donors and raise money. In the first part of this chapter, we examine personal selling's role in the organization, sales force management decisions, and the personal selling process.

The Nature of Personal Selling

Personal selling is one of the oldest professions in the world. The people who do the selling go by many names, including salespeople, sales representatives, agents, district managers, account executives, sales consultants, and sales engineers.

Personal selling
Personal presentations by the firm's sales force for the purpose of making sales and building customer relationships.

Stephen Brashear/ Getty Images

Exhibit 14.1 Professional selling: It takes more than fast talk and a warm smile to sell expensive airplanes. Boeing's real challenge is to win business by building partnerships—day in, day out, year in, year out—with its customers.

People hold many stereotypes of salespeople—including some unfavourable ones. *Salesman* may bring to mind the image of Dwight Schrute, the opinionated Dunder Mifflin paper salesman from the TV show *The Office*, who lacks both common sense and social skills. Or they may think of the real-life "yell-and-sell" TV pitchmen, who hawk everything from the ShamWow to the INSANITY Workout and the Swivel Sweeper in infomercials. However, the majority of salespeople are a far cry from these unfortunate stereotypes.

As the opening IBM story shows, most salespeople are well-educated and well-trained professionals who add value for customers and maintain long-term customer relationships. They listen to their customers, assess customer needs, and organize the company's efforts to solve customer problems. The best salespeople are the ones who work closely with customers for mutual gain. Consider Boeing, the aerospace giant competing in the rough-and-tumble worldwide commercial aircraft market. It takes more than fast talk and a warm smile to sell expensive airplanes:

> Selling high-tech aircraft at US$150 million or more a copy is complex and challenging. A single big sale to an airline, air-freight carrier, government, and military customer can easily run into billions of dollars. Boeing salespeople head up an extensive team of company specialists—sales and service technicians, financial analysts, planners, engineers—all dedicated to finding ways to satisfy a large customer's needs. On the customer side, buying a batch of jetliners involves dozens or even hundreds of decision makers from all levels of the buying organization, and layer upon layer of subtle and not-so-subtle buying influences. The selling process is nerve-rackingly slow—it can take two or three years from the first sales presentation to the day the sale is announced. After getting the order, salespeople must then stay in almost constant touch to keep track of the account's equipment needs and to make certain the customer stays satisfied. The real challenge is to win buyers' business by building day-in, day-out, year-in, year-out partnerships with them based on superior products and close collaboration.

Salesperson

An individual who represents a company to customers by performing one or more of the following activities: prospecting, communicating, selling, servicing, information gathering, and relationship building.

The term **salesperson** covers a wide range of positions. At one extreme, a salesperson might be largely an *order taker*, such as the department store salesperson standing behind the counter. At the other extreme are *order getters*, whose positions demand *creative selling*, *social selling*, and *relationship building* for products and services ranging from appliances, industrial equipment, and airplanes to insurance and IT services. In this chapter, we focus on the more creative types of selling and the process of building and managing an effective sales force.

The Role of the Sales Force

Personal selling is the interpersonal arm of the promotion mix. Advertising consists largely of nonpersonal communication with large groups of consumers. By contrast, personal selling involves interpersonal interactions between salespeople and individual customers—whether face to face, by phone, via email or Twitter, through video or online conferences, or by other means. Personal selling can be more effective than advertising in more complex selling situations. Salespeople can probe customers to learn more about their problems and then adjust the marketing offer and presentation to fit each customer's special needs.

The role of personal selling varies from company to company. Some firms have no salespeople at all—for example, companies that sell only online, or companies that sell through manufacturers' reps, sales agents, or brokers. In most firms, however, the sales force plays a major role. In companies that sell business products and services, such as IBM, DuPont, or Boeing, salespeople work directly with customers. In consumer product companies such as Nestlé or Nike, the sales force plays an important behind-the-scenes role. It works with wholesalers and retailers to gain their support and help them be more effective in selling the company's products to final buyers.

Exhibit 14.2 Salespeople link the company with its customers. To many customers, the salesperson *is* the company.

Digital Vision/Getty Images

Linking the Company with Its Customers The sales force serves as a critical link between a company and its customers. In many cases, salespeople serve two masters—the seller and the buyer. First, they *represent the company to customers*. They find and develop new customers and communicate information about the company's products and services. They sell products by approaching and engaging customers, presenting their offerings, answering objections, negotiating prices and terms, closing sales, and servicing accounts.

At the same time, salespeople *represent customers to the company*, acting inside the firm as "champions" of customers' interests and managing the buyer–seller relationship. Salespeople relay customer concerns about company products and actions back inside to those who can handle them. They learn about customer needs and work with other marketing and nonmarketing people in the company to develop greater customer value.

In fact, to many customers, the salesperson *is* the company—the only tangible manifestation of the company they see. Hence, customers may become loyal to salespeople as well as to the companies and products they represent. This concept of *salesperson-owned loyalty* lends even more importance to the salesperson's customer-relationship-building abilities. Strong relationships with the salesperson will result in strong relationships with the company and its products. Conversely, poor salesperson relationships will probably result in poor company and product relationships.

Given its role in linking the company with its customers, the sales force must be strongly customer-solutions focused. In fact, such a customer-solutions focus is a must not only for the sales force but also for the entire organization.

Coordinating Marketing and Sales Ideally, the sales force and other marketing functions (marketing planners, brand managers, and researchers) should work together closely to jointly create value for customers. Unfortunately, however, some companies still treat sales and marketing as separate functions. When this happens, the separate sales and marketing groups may not get along well. When things go wrong, marketers blame the sales force for its poor execution of what they see as an otherwise splendid strategy. In turn, the sales team blames the marketers for being out of touch with what's really going on with customers. Neither group fully values the other's contributions. If not repaired, such disconnects between marketing and sales can damage customer relationships and company performance.

A company can take several actions to help bring its marketing and sales functions closer together. At the most basic level, it can increase communications between the two groups by arranging joint meetings and spelling out communications channels. It can create opportunities for salespeople and marketers to work together. Brand managers and researchers can tag along on sales calls or sit in on sales planning sessions. In turn, salespeople can sit in on marketing planning sessions and share their firsthand customer knowledge.

A company can also create joint objectives and reward systems for sales and marketing teams or appoint marketing–sales liaisons—people from marketing who "live with the sales force" and help coordinate marketing and sales force programs and efforts. Finally, it can appoint a high-level marketing executive to oversee both marketing and sales. Such a person can help infuse marketing and sales with the common goal of creating value for customers to capture value in return.[2]

Managing the Sales Force LO2

Sales force management

Analyzing, planning, implementing, and controlling sales force activities.

We define **sales force management** as analyzing, planning, implementing, and controlling sales force activities. It includes designing sales force strategy and structure as well as recruiting, selecting, training, compensating, supervising, and evaluating the firm's salespeople. These major sales force management decisions are shown in Figure 14.1 and discussed in the following sections.

Designing the Sales Force Strategy and Structure

Marketing managers face several sales force strategy and design questions. How should salespeople and their tasks be structured? How big should the sales force be? Should salespeople sell alone or work in teams with other people in the company? Should they sell in the field, by phone, or on the Internet? We address these issues next.

The Sales Force Structure   A company can divide sales responsibilities along any of several lines. The structure decision is simple if the company sells only one product line to one industry with customers in many locations. In that case the company would use a *territorial sales force structure*. However, if the company sells many products to many types of customers, it might need a *product sales force structure*, a *customer sales force structure*, or a combination of the two.

Territorial sales force structure

A sales force organization that assigns each salesperson to an exclusive geographic territory in which that salesperson sells the company's full line.

In the **territorial sales force structure**, each salesperson is assigned to an exclusive geographic area and sells the company's full line of products or services to all customers in that territory. This organization clearly defines each salesperson's job and fixes accountability. It also increases the salesperson's desire to build local customer relationships that, in turn, improve selling effectiveness. Finally, because each salesperson travels within a limited geographic area, travel expenses are relatively small. A territorial sales organization is often supported by many levels of sales management positions. For example, individual territory sales reps may report to area managers, who in turn report to regional managers who report to a director of sales.

FIGURE 14.1 Major Steps in Sales Force Management

If a company has numerous and complex products, it can adopt a **product sales force structure**, in which the sales force specializes along product lines. For example, GE employs different sales forces within different product and service divisions of its major businesses. Within GE Infrastructure, for instance, the company has separate sales forces for aviation, energy, transportation, and water-processing products and technologies. No single salesperson can become expert in all of these product categories, so product specialization is required. Similarly, GE Healthcare employs different sales forces for diagnostic imaging, life sciences, and integrated IT products and services. In all, a company as large and complex as GE might have dozens of separate sales forces serving its diverse product and service portfolio.

Using a **customer (or market) sales force structure**, a company organizes its sales force along customer or industry lines. Separate sales forces may be set up for different industries, serving current customers versus finding new ones, and serving major accounts versus regular accounts. Organizing the sales force around customers can help a company build closer relationships with important customers. Many companies even have special sales forces to handle the needs of individual large customers. For example, appliance maker Whirlpool assigns individual teams of salespeople to big retail customers such as Sears, Best Buy, and Home Depot. Each Whirlpool sales team aligns with the large customer's buying team.[3]

When a company sells a wide variety of products to many types of customers over a broad geographic area, it often employs a *complex sales force structure*, which combines several types of organization. Salespeople can be specialized by customer and territory; product and territory; product and customer; or territory, product, and customer. For example, Whirlpool specializes its sales force by customer (with different sales teams for Sears, Best Buy, Home Depot, and smaller independent retailers) *and* by territory for each key customer group (territory representatives, territory managers, regional managers, and so on). No single structure is best for all companies and situations. Each company should select a sales force structure that best serves the needs of its customers and fits its overall marketing strategy.

Product sales force structure
A sales force organization in which salespeople specialize in selling only a portion of the company's products or lines.

Customer (or market) sales force structure
A sales force organization in which salespeople specialize in selling only to certain customers or industries.

Sales Force Size   Once the company has set its structure, it is ready to consider *sales force size*. Sales forces may range in size from only a few salespeople to tens of thousands. Some sales forces are huge—for example, in the United States, PepsiCo employs 36 000 salespeople; American Express, 23 400; GE, 16 400; and Cisco Systems, 14 000.[4] Salespeople constitute one of the company's most productive—and most expensive—assets. Therefore, increasing their numbers will increase both sales and costs.

Many companies use some form of *workload approach* to set sales force size. Using this approach, a company first groups accounts into different classes according to size, account status, or other factors related to the amount of effort required to maintain the account. It then determines the number of salespeople needed to call on each class of accounts the desired number of times.

The company might think as follows: Suppose we have 1000 A-level accounts and 2000 B-level accounts. A-level accounts require 36 calls per year, and B-level accounts require 12 calls per year. In this case, the sales force's *workload*—the number of calls it must make per year—is 60 000 calls

Exhibit 14.3 Sales force structure: Whirlpool specializes its sales force by customer and by territory for each key customer group.

Paul Sancya/AP

[(1000 × 36) + (2000 × 12) = 36 000 + 24 000 = 60 000]. Suppose our average salesperson can make 1000 calls a year. Thus, we need 60 salespeople (60 000 ÷ 1000).

Other Sales Force Strategy and Structure Issues Sales management must also determine who will be involved in the selling effort and how various sales and sales support people will work together.

Outside sales force (or field sales force)
Salespeople who travel to call on customers in the field.

Inside sales force
Salespeople who conduct business from their offices via telephone, online and social media interactions, or visits from prospective buyers.

OUTSIDE AND INSIDE SALES FORCES A company may have an **outside sales force (or field sales force)**, an **inside sales force**, or both. Outside salespeople travel to call on customers in the field. In contrast, inside salespeople conduct business from their offices via telephone, online and social media interactions, or visits from buyers. The use of inside sales has grown in recent years as a result of increased outside selling costs and the surge in online, mobile, and social media technologies.

Some inside salespeople provide support for the outside sales force, freeing them to spend more time selling to major accounts and finding new prospects. For example, *technical sales support people* provide technical information and answers to customers' questions. *Sales assistants* provide research and administrative backup for outside salespeople. They track down sales leads, call ahead and confirm appointments, follow up on deliveries, and answer customers' questions when outside salespeople cannot be reached. Using such combinations of inside and outside salespeople can help serve important customers better. The inside rep provides daily access and support, whereas the outside rep provides face-to-face collaboration and relationship building.

Other inside salespeople do more than just provide support. *Telemarketers* and *online sellers* use the phone, Internet, and social media to find new leads, learn about customers and their business, or sell and service accounts directly. Telemarketing and online selling can be very effective, less costly ways to sell to smaller, harder-to-reach customers. Depending on the complexity of the product and customer, for example, a telemarketer can make from 20 to 33 decision-maker contacts a day, compared with the average of 4 that an outside salesperson can make. In addition, whereas an average business-to-business (B-to-B) field sales call can average close to $600, a routine industrial telemarketing or online contact might average only $20 to $30.[5]

Although the federal government's Do Not Call Registry put a dent in telephone sales to consumers, telemarketing remains a vital tool for most B-to-B marketers. For some smaller companies, telephone and Internet selling may be the primary sales approaches. However, larger companies also use these tactics, either to sell directly to small and midsize customers or to help out with larger ones.

In addition to cost savings, in today's digital, mobile, and social media environments, many buyers are more receptive to—or even prefer—phone and online contact versus the high level of face-to-face contact once required. Many customers are more inclined to gather information online and use the phone, Internet meetings, and social media interactions to engage sellers and close deals. "With virtual meeting software such as GoToMeeting.com and WebEx, communications tools such as Skype, and social media sites such as Twitter, Facebook, and LinkedIn, it's become easier to sell with few if any face-to-face meetings," says an inside sales consultant.[6]

As a result of these trends, telephone and online selling are growing much faster than in-person selling. One study also notes the emergence of the "hybrid sales rep," a modern cross between a field sales rep and an inside rep, who often works from a remote location. Some 41 percent of outside sales activity is now done over the phone or a mobile device, from either a home office, a company office, or on the go.[7]

For many types of products and selling situations, phone or online selling can be as effective as a personal sales call:

Climax Portable Machining and Welding Systems, which manufactures portable maintenance tools for the metal cutting industry, has proven that telephone and online marketing can save money and still lavish attention on buyers. Under the old system, Climax sales engineers spent one-third of their time on the road, training distributor salespeople and accompanying them on calls. They could make about four contacts a day. Now, each of five sales engineers on Climax's inside sales team calls about 30 prospects a day, following up on leads generated by ads, emails, and the company's Facebook, Twitter, YouTube, and other social media sites. Because it takes about five calls to close a sale, the sales engineers update a prospect's profile after each contact, noting the degree of commitment, requirements, next call date, and personal comments. "If anyone mentions he's going on a fishing trip, our sales engineer enters that in the sales information system and uses it to personalize the next call," says Climax's president, noting that this is one way to build good relations.

Another is that the first contact with a prospect includes the sales engineer's business card with his or her picture on it. Climax's customer sales system also gives inside reps instant access to customer information entered by the outside sales force and service people. Armed with all the information, inside reps can build surprisingly strong and personal customer relationships.

Helen King/Corbis Images

Exhibit 14.4 For many types of selling situations, phone or Web selling can be as effective as a personal sales call. At Climax Portable Machine Tools, phone reps build surprisingly strong and personal customer relationships.

Of course, it takes more than friendliness to sell US$15 000 machine tools over the phone (special orders may run as high as US$200 000), but the telephone and online approach works well. When Climax customers were asked, "Do you see the sales engineer often enough?" the response was overwhelmingly positive. Obviously, many people didn't realize that the only contact they had with Climax had been on the phone or Internet.[8]

TEAM SELLING As products become more complex, and as customers grow larger and more demanding, a single salesperson simply can't handle all of a large customer's needs. Instead, most companies now use **team selling** to service large, complex accounts. Sales teams can unearth problems, solutions, and sales opportunities that no individual salesperson could. Such teams might include experts from any area or level of the selling firm—sales, marketing, technical and support services, research and development (R&D), engineering, operations, finance, and others.

Team selling
Using teams of people from sales, marketing, engineering, finance, technical support, and even upper management to service large, complex accounts.

In many cases, the move to team selling mirrors similar changes in customers' buying organizations. Many large-customer companies have implemented team-based purchasing, requiring marketers to employ equivalent team-based selling. When dealing with large, complex accounts, one salesperson can't be an expert in everything the customer needs. Instead, selling is done by strategic account teams, quarterbacked by senior account managers or customer business managers.

Some companies, such as IBM, Xerox, and P&G, have used teams for a long time. As we will discuss later in the chapter, P&G sales reps are organized into Customer Business Development (CBD) teams. Each CBD team is assigned to a major P&G customer, such as Walmart, Safeway, or CVS Pharmacy. The CBD organization places the focus on serving the complete needs of each major customer. It lets P&G "grow business by working as a 'strategic partner' with our accounts," not just as a supplier.[9]

Team selling does have some pitfalls, however. For example, salespeople are by nature competitive and have often been trained and rewarded for outstanding individual performance. Salespeople who are used to having customers all to themselves may have trouble learning to work with and trust others on a team. In addition, selling teams can confuse or overwhelm customers who are used to working with only one salesperson. Finally, difficulties in evaluating individual contributions to the team-selling effort can create some sticky compensation issues.

Exhibit 14.5 Great salespeople: The best salespeople possess intrinsic motivation, disciplined work style, the ability to close a sale, and, perhaps most important, the ability to build relationships with customers.

© Rido/Fotolia

Recruiting and Selecting Salespeople

At the heart of any successful sales force operation is the recruitment and selection of good salespeople. The performance difference between an average salesperson and a top salesperson can be substantial. In a typical sales force, the top 30 percent of the salespeople might bring in 60 percent of the sales. Thus, careful salesperson selection can greatly increase overall sales force performance. Beyond the differences in sales performance, poor selection results in costly turnover. When a salesperson quits, the costs of finding and training a new salesperson—plus the costs of lost sales—can be very high. One sales consulting firm calculates the total costs of a bad sales hire at a whopping US$616 000.[10] Also, a sales force with many new people is less productive, and turnover disrupts important customer relationships.

What sets great salespeople apart from all the rest? In an effort to profile top sales performers, Gallup Consulting, a division of the well-known Gallup polling organization, has interviewed hundreds of thousands of salespeople. Its research suggests that the best salespeople possess four key talents: intrinsic motivation, a disciplined work style, the ability to close a sale, and, perhaps most important, the ability to build relationships with customers.[11]

Super salespeople are motivated from within—they have an unrelenting drive to excel. Some salespeople are driven by money, a desire for recognition, or the satisfaction of competing and winning. Others are driven by the desire to provide service and build relationships. The best salespeople possess some of each of these motivations. They also have a disciplined work style. They lay out detailed, organized plans and then follow through in a timely way.

But motivation and discipline mean little unless they result in closing more sales and building better customer relationships. Super salespeople build the skills and knowledge they need to get the job done. Perhaps most important, top salespeople are excellent customer problem solvers and relationship builders. They understand their customers' needs. Talk to sales executives and they'll describe top performers in these terms: good listeners, empathetic, patient, caring, and responsive. Top performers can put themselves on the buyer's side of the desk and see the world through their customers' eyes. They don't want just to be liked; they want to add value for their customers.

That said, there is no one right way to sell. Each successful salesperson uses a different approach, one that best applies his or her unique strengths and talents. For example, some salespeople enjoy the thrill of a harder sell in confronting challenges and winning people over. Others might apply "softer" talents to reach the same goal. "The key is for sales reps to understand and nurture their innate talents so they can develop their own personal approach and win business *their* way," says a selling expert.[12]

When recruiting, a company should analyze the sales job itself and the characteristics of its most successful salespeople to identify the traits needed by a successful salesperson in their industry. Then it must recruit the right salespeople. The human resources department looks for applicants by getting names from current salespeople, using employment agencies, searching the Internet and online social media, posting ads and notices on its website and industry media, and working through college or university placement services. Another source is to attract top salespeople from other companies. Proven salespeople need less training and can be productive immediately.

Recruiting will attract many applicants from which the company must select the best. The selection procedure can vary from a single informal interview to lengthy testing and interviewing. Many companies give formal tests to sales applicants. Tests typically measure sales aptitude, analytical and organizational skills, personality traits, and other characteristics. But test scores provide only one piece of information in a set that includes personal characteristics, references, past employment history, and interviewer reactions.

Training Salespeople

New salespeople may spend anywhere from a few weeks or months to a year or more in training. After the initial training ends, most companies provide continuing sales training via seminars, sales meetings, and Internet e-learning throughout the salesperson's career. According to one source, North American firms spend billions of dollars on sales training each year. And although training can be expensive, it can also yield dramatic returns. For instance, one study showed that sales training conducted by ADP, an administrative services firm, resulted in a return on investment of nearly 338 percent in only 90 days.[13] In Canada, the Canadian Professional Sales Association (CPSA), in conjunction with Human Resources Skills Development Canada, offers sales training and certification to sales professionals in a wide range of industries, and has trained over 12 000 salespeople.[14]

Training programs have several goals. First, salespeople need to know about customers and how to build relationships with them. Therefore, the training program must teach them about different types of customers and their needs, buying motives, and buying habits. It must also teach them how to sell effectively and train them in the basics of the selling process. Salespeople also need to know and identify with the company, its products, and its competitors. Therefore, an effective training program teaches them about the company's objectives, organization, products, and the strategies of major competitors.

Today, many companies are adding digital e-learning to their sales training programs. Online training may range from simple text- and video-based product training and Internet-based sales exercises that build sales skills to sophisticated simulations that recreate the dynamics of real-life sales calls. One of the most basic forms is virtual instructor-led training (VILT). Using this method, a small group of salespeople at remote locations logs on to a Web conferencing site, where a sales instructor leads training sessions using online video, audio, and interactive learning tools.

Training online instead of on-site can cut travel and other training costs, and it takes up less of a salesperson's selling time. It also makes on-demand training available to salespeople, letting them train as little or as much as needed, whenever and wherever needed. Although most e-learning is Web-based, many companies now offer on-demand training from anywhere via almost any mobile digital device.

Many companies are now using imaginative and sophisticated e-learning techniques to make sales training more efficient—and sometimes even more fun. For example, Bayer HealthCare Pharmaceuticals worked with Concentric Pharma Advertising, a healthcare marketing agency, to create a role-playing simulation video game to train its sales force on a new drug marketing program:

> Most people don't usually associate fast-paced rock music and flashy graphics with online sales training tools. But Concentric Pharma Advertising's innovative role-playing video game—Rep Race: The Battle for Office Supremacy—has all that and a lot more. Rep Race gives Bayer sales reps far more entertainment than the staid old multiple-choice skills tests it replaces. The game was created to help breathe new life into a mature Bayer product—Betaseron, an

Exhibit 14.6 E-training can make sales training more efficient—and more fun. Bayer HealthCare Pharmaceuticals' role-playing video game—Rep Race—helped improve sales rep effectiveness by 20 percent.

18-year-old multiple sclerosis (MS) therapy treatment. The aim was to find a fresh, more active way to help Bayer sales reps apply the in-depth information they learned about Betaseron to actual selling and objections-handling situations. Bayer also wanted to increase rep engagement through interactive learning and feedback through real-time results. Bayer reps liked Rep Race from the start. According to Bayer, when the game was first launched, reps played it as many as 30 times. In addition to its educational and motivational value, Rep Race allowed Bayer to measure sales reps' individual and collective performance. In the end, Bayer calculated that the Rep Race simulation helped improve the Betaseron sales team's effectiveness by 20 percent.[15]

Compensating Salespeople

To attract good salespeople, a company must have an appealing compensation plan. Compensation consists of four elements: a fixed amount, a variable amount, expenses, and fringe benefits. The fixed amount, usually a salary, gives the salesperson some stable income. The variable amount, which might be commissions or bonuses based on sales performance, rewards the salesperson for greater effort and success.

Management must determine what *mix* of these compensation elements makes the most sense for each sales job. Different combinations of fixed and variable compensation give rise to four basic types of compensation plans: straight salary, straight commission, salary plus bonus, and salary plus commission. According to one study of sales force compensation, 18 percent of companies pay straight salary, 19 percent pay straight commission, and 63 percent pay a combination of salary plus incentives. Another study showed that the average salesperson's pay consists of about 67 percent salary and 33 percent incentive pay.[16]

A sales force compensation plan can both motivate salespeople and direct their activities. Compensation should direct salespeople toward activities that are consistent with the overall sales force and marketing objectives. For example, if the strategy is to acquire new business, grow rapidly, and gain market share, the compensation plan might include a larger commission component, coupled with a new-account bonus to encourage high sales performance and new account development. In contrast, if the goal is to maximize current account profitability, the compensation plan might contain a larger base-salary component with additional incentives for current account sales or customer satisfaction.

In fact, more and more companies are moving away from high-commission plans that may drive salespeople to make short-term grabs for business. They worry that a salesperson who is pushing too hard to close a deal may ruin the customer relationship. Instead, companies are designing compensation plans that reward salespeople for building customer relationships and growing the long-run value of each customer.

When times get tough economically, some companies are tempted to cut costs by reducing sales compensation. However, although some cost-cutting measures make sense when business is sluggish, cutting sales force compensation across the board is usually an action of last resort. Top salespeople are always in demand, and paying them less might mean losing them at a time when they are most needed. Thus, short-changing key salespeople can result in short-changing important customer relationships. If the company must reduce its compensation expenses, rather than making across-the-board cuts, companies should continue to pay top performers well while turning loose low performers.

Supervising and Motivating Salespeople

New salespeople need more than a territory, compensation, and training—they need supervision and motivation. The goal of *supervision* is to help salespeople "work smart" by doing the right things in the right ways. The goal of *motivation* is to encourage salespeople to "work hard" and energetically toward sales force goals. If salespeople work smart and work hard, they will realize their full potential—to their own and the company's benefit.

Supervising Salespeople Companies vary in how closely they supervise their salespeople. Many help salespeople identify target customers and set call objectives. Some may also specify how much time the sales force should spend prospecting for new accounts and set other time management priorities. One tool is the weekly, monthly, or annual *call plan* that shows which customers and prospects to call on and which activities to carry out. Another tool is *time-and-duty analysis*. In addition to time spent selling, the salesperson spends time travelling, waiting, taking breaks, and doing administrative chores.

Figure 14.2 shows how salespeople spend their time. On average, active selling time accounts for only 37 percent of total working hours.[17] Companies are always looking for ways to save time—simplifying administrative duties, developing better sales-call and routing plans, supplying more and better customer information, and using phone, email, or Internet conferencing instead of travelling.

Many firms have adopted *sales force automation systems*: computerized, digitized sales force operations that let salespeople work more effectively any time, anywhere. Companies now routinely equip their salespeople with laptops or tablets, smartphones, wireless connections, videoconferencing technologies, and customer-contact and relationship-management software. Armed with these technologies, salespeople can more effectively and efficiently profile customers and prospects, analyze and forecast sales, engage customers, make presentations, prepare sales and expense reports, and manage account relationships. The result is better time management, improved customer service, lower sales costs, and higher sales performance. In all, technology has reshaped the ways in which salespeople carry out their duties and engage customers.

Motivating Salespeople Beyond directing salespeople, sales managers must also motivate them. Some salespeople will do their best without any special urging from management. To

FIGURE 14.2 How Salespeople Spend Their Time

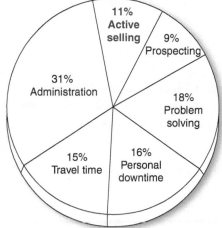

Source: "2014 Sales Performance Optimization Study," CSO Insights, www.csoinsights.com. Used with permission.

them, selling may be the most fascinating job in the world. But selling can also be frustrating. Salespeople often work alone, and they must sometimes travel away from home. They may also face aggressive competing salespeople and difficult customers. Therefore, salespeople often need special encouragement to do their best.

Management can boost sales force morale and performance through its organizational climate, sales quotas, and positive incentives. *Organizational climate* describes the feeling that salespeople have about their opportunities, value, and rewards for a good performance. Some companies treat salespeople as if they are not very important, so performance suffers accordingly. Other companies treat their salespeople as valued contributors and allow virtually unlimited opportunity for income and promotion. Not surprisingly, these companies enjoy higher sales force performance and less turnover.

Sales quota
A standard that states the amount a salesperson should sell and how sales should be divided among the company's products.

Many companies motivate their salespeople by setting **sales quotas**—standards stating the amount they should sell and how sales should be divided among the company's products. Compensation is often related to how well salespeople meet their quotas. Companies also use various *positive incentives* to increase the sales force effort. *Sales meetings* provide social occasions, breaks from the routine, chances to meet and talk with "company brass," and opportunities to air feelings and identify with a larger group. Companies also sponsor *sales contests* to spur the sales force to make a selling effort above and beyond what is normally expected. Other incentives include honours, merchandise and cash awards, trips, and profit-sharing plans.

Evaluating Salespeople and Sales Force Performance

We have thus far described how management communicates what salespeople should be doing and how it motivates them to do it. This process requires good feedback, which means getting regular information about salespeople to evaluate their performance.

Management gets information about its salespeople in several ways. The most important source is *sales reports*, including weekly or monthly work plans and longer-term territory marketing plans. Salespeople also write up their completed activities on *call reports* and turn in *expense reports* for which they are partly or wholly reimbursed. The company can also monitor the sales and profit performance data in the salesperson's territory. Additional information comes from personal observation, customer surveys, and talks with other salespeople.

Using various sales force reports and other information, sales management evaluates the members of the sales force. It evaluates salespeople on their ability to "plan their work and work their plan." Formal evaluation forces management to develop and communicate clear standards for judging performance. It also provides salespeople with constructive feedback and motivates them to perform well.

On a broader level, management should evaluate the performance of the sales force as a whole. Is the sales force accomplishing its customer relationship, sales, and profit objectives? Is it working well with other areas of the marketing and company organization? Are sales force costs in line with outcomes? As with other marketing activities, the company wants to measure its *return on sales investment*.

Selling Digitally: Online, Mobile, and Social Media Tools

The fastest-growing sales trend is the exploding use of online, mobile, and social media tools in selling. New digital sales force technologies are creating exciting new avenues for connecting with and engaging customers in the digital and social media age. Some analysts even predict that the Internet will mean the death of person-to-person selling, as salespeople are ultimately replaced by websites, online social media, mobile apps, video and conferencing technologies, and other tools that allow direct customer contact. "Don't believe it," says one sales expert (see Marketing@Work 14.1).[18] Used properly, online and social media technologies won't make salespeople obsolete; they will make salespeople more productive and effective.

The new digital technologies are providing salespeople with powerful tools for identifying and learning about prospects, engaging customers, creating customer value, closing sales, and nurturing customer relationships. Internet-based technologies can produce big organizational benefits for sales forces. They help conserve salespeople's valuable time, save travel dollars, and give salespeople new vehicles for selling and servicing accounts.

Using the Internet hasn't really changed the fundamentals of selling. "The way to sell is to touch, listen to, and engage customers," says one sales force expert. "Now we do [more of] it online." However, the Internet and social media are dramatically changing the customer buying process. As a result, they are also changing the selling process. In today's digital world, many customers no longer rely as much as they once did on information and assistance provided by salespeople. Instead, they carry out more of the buying process on their own—especially the early stages. Increasingly, they use online and social media resources to analyze their own problems, research solutions, get advice from colleagues, and rank buying options before ever speaking to a salesperson. One study of more than 1400 business buyers found that, on average, buyers completed nearly 60 percent of the buying process before contacting a supplier.[19]

Thus, today's customers have much more control over the sales process than they had in the days when brochures, pricing, and product advice were available only from a sales rep. Customers can now browse corporate sites, blogs, and YouTube videos to identify and qualify sellers. They can hobnob with others buyers on social media such as LinkedIn, Twitter, or Facebook to share experiences, identify solutions, and evaluate products they are considering. According to one study, 55 percent of business buyers now turn to social media when searching for information.[20]

As a result, if and when salespeople do enter the buying process, customers often know almost as much about a company's products as the salespeople do. "It's not just that buyers start the sales process without you," says an analyst, "they typically complete most of the purchase journey before having any contact with sales. And by that point they are far more informed about your business than you are about theirs."[21]

In response to this new digital buying environment, sellers are reorienting their selling processes around the new customer buying process. They are "going where customers are"—social media, Web forums, online communities, blogs—in order to engage customers earlier. They are engaging customers not just where and when they are buying, but also where and when they are learning about and evaluating what they will buy. Salespeople now routinely use digital tools to monitor customer social media exchanges to spot trends, identify prospects, and learn

Exhibit 14.7 Selling and the Internet: Companies use Internet collaboration tools such as Cisco's TelePresence to talk live with customers about products and services.

Courtesy of Cisco

MARKETING@WORK   14.1

B-to-B Salespeople: In This Digital and Social Media Age, Who Needs Them Anymore?

It's hard to imagine a world without salespeople. But according to some analysts, there will be a lot fewer of them a decade from now. With the explosion of the Internet, mobile devices, social media, and other technologies that link customers directly with companies, they reason, who needs face-to-face selling anymore? According to the doubters, salespeople are rapidly being replaced by websites, email, blogs, mobile apps, video sharing, virtual trade shows, social media such as LinkedIn and Facebook, and a host of other digital-age interaction tools.

Research firm Gartner predicts that by 2020, 85 percent of all interactions between businesses will be executed without human intervention, requiring fewer salespeople. Of the 18 million salespeople now employed in the United States, the firm says, there will be only about 4 million left. "The world no longer needs salespeople," one doomsayer boldly proclaims. "Sales is a dying profession and soon will be as outmoded as oil lamps and the rotary phone." Says another, "If we don't find and fill a need faster than a computer, we won't be needed."

So, is business-to-business selling really dying? Will the Internet, mobile technologies, and social media replace the age-old art of selling face to face? To answer these questions, *SellingPower* magazine called together a panel of five sales experts and asked them to weigh in on the future of B-to-B sales. The panel members agreed that technology is radically transforming the selling profession. Today's revolutionary changes in how people communicate are affecting every aspect of business, and selling is no exception.

But is B-to-B selling dead in this Internet age? Don't believe it, says the *SellingPower* panel. Technology, the Internet, and social media won't soon be replacing person-to-person buying and selling. Selling has changed, agrees the

panel, and the technology can greatly enhance the selling process. But it can't replace many of the functions that salespeople perform. "The Internet can take orders and disseminate content, but what it can't do is discover customer needs," says one panellist. "It can't build relationships, and it can't prospect on its own." Adds another panellist, "Someone must define the company's value proposition and unique message and communicate it to the market, and that person is the sales rep."

What is dying, however, is what one panellist calls the account-maintenance role—the order taker who stops by the customer's office on Friday and says, "Hey, got anything for me?" Such salespeople are not creating value and can easily be replaced by automation. However, salespeople who excel at new customer acquisition, relationship management, and account growth with existing customers will always be in high demand.

There's no doubt about it—technology is transforming the profession of selling.

Instead of relying on salespeople for basic information and education, customers can now do much of their own prepurchase research via websites, online searches, social media contacts, and other venues. Many customers now start the sales process online and do their homework about competing products and suppliers before the first sales meeting ever takes place. They don't need basic information or product education; they need solutions. So today's salespeople need "to move into the discovery and relationship-building phase, uncovering pain points and focusing on the prospect's business," says a panellist.

Rather than replacing salespeople, then, technology is augmenting them. Today's salespeople aren't really doing anything fundamentally new. They've always done customer research and social networking. Today, however, they are "doing it on steroids," using a new kit of high-tech digital tools and applications.

Exhibit 14.8   Online selling tools, such as SAP's EcoHub online community-based social media marketplace, are coming into their own in helping to build customer awareness and generate consideration, purchase interest, and sales. But rather than replacing salespeople, such efforts extend their reach and effectiveness.

For example, many companies are moving rapidly into online-community-based selling. Case in point: enterprise-software company SAP, which has set up EcoHub, its own online, community-powered social media marketplace consisting of customers, partners, and almost anyone else who wants to join. The EcoHub community (ecohub.sap.com) has 2 million users in 200 countries and extends across a broad Internet spectrum—a dedicated website, Twitter channels, LinkedIn groups, Facebook fan pages, YouTube channels, Flickr groups, mobile apps, and more. It includes 600 "solution storefronts" where visitors can "easily discover, evaluate, and initiate the purchase of software solutions and services from SAP and its partners." EcoHub also lets users rate the solutions and advice they get from other community members.

SAP was surprised to learn that what it had originally seen as a place for customers to discuss issues, problems, and solutions has turned into a significant point of sale. The information, give-and-take discussions, and conversations at the site draw in customers, even for big-ticket sales. "Some customers are spending US$20 to US$30 million due to EcoHub," says the SAP vice-president who heads up the community.

However, although EcoHub draws in new potential customers and takes them through many of the initial stages of product discovery and evaluation, it doesn't replace SAP's or its partners' salespeople. Instead, it extends their reach and effectiveness. The real value of EcoHub is the flood of sales leads it creates for the SAP and partner sales forces. Once prospective customers have discovered, discussed, and evaluated SAP solutions on EcoHub, SAP invites them to "initiate contact, request a proposal, or start the negotiation process." That's where the person-to-person selling begins.

All this suggests that B-to-B selling isn't dying, it's just changing. The tools and techniques may be different as selling leverages and adapts to selling in the digital and social media age. But the panellists agree strongly that B-to-B marketers will never be able to do without strong sales teams. Salespeople who can discover customer needs, solve customer problems, and build relationships will be needed and successful, regardless of what else changes. Especially for those big-ticket B-to-B sales, "all the new technology may make it easier to sell by building strong ties to customers even before the first sit-down, but when the signature hits the dotted line, there will be a sales rep there."

Sources: Quotes and other information from Robert McGarvey, "All About Us," SellingPower, March 7, 2011, p. 48; Lain Chroust Ehmann, "Sales Up!" SellingPower, January/February 2011, p. 40; James Ledbetter, "Death of a Salesman. Of Lots of Them, Actually," Slate, September 21, 2010, www.slate.com/id/2268122; Sean Callahan, "Is B-to-B Marketing Really Obsolete?" BtoB, January 17, 2011, p. 1; Gerhared Gschwandtner, "How Many Salespeople Will Be Left by 2020?" SellingPower, May/June 2011, p. 7; Brent Adamson, Matthew Dixon, and Nicholas Toman, "The End of Solution Sales," HBR, July–August 2012, pp. 61–68; Scott Gillum, "The Disappearing Sales Process," Forbes, January 7, 2013, www.forbes.com/sites/gyro/2013/01/07/the-disappearing-sales-process; Matt Dixon and Steve Richard, "Solution Selling Is Dead: Why 2013 Is the Year of B2B Insight Selling," Openview, January 4, 2013, http://labs.openviewpartners.com/solution-selling-is-dead-2013-year-of-b2b-insight-selling; and "Getting Started with SAP EcoHub," http://ecohub.sap.com/getting-started, accessed November 2013.

what customers would like to buy, how they feel about a vendor, and what it would take to make a sale. They generate lists of prospective customers from online databases and social networking sites, such as InsideView, Hoovers, and LinkedIn. They create dialogues when prospective customers visit their Web and social media sites through live chats with the sales team. They use Internet conferencing tools such as WebEx, GoToMeeting, or TelePresence to talk live with customers about products and services. They provide videos and other information on their YouTube channels and Facebook pages.

Today's sales forces are also ramping up their own use of social media to engage customers throughout the buying process. A recent survey of business-to-business marketers found that, although they have recently cut back on traditional media and event spending, 68 percent are investing more in social media, ranging from proprietary online customer communities to webinars and Twitter, Facebook, LinkedIn, and YouTube applications. Consider Makino, a leading manufacturer of metal cutting and machining technology:

> Makino complements its sales force efforts through a wide variety of social media initiatives that inform customers and enhance customer relationships. For example, it hosts an ongoing series of industry-specific webinars that position the company as an industry thought leader. Makino produces about three webinars each month and has archived more than 100 on topics ranging from how to get the most out of your machine tools to how metal-cutting processes are done. Webinar content is tailored to specific industries, such as aerospace or medical, and is promoted through carefully targeted banner ads and email invitations. The webinars help to build Makino's customer database, generate leads, build customer relationships, and prepare the way for salespeople by serving up relevant information and educating customers online. Makino also uses Twitter, Facebook, and YouTube to inform customers and prospects about

the latest Makino innovations and events and demonstrate the company's machines in action. "We've shifted dramatically into the electronic marketing area," says Makino's marketing manager. "It speeds up the sales cycle and makes it more efficient—for both the company and the customer. The results have been 'outstanding.'"[22]

Ultimately, online and social media technologies are helping to make sales forces more efficient, cost-effective, and productive. The technologies help salespeople do what good salespeople have always done—build customer relationships by solving customer problems—but do it better, faster, and cheaper.

However, the technologies also have some drawbacks. For starters, they're not cheap. In addition, such systems can intimidate low-tech salespeople or clients. Even more, there are some things you just can't present or teach via the Internet—things that require personal interactions. For these reasons, some high-tech experts recommend that sales executives use online and social media technologies to spot opportunities, provide information, maintain customer contact, and make preliminary client sales presentations but resort to old-fashioned, face-to-face meetings when the time draws near to close a big deal.

The Personal Selling Process LO3

We now turn from designing and managing a sales force to the personal selling process. The **selling process** consists of several steps that salespeople must master. These steps focus on the goal of getting new customers and obtaining orders from them. However, most salespeople spend much of their time maintaining existing accounts and building long-term customer *relationships*. We will discuss the relationship aspect of the personal selling process in a later section.

Steps in the Selling Process

As shown in Figure 14.3, the selling process consists of seven steps: prospecting and qualifying, preapproach, approach, presentation and demonstration, handling objections, closing, and follow-up.

Prospecting and Qualifying The first step in the selling process is **prospecting**—identifying qualified potential customers. Approaching the right customers is crucial to selling success. Salespeople don't want to call on just any potential customers. They want to call on those who are most likely to appreciate and respond to the company's value proposition—those the company can serve well and profitably.

A salesperson must often approach many prospects to get only a few sales. Although the company supplies some leads, salespeople need skill in finding their own. The best source is referrals. Salespeople can ask current customers for referrals and cultivate other referral sources, such as suppliers, dealers, noncompeting salespeople, and Web or other

Selling process
The steps that salespeople follow when selling, which include prospecting and qualifying, preapproach, approach, presentation and demonstration, handling objections, closing, and follow-up.

Prospecting
The sales step in which a salesperson or company identifies qualified potential customers.

FIGURE 14.3 Steps in the Selling Process

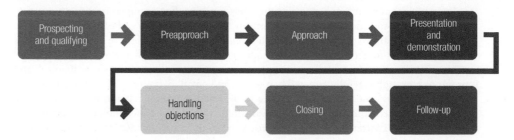

social media contacts. They can also search for prospects in directories or on the Internet and track down leads using the telephone, email, and social media. Or, as a last resort, they can drop in unannounced on various offices (a practice known as *cold calling*).

Salespeople also need to know how to *qualify* leads—that is, how to identify the good ones and screen out the poor ones. Prospects can be qualified by looking at their financial ability, volume of business, special needs, location, and possibilities for growth.

Preapproach Before calling on a prospect, the salesperson should learn as much as possible about the organization (what it needs, who is involved in the buying) and its buyers (their characteristics and buying styles). This step is known as **preapproach**. A successful sale begins long before the salesperson makes initial contact with a prospect. Preapproach begins with good research and preparation. The salesperson can consult standard industry and online sources, acquaintances, and others to learn about the company. He or she can scour the prospect's Web and social media sites for information about its products, buyers, and buying processes. Then the salesperson must apply the research gathered to develop a customer strategy.

The salesperson should set *call objectives*, which may be to qualify the prospect, gather information, or make an immediate sale. Another task is to determine the best approach, which might be a personal visit, a phone call, an email, or a text or tweet. The ideal timing should be considered carefully because many prospects are busiest at certain times of the day or week. Finally, the salesperson should give thought to an overall sales strategy for the account.

Approach During the **approach** step, the salesperson should know how to meet and greet the buyer and get the relationship off to a good start. The approach might take place offline or online, in-person or via digital conferencing or social media. This step involves the salesperson's appearance, opening lines, and follow-up remarks. The opening lines should be positive to build goodwill from the outset. This opening might be followed by some key questions to learn more about the customer's needs or by showing a display or sample to attract the buyer's attention and curiosity. As in all stages of the selling process, listening to the customer is crucial.

Presentation and Demonstration During the **presentation** step of the selling process, the salesperson tells the "value story" to the buyer, showing how the company's offer solves the customer's problems. The *customer-solution approach* fits better with today's relationship marketing focus than does a hard sell or glad-handing approach. The goal should be to show how the company's products and services fit the customer's needs. Buyers today want insights and solutions, not smiles; results, not razzle-dazzle. Moreover, they don't want just products. More than ever in today's economic climate, buyers want to know how those products will add value to their businesses. They want salespeople who listen to their concerns, understand their needs, and respond with the right products and services.

But before salespeople can *present* customer solutions, they must *develop* solutions to present. The solutions approach calls for good listening and problem-solving skills. The qualities that buyers *dislike most* in salespeople

Preapproach
The sales step in which a salesperson learns as much as possible about a prospective customer before making a sales call.

Approach
The sales step in which a salesperson meets the customer for the first time.

Presentation
The sales step in which a salesperson tells the "value story" to the buyer, showing how the company's offer solves the customer's problems.

Exhibit 14.9 Listening to customer needs: Great salespeople know how to sell, but more important, they know how to listen and build strong customer relationships.

Tony Garcia/Getty Images

include being pushy, late, deceitful, unprepared, disorganized, or overly talkative. The qualities they *value most* include good listening, empathy, honesty, dependability, thoroughness, and follow-through. Great salespeople know how to sell, but more important, they know how to listen and build strong customer relationships. According to an old sales adage, "You have two ears and one mouth. Use them proportionally." A classic ad from office products maker Boise Cascade makes the listening point. It shows a Boise salesperson with huge ears drawn on. "With Boise, you'll notice a difference right away, especially with our sales force," says the ad. "At Boise . . . our account representatives have the unique ability to listen to your needs."

Finally, salespeople must also plan their presentation methods. Good interpersonal communication skills count when it comes to making effective sales presentations. However, the current media-rich and cluttered communications environment presents many new challenges for sales presenters. Today's information-overloaded customers demand richer presentation experiences. For their part, presenters now face multiple distractions during presentations from mobile phones, text messages, and other digital competition. As a result, salespeople must deliver their messages in more engaging and compelling ways.

Thus, today's salespeople are employing advanced presentation technologies that allow for full multimedia presentations to only one or a few people. The venerable old sales presentation flip chart has been replaced with sophisticated presentation software, online presentation technologies, interactive whiteboards, digital projectors, and tablet computers.

Handling Objections Customers almost always have objections during the presentation or when asked to place an order. The objections can be either logical or psychological, and are often unspoken. In **handling objections**, the salesperson should use a positive approach, seek out hidden objections, ask the buyer to clarify any objections, take objections as opportunities to provide more information, and turn the objections into reasons for buying. Every salesperson needs training in the skills of handling objections.

Handling objections
The sales step in which a salesperson seeks out, clarifies, and overcomes any customer objections to buying.

Closing After handling the prospect's objections, the salesperson next tries to close the sale. However, some salespeople do not get around to **closing** or don't handle it well. They may lack confidence, feel guilty about asking for the order, or fail to recognize the right moment to close the sale. Salespeople should know how to recognize closing signals from the buyer, including physical actions, comments, and questions. For example, the customer might sit forward and nod approvingly or ask about prices and credit terms.

Closing
The sales step in which a salesperson asks the customer for an order.

Salespeople can use any of several closing techniques. They can ask for the order, review points of agreement, offer to help write up the order, ask whether the buyer wants this model or that one, or note that the buyer will lose out if the order is not placed now. The salesperson may offer the buyer special reasons to close, such as a lower price, an extra quantity at no charge, or additional services.

Follow-up
The sales step in which a salesperson follows up after the sale to ensure customer satisfaction and repeat business.

Follow-Up The last step in the selling process—**follow-up**—is necessary if the salesperson wants to ensure customer satisfaction and repeat business. Right after closing, the salesperson should complete any details on delivery time, purchase terms, and other matters. The salesperson then should schedule a follow-up call after the buyer receives the initial order to make sure proper installation, instruction, and servicing occur. This visit would reveal any problems, assure the buyer of the salesperson's interest, and reduce any buyer concerns that might have arisen since the sale.

Personal Selling and Managing Customer Relationships

The steps in the just-described selling process are *transaction oriented*—their aim is to help salespeople close a specific sale with a customer. But in most cases, the company is not simply seeking a sale. Rather, it wants to engage the customer over the long haul in a mutually profitable *relationship*. The sales force usually plays an important role in customer relationship building. Thus, as shown in Figure 14.3, the selling process must be understood in the context of building and maintaining profitable customer relationships. Moreover, as discussed in a previous section, today's buyers are increasingly moving through the early stages of the buying process themselves, before ever engaging sellers. Salespeople must adapt their selling process to match the new buying process. That means discovering and engaging customers on a relationship basis rather than a transaction basis.

Successful sales organizations recognize that winning and keeping accounts requires more than making good products and directing the sales force to close lots of sales. If the company wishes only to close sales and capture short-term business, it can do this by simply slashing its prices to meet or beat those of competitors. Instead, most companies want their salespeople to practice *value selling*—demonstrating and delivering superior customer value and capturing a return on that value that is fair for both the customer and the company. For example, companies like Procter & Gamble understand that they aren't just selling products to and through their retailer customers. They are partnering with these retail accounts to create more value for final consumers to their mutual benefit. P&G knows that it can succeed only if its retail partners succeed (see Marketing@ Work 14.2).

Unfortunately, in the heat of closing sales, salespeople too often take the easy way out by cutting prices rather than selling value. Sales management's challenge is to transform salespeople from customer advocates for price cuts into company advocates for value. Here's how Rockwell Automation sells value and relationships rather than price:

> Under pressure from Walmart to lower its prices, a condiment producer asked several competing supplier representatives—including Rockwell Automation sales rep Jeff Policicchio—to help it find ways to reduce its operating costs. After spending a day in the customer's plant, Policicchio quickly put his finger on the major problem: Production was suffering because of downtime due to poorly performing pumps on the customer's 32 large condiment tanks. Quickly gathering cost and usage data, Policicchio used his Rockwell Automation laptop value-assessment tool to develop an effective solution for the customer's pump problem.
>
> The next day, as he and competing reps presented their cost-reduction proposals to plant management, Policicchio offered the following value proposition: "With this Rockwell Automation pump solution, through less downtime, reduced administrative costs in procurement, and lower spending on repair parts, your company will save at least $16 268 per pump—on up to 32 pumps—relative to our best competitor's solution." Compared with competitors' proposals, Policicchio's solution carried a higher initial price. However, no competing rep offered more than fuzzy promises about possible cost savings. Most simply lowered their prices.
>
> Impressed by Policicchio's value proposition—despite its higher initial price—the plant managers opted to buy and try one Rockwell Automation pump. When the pump performed even better than predicted, the customer ordered all of the remaining pumps. By demonstrating tangible value rather than simply selling on price, Policicchio not only landed the initial sale but also earned a loyal future customer.[23]

Thus, value selling requires listening to customers, understanding their needs, and carefully coordinating the whole company's efforts to create lasting relationships based on customer value.

MARKETING@WORK   14.2

P&G: It's Not Sales, It's Customer Business Development

For decades, Procter & Gamble has been at the top of almost every expert's A-list of outstanding marketing companies. The experts point to P&G's stable of top-selling consumer brands, or to the fact that year in and year out, P&G is the world's largest advertiser. Consumers seem to agree. You'll likely find at least one of P&G's blockbuster brands in 99 percent of all Canadian and American households; in many homes, you'll find a dozen or more familiar P&G products. But P&G is also highly respected for something else—its top-notch, customer-focused sales force.

P&G's sales force has long been an icon for personal selling at its very best. When it comes to selecting, training, and managing salespeople, P&G sets the gold standard. The company employs a massive sales force of more than 5000 salespeople worldwide. At P&G, however, they rarely call it "sales." Instead, it's "customer business development" (CBD). And P&G sales reps aren't "salespeople"; they're "CBD managers" or "CBD account executives." All this might seem like just so much "corp-speak," but at P&G the distinction goes to the very core of how selling works.

P&G understands that if its customers don't do well, neither will the company. To grow its own business, therefore, P&G must first grow the business of the retailers that sell its brands to final consumers. And at P&G, the primary responsibility for helping customer companies grow falls to the sales force. In P&G's own words, "CBD is more than mere 'selling'—it's a P&G-specific approach which enables us to grow our business by working as a 'strategic partner' (as opposed to just a supplier) with those who ultimately sell our products to consumers." Says one CBD manager, "We depend on them as much as they depend on us." By partnering with each other, P&G and its customers create win-win relationships that help both to prosper.

Most P&G customers are huge and complex businesses—such as Shoppers Drug Mart, Walmart, or The Dollar Store—with thousands of stores and billions of dollars in revenues. Working with and selling to such customers can be a very complex undertaking, more than any single salesperson or sales team could accomplish. Instead, P&G assigns a full CBD team to every large customer account. Each CBD team contains not only salespeople but also a full complement of specialists in every aspect of selling P&G's consumer brands at the retail level.

CBD teams vary in size depending on the customer. For example, P&G's largest customer, Walmart, which accounts for an amazing 20 percent of the company's sales, commands a 350-person CBD team. By contrast, at Dollar General, a U.S.-based discount store, the P&G team consists of about 30 people. Regardless of size, every CBD team constitutes a complete, multifunctional customer service unit. Each team includes a CBD manager and several CBD account executives (each responsible for a specific P&G product category), supported by specialists in marketing strategy, product development, operations, information systems, logistics, finance, and human resources.

To deal effectively with large accounts, P&G salespeople must be smart, well trained, and strategically grounded. They deal daily with high-level retail category buyers who may purchase hundreds of millions of dollars' worth of P&G and competing brands annually. It takes a lot more than a friendly smile and a firm handshake to interact with such buyers. But individual P&G salespeople can't know everything, and thanks to the CBD sales structure, they don't have to. Instead, as members of a full CBD team, P&G salespeople have at hand all the resources they need to resolve even the most challenging customer problems. "I have everything I need right here," says a household care account executive. "If my customer needs help from us with in-store promotions, I can go right down the hall and talk with someone on my team in marketing about doing some kind of promotional deal. It's that simple."

Customer business development involves partnering with customers to

Exhibit 14.10   P&G's customer business development managers know that to grow the company's business, they must first help their retail partners sell P&G's brands.

Jin Lee/Getty Images

jointly identify strategies that create shopper value and satisfaction and drive profitable sales at the store level. When it comes to profitably moving Tide, Pampers, Gillette, or other P&G brands off store shelves and into consumers' shopping carts, P&G reps and their teams often know more than the retail buyers they advise. In fact, P&G's retail partners often rely on CBD teams to help them manage not only the P&G brands on their shelves but also entire product categories, including competing brands.

Wait a minute. Does it make sense to let P&G advise on the stocking and placement of competitors' brands as well as its own? Would a P&G CBD rep ever tell a retail buyer to stock fewer P&G products and more of a competing brand? Believe it or not, it happens all the time. The CBD team's primary goal is to help the customer win in each product category. Sometimes, analysis shows that the best solution for the customer is "more of the other guy's product." For P&G, that's okay. It knows that creating the best situation for the retailer ultimately pulls in more customer traffic,

which in turn will likely lead to increased sales for other P&G products in the same category. Because most of P&G's brands are market-share leaders, it stands to benefit more from the increased traffic than competitors do. Again, what's good for the customer is good for P&G—it's a win-win situation.

Honest and open dealings also help build long-term customer relationships. P&G salespeople become trusted advisers for their retailer-partners, a status they work hard to maintain. "It took me four years to build the trust I now have with my buyer," says a veteran CBD account executive. "If I talk her into buying P&G products that she can't sell or out-of-stocking competing brands that she should be selling, I could lose that trust in a heartbeat."

Finally, collaboration is usually a two-way street—P&G gives and customers give back in return. "We'll help customers run a set of commercials or do some merchandising events, but there's usually a return on investment," explains another CBD manager. "Maybe it's helping us with distribution of a new product or increasing space for fabric care. We're

very willing if the effort creates value for us as well as for the customer and the final consumer." According to P&G, "All customers want to improve their business; it's [our] role to help them identify the biggest opportunities."

Thus, P&G salespeople aren't the stereotypical glad-handers that some people have come to expect when they think of selling. P&G's "salespeople"—its CBD managers—are talented, well-educated, well-trained sales professionals who do all they can to help customers succeed. They know that good selling involves working with customers to solve their problems for mutual gain. They know that if customers succeed, they succeed.

Sources: Based on information from numerous P&G managers; with information from "500 Largest Sales Forces in America," Selling Power, September 2012, pp. 34, 40; "Then and Now: Going to Great Lengths to Get P&G Products into the Hands of Consumers," http://news.pg.com/blog/company-strategy/then-and-now-going-great-lengths-get-pg-products-hands-consumers, accessed June 2013; Cassandra Jowett, "Schulich Grad Finds Her Calling in Customer Business Development at P&G," TalentEgg, January 8, 2013, http://talentegg.ca/incubator/2013/01/08/schulich-grad-finds-calling-customer-business-development-pg; and www.experiencepg.com/jobs/customer-business-development-sales.aspx, accessed November 2013.

Sales Promotion LO4

Personal selling and advertising often work closely with another promotion tool, sales promotion. **Sales promotion** consists of short-term incentives to encourage the purchase or sales of a product or service. Whereas advertising offers reasons to buy a product or service, sales promotion offers reasons to buy *now*.

Sales promotion
Short-term incentives to encourage the purchase or sale of a product or a service.

Examples of sales promotions are found everywhere. A freestanding insert in the Sunday newspaper contains a coupon offering $1 off Meow Mix Tender Centers food for your cat. A Bed Bath & Beyond ad in your favourite magazine offers 20 percent off on any single item. The end-of-the-aisle display in the local supermarket tempts impulse buyers with a wall of Coca-Cola cases—four 12-packs for $12. Buy a new Samsung laptop and get a free memory upgrade. A hardware store chain receives a 10 percent discount on selected Stihl power lawn and garden tools if it agrees to advertise them in local newspapers. In short, sales promotion includes a wide variety of promotion tools designed to stimulate earlier or stronger market response.

The Rapid Growth of Sales Promotion

Sales promotion tools are used by most organizations, including manufacturers, distributors, retailers, and not-for-profit institutions. They are targeted toward final buyers (*consumer promotions*), retailers and wholesalers (*trade promotions*), business customers (*business promotions*), and members of the sales force (*sales force promotions*). Today, in the average consumer packaged-goods company, sales promotion accounts for 60 percent of all marketing budgets.[24]

Exhibit 14.11 Sales promotions are found everywhere. For example, your favourite magazine is loaded with offers like this one that promote a strong and immediate response.

Several factors have contributed to the rapid growth of sales promotion, particularly in consumer markets. First, inside the company, product managers face greater pressures to increase current sales, and they view promotion as an effective short-run sales tool. Second, externally, the company faces more competition, and competing brands are less differentiated. Increasingly, competitors are using sales promotion to help differentiate their offers. Third, advertising efficiency has declined because of rising costs, media clutter, and legal restraints. Finally, consumers have become more deal oriented. In the current economy, consumers are demanding lower prices and better deals. Sales promotions can help attract today's more thrift-oriented consumers.

The growing use of sales promotion has resulted in *promotion clutter*, which is similar to advertising clutter. With so many products being sold on deal these days, a given promotion runs the risk of being lost in a sea of other promotions, weakening its ability to trigger an immediate purchase. Manufacturers are now searching for ways to rise above the clutter; for example, by offering larger coupon values, creating more dramatic point-of-purchase displays, or delivering promotions through new digital media—such as the Internet or mobile phones. One study found that 88 percent of retailers now see digital promotions—including mobile coupons, shopper emails, and online deals—as an important part of their shopper marketing efforts.[25]

In developing a sales promotion program, a company must first set sales promotion objectives and then select the best tools for accomplishing these objectives.

Sales Promotion Objectives

Sales promotion objectives vary widely. Sellers may use *consumer promotions* to urge short-term customer buying or boost customer brand involvement. Objectives for *trade promotions* include getting retailers to carry new items and more inventory, buy ahead, or promote the company's products and give them more shelf space. *Business promotions* are used to generate business leads, stimulate purchases, reward customers, and motivate salespeople. For the sales force, objectives include getting more sales force support for current or new products and getting salespeople to sign up new accounts.

Sales promotions are usually used together with advertising, personal selling, direct marketing, or other promotion mix tools. Consumer promotions must usually be advertised and can add excitement and pulling power to ads. Trade and business sales promotions support the firm's personal selling process.

When the economy tightens and sales lag, it's tempting to offer deep promotional discounts to spur consumer spending. In general, however, rather than creating only short-term sales or temporary brand switching, sales promotions should help to reinforce the product's position and build long-term customer relationships. If properly designed, every sales promotion tool has the potential to build both short-term excitement and long-term consumer engagement and relationships. Marketers should avoid "quick fix," price-only promotions in favour of promotions that are designed to build brand equity. Examples include the various *frequency marketing programs* and loyalty cards that have mushroomed in popularity in recent years. Most hotels, supermarkets, and airlines offer frequent-guest/buyer/flyer programs that give rewards to regular customers to keep them coming back. All kinds of companies now offer rewards programs. Such promotional programs can build loyalty through added value rather than discounted prices.

For example, Shoppers Drug Mart, Canada's largest drugstore chain, has the most successful loyalty program offered by any Canadian retailer. Members of the Optimum program spend 60 percent more on their purchases than nonmembers, and overall, Shoppers generates two-thirds of its nonprescription sales from Optimum cardholders.[26]

Major Sales Promotion Tools

Many tools can be used to accomplish sales promotion objectives. Descriptions of the main consumer, trade, and business promotion tools follow.

Consumer Promotions Consumer promotions include a wide range of tools—from samples, coupons, refunds, premiums, and point-of-purchase displays to contests, sweepstakes, and event sponsorships.

Samples are offers of a trial amount of a product. Sampling is the most effective—but most

Exhibit 14.12 Customer loyalty programs: Canadians are among the highest users of loyalty programs in the world.

Canadian Press

expensive—way to introduce a new product or create new excitement for an existing one. Some samples are free; for others, the company charges a small amount to offset its cost. The sample might be sent by mail, handed out in a store or at a kiosk, attached to another product, or featured in an ad, email, or mobile offer. Samples are sometimes combined into sample packs, which can then be used to promote other products and services. Sampling can be a powerful promotional tool.

Coupons are certificates that save buyers money when they purchase specified products. Most consumers love coupons. Major U.S. consumer packaged goods companies distributed 305 billion coupons with an average face value of $1.53 in 2012. Consumers redeemed more than 2.9 billion of them for a total savings of about $3.7 billion, 27.6 percent higher than five years before.[27] Coupons can promote early trial of a new brand or stimulate sales of a mature brand. However, to combat the increase in coupon clutter, most major consumer goods companies are issuing fewer coupons and targeting them more carefully.

Marketers are also cultivating new outlets for distributing coupons, such as supermarket shelf dispensers, electronic point-of-sale coupon printers, and online and mobile coupon programs. Digital coupons represent today's fastest-growing coupon segment—they can be individually targeted and personalized in ways that print coupons can't. Digital coupons accounted for nearly 9 percent of all coupons redeemed last year; 5.6 percent of all coupons were printed from a computer at home and 1.3 percent were redeemed via smartphone or other mobile devices. According to one study, the number of mobile phone coupon users rose by 66 percent in 2012, following 100 percent growth rates in each of the previous two years.[28] As mobile phones become appendages that many people can't live without, businesses are increasingly eyeing them as prime real estate for coupons, offers, and other marketing messages. For example, in the United States, drugstore chain Walgreens makes coupons available to its customers through several mobile channels:

> Using the Walgreens smartphone app, customers can instantly download coupons ranging in value from 50 cents to $5, good toward anything from health and beauty products to everyday essentials such as diapers. The coupons are conveniently scannable—no clipping or printing

Consumer promotions
Sales promotion tools used to boost short-term customer buying and engagement or enhance long-term customer relationships.

Exhibit 14.13 Mobile coupons: U.S. drugstore chain Walgreens makes coupons available to its customers through several mobile channels.

Walgreens Digital Marketing & Emerging Media Team. Rich Lesperance, Director.

required. Customers simply pull up the coupons on the Walgreens app and cashiers scan them straight from the customer's phone. Walgreens also tweets mobile coupons to customers who check in to any of its 8000 stores nationwide using check-in apps such as Foursquare, Yelp, or Facebook Places. Walgreens has mobile scanning capabilities available at all of its stores, making it the largest retail mobile coupon program in the United States. "Through our mobile application, no matter where people are, they can find an easy way to save next time they come to Walgreens," says the company's president of e-commerce.[29]

Rebates (or *cash refunds*) are like coupons except that the price reduction occurs after the purchase rather than at the retail outlet. The customer sends proof of purchase to the manufacturer, which then refunds part of the purchase price by mail. For example, Toro ran a clever preseason promotion on some of its snowblower models, offering a rebate if the snowfall in the buyer's market area turned out to be below average. Competitors were not able to match this offer on such short notice, and the promotion was very successful.

Price packs (also called *cents-off deals*) offer consumers savings off the regular price of a product. The producer marks the reduced prices directly on the label or package. Price packs can be single packages sold at a reduced price (such as two for the price of one) or two related products banded together (such as a toothbrush and toothpaste). Price packs are very effective—even more so than coupons—in stimulating short-term sales.

Premiums are goods offered either free or at low cost as an incentive to buy a product, ranging from toys included with kids' products to phone cards and DVDs. A premium may come inside the package (in-pack), outside the package (on-pack), or through the mail. For example, over the years, McDonald's has offered a variety of premiums in its Happy Meals—from *Madagascar* characters to Beanie Babies and *Pokémon* toy figures. Customers can visit www.happymeal.com to play games and watch commercials associated with the current Happy Meal sponsor.[30]

Advertising specialties, also called *promotional products*, are useful articles imprinted with an advertiser's name, logo, or message that are given as gifts to consumers. Typical items include T-shirts and other apparel, pens, coffee mugs, calendars, key rings, mouse pads, tote bags, coolers, golf balls, and caps. U.S. marketers spent nearly US$18 billion on advertising specialties in 2011. Such items can be very effective. The "best of them stick around for months, subtly burning a brand name into a user's brain," notes a promotional products expert.[31]

Point-of-purchase (POP) promotions include displays and demonstrations that take place at the point of sale. Think of your last visit to your local convenience store, grocery store, liquor store, or drugstore. Chances are good that you were tripping over aisle displays, promotional signs, "shelf talkers," or demonstrators offering free tastes of featured food products. Unfortunately, many retailers do not like to handle the hundreds of displays, signs, and posters they receive from manufacturers each year. Manufacturers have therefore responded by offering better POP materials, offering to set them up, and tying them in with television, print, or online messages.

Contests, sweepstakes, and *games* give consumers the chance to win something, such as cash, trips, or goods, by luck or through extra effort. A *contest* calls for consumers to submit an entry—a jingle, guess, suggestion—to be judged by a panel that will select the best entries. A *sweepstakes* calls for consumers to submit their names for a drawing. A *game* presents consumers with something—bingo numbers, missing letters—every time they buy, which may or may not help them win a prize.

All kinds of companies use sweepstakes and contests to create brand attention and boost consumer involvement. For example, at the free.ca website, you can find offers ranging from a trip for two from Air Canada to a chance to win a Ford F-150 from Costco.ca. Perhaps Canada's most successful consumer promotion, running for over 25 years, has been Tim Hortons' annual "Roll up the Rim to Win" contest, with prizes ranging from a free cup of coffee to a new car.

Finally, marketers can promote their brands through **event marketing (or event sponsorships)**. They can create their own brand-marketing events or serve as sole or participating sponsors of events created by others. The events might include anything from mobile brand tours to festivals, reunions, marathons, concerts, or other sponsored gatherings. Event marketing is huge, and it may be the fastest-growing area of promotion. Effective event marketing links events and sponsorships to a brand's value proposition.

All kinds of brands now hold events. One week, it might be the National Football League (NFL) filling the southern tip of Times Square with NFL players to promote new NFL jersey designs. The next week, it's a mob of Russian models on the 45th Street island between Broadway and Seventh Avenue in New York City, using it as a fashion runway for Maybelline. But according to one business reporter, energy drink maker Red Bull is the "mother of all event marketers":

Exhibit 14.14 Event marketing: Red Bull hosts hundreds of events each year in dozens of sports around the world, designed to bring the high-octane world of Red Bull to its community of enthusiasts.

Max Rossi/REUTERS

> Event pioneer Red Bull holds hundreds of events each year in dozens of sports around the world. Each event features off-the-grid experiences designed to bring the high-octane world of Red Bull to its community of enthusiasts. The brand even hosts a "Holy S**t" tab on its website, featuring videos of everything from 27-metre ocean cliff dives at its Cliff Diving Series event in Grimstad, Norway, to dare-devil freeskiing feats at its Red Bull Cold Rush event in the Colorado mountain peaks, to absolutely breathtaking wing suit flights at Red Bull events staged in exotic locations from Monterrey, Mexico, to Hunan province, China. The Red Bull Final Descent series is a mountain biking challenge that pushes riders to the brink and back, over some of the most technically challenging terrain in North America. Red Bull events draw large crowds and plenty of media coverage. But it's about more than just the events—it's about customer engagement. It's about creating face-to-face experiences in which customers can actually feel the excitement and live the brand. "It's about deepening and enhancing relationships," says one analyst.[32]

Trade Promotions Manufacturers direct more sales promotion dollars toward retailers and wholesalers (79 percent of all promotions dollars) than to final consumers (21 percent).[33] **Trade promotions** can persuade resellers to carry a brand, give it shelf space, promote it in advertising, and push it to consumers. Shelf space is so scarce these days that manufacturers often have to offer price-offs, allowances, buy-back guarantees, or free goods to retailers and wholesalers to get products on the shelf and, once there, to keep them on it.

Manufacturers employ several trade promotion tools. Many of the tools used for consumer promotions—contests, premiums, displays—can also be used as trade promotions. Or the manufacturer may offer a straight *discount* off the list price on each case purchased during a stated period of time (also called a *price-off*, *off-invoice*, or *off-list*). Manufacturers also may offer an *allowance* (usually so much off per case) in return for the retailer's agreement to feature the manufacturer's products in some way. For example, an advertising allowance compensates retailers for advertising the product, whereas a display allowance compensates them for using special displays.

Manufacturers may offer *free goods*, which are extra cases of merchandise, to resellers who buy a certain quantity or who feature a certain flavour or size. They may also offer *push money*—cash or gifts to dealers or their sales forces to "push" the manufacturer's goods. Manufacturers may give retailers free *specialty advertising items* that carry the company's name, such as pens, calendars, memo pads, flashlights, and tote bags.

Event marketing (or event sponsorships)
Creating a brand-marketing event or serving as a sole or participating sponsor of events created by others.

Trade promotions
Sales promotion tools used to persuade resellers to carry a brand, give it shelf space, and promote it in advertising.

Messe München.

Exhibit 14.15 Some trade shows are huge. At this year's Bauma mining and construction equipment trade show in Munich, Germany, more than 3400 exhibitors from 57 countries presented their latest product innovations to over 530 000 attendees from more than 200 countries.

Business promotions
Sales promotion tools used to generate business leads, stimulate purchases, reward customers, and motivate salespeople.

Business Promotions Companies spend billions of dollars each year on promotion geared toward industrial customers. **Business promotions** are used to generate business leads, stimulate purchases, reward customers, and motivate salespeople. Business promotions include many of the same tools used for consumer or trade promotions. Here, we focus on two additional major business promotion tools: conventions and trade shows and sales contests.

Many companies and trade associations organize *conventions and trade shows* to promote their products. Firms selling to the industry show their products at the trade show. Vendors at these shows receive many benefits, such as opportunities to find new sales leads, contact customers, introduce new products, meet new customers, sell more to present customers, and educate customers with publications and audiovisual materials. Trade shows also help companies reach many prospects that are not reached through their sales forces.

Some trade shows are huge. For example, at the 2015 International Consumer Electronics Show, 3600 exhibitors attracted some 170 000 professional visitors. Even more impressive, at the 2013 Bauma mining and construction equipment trade show in Munich, Germany, more than 3400 exhibitors from 57 countries presented their latest product innovations to over 530 000 attendees from more than 200 countries. Total exhibition space equalled about half a million square metres (more than 127 football fields).[34]

A *sales contest* is a contest for salespeople or dealers to motivate them to increase their sales performance over a given period. Sales contests motivate and recognize good company performers, who may receive trips, cash prizes, or other gifts. Some companies award points for performance, which the receiver can turn in for any of a variety of prizes. Sales contests work best when they are tied to measurable and achievable sales objectives (such as finding new accounts, reviving old accounts, or increasing account profitability).

Developing the Sales Promotion Program

Beyond selecting the types of promotions to use, marketers must make several other decisions in designing the full sales promotion program. First, they must determine the *size of the incentive*. A certain minimum incentive is necessary if the promotion is to succeed; a larger incentive will produce more sales response. The marketer must also set *conditions for participation*. Incentives might be offered to everyone or only to select groups.

Marketers must determine how to *promote and distribute the promotion* program itself. For example, a $2-off coupon could be given out in a package, in an advertisement, at the store, via the Internet, or in a mobile download. Each distribution method involves a different level of reach and cost. Increasingly, marketers are blending several media into a total campaign concept. The *length of the promotion* is also important. If the sales promotion period is too short, many prospects (who may not be buying during that time) will miss it. If the promotion runs too long, the deal will lose some of its "act now" force.

Evaluation is also very important. Marketers should work to measure the returns on their sales promotion investments, just as they should seek to assess the returns on other marketing activities. The most common evaluation method is to compare sales before, during, and after a promotion. Marketers should ask: Did the promotion attract new customers or more purchasing from current customers? Can we hold on to these new customers and purchases? Will the long-run customer relationship and sales gains from the promotion justify its costs?

Clearly, sales promotion plays an important role in the total promotion mix. To use it well, the marketer must define the sales promotion objectives, select the best tools, design the sales promotion program, implement the program, and evaluate the results. Moreover, sales promotion must be coordinated carefully with other promotion mix elements within the overall IMC program.

Have a Heart

To incentivize sales: That is the goal of sales promotions strategies. Most of the time, sales promotions are intended to sell products and generate profit for the company selling them. However, Boston Pizza's annual Heart-Shaped Pizza Valentine's Day promotion has morphed into a bonanza for Boston Pizza Foundation's Future Prospects, which helps youth across the country benefit from positive role models and mentoring programs.

"At Boston Pizza, we believe that access to role models and mentors will help kids thrive and empower them to be all that they can be. That's why Boston Pizza Foundation's Future Prospects partners with organizations that inspire kids to be great," says Cheryl Treliving, executive director of the foundation. "Our annual Valentine's Day promotion has helped us raise and donate more than $5 million since 1993. We are grateful to all of our guests across Canada for their ongoing support and donations."

In this scenario, one of BP's most recognized sales promotions, the heart-shaped Valentine's Day pizza, has converged with its community investment through Future Prospects. Indeed, this is another example of integrating various marketing communications platforms.

"For 23 years we've celebrated Valentine's Day with heart-shaped pizzas, and it's become a tradition for many of our guests," said Steve Silverstone, Boston Pizza International's executive vice-president of marketing, at the campaign launch in 2015. The goal that year was to raise $485 000 for Future Prospects; the actual amount raised, however, was more than $518 000. "It's a way to welcome guests who want to celebrate with loved ones while also supporting an important cause—support of mentorship programs that help youth reach their maximum potential."

QUESTIONS

1. Over the years, Boston Pizza has spurred sales of its menu items with a variety of catchy sales promotions. Go to www.bostonpizza.com and provide examples of current sales promotions.
2. Referring to question 1, categorize the sales promotions according to the various terms used in this chapter.
3. What do you think does more to enhance the BP brand, its heart-shaped pizza or the fundraising promotion it supports? Explain your response.

REVIEWING THE CONCEPTS

 Discuss the role of a company's salespeople in creating value for customers and building customer relationships.

Most companies use salespeople, and many companies assign them an important role in the marketing mix. For companies selling business products, the firm's sales force works directly with customers. Often, the sales force is the customer's only direct contact with the company and therefore may be viewed by customers as representing the company itself. In contrast, for consumer product companies that sell through intermediaries, consumers usually do not meet salespeople or even know about them. The sales force works behind the scenes, dealing with wholesalers and retailers to obtain their support and helping them become more effective in selling the firm's products.

As an element of the promotion mix, the sales force is very effective in achieving certain marketing objectives and carrying out such activities as prospecting, communicating, selling and servicing, and information gathering. But with companies becoming more market oriented, a customer-focused sales force also works to produce both customer satisfaction and company profit. The sales force plays a key role in developing and managing profitable customer relationships.

 Identify and explain the six major sales force management steps.

High sales force costs necessitate an effective sales management process consisting of six steps: designing sales force strategy and structure, recruiting and selecting, training, compensating, supervising, and evaluating salespeople and sales force performance.

In designing a sales force, sales management must address various issues, including what type of sales force structure will work best (territorial, product, customer, or complex structure), sales force size, who will be involved in selling, and how various salespeople and sales support people will work together (inside or outside sales forces and team selling).

Salespeople must be recruited and selected carefully. In recruiting salespeople, a company may look to the job duties and the characteristics of its most successful salespeople to suggest the traits it wants in new salespeople. It must then look for applicants through recommendations of current salespeople, ads, and the Internet and social media, as well as college or university recruitment/place-

ment centres. After the selection process is complete, training programs familiarize new salespeople not only with the art of selling but also with the company's history, its products and policies, and the characteristics of its customers and competitors.

The sales force compensation system helps to reward, motivate, and direct salespeople. In addition to compensation, all salespeople need supervision, and many need continual encouragement because they must make many decisions and face many frustrations. Periodically, the company must evaluate their performance to help them do a better job. In evaluating salespeople, the company relies on information gathered from sales reports, personal observations, customer surveys, and conversations with other salespeople.

The fastest-growing sales trend is the exploding use of online, mobile, and social media tools in selling. New digital sales force technologies are creating exciting new avenues for connecting with and engaging customers in the digital and social media age. Today's sales forces are mastering the use of online, mobile, and social media tools to identify and learn about prospects, engage customers, create customer value, close sales, and nurture customer relationships. Rather than reducing the need for salespeople, online and social media technologies are helping to make sales forces more efficient, cost-effective, and productive. The technologies help salespeople do what good salespeople have always done—build customer relationships by solving customer problems—but do it better, faster, and cheaper.

 Discuss the personal selling process, distinguishing between transaction-oriented marketing and relationship marketing.

Selling involves a seven-step process: prospecting and qualifying, preapproach, approach, presentation and demonstration, handling objections, closing, and follow-up. These steps help marketers close a specific sale and, as such, are transaction oriented. However, a seller's dealings with customers should be guided by the larger concept of relationship marketing. The company's sales force should help orchestrate a whole-company effort in order to develop profitable long-term relationships with key customers based on superior customer value and satisfaction.

The fastest-growing sales trend is the exploding use of online, mobile, and social media tools in selling. The new digital technologies are providing salespeople with powerful tools for identifying and learning about prospects, engaging customers, creating customer value, closing sales, and nurturing customer relationships. Many of today's customers no longer rely as much on assistance provided by salespeople. Instead, increasingly, they use online and social media resources to analyze their own problems, research solutions, get advice from colleagues, and rank buying options before ever speaking to a salesperson. In response, sellers are reorienting their selling processes around the new customer buying process. They are using social media, Web forums, online communities, blogs, and other digital tools to engage customers earlier and more fully. Ultimately, online and social media technologies are helping to make sales forces more efficient, cost effective, and productive.

LO4 **Explain how sales promotion campaigns are developed and implemented.**

Sales promotion campaigns call for setting sales promotion objectives (in general, sales promotions should be *consumer relationship building*); selecting tools; and developing and implementing the sales promotion program by using *consumer promotion tools* (from coupons, refunds, premiums, and point-of-purchase promotions to contests, sweepstakes, and events), *trade promotion tools* (from discounts and allowances to free goods and push money), and *business promotion tools* (conventions, trade shows, and sales contests), as well as determining such things as the size of the incentive, the conditions for participation, how to promote and distribute the promotion package, and the length of the promotion. After this process is completed, the company must evaluate its sales promotion results.

MyMarketingLab

Study, practise, and explore real marketing situations with these helpful resources:

- **Interactive Lesson Presentations:** Work through interactive presentations and assessments to test your knowledge of marketing concepts.
- **Study Plan:** Check your understanding of chapter concepts with self-study quizzes.
- **Dynamic Study Modules:** Work through adaptive study modules on your computer, tablet, or mobile device.
- **Simulations:** Practise decision-making in simulated marketing environments.

DISCUSSION QUESTIONS

1. Describe the roles that a salesperson and the sales force perform in marketing.

2. Compare and contrast the three sales force structures outlined in the chapter. Which structure is most effective?

3. Compare an inside sales force and an outside sales force. Why might a company have both?

4. Discuss how online, mobile, and social media tools are changing the selling function.

5. Define *sales promotion* and discuss its objectives.

6. Discuss the different types of trade sales promotions and distinguish these types of promotions from business promotions.

CRITICAL THINKING EXERCISES

1. Hiring the right people for sales jobs is an important sales management function. Aptitude tests are used often to assist in assessing a candidate's abilities and traits. Search the Internet for information on sales assessment tests and present the characteristics and traits most often assessed.

2. Select a product or service and role-play a sales call— from the approach to the close—with another student. Have one member of the team act as the salesperson

with the other member acting as the customer, raising at least three objections. Select another product or service and perform this exercise again with your roles reversed.

3. Find an example of each type of consumer sales promotion tool. Explain how you obtained the promotion (that is, how did the marketer distribute it to consumers?) and what you think the marketer was trying to achieve with the sales promotion tool.

ONLINE, MOBILE, AND SOCIAL MEDIA MARKETING

Sales promotion has always been an effective tool for influencing behaviour and providing a means for measuring effectiveness. Marketers can measure how many buyers redeem a coupon, enter a contest, receive a premium, or buy bonus packs. But now, new technologies are taking sales promotion to a new level—generating consumer engagement. When AMC Theaters wanted to encourage moviegoers to watch a movie on Sunday, typically a slow day for AMC, the company offered a coupon for $1.00 popcorn and fountain drinks on Facebook for the week prior to a specific Sunday and encouraged respondents to invite their friends to claim a coupon as well. The result? More than 200 000 takers in six days and almost 50 000 of them driving their friends to AMC's fan page as well. Similarly, when Edible Arrangements wanted to acquire fans for its Facebook page and increase awareness for the company, it offered free boxes of chocolate-covered fruit to consumers who entered and "Liked" the page. When the company quickly ran out of free samples, it changed the offer to a coupon and experienced double-digit growth as tens of thousands of customers flooded the stores to redeem the coupon—all in less than a week. When Nintendo Wii wanted to raise awareness and generate excitement for its NBA Jam game, it used an essay contest of "jamisms"; voting was carried out in a bracket style, as in the NBA playoffs. In addition to the 3000 entries, the contest generated buzz and thousands of impressions and new Facebook fans.

QUESTIONS

1. Design a sales promotion campaign using online, mobile, and social media marketing for a small business or organization in your community.

2. Develop a presentation to pitch your campaign to the business or organization and incorporate what you've learned about the selling process.

THINK LIKE A MARKETING MANAGER

During the 2008–2009 recession, Starbucks experienced dwindling profits, resulting in layoffs and store closures. Intensified competition and a growth in consumer frugality as a result of tough economic times were to blame. But rather than lowering prices to match competitors, Starbucks tried various tactics to convince customers that its products offer high value for the premium price. It started a rewards program that offered incentives such as free add-ins to coffee drinks, free in-store refills on drip coffee, complimentary in-store Wi-Fi, and free coffee with the purchase of a pound of coffee beans. The company hoped that such incentives would entice customers to visit more often and to spend more when they visit. Starbucks asserted that, as it gained experience in using the program to gather customer information and track customer purchases, Starbucks Card Rewards would become more effective in achieving its goals. The company's strategy appears to have paid off: In the last quarter of 2014, profits soared by 82 percent.

QUESTIONS

1. Find out what other forms of marketing communications Starbucks uses in Canada and the United States. Does it advertise? Use public relations? What about social media? Is the Starbucks loyalty card program well integrated with these other forms of marketing communications?

2. Starbucks baristas are sales representatives. What other forms of personal selling does—or could—Starbucks use?

3. What other forms of sales promotion could Starbucks use that might provide a sufficient incentive to increase sales while staying true to its premium brand image?

MARKETING ETHICS

Johnson & Johnson agreed to a $2.2 billion settlement over the marketing of its antipsychotic drug Risperdal. Pfizer agreed to a $2.3 billion settlement and Eli Lilly paid $1.4 billion to settle disputes with the U.S. government. GlaxoSmithKline agreed to a $3 million settlement—its fourth settlement with that country's government over the marketing of its products. By U.S. law, pharmaceutical companies are allowed to market their drugs only for uses approved by the nation's Food and Drug Administration (FDA), but doctors may prescribe any approved drug as they see fit. Drug manufacturers have been training their sales forces to educate doctors on non-approved uses and dosages, called "off-label" marketing. Almost 75 percent of the largest pharmaceutical settlements with the U.S. government are for off-label marketing. GlaxoSmithKline even went so far as to have a questionable article ghost-written by a company and later published in a medical journal under the names of academic authors to convince doctors that Paxil was proven effective in treating depression in children, a use that the FDA has not approved. The reported clinical trial was later criticized by the medical community, but doctors probably are not aware of that because a majority of them rely on pharmaceutical companies for information on drugs. Most unlawful practices by the pharmaceutical industry come to light only because an insider—someone in management or a sales rep—blows the whistle. Fortunately, the U.S. Federal False Claim Act provides protection and even incentive for employees to come forward. Pharmaceutical companies settle these types of investigations because even if they plead guilty to criminal charges, which J&J and GlaxoSmithKline did, they don't lose the ability to sell drugs as they would if found guilty after a trial.

QUESTIONS

1. What would you do if you were a pharmaceutical sales rep and were told to promote a drug for off-label use? What protections and incentives are available under the Federal False Claim Act to encourage employees to report illegal behaviour?

2. Research the practice of "off-label" marketing in the Canadian pharmaceutical industry. How does it compare to the situation in the U.S.?

MARKETING BY THE NUMBERS

Brown, Inc. manufactures furniture sold through retail furniture outlets in the southeastern United States. The company has two salespeople who do more than just sell the products—they manage relationships with retail customers to enable them to better meet consumers' needs. The company's sales reps visit retail customers several times per year, often for hours at a time. Brown is considering expanding to other regions of the country and would like to have distribution through 1000 retail customer accounts. To do so, however, the company would have to hire more salespeople. Each salesperson earns $50 000 plus 2 percent commission on all sales. Another alternative is to use the services of sales agents instead of its own sales force. Sales agents would be paid 10 percent of sales.

1. Refer to Appendix 3 to answer this question. Determine the number of salespeople Brown needs if it has 1000 retail customer accounts that need to be called on five times per year. Each sales call lasts approximately 2.5 hours, and each sales rep has approximately 1250 hours per year to devote to customers.

2. At what level of sales would it be more cost efficient for Brown to use its own sales force rather than sales agents? To determine this, consider the fixed and variable costs for each alternative. What are the pros and cons of using a company's own sales force over independent sales agents?

SALESFORCE.COM: HELPING COMPANIES SUPERCHARGE THE SELLING PROCESS

As online, mobile, and social media have proliferated, the nature of business-to-business (B-to-B) selling has changed. In fact, some have predicted the death of the professional salesperson, claiming that today's interactive technologies make it possible to sell products and services to the business customer with little to no human interaction.

But that perspective overlooks one very important characteristic of successful selling: The objective of making a sale and getting customers to purchase again and again is to build solid, enduring customer relationships. And to do that, salespeople are more important than ever. But these days, for salespeople to be effective at everything from prospecting to staying connected to customers between purchases, they must stay abreast of technologies that facilitate the management of customer relationships.

A NEW ERA FOR SALES SUPPORT

Enter Salesforce.com. Marc Benioff started the online company in 1999 to compete in a crowded marketplace of companies that provide support to sales forces both large and small. At first glance, not much differentiated Salesforce.com's system. It seemed to be only one of many that enabled corporate sales representatives to gather and manage information about existing and prospective customers, leading to greater selling productivity.

But Salesforce.com's mission was nothing less than visionary. What made the company different was communicated in the Salesforce.com logo—the word "software" with a red circle around it and a line drawn through it. The company's call-in number was (and still is) "800-NOSOFTWARE." With Salesforce.com, Benioff was declaring the death of expensive packaged customer relationship management (CRM) software—the type peddled by then-industry leaders Siebel and SAP. With its stock symbol, "CRM," Benioff declared early on that Salesforce.com would be *the* force for helping business sales forces manage customer relationships.

Salesforce.com's products were subscription based and accessed through the Web. With nothing to install and no owned software, customers could get up and running quickly and inexpensively. Although that "cloud" model is standard practice for many companies today, it was a radical idea in 1999. But more than just introducing an innovative method for selling software, Benioff was establishing Salesforce.com as an innovative company that would con-

sistently seek new ways to help companies achieve greater sales force efficiency. Since its introduction, Salesforce.com has remained one step ahead of the competition by augmenting its products and services in ways that seem to foreshadow trends in business to business (B-to-B) selling.

During the last 10 years, the company has expanded from its core sales management services to a complete portfolio of Internet-based services that put every aspect of selling and sales management in the cloud. This includes Data.com (B-to-B sales and marketing account and contact data), Database.com (a cloud database), Site.com (cloud-based Internet content management), Desk.com (a social help desk for small business), Work.com (the leading sales performance management platform), and Sales Cloud (the world's number one sales app). A few years ago, Salesforce.com recognized that social media would play a huge role in B-to-B sales. To remain on the cutting edge, Salesforce.com acquired Radian6 (the social media monitoring firm used by more than half of Fortune 500 companies) and launched Chatter (a sort of Facebook for the business world).

The Salesforce.com product portfolio is carefully integrated so that each tool works with every other tool. And whereas each Salesforce.com product has broadened the company's offerings beyond sales force support functions, each also facilitates the sales process. As Salesforce.com puts it, these tools allow companies to "supercharge their sales." Consider how Salesforce.com has helped the following companies achieve better-than-ever customer relationships through selling.

NBCUniversal

NBCUniversal (NBCU) is home to 20 popular media and entertainment brands, including NBC, CNBC, Bravo, Universal, and Telemundo. In the topsy-turvy media world, NBCUniversal has been challenged in recent years by the dramatic changes that have hit the industry, including the growing number of media outlets competing for viewer attention, the increased popularity of online media, and shifts in the nature and type of advertising. Because of NBCU's huge scope, it has perhaps been hit harder by the changes than any other media organization.

NBCU's media empire is so vast that it represents a combined total of more than 2 million ads every year. Managing that many ads across various channels for thousands of advertiser-customers was a daunting task. In fact, at one point, NBCU had more than 250 different portals for viewing information and interactions between the company and the advertisers who purchase its ad space. Managing that kind of interaction was fraught with lost opportunities for providing advertisers with the best way to reach the right customers with the right message.

Salesforce.com, however, has helped NBCU integrate its sales force across its customers. In fact, the portal for managing relationships is now simplified to only one view, allowing all sales reps in every NBCU property to see what all advertisers are doing across all properties. "As business moves into the twenty-first century, you need social collaboration tools to pull everything together," says Eric Johnson, vice-president for sales force effectiveness at NBCU. "Salesforce.com helps capture the collaboration that's happening across the company—to mobilize and grow the business." With the Salesforce.com portfolio of products, NBCU is able to distribute the right social information to account executives at the right time, dramatically improving customer relationships with advertisers. As a result, NBCU has seen big increases in cross-selling.

Salesforce.com tools enable sales reps to manage customer relationships better through more open internal collaboration as well. For example, when the NBCU product team comes up with new advertising and product placement opportunities, it uses Salesforce.com social tools to quickly provide the sales team with everything it needs to sell the new inventory. In this manner, sales reps are more connected than ever. And a better-equipped sales force is a happier sales force. "The collaboration with marketing in the first six months was meteoric," says Dan Sztorc, CNBC account executive. With Salesforce.com, he and his colleagues are continuously connected with each other and with the customers. "We're free to venture out and try different things and take some three-point shots."

NBCU gave all its account executives iPads equipped with a Salesforce.com app that allows them to access all their Salesforce.com tools and other marketing and client information from any place, at any time. Just how successful has NBCU been with Salesforce.com's tools? "The first week we launched this application, we had a 300 percent return on investment," says Johnson. "Social collaboration, social networking—it's here to stay."

GE CAPITAL

In the modern, more social world of business, GE Capital was beginning to realize the importance of building connections with its customers. "The power of the social enterprise in the B-to-B space is that you can really connect with your customers and bring them value in ways

that everyday interactions don't typically allow," says Sigal Zarmi, chief information officer (CIO) of GE Capital. For this reason, GE Capital tapped into Salesforce.com's portfolio of tools.

One tactic that the company employed was building what it calls Access GE, a new collaborative community based on Salesforce.com's Force.com platform. After only five weeks of development, Access GE was launched, providing a thriving community where mid-market CEOs and CFOs could tap into the expertise of their peers as well as that of GE Capital employees. This allows executives at customer organizations to connect with GE and other customers based on similar needs and shared experiences, participating in discussions on topics of mutual interest.

As Access GE allows customers to receive better information more quickly, the power of Salesforce.com's social technologies is boosting collaboration among GE Capital's employees as well. The company's commercial sales team of more than 3100 employees also connects on Chatter to share sales strategies, find internal experts, and uncover opportunities to cross-sell.

How does all this help to sell GE Capital's products and services? Access GE accelerates the time it takes for customers to get answers and information they seek in order to make purchase decisions. "We're connecting customers to GE Capital—and to each other—quickly, efficiently, and socially, building deeper relationships with important clients," explains Zarmi. "That's the power of the social network." All this has helped GE Capital better fulfill its mission to provide financing and expertise that helps its customers' capital go further. With Salesforce.com's help, the company is also developing stronger and deeper connections to its customers, promoting greater employee engagement and collaboration, and achieving growth in ways that it had never before experienced.

MOVING FORWARD WITH NEW PRODUCTS

Based on the success of the customized social tool Access GE, Salesforce.com is expanding its product line. After all, Chatter is a one-to-many communication tool. With Access GE, Salesforce.com recognized the value that its clients could gain by having a many-to-many forum such as Access GE. For this reason, Salesforce.com has introduced Salesforce.com Communities as a branch of Chatter, providing an organized free-for-all for managers and client organizations to meet and collaborate online with each other as well as with company representatives.

Salesforce.com is quick to note that there are risks associated with giving customers an open forum. In addition to sharing valuable positive information, they can air complaints and negative comments to thousands of customers at a time. But the innovative Salesforce.com has embraced that kind of risk from the beginning. With every new technology that it unveils, it focuses on the same trump card to convince reluctant users—productivity enhancements. With Chatter, customer users see an average of 12.5 percent gains in productivity over companies that do not use the B-to-B social network. And Salesforce.com expects that there will be similar productivity gains with Communities as well.

Salesforce.com has remained innovative from the start, keeping ahead of the trends and technologies that are shaping modern B-to-B interactions. In fact, it's so innovative that it was number one on the Forbes list of Most Innovative Companies in 2014 and second only to Tesla in 2015. Its tools are state-of-the-art, providing sales reps with a more accurate and timely infusion of customer information and insight into the sales process than ever before. And it doesn't appear to have any intentions of slowing down. Continuing to invest massive sums in developing and acquiring the technologies that keep it adapting in the ever-evolving marketing environment, Salesforce.com should continue to be a one-stop shop for any company with a sales force. As the company puts it, "With sales for the social enterprise, reps, managers, and execs have everything they need to win deals." Salesforce.com continues to deliver on its promise to supercharge sales.

Sources: Based on information from www.salesforce.com, accessed July 2013. Also see Aaron Ricadela, "Salesforce Is a Cloud Computing King," *Businessweek*, February 14, 2013, www.businessweek.com/articles/2013-02-14/salesforce-is-a-cloud-computing-king; Victoria Barret, "Why Salesforce.com Ranks #1 on Forbes Most Innovative List," *Forbes*, September 12, 2013, www.forbes.com/sites/victoriabarret/2012/09/05/why-salesforce-com-ranks-1-on-forbes-most-innovative-list; and Shel Israel, "Does Salesforce.com Own the Social Enterprise?" *Forbes*, March 20, 2012, www.forbes.com/sites/shelisrael/2012/03/20/does-salesforce-own-the-social-enterprise.

QUESTIONS FOR DISCUSSION

1. When Salesforce.com launched as an Internet-based service, how did that innovation help sales reps to interact better with customers?

2. Describe the differences that Salesforce.com has made for customers NBCU and GE Capital.

3. Consider the selling process. How might any of the Salesforce.com tools described in this case facilitate each step?

4. Looking forward, what products will Salesforce.com need to develop in order to remain on the cutting edge of supporting sales staff with information and collaboration?

© epa european pressphoto agency b.v./Alamy

AFTER STUDYING THIS CHAPTER, YOU SHOULD BE ABLE TO

1 define *direct and digital marketing* and discuss their rapid growth and benefits to customers and companies

2 identify and discuss the major forms of direct and digital marketing

3 explain how companies have responded to the Internet and the digital age with various online marketing strategies

4 discuss how companies use social media and mobile marketing to engage consumers and create brand community

5 discuss the public policy and ethical issues presented by direct marketing

Direct, Online, Social Media, and Mobile Marketing

PREVIEWING THE CONCEPTS

In Chapters 13 and 14, you learned about engaging consumers and communicating customer value through integrated marketing communication, and about four elements of the marketing communications mix: advertising, publicity, personal selling, and sales promotion. In this chapter, we examine direct marketing and its fastest-growing form, digital marketing (online, social media, and mobile marketing). Today, spurred by the surge in Internet usage and buying, and by rapid advances in digital technologies—from smartphones, tablets, and other digital devices to the spate of online social and mobile media—direct marketing has undergone a dramatic transformation. As you read this chapter, remember that although direct and digital marketing are presented as separate tools, they must be carefully integrated with each other and with other elements of the promotion and marketing mixes.

Let's begin by looking at Facebook, a company that markets *only* directly and digitally. The giant online social media network promises to become one of the world's most powerful and profitable digital marketers. Yet, as a money-making marketing company, Facebook is just getting started.

FACEBOOK: GOING ONLINE, SOCIAL, AND MOBILE— AND MAKING MONEY DOING IT

The world is rapidly going online, social, and mobile. And no company is more online, social, and mobile than Facebook. The huge social media network has a deep and daily impact on the lives of hundreds of millions of members around the world. Yet Facebook is now grappling with a crucial question: How can it profitably tap the marketing potential of its massive community to make money without driving off its legions of loyal users?

Facebook is humongous. In little more than 11 years it has signed up more than 1.44 billion members, who combine for over 150 billion friend connections. Some 936 million Facebook members access the site daily and 1.25 billion access it on a mobile device at least once monthly. Together, this army uploads 350 million photos, "Likes" 4.5 billion items, and shares 4.75 billion pieces of content daily.

With that many eyeballs glued to one virtual space for that much time, Facebook has tremendous impact and influence, not just as a sharing community but also as an Internet and mobile gateway. Facebook's power comes not just from its size and omnipresence. Rather, it lies in the deep social connections between users. Facebook's mission is "to give

✔●─ **Practice** on MyMarketingLab
Social Media Metrics

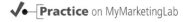
✔●─ **Practice** on MyMarketingLab
Valuing Customers Using the RFM Method

people the power to share and make the world more open and connected." It's a place where friends and family meet, share their stories, display their photos, and chronicle their lives. Hordes of people have made Facebook their digital home 24/7.

By wielding all that influence, Facebook has the potential to become one of the world's most powerful and profitable online marketers. Yet the burgeoning social network is only now beginning to realize that potential. Although Facebook's membership exploded from the very start, CEO Mark Zuckerberg and the network's other idealistic young co-founders gave little thought to making money. In fact, without any help from Facebook, companies themselves were first to discover the social medium's commercial value. Most brands—small and large—have now built their own Facebook pages, gaining free and relatively easy access to the gigantic community's word-of-Web potential. And with the massive number of Likes clicked every day, companies large and small want a piece of that action. At one extreme, The Great Canadian Soap Company in Prince Edward Island has 3300 Facebook Likes. At other extremes, Life is good, Inc. boasts over 2.5 million Likes, and Coca-Cola—the most "Liked" brand on Facebook—has close to 93 million and rising.

As it has matured, however, Facebook has come to realize that it must make its own marketing moves. It's now developing a growing portfolio of products that will let it connect everyone in the world, and it's making money doing it. The social network's first and best bet for converting the value of its massive user base into real dollars is online advertising. In fact, from 2010 to 2014, Facebook's revenues increased from US$2 billion to US$12.5 billion, and advertising accounted for over 90 percent of those revenues. In the first quarter of 2015, advertising revenue soared to US$3.54 billion, with over 70 percent of revenue coming from mobile advertising.

Many online marketers make money through advertising. But Facebook has two unique advantages—unprecedented user data and deep user engagement. Facebook maintains one of the richest collections of user profile data in the world. So ads on Facebook can be carefully targeted, based on user location, gender, age, likes and interests, relationship status, workplace, and education. But Facebook ads do far more than simply capture the right eyeballs. They are "engagement ads" that take advantage of the network's social-sharing power to move people to action. Facebook ads blend in with regular user activities, and users can interact with ads by leaving comments, making recommendations, clicking the Like button, or following a link to a brand-sponsored Facebook page.

Facebook's appeal to both users and advertisers hinges on its ability to target specific kinds of content to well-defined user segments. However, Facebook's former "all things to all people" approach left many users, especially younger ones, visiting Facebook less and shifting time to more specialized competing social networks. To meet that growing threat, Facebook is now pursuing a multi-app strategy of providing "something for any and every individual." According to Zuckerberg, "Our vision for Facebook is to create a set of products that help you share any kind of content you want with any audience you want."

Facebook's first move under this new multi-app strategy was to pay a stunning US$1 billion to acquire Instagram, the surging photo-sharing app. Although Facebook already had its own photo-sharing features, the Instagram acquisition brought a younger, 27-million-strong user base into the Facebook fold. And rather than incorporating Instagram as just another Facebook feature, Facebook has maintained Instagram as an independent brand, with its own personality and user base. Instagram and Facebook customers can choose their desired level of integration, including Instagram membership without a Facebook account. "The fact that Instagram is connected to other services beyond Facebook is an important part of the experience," says Zuckerberg.

Not long after the Instagram acquisition, in its quest to add unique new products and user segments, Facebook announced the creation of Creative Labs, a Facebook division charged with developing single-purpose mobile apps. It also unveiled the new division's first product—Paper, a mobile app that provides easy and personalized access to Facebook's News Feed. Although the core Facebook mobile app already provides access to this content, Paper lets users organize the feed by themes, interests, and sources, serving it all up in a full-screen, distraction-free layout.

On the heels of the Paper launch came another stunning Facebook mega-acquisition. Dwarfing its Instagram deal, Facebook paid a shocking US$19 billion for stand-alone messaging app WhatsApp. Facebook's own Messenger had already grown quickly to 200 million users. But, similar to Instagram, WhatsApp immediately gave Facebook something it could not easily build on its own—an independent brand with more than 450 million registered international users, many of whom were not on Facebook. Facebook also acquired fitness and activity tracking app Moves, which will also continue to operate as a stand-alone brand.

By developing and acquiring such new products and apps, Facebook is doing what it does best—growing its membership and giving its diverse users more ways and reasons to connect and engage. Facebook's fuller portfolio lets users meet their individual needs within the broadening framework of the Facebook family. In turn, more and more-targetable users who spend increased time on the network create more opportunities for Facebook to attract advertising revenues.

Will increased advertising and commercialization alienate loyal Facebook users? Not if it's done right. Recent studies show that online users readily accept—even welcome—well-targeted online advertising and marketing. Tasteful and appropriately targeted offers can enhance rather than detract from the Facebook user experience. Moreover, although Facebook's founders initially opposed running ads or other marketing, worried that marketing might damage Facebook's free (and commercial-free) sharing culture, they've now come to realize that if Facebook doesn't make money, it can't continue to serve its members.

Whatever its future, Facebook seems to have barely scratched the surface. Its new multi-app, multi-segment strategy, combined with its massive, closely knit social structure, gives Facebook staggering potential. Carolyn Everson, Facebook's vice-president of global sales, sums up Facebook's growth potential this way: "I'm not sure the marketing community understands our story yet. We evolve so quickly. We have a saying here: 'We are one percent done with our mission.'"[1]

MANY of the commonly used marketing and promotion tools we've examined in previous chapters were developed in the context of *mass marketing*: targeting broad markets with standardized messages and offers distributed through intermediaries. Today, however, with the trend toward narrower targeting and the surge in digital and social media technologies, many companies are adopting *direct marketing*, either as a primary marketing approach or as a supplement to other approaches. In this section, we explore the exploding world of direct marketing and its fastest-growing form—digital marketing using online, social media, and mobile marketing channels.

Direct and Digital Marketing `LO1`

Direct and digital marketing involve engaging directly with carefully targeted individual consumers and customer communities to both obtain an immediate response and build lasting customer relationships. Companies use direct marketing to tailor their offers

Direct and digital marketing
Engaging directly with carefully targeted individual consumers and customer communities to both obtain an immediate response and build lasting customer relationships.

and content to the needs and interests of narrowly defined segments or individual buyers. In this way, they build customer engagement, brand community, and sales.

For example, Amazon.com interacts directly with customers via its website or mobile app to help them discover and buy almost anything and everything online. Similarly, GEICO interacts directly with customers—by telephone, through its website or phone app, or on its Facebook, Twitter, and YouTube pages—to build individual brand relationships, give insurance quotes, sell policies, or service customer accounts.

The New Direct Marketing Model

Early direct marketers—catalogue companies, direct mailers, and telemarketers—gathered customer names and sold goods mainly by mail and telephone. Today, however, spurred by the surge in Internet usage and buying, and by rapid advances in digital technologies—from smartphones, tablets, and other digital devices to the spate of online social and mobile media—direct marketing has undergone a dramatic transformation.

Direct marketing is often described as direct distribution—as marketing channels that contain no intermediaries. Direct and digital marketing elements are also part of the promotion mix—as an approach for engaging consumers directly and creating brand community. In actuality, direct marketing is both of these things and much more.

Most companies still use direct marketing as a supplementary channel or medium. Thus, most department stores, such as Sears, sell the majority of their merchandise off their store shelves, but they also sell through direct mail, online catalogues, and social media pages. Pepsi's Mountain Dew brand markets heavily through mass-media advertising and its retail partners channel. However, it also supplements these channels with direct marketing. It uses its several brand sites and a long list of social media to engage its customer community in everything from designing their own Mountain Dew lifestyle pages to co-creating advertising campaigns and deciding which limited-edition flavours should be launched or retired. Through such direct interactions, Mountain Dew has created one of the most passionately loyal fan bases of any brand. By one estimate, simply letting fans pick flavours has generated US$200 million in incremental revenues per year for Mountain Dew.[2]

However, for many companies today, direct and digital marketing are more than just supplementary channels or advertising media—they constitute a complete model for doing business. Firms employing this direct model use it as the *only* approach. Companies such as Facebook, Amazon, Google, eBay, Priceline, Netflix, and eLUXE have built their entire approach to the marketplace around direct and digital marketing. Many, like Amazon.com, have employed this model with tremendous success.

Rapid Growth of Direct and Digital Marketing

Direct and digital marketing have become the fastest-growing form of marketing. According to the Direct Marketing Association (DMA), U.S. companies spent almost US$168.5 billion on direct and digital marketing in 2014. As a result, direct-marketing-driven sales now amount to more than US$2 trillion, accounting for 13 percent of the U.S. economy. The DMA estimates

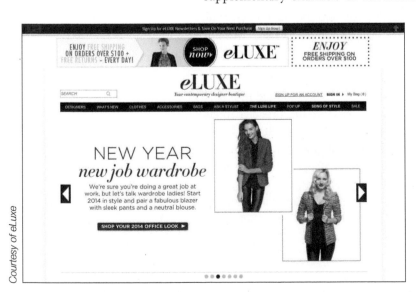

Courtesy of eLuxe

Exhibit 15.1 The new direct marketing model: Companies such as Toronto-based eLUXE have built their entire approach to the marketplace around direct marketing—just visit eluxe.ca.

that direct marketing sales will grow 4.9 percent annually through 2016, compared with a projected 4.1 percent annual growth for total U.S. sales.[3] In Canada, companies spend in excess of $8 billion annually on direct marketing, resulting in approximately $51 billion in sales. While direct mail is still the primary channel of direct marketing (Canadians receive about 1.5 billion pieces of targeted mail each year), response rates have dropped almost 25 percent to under 4 percent.[4]

Direct marketing continues to become more Internet-based, and digital direct marketing is claiming a surging share of marketing spending and sales. For example, in 2014, U.S. marketers spent an estimated US$43 billion on online advertising alone. These efforts generated more than US$260 billion in online consumer spending. Total digital marketing spending—including online display and search advertising, video, social media, mobile, and email—now accounts for the second-largest share of media spending, behind only television. Over the next four years, digital marketing expenditures and digitally driven sales are expected to grow at a blistering 9 percent a year.[5]

Canadian online advertising revenues topped $3.5 billion in 2013, up 14 percent from 2012. French Canadian Internet revenue reached $670 million and represented 19 percent of total Canada Internet ad revenues. Mobile advertising revenues exploded in 2013 a whopping 177 percent, and this growth is part of the reason why digital advertising revenue now exceeds TV advertising revenue. According to a 2013 survey conducted by the Interactive Advertising Bureau of Canada (IAB), the Internet now surpasses television in terms of total weekly time spent by all adults with all media. Canadians in the 18–24 age group now spend approximately 1735 minutes per week on the Internet (compared with 1531 for television), explaining the growing shift in advertising budgets from TV to the Internet.[6]

Benefits of Direct and Digital Marketing to Buyers and Sellers

For buyers, direct and digital marketing are convenient, easy, and private. They give buyers anywhere, any time access to an almost unlimited assortment of goods and a wealth of products and buying information. For example, on its website and mobile app, Amazon.com offers more information than most of us can digest, ranging from top-10 product lists, extensive product descriptions, and expert and user product reviews to recommendations based on customers' previous purchases. Through direct marketing, buyers can interact with sellers by phone or on the seller's site or app to create exactly the configuration of information, products, or services they want and then order them on the spot. Finally, for consumers who want it, digital marketing through online, mobile, and social media provides a sense of brand engagement and community—a place to share brand information and experiences with other brand fans.

For example, Shop.ca provides Canadians with access to millions of products and services across several different product categories offered by a community of retailers and manufacturers, all from the convenience of a single online shopping

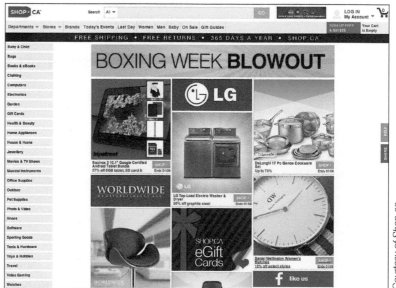

Courtesy of Shop.ca

Exhibit 15.2 Benefits of direct marketing: Competing with giant U.S. retailers, Shop.ca allows Canadian consumers access to millions of products and services offered by Canadian manufacturers and retailers from the convenience of a single shopping site.

site. Launched in 2012, Shop.ca has become the fastest growing retail site in Canada. In 2015, it partnered with Aeroplan to offer even greater value to its customers.

For sellers, direct marketing often provides a low-cost, efficient, speedy alternative for reaching their markets. Today's direct marketers can target small groups or individual customers. Because of the one-to-one nature of direct marketing, companies can interact with customers by phone or online, learn more about their needs, and personalize products and services to specific customer tastes. In turn, customers can ask questions and volunteer feedback.

Direct and digital marketing also offer sellers greater flexibility. They let marketers make ongoing adjustments to prices and programs, or make immediate, timely, and personal announcements and offers. For example, General Electric celebrated National Inventors' Day by asking its Twitter followers for offbeat invention ideas; the company then created illustrations of the best ones, such as a "hand-holding robot."

Especially in today's digital environment, direct marketing provides opportunities for real-time marketing that links brands to important moments and trending events in customers' lives (see Marketing@Work 15.1). It is a powerful tool for moving customers through the buying process and for building customer engagement, community, and personalized relationships.

Forms of Direct and Digital Marketing `LO2`

The major forms of direct and digital marketing are shown in Figure 15.1. Traditional direct marketing tools include face-to-face selling, direct-mail marketing, catalogue marketing, telemarketing, direct-response television marketing, and kiosk marketing. In recent years, however, a dazzling new set of direct digital marketing tools has burst onto the marketing scene, including online marketing (websites, online ads and promotions, email, online videos, and blogs), social media marketing, and mobile marketing. We'll begin by examining the new direct digital and social media marketing tools that have received so much attention lately. Then, we'll look at the still heavily used and very important traditional direct marketing tools. As always, however, it's important to remember that all of these tools—both the new digital and the more traditional forms—must be blended into a fully integrated marketing communications program.

Digital and Social Media Marketing

Digital and social media marketing
Using digital marketing tools such as websites, social media, mobile apps and ads, online video, email, and blogs that engage consumers anywhere, any time via their digital devices.

As noted earlier, **digital and social media marketing** is the fastest-growing form of direct marketing. It uses digital marketing tools such as websites, online video, email, blogs, social media, mobile ads and apps, and other digital platforms to directly engage consumers anywhere, any time via their computers, smartphones, tablets, Internet-ready TVs, and other digital devices. The widespread use of the Internet and digital technologies is having a dramatic impact on both buyers and the marketers who serve them.

FIGURE 15.1 Forms of Direct and Digital Marketing

MARKETING@WORK | 15.1

Real-Time Marketing: Engaging Consumers in the Moment

A funny thing happened during Super Bowl XLVII in New Orleans. Early in the third quarter, the lights in the Mercedes-Benz Superdome suddenly went out. As 71 000 attendees and 106 million viewers restlessly bided their time and scratched their heads, engineers worked feverishly for a full 34 minutes to repair the power outage and bring the lights back on. But whereas the blackout was a disaster for Superdome management and CBS Sports, and an annoyance for players and fans, at least one marketer saw it as an opportunity. Shortly after the blackout began, Nabisco's Oreo brand tweeted out a simple message: "Power out? No problem. You can still dunk in the dark."

That now-famous single tweet, conceived and approved within just minutes, grabbed more attention for Oreo than the brand's extravagant first-quarter "cream versus cookie" spot. Within an hour, the "dunk in the dark" message was retweeted nearly 16 000 times and racked up more than 20 000 Facebook Likes, resulting in tens of millions of favourable exposures. In the following days, Oreo received tons of media coverage, hailing it as "The Brand That Won the Blackout Bowl." Those were pretty impressive results for a one-off joke by a cookie maker.

Oreo's successful Super Bowl one-liner triggered a surge in real-time marketing. Brands of all kinds are now trying to create their own "Oreo moments" by aligning marketing content with real-world events and trending topics through timely tweets, videos, blog entries, and social media posts. Done right, real-time marketing can engage consumers in the moment and make a brand more relevant. Done poorly, however, it can come off as little more than an awkward or inappropriate interruption. According to one observer, "Like Mother Goose's girl with the curl on her forehead, real-time marketing can be very, very good—but when it's bad, it's horrid."

Too often, brands simply toss stand-alone, last-minute ads or messages into social channels, "hoping to catch lightning in a bottle." But hastily prepared or self-serving real-time messages can easily backfire, painting the brand as opportunistic or out of touch. For example, when Hurricane Sandy devastated America's east coast, retailer American Apparel blasted out an email proclaiming a "Hurricane Sandy Sale" ("In case you're bored during the storm, 20% off everything for the next 36 hours"). As might be expected, the Twittersphere lit up with disgust at the retailer's opportunistic pitch, and the company's sentiment scores dropped from 67 to 7 overnight.

Isolated minute-by-minute marketing strikes rarely succeed. Instead, to be consistently successful, real-time marketing must be part of a broader, carefully conceived strategy that makes the brand itself an engaging and relevant part of consumers' lives. According to one marketing strategist, brands must "evolve their entire plan to marketing in a real-time world." Today's smartphone-wielding, social media–saturated customers "are no longer just second-screen viewing—they are second-screen living." Smart brands build agile, ongoing, real-time marketing programs that listen in on the social space and respond with relevant marketing content that blends smoothly with the dynamics of customers' real-time social sharing.

For example, although the Oreo "dunk in the dark" tweet might have seemed off-the-cuff, it was only the latest in a long series of real-time marketing efforts designed to make Oreo a part of consumers' daily conversations. In the months preceding the Super Bowl, Oreo had successfully carried out its "Daily Twist" campaign. Each day for 100 days, the brand posted consumer-inspired Oreo cookie art tied to a relevant event. There was a Mars Rover Landing Oreo (an open-face cookie with tire tracks

Exhibit 15.3 Real-time marketing: Oreo's spectacularly successful "You can still dunk in the dark" tweet triggered a surge in real-time marketing, as brands of all kinds are now trying to create their own "Oreo moments" by aligning marketing content with real-world events and trending topics.

© Ian Dagnall/Alamy Stock Photo

through its red crème filling), a Shin Shin Oreo (a tribute to the Tokyo Zoo's newly born Panda cub), an Elvis Week Oreo (with an Oreo profile of the king of rock 'n' roll), and a Shark Week Oreo (with a jagged bite taken out of it, of course). Among other results of the groundbreaking Daily Twist campaign, Oreo saw a four-fold increase in Facebook shares and watched its Instagram following shoot from 2200 to more than 85 000.

Starbucks, a social media powerhouse with nearly 36 million Facebook fans and 10 million Twitter followers, has long and systematically used real-time marketing to link the brand and what it stands for to current events important to its customers. For example, after Winter Storm Nemo hit the Northeastern United States with heavy snowfall and hurricane-force winds in early 2013, Starbucks Twitter and Facebook promotions offered free coffee to customers in affected areas. "We wanted to make a grand [and timely] gesture," said a Starbucks digital marketer.

On an even grander stage, in the fall of 2013, shortly after bipartisan bickering in Washington resulted in a partial shutdown of the U.S. federal government—furloughing hundreds of thousands of federal employees, closing national

parks, reducing many public health services, and much more—Starbucks launched a #ComeTogether campaign. It began with tweets and Facebook postings by CEO Howard Schultz asking "How can we #cometogether to take care of each other?" and announcing that Starbucks would give a free tall brewed coffee to anyone kind enough to #payitforward and buy the next person in line their favourite beverage. That effort had customers flocking to Starbucks, and tweeting messages like this one: "Bought coffee for the stranger in front of me @Starbucks. Got mine for free. Feels good to #payitforward."

In the next phase of the #ComeTogether campaign, Starbucks distributed a petition via email, social media, and national newspapers urging government officials to reopen government, pay national debts on time, and pass a long-term budget deal. In a single 24-hour period, Starbucks issued two tweets, a Facebook post, an Instagram video, and an email urging customers to sign copies of the petition and bring them to their local Starbucks. Within a day of sending the first tweet, the company had collected more than 1 million signed petitions; only five days later, it tweeted a photo showing an apron-clad Starbucks team member delivering

nearly 2 million petitions to the Capitol Building. In all, the #ComeTogether campaign engaged the Starbucks brand community in positive conversations and actions over an important real-time issue.

Whether connected to a social cause, a trending topic or event, a consumer's personal situation, or something else, the essential concept behind successful real-time marketing is pretty simple: Find or create ongoing connections between the brand and what's happening and important in consumers' lives, then engage consumers genuinely in the moment. One marketing executive suggests that real-time marketers should equate the practice to "meeting somebody in a social gathering—you don't accost them; instead you try to find a commonality of interest."

Sources: Georgia Wells, "Real-Time Marketing in a Real-Time World," *Wall Street Journal,* March 24, 2014, p. R3; Rachel VanArsdale, "Starbucks Real-Time Marketing Asks America to Come Together," October 17, 2013, http://themrsite.com/blog/2013/10/starbucks-real-time-marketing-asks-america-to-come-together; Jeff Dachis, "Stop Whining About Real-Time Marketing," *Advertising Age,* October 10, 2013, http://adage.com/print/ /244665; Christopher Heine, "Ads in Real Time, All the Time," *Adweek,* February 18, 2013, p. 9; Lucia Moses, "Real-Time Marketing," *Adweek,* October 14, 2013, p. 17; Tim Nudd, "Real-Time Rules: Eight Opportunities for Marketing in the Moment, and the Brands That Got It Right," *Adweek,* September 9, 2013, pp. 22–25; and www.360i.com/work/oreo-daily-twist, accessed September 2014.

← ⊙ Simulate on MyMarketingLab **Marketing, the Internet, and the Digital Age** LO3

Online Marketing

Much of the world's business today is carried out over digital networks that connect people and companies. These days, people connect digitally with information, brands, and each other at almost any time and from almost anywhere. The digital age has fundamentally changed customers' notions of convenience, speed, price, product information, service, and brand interactions. As a result, it has given marketers a whole new way to create customer value, engage customers, and build customer relationships.

Digital usage and impact continues to grow steadily. According to a 2014 report, Canada has one of the highest Internet penetration rates in the world, at over 86 percent of households. Canadians also spend an average of 4 hours and 53 minutes per day online using a desktop or laptop. They spend an additional 1 hour and 51 minutes connecting through a mobile device. Worldwide, only 34 percent of the population has Internet access. And 16 percent have access to the mobile Internet, a number that's expected to double over the next five years as mobile becomes an ever more popular way to get online.[7]

As a result, almost half of all Canadian households now regularly shop online at least once a month, and digital buying continues to grow at a healthy double–digit rate. Canadian online retail sales were an estimated $20.6 billion in 2013 and are expected to surpass $34 billion by 2018, as consumers shift their spending from physical to digital stores. Perhaps even more important, although online and digital shopping currently capture less than 10 percent of total retail sales, by one estimate, the Internet influences a staggering 50 percent of total sales—including sales transacted online plus those made in stores but encouraged by online research.[8] And a growing number of consumers armed with smartphones and tablets use them as they shop to find better deals and score price-matching offers.

To reach this burgeoning market, most companies now market online. Some companies operate *only* online. They include a wide array of firms, from *e-tailers* such as Amazon.ca and Expedia.ca that sell products and services directly to final buyers via the Internet to *search engines and portals* (such as Google, Yahoo!, and Bing), *transaction sites* (eBay, Craigslist), *content sites* (the *New York Times* on the Web, TSN.com, and *Encyclopedia Britannica*), and *online social media* (Facebook, YouTube, Pinterest, Instagram, Twitter, and Flickr).

Today, however, it's hard to find a company that doesn't have a substantial online presence. Even companies that have traditionally operated offline have now created their own online sales, marketing, and brand community channels. In fact, **multichannel marketing** companies are having more online success than most online-only competitors.

For example, number two on the list of online retail sites is Staples, the US$23 billion office supply retailer. Staples operates more than 2000 superstores worldwide. But you might be surprised to learn that almost half of Staples' sales are generated online— from its website and mobile app; its presence on social media such as Facebook, Google+, Twitter, YouTube, and LinkedIn; and its own Staples.com community:

> Selling online lets Staples build deeper, more personalized relationships with customers large and small. A large customer, such as GE or P&G, can create lists of approved office products at discount prices and then let company departments or even individuals do their own online and mobile purchasing. This reduces ordering costs, cuts through the red tape, and speeds up the ordering process for customers. At the same time, it encourages companies to use Staples as a sole source for office supplies. Even the smallest companies and individual consumers find 24-hour-a-day online ordering via the Web, Staples mobile app, or social media sites easier and more efficient.
>
> In addition, Staples' online, mobile, and social media efforts complement store sales by engaging customers, enlarging product assortments, offering hot deals, and helping customers find a local store and check stock and prices. In return, local stores promote online buying through in-store kiosks. If customers don't find what they need on the shelves, they can quickly order it via the kiosk. Thus, Staples backs its "make more happen" positioning by offering a full range of contact points and delivery modes— online, social media, mobile, catalogues, phone, and in the store. No online-only or store-only seller can match that kind of call, click, or visit convenience and support. "We're offering more products, more ways to buy, and more great value," summarizes Staples' vice-president of global marketing.[9]

Multichannel marketing
Marketing both through stores and other traditional offline channels and through digital, online, social media, and mobile channels.

Direct digital and social media marketing takes any of the several forms shown in Figure 15.1. These forms include online marketing, social media marketing, and mobile marketing. We discuss each in turn, starting with online marketing.

Exhibit 15.4 Multichannel marketing: More than 43 percent of Staples' sales come from its online marketing operations, including its website and mobile app, its presence on social media, and its own Staples.com community.

Staples the Office Superstore, LLC & Staples, Inc.

Online Marketing

Online marketing

Marketing via the Internet using company websites, online ads and promotions, email, online video, and blogs.

By **online marketing**, we refer to marketing via the Internet using company websites, online advertising and promotions, email marketing, online video, and blogs. Social media and mobile marketing also take place online and must be closely coordinated with other forms of digital marketing. However, because of their special characteristics, we discuss these fast-growing digital marketing approaches in separate sections.

Websites and Branded Web Communities For most companies, the first step in conducting online marketing is to create a website. Websites vary greatly in purpose and content. Some are primarily **marketing websites**, designed to interact with customers to move them closer to a direct purchase or other marketing outcome. For example, MINI USA operates a marketing site at www.MINIUSA.com. Once a potential customer clicks in, the carmaker wastes no time trying to turn the inquiry into a sale, and then into a long-term relationship. The site offers a garage full of useful information and interactive selling features, including fun, detailed descriptions of current MINI models, tools for designing your very own MINI, information on dealer locations and services, and even tools for tracking your new MINI from factory to delivery. After delivery, new owners can check into the MINI online owner's lounge to access technology guides, instructional videos, mobile apps, and service information.

Marketing website

A site that interacts with consumers to move them closer to a direct purchase or other marketing outcome.

Branded community website

A site that presents brand content that engages consumers and creates customer community around a brand.

In contrast, **branded community websites** don't try to sell anything at all. Instead, their primary purpose is to present brand content that engages consumers and creates customer–brand community. Such sites typically offer a rich variety of brand information, videos, blogs, activities, and other features that build closer customer relationships and generate engagement with and between the brand and its customers.

For example, consider ESPN's site. You can't buy anything at ESPN.com. Instead, the site creates a vast branded sports community:

> At ESPN.com, sports fans can access an almost overwhelming repository of sports information, statistics, and game updates. They can customize site content by sport, team, players, and authors to match their own special sports interests and team preferences. The site engages fans in contests and fantasy games (everything from fantasy football, baseball, and basketball to hockey and poker). Sports fans from around the world can participate in discussions with other fans and celebrities before, during, and after sporting events. They can friend and message other users and post comments on message boards and blogs. By downloading various widgets and apps, fans can customize their ESPN experience and carry it with them wherever they go. In all, ESPN's website creates a virtual brand community without walls, a must-have experience that keeps fans coming back again and again.[10]

Creating a website is one thing; getting people to *visit* the site is another. To attract visitors, companies aggressively promote their sites in offline print and broadcast advertising and through ads and links on other sites. But today's Web users are quick to abandon any site that doesn't measure up. The key is to create enough value and engagement to get consumers to come to the site, stick around, and come back again.

At the very least, a website should be easy to use and visually appealing. Ultimately, however, sites must also be *useful*. When it comes to Web browsing and shopping, most people prefer substance over style and function over flash. For example, ESPN's site isn't all that flashy, and it's pretty

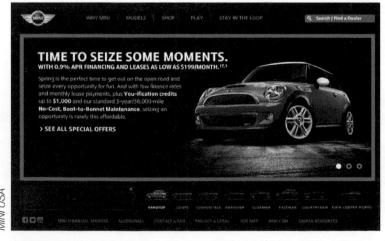

MINI USA

Exhibit 15.5 Marketing websites: Once a potential customer clicks onto the MINI site, the carmaker wastes no time trying to turn the inquiry into a sale, and then into a long-term relationship.

heavily packed and congested. But it connects customers quickly and effectively to all the sports information and involvement they're seeking. Thus, effective websites contain deep and useful information, interactive tools that help find and evaluate content of interest, links to other related sites, changing promotional offers, and entertaining features that lend relevant excitement.

Online Advertising As consumers spend more and more time online, companies are shifting more of their marketing dollars to **online advertising** to build brand sales or attract visitors to their Internet, mobile, and social media sites. Online advertising has become a major promotional medium. The main forms of online advertising are display ads and search-related ads. Together, display and search-related ads account for the largest portion of firms' digital marketing budgets. In 2014, Canadian firms spent almost 90 percent (roughly $3.3 billion) of the total Internet revenue in Canada on these two forms of online advertising.[11]

Online display ads might appear anywhere on an Internet user's screen and are often related to the information being viewed. For instance, while browsing vacation packages on Travelocity.com, you might encounter a display ad offering a free upgrade on a rental car from Enterprise Rent-A-Car. Online display ads have come a long way in recent years in terms of attracting and holding consumer attention. Today's *rich media* ads incorporate animation, video, sound, and interactivity. For example, while browsing sports-related content on your computer or phone, you might see a bright orange Gatorade G Series banner emerge to take over your screen. Your favourite football player then bursts through the banner before the action settles on a stationary click-through display ad showing how some of the world's biggest sports stars use Gatorade Prime to pre-fuel their bodies before games. The action-packed "takeover" ad takes only a few seconds but delivers major impact.[12]

The largest form of online advertising is *search-related ads* (or *contextual advertising*), which accounted for nearly half of all online advertising spending. In search advertising, text-based ads and links appear alongside search engine results on sites such as Google, Yahoo!, and Bing. For example, search Google for "LCD TVs." At the top and side of the resulting search list, you'll see inconspicuous ads for 10 or more advertisers, ranging from Samsung and Dell to Best Buy, Sears, Amazon.ca, Walmart.ca, and Nextag.com. Over 90 percent of Google's US$66 billion in revenues in 2014 came from ad sales. In Canada, online search revenue for 2014 topped $2.1 billion (of the $3.79 billion total Internet revenue). Search is an always-on kind of medium, and the results are easily measured.[13]

A search advertiser buys search terms from the search site and pays only if consumers click through to its site. For instance, type "Coke" or "Coca-Cola" or even just "soft drinks" or "rewards" into your search engine and almost without fail "My Coke Rewards" comes up as one of the top options, perhaps along with a display ad and link to Coca-Cola's official Google+ page. This is no coincidence. Coca-Cola supports its popular online loyalty program largely through search buys. The soft drink giant started first with traditional TV and print advertising but quickly learned that search was the most effective way to bring consumers to its www.mycokerewards.com site to register. Now, any of dozens of purchased search terms will return MyCokeRewards.com at or near the top of the search list.

Email Marketing **Email marketing** remains an important and growing digital marketing tool. "Social media is the hot new thing," says one observer,

Online advertising
Advertising that appears while consumers are browsing online, including display ads, search-related ads, online classifieds, and other forms.

Email marketing
Sending highly targeted, highly personalized, relationship-building marketing messages via email.

Exhibit 15.6 Online display advertising: Gatorade's online "takeover" ad lasts only a few seconds but delivers major impact.

"but email is still the king."[14] By one estimate, over 90 percent of all North American consumers use email every day. What's more, email is no longer limited to PCs and workstations; 65 percent of all emails are now opened on mobile devices. Not surprisingly, then, one study found that email is 40 times more effective at capturing customers than Facebook and Twitter combined. In 2013, marketers sent an estimated 838 billion emails—and yet despite all the email clutter, its low costs mean that email marketing still brings in one of the highest marketing returns on investment. According to the Direct Marketing Association, marketers get a return of $44.25 on every $1 they spend on email. U.S. companies spent almost US$2.1 billion on email marketing in 2014, and it is projected to surpass US$3.1 billion by 2019. In Canada, email marketing revenue jumped from $18 million in 2013 to $19 million in 2014, a growth rate of 8 percent.[15]

When used properly, email can be the ultimate direct marketing medium. Most blue-chip marketers use it regularly and with great success. Email lets these marketers send highly targeted, tightly personalized, relationship-building messages. For example, the National Hockey League sends hypertargeted e-newsletters to fans based on their team affiliations and locations. It sends 62 versions of the e-newsletter weekly—two for each of the 30 teams, tailored to fans in Canada and the United States, respectively, and two generic league e-newsletters for the two countries. Another highly targeted NHL email campaign promotes single-game ticket sales. The emailing consists of 900 different versions covering each of 30 recipient locations and 30 team preferences. For example, a Boston Bruins fan living in Toronto would receive an email with Bruins imagery and information when the Bruins are scheduled to play the Leafs in Toronto. In one year, the email campaign boosted single-game NHL ticket sales by 31 percent over the previous season.[16]

But there's a dark side to the growing use of email marketing. The explosion of **spam**—unsolicited, unwanted commercial messages that clog up our inboxes—has produced consumer irritation and frustration. According to one research company, spam now accounts for 70 percent of all email sent worldwide.[17] Email marketers walk a fine line between adding value for consumers and being intrusive.

To address these concerns, most legitimate marketers now practise *permission-based email marketing*, sending email pitches only to customers who "opt in." Many companies use configurable email systems that let customers choose what they want to get. Amazon.com targets opt-in customers with a limited number of helpful "we thought you'd like to know" messages based on their expressed preferences and previous purchases. Few customers object, and many actually welcome such promotional messages. Amazon.com benefits through higher return rates and by avoiding alienating customers with emails they don't want.

Spam
Unsolicited, unwanted commercial email messages.

Exhibit 15.7 Email can be an effective marketing tool. But there's a dark side—spam, unwanted commercial emails that clog up our inboxes and cause frustration.

Online Videos Another form of online marketing is posting digital video content on brand sites or social media sites such as YouTube, Facebook, and others. Some videos are made for the Web and social media. Such videos range from "how-to" instructional videos and public relations (PR) pieces to brand promotions and brand-related entertainment. Other videos are ads that a company makes primarily for TV and other media but posts online before or after an advertising campaign to extend their reach and impact.

Good online videos can engage consumers by the millions. The online video audience is soaring, with 75 percent of Internet users now streaming video.[18] Marketers hope that some of their videos will go viral. **Viral marketing**, the digital version of word-of-mouth marketing, involves creating videos, ads, and other marketing content that is so infectious that customers will seek them out or pass them along to their friends. Because customers find and pass along the message or promotion, viral marketing can be very inexpensive. And when video or other information comes from a friend, the recipient is much more likely to view or read it.

Viral marketing
The digital version of word-of-mouth marketing: videos, ads, and other marketing content that is so infectious that customers will seek it out or pass it along to friends.

All kinds of videos can go viral, producing engagement and positive exposure for a brand. For example, in one simple but honest McDonald's video, the director of marketing at McDonald's Canada answers an online viewer's question about why McDonald's products look better in ads than in real life by conducting a behind-the-scenes tour of how a McDonald's ad is made. The award-winning three and a half minute video pulled almost 15 million views and 15 000 shares, earning the company praise for its honesty and transparency. As another example, in association with the 2012 London Olympics and 2014 Sochi Winter Olympics, P&G produced three heartwarming two-minute "Proud Sponsors of Moms" videos thanking the moms who helped the athletes reach Olympic heights. These videos also formed the basis for TV ads shown during the Olympics.[19]

At the other extreme, to promote its Shop Your Way rewards program with its free shipping benefit, Kmart posted a TV ad-like video featuring shoppers of all ages exclaiming "ship my pants" (try saying that out loud). "Ship my pants? Right here?" says one surprised shopper. "I just shipped my pants, and it's very convenient," says another. The humorous video wasn't initially aired on TV. But after it pulled in nearly 8 million YouTube views and 38 000 Facebook Likes in only one week, Kmart ran the commercial on selected TV channels.[20]

Sometimes a well-made regular ad can go viral with the help of targeted "seeding." For example, Volkswagen's clever "The Force" Super Bowl LXV ad, featuring a pint-sized Darth Vader using The Force to start a VW Passat, turned viral after a team at VW's ad agency seeded it to selected auto, pop culture, and Star Wars sites the week before the sporting event. By the time the ad aired during the Super Bowl, it had received more than 18 million hits online. By the end of the year, "The Force" had received more than 80 million online views.[21]

Image Courtesy of Sears Brands, LLC and © 2013 Sears Brands, LLC.

Exhibit 15.8 Viral marketing: Kmart's TV ad-like video featuring shoppers of all ages exclaiming "ship my pants" (try saying that out loud) pulled in nearly 8 million YouTube views and 38 000 Facebook likes in only one week.

However, marketers usually have little control over where their viral messages end up. They can seed content online, but that does little good unless the message itself strikes a chord with consumers. For example, why did the seeded VW Darth Vader ad explode virally? Because the sentimental ad appealed to parents—the car's target demographic—who want a responsible suburban family ride. And it appealed to the child inside the parent, who may have once been wowed by *Star Wars* and now wanted a car with a little bit of magic. Says one creative director, "You hope that the creative is at a high enough mark where the seeds grow into mighty oaks. If they don't like it, it ain't gonna move. If they like it, it'll move a little bit; and if they love it, it's gonna move like a fast-burning fire through the Hollywood hills."[22]

Blogs and Other Online Forums Brands also conduct online marketing through various digital forums that appeal to specific special-interest groups. **Blogs** (or weblogs) are online journals where people and companies post their thoughts and other content, usually related to narrowly defined topics. Blogs can be about anything, from politics or baseball to haiku, car repair, or the latest television series. According to one study, there are now more than 31 million blogs in the United States. Many bloggers use social networks such as Twitter and Facebook to promote their blogs, giving them huge reach. Such numbers can give blogs—especially those with large and devoted followings—substantial influence.[23]

Most marketers are now tapping into the blogosphere as a medium for reaching their customer communities. For example, on the Netflix Blog, members of the Netflix team (themselves rabid movie fans) tell about the latest Netflix features, share tricks for getting the most out of the Netflix experience, and collect feedback from subscribers. The Disney Parks Blog is a place to learn about and discuss all things Disney, including a Behind the Scenes area with posts about dance rehearsals, sneak peeks at new construction sites, interviews with employees, and more. Whole Foods Market's Whole Story Blog features videos, images, and posts about healthy eating, recipes, and what's happening inside the store. Clorox's Dr. Laundry blog discusses everything from laundry basics to removing melted crayon from children's clothes, and the Sharpie Blog shares "all the amazing stuff" that people do with Sharpie markers.

Blogs

Online journals where people and companies post their thoughts and other content, usually related to narrowly defined topics.

Sharpie®

Exhibit 15.9 Most marketers are now tapping into the blogosphere as a medium for reaching their customer communities. For example, the Sharpie Blog shares "all the amazing stuff" that people do with Sharpie markers.

Dell has a dozen or more blogs that facilitate "a direct exchange with Dell customers about the technology that connects us all." The blogs include Direct2Dell (the official Dell corporate blog), Dell TechCenter (information technology brought into focus), DellShares (insights for investor relations), Health Care (about the healthcare technology that connects us all), and Education (insights on using technology to enhance teaching, learning, and educational administration). Dell also has a very active and successful YouTube presence that it calls DellVlog, with 7000 videos and more than 52 million video views. Dell bloggers often embed these YouTube videos into blog posts.[24]

Beyond their own brand blogs, many marketers use third-party blogs to help get their messages out. For example, McDonald's systematically reaches out to key "mommy bloggers," those who influence homemakers, who in turn influence their families' eating-out choices:

> McDonald's recently hosted 15 bloggers on an all-expenses-paid tour of its headquarters in Oak Brook, Illinois. The bloggers toured the facilities (including the company's test kitchens), met McDonald's USA president Jan Fields, and had their pictures taken with Ronald at a nearby Ronald McDonald House. McDonald's knows that these mommy bloggers are very important. They have loyal followings and talk a lot about McDonald's in their blogs. So McDonald's is turning the bloggers into believers by giving them a behind-the-scenes view. McDonald's doesn't try to tell the bloggers what to say in their posts about the visit. It simply asks them to write one honest recap of their trip. However, the resulting posts (each acknowledging the blogger's connection with McDonald's) were mostly very positive. Thanks to this and many other such efforts, mommy bloggers around the country are now more informed about and connected with McDonald's. "I know they have smoothies and they have yogurt and they have other things that my kids would want," says one prominent blogger. "I really couldn't tell you what Burger King's doing right now," she adds. "I have no idea."[25]

As a marketing tool, blogs offer some advantages. They can offer a fresh, original, personal, and cheap way to enter into consumer online conversations. However, the blogosphere is cluttered and difficult to control. And although companies can sometimes leverage blogs to engage customers in meaningful relationships, blogs remain largely a consumer-controlled medium. Whether or not they actively participate in the blogs, companies should monitor and listen to them. Marketers can use insights from consumer online conversations to improve their marketing programs.

Social Media Marketing `LO4`

As we've discussed throughout the text so far, the surge in Internet usage and digital technologies and devices has spawned a dazzling array of online **social media** and digital communities. Countless independent and commercial social networks have arisen that give consumers online places to congregate, socialize, and exchange views and information. These days, it seems, almost everyone is buddying up on Facebook or Google+, checking in with Twitter, tuning into the day's hottest videos at YouTube, pinning images on social scrapbooking site Pinterest, or sharing photos with Instagram. And, of course, wherever consumers congregate, marketers will surely follow. Most marketers are now riding the huge social media wave. According to one survey, nearly 90 percent of companies now use social media networks as part of their marketing mixes.[26]

Social media
Independent and commercial online communities where people congregate, socialize, and exchange views and information.

Using Social Media Marketers can engage in social media in two ways: They can use existing social media or they can set up their own. Using existing social media seems the easiest. Thus, most brands—large and small—have set up shop on a host of social media sites. Check the websites of brands ranging from Coca-Cola and Nike to Victoria's Secret or even the NHL's Montreal Canadiens and you'll find links to each brand's Facebook, Google+, Twitter, YouTube, Flickr, Instagram, or other social media pages. Such social media can create substantial brand communities. For example, the Canadiens have 1.57 million Likes on Facebook; Coca-Cola has an eye-popping 93 million and rising.

Some of the major social networks are huge. More than 1.2 billion people access Facebook every month, 3.4 times the combined populations of Canada and the United States. Similarly, Twitter has more than 645 million registered users, and more than 1 billion unique users visit YouTube monthly, watching more than 6 billion hours of video. The list goes on: Google+ has 400 million active users, LinkedIn 240 million, and Pinterest 70 million.[27]

Exhibit 15.10 Thousands of social networking sites have popped up to cater to specific interests, backgrounds, professions, and age groups. At Dogster, 700 000 members set up profiles of their four-legged friends, read doggy diaries, or just give a dog a bone.

Although these large social media networks grab most of the headlines, countless niche social media have also emerged. Niche online social networks cater to the needs of smaller communities of like-minded people, making them ideal vehicles for marketers who want to target special interest groups. There's at least one social media network for just about every interest or hobby. Yub.com and Kaboodle.com are for shopaholics, whereas moms share advice and commiseration at Cafe-Mom.com. GoFISHn, a community of 4000 anglers, features maps that pinpoint where fish are biting and a photo gallery where members can show off their catches. At Dogster, 700 000 members set up profiles of their four-legged friends, read doggy diaries, or just give a dog a (virtual) bone. FarmersOnly.com provides online dating for down-to-earth "country folks" who enjoy "blue skies, living free and at peace in wide open spaces, raising animals, and appreciating nature"—"because city folks just don't get it." myTransponder.com is an online community where pilots find work, students locate flight instructors, and trade-specific advertisers hone in on a hard-to-reach audience of more than 2000 people who love aviation.[28]

Beyond these independent social media, many companies have created their own online brand communities. For example, in Nike's Nike+ running community—consisting of more than 20 million runners who have logged more than 1 billion running miles worldwide—members join together online to upload, track, and compare their performances. Due to its success, Nike has expanded Nike+ to both basketball and general training, each with its own unique community site, app, and corresponding products.[29]

Social Media Marketing Advantages and Challenges Using social media presents both advantages and challenges. On the plus side, social media are *targeted* and *personal*—they allow marketers to create and share tailored brand content with individual consumers and customer communities. Social media are *interactive*, making them ideal for starting and participating in customer conversations and listening to customer feedback. For example, Volvo uses its #Swedespeak Tweetchat platform as a kind of digital focus group to engage customers and obtain immediate input on everything from product features to creating ads. The regular Twitter chats are "creating good conversations," says Volvo's head marketer. "People enjoy being part of [the process]."[30]

Social media are also *immediate* and *timely*. They can be used to reach customers any time, anywhere with timely and relevant content regarding brand happenings and activities. And social media can be very *cost effective*. Although creating and administering social media content can be costly, many social media are free or inexpensive to use. Thus, returns on social media investments are often high compared with those of expensive traditional media such as television or print. The low cost of social media puts them within easy reach of even small businesses and brands that can't afford the high costs of big-budget marketing campaigns.

Perhaps the biggest advantage of social media is its *engagement and social sharing capabilities*. Social media are especially well suited to creating customer engagement and community—

for getting customers involved with the brand and with each other. More than any other channels, social media can involve customers in shaping and sharing brand content and experiences. Consider the "Oreo Cookies vs. Crème" Instagram campaign:

> The two-month Oreo Cookies vs. Crème campaign began with a Super Bowl XLVII ad called "Whisper Fight," in which two men argued in a library over which part of an Oreo cookie they like best—the cookies or the crème. The ad invited consumers to take sides by posting photos they love on social scrapbooking site Instagram with the hashtag #cookiethis or #cremethis. Oreo then selected a number of the photos and worked with artists to create sculptures of the photos made of either cookies or crème. The campaign really got people buzzing about what they like best about Oreos. Prior to the Super Bowl airing, Oreo had about 2200 Instagram followers. Immediately follow-

Exhibit 15.11 Whole Foods Market uses a host of social media to create a Whole Foods lifestyle community. For example, it engages nearly 180 000 brand followers with 59 boards on social scrapbooking site Pinterest.

ing the game, that number had jumped to about 22 000 followers and is now up to more than 87 000. The contest yielded nearly 32 000 fan submissions and 122 sculptures. More than just launching an Instagram page, Oreo launched "an engagement experience," says an Oreo brand manager. Oreo wrapped up the campaign with a series of short, funny online videos accessed by submitting votes for which you like best: cookies or crème. Oreo's answer to the "which is best" question? Not surprisingly, Oreo says it's both.[31]

Social media marketing is an excellent way to create brand communities, places where brand loyalists can share experiences, information, and ideas. For example, Whole Foods Market uses a host of social media to create a Whole Foods lifestyle community where customers can research foods, access recipes, connect with other customers, discuss relevant food-related topics, and link to in-store events. In addition to its very active Facebook, Twitter, YouTube, and Google+ pages, Whole Foods engages nearly 180 000 brand followers with 59 boards on social scrapbooking site Pinterest. Board topics range from "Food Tips and Tricks," "Delicious Art," and "Edible Celebrations" to "Super HOT Kitchens," which is loaded with pictures of captivating kitchens. Whole Foods isn't in the kitchen remodelling business, but cooking and kitchens are a big part of the Whole Foods customer lifestyle.[32]

Social media marketing also present challenges. First, most companies are still experimenting with how to use them effectively, and results are hard to measure. Second, such social networks are largely user controlled. The company's goal in using social media is to make the brand a part of consumers' conversations and their lives. However, marketers can't simply muscle their way into consumers' digital interactions—they need to earn the right to be there. Rather than intruding, marketers must learn to become a valued part of the online experience.

Because consumers have so much control over social media content, even a seemingly harmless social media campaign can backfire. For example, McDonald's launched a Twitter campaign using the hashtag #McDStories, hoping that it would inspire heartwarming stories about Happy Meals. Instead, the effort was hijacked by Twitter users, who turned the hashtag into a "bashtag" by posting less-than-appetizing messages about their bad experiences with the fast-food chain. McDonald's pulled the campaign within only two hours, but the hashtag was still churning weeks later. "You're going into the consumer's backyard. This is their place," warns one social marketer. "Social media is a pressure cooker," says another. "The hundreds of thousands, or millions, of people out there are going to take your idea, and they're going to try to shred it or tear apart and find what's weak or stupid in it."[33]

Integrated Social Media Marketing   Using social media might be as simple as posting some messages and promotions on a brand's Facebook or Twitter pages or creating brand buzz with videos or images on YouTube or Pinterest. However, most large companies are now designing full-scale social media efforts that blend with and support other elements of a brand's marketing strategy and tactics. More than making scattered efforts and chasing Likes and tweets, companies that use social media successfully are integrating a broad range of diverse media to create brand-related social sharing, engagement, and customer community.

Managing a brand's social media efforts can be a major undertaking. For example, Starbucks, one of the most successful social media marketers, manages 51 Facebook pages in the United States (including 43 in other countries); 31 Twitter handles (19 of them international); 22 Instagram names (14 international); plus Google+, Pinterest, YouTube, and Foursquare accounts. Managing and integrating all that social media content is challenging, but the results are worth the investment. Customers can engage with Starbucks digitally without ever setting foot in a store—and engage they do. With almost 36 million fans on its main U.S. page alone, Starbucks is the tenth-largest brand on Facebook. It ranks second on Twitter with 9.96 million followers.

But more than just creating online engagement and community, Starbucks' social media presence drives customer into its stores. For example, in its first big social media promotion, Starbucks offered a free pastry with a morning drink purchase. A million people showed up. Social media "are not just about engaging and telling a story and connecting," says Starbucks' head of global digital marketing. "They can have a material impact on the business."[34]

Mobile Marketing

Mobile marketing

Marketing messages, promotions, and other content delivered to on-the-go consumers through mobile phones, smartphones, tablets, and other mobile devices.

Mobile marketing features marketing messages, promotions, and other content delivered to on-the-go consumers through their mobile devices. Marketers use mobile marketing to engage customers anywhere, any time during the buying and relationship-building processes. The widespread adoption of mobile devices and the surge in mobile Web traffic have made mobile marketing a must for most brands.

With the proliferation of mobile phones, smartphones, and tablets, mobile device penetration is now greater than 100 percent in North America (many people possess more than one mobile device). Almost 68 percent of Canadians own a smartphone, with the vast majority of them using it to access the mobile Internet. They're also avid mobile app users. Indeed, the mobile apps market has exploded: In 2015, there were an estimated 3.1 million apps available worldwide (1.6 million for Android and 1.5 for Apple), and the average Canadian smartphone had approximately 19 apps installed on it.[35]

Most people love their phones and rely heavily on them. According to one study, nearly 90 percent of consumers who own smartphones, tablets, computers, and TVs would give up all of those other screens before giving up their phones. On average, people check their phones 150 times a day—once every six and a half minutes—and spend 58 minutes a day on their smartphones talking, texting, and visiting websites.

Thus, although TV is still a big part of people's lives, mobile is rapidly becoming their "first screen." Away from home, it's their only screen.[36]

For consumers, a smartphone or tablet can be a handy shopping companion. It can provide on-the-go product information, price comparison, advice and reviews from other consumers, and access to instant deals and digital coupons. Not surprisingly, then, mobile devices provide a rich platform for engaging consumers more deeply as they move through the buying process with tools ranging from mobile ads, coupons, and texts to apps and mobile websites.

Mobile advertising spending in Canada and the United States is surging. Almost every major marketer—from P&G and Sears to your local bank or supermarket to nonprofits such as the SPCA—is now integrating mobile marketing into its direct marketing programs. Such efforts can produce very positive outcomes; for example, 49 percent of mobile users search for more information after seeing a mobile ad. Mobile advertising spending in Canada has seen explosive growth, from $427 million in 2013 to $903 million in 2014, representing an annual growth rate of 111 percent.[37]

Companies use mobile marketing to stimulate immediate buying, make shopping easier, enrich the brand experience, or all of these. It lets marketers provide consumers with information, incentives, and choices at the moment they are expressing an interest or when they are in a position to make a buying choice. For example, McDonald's uses mobile marketing to promote new menu items, announce special promotions, and drive immediate traffic at its restaurants. One interactive ad on Pandora's mobile app read "Taste buds. Any size soft drink or sweet tea for $1. Tap to visit site." A tap on the mobile ad took customers to a mobile site promoting McDonald's ongoing summer promotion. Another McDonald's mobile campaign used a word scrabble game to entice customers to try the fast feeder's dollar menu items. Such efforts create both customer engagement and store traffic. Using a game "inside a mobile campaign is all about finding and maintaining engagement," says a McDonald's marketer.[38]

Today's rich media mobile ads can create substantial impact and engagement. For example, HBO ran engaging mobile ads for the season premiere of its *True Blood* series. As consumers browsed their Flixter apps looking for good movies or their Variety apps seeking the latest entertainment news, touches on their screens turned into bloody fingerprints. Blood quickly filled their screens, followed by a tap-to-watch trailer invitation. The spine-chilling *True Blood* mobile ad campaign helped draw 5.1 million viewers to the show's season premiere and increased viewership by 38 percent.[39]

Retailers can use mobile marketing to enrich the customer's shopping experience at the same time as they stimulate buying. For example, Macy's built its "Brasil: A Magical Journey" promotion around a popular and imaginative smartphone app. The campaign featured apparel from Brazilian designers and in-store experiences celebrating Brazilian culture. By using their smartphones to scan Quick Response (QR) codes throughout the store, shoppers could learn about featured fashions and experience Brazilian culture through virtual tours, such as a trip to the Amazon, a visit to Rio de Janeiro during Carnival, or attending a Brazilian soccer match. "Mobile ads aim for 'of-the-moment' targeting, anywhere and everywhere," says one expert, whether it's at the time of a mobile search or in a store during the purchase decision.[40]

Many marketers have created their own mobile online sites, optimized for specific phones and mobile service providers. Others have created useful or entertaining mobile apps to engage customers with their brands and help them shop (see Marketing@Work 15.2). For example, Clorox offers a myStain app that targets young moms with

Exhibit 15.12 Mobile marketing: Macy's "Brasil: A Magical Journey" promotion, built around a popular and imaginative smartphone app, enriched the customer shopping experience while stimulating buying.

Macy's Inc.

MARKETING@WORK 15.2

Mobile Marketing: Customers Come Calling

You're at the local Best Buy checking out portable GPS navigation systems. You've narrowed it down to the latest Garmin nüvi versus a less-expensive competing model, but you're not certain that Best Buy has the best prices. Also, you'd love to know how other consumers rate the two brands. No problem. Just pull out your smartphone and launch your Amazon Mobile app, which lets you browse the brands you're considering, read customer reviews, and compare prices of portable GPS systems sold by Amazon.com and its retail partners. The application even lets you snap a photo or scan a barcode from an item; Amazon.com will then search for a similar item available from Amazon. If Amazon.com offers a better deal, you can make the purchase directly from the app with 1-Click ordering, then track the order until it reaches your doorstep.

Welcome to the world of mobile marketing. Today's smartphones and other mobile devices are changing the way we live—including the way we shop. And as they change how we shop, they also change how marketers sell to us. A growing number of consumers are using their mobile phones as a kind of digital Swiss Army Knife—as a preferred device for texting, browsing the mobile Internet, checking email, watching videos and TV shows, playing games, listening to music, accessing news and information, and socializing. Mobile devices currently account for 50 percent of all Internet time, a number that will continue to grow.

For some, mobile domination has already arrived. For example, for Facebook members who use both its mobile and Web interfaces, time spent per month on the social network's mobile site far exceeds time spent on its classic website. In fact, all by itself, the Facebook app consumes 18 percent of all time spent on mobile devices. Similarly, for Twitter, 60 percent of all traffic is mobile. In all, consumers spend an average of 2 hours and 38 minutes a day socializing and accessing the Internet on their mobile devices—twice the amount of time they spend

eating and about one-third the amount of time they spend sleeping.

Marketers are responding to this massive growth in mobile access and use; the 111 percent jump in Canadian mobile ad spending in 2014 is on par with growth in U.S. spending increases. Mobile phones, tablets, and other mobile devices have become today's brave new marketing frontier, especially for brands courting younger consumers. Mobile devices are very personal, ever-present, and always on. That makes them an ideal medium for obtaining quick responses to individualized, time-sensitive offers. Mobile marketing reaches consumers with the right message in the right place at the right time.

Marketers large and small are weaving mobile marketing into their direct marketing mixes. And the successful campaigns go beyond just giving people a link to buy. They attract attention by providing helpful services, useful information, and entertainment. For example, Tide's Stain Brain app helps customers

find ways to remove stains while out and about. A Sit or Squat app that directs people to nearby public restrooms opens with a splash page for Charmin bathroom tissue. And REI's The Snow Report app gives ski slope information for locations throughout Canada and the United States, such as snow depth, snow conditions, and the number of open lifts. The app helps you share resort information with friends via Twitter and Facebook, and it links you to "Shop REI" for times "when you decide you can't live without a new set of K2 skis or a two-man Hubba Hubba tent."

Beyond helping customers buy, mobile apps provide other helpful services. For example, Target's mobile app lets you keep shopping lists and sends out scannable mobile coupons for groceries and other merchandise: Just hold up your mobile phone at the checkout, and the cashier will scan the barcode off the screen. Zipcar's app lets members find and reserve a Zipcar, honk the horn (so they can find it in a crowd), and even

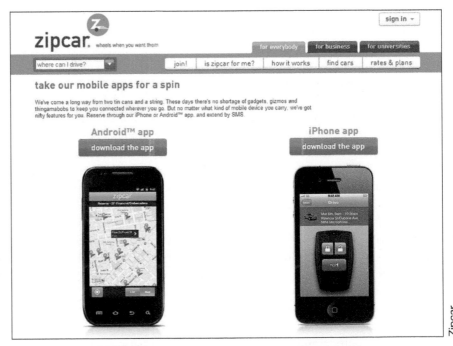

Exhibit 15.13 Mobile marketing: Zipcar's iPhone app lets members find and book a Zipcar, honk the horn (so they can find it in a crowd), and even lock and unlock the doors—all from their phones.

Zipcar

lock and unlock the doors—all from their phones. And with MasterCard's PayPass app, cardholders can pay instantly and securely with their phones at any participating retailer—just "tap, pay, and be on your way."

One of the most effective mobile marketing apps is Kraft's iFood Assistant, which puts "delicious at your fingertips" in the form of easy-to-prepare recipes for food shoppers on the go, how-to videos, a recipe box, and a built-in shopping list. The iFood Assistant app supplies advice on how to prepare thousands of simple but satisfying meals—literally decades' worth of recipes. The app will even give you directions to local stores. Of course, most of the meals call for ingredients that just happen to be Kraft brands. The iFood Assistant app cost Kraft less than US$100 000 to create but has engaged millions of shoppers, providing great marketing opportunities for Kraft and its brands.

As the Amazon example suggests, consumers are increasingly using their phones as in-store shopping aids, and retailers are responding accordingly. For example, Walgreens in the U.S. has created the mobile equivalent of the local newspaper circular. Using new technology, Walgreens knows when participating customers check in to one of its 8000 stores via Foursquare, Yelp, Twitter, Facebook, and a host of other location-based services. The retailer then tweets or texts the customers, sending mobile coupons or directing them to in-store deals with a message such as "Check out the specials on Halls new cough drops in the cold aisle." It's like taking shoppers by the hand and guiding them through the store.

According to one mobile marketing expert, the real advantage to targeting shoppers while they are out and about is the ability to reach consumers when they are closest to buying. "Ask yourself," he says, "are your customers more likely to leave their homes and their pantries . . . to go out and get a sub sandwich . . . or [is it more likely] when they've been out running errands all day, missed lunch, and you sent them a text with an offer for a half-price sub [at a nearby] shop?"

Many consumers are initially skeptical about mobile marketing. But they often change their minds if mobile marketers deliver value in the form of useful brand and shopping information, entertaining content, or discounted prices and coupons for their favourite products and services. Most mobile marketing efforts target only consumers who voluntarily opt in or who download apps. In the increasingly cluttered mobile marketing space, customers just won't do that unless they see real value in it. The challenge for marketers: Develop useful and engaging mobile marketing apps that make customers come calling.

Sources: Chuck Jones, "Mobile Ad Spending Forecast to Increase 4X over the Next 4 Years," *Forbes*, January 4, 2013, www.forbes.com/sites/chuckjones/2013/01/04/mobile-ad-spending-forecast-to-increase-4x-over-the-next-4-years; Greg Sterling, "Report: Nearly 40 Percent of Internet Time Now on Mobile Devices," February 26, 2013, http://marketingland.com/report-nearly-40-percent-of-internet-time-now-on-mobile-devices-34639; Jichél Stewart, "8 Mobile Marketing Trends You Should Track in 2012," *Business 2 Community*, December 18, 2011, www.business2community.com/mobile-apps/8-mobile-marketing-trends-you-should-track-in-2012-0108821; Kunur Patel, "At Walgreens, a Mobile Check-In Acts Like Circular," *Advertising Age*, February 8, 2012, http://adage.com/print/232584; and John Koetsier, "The Mobile War Is Over and the App Has Won," April 3, 2013, http://venturebeat.com/2013/04/03/the-mobile-war-is-over-and-the-app-has-won-80-of-mobile-time-spent-in-apps.

useful on-the-go stain removal solutions. Schwab offers "Schwab to Go," a mobile app that lets customers get up-to-the-minute investment news, monitor their accounts, and make trades at any time from any location. And Starbucks' mobile app lets customers use their phones as a Starbucks card to make fast and easy purchases.

As with other forms of direct marketing, however, companies must use mobile marketing responsibly or risk angering already ad-weary consumers. "If you were interrupted every two minutes by advertising, not many people want that," says a mobile marketing expert. "The industry needs to work out smart and clever ways to engage people on mobiles." The key is to provide genuinely useful information and offers that will make consumers want to engage.

In all, digital direct marketing—online, social media, and mobile marketing—offers both great promise and many challenges for the future. Its most ardent apostles still envision a time when the Internet and digital marketing will replace magazines, newspapers, and even stores as sources for information, engagement, and buying. Most marketers, however, hold a more realistic view. For most companies, digital and social media marketing will remain just one important approach to the marketplace that works alongside other approaches in a fully integrated marketing mix.

Although the fast-growing digital marketing tools have grabbed most of the headlines lately, traditional direct marketing tools are very much alive and still heavily used. We now examine the traditional direct marketing approaches.

Traditional Direct Marketing Forms

The major traditional forms of direct marketing—as shown in Figure 15.1—are face-to-face or personal selling, direct-mail marketing, catalogue marketing, telemarketing, direct-response television (DRTV) marketing, and kiosk marketing. We examined personal selling in depth in Chapter 14. Here, we look into the other forms of traditional direct marketing.

Direct-Mail Marketing

Direct-mail marketing
Marketing that occurs by sending an offer, announcement, reminder, or other item directly to a person at a particular address.

Direct-mail marketing involves sending an offer, announcement, reminder, or other item to a person at a particular address. Using highly selective mailing lists, direct marketers send out millions of mail pieces each year—letters, catalogues, ads, brochures, samples, videos, and other "salespeople with wings." The Direct Marketing Association reports that U.S. marketers spent more than US$45 billion on direct mail in 2013 (including both catalogue and noncatalogue mail), which accounted for 30 percent of all direct marketing spending and generated 31 percent of all direct marketing sales. According to the DMA, every dollar spent on direct mail generates $12.57 in sales. And in Canada, direct-mail spending is estimated to top 1.39 billion in 2016.[41]

Direct mail is well suited to direct, one-to-one communication. It permits high target-market selectivity, can be personalized, is flexible, and allows the easy measurement of results. Although direct mail costs more per thousand people reached than mass media such as television or magazines, the people it reaches are much better prospects. Direct mail has proved successful in promoting all kinds of products, from books, insurance, travel, gift items, gourmet foods, clothing, and other consumer goods to industrial products of all kinds. Charities also use direct mail heavily to raise billions of dollars each year.

Some analysts predict a decline in the use of traditional forms of direct mail in coming years, as marketers switch to newer digital forms, such as email and online marketing, social media marketing, and mobile marketing. The newer digital direct marketing approaches deliver messages at incredible speeds and lower costs compared to the Post Office's "snail mail" pace.

However, even though new digital forms of direct marketing are bursting onto the scene, traditional direct mail is still heavily used by most marketers. Mail marketing offers some distinct advantages over digital forms. It provides something tangible for people to hold and keep, and it can be used to send samples. "Mail makes it real," says one analyst. It "creates an emotional connection with customers that digital cannot. They hold it, view it, and engage with it in a manner entirely different from their [digital] experiences." In contrast, email and other digital forms are easily filtered or trashed. "[With] spam filters and spam folders to keep our messaging away from consumers' inboxes," says a direct marketer, "sometimes you have to lick a few stamps."[42]

Traditional direct mail can be an effective component of a broader integrated marketing campaign. For example, most large companies rely heavily on TV advertising to establish broad customer awareness and positioning. However, companies also use direct mail to break through the clutter of TV advertising. Consider 1-800-GOT-JUNK:

In 1989, Vancouver student Brian Scudamore started a small junk removal service to pay for his

Exhibit 15.14 Creative direct mail campaigns can be a cost-effective way to grow any business.

CIRO CESAR La Opinion Photos/Newscom

university education. In less than 15 years, this small business grew into one of Canada's most successful franchises, now with over 200 locations in three countries. When 1-800-GOT-JUNK decided to test a new direct marketing program to support its North American franchises, it turned to Vancouver-based Kirk Marketing for help. The direct mail creative included a personalized URL (PURL), a die-cut truck, and a scratch card. Created for both the French and English market, the campaign had to work with both Canada Post and the US Postal Service. Franchise owners benefited greatly from the centrally managed data collection done by corporate head office. In fact, one franchise in Austin, Texas, saw an incredible return on investment of over 1000 percent. For every card sent to customers at a cost of $0.50 per card, the franchise made $11.00 in revenue.[43]

Direct mail may be resented as *junk mail* if it's sent to people who have no interest in it. For this reason, smart marketers are targeting their direct mail carefully so as not to waste their money and recipients' time. They are designing permission-based programs that send direct mail only to those who want to receive it.

Catalogue Marketing

Advances in technology, along with the move toward personalized, one-to-one marketing, have resulted in exciting changes in **catalogue marketing**. *Catalog Age* magazine used to define a *catalogue* as "a printed, bound piece of at least eight pages, selling multiple products, and offering a direct ordering mechanism." Today, this definition is sadly out of date.

Catalogue marketing
Direct marketing through print, video, or digital catalogues that are mailed to select customers, made available in stores, or presented online.

With the stampede to the Internet and digital marketing, more and more catalogues are going digital. A variety of online-only cataloguers have emerged, and most print cataloguers have added Web-based catalogues and smartphone catalogue shopping apps to their marketing mixes. For example, apps such as Catalog Spree put a mall full of classic catalogues from retailers such as Macy's, Anthropologie, L.L.Bean, Hammacher Schlemmer, Coldwater Creek, or West Elm only a swipe of the finger away on a smartphone or tablet. And days before the latest Lands' End catalogue arrives in the mail, customers can access it digitally at landsend.com, at social media outlets such as Facebook, or via the Lands' End mobile app. With Lands' End Mobile, says the company, "You're carrying every item we carry."[44]

Digital catalogues eliminate printing and mailing costs. And whereas space is limited in a print catalogue, online catalogues can offer an almost unlimited amount of merchandise. They also offer a broader assortment of presentation formats, including search and video. Finally, online catalogues allow real-time merchandising; products and features can be added or removed as needed, and prices can be adjusted instantly to match demand. Customers can carry digital catalogues anywhere they go, even when shopping at physical stores.

However, despite the advantages of digital catalogues, as your over-stuffed mailbox may suggest, printed catalogues are still thriving. U.S. direct

Catalog Spree, the #1 catalog shopping app for the iPad and iPhone. www.catalogspree.com.

Exhibit 15.15 Digital catalogues: Apps such as Catalog Spree put a mall full of classic catalogues from retailers such as Macy's, Best Buy, Anthropologie, L.L.Bean, Hammacher Schlemmer, or Coldwater Creek only a swipe of the finger away on a smartphone or tablet.

marketers mail out some 12.5 billion catalogues per year—more than 100 per American household. Why aren't companies ditching their old-fashioned paper catalogues in this new digital era? For one thing, paper catalogues create emotional connections with customers that digital sales spaces simply can't. "Glossy catalogue pages still entice buyers in a way that computer images don't," says an analyst.[45]

In addition, printed catalogues are one of the best ways to drive online and mobile sales, making them more important than ever in the digital era. According to one study, 70 percent of online purchases are driven by catalogues. Another study found that 60 percent of consumers who receive a catalogue from a company go online to make a purchase within a week. Catalogue users look at more than double the number of webpages per visit to the company's site than the average visitor and spend twice the amount of time there.[46]

Telemarketing

Telemarketing
Using the telephone to sell directly to customers.

Telemarketing involves using the telephone to sell directly to consumers and business customers. We're all familiar with telephone marketing directed toward consumers, but business-to-business (B-to-B) marketers also use telemarketing extensively. Marketers use *outbound* telephone marketing to sell directly to consumers and businesses. They also use *inbound* toll-free numbers to receive orders from television and print ads, direct mail, or catalogues.

Properly designed and targeted telemarketing provides many benefits, including purchasing convenience and increased product and service information. However, the explosion in unsolicited outbound telephone marketing over the years annoyed many consumers, who objected to the almost daily "junk phone calls."

In Canada, telephone marketing is controlled by the National Do Not Call List. Canadian consumers can reduce the number of telemarketing calls they receive by registering their residential, wireless, fax, or VoIP telephone number through the website at DNCL.gc.ca. The website, maintained by the CRTC, the Canadian Radio-television and Telecommunications Commission, also provides online forms for consumers to register complaints against telemarketers. Canadian marketers must register with the National DNCL, and are required by law to periodically verify that any consumer on the DNCL list is removed from their telemarketing database. Marketers who violate the rules are investigated by the CRTC and can face fines of up to $15 000 per violation. And even when marketers abide by the DNCL rules, they must follow certain procedures when making legal telemarketing calls. For example, at the beginning of a call, telemarketers must tell you why they're calling; they must identify on whose behalf the call is being made; and they must make their calls only within certain calling hours.

Do-not-call legislation has hurt parts of the consumer telemarketing industry. However, two major forms of telemarketing—inbound consumer telemarketing and outbound B-to-B telemarketing—remain strong and growing. Telemarketing also remains a major fundraising tool for nonprofit and political groups. Interestingly, do-not-call regulations appear to be helping some direct marketers more than it's hurting them. Rather than making unwanted calls, many of these marketers are developing "opt-in" calling systems, in which they provide useful information and offers to customers who have invited the company to contact them by phone or email. The opt-in model provides better returns for marketers than the formerly invasive one.

Direct-response television (DRTV) marketing
Direct marketing via television, including direct-response television advertising (or infomercials) and interactive television (iTV) advertising.

Direct-Response Television Marketing

Direct-response television (DRTV) marketing takes one of two major forms: direct-response television advertising and interactive TV (iTV) advertising. Using *direct-response television advertising*, direct marketers air television spots, often 60 or 120 seconds in length, which persuasively describe a product and give customers a toll-free number or a website for ordering. It also includes full 30-minute or longer advertising programs, called *infomercials*, for a single product.

Successful direct-response television advertising campaigns can ring up big sales. For example, little-known infomercial maker Guthy-Renker has helped propel its Proactiv Solution acne treatment and other "transformational" products into power brands that pull in US$1.8 billion in sales annually to 5 million active customers (compare that with only about US$150 million in annual drugstore sales of acne products in the United States). Guthy-Renker now combines DRTV with social media campaigns using Twitter and YouTube to create a powerful integrated direct marketing channel that builds consumer involvement and buying.[47]

DRTV ads are often associated with somewhat loud or questionable pitches for cleaners, stain removers, kitchen gadgets, and nifty ways to stay in shape without working very hard at it. For example, over the past few years yell-and-sell TV pitchmen like Anthony Sullivan (Swivel Sweeper, Awesome Auger) and Vince Offer (ShamWow, Slap-Chop) have racked up billions of dollars in sales of "as seen on TV" products. Brands like OxiClean, ShamWow, and the Snuggie (a blanket with sleeves) have become DRTV cult classics. And infomercial viral sensation PajamaJeans ("Pajamas you live in, Jeans you sleep in") created buzz on everything from YouTube to *The Tonight Show*, selling more than 2 million pairs at $39.95 each, plus $7.95 shipping and handling.[48]

In recent years, however, a number of large companies—from P&G, Disney, Revlon, Apple, and Kodak to Toyota, Coca-Cola, Anheuser-Busch, and even the U.S. Navy—have begun using infomercials to sell their wares, refer customers to retailers, recruit members, or attract buyers to their online, mobile, and social media sites.

A more recent form of direct-response television marketing is *interactive TV (iTV)*, which lets viewers interact with television programming and advertising. Thanks to technologies such as interactive cable systems, Internet-ready smart TVs, and smartphones and tablets, consumers can now use their TV remotes, phones, or other devices to obtain more information or make purchases directly from TV ads. Also, increasingly, as the lines continue to blur between TV screens and other video screens, interactive ads and infomercials are appearing not just on TV, but also on mobile, online, and social media platforms, adding even more TV-like interactive direct marketing venues.

Kiosk Marketing

As consumers become more and more comfortable with digital and touchscreen technologies, many companies are placing information and ordering machines—called *kiosks* (good old-fashioned vending machines but so much more)—in stores, airports, hotels, college and university campuses, and other locations. Kiosks are everywhere these days, from self-service hotel and airline check-in devices, to unmanned product and information kiosks in malls, to in-store ordering devices that let you order merchandise not carried in the store. "Vending machines, which not long ago had mechanical levers and coin trays, now possess brains," says one analyst. Many modern "smart kiosks" are now wireless-enabled. And some machines can even use facial recognition software that lets them guess gender and age and make product recommendations based on that data.[49]

In-store Kodak, Fuji, and HP kiosks let customers transfer pictures from memory cards, mobile phones, and other digital storage devices; edit them; and make high-quality colour prints. Seattle's Best kiosks in grocery, drug, and mass merchandise stores grind and brew fresh coffee beans and serve coffee, mochas, and lattes to on-the-go customers around the clock. Redbox operates more than 35 000 DVD rental kiosks in McDonald's,

Zoom Systems

Exhibit 15.16 **Kiosk marketing:** ZoomShop kiosks automatically dispense an assortment of popular consumer electronics products. This ZoomShop is located in a Macy's store and features Apple products, among others.

Walmart, Walgreens, CVS, Family Dollar, and other retail outlets—customers make their selections on a touchscreen, then swipe a credit or debit card to rent DVDs for less than $2 a day.

ZoomSystems creates small, free-standing kiosks called ZoomShops for retailers ranging from Apple, Sephora, and The Body Shop to Macy's and Best Buy. For example, 100 Best Buy Express ZoomShop kiosks—conveniently located in airports, busy malls, military bases, and resorts—automatically dispense an assortment of portable media players, digital cameras, gaming consoles, headphones, phone chargers, travel gadgets, and other popular products. According to Zoom-Systems, today's automated retailing "offers [consumers] the convenience of online shopping with the immediate gratification of traditional retail."[50]

Public Policy Issues in Direct and Digital Marketing LO5

Direct marketers and their customers usually enjoy mutually rewarding relationships. Occasionally, however, a darker side emerges. The aggressive and sometimes shady tactics of a few direct marketers can bother or harm consumers, giving the entire industry a black eye. Abuses range from simple excesses that irritate consumers to instances of unfair practices or even outright deception and fraud. The direct marketing industry has also faced growing privacy concerns, and online marketers must deal with Internet security issues.

Irritation, Unfairness, Deception, and Fraud

Direct marketing excesses sometimes annoy or offend consumers. For example, most of us dislike direct-response TV commercials that are too loud, long, and insistent. Our mailboxes fill up with unwanted junk mail, our inboxes bulge with unwanted spam, and our computer, phone, and tablet screens flash with unwanted online or mobile display ads, pop-ups, or pop-unders.

Beyond irritating consumers, some direct marketers have been accused of taking unfair advantage of impulsive or less-sophisticated buyers. Television shopping channels, enticing websites, and program-long infomercials targeting television-addicted shoppers seem to be the worst

Canadian Anti-Fraud Centre/Royal Canadian Mounted police

Exhibit 15.17 The Canadian Anti-Fraud Centre provides a wealth of information to help Canadians avoid online scams and telephone fraud.

culprits. They feature smooth-talking hosts, elaborately staged demonstrations, claims of drastic price reductions, "while they last" time limitations, and unequalled ease of purchase to inflame buyers who have low sales resistance.

Fraudulent schemes, such as investment scams or phony collections for charity, have also multiplied in recent years. *Internet fraud*, including identity theft and financial scams, has become a serious problem. The Canadian Anti-Fraud Centre (CAFC) collects information and criminal intelligence on mass marketing fraud (telemarketing), advanced-fee fraud letters (Nigerian letters), Internet fraud, and identity theft complaints from Canadian and American consumers and victims. In 2014, the CAFC received 42 200 complaints of mass marketing fraud, totalling an estimated $75 million in losses.[51]

One common form of Internet fraud is *phishing*, a type of identity theft that uses deceptive emails and fraudulent online sites to fool users into divulging their personal data. For example, consumers may receive an email, supposedly from their bank or credit card company, saying that their account's security has been compromised. The sender asks them to log on to a provided Web address and confirm their account number, password, and perhaps even their social security number. If they follow the instructions, users are actually turning this sensitive information over to scam artists. Although many consumers are now aware of such schemes, phishing can be extremely costly to those caught in the net. It also damages the brand identities of legitimate online marketers who have worked to build user confidence in Web, email, and other digital transactions.

Many consumers also worry about *online and digital security*. They fear that unscrupulous snoopers will eavesdrop on their online transactions and social media postings, picking up personal information or intercepting credit and debit card numbers. Although online shopping has grown rapidly, one study showed that 59 percent of participants were still concerned about identity theft.[52]

Another Internet marketing concern is that of *access by vulnerable or unauthorized groups*. For example, marketers of adult-oriented materials and sites have found it difficult to restrict access by minors. Although Facebook allows no children under age 13 to have a profile, and estimated 40 percent of under-18 Facebook users are actually under 13. Facebook removes 200 000 underage accounts every day. And it's not just Facebook. Young users are logging onto social media such as Formspring, tweeting their locations to the Web, and making friends with strangers on Disney and other games sites. In Canada and the United States, concerned lawmakers are currently debating bills that would help better protect children online. Unfortunately, this requires the development of technology solutions, and as Facebook puts it, "That's not so easy."[53]

Consumer Privacy

Invasion of privacy is perhaps the toughest public policy issue now confronting the direct marketing industry. Consumers often benefit from database marketing; they receive more offers that are closely matched to their interests. However, many critics worry that marketers may know *too* much about consumers' lives and that they may use this knowledge to take unfair advantage of consumers. At some point, they claim, the extensive use of databases intrudes on consumer privacy. Consumers, too, worry about their privacy. Although they are now much more willing to share personal information and preferences with marketers via digital and social media, they are still nervous about it. In one survey, some three-quarters of consumers agreed with the statement, "No one should ever be allowed to have access to my personal data or Web behaviour."[54]

These days, it seems that almost every time consumers post something on social media or send a tweet, visit a website, enter a sweepstakes, apply for a credit card, or order products by phone or online, their names are entered into some company's already bulging database. Using sophisticated computer technologies, direct marketers can mine these databases to "microtarget" their selling efforts. Most marketers have become highly skilled at collecting and analyzing detailed consumer information both online and offline. Even the experts are sometimes surprised by how much marketers can learn. Consider this account by one *Advertising Age* reporter:

> I'm no neophyte when it comes to targeting—not only do I work at *Ad Age*, but I cover direct marketing. Yet even I was taken aback when, as an experiment, we asked the database-marketing company to come up with a demographic and psychographic profile of me. Was it ever spot-on. Using only publicly available information, it concluded my date of birth, home phone number, and political-party affiliation. It gleamed that I was a college graduate, that I was married, and that one of my parents had passed away. It found that I have several bank, credit, and retail cards at "low-end" department stores. It knew not just how long I've lived at my house but how much it costs, how much it was worth, the type of mortgage that's on it, and—within a really close ballpark guess—how much is left to pay on it. It estimated my household income—again nearly perfectly—and determined that I am of British descent.
>
> But that was just the beginning. The company also nailed my psychographic profile. It correctly placed me into various groupings such as: someone who relies more on their own opinions than the recommendations of others when making a purchase; someone who is turned off by loud and aggressive advertising; someone who is family-oriented and has an interest in music, running, sports, computers, and is an avid concert-goer; someone who is never far from an Internet connection, generally used to peruse sports and general news updates; and someone who sees health as a core value. Scary? Certainly.[55]

Some consumers and policy makers worry that the ready availability of information may leave consumers open to abuse. For example, they ask, should online sellers be allowed to plant cookies in the browsers of consumers who visit their sites and use tracking information to target ads and other marketing efforts? Should credit card companies be allowed to make data on their millions of cardholders worldwide available to merchants who accept their cards? Or would it be right for provinces to sell the names and addresses of driver's licence holders, along with height and gender information, allowing apparel retailers to target, say, tall people with special clothing offers?

A Need for Action

In response to these concerns, the Canadian government passed the Personal Information Protection and Electronic Documents Act (PIPEDA) in 2001. It came into full force in 2004. The act is based on four key principles:

- *Consumer knowledge and consent.* Consumers must know that information about them is being gathered and they must provide consent before firms can collect, use, or disclose consumers' personal information.

- *Limitations.* Firms can only collect and use information appropriate to the transaction being undertaken. For example, if a firm needs to mail you something, it can ask for your home address, but it may not request additional information unrelated to this task.

- *Accuracy.* Firms must be sure that the information they gather is recorded accurately. Firms must appoint a privacy officer to be responsible for this task.

- *Right to access.* Finally, individuals have the right to know what information is being held about them. They can also demand that errors in their personal information be corrected, and they may request that their personal information be withdrawn from a firm's database.

In 2009, the Government of Canada announced that it was delivering on its commitment to protect consumers and businesses from the most dangerous and damaging forms of spam. It proposed the Electronic Commerce Protection Act (ECPA), legislation designed to boost confidence in online commerce by protecting privacy and addressing the personal security concerns that are associated with spam, counterfeit websites, and spyware. The proposed legislation also amended PIPEDA, which covers online privacy in detail and contains many provisions relevant to email marketing. Much-needed amendments to PIPEDA finally passed in 2015 with the Digital Privacy Act, which includes business transaction exemptions, mandatory breach notification requirements, enhanced powers for Canada's privacy commissioner, and various other updates.[56]

All of these concerns call for strong actions by marketers to monitor and prevent privacy abuses before legislators step in to do it for them. For example, to head off increased U.S. government regulation, six advertiser groups—the American Association of Advertising Agencies, the American Advertising Federation, the Association of National Advertisers, the Direct Marketing Association, the Interactive Advertising Bureau, and the Network Advertising Initiative—recently issued a set of online advertising principles through the Digital Advertising Alliance. Among other measures, the self-regulatory principles call for online marketers to provide transparency and choice to consumers if Web viewing data is collected or used for targeting interest-based advertising. The ad industry has agreed on an *advertising option icon*—a little "i" inside a triangle—that it will add to most behaviorally targeted online ads—those targeted using third-party information—to tell consumers why they are seeing a particular ad and allowing them to opt out.[57]

Many companies have responded to consumer privacy and security concerns with actions of their own. Still others are taking an industry-wide approach. For example, TRUSTe, a nonprofit self-regulatory organization, works with many large corporate sponsors, including Microsoft, Yahoo!, AT&T, Facebook, Disney, and Apple, to audit privacy and security measures and help consumers navigate the Internet safely. According to the company's website, "TRUSTe believes that an environment of mutual trust and openness will help make and keep the Internet a free, comfortable, and richly diverse community for everyone." To reassure consumers, the company lends its TRUSTe privacy seal to websites, mobile apps, email marketing, and other online and social media channels that meet its privacy and security standards.[58]

The Canadian Marketing Association, which has 800 corporate members, also provides consumers with a wealth of information and smart shopping tips. It posts pages that help consumers know how to deal with online issues such as spam, identifying fraudulent offers, and protecting privacy. Ethical corporations are concerned with poor practices, since they know that direct-marketing abuses will lead to increasingly negative consumer attitudes, lower response rates, and calls for more restrictive provincial and federal legislation. Most direct marketers want the same things that consumers want: honest and well-designed marketing offers targeted only at consumers who will appreciate and respond to them. Direct marketing is just too expensive to waste on consumers who don't want it.

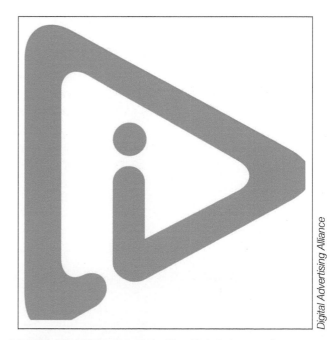

Digital Advertising Alliance

Exhibit 15.18 Consumer privacy: The ad industry has agreed on an *advertising option icon*—a little "i" inside a triangle—that will tell consumers why they are seeing a particular ad and allow them to opt out.

MyBP

Loyalty programs and corporate websites are a perfect match. The programs are easily accessed by loyal customers, visitors, and Web users, and the owner of the site can monitor and manage traffic efficiently and personally. Boston Pizza took its time developing its online customer loyalty program, which was launched in 2014 under the name "MyBP."

"MyBP provides guests with enhanced online ordering tools and also serves as a loyalty platform serving up relevant offers and promotions just for members," explains BP president and CEO Mark Pacinda. "Initially, guests received a free appetizer just for signing up, while other offers are added to user accounts along with personalized communications and better, faster, and easier online ordering tools."

The expansion of MyBP's offerings has been rapid since its inception and continues to provide users with more and more services and value-adds. Most importantly, as a "personalized" portal between true Boston Pizza fans and the company itself, it's designed to truly accumulate and develop a profile of each user. MyBP saves customers' favourite orders and can be prompted to reorder past orders, thus saving time for customers.

As a loyalty program, it tracks orders and offers discounts as more orders accrue in the system. It also offers exclusivity, another important feature of online loyalty programs. As such, enrolling in MyBP automatically exposes the member to MyBP-only communications and promotions.

Of course, the key analytic of any loyalty program is usership. "As of early 2015," Pacinda declared, "more than 188 000 guests had signed up for MyBP."

QUESTIONS

1. Visit www.bostonpizza.com and click on MyBP. Scroll through the various benefits offered, and make note of the ones that appeal to you personally. Explain their value to you.
2. Visit comparable loyalty programs of other casual dining or even quick-service restaurants. How do you feel Boston Pizza's MyBP compares?
3. What features do you think are missing from MyBP that you would like to suggest to the company?

REVIEWING THE CONCEPTS

 Define *direct and digital marketing* and discuss their rapid growth and benefits to customers and companies.

Direct and digital marketing involve engaging directly with carefully targeted individual consumers and customer communities to both obtain an immediate response and build lasting customer relationships. Companies use direct marketing to tailor their offers and content to the needs and interests of narrowly defined segments or individual buyers to build direct customer engagement, brand community, and sales. Today, spurred by the surge in Internet usage and buying, and by rapid advances in digital technologies—from smartphones, tablets, and other digital devices to the spate of online social and mobile media—direct marketing has undergone a dramatic transformation.

For buyers, direct and digital marketing are convenient, easy to use, and private. They give buyers anywhere, any time access to an almost unlimited assortment of products and buying information. Direct marketing is also immediate and interactive, allowing buyers to create exactly the configuration of information, products, or services they desire and then order them on the spot. Finally, for consumers who want it, digital marketing through online, mobile, and social media provides a sense of brand engagement and community—a place to share brand information and experiences with other brand fans. For sellers, direct and digital marketing are powerful tools for building customer engagement and close, personalized, interactive customer relationships. They also offer greater flexibility, letting marketers make ongoing adjustments to prices and programs, or make immediate, timely, and personal announcements and offers.

LO2 Identify and discuss the major forms of direct and digital marketing.

The main forms of direct and digital marketing include traditional direct marketing tools and the new direct digital marketing tools. Traditional direct approaches are face-to-face personal selling, direct-mail marketing, catalogue marketing, telemarketing, DRTV marketing, and kiosk marketing. These traditional tools are still heavily used and very important in most firm's direct marketing efforts. In recent years, however, a dazzling new set of direct digital marketing tools has burst onto the marketing scene, including online marketing (websites, online ads and promotions, email, online videos, and blogs), social media marketing, and mobile marketing.

LO3 Explain how marketers have responded to the Internet and the digital age with various online marketing strategies.

The Internet and digital age have fundamentally changed customers' notions of convenience, speed, price, product information, service, and brand interactions. As a result, they have given marketers a whole new way to create customer value, engage customers, and build customer relationships. The Internet now influences a staggering 50 percent of total sales—including sales transacted online plus those made in stores but encouraged by online research. To reach this burgeoning market, most companies now market online.

Online marketing takes several forms, including company websites, online advertising and promotions, email marketing, online video, and blogs. Social media and mobile marketing also take place online. For most companies, the first step in conducting online marketing is to create a website. The key to a successful website is to create enough value and engagement to get consumers to come to the site, stick around, and come back again.

Online advertising has become a major promotional medium. The main forms of online advertising are display ads and search-related ads. Email marketing is also an important form of digital marketing. Used properly, email lets marketers send highly targeted, tightly personalized, relationship-building messages. Another important form of online marketing is posting digital video content on brand sites or social media. Marketers hope that some of their videos will go viral, engaging consumers by the millions. Finally, companies can use blogs as effective means of reaching customer communities. They can create their own blogs and advertise on existing blogs or influence content there.

 Discuss how companies use social media and mobile marketing to engage consumers and create brand community.

In the digital age, countless independent and commercial social media have arisen that give consumers online places to congregate, socialize, and exchange views and information. Most marketers are now riding this huge social media wave. Brands can use existing social media or they can set up their own. Using existing social media seems the easiest. Thus, most brands—large and small—have set up shop on a host of social media sites. Some of the major social networks are huge; other niche social media cater to the needs of smaller communities of like-minded people. Beyond these independent social media, many companies have created their own online brand communities. More than making just scattered efforts and chasing Likes and tweets, most companies are integrating a broad range of diverse media to create brand-related social sharing, engagement, and customer community.

Using social media presents both advantages and challenges. On the plus side, social media is targeted and personal, interactive, immediate and timely, and cost effective. Perhaps the biggest advantage is its engagement and social-sharing capabilities, making it ideal for creating customer community. On the downside, consumers' dominion over social media content make social media difficult to control.

Mobile marketing features marketing messages, promotions, and other content delivered to on-the-go consumers through their mobile devices. Marketers use mobile marketing to engage customers anywhere, any time during the buying and relationship-building processes. The widespread adoption of mobile devices and the surge in mobile Web traffic have made mobile marketing a must for most brands, and almost every major marketer is now integrating mobile marketing into its direct marketing programs. Many marketers have created their own mobile online sites. Others have created useful or entertaining mobile apps to engage customers with their brands and help them shop.

LO5 **Discuss the public policy and ethical issues presented by direct marketing.**

Although the fast-growing digital marketing tools have grabbed most of the headlines lately, traditional direct marketing tools are very much alive and still heavily used. The major forms are face-to-face or personal selling, direct-mail marketing, catalogue marketing, telemarketing, direct-response television (DRTV) marketing, and kiosk marketing

Direct-mail marketing consists of the company sending an offer, announcement, reminder, or other item to a person at a specific address. Some marketers rely on catalogue marketing—selling through catalogues mailed to a select list of customers, made available in stores, or accessed online. Telemarketing consists of using the telephone to sell directly to consumers. DRTV marketing has two forms: direct-response advertising (or infomercials) and interactive television (iTV) marketing. Kiosks are information and ordering machines that direct marketers place in stores, airports, hotels, and other locations.

Direct marketers and their customers usually enjoy mutually rewarding relationships. Sometimes, however, direct marketing presents a darker side. The aggressive and sometimes shady tactics of a few direct marketers can bother or harm consumers, giving the entire industry a black eye. Abuses range from simple excesses that irritate consumers to instances of unfair practices or even outright deception and fraud. The direct marketing industry has also faced growing concerns about invasion-of-privacy and Internet security issues. Such concerns call for strong action by marketers and public policy makers to curb direct marketing abuses. In the end, most direct marketers want the same things that consumers want: honest and well-designed marketing offers targeted only toward consumers who will appreciate and respond to them.

MyMarketingLab

Study, practise, and explore real marketing situations with these helpful resources:

- **Interactive Lesson Presentations:** Work through interactive presentations and assessments to test your knowledge of marketing concepts.
- **Study Plan:** Check your understanding of chapter concepts with self-study quizzes.
- **Dynamic Study Modules:** Work through adaptive study modules on your computer, tablet, or mobile device.
- **Simulations:** Practise decision-making in simulated marketing environments.

DISCUSSION QUESTIONS

1. List and briefly describe the various forms of direct digital and social media marketing.

2. Compare and contrast a marketing website and a branded community site.

3. Name and describe the two main forms of online advertising.

4. List and briefly describe the major traditional forms of direct marketing.

5. What public policy issues are related to direct and digital marketing?

CRITICAL THINKING EXERCISES

1. In a small group, design and deliver a direct-response television ad (DRTV) for a national brand not normally associated with this type of promotion, such as an athletic shoe, automobile, or food product.

2. Develop a presentation about phishing. In your presentation, define phishing, show three examples (search Google Images for phishing examples), and discuss how consumers and businesses used in scams can protect themselves.

ONLINE, MOBILE, AND SOCIAL MEDIA MARKETING

Mobile marketing is the place to be for small businesses. For example, when rain pounded New Orleans right before its famous Jazz & Heritage Festival, the owner of a local shoe store saw an opportunity. She tweeted about rain boots available at her store, Feet First, and sold out in two hours. Feet First is no stranger to online marketing, what with its website, online shopping cart, and Facebook page, but mobile is where the action is. Employees update the store's Facebook, Twitter, Instagram, Pinterest, Tumblr, and Snapette—a local fashion app—accounts frequently. After all, consumers are increasingly turning to mobile devices to find information and purchase products. The Polkadot Alley, an online store, found that 90 percent of orders come from mobile phones. Even though Yelp's app traffic is a fraction of the site's overall traffic, 45 percent of all Yelp searches come from its mobile app. And with local retailers seeing the advantages of mobile marketing, Google changed its ad platform to accommodate the growth in

mobile ad campaigns. Advertisers not only bid for search words, but also on the searcher's device used to search, their location, and time of day. If it's Saturday before Mother's Day and you use your phone to search for a florist, Emily's Flower Shop kilometre away probably bid 30 percent higher to get its ad at the top of your results list.

QUESTIONS

1. What local businesses in your community are using online, social media, and/or mobile marketing? Interview the owner or manager of one of the businesses to learn how the business uses these marketing activities and its overall level of satisfaction with these activities.

2. Mobile marketing can be confusing for a small business owner. Develop a presentation to deliver to small business owners that describes mobile marketing, its advantages and disadvantages, and examples of how small businesses are using mobile marketing.

THINK LIKE A MARKETING MANAGER

Maestro S.V.P. is an upscale seafood restaurant and oyster bar on trendy St. Laurent Boulevard in Montreal. The clientele of the restaurant is mainly tourists, especially during the summer season, but there are also many regular customers who return again and again because they enjoy the food and the atmosphere, and because they have an oyster shell with their name on it installed on the oyster wall of

fame. The chef is famous for his unique and flavourful seafood sauces, and customers often ask whether they can purchase these sauces to take home. Responding to market demand, the owner has begun packaging and retailing a line of Maestro sauces, such as Havane sauce for tuna, and Porto & Raspberry sauce, which is excellent with mussels. So far, sauces have been sold only from within the restaurant. Lately, the owner has been wondering which forms of Internet marketing might help grow her business.

QUESTIONS

1. If Maestro began the task of creating a customer database, what forms of direct marketing would you recommend it employ to promote its business?

2. Visit the restaurant's website at www.MaestroSVP.com. Would you recommend that the owner include e-commerce capabilities on the site? Explain why or why not.

3. Maestro is a small business and doesn't have a budget for mass-media advertising. Investigate possible opportunities for inexpensive online advertising for Maestro.

4. How is Maestro using social media to promote its business? Be specific. Are there other social media sites you would recommend that it participate in that it's not currently using, and, if so, how should they be used? Are there any niche social network sites that would be appropriate for Maestro?

MARKETING ETHICS

Advertisers pay to have ads placed based on your keyword searches, to track your Web-surfing behaviour, and even to monitor what you post on Facebook or write in Gmail messages. While concerns over privacy mount, the online tracking industry just keeps ramping up. Krux Digital reported that the average visit to a webpage generated 56 instances of data collection, representing a five-fold increase from the previous year. A 2010 investigation by the *Wall Street Journal* found that the 50 most popular U.S. sites installed more than 3000 tracking files on the computer used in the study. The total was even higher—4123 tracking files—for the top 50 sites that are popular with children and teens. Many sites installed more than 100 tracking tools each during the tests. Tracking tools include files placed on users' computers and on websites. Marketers use this information to target online advertisements—but this wouldn't be possible without online-ad auctions. When a user visits a webpage, that information is auctioned among computers to the highest bidder; these bids are based on the user's Internet browsing behaviour. The bidder in such an auction is a technology broker acting on behalf of the advertiser. Real-time bidding makes up 18 percent of the online display ad market, and bids sell for less than $1 per thousand viewers. Web-tracking provides the user data to sell in the auction—and more than 300 companies are gathering this data. Data collectors often share information with each other, called "piggybacking," so they have more information about a website's user than the owner—the ad seller—of a site has. The practice has spread to mobile ads, where consumers receive tailored ads for services in their vicinity. It will eventually spread to Web-enabled televisions as well.

QUESTIONS

1. Write a report explaining how online-ad auctions work and the impact they have on Internet advertising.

2. Critics claim that Internet tracking infringes consumer privacy rights and that the industry is out of control. Should marketers have access to such information? Discuss the advantages and disadvantages of this activity for both marketers and consumers.

MARKETING BY THE NUMBERS

Many companies are realizing the efficiency of telemarketing in the face of soaring sales-force costs. Whereas an average cost of a business-to-business sales call by an outside salesperson is more than $300, the cost of a telemarketing sales call can be as little as $5 to $20. And telemarketers can make 20 to 33 decision-maker contacts per day to a salesperson's four per day. This has gotten the attention of many business-to-business marketers, where telemarketing can be very effective.

QUESTIONS

1. Refer to Appendix 3, Marketing by the Numbers, to determine the marketing return on sales (marketing ROS) and return on marketing investment (marketing

ROI) for Company A and Company B in the chart below. Which company is performing better? Explain.

	Company A (sales force only)	Company B (telemarketing only)
Net sales	$2 000 000	$1 000 000
Cost of goods sold	$ 800 000	$ 500 000
Sales expenses	$ 700 000	$ 200 000

2. Should all companies consider reducing their sales forces in favour of telemarketing? Discuss the pros and cons of this action.

GOOGLE: NEW PRODUCT INNOVATION AT THE SPEED OF LIGHT

Google is wildly innovative. It has topped *Fast Company* magazine's list of the world's most innovative companies, and it regularly ranks among everyone else's top two or three most innovative. Google is also spectacularly successful. Despite formidable competition from giants such as Microsoft and Yahoo!, Google's share in its core business—online search—stands at a decisive 86 percent, more than five times the combined market shares of all other competitors combined. The company also dominates when it comes to paid search advertising, with 86 percent of that online ad segment. And that doesn't include paid search on mobile devices, where Google commands an even greater market share.

But Google has grown to become much more than just an Internet search and advertising company. Google's mission is "to organize the world's information and make it universally accessible and useful." In Google's view, information is a kind of natural resource—one to be mined, refined, and universally distributed. That idea unifies what would otherwise appear to be a widely diverse set of Google projects, such as mapping the world, searching the Internet on a smartphone screen, or even providing for the early detection of flu epidemics. If it has to do with harnessing and using information, Google's got it covered.

AN INNOVATIVE APPROACH TO INNOVATING

Perhaps more than anything else, Google knows how to innovate. At many companies, new product development is a cautious, step-by-step affair that might take a year or two to unfold. In contrast, Google's freewheeling new product development process moves at the speed of light. It implements major new services in less time than it takes competitors to refine and approve an initial idea. For example, a Google senior project manager describes the lightning-quick development of iGoogle, Google's customizable home page:

> It was clear to Google that there were two groups [of Google users]: people who loved the site's clean, classic look and people who wanted tons of information there—email, news, local weather. [For those who wanted a fuller home page,] iGoogle started out with me and three engineers. I was 22, and I thought, "This is awesome." Six weeks later, we launched the first version. The happiness metrics were good, there was healthy growth, and [a few months later], we had [iGoogle fully operational with] a link on Google.com.

Such fast-paced innovation would boggle the minds of product developers at most other companies, but at Google it is standard operating procedure. "That's what we do," says Google's vice-president for search products and user experience. "The hardest part about indoctrinating people into our culture is when engineers show me a prototype and I'm like, 'Great, let's go!' They'll say, 'Oh, no, it's not ready.' I tell them, 'The Googly thing is to launch it early on [as a beta product] and then to iterate, learning what the market wants—and making it great.'" Adds a Google engineering manager, "We set an operational tempo: When in doubt, do something. If you have two paths and you're not sure which is right, take the fastest path."

When it comes to new product development at Google, there are no two-year plans. The company's new product planning looks ahead only four to five months. Google would rather see projects fail quickly than see a carefully planned, long and drawn-out project fail.

Google's famously chaotic innovation process has unleashed a seemingly unending flurry of diverse products, most of which are market leaders in their categories. These include everything from an email service (Gmail), a blog search engine (Google Blog Search), an online payment service (Google Checkout), and a photo-sharing service (Google Picasa) to a universal platform for mobile phone applications (Google Android), a faster-than-anything-else-out-there broadband network (Google Fiber), a cloud-friendly Internet browser (Chrome), projects for mapping and exploring the world (Google Maps and Google Earth), and even an early warning system for flu outbreaks in your area (Flu-Trends). Google claims that FluTrends has identified outbreaks two weeks before the U.S. Centers for Disease Control and Prevention.

COMPETING THROUGH INNOVATION

Not only is Google innovative, but it uses this core competency as a primary competitive weapon. Take some of its recent product introductions. First, there's Google Play. Even though it created the number-one smartphone operating system in the world—Android—Google still could not capture the purchases and activities of all those Android users when it came to apps and entertainment media. Nor could it come close to matching its operating-systems penetration in the tablet market. So Google combined and redesigned everything it had in that department and launched Google Play, an iTunes-like marketplace for apps, music, movies, and games. Although one reviewer claims that this launch "lacks the polish of Apple," he goes on to say that "there should be little doubt … about Google's determination to change that."

A second major product introduction is Google+, an all-purpose social network. With Google+, the search leader fired a shot right over the bow of Facebook. In response, Facebook founder and CEO Mark Zuckerberg put all Facebook employees on "lockdown" alert, working around the clock to copy the best features of Google+ and accelerate development of other Facebook features already being developed. In less than two years' time, Google+ had acquired over 500 million registered members, about half of those who now share their lives on Facebook, making it the second largest social networking site. Like Google Play, Google+ is a cutting-edge product. Such new products put Google into the dash for riches in completely new competitive arenas.

On a smaller scale, Google has added a feature to its mobile search app, Google Now, which has the industry buzzing. Clearly targeting Apple, Google Now features voice recognition that many observers think is even better than Apple's Siri. Based on a branch of artificial intelligence called deep learning, Google's voice recognition feature emulates the way the human brain recognizes patterns and engages in what we call thinking. Although it's extremely complicated and cutting-edge stuff, Google's experts still managed to crank out this feature in only nine months. And they aren't done. Google's experts are fast at work developing *image* recognition capabilities based on the same deep learning technology that will soon make searching images and even video more accurate and intuitive than ever.

INNOVATION WITHOUT BORDERS

With Google's process and culture for innovation, even the sky doesn't seem to be the limit. No product illustrates that better that Google Glass, the wearable smart device that has the whole world talking. Worn like a pair of glasses, Google Glass has a tiny projection screen that hovers in front of the user's face that only the user can see. Voice recognition (the same as found in Google Now) and eye movement recognition provide instant response to the user's every desire and a truly hands-free experience. And that experience is oriented around having the entire virtual world more conveniently accessible than ever before. It remains to be seen just what impact Google Glass will have. But based on reactions thus far, the impact will be nothing short of huge. After using Google Glass for only a few days, *Mashable*'s editor-in-chief, Lance Ulanoff,

dubbed it "the future." Says Ulanoff, "Google Glass could be the next big thing because it's a piece of powerful, yet elegant consumer technology that anyone can use with almost no training."

Google is open to new product ideas from just about any source. What ties it all together is the company's passion for helping people find and use information. Innovation is the responsibility of every Google employee. Google engineers are encouraged to spend 20 percent of their time developing their own "cool and wacky" new product ideas. And all new Google ideas are quickly tested in beta form by the ultimate judges—those who will use them. According to one observer, "Anytime you cram some 20 000 of the world's smartest people into one company, you can expect to grow a garden of unrelated ideas. Especially when you give some of those geniuses one workday a week—Google's famous '20 percent time'—to work on whatever projects fan their passions."

Such thinking sends Google beyond its own corporate boundaries in search of the next wave of big ideas. Google hosted what it called the "Solve For X" conference. The company invited about 50 of the smartest people in the world to tackle some of the world's biggest problems. The emphasis was on "radical." Just how radical were some of the ideas that emerged? How about turning contact lenses into computer monitors with heads-up displays packed full of data? Or how about solving the world's clean water problems through existing desalinization technologies? If that doesn't go far enough for you, how about using magnetic resonance imaging (MRI) technology to put images from the human mind onto a computer screen?

Just the fact that Google organized Solve For X indicates what type of innovator Google is. For Google, innovation is more than a process—it's part of the company's DNA. "Where does innovation happen at Google? It happens everywhere," says a Google research scientist.

If you talk to Googlers at various levels and departments, one powerful theme emerges: Whether they're designing search engines for the blind or preparing meals for their colleagues, these people feel that their work can change the world. The marvel of Google is its ability to continue to instill a sense of creative fearlessness and ambition in its employees. Prospective hires are often asked, "If you could change the world using Google's resources, what would you build?" But here, this isn't a goofy or even theoretical question: Google wants to know because thinking—and building—on that scale is what Google does. After all, this is the company that wants to make available online every page of every book ever published. Smaller-gauge ideas die of disinterest. When it comes to innovation, Google is different. But the difference isn't tangible. It's in the air—in the spirit of the place.

Sources: Robert Hof, "Meet the Guy Who Helped Google Beat Apple's Siri," *Forbes*, May 1, 2013, www.forbes.com/sites/roberthof/2013/05/01/meet-the-guy-who-helped-google-beat-apples-siri; "Covario Finds Q1 Global Paid Search Spending Grew 33 Percent over Last Year," March 28, 2013, www.marketwatch.com/story/covario-finds-q1-global-paid-search-spending-grew-33-percent-over-last-year-2013-03-28; www.karmasnack.com/about/search-engine-market-share, accessed May 2013; Matt Lynley, "Here Are the 17 Radical Ideas from Google's Top Genius Conference That Could Change the World," *Business Insider*, February 11, 2012, www.businessinsider.com/here-are-the-17-radical-ideas-from-googles-top-genius-conference-that-could-change-the-world-2012-2?op=1#ixzz21TPojmMs; Chuck Salter, "Google: The Faces and Voices of the World's Most Innovative Company," *Fast Company*, March 2008, pp. 74–88; "World's 50 Most Innovative Companies," *Fast Company*, March 2013, www.fastcompany.com/section/most-innovative-companies-2013; Lance Ulanoff, "This Is Why Google Glass Is the Future," *Mashable*, May 1, 2013, www.mashable.com/2013/04/30/google-glass-future; and www.google.com, accessed November 2013.

QUESTIONS FOR DISCUSSION

1. Discuss ways in which other companies can use Google's innovativeness to build their own brands and generate sales.

2. How could Google use its innovativeness to succeed in the growing field of mobile marketing?

3. Is there a limit to how big Google's product portfolio can grow? Explain.

4. Will Google be successful in markets where it does not dominate, such as social networks and app/entertainment stores? Why or why not?

Marco Di Lauro/Getty Images

1 discuss how the international trade system and the economic, political-legal, and cultural environments affect a company's international marketing decisions

2 describe three key approaches to entering international markets

3 explain how companies adapt their marketing strategies and mixes for international markets

4 identify the three major forms of international marketing organization

The Global Marketplace

PREVIEWING THE CONCEPTS

You've now learned the fundamentals of how companies develop competitive marketing strategies to create customer value and build lasting customer relationships. In this chapter, we extend these fundamentals to global marketing. Although we discussed global topics in previous chapters—it's difficult to find an area of marketing that doesn't contain at least some international elements—here we'll focus on the special considerations companies face when they market their brands globally. Advances in communication, transportation, and digital technologies have made the world a much smaller place. Today, almost every firm, large or small, faces international marketing issues. In this chapter we'll examine six major decisions marketers make in going global.

To begin our exploration of global marketing, let's look at Coca-Cola, a truly global operation. You'll find a Coca-Cola product within arm's length of almost anyone, anywhere in the world. "We sell moments of happiness, for cents at a time, more than 1.9 billion times a day in more than 200 countries," says the company in its annual report. Like many companies, Coca-Cola's greatest growth opportunities lie in international markets. Here, we examine the company's odyssey into Africa.

COCA-COLA IN AFRICA: "EVERYTHING IS RIGHT THERE TO HAVE IT HAPPEN"

Coca-Cola is one of the world's truly iconic brands—a US$47 billion global powerhouse. It puts Coke products within "an arm's length" of 98 percent of the world's population. Already the world's number one soft drink maker, Coca-Cola is in the midst of a 12-year plan to double its global system revenues by 2020. But achieving such growth won't be easy. The major problem: Soft drink sales growth has lost its fizz in North America and Europe, two of Coca-Cola's largest and most profitable markets. In fact, the U.S. soft drink market has shrunk for five straight years. With sales stagnating in its mature markets, Coca-Cola must look elsewhere to meet its ambitious growth goals.

In recent years, Coca-Cola has sought growth primarily in developing global markets such as China and India, which boast large emerging middle classes but relatively low per capita consumption of Coke. However, both China and India are now crowded with competitors and notoriously difficult for outsiders to navigate. So while Coca-Cola will continue to compete heavily in those countries, it has set its sights on an even more promising long-term growth opportunity—Africa.

Many Western companies view Africa as an untamed final frontier—a kind of no man's land plagued by poverty, political corruption and instability, unreliable transportation, and shortages of fresh water and other essential resources. But Coca-Cola sees plenty of opportunity in Africa to justify the risks. Africa has a growing population of more than 1 billion people and a just-emerging middle class. The number of African households earning at least $5000—the income level where families begin to spend at least half their income on nonfood items—has tripled over the past 30 years to more than a third of the population. "You've got an incredibly young population, a dynamic population," says Coca-Cola CEO Muhtar Kent, "[and] huge disposable income. I mean $1.6 trillion of GDP, which is bigger than Russia, bigger than India."

Coca-Cola is no stranger to Africa. It has operated there since 1929, and it's the only multinational that offers its products in every African country. The company has a dominant 29 percent market share in Africa and the Middle East, as compared with Pepsi's 15 percent share. Coca-Cola's revenues in Africa and the Middle East grew by 4 percent in 2014 (down from 10 percent growth in 2012), far greater than the 0 percent growth in North America and 2 percent decline in Europe.

But there's still plenty of room for Coca-Cola to grow in Africa. For example, annual per capita consumption of Coke in Kenya is just 40 servings, compared with more developed countries like Mexico, where consumption runs at an eye-popping 728 servings per year. So the stage is set for Coca-Cola on the African continent, not just for its flagship Coke brand but also for its large stable of other soft drinks, waters, and juices. Whereas the beverage giant invested US$6 billion in the African market over the past decade, it plans to invest twice that amount during the next 10 years—an effort that includes bottling plants, distribution networks, retailer support, and an Africa-wide promotional campaign called "One Billion Reasons to Believe in Africa."

Marketing in Africa is a very different proposition from marketing in more developed regions. "Africa … is not Atlanta," observes one analyst, "and Coke is, in a sense, sticking its hand into a bees' nest to get some honey." To grow its sales in Africa, beyond just marketing through traditional channels in larger African cities, Coca-Cola is now invading smaller communities with more grassroots tactics. "[Just] being in a country is very easy; you can go and set up a depot in every capital city," says CEO Kent. But in Africa, "that's not what we're about. There's nowhere in Africa that we don't go. We go to every town, every village, every community, every township." In Africa, every small shop in every back alley has become important, as Coca-Cola launches what another analyst describes as "a street-by-street campaign to win drinkers … not yet used to guzzling Coke by the gallon."

For example, take the Mamakamau Shop in Uthiru, a poor community outside Nairobi, Kenya. Piles of trash burn outside the shop and sewage trickles by in an open trench. Besides Coca-Cola products, the shop—known as a duka—also carries everything from mattresses to plastic buckets, all in a room about the size of a small bedroom. Still, proprietor Mamakamau Kingori has earned Coca-Cola's "Gold" vendor status, its highest level, for selling about 72 cola products a day, priced at 30 Kenyan shillings (37 U.S. cents) for a 500-millilitre bottle. Most customers drink the soda in the store while sitting on overturned red crates—they can't afford to pay the bottle deposit. Coca-Cola's Kenyan bottler will reuse the glass bottles up to 70 times.

To earn her "Gold" status, Kingori follows carefully prescribed selling techniques. She uses a red, Coke-provided, refrigerated cooler by the front entrance, protected by a blue cage. Like other mom-and-pop stores in her area, she keeps the cooler fully stocked with

Coke on top, Fanta in the middle, and large bottles on the bottom. Inside the store, she posts red menu signs provided by Coca-Cola that push combo meals, such as a 300-millilitre Coke and a ndazi, a type of local doughnut, for 25 Kenyan shillings.

In Kabira, another poor Nairobi neighbourhood, the crowded streets are lined with shops painted Coke red. The local bottler hires an artist to paint the shops with logos and Swahili phrases like "Burudika na Coke Baridi," meaning "enjoy Coke cold." In countless communities across Africa, whether it's the dukas in Nairobi or tuck shops in Johannesburg, South Africa, small stores play a big role in helping Coca-Cola grow.

Such shops are supplied by a rudimentary but effective network of Coca-Cola distributors. For example, in downtown Nairobi, men in red lab coats load hand-pulled trolleys with 22 to 40 crates of Coke and other soft drinks from Rosinje Distributors, one of 3200 Micro Distribution Centers (MDCs) that Coca-Cola operates in Africa. These centres are the spine of Coca-Cola's African distribution network. For example, the Nairobi plant ships Coke, Fanta, Stoney Ginger Beer, and other Coca-Cola brands to almost 400 area MDCs. From there, crews hustle the products—sometimes a case at a time carried on their heads—to local shops and beverage kiosks. Because of the poor roads crowded with traffic, moving drinks by hand is often the best method. The MDCs help Coca-Cola get its products into remote areas, making them available as people develop a taste for soft drinks and have the income to buy them.

Despite their elemental nature, Coca-Cola's marketing approaches in Africa are proving effective. The company's first rule is to get its products "cold and close." "If they don't have roads to move products long distances on trucks, we will use boats, canoes, or trolleys," says the president of Coca-Cola South Africa. For example, in Nigeria's Makako district—a maze of stilt houses on the Lagos lagoon—women criss-cross the waterways selling Coca-Cola directly from canoes to residents.

There's little doubt that Coca-Cola's increased commitment to Africa will be key to its achieving its global goals. As CEO Muhtar Kent concludes, "Africa is the untold story and could be the big story of the next decade, like India and China were this past decade. . . . Everything is right there to have it happen."[1]

IN THE PAST, many companies paid little attention to international trade. If they could pick up some extra sales via exports, that was fine. But the big market was at home, and it teemed with opportunities. The home market was also much safer. Managers did not need to learn other languages, deal with strange and changing currencies, face political and legal uncertainties, or adapt their products to different customer needs and expectations. Today, however, the situation is much different. Organizations of all kinds, from Coca-Cola and HP to Google, MTV, and even the NBA, have gone global.

Global Marketing Today

Simulate on MyMarketingLab

Global Marketing

The world is shrinking rapidly with the advent of faster digital communication, transportation, and financial flows. Products developed in one country—Samsung electronics, McDonald's hamburgers, Zara fashions, Caterpillar construction equipment, German BMWs, Facebook social networking—have found enthusiastic acceptance in other countries. It would not be surprising to hear about a German businessman wearing an Italian suit meeting an English friend at a Japanese restaurant who later returns home to drink Russian vodka while watching *America's Got Talent* on TV and checking Facebook posts from friends around the world.

PRAKASH SINGH/AFP/Getty Images

Exhibit 16.1 Many companies have now made the world their market. Nearly 60 percent of Apple's sales come from outside the Americas.

International trade has boomed over the past three decades. Since 1990, the number of multinational corporations in the world has more than doubled to more than 63 000. Some of these multinationals are true giants. In fact, of the largest 150 economies in the world, only 77 are countries: The remaining 73 are multinational corporations. Walmart, the world's largest company (based on a weighted average of sales, profits, assets, and market value), has annual revenues greater than the gross domestic product (GDP) of all but the world's 27 largest countries.[2] Despite a dip in world trade caused by the worldwide recession, the world trade of products and services in 2014 was valued at more than US$18.9 trillion.[3]

Many North American companies have long been successful at international marketing: Coca-Cola, McDonald's, Starbucks, Nike, GE, IBM, Apple, Colgate, Caterpillar, Bombardier, and dozens of other firms have made the world their market. In Canada and the United States, names such as Toyota, Nestlé, IKEA, Canon, Adidas, and Samsung have become household words. Other products and services that appear to be North American are, in fact, produced or owned by foreign companies, such as Ben & Jerry's ice cream, Budweiser beer, 7-Eleven, GE and RCA televisions, Carnation milk, Universal Studios, and Motel 6. Michelin, the oh-so-French tire manufacturer, now does 36 percent of its business in North America; J&J, the maker of such familiar products as BAND-AIDs and Johnson's Baby Shampoo, does nearly 56 percent of its business abroad. And America's Caterpillar belongs more to the wider world, with 69 percent of its sales coming from outside the United States.[4]

But as global trade grows, global competition is also intensifying. Foreign firms are expanding aggressively into new international markets, and home markets are no longer as rich in opportunity. Few industries are currently safe from foreign competition. If companies delay taking steps toward internationalizing, they risk being shut out of growing markets in Western and Eastern Europe, China and the Pacific Rim, Russia, India, Brazil, and elsewhere. Firms that stay at home to play it safe might not only lose their chances to enter other markets but also risk losing their home markets. Domestic companies that never thought about foreign competitors suddenly find these competitors in their own backyards.

Ironically, although the need for companies to go abroad is greater today than in the past, so are the risks. Companies that go global may face highly unstable governments and currencies, restrictive government policies and regulations, and high trade barriers. The recently dampened global economic environment has also created big global challenges. In addition, corruption is an increasing problem; officials in several countries often award business not to the best bidder but to the highest briber.

Global firm

A firm that, by operating in more than one country, gains R&D, production, marketing, and financial advantages in its costs and reputation that are not available to purely domestic competitors.

A **global firm** is one that, by operating in more than one country, gains marketing, production, research and development (R&D), and financial advantages that are not available to purely domestic competitors. Because the global company sees the world as one market, it minimizes the importance of national boundaries and develops global brands. The global company raises capital, obtains materials and components, and manufactures and markets its goods wherever it can do the best job.

FIGURE 16.1 Major International Marketing Decisions

For example, U.S.-based Otis Elevator, the world's largest elevator maker, is headquartered in Farmington, Connecticut. However, it offers products in more than 200 countries and achieves 82 percent of its sales from outside the United States. It gets elevator door systems from France, small geared parts from Spain, electronics from Germany, and special motor drives from Japan. It operates manufacturing facilities in the Americas, Europe, and Asia, and engineering and test centres in the United States, Austria, Brazil, China, Czech Republic, France, Germany, India, Italy, Japan, Korea, and Spain. In turn, Otis Elevator is a wholly owned subsidiary of global commercial and aerospace giant United Technologies Corporation.[5] Many of today's global corporations—both large and small—have become truly borderless.

This does not mean, however, that every firm must operate in a dozen countries to succeed. Smaller firms can practise global niching. But the world is becoming smaller, and every company operating in a global industry—whether large or small—must assess and establish its place in world markets.

The rapid move toward globalization means that all companies will have to answer some basic questions: What market position should we try to establish in our country, in our economic region, and globally? Who will our global competitors be and what are their strategies and resources? Where should we produce or source our products? What strategic alliances should we form with other firms around the world?

As shown in Figure 16.1, a company faces six major decisions in international marketing. We discuss each decision in detail in this chapter.

Looking at the Global Marketing Environment

Before deciding whether to operate internationally, a company must understand the international marketing environment. That environment has changed a great deal in recent decades, creating both new opportunities and new problems.

The International Trade System

Canadian companies looking abroad must start by understanding the international *trade system*. When selling to another country, a firm may face restrictions on trade between nations. Governments may charge *tariffs* or *duties*, taxes on certain imported products designed to raise revenue or protect domestic firms. Tariffs and duties are often used to force favourable trade behaviours from other nations. For example, the European Union (EU) recently placed import duties on Chinese solar panels after determining that Chinese companies were selling the panels in EU countries at under-market prices. To retaliate, the very next day, the Chinese government launched an investigation into putting similar duties on EU wine exports to China. The investigation targeted the wine countries of Spain, France, and Italy but spared Germany, which had taken China's side in the solar panel dispute. The message was clear, says an international trade expert: "You don't like our cheap solar panels? Well, we'll make your wine even more expensive."[6]

Exhibit 16.2 Nontariff trade barriers: Walmart and other foreign businesses in China appear to receive unusually close scrutiny and harsh treatment from Chinese authorities, aimed at boosting the fortunes of local Chinese competitors.

Countries may set *quotas*, limits on the amount of foreign imports they will accept in certain product categories. The purpose of a quota is to conserve on foreign exchange and protect local industry and employment. Firms may also encounter *exchange controls*, which limit the amount of foreign exchange and the exchange rate against other currencies.

As well, a company may face *nontariff trade barriers*, such as biases against its bids, restrictive product standards, or excessive host-country regulations or enforcement. For example, foreign businesses in China appear to receive unusually close scrutiny and harsh treatment from Chinese authorities, aimed at boosting the fortunes of local competitors. National and local Chinese regulators recently launched what appeared to be a new wave of protectionism, with the goal of shielding Chinese brands from their Western rivals in a slowing economy. The harshest treatment was reserved for Western retailers such as Walmart. The retailer was first fined for misleading pricing in several of its stores. Next, it paid fines for allegedly selling expired products in the city of Changsha. Then, Chinese regulators in Chongqing accused Walmart of selling regular pork improperly labelled as organic, forcing the chain to temporarily close 13 stores and pay a $573 000 fine. The motives behind these protectionist moves appeared to be more to hinder Walmart's operations in China than to improve the operations of local retailers. As one analyst puts it, "Why go to the effort of getting your own guys to raise their game when you can tear down a foreign guy instead?"[7]

At the same time, certain other forces can *help* trade between nations. Examples include the World Trade Organization (WTO) and various regional free trade agreements.

The World Trade Organization The General Agreement on Tariffs and Trade (GATT), established in 1947 and modified in 1994, was designed to promote world trade by reducing tariffs and other international trade barriers. It established the World Trade Organization (WTO), which replaced GATT in 1995 and now oversees the original GATT provisions. WTO and GATT member nations (currently numbering 161) have met in eight rounds of negotiations to reassess trade barriers and establish new rules for international trade. The WTO also imposes international trade sanctions and mediates global trade disputes. Its actions have been productive. The first seven rounds of negotiations reduced the average worldwide tariffs on manufactured goods from 45 percent to just 5 percent.[8]

The most recently completed negotiations, dubbed the Uruguay Round, dragged on for seven long years before concluding in 1994. The benefits of the Uruguay Round will be felt for many years, as the accord promoted long-term global trade growth, reduced the world's remaining merchandise tariffs by 30 percent, extended the WTO to cover trade in agriculture and a wide range of services, and toughened the international protection of copyrights, patents, trademarks, and other intellectual property. A new round of global WTO trade talks, the

Exhibit 16.3 The WTO promotes trade by reducing tariffs and other international trade barriers. It also imposes international trade sanctions and mediates global trade disputes.

Doha Round, began in Doha, Qatar, in late 2001 and was set to conclude in 2005; however, the discussions continued through 2015.[9]

Regional Free Trade Zones Certain countries have formed *free trade zones* or **economic communities**. These are groups of nations organized to work toward common goals in the regulation of international trade. One such community is the *European Union (EU)*. Formed in 1957, the EU set out to create a single European market by reducing barriers to the free flow of products, services, finances, and labour among member countries and developing policies on trade with nonmember nations. Today, the EU represents one of the world's largest single markets. Currently, it has 28 member countries containing more than half a billion consumers and accounting for almost 20 percent of the world's exports.[10] The EU offers tremendous trade opportunities for non-European firms.

© European Union, 2012

Exhibit 16.4 **Economic communities:** The European Union represents one of the world's single largest markets. Its current member countries contain more than half a billion consumers and account for 20 percent of the world's exports.

Over the past decade and a half, 19 EU member nations have taken a significant step toward unification by adopting the euro as a common currency. Widespread adoption of the euro has decreased much of the currency risk associated with doing business in Europe, making member countries with previously weak currencies more attractive markets. However, the adoption of a common currency has also caused problems as European economic powers such as Germany and France have had to step in to prop up weaker economies such as those of Greece, Portugal, and Cyprus. This recent "euro crisis" has led some analysts to predict the possible breakup of the euro zone as it is now set up.[11]

Economic community

A group of nations organized to work toward common goals in the regulation of international trade.

It is unlikely that the EU will ever go against 2000 years of tradition and become fully integrated. A community with more than two dozen different languages and cultures will always have difficulty coming together and acting as a single entity. Still, with a combined annual GDP of more than US$17 trillion, the EU has become a potent economic force.[12]

In 1994, the *North American Free Trade Agreement (NAFTA)* established a free trade zone among Canada, the United States, and Mexico. The agreement created a single market of 453 million people who produce and consume US$17.8 trillion worth of goods and services annually. Since then, NAFTA has eliminated trade barriers and investment restrictions among the three countries. Total trade among the NAFTA countries nearly tripled from US$288 billion in 1993 to US$1 trillion in 2011.[13]

The Canadian government is working to expand markets for Canadian firms. In 2012, Canada joined the negotiations for the Trans-Pacific Partnership, which includes the U.S., Australia, Brunei, Chile, Japan, Malaysia, New Zealand, Peru, Singapore, Vietnam, and Mexico. Free trade negotiations have also concluded in a deal with the European Union (CETA), which will give Canadian businesses access to one of the most lucrative markets in the world. Canada also has several other free trade agreements with countries around the world.[14]

Each nation has unique features that must be understood. A nation's readiness for different products and services and its attractiveness as a market to foreign firms depend on its economic, political-legal, and cultural environments.

Economic Environment

The international marketer must study each country's economy. Two economic factors reflect the country's attractiveness as a market: its industrial structure and its income distribution.

The country's *industrial structure* shapes its product and service needs, income levels, and employment levels. The four types of industrial structures are as follows:

■ *Subsistence economies:* In a subsistence economy, the vast majority of people engage in simple agriculture. They consume most of their output and barter the rest for simple goods and services. These economies offer few market opportunities. Many African countries fall into this category.

■ *Raw material exporting economies:* These economies are rich in one or more natural resources but poor in other ways. Much of their revenue comes from exporting these resources. Some examples are Chile (tin and copper) and the Democratic Republic of the Congo (copper, cobalt, and coffee). These countries are good markets for large equipment, tools and supplies, and trucks. If there are many foreign residents and a wealthy upper class, they are also a market for luxury goods.

■ *Emerging economies (industrializing economies):* In an emerging economy, fast growth in manufacturing results in rapid overall economic growth. Industrialization typically creates a new rich class and a growing middle class, both demanding new types of imported goods—with more imports of raw textile materials, steel, and heavy machinery, and fewer imports of finished textiles, paper products, and automobiles. As more developed markets stagnate and become increasingly competitive, many companies are now targeting growth opportunities in such emerging markets as Indonesia and Malaysia. And although the BRIC countries—Brazil, Russia, India, and China—used to exemplify emerging economies, among them only India is still seen as a country with significant growth potential.

■ *Industrial economies:* Industrial economies are major exporters of manufactured goods, services, and investment funds. They trade goods among themselves and also export them to other types of economies for raw materials and semifinished goods. The varied manufacturing activities of these industrial nations and their large middle class make them rich markets for all sorts of goods. Examples include Canada, the United States, Japan, and Norway.

The second economic factor is the country's *income distribution.* Industrialized nations may have low-, medium-, and high-income households. In contrast, countries with subsistence economies consist mostly of households with very low family incomes. Still other countries may have households with either very low or very high incomes. Even poor or emerging economies may be attractive markets for all kinds of goods. These days, companies in a wide range of industries—from cars to computers to candy—are increasingly targeting even low- and middle-income consumers in emerging economies.

For example, in India, Ford introduced a new model targeted to consumers who are only now able to afford their first car. In an effort to boost its presence in Asia's third-largest auto market behind Japan and China, Ford introduced the

Namas Bhojani/Namas Bhojani Photography

Exhibit 16.5 Economic environment: In India, Ford's $6600 Figo targets low- to middle-income consumers who are only now able to afford their first car.

Figo, a successful $6600 hatchback designed for a hypothetical twenty-something Indian consumer named Sandeep. Sandeep is a young professional who currently drives a motorcycle. But given his improving means and pending family, he now wants something bigger. "There are huge numbers of people wanting to move off their motorbikes," says Ford's India general manager. As a result, demand is booming in India for cars in the Figo's size and price range. After just two years, the diminutive Figo has become Ford's best-selling car in India and is now also selling well in 50 other emerging markets across Asia and Africa.[15]

Political-Legal Environment

Nations differ greatly in their political-legal environments. In considering whether to do business in a given country, a company should consider factors such as the country's attitudes toward international buying, government bureaucracy, political stability, and monetary regulations.

Some nations are very receptive to foreign firms; others are less accommodating. For example, India has tended to bother foreign businesses with import quotas, currency restrictions, and other limitations that make operating there a challenge. In contrast, neighbouring Asian countries, such as Singapore and Thailand, court foreign investors and shower them with incentives and favourable operating conditions. Political and regulatory stability is another issue. For example, Russia is consumed by corruption and governmental red tape, which the government finds difficult to control, increasing the risk of doing business there. Although most international marketers still find the Russian market attractive, the corrupt climate will affect how they handle business and financial matters.[16]

Companies must also consider a country's monetary regulations. Sellers want to take their profits in a currency of value to them. Ideally, the buyer can pay in the seller's currency or in other world currencies. Short of this, sellers might accept a blocked currency—one whose removal from the country is restricted by the buyer's government—if they can buy other goods in that country that they need or can sell elsewhere for a needed currency. In addition to currency limits, a changing exchange rate can create high risks for the seller.

Most international trade involves cash transactions. Yet many nations have too little hard currency to pay for their purchases from other countries. They may want to pay with other items instead of cash. *Barter* involves the direct exchange of goods or services. For example, Venezuela regularly barters oil, which it produces in surplus quantities, for food on the international market—rice from Guyana; coffee from El Salvador; sugar, coffee, meat, and more from Nicaragua; and beans and pasta from the Dominican Republic. Venezuela has even struck a deal to supply oil to Cuba in exchange for Cuban doctors and medical care for Venezuelans.[17]

Cultural Environment

Each country has its own folkways, norms, and taboos. When designing global marketing strategies, companies must understand how culture affects consumer reactions in each of its world markets. In turn, they must also understand how their strategies affect local cultures.

The Impact of Culture on Marketing Strategy Sellers must understand the ways that consumers in different countries think about and use certain products before planning a marketing program. There are often surprises. For example, the average French man uses almost twice as many cosmetics and grooming aids as his wife. The Germans and the French eat more packaged, branded spaghetti than Italians do. Some 49 percent of

Chinese eat on the way to work. Most North American women let down their hair and take off makeup at bedtime, whereas 15 percent of Chinese women style their hair at bedtime and 11 percent put *on* makeup.[18]

Companies that ignore cultural norms and differences can make some very expensive and embarrassing mistakes. Here are two examples:

> Nike inadvertently offended Chinese officials when it ran an ad featuring LeBron James crushing a number of culturally revered Chinese figures in a kung fu–themed television ad. The Chinese government found that the ad violated regulations to uphold national dignity and respect the "motherland's culture" and yanked the multimillion-dollar campaign. With egg on its face, Nike released a formal apology. Burger King made a similar mistake when it created in-store ads in Spain showing Hindu goddess Lakshmi atop a ham sandwich with the caption "a snack that is sacred." Cultural and religious groups worldwide objected strenuously—Hindus are vegetarian. Burger King apologized and pulled the ads.[19]

Business norms and behaviours also vary from country to country. For example, North American executives like to get right down to business and engage in fast and tough face-to-face bargaining. However, Japanese and other Asian businesspeople often find this behaviour offensive. They prefer to start with polite conversation, and they rarely say no in face-to-face conversations. As another example, firm handshakes are a common and expected greeting in most Western countries; in some Middle Eastern countries, however, handshakes might be refused if offered. Microsoft founder Bill Gates once set off a flurry of international controversy when he shook the hand of South Korea's president with his right hand while keeping his left hand in his pocket, something that Koreans consider highly disrespectful. In some countries, when being entertained at a meal, not finishing all the food implies that it was somehow substandard. In other countries, in contrast, wolfing down every last bite might be taken as a mild insult, suggesting that the host didn't supply enough quantity.[20] North American business executives need to understand these kinds of cultural nuances before conducting business in another country.

By the same token, companies that understand cultural nuances can use them to their advantage in the global markets. For example, as we'll discuss further at the end of this chapter, furniture retailer IKEA's stores are a big draw for up-and-coming Chinese consumers. And IKEA has learned that customers in China want a lot more from its stores than just affordable Scandinavian-designed furniture:

Exhibit 16.6 The impact of culture on marketing strategy: IKEA customers in China want a lot more from its stores than just affordable Scandinavian-designed furniture.

In Chinese, IKEA is known as Yi Jia. Translated, it means "comfortable home," a concept taken literally by the millions of consumers who visit one of IKEA's 11 huge Chinese stores each year. "Customers come on family outings, hop into display beds and nap, pose for snapshots with the decor, and hang out for hours to enjoy the air conditioning and free soda refills," notes one observer. On a typical Saturday afternoon, for example, display beds and other furniture in a huge Chinese IKEA store are occupied, with customers of all ages lounging or even fast asleep. IKEA managers encourage such behaviour, figuring that familiarity with the store will result in later purchasing when shoppers' incomes eventually rise to match their aspirations. "Maybe if you've been visiting IKEA, eating meatballs, hot dogs, or ice cream for 10 years, then maybe you will consider IKEA when you get yourself a sofa," says the company's Asia-Pacific president. Thanks to such cultural understandings, IKEA already captures about 7 percent of the surging Chinese home-furnishings market, and its sales in China increased 20 percent in 2014.[21]

In sum, understanding cultural traditions, preferences, and behaviours can help companies not only avoid embarrassing mistakes but also take advantage of cross-cultural opportunities.

The Impact of Marketing Strategy on Cultures Whereas marketers worry about the impact of global cultures on their marketing strategies, others may worry about the impact of marketing strategies on global cultures. For example, social critics contend that large American multinationals, such as McDonald's, Coca-Cola, Starbucks, Nike, Google, Disney, and Facebook, aren't just globalizing their brands; they are Americanizing the world's cultures. Other elements of American culture have become pervasive worldwide. For instance, more people now study English in China than speak it in the United States. Of the 10 most watched TV shows in the world, 7 are American. If you assemble businesspeople from Brazil, Germany, and China, they'll likely transact in English. And the thing that binds the world's teens together in a kind of global community, notes one observer, "is American culture—the music, the Hollywood fare, the electronic games, Google, Facebook, American consumer brands. The . . . rest of the world is becoming [ever more] like us—in ways good and bad."[22]

"Today, globalization often wears Mickey Mouse ears, eats Big Macs, drinks Coke or Pepsi, and does its computing with Windows," says Thomas Friedman in his book *The Lexus and the Olive Tree: Understanding Globalization.* "Some Chinese kids' first English word [is] Mickey," notes another writer.[23]

Critics worry that, under such "McDomination," countries around the globe are losing their individual cultural identities. Teens in Turkey watch MTV, connect with others globally through Facebook, and ask their parents for more Westernized clothes and other symbols of American pop culture and values. Grandmothers in small European villas no longer spend each morning visiting local meat, bread, and produce markets to gather the ingredients for dinner. Instead, they now shop at Walmart Supercenters. Women in Saudi Arabia see American films, question their societal roles, and shop at any of the country's growing number of Victoria's Secret boutiques. In China, most people never drank coffee before Starbucks entered the market. Now Chinese consumers rush to Starbucks stores "because it's a symbol of a new kind of lifestyle." Similarly, in China, where McDonald's operates more than 80 restaurants in Beijing alone, nearly half of all children identify the chain as a domestic brand.

Such concerns have sometimes led to a backlash against American globalization. Well-known U.S. brands have become the targets of boycotts and protests in some international markets. As symbols of American capitalism, companies such as Coca-Cola, McDonald's, Nike, and KFC have been singled out by antiglobalization protesters in hot spots around the world, especially when anti-American sentiment peaks.

Despite such problems, defenders of globalization argue that concerns about Americanization and the potential damage to American brands are overblown. U.S. brands are doing very well internationally. In the most recent Millward Brown Optimor brand value survey of global consumer brands, 17 of the top 20 brands were American owned, including megabrands such as Apple, Google, IBM, McDonald's, Microsoft,

Exhibit 16.7 The impact of marketing strategy on culture: Nearly half of all children in China identify McDonald's as a domestic brand.

Tomoko Kunihiro

Coca-Cola, GE, Amazon.com, and Walmart.[24] Many iconic American brands are soaring globally. For example, Chinese consumers appear to have an insatiable appetite for Apple iPhones and iPads. When Apple introduced its latest iPhone model in China, demand was so heavy that the company had to abandon sales in some Beijing stores to avert the threat of rioting by mobs of eager consumers. China is now Apple's second biggest market behind the United States. "It's mind-boggling that we can do this well," says Apple CEO Tim Cook.[25]

More fundamentally, the cultural exchange goes both ways: North America gets as well as gives cultural influence. True, Hollywood dominates the global movie market, but British TV originated the programming that was Americanized into such hits as *The Office*, *American Idol*, and *Dancing with the Stars*. Although Chinese and Russian youth are donning NBA superstar jerseys, the increasing popularity of soccer in North America has deep international roots.

Even North American childhood has been increasingly influenced by European and Asian cultural imports. Most kids know all about imports such as Hello Kitty, the Bakugan Battle Brawler, or any of a host of Nintendo or Sega game characters. And J. K. Rowling's so-very-British Harry Potter books have shaped the thinking of a generation of youngsters, not to mention the millions of oldsters who fell under their spell as well. For the moment, English remains the dominant language of the Internet, and having Web access often means that third-world youth have greater exposure to American popular culture. Yet these same technologies let Eastern European students studying in the United States hear webcast news and music from Poland, Romania, or Belarus.

Thus, globalization is a two-way street. If globalization has Mickey Mouse ears, it's also talking on a Samsung mobile phone, buying furniture at IKEA, driving a Toyota Camry, and watching a British-inspired show on a Panasonic plasma TV.

Deciding Whether to Go Global

Not all companies need to venture into international markets to survive. For example, most local businesses need to market well only in their local marketplaces. Operating domestically is easier and safer. Managers don't need to learn another country's language and laws. They don't have to deal with unstable currencies, face political and legal uncertainties, or redesign their products to suit different customer expectations. However, companies that operate in global industries, where their strategic positions in specific markets are affected strongly by their overall global positions, must compete on a regional or worldwide basis to succeed.

Any of several factors might draw a company into the international arena. For example, global competitors might attack the company's home market by offering better products or lower prices. The company might want to counterattack these competitors in their home markets to tie up their resources. The company's customers might be expanding abroad and require international servicing. Or, most likely, international markets might simply provide better opportunities for growth. For example, as we discovered in the story at the start of the chapter, Coca-Cola has emphasized international growth in recent years to offset stagnant or declining U.S. soft drink sales. Today, nearly 60 percent of Coca-Cola's sales come from outside of North America, and the company is making major pushes into 90 emerging markets, such as China, India, and the entire African continent.[26]

Before going abroad, the company must weigh several risks and answer many questions about its ability to operate globally. Can the company learn to understand the preferences and buyer behaviour of consumers in other countries? Can it offer competitively attractive products? Will it be able to adapt to other countries' business cultures and deal effectively with foreign nationals? Do the company's managers have the necessary international experience? Has management considered the impact of regulations and the political environments of other countries?

Deciding Which Markets to Enter

Before going abroad, the company should try to define its international *marketing objectives and policies*. It should decide what *volume* of foreign sales it wants. Most companies start small when they go abroad. Some plan to stay small, seeing international sales as a small part of their business. Other companies have bigger plans, however, seeing international business as equal to or even more important than their domestic business.

The company also needs to choose in *how many* countries it wants to market. Companies must be careful not to spread themselves too thin or expand beyond their capabilities by operating in too many countries too soon. Next, the company needs to decide on the *types* of countries to enter. A country's attractiveness depends on the product, geographical factors, income and population, political climate, and other considerations. In recent years, many major new markets have emerged, offering both substantial opportunities and daunting challenges.

After listing possible international markets, the company must carefully evaluate each one. It must consider many factors. For example, Netflix's decision to expand into European markets such as Germany, France, Italy, and Spain seems like a no-brainer. Netflix needs to grow its subscriber base to cover rapidly rising content costs, and Europe offers huge opportunities. Western Europe boasts 134 million broadband homes, compared with 88 million in the United States. The as-yet-largely-untapped European video-services market is expected to grow by 67 percent to more than $1.1 billion by 2017. Netflix has already entered the U.K. and the Nordic nations, and has become the leading video service in Sweden after only two years.[27]

However, as Netflix considers expanding into new European markets, it must ask some important questions. Can it compete effectively on a country-by-country basis with local competitors? Can it master the varied cultural and buying differences of European consumers? Will it be able to meet environmental and regulatory hurdles in each country? For example, Netflix's expansion has been slow and difficult in Latin America, where e-commerce is less established.

In entering new European markets, Netflix will face many challenges. For example, Europe is now crowded with formidable competitors. More than a dozen local Netflix-like rivals have sprung up there during the past few years—services such as Snap in Germany, Infinity in Italy, and CanalPlay in France have been busy locking in subscribers and content rights. And Amazon.com's Lovefilm is already the leading streaming service in Germany.

Content is another major consideration. Although Netflix is building its own portfolio of international content rights, European competitors already own exclusive in-country rights to many popular U.S. and non-U.S. shows. Netflix may also encounter local regulatory obstacles. Regulations in France, for instance, restrict services like Netflix from airing films until three years after they open nationally in theatres, and video services there are usually required to invest in film production in the country. Despite these challenges, however, Netflix CEO Reed Hastings seems unfazed. "We can still build a very successful business [in these new markets]," he says. Wherever Netflix goes, "I think the key is having unique content, a great reputation, a good value proposition," things at which Netflix excels.

TABLE 16.1	Indicators of Market Potential

Demographic Characteristics

Education

Population size and growth

Population age composition

Geographic Characteristics

Climate

Country size

Population density—urban, rural

Transportation structure and market accessibility

Economic Factors

GDP size and growth

Income distribution

Industrial infrastructure

Natural resources

Financial and human resources

Sociocultural Factors

Consumer lifestyles, beliefs, and values

Business norms and approaches

Cultural and social norms

Languages

Political and Legal Factors

National priorities

Political stability

Government attitudes toward global trade

Government bureaucracy

Monetary and trade regulations

Possible global markets should be ranked on several factors, including market size, market growth, the cost of doing business, competitive advantage, and risk level. The goal is to determine the potential of each market, using indicators such as those shown in Table 16.1. Then the marketer must decide which markets offer the greatest long-run return on investment.

◀◉ Simulate on MyMarketingLab

Managing in a Global Environment

◀◉ Simulate on MyMarketingLab

Global Marketing

Deciding How to Enter the Market LO2

Once a company has decided to sell in a foreign country, it must determine the best mode of entry. Its choices are *exporting*, *joint venturing*, and *direct investment*. Figure 16.2 shows three market entry strategies, along with the options each one offers. As the figure shows, each succeeding strategy involves more commitment and risk but also more control and potential profits.

FIGURE 16.2 Market Entry Strategies

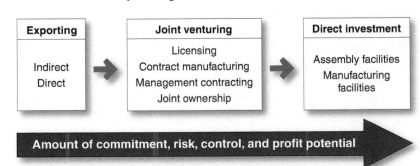

Exporting

The simplest way to enter a foreign market is through **exporting**. The company may passively export its surpluses from time to time, or it may make an active commitment to expand exports to a particular market. In either case, the company produces all its goods in its home country. It may or may not modify them for the export market. Exporting involves the least change in the company's product lines, organization, investments, or mission.

Companies typically start with *indirect exporting*, working through independent international marketing intermediaries. Indirect exporting involves less investment because the firm does not require an overseas marketing organization or network. It also involves less risk. International marketing intermediaries bring know-how and services to the relationship, so the seller normally makes fewer mistakes. Sellers may eventually move into *direct exporting*, whereby they handle their own exports. The investment and risk are somewhat greater in this strategy, but so is the potential return.

Joint Venturing

A second method of entering a foreign market is by **joint venturing**—joining with foreign companies to produce or market products or services. Joint venturing differs from exporting in that the company joins with a host country partner to sell or market abroad. It differs from direct investment in that an association is formed with someone in the foreign country. There are four types of joint ventures: *licensing*, *contract manufacturing*, *management contracting*, and *joint ownership*.

Licensing **Licensing** is a simple way for a manufacturer to enter international marketing. The company enters into an agreement with a licensee in the foreign market. For a fee or royalty payments, the licensee buys the right to use the company's manufacturing process, trademark, patent, trade secret, or other item of value. The company thus gains entry into a foreign market at little risk; at the same time, the licensee gains production expertise or a well-known product or name without having to start from scratch.

In Japan, Budweiser beer flows from Kirin breweries, and Mizkan produces Sunkist lemon juice, drinks, and dessert items. Coca-Cola markets internationally by licensing bottlers around the world and supplying them with the syrup needed to produce the product. Its global bottling partners range from the Coca-Cola Bottling Company of Saudi Arabia to Europe-based Coca-Cola Hellenic, which bottles and markets 136 Coca-Cola brands to 581 million people in 28 countries, from Italy and Greece to Nigeria and Russia.[28]

Licensing has potential disadvantages, however. The firm has less control over the licensee than it would over its own operations. Furthermore, if the licensee is very successful, the firm has given up these profits, and if and when the contract ends, it may find that it has created a competitor.

Exporting
Entering foreign markets by selling goods produced in the company's home country, often with little modification.

Joint venturing
Entering foreign markets by joining with foreign companies to produce or market a product or service.

Licensing
Entering foreign markets through developing an agreement with a licensee in the foreign market.

Exhibit 16.8 Licensing: In Japan, Sunkist lemon juice is produced by Mizkan.

Contract manufacturing
A joint venture in which a company contracts with manufacturers in a foreign market to produce its product or provide its service.

Contract Manufacturing Another option is **contract manufacturing**, in which the company makes agreements with manufacturers in the foreign market to produce its product or provide its service. Sears used this method in opening up department stores in Mexico and Spain, where it found qualified local manufacturers to produce many of the products it sells. The drawbacks of contract manufacturing are decreased control over the manufacturing process and loss of potential profits on manufacturing. The benefits are the chance to start faster, with less risk, and the later opportunity either to form a partnership with or buy out the local manufacturer.

Management contracting
A joint venture in which the domestic firm supplies the management know-how to a foreign company that supplies the capital; the domestic firm exports management services rather than products.

Management Contracting Under **management contracting**, the domestic firm provides the management know-how to a foreign company that supplies the capital. In other words, the domestic firm exports management services rather than products. Hilton uses this arrangement in managing hotels around the world. For example, the hotel chain operates DoubleTree by Hilton hotels in countries ranging from the U.K. and Italy to Peru and Costa Rica, to China, Russia, and Tanzania. The properties are locally owned, but Hilton manages the hotels with its world-renowned hospitality expertise.[29]

Management contracting is a low-risk method of getting into a foreign market, and it yields income from the beginning. The arrangement is even more attractive if the contracting firm has an option to buy some share in the managed company later on. The arrangement is not sensible, however, if the company can put its scarce management talent to better uses or if it can make greater profits by undertaking the whole venture. Management contracting also prevents the company from setting up its own operations for a period of time.

Joint ownership
A cooperative venture in which a company creates a local business with investors in a foreign market, who share ownership and control.

Joint Ownership **Joint ownership** ventures consist of one company joining forces with foreign investors to create a local business in which they share possession and control. A company may buy an interest in a local firm, or the two parties may form a new business venture. Joint ownership may be needed for economic or political reasons. For example, the firm may lack the financial, physical, or managerial resources to undertake the venture alone. Alternatively, a foreign government may require joint ownership as a condition for entry.

Often, companies form joint ownership ventures to merge their complementary strengths in developing a global marketing opportunity. For example, Chrysler's parent company, Fiat, formed a 50/50 joint venture with Chinese state-run Guangzhou Automobile Group (GAC) to produce Jeep vehicles in China. Jeep was one of the first Western auto brands sold in China, and the brand is well recognized and popular there. However, all the Jeeps sold in China have been imported from the United States and subject to steep import tariffs, driving Jeep prices to sky-high levels. For example, before the joint venture, a top-of-the-line Jeep Grand Cherokee sold for as much as $205 000 in China, more than triple its U.S. price. Under the joint venture, once approved, Chrysler and GAC will partner to produce Jeeps in China, avoiding tariffs, reducing production costs, and allowing competitive Jeep prices in the world's largest automotive market.[30]

Joint ownership has certain drawbacks, however. The partners may disagree over investment, marketing, or other policies. Whereas many North American firms like to reinvest earnings for growth, local firms often prefer to take out these earnings; and whereas North American firms emphasize the role of marketing, local investors may rely on selling.

Direct investment
Entering a foreign market by developing foreign-based assembly or manufacturing facilities.

Direct Investment

The biggest involvement in a foreign market comes through **direct investment**—the development of foreign-based assembly or manufacturing facilities. For example, Ford has made direct investments in several Asian countries, including India, China, and Thailand. It recently began building its second facility in India, a US$1 billion state-of-the-art manufacturing and engineering plant that will produce 240 000 cars a year, helping to satisfy Ford's burgeoning demand in India and other Asian markets. Similarly, Honda and Toyota have made substantial direct manufacturing investments in North America. For example, more than 87 percent of the Honda and Acura models sold in North America are made here. "Our fundamental philosophy is to produce where we sell," says a Honda executive.[31]

If a company has gained experience in exporting and if the foreign market is large enough, foreign production facilities offer many advantages. The firm may have lower costs in the form of cheaper labour or raw materials, foreign government investment incentives, and freight savings. The firm may also improve its image in the host country because it creates jobs.

Exhibit 16.9 Direct investment: Ford has made major direct investments in several countries, such as India, China, and Thailand, to help satisfy Ford's burgeoning demand in Asian markets.

SAM PANTHAKY/Getty Images

Generally, a firm develops a deeper relationship with the government, customers, local suppliers, and distributors, allowing it to adapt its products to the local market better. Finally, the firm keeps full control over the investment and therefore can develop manufacturing and marketing policies that serve its long-term international objectives.

The main disadvantage of direct investment is that the firm faces many risks, such as restricted or devalued currencies, falling markets, or government changes. In some cases, a firm has no choice but to accept these risks if it wants to operate in the host country.

Deciding on the Global Marketing Program LO3

Companies that operate in one or more foreign markets must decide how much, if at all, to adapt their marketing strategies and programs to local conditions. At one extreme are global companies that use **standardized global marketing**, essentially using the same marketing strategy approaches and marketing mix worldwide. At the other extreme is **adapted global marketing**. In this case, the producer adjusts the marketing strategy and mix elements to each target market, resulting in more costs but hopefully producing a larger market share and return.

The question of whether to adapt or standardize the marketing strategy and program has been much debated over the years. On the one hand, some global marketers believe that technology is making the world a smaller place, and consumer needs around the world are becoming more similar. This paves the way for global brands and standardized global marketing. Global branding and standardization, in turn, result in greater brand power and reduced costs from economies of scale.

On the other hand, the marketing concept holds that marketing programs will be more effective if tailored to the unique needs of each targeted customer group. If this concept applies within a country, it should apply even more across international markets. Despite global convergence, consumers in different countries still have widely varied cultural backgrounds. They still differ significantly in their needs and wants, spending power, product preferences, and shopping patterns. Because these differences are hard to

Standardized global marketing
An international marketing strategy that basically uses the same marketing strategy and mix in all of the company's international markets.

Adapted global marketing
An international marketing approach that adjusts the marketing strategy and mix elements to each international target market, which creates more costs but hopefully produces a larger market share and return.

◄◉┤**Simulate** on MyMarketingLab

Managing in a Global Environment

◄◉┤**Simulate** on MyMarketingLab

Global Marketing

change, most marketers today adapt their products, prices, channels, and promotions to fit consumer desires in each country.

However, global standardization is not an all-or-nothing proposition. It's a matter of degree. Most international marketers suggest that companies should "think globally but act locally." They should seek a balance between standardization and adaptation, leveraging global brand recognition but adapting their marketing, products, and operations to specific markets. For example, cosmetics giant L'Oréal and its brands are truly global. But the company's outstanding international success comes from achieving a balance that adapts and differentiates brands to make them responsive to local needs while integrating them across world markets to optimize their global impact (see Marketing@Work 16.1). "The best brand organizations drive a single-minded brand purpose and then challenge and empower local marketers to develop the best activation mix to bring that to fruition in every market," says a global branding expert.[32]

Collectively, local brands still account for the overwhelming majority of consumers' purchases. "The vast majority of people still lead very local lives," says a global analyst. "By all means go global, but the first thing you have to do is win on the ground. You have to go local." Another analyst agrees: "You need to respect local culture and become part of it." A global brand must "engage with consumers in a way that feels local to them." Simon Clift, former chief marketing officer at global consumer-goods giant Unilever, put it this way: "We're trying to strike a balance between being mindlessly global and hopelessly local."[33]

McDonald's operates this way: It uses the same basic fast-food look, layout, and operating model in its restaurants around the world but adapts its menu and design to local tastes. For example, McDonald's France uses the power of its global brand and operating model but has redefined itself as a French company that adapts to the needs and preferences of French consumers:

> "France—the land of haute cuisine, fine wine, and cheese—would be the last place you would expect to find a thriving [McDonald's]," opines one observer. Yet the fast-food giant has turned France into its second-most profitable world market. Although a McDonald's in Paris might at first seem a lot like one in Chicago, McDonald's has carefully adapted its French operations to the preferences of local customers. At the most basic level, although a majority of revenues still come from burgers and fries, McDonald's France has changed its menu to please the French palate. For example, it offers up burgers with French cheeses such as chèvre, cantel, and bleu, topped off with whole-grain French mustard sauce. French consumers love baguettes, so McDonald's bakes them fresh in its restaurants and sells them in oh-so-French McBaguette sandwiches. And in response to the growing French trend for healthy eating, the menu in France includes reduced-salt french fries, fresh fruit, and "le Big Mac"—the McDonald's classic but with a whole-wheat-bun option.
>
> But perhaps the biggest difference isn't in the food, but in the design of the restaurants themselves, which have been adapted to suit French lifestyles. For example, French mealtimes tend to be longer, with more food consumed per sitting. So McDonald's has refined its restaurant interiors to create a comfortable, welcoming environment where customers want to linger and perhaps order an additional coffee or dessert. McDonald's even provides table-side service. As a result, the average French McDonald's customer spends about four times what a North American customer spends per visit.[34]

ERIC PIERMONT/AFP/Newscom

Exhibit 16.10 Think globally, act locally: By leveraging the power of its global brand but constantly adapting to the needs and preferences of French consumers and their culture, McDonald's has turned France into its second-most-profitable world market.

MARKETING@WORK 16.1

L'Oréal: "The United Nations of Beauty"

How does a French company successfully market an American version of a Korean skin-beautifier under a French brand name in Australia? Ask L'Oréal, which sells more than $30 billion worth of cosmetics, hair care products, skin care concoctions, and fragrances each year in 150 countries, making it the world's biggest cosmetics marketer. L'Oréal sells its brands globally by understanding how they appeal to varied cultural nuances of beauty in specific local markets. Then it finds the best balance between standardizing its brands for global impact and adapting them to meet local needs and desires.

L'Oréal is as global as a company gets. With offices spread across 130 nations and more than half of its sales coming from markets outside Europe and North America, the company no longer has a clearly defined home market. L'Oréal's well-known brands originated in a half dozen or more different cultures, including French (L'Oréal Paris, Garnier, Lancôme), American (Maybelline, Kiehl's, SoftSheen-Carson, Ralph Lauren, Redkin), British (The Body Shop), Italian (Giorgio Armani), and Japanese (Shu Uemura). The master global marketer is the uncontested world leader in makeup, skin care, and hair colouring, and second only to P&G in hair care.

L'Oréal's global mastery starts with a corps of highly multicultural managers. The company is famous for building global brand teams around managers who have deep backgrounds in several cultures. L'Oréal managers around the world bring diverse cultural perspectives to their brands as if they were, say, German, or American, or Chinese—or all three at once. As explained by one Indian-American-French manager of a team that launched a men's skin care line in Southeast Asia, "I cannot think about things one way. I have a stock of references in different languages: English, Hindi, and French. I read books in three different languages, meet people from different countries, eat food from different [cultures], and so on."

For example, a French-Irish-Cambodian skin care manager noticed that, in Europe, face creams tended to be either "tinted" (considered makeup) or "lifting" (considered skin care). In Asia, however, many face creams combine both traits. Recognizing the growing popularity of Asian beauty trends in Europe, the manager and his team developed a tinted lifting cream for the French market, a product that proved highly successful.

L'Oréal digs deep to understand what beauty means to consumers in different parts of the world. It outspends all major competitors on R&D, painstakingly researching beauty and personal care behaviours unique to specific locales. L'Oréal has set up R&D centres all over the world, perfecting a local observation approach it calls "geocosmetics." This science is fuelled with insights gained through everything from in-home visits to observations made in "bathroom laboratories" equipped with high-tech gadgetry. L'Oréal's research produces precise information about regional beauty and hygiene rituals, as well as about local conditions and constraints that affect the use of its products, such as humidity and temperature:

> How many minutes does a Chinese woman devote to her morning beauty routine? How do people wash their hair in Bangkok? How many brush strokes does a Japanese woman or a French woman use to apply mascara? These beauty rituals, repeated thousands of times, are inherently cultural. Passed on by tradition, influenced by climate and by local living conditions, they strive to achieve an ideal of perfection that is different from one country and from one continent to the next. They provide an incredibly rich source of information for L'Oréal. Behind these rituals, there are physiological realities: fine, straight, and short eyelashes cannot be made up the same way as thick, curled, and long lashes.

L'Oréal uses such detailed insights to create products and positioning for brands in local markets. "Beauty is less and less one size fits all," says a L'Oréal executive in China. "You have to have an answer for very different needs." For example, more than 260 scientists now work in L'Oréal's Shanghai research centre, tailoring products ranging from lipstick to herbal cleaners to cucumber toners for Chinese tastes.

At the same time that understanding the minute details of local customer behaviour helps L'Oréal be responsive to specific market needs, it also lets the company achieve global scale by integrating brands across world cultures. For example, consider Elséve Total Reparação, a hair care line initially developed at L'Oréal's labs in Rio de Janeiro to address specific hair problems described by Brazilian women. In Brazil, more than half of all women have long, dry, dull, and very curly hair, resulting from the humid Brazilian climate, exposure to the sun, frequent washing, and smoothing and straightening treatments. Elséve Total Reparação was an immediate hit in Brazil, and L'Oréal quickly rolled it out to other South American and Latin American markets. The company then tracked down other global locales with climate characteristics and hair care rituals similar to those faced by Brazilian women. Subsequently, L'Oréal launched the brand as Elséve Total Repair in numerous European, Indian, and other Southeast Asian markets, where consumers greeted it with similar enthusiasm.

Such adaptation often plays out across multiple L'Oréal brands—which takes us back to that Korean skin-beautifier sold under a French brand in Australia mentioned in the opening paragraph. Blemish Balm Cream (BB Cream) was originally created by L'Oréal dermatologists in Korea to soothe skin and hide minor blemishes. It quickly became a high-flying Korean brand. However, applying their deep knowledge of skin colours, treatments, and makeup

Getty Image

Exhibit 16.11   Global-local balance: Cosmetics and beauty care giant L'Oréal balances local brand responsiveness and global brand impact, making it "The United Nations of Beauty."

Big Apple image played well with the midprice positioning of the workaday makeup brand globally. The makeover soon earned Maybelline a 20 percent market share in its category in Western Europe. The young urban positioning also hit the mark in Asia, where few women realized that the trendy "New York" Maybelline brand belonged to French cosmetics giant L'Oréal.

Thus, L'Oréal and its brands are truly global. But the company's international success comes from achieving a global-local balance that adapts and differentiates brands in local markets while optimizing their impact across global markets. L'Oréal is one of the few companies that have achieved both local brand responsiveness and global brand integration. When a former CEO once addressed a UNESCO conference, nobody batted an eyelid when he described L'Oréal as "The United Nations of Beauty."

Sources: Based on information from Hae-Jung Hong and Yves Doz, "L'Oréal Masters Multiculturalism," *Harvard Business Review*, June 2013, pp. 114–119; Liza Lin, "L'Oréal Puts on a Happy Face in China," *Bloomberg Businessweek*, April 1–April 7, 2013, pp. 25–26; and www.lorealusa.com/Article. aspx?topcode=CorpTopic_RI_CustomerInnovation and www. lorealusa.com/research-innovation/when-the-diversity-of-types-of-beauty-inspiresscience/stories-of-multicultural-innovations. aspx, accessed September 2014.

worldwide, L'Oréal researchers developed a successful new-generation BB Cream adapted to conditions and skin colours in Canadian and U.S. markets (where BB stands for "beauty balm") and launched it under the Maybelline New York brand. Still not finished, L'Oréal created yet another local version for Europe under the Garnier brand, which it also introduced in other world markets, including Australia.

L'Oréal doesn't just adapt its product formulations globally. It also adapts brand positioning and marketing to international needs and expectations. For example, nearly 20 years ago, the company bought stodgy American makeup producer Maybelline. To reinvigorate and globalize the brand, it moved the unit's headquarters from Tennessee to New York City and added "New York" to the label. The resulting urban, street-smart,

Product

Five strategies are used for adapting product and marketing communication strategies to a global market (see Figure 16.3).[35] We first discuss the three product strategies and then turn to the two communication strategies.

Straight product extension

Marketing a product in a foreign market without making any changes to the product.

Straight product extension means marketing a product in a foreign market without making any changes to the product. Top management tells its marketing people, "Take the product as is and find customers for it." The first step, however, should be to find out whether foreign consumers use that product and what form they prefer.

FIGURE 16.3 Five Global Product and Communications Strategies

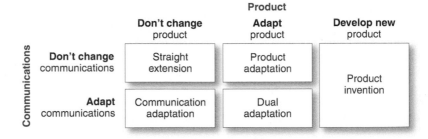

		Product		
		Don't change product	**Adapt** product	**Develop new** product
Communications	**Don't change** communications	Straight extension	Product adaptation	Product invention
	Adapt communications	Communication adaptation	Dual adaptation	

Straight extension has been successful in some cases and disastrous in others. Apple iPads, Gillette razors, Black & Decker tools, and even 7-Eleven Slurpees are all sold successfully in about the same form around the world. But when General Foods introduced its standard powdered JELL-O in the British market, it discovered that British consumers prefer a solid wafer or cake form. Likewise, Philips began to make a profit in Japan only after it reduced the size of its coffeemakers to fit into smaller Japanese kitchens and its shavers to fit smaller Japanese hands. And Panasonic's refrigerator sales in China surged 10-fold in a single year after it shaved the width of its appliances by 15 percent to fit smaller Chinese kitchens.[36] Straight extension is tempting because it involves no additional product development costs, manufacturing changes, or new promotion. But it can be costly in the long run if products fail to satisfy consumers in specific global markets.

Product adaptation involves changing the product to meet local requirements, conditions, or wants. For example, Kraft has adapted its popular Oreo cookie to the unique tastes of consumers all around the world, whether it's mango-and-orange-flavoured Oreos in the Asia Pacific region, green tea Oreos in China, a chocolate and peanut variety in Indonesia, or banana and dulce de leche in Argentina. Chinese Oreos are less sweet than the North American standard; Oreos in India are less bitter.[37]

Product adaptation
Adapting a product to meet local conditions or wants in foreign markets.

As another example, although the North American and European versions of the feisty little Fiat 500 might look a lot alike, Fiat has made stem-to-stern adaptations in its North American model to meet Canadian and U.S. safety standards and buyer expectations. To name just a few modifications, the North American Fiat 500 has a redesigned engine that offers the power demanded by consumers while simultaneously providing the better gas mileage and lower emissions required by the countries' regulations. The gas tank is 40 percent larger to accommodate the longer driving distances that are typical in North America, and there's lots more insulation in the North American car to keep it quiet enough for consumers. Another big difference—the cupholders:

> A silly matter to Europeans, but vital to North Americans, the North American Fiat 500 has an enlarged pod of holders up front to fit bigger drinks, instead of the small European holders, plus two additional holders at the rear of the floor console. The in-car beverage concept is so foreign to Europeans that the 500 design team didn't understand the need for more and bigger holders—until one engineer drew a cartoon of an American wearing one of those gimmick hats that hold two beer cans and have long tubes at straws. Then everybody said, "Ah, yes."[38]

Product invention
Creating new products or services for foreign markets.

Product invention consists of creating something new to meet the needs of consumers in a given country. As markets have gone global, companies ranging from appliance manufacturers and carmakers to candy and soft drink producers have developed products that meet the special purchasing needs of low-income consumers in developing economies. For example, Ford developed the economical, low-priced Figo model especially for entry-level consumers in India; GM created the inexpensive Baojun for China (the name means "treasured horse"). Chinese appliance producer Haier developed sturdier washing machines for rural users in emerging markets, where it found that lighter-duty machines often became clogged with mud when farmers used them to clean vegetables as well as clothes.[39]

FIAT®, FIAT is a registered trademark of FCA Group Marketing S.p.A., used under license by FCA US LLC.

Exhibit 16.12 Product adaptation: The European and North American versions of the feisty little Fiat 500 look pretty much alike. But to meet the preferences of Canadian and U.S. buyers, Fiat adapted the car's interior from stem to stern, including an enlarged pod of bigger cupholders that are so important to North Americans.

Similarly, Finnish mobile phone maker Nokia has created full-featured but rugged and low-cost phones especially designed for the harsher living conditions faced by less-affluent consumers in large developing countries such as India, China, and Kenya. For instance, it developed dustproof keypads, which are crucial in dry, hot countries with many unpaved roads. Some phones have built-in radio antennas for areas where radio is the main source of entertainment. And after learning that poor people often share their phones, the company developed handsets with multiple address books.

Promotion

Companies can either adopt the same communication strategy they use in the home market or change it for each local market. Consider advertising messages. Some global companies use a standardized advertising theme around the world. For example, Chevrolet recently swapped out its American-focused "Chevy Runs Deep" positioning and advertising theme with a more global "Find New Roads" theme. The new theme is one "that works in all markets," says a GM marketing executive. "The theme has meaning in mature markets like the U.S. and Canada as well as emerging markets like Russia and India, where the potential for continued growth is the greatest." The time is right for a more globally consistent Chevy brand message. Chevrolet sells cars in more the 140 countries and had over 20 global vehicle launches last year.[40]

Of course, even in highly standardized communications campaigns, some adjustments might be required for language and cultural differences. For example, in Western markets, fast-casual clothing retailer H&M runs fashion ads with models showing liberal amounts of bare skin. But in the Middle East, where attitudes toward public nudity are more conservative, the retailer runs the same ads digitally adapted to better cover its models.

Global companies often have difficulty crossing the language barrier, with results ranging from mild embarrassment to outright failure. Seemingly innocuous brand names and advertising phrases can take on unintended or hidden meanings when translated into other languages. For example, Interbrand of London, the firm that created household names such as Prozac and Acura, recently developed a brand-name "hall of shame" list, which contained these and other foreign brand names you're never likely to see inside the local Sobeys supermarket: Krapp toilet paper (Denmark), Plopp chocolate (Scandinavia), Crapsy Fruit cereal (France), Poo curry powder (Argentina), and Pschitt lemonade (France). Similarly, advertising themes often lose—or gain—something in the translation. In Chinese, the KFC slogan "finger-lickin' good" came out as "eat your fingers off." And Motorola's Hellomoto ringtone sounds like "Hello, Fatty" in India. Marketers must be watchful to avoid such mistakes, taking great care when localizing their brand names and messages to specific global markets. In important but culturally different markets such as China, finding just the right name can make or break a brand (see Marketing@Work 16.2).

Communication adaptation
A global communication strategy of fully adapting advertising messages to local markets.

Other companies follow a strategy of **communication adaptation**, fully adapting their advertising messages to local markets. Consumer products marketer Unilever does this for many of its brands. For example, whereas ads for Unilever toothpaste brands in Western markets might emphasize anything from whiter teeth or fresher breath to greater sex appeal, ads in Africa take a more basic educational approach, emphasizing the importance of brushing twice a day. And Unilever adapts the positioning, formulation, and appeals for its Sunsilk Lively Clean & Fresh shampoo to serve the varying needs of consumers in different markets. Whereas its standard Western shampoo ads tend to show young women flirtatiously tossing their freshly washed locks over their shoulders, Sunsilk's Lively Clean & Fresh ads in Malaysia show no hair at all. Instead, they feature modern young women wearing tudungs—traditional Muslim

MARKETING@WORK 16.2

Localizing Chinese Brand Names: Very Important but Notoriously Tricky

After a long day's work, an average upscale Beijinger can't wait to dash home, lace on a comfortable pair of Enduring and Persevering, pop the top on a refreshing can of Tasty Fun, then hop into his Dashing Speed and head to the local tavern for a frosty glass of Happiness Power with friends. Translation? In China, those are the brand-name meanings for Nike, Coca-Cola, Mercedes, and Heineken, respectively.

To Westerners, such names sound pretty silly, but to brands doing business in China, the world's biggest and fastest growing consumer market, they are no laughing matter. Perhaps more than anywhere else in the world, brand names in China take on deep significance. Finding just the right name can make or break a brand. "Often, a company's most important marketing decision in China is localizing its name," asserts one global branding analyst. "It's also a notoriously tricky one."

Ideally, to maintain global consistency, the Chinese name should sound similar to the original, while at the same time conveying the brand's benefits in meaningful symbolic terms. Nike's Chinese brand name, Nai ke, does this well. Not only does it sound the same when pronounced in Chinese, its "Enduring and Persevering" meaning powerfully encapsulates the "Just Do It" essence of the Nike brand the world over. Similarly, P&G's Tide is Taizi in China, which translates to "gets out the dirt," a perfect moniker for a tough-acting detergent. Coca-Cola's Chinese name—Kekou ke le—dates all the way back to 1928. It not only sounds much like the English name, but the Chinese symbols also convey happiness in the mouth, a close fit to Coca-Cola's current "open happiness" positioning. Other names that wear well on Chinese ears while also conveying a brand's essence include Lay's snack foods—Le shi ("happy things"); Reebok—Ruibu ("quick steps"); and Colgate—Gau lu jie ("revealing superior cleanliness").

Chinese brand names can convey subtle meanings that might not be apparent to Western sensibilities. For example, "Dashing Speed" seems appropriate enough for an upscale automobile brand like Mercedes. So does BMW's name—Bao Ma—which translates to "Precious Horse." However, in China, "precious" has a feminine connotation, whereas "dashing speed" is more masculine. This works out well for both carmakers, which target different genders among China's upper crust. For instance, BMW is a market leader among affluent Chinese women.

Some brand names translate naturally. For example, when Garnier introduced its Clear shampoo in China, it lucked out. The Chinese word for "clear"—qing—is one of a select few Chinese words with unusually positive associations that are used in many brand names. Garnier added the word yang, which means "flying" or "scattering to the wind." According to the director of Garnier's brand consultancy, the Qing Yang brand name connotes "very light, healthy, and happy—think of hair in the air," just what the brand intends. Other universally positive Chinese words commonly found in brand names include le and xi (happy), li (strength or power), ma (horse), and fu (lucky). Thus, Kia sells one model in China named Qian li ma, or "thousand kilometre horse," suggesting unusual strength.

There was a time when Western companies entering China simply created a brand name that was phonetically similar to the domestic name, even if it had no meaning in the Chinese language. In fact, such obviously foreign looking and sounding names often communicated a sense of Western cachet. For example, Cadillac went with Ka di la ke—a meaningless group of sounds that gave status to the luxury brand. And McDonald's got away with Mai dang lao, a term that sounds like the English version but whose characters translate into gibberish— "wheat," "should," and "labour." Other global companies with short names such as IBM or Gap simply expect consumers to learn their Western names.

Today, however, with so many foreign brands entering the crowded Chinese market, most companies expect more of their Chinese brand names. If Chinese consumers can't pronounce a name or don't know what it stands for, they are much less likely to buy it or talk about it with others, in person or in social media. Instead, with some work, companies can come up with names that will engage and inspire buyers. In China, it's not Subway, it's Sai bai wei—"better than 100 tastes." It's not Marriott but Wan Hao, or "10 000 wealthy elites."

However, finding the right names and characters can be a daunting challenge. Brand-name development in China has become more of a science than an art, involving global branding consultants, computer software, linguistic analysis, and extensive consumer testing. Some global names require careful recrafting. For example, Microsoft had to rethink the introduction of its Bing search engine in China,

Exhibit 16.13 Brand names in China take on deep significance. Coca-Cola's Chinese name, when pronounced, sounds much like the English name, and the Chinese symbols convey "tasty fun" or "happiness in the mouth," a close fit to Coca-Cola's current worldwide "open happiness" positioning.

© Stuwdamdorp/Alamy

where the most common translations of the character pronounced "bing" are words like *defect* or *virus*, not good associations for a digital product. Microsoft changed the name of its product in China to Bi ying, which means "very certain to respond." Still, the brand is having difficulty shaking the resemblance to the original name.

Similarly, S.C. Johnson belatedly renamed its popular Mr. Muscle line of cleaners to Mr. Powerful (Weimeng xiansheng) in China, where Mr. Muscle had a less compelling second meaning—"Mr. Chicken Meat." And French automaker Peugeot thought it had a winning brand name with Biao zhi, only to learn too late that it was too close to *biaozi*, slang for prostitute. It's no surprise that the brand generated more off-colour jokes than sales.

Sources: "Lost in Translation? Pick Your Chinese Brand Name Carefully," *Shanghaiist*, March 28, 2014, http://shanghaiist.com/2014/03/28/hutong-school-pick-your-chinese-brand-name-carefully.php; Michael Wines, "Picking Brand Names in China Is a Business Itself," *New York Times*, November 12, 2011, p. A4; Carly Chalmers, "12 Amazing Translations of Chinese Brand Names," *todaytranslations*, August 27, 2013, www.todaytranslations.com/blog/12-amazing-translations-of-chinese-brand-names; and Angela Doland, "Why Western Companies Like LinkedIn Need Chinese Brand Names," *Advertising Age*, March 5, 2014, adage.com/print/291960.

headscarves that completely cover the hair. To tap the large and growing Malaysian Islamic market, Unilever positions Lively Clean & Fresh directly to the "lifestyle of the tudung wearer" as a remedy for the problem of excess hair and scalp oil that wearing a tudung can cause.[41]

Media also need to be adapted internationally, since media availability and regulations vary from country to country. TV advertising time is very limited in Europe, for instance, ranging from four hours a day in France to none in Scandinavian countries. Advertisers must buy time months in advance, and they have little control over airtimes. However, mobile phone ads are much more widely accepted in Europe and Asia than in Canada and the United States. Magazines also vary in effectiveness. For example, magazines are a major medium in Italy but a minor one in Austria. Newspapers are national in the United Kingdom but only local in Spain.[42]

Unilever plc

Exhibit 16.14 Adapting advertising messages: Whereas Western ads for Unilever toothpaste brands might emphasize whiter teeth, fresher breath, or greater sex appeal, its ads in Africa take a more educational approach, emphasizing healthy teeth.

Price

Companies also face many considerations in setting their international prices. For example, how might Makita price its tools globally? It could set a uniform price globally, but this amount would be too high in poor countries and not high enough in rich ones. It could charge what consumers in each country would bear, but this strategy ignores differences in the actual costs from country to country. Finally, the company could use a standard markup of its costs everywhere, but this approach might price Makita out of the market in some countries where costs are high.

Regardless of how companies go about pricing their products, their foreign prices will probably be higher than their domestic prices for comparable products. An Apple iPad 3 that sells for $499 in the United States goes for $612 in the United Kingdom. Why? Apple faces a *price escalation* problem. It must add the cost of transportation, tariffs, importer margin, wholesaler margin, and retailer margin to its factory price. Depending on these added costs, a product may have to sell for two to five times as much in another country to make the same profit.

To overcome this problem when selling to less-affluent consumers in developing countries, many companies make simpler or smaller versions of their products that can be sold at lower prices. Others have introduced new, more affordable brands in emerging markets. For example, Levi launched the Denizen brand, created for teens and young adults in emerging markets such as China, India, and Brazil who cannot afford Levi's-branded jeans. The name combines the first four letters of *denim* with *zen*, a word with Japanese and Chinese roots that means "meditative state" or "escape from the hustle and bustle of everyday life."[43]

Recent economic and technological forces have had an impact on global pricing. For example, the Internet is making global price differences more obvious. When firms sell their wares online, customers can see how much products sell for in different countries. They can even order a given product directly from the company location or dealer offering the lowest price. This is forcing companies toward more standardized international pricing.

Nelson Ching/Getty Images USA, Inc.

Exhibit 16.15 International pricing: Levi Strauss launched the Denizen brand, created for teens and young adults in emerging markets such as China, India, and Brazil who cannot afford Levi's-branded jeans.

Distribution Channels

An international company must take a **whole-channel view** of the problem of distributing products to final consumers. Figure 16.4 shows the two major links between the seller and the final buyer. The first link, *channels between nations*, moves company products from points of production to the borders of countries within which they are sold. The second link, *channels within nations*, moves products from their market entry points to the final consumers. The whole-channel view takes into account the entire global supply chain and marketing channel. It recognizes that to compete well internationally, the company must effectively design and manage an entire *global value delivery network*.

Channels of distribution within countries vary greatly from nation to nation. There are large differences in the numbers and types of intermediaries serving each country market and in the transportation infrastructure serving these intermediaries. For example, whereas large-scale retail chains dominate the North American scene, most of the retailing in other countries is done by small, independent retailers. In India or Indonesia, millions of retailers operate tiny shops or sell in open markets.

Even in world markets containing similar types of sellers, retailing practices can vary widely. For example, you'll find plenty of Walmarts, Carrefours, Tescos, and other retail

Whole-channel view
Designing international channels that take into account the entire global supply chain and marketing channel, forging an effective global value delivery network.

FIGURE 16.4 Whole-Channel Concept for International Marketing

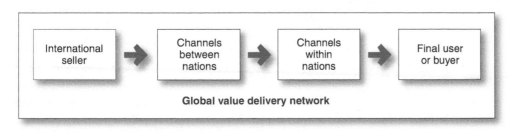

Darcy Holdorf Photography

Exhibit 16.16 Distribution channels vary from nation to nation. Whereas consumer brands sold in Western superstores like Walmart or Target rely largely on self-service, these brands in China hire armies of uniformed in-store promoters to dispense samples and pitch their products in person.

superstores in major Chinese cities. But whereas consumer brands sold in such stores in Western markets rely largely on self-service, brands in China hire armies of uniformed in-store promoters—called "promoter girls" or "push girls"—to dispense samples and pitch their products person to person. In a Beijing Walmart, on any given weekend, you'll find 100 or more such promoters acquainting customers with products from Kraft, Unilever, P&G, Johnson & Johnson, and a slew of local competitors. "Chinese consumers know the brand name through media," says the director of a Chinese retail marketing service, "but they want to feel the product and get a detailed understanding before they make a purchase."[44]

Similarly, as we learned in the story about its ventures in Africa, Coca-Cola adapts its distribution methods to meet local challenges in global markets. For example, in Montevideo, Uruguay, where larger vehicles are challenged by traffic, parking, and pollution difficulties, Coca-Cola purchased 30 small, efficient, three-wheeled ZAP alternative transportation trucks. The little trucks average about one-fifth the fuel consumption and scoot around congested city streets with greater ease. In rural areas, Coca-Cola uses a manual delivery process. In China, an army of more than 10 000 Coca-Cola sales reps makes regular visits to small retailers, often on foot or bicycle. To reach the most isolated spots, the company even relies on teams of delivery donkeys. In Tanzania, 93 percent of Coca-Cola's products are manually delivered via pushcarts and bicycles.[45]

Deciding on the Global Marketing Organization LO4

Companies manage their international marketing activities in at least three different ways: Most companies first organize an export department, then create an international division, and finally become a global organization.

A firm normally gets into international marketing by simply shipping out its goods. If its international sales expand, the company will establish an *export department* with a sales manager and a few assistants. As sales increase, the export department can expand to include various marketing services so that it can actively go after business. If the firm moves into joint ventures or direct investment, the export department will no longer be adequate.

Many companies get involved in several international markets and ventures. A company may export to one country, license to another, have a joint ownership venture in a third, and own a subsidiary in a fourth. Sooner or later it will create *international divisions* or subsidiaries to handle all its international activity.

International divisions are organized in a variety of ways. An international division's corporate staff consists of marketing, manufacturing, research, finance, planning, and personnel specialists. It plans for and provides services to various operating units, which can be organized in one of three ways. They can be *geographical organizations*, with country managers who are responsible for salespeople, sales branches, distributors, and licensees in their respective countries. Or the operating units can be *world product groups*, each responsible for worldwide sales of different product groups. Finally, operating units can be *international subsidiaries*, each responsible for their own sales and profits.

Many firms have passed beyond the international division stage and are truly *global organizations*. For example, consider Reckitt Benckiser (RB), a $15.5 billion European producer of household, health, and personal care products and consumer goods with a stable full of familiar brands (Air Wick, Lysol, Woolite, Calgon, Mucinex, Clearasil, French's, and many others—see www.rb.com):

> RB operates in more than 60 countries. Its top 400 managers represent 53 different nationalities. The company is headquartered in the United Kingdom and its CEO is Indian. Its U.S. business is run by a Dutchman, its Russian business by an Italian, and its Australian business by a Brazilian. "Most of our top managers ... view themselves as global citizens rather than as citizens of any given nation," says RB's chief executive officer.

> RB recently relocated several of its operations to put key marketers in key countries within their regions. For example, it recently moved its Latin American headquarters from Miami to Sao Paulo, Brazil. The company has spent the past decade building a culture of global mobility because it thinks that's one of the best ways to generate new ideas and create global entrepreneurs. And it has paid off. Products launched from 2010 to 2012—all the result of global cross-fertilization—account for 35–40 percent of net revenue. Over the past few years, even during the economic downturn, the company has outperformed its rivals—P&G, Unilever, and Colgate—in growth.[46]

Exhibit 16.17 European household, health, and consumer-goods producer Reckitt Benckiser has a truly global organization. "Most of our top managers . . . view themselves as global citizens rather than as citizens of any given nation."

Reckitt Benckise

Global organizations don't think of themselves as national marketers that sell abroad but as global marketers. The top corporate management and staff plan worldwide manufacturing facilities, marketing policies, financial flows, and logistical systems. The global operating units report directly to the chief executive or the executive committee of the organization, not to the head of an international division. Executives are trained in worldwide operations, not just domestic *or* international operations. Global companies recruit management from many countries, buy components and supplies where they cost the least, and invest where the expected returns are greatest.

Today, major companies must become more global if they hope to compete. As foreign companies successfully invade their domestic markets, companies must move more aggressively into foreign markets. They will have to change from companies that treat their international operations as secondary to companies that view the entire world as a single borderless market.

BP USA

If the main goal of companies is to increase wealth, then at some point along that growth trajectory an international opportunity will beckon. For Vancouver-based Boston Pizza, the notion of expanding into the United States appeared to be a no-brainer. Stable economy, federal trade partners, trade agreement, and of course the shared cultural love for pizza and sports bars—all factored into the mix. BP began this expansion in 1998 with a location in Arizona, and has since grown to over 50 restaurants. However, don't cross the border looking for "Boston Pizza"—you won't find any of them.

The chain was rebranded as "Boston's The Gourmet Pizza" in order to emphasize and "communicate the superior product offering," according to a company statement. Subtle perhaps, especially when, except for the sign hanging outside, the restaurants look the same. However, therein lies one of the important considerations when planning an expansion into international markets, even those as similar as Canada and the United States: Know your market.

In a sea of billion-dollar pizza brands dominated by Dominos and Pizza Hut, it was important for the brand to differentiate itself in the United States within its very name. Several other socio-geographical influencers have helped give Boston's its own uniquely American feel, while still maintaining the values instilled by its parent Canadian company.

QUESTIONS

1. Visit www.bostons.com and www.bostonpizza.com. Open up the "Menu" link in both websites and compare and contrast the food items offered. Make note of items that aren't shared between the two chains, and speculate as to why this is so.
2. Despite sharing the world's longest peaceful international border, there are differences in the socio-cultural makeup of Canada and the United States. Identify the most obvious differences, and determine whether these have anything to do with the differences in product offerings or promotional tactics on either side of the border.

REVIEWING THE CONCEPTS

 LO1 **Discuss how the international trade system and the economic, political-legal, and cultural environments affect a company's international marketing decisions.**

A company must understand the *global marketing environment*, especially the international trade system. It should assess each foreign market's *economic, political-legal,* and *cultural characteristics.* The company can then decide whether it wants to go abroad and consider the potential risks and benefits. It must decide on the volume of international sales it wants, how many countries it wants to market in, and which specific markets it wants to enter. These decisions call for weighing the probable returns against the level of risk.

 LO2 **Describe three key approaches to entering international markets.**

The company must decide how to enter each chosen market—whether through *exporting, joint venturing,* or *direct investment.* Many companies start as exporters, move to joint ventures, and finally make a direct investment in foreign markets. In *exporting*, the company enters a foreign market by sending and selling products through international marketing intermediaries (indirect exporting) or the company's own department, branch, or sales representatives or agents (direct exporting). When establishing a *joint venture*, a company enters foreign markets by joining with foreign companies to produce or market a product or service. In *licensing*, the company enters a foreign market by contracting with a licensee in the foreign market and offering the right to use a manufacturing process, trademark, patent, trade secret, or other item of value for a fee or royalty.

 LO3 **Explain how companies adapt their marketing strategies and mixes for international markets.**

Companies must also decide how much their marketing strategies and their products, promotion, price, and channels should be adapted for each foreign market. At one extreme, global companies use *standardized global marketing* worldwide. Others use *adapted global marketing*, in which they adjust the marketing strategy and mix to each target market, bearing more costs but hoping for a larger market share and return. However, global standardization is not an all-or-nothing proposition. It's a matter of degree. Most international marketers suggest that companies should "think globally but act locally"—that they should seek a balance between globally standardized strategies and locally adapted marketing mix tactics.

 LO4 **Identify the three major forms of international marketing organization.**

The company must develop an effective organization for international marketing. Most firms start with an *export department* and graduate to an *international division.* A few become *global organizations*, with worldwide marketing planned and managed by the top officers of the company. Global organizations view the entire world as a single, borderless market.

MyMarketingLab

Study, practise, and explore real marketing situations with these helpful resources:

- **Interactive Lesson Presentations:** Work through interactive presentations and assessments to test your knowledge of marketing concepts.
- **Study Plan:** Check your understanding of chapter concepts with self-study quizzes.
- **Dynamic Study Modules:** Work through adaptive study modules on your computer, tablet, or mobile device.
- **Simulations:** Practise decision-making in simulated marketing environments.

DISCUSSION QUESTIONS

1. Explain what is meant by the term *global firm* and list the major decisions involved in international marketing.

2. Discuss the four types of country industrial structures and the opportunities each offers to international marketers.

3. Discuss the three ways to enter foreign markets. Which is the best?

4. Discuss the strategies used for adapting products to a global market. Which strategy is best?

5. Discuss how companies manage their international marketing activities.

CRITICAL THINKING EXERCISES

1. Canada has a number of free trade agreements (FTAs) with several countries. Visit the Government of Canada website "Foreign Affairs, Trade and Development Canada" (www.international.gc.ca/trade-agreements-accords-commerciaux/agr-acc/fta-ale.aspx?lang=eng) and examine one of the FTAs currently in force. To what extent does this FTA allow Canadian businesses to export their products to the foreign country? Are there industries in Canada that may be hurt by this agreement? Why or why not?

2. What is a *free trade zone*? Give an example of a free trade zone and research how successful it has been.

3. One way to analyze the cultural differences among countries is to conduct a Hofestede analysis. Visit www.geert-hofstede.com to learn what this analysis considers. Develop a presentation explaining how three countries of your choice differ from Canada.

ONLINE, MOBILE, AND SOCIAL MEDIA MARKETING

With a population of 143 million, 60 million of whom are Internet users, Russia is emerging as the next big e-commerce frontier. Although online sales currently make up less than 2 percent of retail sales in Russia, they are projected to increase to 5 percent—that's $36 billion—by 2015. That fact has caught the attention of global e-commerce firms like Amazon and eBay, as well as China's equivalent of Amazon, Alibaba. The leading local online retailer in Russia is Ozon Group, often referred to as "Russia's Amazon." Ozon's 2014 sales were close to $500 million, representing an almost 70 percent increase in just two years. There are obstacles to e-commerce in Russia, however. The majority of consumers don't have credit cards because many don't trust them to pay for purchases online or offline, making Russia a heavily cash-based marketplace. Delivery is another problem. To combat these barriers, Ozon developed its own courier system. Drivers not only collect cash payments; they even offer style advice on apparel orders when delivered! Meanwhile, Russian consumers ordering items from international e-commerce sites such as Amazon may never receive their packages. In fact, officials at Moscow airport reported having 500 metric tons of unprocessed packages in one month alone. Seeing an opportunity for revenue, Russia's Customs Service is considering import duties on packages ordered from foreign websites.

QUESTIONS

1. What types of barriers are present in Russia that might slow the expansion of international e-commerce there?

2. Suggest the best ways companies such as eBay and Amazon can enter this market.

THINK LIKE A MARKETING MANAGER

When you consider Canadian exporters, you might think about our rich natural resources such as lumber and oil. However, you might be surprised to learn that one of our key sources of export strength in recent years has been in the financial services and insurance sector. For example, TD Canada Trust operates nearly 1300 locations across the east coast of the United States for Canadian travellers and American customers alike. The Canadian banking system has often been praised for being one of the safest in the world and has been ranked at number one by the World Economic Forum for several years running. It's no wonder that there are enormous opportunities for global growth.

QUESTIONS

1. Other than the TD example, choose a Canadian bank or insurance company and research its worldwide locations. How many countries does the company operate in?

2. Based on the information you found, what adaptations has the firm made when entering other countries?

MARKETING ETHICS

India's Supreme Court delivered what might be the final nail in the coffin of pharmaceutical innovation in India by rejecting Novartis's attempt to win patent protection for a potentially life-saving drug. The ruling came after more than six years of legal battles. Other multinational pharmaceutical companies have suffered setbacks related to patents as well. Bayer's patent for its expensive cancer drug was revoked after being challenged by an Indian generic drug manufacturer, and Bayer was even ordered to issue a licence to the Indian company so that it could copy Bayer's drug and sell it for one-thirtieth the price Bayer charged. Roche also had a patent revoked after challenges from local companies and health organizations. India reluctantly agreed to offer patent protection after joining the World Trade Organization in 1995, but it seems reluctant to grant or maintain patent protection to multinational pharmaceutical firms.

India is a fast-growing market, with pharmaceuticals demand expected to reach almost US$50 billion by 2020 from its current US$11 billion. However, this market is dominated by low-cost Indian generic drug producers, and India's government seems bent on protecting that industry. The Supreme Court ruling was praised by public-health advocacy groups, such as Médécins Sans Frontieres (MSF), who see it as a way to get low-cost drugs in India and other developing nations; India is, in fact, the largest supplier of low-cost HIV and other drugs to these nations. Novaritis's drug, Glivec, costs almost US$2000 per month compared with US$200 per month for comparable generic versions in India, which didn't help the company's case. However, the company claims that 95 percent of 16 000 patients taking Glivec in India receive it free of charge through a company support program.

QUESTIONS

1. Debate both sides of this issue. Should pharmaceutical companies be granted patents in less-developed countries?

2. Discuss another example of multinational companies having difficulty expanding into India.

MARKETING BY THE NUMBERS

Colleges and universities in the United States offering graduate degrees enjoyed double-digit growth for nearly a decade, particularly from Chinese applicants. But that's changing. Applications from Chinese students declined 5 percent for the 2013–2014 academic year, dropping the overall graduate school application growth rate from foreign students to just 1 percent. This has schools that offer business, engineering, life sciences, and physical and earth sciences graduate degrees wondering how they will fill their classrooms. One bright spot is applications from Brazilians, which increased 24 percent because of a push by the Brazilian government to boost advanced degrees from U.S. schools. Brazil is currently the sixth largest economy in the world, but not enough of its citizens hold advanced degrees, which threatens the country's future growth. Many U.S. schools are wondering if this market is worthy of more marketing efforts to replace the lost Chinese applicants.

QUESTIONS

1. Develop a relevant demographic profile of Brazil to present to an American graduate school director to inform him or her about this potential market of students.

2. Is this an attractive market for American graduate programs? Refer to Appendix 3: Marketing by the Numbers and use outside resources if necessary to develop a market-potential estimation.

END-OF-CHAPTER CASE

IKEA: MAKING LIFE BETTER FOR THE WORLD'S MANY PEOPLE

Walmart may be the biggest retailer in the world, but IKEA is the largest furniture retailer. In a recent year more than 770 million shoppers flocked to the Scandinavian retailer's 338 huge stores in 41 countries, generating revenues of more than US$36 billion. That's an average of over US$106 million per store per year, about two and a half times the average sales of a Walmart store. From Beijing to Moscow to Winnipeg, customers pour into IKEA's stores for simple, practical furniture at affordable prices. IKEA is big and getting bigger—its sales have doubled during the past decade. But it's also practical and methodical, growing by only 20 or so superstores each year.

Even these big numbers don't begin to illustrate the impact that IKEA has had on consumers all over the world. Far more than just a big furniture chain, IKEA has achieved global growth and success by connecting with consumers of all nationalities and cultures. IKEA has excelled as a curator of people's lifestyles. Consumers around the world flock to IKEA to signal that they have arrived, that they both have good taste and recognize value. In fact, without IKEA, many people in the world would have little access to affordable, contemporary products for their homes. IKEA's mission is to "create a better everyday life for the many people." It accomplishes this seemingly impossible mission by striking just the right balance between global brand standardization and catering to the local cultural differences in markets around the world.

A STANDARDIZED GLOBAL BRAND

In the 1940s, Ingvar Kamprad developed what became known as the "IKEA Concept." He was a native of Småland, Sweden, where the soil was poor and the people had a reputation for working hard, living frugally, and making the most of limited resources. The IKEA concept is founded on those characteristics—"offering a wide range of well-designed, functional home furnishing products at prices so low that as many people as possible will be able to afford them."

Some aspects of IKEA's products are consistent in all markets. For starters, its products are rooted in Swedish contemporary design. The classic, simple lines of IKEA design produce timeless products that few companies in any industry can match. For example, POANG—an upholstered chair based on a laminated, bentwood frame with only two front legs—was created in 1976 but remains one of the company's best-selling lines today. The same

holds true for the BILLY bookcase. In fact, most of IKEA's best-selling products have been around for years. And that's how IKEA intends customers to enjoy them—for years.

Low price is a key common component of IKEA's products. The benchmark for every IKEA product is half the price of similar products from competitors. And with its relentless focus on cost-cutting, IKEA can keep the price of a product constant or even reduce it over time. Selling the same products in every market achieves scale that contributes to IKEA's low-cost structure. So does its "flat-pack" approach—designing furniture so that it can be packed and sold in pieces and assembled by customers at home.

IKEA stores around the world also share a standard design. For starters, they are huge. At an average size of 300 000 square feet, they're about 50 percent larger than the average Walmart Supercenter. These large stores let IKEA achieve another aspect of its global brand concept—a one-stop home shopping experience that includes furniture, appliances, and household goods for every room. Although such massive size may be overwhelming to some consumers, IKEA's stores are organized in three main sections. Its *showrooms* are set up in a series of rooms that not only show off each product, but also put the product in an actual room context, giving customers ideas for how they might use the product in their homes. The *marketplace* section contains the small items—everything from desk lamps to kitchen utensils—also organized by area of the home. The *warehouse* allows customers to pull their own furniture items in flat-pack boxes and cart them out. One main thoroughfare weaves its way clockwise through the store from one area to the next, a design that encourages customers to see the store in its entirety. Parents can drop their children in the Småland play area and the entire family can eat in the three-meal-a-day restaurant or the snack bar, making it easy to hang around and shop for hours.

LISTENING, UNDERSTANDING, AND ADAPTING

Although most of IKEA's standardized formula works in every market, the company has learned that one size does not fit all when it comes to global customers. So IKEA tweaks its marketing mix in different markets to better meet local consumer needs. The retailer seeks constant feedback from customers in stores, and it visits thousands more each year through in-home visits, observing how consumers live and asking about their dreams and challenges.

When the first U.S. IKEA store opened in Philadelphia in 1985, the beds that it carried were the same as those offered in its other world markets. But Americans weren't buying them, and sales suffered. As IKEA opened more U.S. stores, it worked to figure out the American style of sleeping. It learned that height, firmness, and maximum size are key bed characteristics sought by U.S. consumers. So, IKEA altered the composition of its mattresses and added king-size beds to the mix. Then, it altered the presentation and promotion of these products so that the concept was clear. Not surprisingly, its sleep product lines really took off.

A more recent change that came about from listening to consumers in North America and certain other markets is the offering of more services. Whereas picking, pulling, hauling, and assembling still works for most people, for others it was all just too much trouble. IKEA now offers flat-rate pricing on pulling orders and home delivery. It even maintains a list of contractors in each market whom customers can call on to assemble the items in their homes.

Some markets have required more changes. As IKEA has expanded into Asia, for example, it has learned that customer needs vary substantially from those in Europe and North America. Take China, for example. With some of the largest cities in the world, China has no shortage of customers. But most of China's 1.3 billion people don't buy home furnishings. So IKEA focuses instead on China's exploding middle class—"the many people" in growing urban populations who are more educated and fall into the 25-to-35 age range. For this reason, IKEA stores in China are located closer to city centres, rather than in the suburbs, and are located near a light-rail transportation line.

Some of the changes for IKEA China are based on the fundamental principle of stocking products that people in a given area will buy. In the United States, but not in China, mattresses are firmer. Whereas IKEA stores in China carry the same number of products as those in other parts of the world—most of them from the standard IKEA range—in China the company also stocks rice cookers and chopsticks. And when it stocked 250 000 placemats commemorating the year of the rooster, they sold out in weeks.

In massive city centres such as Beijing and Shanghai, home ownership among the middle class has gone from nearly zero to about 70 percent in the past 15 years or so. Because virtually all new homeowners have little sense of how to furnish and decorate a home, they are eager to learn from the West. However, not everything that works in more developed parts of the world works in China. For one thing, the average living space in China's crowded cities is much smaller than in Europe and North America. An average Chinese family lives in a small apartment in a high-rise building, often with multigenerational family members. So in China, IKEA focuses on products geared toward saving space and organizing a household. And it helps consumers figure out how to live smart and organize in small living spaces.

Pricing in China is somewhat of a paradox. Chinese customers are attracted to IKEA's design and the comprehensive selection, so that's where IKEA puts its emphasis in terms of positioning. But at the same time, in emerging markets like China, low prices are the norm, and IKEA must cut prices drastically to remain competitive. When it first opened its doors in China more than a decade ago, IKEA found that its products were more expensive than those of local, low-priced firms. Competitors began selling copies of IKEA's designs at a fraction of the cost. Using its cost-cutting expertise, however, IKEA has brought prices in China down by more than 50 percent over the past 10 years. The classic Klippan sofa, for example, now costs only $160, a third of what it did a decade ago (the same sofa costs $470 in Sweden).

Another challenge in selling furniture in the world's most populated country is that there are significant differences across the country's many regions. For example, in some regions, apartments have smaller rooms. Thus, IKEA designs showrooms in those areas to reflect the smaller size. Apartment buildings throughout China have balconies. But in northern China, balconies are widely used for food storage, whereas in southern China, they double as laundries. IKEA showrooms in these regions reflect such differences and regional needs.

The Chinese market features another unusual characteristic—gawkers. China's stores boast more traffic than IKEAs in any other part of the world (the Beijing store pulls in 28 000 customers on a Saturday—a strong week for a European store). But the majority of visitors are just hanging out and looking. Actually, many of them are there to enjoy the air conditioning, a cheap meal, and a place to relax in comfort. People often lounge for extended periods in showrooms, just as they would in their own living rooms. Some will even pull back the covers on an IKEA bed, take off their shoes, and hunker down for a good nap. Whereas this kind of behaviour would get customers kicked out of IKEAs in any other market, management recognizes that with China's rapidly growing middle class, allowing such behaviour is an investment in the future.

IKEA plans to expand its number of stores in China from 11 to 40 during the next seven years. But China is just an illustration of IKEA's strategy throughout the world. The company also plans to double its number of stores in the United States during the same period. And as IKEA continues to grow in existing markets, it is also eyeing new markets with vast, untapped potential. IKEA is currently laying the groundwork in India, where it plans 25 stores. Having doubled sales in the past decade, IKEA plans to double them again by 2020. And that's based on the same methodical growth of 20 to 25 new stores.

With its keen ability to understand the cultural differences of each market and to adapt its marketing mix accordingly, there doesn't seem to be much standing in IKEA's way.

Sources: Based on information from www.ikea.com/ms/en_US/about_ikea/index.html, accessed August, 2013. Also see Anna Ringstrom, "IKEA Turns the Global Local for Asia Push," *Reuters*, March 6, 2013, www.reuters.com/article/2013/03/07/us-ikea-expansion-idUSBRE92606220130307; Walter Loeb, "IKEA Is a World-Wide Wonder," *Forbes*, December 5, 2012, www.forbes.com/sites/walterloeb/2012/12/05/ikea-is-a-world-wide-wonder; Jenna Goudreau, "How IKEA Leveraged the Art of Listening to Global Dominance," *Forbes*, January 30, 2013, www.forbes.com/sites/jennagoudreau/2013/01/30/how-ikea-leveraged-the-art-of-listening-to-global-dominance; Pan Kwan Yuk, "IKEA in China: Turning Gawkers into Consumers," *Financial Times*, April 4, 2013, http://blogs.ft.com/beyond-brics/2013/04/04/ikea-in-china-turning-gawkers-into-consumers/?Authorised=false#axzz2VAi2u6c8; and Jens Hansegard, "IKEA Taking China by Storm," *Wall Street Journal*, March 26, 2012, http://online.wsj.com/article/SB10001424052702304636404577293083481821536.html.

QUESTIONS FOR DISCUSSION

1. Does IKEA have a truly global strategy, or just a series of regional strategies? Explain.

2. Discuss IKEA's global strategy in terms of the five global product and communications strategies.

3. If IKEA can sell a sofa in China for $160, why doesn't it sell the product at that low price in all its markets?

4. Can competitors easily duplicate IKEA's strategy? Why or why not?

5. Should IKEA expand more rapidly than 20 to 25 stores per year? Explain.

General Company Information: Boston Pizza

Introduction

It is unlikely that Greek immigrant–cum-Edmontonian Gus Agioritis had envisioned a dominant international restaurant chain when he opened the first Boston Pizza & Spaghetti House in 1964. It might even be difficult for current owners Jim Treliving and George Melville to admit they'd foreseen the wave of popularity that would wash across Canada, and begin U.S. and Mexican penetration, when they opened 19 stores in the early 1970s. And yet all three entrepreneurs took a simple idea and grew it, with the help of hundreds of other like-minded entrepreneurs along the way.

Today, Canada's leading casual dining brand has become a household name, associated with family, fun, food, and, oh yes—sports. It is, in fact, that equal and powerful balance between family dining and sports bar that stands as one of Boston Pizza's key differentiating characteristics.

Having celebrated its 50th anniversary in 2014, Boston Pizza has crossed a significant milestone and is poised for an encore. Certainly, the pieces are in place for a second successful semicentennial, based on the accomplishments within those first 50 years:

- $1 billion in annual sales, 2014
- 40 million guests served, 2014
- 370+ stores, 2014
- 3 countries of operation (Canada, U.S., and Mexico)
- 2 distinct product offerings: family dining and sports bar
- 100 menu items
- Platinum member of "Canada's 50 Best Managed Companies," 21 consecutive years

But while these milestones bear witness to a company that knows how to make money, there's a softer, gentler side to BP as well. The Boston Pizza Foundation, which has raised and donated over $20 million toward partner charities in Canada and around the world, demonstrates that the company is pretty good at making friends, too.

Add to these accomplishments BP's innovative financial engine, called the Boston Pizza Royalties Income Fund, and you get the sense that the current state of the organization is well equipped to move into the future.

Corporate Structure

Boston Pizza International Inc. (BPI), headquartered in Richmond, B.C., owns and operates three stores in Canada, but is the franchisor for over 370 stores across Canada. BPI is the operational brains and engine of the brand. That said, Boston Pizza Royalties Income Fund, a trust fund set up in 2002, actually owns all BP trademark rights, and licenses them exclusively to BPI in exchange for a 5.5 percent monthly royalty on all BP franchise sales.

The trust does what trust funds are designed to do—it creates consistent cash flow for investors without bearing the risk, burden, costs, or capital expenditure requirements of a company. BPI does all that. The fund has not missed a month of paid-out cash distributions since its inception in 2002.

Boston Pizza International Inc. is co-owned and co-chaired by Jim Treliving and George Melville, who established the partnership that started it all in the 1970s. Together they form the nucleus of the executive team, joined by president and CEO Mark Pacinda.

Development of a Brand

Truly entrepreneurial in its culture, Boston Pizza began as a simple pizza and spaghetti house in Edmonton before quickly catching on as a business model that was scalable and soon adopted by a number of franchisees in Alberta and B.C.

In 1968 the original visionary, Gus Agioritis, willingly handed the keys over to Jim Treliving, an RCMP officer who convinced his accounting buddy George Melville to join his business enterprise. By 1973 the two, who had dreamed of starting a business, liked the idea that Boston Pizza was a proven model and were prepared to turn it into a national brand. Ten years later, by then owners of 19 restaurants, they pushed all their chips into the middle of the table and bought out all the franchisees in order to become the franchisor and begin reselling the individual franchise licences. Boston Pizza International Inc. became the company co-owned by Treliving and Melville.

BP's first big break, like most in business, was neither handed to them nor a stroke of good luck. It was, in fact, a combination of foresight, hustle, and diplomacy that led to BP's becoming the official pizza supplier of the Vancouver World Exposition 1986. Expo 86 exposed Boston Pizza not only to travellers from around Canada but to folks from around the world. It also grossed $8 million in sales for Boston Pizza.

Expo 86 proved to be one of the most pivotal points along the timeline of the brand. Additional franchises were granted, and soon a long, steady succession of milestones would occur.

1993: 25 Year Award from International Franchise Association

1994: Named one of Canada's Best Managed Companies by Financial Post (which it has earned every year since)

1996: 100th store opens in Cold Lake, Alberta.

1998: Regional office in Ontario opens, beginning an eastern Canadian expansion

1998: Two locations open in the U.S., named "Boston's The Gourmet Pizza."

1999: Jim Treliving and George Melville earn the Ernst & Young Entrepreneur of the Year Award for commitment to hospitality and tourism.

2002: Boston Pizza Royalties Income Fund is created and begins trading on the TSX under the symbol BPF.UN, following the initial public offering on July 17.

2004: Boston Pizza celebrates its 40th anniversary and begins expansion into Quebec with the opening of a corporate office in Laval.

2005: Boston Pizza locations across Canada serve more than 30 million customers, and the 200th location opens in Kitchener, Ontario.

2006: Boston Pizza opens its first locations in Newfoundland and P.E.I., making Boston Pizza a truly coast-to-coast operation.

2013: The 350th Boston Pizza location opens in Devon, Alberta.

2014: A record 85 000 pizzas are served in Canada on August 12 to celebrate the brand's 50th anniversary.

Two-Model Concept

From the beginning, BP has focused strategically on two markets, which offer considerable crossover: family dining and sports enthusiasts. The restaurant–sports bar concept is a key differentiator among other competitors in the family dining space, both in Canada and the United States.

"We are a nation of sports fans, so nothing draws Canadians together like sports," offers president and CEO Mark Pacinda. "We have always gathered together to watch sports; whether it's hockey, football, baseball, the Olympics, or a world championship fight in boxing, we gather together socially and make it into an occasion. Boston Pizza offers that comfortable but lively gathering place, with big beautiful HD screens and a menu with over 100 items to choose from."

While the sports bar side of a Boston Pizza restaurant offers a lively sports environment, the family dining side provides that comfortable and familiar setting, complete with crayons, colouring, and kids' meals, to round out the family experience.

Strategically, the two-model concept stretches Boston Pizza's traffic wider than most family dining restaurants as well. "We do very well for lunch and dinner, as you would expect from a family restaurant," asserts Pacinda. "But the sports bar opens us up to late-night dining and social gathering as well. So we really have three key 'dayparts,' which provide the BP experience for our guests as well as three tremendous sales opportunities for our franchisees."

Strategic Direction

Boston Pizza's main growth opportunities remain in developing the brand in Canada. While this may sound redundant, given the fact that there are already over 370 locations across all provinces and territories, shifts in demographics and consumer behaviour with regard to dining have forced BP to explore new dining formats, which has in turn opened new doors—literally.

"Traditionally the company has built these large 5000 square foot, square-box restaurants primarily in the suburbs," begins director of communications Perry Schwartz. "But the burbs are by and large built out, so the new opportunity for us is in finding smaller scale spaces in communities that are underserved by our brand." He cites recent examples of newer, smaller stores opening in Trenton, Ontario, and in the SAIT Polytechnic Campus in Calgary, as examples of this new direction. "How we get from 370 stores in this country to 500 stores is probably along that path."

BP's growth along that, or any path, will not of course proceed without obstacles—growth never does. For as BP seizes opportunities for touchpoints to more deeply weave its brand into the fabric of Canadian dining, others have similar ideas. "There's a convergence of quick service and fine dining toward the middle," claims Schwartz. "McDonald's and Tim Hortons have done a good job of creating an ambience in their stores that makes them an inviting place now to go for dinner. At the same time, some of the higher-end places are offering more mainstream menu items. So that space we've had, as sort of the casual fine dining, has become more blurred."

Four Pillars Strategy

Regardless of size and location of new restaurants, or challenges by competitors, Boston Pizza will no doubt adhere to its long-standing four pillars strategy as a checklist for all strategic decisions. The four pillars are as follows:

1. A Commitment to Continually Improving the Guest Experience

Boston Pizza has over 50 years of focus and effort toward improving the experience of our restaurant guests. A vibrant, colourful design in a casual and comfortable dining atmosphere, combined with a menu that features old favourites and new taste sensations, keeps guests coming back for more.

2. A Commitment to Building the Boston Pizza Brand

Having a strong and recognizable brand that consumers trust and want to do business with creates value for all stakeholders.

3. A Commitment to Franchisee Profitability

The best way to ensure the success of the Boston Pizza Royalties Income Fund, Boston Pizza International Inc., and the Boston Pizza brand is to ensure the success of Boston Pizza franchisees.

4. A Commitment to Being Involved in Our Communities

Boston Pizza franchisees, staff, and management have always made community involvement a key priority through engaging sports teams and civic groups, volunteering time, and donating funds to support a variety of local and national causes.

With the four pillars to support them strategically, an experienced franchisor team with a proven franchising model, and a truly proven and popular national brand, Boston Pizza would appear to be poised to maintain its position as Canada's favourite family dining location.

Questions

1. What is Boston Pizza's biggest opportunity? What forces in the micro- and macroenvironments have created this opportunity?

2. How would you suggest Boston Pizza apply its four pillars strategy toward taking advantage of the opportunity cited in question 1?

3. How can Boston Pizza leverage the proven four pillars strategy toward thwarting the efforts of competitors to encroach on the position of "Canada's favourite family restaurant"?

Abbreviated Sample Marketing Plan: Boston Pizza

This appendix provides a sample marketing plan for a new product offered by Boston Pizza. Deciding on a new product is no small feat, and it's a decision that is not made lightly. Although its main product is in its name, Boston Pizza continually monitors trends, listens to its customers, and updates its menu accordingly. Over its first 50 years, BP's menu has grown from pizza and spaghetti to a wide range of appetizers and main courses, expanding far beyond the original product offering as the demands of its customers have evolved. This is typically the origin of a new product idea for Boston Pizza, which must keep with the times in order to stay in business. But how are new product ideas fully developed, and how do they come to market?

Although a SWOT analysis appears several pages into a marketing plan, it's actually one of the first tasks required in product development. The determination of a new product idea either results from, or is validated by, a thorough SWOT analysis, followed by brainstorming ideas based on what the SWOT analysis reveals. For instance, if Boston Pizza were faced with a competitive threat, whereby fast-casual, quick-service, and family restaurants had introduced a product type that BP didn't currently carry, it would compel the marketing team to at least consider its suitability for BP's menu.

This situation might be compounded by a social opportunity identified by demand among BP's target market for a similar product. However, there may be hindrances exposed through the SWOT process as well, such as a specific weakness that BP would have to fix in order to proceed in developing the product idea. The main takeaway is that a thorough SWOT analysis is one of the first steps toward discovering an appropriate new-product idea.

After executing a SWOT analysis, the new-product development process must be deep and rigorous. While Boston Pizza may introduce several new menu items in any given year, none of them arrive on a guest's table without having been subjected to the checkpoints in this process. We recommend that you review Chapter 8, Developing and Managing Products and Services, as you go through the following example. The steps covered in that chapter, coupled with management's thorough analysis of Boston Pizza's current situation, can provide a number of plausible new product ideas.

Finally, whatever the new product idea is, management must ensure that it's consistent with the Boston Pizza brand—an intangible quality that speaks to the essence of the company. Typical Boston Pizza offerings exemplify such descriptors as *family-oriented*, *high quality*, *hearty*, and *delicious*. That's why nachos and wings make it in while other offerings, despite being trendy and healthy, would not make the cut.

What follows is marketing plan for a hypothetical new-product launch for Boston Pizza. This plan is structured using sections and sequencing similar to those of an actual marketing plan, but in no way are these reflective of Boston Pizza's objectives or strategies, which remain confidential. As such, everything that follows should be treated as a guideline only. The sample in part draws from the primary and secondary research used in the creation of the text's end-of-chapter comprehensive cases, but, again, it's not intended to represent Boston Pizza's actual marketing plan. It is deliberately hypothetical, and intended purely as an example of applying theory to an actual company. Furthermore, in the interest of confidentiality and for simplicity, this sample is abbreviated; it features only the most vital material required to demonstrate the look, feel, and comprehensiveness of a marketing plan and excludes much of the finer detail that would otherwise be included.

Marketing Plan for Boston Pizza Product Launch—GlutenWise Burgers

Executive Summary

This section summarizes the main goals, recommendations, and points. It serves as an overview for senior managers who will read and approve the marketing plan. For management convenience, a table of contents generally follows this section.

Boston Pizza is Canada's leading casual dining restaurant, with a network of over 370 franchised locations scattered across every province and territory in Canada. It's known for being a family dining restaurant as well as for having a vibrant, energetic sports bar component—a dual concept under one roof that has proven to be one of its differentiating competitive advantages. And rather than adhering to a single-sentence mission, Boston Pizza is governed by what it calls its four pillars strategy: a commitment to guest experience, brand, franchise profitability, and community involvement. This four-pronged commitment helps bring in 40 million diners per year, and in 2014, it pushed total sales past $1 billion.

Despite its popularity, Boston Pizza refuses to rest on its success. After all, its four pillar strategy commits the company to constantly raise the bar in all aspects of its business; it's in constant pursuit of ways to improve upon what it does. Recent market analysis (detailed within the SWOT analysis section of the marketing plan) revealed two key findings. First, the gluten-intolerant market in Canada continues to grow. Second, other leading casual dining, fast casual, and even quick service restaurants have expanded their menu offerings to satisfy this demand, including the addition of a gluten-free burger option.

One of Boston Pizza's strengths is its established "GlutenWise" menu, catering to the gluten intolerant and even the celiac population. However, the absence of a burger within this category could be viewed as a liability, or at the very least a weakness. It is therefore proposed that BP introduce a burger into its GlutenWise menu. This is the subject of the marketing plan that follows.

The Boston Pizza GlutenWise Burger won't just be a burger sitting on a gluten-free bun. In true BP tradition, it will be hearty, healthy, substantial, and delicious. The "basic" burger won't be very basic at all—it will be a half-pound, 100 percent prime rib beef burger sandwiched between the best tasting, most texturally pleasant gluten-free bun made in Canada. This claim will be supported by the key multi-tiered promotional strategy built around a national gluten-free bun contest.

To remain consistent with the choice BP diners have come to expect, the burger will also be fully customizable. Pricing will be in alignment with Boston Pizza's current strategy of delivering value for customers' money. A combination of customer-based value and cost-plus pricing strategy is recommended, similar to that used in the pricing of BP's GlutenWise Pizza. However, the option to *not* include a price premium is suggested as well.

While distribution of the BP GlutenWise Burger will be through the existing network of over 370 franchised stores across Canada, the challenge will be in creating and sustaining an efficient supply chain for the bun itself. Either in-house production will be made feasible or a centrally operated gluten-free baking facility will be awarded an exclusive baking contract based on a national search for the facility offering both baking and shipping capabilities.

As with BP's other GlutenWise menu items, sales and financial objectives are not as important as simply providing healthy, safe, and delicious food options for BP's diet-sensitive customers. Thus, the main marketing objective of the GlutenWise Burger is to fill a significant void in the restaurant's GlutenWise menu, but to do so in a way that is delicious and affordable. It must be on-brand in terms of outstanding value and flavour.

Current Marketing Situation

In this section, marketing managers discuss the overall market, identify the market segments they will target, and provide information about the company's current situation.

Boston Pizza is Canada's leading casual dining restaurant, with a network of over 370 franchised locations. It continues to be responsive to its customers, communities, and franchisees through a steadfast four pillar strategy focused on building a powerful restaurant brand. Having celebrated its 50th year in 2014, BP is poised to make further inroads into Canada's casual dining space by continuing to grow in numbers and market share.

Canada's population continues to evolve as the density of baby boomers pushes through BP's target market lens, giving way to Gen X, Y, and Z—those born between 1966 and 1996. The older of these cohorts (Gen X) often have older children, while the early-born Gen Zs are still in university. Either way, BP's market is composed of sophisticated consumers with high expectations for value.

While holding down the position of Canada's favourite family/casual dining restaurant, that category is quickly becoming blurred as quick-service restaurants like Tim Hortons stretch upmarket while higher end restaurants stretch downward. The result is a convergence of competitors for which BP must be prepared. As well, macroeconomic conditions continue to affect the bottom line of discretionary-dependent businesses in the hospitality space, so BP must be prepared and responsive to Canada's somewhat volatile economy. Regulations regarding nutritional guidelines continue to evolve, necessitating close monitoring by firms like Boston Pizza. Finally, technological factors continue to advance efficiencies in all industries. It is vital that BP monitor these trends as well in order to ensure that it's taking advantage of the most beneficial tech advantages.

The most compelling trend driving the decision to introduce a GlutenWise Burger is the rapid growth of the gluten-intolerant (GI) market. Once thought to be comprised solely of those afflicted with celiac disease—a segment representing just 1 percent of the population—the GI segment has grown to include over 10 percent of the population. This has created a demand, which has, in turn, driven the development of gluten-free products. More and more food-producing companies are striving to develop or acquire assets, which include gluten-free (GF) capability. Finally, this competitive force has spurred technological advancement around producing GF products.

Market Description

Describing the targeted segments in detail provides context for the marketing strategies and detailed action programs discussed later in the plan.

Since Boston Pizza is a two-concept dining experience, it benefits from two distinct target markets that provide steady traffic over three distinct dayparts. Being Canada's leading casual family dining restaurant, BP's primary target market is families comprising young to early-middle-aged parents with infant to teenaged children. These families are active and busy with preschool, school, after-school, and extracurricular activities. There are likely two incomes to the household, but together they're unlikely to exceed a total of $100 000 annually. The parents of these families are value driven and time-starved, but they like the idea of family/social outings for dinner and find comfort in familiar consumer brands. When dining out, they also prefer restaurants in nearby shopping areas that have parking and other amenities. More than anything, these parents seek hearty and healthy food in a clean, comfortable, safe environment where families feel welcome and the dollar stretches far. The family segment fills the tables and booths of the typical Boston Pizza restaurant during the busy dinner daypart.

BP's second target market are sports enthusiasts, both male and female, who love the idea of getting together with friends to watch a sporting event on a big-screen TV while enjoying that same renowned Boston Pizza food and hospitality. This market ranges anywhere from entry legal drinking age (varying from province to province) on up. They're less likely to have young children, but recent studies are showing Gen Y and Gen Z customers bringing their parents in to enjoy a sporting event among friends at Boston Pizza.

Like the family segment, these sports enthusiasts are value-motivated and enjoy the convenience and access of Boston Pizza. They're extremely sociable, preferring to view sporting events among friends (and sometimes even like-minded strangers) rather than in private. This group is also often active in recreational or organized sports and finds the friendly sports-themed environment at Boston Pizza to be comforting, supportive, and equally invested in its love of sports.

Product Review

The product review summarizes the main features for all the company's products, organized by product line, type of customer, market, or order of product introduction.

Boston Pizza's product mix is a vast menu offering, with over 100 unique choices among its starters, entrees, desserts, and beverages. However, given that it's a restaurant, a large part of BP's product offering comes in the form of a service. To that end, BP's value proposition is a total dining experience featuring delicious, ample servings, prepared professionally and presented in a friendly and enthusiastic manner.

Boston Pizza falls into the casual family dining and sports bar categories of the hospitality industry, and as such, its customers make a conscious decision when dining out. That distinguishes Boston Pizza's offerings as consumer shopping products, which are nondurable in that the products made (food and beverage items) are used and consumed once. This is one of the unique traits of restaurants, along with the fact that most, aside from quick service restaurants, rely on a combination of goods and the service of hospitality to create and maintain some sort of competitive advantage.

As Canadians' demand for new food choices and experiences grows, the number of menu offerings at Boston Pizza is growing as well. BP's GlutenWise line of products is a good example of this responsiveness. First introduced in 2010, the GlutenWise menu has evolved to the point where numerous choices are available for pizza served on gluten-free crust or pasta using a gluten-free fusilli.

Table 1 represents BP's current GlutenWise menu offerings, following along the same product lines as BP's overarching product-mix structure of pizza, pasta, starters, salads, and mains. Absent from the GlutenWise menu offerings, but present in Boston Pizza's regular menu, is the category of burgers. This void is to be filled with the introduction of the BP GlutenWise Burger and its respective product line options, indicated in red in Table 1.

TABLE 1   Boston Pizza GlutenWise Menu

Pizza	Pasta	Starters	Salads	Burgers and Mains
Cheeses:	■ Tomato Marinara	Wings:	■ Grilled Chicken Pecan	Mains
■ Mozzarella	■ Creamy Alfredo	■ Naked	■ Spinach Salad	■ Slow Roasted Pork Ribs
■ Cheddar	■ Beef Bolognese	■ Mild	■ Mediterranean Salad	■ Lemon Baked Salmon Fillet
■ Feta	■ Fifty-Fifty	■ Medium	■ GlutenWise Caesar	■ New York Striploin Steak
		■ Hot	■ Chopped Chicken	
Toppings:	Proteins:	■ Thai Chili	■ Garden Greens	
■ Genoa salami	■ Chicken	■ Honey Garlic		Burgers
■ Pepperoni	■ Shrimp	■ Salt and Pepper Dry Rub	Dressings:	■ Double Bacon BBQ
■ Smoked ham	■ Salmon		■ Poppy seed	■ Prime Rib
■ Smoked bacon	■ Cheese		■ Ranch	■ Spicy Perogy
■ Green peppers			■ House	■ Pepperoni and Bacon Pizza
■ Banana peppers			■ Citrus	
■ Jalapeno peppers			■ Raspberry	
■ Fresh mushrooms			■ Mediterranean	
■ Tomatoes				
■ Olives				
■ Onions				
■ Chicken				
■ Spicy chicken				
■ Shrimp				
■ Taco beef				
■ Spicy Italian sausage				
■ Anchovies				
■ Sun-dried tomatoes				
■ Spinach				
■ Pineapple				
■ Red pepper				

Competitive Review

The purpose of a competitive review is to identify key competitors, describe their market positions, and briefly discuss their strategies.

The restaurant/hospitality industry is a competitive landscape best described as a monopolistic competition. That landscape features several types of competitors, and they differentiate widely. Statistics Canada divides the industry into a) full service restaurants, b) limited service restaurants, c) special food services, and d) drinking places.

While Boston Pizza falls into the category of full service restaurants, an emerging trend in the industry is beginning to pit limited service restaurants, also known as quick service restaurants (QSR), against the casual dining space occupied by Boston Pizza. As such, fellow Canadian-based juggernaut Tim Hortons, a QSR market leader, is beginning to encroach upon the casual dining space by offering more menu items and creating more full meal-friendly dining experiences. Indeed, Tim Hortons and McDonalds are now vying for BP's average customer more than many full service restaurants are.

At the same time, upscale fine-dining establishments have had to deal with declining sales and patronage by downmarket stretching in order to provide more basic and value-priced menu options. Over time, this trend has single-handedly created a new full service category known as "premium casual," led in Canada by brands such as Earls and Joey.

Nevertheless, the incursion of both upmarket and downmarket establishments into BP's casual dining sector of full service restaurants is concerning, and provides a competitive rationale as to why a GlutenWise Burger product on BP's menu is an essential addition to protect its position.

We'll use Porter's five forces of competition framework (developed by Harvard School of Business economist Michael Porter) as a convenient tool for identifying BP's competitors. The framework begins with *direct competitors*: those most similar in product and target market. *Substitutes* follow, defined as competitors that satisfy the same need but by different means. *Entry barriers* describe the ease or difficulty of entering the market. *Supplier power* and *buyer power* identify supply chain and channel partners that aren't competing for market share, but rather attempting to gain advantage in price negotiations.

Table 2 identifies, describes, and provides examples of specific competitors in these categories.

TABLE 2   Boston Pizza's Porter Five Forces Overview

Porter Five-Force Category	Primary Examples	Description
Direct Competitors	Pizza Hut, Montana's, Swiss Chalet, Smitty's, Ricky's, Denny's, Kelsey's, Eastside Mario's	The casual/family dining category has become incredibly competitive as brands such as those listed vie for increased share of a growing market. Some of the brands listed are owned by larger corporate entities (e.g., Cara Operations owns Montana's, Swiss Chalet, Milestones, Kelsey's, and Harvey's).
Substitutes	Fast Casual: Tim Hortons, McDonalds, Harvey's, Burger King	Fast casual is undergoing a sector-wide repositioning, demonstrated by tangible and intangible developments. Tim Hortons and McDonalds stores, for instance, have been renovated to include fireplaces and cleaner, more family-friendly settings.
	Premium Casual: Earls, Cactus Club, The Keg, Milestones, Saltlik, Moxie's	While targeting slightly different consumers, premium casual is a rapidly growing space, benefitting from demo-socio trends of Canadians eating out more often.
Entry Barriers	N/A	Entry barriers to opening a new restaurant independently are relatively low. Hundreds are opened every year in Canada. The success rate, however, is also relatively low, due largely to the dominance of national brands listed above. Thus, despite the ease of entry, the difficulty of sustaining profitability is enough of a deterrent to keep entry barriers high.
Supplier Power	Food producers contributing to preparation of all BP menu items	Supplier power is high, since in many cases the ingredients required for the preparation of BP's products have long supply chains leading back to food producers and raw agricultural growers.
Buyer Power	End consumers	Boston Pizza is a B-to-C-oriented business, meaning that buyer power can occur only with massive rejection of Boston Pizza's faithful. It is not reliant upon corporate sales (B-to-B), and thus buyer power is low.

TABLE 3   Boston Pizza SWOT Analysis

	Strengths	Weaknesses
Marketing	■ Established and trusted brand	■ No current gluten-free burger
	■ Extensive franchise channels	■ Cynicism toward a "GlutenWise" line as being insufficient for sufferers of celiac disease
	■ Established GlutenWise line	
	■ Support of Canadian Celiac Association	
	■ Director of Culinary and Master Chef Michael Gray	
Management	■ Owner/management structure	
	■ Experience of senior management	
	■ Economies of scale in store operations	
Financial	■ Strong financial prerequisites of franchisees	
	■ Support of Boston Pizza Royalty Income Trust	
	Opportunities	**Threats**
Demographic	■ Growing target market	
	■ Growing demand for GF diet	
Economic		■ Volatility of Canadian economy
Natural		■ Drought conditions affecting crop growth, increasing costs
Technological	■ Breakthroughs in GF baking techniques	
Political-Legal		■ Canadian Food Inspection Agency monitoring gluten-free food production and claims made
Cultural	■ Increasing awareness of the health benefits of a GF diet	
	■ Values placed on brand recognition	

Swot Analysis

SWOT analysis is the most commonly used tool for marketing planning, as it identifies internal forces of the microenvironment (strengths and weaknesses) and external forces of the macroenvironment (opportunities and threats). SWOT analysis findings can be plotted in a matrix or in point form. Internal forces are subdivided into marketing, management, and financial, while external forces are subdivided by macroenvironments: demographic, economic, natural, technological, political, and cultural.

Despite the competitive forces analyzed in the preceding section, Boston Pizza remains well positioned to ward off threats and leverage its strengths toward available environmental opportunities. At the same time, it must acknowledge and shore up weaknesses, which could hinder its ability to successfully launch the GlutenWise Burger. Table 3 outlines the major environmental forces impacting Boston Pizza.

Strengths

Strengths are internal capabilities that can help the company reach its objectives.

Boston Pizza's recognizable and trusted brand is its most valuable strength. The familiar BP storefront is a warm invitation to time-strapped, value-conscious parents as well as sports enthusiasts. They all know and enjoy the wide selection of hearty, healthy, and delicious menu choices, and the friendly and enthusiastic environment.

The fact that BP has an established menu catering to gluten-sensitive people is also a strength. The GlutenWise line was introduced in 2010 and has stood the test of time. Michael Gray, BP's head chef and director of culinary, constantly surveys the environment and is thus aware of food trends and compatible suppliers. Despite infrequent criticisms of the authenticity of a "GlutenWise" food option, the Canadian Celiac Association has endorsed BP's line of gluten-free offerings.

Weaknesses

Weaknesses are internal elements that may interfere with the company's ability to achieve its objectives.

Perhaps BP's only weakness in its menu is the driver behind the marketing plan for this product proposal. Gluten-free burgers are now available at several Canadian fine-dining and premium casual eateries. And while this is a competitive threat, it is a factor whose origin is completely under BP's control. It must introduce a GlutenWise Burger both to broaden its appeal to the gluten-intolerant market and to keep pace with its competitors.

Opportunities

Opportunities are external elements that the company may be able to exploit to its advantage.

With the 2010 introduction of its GlutenWise line of pizzas, salads, and mains, Boston Pizza acknowledged the growing population of Canadians afflicted with some form of intolerance to gluten and satisfied the needs of this gluten-intolerant market. It is a market that continues to grow.

The other dominant opportunity compelling BP to proceed with a GlutenWise Burger is the growing sophistication of the gluten-free food production industry. This technological opportunity is founded on the growing needs of the market, which has sparked advances in GF baking techniques and resulted in products, such as hamburger buns, that are enjoyable to consumers.

Threats

Threats are current or emerging external elements that could potentially challenge the company's performance.

The single biggest threat facing BP in its absence of a gluten-free burger is the fact that many of its direct competitors have already gone to market with one. This was outlined in the earlier Competitive Review section.

While it's true that economic, natural, and political-legal forces could negatively impact Boston Pizza, those same forces would have similar effects on BP's competition, and are thus not detailed here.

Objectives

Objectives should be defined in specific, measurable, attainable, realistic, and time-bound (SMART) terms so that management can measure progress and plan corrective action if needed to stay on track. (Note that, in the interest of respecting Boston Pizza's competitive confidentiality, specific sales and volume projections for this product launch are not included.)

Boston Pizza has accomplished remarkable growth in its first 50 years. With over 370 stores across Canada, not to mention significant penetration into the United States and

Mexico, BP has become the go-to destination for tens of millions of diners and sports fans every year. There are a number of areas for continued growth, but as implied by BP's four pillars strategy, growth can be achieved only when it demonstrates a commitment to any combination of guest experience, brand, franchise profitability, and community involvement.

We've seen that the space for a GlutenWise Burger menu offering beckons. Consumer demand is growing, competition is reacting, and BP has an established product line upon which to create a natural extension of a burger.

Throughout the process of adding the GlutenWise Burger, the main objective is to adhere to the four pillar strategy. The new burger will enhance guest experience—particularly those with gluten sensitivity. It will build on BP's already strong brand. Sales, though uncertain until a full marketing plan has been implemented, are bound to increase—satisfying franchisee profitability. Finally, the GlutenWise Burger will further ingratiate BP with the Canadian Celiac Association and other health-conscious Canadian groups and associations.

Marketing Strategy

Beginning with a positioning statement and a statement of value proposition, the following pages summarize recommended strategies for Boston Pizza using the conventional marketing mix elements—product, price, distribution, and promotion—along with integrated marketing communications (IMC).

Positioning

A positioning built on meaningful differentiation, and supported by appropriate strategy and implementation, can help the company build competitive advantage.

Boston Pizza is Canada's favourite family dining and sports bar restaurant, appealing to people of all ages by offering a wide variety of delicious menu items in a familiar and fun setting.

Product Strategy

Despite having over 100 offerings currently on the Boston Pizza menu, there is still room for expansion, but only when a need is discovered. As has been identified throughout this plan, the absence of a GlutenWise Burger is a conspicuous gap that must be filled.

Consistent with BP's current burger menu items, the GlutenWise Burger will be a hearty and delicious half-pound, all-prime-rib-beef burger, grilled to perfection and perched on a gluten-free bun that will be deemed to be the best GF bun in Canada. While Boston Pizza has been widely celebrated for its GlutenWise line, including kudos from the president of the Canadian Celiac Association, it won't compromise flavour simply to add a menu item. Boston Pizza will acknowledge the difficulty faced by Canada's gluten-sensitive customers in finding baked goods that are both delicious and texturally pleasant.

Although a growing number of GF buns are commercially available, BP will launch a nationwide search for the "Best GF Bun in Canada" that will not only result in a delicious component of the GlutenWise Burger, but will also provide the catalyst for the GlutenWise Burger promotional strategy. An incredible tasting gluten-free bun will become a distinct competitive advantage. BP will therefore need to ensure ownership and confidentiality of the bun's recipe while at the same time honouring, celebrating, and rewarding the winner of the national competition. (Details on the best-bun contest follow in the Promotion Strategy section.)

The GlutenWise Burger will be available in the same varieties as its non-gluten-free counterparts: Double Bacon Barbecue, Prime Rib, Spicy Perogy, and Pepperoni and

Bacon Pizza Burger (which will be made using BP's gluten-free pizza crust). And as BP's culinary team continues to bring forward innovative and delicious new burger offerings to the menu, a similar GlutenWise option will be delivered simultaneously.

Pricing Strategy

With BP's customer-based value pricing evident throughout its menu, customers feel that they're getting their money's worth and more. The current lineup of burgers ranges from $12.25 for the Prime Rib Burger to $14.25 for the Double Bacon, Spicy Perogy, and Pizza Burgers. All varieties of burger come with a chosen side dish. While priced higher than the average quick service restaurant burger combo, BP's burgers are in fact priced lower than most of its competitors' versions in the casual dining and premium casual dining categories.

With its GlutenWise Burgers, Boston Pizza may choose to use a cost-based pricing strategy as it has done with its pizzas, for which it charges one dollar extra per personal-sized pizza to account for the additional costs in producing a gluten-free crust. Or, providing that the costs of production are recoverable without a price increase, BP may choose to hold the price consistent with that of its other non-gluten-free menu offerings.

If the latter decision is made, it is recommended that BP remove the price premium placed on all GlutenWise items and use this as both a competitive advantage and a promotional strategy. A sort of "penalty free" pricing/promo strategy might be a fun way to demonstrate BP's price leadership in the gluten-free space.

Costs of the gluten-free bun will not be known until the "Best GF Bun" is named and production thereof can be finalized. At such time BP will use its considerable buying power, brand equity, and current supplier network to procure the best ingredients at the best price in order to keep costs of production minimal.

Distribution Strategy

With its 370-plus locations across Canada, Boston Pizza is well equipped to manage the distribution of its GlutenWise Burger through the exact same direct marketing channels already in place. Like the existing GlutenWise menu, the burger items will be available both in-store and by delivery.

The actual supply chain of the GlutenWise Burger bun will be based on the winning recipe in its "Best GF Bun" competition. Once that is determined, an efficient production process will need to be developed. If the buns can be prepared in-house (as is the case with BP's GlutenWise pizza dough), then ingredients will be sourced from suppliers and logistics established accordingly. If, however, for whatever reason the buns must be prepared externally, then a different supply chain process will be put in place.

Promotion/Integrated Marketing Communications (IMC) Strategy

The most exciting component of the GlutenWise Burger launch, aside from the burger itself, will be the integrated marketing communications program built around the aforementioned "Best GF Bun" contest. This truly integrated, multitiered program will work as follows.

Sales Promotions/Public Relations/Online

Working with its creative partner and public relations agency, BP will use conventional and social media to roll out the "Best GF Bun" contest, explaining its rules, regulations, and process. Starting with fairly low-key and subtle messaging, the contest itself will invite any and all Canadians interested in developing a gluten-free bun to submit recipes to BP online within a stated time period. Boston Pizza will specifically seek out media attention using strategically crafted and disseminated media releases.

BP's head chef Michael Gray will then oversee the selection of a shortlist of recipes, of which prototypes will be developed while strictly adhering to Canada Food Inspection Agency regulations and the Canadian Celiac Association's policy for gluten-free baking.

Through the course of a taste-testing period, gluten-sensitive customers will be chosen randomly at various stores throughout Canada to participate in taste-testing. Their feedback will be submitted online through Boston Pizza's smartphone app. Again, publicity will be a key promotional tactic to drive attention to the "Best GF Bun" contest.

Using the taste-testing results, a winning recipe will be named and widely promoted through public relations. The creator of the recipe will be widely celebrated and financially rewarded. He or she will have committed to media opportunities in advance and will thus fulfill those obligations as part of the contest rules.

Ultimately, Boston Pizza's GlutenWise Burger product launch will take place across Canada, and will be connected with BP's existing "We'll Make You a Fan" positioning at the commencement of a new NHL season.

Advertising

Mainstream media advertising will not occur until the winning recipe has been chosen, production logistics are finalized, and the new product is ready for full release. Once the menu revisions have been made across all print and digital collateral pieces, a television, print, outdoor, and radio campaign will commence, celebrating the new GlutenWise Burger using a variety of appeals that chronicle the "Best GF Bun" contest.

Personal Selling

All BP front-of-house staff will be fully educated to speak accurately about the development of the GF bun and to help promote sales of the bun while serving customers of Boston Pizza.

Action Programs

Action programs help the marketing department convert strategies into actual activities that will see the strategies executed. Specific attention is given here to the execution of the marketing communication programs described above. These implementation plans are usually laid out in Gantt chart form so that a project management approach can be utilized.

The following is a high-level visual representation of the key strategies and sequencing required to develop and implement BP's GlutenWise Burger. A full Gantt chart depicting specific steps of the program will be developed and executed upon acceptance of the GlutenWise Burger product introduction.

Strategy	May	June	July	Aug.	Sept.	Oct.	Nov.
Product							
■ Development	▓	▓	▓	▓			
■ Production					▓		
■ Launch						▓	
Promotion							
■ Contest Launch	▓						
■ Contest Execution		▓	▓				
■ Contest Conclusion				▓			

Budget and Income Statement

Controls help management assess results after their plan has been implemented, identify any problems or performance variations, and initiate corrective action. (Note that Boston Pizza reserves the right to withhold sales and costs information that would normally be discussed in this section of a marketing plan. Therefore, the content that follows provides only limited and discussion-based references to sales.)

Upon approval of the GlutenWise Burger product line, a pro forma income statement will be developed. Prior to approval, and without knowing specific ingredients of the as-yet-undetermined GF burger bun recipe, it is difficult to calculate Cost of Goods Sold. In turn, without COGS, it is impossible at this point to prepare an accurate profit-and-loss statement. However, as stated in the SWOT analysis section of this plan, there is a growing trend in demand for gluten-free menu items at restaurants. Furthermore, according to a recent survey, more than 20 percent of those participating in a study regarding restaurant burger consumption indicated that the availability of a gluten-free alternative was important. Thus, it is reasonably assumed that the GlutenWise Burger will be profitable.

Marketing Controls

While the main objective of the GlutenWise Burger launch has more to do with brand than with sales, ongoing sales analysis and primary research will be conducted to monitor expectations against actual consumption of the new product.

Marketing by the Numbers

Marketing managers are facing increased accountability for the financial implications of their actions. This appendix provides a basic introduction to measuring marketing financial performance. Such financial analysis guides marketers in making sound marketing decisions and in assessing the outcomes of those decisions.

The appendix is built around a hypothetical manufacturer of consumer electronics products—HD. The company is introducing a device that plays videos and television programming streamed over the Internet on multiple devices in a home, including high-definition televisions, tablets, and mobile phones. In this appendix, we will analyze the various decisions HD's marketing managers must make before and after the new product launch.

The appendix is organized into *three sections*. The *first section* introduces pricing, break-even, and margin analysis assessments that will guide the introduction of HD's new product. The *second section* discusses demand estimates, the marketing budget, and marketing performance measures. It begins with a discussion of estimating market potential and company sales. It then introduces the marketing budget, as illustrated through a *pro forma* profit-and-loss statement followed by the actual profit-and-loss statement. Next, we discuss marketing performance measures, with a focus on helping marketing managers to better defend their decisions from a financial perspective. In the *third section,* we analyze the financial implications of various marketing tactics.

Each of the three sections ends with a set of quantitative exercises that provide you with an opportunity to apply the concepts you learned to situations beyond HD.

Pricing, Break-Even, and Margin Analysis

Pricing Considerations

Determining price is one of the most important marketing mix decisions. The limiting factors are demand and costs. Demand factors, such as buyer-perceived value, set the price ceiling. The company's costs set the price floor. In between these two factors, marketers must consider competitors' prices and other factors such as reseller requirements, government regulations, and company objectives.

Most current competing Internet streaming products sell at retail prices between $100 and $500. We first consider HD's pricing decision from a cost perspective. Then, we consider consumer value, the competitive environment, and reseller requirements.

Determining Costs

Recall from Chapter 10 that there are different types of costs. **Fixed costs** do not vary with production or sales level and include costs such as rent, interest, depreciation, and clerical and management salaries. Regardless of the level of output, the company must pay these costs. Whereas total fixed costs remain constant as output increases, the fixed cost per unit (or average fixed cost) will decrease as output increases because the total fixed costs are spread across more units of output. **Variable costs** vary directly with the level of production and include costs related to the direct production of the product

Fixed costs
Costs that do not vary with production or sales level.

Variable costs
Costs that vary directly with the level of production.

(such as costs of goods sold—COGS) and many of the marketing costs associated with selling it. Although these costs tend to be uniform for each unit produced, they are called variable because their total varies with the number of units produced. **Total costs** are the sum of the fixed and variable costs for any given level of production.

HD has invested $10 million in refurbishing an existing facility to manufacture the new video streaming product. Once production begins, the company estimates that it will incur fixed costs of $20 million per year. The variable cost to produce each device is estimated to be $125 and is expected to remain at that level for the output capacity of the facility.

Setting Price Based on Costs

HD starts with the cost-based approach to pricing discussed in Chapter 10 . Recall that the simplest method, **cost-plus pricing** (or **markup pricing**), simply adds a standard markup to the cost of the product. To use this method, however, HD must specify expected unit sales so that total unit costs can be determined. Unit variable costs will remain constant regardless of the output, but *average unit fixed costs* will decrease as output increases.

To illustrate this method, suppose HD has fixed costs of $20 million, variable costs of $125 per unit, and expects unit sales of 1 million players. Thus, the cost per unit is given by:

$$\text{Units cost} = \text{variable cost} + \frac{\text{fixed costs}}{\text{unit sales}} = \$125 + \frac{\$20,000,000}{1,000,000} = \$145$$

Note that we do *not* include the initial investment of $10 million in the total fixed cost figure. It is not considered a fixed cost because it is not a *relevant* cost. **Relevant costs** are those that will occur in the future and that will vary across the alternatives being considered. HD's investment to refurbish the manufacturing facility was a one-time cost that will not reoccur in the future. Such past costs are *sunk costs* and should not be considered in future analyses.

Also notice that if HD sells its product for $145, the price is equal to the total cost per unit. This is the **break-even price**—the price at which unit revenue (price) equals unit cost and profit is zero.

Suppose HD does not want to merely break even but rather wants to earn a 25% markup on sales. HD's markup price is:[1]

$$\text{Markup price} = \frac{\text{unit cost}}{(1 - \text{desired return on sales})} = \frac{\$145}{1 - 0.25} = \$193.33$$

This is the price at which HD would sell the product to resellers such as wholesalers or retailers to earn a 25% profit on sales.

Another approach HD could use is called **return on investment (ROI) pricing** (or **target-return pricing**). In this case, the company *would* consider the initial $10 million investment, but only to determine the dollar profit goal. Suppose the company wants a 30% return on its investment. The price necessary to satisfy this requirement can be determined by:

$$\text{ROI price} = \text{unit cost} + \frac{\text{ROI} \times \text{investment}}{\text{unit sales}} = \$145 + \frac{0.3 \times \$10,000,000}{1,000,000} = \$148$$

That is, if HD sells its product for $148, it will realize a 30% return on its initial investment of $10 million.

In these pricing calculations, unit cost is a function of the expected sales, which were estimated to be 1 million units. But what if actual sales were lower? Then the unit cost would be higher because the fixed costs would be spread over fewer units, and the realized percentage

Total costs
The sum of the fixed and variable costs for any given level of production.

Cost-plus pricing (or markup pricing)
A standard markup to the cost of the product.

Relevant costs
Costs that will occur in the future and that will vary across the alternatives being considered.

Break-even price
The price at which total revenue equals total cost and profit is zero.

Return on investment (ROI) pricing (or target-return pricing)
A cost-based pricing method that determines price based on a specified rate of return on investment.

markup on sales or ROI would be lower. Alternatively, if sales are higher than the estimated 1 million units, unit cost would be lower than $145, so a lower price would produce the desired markup on sales or ROI. It's important to note that these cost-based pricing methods are *internally* focused and do not consider demand, competitors' prices, or reseller requirements. Because HD will be selling this product to consumers through wholesalers and retailers offering competing brands, the company must consider markup pricing from this perspective.

Setting Price Based on External Factors

Whereas costs determine the price floor, HD also must consider external factors when setting price. HD does not have the final say concerning the final price of its product to consumers—retailers do. So it must start with its suggested retail price and work back. In doing so, HD must consider the markups required by resellers that sell the product to consumers.

In general, a dollar **markup** is the difference between a company's selling price for a product and its cost to manufacture or purchase it. For a retailer, then, the markup is the difference between the price it charges consumers and the cost the retailer must pay for the product. Thus, for any level of reseller:

$$\text{Dollar markup} = \text{selling price} - \text{cost}$$

Markups are usually expressed as a percentage, and there are two different ways to compute markups—on *cost* or on *selling price*:

$$\text{Markup percentage on cost} = \frac{\text{doller markup}}{\text{cost}}$$

$$\text{Markup percentage on selling price} = \frac{\text{dollor markup}}{\text{selling price}}$$

To apply reseller margin analysis, HD must first set the suggested retail price and then work back to the price at which it must sell the product to a wholesaler. Suppose retailers expect a 30% margin and wholesalers want a 20% margin based on their respective selling prices. And suppose that HD sets a manufacturer's suggested retail price (MSRP) of $299.99 for its product.

HD selected the $299.99 MSRP because it is lower than most competitors' prices but is not so low that consumers might perceive it to be of poor quality. And the company's research shows that it is below the threshold at which more consumers are willing to purchase the product. By using buyers' perceptions of value and not the seller's cost to determine the MSRP, HD is using **value-based pricing**. For simplicity, we will use an MSRP of $300 in further analyses.

To determine the price HD will charge wholesalers, we must first subtract the retailer's margin from the retail price to determine the retailer's cost ($300 − ($300 × 0.30) = $210). The retailer's cost is the wholesaler's price, so HD next subtracts the wholesaler's margin ($210 − ($210 × 0.20) = $168). Thus, the **markup chain**; representing the sequence of markups used by firms at each level in a channel for HD's new product is:

Suggested retail price:	$300
minus retail margin (30%):	− $ 90
Retailer's cost/wholesaler's price:	$210
minus wholesaler's margin (20%):	− $ 42
Wholesaler's cost/HD's price:	$168

By deducting the markups for each level in the markup chain, HD arrives at a price for the product to wholesalers of $168.

Markup
The difference between a company's selling price for a product and its cost to manufacture or purchase it.

Value-based pricing
Offering just the right combination of quality and good service at a fair price.

Markup chain
The sequence of markups used by firms at each level in a channel.

Break-Even and Margin Analysis

The previous analyses derived a value-based price of $168 for HD's product. Although this price is higher than the break-even price of $145 and covers costs, that price assumed a demand of 1 million units. But how many units and what level of dollar sales must HD achieve to break even at the $168 price? And what level of sales must be achieved to realize various profit goals? These questions can be answered through break-even and margin analysis.

Determining Break-Even Unit Volume and Dollar Sales

Based on an understanding of costs, consumer value, the competitive environment, and reseller requirements, HD has decided to set its price to wholesalers at $168. At that price, what sales level will be needed for HD to break even or make a profit on its product? **Break-even analysis** determines the unit volume and dollar sales needed to be profitable given a particular price and cost structure. At the break-even point, total revenue equals total costs and profit is zero. Above this point, the company will make a profit; below it, the company will lose money. HD can calculate break-even volume using the following formula:

Break-even analysis
Analysis to determine the unit volume and dollar sales needed to be profitable given a particular price and cost structure.

$$\text{Break-even volume} = \frac{\text{fixed costs}}{\text{price} - \text{unit variable cost}}$$

The denominator (price − unit variable cost) is called **unit contribution** (sometimes called contribution margin). It represents the amount that each unit contributes to covering fixed costs. Break-even volume represents the level of output at which all (variable and fixed) costs are covered. In HD's case, break-even unit volume is:

Unit contribution
The amount that each unit contributes to covering fixed costs—the difference between price and variable costs.

$$\text{Break-even volume} = \frac{\text{fixed costs}}{\text{price} - \text{variable ost}} = \frac{\$20,000,000}{\$168 - 125} = 465,116.2 \text{ units}$$

Thus, at the given cost and pricing structure, HD will break even at 465,117 units.

To determine the break-even dollar sales, simply multiply unit break-even volume by the selling price:

$$\text{BE sales} = \text{BE}_{\text{vol}} \times \text{price} = 465,117 \times \$168 = \$78,139,656$$

Another way to calculate dollar break-even sales is to use the percentage contribution margin (hereafter referred to as **contribution margin**), which is the unit contribution divided by the selling price:

Contribution margin
The unit contribution divided by the selling price.

$$\text{Contribution margin} = \frac{\text{price} - \text{variable cost}}{\text{price}} = \frac{\$168 - \$125}{\$168} = 0.256 \text{ or } 25.6\%$$

Then,

$$\text{Break-even sales} = \frac{\text{fixed costs}}{\text{contribution margin}} = \frac{\$20,000,000}{0.256} = \$78,125,00$$

Note that the difference between the two break-even sales calculations is due to rounding.

Such break-even analysis helps HD by showing the unit volume needed to cover costs. If production capacity cannot attain this level of output, then the company should not launch this product. However, the unit break-even volume is well within HD's capacity. Of course, the bigger question concerns whether HD can sell this volume at the $168 price. We'll address that issue a little later.

Understanding contribution margin is useful in other types of analyses as well, particularly if unit prices and unit variable costs are unknown or if a company (say, a retailer) sells many products at different prices and knows the percentage of total sales variable costs represent. Whereas unit contribution is the difference between unit price and unit variable costs, total contribution is the difference between total sales and total variable costs. The overall contribution margin can be calculated by:

$$\text{Contribution margin} = \frac{\text{total sales} - \text{total variable costs}}{\text{total sales}}$$

Regardless of the actual level of sales, if the company knows what percentage of sales is represented by variable costs, it can calculate contribution margin. For example, HD's unit variable cost is $125, or 74% of the selling price ($125 ÷ $168 = 0.74). That means for every $1 of sales revenue for HD, $0.74 represents variable costs, and the difference ($0.26) represents contribution to fixed costs. But even if the company doesn't know its unit price and unit variable cost, it can calculate the contribution margin from total sales and total variable costs or from knowledge of the total cost structure. It can set total sales equal to 100% regardless of the actual absolute amount and determine the contribution margin:

$$\text{Contribution margin} = \frac{100\% - 74\%}{100\%} = \frac{1 - 0.74}{1} = 1 - 0.74 = 0.26 \text{ or } 26\%$$

Note that this matches the percentage calculated from the unit price and unit variable cost information. This alternative calculation will be very useful later when analyzing various marketing decisions.

Determining "Break Even" for Profit Goals

Although it is useful to know the break-even point, most companies are more interested in making a profit. Assume HD would like to realize a $5 million profit in the first year. How many must it sell at the $168 price to cover fixed costs and produce this profit? To determine this, HD can simply add the profit figure to fixed costs and again divide by the unit contribution to determine unit sales:

$$\text{Unit volume} = \frac{\text{fixed cost} + \text{profit goal}}{\text{price} - \text{variable cost}} = \frac{\$20{,}000{,}000 + \$5{,}000{,}000}{\$168 - \$125} = 581{,}395.3 \text{ units}$$

Thus, to earn a $5 million profit, HD must sell 581,396 units. Multiply by price to determine dollar sales needed to achieve a $5 million profit:

$$\text{Dollar sales} = 581{,}396 \text{ units} \times \$168 = \$97{,}674{,}528$$

Or use the contribution margin:

$$\text{Sales} = \frac{\text{fixd cost} + \text{profit goal}}{\text{contribution margin}} = \frac{\$20{,}000{,}000 + \$5{,}000{,}000}{0.256} = \$97{,}656{,}250$$

Again, note that the difference between the two break-even sales calculations is due to rounding.

As we saw previously, a profit goal can also be stated as a return on investment goal. For example, recall that HD wants a 30% return on its $10 million investment. Thus, its absolute profit goal is $3 million ($10,000,000 × 0.30). This profit goal is treated the same way as in the previous example:[2]

$$\text{Unit volume} = \frac{\text{fixed cost} + \text{profit goal}}{\text{price} - \text{variable cost}} = \frac{\$20{,}000{,}000 + \$3{,}000{,}000}{\$168 - \$125} = 534{,}884 \text{ units}$$

$$\text{Dollar sales} = 534{,}884 \text{ units} \times \$168 = \$89{,}860{,}512$$

Or

$$\text{Dollar sales} = \frac{\text{fixed cost} + \text{profit goal}}{\text{contribution margin}} = \frac{\$20,000,000 + \$3,000,000}{0.256} = \$89,843,750$$

Finally, HD can express its profit goal as a percentage of sales, which we also saw in previous pricing analyses. Assume HD desires a 25% return on sales. To determine the unit and sales volume necessary to achieve this goal, the calculation is a little different from the previous two examples. In this case, we incorporate the profit goal into the unit contribution as an additional variable cost. Look at it this way: If 25% of each sale must go toward profits, that leaves only 75% of the selling price to cover fixed costs. Thus, the equation becomes:

$$\text{Unit volume} = \frac{\text{fixed cost}}{\text{price} - \text{variable cost} - (0.25 \times \text{price})} \text{ or } \frac{\text{fixed cost}}{(0.75 \times \text{price}) - \text{variable cost}}$$

So,

$$\text{Unit volume} = \frac{\$20,000,000}{(0.75 \times \$168) - \$125} = 20,000,000 \text{ units}$$

$$\text{Dollar sales necessary} = 20,000,000 \times \text{units} \times \$168 = \$3,360,000,000$$

Thus, HD would need more than $3 billion in sales to realize a 25% return on sales given its current price and cost structure! Could it possibly achieve this level of sales? The major point is this: Although break-even analysis can be useful in determining the level of sales needed to cover costs or to achieve a stated profit goal, it does not tell the company whether it is *possible* to achieve that level of sales at the specified price. To address this issue, HD needs to estimate demand for this product.

Before moving on, however, let's stop here and practice applying the concepts covered so far. Now that you have seen pricing and break-even concepts in action as they relate to HD's new product, here are several exercises for you to apply what you have learned in other contexts.

Marketing by the Numbers Exercise Set One

Now that you've studied pricing, break-even, and margin analysis as they relate to HD's new-product launch, use the following exercises to apply these concepts in other contexts.

1.1 Elkins, a manufacturer of ice makers, realizes a cost of $250 for every unit it produces. Its total fixed costs equal $5 million. If the company manufactures 500,000 units, compute the following:
  a. unit cost
  b. markup price if the company desires a 10% return on sales
  c. ROI price if the company desires a 25% return on an investment of $1 million

1.2 A gift shop owner purchases items to sell in her store. She purchases a chair for $125 and sells it for $275. Determine the following:
  a. dollar markup
  b. markup percentage on cost
  c. markup percentage on selling price

1.3 A consumer purchases a coffee maker from a retailer for $90. The retailer's markup is 30%, and the wholesaler's markup is 10%, both based on selling price. For what price does the manufacturer sell the product to the wholesaler?

1.4 A lawn mower manufacturer has a unit cost of $140 and wishes to achieve a margin of 30% based on selling price. If the manufacturer sells directly to a retailer who then adds a set margin of 40% based on selling price, determine the retail price charged to consumers.

1.5 Advanced Electronics manufactures DVDs and sells them directly to retailers who typically sell them for $20. Retailers take a 40% margin based on the retail selling price. Advanced's cost information is as follows:

DVD package and disc	$2.50/DVD
Royalties	$2.25/DVD
Advertising and promotion	$500,000
Overhead	$200,000

Calculate the following:
a. contribution per unit and contribution margin
b. break-even volume in DVD units and dollars
c. volume in DVD units and dollar sales necessary if Advanced's profit goal is 20% profit on sales
d. net profit if 5 million DVDs are sold

Demand Estimates, the Marketing Budget, and Marketing Performance Measures

Market Potential and Sales Estimates

HD has now calculated the sales needed to break even and to attain various profit goals on its new product. However, the company needs more information regarding demand in order to assess the feasibility of attaining the needed sales levels. This information is also needed for production and other decisions. For example, production schedules need to be developed and marketing tactics need to be planned.

The **total market demand** for a product or service is the total volume that would be bought by a defined consumer group in a defined geographic area in a defined time period in a defined marketing environment under a defined level and mix of industry marketing effort. Total market demand is not a fixed number but a function of the stated conditions. For example, next year's total market demand for this type of product will depend on how much other producers spend on marketing their brands. It also depends on many environmental factors, such as government regulations, economic conditions, and the level of consumer confidence in a given market. The upper limit of market demand is called **market potential**.

One general but practical method that HD might use for estimating total market demand uses three variables: (1) the number of prospective buyers, (2) the quantity purchased by an average buyer per year, and (3) the price of an average unit. Using these numbers, HD can estimate total market demand as follows:

$$Q = n \times q \times p$$

where

Q = total market demand
n = number of buyers in the market
q = quantity purchased by an average buyer per year
p = price of an average unit

Total market demand
The total volume that would be bought by a defined consumer group in a defined geographic area in a defined time period in a defined marketing environment under a defined level and mix of industry marketing effort.

Market potential
The upper limit of market demand.

Chain ratio method
Estimating market demand by multiplying a base number by a chain of adjusting percentages.

A variation of this approach is the **chain ratio method**. This method involves multiplying a base number by a chain of adjusting percentages. For example, HD's product is designed to stream high-definition video on high-definition televisions as well as play other video content streamed from the Internet to multiple devices in a home. Thus, consumers who do not own a high-definition television will not likely purchase this player. Additionally, only households with broadband Internet access will be able to use the product. Finally, not all HDTV-owning Internet households will be willing and able to purchase this product. HD can estimate U.S. demand using a chain of calculations like the following:

Total number of U.S. households

$\times$ The percentage of HDTV-owning U.S. households with broadband Internet access

$\times$ The percentage of these households willing and able to buy this device

The U.S. Census Bureau estimates that there are approximately 113 million households in the United States.[3] HD's research indicates that 60 percent of U.S. households own at least one HDTV and have broadband Internet access. Finally, the company's research also revealed that 30 percent of households possess the discretionary income needed and are willing to buy a product such as this. Then, the total number of households willing and able to purchase this product is:

$$113 \text{ million households} \times 0.60 \times 0.30 = 20.34 \text{ million households}$$

Households only need to purchase one device because it can stream content to other devices throughout the household. Assuming the average retail price across all brands is $350 for this product, the estimate of total market demand is as follows:

$$20.34 \text{ million households} \times 1 \text{ device per household} \times \$350 = \$7,119,000,000$$

This simple chain of calculations gives HD only a rough estimate of potential demand. However, more detailed chains involving additional segments and other qualifying factors would yield more accurate and refined estimates. Still, these are only *estimates* of market potential. They rely heavily on assumptions regarding adjusting percentages, average quantity, and average price. Thus, HD must make certain that its assumptions are reasonable and defendable. As can be seen, the overall market potential in dollar sales can vary widely given the average price used. For this reason, HD will use unit sales potential to determine its sales estimate for next year. Market potential in terms of units is 20.34 million (20.34 million households $\times$ 1 device per household).

Assuming that HD forecasts it will have a 3.66% market share in the first year after launching this product, then it can forecast unit sales at 20.34 million units $\times$ 0.0366 = 744,444 units. At a selling price of $168 per unit, this translates into sales of $125,066,592 (744,444 units $\times$ $168 per unit). For simplicity, further analyses will use forecasted sales of $125 million.

This unit volume estimate is well within HD's production capacity and exceeds not only the break-even estimate (465,117 units) calculated earlier, but also the volume necessary to realize a $5 million profit (581,396 units) or a 30% return on investment (534,884 units). However, this forecast falls well short of the volume necessary to realize a 25% return on sales (20 million units!) and may require that HD revise expectations.

To assess expected profits, we must now look at the budgeted expenses for launching this product. To do this, we will construct a pro forma profit-and-loss statement.

The Profit-and-Loss Statement and Marketing Budget

All marketing managers must account for the profit impact of their marketing strategies. A major tool for projecting such profit impact is a **pro forma** (or **projected**) **profit-and-loss statement** (also called an **income statement** or **operating statement**). A pro forma statement shows projected revenues less budgeted expenses and estimates the projected net profit for an organization, product, or brand during a specific planning period, typically a year. It includes direct product production costs, marketing expenses budgeted to attain a given sales forecast, and overhead expenses assigned to the organization or product. A profit-and-loss statement typically consists of several major components (see **Table A3.1**):

Pro forma (or **projected**) **profit-and-loss statement** (or **income statement or operating statement**) A statement that shows projected revenues less budgeted expenses and estimates the projected net profit for an organization, product, or brand during a specific planning period, typically a year.

- *Net sales*—gross sales revenue minus returns and allowances (for example, trade, cash, quantity, and promotion allowances). HD's net sales for 2014 are estimated to be $125 million, as determined in the previous analysis.

- *Cost of goods sold*—(sometimes called *cost of sales*)—the actual cost of the merchandise sold by a manufacturer or reseller. It includes the cost of inventory, purchases, and other costs associated with making the goods. HD's cost of goods sold is estimated to be 50% of net sales, or $62.5 million.

- *Gross margin (or gross profit)*—the difference between net sales and cost of goods sold. HD's gross margin is estimated to be $62.5 million.

- *Operating expenses*—the expenses incurred while doing business. These include all other expenses beyond the cost of goods sold that are necessary to conduct business. Operating expenses can be presented in total or broken down in detail. Here, HD's estimated operating expenses include *marketing expenses* and *general and administrative expenses*.

Marketing expenses include sales expenses, promotion expenses, and distribution expenses. The new product will be sold through HD's sales force, so the company budgets $5 million for sales salaries. However, because sales representatives earn a 10% commission on sales, HD must also add a variable component to sales expenses of $12.5 million

TABLE A3.1 Pro Forma Profit-and-Loss Statement for the 12-Month Period Ended -December 31, 2014			
			% of Sales
Net Sales		$ 125,000,000	100 %
Cost of Goods Sold		62,500,000	50 %
Gross Margin		$ 62,500,000	50 %
Marketing Expenses			
Sales expenses	$ 17,500,000		
Promotion expenses	15,000,000		
Freight	12,500,000	45,000,000	36 %
General and Administrative Expenses			
Managerial salaries and expenses	$ 2,000,000		
Indirect overhead	3,000,000	5,000,000	4 %
Net Profit before Income Tax		$ 12,500,000	10 %

(10% of $125 million net sales), for a total budgeted sales expense of $17.5 million. HD sets its advertising and promotion to launch this product at $10 million. However, the company also budgets 4% of sales, or $5 million, for cooperative advertising allowances to retailers who promote HD's new product in their advertising. Thus, the total budgeted advertising and promotion expenses are $15 million ($10 million for advertising plus $5 million in co-op allowances). Finally, HD budgets 10% of net sales, or $12.5 million, for freight and delivery charges. In all, total marketing expenses are estimated to be $17.5 million + $15 million + $12.5 million = $45 million.

General and administrative expenses are estimated at $5 million, broken down into $2 million for managerial salaries and expenses for the marketing function and $3 million of indirect overhead allocated to this product by the corporate accountants (such as depreciation, interest, maintenance, and insurance). Total expenses for the year, then, are estimated to be $50 million ($45 million marketing expenses + $5 million in general and administrative expenses).

- *Net profit before taxes*—profit earned after all costs are deducted. HD's estimated net profit before taxes is $12.5 million.

In all, as Table A3.1 shows, HD expects to earn a profit on its new product of $12.5 million in 2014. Also note that the percentage of sales that each component of the profit-and-loss statement represents is given in the right-hand column. These percentages are determined by dividing the cost figure by net sales (that is, marketing expenses represent 36% of net sales determined by $45 million ÷ $125 million). As can be seen, HD projects a net profit return on sales of 10% in the first year after launching this product.

Marketing Performance Measures

Now let's fast-forward a year. HD's product has been on the market for one year and management wants to assess its sales and profit performance. One way to assess this performance is to compute performance ratios derived from HD's **profit-and-loss statement** (or **income statement** or **operating statement**).

Profit-and-loss statement (or income statement or operating statement)
A statement that shows actual revenues less expenses and net profit for an organization, product, or brand during a specific planning period, typically a year.

Whereas the pro forma profit-and-loss statement shows *projected* financial performance, the statement given in **Table A3.2** shows HD's *actual* financial performance based on actual sales, cost of goods sold, and expenses during the past year. By comparing the profit-and-loss statement from one period to the next, HD can gauge performance against goals, spot favorable or unfavorable trends, and take appropriate corrective action.

The profit-and-loss statement shows that HD lost $1 million rather than making the $12.5 million profit projected in the pro forma statement. Why? One obvious reason is that net sales fell $25 million short of estimated sales. Lower sales translated into lower variable costs associated with marketing the product. However, both fixed costs and the cost of goods sold as a percentage of sales exceeded expectations. Hence, the product's contribution margin was 21% rather than the estimated 26%. That is, variable costs represented 79% of sales (55% for cost of goods sold, 10% for sales commissions, 10% for freight, and 4% for co-op allowances). Recall that contribution margin can be calculated by subtracting that fraction from one (1 − 0.79 = 0.21). Total fixed costs were $22 million, $2 million more than estimated. Thus, the sales that HD needed to break even given this cost structure can be calculated as:

$$\text{Break-even sales} = \frac{\text{fixed costs}}{\text{contribution margin}} = \frac{\$22,000,000}{0.21} = \$104,761,905$$

If HD had achieved another $5 million in sales, it would have earned a profit.

Although HD's sales fell short of the forecasted sales, so did overall industry sales for this product. Overall industry sales were only $2.5 billion. That means that HD's **market share** was 4% ($100 million ÷ $2.5 billion = 0.04 = 4%), which was higher than forecasted. Thus, HD attained a higher-than-expected market share but the overall market sales were not as high as estimated.

Market share
Company sales divided by market sales.

TABLE A3.2 Profit-and-Loss Statement for the 12-Month Period Ended December 31, 2014			
			% of Sales
Net Sales		$100,000,000	100 %
Cost of Goods Sold		55,000,000	55 %
Gross Margin		$ 45,000,000	45 %
Marketing Expenses			
Sales expenses	$15,000,000		
Promotion expenses	14,000,000		
Freight	10,000,000	39,000,000	39 %
General and Administrative Expenses			
Managerial salaries and expenses	$ 2,000,000		
Indirect overhead	5,000,000	7,000,000	7 %
Net Profit before Income Tax		($ 1,000,000)	(−1 %)

Analytic Ratios

The profit-and-loss statement provides the figures needed to compute some crucial **operating ratios**—the ratios of selected operating statement items to net sales. These ratios let marketers compare the firm's performance in one year to that in previous years (or with industry standards and competitors' performance in that year). The most commonly used operating ratios are the gross margin percentage, the net profit percentage, and the operating expense percentage. The inventory turnover rate and return on investment (ROI) are often used to measure managerial effectiveness and efficiency.

Operating ratios
The ratios of selected operating statement items to net sales.

The **gross margin percentage** indicates the percentage of net sales remaining after cost of goods sold that can contribute to operating expenses and net profit before taxes. The higher this ratio, the more a firm has left to cover expenses and generate profit. HD's gross margin ratio was 45%:

Gross margin percentage
The percentage of net sales remaining after cost of goods sold—calculated by dividing gross margin by net sales.

$$\text{Gross margin percentage} = \frac{\text{gross margin}}{\text{net sales}} = \frac{\$45,000,000}{\$100,000,000} = 0.45 = 45\%$$

Note that this percentage is lower than estimated, and this ratio is seen easily in the percentage of sales column in Table A3.2 . Stating items in the profit-and-loss statement as a percent of sales allows managers to quickly spot abnormal changes in costs over time. If there was previous history for this product and this ratio was declining, management should examine it more closely to determine why it has decreased (that is, because of a decrease in sales volume or price, an increase in costs, or a combination of these). In HD's case, net sales were $25 million lower than estimated, and cost of goods sold was higher than estimated (55% rather than the estimated 50%).

Net profit percentage
The percentage of each sales dollar going to profit—calculated by dividing net profits by net sales.

The **net profit percentage** shows the percentage of each sales dollar going to profit. It is calculated by dividing net profits by net sales:

$$\text{Net profit percentage} = \frac{\text{net profit}}{\text{net sales}} = \frac{-\$1,000,000}{\$100,000,000} = -0.01 = -1.0\%$$

This ratio is easily seen in the percent of sales column. HD's new product generated negative profits in the first year, not a good situation given that before the product launch net profits before taxes were estimated at more than $12 million. Later in this appendix, we will discuss further analyses the marketing manager should conduct to defend the product.

Operating expense percentage
The portion of net sales going to operating expenses—calculated by dividing total expenses by net sales.

The **operating expense percentage** indicates the portion of net sales going to operating expenses. Operating expenses include marketing and other expenses not directly related to marketing the product, such as indirect overhead assigned to this product. It is calculated by:

$$\text{Operating expense percentage} = \frac{\text{total expenses}}{\text{net sales}} = \frac{\$46,000,000}{\$100,000,000} = 0.46 = 46\%$$

This ratio can also be quickly determined from the percent of sales column in the profit-and-loss statement by adding the percentages for marketing expenses and general and administrative expenses (39% + 7%). Thus, 46 cents of every sales dollar went for operations. Although HD wants this ratio to be as low as possible, and 46% is not an alarming amount, it is of concern if it is increasing over time or if a loss is realized.

Inventory turnover rate
(or **stockturn rate**)
The number of times an inventory turns over or is sold during a specified time period (often one year)—calculated based on costs, selling price, or units.

Another useful ratio is the **inventory turnover rate** (also called **stockturn rate** for resellers). The inventory turnover rate is the number of times an inventory turns over or is sold during a specified time period (often one year). This rate tells how quickly a business is moving inventory through the organization. Higher rates indicate that lower investments in inventory are made, thus freeing up funds for other investments. It may be computed on a cost, selling price, or unit basis. The formula based on cost is:

$$\text{Inventory turnover rate} = \frac{\text{cost of goods sold}}{\text{average inventory at cost}}$$

Assuming HD's beginning and ending inventories were $30 million and $20 million, respectively, the inventory turnover rate is:

$$\text{Inventory turnover rate} = \frac{\$55,000,000}{(\$30,000,000 + \$20,000,000)/2} = \frac{\$55,000,000}{\$25,000,000} = 2.2$$

That is, HD's inventory turned over 2.2 times in 2014. Normally, the higher the turnover rate, the higher the management efficiency and company profitability. However, this rate should be compared to industry averages, competitors' rates, and past performance to determine if HD is doing well. A competitor with similar sales but a higher inventory turnover rate will have fewer resources tied up in inventory, allowing it to invest in other areas of the business.

Return on investment (ROI)
A measure of managerial effectiveness and efficiency—net profit before taxes divided by total investment.

Companies frequently use **return on investment (ROI)** to measure managerial effectiveness and efficiency. For HD, ROI is the ratio of net profits to total investment required to manufacture the new product. This investment includes capital investments in land, buildings, and equipment (here, the initial $10 million to refurbish the manufacturing facility) plus inventory costs (HD's average inventory totaled $25 million), for a total of $35 million. Thus, HD's ROI for this product is:

$$\text{Return on investment} = \frac{\text{net profit before taxes}}{\text{investment}} = \frac{-\$1,000,000}{\$35,000,000} = -0.286 = -2.86\%$$

ROI is often used to compare alternatives, and a positive ROI is desired. The alternative with the highest ROI is preferred to other alternatives. HD needs to be concerned with the ROI realized. One obvious way HD can increase ROI is to increase net profit by reducing expenses. Another way is to reduce its investment, perhaps by investing less in inventory and turning it over more frequently.

Marketing Profitability Metrics

Given the previous financial results, you may be thinking that HD should drop this new product. But what arguments can marketers make for keeping or dropping this product? The obvious arguments for dropping the product are that first-year sales were well below expected levels and the product lost money, resulting in a negative return on investment.

So what would happen if HD did drop this product? Surprisingly, if the company drops the product, the profits for the total organization will decrease by $4 million! How can that be? Marketing managers need to look closely at the numbers in the profit-and-loss statement to determine the *net marketing contribution* for this product. In HD's case, the net marketing contribution for the product is $4 million, and if the company drops this product, that contribution will disappear as well. Let's look more closely at this concept to illustrate how marketing managers can better assess and defend their marketing strategies and programs.

Net Marketing Contribution

Net marketing contribution (NMC), along with other marketing metrics derived from it, measures *marketing* profitability. It includes only components of profitability that are controlled by marketing. Whereas the previous calculation of net profit before taxes from the profit-and-loss statement includes operating expenses not under marketing's control, NMC does not. Referring back to HD's profit-and-loss statement given in Table A3.2 , we can calculate net marketing contribution for the product as:

$$\text{NMC} = \text{net sales} - \text{cost of goods sold} - \text{marketing expenses}$$
$$= \$100 \text{ million} - \$55 \text{ million} - \$41 \text{ million} = \$4 \text{ million}$$

Net marketing contribution (NMC)
A measure of marketing profitability that includes only components of profitability controlled by marketing.

The marketing expenses include sales expenses ($15 million), promotion expenses ($14 million), freight expenses ($10 million), and the managerial salaries and expenses of the marketing function ($2 million), which total $41 million.

Thus, the product actually contributed $4 million to HD's profits. It was the $5 million of indirect overhead allocated to this product that caused the negative profit. Further, the amount allocated was $2 million more than estimated in the pro forma profit-and-loss statement. Indeed, if only the estimated amount had been allocated, the product would have earned a *profit* of $1 million rather than losing $1 million. If HD drops the product, the $5 million in fixed overhead expenses will not disappear—it will simply have to be allocated elsewhere. However, the $4 million in net marketing contribution *will* disappear.

Marketing Return on Sales and Investment

To get an even deeper understanding of the profit impact of marketing strategy, we'll now examine two measures of marketing efficiency—*marketing return on sales* (marketing ROS) and *marketing return on investment* (marketing ROI).[4]

Marketing return on sales (or **marketing ROS**) shows the percent of net sales attributable to the net marketing contribution. For our product, ROS is:

Marketing return on sales
(or **marketing ROS**)
The percent of net sales attributable to the net marketing contribution—calculated by dividing net marketing contribution by net sales.

$$\text{Marketing ROS} = \frac{\text{net marketing contribution}}{\text{net sales}} = \frac{\$4,000,000}{\$100,000,000} = 0.04 = 4\%$$

Thus, out of every $100 of sales, the product returns $4 to HD's bottom line. A high marketing ROS is desirable. But to assess whether this is a good level of performance, HD must compare this figure to previous marketing ROS levels for the product, the ROSs of other products in the company's portfolio, and the ROSs of competing products.

Marketing return on investment (or **marketing ROI**) measures the marketing productivity of a marketing investment. In HD's case, the marketing investment is represented by $41 million of the total expenses. Thus, marketing ROI is:

$$\text{Marketing ROI} = \frac{\text{net marketing contribution}}{\text{marketing expenes}} = \frac{\$4,000,000}{\$41,000,000} = 0.0976 = 9.76\%$$

As with marketing ROS, a high value is desirable, but this figure should be compared with previous levels for the given product and with the marketing ROIs of competitors' products. Note from this equation that marketing ROI could be greater than 100%. This can be achieved by attaining a higher net marketing contribution and/or a lower total marketing expense.

In this section, we estimated market potential and sales, developed profit-and-loss statements, and examined financial measures of performance. In the next section, we discuss methods for analyzing the impact of various marketing tactics. However, before moving on to those analyses, here's another set of quantitative exercises to help you apply what you've learned to other situations.

Marketing by the Numbers Exercise Set Two

2.1 Determine the market potential for a product that has 20 million prospective buyers who purchase an average of 2 per year and price averages $50. How many units must a company sell if it desires a 10% share of this market?

2.2 Develop a profit-and-loss statement for the Westgate division of North Industries. This division manufactures light fixtures sold to consumers through home improvement and hardware stores. Cost of goods sold represents 40% of net sales. Marketing expenses include selling expenses, promotion expenses, and freight. Selling expenses include sales salaries totaling $3 million per year and sales commissions (5% of sales). The company spent $3 million on advertising last year, and freight costs were 10% of sales. Other costs include $2 million for managerial salaries and expenses for the marketing function and another $3 million for indirect overhead allocated to the division.
   a. Develop the profit-and-loss statement if net sales were $20 million last year.
   b. Develop the profit-and-loss statement if net sales were $40 million last year.
   c. Calculate Westgate's break-even sales.

2.3 Using the profit-and-loss statement you developed in question 2.2b, and assuming that Westgate's beginning inventory was $11 million, ending inventory was $7 million, and total investment was $20 million including inventory, determine the following:
   a. gross margin percentage
   b. net profit percentage
   c. operating expense percentage
   d. inventory turnover rate
   e. return on investment (ROI)
   f. net marketing contribution
   g. marketing return on sales (marketing ROS)
   h. marketing return on investment (marketing ROI)
   i. Is the Westgate division doing well? Explain your answer.

Financial Analysis of Marketing Tactics

Although the first-year profit performance for HD's new product was less than desired, management feels that this attractive market has excellent growth opportunities. Although the sales of HD's product were lower than initially projected, they were not unreasonable given the size of the current market. Thus, HD wants to explore new marketing tactics to help grow the market for this product and increase sales for the company.

For example, the company could increase advertising to promote more awareness of the new product and its category. It could add salespeople to secure greater product distribution. HD could decrease prices so that more consumers could afford its product. Finally, to expand the market, HD could introduce a lower-priced model in addition to the higher-priced original offering. Before pursuing any of these tactics, HD must analyze the financial implications of each.

Increase Advertising Expenditures

HD is considering boosting its advertising to make more people aware of the benefits of this device in general and of its own brand in particular. What if HD's marketers recommend increasing national advertising by 50% to $15 million (assume no change in the variable cooperative component of promotional expenditures)? This represents an increase in fixed costs of $5 million. What increase in sales will be needed to break even on this $5 million increase in fixed costs?

A quick way to answer this question is to divide the increase in fixed cost by the contribution margin, which we found in a previous analysis to be 21%:

$$\text{Increase in sales} = \frac{\text{increase in fixed cost}}{\text{contribution margin}} = \frac{\$5,000,000}{0.21} = \$23,809,524$$

Thus, a 50% increase in advertising expenditures must produce a sales increase of almost $24 million to just break even. That $24 million sales increase translates into an almost 1 percentage point increase in market share (1% of the $2.5 billion overall market equals $25 million). That is, to break even on the increased advertising expenditure, HD would have to increase its market share from 4% to 4.95% ($123,809,524 ÷ $2.5 billion = 0.0495 or 4.95% market share). All of this assumes that the total market will not grow, which might or might not be a reasonable assumption.

Increase Distribution Coverage

HD also wants to consider hiring more salespeople in order to call on new retailer accounts and increase distribution through more outlets. Even though HD sells directly to wholesalers, its sales representatives call on retail accounts to perform other functions in addition to selling, such as training retail salespeople. Currently, HD employs 60 sales reps who earn an average of $50,000 in salary plus 10% commission on sales. The product is currently sold to consumers through 1,875 retail outlets. Suppose HD wants to increase that number of outlets to 2,500, an increase of 625 retail outlets. How many additional salespeople will HD need, and what sales will be necessary to break even on the increased cost?

One method for determining what size sales force HD will need is the **workload method**. The workload method uses the following formula to determine the sales force size:

$$NS = \frac{NC \times FC \times LC}{TA}$$

Workload method
An approach to determining sales force size based on the workload required and the time available for selling.

where

$$NS = \text{number of salespeople}$$
$$NC = \text{number of customers}$$
$$FC = \text{average frequency of customer calls per customer}$$
$$LC = \text{average length of customer call}$$
$$TA = \text{time an average salesperson has available for selling per year}$$

HD's sales reps typically call on accounts an average of 20 times per year for about 2 hours per call. Although each sales rep works 2,000 hours per year (50 weeks per year × 40 hours per week), they spend about 15 hours per week on nonselling activities such as administrative duties and travel. Thus, the average annual available selling time per sales rep per year is 1,250 hours (50 weeks × 25 hours per week). We can now calculate how many sales reps HD will need to cover the anticipated 2,500 retail outlets:

$$NS = \frac{2,500 \times 20 \times 2}{1,250} = 80 \, \text{salespeople}$$

Therefore, HD will need to hire 20 more salespeople. The cost to hire these reps will be $1 million (20 salespeople × $50,000 salary per sales person).

What increase in sales will be required to break even on this increase in fixed costs? The 10% commission is already accounted for in the contribution margin, so the contribution margin remains unchanged at 21%. Thus, the increase in sales needed to cover this increase in fixed costs can be calculated by:

$$\text{Increase in sales} = \frac{\text{increase in fixed cost}}{\text{contribution margin}} = \frac{\$1,000,000}{0.21} = \$4,761,905$$

That is, HD's sales must increase almost $5 million to break even on this tactic. So, how many new retail outlets will the company need to secure to achieve this sales increase? The average revenue generated per current outlet is $53,333 ($100 million in sales divided by 1,875 outlets). To achieve the nearly $5 million sales increase needed to break even, HD would need about 90 new outlets ($4,761,905 ÷ $53,333 = 89.3 outlets), or about 4.5 outlets per new rep. Given that current reps cover about 31 outlets apiece (1,875 outlets ÷ 60 reps), this seems very reasonable.

Decrease Price

HD is also considering lowering its price to increase sales revenue through increased volume. The company's research has shown that demand for most types of consumer electronics products is elastic—that is, the percentage increase in the quantity demanded is greater than the percentage decrease in price.

What increase in sales would be necessary to break even on a 10% decrease in price? That is, what increase in sales will be needed to maintain the total contribution that HD realized at the higher price? The current total contribution can be determined by multiplying the contribution margin by total sales:[5]

$$\text{Current total contribution} = \text{contribution margin} \times \text{sales}$$
$$= 0.21 \times \$100 \, \text{million} = \$21 \, \text{million}$$

Price changes result in changes in unit contribution and contribution margin. Recall that the contribution margin of 21% was based on variable costs representing 79% of sales. Therefore, unit variable costs can be determined by multiplying the original price by this percentage: $168 × 0.79 = $132.72 per unit. If price is decreased by 10%, the new price is $151.20. However, variable costs do not change just because price decreased, so the contribution and contribution margin decrease as follows:

	Old	New (reduced 10%)
Price	$168	$151.20
− Unit variable cost	$132.72	$132.72
− Unit contribution	$35.28	$18.48
Contribution margin	$35.28/$168 = 0.21 or 21%	$18.48/$151.20 = 0.12 or 12%

So a 10% reduction in price results in a decrease in the contribution margin from 21% to 12%.[6] To determine the sales level needed to break even on this price reduction, we calculate the level of sales that must be attained at the new contribution margin to achieve the original total contribution of $21 million:

New contribution margin × new sales level = original total contribution

So,

$$\text{New sales level} = \frac{\text{original contribution}}{\text{new contribution margin}} = \frac{\$21,000,000}{0.12} = \$175,000,000$$

Thus, sales must increase by $75 million ($175 million − $100 million) just to break even on a 10% price reduction. This means that HD must increase market share to 7% ($175 million ÷ $2.5 billion) to achieve the current level of profits (assuming no increase in the total market sales). The marketing manager must assess whether or not this is a reasonable goal.

Extend the Product Line

As a final option, HD is considering extending its product line by offering a lower-priced model. Of course, the new, lower-priced product would steal some sales from the higher-priced model. This is called **cannibalization**—the situation in which one product sold by a company takes a portion of its sales from other company products. If the new product has a lower contribution than the original product, the company's total contribution will decrease on the cannibalized sales. However, if the new product can generate enough new volume, it is worth considering.

Cannibalization
The situation in which one product sold by a company takes a portion of its sales from other company products.

To assess cannibalization, HD must look at the incremental contribution gained by having both products available. Recall in the previous analysis we determined that unit variable costs were $132.72 and unit contribution was just over $35. Assuming costs remain the same next year, HD can expect to realize a contribution per unit of approximately $35 for every unit of the original product sold.

Assume that the first model offered by HD is called HD1 and the new, lower-priced model is called HD2. HD2 will retail for $250, and resellers will take the same markup percentages on price as they do with the higher-priced model. Therefore, HD2's price to wholesalers will be $140 as follows:

Retail price:	$ 250
minus retail margin (30%):	−$ 75
Retailer's cost/wholesaler's price:	175
minus wholesaler's margin (20%):	−$ 35
Wholesaler's cost/HD's price	$ 140

If HD2's variable costs are estimated to be $120, then its contribution per unit will equal $20 ($140 − $120 = $20). That means for every unit that HD2 cannibalizes from

HD1, HD will *lose* $15 in contribution toward fixed costs and profit (that is, contribution$_{HD2}$ − contribution$_{HD1}$ = $20 − $35 = −$15). You might conclude that HD should not pursue this tactic because it appears as though the company will be worse off if it introduces the lower-priced model. However, if HD2 captures enough *additional* sales, HD will be better off even though some HD1 sales are cannibalized. The company must examine what will happen to *total* contribution, which requires estimates of unit volume for both products.

Originally, HD estimated that next year's sales of HD1 would be 600,000 units. However, with the introduction of HD2, it now estimates that 200,000 of those sales will be cannibalized by the new model. If HD sells only 200,000 units of the new HD2 model (all cannibalized from HD1), the company would lose $3 million in total contribution (200,000 units × −$15 per cannibalized unit = −$3 million)—not a good outcome. However, HD estimates that HD2 will generate the 200,000 of cannibalized sales plus an *additional* 500,000 unit sales. Thus, the contribution on these additional HD2 units will be $10 million (i.e., 500,000 units × $20 per unit = $10 million). The net effect is that HD will gain $7 million in total contribution by introducing HD2.

The following table compares HD's total contribution with and without the introduction of HD2:

	HD1 Only	HD1 and HD2
HD1 contribution	600,000 units × $35 = $21,000,000	400,000 units × $35 = $14,000,000
HD2 contribution	0	700,000 units × $20 = $14,000,000
Total contribution	$21,000,000	$28,000,000

The difference in the total contribution is a net gain of $7 million ($28 million − $21 million). Based on this analysis, HD should introduce the HD2 model because it results in a positive incremental contribution. However, if fixed costs will increase by more than $7 million as a result of adding this model, then the net effect will be negative and HD should not pursue this tactic.

Now that you have seen these marketing tactic analysis concepts in action as they related to HD's new product, here are several exercises for you to apply what you have learned in this section in other contexts.

Marketing by the Numbers Exercise Set Three

3.1 Alliance, Inc. sells gas lamps to consumers through retail outlets. Total industry sales for Alliance's relevant market last year were $100 million, with Alliance's sales representing 5% of that total. Contribution margin is 25%. Alliance's sales force calls on retail outlets and each sales rep earns $50,000 per year plus 1% commission on all sales. Retailers receive a 40% margin on selling price and generate average revenue of $10,000 per outlet for Alliance.

a. The marketing manager has suggested increasing consumer advertising by $200,000. By how much would dollar sales need to increase to break even on this expenditure? What increase in overall market share does this represent?

b. Another suggestion is to hire two more sales representatives to gain new consumer retail accounts. How many new retail outlets would be necessary to break even on the increased cost of adding two sales reps?

c. A final suggestion is to make a 10% across-the-board price reduction. By how much would dollar sales need to increase to maintain Alliance's current contribution? (See endnote 6 to calculate the new contribution margin.)

d. Which suggestion do you think Alliance should implement? Explain your recommendation.

3.2 PepsiCo sells its soft drinks in approximately 400,000 retail establishments, such as supermarkets, discount stores, and convenience stores. Sales representatives call on each retail account weekly, which means each account is called on by a sales rep 52 times per year. The average length of a sales call is 75 minutes (or 1.25 hours). An average salesperson works 2,000 hours per year (50 weeks per year × 40 hours per week), but each spends 10 hours a week on nonselling activities, such as administrative tasks and travel. How many salespeople does PepsiCo need?

3.3 Hair Zone manufactures a brand of hair-styling gel. It is considering adding a modified version of the product—a foam that provides stronger hold. Hair Zone's variable costs and prices to wholesalers are:

	Current Hair Gel	New Foam Product
Unit selling price	2.00	2.25
Unit variable costs	.85	1.25

Hair Zone expects to sell 1 million units of the new styling foam in the first year after introduction, but it expects that 60% of those sales will come from buyers who normally purchase Hair Zone's styling gel. Hair Zone estimates that it would sell 1.5 million units of the gel if it did not introduce the foam. If the fixed cost of launching the new foam will be $100,000 during the first year, should Hair Zone add the new product to its line? Why or why not?

Endnotes

CHAPTER 1

1. Kelly Gadzala, "Joe Keeps It Fresh," *Strategy*, October 5, 2011, http://strategyonline.ca/2011/10/05/joe-keeps-it-fresh; Megan Durisin, "Can Canada's Joe Fresh Save JCPenney?" *Financial Post*, March 15, 2013, http://business.financialpost.com/2013/03/16/can-canadas-joe-fresh-save-jcpenney; Jessica Allen, "Backstage with Joe Mimran: The Joe Fresh Designer—and Canadian Fashion Mogul—on What Inspired His 2013 Spring Collection," *Maclean's*, October 26, 2012, www2.macleans.ca/2012/10/26/backstage-with-joe-mimran; Hollie Shaw, "Brands Like Joe Fresh, President's Choice Set Loblaw Apart, Weston Tells AGM," *Financial Post*, May 3, 2012, http://business.financialpost.com/2012/05/03/brands-like-joe-fresh-presidents-choice-set-loblaw-apart-weston-tells-agm; information from www.joefresh.com and www.loblaws.ca; Jeanne Beker, "Joe Fresh Announces $1-Million Investment in Canada's Fashion Future," *Globe and Mail*, March 23, 2015, www.theglobeandmail.com/news/national/joe-fresh-announces-1-million-investment-in-canadas-fashion-future/article23575882; "Aldo Group Makes a Deal to Design Shoe Line for Joe Fresh," *CBC News*, March 26, 2015, www.cbc.ca/news/business/aldo-group-makes-deal-to-design-shoe-line-for-joe-fresh-1.3010625; and Kristin Rushowy, "Joe Fresh Losing Founder Joe Mimran," *Toronto Star*, March 16, 2015, www.thestar.com/news/gta/2015/03/16/joe-fresh-losing-founder-joe-mimran.html.

2. See Keith O'Brien, "How McDonald's Came Back Bigger Than Ever," *New York Times*, May 4, 2012, www.nytimes.com/2012/05/06/magazine/how-mcdonalds-came-back-bigger-than-ever.html?pagewanted=all; Heather Kelly, "Facebook Mobile Users Surpass Desktop Users for First Time," *CNN Tech*, January 31, 2013, www.cnn.com/2013/01/30/tech/social-media/facebook-mobile-users; and "Global 500," *Fortune*, July 22, 2013, p. 134.

3. See Philip Kotler and Kevin Lane Keller, *Marketing Management*, 14th ed. (Upper Saddle River, NJ: Prentice Hall, 2012), p. 5.

4. The American Marketing Association offers the following definition: "Marketing is the activity, set of institutions, and processes for creating, communicating, delivering, and exchanging offerings that have value for customers, clients, partners, and society at large." See www.marketingpower.com/_layouts/Dictionary.aspx?dLetter=M, accessed November 2013.

5. See "50 Years of Helping Customers Save Money and Live Better," Walmart Annual Report, www.walmartstores.com/sites/annual-report/2012/WalMart_AR.pdf, March 2013, p. 5; Dan Sewell, "Kroger CEO Often Roams Aisles, Wielding Carte Blanche," *Journal Gazette* (Fort Wayne, IN), November 15, 2010, www.journalgazette.net/article/20101115/BIZ/311159958/-1/BIZ09; Christine Birkner, "10 Minutes with Ashlee Yingling," *Marketing News*, May 31, 2013, pp. 24–28; and "McDonald's Listening Tour," www.aboutmcdonalds.com, accessed July 2013.

6. See Theodore Levitt's classic article, "Marketing Myopia," *Harvard Business Review*, July–August 1960, pp. 45–56. For more recent discussions, see Lance A. Bettencourt, "Debunking Myths About Customer Needs," *Marketing Management*, January/February 2009, pp. 46–51; N. Craig Smith, Minette E. Drumright, and Mary C. Gentile, "The New Marketing Myopia," *Journal of Public Policy & Marketing*, Spring 2010, pp. 4–11; and Roberto Friedmann, "What Business Are You In?" *Marketing Management*, Summer 2011, pp. 18–23.

7. See J. J. McCorvey, "Bird of Play," *Fast Company*, December 2012/January 2013, pp. 100–107+; and www.angrybirds.com, accessed November 2013.

8. "Henry Ford, Faster Horses, and Market Research," *Research Arts*, January 25, 2011, www.researcharts.com/2011/01/henry-ford-faster-horses-and-market-research.

9. See Michael E. Porter and Mark R. Kramer, "Creating Shared Value," *Harvard Business Review*, January–February 2011, pp. 63–77; Vivian Gee, "Creating Shared Value," *Huffington Post*, January 29, 2012, www.huffingtonpost.com/vivian-gee/creating-shared-value_1_b_1240228.html; and "Shared Value," www.fsg.org, accessed October 2013.

10. Michael Krauss, "Evolution of an Academic: Kotler on Marketing 3.0," *Marketing News*, January 30, 2011, p. 12.

11. Based on information from RBC's website, "Community and Sustainability," www.rbc.com/community-sustainability/index.html, accessed April 5, 2015.

12. Based on information from www.weber.com, accessed May 2013.

13. See "JetBlue Airways Awarded Eighth Consecutive Customer Satisfaction J.D. Power and Associates Honor," June 13, 2012, http://blog.jetblue.com/index.php/2012/06/13/jetblue-airways-awarded-eighth-consecutive-customer-satisfaction-j-d-power-and-associates-honor; Kelly Liyakasa, "Customer Experience Is Critical in Net Promoter Benchmarks," *CRM Magazine*, June 2012, www.destinationcrm.com/Articles/Columns-Departments/Insight/Customer-Experience-Is-Critical-in-Net-Promoter-Benchmarks-82569.aspx; and http://experience.jetblue.com, www.jetblue.com/about, and http://blog.jetblue.com, accessed November 2013.

14. "Passengers Tolerate Higher Costs and Fees of Traveling as Airline Satisfaction Continues to Improve, but Still Trails Other Industries," www.jdpower.com/ja/node/4611, accessed April 2015.

15. Ron Ruggless, "Panera Loyalty Program Approaches 10M Members," *Nation's Restaurant News*, March 8, 2012, http://nrn.com/article/panera-loyalty-program-approaches-10m-members; and http://mypanera.panerabread.com, accessed November 2013.

16. For more information, see www.apple.com/usergroups and www.webernation.com, accessed November 2013.

17. Based on information from Noreen O'Leary, "Hertz Learns Value of Sharing in Purchase Cycle," *Adweek*, May 30, 2012;

"Hertz Fans Share It Up! on Facebook," *PRNewswire*, April 11, 2012, www.prnewswire.com/news-releases/hertz-fans-share-it-up-on-facebook-146987185.html; "The Top 10 Social Media Success Stories of 2012 & What We Can Learn from Them," *Social Media Strategies Summit Blog*, November 28, 2012, http://socialmediastrategiessummit.com/blog/the-top-10-social-media-success-stories-of-2012-what-we-can-learn-from-them; and www.Hertz.com, accessed November 2013.

18. Gordon Wyner, "Getting Engaged," *Marketing Management*, Fall 2012, pp. 4–10. For more discussion on customer engagement, see Don E. Schultz, "Social Media's Slippery Slope," *Marketing Management*, February 2013, pp. 20–21.

19. See mystarbucksidea.force.com, accessed November 2013.

20. "2013 USA Today Facebook Super Bowl Ad Meter," http://admeter.usatoday.com, accessed May 2013; Christopher Heine, "Frito-Lay Likes the Data from Doritos' 'Crash the Super Bowl,'" *Adweek*, February 7, 2013, www.adweek.com/news/technology/frito-lay-likes-data-doritos-crash-super-bowl-147127; and www.crashthesuperbowl.com, accessed May 2013.

21. See Gavin O'Malley, "Entries Pour in for Heinz Ketchup Commercial Contest," August 13, 2007, http://publications.mediapost.com; and www.youtube.com/watch?v=JGY-ubAJSyI, accessed November 2013.

22. "Stew Leonard's," *Hoover's Company Records*, July 15, 2012, www.hoovers.com; and www.stew-leonards.com/html/about.cfm, accessed November 2013.

23. Graham Brown, "MobileYouth Key Statistics," March 28, 2008, www.mobileyouth.org/?s=MobileYouth+Key+Statistics. For interesting discussions of customer lifetime value, see Norman W. Marshall, "Commitment, Loyalty, and Customer Lifetime Value: Investigating the Relationships Among Key Determinants," *Journal of Business & Economics Research*, August 2010, pp. 67–85; and Christian Gronroos and Pekka Helle, "Return on Relationships: Conceptual Understanding and Measurement of Mutual Gains from Relational Business Engagements," *Journal of Business & Industrial Marketing*, Vol. 27, No. 5, 2012, pp. 344–359.

24. Based on quotes and information from Brad Stone, "What's in the Box? Instant Gratification," *Bloomberg Businessweek*, November 29–December 5, 2010, pp. 39–40; JP Mangalindan, "Amazon's Prime and Punishment," *CNNMoney*, February 21, 2012, http://tech.fortune.cnn.com/2012/02/21/prime-and-punishment; Marcus Wohlsen, "Why Amazon Prime Could Soon Cost You Next to Nothing," *Wired*, March 13, 2013, www.wired.com/business/2013/03/amazon-prime-could-soon-cost-next-to-nothing; and www.amazon.com/gp/prime/ref=footer_prime, accessed November 2013.

25. For more discussions on customer equity, see Roland T. Rust, Valerie A. Zeithaml, and Katherine N. Lemon, *Driving Customer Equity* (New York: Free Press, 2000); Rust, Lemon, and Zeithaml, "Return on Marketing: Using Customer Equity to Focus Marketing Strategy," *Journal of Marketing*, January 2004, pp. 109–127; Dominique M. Hanssens, Daniel Thorpe, and Carl Finkbeiner, "Marketing When Customer Equity Matters," *Harvard Business Review*, May 2008, pp. 117–124; Christian Gronroos and Pekka Helle, "Return on Relationships: Conceptual Understanding and Measurement of Mutual Gains from Relational

Business Engagements," *Journal of Business &; Industrial Marketing*, Vol. 27, No. 5, 2012, pp. 344–359; and Peter C. Verhoef and Katherine N. Lemon, "Successful Customer Value Management: Key Lessons and Emerging Trends," *European Management Journal*, February 2013, p. 1.

26. This example is adapted from information found in Rust, Lemon, and Zeithaml, "Where Should the Next Marketing Dollar Go?" *Marketing Management*, September–October 2001, pp. 24–28; with information from Dan Slater, "She Drives a Cadillac," *Fast Company*, February 2012, pp. 26–28; and Jeff Bennett and Joseph B. White, "New Cadillac, Old Dilemma," *Wall Street Journal*, March 27, 2013, p. B1.

27. Based on Werner Reinartz and V. Kumar, "The Mismanagement of Customer Loyalty," *Harvard Business Review*, July 2002, pp. 86–94. Also see Stanley F. Slater, Jakki J. Mohr, and Sanjit Sengupta, "Know Your Customer," *Marketing Management*, February 2009, pp. 37–44; and Crina O. Tarasi, et al., "Balancing Risk and Return in a Customer Portfolio," *Journal of Marketing*, May 2011, pp. 1–17.

28. "Infographic: The 2014 Canadian Smartphone Market," http://catalyst.ca/infographic-2014-canadian-smartphone-market.

29. Mobile facts from "Voice: One Screen to Rule Them All," *Adweek*, February 13, 2013, www.adweek.com/print/147137; and "Social Networking Eats Up 3+ Hours per Day for the Average American User," *MarketingCharts*, January 9, 2013, www.marketingcharts.com/wp/interactive/social-networking-eats-up-3-hours-per-day-for-the-average-american-user-26049.

30. Data from "Our Mobile Planet: Canada—Understanding the Mobile Consumer," *Ipsos Media CT*, May 2013.

31. For these and other examples, see "The State of Online Branded Communities," *Comblu*, November 2012, p. 17, http://comblu.com/thoughtleadership/the-state-of-online-branded-communities-2012.

32. See Stuart Feil, "How to Win Friends and Influence People," *Adweek*, September 12, 2013, pp. S1–S7; and Joe Mandese, "Carat Projects Digital at One-Fifth of All Ad Spend, Beginning to Dominate Key Markets," *MediaPost News*, March 20, 2013, www.mediapost.com/publications/article/196238/carat-projects-digital-at-one-fifth-of-all-ad-spen.html#axzz2PsYL9uFf.

33. Christopher Heine, "Brands Favor Social Shares Over Likes: Chatter Is the Key," *Adweek*, April 1, 2013, www.adweek.com/print/148256.

34. Stuart Feil, "How to Win Friends and Influence People: What Brands Are Doing for Their Social Followers," *Adweek*, pp. S1–S7; and www.youtube.com/watch?v=yeICGBk1ZsA, accessed November 2013.

35. "Infographic: The 2014 Canadian Smartphone Market," http://catalyst.ca/infographic-2014-canadian-smartphone-market.

36. See Applebaum, "Mobile Magnetism," p. S7; and Brian Quintion, "2012 PRO Award Winner: Catapult Action Biased Marketing for Mars Petcare," *Chief Marketer*, August 3, 2012, www.chiefmarketer.com/agencies/2012-pro-award-winner-catapult-action-biased-marketing-for-mars-petcare-03082012. PEDIGREE® is a registered trademark of Mars, Incorporated. The trademark is

used with permission. Mars, Incorporated is not associated with Pearson Education, Inc. The image of the PEDIGREE® Advertisement is printed with permission of Mars, Incorporated.

37. See John Gerzema, "How U.S. Consumers Are Steering the Spend Shift," *Advertising Age*, October 11, 2010, p. 26; and Gregg Fairbrothers and Catalina Gorla, "The Decline and Rise of Thrift," *Forbes*, April 23, 2012, www.forbes.com/sites/greggfairbrothers/2012/04/23/the-decline-and-rise-of-thrift.

38. See Matt Townsend, "Why Target's Cheap-Chic Glamour Is Fading," *Bloomberg Businessweek*, September 26, 2012, pp. 30–31; and "Our Mission," http://sites.target.com/site/en/company/page.jsp?contentId=WCMP04-031699, accessed August 2013.

39. "Bust a Move for Breast Health Delivers Unforgettable Day and Important Funds for Breast Health," *Canadian Newswire*, March 24, 2012, www.newswire.ca/en/story/943491/bust-a-move-for-breast-healthtm-delivers-unforgettable-day-and-important-funds-for-breast-health; Jeremy Webb, "Martin Adds Giggles to Bust a Move," *The Chronicle Herald*, April 1, 2012, http://thechronicleherald.ca/artslife/79808-martin-adds-giggles-bust-move; Tara Bradbury, "Bust a Move Breaks the Bank," *The Telegram*, April 2, 2012, www.thetelegram.com/News/Local/2012-04-02/article-2944894/Bust-a-Move-breaks-thebank/1; Patricia Kozicka, "Hundreds Bust a Move for Breast Health," *Global News*, March 24, 2012, http://globalnews.ca/news/226315/hundreds-bust-a-move-for-breast-health; Caley Ramsay, "Bust a Move Draws Hundreds in the Name of Breast Health," *Global News*, March 21, 2015, http://globalnews.ca/news/1896012/bust-a-move-draws-hundreds-in-the-name-of-breast-health; and information at www.bustamove.ca.

40. "Leading National Advertisers," *Advertising Age*, June 21, 2010, 10–12; Bill Curry, "Tory Government Hiked Ad Spending to Promote Stimulus Projects," *Globe and Mail*, January 4, 2012, www.theglobeandmail.com/news/politics/tory-government-hiked-ad-spending-to-promote-stimulus-projects/article1357867; and information from Public Works and Government Services Canada, www.tpsgc-pwgsc.gc.ca/pub-adv/rapports-reports/2011-2012/deppub-advexp-eng.html. For more on social marketing, see Philip Kotler, Ned Roberto, and Nancy R. Lee, *Social Marketing: Improving the Quality of Life*, 2nd ed. (Thousand Oaks, CA: Sage Publications, 2002).

41. Quotes and information found at www.patagonia.com/web/us/-contribution/patagonia.go?assetid=2329, accessed November 2013.

CHAPTER 2

1. See "Christie Projection Mapping Display Transforms Canada's Parliament Hill Centre Block into Virtual Storybook," press release published by Christie Digital, February 27, 2013; "Branham 300 NOW Spotlight Company: Christie Digital Systems Canada," published by Branham Group Inc., Ottawa, September 2011; and information from ChristieDigital.com, media articles about Christie, and Facebook.com/ChristieDigital.

2. Mission statements are from Indigo Books & Music at www.chapters.indigo.ca/our-company/mission, accessed August 2013, and Under Armour at www.uabiz.com/company/mission.cfm, accessed August 2013.

3. Based on information from a customer case study on Buffalo Wild Wings written by advertising agency 22squared and published on its website in 2012; and information from the Buffalo Wild Wings website at buffalowildwings.com and .ca, accessed April 2015.

4. "Heinz Agrees to Buy 80% Stake in Brazil's Quero Brand Owner," by Chris Burritt and Matthew Boyle, published on BloombergBusiness.com March 3, 2011; and "Heinz Opens State-of-the-Art Infant Cereal Factory in China," a press release published on Heinz.com December 2, 2014.

5. The following discussion is based in part on a document called "The Experience Curve Reviewed," published by Boston Consulting Group and available on its website at BCG.com/documents/file13904.pdf, accessed April 2015.

6. Lisa Richwine, "Disney Earnings Beat Despite Shaky Economy," Reuters.com, February 8, 2012; and The Walt Disney Company Annual Report 2013.

7. H. Igor Ansoff, "Strategies for Diversification," *Harvard Business Review*, September–October 1957, pp. 113–124.

8. Facts in this and the following paragraphs are based on information found in Tess Steins, "Starbucks Details Plans for Energy Drink, International Expansion," *Wall Street Journal*, March 21, 2012; David A. Kaplan, "Strong Coffee," *Fortune*, December 12, 2011, pp. 101–115; Jon Carter, "Starbucks: For Infusing a Steady Stream of New Ideas to Revise Its Business," *Fast Company*, March 2012, pp. 112+; "Starbucks CEO Howard Schultz Opens Annual Meeting of Shareholders," *Wireless News*, March 25, 2013; and www.starbucks.com, accessed April 2015.

9. See Michael E. Porter, *Competitive Advantage: Creating and Sustaining Superior Performance* (New York: Free Press, 1985); and Michael E. Porter, "What Is Strategy?" *Harvard Business Review*, November–December 1996, pp. 61–78. Also see "The Value Chain," www.quickmba.com/strategy/value-chain, accessed July 2013; and Philip Kotler and Kevin Lane Keller, *Marketing Management*, 14th ed. (Upper Saddle River, NJ: Prentice Hall, 2012), pp. 34–35 and pp. 203–204.

10. Nirmalya Kumar, "The CEO's Marketing Manifesto," *Marketing Management*, November–December 2008, pp. 24–29; and Tom French and others, "We're All Marketers Now," McKinsey Quarterly, July 2011, www.mckinseyquarterly.com/Were_all_marketers_now_2834.

11. Rebecca Ellinor, "Crowd Pleaser," *Supply Management*, December 13, 2007, pp. 26–29; and information from www.loreal.com/_en/_ww/html/suppliers/index.aspx, accessed August 2009.

12. See www.nikebiz.com/company_overview, accessed April 2009.

13. "100 Leading National Advertisers," *Advertising Age*, June 25, 2012, p. 14.

14. The four *P*s classification was first suggested by E. Jerome McCarthy, *Basic Marketing: A Managerial Approach* (Homewood, IL: Irwin, 1960). For the four *C*s, other proposed classifications, and more discussion, see Robert Lauterborn, "New Marketing Litany: 4P's Passé C-Words Take Over," *Advertising Age*, October 1, 1990, p. 26; Phillip Kotler, "Alphabet Soup," *Marketing Management*,

March–April 2006, p. 51; Nirmalya Kumer, "The CEO's Marketing Manifesto," *Marketing Management*, November/ December 2008, pp. 24–29; Richard Ettenson and others, "Rethinking the 4 Ps," *Harvard Business Review*, January–February 2013, p. 26; and Roy McClean, "Marketing 101—4 C's versus the 4 P's of Marketing," www.customfitfocus.com/marketing-1.htm, accessed March 2015.

15. Mike Linton, "Why Do Chief Marketing Officers Have a Short Shelf Life?" Forbes magazine online, May 15, 2009.

16. Grant Surridge, "Marketers of the Year: Duncan Fulton Retells Sport Chek's Story," Strategy magazine online, December 7, 2012; Chris Daniels, "The Meteoric Rise of Duncan Fulton," Marketing magazine online, November 24, 2011; and Canadian Tire corporate website, accessed March 2015.

17. Kristin Laird, "Marketing's Barriers to ROI," *Marketing* magazine, December 4, 2008.

18. Kristin Laird, "Social Media Week: ROI vs. Value," *Marketing* magazine, February 16, 2012.

19. For a full discussion of this model and details on customer-centred measures of return on marketing investment, see Roland T. Rust, Katherine N. Lemon, and Valerie A. Zeithaml, "Return on Marketing: Using Customer Equity to Focus Marketing Strategy," *Journal of Marketing*, January 2004, pp. 109–127; Roland T. Rust, Katherine N. Lemon, and Das Narayandas, *Customer Equity Management* (Upper Saddle River, NJ: Prentice Hall, 2005); Roland T. Rust, "Seeking Higher ROI? Base Strategy on Customer Equity," *Advertising Age*, September 10, 2007, pp. 26–27; Andreas Persson and Lynette Ryals, "Customer Assets and Customer Equity: Management and Measurement Issues," *Marketing Theory*, December 2010, pp. 417–436; and Kirsten Korosec, "'Tomāto, Tomäto'? Not Exactly," *Marketing News*, January 13, 2012, p. 8.

20. "Marketing Strategy: Diageo CMO: 'Workers Must Be Able to Count,'" *Marketing Week*, June 3, 2010, p. 5. Also see Art Weinstein and Shane Smith, "Game Plan: How Can Marketers Face the Challenge of Managing Customer Metrics?" *Marketing Management*, Fall 2012, pp. 24–32; and Francis Yu, "Why Is It So Hard to Prove ROI When Data and Metrics Are So Abundant?" *Advertising Age*, October 15, 2012, p. 27.

CHAPTER 3

1. Quotes and other information from or adapted from Andrew Saunders, "Paul Polman of Unilever," *Management Today*, March 2011, pp. 42–47; Adi Ignatius, "Captain Planet," *Harvard Business Review*, June 2012, pp. 2–8; and information found on Unilever's websites, unilever.ca and unileverusa.com, accessed June 2015.

2. Information from Sierra Club website at SierraClub.org, and from nonprofit organization Public Citizen's website at Citizen.org, accessed June 2015.

3. "McDonald's Launches Marketing for 'Favorites Under 400 Calories' Platform," *Advertising Age*, July 24, 2012. Additional information from www.mcdonalds.com/us/en/food/meal_bundles/favoritesunder400.html, and financial information about the company from AboutMcDonalds.com, accessed June 2015.

4. Chris Snowdon, "Absurd Prohibition of Toy Advertising Will Lead to Higher Prices," April 11, 2013. BBC Radio program, published and available on the website of the Institute of Economic Affairs (iae.org.uk).

5. Jeff Gray, "Rogers Violated False-Advertising Rules with 'Fewest Dropped Call' Claims, Court Hears," *Globe and Mail*, May 13, 2013.

6. "Bell Canada to Pay $10 Million Fine for Misleading Ads," *Canadian Press*, June 29, 2011.

7. Brent Kendall, "Skechers Settles with FTC Over Deceptive Advertising of Toning Shoes," *Wall Street Journal*, May 17, 2012, p. B3; and "Challenging Deceptive Advertising and Marketing" and information from www.ftc.gov, accessed June 2015.

8. Based on information from Ted Burnham, "Nutella Maker May Settle Deceptive Ad Lawsuit for $3 Million," *NPR*, April 26, 2012, http://www.npr.org/blogs/thesalt/2012/04/26/151454929/ nutella-maker-may-settle-deceptive-ad-lawsuit-for-3-million; and https://nutellaclassactionsettlement.com, accessed June 2015.

9. "Environmental Claims: A Guide for Industry and Advertisers," published by the Competition Bureau and available on its website at CompetitionBureau.gc.ca.

10. Emma Hall, "Green Murder," *Marketing*, October 29, 2007, p. 11.

11. Theodore Levitt, "The Morality (?) of Advertising," *Harvard Business Review* (July–August 1970), pp. 84–92.

12. Adapted from David Suzuki, "We All Pay for Technology," *Niagara Falls Review*, March 15, 2007, p. A4. For more discussion, see Joseph Guiltinan, "Creative Destruction and Destructive Creations: Environmental Ethics and Planned Obsolescence," *Journal of Business Ethics* (May 2009), pp. 19–28.

13. See "Law Targets Obsolete Products," April 22, 2013, *The Connexion*, www.connexionfrance.com/Planned-obsolescence-obsolete-products-iPod-washing-machine-printers-14655-view-article.html, accessed June 2015.

14. Rob Walker, "Replacement Therapy," *Atlantic Monthly*, September 2011, p. 38.

15. Information from Adbusters.org.

16. The Story of Stuff project is online at StoryOfStuff.org.

17. Information from Transport for London website, tfl.gov.uk.

18. Emailvision Survey: Bombarding Consumers with Marketing Creates Brand Resentment, *Wireless News*, January 24, 2013.

19. Vitaly Pecherskiy, "Trends That Gave Rise to Native Advertising," *Marketing* magazine online, April 7, 2015.

20. Jeff Beer, "Loblaw Goes Fishing in Sustainable Waters," *Marketing* magazine online, February 4, 2010.

21. Ross Gordon, Marylyn Carrigan, and Gerard Hastings, "A Framework for Sustainable Marketing," *Marketing Theory*, 11 (2011), p. 143.

22. Information from BullfrogPower.com.

23. See Philip Kotler, "Reinventing Marketing to Manage the Environmental Imperative," *Journal of Marketing*, July 2011, pp. 132–135; and Kai Ryssdal, "Unilever CEO: For Sustainable

Business, Go against 'Mindless Consumption,'" *Marketplace*, June 11, 2013, www.marketplace.org/topics/sustainability/consumed/unilever-ceo-paul-polman-sustainble-business.

24. SC Johnson.

25. Based on information in Drew Winter, "Honda Workers Eliminate Landfill Waste," *WardsAuto*, August 1, 2011, http://wardsauto.com/news-amp-analysis/honda-workers-eliminate-landfill-waste; and Jim Motavalli, "Automakers Work to Achieve Zero-Waste Goals," *New York Times*, March 1, 2013, http://wheels.blogs.nytimes.com/2013/03/01/automakers-work-to-achieve-zero-waste-goals.

26. See Alan S. Brown, "The Many Shades of Green," *Mechanical Engineering*, January 2009, and information from IBM.com and the website of the American Society of Mechanical Engineers (asme.org).

27. Based on information from Simon Houpt, "Beyond the Bottle: Coke Trumpets Its Green Initiatives," *Globe and Mail*, January 13, 2011; Marc Gunther, "Coca-Cola's Green Crusader," *Fortune*, April 28, 2008, p. 150; "Coca-Cola to Install 1,800 CO2 Coolers in North America," April 30, 2009, www.r744.com/articles/2009-04-30-coca-cola-to-install-1800-co2-coolers-in-north-america.php; and Coca-Cola's "Position Statement on Climate Protection," January 1, 2012, www.coca-colacompany.com.

28. Based on information from "Walmart," *Fast Company*, March 2010, p. 66; "Walmart Eliminates More Than 80 Percent of Its Waste in California That Would Otherwise Go to Landfills," March 17, 2011 (press release published on WalmartStores.com); Jack Neff, "Why Walmart Has More Green Clout Than Anyone," *Advertising Age*, October 15, 2007, p. 1; Denise Lee Yohn, "A Big, Green, Reluctant Hug for Retailing's 800-lb. Gorilla," *Brandweek*, May 5, 2008, p. 61; Edward Humes, *Force of Nature: The Unlikely Story of Walmart's Green Revolution* (New York: HarperCollins, 2011); Jack Neff, "For Walmart, Sustainability Is Slow Going," *Advertising Age*, April 23, 2012, p. 6; and Walmart's webpage titled "Environmental Sustainability," http://walmartstores.com/sustainability, accessed July 2015.

29. Quote from Austin Carr, "Nike: The No. 1 Most Innovative Company of 2013," *Fast Company*, March 2013.

30. Information from Eleftheria Parpis, "Must Love Dogs," *Adweek online*, February 18, 2008; and information from Pedigree.com, accessed July 2015.

31. Information from Puma.com, accessed July 2015.

32. Information from Nau.com, accessed July 2015.

33. Example based on information from Kelly Voelker, "Social Media's Role in Issue Management," *SlideShare*, April 7, 2010, www.slideshare.net/socialmediaorg/blogwell-cincinnatti-social-media-case-study-graco-presented-by-kelly-voelker; and David Grant, "Moms a-Twitter over Graco's Stroller Recall Response," *Christian Science Monitor*, January 10, 2010, www.csmonitor.com/Business/2010/0121/Moms-a-Twitter-over-Graco-s-stroller-recall-response.

34. See Transparency International, "Bribe Payers Index 2011," http://bpi.transparency.org/bpi2011, and "Global Corruption Barometer 2010/2011," http://gcb.transparency.org/gcb201011.

Also see Michael Montgomery, "The Cost of Corruption," AmericanRadioWorks, http://americanradioworks.publicradio.org/features/corruption, accessed July 2015.

35. David A. Lubin and Daniel C. Esty, "The Sustainability Imperative," *Harvard Business Review*, May 2010, pp. 41–50; and Roasbeth Moss Kanter, "It's Time to Take Full Responsibility," *Harvard Business Review*, October 2010, p. 42.

36. "Why Companies Can No Longer Afford to Ignore Their Social Responsibilities," *Time*, May 28, 2012, http://business.time.com/2012/05/28/why-companies-can-no-longer-afford-to-ignore-their-social-responsibilities.

CHAPTER 4

1. Based on information from Ashley Vance, "Microsoft Sees a New Image of Itself in Windows 8," *Business Week*, October 29, 2012, pp. 41–42: Rolfe Winkler, "Microsoft's Marriage Made in Dell," *Wall Street Journal*, February 6, 2013, p. C14; Spencer Jakab, "Microsoft Holds More Than Meets the Eye," *Wall Street Journal*, January 23, 2013, p. C1; Rolfe Winkler, "Microsoft's Same Old New Problem," *Wall Street Journal*, January 25, 2013, p. C10; Ashlee Vance and Dina Bass, "Microsoft's Office 2013 Is Software for the Cloud," *Bloomberg Businessweek*, January 29, 2013, www.businessweek.com/articles/2013-01-29/microsofts-old-software-comes-with-a-new-image; Haydn Shaughnessy, "Here's How Microsoft Plans on Expanding Its Device and OS Business," *Forbes*, April 25, 2013, www.forbes.com/sites/haydnshaughnessy/2013/04/25/heres-how-microsoft-plans-on-expanding-its-device-and-os-business/?ss=strategies-solutions; Ritsuko Ando and Bill Rigby, "Microsoft Swallows Nokia's Phone Business for $7.2 Billion," September 3, 2013, www.reuters.com/article/2013/09/03/us-microsoft-nokia-idUSBRE98202V20130903; and annual reports and other information from www.microsoft.com/investor/default.aspx, accessed November 2013.

2. Information from www.ikea.com, accessed November 2013.

3. Information from Robert J. Benes, Abbie Jarman, and Ashley Williams, "2007 NRA Sets Records," www.chefmagazine.com, accessed September 2007; and www.thecoca-colacompany.com/dynamic/press_center and www.cokesolutions.com, accessed November 2013.

4. See www.lifeisgood.com/#!/playmakers, accessed November 2013.

5. World POPClock, U.S. Census Bureau, at www.census.gov/popclock, accessed May 2013. This site provides continually updated projections of the U.S. and world populations.

6. Statistics Canada, "Population Projections for Canada, Provinces and Territories," www.statcan.gc.ca/pub/91-520-x/2010001/aftertoc-aprestdm1-eng.htm, accessed May 2015.

7. Daniel Stoffman, "Completely Predictable People," *Report on Business*, November 1990, pp. 78–84; David Foot and Daniel Stoffman, *Boom, Bust and Echo* (Toronto: Macfarlane Walter & Ross, 1996), 18–22.

8. See Wayne Friedman, "Ad Dollars Shift as Boomers Age," *Media Daily News*, July 5, 2012, www.mediapost.com/publications/article/178187/#axzz2S9pYRPYV; "The 50+ Demo Is Soaring," *AARP*, http://advertise.aarp.org/insights, accessed November 2013; and http://www.immersionactive.com/resources/size-wealth-spending-50-consumers.

9. See "Keeping Up with the Baby Boomers," *MarketWatch*, March 20, 2012, www.marketwatch.com/story/keeping-up-with-the-baby-boomers-2012-03-20.

10. See www.eldertreks.com, accessed November 2013.

11. For more discussion, see Bernadette Turner, "Generation X … Let's GO!" *New Pittsburgh Courier*, March 2–March 8, 2011, p. A11; Piet Levy, "Segmentation by Generation," *Marketing News*, May 15, 2011, pp. 20–23; and Leonard Klie, "Gen X: Stuck in the Middle," *Customer Relationship Management*, February 2012, pp. 24–29.

12. Julie Jargon, "DQ Dips into Humor," *Wall Street Journal*, May 26, 2011, p. B6; and "Dairy Queen and Subway Top Lists of Most Effective QSR Advertising," *Quick Serve Leader*, http://quickserveleader.com/article/dairy-queen-and-subway-top-lists-most-effective-qsr-advertising, accessed March 2013.

13. Piet Levy, "Segmentation by Generation," p. 23. Also see Sarah Mahoney, "Struggling, Gen Y Redefines Wants, Needs," *Marketing Daily*, March 5, 2012, www.mediapost.com/publications/article/169424/struggling-gen-y-redefines-wants-needs.html?print; and Greg Petro, "Millennial Engagement and Loyalty—Make Them Part of the Process," *Forbes*, March 21, 2013, www.forbes.com/sites/gregpetro/2013/03/21/millennial-engagement-and-loyalty-make-them-part-of-the-process.

14. See Dale Buss, "Hamsterbranding: Kia and Chevy Know How to Score with Millennials," *BrandChannel*, July 30, 2012, www.brandchannel.com/home/post/2012/07/30/Kia-Hamsters-Millennials-073012.aspx; Kurt Earnst, "Kia Bares Its 2014 Soul, Offering a Better Ride," *Christian Science Monitor*, March 28, 2013, www.csmonitor.com/Business/In-Gear/2013/0328/Kia-bares-its-2014-Soul-offering-a-better-ride Kia Motors America; and www.youtube.com/watch?v=o0B5vuAYk94 and www.kia.com/us/#/soul/videos, accessed November 2013.

15. See Heather Chaet, "The Tween Machine," *Adweek*, June 25, 2012, www.adweek.com/print/141357; and www12.statcan.ca/census-recensement/2011/as-sa/98-311-x/2011001/tbl/tbl2-eng.cfm, accessed May 2015.

16. The first quote is from Cynthia Boris, "Generation Z: If They're Awake, They're Online," *Marketing Pilgrim*, March 20, 2013, www.marketingpilgrim.com/2013/03/generation-z-if-theyre-awake-theyre-online.html. For the second quote and an excellent overall summary of Generation Z and its brand implications, see "Gen Z: Digital in Their DNA," *JWT*, April 2012, www.jwtintelligence.com/wp-content/uploads/2012/04/F_INTERNAL_Gen_Z_0418122.pdf.

17. See "GenZ: Digital in Their DNA"; and Shannon Bryant, "'Generation Z' Children More Tech-Savvy; Prefer Gadgets, Not Toys," *Marketing Forecast*, April 3, 2013, www.marketingforecast.com/archives/23277.

18. Robert Klara, "It's Not Easy Being Tween," *Adweek*, June 27, 2012, www.adweek.com/print/141378.

19. See "Netflix 'Just for Kids' Now on iPad," October 1, 2012, http://blog.netflix.com/2012/10/netflix-just-for-kids-now-on-ipad.html; and http://movies.netflix.com/Kids, accessed November 2013.

20. Heather Chaet, "The Tween Machine," *Adweek*, June 25, 2012, www.adweek.com/print/141357.

21. Statistics Canada, "Study: Generational Change in Paid and Unpaid Work—2010," *The Daily*, July 12, 2011, www.statcan.gc.ca/daily-quotidien/110712/dq110712c-eng.htm; 2011 census data, www12.statcan.gc.ca/census-recensement/2011/as-sa/98-312-x/98-312-x2011003_1-eng.cfm; www12.statcan.gc.ca/census-recensement/2011/as-sa/98-312-x/98-312-x2011003_2-eng.cfm; and http://www12.statcan.gc.ca/census-recensement/2011/as-sa/98-312-x/98-312-x2011001-eng.cfm.

22. "Women Outnumber Men in Canadian Workforce," *Canadian Press*, September 2009, www.ctv.ca/CTVNews/Canada/20090905/women_workforce_090905, accessed June 2012; Statistics Canada, "Women in Canada: Paid Work—2009," *The Daily*, December 9, 2010, www.statcan.gc.ca/daily-quotidien/101209/dq101209a-eng.htm.

23. See Marissa Miley and Ann Mack, "The New Female Consumer: The Rise of the Real Mom," *Advertising Age*, November 16, 2009, p. A1; and Christine Birkner, "Mom's the Word," *Marketing News*, May 15, 2011, p. 8.

24. Tavia Grant, "Stuck in Place: Canada's Mobility Problem," *Globe and Mail*, June 2012, www.theglobeandmail.com/report-on-business/economy/canada-competes/stuck-in-place-canadas-mobility-problem/article4237314.

25. Statistics Canada, "2011 Census: Population and Dwelling Counts," *The Daily*, February 8 2012, www.statcan.gc.ca/daily-quotidien/120208/dq120208a-eng.htm.

26. Mary C. Noonan and Jennifer L. Glass, "The Hard Truth about Telecommuting," *Monthly Labor Review*, June 2012, www.bls.gov/opub/mlr/2012/06/art3full.pdf.

27. See "About WebEx," www.webex.com/about-webex/index.html, accessed November 2013; "What Is Cloud Computing?" www.salesforce.com/cloudcomputing, accessed November 2013; and www.regus.com and http://grindspaces.com, accessed November 2013.

28. Statistics Canada, "Educational Attainment of the Population Aged 25 to 64, Off-Reserve Aboriginal, Non-Aboriginal, and Total Population, Canada, Provinces and Territories, 2009, 2010 and 2011," www.statcan.gc.ca/pub/81-582-x/2012001/tbl/tbld6.3-eng.htm, accessed June 2012.

29. *CBC News*, "Labour Shortage 'Desperate,' Chamber Says," February 2012, www.cbc.ca/news/business/story/2012/02/08/canada-labourshortage.html; and Human Resources and Skills Development Canada, "Looking Ahead: A 10-Year Outlook for the Canadian Labour Market (2008–2017)," November 2008, www23.hrsdc.gc.ca/l.3bd.2t.1ilshtml@-eng.jsp?lid=1&fid=1&lang=en#ExecutiveSummary.

30. Statistics Canada, "Visible Minority Population and Top Three Visible Minority Groups, Selected Census Metropolitan Areas," http://www12.statcan.gc.ca/nhs-enm/2011/as-sa/99-010-x/2011001/tbl/tbl2-eng.cfm; and www.statcan.gc.ca/pub/12-581-x/2012000/pop-eng.htm#t03.

31. "New Initiative Aims to 'Imagine a Future' for One Million Black Girls over the Next Three Years," press release, July 2012, www.myblackisbeautiful.com/press/imagine_a_future_release.php; "Procter & Gamble's My Black Is Beautiful Honored with City of Cincinnati Proclamation," *PR Newswire*, May 21, 2010; and

information from www.myblackisbeautiful.com, accessed November 2013.

32. "America's LGBT 2012 Buying Power Projected at $790 Billion," *Echelon Magazine*, March 27, 2012, www.echelonmagazine.com/index.php?id=2597&title=America%60s_LGBT_2012_Buying_Power_Projected_at_$790_Billion.

33. Statistics Canada, "2006 Census: Family Portrait: Continuity and Change in Canadian Families and Households in 2006: Highlights," www12.statcan.ca/census-recensement/2006/as-sa/97-553/p1-eng.cfm, April 2009; and www12.statcan.gc.ca/census-recensement/2011/as-sa/98-312-x/98-312-x2011001-eng.cfm.

34. See Brandon Miller, "And the Winner Is …" *Out Traveler*, Winter 2008, pp. 64–65; Tanya Irwin, "American Airlines, GayCities Partner for Promo," *Marketing Daily*, January 15, 2012, www.mediapost.com/publications/article/165789/american-airlines-gaycities-partner-for-promo.html; Leanne Italie, "Gay-Themed Ads Are Becoming More Mainstream," *Huffington Post*, March 6, 2013, www.huffingtonpost.com/2013/03/06/gay-themed-ads-mainstream-_n_2821745.html; and www.aa.com/rainbow, accessed November 2013.

35. Based on information from "50 Most Innovative Companies: Azul—For Converting Bus Riders into Frequent Fliers," www.fastcompany.com/most-innovative-companies/2011/profile/azul.php; "Azul CEO Neeleman on Brazil, U.S. Airline Industry," *Bloomberg Businessweek*, December 14, 2012, www.businessweek.com/videos/2012-12-14/azul-ceo-neeleman-on-brazil-u-dot-s-dot-airline-industry; and www.voeazul.com.br, accessed November 2013.

36. Statistics Canada, "Income in Canada—2010," www.statcan.gc.ca/pub/75-202-x/75-202-x2010000-eng.htm, accessed June 2012; Statistics Canada, "Study: High Income Canadians," September 2007, www.statcan.gc.ca/daily-quotidien/070924/dq070924a-eng.htm, accessed April 2009; "2006 Census: Earnings, Income, and Shelter Costs," May 2008, www.statcan.gc.ca/daily-quotidien/080501/dq080501a-eng.htm, accessed April 2009; and "Census Release Topics," www12.statcan.ca/census-recensement/2006/rt-td/index-eng.cfm, accessed April 2009.

37. See "Warm Weather Puts Chill on Brands' Winters," *Advertising Age*, February 19, 2012, http://adage.com/print/232824; Alex Taylor III, "Toyota's Comeback Kid," *Fortune*, February 27, 2012, pp. 72–79; and Rick Newman, "Toyota's Back in the Fast Lane," *US News*, February 6, 2013, www.usnews.com/news/blogs/rick-newman/2013/02/06/toyotas-back-in-the-fast-lane.

38. The 2030 Water Resources Group, www.2030wrg.org, accessed June 2013; and "The World's Water," *Pacific Institute*, www.worldwater.org/data.html, accessed July 2013.

39. Information from www.timberland.com and http://earthkeepers.timberland.com/?camp=S:G:SPC:timberland_earthkeepers:TBL#/howweact, accessed June 2013.

40. See Maid Napolitano, "RFID Surges Ahead," *Materials Handling*, April 2012, pp. S48–S50; Walter Loeb, "Macy's Wins with Technology," *Forbes*, July 10, 2013, www.forbes.com/sites/walterloeb/2012/07/10/macys-wins-with-technology; and "Burberry Introduces Smart Personalization for Shoppers," *Integer*, March 25, 2013, http://shopperculture.integer.com/2013/03/burberry-introduces-smart-personalization-for-shoppers.html.

41. See "A $1 Billion Project to Remake the Disney World Experience, Using RFID," www.fastcodesign.com/1671616/a-1-billion-project-to-remake-the-disney-world-experience-using-rfid#1; and Brooks Barnes, "At Disney Parks, a Bracelet Meant to Build Loyalty (and Sales)," *New York Times*, January 7, 2013, p. B1.

42. See "Warby Parker—Stylish Buy One Give One Eyewear Helps Restore Vision and Hope," *Shop with Meaning*, http://shopwithmeaning.org/warby-parker-glasses-stylish-buy-one-give-one-eyewear, accessed June 2013; and "Warby Parker: Do Good," www.warbyparker.com/do-good/#home, accessed November 2013.

43. John Biggs, "Three Things Warby Parker Did to Launch a Successful Lifestyle Brand," *TechCrunch*, May 7, 2013, http://techcrunch.com/2013/05/07/the-three-things-warby-parker-did-to-launch-a-successful-lifestyle-brand.

44. See "The Growth of Cause Marketing," www.causemarketingforum.com/site/c.bkLUKcOTLkK4E/b.6452355/apps/s/content.asp?ct=8965443, accessed July 2013.

45. See "10 Crucial Consumer Trends for 2010," *Trendwatching.com*, http://trendwatching.com/trends/pdf/trendwatching%202009-12%2010trends.pdf; and "The F-Factor," *Trendwatching.com*, May 2011, http://trendwatching.com/trends/pdf/trendwatching%202009-12%2010trends.pdf.

46. Sherry Turkle, "The Flight from Conversation," *New York Times*, April 21, 2013, www.nytimes.com/2012/04/22/opinion/sunday/the-flight-from-conversation.html?pagewanted=all&_r=2&.

47. "The F-Factor," *Trendingwatching.com*, p. 1.

48. "Survey Measures the 'Olympic Effect' on National Pride," March 2010, www.historica-dominion.ca/node/1003, accessed June 2012.

49. www.lohas.com, accessed November 2013.

50. www.gogoquinoa.com, accessed May 2015.

51. "U.S. Organic Market Surpasses $31 Billion in 2011," *What's New in Organic*, July 2012, www.ota.com/pics/documents/WhatsNews-54c.pdf.

52. Michael Valpy, "Religious Observance Continues to Decline," *Globe and Mail*, March 19, 2003; Statistics Canada, "Who's Religious?" www.statcan.gc.ca/pub/11-008-x/2006001/9181-eng.htm, accessed June 2012; and Statistics Canada, "2011 National Household Survey: Immigration, Place of Birth, Citizenship, Ethnic Origin, Visible Minorities, Language and Religion," www.statcan.gc.ca/daily-quotidien/130508/dq130508b-eng.htm.

53. For more discussion, see Diana Butler Bass, "The End of Church," *Huffington Post*, February 18, 2012, www.huffingtonpost.com/diana-butler-bass/the-end-of-church_b_1284954.html.

54. Paula Forbes, "Taco Bell Ad: Thank You for Suing Us," January 28, 2011, *Eater*, http://eater.com/archives/2011/01/28/taco-bell-ad-thanks-firm-for-law-suit.php; "Law Firm Voluntarily Withdraws Class-Action Lawsuit Against Taco Bell," April 19, 2011, http://money.msn.com/business-news/article.aspx?feed=BW&date=20110419&id=13327023; Bruce Horovitz, "Taco Bell Comes Out of Its Shell to Ring in New Menu," *USA Today*,

February 20, 2012, www.usatoday.com/money/industries/food/ story/2012-02-20/taco-bell/53157494/1; and www.tacobell.com/ nutrition/foodfacts/BeefQuality, accessed July 2013.

CHAPTER 5

1. Based on information found in Natalie Zmuda, "Pepsi Tackles Identity Crisis After Fielding Biggest Consumer-Research Push in Decades," *Advertising Age*, May 7, 2012, pp. 1, 14; Martinne Geller, "Pepsi Pushing People to 'Live for Now,'" *Reuters*, April 30, 2012, www.reuters.com/article/2012/04/30/us-pepsi-idUSBRE83T0EP20120430; Natalie Zmuda, "Pepsi Debuts First Global Campaign," *Advertising Age*, April 30, 2012, http://adage. com/article/print/234379; Jen Chaney, "Beyoncé, Now Brought to You by Pepsi," *Washington Post*, December 10, 2012; Ravi Balakrishnan, "Is the 'Right Here Right Now' Campaign a Game Changer for Pepsi?" *The Economic Times (Online)*, February 6, 2012, http://articles.economictimes.indiatimes.com/2013-02-06/ news/36949962_1_homi-battiwalla-pepsico-india-surjo-dutt; and Natalie Zmuda, "Pepsi Puts the Public in Super Bowl Spot," *Advertising Age*, January 7, 2013, p. 10.

2. Sheilynn McCale, "Apple Has Sold 300M iPods, Currently Holds 78 Percent of the Music Player Market," *The New Web*, October 4, 2011, http://thenextweb.com/apple/2011/10/04/ apple-has-sold-300m--ipods-currently-holds-78-of-the-music-player-market/; "iPod Still Has 70% of the MP3 Player Market," *MacTech*, July 24, 2012, www.mactech.com/2012/07/24/ipod-still-has-70-mp3-player-market; and "Apple iPhone 5 and Stunning New iPods Set Stage for Strongest December Quarter Ever," *Forbes*, September 12, 2012, www.forbes.com.

3. Helen Leggatt, "IBM: Marketers Suffering from Data Overload," *BizReport*, October 12, 2011, www.bizreport.com/2011/10/ibm-marketers-suffering-data-overload.html#; Carey Toane, "Listening: The New Metric," *Strategy*, September 2009, p. 45; and Margarita Tartakovsky, "Overcoming Information Overload," *PsychCentral*, January 21, 2013, http://psychcentral.com/blog/archives/2013/ 01/21/overcoming-information-overload.

4. Piet Levy, "A Day with Stan Sthanunathan," *Marketing News*, February 28, 2011, pp. 11+.

5. See www.walmartstores.com/Suppliers/248.aspx and http:// retaillinkblog.com/what-is-walmarts-retail-link-system/3, accessed November 2013.

6. Alicia Androich, "Indigo Launches Plum Rewards to Connect with Customers," *Marketing magazine*, April 6, 2011, www. marketingmag.ca/news/marketer-news/indigo-launches-plum-rewards-toconnect-with-customers-25608; and "Infusion Case Study: Indigo Customer Database," www.infusion.com/PDF/ Cases/Infusion-RetailandServices-IndigoCustomerDatabase.pdf.

7. Based on information from Adam Ostrow, "Inside the Gatorade's Social Media Command Center," June 6, 2010, http://mashable.com/2010/06/15/gatorade-sical-media-mission-control/; Valery Bauerlein, "Gatorade's 'Mission': Using Social Media to Boost Sales," *Wall Street Journal Asia*, September 15, 2010, p. 8; and Natalie Zmuda, "Gatorade: We're Necessary Performance Gear," *Advertising Age*, January 2, 2012.

8. Example based on information from Michal Lev-Ram, "Samsung's Road to Mobile Domination," *Fortune*, February 4,

2013, pp. 99–101; Jason Gilbert, "Samsung Mocks iPhone 5, Apple Fanboys Again in New Galaxy S3 Commercial," *Huffington Post*, September 1, 2012, www.huffingtonpost.com/2012/09/20/ samsung-mocks-iphone-5-commercial_n_1898443.html; and Suzanne Vranica, "Tweets Spawn Ad Campaigns," *Wall Street Journal*, October 22, 2012, p. B5.

9. Irena Slutsky, "'Chief Listeners Use Technology to Track, Sort Company Mentioned," *Advertising Age*, August 30, 2010, http:// adage.com/digital/article?article_id=145618; also see Tina Sharkey, "Who Is Your Chief Listening Officer?" *Forbes*, March 3, 2012, www.forbes.com/sites/tinasharkey/2012/03/13/who-is-your-chief-listening-officer.

10. Adam Lashinsky, "The Secrets Apple Keeps," *Fortune*, February 6, 2012, pp. 85–94.

11. George Chidi, "Confessions of a Corporate Spy," *Inc.*, February 2013, pp. 72–77.

12. See http://biz.yahoo.com/ic/101/101316.html, accessed July 2013; Josh Kohn-Lindquist, "A Monstrous SWOT: Big Growth at a Cheaper Price," *The Motley Fool*, November 15, 2012, http:// beta.fool.com/joryko/2012/11/15/monster-swot/16557; and www.statista.com/statistics/275163/red-bulls-number-of-cans-sold-worldwide, accessed August 2015.

13. For more on research firms that supply marketing information, see Jack Honomichl, "2012 Honomichl Top 50," special section, *Marketing News*, June 2012. Other information from www.nielsen. com/us/en/measurement/retail-measurement.html and http:// thefuturescompany.com/what-we-do/us-yankelovich-monitor, accessed September 2013.

14. See www.symphonyiri.com/?TabId=159&productid=83, accessed November 2013.

15. See Jennifer Reingold, "Can P&G Make Money in Places Where People Earn $2 a Day?" *Fortune*, January 17, 2011, pp. 86–91; and C. K. Prahalad, "Bottom of the Pyramid as a Source of Breakthrough Innovations," *Journal of Product Innovation Management*, January 2012, pp. 6–12.

16. For more discussion of online ethnography, see Pradeep K. Tyagi, "Webnography: A New Tool to Conduct Marketing Research," *Journal of American Academy of Business*, March 2010, pp. 262–268; Robert V. Kozinets, "Netnography: The Marketer's Secret Weapon," March 2010, http://info.netbase.com/rs/netbase/ images/Netnography_WP; and http://en.wikipedia.org/wiki/ Online_ethnography, accessed December 2013.

17. Example adapted from information found in "My Dinner with Lexus," *Automotive News*, November 29, 2010, www.autonews. com/apps/pbcs.dll/article?AID=/20101129/RETAIL03/ 311299949/1292; and "An Evening with Lexus," YouTube video, www.youtube.com/watch?v=LweS8EScADY, accessed December 2013.

18. See "Internet World Stats," accessed March 2015, www. internetworldstats.com/stats14.htm#north.

19. For more information, see www.focusvision.com and www. youtube.com/watch?v=PG8RZl2dvNY, accessed November 2013.

20. Derek Kreindler, "Lexus Soliciting Customer Feedback with Lexus Advisory Board," August 24, 2010, *Automotive News*, www.

autoguide.com/auto-news/2010/08/lexus-soliciting-customer-feedback-with-lexus-advisory-board.html; "20,000 Customers Sign Up for the Lexus Advisory Board," August 30, 2010, www.4wheelsnews.com/20000-customers-signed-up-for-the-lexus-advisory-board; and www.lexusadvisoryboard.com, accessed November 2013.

21. For more discussion of online behavioural and social tracking and targeting, see Amit Avner, "How Social Targeting Can Lead to Discovery," *Adotas*, February 7, 2012, www.adotas.com/2012/02/how-social-targeting-can-lead-to-discovery; Edward Wyatt and Tanzina Vega, "Conflict over How Open 'Do Not Track' Talks Will Be," *New York Times*, March 30, 2012, p. B3; Thomas Claburn, "Microsoft Finds People Want More Privacy Control," *Informationweek–Online*, January 24, 2013, www.informationweek.com/windows/security/microsoft-finds-people-want-more-privacy/240146932; and Lisa M. Thomas, "We Know Where You've Been: Emerging Rules in Online Behavioral Advertising," *Computer and Internet Lawyer*, February 2013, pp. 16–19.

22. Based on information from "Time Warner Opens NYC Neuromarketing Lab," *Neuromarketing*, January 26, 2012, www.neurosciencemarketing.com/blog/articles/new-labs.htm; Amy Chozick, "These Lab Specimens Watch 3-D Television," *New York Times*, January 25, 2012, p. B3; and Sam Thielman, "Time Warner's Media Lab Knows What You Like to Watch," *Adweek*, February 4, 2013, www.adweek.com/news/technology/time-warner-s-media-lab-knows-what-you-watch-147045. Also see www.timewarnermedialab.com.

23. Jessica Tsai, "Are You Smarter Than a Neuromarketer?" *Customer Relationship Management*, January 2010, pp. 19–20.

24. See "NeuroFocus Received Gran Ogilvy Award from the Advertising Research Foundation," *PRNewswire*, April 2, 2009, www.neurofocus.com/news/ogilvy_neurofocus.htm; and Adam L. Penenberg, "NeuroFocus Uses Neuromarketing to Hack Your Brain," *Fast Company*, August 8, 2011, www.fastcompany.com/magazine/158/neuromarketing-intel-paypal.

25. Melinda Mattos, "A Fresh Start for Sobeys," *Strategy*, December 1, 2010, http://strategyonline.ca/2010/12/01/moysobeys-20101201/; and information from www.sobeyscorporate.com.

26. "1-800-Flowers.com Customer Connection Blooms with SAS Business Analytics," www.sas.com/success/1800flowers.html, accessed September 2013.

27. See www.pensketruckleasing.com/leasing/precision/precision_features.html, accessed November 2013.

28. Based on information in Ann Zimmerman, "Small Business; Do the Research," *Wall Street Journal*, May 9, 2005, p. R3; with additional information and insights from John Tozzi, "Market Research on the Cheap," *BusinessWeek*, January 9, 2008, www.businessweek.com/smallbiz/content/jan2008/sb2008019_352779.htm; "Understanding the Basics of Small Business Market Research," *All Business*, www.allbusiness.com/marketing/market-research/2587-1.html#axzz2K8T92eOR, accessed February 2013; and www.bibbentuckers.com, accessed September 2013.

29. For some good advice on conducting market research in a small business, search "conducting market research" at www.sba.

gov or see "Researching Your Market," *Entrepreneur*, www.entrepreneur.com/article/43024-1, accessed November 2013.

30. See "Top 25 Global Market Research Organizations," *Marketing News*, August 31, 2012, pp. 16+; and www.nielsen.com/us/en/about-us.html and www.nielsen.com/global/en.html?worldWideSelected=true, accessed November 2013.

31. For these and other examples, see "From Tactical to Personal: Synovate's Tips for Conducting Marketing Research in Emerging Markets," *Marketing News*, April 30, 2011, pp. 20–22. Internet stats are from www.internetworldstats.com, accessed March 2015.

32. Subhash C. Jain, *International Marketing Management*, 3rd ed. (Boston: PWS-Kent, 1990), p. 338. For more discussion on international marketing research issues and solutions, see Warren J. Keegan and Mark C. Green, *Global Marketing*, 6th ed. (Upper Saddle River, NJ: Prentice Hall, 2011), pp. 170–201.

33. See Andrew Roberts, "In Some Stores, All Eyes Are on You," *Bloomberg Businessweek*, December 10, pp. 32–33; and Emma K. McDonald, Hugh N. Wilson, and Unut Konus, "Better Customer Insight—In Real Time," *Harvard Business Review*, September 2012, pp. 102–107.

34. Tina Sharkey, "Who Is Your Chief Listening Officer?" *Forbes*, March 13, 2012, www.forbes.com/sites/tinasharkey/2012/03/13/who-is-your-chief-listening-officer.

35. Juan Martinez, "Marketing Marauders or Consumer Counselors?" *CRM Magazine*, January 2011, www.destinationcrm.com. Also see Laure McKay, "Eye on Customers: Are Consumers Comfortable with or Creeped Out by Online Data Collection Tactics?" *CRM Magazine*, January 2011, www.destinationcrm.com; Ki Mae Heussner, "Whose Life Is It, Anyway?" *Adweek*, January 16, 2012, pp. 22–26; and Ted Gotsch, "'Do Not Track' Privacy Effort Can Mislead Public, Experts Say," *Cybersecurity Policy Report*, November 5, 2012.

36. Thomas Clayburn, "Microsoft Finds People Want More Privacy Control," *Informationweek–Online*, January 24, 2013, www.informationweek.com/windows/security/microsoft-finds-people-want-more-privacy/240146932.

37. "ICC/ESOMAR International Code of Marketing and Social Research Practice," www.esomar.org/index.php/codes-guidelines.html, accessed July 2013. Also see "Respondent Bill of Rights," www.mra-net.org/ga/billofrights.cfm, accessed December 2013.

38. "FTC Complaint Charges Deceptive Advertising by POM Wonderful," September 27, 2010, www.ftc.gov/opa/2010/09/pom.shtm; Chris MacDonald, "Fruit Juice Ads and Sour Grapes," *Canadian Business*, July 16, 2012, p. 17; Ashley Post, "FTC Issues Final Ruling Against POM Wonderful," *Inside Counsel. Break News*, January 17, 2013; and Andrew Zajac, "POM Wonderful Loses Bid to Block FTC Deceptive-Ad Claims, *Bloomberg Business*, January 30, 2015, www.bloomberg.com/news/articles/2015-01-30/pom-wonderful-loses-bid-to-block-ftc-deceptive-ad-claim.

CHAPTER 6

1. Based on information found in Tom Foster, "The GoPro Army," *Inc.*, January 26, 2012, www.inc.com/magazine/201202/the-gopro-army.html; Tom Foster, "How GoPro Measures Social

Engagement," *Inc.*, January 26, 2012, www.inc.com/
magazine/201202/the-bare-truth-gopro-social-engagement.html;
Peter Burrows, "GoPro's Incredible Small, Durable Camcorder,"
Bloomberg Businessweek, June 30, 2011, www.businessweek.com/
magazine/gopros-incredible-small-durable-camcorder-07012011.
html; Casey Newton, "GoPro Positioned to Grab Big Slice of
Global Market," *San Francisco Chronicle*, May 6, 2011, p. D1; Peter
Burrows, "GoPro Widens the View of Its Customer Base,"
Bloomberg Businessweek, October 23, 2012, pp. 43–44; Tim
Peterson, "GoPro Boosts Sales via Snap and Share," *Adweek*,
January 2013, pp. 12–13; Tom Huddleston, "GoPro Rides Big
Wave of Camera Sales, but Shares Wipeout," *Fortune*, February 5,
2015, http://fortune.com/2015/02/05/gopro-earnings-revenue-
swells; and www.GoPro.com and http://-gopro.com/about-us,
accessed September 2013.

2. Consumer expenditure figures from www.cia.gov/library/
publications/the-world-factbook/geos/us.html. Population figures
from the World POPClock, U.S. Census Bureau, www.census.
gov/main/www/popclock.html, accessed March 2013. This site
provides continually updated projections of U.S. and world
populations.

3. Nicholas Köhler, "Canadians Feel like They're on Top of the
World," *Macleans.ca*, www2.macleans.ca/2011/12/19/on-top-of-
the-world-2, accessed April 16, 2012.

4. The Centre for Canadian Studies, "The Political Voice of
Canadian Regional Identities," 2001, http://culturescope.ca/ev_
en.php?ID=9417_201&ID2=DO_TOPIC, accessed September
2006.

5. *CBC News*, "Aboriginal People Could Number 2.2M by 2031,"
December 7, 2011, www.cbc.ca/news/canada/story/2011/12/07/
aboriginalpopulation-forecast.html.

6. James Murray, "Quality Market Launches New Online Store
That Is Easy and Fun!" April 15, 2012, http://netnewsledger.
com/2012/04/15/quality-market-launches-new-onlinestore-that-
is-easy-and-fun.

7. Statistics Canada, "Study: Canada's Visible Minority Population
in 2017," *The Daily*, March 22, 2005; and "Canada Welcomes
Highest Number of Legal Immigrants in 50 Years While Taking
Action to Maintain the Integrity of Canada's Immigration System,"
February 13, 2011, www.cic.gc.ca/english/department/media/
releases/2011/2011-02-13.asp.

8. Huixia Sun, "Chinese Websites Beat Economic Blues,"
Vancouver Sun, May 15, 2009; and Chris Powell, "New Chinese
Canadians Prefer Internet to TV: Diversity Study," *Marketing
magazine*, April 2008.

9. Statistics Canada, "2006 Census Data Products," www12.
statcan.ca/census-recensement/2006/dp-pd/index-eng.cfm,
accessed May 2009.

10. Eleftheria Parpis, "Goodbye Color Codes," *Adweek*, September
27, 2010, pp. 24–25; "Ethnic Marketing: McDonald's Is Lovin' It,"
Bloomberg BusinessWeek, July 18, 2010, pp. 22–23; Stuart Elliott,
"Mosaic Marketing Takes a Fresh Look at Changing Society," *New
York Times*, July 18, 2011, p. B3; "Ethnic Advertising: One
Message or Many?," *The Economist*, December 31, 2011; and Alex
Frias, "5 Tips to Refresh Your Multicultural Marketing Strategy in

2013," *Forbes*, February 8, 2013, www.forbes.com/sites/theyec/
2013/02/08/5-tips-to-refresh-your-multicultural-marketing-
strategy-in-2013.

11. Adam Bluestein, "Make Money in 2013 (and Beyond)," *Inc.*,
December 2012/January 2013, pp. 58–65, here p. 64.

12. Based on information from Julie Liesse, "The Big Idea,"
Advertising Age, November 28, 2011, pp. C4–C6; and "Philips's
'Wake up the Town,'" www.ketchum.com/philips's-"wake-town,"
accessed July 2013.

13. Eve Tahmincioglu, "Majority of Dads Say They Do the
Grocery Shopping," *Life Inc.*, June 15, 2012, http://lifeinc.today.
com/_news/2012/06/15/12238737-majority-of-dads-say-they-
do-the-grocery-shopping?lite; Samantha Murphy, "Stereotype
Debunked: Women Buy More Technology Than Men," http://
mashable.com/2012/01/09/women-and-technology, January 9,
2012; and Chris Slocumb, "Women Outspend Men 3 to 2 on
Technology Purchases," ClarityQuest, January 3, 2013, www.
clarityqst.com/women-outspend-men-3-to-2-on-technology-
purchases.

14. Laura A. Flurry, "Children's Influence in Family Decision
Making: Examining the Impact of the Changing American
Family," *Journal of Business Research*, April 2007, pp. 322–330; and
"Tween Years Prove to Be Rewarding for Toymakers," *USA Today*,
December 22, 2010, p. 1B. Also see Michael R. Solomon, Judith
L. Zaichkowsky, and Rosemary Polegato, *Consumer Behaviour:
Buying, Having, and Being*, 5th Canadian edition (Toronto: Pearson
Canada, 2011).

15. Information on Acxiom's Personicx segmentation system from
www.acxiom.com/Ideas-and-Innovation/Self-Assessment-Tools,
accessed November 2013.

16. Quotes from www.mooresclothing.com/mor/index.jsp.19.

17. See Stuart Elliott, "Penney's New Approach Takes Target-Like
Tack," *New York Times*, January 25, 2012; and Laura Heller,
"Mission Accomplished: J.C.Penney Was the Most Interesting
Retailer of 2012," *Forbes*, February 8, 2013, www.forbes.com/
sites/lauraheller/2013/02/08/mission-accomplished-jcpenney-
was-the-most-interesting-retailer-of-2012.

18. REI information from www.rei.com/aboutrei/about_rei.html
and other pages at the www.rei.com site, accessed September 2013.

19. See www.thebenjamin.com/DreamDog.aspx, www.dogtv.com,
and www.neuticles.com/faq.php, accessed September 2013.

20. See Jennifer Aaker, "Dimensions of Measuring Brand
Personality," *Journal of Marketing Research*, August 1997, pp. 347–
356; and Kevin Lane Keller, *Strategic Brand Management*, 3rd ed.
(Upper Saddle River, New Jersey, 2008), pp. 66–67. For more on
brand personality, see Lucia Malär, Harley Kromer, Wayne D.
Hoyer, and Bettina Nyffenegger, "Emotional Brand Attachment
and Brand Personality: The Relative Importance of the Actual and
the Ideal Self," *Journal of Marketing*, July 2011, pp. 35–52; and Jack
Neff, "Just How Well-Defined Is Your Brand's Ideal?" *Advertising
Age*, January 16, 2012, p. 4.

21. See www.skullcandy.com, www.skullcandy.com/blog, and
http://investors.skullcandy.com/index.cfm, accessed September
2013.

22. See Abraham H. Maslow, "A Theory of Human Motivation," *Psychological Review*, 50 (1943), pp. 370–396. Also see Maslow, *Motivation and Personality*, 3rd ed. (New York: HarperCollins Publishers, 1987); and Michael R. Solomon, *Consumer Behavior*, 9th ed. (Upper Saddle River, NJ: Prentice Hall, 2011), pp. 135–136.

23. Ellen Moore, "Letter to My Colleague: We Can Do Better," *Adweek*, December 22, 2010, www.adweek.com/news/advertising-branding/letter-my-colleagues-we-can-do-better-104084.

24. For more reading, see Lawrence R. Samuel, *Freud on Madison Avenue: Motivation Research and Subliminal Advertising in America* (Philadelphia: University of Pennsylvania Press, 2010); Charles R. Acland, *Swift Viewing: The Popular Life of Subliminal Influence* (Duke University Press, 2011); and Christopher Shea, "The History of Subliminal Ads," *Wall Street Journal*, February 15, 2012, http://blogs.wsj.com/ideas-market/2012/02/15/the-history-of-subliminal-ads.

25. Example based on information found in John Berman, "Shrek Boosts Vidalia Onion Sales," June 29, 2010, http://abcnews.go.com/WN/shrek-boosts-vidalia-onion-sales/story?id=11047273; and "Vidalia Onion Committee Cinches Triple Crown of National Marketing Awards," October 20, 2011, www.vidaliaonion.org/news/vidalia_onion_committee_cinches_triple_crown_of_national_marketing_awards. Vidalia® is a registered certification mark of Georgia Department of Agriculture.

26. See Leon Festinger, *A Theory of Cognitive Dissonance* (Stanford, CA: Stanford University Press, 1957); Cynthia Crossen, "'Cognitive Dissonance' Became a Milestone in the 1950s Psychology," *Wall Street Journal*, December 12, 2006, p. B1; and Anupam Bawa and Purva Kansal, "Cognitive Dissonance and the Marketing of Services: Some Issues," *Journal of Services Research*, October 2008–March 2009, p. 31.

27. The following discussion draws from the work of Everett M. Rogers. See his *Diffusion of Innovations*, 5th ed. (New York: Free Press, 2003).

28. Nick Bunkley, "Hyundai, Using a Safety Net, Wins Market Share," *New York Times*, February 5, 2009; and Noreen O'Leary, "Chevy Launches 'Love It or Return It' Promo," *Adweek*, July 10, 2012, www.adweek.com/news/advertising-branding/chevy-launches-love-it-or-return-it-promo-141772.

29. Based on Rogers, *Diffusion of Innovation*, p. 281. For more discussion, see http://en.wikipedia.org/Everett_Rogers, accessed November 2013.

30. "High Definition Is the New Normal," *Nielsen Wire*, October 17, 2012, http://blog.nielsen.com/nielsenwire/media_entertainment/high-definition-is-the-new-normal.

31. See www.omnexus.com/sf/dow/?id=plastics, accessed March 2010; and http://plastics.dow.com, accessed September 2013.

32. This classic categorization was first introduced in Patrick J. Robinson, Charles W. Faris, and Yoram Wind, *Industrial Buying Behavior and Creative Marketing* (Boston: Allyn & Bacon, 1967). Also see James C. Anderson, James A. Narus, and Das Narayandas, *Business Market Management*, 3rd ed. (Upper Saddle River, NJ: Prentice Hall, 2009), Chapter 3; and Philip Kotler and Kevin Lane Keller, *Marketing Management*, 14th ed. (Upper Saddle River, NJ: Prentice Hall, 2012), Chapter 7.

33. Based on information from "Six Flags Entertainment Corporation: Improving Business Efficiency with Enterprise Asset Management," July 12, 2012, http://www-01.ibm.com/software/success/cssdb.nsf/CS/LWIS-8W5Q84?OpenDocument&Site=default&cty=en_us; and www-01.ibm.com/software/tivoli/products/maximo-asset-mgmt, accessed November 2013.

34. Information accessed at Industry Canada's Small Business Research and Statistics website, www.ic.gc.ca/eic/site/sbrp-rppe.nsf/eng/rd02456.html; and Great Little Box Company website, www.greatlittlebox.com.

35. Robinson, Faris, and Wind, *Industrial Buying Behavior*, p. 14. Also see Kotler and Keller, *Marketing Management*, pp. 197–203.

36. See https://homedepotlink.homedepot.com/en-us/Pages/default.aspx, accessed May 2013.

37. For this and other examples, see "10 Great Web Sites," *BtoB Online*, September 13, 2010. Other information from www.shawfloors.com/About-Shaw/Retailer-Support, accessed November 2013.

CHAPTER 7

1. Based on information from Peter Himler, "Liquid Gold," *Forbes*, January 7, 2013; "P&G's Detergents (Tide, Ariel) More Valuable Than Gillette Razors," *Trefis*, June 10, 2010; Dan Monk, "Procter & Gamble Washing Out Rivals with Tide Pods, Analyst Says," *Business Courier*, September 7, 2012 (online at www.bizjournals.com); and information from Procter & Gamble's website, PG.com, July 2015.

2. Elizabeth Hames, "The Beer Up Here," *Canadian Business*, March 18, 2013, pp. 8–9; Josh Rubin, "What's Brewing: Yukon Gold Beer Brings Northern Exposure," *Toronto Star*, May 7, 2015; and Yukon Brewing's website, YukonBeer.com, accessed July 2015.

3. Joel Stein, "The Men's 'Skin Care' Product Boom," *Time*, October 30, 2010; Kristen Vinakmens, "Beauty Forecast 2013," *Cosmetics*, January/February 2013, p. 56; Noreen O'Leary, "Talk to Her," *Adweek*, February 27, 2012; Andrew Adam Newman, "Axe Adds Fragrance for Women to Its Lineup," *New York Times*, January 8, 2012; and information from axeanarchy.axe.us and www.menaji.com, accessed July 2015.

4. Elisabeth A. Sullivan, "H.O.G.: Harley-Davidson Shows Brand Strength as It Navigates Down New Roads—and Picks Up More Female Riders Along the Way," November 1, 2008, p. 8; "Harley-Davidson Hosts Special Rides to Kick Off Women Riders Month," *PR Newswire*, March 23, 2009; and information from Harley-Davidson's website, investor.harley-davidson.com, accessed July 2015.

5. Example from Richard Baker, "Retail Trends—Luxury Marketing: The End of a Mega-Trend," *Retail*, June/July 2009, pp. 8–12.

6. Eve Lazarus, "Coast Capital Singing a Chinese Song," *Marketing magazine online*, July 24, 2007.

7. Kristin Laird, "Hyundai Harnesses Star Power in Quebec," *Marketing Daily*, March 28, 2008.

8. See vfc.com/brands, accessed July 2015.

9. Information from TrekBikes.com, accessed July 2015.

10. Brian Wansink and Sea Bum Park (2000), "Comparison Methods for Identifying Heavy Users," *Journal of Advertising Research*, 40(4) (July/August), pp. 61–72.

11. "Paying It Forward: How Mobile Wallet Apps Are Changing Consumer Habits," Nielsen.com, June 24, 2015.

12. Evra Taylor, "The Pink Dollar Is at Par," *Marketing* magazine, July 9, 2012, pp. 23–27; and Evra Taylor, "Is Canada's Lesbian, Gay, Bisexual and Transgender Community Worth Pursuing?" *Marketing* magazine, July 9, 2012, p. 70.

13. Information from starbucksfs.com and starbucksocs.com, accessed July 2015.

14. See "Coca-Cola Launches Global Music Effort to Connect with Teens," *Advertising Age*, March 3, 2011; "Coca-Cola's London 2012 Game Plan: Woo Teens Through Music, Parents Through Sustainability," *BrandChannel*, September 29, 2011; Mark Miller, "Coca-Cola Music Strategy Strengthened by $10M Spotify Stake," *Brand Channel*, November 15, 2012; and David Moth, "Coca-Cola Reveals Lessons Learned from Its London Olympics Marketing," February 6, 2013, Econsultancy.com (blog).

15. See Michael Porter, *Competitive Advantage* (New York: Free Press, 1985), pp. 4–8, 234–236. For more recent discussions, see Kenneth Sawka and Bill Fiora, "The Four Analytical Techniques Every Analyst Must Know: 2. Porter's Five Forces Analysis," *Competitive Intelligence magazine*, May–June 2003, p. 57; and Philip Kotler and Kevin Lane Keller, *Marketing Management*, 14th ed. (Upper Saddle River, NJ: Prentice Hall, 2012), p. 232.

16. Brad van Auken, "Leveraging the Brand: Hallmark Case Study," January 11, 2008, published on BrandStrategyInsider.com; "Hallmark Breaks Out of Special-Occasion Mold," *Advertising Age*, July 6, 2011; and information from Hallmark.com, accessed July 2015.

17. Rich Chamberlain, "Sabian Marks Rush Anniversary with New Paragons," *Rhythm* magazine, June 23, 2015; Kathleen Martin, "Global Cymbals," *Marketing*, March 22, 2004, p. 13; and information from Sabian's website at Sabian.com.

18. Piyush Shah, "Busting Myths in Location-Based Mobile Advertising: Perceptions, Paradoxes and Possibilities," MediaPost.com, August 14, 2015; Lauren Johnson, "4 Location-Based Marketing Tactics That Are Working: Payments, Beacons, and Coupons Are Top Priorities," AdWeek.com, August 4, 2014; and information from Groupon.com, Foursquare.com, CheckPoints.com, and Shopkick.com.

19. Abbey Klaassen, "Harley-Davidson Breaks Consumer-Created Work from Victors & Spoils," *Advertising Age*, February 14, 2012.

20. Michael Myser, "Marketing Made Easy," *Business 2.0*, June 2006, pp. 43–44.

21. See Bobby J. Calder and Steven J. Reagan, "Brand Design," in Dawn Iacobucci, ed., *Kellogg on Marketing* (New York: John Wiley & Sons, 2001), p. 61. For more discussion, see Philip Kotler and Kevin Lane Keller, *Marketing Management*, 13th ed. (Upper Saddle River, NJ: Prentice Hall, 2009), pp. 315–316.

CHAPTER 8

1. "Corning Gorilla Glass Helps Meizu Make Its Slimmest Smartphone Yet," published on Thomson Reuters One and MarketWatch July 7, 2015; Connie Guglielmo, "Working with Innovators from Thomas Edison to Steve Jobs, Corning Finds a Glass Fix," *Forbes*, September 23, 2013; David Lidsky, "Corning: For Becoming the 800-Pound Gorilla of the Touch-Screen Business," *Fast Company*, February 11, 2013; Bryan Gardiner, "Glass Works: How Corning Created the Ultrathin, Ultrastrong Material of the Future," *Wired*, September 24, 2012; Charles Schelle, "Steve Jobs' Biographer Isaacson Shares Tales of Apple Founder's Genius," *Sarasota Patch*, January 16, 2013; and information from Corning.com and CMOG.org.

2. Danny Kucharsky, "Friendly Funerals," *Marketing*, April 10, 2006, pp. 17–18.

3. Gwyn Topham, "Sir Richard Branson's Setbacks: From Virgin Cola to Virgin Brides," *Guardian* online, October 6, 2014; Richard Branson, "What Makes You So Special?" *Canadian Business*, August 12, 2013, p. 28.

4. Barry Curewitz, "Want New Products That Get Noticed? Change the Process," *Advertising Age*, October 1, 2007.

5. For more about the diffusion of innovations theory and the technology adoption life cycle, see any edition of Geoffrey A. Moore, *Crossing the Chasm* (New York: HarperCollins, 1991); and Everett M. Rogers, *Diffusion of Innovations* (New York: The Free Press, originally published 1962).

6. Based on information from "Hack Week @ Twitter," January 25, 2012, blog.twitter.com/2012/01/hack-week-twitter.html; "Twitter's 'Hack Week,' 7 Days for New Ideas," *Mashable*, January 26, 2012; "Hack Week: Efficiency Edition," April 26, 2012, http://blog.twitter.com/2012/04/hack-week-efficiency-edition.html; and "Twitter's 'Hack Week,' 7 Days for New Ideas," *Mashable* video published on YouTube.

7. Andrew Abbott, "Announcing the PayPal Mobile App Challenge Winners!" TopCoder.com, February 8, 2011.

8. For a more comprehensive discussion of marketing strategies over the course of the product life cycle, see Philip Kotler and Kevin Lane Keller, *Marketing Management*, 9th Canadian ed., Chapter 10.

9. Angelina Chapin, "Guitar Hero (2005–2011)," *Canadian Business*, March 14, 2011, p. 25.

10. Alex Davies, "Volvo Will Test Self-Driving Cars with Real Customers in 2017," *Wired* online, February 23, 2015; Michael McCullough, "Look, Ma, No Hands!" *Canadian Business*, August 2014, pp. 10–11.

11. Based on information from "Nest Labs Introduces the World's First Learning Thermostat," press release published on Nest.com, October 25, 2011; Katie Fehrenbacher, "'Hundreds of Thousands' of Nest Learning Thermostats Sold," *GigaOM*, September 4, 2012.

12. Rebecca Harris, "Nice Package," *Marketing*, April 9, 2012, pp. 26–31.

13. Rebecca Harris, "Nice Package," *Marketing*, April 9, 2012, pp. 26–31; and information provided by Petcurean.

14. Sustainable Packaging Coalition, SustainablePackaging.org.

15. Katharine Earley, "How Are Companies Applying Circular Thinking to Packaging?" *Guardian* online, July 1, 2015.

16. Jeff Beer, "Oreos's Chinese Twist," *Canadian Business*, December 10, 2012, pp. 66–67.

17. Chad Brooks, "Lost in Translation: 8 International Marketing Fails," *Business News Daily* online, October 7, 2013.

18. Statistics Canada annual data for 2014.

19. John Greenwood, "The Services Industry: Canada's Secret Economic Playground?" *Maclean's* online, April 1, 2015.

20. See James L. Heskett, W. Earl Sasser, Jr., and Leonard A. Schlesinger, *The Service Profit Chain: How Leading Companies Link Profit and Growth to Loyalty, Satisfaction, and Value* (New York: Free Press, 1997); and Heskett, Sasser, and Schlesinger, *The Value Profit Chain: Treat Employees Like Customers and Customers Like Employees* (New York: Free Press, 2003). Also see John Marshall and Dave Mayer, "Activate a Brand Internally," *Marketing Management*, Winter 2012, pp. 37–44.

21. Sarah Barmak & Graham F. Scott, "Yes, We Sell No Bananas," *Canadian Business*, October 1, 2012.

22. Adapted from Sarah Kessler, "The Future of the Hotel Industry and Social Media," *Mashable!*, October 19, 2010; and Jeff Williams, "Marriott's SM Team Gets It," *HD Leader*, September 14, 2010.

CHAPTER 9

1. "Crave More Staked New Ground with Custom Execution," *Marketing*, January 2015, p. 34; Chris Powell, "Behind the Scenes of the Rogers/Loblaw 'Crave More' Campaign," *Marketing* online, September 24, 2014; Ashley Csanady, "Loblaws Launches Social Network to Attract More Foodies," Canada.com, September 19, 2014; Kristen Mogg, "Loblaws Revamps President's Choice Marketing," My Private Brand (mypbrand.com), September 18, 2014; Mai Nguyen, "Loblaw's 'Crave More' Campaign Aims President's Choice at Foodie Culture," *Canadian Business* online, September 18, 2014; "Canada's Top Food Brand, President's Choice®, Modernizes Message to Reflect Today's Broader Customer Cravings," press release published on Canada Newswire, September 18, 2014; Susan Krashinsky, "Loblaw Targets Food-Savvy Canadians in Major Marketing Overhaul," *Globe and Mail* online, September 17, 2014; and information from AdForum.com, SapientNitro.com, and PresidentsChoice.ca.

2. Jonathan Salem Baskin, "Our Measurement Problem Begins with Definitions," AdAge.com, May 17, 2010.

3. Marty Neumeier, *The Brand Gap* (Berkeley, CA: New Riders, 2006).

4. "The Feud: Nestlé vs. Cadbury," *Canadian Business*, October, 2012, p. 37.

5. "Study Shows Kids Prefer Food in McDonald's Wrappers," MarketingMag.ca, August 8, 2007.

6. Jack Trout, "'Branding' Simplified," *Forbes*, April 19, 2007, www.forbes.com.

7. Susan Fournier, "Consumers and Their Brands: Developing Relationship Theory in Consumer Research," *Journal of Consumer Research*, March 1998.

8. Kevin Roberts, *Lovemarks: The Future Beyond Brands* (New York: powerHouse Books, 2004).

9. "Chuck Hughes, Celebrity Chef: On His Personal Brand, His New Show and What He Really Does on His Days Off," *Canadian Business*, July 16, 2012, pp. 65–66; Mishki Vaccaro, "Chuck Hughes Becomes the First Canadian Chef to Beat Bobby Flay on Iron Chef," *Toronto Life* online, March 21, 2011;

10. Deborah Aarts, "Interview: Second Cup CEO Alix Box on Reinventing an Outdated Brand," *Canadian Business* online, December 11, 2014; Russ Martin, "Something New Is Brewing at Second Cup," *Marketing* online, December 4, 2014; and "Second Cup Coffee Co Introduces Innovative Café of the Future," press release published on Canada Newswire, December 4, 2014.

11. For more on Young & Rubicam's BrandAsset Valuator, see W. Ronald Lane, Karen Whitehill King, and Tom Reichert, *Kleppner's Advertising Procedure*, 18th ed. (Upper Saddle River, NJ: Pearson Prentice Hall, 2011), pp. 83–84; and Young & Rubicam's website, YR.com/BAV.

12. All information from BestGlobalBrands.com and Interbrand's Best Canadian Brands 2014.

13. Ted Matthews, *Brand: It Ain't the Logo*, Instinct Brand Equity Coaches Inc., 2012.

14. "Best Buy Canada Chooses Desjardins to Manage Its Private Label Credit Card Portfolio," press release published on Canada Newswire, January 7, 2015.

15. Claire Brownell, "DSS Group Inc Deal Has Helped Put Fizz Back in Cott Corp's Shares," *Financial Post* online, March 17, 2015; Cott Corporation Annual Report 2014; and information from Cott.com.

16. Michael Stone, "Licensing Expo: Fun and Games in 3-D from Las Vegas," AdAge.com, June 12, 2015.

17. Chris Powell, "Elle Canada Partners with Sally Hansen on Co-Branded Report," *Marketing* online, July 14, 2015.

18. David Welch, "Kraft's Planters Heads for the Peanut Butter Aisle," Bloomberg.com, March 8, 2012; Tim Nudd, "Ad of the Day: Planters Mr. Peanut's Stunt Double Takes a Beating for Kraft Brand's New Peanut Butter," AdWeek.com, June 24, 2011.

19. Ashley Rodriguez, "Apparel Wholesaler Gildan Takes On Hanes, Fruit of the Loom," AdAge.com, May 26, 2015; Canadian Press, "Gildan Activewear Makes Super Bowl Play with TV Spot," *Marketing magazine*, February 5, 2013; Jeff Beer, "Out of the Closet: Why Gildan Went Big on TV," *Marketing magazine*, March 14, 2013.

20. Lee Hee Jung and Kang Myung Soo, "The Effect of Brand Experience on Brand Relationship Quality," *Academy of Marketing Studies Journal*, 2012, 16(1), pp. 87–98.

21. "While TV Gets Auto Ad Dollars; Social Is the Critical Inflection Point in Purchase Decisions," *Business Wire*, February 21, 2013.

22. Robert Klara, "Five Famous Female Frontwomen," AdWeek.com, February 26, 2013; and Old Time Radio Catalogue, OTRCat.com.

23. Danny Kucharsky, "Record-Breaking Stunt Ushers New Footcare Brand into Canada," *Marketing* online, June 25, 2015; and "Amopé PediPerfect Sets the Guinness World Records Title for Most Pedicures Given in 8 Hours," press release published on Canada Newswire, June 11, 2015.

24. Emma Hall, "New Benetton Ads Confront Prejudice, but Don't Shock," AdAge.com, January 23, 2013.

25. Kevin Roberts, *Lovemarks: The Future Beyond Brands* (New York: powerHouse Books, 2004).

26. Mark Thomson, "The Power of a Good Brand Story," BrandChannel.com, October 25, 2004.

27. Rebecca Harris, "Farmers Sing Potato Praises for Cavendish Farms," *Marketing magazine*, January 15, 2013; Chris Powell, "Cavendish Farms Chooses Yield and Cairns O'Neil," *Marketing magazine*, May 29, 2012; and information from CavendishFarms.com and YieldBranding.com.

28. "The Power of Story," *Marketing magazine*, September 12, 2012, p. 19.

29. Anthony Mullen, "Emerging Technologies Demand New Marketing Fundamentals," AdAge.com, March 4, 2013.

30. Brian Solis, *Engage!* (New York: John Wiley & Sons, 2010).

31. *The MediaBrix Social and Mobile Gaming Report*, MediaBrix.com, March 2013; and James Dohnert, "Social and Mobile Gaming Ads Offer 20 Percent Engagement Rates," ClickZ.com, March 4, 2013.

32. Nicola Kemp, "Beyond the Narcissism: Six Trends Defining the Next Decade of Social Media," *Marketing* magazine (U.K.) online, June 22, 2015.

CHAPTER 10

1. Bryan Pearson, "Framing the In-Store Vision Online: What Warby Parker Can Teach Digital Merchants (Part 2)," Forbes.com, July 7, 2015; Douglas MacMillan, Eyeglass Retailer Warby Parker Valued at $1.2 Billion," *Wall Street Journal* blogs (Blogs.WSJ.com), April 30, 2015; Drake Baer, "Why Warby Parker Invited 20,000 Customers to Their Apartment," *Fast Company*, May 10, 2013; Vanessa O'Connell, "Warby Parker Co-Founder Says Initial Vision Was All About Price," *Wall Street Journal*, July 18, 2012; Nina Strochlic, "Warby Parker Thrives by Giving Away Glasses Whenever It Sells a Pair," *The Daily Beast*, May 7, 2013; and information from Warby Parker.

2. For more on the importance of sound pricing strategy, see Thomas T. Nagle, John Hogan, and Joseph Zale, *The Strategy and Tactics of Pricing: A Guide to Growing More Profitably*, 5th ed. (Upper Saddle River, NJ: Prentice Hall, 2011), Chapter 1.

3. Anne Marie Chaker, "For a Steinway, I Did It My Way," *Wall Street Journal*, May 22, 2008; and information from the Steinway Piano Gallery Toronto.

4. Patrick Collinson, "Ryanair Takes Aim at Price Comparison Websites," *Guardian* online, July 27, 2015; and information from Ryanair.com.

5. "Cineplex Brings VIP Cinemas and UltraAVX to Downtown Edmonton," press release published on Marketwired.com, January 22, 2015.

6. "Shomi Expands to Anyone in Canada with Internet Connection, Not Just TV Subscribers," *Canadian Press*, May 27, 2015; Brad Oswald, "Netflix, Crave TV, Shomi Go to War Online to Capture Canadians Who Want U.S. Programming," *Winnipeg Free Press* online, February 21, 2015; and Michael Oliveira, "Review: Is Shomi a Better Streaming Service Than Netflix?" *Canadian Press*, November 5, 2014.

7. Joseph Weber, "Over a Buck for Dinner? Outrageous," *BusinessWeek*, March 9, 2009, p. 57; and Tom Mulier and Matthew Boyle, "Dollar Dinners from ConAgra's Threatened by Costs," *Bloomberg Businessweek*, August 19, 2010.

8. Jens Hansegard, "IKEA Taking China by Storm," *Wall Street Journal*, March 26, 2012; Mei Fong, "IKEA Hits Home in China: The Swedish Design Giant, Unlike Other Retailers, Slashes Prices for the Chinese," *Wall Street Journal*, March 3, 2006, p. B1; and Anna Ringstrom, "One Size Doesn't Fit All: IKEA Goes Local for China, India," *Globe and Mail*, March 7, 2013.

9. Matthew Boyle, "Unilever: Taking on the World, One Stall at a Time," *Bloomberg Businessweek*, January 7, 2013, pp. 18–20.

10. Mark Ritson, "Should You Launch a Fighter Brand?" *Harvard Business Review*, October 2009.

11. See the Competition Act, Sections 34–38, http://laws.justice.gc.ca/en/C-34.

12. Jim Middlemiss, "Don't Get Caught Offside in Rule Changes," *Financial Post*, March 23, 2009.

CHAPTER 11

1. Based on information from Greg Satell, "What Neflix's 'House of Cards' Means for the Future of TV," *Forbes*, March 4, 2013; Greg Bensinger, "Netflix Posts Surprise Profit," *Wall Street Journal*, January 23, 2013; Stu Woo, "Under Fire, Netflix Rewinds DVD Plan," *Wall Street Journal*, October 11, 2011, p. A1; Ronald Grover and Cliff Edwards, "Can Netflix Find Its Future by Abandoning Its Past?" *Bloomberg Businessweek*, September 26–October 2, 2011, pp. 29–30; Stu Woo and Ian Sherr, "Netflix Recovers Subscribers," *Wall Street Journal*, January 26, 2012, p. B1; Dan Mitchell, "Why Netflix Can't Keep Winning," *Fortune*, January 22, 2013.

2. Eve Lazarus, "Branching Out," *Marketing magazine*, October 20, 2003, p. 29.

3. All information from Caterpillar.com.

4. Christopher Loudon, "The Sun Life," *Marketing magazine*, March 1, 2010, pp. 27–32.

5. Mark Ritson, "Why Retailers Call the Shots," *Marketing*, February 18, 2009, p. 24; Kim Bhasin, "Costco Kicks Out Coke and Replaces It with Pepsi in Food Courts," *Business Insider*, February 15, 2013.

6. "Fashion Forward; Inditex," *The Economist*, March 24, 2012, pp. 63–64; Suza Hansen, "How Zara Grew into the World's Largest Fashion Retailer," *New York Times*, November 9, 2012; and information from the Inditex Press Dossier, www.inditex.com/en/press/information/press_kit.

7. Boston Pizza website, BostonPizza.com.

8. Paul Eisensten, "Toyota Tops in Supplier Relations—Just Barely," *The Detroit Bureau*, May 23, 2011.

9. Bert Helm, "At KFC, a Battle Among the Chicken-Hearted," *Bloomberg Businessweek*, August 16–August 29, 2010, p. 19; and Diane Brady, "YUM's Big Game of Chicken," *Bloomberg Businessweek*, March 29, 2012, pp. 64–69.

10. Beth Negus Viveiros, "Mattel Uses Web to Boost Retail Sales and Bond with Collectors," *Chief Marketer*, September 23, 2012.

11. Kyle Stock, "Stihl Chain Saws Thrive Outside the Big Box," Bloomberg.com, April 24, 2014.

12. Information from LeeValley.com and VeritasTools.ca.

13. "Logistics Costs Remain High in China: Report," *WantChina Times.com*, February 16, 2013.

14. Julie Jargon, "Asia Delivers for McDonald's," *Wall Street Journal*, December 13, 2011; "Feel Like a Burger? Dial M for McDonald's Japan," *Asia Pulse*, January 23, 2012; and information from McDonald's annual reports.

15. "Best Year for Supply Chain and Logistics Since Great Recession According to 26th Annual State of Logistics Report," press release published by the Council of Supply Chain Management Professionals (CSCMP), June 23, 2015; and information from the Canadian Supply Chain Management Association's website, SCMANational.ca.

16. William B. Cassidy, "Walmart Squeezes Costs from Supply Chain," *Journal of Commerce*, January 5, 2010; and "Walmart to Save $150 Million Thanks to Sustainability Programs," *Triple Pundit*, October 16, 2012.

17. Laura Cameron, "The Big Money in Slow Shipping," *Canadian Business*, May 10, 2010, p. 22.

18. Bill Mongrelluzzo, "Supply Chain Expert Sees Profits in Sustainability," *Journal of Commerce*, March 11, 2010; SC Johnson example from "SC Johnson Reduces Greenhouse Gasses by the Truckload," press release published by SC Johnson, November 28, 2007; also see "SC Johnson Named Recipient of 2012 SmartWay Excellence Award by the United States Environmental Protection Agency," *PRNewswire*, October 12, 2012.

19. Ted LaBorde, "Home Depot Opens New Record Limited Distribution Center in Westfield," masslive.com, December 14, 2010; "Home Depot Distribution Efficiencies Improve In-Stock Positions," *Retailed Info Systems News*, November 21, 2011, http://risnews.edgl.com/retail-best-practices/Home-Depot-Distribution-Efficiencies-Improve-In-Stock-Positions76905; and www.homedepot.com.

20. Julianne Pepitone, "Amazon Buys Army of Robots," *CNNMoney*, March 20, 2012; "Rise of the Orange Machines," *Bloomberg Businessweek*, November 15–November 21, 2010, p. 47; and Evan West, "These Robots Play Fetch," *Fast Company*, July–August 2007, pp. 49–50.

21. "Toshiba Laptop Repair," May 2013, http://pressroom.ups.com/Video/Toshiba+Laptop+Repair; and www.thenewlogistics.com and www.ups.com/content/us/en/about/facts/worldwide.html.

CHAPTER 12

1. Farhad Manjoo, "Dot Convert," *Fast Company*, December 2012/January 2013, pp. 113–116+; Emily Jane Fox, "Walmart: The $200 Billion Grocer," *CNNMoney*, January 31, 2013; John Huey, "Wal-Mart: Will It Take Over the World?" *Fortune*, January 30, 1998, pp. 52–61; Michael Barbano and Stuart Elliott, "Clinging to Its Roots, Wal-Mart Steps Back from an Edgy, New Image," *New York Times*, December 10, 2006; Geoff Colvin, "Wal-Mart's Makeover," *Fortune*, December 26, 2011, pp. 50–55; "Global 500: The World's Largest Corporations," *Fortune*, July 22, 2013, pp. 133+; "Canada's Top Companies by Industry," *Globe and Mail*, July 3, 2013; Hollie Shaw, "Walmart Canada Gaining Ground in Retail Food Fight," *Financial Post*, November 13, 2014; and Walmart Canada's corporate website, walmartcanada.ca.

2. Information from Statistics Canada and the Retail Council of Canada.

3. Carol Toller, "Nordstrom Is Always Right," *Canadian Business*, March 2015, pp. 59–62; Paula McCooey, "Nordstrom Boss 'Overwhelmed' by Reception at Ottawa Opening," *Ottawa Citizen*, published online March 6, 2015; and Nordstrom history from Nordstrom.com.

4. Susana Silva, "Pet Valu Opens New Location in Binbrook," *The Sachem & Glanbrook Gazette*, www.sachem.ca, June 4, 2013.

5. Based on information from Maureen Morrison, "Fast-Casual Burger Joints Snag a Seat at the Table," *Advertising Age*, September 26, 2011; Karen Weise, "Behind Five Guys' Beloved Burgers," *Bloomberg Businessweek*, August 11, 2011; Monte Burke, "Five Guys Burgers: America's Fastest Growing Restaurant Chain," *Forbes*, August 6, 2012; and the websites aboutmcdonalds.com and fiveguys.com.

6. Kristin Laird, "Sport Chek Turns Digital Focus In-Store with New Retail Concept," *Marketing magazine* online, January 29, 2013; and "Sport Chek Changes the Game with Retail Lab in Toronto," press release issued by FGL Sports on Canada Newswire, January 28, 2013.

7. Courtenay Edelhart, "Malls Can't Take Customers for Granted as New Outdoor Centers Pop Up," *McClatchy-Tribune Business News*, January 16, 2010; Eric Schwartzberg, "Lifestyle Centers Draw Retailers, Shoppers," *The Oxford Press*, November 21, 2011; and "It's the End of the Mall as We Know It," *Real Estate Weekly*, February 22, 2013.

8. Ted Salter, "The Future of Retail: How Consumer Behaviour Is Changing Businesses," *Canadian Retailer*, Summer 2015, pp. 16–18.

9. Rupal Parekh, "Test Driving BMW's First Concept Store in Paris," *Advertising Age*, June 1, 2012.

10. Mark Brown, "Location, Location, Location," *Canadian Business*, Summer 2014, pp. 12–13.

11. Ivor Tussell, "The Internet of You," *Canadian Business*, July 2014, pp. 43–44; and information from Nymi.com.

12. Alex Brownsell, "Shoppable Media: How Commerce Is Set to Revolutionise Global Media," MandMGlobal.com, November 12, 2014; and "Shoppable Media, In-Store Technology and Physical Presences for Online Stores," AdAge.com, January 9, 2013.

13. Natalie Galiordi, "Intel's Interactive Display Spices Up the Customer Experience," KioskMarketPlace.com, January 30, 2013.

14. Ted Salter, "The Future of Retail: How Consumer Behaviour Is Changing Businesses," *Canadian Retailer*, Summer 2015, pp. 16–18.

15. Amy Callahan, "5 Marketing Blunders to Avoid in Your Next Social Shopper Marketing Campaign," HuffingtonPost.com, July 28, 2015; and Alicia Androich, "Shopper Marketing: Around and Around We Go," *Marketing magazine*, June 7, 2012.

16. Statistics Canada, Canadian Internet Use Survey 2012.

17. "Shoptiques.com Launces Its Boutique Retail Platform un Canada," press release, PRNewswire.com, August 12, 2015.

18. Vijay Kumar, "Canadians Prefer Online Shopping to Retail Shopping," *International Business Times*, ibtimes.com, January 24, 2013.

19. Chris Powell, "GroupM Gets Inside the 'Showrooming' Trend," *Marketing magazine*, August 22, 2012.

20. Steve Olenski, "The Number One Mistake Retail Brands Make When It Comes to Twitter," *Forbes*, January 24, 2013.

21. Ted Salter, "The Future of Retail: How Consumer Behaviour Is Changing Businesses," *Canadian Retailer*, Summer 2015, pp. 16–18.

22. Manisha Krishnan, "Game of Thrones Pop-Up Shop in Toronto Draws Devoted Fans," TheStar.com, April 6, 2015.

23. Information from GreeningRetail.ca.

24. Information from Staples.com.

25. Eva Friede, "Aritzia Puts On the Ritz for Downtown Montreal Launch," MontrealGazette.com, May 8, 2015; Stefania Moretti, "An Empire State of Mind," *Canadian Business*, March 18, 2013, pp. 36–39; and information from Aritzia.com.

26. Ben Hanuka, "The Dangerous Mistake U.S. Retailers Make in Canada," HuffingtonPost.ca, March 5, 2014.

27. Statistics Canada, Annual Wholesale Trade 2012.

28. Grainger facts and other information from "Grainger: Beyond the Box Fact Book"; and other information from Grainger.com.

29. Information from McKesson.com.

CHAPTER 13

1. Information from http://cassies.ca/entry/viewcase/7162, accessed March 22, 2013; Susan Krashinsky, "AutoTrader.ca Spot Nabs Top Prize at Cassies," *Globe and Mail*, January 28, 2013, www.theglobeandmail.com/report-on-business/industry-news/marketing/autotraderca-spot-nabs-top-prize-at-cassies/article7931743; Val Maloney, "How a Content Experiment Drove Trips to Autotrader.ca," *Media in Canada*, February 6, 2015, http://mediaincanada.com/2015/02/06/how-a-content-experiment-drove-trips-to-autotrader-ca; and autoTRADER.ca Partners with CO-OP Advertising for Road Ahead," CNW Newswire, February 23, 2015, www.newswire.ca/en/story/1491529/autotrader-ca-partners-with-co-op-advertising-for-road-ahead.

2. For other definitions, see www.marketingpower.com/_layouts/-Dictionary.aspx, accessed November 2013.

3. Statistics from www.statista.com/statistics/265717/distribution-of-advertising-spending-worldwide-by-medium, accessed September 2015.

4. Chris Anderson, "The 'Angry Birds in Space' Video Marketing Campaign," *The Video Marketer*, March 22, 2012, http://blog.wooshii.com/the-angry-birds-in-space-video-marketing-campaign; and "Samsung, Wieden & Kennedy Rule Ad Age's 2013 Viral Video Awards," *Advertising Age*, April 16, 2013, http://adage.com/print/240900.

5. This example is based on information from Stuart Elliott, "Ad for Method Celebrates the Madness," *New York Times*, March 12, 2012, p. B1; and "Method Brings 'Clean Happy' Campaign to TV," *Business Wire*, March 4, 2013, www.businesswire.com/news/home/20130304005445/en/Method-Brings-%E2%80%9CClean-Happy%E2%80%9D-Campaign-TV.

6. See Jon Lafayette, "4A's Conference: Agencies Urged to Embrace New Technologies," *Broadcasting & Cable*, March 8, 2011, www.broadcastingcable.com/article/464951-4A_s_Conference_Agencies_Urged_To_Embrace_New_Technologies.php; David Gelles, "Advertisers Rush to Master Fresh Set of Skills," *Financial Times*, March 7, 2012, www.ft.com/intl/cms/s/0/8383bbae-5e20-11e1-b1e9-00144feabdc0.html#axzz1xUrmM3KK; and Steve McKee, "Integrated Marketing: If You Knew It, You'd Do It," *Bloomberg Businessweek*, May 10, 2012, www.businessweek.com/articles/2012-05-10/integrated-marketing-if-you-knew-it-youd-do-it#p2.

7. See "Thrill of the Chase: Coca-Cola Invites Fans to Shape Storyline of Big Game Ad," *Coca-Cola Journey*, January 25, 2013, www.coca-colacompany.com/stories/thrill-of-the-chase-coca-cola-invites-fans-to-shape-storyline-of-big-game-ad; Dale Buss, "Super Bowl Ad Watch: Crowdsourcing Peaks with Coke's 'Mirage' Campaign, *BrandChannel*, January 22, 2013, www.brandchannel.com/home/post/2013/01/22/SuperBowl-Coke-012213.aspx; and Natalie Zmuda, "Watching the Super Bowl from Coca-Cola's War Room(s)," *Advertising Age*, February 4, 2013, http://adage.com/print/239582.

8. Frank Pallotta, "Super Bowl XLIX Posts the Largest Audience in TV History," *CNN.com*, February 2, 2015, http://money.cnn.com/2015/02/02/media/super-bowl-ratings; "Update: Oscar Ratings Down 16%, Lowest in Six Years," Variety.com, February 23, 2015, http://variety.com/2015/tv/ratings/oscar-ratings-abc-telecast-down-10-in-overnights-to-four-year-low-1201439543; Lisa de Moraes, "Full 2014–2015 TV Season Series Rankings: Football & 'Empire' Ruled," Deadline.com, May 21, 2015, http://deadline.com/2015/05/2014-15-full-tv-season-ratings-shows-rankings-1201431167; and Lara O'Reilly, "Pepsi Tells Us Why a Super Bowl Ad Should Never Just Be a One-Off," *BusinessInsider.com*, January 30, 2015, www.businessinsider.com/pepsi-2015-super-bowl-plans-2015-1.

9. See discussions at Mike Ishmael, "The Cost of a Sales Call," October 22, 2012, http://4dsales.com/the-cost-of-a-sales-call; Jeff Green, "The New Willy Loman Survives by Staying Home," *Bloomberg Businessweek*, January 14–January 20, 2013, pp. 16–17; and "What Is the Real Cost of a B2B Sales Call?" www.marketing-playbook.com/sales-marketing-strategy/what-is-the-real-cost-of-a-b2b-sales-call, accessed October 2013.

10. Jack Neff, "Unilever Ad Spending Hits New Heights," *Advertising Age*, January 23, 2013, http://adage.com/print/239348.

11. Statistics from www.statista.com, accessed June 2015.

12. Bill Curry, "Tory Government Hiked Ad Spending to Promote Stimulus Projects," *Globe and Mail*, January 4, 2012, www.theglobeandmail.com/news/politics/tory-government-hiked-ad-spending-to-promote-stimulusprojects/article2291855; Bruce Cheadle, "Government Spending $13.5 Million in Ad Blitz in April and May," *Globe and Mail*, April 27, 2015, www.theglobeandmail.com/news/politics/government-spending-135-million-in-ad-blitz-in-april-and-may/article24138431.

13. "Walmart Gets Boost from Local-Price-Comparison Ads," *Advertising Age*, June 25, 2013, www.adage.com/print/242755.

14. "Take the Bing It On Challenge," September 6, 2012, www.bing.com/blogs/site_blogs/b/search/archive/2012/09/06/challenge-announce.aspx; and "Take the Bing It On Challenge at a Microsoft Store Near You," May 10, 2013, www.bing.com/blogs/site_blogs/b/search/archive/2013/05/10/take-the-bing-it-on-challenge-at-a-microsoft-store-near-you.aspx.

15. For this and other examples of comparative advertising, see "Kraft, Sara Lee Call Truce in Weiner War," *Chicago Tribune*, September 8, 2011; "What Marketers Can Learn from the Great Weiner War," *Advertising Age*, August 17, 2011, http://adage.com/print/229299; and Gabriel Beltrone, "Creatives Discuss How to Be Provocative and Effective," *Adweek*, May 8, 2012, www.adweek.com/print/140140.

16. For more on setting promotion budgets, see W. Ronald Lane, Karen Whitehill King, and J. Thomas Russell, *Kleppner's Advertising Procedure*, 18th ed. (Upper Saddle River, NJ: Prentice Hall, 2011), Chapter 6.

17. See Jean Halliday, "Thinking Big Takes Audi from Obscure to Awesome," *Advertising Age*, February 2, 2009, http://adage.com/print?article_id=134234; Chad Thomas and Andreas Cremer, "Audi Feels a Need for Speed in the U.S.," *Bloomberg BusinessWeek*, November 22, 2010, p. 1; Tito F. Hermoso, "Watch Out for Audi," *BusinessWorld*, June 15, 2011, p. 1; and Carey Vanderborg, "Audi Looks to Top BMW and Mercedes in 2013 with A3 Sedan," *International Business Times*, March 13, 2013, www.ibtimes.com/audi-looks-top-bmw-mercedes-2013-a3-sedan-photo-1123549#.

18. "Forget the Bundle, Consumers Have an Appetite for Choice," *Videomind*, December 16, 2011, http://videomind.ooyala.com/blog/forget-bundle-consumers-have-appetite-choice; and "Number of Magazine Titles," www.magazine.org/ASME/EDITORIAL_TRENDS/1093.aspx, accessed July 2012.

19. "Results of 4A's 2011 Television Production Cost Survey," January 22, 2013, www.aaaa.org/news/bulletins/pages/tvprod_01222013.aspx; Brian Steinberg, "TV Ad Prices," *Advertising Age*, October 21, 2012, http://adage.com/printl/237874/; and Claire Groden, "This Is How Much a 2016 Super Bowl Ad Costs," *Fortune.com*, August 6, 2015, http://fortune.com/2015/08/06/super-bowl-ad-cost.

20. Information from Television Bureau of Canada, "TV Basics: 2014-2015," http://www.tvb.ca/page_files/pdf/infocentre/tvbasics.pdf.

21. "Advertising in the U.S.: Synovate Global Survey Shows Internet, Innovation and Online Privacy a Must," December 3, 2009, www.synovate.com/news/article/2009/12/advertising-in-the-us-synovate-global-survey-shows-internet-innovation-and-online-privacy-a-must.html; and "Disconnect: Marketers Say TV Ads More Effective in General, Yet Traditional Spots 'Dissatisfy,'" *TVexchanger.com*, February 16, 2012, www.tvexchanger.com/interactive-tv-news/disconnect-marketers-say-tv-ads-more-effective-in-general-yet-traditional-spots-dissatisfy.

22. Jared Sternberg, "The DVR Ate My Ad—A Lot More People Fast-Forward Through TV Commercials Than You Think," *The Sternberg Report*, April 5, 2011, http://thestarryeye.typepad.com/sternberg/2011/04/the-dvr-ate-my-ad-a-lot-more-people-fast-forward-through-commercials-than-you-think.html; Brian Stelter, "On Sundays, the DVR Runneth Over," *New York Times*, April 20, 2012, p. C1; and David Goetzl, "TV Spending Nears $80 Billion, DVR Penetration Chasing 50%," *Media Post*, April 22, 2013, www.mediapost.com/publications/article/198659/#axzz2TrrvRBkB; and Information from Television Bureau of Canada, "TV Basics: 2014-2015," http://www.tvb.ca/page_files/pdf/infocentre/tvbasics.pdf.

23. Abe Sauer, "Announcing the 2015 Brandcameo Product Placement Award Winners," *BrandChannel*, February 20, 2015, http://brandchannel.com/2015/02/20/announcing-the-2015-brandcameo-product-placement-awards; and Abe Sauer, "Product Placement Watch: Every Brand in the Entourage Movie," *BrandChannel*, June 3, 2015, http://brandchannel.com/2015/06/03/entourage-product-placement.

24. Andrew Hampp, "Web Series Shows a Bit of Quality Can Help Sell 'Crap,'" *Advertising Age*, January 11, 2010, p. 10; "Ford Introduces All-New Fusion with Groundbreaking Transmedia Campaign," *Marketing Weekly News*, July 14, 2012, p. 277; and Beecher Tuttle, "IKEA's Hit Web Show: An Entertaining Ad," *Wall Street Journal*, September 7, 2012, http://online.wsj.com/article/SB10000872396390444358404577609932125128046.html.

25. James Montgomery, "What's the Deal with the Trivago Guy? Meet TV's Sloppy, Sexy Pitchman," *RollingStone.com*, July 31, 2014, www.rollingstone.com/culture/news/whats-the-deal-with-the-trivago-guy-meet-tvs-sloppy-sexy-pitchman-20140731.

26. For facts and more examples, see Bruce Horovitz, Laura Petrecca, and Gary Strauss, "Super Bowl AdMeter Winner: Score One for the Doritos Baby," *USA Today*, February 7, 2012; Laura Petrecca, "Doritos AdMeter Winners Each Receive a $1 Million Bonus," *USA Today*, February 8, 2012; "2013 USA Today Facebook Super Bowl Ad Meter," http://admeter.usatoday.com, accessed May 2013; Christopher Heine, "Frito-Lay Likes the Data from Doritos' 'Crash the Super Bowl,'" *Adweek*, February 7, 2013, www.adweek.com/news/technology/frito-lay-likes-data-doritos-crash-super-bowl-147127; and www.crashthesuperbowl.com, accessed June 2013.

27. Quotes and other information from Lauren Drell, "User Generated Content: Lessons from 4 Killer Ad Campaigns," *American Express Open Forum*, January 28, 2013, https://www.openforum.com/articles/lessons-from-4-killer-ugc-campaigns; and http://thesweatlife.lululemon.com, accessed October 2013.

28. Michael Bourne, "Sailing the 14 Social C's," *Mullen*, February 12, 2012, www.mullen.com/sailing-the-14-social-cs.

29. Antony Young, "Get Beyond the 30-Second Ad: In a World of Many Platforms, It's a Must," *Advertising Age*, April 12, 2013,

http://adage.com/article/cmo-strategy/30-ad-a/240857; and "The Weather Channel's Innovative Mobile Advertising," April 4, 2013, http://talkingnewmedia.blogspot.com/2013/04/the-weather-channels-innovative-mobile.html.

30. Brian Steinberg, "Viewer-Engagement Rankings Signal Change for TV Industry," *Advertising Age*, May 10, 2010, p. 12. For more on measuring engagement, see Kirby Thornton, "Neilsen Engages Twitter for TV Insights," *Media Is Power*, March 21, 2013, www.mediaispower.com/nielsen-engages-twitter-for-tv-insights/#sthash.yOJpbk51.ggCAZYJ5.dpbs; and "New Data Correlates Social Engagement with Traditional Radio Ratings," *PR Newswire*, April 10, 2013, www.prnewswire.com/news-releases/202264391.html.

31. Tavis Coburn, "Mayhem on Madison Avenue," *Fast Company*, January 2011, pp. 110–115.

32. Joe Tripoti, "Coca-Cola Marketing Shifts from Impressions to Expressions," April 27, 2011, http://blogs.hbr.org/cs/2011/04/coca-colas_marketing_shift_fro.html; and Devon Glenn, "Coca-Cola on Social Content: 'Expressions Are More Valuable Than Impressions,'" *Social Times*, September 11, 2012, http://socialtimes.com/coca-cola-on-social-content-expressions-are-more-valuable-than-impressions_b104547. Also see Paul Dunay, "Engagement Advertising: The Future of Brand Advertising?" *Forbes*, March 12, 2013, www.forbes.com/sites/gyro/2013/03/12/engagement-advertising-the-future-of-brand-advertising.

33. See "Nielsen: Most Tablet/Smartphone Users Watch TV at Same Time," *Electronista*, April 5, 2012, www.electronista.com/articles/12/04/05/simultaneous.use.prevalent.in.us.market.

34. *Forbes* and *Bloomberg Businessweek* cost and circulation data, http://bloombergmedia.com/pdfs/bbw_rates.pdf and www.forbesmedia.com, accessed November 2013.

35. For these and other examples, see Christopher Heine, "Lexus Nabs 100K Video Views on Facebook—in 10 Minutes," *Adweek*, January 23, 2013, www.adweek.com/news/technology/print/146726; and Matt McGee, "Oreo, Audi, and Walgreens Newsjack Super Bowl 'Blackout Bowl,'" *Marketing Land*, February 3, 2013, http://marketingland.com/oreo-audi-walgreens-market-quickly-during-super-bowl-blackout-32407.

36. Information on advertising agency revenues from "Agency Report," *Advertising Age*, April 28, 2014, pp. 8+.

37. Based on Glen Broom and Bey-Ling Sha, *Cutlip & Center's Effective Public Relations*, 11th ed. (Upper Saddle River, NJ: Prentice Hall, 2013), Chapter 1.

38. Information from Dairy Farmers of Canada, www.dairyfarmers.ca/news-centre/campaigns/recharge-with-milk; Melissa Malcolm, "Success Is Built with Chocolate Milk," *Dairy Foods*, February 2014, pp. 15–17; Polly Elmore, "Promoting Chocolate Milk as an Energy Drink," *PR Works*, February 3, 2014, http://prwrks.com/promoting-chocolate-milk-as-an-energy-drink; and http://gotchocolatemilk.com, accessed September 2014.

39. See Geoffrey Fowler and Ben Worthen, "Buzz Powers iPad Launch," *Wall Street Journal*, April 2, 2010; "Apple iPad Sales Top 2 Million Since Launch," *Tribune-Review* (Pittsburgh), June 2, 2010; "PR Pros Must Be Apple's iPad as a True Game-Changer," *PRweek*, May 2010, p. 23; Yukari Iwatani Kane,

"Apple's iPad 2 Chalks Up Strong Sales in Weekend Debut," *Wall Street Journal*, March 14, 2011, http://online.wsj.com/article/SB10001424052748704027504576198832667732862.html; and "Apple Launches New iPad," March 7, 2012, www.apple.com/pr/library/2012/03/07Apple-Launches-New-iPad.html.

40. Sarah Skerik, "An Emerging PR Trend: Content PR Strategy and Tactics," *PR Newswire*, January 15, 2013, http://blog.prnewswire.com/2013/01/15/an-emerging-pr-trend-content-pr-strategy-tactics.

41. Example based on information from Julie Liesse, "The Big Idea," *Advertising Age*, November 28, 2011, pp. C4–C6; and www.wrangler.com/store/WRG_STORE_US/en_US/style/92nb0bt.html, accessed November 2013.

CHAPTER 14

1. Portions based on information found in Jesi Hempel, "IBM's All-Star Salesman," *Fortune*, September 26, 2008, http://money.cnn.com/2008/09/23/technology/hempel_IBM.fortune/index.htm; and www.03.ibm.com/employment/jobs/softwaresales and www-03.ibm.com/ibm/history/ibm100/us/en/icons/ibmsales, accessed November 2013.

2. See Philip Kotler, Neil Rackham, and Suj Krishnaswamy, "Ending the War Between Sales and Marketing," *Harvard Business Review*, July–August 2006, pp. 68–78; Elizabeth A. Sullivan, "The Ties That Bind," *Marketing News*, May 15, 2010; Allan Mayer, "Improving the Relationships Between Sales and Marketing," *OneAccord*, May 30, 2012, www.oneaccordpartners.com/blog/bid/132539; and Philip Kotler and Kevin Lane Keller, *Marketing Management*, 14th ed. (Upper Saddle River, NJ: Prentice Hall, 2012), p. 554.

3. See Henry Canaday, "How One Enterprise Sales Force Works with Channels Partners to Maintain and Build Sales," *Selling Power*, May 13, 2013, www.sellingpower.com/enterprise-sales.

4. "Selling Power 500: The Largest Sales Force in America," *Selling Power*, July/August/September 2013, p. 32.

5. See discussions in Mike Ishmael, "The Cost of a Sales Call," October 22, 2012, http://4dsales.com/the-cost-of-a-sales-call; Jeff Green, "The New Willy Loman Survives by Staying Home," *Bloomberg Businessweek*, January 14–January 20, pp. 16–17; and "What Is the Real Cost of a B2B Sales Call?" www.marketing-playbook.com/sales-marketing-strategy/what-is-the-real-cost-of-a-b2b-sales-call, accessed April 2013.

6. Green, "The New Willy Loman Survives by Staying Home," pp. 16–17.

7. Quote and facts from Jim Domanski, "Special Report: The 2012 B@B Tele-Sales Trend Report," www.salesopedia.com/downloads/2012%20B2B%20Tele-Sales%20Trend%20Special%20Reportl.pdf, accessed July 2013.

8. See "Case Study: Climax Portable Machine Tools," www.selltis.com/productCaseStudiesClimaxPortableMachineTools.aspx; and www.climaxportable.com, accessed November 2013.

9. "Customer Business Development," www.experiencepg.com/jobs/customer-business-development-sales.aspx, accessed November 2013.

10. Scott Fuhr, "Good Hiring Makes Good Cents," *Selling Power*, July/August/September 2012, pp. 20–21.

11. For this and more information and discussion, see www. gallupaustralia.com.au/consulting/118729/sales-force-effectiveness. aspx, accessed July 2012; Lynette Ryals and Iain Davies, "Do You Really Know Who Your Best Salespeople Are?" *Harvard Business Review*, December 2010, pp. 34–35; "The 10 Skills of Super Salespeople," www.businesspartnerships.ca/articles/the_10_skills_ of_super_salespeople.phtml, accessed July 2012; and "Profile of a Super Seller," *Selling Power*, October/November/December 2012, pp. 12–13.

12. Barbara Hendricks, "Strengths-Based Selling," February 8, 2011, www.gallup.com/press/146246/Strengths-Based-Selling. aspx.

13. Corporate Visions, Inc., "ADP Case Study," http:// corporatevisions.com/v5/documents/secure_downloads/CVI_ caseStudy_ADP.pdf, accessed June 2013; and Henry Canaday, "Higher Expectations," *Selling Power*, November/December 2011, pp. 50–51.

14. Website of the Canadian Professional Sales Association, www. cpsa.com.

15. Based on information found in Sara Donnelly, "Staying in the Game," *Pharmaceutical Executive*, May 2008, pp. 158–159; Bayer Healthcare Pharmaceuticals, Inc., "Improving Sales Force Effectiveness: Bayer's Experiment with New Technology," 2008, www.icmrindia.org/casestudies/catalogue/Marketing/MKTG200. htm; Tanya Lewis, "Concentric," *Medical Marketing and Media*, July 2008, p. 59; www.hydraframe.com/mobile/project_reprace.htm, accessed July 2012; Andrew Tolve, "Pharma Sales: How Simulation Can Help Reps Sell," *Eye for Pharma*, March 28, 2012, http:// social.eyeforpharma.com/sales/pharma-sales-how-simulation-can- help-reps-sell; and Dario Priolo, "Nine Trends in Sales Force Effectiveness and Learning and Development for 2013," *The Richardson Sales Excellence Review*, December 19, 2012, http:// blogs.richardson.com/2012/12/19/nine-trends-in-sales-force- effectiveness-and-learning-development-for-2013.

16. For this and more discussion, see Joseph Kornak, "07 Compensation Survey: What's It All Worth?" *Sales & Marketing Management*, May 2007, pp. 28–39; William L. Cron and Thomas E. DeCarlo, *Dalrymple's Sales Management*, 10th ed. (New York: John Wiley & Sons Inc., 2009), p. 303; Ken Sundheim, "How Sales Professionals Are Paid," *Salesopedia*, www.salesopedia.com/ compensation-compensationdesign, accessed July 2013; and Alexander Group, "2013 Sales Compensation Trends Survey Results," January 4, 2013, www.alexandergroup.com/resources/ survey-findings.

17. See Louis Columbus, "Top-Five Focus Areas for Improving Sales Effectiveness Initiatives," *Accenture*, 2013, www.accenture. com/SiteCollectionDocuments/PDF/Accenture-Top-Five- Improvements-Sales-Effectiveness.pdf; and "2014 Sales Performance Optimization Study," CSO Insights, www.csoinsights. com/Publications.

18. Lain Chroust Ehmann, "Sales Up!" *Selling Power*, January/ February 2011, p. 40. Also see Scott Gillum, "The Disappearing Sales Process," *Forbes*, January 7, 2013, www.forbes.com/sites/ gyro/2013/01/07/the-disappearing-sales-process; and Matt Dixon

and Steve Richard, "Solution Selling Is Dead: Why 2013 Is the Year of B2B Insight Selling," *Openview*, http://labs. openviewpartners.com/solution-selling-is-dead-2013-year-of- b2b-insight-selling.

19. Brent Adamson, Matthew Dixon, and Nicholas Toman, "The End of Solution Sales," *Harvard Business Review*, July–August 2012, pp. 61–68.

20. Barbara Giamanco and Kent Gregoire, "Tweet Me, Friend Me, Make Me Buy," *Harvard Business Review*, July–August 2012, pp. 88–94.

21. Giamanco and Gregoire, "Tweet Me, Friend Me, Make Me Buy," p. 90.

22. Based on information from Elizabeth A. Sullivan, "B-to-B Marketers: One-to-One Marketing," *Marketing News*, May 15, 2009, pp. 11–13. Also see Henry Canaday, "A Socially Salable World," *Selling Power*, April/May/June 2012, pp. 46–50; and Green, "The New Willy Loman Survives by Staying Home," pp. 16–17. For more on Makino's social networking efforts, see www.facebook.com/MakinoMachine, www.youtube.com/user/ MakinoMachineTools, and http://twitter.com/#!/makinomachine, accessed November 2013.

23. Example based on information from James C. Anderson, Nirmalya Kumar, and James A. Narus, "Become a Value Merchant," *Sales & Marketing Management*, May 6, 2008, pp. 20–23; and "Business Market Value Merchants," *Marketing Management*, March/April 2008, pp. 31+. For more discussion and examples, see Heather Baldwin, "Deeper Value Delivery," *Selling Power*, September/October 2010, p. 16; and Thomas P. Reilly, "Value- Added Selling Is Smart," *Selling Power*, June 27, 2012, www. sellingpower.com/content/article.php?a=8917.

24. Kantar Retail, *Making Connections: Trade Promotion Integration Across the Marketing Landscape* (Wilton, CT: Kantar Retail, July 2012), p. 5.

25. Kantar Retail, *Making Connections: Trade Promotion Integration Across the Marketing Landscape*, p. 6.

26. "Shoppers Drug Mart Tightens up Optimum Rewards," *Canadian Press*, June 18, 2010.

27. NCH Marketing Services, "NCH Annual Topline U.S. CPG Coupon Facts Report for Year-End 2012," January 2013, www2. nchmarketing.com/ResourceCenter/assets/0/22/28/76/226/457/ 735949da63a14f209014dd04c27f1472.pdf.

28. See NCH Marketing Services, "NCH Annual Topline U.S. CPG Coupon Facts Report for Year-End 2012"; "Mobile Spurs Digital Coupon User Growth," *eMarketer*, January 31, 2013, www. emarketer.com/Article/Mobile-Spurs-Digital-Coupon-User- Growth/1009639; and Laurie Sullivan, "Digital Coupons Impact New Product Awareness, Brand Recall," *Online Media Daily*, May 9, 2013, www.mediapost.com/publications/article/199931/ #axzz2TNtmqZwq.

29. Based on information from "Walgreens Brings Mobile Couponing and Exclusive Offers to Smartphone Users Beginning Black Friday," November 17, 2011, http://news.walgreens.com/ article_display.cfm?article_id=5504; Kunar Patel, "At Walgreens, a Mobile Check-In Acts Like a Circular," *Advertising Age*, February 8, 2012, http://adage.com/print/232584; and www.walgreens.com/topic/apps/learn_about_mobile_browser_app.jsp, accessed June 2013.

30. See www.happymeal.com/en_US, accessed July 2013.

31. See "2011 Estimate of Promotional Products Distributor Sales," www.ppai.org/inside-ppai/research/Documents/2011%20SalesVolume%20Sheet.pdf, accessed July 2012.

32. Based on information found in Patrick Hanlon, "Face Slams: Event Marketing Takes Off," *Forbes*, May 9, 2012, www.forbes.com/sites/patrickhanlon/2012/05/09/face-slams-event-marketing-takes-off; and www.redbull.com/en/events and www.redbull.com/cs/Satellite/en_INT/RedBull/HolyShit/011242745950125, accessed June 2013. The referenced wing suit flying video can be found at http://player.vimeo.com/video/31481531?autoplay=1.

33. Kantar Retail, *Making Connections: Trade Promotion Integration Across the Marketing Landscape*, p. 10.

34. See "CES 2015: The Final Word," www.cnet.com/news/ces-2015-the-final-word; "Bauma 2013 Records Highest Ever Attendance," *Construction Week*, April 22, 2013, www.constructionweekonline.com/article-22027-bauma-2013-records-highest-ever-attendance/#.UZPTULXYdyI; and "Bauma 2013 Equipment Show Sees Record Attendance of 530,000," *CMBOL*, April 23, 2013, www.cmbol.com/news/detail/2013/04/2013042314194724.shtm.

CHAPTER 15

1. Based on information from Sarah Kessler, "With Paper, Facebook Stops Trying to Be Everything for Everyone," *Fast Company*, January 30, 2014, www.fastcompany.com/3025762/with-paper-facebookstops-trying-to-be-everything-for-everyone; Josh Constine, "Zuck Says Ads Aren't the Way to Monetize Messaging," *Techcrunch*, February 19, 2014, http://techcrunch.com/2014/02/19/whatsapp-will-monetize-later; Shayndi Raice and Spencer E. Ante, "Insta-Rich: $1 Billion for Instagram," *Wall Street Journal*, April 10, 2012, http://online.wsj.com/news/articles/SB10001424052702303815404577333840377381670; "Facebook's Sales Chief: Madison Avenue Doesn't Understand Us Yet," *Advertising Age*, April 29, 2011, www.adage.com/print/227314/; Craig Smith, "By the Numbers: 105 Amazing Facebook User Statistics," *Digital Marketing Ramblings*, March 13, 2014, http://expandedramblings.com/index.php/by-thenumbers-17-amazing-facebook-stats/#.U2F1gtxH38u; "Facebook's Revenue and Net Income from 2007 to 2014 (in Million U.S. Dollars)," *Statista.com*, www.statista.com/statistics/277229/facebooks-annual-revenue-and-net-income; Ben Popper, "More Than 70 Percent of Facebook's $3.45 Billion Revenue Is Now Mobile," *TheVerge.com*, April 22, 2015, www.theverge.com/2015/4/22/8470633/facebook-q1-2015-earnings-report; and www.facebook.com, www.instagram.com, and www.whatsapp.com, accessed September 2014.

2. ComBlu, "The State of Online Branded Communities," http://comblu.com/downloads/ComBlu_StateOfOnlineCommunities_2012.pdf, November 2012, p. 17; and www.mountaindew.com, accessed November 2013.

3. For these and other direct marketing statistics in this section, see Direct Marketing Association, *The DMA 2014 Statistical Fact Book*, 36th ed., April 2014; and a wealth of other information at www.the-dma.org, accessed September 2014.

4. See Direct Marketing media kit, accessed at www.dmn.ca/2012%20Media%20Kit_DM.pdf; and "Marketing Facts 2013: Statistics and Trends for Marketing in Canada," Canadian Marketing Association, 2012.

5. Ginger Conion, "Outlook 2014: Marketing Spending to Rise," *Direct Marketing News*, January 10, 2014, www.dmnews.com/outlook-2014-marketing-spending-to-rise/article/328925; Thad Reuter, "U.S. e-Commerce to Grow to 13% in 2013," *Internet Retailer*, March 13, 2013, https://www.internetretailer.com/2013/03/13/us-e-commerce-grow-13-2013; Sucharita Mulpuru, "US Online Retail Forecast, 2012 to 2017," March 13, 2013, www.forrester.com/US+Online+Retail+Forecast+2012+To+2017/fulltext/-/E-RES93281?objectid=RES93281; "Marketing Fact Pack 2014," *Advertising Age*, December 30, 2013, p. 14; and "Monthly and Annual Retail Trade," U.S. Census Bureau, www.census.gov/retail, accessed September 2014.

6. "Digital Overtakes TV for Largest Share of Ad Spend in Canada," Interactive Advertising Bureau of Canada, http://iabcanada.com/digital-overtakes-tv-for-largest-share-of-ad-spend-in-canada; and "2013: Unearthing Internet Time," Interactive Advertising Bureau of Canada, www.iabcanada.com/files/Dec-2013-CMUST-Leavebehind.pdf.

7. Melody McKinnon, "Canadian Digital, Social and Mobile Statistics on a Global Scale 2014," http://canadiansinternet.com/canadian-digital-social-mobile-statistics-global-scale-2014; "Global Mobile Statistics 2013," *MobiThinking*, March 2013, http://mobithinking.com/mobile-marketing-tools/latest-mobile-stats/a#smartphonepenetration; and www.internetworldstats.com/stats.htm, accessed July 2013.

8. Hollie Shaw, "Online Retail Sales to Hit $34 Billion in Canada by 2018," *Financial Post*, July 23, 2013, http://business.financialpost.com/news/retail-marketing/online-retail-sales-to-hit-40-billion-in-canada-by-2018; and "At the #NRF13: Web-Influenced Purchases Drive Retail Sales," *Review Trackers*, January 15, 2013, www.reviewtrackers.com/nrf13-web-influenced-purchases-drive-retail-sales-both-online-offline.

9. See Paul Davidson, "Staples Closing 225 Stores, Strengthens Online Focus," *USA Today*, March 7, 2014, www.usatoday.com/story/money/business/2014/03/06/staples-closings/6114525; "Staples Aims to Change Image with New Slogan," *Boston Globe*, January 3, 2014; and annual reports and other information found at www.staples.com, accessed September 2014.

10. See ComBlu, "The State of Online Branded Communities," http://comblu.com/downloads/ComBlu_StateOfOnlineCommunities_2012.pdf, November 2012, p. 19; "Why Join an Online Brand Community?" *Marketing Charts*, October 17, 2013, www.marketingcharts.com/wp/online/why-join-an-online-brand-community-37429; and www.espn.com, accessed November 2014.

11. "2014 Actual + 2015 Estimated Canadian Internet Advertising Revenue Survey—Detailed Report," Interactive Advertising Bureau of Canada, https://iabcanada.com/wp-content/uploads/2015/08/IAB-Canada-Internet-AdRev-Survey-2014-15-Jun-2915-waddendum2.pdf.

12. See "IAC Internet Advertising Competition: Best Rich Media Online Ad," www.iacaward.org/iac/winners_detail.asp?yr=all&

award_level=best&medium=Rich%20media%20Online%20Ad; and "Gatorade—Prime Rich Media Takeover," www.iacaward.org/iac/winner.asp?eid=10379, both accessed July 2013.

13. "2014 Actual + 2015 Estimated Canadian Internet Advertising Revenue Survey—Detailed Report," Interactive Advertising Bureau of Canada, https://iabcanada.com/wp-content/uploads/2015/08/IAB-Canada-Internet-AdRev-Survey-2014-15-Jun-2915-waddendum2.pdf; and Google 2015 Financial Tables, https://investor.google.com/financial/tables.html, accessed September 2015.

14. "Social Media Is the Hot New Thing, but Email Is Still the King," *Advertising Age*, September 30, 2013, p. 18.

15. See Nora Aufreiter et al., "Why Marketers Should Keep Sending You Emails," January 2014, www.mckinsey.com/Insights/Marketing_Sales/Why_marketers_should_keep_sending_you_emails; Niti Shah, "18 Email Marketing Stats That'll Make You Better at Your Job," *HubSpot*, December 5, 2013, http://blog.hubspot.com/marketing/email-marketing-stats-list; Amy Gesenhues, "Report: Marketing Emails Opened on Mobile Devices Jumped 61% to 65% in Q4 2013," January 23, 2014, http://marketingland.com/report-65-of-marketing-emails-were-opened-on-mobile-devicesin-q4-2013-71387; "E-Mail Marketing Spending in the United States from 2014 to 2019 (in Billion U.S. Dollars)," *Statista.com*, www.statista.com/statistics/266624/ e-mail-marketing-expenditure-in-the-united-states; and "2014 Actual + 2015 Estimated Canadian Internet Advertising Revenue Survey—Detailed Report," Interactive Advertising Bureau of Canada, https://iabcanada.com/wp-content/uploads/2015/08/IAB-Canada-Internet-AdRev-Survey-2014-15-Jun-2915-waddendum2.pdf.

16. See Elizabeth A. Sullivan, "Targeting to the Extreme," *Marketing News*, June 15, 2010, pp. 17–19; and Dianna Dilworth, "NHL Scores Goal with Single Game Ticket Sales to Far-Flung Loyal Hockey Fans," *Direct Marketing*, July 1, 2012, www.dmnews.com/article/246912/#. For more examples of outstanding email marketing campaigns, see "Marketing Sherpa Email Awards 2013," *Marketing Sherpa*, www.meclabs.com/training/misc/emailsummit/sherpa/Email_Awards_2013.pdf.

17. Jeff Goldman, "Spam Down, Phishing Up in March 2013," *eSecurity Planet*, April 23, 2013, www.esecurityplanet.com/network-security/spam-down-phishing-up-in-march-2013.html.

18. Linda Moses, "Online Video Ads Have Higher Impact Than TV Ads," *Adweek*, May 1, 2013, www.adweek.com/print/148982.

19. For these and other examples, see "Samsung, Wieden & Kennedy Rule Ad Age's 2013 Viral Video Awards," *Advertising Age*, April 16, 2013, http://adage.com/article/240900/; and Alexander Coolidge, "P&G Aims for Moms' Heart with Latest 'Thank You' Ad," *USA Today*, January 8, 2014, www.usatoday.com/story/money/business/2014/01/08/pg-olympics-thank-you-ad/4380229.

20. Laura Heller, "'Ship My Pants': Kmart's Unexpected Viral Hit," *Forbes*, April 15, 2013, www.forbes.com/sites/lauraheller/2013/04/15/ship-my-pants-kmarts-unexpected-viral-hit; Ron Dicker, "Kmart Makes Merry Mischief Again with 'Ship My Pants,' Dickens Style," *Huffington Post*, December 13, 2013,

www.huffingtonpost.com/2013/12/13/kmart-ship-my-pants-dickens-christmas-carol_n_4440133.html; and www.youtube.com/watch?v=I03UmJbK0lA, accessed September 2014.

21. Michael Learmonth, "Fresh Numbers: Honda Won Super Bowl Before It Even Began," *Advertising Age*, February 6, 2012, http://adage.com/print/232543.

22. David Gelles, "The Public Image: Volkswagen's 'The Force' Campaign," *Financial Times*, February 22, 2011, p. 14; and Troy Dreier, "The Force Was Strong with This One," *Streaming Media magazine*, April/May 2011, pp. 66–68. Also see Thales Teixeira,"The New Science of Viral Ads," *Harvard Business Review*, March 2012, pp. 25–28.

23. "State of the Blogging World in 2012," *New Media Expo Blog*, July 25, 2012, www.blogworld.com/2012/07/25/state-of-the-blogging-world-in-2012.

24. See http://en.community.dell.com/dell-blogs/default.aspx and www.youtube.com/user/DellVlog, accessed September 2014.

25. Based on information found in Keith O'Brien, "How McDonald's Came Back Bigger Than Ever," *New York Times*, May 6, 2012, p. MM44.

26. Stuart Feil, "How to Win Friends and Influence People," *Adweek*, September 10, 2013, pp. S1–S2.

27. http://newsroom.fb.com/company-info; www.youtube.com/yt/press/statistics.html; and www.statisticbrain.com/twitter-statistics, accessed September 2014.

28. For these and other examples, see www.yub.com, www.kaboodle.com, www.gofishn.com, www.dogster.com, www.farmersonly.com, www.myTransponder.com, and www.cafemom.com, all accessed November 2013.

29. See http://nikeinc.com/news/nike-coach-feature-motivates-runners-with-customized-training-plans and www.nikeplus.com, accessed June 2013.

30. Karl Greenberg, "Volvo Uses Twitter Chat for Digital Focus Groups," *Marketing Daily*, May 29, 2013, www.mediapost.com/publications/article/201309/#axzz2UsMXTPXB.

31. Based on information found at Tim Nudd, "Online Test Just Wants to Make You Happy," *Adweek*, March 18, 2013, www.adweek.com/adfreak/oreo-wraps-cookie-vs-creme-campaign-dozens-goofy-videos-148017; and Lisa Lacy, "Oreo to Fans: Cookie or Crème?" *ClickZ*, February 7, 2013, www.clickz.com/clickz/news/2241725/oreo-to-fans-cookie-or-creme.

32. See "The State of Online Branded Communities," *Comblu*, November 2012, p. 17, http://comblu.com/thoughtleadership/the-state-of-online-branded-communities-2012; and http://pinterest.com/wholefoods, accessed November 2013.

33. Example and quotes from Kashmir Hill, "#McDStories: When a Hashtag Becomes a Bashtag," *Forbes*, January 24, 2012, www.forbes.com/sites/kashmirhill/2012/01/24/mcdstories-when-a-hashtag-becomes-a-bashtag; Gabriel Beltrone, "Brand #Fail," *Adweek*, May 15, 2012, www.adweek.com/news/advertising-branding/brand-fail-140368; Michael Bourne, "Sailing of 14 Social Cs," *Mullen Advertising*, February, 13, 2012, www.mullen.com/sailing-the-14-social-cs; and "#Bashtag: Avoiding User

Outcry in Social Media," *WordStream*, March 8, 2013, www. wordstream.com/blog/ws/2013/03/07/bashtag-avoiding-social-media-backlash.

34. Melissa Allison, "Re-Creating the Coffee Klatch Online," *Raleigh News & Observer*, May 6, 2013, p. 1D; and www.facebook. com/Starbucks, https://twitter.com/Starbucks, and www. socialbakers.com/statistics/twitter/profiles/brands, accessed September 2015.

35. "Infographic: The 2015 Canadian Smartphone Market," http://catalyst.ca/infographic-2015-canadian-smartphone-market; and "Number of Apps Available in Leading App Stores as of July 2015," www.statista.com/statistics/276623/number-of-apps-available-in-leading-app-stores.

36. Jonathan Nelson, "Voice: One Screen to Rule Them All," *Adweek*, February 13, 2013, p. 15; Stephen Willard, "Study: People Check Their Cell Phones Every Six Minutes, 150 Times a Day," *Elite Daily*, February 11, 2013, http://elitedaily.com/news/world/ study-people-check-cell-phones-minutes-150-times-day; and John Fetto, "Americans Spend 58 Minutes a Day on Their Smartphones," *Experian*, May 28, 2013, www.experian.com/blogs/ marketing-forward/2013/05/28/americans-spend-58-minutes-a-day-on-their-smartphones.

37. "2014 Actual + 2015 Estimated Canadian Internet Advertising Revenue Survey—Detailed Report," Interactive Advertising Bureau of Canada, https://iabcanada.com/wp-content/ uploads/2015/08/IAB-Canada-Internet-AdRev-Survey-2014-15-Jun-2915-waddendum2.pdf.

38. See Lauren Johnson, "McDonald's Beefs Up Advertising Strategy with Mobile Game," *Mobile Marketer*, March 28, 2013, www.mobilemarketer.com/cms/news/advertising/12447.html; and Rimma Kats, "McDonald's Beefs up Mobile Efforts via Targeted Campaign," *Mobile Marketing*, August 16, 2013, www. mobilemarketer.com/cms/news/advertising/13553.html.

39. Adapted from Giselle Tsirulnik, "Most Impressive Mobile Advertising Campaigns in 2010," December 29, 2010, www. mobilemarketer.com/cms/news/advertising/8617.html.

40. "Location, Location, Location," *Adweek*, February 13, 2012, pp. M9–M11. For the Macy's and other examples, see Michael Applebaum, "Mobile Magnetism," *Adweek*, June 24, 2012, p. S7.

41. See "Stats & Facts: Direct Marketing," CMO Council, www. cmocouncil.org/facts-stats-categories.php?view=all&category= directmarketing, accessed September 2014; and "National Ad Spending in Canada in 2011 and 2016, by Media Channel (in Million Canadian Dollars), *Statista.com*, http://www.statista.com/ statistics/235203/national-ad-spending-in-canada.

42. Julie Liesse, "When Times Are Hard, Mail Works," *Advertising Age*, March 30, 2009, p. 14; Paul Vogel, "Marketers Are Rediscovering the Value of Mail," *Deliver magazine*, January 11, 2011, www.delivermagazine.com/2011/01/marketers-are-rediscovering-the-value-of-mail; and "The Resurrection of Direct Mail in 2012," *PRWeb*, www.prweb.com/releases/Direct-mail/ Resurection/prweb9301877.htm, accessed July 2012.

43. Information obtained from www.1800gotjunk.com/ca_en/ about/press_room.aspx and www.kirkmarketing.com/case-studies/1-800-got-junk, accessed February 2013.

44. See "Catalog Spree Survey Shows 89.8 Percent of Shoppers Prefer Digital Catalogs," April 19, 2012, http://catalogspree.com/ catalog-spree-survey-shows-89-8-percent-of-shoppers-prefer-digital-catalogs; and www.landsend.com/mobile/index.html and http://catalogspree.com, accessed November 2013.

45. Jeffrey Ball, "Power Shift: In Digital Era, Marketers Still Prefer a Paper Trail," *Wall Street Journal*, October 16, 2009, p. A3; Jennifer Valentino-DeVries, "With Catalogs, Opt-Out Policies Vary," *Wall Street Journal*, April 13, 2011, p. B7; Lois Geller, "Why Are Printed Catalogs Still Around?" *Forbes*, October 10, 2012, www.forbes. com/sites/loisgeller/2012/10/16/why-are-printed-catalogs-still-around; and *The DMA 2012 Statistical Fact Book*.

46. Ball, "Power Shift: In Digital Era, Marketers Still Prefer a Paper Trail"; "Report: Catalogs Increasingly Drive Online Sales," RetailCustomerExperience.com, March 17, 2010, www. retailcustomerexperience.com/article/21521/Report-Catalogs-increasingly-drive-online-sales; and "Catalogs Drive Online Sales, Says MarketReach Research," February 19, 2013, www.dma.org. uk/news/catalogues-drive-online-sales-says-marketreach-research.

47. See Rachel Brown, "Perry, Fischer, Lavigne Tapped for Proactiv," *WWD*, January 13, 2010, p. 3; Rahul Parikh, "Proactiv's Celebrity Shell Game," Salon.com, February 28, 2011, www.salon. com/2011/02/28/proactiv_celebrity_sham; "Three Proactiv Social Media Campaigns Named Finalists for PR News' Social Media Icon Awards," *PRNewswire*, April 17, 2013; and www.proactiv. com, accessed November 2013.

48. Mercedes Cardona, "Hampton's PajamaJeans Go Viral with DRTV Campaign," *Direct Marketing News*, December 2011, p. 17; and http://ec2-54-245-244-125.us-west-2.compute.amazonaws. com/ad/7IOT/pajama-jeans, November 2013.

49. Stephanie Rosenbloom, "The New Touch-Face of Vending Machines," *New York Times*, May 25, 2010, www.nytimes. com/2010/05/26/business/26vending.html; "Automating Retail Success," www.businessweek.com/adsections/2011/pdf/111114_ Verizon3.pdf, accessed July 2012; and "The Kiosk and Self-Service Top Five," *Kiosk Marketplace*, April 17, 2013, www. kioskmarketplace.com/article/211559.

50. "Best Buy: Consumer Electronics Retailing on the Go," www.zoomsystems.com/our-partners/partner-portfolio; and www.zoomsystems.com/about-us/company-overview, accessed April 2013.

51. See Canadian Anti-Fraud Centre, www.antifraudcentre-centreantifraude.ca/reports-rapports/2014/ann-ann-eng.htm#a2.

52. See Molly Bernhart Walker, "America's Less Concerned About Internet Security," *FierceGovernmentIT*, May 10, 2012, www. fiercegovernmentit.com/story/americans-less-concerned-about-internet-security/2012-05-10.

53. See Susan Dominus, "Underage on Facebook," *MSN Living*, March 15, 2012; http://living.msn.com/family-parenting/ underage-on-facebook-5; Josh Wolford, "Facebook Still Has a Big Problem with Underage Users, and They Know It," *WebProNews*, January 24, 2013, www.webpronews.com/facebook-still-has-a-big-problem-with-underage-users-and-they-know-it-2013-01.

54. Hadley Malcolm, "Millennials Don't Worry About Online Privacy," *USA Today*, April 21, 2013.

55. Based on information from Michael Bush, "My Life, Seen Through the Eyes of Marketers," *Advertising Age*, April 26, 2010, http://adage.com/print/143479.

56. "Anti-Spam Laws in Canada," *Email Marketing Reports*, www.email-marketing-reports.com/canspam/Canada, accessed July 2009; "Government of Canada Protects Canadians with the Electronic Commerce Protection Act," Industry Canada News Release, April 24, 2009, www.ic.gc.ca/eic/site/ic1.nsf/eng/04595.html, accessed July 2009; and "Long-Awaited PIPEDA Amendments Become Law," June 23, 2015, www.torys.com/insights/publications/2015/06/long-awaited-pipeda-amendments-become-law.

57. See "Facebook to Make Targeted Ads More Transparent for Users," *Advertising Age*, February 4, 2013, http://adage.com/article/239564; and www.aboutads.info, accessed November 2013.

58. Information on TRUSTe from www.truste.com, accessed November 2013.

CHAPTER 16

1. Based on information from Monica Mark, "Coca-Cola and Nestlé Target New Markets in Africa," *The Guardian*, May 4, 2012, www.guardian.co.uk/world/2012/may/04/coca-cola-nestle-markets-africa; Duane Stanford, "Africa: Coke's Last Frontier," *Bloomberg Businessweek*, November 1, 2010, pp. 54–61; Annaleigh Vallie, "Coke Turns 125 and Has Much Life Ahead," *Business Day*, May 16, 2011, www.businessday.co.za/articles/Content.aspx?id_142848; "Coca-Cola Makes Big Bets on Africa's Future," *Trefis*, May 25, 2012, www.trefis.com/stock/ko/articles/123022/coca-cola-makes-big-bets-on-africas-future/2012-05-25; "Deloitte on Africa," Deloitte, www.deloitte.com/assets/Dcom-SouthAfrica/Local%20Assets/Documents/rise_and_rise.pdf, accessed July 2013; and Coca-Cola annual reports and other information from http://assets.coca-colacompany.com/71/c1/e7da9f524671bde9899c005cacc0/2014-annual-report-operating-group-pdf.pdf, accessed September 2015.

2. Data from "Fortune 500," *Fortune*, May 2013, http://money.cnn.com/magazines/fortune/fortune500/; Christopher Stolarski, "The FDI Effect," Marquette University Research and Scholarship 2011, www.marquette.edu/research/documents/discover-2011-FDI-effect.pdf; and "List of Countries by GDP: List by the CIA World Factbook," Wikipedia, http://en.wikipedia.org/wiki/List_of_countries_by_GDP_ (nominal), accessed November 2013.

3. "Modest Trade Recovery to Continue in 2015 and 2016 Following Three Years of Weak Expansion," WTO Press Release, April 14, 2015, https://www.wto.org/english/news_e/pres15_e/pr739_e.htm.

4. Information from www.michelin.com/corporate, www.jnj.com, and www.caterpillar.com, accessed November 2013.

5. See www.otisworldwide.com/d1-about.html and UTC Annual Report 2012, http://2012ar.utc.com/assets/pdfs/UTCAR12_Full_Report.pdf, accessed July 2013.

6. Rob Schmitz, "Trade Spat Between China and EU Threatens Exports of Solar Panels, Wine," *Marketplace*, June 6, 2013, www.marketplace.org/topics/world/trade-spat-between-china-and-eu-threatens-exports-solar-panels-wine.

7. See Dexter Roberts and Michael Wei, "China's New Protectionism," *Bloomberg Businessweek*, October 27, 2011, www.businessweek.com/magazine/chinas-new-protectionism-10272011.html; and Arun Sudhaman, "Walmart Brings in PR Counsel in China," *The Holmes Report*, April 24, 2012, www.holmesreport.com/news-info/11755/WalMart-Brings-In-PR-Counsel-In-China.aspx.

8. "What Is the WTO?" www.wto.org/english/thewto_e/whatis_e/what_we_do_e.htm, accessed November 2013.

9. "Mexico Confident as WTO Leadership Race Wraps Up," *Economic Times*, May 6, 2013, http://economictimes.indiatimes.com/news/international-business/mexico-confident-as-wto-leadership-race-wraps-up/articleshow/19918085.cms; *WTO Annual Report 2012*, www.wto.org/english/res_e/publications_e/anrep12_e.htm, accessed May 2013; and World Trade Organization, "10 Benefits of the WTO Trading System," www.wto.org/english/thewto_e/whatis_e/10ben_e/10b00_e.htm, accessed November 2013.

10. "The EU at a Glance," http://europa.eu/about-eu/index_en.htm; and "EU Statistics and Opinion Polls," http://europa.eu/documentation/statistics-polls/index_en.htm, accessed November 2013.

11. "Economic and Monetary Affairs," http://europa.eu/pol/emu/index_en.htm, accessed October 2013; Dan O'Brien, "Risk of Euro Break-Up Now Higher Than Ever Before," *The Irish Times*, April 5, 2013, www.irishtimes.com/business/economy/europe/risk-of-euro-break-up-now-higher-than-ever-before-1.1349443; and "European Union: The Euro," http://europa.eu/about-eu/basic-information/money/euro, accessed November 2013.

12. Trading Economics, www.tradingeconomics.com/european-union/gdp, accessed June 2015.

13. Statistics and other information from CIA, *The World Factbook*; and Office of the United States Trade Representative, "Joint Statement from 2012 NAFTA Commission Meeting," April 2012, www.ustr.gov/about-us/press-office/press-releases/2012/april/joint-statement-2012-nafta-commission-meeting.

14. Government of Canada Foreign Affairs, Trade and Development Canada, www.international.gc.ca/trade-agreements-accords-commerciaux/agr-acc/fta-ale.aspx?lang=eng.

15. Example based on information found in Bruce Einhorn, "Alan Mulally's Asian Sales Call," *Bloomberg BusinessWeek*, April 12, 2010, pp. 41–43; "Ford, Volkswagen Eye Up North India to Set Up New Facilities," *Businessline*, December 8, 2010, p. 1; and "Ford to Tag New Figo 2012 Less by INR 16,000," *Crazy About Cars*, March 9, 2012, www.carzy.co.in/blog/car-news/ford-tag-figo-2012-inr-16000.html.

16. See "2012 Investment Climate Statement—Russia," U.S. Bureau of Economic and Business Affairs, May 2013, www.state.gov/e/eb/rls/othr/ics/2012/191223.htm; and "Welcome to the U.S. Commercial Service in Russia," http://export.gov/russia, accessed November 2013.

17. Laurent Belsie, "What Will Venezuela Do with Its Oil?" *Christian Science Monitor*, March 6, 2013, www.csmonitor.com/Environment/2013/0307/What-will-Venezuela-do-with-its-oil-Top-five-energy-challenges-after-Chavez/Oil-bartering; and

International Reciprocal Trade Association, www.irta.com/modern-trade-a-barter.html, accessed November 2013.

18. For these and other examples, see Emma Hall, "Do You Know Your Rites? BBDO Does," *Advertising Age*, May 21, 2007, p. 22.

19. Jamie Bryan, "The Mintz Dynasty," *Fast Company*, April 2006, pp. 56–61; Viji Sundaram, "Offensive Durga Display Dropped," *India-West*, February 2006, p. A1; and Emily Bryson York and Rupal Parekh, "Burger King's MO: Offend, Earn Media, Apologize, Repeat," *Advertising Age*, July 8, 2009, http://adage.com/print?article_id=137801.

20. For these and other examples, see Bill Chappell, "Bill Gates' Handshake with South Korea's Park Sparks Debate," *NPR*, April 23, 2013, www.npr.org/blogs/thetwo-way/2013/04/23/178650537/bill-gates-handshake-with-south-koreas-park-sparks-debate; "Managing Quality Across the (Global) Organization, Its Stakeholders, Suppliers, and Customers," Chartered Quality Institute, www.thecqi.org/Knowledge-Hub/Knowledge-portal/Corporate-strategy/Managing-quality-globally, accessed October 2013.

21. Quotes and other information found in David Pierson, "Beijing Loves IKEA—but Not for Shopping," *Los Angeles Times*, August 25, 2009, http://articles.latimes.com/2009/aug/25/business/fi-china-ikea25; Michael Wei, "In IKEA's China Stores, Loitering Is Encouraged," *Bloomberg Businessweek*, November 1, 2010, pp. 22–23; Jens Hansegard, "Ikea Taking China by Storm," *Wall Street Journal*, March 2012, http://online.wsj.com/article/SB10001424052702304636404577293083481821536.html; Pan Kwan Yuk, "IKEA in China: Turning Gawkers into Customers," *BeyondBrics*, April 4, 2013, http://blogs.ft.com/beyond-brics/2013/04/04/ikea-in-china-turning-gawkers-into-consumers/?#axzz2SobYFh98; and "IKEA Sees Full-Year Sales Jump 11% on Russia, China Boost," RT.com, September 10, 2015, http://www.rt.com/business/314906-ikea-sales-increase-stores.

22. Andres Martinez, "The Next American Century," *Time*, March 22, 2010, p. 1.

23. Thomas L. Friedman, *The Lexus and the Olive Tree: Understanding Globalization* (New York: Anchor Books, 2000); and Michael Wei and Margaret Conley, "Global Brands: Some Chinese Kids' First Word: Mickey," *Bloomberg Businessweek*, June 19, 2011, pp. 24–25.

24. "BrandZ Top 100 Most Valuable Global Brands 2013," Millward Brown Optimor, www.millwardbrown.com/brandz/2013/Top100/Docs/2013_BrandZ_Top100_Chart.pdf, accessed November 2013.

25. See Kim-Mai Cutler, "Apple's Chinese iPhone Sales 'Mind-Boggling,' Bring China Revenues to $7.9 Billion," *Tech Crunch*, April 24, 2012, http://techcrunch.com/2012/04/24/apples-iphone-sales-in-china-are-up-by-fivefold-from-a-year-ago; Nick Wingfield, "Apple Profit Rises on Higher iPhone and iPad Sales," *New York Times*, April 24, 2012, p. B1; and Chuck Jones, "Apple's iPhone Share Continues to Increase in Urban China," *Forbes*, February 26, 2013, www.forbes.com/sites/chuckjones/2013/02/26/apples-iphone-share-continues-to-increase-in-urban-china.

26. William J. Holstein, "How Coca-Cola Manages 90 Emerging Markets," *Strategy+Business*, November 7, 2011, www.strategy-business.com/article/00093?gko=f3ca6; "2012 Annual Report,"

www.coca-colacompany.com/investors/annual-other-reports; and other financial and review data from www.coca-colacompany.com/our-company, accessed November 2013.

27. This Netflix example is based on information found in Sam Schechner, "Europe's Media Giants Prep for Netflix Landing," *Wall Street Journal*, January 29, 2014, http://online.wsj.com/news.

28. See www.coca-colahellenic.com/aboutus, accessed November 2013.

29. See http://en.wikipedia.org/wiki/Doubletree, accessed November 2013.

30. Mike Ramsey and Christina Rogers, "Chrysler's Jeep Faces Uphill Climb in China," *Wall Street Journal*, May 10, 2013, p. B4.

31. "Ford India Lays Foundation Store for Sanand Plant," March 22, 2012, www.drivingford.in/tag/ford-india-plant; Alan Ohnsman, "Major Auto Production at Toyota, Honda Boosts U.S. Economy," July 17, 2012, www.autonews.com; and Aradhana Aravindan, "Ford Looks to Ride Emerging Market Mini-SUV Boom in India," *Reuters*, June 17, 2013, www.reuters.com/article/idUSBRE95G0RJ20130617.

32. Marc de Swaan Arons, "There Is Absolutely a Need for One Single Global Vision," *Marketing News*, September 30, 2011, p. 30.

33. Quotes from Andrew McMains, "To Compete Globally, Brands Must Adapt," *Adweek*, September 25, 2008, www.adweek.com; Pankaj Ghemawat, "Regional Strategies for Global Leadership," *Harvard Business Review*, December 2005, pp. 97–108; Eric Pfanner, "The Myth of the Global Brand," *New York Times*, January 11, 2009, www.nytimes.com; and de Swaan Arons, "There Is Absolutely a Need for One Single Global Vision," p. 30. Also see Pankej Ghemawat, "Finding Your Strategy in the New Landscape," *Harvard Business Review*, March 2010, pp. 54–60.

34. Based on information from Lucy Fancourt, Bredesen Lewis, and Nicholas Majka, "Born in the USA, Made in France: How McDonald's Succeeds in the Land of Michelin Stars," Knowledge@Wharton, January 3, 2012, http://knowledge.wharton.upenn.edu/article.cfm?articleid=2906; and Richard Vines and CarolineConnan, "McDonald's Wins over French Chef with McBaguette Sandwich," *Bloomberg*, January 15, 2013, www.bloomberg.com/news/2013-01-15/mcdonald-s-wins-over-french-chef-with-mcbaguette-sandwich.html.

35. See Warren J. Keegan and Mark C. Green, *Global Marketing*, 7th ed. (Upper Saddle River, NJ: Prentice Hall, 2013), pp. 303–308.

36. Toshiro Wakayama, Junjiro Shintaku, and Tomofumi Amano, "What Panasonic Learned in China," *Harvard Business Review*, December 2012, pp. 109–113.

37. For these and other examples, see Bruce Einhorn, "There's More to Oreo Than Black and White," *Bloomberg Businessweek*, May 3, 2012, www.businessweek.com/articles/2012-05-03/theres-more-to-oreo-than-black-and-white.

38. James R. Healey, "Fiat 500: Little Car Shoulders Huge Responsibility in U.S.; Retro Cutie Had to Be Redone from Inside Out for Sale Here," *USA Today*, June 1, 2011, p. B1; and "New 2012 Fiat 500 Named 'Best Car' in Travel + Leisure Annual Design Awards Issue," *PRNewswire*, February 15, 2012.

39. See "Easier Said Than Done," *The Economist*, April 15, 2010, www.economist.com/node/15879299; and Normandy Madden, "In China, Multinationals Forgo Adaptation for New-Brand Creation," *Advertising Age*, January 17, 2011, p. 10.

40. Jeffrey N. Ross, "Chevrolet Will 'Find New Roads' as Brand Grows Globally: Aligns Around the World Behind Singular Vision," January 8, 2013, http://media.gm.com/media/us/en/gm/news.detail.html/content/Pages/news/us/en/2013/Jan/0107-find-new-roads.html.

41. Emma Hall, "Marketers, Agencies Eye Booming Africa for Expansion," *Advertising Age*, June 13, 2011, p. 28; and Liz Gooch, "The Biggest Thing Since China: Global Companies Awake to the Muslim Consumer, and Marketers Follow Suit," *International Herald Tribune*, August 12, 2010, p. 1.

42. See George E. Belch and Michael A. Belch, *Advertising and Promotion: An Integrated Marketing Communications Perspective*, 8th ed. (New York: McGraw-Hill, 2011), Chapter 20; Shintero Okazaki and Charles R. Taylor, "What Is SMS Advertising and Why Do Multinationals Adopt It?" *Journal of Business Research*, January 2008, pp. 4–12; and Warren J. Keegan and Mark C. Green, *Global Marketing*, 7th ed. (Upper Saddle River, NJ: Prentice Hall, 2013), pp. 398–400.

43. For these and other examples, see Normandy Madden, "In China, Multinationals Forgo Adaptation for New-Brand Creation," *Advertising Age*, January 17, 2011, p. 10; Cristina Drafta, "Levi Strauss Targets Asia with Denizen," *EverythingPR*, May 16, 2011, www.pamil-visions.net/denizen/228239; and www.levistrauss.com/brands/denizen, accessed October 2013.

44. Anita Chang Beattie, "Catching the Eye of a Chinese Shopper," *Advertising Age*, December 10, 2013, pp. 20–21.

45. See "Coca-Cola Rolls Out New Distribution Model with ZAP," ZAP, January 23, 2008, www.zapworld.com/zap-coca-cola-truck; Jane Nelson, Eriko Ishikawa, and Alexis Geaneotes, "Developing Inclusive Business Models: A Review of Coca-Cola's Manual Distribution Centers in Ethiopia and Tanzania," Harvard Kennedy School, 2009, www.hks.harvard.edu/m-rcbg/CSRI/publications/other_10_MDC_report.pdf; and "How Coca-Cola's Distribution System Works," *Colalife*, December 19, 2010, www.colalife.org/2010/12/19/how-coca-colas-distribution-system-works. For some interesting photos of Coca-Cola distribution methods in third-world and emerging markets, see www.flickr.com/photos/73509998@N00/sets/72157594299144032, accessed October 2013.

46. Based on information found in Bart Becht, "Building a Company Without Borders," *Harvard Business Review*, April 2010, pp. 103–106; "From Cincy to Singapore: Why P&G, Others Are Moving Key HQs," *Advertising Age*, June 10, 2012, http://adage.com/print/235288; G. A. Chester, "3 Things to Love About Reckett Benckiser," *Daily Finance*, June 19, 2013, www.dailyfinance.com/2013/06/19/3-things-to-love-about-reckitt-benckiser; and www.rb.com/Investors-media/Investor-information, accessed November 2013.

Glossary

Adapted global marketing An international marketing approach that adjusts the marketing strategy and mix elements to each international target market, which creates more costs but hopefully produces a larger market share and return.

Administered VMS A vertical marketing system that coordinates successive stages of production and distribution, not through common ownership or contractual ties, but through the size and power of one of the parties.

Adoption process The mental process through which an individual passes from first hearing about an innovation to final adoption.

Advertising Any paid form of non-personal presentation and promotion of ideas, goods, or services by an identified sponsor.

Advertising agency A marketing services firm that assists companies in planning, preparing, implementing, and evaluating all or portions of their advertising programs.

Advertising budget The dollars and other resources allocated to a product or company advertising program.

Advertising media The vehicles through which advertising messages are delivered to their intended audiences.

Advertising objective A specific communication *task* to be accomplished with a specific *target* audience during a specific period of *time*.

Advertising strategy The strategy by which the company accomplishes its advertising objectives. It consists of two major elements: creating advertising messages and selecting advertising media.

Affordable method Setting the advertising budget at the level management thinks the company can afford.

Age and life-cycle segmentation Dividing a market into different age and life-cycle groups.

Agent A representative, either of a buyer or a seller, who performs only a few functions and does not take title to goods.

Allowance Promotional money paid by manufacturers to retailers in return for an agreement to feature the manufacturer's products in some way.

Approach The step in the selling process in which the salesperson meets the customer for the first time.

Attitude A person's consistently favourable or unfavourable evaluations, feelings, and tendencies toward an object or an idea.

Baby boomers The 9.8 million Canadians born during the baby boom following World War II and lasting until the mid-1960s.

Behavioural segmentation Dividing a market into segments based on consumer knowledge, attitudes, uses, or responses to a product.

Behavioural targeting Using online consumer tracking data to target advertisements and marketing offers to specific consumers.

Belief A descriptive thought that a person holds about something.

Benefit segmentation Dividing the market into segments according to the different benefits that consumers seek from the product.

Blogs Online journals where people post their thoughts, usually on a narrowly defined topic.

Brand A name, symbol, icon, design, or a combination of these, that identifies the maker or marketer of a product.

Brand advocates Customers, employees, and others who willingly and voluntarily promote their favourite brands.

Brand ambassador A real person who, under contract with the brand's marketing organization, acts as a spokesperson for the brand.

Brand characters Lifelike brand icons, or mascots, that can move speak, and interact, and that have personality traits.

Brand content management Creating, inspiring, and sharing brand messages and conversations with and among consumers across a fluid mix of paid, owned, earned, and shared channels.

Brand engagement The interaction between consumers and brands, based on the emotional connection consumers feel toward the brand.

Brand equity The dollar amount attributed to the value of the brand, based on all the intangible qualities that create that value.

Brand extensions Extending an existing brand name to new product categories.

Brand icons Objects with distinct shapes, colours, or patterns that are associated with the brand.

Brand personality The sum total of all the attributes of a brand, and the emotions it inspires in the minds of consumers.

Branded content (content marketing) Any form of information or story written and produced by a brand marketer, with the brand clearly and prominently featured.

Branded community website A site that presents brand content that engages consumers and creates customer community around a brand.

Branded entertainment A form of entertainment, usually video, that is created with the cooperation or financial support of a marketer.

Break-even pricing (or target return pricing) Setting price to break even on the costs of making and marketing a product, or setting price to make a target return.

Broker A wholesaler that does not take title to goods and whose function is to bring buyers and sellers together and assist in negotiation.

Business analysis A review of the sales, costs, and profit projections for a new product to find out whether these factors satisfy the company's objectives.

Business buyer behaviour The buying behaviour of the organizations that buy goods and services for use in the production of other products and services or to resell or rent them to others at a profit.

Business buying process The decision process by which business buyers determine which products and services their organizations need to purchase and then find, evaluate, and choose among alternative suppliers and brands.

Business portfolio The collection of businesses and products that make up the company.

Business promotions Sales promotion tools used to generate business leads, stimulate purchases, reward customers, and motivate salespeople.

Buying centre   All the individuals and units that play a role in the purchase decision-making process.

By-product pricing   Setting a price for by-products to make the main product's price more competitive.

Captive-product pricing   Setting a price for products that must be used along with a main product, such as blades for a razor and games for a video-game console.

Catalogue marketing   Direct marketing through print, video, or digital catalogues that are mailed to select customers, made available in stores, or presented online.

Category killer (or big box store)   A giant specialty store that carries a very deep assortment of a particular line.

Causal research   Marketing research to test hypotheses about cause-and-effect relationships.

Channel conflict   Disagreement among marketing channel members over goals, roles, and rewards.

Channel level   A layer of intermediaries that performs some work in bringing the product and its ownership closer to the final buyer.

Closing   The step in the selling process in which the salesperson asks the customer for an order.

Co-branding   The practice of using the established brand names of two different companies on the same product.

Cognitive dissonance   Buyer discomfort caused by postpurchase conflict.

Commercialization   The full-scale introduction of the new product into the market.

Commercial online databases   Computerized collections of information available from online commercial sources or via the Internet.

Communication adaptation   A global communication strategy of fully adapting advertising messages to local markets.

Competition-based pricing   Setting prices based on competitors' strategies, prices, costs, and market offerings.

Competitive advantage   An advantage over competitors gained by offering greater customer value, either through lower prices or by providing more benefits that justify higher prices.

Competitive marketing intelligence   The systematic collection and analysis of publicly available information about consumers, competitors, and developments in the marketing environment.

Competitive-parity method   Setting the promotion budget to match competitors' outlays.

Competitive review   The purpose of a competitive review is to identify key competitors, describe their market positions, and briefly discuss their strategies.

Concentrated (niche) marketing   A market-coverage strategy in which a firm goes after a large share of one or a few segments or niches.

Consumer activism   An organized movement of citizens and government agencies to improve the rights and power of buyers in relation to sellers.

Consumer buyer behaviour   The buying behaviour of final consumers—individuals and households that buy goods and services for personal consumption.

Consumer-generated marketing   Brand exchanges created by consumers themselves—both invited and uninvited—by which consumers are playing an increasing role in shaping their own brand experiences and those of other consumers.

Consumer market   All the individuals and households that buy or acquire goods and services for personal consumption.

Consumer-oriented marketing   The philosophy of sustainable marketing that holds that the company should view and organize its marketing activities from the consumer's point of view.

Consumer products   Products purchased by consumers for their personal (i.e., non-business) use.

Consumer promotions   Sales promotion tools used to boost short-term customer buying and involvement or to enhance long-term customer relationships.

Consumer-to-business (C2B) online marketing   Online exchanges in which consumers search out sellers, learn about their offers, initiate purchases, and sometimes even drive transaction terms.

Consumer-to-consumer (C2C) online marketing   Online exchanges of goods and information between final consumers.

Contract manufacturing   A joint venture in which a company contracts with manufacturers in a foreign market to produce its product or provide its service.

Contractual VMS   A vertical marketing system in which independent firms at different levels of production and distribution work together under contract.

Convenience product   A consumer product that customers usually buy frequently, immediately, and with a minimum of comparison and buying effort.

Convenience store   A small store, located near a residential area, that is open long hours or seven days a week and carries a limited line of high-turnover convenience goods.

Corporate chains   Two or more outlets that are commonly owned and controlled.

Corporate VMS   A vertical marketing system that combines successive stages of production and distribution under single ownership—channel leadership is established through common ownership.

Cost-based pricing   Setting prices based on the costs for producing, distributing, and selling the product plus a fair rate of return for effort and risk.

Cost-plus pricing (or markup pricing)   Adding a standard mark-up to the cost of the product.

Creative concept   The compelling "big idea" that will bring the advertising-message strategy to life in a distinctive and memorable way.

Cross-cultural marketing   Including ethnic themes and cross-cultural perspectives within a brand's mainstream marketing, appealing to consumer similarities across subcultures rather than differences.

Crowdsourcing   Inviting broad communities of people such as customers, employees, independent scientists and researchers, and even the public at large, into the new product innovation process.

Cultural environment   Institutions and other forces that affect society's basic values, perceptions, preferences, and behaviours.

Culture   The set of basic values, perceptions, wants, and behaviours learned by a member of society from family and other important institutions.

Customer-engagement marketing   Making the brand a meaningful part of consumers' conversations and lives by fostering direct and continual customer involvement in shaping brand conversations, experiences, and community.

Customer equity   The total combined customer lifetime values of all of the company's customers.

Customer insights   Fresh understandings of customers and the marketplace derived from marketing information that becomes the basis for creating customer value and relationships.

Customer lifetime value   The value of the entire stream of purchases that the customer would make over a lifetime of patronage.

Customer (or market) sales force structure   A sales force organization in which salespeople specialize in selling only to certain customers or industries.

Customer-perceived value   The customer's evaluation of the difference between all the benefits and all the costs of a market offering relative to those of competing offers.

Customer relationship management (CRM)   The overall process of building and maintaining profitable customer relationships by delivering superior customer value and satisfaction.

Customer satisfaction   The extent to which a product's perceived performance matches a buyer's expectations.

Customer value-based pricing   Setting price based on buyers' perceptions of value rather than on the seller's cost.

Customer-value marketing   A principle of sustainable marketing that holds that a company should put most of its resources into customer-value-building marketing investments.

Decline stage   The product life-cycle stage in which a product's sales decline.

Deficient products   Products that have neither immediate appeal nor long-run benefits.

Demand curve   A curve that shows the number of units the market will buy in a given time period, at different prices that might be charged.

Demands   Human wants that are backed by buying power.

Demographic segmentation   Dividing the market into segments based on variables such as age, gender, family size, life cycle, household income (HHI), occupation, education, ethnic or cultural group, and generation.

Demography   The study of human populations in terms of size, density, location, age, gender, race, occupation, and other statistics.

Department store   A retail store that carries a wide variety of product lines, each operated as a separate department managed by specialist buyers or merchandisers.

Derived demand   Business demand that ultimately comes from (derives from) the demand for consumer goods.

Descriptive research   Marketing research to better describe marketing problems, situations, or markets.

Desirable products   Products that give both high immediate satisfaction and high long-run benefits.

Differentiated (segmented) marketing   A market-coverage strategy in which a firm decides to target several market segments and designs separate offers for each.

Differentiation   Actually differentiating the market offering to create superior customer value.

Diffusion of innovations theory   A social sciences theory that divides members of a social group into segments according to how likely they are to adopt a new idea.

Digital and social media marketing   The use of digital marketing tools such as websites, social media, mobile apps and ads, online video, email, and blogs to engage carefully targeted individual consumers and customer communities via their digital devices to obtain an immediate response and build lasting customer relationships.

Direct investment   Entering a foreign market by developing foreign-based assembly or manufacturing facilities.

Direct-mail marketing   Marketing that occurs by sending an offer, announcement, reminder, or other item directly to a person at a particular address.

Direct and digital marketing   Engaging and interacting directly with carefully targeted individual consumers and consumer communities to both obtain an immediate response and cultivate lasting customer relationships.

Direct marketing channel   A marketing channel that has no intermediary levels.

Direct-response television marketing   Direct marketing via television, including direct-response television advertising (or infomercials) and interactive television (iTV) advertising.

Discount   A straight reduction in price on purchases during a stated period of time or on larger quantities.

Discount store   A retail operation that sells standard merchandise at lower prices by accepting lower margins and selling at higher volume.

Disintermediation   The cutting out of marketing channel intermediaries by product or service producers, or the displacement of traditional resellers by radical new types of intermediaries.

Diversification   A strategy for company growth through starting up or acquiring businesses outside the company's current products and markets.

Downsizing   Reducing the business portfolio by eliminating products or business units that are not profitable or that no longer fit the company's overall strategy.

Drop shipper   An intermediary that takes orders and payment from the customer, then arranges to have the merchandise shipped to the customer directly from the supplier.

Dynamic pricing   Adjusting prices continually to meet the characteristics and needs of individual customers and situations.

Economic community   A group of nations organized to work toward common goals in the regulation of international trade.

Economic environment   Economic factors that affect consumer buying power and spending patterns.

Email marketing   Sending highly targeted, tightly personalized, relationship-building marketing messages via email.

Environmentalism   An organized movement of concerned citizens, businesses, and government agencies to protect and improve people's current and future living environment.

Environmental sustainability   A management approach that involves developing strategies that both sustain the environment and produce profits for the company.

E-procurement   Purchasing through electronic connections between buyers and sellers—usually online.

Ethnographic research   A form of observational research that involves sending trained observers to watch and interact with consumers in their "natural habitat."

Event marketing (or event sponsorships)   Creating a brand-marketing event or serving as a sole or participating sponsor of events created by others.

Exchange   The act of obtaining a desired object from someone by offering something in return.

Exclusive distribution   A distribution strategy in which the marketer gives the rights to distribute its products to only one retailer, or to only one retailer in a particular geographic territory.

Execution style   The approach, style, tone, words, and format used for executing an advertising message.

Experimental research   Gathering primary data by selecting matched groups of subjects, giving them different treatments, controlling related factors, and checking for differences in group responses.

Exploratory research   Marketing research to gather preliminary information that will help define the problem and suggest hypotheses.

Exporting   Entering foreign markets by selling goods produced in the company's home country, often with little modification.

Factory outlet   An off-price retailing operation that is owned and operated by a manufacturer and normally carries the manufacturer's surplus, discontinued, or irregular goods.

Fad   A temporary period of unusually high sales driven by consumer enthusiasm and immediate product or brand popularity.

Fashion   A currently accepted or popular style of design, colour, or theme.

Fixed costs (overhead)   Costs that do not vary with production or sales level.

Focus group interviewing   Personal interviewing that involves inviting six to ten people to gather for a few hours with a trained interviewer to talk about a product, service, or organization. The interviewer "focuses" the group discussion on important issues.

Follow-up   The last step in the selling process in which the salesperson follows up after the sale to ensure customer satisfaction and repeat business.

Franchise   A contractual association between a manufacturer, wholesaler, or service organization (a franchisor) and independent businesspeople (franchisees) who buy the right to own and operate one or more units in the franchise system.

Franchise organization   A marketing system that links several stages in the production and distribution process and controls operations from a central head office.

Gender segmentation   Dividing a market into different segments based on gender.

General merchandise store   A store that sells a broad selection of merchandise where people can purchase all their general goods.

Generation X   The 7 million Canadians born between 1967 and 1976 in the "birth dearth" following the baby boom.

Generation Z   People born after 2000 (although many analysts include people born after 1995) who make up the kid, tween, and teen markets.

Geographical pricing   Setting prices for customers located in different parts of the country or the world.

Geographic segmentation   Dividing a market into different geographical units, such as global regions, countries, regions within a country, provinces, cities, or even neighbourhoods.

Global firm   A firm that, by operating in more than one country, gains R&D, production, marketing, and financial advantages in its costs and reputation that are not available to purely domestic competitors.

Good-value pricing   Offering just the right combination of quality and good service at a fair price.

Group   Two or more people who interact to accomplish individual or mutual goals.

Growth–share matrix   A portfolio-planning method that evaluates a company's strategic business units (SBUs) in terms of its market growth rate and relative market share. SBUs are classified as stars, cash cows, question marks, or dogs.

Growth stage   The product life-cycle stage in which a product's sales start climbing quickly.

Handling objections   The step in the selling process in which the salesperson seeks out, clarifies, and overcomes customer objections to buying.

Horizontal marketing system   An arrangement in which two or more companies that operate at the same channel level join together to follow a new marketing opportunity.

Household income (HHI) segmentation   Dividing a market into different income segments.

Idea generation   The systematic search for new-product ideas.

Idea screening   Screening new-product ideas to spot good ideas and drop poor ones as soon as possible.

Independent off-price retailer   An off-price retailer that is either independently owned and run or a division of a larger retail corporation.

Indirect marketing channel   A marketing channel containing one or more intermediary levels.

Individual marketing (mass customization)   Tailoring products and marketing programs to the needs and preferences of individual customers.

Industrial product   A product bought by individuals and organizations for further processing or for use in conducting a business.

Innovative marketing   A principle of sustainable marketing that requires that a company seek real product and marketing improvements.

Inside sales force   Salespeople who conduct business from their offices via telephone, online and social media interactions, or visits from prospective buyers.

Integrated marketing communications (IMC)   Carefully integrating and coordinating the company's many communications channels to deliver a clear, consistent, and compelling message about the organization and its products.

Intensive distribution   A marketing strategy in which the product is stocked in as many outlets as possible.

Intermarket (cross-market) segmentation   Forming segments of consumers who have similar needs and buying behaviour even though they are located in different countries.

Internal databases   Electronic collections of consumer and market information obtained from data sources within the company network.

Internal marketing   Orienting and motivating customer-contact employees and supporting service people in working as a team to provide customer satisfaction.

Introduction stage   The product life-cycle stage in which the new product is first distributed and made available for purchase.

Joint ownership   A cooperative venture in which a company creates a local business with investors in a foreign market, who share ownership and control.

Joint venturing   Entering foreign markets by joining with foreign companies to produce or market a product or service.

Just-in-time logistics systems   A type of inventory management system in which only small inventories of parts or merchandise are held, and new stock arrives "just in time" when it is needed.

Learning   Changes in an individual's behaviour arising from experience.

Licensing of brands   Entering foreign markets through developing an agreement with a licensee in the foreign market.

Licensing (joint ventures)   Entering foreign markets through developing an agreement with a licensee in the foreign market.

Lifestyle   A person's pattern of living as expressed in his or her activities, interests, and opinions.

Line extensions   Extending an existing brand name to new forms, colours, sizes, ingredients, or flavours of an existing product category.

Local marketing   A small group of people who live in the same city, or neighbourhood, or who shop at the same store.

Logistics management (supply chain management)   Planning, implementing, and controlling the physical flow of materials, final goods, and related information from points of origin to points of consumption to meet customer requirements at a profit.

Macroenvironment   The larger societal forces that affect the microenvironment—demographic, economic, natural, technological, political, and cultural forces.

Madison & Vine   A term that has come to represent the merging of advertising and entertainment in an effort to break through the clutter and create new avenues for reaching customers with more engaging messages.

Management contracting   A joint venture in which the domestic firm supplies the management know-how to a foreign company that supplies the capital; the domestic firm exports management services rather than products.

Market   The set of all actual and potential buyers of a product or a service.

Market development   A strategy for company growth by identifying and developing new market segments for current company products.

Market offerings   Some combination of products, services, information, or experiences offered to a market to satisfy a need or want.

Market penetration   A strategy for company growth by increasing sales of current products to current market segments without changing the product.

Market-penetration pricing   Setting a low initial price for a new product in order to attract a large number of buyers and a large market share.

Market segment   A group of customers who respond in a similar way to a given set of marketing efforts.

Market segmentation   Dividing a market into distinct groups of buyers who have different needs, characteristics, or behaviours, and who might require separate products or marketing programs.

Market-skimming pricing (or price skimming)   Setting a high price for a new product to skim maximum revenues layer by layer from the segments willing to pay the high price; the company makes fewer but more profitable sales.

Market targeting   The process of evaluating each market segment's attractiveness and selecting one or more segments to enter.

Marketing   The process by which companies create value for customers and build strong customer relationships to capture value from customers in return.

Marketing channel (or distribution channel)   A set of interdependent organizations that help make a product or service available for use or consumption by the consumer or business customer.

Marketing channel design   Designing effective marketing channels by analyzing customer needs, setting channel objectives, determining the types and responsibilities of channel members, and making decisions about international distribution channels.

Marketing concept   The marketing management philosophy that holds that achieving organizational goals depends on knowing the needs and wants of target markets and delivering the desired satisfactions better than competitors do.

Marketing control   The process of measuring and evaluating the results of marketing strategies and plans and taking corrective action to ensure that objectives are achieved.

Marketing environment   The actors and forces outside marketing that affect marketing management's ability to build and maintain successful relationships with target customers.

Marketing Implementation   The process that turns marketing strategies and plans into marketing actions to accomplish strategic marketing objectives.

Marketing information system (MIS)   People and procedures dedicated to assessing information needs, developing the needed information, and helping decision makers use the information to generate and validate actionable customer and market insights.

Marketing intermediaries   Firms that help the company to promote, sell, and distribute its goods to final buyers.

Marketing management   The art and science of choosing target markets and building profitable relationships with them.

Marketing mix   The set of controllable, tactical marketing tools—product, price, place, and promotion—that the firm blends to produce the response it wants in the target market.

Marketing myopia   The mistake of paying more attention to the specific products a company offers than to the benefits and experiences produced by these products.

Marketing research   The systematic design, collection, analysis, and reporting of data relevant to a specific marketing situation facing an organization.

Marketing strategy   The marketing logic by which the company hopes to create customer value and achieve profitable customer relationships.

Marketing strategy development   Designing an initial marketing strategy for a new product based on the product concept.

Marketing website   A website that engages consumers in interactions that will move them closer to a direct purchase or other marketing outcome.

Maturity stage   The product life-cycle stage in which sales growth slows or levels off.

Microenvironment   The actors close to the company that affect its ability to serve its customers—the company, suppliers, marketing intermediaries, customer markets, competitors, and publics.

Micromarketing   The practice of tailoring products and marketing programs to the needs and wants of specific individuals and local customer segments—includes *local marketing and individual marketing*.

Millennials (or Generation Y)   The 10.4 million children of the Canadian baby boomers, born between 1977 and 2000.

Mission statement   A statement of the organization's purpose—what it wants to accomplish in the larger environment.

Mobile marketing Marketing messages, promotions, and other content delivered to on-the-go consumers through mobile phones, smartphones, tablets, and other mobile devices.

Modified rebuy A business buying situation in which the buyer wants to modify product specifications, prices, terms, or suppliers.

Motive (drive) A need that is sufficiently pressing to direct the person to seek satisfaction of the need.

Multibranding A brand development strategy in which the same manufacturer produces many different brands in the same product category.

Multichannel (hybrid) distribution system A distribution system in which a single firm sets up two or more marketing channels to reach one or more market segments.

Multichannel marketing Marketing both through stores and other traditional offline channels and through digital, online, social media, and mobile channels.

Multimodal (or intermodal) transportation Combining two or more modes of transportation.

National brand (or manufacturer's brand) A brand created and owned by the manufacturer of the product.

Natural environment The physical environment and the natural resources that are needed as inputs by marketers or that are affected by marketing activities.

Needs States of felt deprivation.

New product A good, service, or idea that is perceived by some potential customers as new.

New-product development The development of original products, product improvements, product modifications, and new brands through the firm's own product-development efforts.

New task A business buying situation in which the buyer purchases a product or service for the first time.

Objective-and-task method Developing the promotion budget by (1) defining specific objectives, (2) determining the tasks that must be performed to achieve these objectives, and (3) estimating the costs of performing these tasks. The sum of these costs is the proposed promotion budget.

Observational research Gathering primary data by observing relevant people, actions, and situations.

Occasion segmentation Dividing the market into segments according to occasions when buyers get the idea to buy, actually make their purchase, or use the purchased item.

Off-price retailer A retailer that buys at less-than-regular wholesale prices and sells at less than retail.

Online advertising Advertising that appears while consumers are browsing the Web, including display ads, search-related ads, online classifieds, and other forms.

Online focus groups Gathering a small group of people online with a trained moderator to chat about a product, service, or organization and to gain qualitative insights about consumer attitudes and behaviour.

Online marketing Marketing via the Internet using company websites, online ads and promotions, email, online video, and blogs.

Online marketing research Collecting primary data online through Internet surveys, online focus groups, Web-based experiments, or tracking consumers' online behaviour.

Online social networks Online social communities—blogs, social networking websites, or even virtual worlds—where people socialize or exchange information and opinions.

Opinion leader Person within a reference group who, because of special skills, knowledge, personality, or other characteristics, exerts social influence on others.

Optional-product pricing The pricing of optional or accessory products along with a main product.

Outside sales force (or field sales force) Salespeople who travel to call on customers in the field.

Packaging The activities of designing and producing the container or wrapper for a product.

Partner relationship management Working closely with partners in other company departments and outside the company to jointly bring greater value to customers.

Percentage-of-sales method Setting the promotion budget at a certain percentage of current or forecasted sales, or as a percentage of the unit sales price.

Perception The process by which people select, organize, and interpret information to form a meaningful picture of the world.

Personal selling Personal customer interactions by the firm's sales force for the purpose of making sales and building customer relationships.

Personality The unique psychological characteristics that distinguish a person or group.

Pleasing products Products that give high immediate satisfaction but may hurt consumers in the long run.

Political environment Laws, government agencies, and pressure groups that influence and limit various organizations and individuals in a given society.

Portfolio analysis The process by which management evaluates the products and businesses that make up the company.

Positioning Arranging for a market offering or product to occupy a clear, distinctive, and desirable place relative to competing products in the minds of target consumers.

Positioning statement A statement that summarizes company or brand positioning—it takes this form: To (target segment and need) our (brand) is (concept) that (point of difference).

Preapproach The step in the selling process in which the salesperson learns as much as possible about a prospective customer before making a sales call.

Presentation The step in the selling process in which the salesperson tells the "value story" to the buyer, showing how the company's offer solves the customer's problems.

Price The amount of money charged for a product or a service, or the sum of the values that customers exchange for the benefits of having or using the product or service.

Price elasticity A measure of the sensitivity of demand to changes in price.

Primary data Information collected for the specific purpose at hand.

Private brand (store brand, private label) Brand names applied by the marketer to products manufactured for them under contract.

Product Anything that can be offered to a market for attention, acquisition, use, or consumption that might satisfy a want or need.

Product adaptation Adapting a product to meet local conditions or wants in foreign markets.

Product bundle pricing Combining several products and offering the bundle at a reduced price.

Product concept (new product development) A detailed version of the new-product idea stated in meaningful consumer terms.

Product concept (as a marketing management orientation) The idea that consumers will favour products that offer the most quality, performance, and features and that the organization should therefore devote its energy to making continuous product improvements.

Product development Developing the product concept into a physical product to ensure that the product idea can be turned into a workable market offering. Also a strategy for company growth by offering modified or new products to current market segments.

Product invention Creating new products or services for foreign markets.

Product life cycle The course of a product's sales and profits over its lifetime. It involves five stages: product development, introduction, growth, maturity, and decline.

Product line A group of products that are closely related because they function in a similar manner, are sold to the same customer groups, are marketed through the same types of outlets, or fall within given price ranges.

Product line pricing Setting the price steps between various products in a product line based on cost differences between the products, customer evaluations of different features, and competitors' prices.

Product–market expansion grid A portfolio-planning tool for identifying company growth opportunities through market penetration, market development, product development, or diversification.

Product mix (or product portfolio) The set of all product lines and items that a company markets.

Product position The way the product is defined by consumers on important attributes—the place the product occupies in consumers' minds relative to competing products.

Product quality The characteristics of a product or a service that bear on its ability to satisfy stated or implied customer needs.

Product sales force structure A sales force organization in which salespeople specialize in selling only a portion of the company's products or lines.

Product value analysis Carefully analyzing a product's or service's components to determine whether they can be redesigned and made more effectively and efficiently to provide greater value.

Production concept The idea that consumers will favour products that are available and highly affordable and that the organization should therefore focus on improving production and distribution efficiency.

Promotion mix (or marketing communications mix) The specific blend of promotion tools that the company uses to persuasively communicate customer value and build customer relationships.

Promotional pricing Temporarily pricing products below the list price and sometimes even below cost to increase short-run sales.

Prospecting The step in the selling process in which the salesperson or company identifies qualified potential customers.

Psychographic segmentation Dividing a market into different segments based on social class, lifestyle, or personality characteristics.

Psychological pricing Pricing that considers the psychology of prices and not simply the economics; the price is used to say something about the product.

Public Any group that has an actual or potential interest in or impact on an organization's ability to achieve its objectives.

Public relations (PR) Building good relations with the company's various publics by obtaining favourable publicity, building up a good corporate image, and handling or heading off unfavourable rumours, stories, and events.

Pull strategy A promotion strategy that calls for spending a lot on advertising and consumer promotion to induce final consumers to buy the product, creating a demand vacuum that "pulls" the product through the channel.

Push strategy A promotion strategy that calls for using the sales force and trade promotion to push the product through channels. The producer promotes the product to channel members who in turn promote it to final consumers.

Rack jobber A wholesaler that buys merchandise and resells it on "racks" inside a retail store, in partnership with the retailer.

Reference prices Prices that buyers carry in their minds and refer to when they look at a given product.

Retailer A business that primarily sells products and services to consumers.

Retailing The business of selling goods or services to consumers for their personal use.

Return on advertising investment The net return on advertising investment divided by the costs of the advertising investment.

Return on marketing investment (or marketing ROI) The net return from a marketing investment divided by the costs of the marketing investment.

Sales force management Analyzing, planning, implementing, and controlling sales force activities.

Sales promotion Short-term incentives to encourage the purchase or sale of a product or a service.

Sales quota A standard that states the amount a salesperson should sell and how sales should be divided among the company's products.

Salesperson An individual who represents a company to customers by performing one or more of the following activities: prospecting, communicating, selling, servicing, information gathering, and relationship building.

Salutary products Products that have low appeal but may benefit consumers in the long run.

Sample A segment of the population selected for marketing research to represent the population as a whole.

Secondary data Information that already exists somewhere, having been collected for another purpose.

Segmentation Dividing a market into distinct groups with distinct needs, characteristics, or behaviours that might require separate marketing strategies or mixes.

Segmented pricing Selling a product or service at two or more prices, where the difference in prices is not based on differences in costs.

Selective distribution A distribution strategy in which the marketer selects a set of retailers that specialize in their product category.

Selling concept The idea that consumers will not buy enough of the firm's products unless it undertakes a large-scale selling and promotion effort.

Selling process The steps that salespeople follow when selling, which include prospecting and qualifying, preapproach, approach, presentation and demonstration, handling objections, closing, and follow-up.

Sense-of-mission marketing A principle of sustainable marketing that holds that a company should define its mission in broad social terms rather than narrow product terms.

Service An activity, benefit, or satisfaction offered for sale that is essentially intangible and does not result in the ownership of anything.

Service inseparability A major characteristic of services—they are produced and consumed at the same time and cannot be separated from their providers.

Service intangibility A major characteristic of services—they cannot be seen, tasted, felt, heard, or smelled before they are bought.

Service perishability A major characteristic of services—they cannot be stored for later sale or use.

Service–profit chain The chain that links service firm profits with employee and customer satisfaction.

Service retailer A retailer whose product line is actually a service; examples include hotels, airlines, banks, restaurants, and many others.

Service variability A major characteristic of services—their quality may vary greatly, depending on who provides them and when, where, and how.

Share of customer The portion of the customer's purchasing that a company gets in its product categories.

Shopper marketing Using point-of-sale promotions and advertising to extend brand equity to "the last mile" and encourage favourable in-store purchase decisions.

Shopping centre A group of retail businesses built on a site that is planned, developed, owned, and managed as a unit.

Shopping product Less frequently purchased consumer products and services that shoppers compare carefully on suitability, quality, price, and style.

Social class Relatively permanent and ordered divisions in a society whose members share similar values, interests, and behaviours.

Social media Independent and commercial online communities where people congregate, socialize, and exchange views and information.

Societal marketing A principle of sustainable marketing that holds that a company should make marketing decisions by considering consumers' wants, the company's requirements, consumers' long-run interests, and society's long-run interests.

Societal marketing concept The idea that a company's marketing decisions should consider

consumers' wants, the company's requirements, consumers' long-run interests, and society's long-run interests.

Spam Unsolicited, unwanted commercial email messages.

Specialty product A consumer product with unique characteristics or brand identification for which a significant group of buyers is willing to make a special purchase effort.

Specialty store A retail store that carries a narrow product line with a deep assortment within that line.

Standardized global marketing An international marketing strategy that basically uses the same marketing strategy and mix in all of the company's international markets.

Straight product extension Marketing a product in a foreign market without making any changes to the product.

Straight rebuy A business buying situation in which the buyer routinely reorders something without any modifications.

Strategic planning The process of developing and maintaining a strategic fit between the organization's goals and capabilities and its changing marketing opportunities.

Style A basic and distinctive mode of expression.

Subculture A group of people with shared value systems based on common life experiences and situations.

Supermarket A large, low-cost, low-margin, high-volume, self-service store that carries a wide variety of grocery and household products.

Superstore A store much larger than a regular supermarket that offers a large assortment of routinely purchased food products, nonfood items, and services.

Supplier development Systematic development of networks of supplier-partners to ensure an appropriate and dependable supply of products and materials for use in making products or reselling them to others.

Survey research Gathering primary data by asking people questions about their knowledge, attitudes, preferences, and buying behaviour.

Sustainable marketing A philosophy of socially and environmentally responsible marketing that meets the present needs of consumers and busi-

nesses while also preserving or enhancing the ability of future generations to meet their needs.

Sustainable packaging Packaging that meets the requirements of the product while minimizing the environmental, economic, and social impacts of the product and its package.

SWOT analysis An overall evaluation of the company's strengths (S), weaknesses (W), opportunities (O), and threats (T).

Systems selling (or solutions selling) Buying a packaged solution to a problem from a single seller, thus avoiding all the separate decisions involved in a complex buying situation.

Target costing Pricing that starts with an ideal selling price, and then targets costs that will ensure that the price is met.

Target market A set of buyers sharing common needs or characteristics that the company decides to serve.

Targeting The process of evaluating each market segment's attractiveness and selecting one or more segments to enter.

Team selling Using teams of people from sales, marketing, engineering, finance, technical support, and even upper management to service large, complex accounts.

Technological environment Forces that create new technologies, creating new product and market opportunities.

Technology Adoption Life Cycle A marketing theory that proposes that when marketing a technology product, marketers must cross a chasm, or significant gap, between members of the early adopters segment and members of the early majority segment, before a new product will become successful.

Telemarketing Using the telephone to sell directly to customers.

Territorial sales force structure A sales force organization that assigns each salesperson to an exclusive geographic territory in which that salesperson sells the company's full line.

Test marketing The stage of new-product development in which the product and marketing program are tested in realistic market settings.

Third-party logistics (3PL) provider An independent logistics provider that performs any or all of the functions required to get its client's product to market.

Total costs The sum of the fixed and variable costs for any given level of production.

Touchpoints Advertising, marketing communications, personal experience with the brand, word of mouth, social media, company and brand websites, store displays, and anything else that brings a consumer into contact with a brand.

Trade promotions Sales promotion tools used to persuade resellers to carry a brand, give it shelf space, promote it in advertising, and push it to consumers.

Undifferentiated (mass) marketing A market-coverage strategy in which a firm decides to ignore market segment differences and go after the whole market with one offer.

Unsought product A consumer product that the consumer either does not know about or knows about but does not normally think of buying.

Value-added pricing Attaching value-added features and services to differentiate a company's offers and charging higher prices.

Value chain The series of internal departments that carry out value-creating activities to design, produce, market, deliver, and support a firm's products.

Value delivery network The network made up of the company, suppliers, distributors, and, ultimately, customers who partner with each other to improve the performance of the entire system.

Value proposition The full positioning of a brand—the full mix of benefits upon which it is positioned.

Variable costs Costs that vary directly with the level of production.

Vertical marketing system (VMS) A distribution channel structure in which producers, wholesalers, and retailers act as a unified system. One channel member owns the others, has contracts with them, or has so much power that they all cooperate.

Viral marketing The digital version of word-of-mouth marketing: videos, ads, and other marketing content that is so infectious that customers will seek it out or pass it along to friends.

Wants The form human needs take as shaped by culture and individual personality.

Warehouse club An off-price retailer that sells a limited selection of brand-name grocery items, appliances, clothing, and other goods at deep discounts to members who pay annual membership fees.

Whole-channel view Designing international channels that take into account the entire global supply chain and marketing channel, forging an effective global value delivery network.

Wholesalers Companies whose primary business is wholesaling.

Wholesaling All activities involved in selling goods and services to those buying for resale or business use.

Word-of-mouth influence The impact of the personal words and recommendations of trusted friends, associates, and other consumers on buying behaviour.

Indexes

Subject Index